Let's Go writers travel on your budget.

"Guides that penetrate the veneer of the holiday brochures and mine the grit of real life."

—*The Economist*

"The writers seem to have experienced every rooster-packed bus and lunar-surfaced mattress about which they write."

—*The New York Times*

"All the dirt, dirt cheap."

—*People*

Great for independent travelers.

"The guides are aimed not only at young budget travelers but at the independent traveler; a sort of streetwise cookbook for traveling alone."

—*The New York Times*

"A guide should tell you what to expect from a destination. Here *Let's Go* shines."

—*The Chicago Tribune*

"An indispensible resource, *Let's Go*'s practical information can be used by every traveler."

—*The Chattanooga Free Press*

Let's Go is completely revised each year.

"A publishing phenomenon...the only major guidebook series updated annually. *Let's Go* is the big kahuna."

—*The Boston Globe*

"Unbeatable: good sight-seeing advice; up-to-date info on restaurants, hotels, and inns; a commitment to money-saving travel; and a wry style that brightens nearly every page."

—*The Washington Post*

All the important information you need.

"*Let's Go* authors provide a comedic element while still providing concise information and thorough coverage of the country. Anything you need to know about budget traveling is detailed in this book."

—*The Chicago Sun-Times*

"*Let's Go* guidebooks take night life seriously."

—*The Chicago Tribune*

Let's Go Publications

Let's Go: Alaska & the Pacific Northwest 2002
Let's Go: Amsterdam 2002 **New Title!**
Let's Go: Australia 2002
Let's Go: Austria & Switzerland 2002
Let's Go: Barcelona 2002 **New Title!**
Let's Go: Boston 2002
Let's Go: Britain & Ireland 2002
Let's Go: California 2002
Let's Go: Central America 2002
Let's Go: China 2002
Let's Go: Eastern Europe 2002
Let's Go: Egypt 2002 **New Title!**
Let's Go: Europe 2002
Let's Go: France 2002
Let's Go: Germany 2002
Let's Go: Greece 2002
Let's Go: India & Nepal 2002
Let's Go: Ireland 2002
Let's Go: Israel 2002
Let's Go: Italy 2002
Let's Go: London 2002
Let's Go: Mexico 2002
Let's Go: Middle East 2002
Let's Go: New York City 2002
Let's Go: New Zealand 2002
Let's Go: Paris 2002
Let's Go: Peru, Ecuador & Bolivia 2002
Let's Go: Rome 2002
Let's Go: San Francisco 2002
Let's Go: South Africa with Southern Africa 2002
Let's Go: Southeast Asia 2002
Let's Go: Southwest USA 2002 **New Title!**
Let's Go: Spain & Portugal 2002
Let's Go: Turkey 2002
Let's Go: USA 2002
Let's Go: Washington, D.C. 2002
Let's Go: Western Europe 2002

Let's Go *Map Guides*

Amsterdam
Berlin
Boston
Chicago
Dublin
Florence
Hong Kong
London
Los Angeles
Madrid
New Orleans
New York City
Paris
Prague
Rome
San Francisco
Seattle
Sydney
Venice
Washington, D.C.

AUSTRALIA

2002

Krishnan Unnikrishnan editor
Loran C. Fredric associate editor
Gretchen Puttkamer associate editor

researcher-writers
Steve Collins
Alice Farmer
John Fiore
Nathan Foley-Mendelssohn
Christine Monta
Matthew Shea O'Hare
Meredith Osborn
Johs Pierce
Jevan Soo

Nathaniel Popper managing editor
Brooks Newkirk map editor

St. Martin's Press New York

HELPING LET'S GO If you want to share your discoveries, suggestions, or corrections, please drop us a line. We read every piece of correspondence, whether a postcard, a 10-page email, or a coconut. Please note that mail received after May 2002 may be too late for the 2003 book, but will be kept for future editions. **Address mail to:**

Let's Go: Australia
67 Mount Auburn Street
Cambridge, MA 02138
USA

Visit Let's Go at **http://www.letsgo.com,** or send email to:

feedback@letsgo.com
Subject: "Let's Go: Australia"

In addition to the invaluable travel advice our readers share with us, many are kind enough to offer their services as researchers or editors. Unfortunately, our charter enables us to employ only currently enrolled Harvard students.

Maps by David Lindroth copyright © 2002, 2001, 2000, 1999, 1998, 1997, 1996, 1995, 1994, 1993, 1992, 1991, 1990, 1989, 1988 by St. Martin's Press.

Distributed outside the USA and Canada by Macmillan.

Let's Go: Australia Copyright © 2002 by Let's Go, Inc. All rights reserved. Printed in the United States of America. No part of this book may be used or reproduced in any manner whatsoever without written permission except in the case of brief quotations embodied in critical articles or reviews. Let's Go is available for purchase in bulk by institutions and authorized resellers. For information, address St. Martin's Press, 175 Fifth Avenue, New York, NY 10010, USA.

ISBN: 0-312-27028-3

First edition
10 9 8 7 6 5 4 3 2 1

Let's Go: Australia is written by Let's Go Publications, 67 Mount Auburn Street, Cambridge, MA 02138, USA.

Let's Go® and the thumb logo are trademarks of Let's Go, Inc.
Printed in the USA on recycled paper with biodegradable soy ink.

ADVERTISING DISCLAIMER All advertisements appearing in Let's Go publications are sold by an independent agency not affiliated with the editorial production of the guides. Advertisers are never given preferential treatment, and the guides are researched, written, and published independent of advertising. Advertisements do not imply endorsement of products or services by Let's Go, and Let's Go does not vouch for the accuracy of information provided in advertisements.

If you are interested in purchasing advertising space in a Let's Go publication, contact: Let's Go Advertising Sales, 67 Mount Auburn St., Cambridge, MA 02138, USA.

CONTENTS

MAPS

INDONESIA
TIMOR SEA
Darwin
PAPUA NEW GUINEA
CORAL SEA
INDIAN OCEAN
GREAT BARRIER REEF
NORTHERN TERRITORY pp. 235-286
QUEENSLAND pp. 284-404
Tropic of Capricorn
WESTERN AUSTRALIA pp. 607-669
SOUTH AUSTRALIA pp. 405-459
Brisbane
NEW SOUTH WALES pp. 91-234
Perth
Adelaide
Sydney
Canberra
ACT pp. 79-90
Melbourne
0
500 miles
0
500 kilometers
SOUTHERN OCEAN
VICTORIA pp. 499-606
TASMANIA pp. 460-498
Hobart
TASMAN SEA
N
Australia: Chapters

Hospital
Bus Station
Church
Hotel/Hostel
Police
Airport
Synagogue
Food & Drink
Post Office
Train Station
Mountain
Pubs/Nightlife
Tourist Office
Highway
Adult Entertainment
Clubs
Bank
National Park
Winery
Camping
Embassy
Beach
Ranger Station
General/Services
Ferry Landing
Shipwreck
N
The Let's Go thumb always points NORTH.

-10
0
10
20
30
40
°Celsius
°Fahrenheit
30
40
50
60
70
80
90
100
110
120

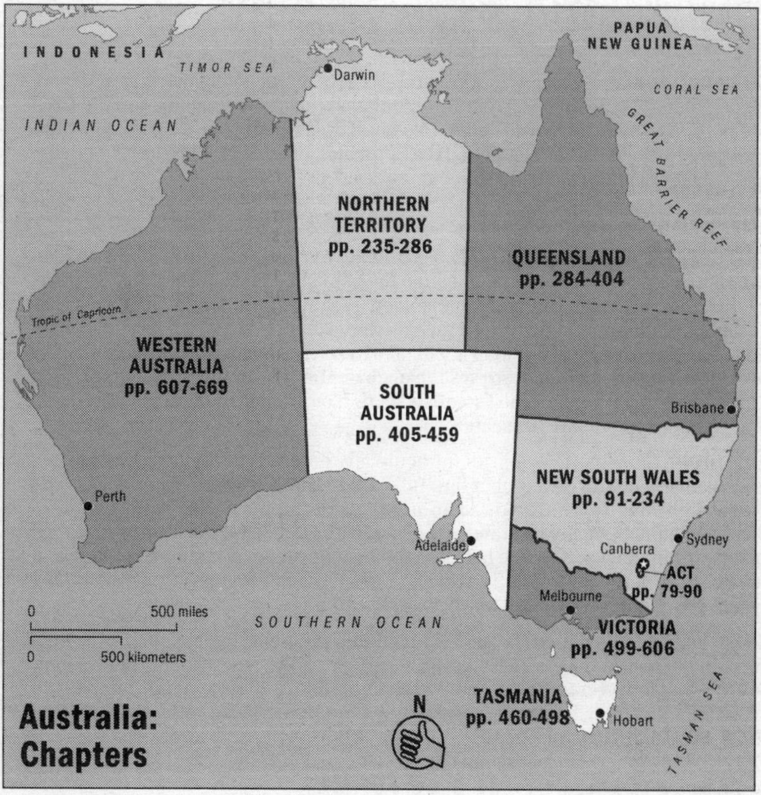

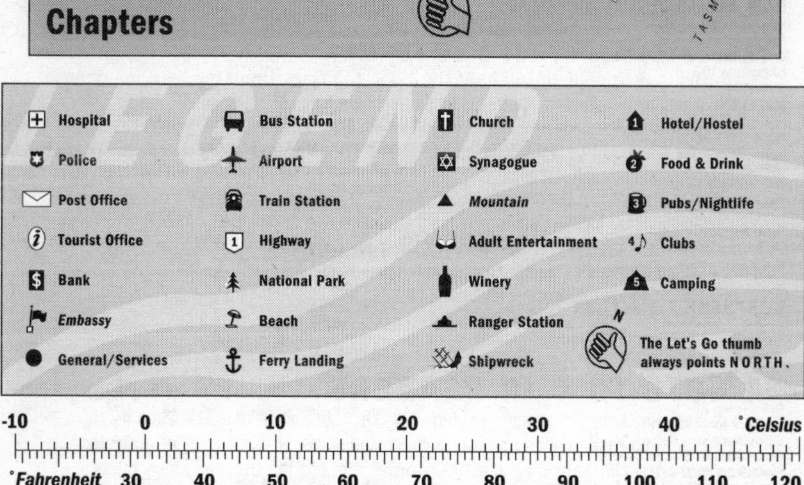

100 meters (m) = 328 feet (ft.) **500m = 1640 ft. = 0.31 miles (mi.)**
1 kilometer (km) = 0.625 mi. **50km = 31.25 mi.** **1 hectare (ha) = 2.47 acres**

HOW TO USE THIS BOOK

Enter into *Let's Go: Australia 2002's* Dreaming

Our "Ancestor Spirits" have come to this Earth in human and other forms (including associate editors, proofers, Research-Writers, etc.), giving not only the land, plants, and animals their current form, but also this book. Eagerly coming from the Spirits of the Land Down Under, this book passes into your welcoming hands. Timeless, with no end or beginning, the Spirits understand the importance of educating and orientating you through our stories.

THE STORY

THE CREATION. These *djang* sites are where the Spirits originally passed through, took shape, or entered or exited the book. The first site, **Discover Australia,** of this book provides you with an overview of travel in Australia, including **Suggested Itineraries** that allow you to recreate the paths of the Spirits unveiling what you shouldn't miss and how long it will take to see it. The **History & Culture** chapter provides you with a original stories the uncover the rich art, culture, and tradition of the Land Down Under. The **Essentials** section outlines the practical information you will need to prepare for search.

THE JOURNEY. Nine R-W spirits miraculously entered Australia's seven states and reemerged with seven chapters full of important stories, experiences, and spirit sightings to guide you. The heart of the book is the eight chapters arranged alphabetically by **state** or **territory,** with the **capital city** always first. The black tabs in the margins will help you to navigate between chapters quickly and easily. In order to help you in travels, Let's Go has provided thumbs-up (☒), where the Spirits were particularly moved.

THE GHOSTS. The appendix (p. 626) contains the lonely spirits unable to take form in the rest of the book. However, these spirits are no less important to your journey—useful temperature conversions, a list of holidays and festivals, a phrasebook of **beer terminology** and handy phrases in **'strine**—exist to help you enjoy the finer points of life.

A FEW NOTES ABOUT LET'S GO FORMAT

A few terms may appear throughout the book that may seem unclear; many are just Australian lingo. **Return,** as in "4km return," means round-trip. All listed prices are in **Australian dollars,** unless otherwise noted. In hostel listings, you'll often see something at the end like **YHA, VIP,** or **NOMADS.** These hostels give discounts (usually $1 per night) to people carrying that type of card (p. 43). **BYO** means you are allowed to "**B**ring **Y**our **O**wn" alcohol into a restaurant; sometimes these places charge **corkage** fees. **Licensed** restaurant sells alcohol. If you're not sure where or what something is check out the **Index** or the **Glossary.**

After experiencing the *Let's Go: Australia 2002* Dreaming, keep the Spirits alive and pass the Dreaming on to others.

A NOTE TO OUR READERS The information for this book was gathered by *Let's Go* researchers from May through August of 2001. Each listing is based on one researcher's opinion, formed during his or her visit at a particular time. Those traveling at other times may have different experiences since prices, dates, hours, and conditions are always subject to change. You are urged to check the facts presented in this book beforehand to avoid inconvenience and surprises.

ABOUT LET'S GO

FORTY-TWO YEARS OF WISDOM

For over four decades, travelers crisscrossing the continents have relied on *Let's Go* for inside information on the hippest backstreet cafes, the most pristine secluded beaches, and the best routes from border to border. *Let's Go: Europe*, now in its 42nd edition and translated into seven languages, reigns as the world's bestselling international travel guide. In the last 20 years, our rugged researchers have stretched the frontiers of backpacking and expanded our coverage into the Americas, Australia, Asia, and Africa (including the new *Let's Go: Egypt* and the more comprehensive, multi-country jaunt through *Let's Go: South Africa & Southern Africa*). Our new-and-improved City Guide series continues to grow with new guides to perennial European favorites Amsterdam and Barcelona. This year we are also unveiling *Let's Go: Southwest USA*, the flagship of our new outdoor Adventure Guide series, which is complete with special roadtripping tips and itineraries, more coverage of adventure activities like hiking and mountain biking, and first-person accounts of life on the road.

It all started in 1960 when a handful of well-traveled students at Harvard University handed out a 20-page mimeographed pamphlet offering a collection of their tips on budget travel to passengers on student charter flights to Europe. The following year, in response to the instant popularity of the first volume, students traveling to Europe researched the first full-fledged edition of *Let's Go: Europe*. Throughout the 60s and 70s, our guides reflected the times—in 1969, for example, we taught you how to get from Paris to Prague on "no dollars a day" by singing in the street. In the 90s we focused in on the world's most exciting urban areas to produce in-depth, fold-out map guides, now with 20 titles (from Hong Kong to Chicago) and counting. Our new guides bring the total number of titles to 57, each infused with the spirit of adventure and voice of opinion that travelers around the world have come to count on. But some things never change: our guides are still researched, written, and produced entirely by students who know first-hand how to see the world on the cheap.

HOW WE DO IT

Each guide is completely revised and thoroughly updated every year by a well-traveled set of nearly 300 students. Every spring, we recruit over 200 researchers and 90 editors to overhaul every book. After several months of training, researcher-writers hit the road for seven weeks of exploration, from Anchorage to Adelaide, Estonia to El Salvador, Iceland to Indonesia. Hired for their rare combination of budget travel sense, writing ability, stamina, and courage, these adventurous travelers know that train strikes, stolen luggage, food poisoning, and marriage proposals are all part of a day's work. Back at our offices, editors work from spring to fall, massaging copy written on Himalayan bus rides into witty, informative prose. A student staff of typesetters, cartographers, publicists, and managers keeps our lively team together. In September, the collected efforts of the summer are delivered to our printer, who turns them into books in record time, so that you have the most up-to-date information available for your vacation. Even as you read this, work on next year's editions is well underway.

WHY WE DO IT

We don't think of budget travel as the last recourse of the destitute; we believe that it's the only way to travel. Our books will ease your anxieties and answer your questions about the basics—so you can get off the beaten track and explore. Once you learn the ropes, we encourage you to put *Let's Go* down and strike out on your own. You know as well as we that the best discoveries are often those you make yourself. When you find something worth sharing, please drop us a line. We're Let's Go Publications, 67 Mount Auburn St., Cambridge, MA 02138, USA (feedback@letsgo.com). For more info, visit our website, www.letsgo.com.

RESEARCHER-WRITERS

Steve Collins *ACT, Southern and Coastal NSW, and Victoria Ski Fields*

Ranger Steve C. jumped into his research head first, only to resurface a short time ago. To our delight, though his investigative skills might have caused intermittent disappearances in the bush, he returned outstanding copy.

Alice Farmer *South Australia and Great Ocean Road, Victoria*

The fabulous and dedicated Miss Alice left no stone unturned and no rental car unharmed in her trip through Australia. Despite a few too many trips to the wineries, this former *Let's Go* Managing Editor always churned out stellar copy. This shining star was so bright, she even caused a few blackouts in Victoria.

John Fiore *Northern Territory and the Kimberley, WA*

As a former *Let's Go* Map Manager and office Superstar, we knew we could trust John to explore the untouched, uncharted, and unrevealed outback. Along the track, he discovered...well, the places *to put on* the map. With a keen eye, and often a pen in his hand, John unfortunately sometimes forgot to look up.

Nathan Foley-Mendelssohn *Western Australia*

An editor of *Let's Go: California 2001*, while Nate opted to get out of the office he stuck to his love for a western coast. Though a man a few words, we soon found out that Nate is a man of many actions. The question remains: did he really go to Ningaloo Blue or did he spend his money more wisely somewhere else?

Christine Monta *Melbourne, Victoria, and Far West New South Wales*

Guarana-guzzling Agent X conquered Australia with surprising ease and confidence. A straight-up, no-fuss researcher, Ms. X came as a blessing. Scantily clad each night in a *Let's Go* wool hat to battle the Victorian winter, the girl's even got style. Priscilla? Step aside—Chrissy is the true Queen of the Desert.

Matthew Shea O'Hare *Southern Queensland*

Oh, oh, Matty O. Mr. O'Hare, sometimes forgetful of the time difference, never failed to keep in touch with the editors back home. A veteran to Oz, Matty was eager to return to the land down under for one last hurrah. A upstanding young man and a navigator of the nightlife, he was a valued member of Oz 2002.

Meredith Osborn *Northern Queensland*

Overwhelmed by the beer chugging backpackers on the coast, Meredith turned inland and found solace in the outback. She battled undeveloped roads like a true jilleroo, never disheartened, even if the only thing she came upon was another cattle station or outback pub. From wherever her inspiration hailed, she managed to capture the essence of life on the road.

Johs Pierce *Tasmania and Gippsland, Victoria*

The Editor of *Let's Go: Britain & Ireland 2001*, Johs opted for a whirl around the colonies this year, giving the Tasmanian devil a run for his money in the process. In Tasmania, headlines heralded the arrival of our beer-swilling winner of the most easy-going researcher award.

Jevan Soo *Sydney and Northern New South Wales*

After finally learning how to order a coffee in Oz, Jevan was ready to be an RW star. Crack-free and always wearing a smile, he ventured to seaside ports, to his "own private circle of hell," to outback nothingness, and yes, the Mothership, Sydney. Who could ask for anything more? We sure couldn't.

ACKNOWLEDGMENTS

The Let's Go 2002 series is dedicated to the memory of Haley Surti

TEAM OZ 2002 THANKS: To the most hardcore RWs in the Southern Hemisphere; Nathaniel for taking care of us, mappin' Brooks; our AUS/NZ pod—hardcore Holly, calm Chris, and seductive Sharmi; SEAS; Production Gods and Goddess Jen, Caleb, and Melissa; fourth floor love; to Anne Chisholm, the glue of LG; and the precious flip 'n' tucks.

KU: To an unbelievable bookteam—only pure love for Gretchen (and to SEAS for splitting her), Loran, and the RW's who dove head first into Oz. To the best pod in LG for the chaos; HF and CC for setting us straight in hard times; SS for the wall of love. To Sarah R. for introducing me to Mama Go. To understanding from the Pudding (and Greg) and FAP. To AJ, Anand, and TRJ. To Aaliyah (& DD), Lisa F., ECG, BL, JRS, SAP, HRST and July 4th crew. To my cousins in Oz, who got me hooked. To all the love I missed (you know what I mean) in Ashland and H-town. To the continuous support and unconditional love from Amma, Acha, Ramu, and Ammu. **For Haley.**

LCF: To Krishnan and Gretchen for putting up with my antics; Sandra for being there no matter what; JDM II for lots of laughs, crazy times, unreal stories, and the ray gun; big ups to the SCC (Daniel, James, TDP, Brandon, and all tha rest) for 'dem times in Funky Town; Asher for those sprints; Dan for the networking; Eric for being chill; Gene for the talk; Nin Nin, Robert, and Carl, I'll see you soon; Nana Marge, I miss you; the McGee's for all the help; HRFC, I have a pet kangaroo; Awol for sippin' on that Kris; Mom and Dad, for missing me but understanding, I love you both.

GCP: To K and L for late night havoc from the start; to (my first, but not only) love: SEAS, sorry to be MIA in the last stretch; the RWs for their endurance. Thanks to Lize for being my best critic; to Lizzy for motivating the crazy girl in me; to the roomies who I know will always be there, you are the best. Much love to the boy in Coogee for believing in me and laughing with me. Last, to the millennium family: for letting me explore the world, for guiding me but not directing me, and always trusting my stubborn ways.

Editor
Krishnan Unnikrishnan
Associate Editors
Loran C. Fredric, Gretchen C. Puttkamer
Managing Editor
Nathaniel Popper
Map Editor
Brooks Newkirk

Publishing Director
Sarah P. Rotman
Editor-in-Chief
Ankur N. Ghosh
Production Manager
Jen Taylor
Cartography Manager
Dan Barnes
Design & Photo Manager
Vanessa Bertozzi
Editorial Managers
Amélie Cherlin, Naz F. Firoz, Matthew Gibson, Sharmi Surianarain, Brian R. Walsh
Financial Manager
Rebecca L. Schoff
Marketing & Publicity Managers
Brady R. Dewar, Katharine Douglas, Marly Ohlsson
New Media Manager
Kevin H. Yip
Online Manager
Alex Lloyd
Personnel Manager
Nathaniel Popper
Production Associates
Steven Aponte, Chris Clayton, Caleb S. Epps, Eduardo Montoya, Melissa Rudolph
Some Design
Melissa Rudolph
Office Coordinators
Efrat Kussell, Peter Richards

Director of Advertising Sales
Adam M. Grant
Senior Advertising Associates
Ariel Shwayder, Kennedy Thorwarth
Advertising Associate
Jennie Timoney
Advertising Artwork Editor
Peter Henderson

President
Cindy L. Rodriguez
General Manager
Robert B. Rombauer
Assistant General Manager
Anne E. Chisholm

INDONESIA
Melville Island
Bathurst Island
TIMOR SEA
Darwin
ARNHE
Katherine
INDIAN OCEAN
Wyndham
Kununurra
THE KIMBERLEY
Derby
Halls Creek
Broome
Fitzroy Crossing
Tennant Creek
NORTH
TERRI
GREAT SANDY DESERT
Port Hedland
Onslow
Exmouth
Tom Price
Alice Springs
MACDONNEL
GIBSON DESERT
Uluru
(Ayers Rock)
WESTERN
AUSTRALIA
Carnarvon
Shark Bay
Denham
GREAT VICTORIA DESERT
SOUT
AUST
Geraldton
NULLARBOR PLAIN
Kalgoorlie-Boulder
Coolgardie
Norseman
Perth
Fremantle
GREAT AUSTRALIAN BIGHT
Bunbury
Esperance
Augusta
Albany
SOUTHERN OCEAN
N
0
200 miles
0
200 kilometers
Australia

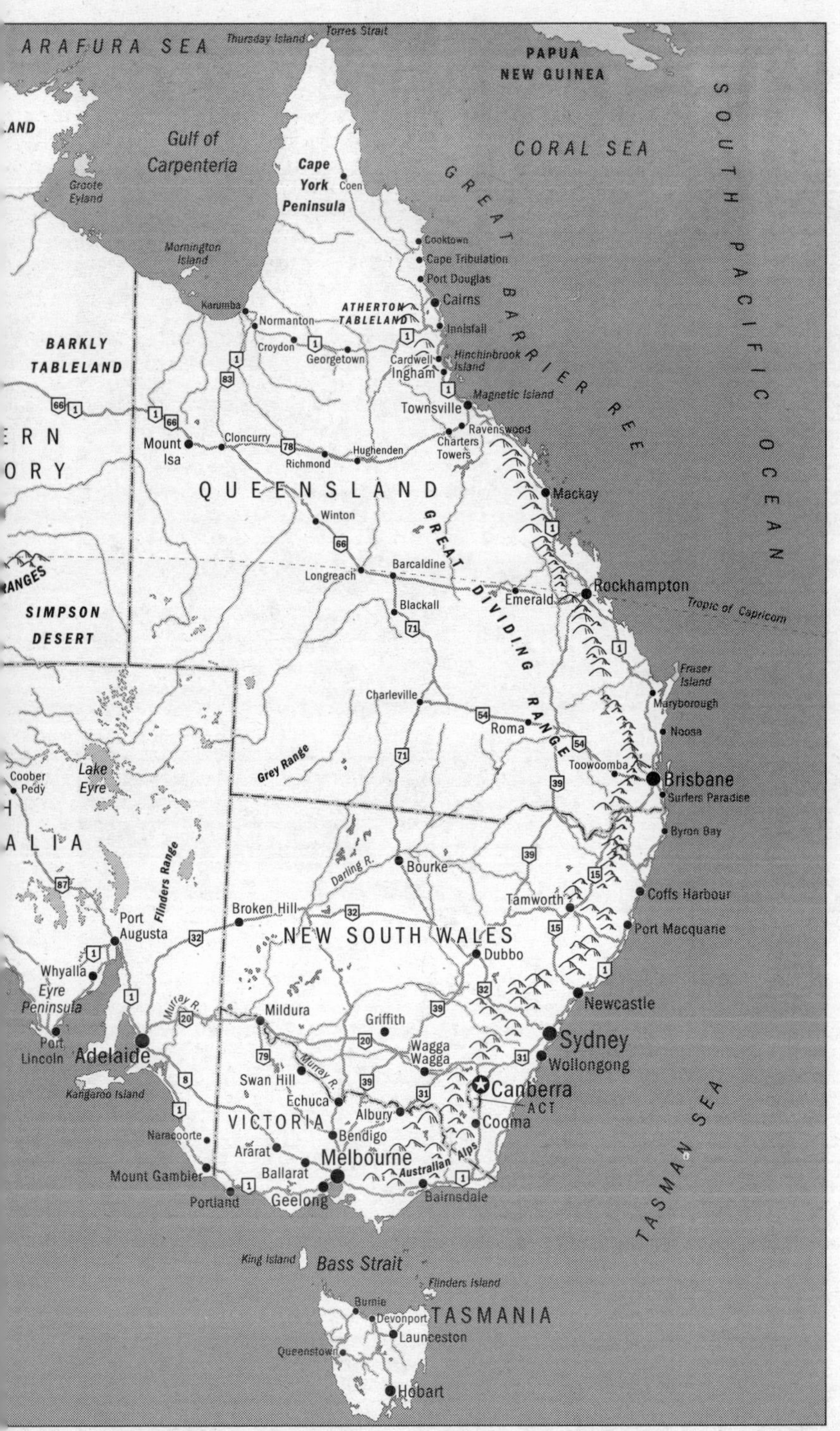

ARAFURA SEA
Thursday Island
Torres Strait
PAPUA
NEW GUINEA
CORAL SEA
SOUTH PACIFIC OCEAN
Gulf of
Carpenteria
Groote
Eyland
Mornington
Island
Cape
York
Peninsula
Coen
GREAT BARRIER REEF
Cooktown
Cape Tribulation
Port Douglas
Cairns
ATHERTON
TABLELAND
Innisfail
Karumba
Normanton
Croydon
Georgetown
Cardwell
Hinchinbrook
Island
Ingham
BARKLY
TABLELAND
Magnetic Island
Townsville
Ravenswood
Charters
Towers
Mount
Isa
Cloncurry
Richmond
Hughenden
QUEENSLAND
Mackay
Winton
GREAT DIVIDING RANGE
Barcaldine
Longreach
Rockhampton
Emerald
Tropic of Capricorn
Blackall
SIMPSON
DESERT
Fraser
Island
Maryborough
Charleville
Roma
Noosa
Toowoomba
Brisbane
Surfers Paradise
Grey Range
Coober
Pedy
Lake
Eyre
Byron Bay
Bourke
Darling R.
Flinders Range
Coffs Harbour
Tamworth
Broken Hill
Port
Augusta
NEW SOUTH WALES
Port Macquarie
Dubbo
Whyalla
Eyre
Peninsula
Newcastle
Murray R.
Mildura
Griffith
Port
Lincoln
Adelaide
Sydney
Wagga
Wagga
Wollongong
Swan Hill
Murray R.
Canberra
Kangaroo Island
Echuca
ACT
Albury
Cooma
VICTORIA
Bendigo
Naracoorte
Ararat
Melbourne
Australian Alps
Mount Gambier
Ballarat
Portland
Geelong
Bairnsdale
TASMAN SEA
King Island
Bass Strait
Flinders Island
Burnie
Devonport
TASMANIA
Launceston
Queenstown
Hobart

Mooooore Room.

Real American Airlines deals for students and faculty, online at StudentUniverse. Earn AAdvantage miles and enjoy *more room throughout Coach only on American**.

StudentUniverse.com

featuring AmericanAirlines

800.272.9676

RESTRICTIONS: A portion of or all travel may be on American Eagle, American's regional airline affiliate. American Airlines, American Eagle and AAdvantage are marks of American Airlines, Inc. American Airlines reserves the right to change AAdvantage program rules, regulations, travel awards and special offers at any time without notice, and to end the AAdvantage program with six months notice. American Airlines is not responsible for products or services by other participating companies. *Only American has removed rows of seats throughout Coach to provide more room for more Coach passengers than any other airline. Now available on all two-class aircraft; three-class aircraft reconfiguration in progress; not available on American Eagle.

DISCOVER AUSTRALIA

For the indigenous people, the stark terrain of the Land Down Under, which had scared so many others, was actually a vibrant landscape carved and populated by sacred spirits: the deserts, canyons, rainforests, and valleys were embodied by these Dreaming creatures. The British convicts who settled this land were sent against their will into presumed desolation, a vast emptiness on the other side of the world. But the Aboriginals who had occupied Australia for thousands of years respected and honored its natural beauty. The Australia of myth is big, hot, and empty, but the reality, like the Dream, presents endless possibility. The outback—the *never never*—is only a little distant from the populated coasts, allowing travelers to zig zag between the underwater majesty of the Great Barrier Reef and the eerily calm beauty of the Red Centre, or seek a middle ground in the 37,000 kilometers of pristine beach. In Australia the ends of exploration are left to the limits of the individual. You can splice the mystery of the outback with a coastal journey or completely live it with a rugged bushwalk through Tasmanian wilderness or a solitary drive on the world's longest straight-away. This problem-free paradise promises that you will be left alone as much as you want; the people aren't pushy, and the great cities are welcoming oases of civilization in which you will never feel left out. In the end, Australia is not for someone else, it is for you—to lose and find yourself, to make it up as you go along, to travel in a pure sense that more trafficked travel destinations can no longer offer. Visitors come for a full view of it all—the outback, the coast, the Aboriginal lore, the modern culture—and leave with at least a glimpse of themselves. Australia used to be on the other side of what early explorers deemed a flat world; fear prevented them from heading over the oceans. But today we know the world is round. *Never never?* Now.

FACTS AND FIGURES

CAPITAL: Canberra

HUMAN POPULATION: 18.6 million

SHEEP POPULATION: 37 million

NUMBER OF BEACHES: About 7000

WEST-TO-EAST DISTANCE: 4000km

PERCENT LARGER THAN BRITAIN, ITS FORMER COLONIALIST RULER: 3152%

PERCENT OF THE WORLD'S OPALS: 90%

BEER PER AUSTRALIAN: 96L beer/yr.

KINDS OF KANGAROOS: 60

AMOUNT OF FOLIAGE KOALAS MUST EAT EACH DAY TO SURVIVE: 9kg (about 20lb.)

AMOUNT OF DAMAGE TO CROPS CAUSED BY RABBITS EACH YEAR: over AUS $1 billion

MOST VALIANT ATTEMPT TO KEEP THE BITCHES OFF EWE: World's longest fence (5,531km/3,435 mi.) keeps Queensland's dingoes in the north away from sheep in the south.

NUMBER OF ABBREVIATIONS ENDING IN THE SOUND "EE": Infinite—midgie, bluey, barbie, esky, dummy, mozzie...

WHEN TO GO

Australia is big. Really big. When to travel depends on where you want to go and what you want to do. Crowds and prices of everything from flights to hostel bunks tend to be directly proportional to the quality of the weather.

In the south, the **seasons** of the temperate climate zone are reversed from those in the Northern Hemisphere. Summer lasts from December to February, autumn from March to May, winter from June to August, and spring from September to November. In general, Australian winters are mild, comparable to the southern U.S. or southern Europe; snow is infrequent except in the mountains, though in winter it's far too cold to have much fun at the beach. The north is an entirely different story—many people forget that over one-third of Australia is in the tropics, where it's always hot. Seasons here are defined not by the almost-constant temperature but by the wildly varying precipitation. **"The Wet"** lasts from November to April, and **"the Dry"** is from May to October (p. 253). During the Wet, heavy downpours and violent storms plague Australia, especially on the north coast. During the Dry, nearly every section of Australia endures a drought. Traveling in the Wet is not recommended for the faint of heart; the heavy rains, washing out unsealed roads, make driving a challenge in non-urban areas.

Diving on the Great Barrier Reef is seasonal as well; January and February are rainy months, and the water is clearest between April and October. The toxic box jellyfish is most common around the east coast between October and April. Ski season in New South Wales and Victoria runs from late June to September, and the famous wildflowers of Western Australia bloom from September to December. For help planning when and where to go, read below, and see the chart of **temperature and rainfall** data and the list of major **holidays and festivals** on p. 672.

THINGS TO DO

Australia's abundant wilderness and unique geography could keep almost any traveler busy for years. Every topography and natural wonder can be explored on the continent, from rainforests abuzz with the chatter of wildlife to eerily quiet red deserts, from jagged mountains to tamed beaches. This chapter offers a brief glimpse at some of its more popular attractions. For more specific regional attractions, see the **Highlights of the Region** section at the beginning of each chapter.

SAND AND SURF

Great beaches are everywhere—Australia is an island continent, after all. Beachlife can mean lounging in the sun with cool drinks and swarms of happy sunbathers or quiet solitude among expansive dunes and gently lapping waves. **Bondi** and **Coogee** beaches in **Sydney** (p. 94) are crowded and glamorous. The ocean off Queensland's **Fraser Island** (p. 337) lets you look at pristine beauty but not touch. **Whitehaven Beach** in the **Whitsunday Islands** (p. 357) paints perfect white sand against azure waters. The green hills at Broome's **Cable Beach** (p. 656) tumble softly into the Indian Ocean.

Surf's up in the land down under, and the east coast takes center stage. The waves at **Surfers Paradise** (p. 314) are perfect for beginners, and a little farther south, **Coolongatta** (p. 312) is the place for pros, **Duranbah** for fast waves, **Kirra** and **Snapper Rocks** for some of the best surfing in the world. In New South Wales, **Byron Bay** (p. 189) and Newcastle's **Nobby's Beach** (p. 156) are among the country's most popular spots, whereas **Lennox Head** (p. 196) is home to one of the longest right-hand breaks in the world. On the southern coast, Victoria's **Bell's Beach** in Torquay (p. 544) hosts the annual Rip Curl Classic. Though not as popular as the east coast's veritable surfing carnivals, the crowds love **Yallingup** (p. 625) in Western Australia and Bruny Island's **Cloudy Bay** (p. 473) in Tasmania.

SCUBA DIVING

Whether you're a seasoned scuba diver or a determined beginner, you've probably got "see the Great Barrier Reef" scrawled on your list of things to do in your lifetime. And for good reason—off the coast of Queensland, the 2000km reef system encompasses hundreds of islands and cays and thousands of smaller coral reefs, rendering the marine wonderland available to anyone. Most choose to venture out from **Cairns** (p. 373), the main gateway to the reef. Further south, on the doorstep of the reef, the sunken **S.S. Yongala** near **Townsville** (p. 361) is one of the best wreck dives in the world. **Airlie Beach** (p. 353) draws backpackers ready to leave the bars for the thrill of the reefs. Though the Great Barrier Reef is quintessential, most coasts have good diving spots. In New South Wales, the diving in **Batesman's Bay** (p. 205) is second only to the Reef. In South Australia, **Innes National Park** (p. 443) yields access to the Southern Ocean's depths. In Western Australia, giant whale sharks patrol **Ningaloo Reef** in **Exmouth** (p. 648), making for an exhilarating dive. For those looking to learn how to dive, the cheapest certification courses can be found in Queensland at **Hervey Bay** (p. 334), **Bundaberg** (p. 340), and **Magnetic Island** (p. 365). For additional diving information, see **The Great Barrier Reef** (p. 287).

THE OUTBACK

The draw of the outback is mythical, yet magnetic. Geographically confined by the continent's more developed coasts, Australia's outback seems like the most never-ending place on earth. Every year, both travelers and Aussies take on the *never never*, hoping to find a little piece of adventure and a lot of peace of mind. In the west, the red dust and bushland of the **Pilbara** (p. 649) extend limitlessly on every horizon. During the Dry season, the **Kimberley** (p. 655) opens to the insanely courageous who rumble along the **Gibb River Road** (p. 664), the roughest but most stunning drive in the world. In the Northern Territory, **Kakadu National Park** (p. 249) is a gateway to another world of thundering waterfalls, snapping crocs, and mystical beauty. The Aboriginal homeland **Arnhem Land** (p. 258) is the essence of the outback, yet virtually inaccessible. In Australia's Red Centre, imposing **Uluru (Ayers Rock)** (p. 284) keeps a dignified 360° watch over the rest of the outback. Its cousin **Kata Tjuta** (p. 286) revels in solitude, yielding its more poignant beauty only to those who haven't gone Rock-crazy. Down into South Australia, **Coober Pedy** (p. 451) playfully affirms the Down Under mentality—scorching temperatures force residents to carve their homes underground. The **Nullarbor** (p. 457 and p. 640) is a desolate blight, perfect for true solitude. For travelers who won't make it out of the east, Queensland's outback **mining towns** (p. 393) and New South Wales's **Broken Hill** (p. 229) are on the fringe but offer a taste of what lies within.

NATIONAL PARKS AND UNTAMED WILD

Australia has a national park around every corner. The parks preserve all types of terrain—from rainforest to desert, from mountain to coast. Hands-down, the Northern Territory has the best national parks in Australia. The itinerary-topping **Uluru (Ayers Rock)** (p. 284) and timeless **Kakadu** (p. 249) ensure the other (some say better) Territory parks stay more pristine and untrammeled. The **Macdonnell Ranges** (p. 276) have some of the continent's best hiking, and just next door is the spectacular **Kings Canyon** (p. 280). Up the track, the write-home-to-Ma lookouts of **Nitmiluk (Katherine Gorge)** (p. 264) are equalled by the surprising waterfalls of **Litchfield** (p. 260). In Queensland, lush rainforest complements the nearby reef from the tip of **Cape York** (p. 395) all the way down to **Eungella** (p. 351). In New South Wales, the **Blue Mountains** (p. 134) attracts avid abseilers and in winter **Kosciuszko** (p. 211) becomes a warren of ski bunnies and bums. **Wilsons Promontory** (p. 592) in Victoria is the most beautiful part of the southern coast. Tasmania is Australia's hiking mecca; the **Overland Track** (p. 480) is one of the best bushwalks in the world. South Australia's **Flinders Ranges** (p. 444) cater to the truly hardcore. Struggling not to be denied, Western Australia showcases marine life—whales and dolphins defend the hype behind **Bunbury** (p. 623) and **Monkey Mia** (p. 645).

ABORIGINAL CULTURE

Aboriginals traditionally see a strong connection between the earth and its inhabitants. During the "Dreaming," they believe, spirits carved the canyons and gorges and came to life as animals and trees. The spirituality of the Aboriginals will never be fully incorporated in modern Australian culture, but the significance of their people and beliefs is everywhere. In New South Wales, **Mungo National Park** (p. 234) records the earliest Aboriginal presence. Sacred regions and timeless rock art sites penetrate from **Tasmania** (p. 460) in the far south to **Kakadu National Park** (p. 249) in the Northern Territory's Top End. Though lore has become popular among tourists, increasing the chances of glitz overwhelming tradition, **Tjapukai** (p. 382) near Cairns, **Brambuk Living Cultural Centre** (p. 556) in Grampians National Park, and **Warradjan Aboriginal Cultural Centre** (p. 250) in Kakadu National Park all present intelligent and fair histories of "Dreaming" stories and European interaction. Modern Aboriginal art can be found in small galleries in larger cities, but the **National Gallery** in Canberra (p. 79) has the continent's best collection.

CITY SIGHTS

Australia's mythical outback spirit and dominant rugged beauty might have made it easy for travelers to bypass city life altogether. But, Australia's cosmopolitan meccas shine from under the veneer of obscurity. **Sydney** (p. 94) thrives under several influences—the city center demonstrates European roots; Haymarket is the city's fast-growing Chinatown; bohemian Glebe speaks up for university life; and the sands of Bondi play home to the beach crowd. Melding international culture with a typical Aussie laid-back attitude, **Melbourne** (p. 500) offers more style than Sydney with less hype. With incredible nightlife, a chill daytime cafe society, and a bustling budget food scene, all as backdrop to the mad and venerable Melbourne Cricket Ground, Melbourne is truly the continent's best city. **Canberra** (p. 79), the orderly capital, gives travelers a sense of Aussie business and government. Like the smooth jazz notes of its clubs, **Brisbane** eases coastal backpackers into urban culture. **Hobart** is a civilized bastion in the Tasmanian wild. The antithesis of a tourist trap, the country town of **Adelaide** lives at a slower pace. Farther from the east, **Perth** (p. 607) and **Darwin** (p. 238) grant relaxing coastal stretches and hopping nightlife on the other edge of the *never never*.

WINE

Though not known for its cuisine, Australia has recently acquired an international reputation for the quality of its victual spirits. All throughout Australia, scores of tiny boutique vineyards dot random small towns and river banks. Just follow your nose and keep your wallet in your pocket—most wine tastings are absolutely free. The premier, and most touristed, wine region is New South Wales's **Hunter Valley** (p. 146). West across the Victoria border, **Rutherglen** (p. 585) is smaller but it's proximity to the **Milawa Cheese Region** (p. 584) will whet your *fromage*-inclined palette. Just south, the **Yarra Valley** (p. 537) is Victoria's best donation to the wine scene. At the end of the wine trail, South Australia's **Barossa** (p. 431) and **Clare Valleys** (p. 435) rival the quality of the Hunter without the hype.

LET'S GO PICKS

HARDEST TOWN TO FIND ON A MAP: The asbestos-ridden "town" of **Wittenoom, WA** (p. 653).

MOST HAREM-LIKE SETTING: The mating whales off the coast of Augusta, WA (p. 628), or the lounge of comfort in Solar Couch Cafe, **Newcastle, NSW** (p. 160).

BEST FACE-LIFT: The dreaded neighbor's house in **St. Kilda, VIC** (p. 516) or the $2.5 million renovations to the **Kalgoorlie, WA** brothel scene (p. 639).

BEST UNDERGROUND SCENE: The underground city of **Coober Pedy, SA** (p. 451) or the never-ending thump of clubs all over **Melbourne, VIC** (p. 531).

BEST MEAT PIE: The Pinnacle Hotel, **Pinnacle, QLD** (p. 351) or a different type of meat at The Beat in **Brisbane, QLD** (p. 306).

BEST OXYMORON: The dry rainforest in **Long Point, NSW** (p. 154).

BEST WAYS TO GET HIGH: Atop Australia's highest peak, **Mt. Kosciuszko, VIC** (p. 208) or above the smoky clouds in **Nimbin, NSW** (p. 187).

BEST PLACE TO GET WRECKED: At the best wreck dive in the world, the *S.S. Yongala*, off **Townsville, QLD** (p. 361), or for free in the wine vineyards of the **Barossa Valley, NSW** (p. 431).

BEST PARTY OUT OF THE CLOSET: The world-famous, utterly insane, party of a lifetime at the **Sydney Gay and Lesbian Mardi Gras** (p. 126).

BEST PLACE TO TAKE A LOAD OFF: In the state-of-the-art toilets of **Halls Creek, WA** (p. 662) or relaxing at Wineglass Bay, **Freycinet National Park, TAS** (p. 495).

BEST COUNTRY TO VISIT: Australia, that big continent in the South Pacific.

SUGGESTED ITINERARIES

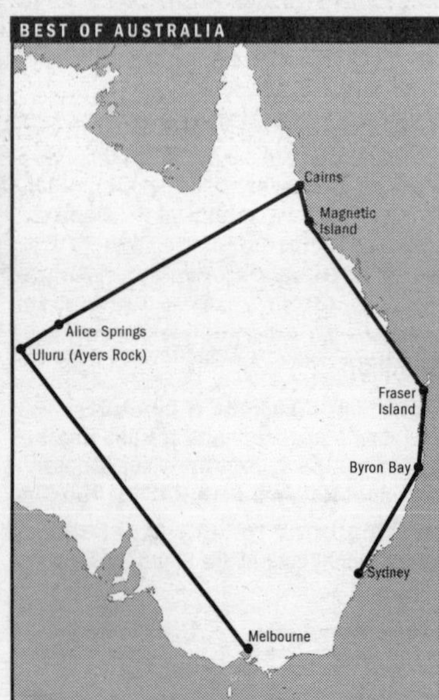

BEST OF AUSTRALIA (3 WEEKS). Cosmopolitan **Sydney** (p. 94) begins this tour of the continent's highlights. Heading north up the coast, get a taste of the surf before having your aura read in **Byron Bay** (p. 189). Hop into Queensland and across to the constantly-changing sand dunes of **Fraser Island** (p. 337). Check out what you came to Oz for, the Great Barrier reef, on a dive from **Magnetic Island** (p. 365) before heading farther north to **Cairns** (p. 373). Perhaps snorkel a day or two or check out the World Heritage rainforest before catching a flight to the Northern Territory's **Alice Springs** (p. 270). From this most famous of Outback towns, it's just a short trip to the most famous of Australian icons: **Uluru (Ayers Rock)** (p. 283) and **Kata Tjuta (the Olgas)** (p. 283). From Alice, fly to **Melbourne** (p. 500), the cultural heart of Oz. To make a loop, bus directly back to Sydney or reverse the All Points South itinerary.

SUN, SURF, AND SHOUTS (3-4 WEEKS). The beaches and nightlife of **Sydney** (p. 94) set a high standard from the start, and the vineyards of the **Hunter Valley** (p. 146) bring an air of sophistication to the effort of getting housed. People like to tie one on in **Coffs Harbour** (p. 178), while chill **Byron Bay** (p. 189) brings surfing and relaxation. For those who want to learn how to party, **Surfers Paradise** (p. 314) offers a crash course that will serve you well up the coast. **Brisbane's** (p. 293) smoky jazz clubs are a debonair break from backpacker culture. For a return to natural beauty, travel off the coast to the gorgeous beaches of **Fraser** (p. 337) and **Great Keppel Islands** (p. 346). After recuperating from a big night in **Airlie Beach** (p. 346), go scuba diving or sailing to the **Whitsunday Islands** (p. 357). The next necessary stops, **Townsville** (p. 360) and **Magnetic Island** (p. 365) promise not only a vacation where the sun is always shining, but also some of the cheapest and best diving on the Great Barrier Reef. **Mission Beach** (p. 369) maintains a long sliver of sparkling white silica and popular diving charters. Tropical **Cairns** (p. 373) sums the whole coastal route with unlimited diving, adventure activities, and hearty backpacker nightlife. If you've got another day, investigate the rainforests and less crowded reef just north in **Port Douglas** (p. 387).

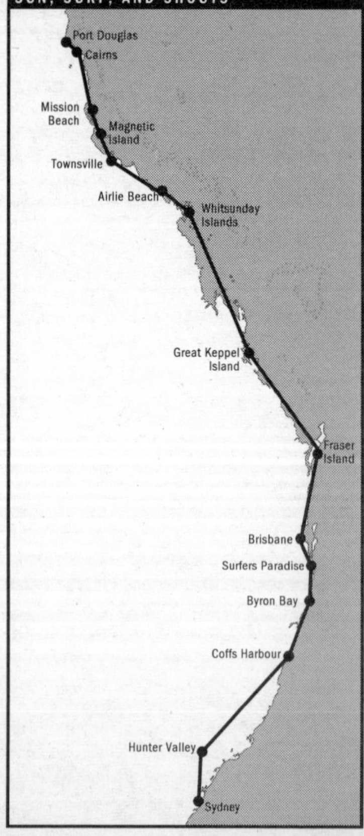

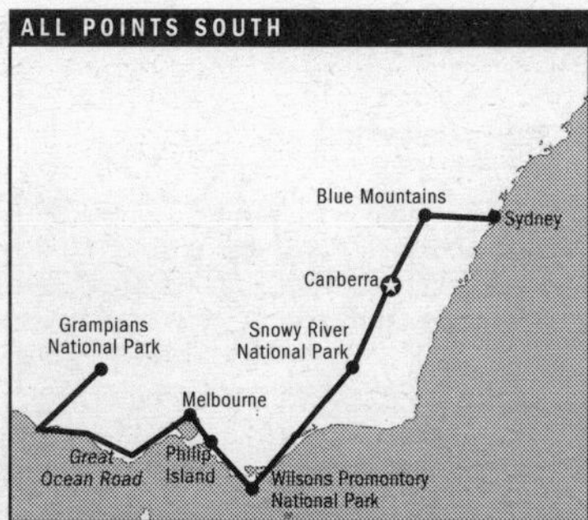

ALL POINTS SOUTH (2 WEEKS). After exploring **Sydney** (p. 94), head out for some abseiling and sightseeing in the **Blue Mountains** (p. 134). The nation's capital, **Canberra** (p. 79), offers insights into the higher cultural, and lower political, aspects of the country. Stop to do some hiking in the rugged **Snowy River National Park** (p. 601) on your way to the coastal wonders of **Wilsons Promontory National Park** (p. 592). Stop at **Philip Island** (p. 538) to watch the adorable penguins at dusk before sliding west into **Melbourne** (p. 500) for an injection of funk, nightlife, and cafe culture. Further west, fall in love with the **Great Ocean Road** (p. 543) before taking a break for another natural high, the jagged peaks of **Grampians National Park** (p. 556).

WILD WILD WEST
The Kimberley
Broome
Exmouth
Karijini National Park
Shark Bay & Monkey Mia
Geraldton
The Pinnacles
Rottnest Island
Perth
Fremantle

WILD WILD WEST (2-3 WEEKS). This itinerary is particularly ideal between August and November when Western Australia is carpeted in wildflowers. Base yourself in **Perth** (p. 607) while you get lost in the history of **Fremantle** (p. 617), bike around beautiful **Rottnest Island** (p. 621), and daytrip out to the eerie limestone pillars rising from the dunes at the **Pinnacles** (p. 642). Heading north, learn to windsurf in **Geraldton** (p. 642), before frolicking with the dolphins of **Monkey Mia** (p. 645) in Western Australia's only World Heritage Area, **Shark Bay** (p. 645). Dive into the ocean off of **Exmouth** (p. 648), then swim in the plunge pools within the red gorges of **Karijini National Park** (p. 653). The wayward tourist destination of **Broome** (p. 656) entices backpackers with pristine beaches and serves as a gateway to the indescribable wilderness adventure that is **The Kimberley** (p. 655).

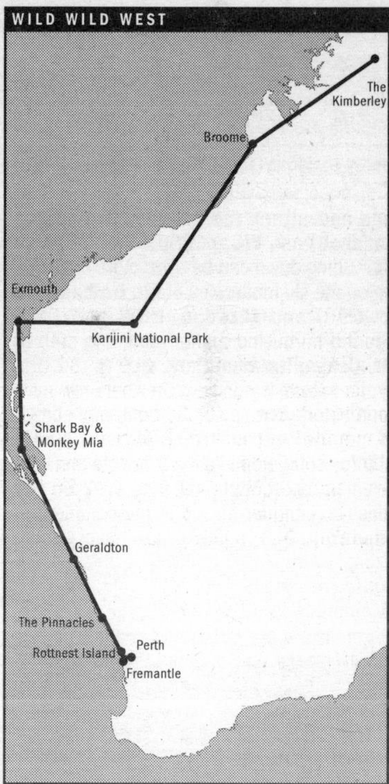

DEVIL-BE-DAMNED ADVENTURE (UP TO A LIFETIME). Think you're hardcore? Think again. Start just outside of **Perth, WA** (p. 607) to hike the 964km **Bibbulman Track** (p. 623) to **Albany, WA** (p. 632). Now prepare for the grueling desert haul crossing the **Nullarbor Plain** from **Norseman, WA** (p. 636) to **Ceduna, SA** (p. 456). Stretch your

DEVIL-BE-DAMNED ADVENTURE

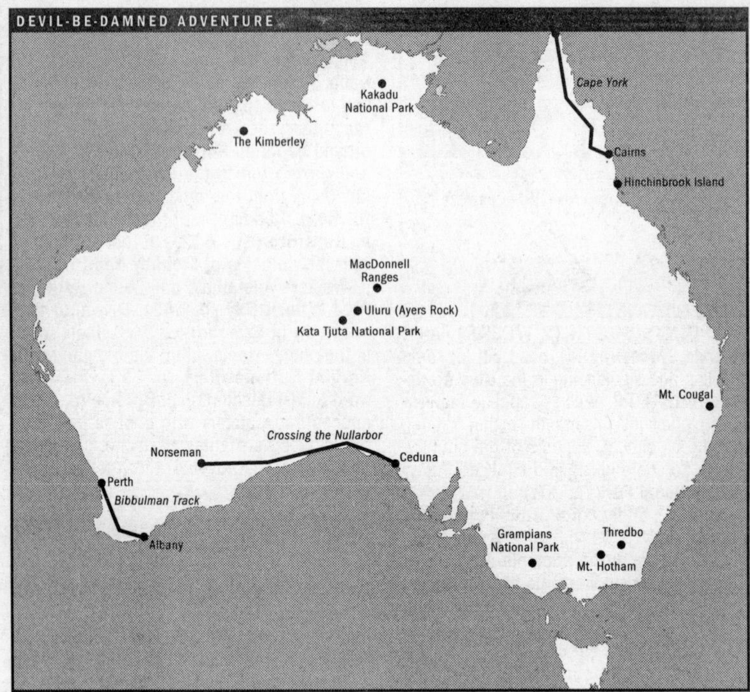

legs and attack the hikes of **Grampians National Park, VIC** (p. 556). Tired of climbing? Going down can be even more challenging on the ski mountains of **Mt. Hotham, VIC** (p. 590) and **Thredbo, NSW** (p. 208). Headed north, the most daring can stop at **Mt. Cougal National Park, QLD** (p. 322) to try the natural waterslide. Go where few have gone before, but be sure to book way ahead, to mountaineer on **Hinchinbrook Island, QLD** (p. 369). Hop in a 4WD vehicle and continue up the coast—ALL THE WAY up the coast—to conquer the tip of the continent at **Cape York, QLD** (p. 395). Now travel west to the **MacDonnell Ranges, NT** (p. 276) to tackle more hikes. The next stop is pretty much on the beaten track, but if you think a sunset at **Uluru (Ayers Rock), NT** (p. 283) isn't worth a detour, then you've clearly never been there. Return to the wilderness at Australia's largest national park and every outdoor enthusiast's dream: **Kakadu National Park, NT** (p. 249). Finally, round out your trip on the severe turn-offs and ruts of the **Gibb River Road** (p. 664) in **The Kimberley, WA** (p. 655). We hope you survived. Only now does *Let's Go* recognize you as hardcore!

HISTORY AND CULTURE

HISTORY

BEFORE EUROPEAN SETTLEMENT

THE PEOPLE. Most **Aboriginal** people believe that their occupation of Australia is timeless. By some estimates, the native people of Australia have inhabited the island continent for as long as 100,000 years and had settled across most of the continent by 30,000 years ago. During the Aboriginal occupation of Australia, massive environmental changes occurred, including great variations in temperature and rainfall, the extinction of animal species, and shifts in sea level. Although it is hard to uncover aspects of culture other than stone tools, archaeologists have unveiled evidence of ancient art, complex burial practices, and Stone-age boomerangs. Estimates of the Aboriginal population of Australia just prior to European colonization vary widely, from 300,000 to over one million. The Aboriginal people were **hunters and gatherers,** migrating seasonally in search of food. Men usually hunted large game, while women gathered vegetables. The large prey was divided among band members, while smaller food was kept for the family. Although Aborigines did not farm, they did increase the land's productivity by setting controlled fires (see **Burn, Baby, Burn,** p. 254) which replaced nutrients in the soil and allowed germination of seeds that opened only under intense heat.

TRIBAL LIFE. The Aboriginal people formed tribes, largely based on territorial claims. While language did not determine the boundaries of these tribes, it has been estimated that there were more than 200 languages, with up to 600 dialect groups. Most Aborigines could speak at least two different languages. Within their tribes, Aborigines divided into smaller groups, called bands, which were made up of two or three different families. Aborigines were generally accepting of polygamy, and families used inter-band marriages to solidify communities.

COMMUNITY AND SOCIAL STRUCTURE. Aborigines, because of the nomadic nature of their lives, did not develop a system of private land ownership. Instead, a sort of unwritten charter tied together a particular tribe and the territory they covered in their travels, known as a "range." The relationship between these caretakers and their areas was considered one of reciprocal responsibility. Along with strong ties to the land, there was a strong cultural emphasis on expansion through personal relationships such as kinship, marriage, and ceremony.

THE DREAMING. Aborigines believe the world was created during the Dreaming, or Creation Time, a mythological period of time with no beginning or end, when the acts and deeds of

45,000,000 BC
The link between Australia and Antarctica and Gondwanaland separates, isolating Australian fauna from placental mammals.

15,000,000 BC
Australia experiences the first of many Ice Ages that expose a land bridge between Australia and Asia, allowing for the exchange of animals and plants.

2,000,000 BC
The Australian and Asian tectonic plates collide, giving rise to the major mountain ranges in Australia.

100,000 BC
Aborigines migrate from Southeast Asia.

10,000 BC
Rising sea levels fill the Bass Strait, preventing the spread of dingoes to Tasmania and stimulating the growth of the Great Barrier Reef.

115 AD
Claudius Ptolemy, a Greek-Egyptian astronomer and geographer, theorizes that there must be a vast continent east of Africa in the southern hemisphere.

1400s
The Chinese and Arabs document a large island south of Asia; later, Portuguese sailors speak of *terra Australis incognita* ("unknown southern land").

1600s
Dutch vessels accidently encounter the west coast of Australia.

1606
While the Dutch ship *Duyfken* was exploring Cape York Peninsula, the first Europeans come in contact with Australian Aborigines.

1642
Abel Tasman locates Tasmania.

1688
William Dampier explores the west coast.

1768
Captain Cook is issued orders to "take possession of convenient situations in the name of the King with the consent of the natives...or if you find the country uninhabited Take Possession for His Majesty."

April 28, 1770
Captain Cook discovers and names Botany Bay after the diverse flora.

May 13, 1787
The First Fleet of convicts leave England.

January 20, 1788
The First Fleet lands in Botany Bay.

powerful ancestral beings shaped the land and populated it with humans, animals, and plants. There are three categories of land in Aboriginal culture: ceremonial sites, *djang* (Dreaming), and *djang andjamun* (Sacred Dreaming). Ceremonial sites are now used for burials, rites of passage, and other events. At *djang* sites, a creator passed through, took shape, or entered or exited the Earth, leaving the site safe to visit. *Djang andjamun* sites, however, where the ancestor still lingers, are considered spiritual hazard zones. Laws prohibit entry to the latter group of sites. Because features of the land are linked to the ancestors, it is not an inherited possession, but a sacred site.

The Dreamtime stories defined the Aborigines' interactions with each other and the environment. The relationships of social units and their geographic home were determined by interactions of Traveling Dreaming Beings and localized Dreaming Beings. In ceremonies, Aborigines celebrated, integrated, and regenerated the travels of the Dreamings, bringing together social groups, the land, resources, and languages, and uniting the timeless Dreaming and the present. For more info on the Dreaming, flip through **Kakadu National Park,** p. 249.

EUROPEAN SETTLEMENT

COLONIZATION

TAKE A LOOK. Although Australia is often inextricably linked with Britain, the British were not the first outsiders to stumble upon the continent. **Chinese** explorers were almost certainly among the first non-Aborigines to arrive. **Portuguese** sailors in the 15th century were also aware of the existence of a *terra australis incognita* ("unknown southern land"). The Spanish, too, visited Australia in the early 1600s. Dutch explorers included a misshapen Australia on 16th century maps, and left a memorial at Shark Bay (see p. 645) in 1616 proving their discovery. It was not until 1642 that **Abel Tasman,** a Dutch explorer under the commission of Governor **Anthony van Diemen** of the Dutch Indies, sailed south to spot the rest of Australia—a "new" southern island. Although he modestly dubbed it Van Diemen's Land, it nonetheless came to be known as Tasmania. Tasman explored Australia's coast but never established a settlement.

TAKE A CLOSER LOOK. As early as 1573 occasional English documents suggested exploring the southern hemisphere. The move to colonize did not come until **William Dampier,** an English pirate who explored the Australian coast in 1688, published his records, *Voyages*, and persuaded the English Admiralty to let him return. In 1699-1700, he explored the coastline extensively, but his evaluation was so harsh that little interest was generated for settlement. In 1770, while observing the transit of Venus across the sun, the English captain **James Cook** in his ship *Endeavour*, explored the eastern coast of what would become Australia. The other sides of the island continent had all been mapped, but the Great Barrier Reef had previously deterred explorers from the east. Cook and his crew of astronomers and scientists discovered and named **Botany Bay,** and returned to England with stories of strange animals and plants.

SETTLE DOWN. The motives for the British colonization of Australia have been a matter of debate. The traditional explanation is that Britain needed to solve the problem of overcrowding in its prisons. Another explanation suggests that the English hoped to establish a base for a global navy with plentiful natural resources—particularly timber—and an available work force, particularly prisoners. In any case, the prisons in London were full, and Australia, by all accounts, was empty. Preparations for convict settlement began in 1786. On May 13, 1787, the 11-ship **First Fleet** left from England with its unwilling cargo. **Lord Sydney,** the British home secretary, appointed **Arthur Phillip** to command the fleet. About 730 convicts were on board, with more than 250 others who were mostly wardens and their families. The fleet arrived at Botany Bay on January 20, 1788 after a grueling eight-month voyage. When the local resources were deemed insufficient for a colony, Commander Phillip headed north to Port Jackson. The English flag was raised on January 26, on the spot where Sydney stands today.

CONVICT(ION)S AND PERSISTENCE

LET'S GO AGAINST OUR WILL. Upon arrival in Australia, the convicts and their guards faced a foreign, unyielding land. And, to put it lightly, the first years of the colony went poorly: half the workforce was occupied guarding the other half; livestock escaped into the bush; relations with Aborigines deteriorated; most subsequent supply ships wrecked; the land seemed impossibly inhospitable. The convicts were mostly undesirables from the slums of London deported to Australia for small crimes (see **Budget Travel in the Old Days,** p. 15), and had no agricultural experience. Moreover, the seeds and cuttings that the fleet had so carefully carried across the sea did not thrive in the strange climate. Captain Phillip's grand plans for 200-foot-wide streets had to be scrapped; the colony had only manpower. No mill or team of cattle would be available for over eight years.

EARLY ABORIGINAL INTERACTION. Australia's history of white settlement is, as often is the case, partly a history of genocide. When the British landed in Australia and claimed the land for the Crown, they did so under a doctrine of **terra nullius,** (empty land), which meant either that there were no people on the continent, or that inhabitants were mere occupants, and did not actually own the land. This doctrine gave the British free reign (or so they rationalized) to take what land they wished, without the hassle of treaties or agreements. Most Aborigines were displaced, if not eradicated; European settlement disrupted hunting territories, destroyed watering holes, and brought influenza, measles, smallpox, tuberculosis, and venereal diseases. Many Aboriginal children were kidnapped and forced into assimilation programs, a practice not officially ended until the twentieth century (see **Stolen Children,** p. 18). Some Europeans even took to deliberately and savagely killing the Aborigines. The history of Aboriginal and white interaction in Tasmania, where the Aborigines had remained isolated for over thousands of years, is particularly horrid; systematic genocide of the Aboriginal population caused their near-complete disappearance within 70 years of contact.

January 26, 1788
The First Fleet relocates to Port Jackson–the site of Sydney.

1792
Arthur Phillip becomes the first governor of New South Wales.

1808
John Macarthur takes governship from William Bligh.

1809
The Imperial Government appoints Colonel Macquarie as governor; after more fighting, Macquarie extends full citizenship to convicts who served their sentence.

1851
The discovery of gold in Victoria, Ballarat's population grew from 300 to 10,000 in 3 months.

1854
Miners in Ballarat revolt against the high miner licensing fees.

1855
New South Wales and Victoria become the first states in Australia.

January 1868
The last convict ship arrives in Australia.

April 26, 1879
The world's second national park is created near Port Hacking, NSW.

1900
A outbreak of the bubonic plague strikes Sydney.

January 1, 1901
Commonwealth of Australia is founded.

1901
The 1901 Act prohibits permanent settlement by non-Europeans.

1902
Australia grants suffrage to women.

1905
Non-aboriginal population reaches 4 million.

1906
World's first feature length movie is made.

1914
Australia delivers the first Allied shot in WWI.

April 25, 1915
ANZAC Day
The most devastating day of battle for Australia in WWI; 2000 members of ANZAC were killed at Gallipoli.

1918
Non-aboriginal population reaches 5 million.

1927
Canberra becomes the official capital.

1927
Rev. Flynn establishes the Flying Doctor Service.

1928
Bert Hinkler flies solo from Britain to Australia in record time; Charles Kingsford Smith and Charles Uln achieve the first trans-Pacific flight.

1929
The Great Depression settles in.

POWER POLITICS. Arthur Phillip, the first governor of New South Wales, saw the colonists through troubled times before returning to England in 1792. After some time, a growing number of convicts were finishing their sentences and looking for a piece of the power pie. The **New South Wales Corps,** a group of officers that assigned jobs to the convicts and maintained order, became engaged in a power struggle with Australia's governors to curb the growing influence of former convicts. The tension came to a climax in 1808 when **John Macarthur,** a former officer of the Corps, forced **William Bligh** from the governorship. In 1809, the imperial government appointed **Colonel Lachlan Macquarie** to the position of governor. Macquarie fought with officers and English citizens who had come to Australia due to the promise of large land grants (and influence). Eventually, Macquarie extended full citizenship to convicts who served their seven years and remained in Australia.

EXPANSION

THE NEVERENDING STORY. The costs for maintaining convict colonies became an increasingly onerous economic burden for England, since most were not self-supporting (and were located halfway around the world). The transportation of convicts lasted for almost exactly 80 years. After 1815, as more convicts continued arriving, the government began hiring convicts to private employers to lighten the load. Abolitionist crusades in the 1830s convinced some that the practice smelled suspiciously of **slavery.** In 1840, the practice was abolished, and almost no more convicts were sent to eastern Australia. However, a steady stream continued to pour into Tasmania and, in 1850, convicts began to arrive in Western Australia. Finally, in January 1868, the last convict ship arrived in Australia. In all, approximately 160,500 convicts had been sent to Australia.

WORTH A SHOT. England also encouraged settler migration with **land grants** until 1831, and offered cheap passage for women to equalize the gender imbalance. **Wool** was Australia's major export, and by 1845, **sheep farming** was the most profitable business in the country. Despite land grants and economic improvements, the population remained stagnant. The discovery of **gold** in 1851 accomplished what the promise of land could not. At the end of 1851, the non-Aboriginal population numbered around 450,000, eight times that of a quarter-century earlier. Ten years later, the number was 1,150,000. The fierce competition for gold inevitably led to conflict, Australia's closest brush with civil war. During the 1854 **Eureka Stockade Rebellion,** miners in **Ballarat,** Victoria (see **Our Proudest Defeat,** p. 566), formed a collective and built a stockade to protest miner licensing fees. Government forces crushed the uprising in a violent fifteen-minute melee that cost two dozen miners their lives. The rest of Australia was outraged, and the mining fee was lifted.

HOW WIDE IS IT? Four of the six states (the Northern Territory is not a state) were formed between 1829 and 1859. The English parliament first ratified New South Wales' and Victoria's constitutions in 1855, bringing **self-government** to Australia for the first time, and giving the country a more cohesive feel. Previous to the formation of a central government, each individual colony had little to do with other colonies and instead communicated directly with London. Australia's rail system is a classic case of colonial confusion: in the 19th century, when the country's original six colonies started building railroad tracks, each colony conferred with London instead of its neighbors. By 1901, the year of Australian federation, railroads in the six areas of the country had tracks of six different widths.

TWENTIETH CENTURY

UNIFICATION AND SEGREGATION

FEDERATION. The Commonwealth of Australia was founded on January 1, 1901. Federation had been a difficult process for Australia; the new constitution was only ratified after a decade of debate among the six different colonies over issues such as representation and tax collection. The six states of Australia were (and are) New South Wales, Victoria, Queensland, South Australia, Western Australia, and Tasmania. The Northern Territory and the Australian Capital Territory are two self-governing territories within Australia that still do not have state status. The new national government gradually consolidated its power over the states. As a compromise between Sydney and Melbourne, the capital was located in a brand-new city between the two. **Canberra** formally became the nation's capital in 1927. For more on the federation, see **Government,** p. 17.

SUFFRAGE. The year after federation, Australia became only the second country in the world, after New Zealand, to grant federal **suffrage to women.** In 1921, **Edith Dircksey Cowan** of Western Australia became the first female in a state parliament in Australia. Her only predecessor in the British Empire was Lady Astor who served in the House of Commons in 1919.

RACE. Despite the progressive moves forward in gender relations, Australia still had a ways to go. When convicts stopped arriving, Europeans began encouraging the immigration of Chinese laborers. Race-based immigration restrictions were soon adopted, especially when **Chinese immigrants** started working the goldfields. In 1879, an Intercolonial Trade Union Congress, one of the first national meetings with representatives from all of the states, published a warning that Chinese immigration "supplanted white labor, and would leave no work or hope for the rising generation, who would fill the jails in consequence." By 1888, the "Chinese question" had emerged onto the political front stage, and a Queensland journal first coined the rallying cry **"White Australia."** In 1896, immigration restrictions were extended to include all non-whites. With Federation came the **Immigration Restriction Act of 1901,** which required immigrants to pass a 50-word dictation test in any European language chosen at the discretion of the immigration officers.

WORLD WAR

WWI. At the outset of **World War I,** Australia's Prime Minister declared support for the mother country, saying: "Our duty is quite clear—to gird up our loins and remember that we are Brit-

1939
In WWII, Australia again delivers the first Allied shot; bushfires surge over millions of hectares, destroying buildings and killing over 70 people, on the horrific Black Friday.

February 19, 1942
The Japanese first bomb Darwin.

1951
An assimilation policy is implemented to educate detribalized Aborigines and any part-Aborigines (regardless of their wishes).

September 1, 1951
Australia, New Zealand, and the US sign the **ANZUS** military pact.

1954
Queen Elizabeth II becomes the first reigning monarch to tour Australia.

1956
Melbourne hosts the Olympic Games.

1958
Qantas becomes the first round-the-world passenger. airline service.

May 1965
The **ANZUS** agreement pulls Australia into the Vietnam conflict.

May 1965
The **ANZUS** agreement pulls Australia into the Vietnam conflict.

January 9, 1967 Ronald Ryan is the last man to be executed in Australia.

1967 Australia severs currency link with Britain.

1969 Australian students storm US Consulate, protesting Vietnam.

1973 "White Australia" policy formally dismantled; the Sydney Opera House, funded by lotteries, opens.

Dec. 25, 1974 Cyclone Tracy levels Darwin.

1995 Protesting the French nuclear weapons testing in the South Pacific, dissidents bomb French Consulate.

May 1997 Government-owned Telstra is sold to raise money to clean the environment.

November 6, 1999 Australians vote to not become a republic and officially keep ties with the British Crown.

March 28, 2000 Australians "Walk for Aboriginal Reconciliation" seeking an official apology.

2000 Sydney hosts the Summer Olympics.

ons." About 330,000 Australians girded up their loins and 60,000 lost their lives. About 165,000 more soldiers were wounded. While these figures pale in comparison to casualties from other countries, they were a shocking percentage of the country's relatively small population. The single worst day of battle was April 25, 1915, when 2000 members of the **Australian and New Zealand Army Corps** (ANZAC) were killed at **Gallipoli,** Turkey, initiating a campaign that eventually took 8500 Australian lives and forced evacuation of the troops. Australia celebrates **Anzac Day** (April 25) each year to remember the heroism of these troops. Economically, though, the war helped industries by opening Western markets to Australian exports.

WWII. A generation later, **World War II** allowed Australia to reiterate its commitment to Great Britain and its allies. The Royal Australian Air Force defended Great Britain, while other troops won victories at Tobruk and El-Alamein in North Africa. After the Japanese attack on the United States' Pearl Harbor (Dec. 7, 1941) and the fall of British-protected Singapore (Feb. 15, 1942), Australian citizens became increasingly concerned about safety on their own shores. On February 19, 1942, **Darwin,** the capital of the Northern Territory, suffered the first of many destructive bombings by the Japanese. The US, with its commitment to the Pacific theater, became a closer ally to Australia than the more distant Britain. Over the course of the war, about 30,000 Australian soldiers died fighting.

AFTERMATH AND ALLIANCE

HELL NO. After 1945, the country enjoyed a time of relative peace and prosperity marked by rapid immigration; in the thirty years following the end of the war, the population nearly doubled from seven million to 13.5 million. In the meantime, Australia and American formalized relations in 1951 with the signing of the **Australia-New Zealand-United States (ANZUS)** pact. When the United States became embroiled in the **Vietnam** conflict, Australians were conscripted to serve, touching off a slow-gathering storm of anti-war protest. Violent protests broke out among university students in Sydney and Melbourne in 1968, just as anti-war protests were heating up in the US as well. Dissent culminated in 1969, when Australian students stormed the US consulate in Melbourne.

MONEY MATTERS. In 1967, Australia broke its currency link with Britain by deciding not to devalue the pound sterling. Within the same year, **Japan** replaced the United Kingdom as the primary recipient of Australian exports, and eventually passed the United States to become Australia's largest supplier of imports by 1984. Australia today is a member of the **Asia Pacific Economic Cooperation (APEC)** forum.

GIVE A HOOT. The 1970s also saw the beginnings of **environmental activism** in Australia, echoing movements the world over. The first case to create a nationwide impact was a disagreement over **Lake Pedder** in Tasmania. Despite protests, a hydroelectric dam was erected in 1973. The loss galvanized environmentalists to organize and protest, and eventually to put the Green party in power in Tasmania in 1989.

BUDGET TRAVEL IN THE OLD DAYS In the late 18th and early 19th centuries, it didn't take much to win a free trip to Australia, as long as you didn't mind traveling aboard a convict ship. Most of the convicts were guilty of petty thievery—and of being poor, ill-connected, and often Irish. Many had originally been sentenced to death, with those sentences commuted to "transportation beyond the seas" and seven years' service upon arrival. Records show that the disappearance of one coffee pot, one guinea, 28 lb. of hair powder, six live turkeys, five woolen blankets, one piece of yellow canvas, three petticoats, 11 yards of printed cotton, 8 lb. of cheese, or one sheep was enough to send a convict to Australia. One man was convicted of destroying 12 cucumber plants, while another "unlawfully cut down one maiden ash timber tree." One woman was convicted of "spoiling, burning, and defacing the garment of a female." Another woman received a sentence of death, commuted to Australian transportation, for stealing two linen aprons. A boy, age 11, was shipped out for stealing one pair of silk stockings. A stiff price to pay for that smooth, silky feel...

CURRENT EVENTS

DAMN REPUBLICANS

WHAT HAPPENED. The most ground-breaking political news of the '90s was when Queen Elizabeth won her first election. On November 6, 1999, in response to a **national referendum vote,** 55% of Australians voted to officially keep ties with the British Crown and not become a republic. Under the reforms proposed, the duties of monarch would have been performed by a non-political President appointed by a two-thirds vote of the parliament. Despite a strong Republican sentiment in the country, the Australian people voted to continue as a constitutional monarchy rather than have an parliament-appointed president. Some believe that the vote was evidence of a break between a forward-looking urban middle class who supported the republic and rural voters and workers who were hostile to any change. Others instead point to Australians' preference for a democratically elected president and a general distrust of politicians. But almost all agree that the referendum did not resolve the debate once and for all.

...AND WHY. In November 11, 1975, the Governor General, acting in response to a deadlock over government finances, exercised his right to dissolve parliament in times of crisis. The deadlock occurred after two states replaced outgoing Labor members of parliament with Liberals, swaying the balance in their favor. The Governor General responded by dismissing the Labor Prime Minister, **Edward Gough Whitham,** and appointing **Malcolm Fraser,** a Liberal, to lead. This act shocked the Australian people and raised popular support for **republicanism,** a movement geared toward gaining full independence from the British Crown. In the election a year after the dissolution, the Liberals under Fraser were voted into power anyway, and remained there for eight years.

In 1983, the Labor Party once again took control of parliament under Prime Minister **Bob Hawke,** who retained power for four terms. He was succeeded by **Paul Keating,** also a member of the Labor Party, who tried to use the Labor dominance to improve economic relations with Asia and transform Australia into a republic. In 1996, after 13 years of uninterrupted Labor rule, the Liberals finally regained control of parliament under **John Howard,** a social conservative and constitutional monarchist. His platform included industrial relations reform and the reversal of some of the more liberal policies of the Labor administration. On February 13, 1998, a constitutional convention voted overwhelmingly in favor of severing Australia's 210-year-old links to the British monarchy and making the country a republic. Many republicans who had favored election of a president by popular ballot compromised, and accepted a proposal by the Australian Republican Movement to have the president elected by parliament. And so, the national referendum was born.

THE FIGHT OVER THE FLAG On September 3, 1901, the first **Australian flag** flew over the Exhibition Building in Melbourne, the winner of a design contest that had attracted 32,823 entries from all over the world. The blue flag has the Union Jack in the upper left corner, with the star of Australia underneath, today with seven points, one for each state or territory in the federation. The Southern Cross star formation is to the right. Since then, much debate has ensued over whether the flag is an appropriate national symbol for Australia. Criticism of the current flag include its similarity to other flags (especially New Zealand's) and the Union Jack's implication of subordination or loyalty to Britain. The main argument for the current flag is that thousands of men and women fought and died under it, giving it historical value. Many others simply find nothing wrong with the flag. However, recent polls show that support for a new flag is increasing. Throughout the past 15 years, over 50,000 new designs have been submitted to Ausflag, the lead organization fighting the current flag.

NEWS BRIEFS

GUN CONTROL AND FIRE SAFETY. On April 28, 1996, at **Port Arthur,** Tasmania (see **Recent News,** p. 471), deranged citizen Martin Bryant shot and killed 35 strangers. The event fueled Australia's gun-control movement, and led to a much-touted plan to ban rapid-fire weapons. The issue is still a sensitive one, so be wary of any politically-charged remarks you make, especially in the Port Arthur area. In June 2000, a hostel in **Childers,** Queensland (see **Hostel Fire,** p. 342) burned down, resulting in the death of 15 backpackers. Though investigators have suspected arson was the cause of the fire at the old wooden pub, the tragedy has nevertheless drawn attention to the need for official guidelines—especially for strict fire regulations—over the hostel industry.

ENVIRONMENT. For the most part, Australia has shown an intense commitment to the preservation of its natural beauty, and the environment in general. In 1995, French President Jacques Chirac decided to sponsor **nuclear weapons testing** in the South Pacific. Protesters fire-bombed the French consulate in Perth, and demonstrations were held all over the country. In May 1997, the Australian government funded a $1.3 billion project to clean up the Murray and Darling Rivers, by selling **Telstra,** the previously state-owned telecommunications company. Recent protests about a **uranium mining** project on Aboriginal lands in Kakadu National Park, reveal two of the most important issues in contemporary Australian politics: race and the environment. The question of native land rights and government intervention remains unanswered (see **Land Rights,** p. 18).

ECONOMY. Despite struggling with racism, Australia for the most part has increasingly emphasized its role as a member of the Pacific economic and security community. International trade is vital to Australia's economy, particularly within the region; hence, the **Asian currency crisis** that began in the summer of 1997 has had damaging spillover effects. While Australia's economy has not collapsed, its dollar's value has spiraled downward and exports to Asia have declined.

POLITICS. Pauline Hanson, a former Queensland member of the federal parliament, has received a great deal of negative press for her inflammatory political platform as a reactionary conservative and the leader of the **One Nation Party.** The party supports isolationist policies, charges that Asian interests have corrupted Australian business, calls for strict limits on immigration, and challenges social programs for Aborigines arguing that they represent unfair preferences. Hanson did not regain her seat in parliament in the general election at the end of 1998, and the One Nation Party has little power in the national legislature today. Some analysts have predicted a resurgence in the party's political standing within the next few years, and nationwide polls still show a substantial population of supporters.

THE PEOPLE

POPULATION COMPOSITION. The Commonwealth of Australia is home to 19.2 million people. Immigration has defined the narrative of the Australian population, as more than 20% of the current population was born overseas. The **White Australia Policy** (see p. 5) created a fairly homogenous population. In 2000, whites made up 92% of the population while Aborigines comprised less than 2%. In recent years, Asian immigration has accelerated. Asians now account for just under 7% of the Australian population. **English** (better known as **'Strine**; see p. 670) is Australia's only national language and is spoken in 85% of Australian homes. Virtually 100% of the population is **literate.**

RELIGION. The religious composition of the population generally reflects the immigrant's backgrounds. Just over 75% of Australians declare themselves **Christians.** Roman Catholics make up about 26% of the population, Anglicans account for 26%, and other Christian denominations make up 24%. **Non-Christian** religions comprise 11%, with Buddhism, Muslim, and Judaism leading the list. Roughly 10% of Australians reject organized religion.

DEMOGRAPHICS. Australia's population density is 2.5 people per square kilometer. In comparison, the United States squeezes 28.2 people in an average square kilometer, and, for a particularly tight fit, the United Kingdom has 243.6 people per square kilometer. Eighty-five percent of Australians live in urban areas, and the suburbs are still growing. The vast majority live on or relatively near the coasts, particularly the east coast—some theories point to the vast, inhospitable desert in the center of the country as the reason for this coastal population concentration.

GOVERNMENT

REPRESENTATION. Australia's government is a constitutional monarchy in which federal and state governments share power. The British monarch is Australia's official head of state, and appoints a **Governor General** to exercise authority. The Governor General primarily stands as a symbol of Australia's commonwealth status. **Peter Hollingworth** replaced **Sir William Deane** as the Governor General in July 2001. The **Federal Parliament** is a bicameral legislature comprised of the **House of Representatives,** in which representation of each state and territory is determined by population, and the **Senate,** consisting of 12 delegates from each state and two from each territory. Voter participation is nearly 90%, partly due to a system of compulsory voting, under which eligible voters who abstain can be fined. Voting is **preferential,** meaning that a voter ranks all the candidates in order of preference.

LEGISLATION. The Governor General appoints the leader of the majority party in the House of Representatives to the position of **Prime Minister.** The Prime Minister then acts as the head of the legislative body. Supreme judicial power rests in the seven-person **High Court.** This body may declare legislative and executive actions unconstitutional. Most appointments and decisions under the jurisdiction of the Governor General, including **cabinet** members and High Court judges, are made with the advice of the Prime Minister. State governments are particularly strong and active, with a structure like that of the central government. Each state has its own Governor General, who is advised by a Premier and cabinet, and a legislative body to make laws. The federal government defers many duties to the state governments, and thus laws and policies can vary greatly from state to state.

LABOR AND LIBERAL. The two main parties in the federal parliament are the **Labor Party** and the **Liberal Party.** The Liberal Party currently holds the most power in parliament, led by Prime Minister **John Howard.** The Labor Party advocates the recognition of Aboriginal lands, socialist economic policies, and severing ties with the English monarchy in order to form an Australian republic. The party's former leader, **Paul Keating,** a staunch advocate for Australia's becoming a republic, was

Australia's Prime Minister until 1996. (Australia's elections take place every three years.) That year's election brought a new Liberal majority, and **Kim Beazley** took over the reigns. Its platforms advocate free enterprise, conservative financial policies, and a strong relationship with the British Commonwealth. These two parties were most responsible for the debate over turning Australia into a republic.

OTHER POLITICAL PARTIES. Several smaller parties hold some weight in parliament, including the **National Party,** which often forms a coalition with the Liberals. The **Green Party** is very active in the **Tasmanian** state government and fights for liberal platforms and environmental concerns. The **Australian Democrats,** holding a moderate socialist agenda, have maintained a small faction in the Senate. The **One Nation Party** also had a controversial stint in Parliament (see **Current Events,** p. 15).

ABORIGINAL RIGHTS

GRIEVANCES

STOLEN CHILDREN. In the early 1800s, some missionaries began to try to make Aborigines "employable" by converting them to Christianity and teaching them European skills and customs. Some of the program leaders decided that this was impossible if Aboriginal children were raised by Aboriginal parents, and the children were moved out of their homes to live with European families. This removal became state policy in New South Wales in 1883 and, astonishingly, was not officially discontinued until 1969. Aborigines refer to these children as "taken" or "stolen," and it is estimated that there may be 100,000 people of Aboriginal descent today who do not know their families or the communities of their birth. Many are still seeking restitution or merely an overdue government apology.

GROWING DISSENT. The land rights issue has become a hot topic in Australia during the last few decades, as Aboriginal peoples demand land rights and compensation for the loss of land and the abuse they have endured. In 1933, the Aboriginal population of Australia hit a low of 73,828. By 1981 this had risen to just over 171,000, and the most recent census (1996) counted 353,000 Aborigines, making up two percent of the total population. Finally, Aborigines have gathered enough clout to band together and organize politically to fight for their rights. Some Australians of European descent—particularly those with mining and other industry interests—vehemently defend their control of the land. The courts and the government have taken up the issue, and legal developments and legislation continue to fuel the controversy.

LAND RIGHTS

NATIVE TITLE. In 1966, the **Gurindji** Aboriginal people from the Northern Territory formed the first Aboriginal-owned and -operated cattle station, **Daguragu.** Although it took a long and difficult 20 years, the Gurindji were officially given permanent title to the land in a 1986 court decision. This Aboriginal legal success paved the way for the controversial **Mabo** decision in 1992. The Mabo case originated with a claim by Koiki (Eddie) Mabo, a Torres Straits Islander who successfully argued for the return of Murray Island to the Mer people (its original inhabitants) through the legal system. The High Court struck down the legal fiction of *terra nullius*, recognizing that the principle of native title–defined as the traditional Aboriginal right of access, use, or occupation of the land—had existed before the arrival of the British. The Mabo decision, however, left ambiguities as to where and to whom native title was applicable, and as to what exactly it meant. The **Native Title Act** of 1993 sought to clarify the decision by establishing guidelines to reassure farmers, miners, and conservatives that the Aborigines could not claim Native Title to the whole continent. It also set out a means of compensating Aborigines, placed limitations on future acts affecting Native Title land and waters, and created a Land Fund to help Aboriginal and Torres Strait Islanders acquire and manage land.

ONGOING DISPUTES. The effectiveness of the Act is still in doubt. Many believe that it was a token gesture, granting few substantial new rights to Aborigines and leaving many of the ambiguities in place. Several amendments have been proposed, partly in response to the issues emerging from the 1996 **Wik** case. In December of 1996, the Wik and Thayorre peoples of western Cape York obtained a ruling that a **pastoral lease** (where the Crown rents land to a farmer for a long, long time) does not necessarily require Aborigines who are living on that land to leave. In fact, both farmer and Aborigines can claim rights to the same land under Australian law. A pastoral lease can co-exist with Native Title. In the case of conflict, however, the former takes precedence, thus limiting the practical implementation of Native Title throughout the 42% of Australia that is under pastoral lease.

FURTHER SETBACKS. Following the Court's decision, the government developed a **10-point plan on Native Title** that eliminated Native Title in certain circumstances. The **Native Title Amendment Bill of 1997** incorporates this plan and has been resoundingly condemned by Aboriginal leaders and their supporters. Other bills related to Aboriginal land rights are currently under consideration, and new cases continue to come before the High Court. Each bill attempts to clarify the one before, but it is clear that the Aborigines' struggle for land rights is far from over. Some Aboriginal leaders used the Sydney Olympics to attract international attention to their grievances. For updated information on Aboriginal political events and Native Title claims, check out the web site of the Aboriginal and Torres Strait Islander Commission at www.atsic.gov.au, and that of the Australian Institute for Australian and Torres Strait Islander Studies at www.aiatsis.gov.au.

RECONCILIATION. Indigenous people continue to experience poorer health, limited employment opportunities, and educational disadvantages. Aborigines often face prejudice when trying to rent a home, find a job, thumb a cab, and other everyday activities which many citizens take for granted. Official efforts have been made to eliminate the prejudice including the **Racial Discrimination Act of 1975,** and there has been progress towards recognizing the culture, history, and rights of the Aborigines. In 1991 the Council for Aboriginal Reconciliation was established to help foster a national dialogue on reconciliation. In December of 2000, the council released a report recommending that the Australian government draft a treaty to deal with the past treatment of indigenous peoples. The government currently pays "welfare" to anyone of Aboriginal descent. On March 28, 2000, a quarter of a million people marched in support of Australia's Aborigines. The "Walk for Aboriginal Reconciliation" across Sydney's Harbour Bridge was in hope of receiving an official apology from Prime Minister John Howard on behalf of the Australian government and people. Yet despite these recommendations, civil protests, and the government's recognition of the injustice, an official apology has not been made.

CULTURE

ARTS

While Australians might identify better with a national athlete than a native artist, art in Australia is slowly becoming part of a strong national identity. In a country where the national identity has been somewhat thwarted by its history, art serves as a way for people to express their heritage and experience. Historically, European arts exerted a strong influence on non-Aboriginal Australian artists and writers, and the artists responded by focusing particularly on their relationship with their unique—some might say solitary—landscape and climate. Though modern artists are branching out to explore new themes, the most popular national arts are still those that depict traditional themes, sustain an Australian mythology, or explore some facet of the nation's cultural and natural heritage. Where Aborigines were once discriminated against and overlooked by a predominantly white society, Aboriginal art has become one of Australia's cultural icons.

LITERATURE

THE FIRST FORMS. Even before Europeans settled in Australia, the Aboriginal people developed a rich **oral tradition.** By mixing song, dance, and the spoken word, the Aborigines could pass on stories and religious expressions through generations. Many Aboriginal groups named objects and animals by the actual sound that they made, helping young children to not only learn traditional stories, but to also learn to distinguish aspects of their environment. Although modern writers like **Sally Morgan** in her book *My Place* and **Paddy Roe** in *Gularabulu* have tried to capture some of this oral tradition on paper, the artistry of the original storytellers will never be fully recreated.

HISTORICAL AND EARLY WORKS. During the early 19th century, the Australian literary world began to expand through the creative efforts of newly settled Europeans. Most of the works were in the form of short written histories and accounts of pioneer life. A few writers wove themes of convict exile and settler life into their poetry. **Barron Field,** an author with a more fertile mind than his arid name suggests, wrote the first volume of Australian poetry entitled *First Fruits of Australian Poetry*. During the 1870s, popular poet **Adam Lindsay Gordon** wrote *Bush Ballads and Galloping Rhymes*, evoking Australian camaraderie and stoicism.

Australian literature found a wider audience with the **The Bulletin,** a literary journal founded in Sydney in 1880. It started a tradition of publishing new and original works, encouraging local artists and writers. *The Bulletin's* contributions to literature continued through the 20th century, but as its politics became conservative and anachronistic, sales fell. The journal became *The Bulletin with Newsweek* under new ownership, but its significance has faded in the past three decades.

Possibly the first uniquely Australian literature was the **bush ballad,** a form of poetry frequently published in *The Bulletin* that celebrated the working man and the superiority of life in the bush. The most famous of these ballads is **Banjo Paterson's** *Waltzing Matilda*, a song often considered even more representative of the independent Australian pride than the national anthem (see p. 400). A strong division existed between popular and intellectual poetry; intellectual poets were often seen as too pseudo-European. At the end of 1800s, some poets began to shift their focus from the landscape of bush ballads to more urban concepts. More recently, **Judith Wright** has led a movement towards a re-examination of colonial literature, establishing a continuity of identity with the poets of the past. **A.D. Hope's** *Australia* condemns the country's insularity but still expresses hope for the future. In recent years the prose style has diversified with increased overseas influences, and short stories today explore social issues and express the realities of urban life.

THE AUSTRALIAN NOVEL. Modern written literature has a complicated history, in part because many of the early novelists spent most of their adult lives outside Australia. **Henry Savory** wrote the first Australian novel, *Quintus Servinton*, in 1831. Like other early novelists, he struggled with the mindset of most Australians accustomed to a life shadowed by the British penal system. The convict experience had a profound presence in Australian literature and history. **Marcus Clarke's** *His Natural Life* (1869), centered around the fictional Australian character who symbolized independent ruggedness and rough manners of early inhabitants. The most famous Australian work is *Voss* (1957), by Nobel Prize-winner **Patrick White.** A love story about the idiosyncrasies of Australia 150 years ago—the vacancy at the center, life on the perimeter, urban residents' (particularly male) obsession with the bush—the same concepts the occupy authors and readers today.

CULTURE AND IDENTITY. The tradition and misogyny in early bush ballads and short stories provoked a conflict between male and female writers in the 20th century. Among the better-known female writers is **Miles Franklin,** author of *My Brilliant Career* (1901), a book influenced by her rejection of traditional female roles as wife and mother to work as a journalist and feminist in Sydney. Today's names in literature still introspectively examine the meaning of being Australian, although context increasingly varies. **Peter Carey** is best known as the author of *Bliss* (1981), a humorous exploration of the Australian national character, as well as his particularly dark satire, *Oscar and Lucinda* (1988), which won the Booker prize for fiction. **Tim Winton,** a Western Australian short-story writer and novelist, has won several distinguished awards for his portrayal of the everyday lives of the Westralians. Both Carey and Winton write with concern for the effects of colonialism on the Australian environment and people. The attention given to "ethnic" writing, Aboriginal literature, and song-cycles has also been growing in the 20th century. A growing number of **Aboriginal writers** are beginning to gain national recognition. The anthology *Paperbark* provides a sample of Aboriginal literature.

POPULAR MUSIC

Australia's early colonial period relied heavily on British folk music, with lively fiddle and drum bushdances held in cleared-out sheep-shearing sheds. Popular music of the last few decades was greatly influenced first by British rock and later by American New Wave and Alternative music. More recently, some Aboriginal sounds have come in vogue. You can now find virtually any music from around the world in Australia. Oz's youth radio, **JJJ (Triple J),** plays contemporary local music, and is always promoting new acts. Many of the nightlife spots mix everything from top-40 hits to alternative music, to the techno artists of the European disco scene.

AMERICAN INVASION. US soldiers brought big band jazz to Australia during WWI, and the American music has found increasingly firm footing. Don Burrows and Graeme Bell were inspired leaders of big and small groups in the '60s, establishing an **Australian jazz** scene that gained mainstream attention with the likes of too-hip singer Vince Jones, instrumental wizard James Morrison, and genius pianist Paul Gabowsky in the '80s.

ROCK AND ROLL. The Australian pop of the late '50s was epitomized by rocker **Johnny O'Keefe** whose sound, inspired by the musical blend emerging from the American south, took the country by storm. Television hit Australia at the same time as rock and roll, creating a booming youth culture based around shows like **Australian Bandstand.** Influenced by groups like Peter, Paul, and Mary, a lively folk music scene thrived at the same time.

HARD ROCK AND NEW WAVE. In the late '70s, **AC/DC** hit the charts with blues-influenced heavy metal grown out of pub culture. After making it big, the group moved its headquarters to Europe. They are no longer considered truly Australian (especially since they were originally Scottish immigrants). Refusing to emulate American and English sounds, **Cold Chisel, Goanna,** and **Australian Crawl** gained local fame with Aussie-themed hits that still get radio airtime.

The '80s saw the advent of bands like **Midnight Oil,** a group born out of hard rock pub culture and known for its support of social causes. While many popular Australian bands never managed to sell their sound outside of Australia, there are a few notable exceptions. **Men At Work** came from the land down under with a Vegemite sandwich to break into the American music scene for a short while. Following in their quickly disappearing footsteps, **Crowded House** briefly became a well-known international band at the height of New Wave. **INXS** became one of the most successful Australian bands, but a recently planned comeback tour was cut short by the suicide of lead singer Michael Hutchence.

Today's Australian music is very diverse, influenced by grunge and world music. Recently **Savage Garden** flew to the moon and back, leaping onto the international pop scene, while **Nick Cave and the Bad Seeds** carry a fair-sized European following. Both **Kylie Minogue** and **Natalie Imbruglia** graduated from the Australian TV show *Neighbours* to take a shot at pop music.

BUSH ROCK AND COUNTRY. Aboriginal groups have just recently entered the mainstream music culture. **Yothu Yindi,** a band out of Arnhem Land in the Northern Territory, has combined Aboriginal musical styles with dance music and rock, and respects Midnight Oil's tradition of using the spotlight to further political causes. *The Australia Post* has recently honored the band with a national stamp. Other similarly politicized Aboriginal "bush rock" groups are the **Coloured Stones,** the **Warumpi Band,** and **Archie Roach,** whose country-influenced tunes reflect on his background as a "stolen child" and the problems of Aborigines in urban Australia.

Country music is big in Australia, and is celebrated at an annual **Country Music Festival** in Tamworth, the "country capital" of Australia (see p. 150). The music takes its cues from its American counterpart, but is strongly influenced by the peculiarities of Australian rural life. **Slim Dusty** is the style's founding father, having sold over three million albums since he began songwriting at age 12. He roused crowds at the closing ceremonies of the Sydney Olympics, leading the crowd in a sing along of "Waltzing Matilda."

VISUAL ARTS

ABORIGINAL PAINTING. The nation's original visual art, although its intent was not exclusively artistic but educational and spiritual, dates back over 80,000 years. Combining intricate colors in a dot-form, Aboriginal art has become iconoclastic, in both authentic portrayals and in the world of marketing tourism. Before the 1970s, public perception of Aboriginal art was restricted to "bark paintings"—paintings on strips of eucalyptus that were traditionally ceremonial and generally destroyed during or after the ceremony. After becoming collector's items in the 1940s, bark paintings have since been widely reproduced. During the 1970s, other forms of Aboriginal art, such as mural art, body painting, and rock painting, were rediscovered and became popular, partly because of government support.

ART IN MODERN TIMES. Visual arts of the modern era began, much like other arts, with a search for Australian identity. Especially in the work of early Australian impressionists such as **Tom Roberts** (1856-1931), whose *Break Away* depicts the red, dry, dusty land of the cattle station, and **Frederick McCubbin** (1850-1917), whose *Lost Child* portrays the thin forests of smoky green gum trees. Later landscape paintings by artists like **Hans Heysen, Robert Juniper,** and **Russell Drysdale** focused on similar natural features, with a greater variety of style, color, and mood. **Sidney Nolan's** series on Ned Kelly illustrates the folk hero's exploits, final capture, and execution. Completed between 1945 and 1954, these pieces are on display in Australia's National Galleries (see **Canberra,** p. 86 and **Glenrowan,** p. 582). Nolan has also done emotional and provocative series on the Eureka Stockade, Gallipoli and drought. Other prominent contemporary artists include **John Perceval,** expressionist **Albert Tucjer,** abstract artist **John Colburn,** and **Arthur Boyd,** who depicts popular figures of Australian legend. Younger Australian painters such as **Mandy Martin, Susan Norrie,** and **Neil Taylor** have flooded the scene with eclectic collections and explorations of post-industrial Australia.

FILM

"EARLY" WORKS. Although responsible for producing the world's first feature length film—*The Story of the Kelly Gang* in 1906—the Australian cinema industry was fairly inactive until the 1970s when the federal government created the **Australian Film Development Corporation** (later called the **Australian Film Commission**) to fund original Australian films. In the last few decades, the rest of the world has begun giving greater respect to Australian talent in the film industry. The **Australian Film School** opened in 1973 and began training the likes of **Gillian Armstrong, Paul Cox,** and **Bruce Beresford.** In 1976, **Peter Weir's** acclaimed *Picnic at Hanging Rock* hit the international scene, followed by *Gallipoli* in 1980 (which starred Australian-born and bred superstar **Mel Gibson**). Other popularly recognized and appreciated Australian films of this time period include **Phillip Noyce's** *Newsfront* and **Gillian Armstrong's** *My Brilliant Career.* The '80s brought the *Mad Max* trilogy as well as the *The Year of Living Dangerously.* Australia has created a spate of hits in the past ten years that include *Strictly Ballroom, Death in Brunswick,*

AUSSIE STARS IN NORTHERN SKIES Several Australian movie directors and actors have found international success recently. **Geoffrey Rush,** after being nominated for a best actor Oscar for Australian-made *Shine*, endeared himself to audiences in *Shakespeare in Love*, only to play the Oscar-nominated role of The Marquis de Sade in *Quills*. Aussie-lass **Cate Blanchett** recently starred in *Elizabeth*, and **Peter Weir** directed *The Truman Show*. Sydney was the prominent backdrop for last summer's blockbuster *Mission Impossible II* starring Tom Cruise who recently separated from Aussie **Nicole Kidman,** who has reinvented herself as a sultry siren in *Moulin Rouge*. **George Lucas,** the producer of *Star Wars* has chosen Australia as the film set for parts two and three of the new prequel trilogy. In the Australian spirit of the independent macho man, **Russell Crowe** played a tough cop in *L.A. Confidential*, alongside fellow Aussie, **Guy Pierce,** who continues to forget himself as Leonard Shelby in *Memento*. Crowe followed with a courageous role in the critically-acclaimed *The Insider*, and then led the Oscar-sweep for the 2000 hit *Gladiator*. The only Aussie who can beat that is *Braveheart* himself, although his Hollywood son, **Heath Ledger** (*10 Things I Hate About You, A Knight's Tale)* in *The Patriot*, could possibly fill old Mel's shoes quite nicely.

Muriel's Wedding, *The Adventures of Priscilla, Queen of the Desert* and *Shine*. The same Australian creative team and Australian director **Baz Luhrmann** that produced *Strictly Ballroom* also produced the well-received modern interpretation of *Romeo and Juliet* and the recent *Moulin Rouge*.

While Australia jumps into the international movie-scene with Sydney sometimes being referred to as 'the next Hollywood,' domestic hits continue to attract large audiences. Check out *Chopper*, a true story about an Aussie who literally got away with murder, or *The Dish*, about Australia's own involvement in the US's achievement of putting man on the moon (visit the real 'dish' in NSW, p. 222). *Bootmen*, starring the extremely talented **Adam Garcia** (*Coyote Ugly)*, has a great mix of love, drama, tears, and extreme dance, to keep you intrigued with both Australian culture, artistry, and rising international talent.

FOOD AND DRINK

THE BASICS

WHAT ARE YOU EATING? Australians eat four meals a day: breakfast, lunch, dinner and beer. Aussies hardly ever eat their **"brekkie"** out, and most restaurants don't open until noon except in the larger cities. An interesting part of brekkie that Aussies enjoy is spaghetti, along with the traditional eggs, toast, and sausage. The evening meal is sometimes called **"tea,"** but shouldn't be confused with the diminutive British version; it's the largest meal of the day. Beware of ordering only an **"entree,"** an appetizer in Australia. A **"cuppa"**—tea or coffee—should tide you over between meals. The pub is the place to go to relax and grab a quick bite to eat. And whatever the country may lack in gourmet cuisine it makes up for in delectable beer. **Tipping** in Australian restaurants and pubs is rare and never expected. **Vegetarians** shouldn't go hungry despite Australia's meat-hungry reputation. Trendy urban eateries frequently cater to special diets, but traditional establishments rarely will.

WHERE AND HOW TO EAT. As is to be expected from the island-continent, **seafood** is a highlight, although all meats can be found. From the British come cholesterol-heavy **pub meals,** such as steak and eggs, and the Aussie institution of **fish'n'chips.** A popular meal for families on Friday nights, the fish is fried, battered, rolled in newspaper, and served with British-style chips (thick french fries). **Chook** (chicken) is often substituted for fish to create much-needed variety. **"Chippers"** are the quintessential Aussie eateries, and most specialize in **takeaway** (take-out).

KEEP YOUR KIWIS OFF! Sweet and white, creamy and light, **pavlova** is, was, and forever shall be *the* Australian dessert. Some consider the ability to make this chewy meringue covered in whipped cream and fresh fruit a prerequisite for marriage–if one's spouse can't make a decent pav, he or she just isn't fit to bring little Aussies into the world. The term "pavlova" is of debatable origin. Rather, its origin has been debated. Let's set the record straight. The delectable dessert came into existence in 1935 when the chef of Perth's Esplanade Hotel, Bert Sachse, decided to create a new dish in honor of their famous Russian guest: the ballerina Anna Pavlova. Nevertheless, some poor misguided souls in neighboring New Zealand seem to believe that *they* invented the dessert. Utter hogwash.

AUSTRALIAN "CUISINE"

WATCH WHAT YOU EAT. Australia's origin as a convict colony didn't endow the country with a subtle palate. **Meat pies** are the ultimate Australian fare. Inexplicably popular, these doughy shells contain meat of dubious origin and often a mushy vegetable filling. Most consumers douse them in **tomato sauce** (a sweet ketchup-like concoction) to disguise the taste. Let us say again—tomato sauce is not ketchup. Use Australian condiments sparingly until you are familiar with them. Aussie mustard delivers a horseradishy kick, and the infamous **Vegemite,** a yeasty by-product of the beer-brewing process, should be scraped thinly rather than spread liberally.

SPICE UP YOUR DIET. Australia may suffer from a reputation of having a notoriously dull national cuisine, but it has been remarkably successful at adding layers of flavor with each wave of immigration. Recent European and Middle Eastern arrivals have spiced up Australian menus with Greek souvlaki, Italian pasta, and Lebanese tabbouleh. The cheapest way to sample these flavors is at any of numerous takeaway joints. Influxes of immigrants from Asian and Pacific countries have added further variety. Chinese dishes first arrived with Chinese gold prospectors in the 1850s and have so infiltrated the menu that even their names have taken a uniquely Australian twist: **"dim sims"** are Australian *dim sum.* Japanese, Thai, Malay, and Vietnamese restaurants also are abundant, particularly in Darwin and cosmopolitan centers in the southeast.

NOT UNTIL YOU FINISH DINNER. Australia has plentiful pickings when it comes to fruit for desserts; its tropical north supports fruit industries that other western countries can only fantasize about. Travelers from fruit-deprived countries will encounter exotic offerings such as custard apples, lychees, passionfruit, star fruit, coconuts, mangoes, and pineapples. Queensland is the main fruit-producing region. Of the typical prepared desserts, there's the ubiquitous **lamington**—a coconut-covered chunk of pound cake dipped in chocolate, and the festive **pavlova** meringue (see **Keep Your Kiwis Off!,** above).

BUSH TUCKER

THE REAL THING. Coastal Aborigines have eaten crayfish, **yabbies** (freshwater shrimp), and fish for centuries, and the first English settlers rapidly followed suit. But in the harsh environments of the bush, Aboriginal foragers exploited food resources that early colonists found a little too unorthodox to stomach. **Witchetty grubs** are the most well-known of the bush foods that make some first-timers twinge. If you want to sample **goanna** or **ants,** however, you might have to catch dinner yourself or join one of the Red Centre tours that feature real bush tucker.

FOR THE TOURISTS. These days the appeal of bush tucker has grown and is no longer limited to the adventurous and brave of heart (read: tourist). Australia has recently discovered a taste for is own "exotic" indigenous food. And "bush tucker" is the new urban catch phrase. Each year, more restaurants spring up offering hip urban menus that incorporate Aboriginal wild foods like bunya nuts, Kakadu plums, and wild rosella flowers with specialty meats such as kangaroo filet, crocodile meat, Northern Territory buffalo, and wild magpie geese.

MORE THAN JUST DRINKIN'

COFFEE. In Australia, ordering drinks is an art that takes time to perfect. Nothing better illustrates this than ordering a simple cup of coffee. In fact, it might sound bizarre to some, but ordering "just coffee" is nearly impossible. Though they are a long way from Italy, Australia's major cities harbor a cappucino culture that can deliver caffeine into your bloodstream in more ways than there are letters in cappucino. If you need some help ordering, see the guide to **Coffee Confusion** on p. 115. Whatever you do, don't let any Aussie know that you needed to ask for directions.

BEER. Let's move on to the more important skill of choosing a beer. A close association (if not love) exists between Australia and **beer,** and with good reason. Australia produces some of the world's best brews, and Australians over the legal drinking age of 18 consume it readily (we can't speak for those under the legal age). Some Australians despise **Fosters,** which owes its international name-recognition to saturation advertising. Much like the footy teams, each state has a beer "mascot," a locally brewed and distributed piece of state pride. Queensland makes **XXXX** ("four-x"), but **Victoria Bitter,** known as "VB," is tipped back a bit more by the locals. **Cooper's Ale,** from South Australia, is a terrific drop-brewed beer in the bottle (roll the bottle back and forth for 30 seconds to mix the sediment left in every bottle) and promises a different taste with each sip. **Touhey's New** is a popular brew from NSW, while **Melbourne Bitter** from its southerly neighbor, has a large following as well. While many beers have a relatively high alcoholic content (around 5%), there has been a recent trend toward "light" beers, which have less alcohol (not fewer calories). **Strongbow,** Australia's favorite cider, is quietly gaining popularity in pubs as a potent and tasty alternative, but many Aussie blokes wouldn't be seen dead holding a stubbie of it (the favorite excuse is "I was holding it for my girlfriend"). Beer unequivocally prevails, even though a popular choice are mixed canned-drinks and malt brews (like Jack Daniels and Cola) found in all liquor stores. The best place to share a coldie with your mates is the omnipresent Aussie **pub.** Traditional payment etiquette is the **shout,** in which drinking mates alternate rounds. If the beach is more your style, throw a **slab** (24 containers of beer) in the **Esky** (ice chest). For more beer terminology, consult the **glossary,** p. 670.

WINE. Simply put, Australian **wines** rival the best wines in the world. Overseas export started soon after the first vineyards began to produce wine in the early 1800s, and the industry has gained renown after a post-WWII influx of European talent. The **Hunter Valley** (see p. 146), the **Barossa** and **Clare Valleys** (see p. 431), the **Swan** and **Margaret Rivers** (see p. 624), and the **Derwent** and **Tamar Valleys** (see p. 475), possess some of the best Aussie vineyards. Many cafes and low-end restaurants advertise that they are **BYO,** or "bring your own." Though typically not licensed to serve alcohol, these establishments permit patrons to furnish their own bottle of wine with the meal and charge only a small **corkage fee,** if anything.

SPORT

WHERE TO FIND IT. Australians take sport very seriously. Sport has often been referred to as the national identity. The 1956 Melbourne Olympics inaugurated national television broadcasting in Australia, and televisions in public places have been tuned to sporting events ever since. While the big event on everyone's calendar in late 2000 was the Sydney Olympics, the national team-sports melodrama extends year-round. You can't walk into a bar without a sports event from somewhere in Oz on TV. Unfortunately, much of it revolves around gambling (see **That's What It's All About,** p. 307). In winter, Western Australia, South Australia, and Victoria catch **footy fever** for **Australian Rules Football,** while New South Wales and Queensland traditionally follow **rugby.** In summer, **cricket** is the spectator sport of choice across the nation. Star Aussie Rules football players and top cricketers enjoy hero status. Tune in to H. G. Nelson and Roy Slaven's Sunday afternoon Triple-J radio show *This Sporting Life* for a taste of Aussie sport culture.

WHAT IS IT? Even if you missed the Olympics, cricket seems eternally confusing, or Aussie Rules Football is still incomprehensible, just join in the crowds, cheer for the home team, and remember the old adage that many an Australian sports fan takes to heart: **It's all fun and games until somebody loses an eye—then it's sport.**

CRICKET. The uninitiated may have trouble making sense of a sport where people can "bowl a maiden over of five flippers and a googly," but visitors won't be able to avoid the enthusiasm. Two teams of 11 players face off in a contest that can last anywhere from an afternoon to five days. Each summer, **international cricket** overshadows the national competition. A "test match" is not just a scrimmage; it is the most lengthy and serious form of international cricket. In 1877, Australia's cricket team headed to England for its first international test against the mother country, and, surprisingly, the colonials won. The Australians, as a shocked English reporter wrote, had "taken off with the ashes" of English cricket. Ever since then, British and Australian Test teams have been in noble contest for **"the Ashes"** (the trophy is a small, symbolic urn) with other British colonial countries such as India, Pakistan, and South Africa joining in the competition.

In December and January, different international teams arrive for a **full tour,** consisting of five test matches, one each in Melbourne, Sydney, Perth, Adelaide, and Brisbane. The five-day tests are accompanied by smaller, titillating one-day matches, and are over by February, in time for the country to turn its attention to **national cricket** and the Sheffield Shield finals in March.

AUSTRALIAN RULES FOOTBALL. How to play? Good question. In Victoria, South Australia, and Western Australia, the **Australian Football League (AFL)** teams fill the winter void that the end of the cricket season leaves. Played on cricket ovals, the game was originally designed (if there is any actual design involved) to keep cricket players in shape in the off-season. Teams attempt to get the red leather ball from one end of the field to the other and kick it through the opposing team's posts to score. Each team of 18 players defends three sets of posts for four 20-minute quarters: six points are earned for scoring in the middle goal, and one point for reaching either side goal. Confused yet? Just wait until you actually see a match.

The basic move in AFL is the **punt,** used for both passing and scoring; good players can punt the ball over 70m. The best move to make, though, is the **mark.** If a player can catch the ball on the kick before it bounces, he is entitled to unobstructed possession of that ball. Consequently, just after a kick, the players all pack together and run, jump, and soar (though not gracefully) under and over each other, in a effort to snatch the ball from the sky. The AFL grand final, in early September, is a marvelous spectacle at the home of Australian sport, the **MCG** (**Melbourne Cricket Ground,** see p. 529).

RUGBY. According to legend, **rugby** was born one glorious day in 1823 when one inspired (or perhaps frustrated) student in Rugby, England, picked up a soccer ball and ran it into the goal. Since then, rugby has evolved (or devolved) into an intricately punishing game, with two variants: **rugby union** involving 15-man teams, and **rugby league** with 13-man teams. Despite the international reputation of the national union team, the **Wallabies,** rugby union sometimes carries a muted following. Since they defeated France to win the World Cup in 1999, though, rugby union has grown in popularity. Matches such as the **Super 12** tournament and **Tri-nation** series (Australia, South Africa, and New Zealand) often pack stadiums and pubs. Part of the Tri-nation series, the **Bledisloe Cup** (first played in 1931) perpetuates a healthy animosity with Australia's down-under cousin, New Zealand.

Rugby league attracts a much larger following, especially in New South Wales and Queensland. The national league competition culminates in the **National Rugby League (NRL) final** in September. The only match that comes close to the intensity or popularity of the NRL final is the **State of Origin** series in June, when Queensland takes on New South Wales. Both games promise a mix of blood, mud, and plenty of drinking. For all the rugby action you can handle (if you're tough enough), check out www.rugbyworld.com.

OTHER SPORT. Australia sport is not only cricket shots or footy marks. Melbourne hosts one of tennis' Grand Slam events, the **Australian Open,** each January. Grassy tennis courts, bowling greens, and golf courses pepper the cities coast-to-coast. Most towns also have a horse racing track, and on the first Tuesday in November, the entire country stops to watch jockeys jockey for the prestigious **Melbourne Cup**, where fashionable and outlandish attire sometimes appears more important than the race. On Boxing Day, even as the Melbourne cricket Test gets underway, half of Australia's amateur sailing community fills Sydney Harbour with billowing white sails to begin the **Sydney-to-Hobart yacht race,** the highlight in a full calendar of water sports. Australia is famous for its **surfing,** which for some is a competitive sport in addition to a great way to spend a summer morning. People attempt to surf virtually everywhere, but especially up and down the east coast.

ENVIRONMENT

Simply put, Australia has benefited from millions of years of isolation on a very large island. The sheltered existence has helped breed some of the world's most peculiar plants and animals. When plants and animals landed on a continent nearly devoid of competition, they grew fast from a limited number of ancestral groups. However, Australia's inevitable contact with the outside has presented an enormous challenge to its unique biology. The introduction of animals and colonization by Europeans upset Australia's delicate ecology. It is estimated that 13 species of mammals and one species of bird have already become extinct since European settlement. In recent years, environmental policy has begun to recognize the importance of protecting Australia's precious biodiversity.

PLANTS

STRANGE GROWTHS IN SECRET PLACES. There is one plant you are guaranteed to find in Australia. Dominating forests from coast to coast, the **eucalypts,** also known as **gum trees,** amaze biologists with their successful adaptation to diverse environments, taking on many different shapes and sizes across the continent. The majestic **karri** soars to over 50m in ancient stands along well-watered valleys, while the **mallee** gum tends to grow in stunted copses across scrubland, like that of western Victoria. The characteristically bulging trunk and splayed branches of the **boab** mark the horizon, particularly in the arid Kimberley of Western Australia. In the drier areas of the southeast, a common species of the **acacia** tree (which has over 600 species), known as the **golden wattle,** is distinguished by its fragrant flowers. Perhaps the most unusual—and most rare—tree is the **Wollemi pine.** The pine was discovered by scientists a few years ago, who had previously thought that the species was extinct (see **Wollemi National Park,** p. 145).

BRING ME A SHRUBBERY. Gums aren't the only plant dominating the landscape. Other regulars in the bush and coastal thickets include **banksias, tea trees,** and **grevillias.** Feathery and almost pine-like in appearance, **casuarinas** also exist in multiple habitats. In temperate, rain-fed stretches of Victoria and Tasmania, valleys of tall, dinosaur-era **tree ferns** are dwarfed by towering **mountain ash,** the tallest flowering plant in nature. A remarkable feature found along parts of Australia's tropical coasts, the **mangrove** has adapted readily to its unfavorable environment, and stilt-like trunks cling tenaciously to the briny mud of alluvial swamps. Meanwhile, Australia has wide swaths of land that grow nary a tree. The arid outback is dominated by dense tufts of **spinifex** grasses. Another common plant is the **saltbush,** a hearty shrub that grows in soil too salty for other plants and that has been pivotal in converting harsh habitats to livestock pastures.

FLOWER POWER. Although Australia has a tough plant life, wildflowers are abundant in more fertile areas. Western Australia is home to **swamp bottlebrush, kangaroo paw,** and **Ashby's banksia,** along with nearly 10,000 other species. Yellow and pink **everlastings** cover fields across the country, to the delight of casual wildflower viewers, but rare **spider orchids** hidden in the forests reveal themselves only to the most dogged of investigators. The **Sturt pea** adds a distinctive splash of red and black to the inland deserts of South Australia and Western Australia. Elsewhere, **orchids** and **begonias** provide extra visual garnish.

ANIMALS

When most people think of Australia, they picture kangaroos and cuddly koalas. But the country has much more to offer than those tourist symbols. Between 200,000 and 300,000 species of animals call Australia home. While most of these are insects, many larger and more exotic creatures make the island continent their breeding ground. Marsupials, of course, are the stars of the Australian menagerie. Marsupials had few mammalian competitors on the continent and inhabited many different ecosystems. Thus, early naturalists named marsupials by the habitat in which other mammals would be found; the koala is not a bear; the marsupial "rat" is not a rat; the marsupial "cat" and "mole" are more closely related to each other than their given names would suggest.

KANGAROOS. Bounding about everywhere, kangaroos are synonymous with Australia and, like most indigenous Australian mammals, they are marsupials. At any time after the age of two, a female kangaroo is likely to have one offspring in the womb, one living in the pouch, and one making occasional visits to the pouch. This style of reproduction, combined with the kangaroo's ability to suspend gestation for up to two years, ensures survival in harsh desert environments, but also results in a markedly lower life span for females. Kangaroos have thrived on the fringes of human communities since colonization, leading the Australian government to conduct an annual program of kangaroo culling.

Kangaroos travel in groups known as mobs, which can have over 20 members. The many species are in two basic groups: grey kangaroos and the larger and more aggressive red kangaroos. Male red 'roos can grow to be 3m long, nose to tail, and are capable of propelling themselves nearly 9m at a single bound. Contrary to popular myth, kangaroos do not feed marmalade sandwiches to small bears or send their young out to play with tree-dwelling pigs and tail-bouncing tigers. The kangaroo's look-alike cousin, the wallaby, is another common outback critter. Other native marsupials include wombats, possums, bandicoots, and quolls.

KOALAS. Australia's other most-loved marsupials live on and among the leaves of certain eucalypt trees. Sleeping an average 18 out of every 24 hours and existing on a diet made up exclusively of the intoxicating and semi-toxic eucalyptus leaves (with the nutrition equivalent of cardboard), the koala lives every college student's dream. It has little energy for hunting, gathering, or even moving. Seeing a koala is often just a matter of being patient enough to scan the treetops for a familiar furball, or impatient enough to find the nearest zoo or nature preserve.

MONOTREMES. Australia's list of peculiar mammals does not end with marsupials. Two families of **monotremes,** or egg-laying mammals, call Australia home. **Echidnas** are small ant-eaters that resemble porcupines with protruding snouts. When threatened, the echidna buries itself in the ground, leaving only long spines exposed. The **platypus** sports a melange of zoological features: the bill of a duck, the fur of an otter, the tail of a beaver, and webbed claws. So outrageous did this anatomy seem to colonists that early naturalists refused to consider stuffed specimens real (see **Magnificent Mammalian Monotreme,** p. 29).

REPTILES. The most fearsome reptiles, saltwater crocodiles **("salties")** actually live in both brine and freshwater and grow to lengths of 7m. For a primer on discriminating between the salty and its less threatening freshwater relative—and avoiding becoming croc fodder—take a look at freshies and salties, p. 247. In addition to its crocodiles, Australia's reptiles include aggressive **goannas** (see **I'm-A Goanna Get Ya!,** below), and a wide array of **poisonous snakes,** including the **taipan, smooth snake, tiger snake, brown snake,** and the **death adder** (for advice on what to do in the case of an adverse meeting with one of these nasties, see p. 53).

I'M-A GOANNA GET YA! Goannas are large lizards, growing up to 3 or 4 meters. Should you encounter one, the old maxim applies: it's more afraid of you than the other way 'round. Be aware, however, that goannas protect themselves from danger by scurrying up trees, and if a scared goanna comes running toward you (away from whatever scared it), there's the off-chance that it will try to seek refuge on you! Crouch down or lie flat to avoid being climbed. Once your pursuer realizes you're not a tree and offer no protection, it should leave you alone.

BIRDS. Outshining Australia's mammals in vividness of color is the continent's tremendous diversity of **birds.** The **emu** is related to other flightless birds such as the African ostrich and the extinct moa of New Zealand. Flightless hordes of **little** (or **fairy**) **penguins** can be spotted at sites on the south coast, where they wade ashore each night. Australia's flight-endowed birds include noisy flocks of **galahs,** colorful **rainbow lorikeets,** and large **cassowaries.** Songs and poems have immortalized the unmistakable laugh of the **kookaburra.** Both **crimson rosellas** and **cockatoos** are common in the southeast.

MEGAFAUNA. Giant marsupials once roamed the landscape of prehistoric Australia. Now extinct, these megafauna included towering relatives of kangaroos called diprotodons. The megafauna died off soon after the arrival of humans, due to hunting or climatic changes (see **Cenozoic Megafauna,** p. 234). The **thylacine,** or **Tasmanian tiger,** is a more recent loss. Resembling a large wolf with stripes, the predator was driven to the edge of extinction by competition with dingoes, then hunted by white settlers who feared for livestock. One infamous marsupial carnivore has survived, however. Fierce in temperament, **Tasmanian devils** are nocturnal scavengers. They also hunt small prey and have been known to kill livestock with their powerful jaws (see **Marsupials from Hell,** p. 478).

PESTS. Humans have been responsible for the introduction of animals to Australia since prehistoric times, and many are now considered pests. The **dingo,** a lithe, wild canine with a vicious bite but no bark, crossed the Timor Sea with ancestors of Aboriginal populations several thousand years ago. The creatures mainly hunt small, wild prey, but may also menace livestock (ranchers detest them and kill those they encounter near their flocks). Although dingoes pose little threat to adults, they are can injure and even kill, children. The massive overpopulation of **rabbits,** purportedly introduced to Australia to provide practice targets for marksmen (see **Believe It Or Not,** p. 542), has become one of Australia's gravest wildlife problems. Accidental introductions such as European **rats** and **Cane toads** present serious threats to native fauna as well.

LIVESTOCK. More recent (and intentional) arrivals accompanied European colonists to help settle the land. Domesticated **cattle** and **sheep** have always been of tremendous economic importance in Australia, with ranches across the continent. These species have had a dramatic impact on the landscape and ecological balance of the nation; vast tracts have been converted to pasture to support the meat industry. In recent years, the farming of non-native **honeybees** has also become a growing part of the economy.

MAGNIFICENT MAMMALIAN MONOTREME

Oh yes, we're talking about that milk-bearing, web-footed wonder, the platypus. The result of an evolutionary mix-and-match game, these furry water dwellers have been swimming around for at least 190 million years. In addition to anatomical non-sequiters such as a duck's bill and a beaver's tail, the male platypus also has a venomous spur under its ankle. Both genders have an all-purpose cloaca, an organ usually found in birds and reptiles. Solid waste, urine, sperm and eggs are all released from this one hole (hence "monotreme"). The platypus swims with its eyes, ears and nostrils shut, but uses special sensors on its bill to detect the electrical signals of other, potentially tasty animals. These timid creatures inhabit eastern waters from Tasmania up to Cooktown and are quite common in the bends of creeks within the Atherton Tablelands.

MARINE LIFE

THE GREAT BARRIER REEF. Fur seals, elephant seals, and sea lions populate Australia's southern shores during summer breeding seasons, but it's the Great Barrier Reef that makes Australia's sea life unique. It's also one of Australia's biggest tourist draws and a diving wonderland. A comprehensive overview on **diving and snorkeling** the reef is in the introduction to the Queensland chapter (see **The Great Barrier Reef,** p. 287). The longest coral formation in the world, it is actually a series of many reefs that stretches more than 2000km along the eastern coast of Queensland from the Tropic of Capricorn to Papua New Guinea. Although adult **coral polyps** are sedentary, corals actually belong to the animal kingdom. Thus, the Great Barrier Reef is the only community of animals visible to the eye from space.

Corals rely on sunlight filtering down from the ocean surface and cannot grow at depths greater than 50m. Reef accumulates whenever a coral polyp dies and leaves behind its skeletal legacy of calcium carbonate. As layers of limestone build, the reef rises toward the surface. Once the coral reaches the top of the waves, the surf pounds it into sand-size bits. Add some more years and the bits form a little mound, called a **cay,** that sticks out of the water. Birds come along, land on the cay, and ingloriously deposit seeds from the mainland, and vegetation turns the cay into an island. Sea turtles and birds come to nest, and soon a whole ecosystem has literally risen from the water. Colonies of coral grow by asexual reproduction, but new colonies propagate by **sexual reproduction**—quite a feat for creatures fixed to one spot, see p. 383.

CORAL. Coral reefs take a number of different forms. Closest to the shore are **patch reefs,** comprised of patches of **hard** and **soft coral.** The former is often dried, bleached and sold to tourists in shops. Beware of national marine park rules against removing living creatures from the sea and customs fines up to $500 for removing any piece of a coral reef. Soft corals, however, lose their shape and turn to sludge when taken out of water. Long, slender **sea whips** and delicate, intricate **fan corals** are some of the most plentiful and beautiful soft corals. Hard corals come in hues ranging from purple to emerald to red, and are mostly categorized as either branched, boulder, or plate coral. The fast-growing **branched coral** is named for its appearance; its most common varieties are the thin, brittle **needle coral,** the antler-like **stag coral,** and **finger coral. Boulder coral** is sturdier and slower-growing, including the **honey-comb, golfball** and **brain boulders;** in areas where cyclones are frequent, these are the species that tend to survive. **Plate corals,** such as **sheet** and **table corals** look like they sound.

Further out than the patch reefs are **fringe reefs,** which contain the same types of coral. Their arrangement in circular patterns deeply entrenched in the sea floor means that they frequently fill with silt, clouding visibility for divers. The far outer reef is made up of 710km of **ribbon reef;** this includes some of Australia's best diving, but is accessible only to boats that venture out for four days or longer.

FISH AND MAMMALS. The reef also houses a spectacular variety of colorful, sometimes otherworldly fish, from the enormous **potato cod** to the **fusaleres,** a family of fish that change color at night. The **parrotfish** eats bits of coral by cracking it in its beak-like mouth, and at night envelops itself in a protective mucus sac, a phenomenon that might be a highlight of a night dive. If you're diving, taking a **briefing course** on marine life is an excellent way to familiarize yourself with what you'll see. While it's impossible to memorize every species, many shops sell **fish identification cards** that you can take down with you. A few terms to know: the **wrasse** is a long, slender, cigar-like fish; **angel** and **surgeon fish** have similar oblong shapes, but the surgeon has a razor-sharp barb close to its tail; the **butterfly** and **bat fish** are round, but the latter is a larger and has a black stripe across the eye. Despite Australia's reputation for **sharks,** only grey **reef sharks** (and the very occasional **tiger shark**) are seen around the Reef and are typically harmless when unprovoked. Besides fish, the reef houses **turtles, porpoises, dolphins,** and **whales,** as well as **echinoderms:** sea cucumbers, sea stars, feather stars, and brittle stars.

POISONOUS SEA CREATURES. If an Aussie is somewhat scared of something, that means you should probably be terrified. If you're told that the unidentified creature you're holding is a **nasty**—drop it. Better yet, **don't touch unfamiliar objects.** Many benign-looking creatures are poisonous, some even deadly. The most infamous nasty is the **box jellyfish,** a near-transparent creature which tends to live near the coast, particularly near river mouths or estuaries. Its up-to-3m tentacles contain a toxin that can kill you within three minutes; carrying a vinegar-based antivenom is wise. The best option is to avoid coastal diving (and swimming) altogether during box jellyfish season (Oct.-Apr.) and to obey all posted warnings. The **cone shell** has brightly patterned shells that look as though they would make excellent souvenirs, but the stingers inside are packed with enough venom to kill an adult human. The **stone fish** lies motionless and camouflaged against the coral, waiting for prey. If you're unlucky enough to step on its poison-filled spines, seek medical attention pronto. It takes a lot of weight to step on one of these and get hurt, so it is dangerous only in shallow water. **Sting rays, lion fish,** and **sea snakes** are all poisonous as well, but aren't likely to attack except in retaliation. Some nasties are irritating but not deadly. If you pick up the inert **sea urchin,** you may get small pieces of its spines embedded in your skin, causing swelling and pain. A prick from the **crown of thorns,** a type of sea star, will send a low-grade poison into your bloodstream. However, its effects on the reef itself are far worse, as it feeds on coral. A recent population explosion has led to the legalized removal of sea stars by dive boats.

ESSENTIALS

FACTS FOR THE TRAVELER

CLIMATE

HIGH SEASON. Winter (June-Aug.) is peak travel season in Australia. During these months, you must book accommodations and tours months in advance especially in the Top End, the Red Centre, most of Western Australia, and Northern Queensland. In fact, in these regions during the pleasant months of Apr.-Sept., many hostels and resorts will charge higher prices especially during Australian school holidays. If possible, avoid the end of Dec. (after Boxing Day) and the month of January when Australians take their summer vacations—expect all accommodations to be scarce and charging higher fares.

LOW SEASON. Sweltering heat, fierce sunlight, and uncomfortable humidity characterize the months from October to March in northern Western Australia and the Northern Territory. Many outdoor activities are near impossible. However, during the Wet (Nov.-Apr.), floodwaters, lush vegetation growth, and swelling waterfalls can be quite enjoyable in Darwin, Kakadu National Park, and the Kimberley. Nevertheless, the Australian summer is a time to visit the southern states of Victoria, New South Wales, South Australia, southern Western Australia, and Tasmania.

TIME ZONES

Time zones in Australia can be a bit confusing, especially when only certain states across the continent observe Daylight Savings Time (late October to late March), marking the official beginning of summer. This means that Australia's times zones follow state borders both vertically and horizontally. Greenwich Mean Time (GMT) is not affected by Daylight Savings Time (DST), providing a standard to calculate differences in time zones. The rows on the left represent where you are. The columns across the top represent where you wish to know the time. To calculate the time in a different zone, simply add or subtract the difference in hours between the two places. For example, if it is noon in GMT, then it is 10pm in Victoria. Remember that the date is affected in some cases—Australia is ahead of the Western Hemisphere, so Monday evening in New York is Tuesday morning in Sydney. All regions that observe DST have an asterisk. Therefore, during DST if you start in a row with an asterisk, you must subtract 1 hour. If you end in a column with an asterisk, you must add 1 hour. For example, during DST if it is noon in GMT, then it is 11pm in Victoria. In 2002, all states in Australia begin DST at 2am on October 27, while Tasmania begins its observation on October 6. DST ends March 30, 2003.

London is 1 hour ahead of GMT from the last Sunday in March to the last Sunday in October due to DST. **New York City** is normally 5 hours behind GMT. However, from the first Sunday in April to the last Sunday in October, NYC is only 4 hours behind GMT due to DST.

	GMT	WA	NT	SA*	QLD	ACT, NSW, TAS, VIC*
Greenwich Mean Time		+8	+9.5	+9.5	+10	+10
Western Australia	-8		+1.5	+1.5	+2	+2
Northern Territory	-9.5	-1.5		0	+0.5	+0.5
Southern Australia*	-9.5	-1.5	0		+0.5	+0.5
Queensland	-10	-2	-0.5	-0.5		0
ACT, New South Wales, Tasmania, Victoria*	-10	-2	-0.5	-0.5	0	

DOCUMENTS AND FORMALITIES

ENTRANCE REQUIREMENTS. Unlike during the convict era, a criminal record is no longer required for entry into Australia.

Passports (p. 34). Required for all visitors.

Visas (p. 35). Required of all citizens except holders of Australian and New Zealand passports.

Working Visa (p. 35). Required for all foreigners planning to work in Australia.

Inoculations (p. 44). Only necessary for those who come from or have just visited yellow fever-infected areas (parts of South America and Central Africa).

Driving Permit (p. 70). Recommended; required for many car rental agencies.

AUSTRALIAN CONSULAR SERVICES ABROAD

Canada: High Commission, 50 O'Connor St. #710, **Ottawa,** ON K1P 6L2 (☎613-783-7665; fax 236-4376; www.ahc-ottawa.org).

Ireland: Fitzwilton House, 2nd floor, Wilton Tce., **Dublin** 2 (☎01 676 1517; fax 661 3576; www.australianembassy.ie).

New Zealand: High Commission, 72-78 Hobson St., P.O. Box 4036, **Wellington** (☎04 473 6411; fax 498 7118). Consulate, Union House, 7th-8th floor, 132-138 Quay St., (Private Bag 92023) **Auckland,** (☎09 303 2429; fax 377 0798).

South Africa: High Commission, 292 Orient St., Arcadia, **Pretoria** 0083; Private Bag X150, Pretoria 0001. (☎012 342 3740; fax 342 4222).

United Kingdom: High Commission, The Strand, **London** WC2B 4LA (☎171 379 4334; fax 465 8218; www.australia.org.uk). Consulate, Chatsworth House, Lever St., **Manchester** MI 2QL (☎161 228 1344; fax 236 4074).

United States: Visa requests should go to Washington, D.C. or Los Angeles. Embassy, 1601 Massachusetts Ave. NW, **Washington, D.C.** 20036 (☎202-797-3000; fax 797-3168; www.austemb.org). Consulate, 150 E. 42nd St., 34th fl., **New York,** NY 10017 (☎212-351-6500; fax 351-6501). Consulate, 2049 Century Park E, 19th floor, **Los Angeles,** CA 90067 (visas ☎310-229-4840, general 229-4800; fax 277-5620).

EMBASSIES AND CONSULATES IN AUSTRALIA

Canada: High Commission (☎02 6270 4000; fax 6273 4081), Commonwealth Ave., **Canberra** ACT 2600. Consulate, Level 5, Quay West Building, 111 Harrington St., **Sydney** NSW 2000 (☎02 9364 3000; fax 9364 3098). Consulate, 267 St. George's Tce., **Perth** WA 6000 (☎08 9322 7930; fax 9261 7706). Consulate, 123 Camberwell Rd. **Hawthorn East** VIC 3123 (☎03 9811 9999; fax 9811 9969).

Ireland: Embassy, 20 Arkana St., Yarralumla, **Canberra** ACT 2615 (☎02 6273 3022; fax 6273 3741). Consulate, P.O. Box 250, **Floreat Forum** WA 6014 (☎/fax 08 9385 8247). Consulate, Level 30, 400 George St. **Sydney** NSW 2000 (☎02 9231 6999; fax 9231 6254).

New Zealand: High Commission, Commonwealth Ave., **Canberra** ACT 2600 (☎02 6270 4211; fax 6273 3194). Consulate, GPO Box 365 (Level 10, 55 Hunter St.), **Sydney** NSW 1041 (passport ☎02 9223 0222, visa 9223 0144; fax 9221 7836).

South Africa: High Commission, State Circle, Yarralumla, **Canberra** ACT 2600 (☎02 6273 2424; fax 6273 3543).

United Kingdom: High Commission, Commonwealth Ave., Yarralumla, **Canberra** ACT 2600 (☎02 6270 6666; fax 6273 3236). Consulate, 17th floor, 90 Collins St., **Melbourne** VIC 3000 (☎03 9650 4155; fax 9650 3699). Consulate, Level 26, Allendale Square, 77 St. George's Tce., **Perth** WA 6000 (☎08 9221 5400; fax 9221 2344). Consulate, Level 16, The Gateway, 1 Macquarie Pl., **Sydney** NSW 2000 (☎02 9247 7521; fax 9251 6201).

United States: Embassy, Moonah Pl., Yarralumla, **Canberra** ACT 2600 (☎02 6214 5600; fax 6214 5970). Consulate, Level 59, MLC Centre, 19-29 Martin Pl., **Sydney** NSW 2000 (☎02 9373 9200; fax 9373 9184). Consulate, 553 St. Kilda Rd., **Melbourne** VIC 3004 (☎03 9526 5900; fax 9510 4646). Consulate, 13th floor, 16 St. George's Tce., **Perth** WA 6000 (☎08 9231 9400; fax 9231 9444).

PASSPORTS

REQUIREMENTS. All visitors need valid passports to enter Australia and return home. Australia prohibits entrance if the holder's passport expires in under six months; returning home with an expired passport is illegal and may result in a fine.

PHOTOCOPIES. Be sure to photocopy the page of your passport with your photo, passport number, and other identifying information, as well as any visas, travel insurance policies, plane tickets, or traveler's check serial numbers. Carry one set of copies in a safe place, apart from the originals, and leave another set at home. Consulates also recommend that you carry an expired passport or an official copy of your birth certificate in a part of your baggage separate from other documents.

LOST PASSPORTS. Your passport is a public document belonging to your nation's government. You may have to surrender it to a foreign government official, but if you don't get it back in a reasonable amount of time, inform the nearest embassy or consulate of your home country. If you lose your passport, immediately notify the local police and the nearest embassy or consulate of your home government. To expedite its replacement, you will need to know all information previously recorded and show ID and proof of citizenship. A replacement may take weeks to process, and it may be valid only for a limited time. Any visas stamped in your old passport will be irretrievably lost. In an emergency, ask for immediate temporary traveling papers that will permit you to re-enter your home country.

NEW PASSPORTS. File any new passport or renewal applications well in advance of your departure date. Most passport offices offer rush services for a steep fee. Citizens living abroad who need a passport or renewal should contact the nearest consular service of their home country.

Canada: Canadian Passport Office, Department of Foreign Affairs and International Trade, Ottawa, ON K1A OG3 (☎819-994-3500 or ☎800-567-6868; www.dfait-maeci.gc.ca/passport). Applications available at passport offices, Canadian missions, and post offices. Passports CDN$60; valid for 5 years (non-renewable).

Ireland: Department of Foreign Affairs, Passport Office, Molesworth St., Dublin 2 (☎01 671 1633; www.irlgov.ie/iveagh), or the Passport Office, Irish Life Building, 1A South Mall, Cork (☎021 494 4700). Applications available at a *Garda* station or post office, or request one from a passport office. Passports IR£45; valid for 10 years. Under 18 or over 65 IR£10; valid for 3 years.

New Zealand: Passport Office, Department of International Affairs, P.O. Box 10526, Wellington, New Zealand (☎0800 22 50 50 or ☎4 474 8000; fax 474 8002; www.passports.govt.nz). Standard processing time is 10 working days. Passports NZ$80; valid for 10 years. Children NZ$40; valid for 5 years. 3 day "urgent service" NZ$160; children NZ $120. Callout service NZ$330; children $290.

South Africa: Passports are issued only in Pretoria, but all applications must still be submitted or forwarded to the nearest South African consulate. Processing time is 3 months or more. For more information, check out http://usaembassy.southafrica.net/VisaForms/Passport/Passport2000.html. Passports around ZAR190; valid for 10 years. Under 16 around ZAR80; valid for 5 years.

United Kingdom: Info ☎0870 521 0410; www.ukonline.gov.uk. Get an application from a passport office, main post office, travel agent, or online (for UK residents only) at www.ukpa.gov.uk/forms/f_app_pack.htm. Then apply by mail or in person at a passport office. Passports UK£28; valid for 10 years. Under 15 UK£14.80; valid for 5 years.

The process takes about 4 weeks; faster service (by personal visit to the offices listed above) costs an additional £12.

United States: Info ☎202-647-0518; www.travel.state.gov/passport_services.html. Apply at any federal or state courthouse, authorized post office, or US Passport Agency (in most major cities); see the "US Government, State Department" section of the telephone book or a post office for addresses. Processing takes 3-4 weeks. New passports US$60; valid for 10 years. Under 16 US$40; valid for 5 years. Passports may be renewed by mail or in person for US$40. Add US$35 for 3-day expedited service.

VISAS, ETA, AND WORK PERMITS

VISAS. Australia **requires all visitors** except Australian citizens and New Zealand passport holders to have a visa. You can obtain an **Electronic Travel Authority (ETA)** while purchasing your ticket at a travel agency or at the airport ticket counter. The Australian Government has also now made it possible to arrange an ETA over the Internet (www.eta.immi.gov.au). Quick and simple, the fully-electronic ETA replaces a standard visa. It allows three months on each visit within a one-year period. The ETA is free for those staying less than three months. To extend a visit over three months, contact the nearest office of the Department of Immigration and Multicultural Affairs in Australia before the end of your 3 month stay period. There is no provision for obtaining a further ETA when you are in Australia. For more info, contact the nearest **Australian Tourist Commission (ATC)** branch (see p. 37). Standard **visas** (US$40) may be obtained from the nearest Australian high commission, embassy, or consulate. If you register in person, it will take two days to process; allow 21 working days by mail. Rates on extending your ETA or visa depend on length of desired stay and type of visa; an application to extend a standard visa is AUS$150. Contact the **Department of Immigration and Multicultural Affairs** at their toll-free inquiries line (☎13 18 81) before your stay period expires. Otherwise, contact an Australian consulate or embassy (see p. 33).

US citizens can take advantage of the **Center for International Business and Travel** (**CIBT;** ☎800-929-2428), which secures visas for travel to almost all countries for a variable service charge. Between the hours of 8:30am and 8pm (M-F) email to customerservice@cibt.com will be returned within two hours.

Be sure to double-check on entrance requirements at the nearest embassy or consulate of Australia for up-to-date info before departure. US citizens can also consult www.pueblo.gsa.gov/cic_text/travel/foreign/foreignentryreqs.html.

WORK PERMITS. Eighteen to twenty-five year olds from Canada, Ireland, Japan, Korea, Malta, the Netherlands, the UK, and Germany are eligible for a **working holiday visa,** granted only under certain conditions for a fee of AUS$150. Any work done in Australia must be solely to support your vacation. You must show either a return ticket or sufficient funds to leave the country, as well as the skills to obtain a job. Students going to Australia to study abroad are almost guaranteed a working visa that allows for 20 hours per week of work. To obtain a **student visa,** you must complete an application form, pay the application charge, have a confirmation of enrollment issued by a registered provider, and meet health and character requirements. Working and studying visas vary according to your plans; contact the Australian embassy or consulate in your home country with questions. For more information, see **Work,** p. 76, or go to www.immi.gov.au for a full list of rules.

IDENTIFICATION

When you travel, always carry two or more forms of identification on your person, including at least one photo ID; a passport combined with a driver's license or birth certificate is usually adequate. Many establishments, especially banks, require several IDs to cash traveler's checks. Never carry all your forms of ID together; split them up in case of theft or loss. It is useful to bring extra passport-size photos to affix to the various IDs or passes you may acquire along the way.

STUDENT AND TEACHER IDENTIFICATION. The **International Student Identity Card (ISIC),** the most widely accepted form of student ID, provides discounts on sights, accommodations, food, and transportation. Present the card wherever you go, and ask about discounts even when none are advertised. The ISIC is preferable to an institution-specific card (such as a university ID) because it is more likely to be recognized (and honored) abroad. All cardholders have access to a 24-hour emergency helpline for medical, legal, and financial emergencies (in North America call ☎877-370-ISIC, elsewhere call US collect ☎+1 715-345-0505, UK collect +44 20 8762 8110, or France collect +33 155 633 144), and holders of US-issued cards are also eligible for insurance benefits (see **Insurance,** p. 46). Many student travel agencies issue ISICs, including STA Travel in Australia and New Zealand; Travel CUTS in Canada; USIT in the Republic of Ireland and Northern Ireland; SASTS in South Africa; Campus Travel and STA Travel in the UK; Council Travel (www.counciltravel.com/idcards/default.asp) and STA Travel in the US (see p. 61). The card is valid from September of one year to December of the following year. Applicants must be degree-seeking students of a secondary or post-secondary school and must be at least 12 years of age. Because of the proliferation of fake ISICs, some services (particularly airlines) require additional proof of student identity, such as a school ID or a letter attesting to student status, signed by your registrar and stamped with your school seal. The **International Teacher Identity Card (ITIC)** offers the same insurance coverage as well as similar but limited discounts. Both cards cost AUS$16.50, CDN$16.50 or US$22. For more info, contact the **International Student Travel Confederation (ISTC),** Herengracht 479, 1017 BS Amsterdam, Netherlands (☎+31 20 421 28 00; fax 421 28 10; istcinfo@istc.org; www.istc.org).

YOUTH IDENTIFICATION. The International Student Travel Confederation issues a discount card to travelers 26 years or under who are not students. This one-year **International Youth Travel Card** (**IYTC;** formerly the **GO 25** Card) offers many of the same benefits as the ISIC. Most places that sell ISIC also sell the IYTC (US$22).

ISICONNECT SERVICE. If you wish to consolidate all your means of communication, you can activate your ISIC's ISIConnect service which gives you access to different methods of keeping in touch via phone, fax, and Internet, including: a universal calling card; a voicemail box; faxmail service; email capabilities, including a service that reads your email to you over the phone; an online "travel safe" for storing (and faxing) important documents; a 24hr. emergency help line (via phone or ISIConnect@ekit.com) offering medical and legal referrals. To activate the card, visit www.isiconnect.ekit.com or in Australia call ☎1800 114 478.

DISCOUNTS. "Concessions" is the Australian catch-all phrase for discounts always given to specific groups, most often students and senior citizens. However, it may be limited to holders of specific Australian concession cards. "Pensioners" are Australian senior citizens, and discounts for pensioners may or may not apply to non-Australians who otherwise fit the bill. Student discounts often require that you show an ID and may only apply to Australian University students, or even to university students within the particular state. Discounts on accommodations are regularly given to VIP, YHA, ISIC, or NOMADS card holders. Play it safe and carry a couple forms of ID with you at all times.

CUSTOMS

Because of the isolation afforded by being an island nation, Australia has been able to avoid some of the pests and diseases that plague other countries. Dedicated to protecting its shores, the Customs Bureau has recently set aside AUS$239 million to prevent Foot and Mouth Disease from coming to Australia. As always, with increased tourism, there is an increased risk of contamination from imported goods. Customs is therefore taken extremely seriously. Articles subject to quarantine may include live animals, food, animal products, plants, plant products, and protected wildlife. These articles are not automatically forbidden, but they will undergo a **quarantine inspection.** Camping equipment is also subject to a quarantine inspection, so be prepared to declare these items as well. Don't risk large fines or hassles when entering Australia—throw out questionable items in the big customs bins as you leave the plane, and declare anything about which you have the slightest suspicion. The beagles in orange smocks know their stuff, and they WILL find you out. If you must bring your **pets** with you, contact the **Australian Quarantine and Inspections Service,** GPO Box 858, Canberra, ACT 2601 (☎02 6272 3933; animal-live@aqis.gov.au) to obtain a permit. Pick up **Customs Information for Travellers** at an Australian consulate or any travel agency for more info. Australia expressly forbids the entry of drugs, steroids, and weapons.

Visitors over 18 may bring into Australia up to 1125ml alcohol, 250 cigarettes, and 250g tobacco **duty-free.** For other goods intended as gifts, the allowance is AUS$400 (over 18) or AUS$200 (under 18).

Upon returning home, you must declare articles acquired abroad and pay a **duty** on the value of articles that exceeds the allowance established by your country's customs service. Goods bought at **duty-free** shops abroad are not exempt from duty tax at your return; you must declare these items as well. "Duty-free" merely means that you need not pay a tax in the country of purchase. Australia recently implemented a **Tourist Refund Scheme** (TRS) that refunds the **Goods and Services Tax** (GST) on items bought in Australia (see **Taxes and Tipping,** p. 41). For more information on customs requirements, contact the following information centers:

Australia: Australian Customs National Information Line (in Australia ☎1300 363 263, from elsewhere ☎02 6275 6666; www.customs.gov.au).

Canada: Canadian Customs, 2265 St. Laurent Blvd., Ottawa, ON K1G 4K3 (24hr. ☎800-461-9999) or from outside Canada: ☎204-983-3500; 506-636-5064; www.ccra-adrc.gc.ca).

Ireland: Customs Information Office, Irish Life Centre, Lower Abbey St., Dublin 1 (☎01 878 8811; fax 878 0836; taxes@revenue.iol.ie; www.revenue.ie).

New Zealand: New Zealand Customhouse, 17-21 Whitmore St., Box 2218, Wellington (☎04 473 6099, general 09 300 5399 or 0800 428 786; fax 473 7370; www.customs.govt.nz).

South Africa: Commissioner for Customs and Excise, Private Bag X47, Pretoria 0001 (☎012 314 9911; fax 328 6478; www.gov.za).

United Kingdom: Her Majesty's Customs and Excise, Passenger Enquiry Team, Wayfarer House, Great South West Rd., Feltham, Middlesex TW14 8NP (☎020 8910 3744; National Advice Service: 0845 010 9000; www.hmce.gov.uk).

United States: US Customs Service, 1300 Pennsylvania Ave. NW, Washington, D.C. 20229 (☎202-927-1000; fax 354-1010; www.customs.gov).

TOURIST BOARDS

The government-sponsored **Australian Tourist Commission** promotes tourism internationally, distributing literature and sponsoring helplines. The ATC carries books, magazines, and fact sheets for backpackers, younger people, disabled travelers, and others with special concerns. For more information on events and domestic travel, check out www.australia.com and www.atc.net.au. Contact these office affiliates in the nearest location:

Australia (Head Office): Level 4, 80 William St., Wolloomooloo, NSW 2011; Postal Address: GPO Box 2721, Sydney 1006 (☎02 9360 1111; fax 9331 6469).

New Zealand: Level 13, 44-48 Emily Pl., P.O. Box 1666 Auckland 1 (☎09 379 9594 or 0800 65 03 03; fax 307 3117).

United Kingdom: Gemini House, 10-18 Putney Hill, London SW15 6AA (☎20 8780 2229; fax 8780 1496).

U.S./Canada: 2049 Century Park East, Suite 1920, Los Angeles, CA 90067 (☎310-229-4870 or 800-333-4305; fax 310-552-1215).

MONEY

No matter how low your budget, you should keep handy a larger amount of cash than usual. Carrying it around is risky but necessary; personal checks are seldom accepted and even traveler's checks may not be accepted in some locations.

***LET'S GO: AUSTRALIA* LISTS ALL PRICES IN AUSTRALIAN DOLLARS UNLESS OTHERWISE STATED**

CURRENCY AND EXCHANGE

The Australian currency is in dollars and cents. Notes come in \$5, \$10, \$20, \$50, and \$100 denominations, and coins in 5¢, 10¢, 20¢, 50¢, \$1, and \$2 denominations. The currency chart below is based on August 2001 exchange rates between local currency and US dollars (US\$), Canadian dollars (CDN\$), British pounds (UK£), Irish pounds (IR£), Australian dollars (AUS\$), New Zealand dollars (NZ\$), South African Rand (ZAR), and European Union euros (EUR€). Check a large newspaper or the currency calculator on our website (www.letsgo.com) for the latest exchange rates.

CURRENCY

US\$1 = AUS\$1.87	**AUS\$1= US\$0.54**
CDN\$1 = AUS\$1.21	**AUS\$1= CDN\$0.82**
UK£1 = AUS\$2.71	**AUS\$1= UK£0.37**
IR£1 = AUS\$2.17	**AUS\$1= IR£0.46**
NZ\$1 = AUS\$0.83	**AUS\$1= NZ\$1.21**
ZAR1 = AUS\$0.22	**AUS\$1= ZAR4.47**
EUR€ = AUS\$1.71	**AUS\$1= EUR€0.58**

As a general rule, it's cheaper to convert money in Australia. It's good to bring enough foreign currency to last for the first 24 to 72 hours of a trip to avoid being penniless after banking hours or on a holiday. In the U.S., **International Currency Express** (☎888-278-6628; www.foreignmoney.com) will deliver foreign currency for over 120 countries or traveler's checks overnight to your home (US\$15) or second-day (US\$12) at competitive exchange rates.

Watch out for commission rates, and check newspapers for the standard rate of exchange. When changing money abroad, try to go only to banks or bureaus of change that have at most a 5% margin between their buy and sell prices. The largest and most widespread banks in Australia are ANZ, Commonwealth, National, and Westpac. Since you lose money with every transaction, **convert large sums** (unless the currency is depreciating rapidly), **but no more than you'll need.** Using an ATM card or a credit card (see p. 39) often gets you the best possible rates as well.

If you use traveler's checks or bills, carry some in small denominations (the equivalent of US\$50 or less) for times when you are forced to exchange money at disadvantageous rates, but bring a range of denominations, since charges may be levied per check cashed. Store your money in a variety of forms; ideally, you will at any given time be carrying some cash, some traveler's checks, and an ATM (see p. 40) and/or credit card (p. 39).

BUT I WANNA PAY MORE!

On July 1, 2000, Australia implemented a new 10% Goods and Services Tax (GST). Much of Australia was at unrest when the GST began, as prices increased. Some establishments, however, have kept prices the same, paying for the tax out of their own pockets. Prices in this book could differ from the actual current price by up to 10% as establishments still adjust. For more info, see **Tipping and Taxes,** p. 41.

TRAVELER'S CHECKS

Traveler's checks (**American Express** and **Visa** are the most recognized) are one of the safest and least troublesome means of carrying funds, since they can be refunded if stolen. Several agencies and banks sell them, usually for face value plus a small commission. Members of the American Automobile Association, and some banks and credit unions, can get American Express checks commission-free (see **Driving Permits and Insurance,** p. 70). Each agency provides refunds if checks are lost or stolen, and many provide additional services, like toll-free refund hotlines, emergency message services, and stolen credit card assistance.

While traveling, keep check receipts and a record of which checks you've cashed separate from the checks themselves. Also leave a list of check numbers with someone at home. Never countersign checks until you're ready to cash them, and always bring your passport with you to cash them. If your checks are lost or stolen, immediately contact a refund center (of the company that issued your checks) to be reimbursed; they may require a police report verifying the loss or theft. Less-touristed, rural areas may not have refund centers at all, so you might have to wait to be reimbursed. Ask about toll-free refund hotlines and the location of refund centers when purchasing checks, and always carry emergency cash.

American Express: For lost cheques call ☎1800 251 902 in Australia; in New Zealand ☎0800 441 068; in the UK ☎0800 521 313; in the US and Canada ☎800-221-7282. Elsewhere call US collect ☎+1 801 964-6665; www.aexp.com. Traveler's cheques are available in Australia at 1-4% commission at AmEx offices and banks, commission-free at AAA offices (see p. 68). *Cheques for Two* can be signed by either of 2 people.

Citicorp: In the US and Canada call ☎800-645-6556; in Europe, the Middle East, or Africa call the UK ☎+44 20 7508 7007; elsewhere call US collect ☎+1 813-623-1709. Traveler's checks available in 7 currencies at 1-2% commission. Call 24hr.

Thomas Cook MasterCard: In the US and Canada call ☎800-0223-7373; in the UK call ☎0800 622 101; elsewhere call UK collect ☎+44 1733 31 89 50. Checks available in 13 currencies at 2% commission. Thomas Cook offices cash checks commission-free.

Visa: In the US call ☎800-227-6811; in the UK call ☎0800 895 078; elsewhere call UK collect ☎+44 1733 31 89 49. Call for the location of their nearest office.

CREDIT CARDS

Credit cards are generally accepted in all but the smallest businesses in Australia. Credit cards often offer superior exchange rates—up to 5% better than the retail rate used by banks and other currency exchanges. Credit cards may also offer services such as insurance or emergency help and are sometimes required to reserve hotel rooms or rental cars. **MasterCard** and **Visa** are the most welcomed; **American Express** cards work at some ATMs and at AmEx offices and major airports.

Credit cards are also useful for **cash advances,** which allow you to withdraw cash from associated banks and ATMs throughout Australia instantly. However, transaction fees for all credit card advances (up to US$10 per advance, plus sometimes a 2-3% extra on foreign transactions after conversion) tend to make credit cards a more costly way of withdrawing cash than ATMs or traveler's checks. In an emergency, however, the transaction fee may prove worth the cost. To be eligible for an advance, you'll need to get a **Personal Identification Number (PIN)** from your credit card company (see **Cash (ATM) Cards,** below).

CREDIT CARD COMPANIES. **Visa** (US ☎800-336-8472) and **MasterCard** (US ☎800-307-7309) are issued in cooperation with banks and other organizations. **American Express** (US ☎800-843-2273) has an annual fee of up to US$55. AmEx cardholders may cash personal checks at offices abroad, access an emergency medical and legal assistance hotline (24hr.; in North America call ☎800-554-2639, elsewhere call US collect ☎+1 202 554-2639), and enjoy American Express Travel Service benefits (including plane, hotel, and car rental reservation changes; baggage loss and flight insurance; mailgram and international cable services; held mail). The **Discover Card** (in US call ☎807-347-2683, elsewhere call US ☎+1 801-902-3100) offers small cash-back bonuses on most purchases, but it is not readily accepted in Australia.

CASH (ATM) CARDS

Cash cards—popularly called ATM cards—are widespread in Australia. Depending on the system that your home bank uses, you can most likely access your personal bank account from abroad. ATMs get the same wholesale exchange rate as credit cards, but there is often a limit on the amount of money you can withdraw per day (around US$500), and computer networks sometimes fail. There is typically also a surcharge of US$1-5 per withdrawal. Be sure to memorize your PIN code in numeric form since machines often don't have letters on their keys. Also, if your PIN is longer than four digits, ask your bank whether you need a new number.

ELECTRONIC BANKING. The two major international money networks are **Cirrus** (US ☎800-424-7787) and **PLUS** (US ☎800-843-7587). To locate ATMs around the world, call the above numbers, or consult www.visa.com/pd/atm or www.mastercard.com/atm. **Cirrus** is the most widespread ATM network in Australia; **PLUS** is almost as good, and **Visa** is probably third best. **Mastercard** and **American Express** are found less often but are possible to use. **NYCE** is not found in Australia. Though ATMs are increasingly prevalent in smaller towns and rural areas, they are scarce in northern Western Australia and more remote interior areas.

Visa TravelMoney (for emergency assistance in Australia, call ☎0800 125 161) is a system allowing you to access money from any Visa ATM, common throughout Australia. You deposit an amount before you travel (plus a small administration fee), and you can withdraw up to that sum. The cards, which give you the same favorable exchange rate for withdrawals as a regular Visa, are especially useful if you plan to travel through many countries. Check with your local bank to see if it issues TravelMoney cards. **Road Cash** (US ☎877-762-3227; www.roadcash.com) issues cards in the US with a minimum US$300 deposit. However, they also charge for international withdrawls ($2- 3).

EFTPOS. Electronic Funds Transfer at Point Of Sale (EFTPOS) is an extremely common way for Australians to pay for goods. ATM cards (from Australian banks only) swiped at the register work as debit cards, withdrawing money directly from your bank account. Most establishments offer EFTPOS with a cash-back option. Since most Australian banks charge customers for each transaction, using EFTPOS to purchase goods while using the cash-back option allows for fewer transactions. EFTPOS is useful for travelers because it means they can carry less cash and not have to worry about credit card bills. If you'll be in Australia for a while, the convenience of this service, among other reasons, may justify opening an Australian bank account. The most widespread banks in Australia are ANZ, Commonwealth, National, and Westpac, and most offer online banking as well. A permanent Australian address and two or three forms of identification are required to open an account; your home driver's license and your passport are the most sure-fire bets. Banks accept cash or traveler's checks to open an account. You can expect the bank to perform a routine check on your credit history. Bringing along home bank statements from the last three months can expedite the process enormously; accounts can be ready in as little as an hour.

GETTING MONEY FROM HOME

AMERICAN EXPRESS. Cardholders can withdraw cash from their checking accounts at any of AmEx's major offices and many representative offices (up to US$1000 every 21 days outside of the US). These "Express Cash" withdrawals from any AmEx ATM in Australia are automatically debited from the cardholder's checking account or line of credit. AmEx Green card holders may withdraw up to US$1000 in any seven-day period (2% transaction fee; minimum US$3, maximum US$20). To enroll in Express Cash, card members may call ☎800-227-4669 in the US; elsewhere call the US collect ☎+1 336-393-1111. The AmEx national number in Australia is ☎0800 230 100.

WESTERN UNION. Travelers from the US, Canada, and the UK can wire money abroad through Western Union's international money transfer services. In the US, call ☎800-325-6000; in Canada, ☎800-235-0000; in the UK, ☎0800 83 38 33; in Australia, ☎1800 501 500. The rates for sending cash are generally US$10-11 cheaper than with a credit card, and the money is usually available within an hour. To locate the nearest Western Union location consult www.westernunion.com.

FEDERAL EXPRESS. Some people choose to send money abroad in cash via FedEx to avoid transmission fees and taxes. While FedEx is reasonably reliable, note that this method is illegal. For FedEx in the US and Canada call ☎800-463-3339; in the UK, ☎0800 12 38 00; in Ireland, ☎0800 53 58 00; in Australia, ☎13 26 10; in New Zealand, ☎0800 733 339; in South Africa, ☎021 551-7610.

US STATE DEPARTMENT (US CITIZENS ONLY). In dire emergencies only, the US State Department will forward money within hours to the nearest consular office, which will then disburse it according to instructions for a US$15 fee. If you wish to use this service, you must contact the Overseas Citizens Service division of the US State Department (☎202-647-5225; nights, Sundays, and holidays ☎202-647-4000).

COSTS AND TIPS FOR STAYING ON BUDGET

The cost of your trip will vary considerably depending on where you go, how you travel, and where you stay. The single biggest cost of your trip will probably be your round-trip (return) **airfare** to Australia (see p. 58). A **railpass** (or **bus pass**) would be another major pre-departure expense as well as **domestic airfare** for travel within Australia (see p. 63). Before you go, spend some time calculating a reasonable per-day **budget** that will meet your specific needs. To give you a general idea, a bare-bones day in Australia (sleeping in hostels, buying food at supermarkets) would cost about US$20-30; a slightly more comfortable day (sleeping in hostels and the occasional budget hotel, eating one meal a day at a restaurant, going out at night) would run around US$40-50; for a luxurious day, the sky's the limit. Don't forget to factor in emergency reserve funds (at least US$200) when planning how much money you'll need.

Considering that saving just a few dollars a day over the course of your trip might pay for days or weeks of additional travel, the art of penny-pinching is well worth learning. Learn to take advantage of freebies: for example, **museums** will typically be free once a week or once a month, and cities often host free open-air **concerts** and/or **cultural events** (especially in the summer). Bring a **sleepsack** (see p. 47) to save on sheet charges in hostels, and do your **laundry** in the sink (unless you're explicitly prohibited from doing so). You can split **accommodations** costs (in hotels and some hostels) with trustworthy fellow travelers; multi-bed rooms almost always work out cheaper per person than singles. The same principle will also work for cutting down on the cost of **restaurant** meals. You can also buy food in **supermarkets** instead of eating out; you'd be surprised how tasty (and cheap) simple bread can be with cheese or spread.

With that said, don't go overboard with your budget obsession. Staying within your budget is important, but don't do so at the expense of your sanity or health.

TIPPING AND TAXES

In Australia, tipping is not required at restaurants, bars, taxis, or hotels—service workers are fully salaried and do not rely on tips for income. Tips are occasionally left at more expensive restaurants, if you think the service was exceptionally good. In this case, 10% is more than sufficient. Taxes are already included in the bill, so only pay the advertised price.

On July 1, 2000, Australia implemented a **10% Goods and Services Tax (GST).** Some retail goods such as basic foods and medicines are not subject to the new tax. To offset some of the GST price increases, the country's wholesale sales tax was reduced. As part of The New Tax System, the Government also introduced a **Tourist Refund Scheme (TRS).** Under the TRS, tourists and Australian overseas travelers may be entitled to a refund of the goods and services tax (GST) and of the **Wine Equalisation Tax (WET)** on purchases of goods bought from Australian retailers. The refund is only good for GST and/or WET paid on purchases of AUS$300 or more. The GST refund is calculated by dividing the total amount (after tax) of the purchase by 11. The WET refund is 14.5% of the price paid for wine. Travelers can claim the refund from customs officers when departing Australia by presenting tax receipts from retailers along with a valid passport and proof of travel at TRS booths in international airports or cruise terminals. For more information on the TRS, see the Australia Customs service web page (www.customs.gov.au).

SAFETY AND SECURITY

EMERGENCY PHONE NUMBER	Anywhere in Australia, dial ☎**000.**

Although Australia is a relatively safe country, it is always important to keep personal safety in mind. Tourists are particularly vulnerable to crime because they often carry large amounts of cash and are not as street savvy as locals. To avoid unwanted attention, try to blend in as much as possible. The gawking camera-toter is a more obvious target than the low-profile traveler. Familiarize yourself with your surroundings before setting out; if you must check a map on the street, duck into a cafe or shop. If you are traveling alone, be sure that someone at home knows your itinerary and **never admit that you're traveling alone.** The **Australian Department of Foreign Affairs and Trade** (☎02 6261 1111) offers travel information and advisories at their website (www.dfat.gov.au).

GENERAL PRECAUTIONS

EXPLORING. Extra vigilance is always wise, but there is no need for panic when exploring a new city or region. Find out about unsafe areas from tourist offices, from the manager of your hotel or hostel, or from a local whom you trust. You may want to carry a **whistle** to scare off attackers or attract attention; memorize the emergency number of the city or area. Anywhere in Australia, **dial ☎000 for emergency medical help, police, or fire.** Whenever possible, *Let's Go: Australia* warns of unsafe neighborhoods and areas.

SELF DEFENSE. There is no sure-fire set of precautions that will protect you from all of the situations you might encounter when you travel. A good self-defense course will give you more concrete ways to react to different types of aggression. **Prepare & IMPACT Personal Safety** (www.prepareinc.com) can refer you to local self-defense courses in the United States (☎800-345-5425). Workshops (2-3hr.) start at US$50, and full courses run US$350-500. Both women and men are welcome. Their Australian affiliate can be reached at Worth Defending, c/o Sharon Dane, 0417 77 1218 or 07 3311 5378; worthdefending@mbox.com.au, P.O. Box 734, Mudgeerab QLD 4213.

PROTECTING YOUR VALUABLES. To prevent easy theft, don't keep all your valuables (money, important documents) in one place. **Photocopies** of important documents allow you to recover them in case they are lost or filched. Carry one copy separate from the documents and leave another copy at home. Label every piece of luggage both inside and out. **Don't put a wallet with money in your back pocket.** Never count your money in public, and carry as little as possible. If you carry a purse, buy a sturdy one with a secure clasp, and carry it crosswise on the side, away from the street with the clasp against you. Secure packs with small combination padlocks which slip through the two zippers. A **money belt** is the best way to carry cash; you can buy one at most camping supply stores. A nylon, zippered pouch with a belt that sits inside the waist of your pants or skirt combines conve-

TRAVEL ADVISORIES. The following government offices provide travel information and advisories by telephone, by fax, or via the web:

Australian Department of Foreign Affairs and Trade: ☎02 6261 1111; www.dfat.gov.au.

Canadian Department of Foreign Affairs and International Trade (DFAIT): In Canada call ☎800-267-8316, elsewhere call ☎+1 613-944-4000; www.dfait-maeci.gc.ca. Call for their free booklet, *Bon Voyage...But.*

New Zealand Ministry of Foreign Affairs: ☎04 494 8500; fax 494 8506; www.mft.govt.nz/trav.html.

United Kingdom Foreign and Commonwealth Office: ☎020 7008 0232; fax 7008 0155; www.fco.gov.uk.

US Department of State: ☎202-647-5225, automatic faxback 202-647-3000; http://travel.state.gov. For *A Safe Trip Abroad,* call 202-512-1800.

nience and security. A **neck pouch** is equally safe, although far less accessible. Refrain from pulling out your neck pouch in public; if you must, be very discreet. Avoid keeping anything precious in a fanny-pack (even if it's worn on your stomach): your valuables will be highly visible and easy to steal. Keep some money separate from the rest to use in an emergency or in case of theft.

BOWLS, BOOZE, AND BUTTS. Australia has fairly strict drug laws, and **illegal drugs** are best avoided altogether. There is a debate currently ensuing over whether or not to legalize marijuana, but for now it is illegal. Australia does not differentiate between "hard" drugs and more mainstream ones such as marijuana; all are illegal to possess in any quantity. If you carry **prescription drugs** while you travel, take a copy of the prescription with you to show at customs.

Very strict **drunk-driving** (or "drink-driving" as Aussies say) laws apply, and most states operate frequent random breath-testing. The maximum legal blood-alcohol limit for drivers is .05%. For learner drivers, P-plate holders, and drivers under 25 who have had their licence for less than three years, the maximum blood-alcohol limit is .02%. You must be 18 to purchase alcohol or consume it in public.

Smoking is prohibited in government buildings and on most public transportation in Australia, including domestic flights. Some international airlines even prohibit smoking while flying in Australian airspace.

HEALTH

In the event of a serious illness or emergency, call **☎000 from any phone**—this is a free call—to connect to police, an ambulance, or the fire department.

Common sense is the simplest prescription for good health on the road. Travelers complain most often about their feet and their gut, so take precautionary measures: drink lots of fluids to prevent dehydration and constipation, wear sturdy, broken-in shoes and clean socks, and use talcum powder to keep your feet dry.

BEFORE YOU GO

Preparation can help minimize the likelihood of contracting a disease and maximize the chances of receiving effective health care in the event of an emergency.

For minor health problems, bring a compact **first-aid kit** (p. 48). **Contact lens** wearers should bring an extra pair, extra solutions, a copy of the prescription, eyedrops, and a pair of glasses. Those who use heat disinfection might consider switching to chemical cleansers for the trip, but check with your lens dispenser to see if it's safe to switch; some lenses may be damaged by a chemical system.

In your **passport,** write the names of any people you wish to be contacted in case of a medical emergency, and also list any **allergies** or medical conditions you would want doctors to be aware of. Allergy sufferers might want to obtain a full supply of any necessary medication before the trip. Matching a prescription to a foreign equivalent is not always easy, safe, or possible. Carry up-to-date, legible prescriptions or a statement from your doctor stating the medication's trade name, manufacturer, chemical name, and dosage. While traveling, be sure to keep all medication with you in your carry-on luggage. Australian pharmacies, called chemists, can fill most prescriptions written by an Australian doctor.

IMMUNIZATIONS. Take a look at your immunization records before you go. Travelers over two years old should be sure that the following vaccines are up to date: MMR (for measles, mumps, and rubella); DTaP or Td (for diptheria, tetanus, and pertussis); OPV (for polio); HbCV (for haemophilus influenza B); HBV (for hepatitus B). Check with a doctor for guidance through this maze of injections. For more information, contact the US **Centers for Disease Control and Prevention** (**CDC;** ☎877-FYI-TRIP; www.cdc.gov/travel), which maintains an international fax information service and an international travelers hotline (☎404-332-4559).

INOCULATION REQUIREMENTS. Vaccinations are not required unless you have visited a yellow fever infected country or zone within six days prior to arrival. You do not need any other health certificate to enter Australia.

MEDICAL ASSISTANCE ON THE ROAD. If you are concerned about being able to access medical support while traveling, there are special support services you may employ. The *MedPass* from **GlobalCare, Inc.,** 2001 Westside Pkwy., #120, Alpharetta, GA 30004, USA (☎800-860-1111; fax 770-475-0058; www.globalems.com), provides 24hr. international medical assistance, support, and medical evacuation resources. The **International Association for Medical Assistance to Travelers** (**IAMAT;** US ☎716-754-4883, Canada ☎416-652-0137, New Zealand ☎03 352 20 53; www.sentex.net/~iamat) has free membership, lists English-speaking doctors worldwide, and offers detailed info on immunization requirements and sanitation. If your regular **insurance** policy (p. 46) does not cover travel abroad, you may wish to purchase additional coverage.

MEDICAL CONDITIONS. Those with medical conditions (e.g. diabetes, allergies to antibiotics, epilepsy, heart conditions) may want to obtain a stainless steel **Medic Alert** identification tag (US$35 the first year, $20 annually thereafter), which identifies the condition and gives a 24-hour information number. Contact the Medic Alert Foundation, 2323 Colorado Ave, Turlock, CA 95382 (☎888-633-4298; www.medicalert.org). Throughout Australia, the Medic Alert number is ☎0800 88 22 22 (www.medicalert.com.au). Diabetics can contact the **American Diabetes Association,** 1071 N. Beauregard St, Alexandria, VA 22311 (☎800-342-2383; www.diabetes.org), to get a copy of "Travel and Diabetes" and a diabetic ID card, which has messages in 18 languages explaining the carrier's diabetic status.

If you are **HIV** positive, contact the Bureau of Consular Affairs, #6831, Department of State, Washington, D.C. 20520 (☎202-647-1488; auto-fax 647-3000; http://travel.state.gov). Travelers applying for a permanent visa must first be tested for HIV and AIDS; tests taken in the US are acceptable.

JET LAG. Many travelers to Australia will arrive after a flight of over 12 hours. In such cases, jet lag can be rather severe and take a few days to overcome. To minimize the effects of jet lag, "reset" your body's clock by adopting the time of your destination as soon as you board the plane. While it may be tempting to sleep, some say it is best to force yourself to make it at least through the early evening. If you will be arriving in the morning, one strategy is to stay up all night before your departure and sleep on the plane. On long flights, search for an open row for a better sleep. Some travelers also take herbal supplements such as melatonin (or a few glasses of free in-flight wine) to help reset their body clocks.

ENVIRONMENTAL HAZARDS

HEAT EXHAUSTION AND DEHYDRATION. Heat exhaustion, characterized by dehydration and salt deficiency, can lead to fatigue, headaches, and wooziness. Avoid heat exhaustion by drinking plenty of clear fluids and eating salty foods like crackers. Always drink enough liquids to keep your urine clear. Alcoholic beverages, coffee, strong tea, and caffeinated sodas are dehydrating. Wear a hat, sunglasses, and a lightweight longsleeve shirt in hot sun, and take time to acclimate to a hot destination before seriously exerting yourself. Continuous heat stress can eventually lead to **heatstroke,** characterized by rising body temperature, severe headache, and cessation of sweating. Heatstroke is rare but serious, and victims must be cooled off with wet towels and taken to a doctor as soon as possible.

SUNBURN. Since there is so much outdoor fun in Australia, apply sunscreen liberally and often to avoid burns and lower the risk of skin cancer, a disease which is no stranger to Australia. Queensland has the highest rate of skin cancer cases in the world. The sun is very strong; if you don't usually burn, still wear sunscreen, at least for the first few days of exposure. If you are planning on spending time near water, in the desert, or in the snow, you are at risk of getting burned, even when it is cloudy. If sunburned, drink more fluids than usual and apply Calamine or an aloe-based lotion.

HYPOTHERMIA AND FROSTBITE. A rapid drop in body temperature is the clearest warning sign of overexposure to cold. Victims may also shiver, feel exhausted, have poor coordination or slurred speech, hallucinate, or suffer amnesia. Seek medical help, and *do not let hypothermia victims fall asleep*—their body temperature will continue to drop, and they may die. To avoid hypothermia, keep dry, wear layers, and stay out of the wind. In wet weather, wool and synthetics such as pile retain heat. Most other fabric, especially cotton, will make you colder. The Australian climate is fairly temperate for most of the year, but during the winter months, especially in areas like the Snowy Mountains, it can get cold. When the temperature is below freezing, watch for **frostbite.** If a region of skin turns white, waxy, and cold, do not rub the area. Drink warm beverages, get dry, and slowly warm the area with dry fabric or steady body contact until a doctor can be found.

INSECT, ANIMAL AND FOOD-BORNE DISEASES. Many diseases are transmitted by insects—mainly mosquitoes, fleas, ticks, and lice. Be aware of insects in wet or forested areas (such as northern Queensland and Kakadu, NT), while hiking, and especially while camping. **Mosquitoes** are most active from dusk to dawn. Use insect repellents, such as DEET. Wear long pants and long sleeves (fabric need not be thick or warm; tropic-weight cottons can keep you comfortable in the heat) and buy a mosquito net. Wear shoes and socks, and tuck long pants into socks. Soak or spray your gear with permethrin, licensed in the U.S. for use on clothing. Natural repellents can be useful supplements: taking vitamin B-12 pills regularly can make you smelly to insects, as can garlic pills. Calamine lotion or topical cortisones (like Cortaid) may stop insect bites from itching, as can a bath with a half-cup of baking soda or oatmeal. **Encephalitis** is a rarely occurring disease transmitted in regions of WA by mosquitoes. Carriers breed annually north of Port Hedland between Feb. and Apr. Symptoms include headaches, neck stiffness, and nausea. **Ross River and Barmah Forest Virus (epidemic polyarthritis)** is a disease transmitted by mosquitoes in regions of Victoria. Symptoms include fever, aching joints and sometimes small purple blotches that look like bruises. Full recovery can take up to several months to complete. **Ticks**—responsible for Lyme and other diseases—can be particularly dangerous in rural and forested regions. While walking, pause periodically to brush off ticks from exposed parts of your body using a fine-toothed comb. Do not try to remove ticks by burning them.

Prevention is the best cure for food- and water-borne diseases: be sure that everything you eat is cooked properly and that the water you drink is clean. To purify your own water, bring it to a rolling boil or treat it with **iodine tablets,** available at any camping goods store. Other culprits are raw shellfish, unpasteurized milk, and sauces containing raw eggs. Always wash your hands before eating, or bring a quick-drying purifying liquid hand cleaner.

AIDS, HIV, STDS

Acquired Immune Deficiency Syndrome (AIDS) is a growing problem around the world. The World Health Organization estimates that there are around 36 million people infected with the HIV virus, and women now represent 42% of all new HIV infections. In Australia, 20,400 adults are currently diagnosed with HIV—0.15% of the population. Since the start of the AIDS epidemic, 8300 cases of AIDS have been recorded. Visitors or students applying for a permanent or long-term visa will be tested for AIDS. Contact the Australian consulate for details about the AIDS and HIV policies regarding permanent and temporary entrance to the country.

Sexually transmitted diseases (STDs) such as gonorrhea, chlamydia, genital warts, syphilis, and herpes are easier to catch than HIV, and some can be just as deadly. **Hepatitis B** and **C** are also serious sexually transmitted diseases. Warning signs for STDs include: swelling, sores, bumps, or blisters on the sex organs, rectum, or mouth; burning and pain during urination and bowel movements; itching around sex organs; swelling or redness in the throat; or flu-like symptoms with fever, chills, and aches. If these symptoms develop, see a doctor immediately. When having sex, condoms may protect you from certain STDs, but oral or even tactile contact can lead to transmission.

WOMEN'S HEALTH

Women travelers may be vulnerable to **urinary tract** and **bladder infections,** common and uncomfortable bacterial diseases that cause a burning sensation and painful and frequent urination. To minimize risk, drink plenty of vitamin-C-rich juice and clean water and urinate frequently, especially after intercourse. Untreated, these infections can lead to kidney infections, sterility, and even death.

Tampons and **pads** are sometimes hard to find when traveling, especially in Australia's less populated areas like parts of the Northern Territory, so it may be advisable to take supplies along. **Reliable contraceptive devices** may also be difficult to find. Women on the pill should bring enough to allow for possible loss or extended stays. Bring a prescription, since forms of the pill vary a good deal.

INSURANCE

Travel insurance generally covers four basic areas: medical/health problems, property loss, trip cancellation/interruption, and emergency evacuation. Although your regular insurance policies may well extend to travel-related accidents, you may consider purchasing travel insurance if the cost of potential trip cancellation/interruption is greater than you can absorb.

Be aware that many **medical insurance** policies (especially university policies) often cover costs incurred abroad; check with your provider. **US Medicare does not cover foreign travel.** Australia's national health insurance scheme, Medicare, is available for travelers from New Zealand, the United Kingdom, Ireland, Malta, Sweden, Italy, Finland, and the Netherlands. Visitors from these places can enroll at any Medicare office in Australia. Canadians are protected by their home province's health insurance plan for up to 90 days after leaving the country; check with the provincial Ministry of Health or Health Plan Headquarters for details.

ISIC and **ITIC** provide basic insurance benefits, including US$100 per day of in-hospital sickness for a maximum of 60 days, US$3000 of accident-related medical reimbursement, and US$25,000 for emergency medical transportation (see **Identification,** p. 35). Cardholders have access to a toll-free 24hr. helpline whose multilingual staff can provide assistance in medical, legal, and financial emergencies overseas. (US and Canada ☎877-370-4742, elsewhere call US collect ☎+1 715-345-

0505). **American Express** (☎800-528-4800) grants most cardholders automatic car rental insurance (collision and theft, but not liability). AmEx also includes accidental death and dismemberment coverage of US$100,000 when you purchase the flight, train, boat, or bus ticket with the card.

Prices for travel insurance purchased separately generally run about US$50 per week for full coverage, while trip cancellation/interruption may be purchased separately at a rate of about US$5.50 per US$100 of coverage. **Homeowners' insurance** (or your family's coverage) often covers theft during travel and loss of travel documents (passport, plane ticket, railpass, etc.) up to US$500.

INSURANCE PROVIDERS. **Council** and **STA** (see p. 46 for complete listings) offer a range of plans that can supplement your basic coverage. Other private insurance providers in the US and Canada include: Access America (☎800-284-8300); Berkely Group/Carefree Travel Insurance (☎800-323-3149; www.berkely.com); Globalcare Travel Insurance (☎800-821-2488; www.globalcare-cocco.com); Travel Assistance International (☎800-821-2828; www.worldwide-assistance.com). Providers in the UK include Campus Travel (☎01865 258 000) and Columbus Travel Insurance (☎020 7375 0011). Additionally, for Australia specific information, contact **Travel Insurance on the Net** (☎02 6293 3764; www.travelinsurance.com.au), which offers Smart Cover, Worldcare Assist, Australia Visitors Travel Insurance, and Travel Insurance, the complete insurance coverage.

PACKING

Pack light: lay out only what you absolutely need, then take half the clothes and twice the money. The less you have, the less you have to lose (or store, or carry on your back). Save any extra space left for souvenirs or items you pick up along the way. If you plan to do a lot of hiking, see **Camping And The Outdoors,** p. 51.

LUGGAGE. Toting a suitcase or trunk is fine if you plan to stay in one or two cities and explore from there, but a very bad idea if you're going to be trekking through the Kimberly or hiking through the rainforest. A small backpack, rucksack, or courier bag may be useful as a daypack for sight-seeing expeditions; it doubles as an airplane carry-on. An empty, lightweight duffel bag packed inside your luggage may also be useful. Once abroad you can fill your luggage with purchases and keep your dirty clothes in the duffel. For advice on backpacks, see p. 52.

CLOTHING. No matter if it's the Wet or the Dry, it's always a good idea to bring a **warm jacket** or wool sweater, a **rain jacket** (Gore-Tex® is both waterproof and breathable), sturdy shoes or **hiking boots,** and **thick socks. Flip-flops** or waterproof sandals are crucial for grubby hostel showers. You may also want to add one outfit beyond the jeans and t-shirt uniform, and maybe a nicer pair of shoes if you plan to do any clubbing in the bigger cities.

SLEEPSACKS. Many hostels require that you either provide your own linen or rent sheets from them. Save cash by making your own sleepsack: fold a full-size sheet in half the long way, then sew it closed along the long side and one of the short sides. Keep in mind that some hostels in larger cities prohibit sleeping bags.

WASHING CLOTHES. *Let's Go* attempts to provide info on laundromats in the Practical Information and hostel listings. Most cities have laundromats, but sometimes it may be cheaper and easier to use a sink. Bring a small bar or tube of detergent soap, a small rubber ball to stop up the sink, and a travel clothes line.

ELECTRIC CURRENT. In Australia, electricity is 220/240 volts, and AC is 50Hz, enough to fry 110V North American appliances. 220V electrical appliances don't like 110V current, either. Hardware stores sell adapters (to change the shape of the plug) and converters (to change the voltage). Don't make the mistake of using only an adapter (unless appliance instructions explicitly state otherwise).

FIRST-AID KIT. For a basic first-aid kit, pack: contact lenses, bandages, pain reliever, antibiotic cream, a thermometer, a Swiss Army knife, tweezers, moleskin, decongestant, motion-sickness remedy, diarrhea or upset-stomach medication (Pepto Bismol), an antihistamine, sunscreen, insect repellent, and burn ointment.

OTHER USEFUL ITEMS. An umbrella; sealable plastic bags (for damp clothes, soap, food, shampoo, and other spillables); an alarm clock; waterproof matches; sun hat; sunglasses; pocketknife; plastic water bottle; compass; towel; padlock; whistle; flashlight; earplugs; electrical tape (for patching tears); garbage bags; a small calculator for currency conversion; a pair of flip-flops for the shower; a money-belt for carrying valuables; deodorant; razors; tampons; condoms.

ACCOMMODATIONS

HOTELS

While **hotels** in large cities are similar to those in the rest of the world, "hotels" in rural Australia, particularly in Victoria and New South Wales, are simple furnished rooms above local pubs. Some resemble fancy Victorian-era lodging with grand back staircases, high tin ceilings, and wrap-around verandas. A simple breakfast may be included and there's occasionally a common kitchen. Others have been converted to long-term worker housing, and are thus less conducive to brief overnight stays. Singles in these hotels usually cost AUS$15-30. This generally includes a towel, a shared bathroom, and a private bedroom (no bunks, usually). The pubs are fully functional downstairs, so it's a good idea to choose a quieter one if you're fond of tucking in early. **Motels** in Australia are accommodations with parking.

HOSTELS

In Australia, a "youth hostel" is more commonly known as a "backpackers." Hostels are generally dorm-style accommodations, often in single-sex large rooms with bunk beds, although most hostels do offer private rooms or doubles for families and couples. They sometimes have kitchens and utensils for your use, bike rentals, storage areas, and laundry facilities. Remember that crime occurs in even the most demure-looking hostel; bring your own **padlock** for your storage locker. Many hostels allow guests to leave valuables in a safe at the front desk. Some hostel owners provide transportation to and from bus stations and airports. In Australia, a bed in a hostel will average around AUS$15-20. A **VIP** discount card offered by Backpackers Resorts International gets AUS$1 off per night at many hostels. *Let's Go* designates these hostels with a VIP at the end of the listing. The two most common hostel chains in Australia are YHA and Nomads (see below). A list of many hostels, regardless of affiliation, can be found at www.hostels.com.

A HOSTELER'S BILL OF RIGHTS. There are certain standard features that we do not include in our hostel listings. Unless we state otherwise, you can expect that every hostel has: no lockout, no curfew, free hot showers, secure storage, and no key deposit.

HOSTELLING INTERNATIONAL. Joining the youth hostel association in your own country (listed below) automatically grants you membership privileges in **Hostelling International (HI),** a federation of national hosteling associations. Australia's over 140 **YHAs** are members of HI, and some in larger cities accept reservations via the **International Booking Network** (Australia ☎02 9261 1111; Canada ☎800-663-5777; England and Wales ☎1629 58 14 18; Northern Ireland ☎1232 32 47 33; Republic of Ireland ☎01 830 1766; New Zealand ☎09 379 9808; Scotland ☎8701 55 32 55; US ☎800-909-4776; www.hostelbooking.com.) HI's umbrella organization's web page (www.iyhf.org), which lists the web addresses and phone numbers of all national associations, is a great place to begin researching hostelling in a specific region. Most student travel agencies (see p. 58) sell HI cards. The prices listed are valid for **one-year memberships** unless otherwise noted.

Your gateway to Australia!

We invented backpacking...

YHA is the world's leading budget accommodation network. We offer you 150 of the best places to stay in Oz – from the beach to the bush to the cities.

Great hostels!

- Affordable, secure, friendly
- 24-hour access
- Informed staff for travel tips
- Free hostel-to-hostel reservation
- Open to all ages

Get a bed online...

Want to have a place to stay confirmed before you leave home?

Go to www.yha.com

1 > Pick your hostel
2 > Fill in the form
3 > Hit the SEND button

Done! It's that easy!

For HI membership in the US call (202) 783 6161

YHA Australia, Hostelling International and the YHA and HI house and tree logos are Registered Trademarks of YHA Australia Incorporated – Level 3, 10 Mallett Street, Camperdown NSW 2050 Australia

Great value Accommodation/Coach Passes available online

www.yha.com

Australian Youth Hostels Association (AYHA), Level 3, 10 Mallett St., Camperdown NSW 2050 (☎02 9565 1699; fax 9565 1325; www.yha.org.au). AUS$52, under 18 AUS$16.

Hostelling International-Canada (HI-C), 400-205 Catherine St., Ottawa, ON K2P 1C3 (☎800-663-5777 or 613-237-7884; fax 237-7868; info@hostellingintl.ca; www.hostellingintl.ca). CDN$35, under 18 free.

An Óige (Irish Youth Hostel Association), 61 Mountjoy St., Dublin 7 (☎01 830 4555; fax 830 5808; anoige@iol.ie; www.irelandyha.org). IR£10, under 18 IR£4.

Youth Hostels Association of New Zealand (YHANZ), P.O. Box 436, 193 Cashel St., 3rd Floor Union House, Christchurch 1 (☎03 379 9970; fax 365 4476; info@yha.org.nz; www.yha.org.nz). NZ$40, under 17 free.

Hostels Association of South Africa, 3rd fl. 73 St. George's St. Mall, P.O. Box 4402, Cape Town 8000 (☎021 424 2511; info@hisa.org.za; www.hisa.org.za). ZAR45.

Scottish Youth Hostels Association (SYHA), 7 Glebe Crescent, Stirling FK8 2JA (☎01786 89 14 00; fax 89 13 33; www.syha.org.uk). UK£6.

Youth Hostels Association (England and Wales) Ltd., Trevelyan House, 8 St. Stephen's Hill, St. Albans, Hertfordshire AL1 2DY, UK (☎0870 870 8808; fax 01727 84 41 26; www.yha.org.uk). UK£12.50, under 18 UK£6.25, families UK£25.

Hostelling International Northern Ireland (HINI), 22-32 Donegall Rd., Belfast BT12 5JN, Northern Ireland (☎02890 31 54 35; fax 43 96 99; info@hini.org.uk; www.hini.org.uk). UK£10, under 18 UK£6.

Hostelling International-American Youth Hostels (HI-AYH), 733 15th St. NW, #840, Washington, D.C. 20005 (☎202-783-6161; fax 783-6171; hiayhserv@hiayh.org; www.hiayh.org). US$25, under 18 free.

NOMADS. Another large hosteling chain in Australia is NOMADS Backpackers. Though it has only about one third as many locations as YHA, the services and amenities are similar. You don't have to be a member to stay at a NOMADS hostel. Their website (www.nomadsworld.com) not only lists all hostels, but also gives advice on finding work. Bookings can be made through the respective hostel or by calling. The NOMADS Adventure Card (AUS$25) offers discount international calling, cheaper rates at many Internet cafes, and either $1 off per night or 7th night free at NOMADS. For reservations, call ☎1800 819 883 (from overseas, ☎+61 8 8224 7633; fax 8363 7968), or bookings@nomadsworld.com.

BED AND BREAKFASTS

For a cozy alternative to impersonal hotel rooms, B&Bs (private homes with rooms available to travelers) range from the acceptable to the sublime. Hosts will sometimes go out of their way to be accommodating by giving personalized tours or offering home-cooked meals. On the other hand, many B&Bs do not provide phones, TVs, or private bathrooms. Rooms in B&Bs generally cost AUS$40-80 for a single and AUS$60-100 for a double but are more expensive in touristed areas.

Several travel guides and reservation services specialize in B&Bs. Check out www.babs.com.au for a list of Australian B&Bs. **Bed and Breakfast Australia,** PO Box 448 Homebush St., Sydney NSW, 2140 (☎02 9763 5833; fax 02 9763 1677; bnb@bedandbreakfast.com.au) can plan itineraries and make advance bookings.

UNIVERSITIES

Many **colleges and universities** open their residence halls to travelers when school is not in session—some do so even during term-time. These dorms are often close to student areas—good sources for information on things to do—and are usually very clean. Getting a room may take a couple of phone calls and require advanced planning, but rates tend to be low. *Let's Go* lists colleges that rent dorm rooms among the accommodation listings for appropriate cities.

Typical university holidays include most of September and the summer break from late November to late February. Easter break lasts for two weeks, while winter break encompasses the first two weeks of July. The Universities of Canberra, Sydney, and Queensland, as well as Flinders University of South Australia, Melbourne University, and Monash and LaTrobe Universities in Melbourne are among those occasionally offering accommodation. No one policy covers all institutions. Contact the universities directly; the Australian Tourist Commission has contact info at www.australia.com, under "Traveller's Resources," then "Special Interest Fact Sheets," then "Student Travel." Demand is high, so book ahead.

HOME EXCHANGE AND RENTALS

Home exchanges offer the opportunity to live like a native and to cut down dramatically on accommodation fees—usually only an administration fee is paid to the exchange service. Once you join or contact one of the exchange services listed below, it is then up to you to decide with whom you would like to exchange homes. Most companies have pictures of member's homes and information about the owners. A great site with many exchange companies is http://garlic.aitec.edu.au/~bwechner/Documents/Travel/Lists/HomeExchangeClubs.html. Home rentals are much more expensive than exchanges, but can be cheaper than comparably-serviced hotels. Both home exchanges and rentals are ideal for families with children or travelers with special dietary needs; you often get your own kitchen, maid service, TV, and telephones.

HomeLink International, P.O. Box 1388, Byron Bay, NSW 2481 (☎02 6680 8071; fax 6680 8073; homelink@nor.com.au; www.homelink.org). 25 offices worldwide; contact the one in your home country to facilitate home exchange. Listing of 11,000 homes worldwide, and 400 homes throughout Australia. Paid subscribers have access to a comprehensive web page; on-line registration available.

Latitudes Home Exchange, P.O. Box 478, Mt. Lawley, WA 6050 (☎08 9328 7408; fax 9328 7629; www.home-swap.com). Offers temporary home exchange for 1 month-2 years. Computerized matching service (USD$75 lifetime membership; USD$385 fee when the member approves a match) or directory listings (USD$75 per year).

Intervac International Home Exchange, has home exchanges in 34 countries. Check out www.intervac.com to find your home country listing.

CAMPING AND THE OUTDOORS

If your travels take you to Australia when the weather is agreeable, camping is by far the cheapest way to go. The ubiquitous caravan parks offer sites without power for campers, and some hostels have camping facilities or at least allow guests to pitch tents in the yard. Unpowered campsites can vary in price from free to AUS$20 for a prime spot during Christmas holidays. The flexibility of camping allows you to access the more remote corners of the country's numerous wilderness areas, including most of the 14 World Heritage Sites in Australia.

World Heritage Sites have been determined to have significant ecological or cultural value for the world. Some of the World Heritage Sites in other countries are the Acropolis, Stonehenge, the Serengeti, and Yellowstone. Australia's include **The Great Barrier Reef, Fraser Island** in Queensland; **Kakadu National Park** and **Uluru** (Ayers Rock in Kata Tjuta National Park) in Northern Territory; **Lord Howe Island Group, Blue Mountains,** and **Willandra Lakes Region** in New South Wales; **Shark Bay** in Western Australia; as well as the Tasmanian wilderness, Heard and McDonald Islands, Macquarie Island, fossil sites in Queensland and South Australia, and the wet tropics and rainforest reserves of Queensland. For more information on World Heritage Sites, check out www.unesco.org/whc/nwhc/pages/sites/main.htm.

ESSENTIALS

USEFUL PUBLICATIONS AND WEB RESOURCES

Other publications about camping and hiking are available from the **NSW National Parks and Wildlife Service Head Office,** Level 1, 43 Bridge St., Hurstville NSW 2220 (☎02 9585 6333; fax 9585 6527; feedback@npws.nsw.gov.au; www.npws.nsw.gov.au; open M-F 9am-5pm). **Australia Outdoor Connection** (http://flinders.com.au/home.htm) is sponsored by Flinders Camping in Adelaide which provides camping and environmental information and links. For **topographical maps of Australia,** contact the Australian Surveying & Land Information Group (☎02 6201 4201 or 0800 80 01 73; www.auslig.gov.au), or write to P.O. Box 2, Belconnen, ACT 2616. AUSLIG publishes over 500 maps (most $7.50, plus shipping).

CAMPING AND HIKING EQUIPMENT

WHAT TO BUY...

Good camping equipment is both sturdy and light. Camping equipment is generally more expensive in Australia than in North America, so if you have your own, you might want to bring it with you. However, customs officials will inspect used camping equipment to be sure that it is clean and free of any dirt or foreign soil.

Sleeping Bag: Most good sleeping bags are rated by "season," or the lowest outdoor temperature at which they will keep you warm ("summer" means 30-40°F at night and "four-season" or "winter" often means below 0°F). Sleeping bags are made either of down (warmer and lighter, but more expensive, and miserable when wet) or of synthetic material (heavier, more durable, and warmer when wet). Prices vary, but might range from US$80-150 for a summer synthetic to US$150-250 for a good down winter bag. **Sleeping bag pads,** including foam pads (US$10-20) and air mattresses (US$15-50) cushion your back and neck and insulate you from the ground. **Therm-A-Rest** brand self-inflating sleeping pads are part foam and part air-mattress and inflate when you unroll them, but are costly at US$45-80. Bring a **"stuff sack"** (US$5-15) or plastic bag to store your sleeping bag and keep it dry.

Tent: The best tents are free-standing, with their own frames and suspension systems; they set up quickly and only require staking in high winds. Low-profile dome tents are the best all-around. When pitched, their internal space is almost entirely usable, which means little unnecessary bulk. If you're traveling by car, go for the bigger tent, but if you're hiking, stick with a smaller tent that weighs no more than 5-6 lbs (2-3kg). Seal the seams of your tent with waterproofer, and make sure it has a rain fly. Good 2-person tents start at US$90; 4-person tents at US$300.

Backpack: If you intend to do a lot of hiking, you should have a frame backpack. **Internal-frame packs** mold better to your back, keep a lower center of gravity, and can flex adequately to allow you to hike difficult trails that require a lot of bending and maneuvering. **External-frame packs** are more comfortable for long hikes over even terrain since they keep the weight higher and distribute it more evenly. Whichever you choose, make sure your pack has a strong, padded hip belt, which transfers the weight from the shoulders to the legs. Any serious backpacking requires a pack of at least 4000 cubic inches (16,000cc). Allow an additional 500 cubic inches for your sleeping bag in internal-frame packs. Sturdy backpacks cost anywhere from US$150-450. This is one area where it doesn't pay to economize—cheaper packs may be less comfortable, and the straps are more likely to fray or rip. Before you buy any pack, insist on filling it with something heavy and walking around the store to get a sense of how it distributes weight before buying. A **waterproof backpack cover** will prove invaluable. Otherwise, plan to store all of your belongings in sealable plastic bags inside your backpack.

Boots: Get hiking boots with good **ankle support** appropriate for the terrain you plan to hike. Your boots should fit snugly and comfortably over one or two wool socks and a thin liner sock. Break in boots properly by wearing them for several weeks to spare yourself painful and debilitating blisters, and spray them with a waterproofing agent.

Other Necessities: Raingear either in two pieces, a top and pants, or a poncho is absolutely essential, even when a destination is reputed to be sunny. **Synthetics,** like polypropylene tops, socks, and long underwear, along with a pile jacket, will keep you warm even when wet. Plastic water bottles keep water cooler than metal ones do, and are virtually shatter- and leak-proof. Large, collapsible **water sacks** will significantly improve your lot in primitive campgrounds and weigh practically nothing when empty. Bring **water-purification tablets** (US$5 for 50 tablets) for when you can't boil water. Though most campgrounds provide campfire sites, you may want to bring a small **metal grate** or **grill** of your own. For those places that forbid fires or the gathering of firewood, you'll need a **camp stove.** A classic Coleman stove starts at about US$40. You will need to purchase a **fuel bottle** and fill it with propane to operate it. A **first aid kit** (see p. 48), **pocket knife, insect repellent, calamine lotion,** and **waterproof matches** or a **lighter** are other essential camping items.

...AND WHERE TO BUY IT

The mail-order/online companies listed below offer lower prices than many retail stores, but a visit to a local camping or outdoors store will give you a good sense of the look and weight of certain items.

Campmor, Upper Saddle River, NJ USA (US ☎800-525-4784; from abroad call US ☎+1 201-825-8300; www.campmor.com).

Discount Camping, 880 Main North Rd., Pooraka, South Australia 5095, Australia (☎08 8262 3399; fax 08 8260 6240; www.discountcamping.com.au).

Eastern Mountain Sports (EMS), 327 Jaffrey Rd., Peterborough, NH 03458, USA (US☎888-463-6367; www.shopems.com)

L.L. Bean, Freeport, ME USA (US and Canada ☎800-441-5713; UK ☎0800 891 297; elsewhere, call US ☎+1 207-552-3028; www.llbean.com).

Mountain Designs, P.O. Box 87, Kelvin Grove, Queensland 4059, Australia (☎07 3856 2344; www.mountaindesign.com.au).

Recreational Equipment, Inc. (REI), Sumner, WA USA (☎800-426-4840; www.rei.com).

YHA Adventure Shop, 16-18 Lugdate Hill, London, EC4M 7DR, UK (☎020 7329 4578). The main branch of one of Britain's largest outdoor equipment suppliers.

WILDERNESS SAFETY

Stay warm, stay dry, and stay hydrated. The vast majority of life-threatening wilderness situations result from a breach of this simple dictum. On any hike, however brief, you should pack enough equipment to keep you alive should disaster befall. This includes **raingear,** a **hat, mittens,** a **first-aid kit,** a **reflector,** a **whistle, high energy food,** and extra **water.** Dress in warm layers of **synthetic materials** designed for the outdoors, or **wool.** Pile fleece jackets and Gore-Tex® raingear are excellent choices. Never rely on **cotton** for warmth. This "death cloth" will be absolutely useless should it get wet. Make sure to check all equipment for any defects before setting out, and see **Camping and Hiking Equipment,** p. 52, for more information.

Check **weather forecasts** and pay attention to the skies when hiking. Weather patterns can change suddenly. Whenever possible, let someone know when and where you are going hiking—either a friend, your hostel, a park ranger, or a local hiking organization. Do not attempt a hike beyond your ability—you may be endangering your life.

See **Health,** p. 43, for info on outdoor ailments such as heatstroke, hypothermia, giardia, rabies, and insects, as well as basic medical concerns and first-aid.

For **further reading,** consult *How to Stay Alive in the Woods* by Bradford Angier (Macmillan, US$8).

DANGEROUS WILDLIFE

When Gondwanaland split up into continents ages ago, Australia got more than its fair share of extremely dangerous animal life. With a few precautions, travelers should be able to avoid the nastiest creatures, but hospitals do stock anti-venoms. If you get bitten or stung, it is best to take the offending creature to the hospital with you (if you are not in danger of being bitten or stung again) so that doctors can administer the correct anti-venom.

Sea life can be deadly during certain times of year, and warnings to stay out of the water should be strictly observed. The most notorious of these beasts is the **box jellyfish,** which inhabits the waters on the Top End from October to April, and the northern shores on both the west and east coast from November to April. Swimming on beaches north of Rockhampton QLD during these months is forbidden (see p. 380). If stung, your chances of surviving are virtually zero; the pain alone causes immediate shock. Box jellyfish that have washed up on shore are still dangerous, so walking barefoot at the water's edge is discouraged. The sting is potentially lethal to adults, and almost certainly lethal to children. Most beaches where the box jellyfish are a concern have netted areas for swimming. The **stonefish** and **blue-ringed octopus** also present danger at the beach. **Sharks** are common to some Australian shores, but lifeguards at heavily visited beaches keep a good look out—don't swim outside the red and yellow flagged areas.

Freshwater and saltwater **crocodiles** present another water and water's-edge hazard in north and northwest Australia. "Salties" are the more dangerous of the two. They can be found in fresh and salt water, are hard to see, and attack without provocation. Heed local warning signs; don't swim or paddle in streams, lakes, the ocean, or other natural waterways, and keep kids away from the water's edge. "Freshies" are found in freshwater and will not attack unless provoked, but they are also hard to see, and you may provoke one without knowing it's there.

Snakes are perhaps the most feared Australian animals, and while most hikers will never run across these venomous slitherers, there are certain precautions and safety information that travelers should know. Several species of poisonous snakes live in Australia; most are scared enough of humans that they will slide away at the sound of tramping feet. If cornered, though, a few might attack in self-defense. To prevent a bite, wear boots and long pants when walking through the wilderness, and never approach, attempt to step over, or try to kill a snake. Instead, walk around it at a safe distance. If bitten, tightly wrap the wounded area and work the bandage down to the tip of the limb and back up to the next joint to help slow the spread of venom. If possible, keep the infected area immobile, and seek medical attention immediately. Do not try to suck out the venom or clean the bite. Don't panic—most snake bites can be treated effectively.

The two most dangerous **spiders** in Australia are the funnel-web (found in eastern Australia including Tasmania) and the redback (common throughout Australia, particularly in urban areas). Stinging **insects** abound in Australia, including the bull-ant, wasp, bee, and bush-tick, and although these may hurt a lot, they are not life-threatening. If you know that you are allergic to bee stings or other insect bites, carry your own epinephrine kit. After a period of time in the bush, check for lumps on your skin to find and remove bush-ticks.

CARAVANS AND CAMPERVANS

Caravanning is popular in Australia, where most campgrounds double as caravan parks, consisting of both tent sites and powered sites for caravans. On-site caravans (also called on-site vans) are a frequent feature at caravan parks and are anchored permanently to the site and rented out. "Cabins" at caravan parks are often analogous to an on-site van, with a toilet inside.

There is a distinction between **caravans** and **campervans (RVs).** The former is pulled as a trailer, while the latter has its own cab. Renting a caravan is more expensive than tenting or hosteling, but cheaper than renting a car and staying in hotels. The convenience of bringing along your own bedroom, bathroom, and kitchen makes it an attractive option, especially for older travelers and families.

It's not difficult to arrange a campervan rental, although you should start gathering information several months before departure. Rates vary widely by region, season (Dec.-Feb. are the most expensive months), and type of van. It always pays to contact several different companies to compare vehicles and prices. **Hertz** (☎800-654-3001) is a US firm which arranges caravan rentals in Australia. **Maui Rentals** (☎02 9556 6100; fax 9556 3900; www.maui-rentals.com) and **Britz Campervan Rentals and Tours** (☎03 8379 8890; www.britz.com.au) rent RVs in Australia.

KEEPING IN TOUCH

MAIL

SENDING MAIL TO AUSTRALIA

Mark envelopes "air mail" or "par avion" to avoid having letters sent by sea.

Canada: Allow 4-10 days for regular airmail to Australia. Postcards and letters up to 20g cost CDN$1.05; packages up to 0.5kg CDN$10.20, up to 2kg CDN$34.00. www.canadapost.ca/CPC2/common/rates/ratesgen.html#international.

Ireland: Allow 5-7 days for regular airmail to Australia. Postcards and letters up to 25g cost IR£0.45. Add IR£2.60 for Swiftpost International (one day faster). www.anpost.ie.

Japan: Allow 4-5 days for regular airmail to Australia. Postcards 70¥; letters up to 20g 90¥, up to 50g 160¥; packages up to 0.5kg 780¥, up to 2kg cost 2,150¥.

New Zealand: Allow approximately 7 days for regular airmail to Australia. Postcards NZ$1.50. Letters up to 20g cost NZ$1.50-2.00; small parcels up to 0.5kg NZ$6.89-24, up to 2kg NZ$15.09-39. www.nzpost.co.nz/nzpost/inrates.

UK: Allow 4-8 days for airmail to Australia. Letters up to 20g cost UK£0.65; packages up to 0.5kg UK£4.95, up to 2kg UK£19.20. UK Swiftair delivers letters a day faster for an extra UK£2.85. www.royalmail.co.uk/calculator.

US: Allow 7-10 days for regular airmail to Australia. Postcards/aerogrammes cost US70¢; letters under 1 oz. US80¢; packages under 1 lb. cost US$14.50. **US Global Priority Mail** delivers small/large flat-rate envelopes to Australia in 4 business days for US$5/9. http://ircalc.usps.gov.

Additionally, **Federal Express** (Australia ☎13 26 10; US and Canada ☎800-247-4747; New Zealand ☎0800 73 33 39; UK ☎0800 12 38 00; www.fedex.com) handles express mail services from most of the above countries to Australia; they can get a letter from New York to Sydney in three business days for US$30.98. Rates among non-US locations are prohibitively expensive (e.g. London to Sydney costs $44.70).

RECEIVING MAIL IN AUSTRALIA

There are several ways to arrange pickup of letters sent to you by friends and relatives while you are abroad.

General Delivery: Mail can be sent via **Poste Restante** (General Delivery) to almost any city or town in Australia with a post office. Address *Poste Restante* letters as in the following example: Krigrelor FREPUTUNN, Poste Restante, London SW1, United Kingdom. The mail will go to a special desk in the central post office unless you specify a post office by street address or postal code. It's best to use the largest post office, since mail may be sent there regardless. Poste Restante mail is usually held for only 30 days; bring your passport or other photo ID for pick up. If the clerks insist that there is nothing for you, have them check under your first name as well. *Let's Go* lists post offices in the **Practical Information** section for each city and most towns.

American Express: AmEx travel offices around the world offer a free **Client Letter Service** (mail held up to 30 days and forwarded upon request) for cardholders who contact them in advance. Address letters in the same way shown above. Some offices will offer service to non-cardholders (especially AmEx Traveler's Cheque holders), but call ahead to make sure. *Let's Go* lists AmEx office locations for most large cities in **Practical Information** sections. A complete list is available from AmEx (in the US ☎800-528-4800, in Australia ☎1800 230 100, or visit www.americanexpress.com).

SENDING MAIL HOME FROM AUSTRALIA

General post offices (GPO) are usually open Monday through Friday from 9am to 5pm. Larger branches sometimes have extended hours and are also open on Saturday mornings. Domestic letters require AUS45¢ and take up to two business days.

Airmail letters (up to 50g) from major cities in Australia to North America average 4-6 days (AUS$1.50); to New Zealand, 4-5 days (AUS$1); to Japan 3-4 days $AU1; to the UK or Ireland, 4-5 days (AUS$1.50); to South Africa, 5-6 days (AUS$1.50). **Postcards** to any destination cost AUS$1. **Aerogrammes,** printed sheets that fold into envelopes and travel via airmail, are available at post offices (AUS78¢). Most post offices will charge exorbitant fees or refuse to send aerogrammes with enclosures. **Surface mail** is by far the cheapest and slowest way to send mail. It takes two to four months to cross the Pacific and one to three months to cross the Atlantic—appropriate for sending large quantities of items you won't need for a while.

TELEPHONES

CALLING HOME FROM AUSTRALIA

Increasing competition is beating out the calling card as the best way to call home. Cheap international calling stores such as Global Gossip appear in the major cities. Prepaid phone cards can be bought and used throughout Australia, usually at cheaper rates than the regular international carriers, though sometimes these cards have restrictions on what times you can place calls. A newer and possibly better option is to purchase your own mobile phone in Australia ($80-160). Once you own the phone, international calls can be expensive and usually require prepaid phone cards; however, incoming calls are usually free (check before purchasing the phone), so people at home can call you, and you don't have to pay the bill. Shop around while you're down there, as prices drop and incredible deals appear unexpectedly. Throughout Australia, though, a **calling card** might be your most convenient option. To obtain a calling card or to call home with one contact your national telecommunications service provider before leaving home:

You can usually make **direct international calls** from pay phones, but if you aren't using a calling card you may need to drop your coins as quickly as your words.

COMPANY	TO OBTAIN A CARD, DIAL:	TO CALL ABROAD, DIAL:
AT&T (US)	800-222-0300	1800 881 011
British Telecom Direct	800 34 51 44	0800 881 441
Canada Direct	800-668-6878	1800 881 150
Ireland Direct	800 40 00 00	1800 881 353
MCI (US)	800-444-3333	1800 881 100
New Zealand Direct	0800 00 00 00	1800 881 640
Sprint (US)	800-877-4646	1800 881 877
Telkom South Africa	10 219	1800 881 270
Telstra Australia	13 22 00	13 22 00

PLACING INTERNATIONAL CALLS. To call Australia from home or to call home from Australia, dial:

1. The **international dialing prefix.** To dial out of **Australia,** dial 0011; **Canada** or the **US,** 011; the **Republic of Ireland, New Zealand,** or the **UK,** 00; **South Africa,** 09.
2. The **country code** of the country you want to call. To call **Australia,** dial 61; **Canada** or the **US,** 1; the **Republic of Ireland,** 353; **New Zealand,** 64; **South Africa,** 27; the **UK,** 44.
3. The **city/area code.** *Let's Go* lists the city/area codes for cities and towns in Australia opposite the city or town name, next to a ☎. If the first digit is a zero (e.g., 020 for London), omit the zero when calling from abroad (e.g., dial 20 from Canada to reach London).
4. The **local number.**

Prepaid phone cards and occasionally major credit cards can be used for direct international calls, but they are less cost-efficient. Although incredibly convenient, in-room hotel calls invariably include an arbitrary and sky-high surcharge.

The expensive alternative to dialing direct or using a calling card is using an international operator to place a **collect call;** sometimes in an emergency, though, this is the only way to reach home. An operator from your home nation can be reached by dialing the appropriate service provider listed above, and they will typically place a collect call even if you don't possess one of their phone cards.

CALLING WITHIN AUSTRALIA

Public phones are easy to find nearly everywhere you go in Australia. Some phone booths in Australia are coin-operated, some are phone-card operated, and some accept either coins or phone cards. Local calls from phone booths cost AUS40¢. In addition to phone booths, public phones (often small blue or orange boxes) can sometimes be found in bars and hotels, and local calls on these often cost AUS50¢.

Australia has two main telecommunications companies: Optus and Telstra. Telstra rules every local market and much long-distance, while Optus concentrates on mobile phone service and long-distance. **Pre-paid phonecards** are available in $5, $10, $20, and $50 denominations from many newsagents and pharmacies. Most must be inserted into the phone, whereas others have a toll-free access telephone number and a personal identification number (PIN). As phone cards have grown in popularity, so have the number of booths accepting cards only. Therefore, if heading to a remote area, it might be best to have both types of cards. A few public phones (at airports, city center locations, and major hotels) even take **credit cards.**

For **directory assistance,** you can call ☎013 from any public phone at no charge. Six-digit phone numbers beginning with **13** are information numbers that can be dialed from anywhere in Australia for the price of a local call. Numbers beginning with **1300** operate similarly. Numbers beginning **1800 or 0800** are **toll-free.**

Mobile phones are everywhere in urban Australia. Mobile phone numbers are either nine or 10 digits; the nine-digit phone numbers begin 01* and ten-digit numbers begin 04**. Usually the caller picks up the charges when calling a mobile phone, and charges run about AUS80¢ per minute. Some hotel owners ask guests to register their mobile phones when they check in.

Long-distance calls within Australia use STD (Subscriber Trunk Dialing) services. You must dial an **area code** (listed above) before the eight-digit number.

EMAIL AND INTERNET

Finding Internet access in Australia is simple. Most big cities have **Internet shops** that also offer discounted international calling. These coffee-less counterparts to **cybercafes** offer access from as low as **free** to as high as $8 per hour. Coin-operated Internet kiosks are an expensive (usually $2 per 10min.) yet common option in cities and many hostels. In addition, virtually all public libraries now offer free access to the web, though sometimes you are restricted from checking email or must have a prior reservation. *Let's Go* lists Internet access options in the **Practical Information** section of towns and cities. Other Internet access points in Australia can be found at www.gnomon.com.au/publications/netaccess.

Free web-based email providers include Hotmail (www.hotmail.com) and Yahoo! Mail (www.yahoo.com). Most internet search engines have affiliated free email service. If you have a Telnet account, you can forward that email to the web-based account. Travelers who have the luxury of a laptop with them can use a **modem** to call an Internet service provider. Some Internet providers also have access phone numbers in other countries so you only need pay for a local call; contact your own provider for more information. Otherwise, long-distance phone cards specifically intended for such calls can defray normally high phone charges. Check with your long-distance phone provider to see if they offer this option.

ESSENTIALS

GETTING THERE

BY PLANE

When it comes to airfare, a little effort can save you a bundle. The key is to hunt around, be flexible, and persistently ask about discounts. Students, seniors, and those under 26 should never pay full price for a ticket.

AIRFARES

Airfares to Australia peak between Dec. and Feb.; holidays (see p. 672) are also expensive. The cheapest times to travel are between Sept. and Nov. Midweek (M-Th morning) round-trip flights run US$40-50 cheaper than weekend flights, but they are generally more crowded and less likely to permit frequent-flier upgrades. Traveling with an "open return" ticket can be pricier than fixing a return date when buying the ticket. Round-trip flights are by far the cheapest; "open-jaw" (arriving in and departing from different cities, e.g. Los Angeles-Sydney and Melbourne-Sydney) tickets tend to be pricier. Patching one-way flights together is the most expensive way to travel. Flights between Australia's regional hubs—Sydney, Brisbane, Melbourne—will tend to be cheaper.

If Australia is only one stop on a more extensive globe-hop, consider a round-the-world (RTW) ticket. Tickets usually include at least 5 stops and are valid for about a year; prices range US$1200-5000. Try **Northwest Airlines/KLM** (US ☎800-447-4747; www.nwa.com) or **Star Alliance,** a consortium of 22 airlines including United Airlines (US ☎800-241-6522; www.star-alliance.com).

Boarding: Whenever flying internationally, pick up tickets for international flights well in advance of the departure date, and confirm by phone within 72hr. of departure. Most airlines require that passengers arrive at the airport at least 2hr. before departure. One carry-on item and 2 pieces of checked baggage under 20kg (44 lb.) is the norm.

Fares: The privilege of spending 24hr. or more on a plane doesn't come cheap. Full-price round-trip fares to Australia from the US or Canada depending upon which coast of each continent you are heading to and from can run between US$900 and $2000; from the UK, 500£/1100£; from New Zealand 400NZ$/700NZ$.

BUDGET AND STUDENT TRAVEL AGENCIES

While knowledgeable agents specializing in flights to Australia can make your life easy and help you save, they may not spend the time to find you the lowest possible fare—they get paid on commission. Travelers holding **ISIC and IYTC cards** (see p. 36) qualify for big discounts from student travel agencies. Most flights from budget agencies are on major airlines, but in peak season some may sell seats on less reliable chartered aircraft.

usit world (www.usitworld.com). Over 50 **usit campus** branches in the UK (www.usitcampus.co.uk), including 52 Grosvenor Gardens, **London** SW1W 0AG (☎0870 240 10 10); **Manchester** (☎0161 273 1880); **Edinburgh** (☎0131 668 3303). Nearly 20 **usit NOW** offices in Ireland, including 19-21 Aston Quay, O'Connell Bridge, **Dublin** 2 (☎01 602 1600; www.usitnow.ie), and **Belfast** (☎02 890 327 111; www.usitnow.com). Offices also in Athens, Auckland, Brussels, Frankfurt, Johannesburg, Lisbon, Luxembourg, Madrid, Paris, Sofia, and Warsaw.

Council Travel (www.counciltravel.com). Countless US offices, including branches in Atlanta, Boston, Chicago, L.A., New York, San Francisco, Seattle, and Washington, D.C. Check the website or call ☎800-2-COUNCIL (226-8624) for the office nearest you. Australian offices include: 39 Lake St, **Cairns** (☎07 4041 4500); 315 Wellington St., **Perth** (☎08 9321 8330); Level 8, 92 Pitt St., **Sydney** (☎02 9232 8444).

CTS Travel, 44 Goodge St., **London** W1T 2AD (☎0207 636 0031; fax 0207 637 5328; ctsinfo@ctstravel.co.uk).

CALL 1-800-2COUNCIL
CLICK www.counciltravel.com
VISIT one of our 75 retail locations

Adventures in Australia

Budget Airfares

Circle Pacific Airfares

Airpasses

Buspasses

Adventure Trips

Sea Kayaking Trips

Walking Trips

Learn to Dive Trips

Travel Insurance

Experienced Travel Counselors

USA

SAN DIEGO
7 Horton Plaza
619-544-0800

SAN FRANCISCO
785 Market St. #1710
415-247-1800

SEATTLE
715 Broadway Ave. East
206-322-0396

STANFORD UNIVERSITY
Tresidder Union
2nd Floor
650-470-0050

CANADA

CALGARY
815 10th Ave. SW
403-262-6632

EDMONTON
8103 104th St.
780-439-3096

LONDON
685 Richmond St. #101
519-667-9993

OTTAWA
73 Clarence St.
613-244-1113

TORONTO
381 King St. West
416-345-9726

VANCOUVER
1516 Duranleau St.
Granville Island
604-659-3350

THE ADVENTURE TRAVEL COMPANY
A division of Travel CUTS

www.atcadventure.com

STA Travel, 7890 S. Hardy Dr., Suite 110, Tempe AZ 85284 (24hr. reservations and info ☎800-777-0112; www.statravel.com). A student and youth travel organization with countless offices worldwide (check their website), including US offices in Boston, Chicago, L.A., New York, San Francisco, Seattle, and Washington, D.C. Ticket booking, travel insurance, railpasses, and more. In the UK, walk-in office 11 Goodge St., **London** W1T 2PF or call ☎0870 160 6070. In New Zealand, 10 High St., **Auckland** (☎09 309 0458). In Australia, 366 Lygon St., **Melbourne** VIC 3053 (☎03 9349 4344).

StudentUniverse, 545 Fifth Ave., Suite 640, New York, NY 10017 (toll-free customer service ☎800-272-9676, outside the US 212-986-8420; help@studentuniverse.com; www.studentuniverse.com), is an online student travel service offering discount ticket booking, travel insurance, railpasses, destination guides, and much more. Customer service line open M-F 9am-8pm and Sa noon-5pm EST.

Travel CUTS (Canadian Universities Travel Services Limited), 187 College St., **Toronto,** ON M5T 1P7 (☎416-979-2406; fax 979-8167; www.travelcuts.com). 60 offices across Canada. Also in the UK, 295-A Regent St., **London** W1R 7YA (☎0207-255-1944).

ESSENTIALS

COMMERCIAL AIRLINES VIA INTERNET

Many airline sites offer special last-minute deals. The Internet is one of the best places to look for travel bargains—it's fast, convenient, and you can spend as long as you like exploring options without driving your travel agent insane.

Commercial airlines' lowest regular offer is the **APEX** (Advance Purchase Excursion) fare, which provides confirmed reservations and allows "open-jaw" tickets. Generally, reservations must be made seven to 21 days ahead of departure, with seven- to 14-day minimum-stay and up to 90-day maximum-stay restrictions. These fares carry hefty cancellation and change penalties (fees rise in high season). Book peak-season APEX fares early; by October you may have a hard time getting your desired departure date. Use **Microsoft Expedia** (msn.expedia.com) or **Travelocity** (www.travelocity.com) to get an idea of the lowest published fares, then use the resources outlined here to try to beat them.

Popular carriers to Australia include **Air New Zealand** (www.airnewzealand.co.nz), **British Airways** (www.britishairways.com), **Cathay Pacific** (www.cathaypacific.om), **South African Airlines** (www.saa.co.za) and **United Airways** (www.united.com), most of which have daily nonstop flights from Los Angeles to Sydney. **Qantas** (www.qantas.com.au) is Australia's main airline and has the most international connections. Other sites that do the legwork and compile the deals for you: www.bestfares.com, www.onetravel.com, www.lowestfare.com, and www.travelzoo.com.

STA (www.statravel.com), **Council** (www.counciltravel.com), and **StudentUniverse** (www.studentuniverse.com) provide quotes on student tickets, while **Expedia** and **Travelocity** offer full travel services. **Priceline** (www.priceline.com) allows you to specify a price, and obligates you to buy any ticket that meets or beats it; be prepared for antisocial hours and odd routes. **Skyauction** (www.skyauction.com) allows you to bid on both last-minute and advance-purchase tickets. **TravelHUB** (www.travelhub.com) is a directory of travel agents that includes a searchable database of fares.

An indispensable resource on the Internet is the *Air Traveler's Handbook* (www.cs.cmu.edu/afs/cs/user/mkant/Public/Travel/airfare.html), a comprehensive listing of links to everything you need to know before you board a plane.

Just one last note—to protect yourself, make sure that the site you use has a secure server before handing over any credit card details. Happy hunting!

OTHER CHEAP ALTERNATIVES

AIR COURIER FLIGHTS. Couriers help transport cargo on international flights by guaranteeing delivery of the baggage claim slips from the company to a representative overseas. Generally, couriers must travel light (carry-ons only) and deal with complex restrictions on their flight. Most flights are round-trip with short

StudentUniverse.com Real Travel Deals

800.272.9676

fixed-length stays and a limit of a single ticket per issue. Most of these flights also operate only out of the biggest cities, like New York. Generally, you must be over 21 (in some cases 18), have a valid passport, and procure your own visa. Groups such as the **Air Courier Association** (☎800-282-1202; www.aircourier.org) and the **International Association of Air Travel Couriers** (☎561-582-8320; www.courier.org) provide their members with lists of opportunities and courier brokers worldwide for an annual fee. For travel to Australia, however, courier options are limited.

TICKET CONSOLIDATORS. Ticket consolidators, or **"bucket shops,"** buy unsold tickets in bulk from commercial airlines and sell them at discounted rates. The best place to look is in the Sunday travel section of any major newspaper, where many bucket shops place tiny ads. Call quickly, as availability is typically extremely limited. Not all bucket shops are reliable establishments, so insist on a receipt that gives full details of restrictions, refunds, and tickets, and pay by credit card (in spite of the 2-5% fee) so you can stop payment if you never receive your tickets. For **more information,** check the website **Consolidators FAQ** (www.travel-library.com/air-travel/consolidators.html), **Air Travel Advisory Bureau** (☎0207-636-5000; www.atab.co.uk) or the book *Consolidators: Air Travel's Bargain Basement*, by Kelly Monaghan (Intrepid Traveler, US$8).

GETTING AROUND

BY PLANE

Because Australia is so large, many travelers, even many budget travelers, take a domestic flight at some point while touring the country. Qantas and Ansett Australia (recently acquired by Air New Zealand) are the two major domestic carriers. Oz Experience (p. 66) and Qantas offer an Air-Bus Pass with which travelers can fly one-way, and bus back (or vice versa) around Australia. Passes are valid for six months with unlimited stops; all dates can be changed.

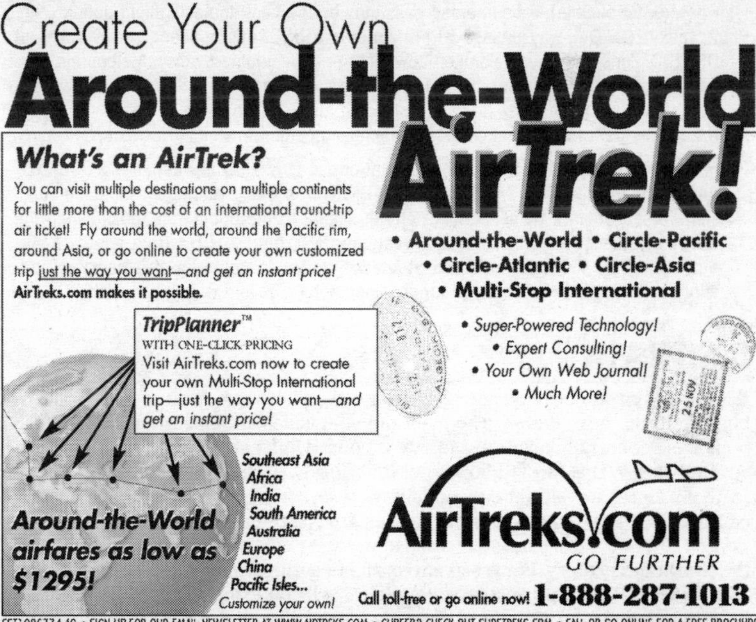

Self-Drive Holiday Specialists
http://www.getaboutoz.com

Ensuring You Get The Best Choice at the Best Price

- Economy cars
- Campervans / Motorhomes
- Taragos / Mini buses
- 4WD Vehicles / Bushcampers
- Station Wagons /Camping Equipment
- New Zealand Bookings
- On-line Accommodation

One Way & 4WD Rentals Australia
Website www.onewayrentals.com
Call Toll Free within Australia
1800 656 899
Shop 2, 171 William St, Darlinghurst NSW 2011
Ph: (61) 2 9380 5536 Fax: (61) 2 9361 6998
E-mail: enquiries@getaboutoz.com

Qantas: (www.qantas.com.au) Reservations ☎13 13 13 in Australia, ☎800-227-4500 in the U.S. and Canada, ☎0845 7 747 767 in the UK. Qantas boomerang passes allow travelers to change flight dates free of charge on domestic flights; cities can be changed for $50. For international travelers (with the exception of New Zealanders and Fijians, who are not eligible), a boomerang pass may be the best domestic flight option (min. 2, max. 10). One-way passes within zones are US$160, between zones starts at US$190. Zones are roughly broken down into east (including Sydney, Melbourne, Brisbane, Cairns, and Adelaide), central (including Ayers Rock, Alice Springs, and Darwin), west (including Perth), New Zealand (including Auckland), and South Pacific (including Nadi). The first two segments must be purchased before arriving in Australia.

Ansett Airlines: (www.ansett.com.au) Reservations ☎13 13 00 in Australia, ☎800-262-2468 in the U.S., 0208 741 2299 in the UK. With a wink at monopolistic price collusion, Ansett offers a domestic flight option similar to the boomerang pass called the G'day airpass (with only an east, west, and NZ zone, $155 within zones, $195 between). Has the most extensive domestic routes in Australia and New Zealand, although it flies internationally to Japan, Hong Kong, Fiji, and Bali, Indonesia.

BY TRAIN

Each state runs its own rail service, and transfers between services may require a bus trip to the next station. The main rail companies are **Countrylink** (☎13 22 32; bookings@countrylink.nsw.gov.au; www.countrylink.nsw.gov.au), based in New South Wales, **V/Line** (☎13 61 96; www.vline.vic.gov.au) in Victoria, **Queensland Rail** (☎13 22 32; res.traveltrain@qr.com.au; www.qr.com.au) in Queensland, **Westrail** (☎13 10 53; www.wagr.wa.gov.au) in Western Australia, and **Great Southern Railways** (☎13 21 47; salesagent@gsr.com.au; www.gsr.com.au) in South Australia and the Northern Territory. For reservations and ticketing from the US, call ☎800-423-2880. Wheelchair access on interstate trains can be poor, as the corridors are often too narrow. Some larger stations provide collapsible wheelchairs, but not all do. Also, some stations have platforms which make it difficult to disembark.

The **Austrail Pass** allows unlimited travel over consecutive days within a given period (14 days US$363, 21 days US$473, 30 days US$569). The **Austrail Flexipass** allows you to purchase 8 (US$303), 15 (US$435), 22 (US$611), or 29 (US$792) traveling days to be used over a six-month period. Both passes are only available to non-Australians and must be bought overseas. Rail Australia has agents in the US (☎800-423-2880), Canada (☎416-322-1034), New Zealand (☎09 639 0515), South Africa (☎021 419 9382), Japan 03 3818 5671, and the UK (☎87075 002 22). The **East Coast Discovery Pass** allows unlimited stops in one direction on the Eastern Seaboard within six months (Sydney-Cairns US$136, Melbourne-Cairns US$181). For information on more passes, go to www.railpage.org.au/pass.html.

BY BUS

Buses cover more of the desolate intermediate landscape of Australia than do trains. Buses run regularly to major cities, but journeys off the beaten track may require a wait of a few days. It may be more cost efficient to buy a kilometer or multi-day pass if you are planning on doing a large amount of travel by bus.

GREYHOUND PIONEER. Greyhound (☎13 20 30; outside Australia, ☎+61 7 3258 1930) covers the whole country, with dozens of travelpass options. Seven- to 21-day passes allow you to travel on any Greyhound route within 30 to 60 days, depending on the length of your pass; days of travel do not have to be consecutive. These passes cost between AUS$672 and AUS$1325. The **Aussie Explorer Pass** allows you to predetermine a route and take up to 12 months to get there, while an **Aussie Kilometer Pass** lets you choose a number of kilometers to be used on any Greyhound route (minimum 2000km, AUS$281). Most of these passes can be used to take **Greyhound Pioneer Tours,** which offer combinations of tours for National Parks and scenic spots in Central Australia, Western Australia, and the Top End.

MCCAFFERTY'S COACHLINES. McCafferty's (☎13 14 99; infomcc@mccaffertys.com.au; www.mccaffertys.com.au) runs through most of the country, with the exception of Western Australia. **Travel Australia** passes are valid for 6 to 12 months

(up to AUS$1116), and let travelers ride with unlimited stops one way along any of seven predetermined routes. Passes can be purchased from a local travel agent or at any McCafferty's terminal. A 10% discount is available for international students, pensioners, and backpacker card holders; the discount is 15% if the purchase is made outside of Australia. McCafferty's also offers an **Australian Roamer** pass, which allows long-distance travelers to pay by the kilometer (2000km AUS$239, 10,000km AUS$915); the Roamer pass is available only to backpacker card and ISIC card holders. Non-Australians are also able to get the **Discover Australia Day Pass,** but it must be purchased before arrival in Australia. Allowing for unlimited travel on the McCafferty's network for a set number of days within the life of the pass, you can choose among many options between 7 (AUS$693) and 30 (AUS$1643) days worth of travel within a range of 30 to 60 days.

OZ EXPERIENCE. This popular bus company offers backpacker packages with a lot of flexibility and charismatic drivers who double as tour guides. The packages must be purchased for predetermined routes (cheaper if bought outside of Australia), and travelers can usually take up to six months to finish with unlimited stopovers. Be prepared for a younger, more party-heavy crowd. 5% YHA discount. (☎ 02 8356 1766 or 1300 30 00 28; www.ozexperience.com. Shop 401, Kingsgate Shopping Centre, Darlinghurst Rd., Kings Cross, Sydney NSW 2011.)

BY CAR

Some regions of Australia are virtually inaccessible without a car, and in many sparsely populated areas public transportation options are simply inadequate. One of the major dilemmas of traveling in Australia, at least beyond the main coastal cities, is that the road system is in many areas basic and often poorly maintained. To travel on most outback roads and in many national parks, you will often need a **four-wheel-drive (4WD),** which unfortunately can double the cost of renting or buying. Shopping around well ahead of time is advisable.

ON THE ROAD

Australians drive on the **left side** of the road. In unmarked intersections, a driver must yield to vehicles entering the intersection from the right. In some big cities, right turns often must take place from the farthest left lane, after the light has already turned red—keep your eyes peeled for signs to that effect. By law, **seat belts** must be worn. Children under 40 lb. should ride only in a special kind of carseat, available for a small fee at most car rental agencies. The speed limit in most cities is 60kph (35mph) and on highways 100 or 110kph (62 or 68mph). Radar guns are often used to patrol well-traveled roads; sly speed cameras nab offenders on less populated paths. **Petrol (gasoline)** prices vary by state, but average about AUS88¢-1.05¢ per liter in cities and from AUS90¢-$1.15 per liter in outlying areas.

PRECAUTIONS. When traveling in the summer or in the outback, bring substantial amounts of water (a suggested 5L of **water** per person per day) for drinking and for the radiator. For long outback drives, travelers should register with police before beginning the trek, and again upon arrival at the destination. Check with the local automobile club for details. In the north, **four-wheel-drive (4WD)** is essential for seeing the parks, particularly in the Wet, when dirt roads turn to mud. When traveling in the outback or for long distances, make sure tires are in good repair and have enough air, and get good maps. A **compass** and a **car manual** can also be very useful. You should always carry a **spare tire** and **jack, jumper cables, extra oil, flares, a torch (flashlight),** and **heavy blankets** (in case your car breaks down at night or in the winter). If you don't know how to **change a tire,** learn before heading into the outback. Blowouts on dirt roads are exceedingly common. If you do have a breakdown, **stay with your car;** if you wander off, there's less likelihood trackers will find you.

DANGERS. Australia's highway system can be tough, and road conditions are not consistent. Find out ahead of time whether roads are sealed, especially if you're driving a conventional vehicle. Unsealed roads dominate rural Australia, ranging from smooth, hard-packed sand to an eroded mixture of mud, sand, and stones. Locals are a good source of information on the road conditions in the immediate

vicinity. When driving on unsealed roads, call regional tourist boards ahead of time for road conditions, especially in the North, as the wet season sometimes makes roads impassible for months after the rains stop. Furthermore, you should allow at least twice as much time as you would for travel on paved roads. One can skid on gravel almost as badly as on ice.

Kangaroos are a serious danger to drivers; they may be cute, but they are large and will jump in front of or into the side of cars. Dusk and dawn are particularly dangerous times when 'roos are usually hopping about.

CAR ASSISTANCE. The **Australian Automobile Association (AAA)** is the national umbrella organization for all of the local automobile organizations. You won't often see it called the AAA, though; in most states, the local organization is called the **Royal Automobile Club (RAC).** In New South Wales and the ACT, it's the **National Royal Motorist Association (NRMA).** In the Northern Territory, it's the **Automobile Association of the Northern Territory (AANT).** Services—from breakdown assistance to map provision—are similar to those offered by automobile associations in other countries. Most overseas organizations have reciprocal membership with AAA (including AAA in the US; AA and RAC in the UK; NZAA in New Zealand; AASA in South Africa). Bring proof of your membership to Australia, and you'll be able to use AAA facilities free of charge. To join in the US, dial ☎800 222 4357. **AAA roadside assistance** can be reached at ☎13 11 11, and ☎08 8941 0611 in the Northern Territory. It's possible to join AAA through any state's organization. *Let's Go* lists the location of the state automobile organization in each state introduction.

RENTING

Although the cost of renting a car can be prohibitive for an individual traveler, rentals can become cost-efficient when traveling with a group.

RENTAL AGENCIES. There are three basic categories: multinational companies with hundreds of branches, national companies with tens of branches, and local agencies which serve only one city or region. Budget, Hertz, Avis, National and Thrifty are Australia's largest multinational companies. You can generally make reservations before you leave by calling their offices in your home country. However, occasionally the price and availability information they give doesn't jive with what the local offices in Australia will tell you. Try checking with both numbers to make sure you get the best price and accurate information. Local desk numbers are included in town listings; for home-country numbers, call your toll-free directory or check the web. The larger national companies are Delta and Britz. These complement dozens of smaller local agencies, which usually have lower prices. Australia numbers and web addresses are listed below:

Avis (☎02 9353 9000, nationwide ☎13 63 33; www.avis.com). YHA member discounts available; quote code P081600 when making reservations.

Britz (☎800 331 454; www.britz.com) Offer super saver discounts around Australia.

Budget (☎03 9206 3333, nationwide ☎1300 36 28 48; www.budget.com.au). YHA discounts available; quote code E013609.

Delta (☎1300 131 390; www.deltaeuropcar.com.au).

Hertz (☎03 9698 2555, nationwide ☎13 30 39; www.hertz.com). YHA discounts available; quote CDP code 317961.

Thrifty (☎1300 36 72 27; www.thrifty.com.au).

To rent a car from most establishments, you need to be at least 21 years old. Some agencies require renters to be 25, and most charge those aged 21-24 an additional insurance fee (around AUS$10-22 per day). Policies and prices vary greatly. Small local operations occasionally rent to people under 21, but be sure to ask about the insurance coverage and deductible, and always check the fine print.

COSTS AND INSURANCE. Rental car prices start at around AUS$45 a day from national companies and AUS$30 from local agencies. Expect to pay more for larger cars and for 4WD. Cars with **automatic transmission** can cost up to AUS$15 a day more than standard manuals (stick shift), and in Western Australia, Northern Territory, and more remote areas of the eastern states, automatic transmission is hard to find at all. It is virtually impossible to find an automatic 4WD.

Many rental packages offer unlimited kilometers, while others offer 100-200km per day with a surcharge of approximately AUS25¢ per kilometer after that. Return the car with a full tank of petrol to avoid high fuel charges at the end. Be sure to ask whether the price includes **insurance** against theft and collision. Remember that if you are driving a conventional vehicle on an **unsealed road** (Australian for unpaved) in a rental car, you are almost never covered by insurance; ask about this before leaving the rental agency. Beware that cars rented on an **American Express** or **Visa/Mastercard Gold or Platinum** credit cards in Australia might *not* carry the automatic insurance that they would in some other countries; check with your credit card company. Insurance plans almost always come with an **excess** (or deductible) of around AUS$1000 for conventional vehicles; excess ranges up to around AUS$2500 for younger drivers and for 4WD. This means you pay for all damages up to that sum, unless they are the fault of another vehicle. The excess you will be quoted applies to collisions with other vehicles; collisions with non-vehicles, such as trees or kangaroos, ("single-vehicle collisions") will cost you even more. The excess can often be reduced or waived entirely if you pay an additional charge, between AUS$5-20 per day.

National chains often allow one-way rentals, picking up in one city and dropping off in another. However, there is usually a minimum hire period and sometimes an extra drop-off charge of several hundred dollars.

BUYING AND SELLING USED CARS

Buying used cars and then reselling them is popular among long-term travelers or those too young to rent. Automotive independence costs around AUS$1600-5000. However, used car dealers have been know to rip off foreigners, especially backpackers. Research prices, or ask a trustworthy Aussie about reasonable prices; some people recommend bringing an Aussie along when purchasing the car. Buying from a private owner or fellow traveler is often a cheaper alternative. In many cities, hundreds of private sellers rent space at used car lots, as buyers stroll around and haggle. Hostel or university bulletin boards are another good bet. In Sydney, check the *Weekly Trading Post* on Thursdays for used car advertisements, and the *Daily Telegraph Mirror* and *Sydney Morning Herald* on Saturdays. When selling a car back, consider the high tourist season for the region you're in. Vehicles are also easier to sell if they are registered in the state where they are being sold—new owners need to register the car, and some states don't allow registration transfer by mail. If you buy a car privately, check the registration papers against the license of the person who is selling the car.

WHAT TO LOOK FOR. The **Ford Falcon, Holden Kingswood,** and **Holden Commodore** are among the popular large cars, while the **Toyota Corolla** and **Mazda 626** have cornered much of the small-car market. Those who buy campervans report having the most luck with **Toyota.** Buying popular automobiles can pay off if you end up needing parts in the middle of nowhere. Holden, Ford, Nissan, Toyota, Mazda, and Mitsubishi are all fairly safe bets. Keep in mind the low resale value of used cars—you probably won't turn a profit or finance your ticket home at the end of your trip. Another option is to purchase a car from a dealer who guarantees to buy the car back at the end of your trip. Be wary of small print when examining **buy-back deals.**

Before buying a used car, check with the local branch of the AAA, as states have varying requirements for a transfer of ownership, and local organizations can advise you on how to get your money's worth. The NRMA in New South Wales publishes *International Tourists Car Buying Advice* and *Worry-free Guide to*

Buying a Car. In Victoria, all cars are required to carry a Road Worthiness Certificate, and it's probably unwise to purchase a car without one. Local auto clubs also do mechanical inspections (NRMA inspections ☎1300 362 802).

BEFORE YOU BUY. When buying a car, call the **Register of Encumbered Vehicles** to confirm that a vehicle is unencumbered—that it has not been reported as stolen and has no outstanding financial obligations nor traffic warrants. For cars registered in NSW, VIC, ACT, QLD, or NT, dial ☎02 9600 0022 or ☎1800 42 49 88; in TAS, dial ☎03 6233 5201; in SA, dial ☎13 10 84; in WA, dial ☎1300 30 40 24. You'll need to provide the registration-, engine-, and VIN/chassis-numbers of the vehicle. In New South Wales, a car must have a pink inspection certificate to guarantee that it is roadworthy. It is valid for 20 days—available at most service stations.

INSURANCE AND REGISTRATION. **Third-party personal injury insurance,** sometimes called a green slip, is automatically included with every registered vehicle. In the event of an accident, this covers any person who may be injured except the driver at fault, but does not cover damage or repairs to any cars or property. Even travelers trying to save money should consider purchasing additional insurance. **Third-party property damage insurance** covers the cost of repair to other people's cars or property if you're responsible for an accident. **Full comprehensive insurance,** which covers damage to all vehicles, including your own, is more expensive, but provides more peace of mind. Within two weeks after purchase, you'll need to **register** the car in your name at the Motor Vehicle Registry. Although requirements vary between states, re-registration costs about AUS$15, and must be completed within about two weeks. The local automobile organization can always help.

If you rent, lease, or borrow a car, you will need a **green card,** or **International Insurance Certificate,** to prove that you have liability insurance. Obtain it through the car rental agency; most include coverage in their prices. If you lease a car, you can obtain a green card from the dealer. Some travel agents offer the card; it may also be available at border crossings. Verify whether your auto insurance applies abroad; even if it does, you will still need a green card to certify this to foreign officials. If you have a collision abroad, the accident will show up on your domestic records if you report it to your insurance company. Rental agencies may require you to purchase theft insurance in countries that they consider to have a high risk of auto theft. Ask your rental agency about Australia.

INTERNATIONAL DRIVING PERMITS

If you plan to drive a car while in Australia, your home country's driver's license will suffice. After driving in the same state for three months, you must have an International Driving Permit (IDP). If your home country's driver's license is not printed in English, you must have an English translation with you. Your IDP, valid for one year, must be issued in your own country before you depart; AAA affiliates cannot issue IDPs valid in their own country. You must be 18+ to receive the IDP. A valid driver's license from your home country must always accompany the IDP. An application for an IDP usually needs to include one or two photos, a current local license, an additional form of identification, and a fee. To apply, contact the national or local branch of your home country's Automobile Association.

Canada:(www.caa.ca/CAAInternet/travelservices/internationaldocumentation/idp-travel.htm) Permits CDN$10.

Ireland:(www.aaireland.ie/travel/id_permit.htm) Permits IR£4.

New Zealand:(www.nzaa.co.nz/cg/MainMenu) Permits NZ$10.

South Africa:(www.aasa.co.za/holiday/perm.html) Permits ZAR45.

UK:(www.theaa.co.uk/motoringandtravel/idp/) Permits UK£4.

US:(www.aaa.com/aaa/240/sne/travel/idpc.html) Permits US$10.

BY BICYCLE

Australia has many **bike tracks** to attract cyclers. Much of the country is flat, and road bikers can travel long distances without needing to huff and puff excessively. In theory, bicycles can go on **buses and trains,** but most major bus companies require you to disassemble your bike and pay a flat AUS$15 fee. You may not be allowed to bring your bike into train compartments.

The **Bicycle Federation of Australia (BFA),** GPO Box 3222, Canberra, ACT 2601 (☎03 9827 4453; secretary@bfa.asn.au; www.bfa.asn.au), a nonprofit bicycle advocacy group, publishes *Australian Cyclist* magazine and has a list of regional bicycling organizations on its web page. Member groups include the Pedal Power ACT (☎02 6248 7990), Bicycle Institute of South Australia (☎08 8271 5824), Bicycle Transportation Alliance (Western Australia, ☎08 9420 7210), Bicycle New South Wales (☎02 9283 5200), Bicycle Tasmania (☎03 6233 6619), Victoria Bicycle Association (jch@sci.vu.edu.au), and the Bicycle Institute of Queensland (☎07 3844 1144), among others. Some of these organizations focus more on daytrips and short excursions than on long-distance riding, but they are a place to begin.

Safe and secure cycling requires a quality helmet and lock. A good **helmet** costs about AUS$40—much cheaper than critical head surgery. Helmets are required by law in Australia. Travel with good **maps** from the state Automobile Associations.

BY THUMB

LET'S GO DOES NOT RECOMMEND HITCHHIKING. *Let's Go* strongly urges you to seriously consider the risks before you choose to hitch. We do not recommend hitching as a safe means of transportation, and none of the information printed here is intended to do so.

Given the infrequency of public transportation to several popular destinations, travelers often need to find other ways to get where they're going. Hostels frequently have message boards where those seeking rides and those seeking to share the cost of gas can meet up. If you are looking to travel with a stranger, carless travelers report having a good deal of luck meeting willing drivers in roadhouses. This arrangement gives them an opportunity to size up potential lifts before accepting a ride. On the east coast, backpacker traffic moves from Sydney to Brisbane (and possibly as far north as Cairns, see p. 287), and those who go with the flow are sure to make friends who have wheels.

Standing on the side of the highway with your thumb out is much more dangerous than making a new friend at your hostel. Safety issues are always imperative, even when you're traveling with another person. Hitching (Australian for hitchhiking) means risking assault, sexual harassment, and unsafe driving, all while entrusting your life to a random person who happens to stop beside you on the road. If you're a woman traveling alone, don't hitch. It's too dangerous. A man and a woman are a safer combination; two men will have a harder time finding a ride, as drivers also must be careful. Avoid getting in the back of a two-door car (there is little chance of escape if in trouble), and never let go of your backpack. Hitchhiking at night can be particularly dangerous. Don't accept a ride that you are not entirely comfortable with. If you ever feel threatened, insist on being let off, but keep in mind that the vast distances between towns on some stretches of highway increase your chance of being left literally in the middle of nowhere.

If you decide to hitch, choose a spot on the side of the road with ample space for a car to pull over, where traffic is not moving too fast. The edges of town are ideal as people have not yet accelerated to highway speed. Dress nicely and keep your backpack in full view, as it tells people you're a backpacker and justifies your reason for hitching. A sign with your destination marked in large letters can also help.

SPECIFIC CONCERNS

WOMEN TRAVELERS

Women exploring on their own inevitably face some additional safety concerns, but it's easy to be adventurous without taking undue risks. If you are concerned, consider staying in hostels which offer single rooms that lock from the inside or in religious organizations with rooms for women only. Communal showers in some hostels are safer than others; check them before settling in. Stick to centrally located accommodations and avoid solitary late-night treks or metro rides.

Conditions for women in Australia have improved greatly in recent years, but vestiges of a male-dominated culture remain. Outback pubs, especially, can be chauvinistic and uncomfortable places to some. In general, though, it is safe for women to travel alone in Australia.

Always carry extra money for a phone call, bus, or taxi. **Hitching** is never safe for lone women, or even for two women traveling together. Choose train compartments occupied by women or couples; ask the conductor to put together a women-only compartment if there isn't one. Look as if you know where you're going and approach older women or couples for directions if you're lost or uncomfortable.

Generally, the less you look like a tourist, the better off you'll be. Dress conservatively, especially in rural areas. Trying to fit in can be effective, but dressing to the style of an obviously different culture may cause you to be ill at ease and a conspicuous target. Wearing a conspicuous **wedding band** may help prevent unwanted overtures. Some travelers report that carrying pictures of a "husband" or "children" is extremely useful to help document marriage status. Even a mention of a husband waiting back at the hotel may be enough in some places to discount your potentially vulnerable, unattached appearance.

Your best answer to verbal harassment is no answer at all; feigning deafness, sitting motionless, and staring straight ahead at nothing in particular will do a world of good that reactions usually don't achieve. The extremely persistent can sometimes be dissuaded by a firm, loud, and very public "Go away!" Don't hesitate to seek out a police officer or a passerby if you are being harassed. Memorize the emergency numbers (☎000), and consider carrying a whistle or airhorn on your keychain. A self-defense course will not only prepare you for a potential attack, but will also raise your level of awareness of your surroundings as well as your confidence (see **Self Defense,** p. 42). Also be sure you are aware of the health concerns that women face when traveling (see **Women's Health,** p. 46).

TRAVELING ALONE

There are many benefits to traveling alone, including independence and greater interaction with locals. On the other hand, any solo traveler is a more vulnerable target of harassment and street theft. Lone travelers need to be well-organized and look confident at all times. Try not to stand out as a tourist, and be especially careful in deserted or very crowded areas. If questioned, never admit that you are traveling alone. Maintain regular contact with someone at home who knows your itinerary. For more tips, pick up *Traveling Solo* by Eleanor Berman (Globe Pequot Press, US$17) or subscribe to **Connecting: Solo Travel Network,** 689 Park Road, Unit 6, Gibsons, BC V0N 1V7 (☎604-886-9099; www.cstn.org; membership US$28).

Alternatively, several services link solo travelers with companions who have similar travel habits and interests; for a bi-monthly newsletter for single travelers seeking a travel partner (subscription US$48), contact the **Travel Companion Exchange,** P.O. Box 833, Amityville, NY 11701 (☎ 800-392-1256; www.whytravelalone.com).

OLDER TRAVELERS

Senior citizens are eligible for a wide range of discounts on transportation, museums, movies, theaters, concerts, restaurants, and accommodations. If you don't see a senior citizen (or "pensioner") price listed, ask, and you may be delightfully surprised. The books *No Problem! Worldwise Tips for Mature Adventurers*, by Janice Kenyon (Orca Book Publishers; US$16) and *Unbelievably Good Deals and Great Adventures That You Absolutely Can't Get Unless You're Over 50*, by Joan Rattner Heilman (NTC/Contemporary Publishing; US$13) are both excellent resources. **Elderhostel,** 11 Ave. de Lafayette, Boston, MA 02111 (☎877-426-8056; www.elderhostel.org), organizes 1- to 4-week "educational adventures" in Australia on varied subjects for those 55+.

BISEXUAL, GAY, AND LESBIAN TRAVELERS

The profile of bisexual, gay, and lesbian community in Australia has risen in recent years, most notably in the popularity of the **gay and lesbian Mardi Gras** in Sydney each year, which is now the largest gay and lesbian gathering in the world (see p. 126). Though pockets of discrimination exist everywhere, the east coast is especially gay-friendly—Sydney ranks in the most gay-friendly cities on earth. The farther into the country you get, the more homophobia you may encounter. Homosexual acts are now legal in every state except Tasmania.

Gay and Lesbian Tourism Australia (GALTA) is a nonprofit nationwide network of tourism industry professionals who are dedicated to the welfare and satisfaction of gay and lesbian travelers to, from, and within Australia. They can be reached at ☎08 8379 7498 or on the web at www.galta.com.au. Listed below are relevant contact organizations, mail-order bookstores, and publishers:

Gaytravel Net Australia (www.gaytravel.net.nz/aus).

Gay/Lesbian Visitor Information Sydney, P.O. Box 7, Darlinghurst NSW 2010 (☎02 9331 1333; fax 9331 1199; pride@rainbow.net.au).

Silke's Travel. (☎02 8347 2000; www.silkes.com.au). Travel agency that specializes in planning gay and lesbian holidays.

Friend's of Dorothy Travel, 2nd Floor, 77 Oxford St., Darlinghurst NSW (☎02 9360 3616; www.fod.com.au/travel). Gay and lesbian owned travel agency.

International Lesbian and Gay Association (ILGA), 81 rue Marché-au-Charbon, B-1000 Brussels, Belgium (☎+32 2 502 2471; www.ilga.org). Provides political information, such as homosexuality laws of individual countries.

FURTHER READING: BISEXUAL, GAY, & LESBIAN.

G'Day Guide/G'day Accommodation Guide, a guide for gay travelers to Australia (published May and December; contact 4 Baker St., St. Kilda, VIC 3182).

Spartacus International Gay Guide 2001-2002. Bruno Gmunder Verlag (US$33).

Ferrari Guides' Gay Travel A to Z, Ferrari Guides' Men's Travel in Your Pocket, and *Ferrari Guides' Inn Places.* Ferrari Publications (US$16-20). Purchase the guides online at www.ferrariguides.com.

The Gay Vacation Guide: The Best Trips and How to Plan Them, Mark Chesnut. Citadel Press (US$15).

TRAVELERS WITH DISABILITIES

Travelers with disabilities should inform airlines and hotels of their disabilities when making arrangements for travel; some time may be needed to prepare special accommodations. Call ahead to restaurants, hotels, parks, and other facilities to find out about the existence of ramps, the widths of doors, the dimensions of elevators, etc. **Guide dog owners** should inquire as to the quarantine policies of each destination country. At the very least, they will need to provide a certificate of immunization against rabies. After the 2000 Sydney Olympics and Paralympics, many locations in Australia (particularly the east) became wheelchair accessible, and budget options for the disabled are increasingly available. The following organizations provide information or publications that might be of assistance:

National Information Communication Network (NICAN), P.O. Box 407, Curtin ACT 2605 (☎02 6285 3713; fax 02 6285 3714; www.nican.com.au). National database of accommodations, recreation, tourism, sport and arts for the disabled.

Australian Quadriplegic Association, Letterbox 40 184 Bourke Rd., Alexandria, NSW 2015 (☎02 9661 8855; fax 02 9661 9598; www.aqa.com.au). Network of community services for individuals with spinal cord injuries.

IDEAS, P.O. Box 479, Tamut NSW 2720 (☎02 6947 3377 or 1800 029 904; www.ideas.org.au). Provides info about the needs and rights of people with disabilities.

Travelers Aid Disability Access (TADAS), Level 2, 169 Swanston St., Melbourne VIC 3000 Australia (☎03 9654 7690; fax 03 9654 1926; home.vicnet.net.au/~tadas). Support and information for people visiting Melbourne.

Accessibility.com.au, the access information supermarket, provides information about accessible opportunities in Sydney.

Wheelabout Van Rental, P.O. Box 3180, Erina NSW 2250 Australia (☎02 4367 0900; fax 4365 5840; www.wheelabout.com). Wheelchair accessible van rentals and sales.

FURTHER READING AND WEBSITES

Easy Access Australia by Bruce Cameron (order at www.vicnet.net.au/~bruceeaa).

The Wheelie's Handbook of Australia by Colin and Diane James (order at home.vicnet.net.au/~wheelies/?S=A).

The **Green Book** (http://members.nbci.com/thegreenbook/home.html) has a partial listing of disabled-access accommodations and sights in Australia.

MINORITY TRAVELERS

Australia is a generally tolerant and diverse country, but fear of losing jobs to **Asian** immigrants has inflamed racism in some areas. This may well extend to Asian travelers. White Australians are often described as racist in their attitudes toward the **Aborigines,** and this assessment is not unfounded. Black travelers are likely to get a few stares in smaller towns and may encounter some hostility in outback areas but will probably not be discriminated against in cities. As always, cities tend to be more tolerant; don't let this dissuade you from venturing off the beaten track. *Let's Go* asks that its researchers exclude from the guides establishments that discriminate. Contact us if you encounter discrimination in any establishment we list.

TRAVELERS WITH CHILDREN

Family vacations often require that you slow your pace, and always require that you plan ahead. When deciding where to stay, remember the special needs of young children; if you pick a B&B or a small hotel, call ahead and make sure it's child-friendly. If you rent a car, make sure the rental company provides a car seat for younger children. **Be sure that your child carries ID** in case of an emergency or in case he or she gets lost, and arrange a meeting spot in case of separation.

Virtually all museums and tourist attractions in Australia have a children's rate. Children under two generally fly for 10% of the adult airfare on international flights (this does not necessarily include a seat). International fares are usually discounted 25% for children from two to 11. Finding a private place for **breast feeding** is often a problem while traveling, so plan accordingly.

DIETARY CONCERNS

Despite the prevalence of meat pies, **vegetarians** should have little problem finding suitable cuisine in Australia. Most restaurants have vegetarian selections on their menus and some cater specifically to vegetarians. *Let's Go* notes restaurants with good vegetarian selections in city listings. For more information, visit the **Australian Vegetarian Society,** (www.moreinfo.com.au/avs). For a vegetarian shopping guide and listings of vegetarian restaurants, consult *The Vegetarian Traveler:*

FURTHER READING: TRAVELERS WITH CHILDREN.

Backpacking with Babies and Small Children, Goldie Silverman. Wilderness Press (US$10).

How to take Great Trips with Your Kids, Sanford and Jane Portnoy. Harvard Common Press (US $10).

Have Kid, Will Travel: 101 Survival Strategies for Vacationing With Babies and Young Children, Claire and Lucille Tristram. Andrews McMeel Publishing (US$9).

Adventuring with Children: An Inspirational Guide to World Travel and the Outdoors, Nan Jeffrey. Avalon House Publishing (US$15).

Trouble Free Travel with Children, Vicki Lansky. Book Peddlers (US$9).

ESSENTIALS

Where to Stay if You're Vegetarian, by Jed and Susan Civic (Larson Publications; US$16). Travelers who keep **kosher** should contact synagogues in larger cities for information on kosher restaurants; your own synagogue may have access to lists of Jewish institutions in Australia. If your observance is strict, you may have to prepare your own food on the road. A good resource is the *Jewish Travel Guide*, by Michael Zaidner (Vallentine Mitchell; US$17).

ALTERNATIVES TO TOURISM

STUDYING ABROAD

Foreign study programs vary in expense, academic quality, living conditions, degree of contact with local students, and exposure to local culture. High school students can usually find exchange programs. For university students, most American undergraduates enroll in programs sponsored by U.S. universities. However, some local universities can be much cheaper than an American university program, though it can be hard to receive academic credit (and sometimes housing). Schools that offer study abroad programs to foreigners are listed below. For a more complete list, check out www.studyabroadlinks.com/search/Australia.

American Institute for Foreign Study, College Division, River Plaza, 9 West Broad St., Stamford, CT 06902, USA (☎800-727-2437, ext. 5163; www.aifsabroad.com). Organizes programs for high school and college study in universities in Australia.

Arcadia University for Education Abroad, 450 S. Easton Rd., Glenside, PA 19038, USA (☎866-927-2234; www.arcadia.edu/cea). Operates programs in Australia. Costs range from $2400 (summer) to $20,000 (full-year).

Association of Commonwealth Universities (ACU), John Foster House, 36 Gordon Sq., London WC1H OPF (☎+44 020 7380 6700; www.acu.ac.uk). Publishes information about Commonwealth universities including Australia.

Council on International Educational Exchange (CIEE), 633 3rd Ave. 20th floor, New York, NY 10017-6706, USA (☎888-268-6245 or 800-407-8839; www.ciee.org/study) sponsors work, volunteer, academic, and internship programs in Australia.

School for International Training, College Semester Abroad, Admissions, Kipling Rd., P.O. Box 676, Brattleboro, VT 05302, USA (☎800-336-1616; www.sit.edu). Semester- and year-long programs in Australia run US$10,600-13,700. Also runs the **Experiment in International Living** (☎800-345-2929; fax 802-258-3428; eil@worldlearning.org). 3- to 5-week summer programs that offer high-school students cross-cultural homestays, community service, and ecological adventure and cost US$1900-5000.

Institute for Study Abroad, Butler University (ISA), (☎800-858-0229 or 317-940-9336; www.isabutler.org). A semester abroad program that is affiliated with the major universities of Australia. The ISA program takes care of applications to the universities, visas, housing, and provides personal guidance while abroad. US$40 application fee.

International Association for the Exchange of Students for Technical Experience (IAESTE), 10400 Little Patuxent Pkwy. #250, Columbia, MD 21044-3510, USA (☎410-997-2200; www.aipt.org). 8- to 12-week programs in Australia for college students who have completed 2 years of technical study. US$25 application fee.

University of Melbourne, International Center, Parkville, VIC 3010 ☎03 8344 6890; www.unimelb.edu.au/international/sabroad.html). Semester abroad offerings in 10 academic disciplines, including campus housing 10min. from the city center.

University of New South Wales, Level 16 Matthews Building, UNSW Kensington, Sydney NSW ☎02 9385 3179; www.studyabroad.unsw.edu.au). UNSW aside from semester offerings, hosts 6-week study programs during Northern Hemisphere summer for undergraduates, graduate students, and adults. To find out more about courses in Australian history, Outback art, biogeography, and screen acting (among others).

FURTHER READING & RESOURCES: STUDYING ABROAD.

StudyAbroad.Com Program Search (www.studyabroad.com).

Academic Year Abroad 2001-2002. Institute of International Education Books (US$47).

Vacation Study Abroad 2000-2001. Institute of International Education Books (US$43).

Peterson's Study Abroad 2001. (Peterson's, US$30).

Peterson's Summer Study Abroad 2001. (Peterson's, US$30).

WORKING

There's no better way to immerse yourself in a foreign land than to become part of its economy. Call the Consulate or Embassy of Australia to get more information about work permits. Working holiday visas are intended to allow visitors to supplement their vacation funds for up to a year and do not allow full time work for more than three months. For more information, see **Work Permits,** p. 35. While working in Australia technically requires a permit, travelers can generally find jobs in cities and towns if they are willing to try their hands at menial clerical work or seasonal jobs like fruit picking, collecting for charity, or working on a sheep station. For **work** options around the country, consult the index.

If you are a **U.S. citizen** and a full-time student at a U.S. university, the simplest way to get a job abroad is through work permit programs run by **Council on International Educational Exchange (Council)** and its member organizations. For a US$400 application fee, Council can procure three- to six-month work permits for Australia and a handbook to help you find work and housing (plus US$106 visa application fee; ☎888-268-6245).

The **Commonwealth Employment Service's** offices and backpacker magazines or hostels usually have info on seasonal work. If you are planning to work for an extended period of time or want to open a bank account in Australia, you should apply for a Tax File Number. These are not required, but without one, tax will be withheld at the highest rate. Contact the Australian Taxation Office.

Willing Workers on Organic Farms (WWOOF) grants a cheap opportunity to live and learn on organic farms. Membership (AUS$45) in WWOOF allows you to receive a handbook of WWOOF partners throughout Australia. There can be stipulations on minimum stays and work expected from a WWOOFer, but each site has its own expectations. Bed and board are provided in exchange. Memberships can be purchased from Melbourne Student Uni Travel, 440 Elizabeth St. (☎03 9662 4666) or many other places throughout Australia (see www.wwoof.com.au/agents.html).

VOLUNTEERING

Throughout Australia, small organic farms agree to sponsor volunteers in exchange for a few hours of work each day. See **WWOOF,** above. Volunteer jobs are readily available almost everywhere. You may receive room and board in exchange for your labor. You can sometimes avoid the high application fees charged by the organizations that arrange placement by contacting the individual workcamps directly; check with the organizations.

Australian Trust for Conservation Volunteers, Box 423, Ballarat VIC 3353 (☎03 5333 1483 or nationwide ☎1800 032 501; info@conservationvolunteers.com.au; www.atcv.com.au), offers travel volunteer packages (6 weeks, AUS$840) that include service opportunity as well as accommodations, food, and project-related transport.

Habitat for Humanity International, 121 Habitat St., Americus, GA 31709, USA (☎800-422-4828; www.habitat.org/intl/). Offers international opportunities in Australia to live with and build houses in a host community.

Involvement Volunteers, P.O. Box 218, Port Melbourne VIC 3207 (☎03 9646 5504; ivworldwide@volunteering.org.au; www.volunteering.org.au), offers volunteering options in Australia as well as New Zealand, Fiji, Malaysia, Japan, and several other areas that might be accessible on your way into or out of the country.

Service Civil International Voluntary Service (SCI-IVS), 814 NE 40th St., Seattle, WA 98105, USA (☎/fax 206-545-6585; www.sci-ivs.org). Arranges placement in workcamps in Australia for those 18+. Registration fee US$65-150.

ESSENTIALS

THE WORLD WIDE WEB

Almost every aspect of budget travel (with the most notable exception, of course, being experience) is accessible via the web. Within 10min. at the keyboard, you can make a reservation at a hostel, get advice on travel hotspots from other travelers who have just returned from Australia, or find out exactly how much a train from Melbourne to Cairns costs.

Listed here are some budget travel sites to start off your surfing; other relevant web sites are listed throughout the book. Because website turnover is high, use search engines (such as www.google.com) to strike out on your own.

THE ART OF BUDGET TRAVEL

How to See the World: www.artoftravel.com. A compendium of great travel tips, from cheap flights to self defense to interacting with local culture.

Rec. Travel Library: www.travel-library.com. A fantastic set of links for general information and personal travelogues.

Lycos: cityguide.lycos.com. General introductions to cities and regions throughout Australia, accompanied by links to applicable histories, news, and local tourism sites.

INFORMATION ON AUSTRALIA

Atevo Travel: www.atevo.com/guides/destinations. Detailed introductions, travel tips, and suggested itineraries.

Australia Tourist Commission: www.australia.com. The website has information about Australia and travel including climate, economy, health, and safety concerns.

Australian Tourism Net: www.atn.com.au. The Australian Tourism Net, has tons of service listings and Oz facts.

Australian Whitepages: www.whitepages.com.au. If you ever need a phone number or address, this is the place.

CIA World Factbook: www.odci.gov/cia/publications/factbook/index.html. Tons of vital statistics on Australia's geography, government, economy, and people.

Embassy of Australia: www.austemb.org. The website of the Australian Embassy has facts about Australia and travel information related to Australian law and politics.

MyTravelGuide: www.mytravelguide.com. Country overviews, with everything from history to transportation to live web cam coverage of Australia.

PlanetRider: www.planetrider.com. A subjective list of links to the "best" websites covering the culture and tourist attractions of Australia.

TravelPage: www.travelpage.com. Links to official tourist office sites in Australia.

World Travel Guide: www.travel-guides.com/navigate/world.asp. Helpful practical info.

AND OUR PERSONAL FAVORITE...

Let's Go: www.letsgo.com. Our constantly expanding website features photos and streaming video, online ordering of all our titles, info about our books, a travel forum buzzing with stories and tips, and links that will help you find everything you ever wanted to know about Australia.

AUSTRALIAN CAPITAL TERRITORY

Carved out of New South Wales in 1908, the Australian Capital Territory (ACT), designed and constructed at the beginning of the 20th century, was a geographic and political compromise between Sydney and Melbourne in the competition to host the capital of the newly-federated Australia. Although it is not a fully-qualified state, the center of the territory—Canberra—is the political heart of the country. Home to commuters and suburban shopping areas, neatly-designed satellite towns creep outward from Canberra into the bush. The ACT's combination of a cosmopolitan center and outlying natural refuges promises visitors a capital look at high culture and government at an easygoing pace.

CANBERRA ☎02

For a city that is home to 320,000 people and the government of an entire continent, Canberra's streets are, for the most part, amazingly quiet. Wide avenues, huge tracts of green spaces, and modern architecture offer a utopian vision of metropolis; yet it feels empty, as if someone expected a lot more people to show up. The city houses a myriad of tourist attractions from space centers to dinosaur museums and it is all beautifully planned, but there is a shortage of tourists to see it all. The unique city was designed by Walter Burley Griffin, student of Frank Lloyd Wright. The American architect's proposal was selected from a pool of 137 competitors before construction began in 1913. The first Canberra Parliament convened in 1927; since then, life has picked up pace a bit, but even today Canberra keeps a low profile and a refined lifestyle to match. Canberra is both a national exhibition and the international face of the Australian political body. Regardless of its dull reputation, Canberra's blend of culture and class qualifies it as one of Australia's most underrated destinations.

CANBERRA HIGHLIGHTS

MT.AINSLIE. Take in the expansive city views from Mt. Ainslie (p. 86).

QUESTION TIME. Don't miss the political antics when the Parliamentary floor is opened to questions from the public (p. 86).

AUSTRALIAN WAR MEMORIAL. Works by prominent Australian artists depict scenes of wartime life (p. 87).

INTERCITY TRANSPORTATION

BY PLANE. Located in Pialligo, 7km east of the city center, the **Canberra International Airport** is an easy ride by car. From Commonwealth Ave., take Parkes Way east past the roundabout at Kings Ave. The name of the road changes first to Morshead Dr., then to Pialligo Ave., en route to the airport. On weekdays, **Deane's Buslines** operates the **Air Liner** (☎6299 3722), a shuttle service that transports passengers between the airport and the City Interchange (20min., 14 per day, $5).

For weekend transit, a **taxi** (13 22 27) is your best bet. ($17 one-way from the city center.) The airport only handles domestic flights to four cities; all international travel requires a stop in Sydney. **Virgin Blue Airlines** (☎13 67 89) is quickly becoming a major player in the Canberra travel market, offering competitive service and super low prices to Brisbane (1¾hr., 1 per day, $248). Both **Qantas** (☎13 13 13) and **Ansett** (☎13 13 00) connect Canberra to: Adelaide (1½hr., 2-4 per day, $375); Brisbane (2hr., 4 per day, $418); Melbourne (1hr., 10 per day, $198); Sydney (50min., 24 per day, $198). To get the best fares, book at least 14 days in advance.

BY TRAIN. The **Canberra Railway Station,** on the corner of Wentworth Ave. and Mildura St. in Kingston, 6km from the city center, is on ACTION bus route #39 (bus to Civic 25min., at least 1 per hr.). Alternatively, a taxi ride to the city will cost $12-14. The station houses little more than a **Countrylink** office. (☎13 22 32 or 6239 7039. Open M-Sa 6:20am-5:30pm, Su 10:30am-5:30pm.) **Trains** leave for Brisbane (24hr., 1 per day, $128) via Sydney (4hr., 3 per day, $47). **Train/coach** runs to: Bega (3½hr., 1 per day, $33); Cooma (1¼hr., 1-2 per day, $17); Goulburn (1¼hr., 3 per day, $13); Melbourne (8½hr., 1 per day, $90); Wollongong via Moss Vale (4hr., 1 per day, $38). Fourteen-day, seven-day, and two-day advance purchases yield discounted prices.

ACT

BY BUS. Intercity **buses** are at **Jolimont Tourist Centre,** 65-67 Northbourne Ave., just north of Alinga St. in Civic. (Open daily 6am-10:30pm; winter 5am-10:30pm.) Self-service coin lockers cost $4 per day. The ticketing office for Greyhound/McCafferty's stores bags for the day ($2 per piece of luggage). Several bus companies, both major domestic airlines, and Countrylink have desks in the building.

Greyhound Pioneer (☎13 20 30) and **McCafferty's** (☎13 14 99) provide service to: Adelaide (17hr., 2 per day, $121); Albury (5-6hr., 4 per day, $33); Goulburn (1hr., 5 per day, $23); Griffith (6hr., 2 per day, $46); Gundagai (1¾hr., 4 per day, $26); Melbourne (8-10hr., 4 per day, $59); Parramatta (3½hr., 9 per day, $36); Sydney (4-5hr., 11 per day, $36); Wagga Wagga (3hr., 2 per day, $33). From June to October buses run to: the snowfields at Cooma (1½hr., 3 per day, $36); Perisher Blue via the Skitube (2¾hr., 2 per day, $51); Thredbo (3½hr., 2 per day, $52) via Jindabyne (2¼hr., 3 per day, $43). **Murrays** (☎13 22 51) also runs to: Bateman's Bay (2½hr., 1 per day, $24); Goulburn (1¼hr., 1 per day, $15); Narooma (4¼hr., 1-2 per day, $36); Sydney (4hr., 4 per day, $35); Wollongong (3½hr., 1 per day, $24); as well as ski-season service to Cooma (1¼hr., 1-2 per day, $27); Jindabyne (3¼hr., 1-2 per day, $27); Perisher Blue (3hr., 1-2 per day, $27); Thredbo (3hr., 1-2 per day, $33). McCafferty's and Murray's offer great deals on **ski packages** which include return transport, lift tickets, ski rental, and park entrance for $100. **Transborder Express** (☎6241 0033) runs to Yass (1hr., 1-4 per day, $12).

BY CAR. The **NRMA automobile club,** 92 Northbourne Ave., is the place to turn for road service or car problems. (☎13 21 32. Open M-F 9:30am-5pm.) For 24hr. **emergency road service,** call 13 11 11. **Avis,** 17 Lonsdale St. (☎6249 6088; open M-F 8am-6pm, Sa 8am-2pm, Su 8am-1pm); **Budget** (☎13 27 27; open M-F 8am-5pm, Sa 8am-noon), on the corner of Mort and Girraween St.; **Delta Europcar,** 74 Northbourne Ave. (☎13 13 90; open M-F 8am-5:30pm, Sa 8am-4pm); **Hertz,** 32 Mort St. (☎6257 4877; open M-F 8am-6pm, Sa 8am-3pm); **Thrifty,** 29 Lonsdale St. (☎6247 7422; open M-F 8am-5:30pm, Sa-Su 8am-5pm), all have offices in Braddon and at the airport. Local outfit **Value Rent-a-Car,** in the Rydges Capital Hill Hotel on Canberra Ave. and National Circuit, charges $35 per day and $195 weekly. (☎1800 629 561. Open M-F 8am-6pm, Sa-Su for pickup and drop-off only.)

ORIENTATION

Lake Burley Griffin, formed by the damming of the Molonglo River, splits Canberra in two; on each side is a central hill with concentric roads leading outwards. **Commonwealth Ave.** spans the lake to connect these points.

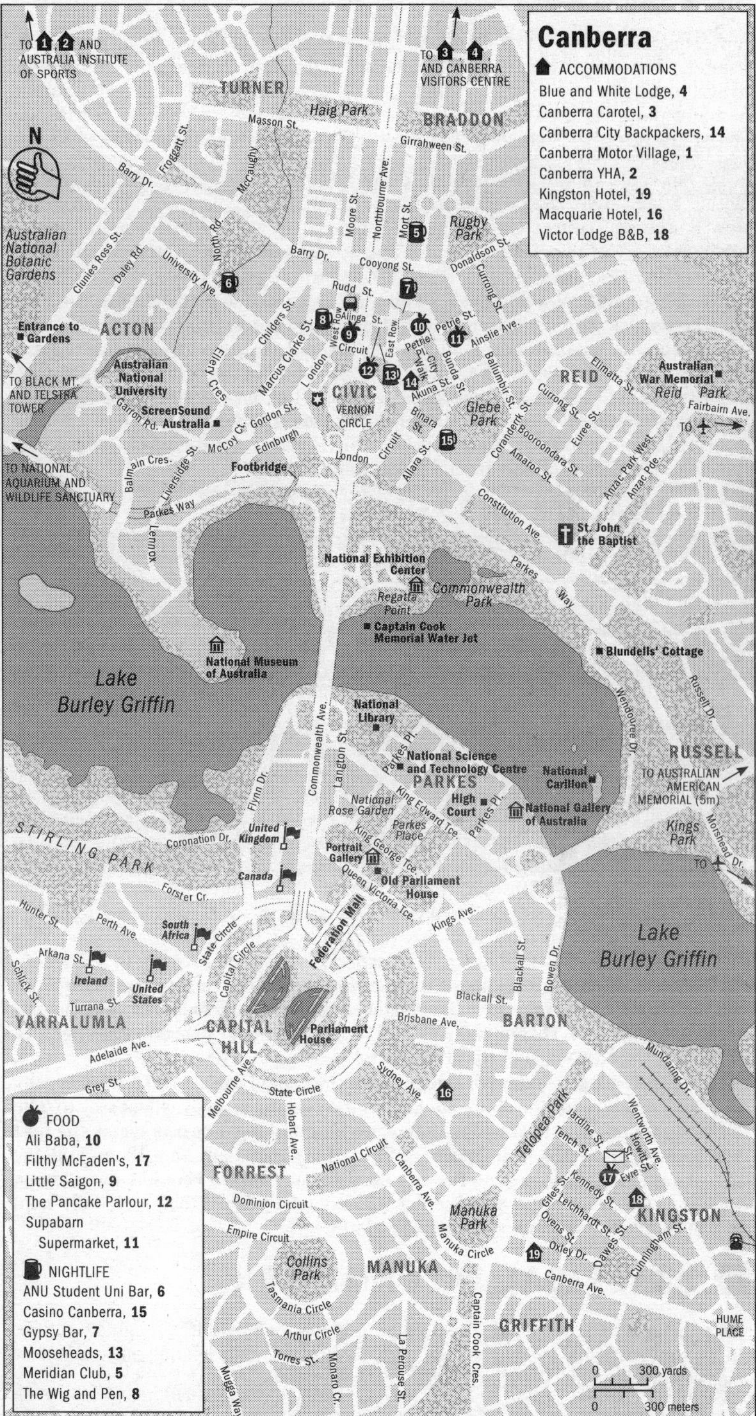
Canberra
ACCOMMODATIONS
Blue and White Lodge, 4
Canberra Carotel, 3
Canberra City Backpackers, 14
Canberra Motor Village, 1
Canberra YHA, 2
Kingston Hotel, 19
Macquarie Hotel, 16
Victor Lodge B&B, 18
FOOD
Ali Baba, 10
Filthy McFaden's, 17
Little Saigon, 9
The Pancake Parlour, 12
Supabarn Supermarket, 11
NIGHTLIFE
ANU Student Uni Bar, 6
Casino Canberra, 15
Gypsy Bar, 7
Mooseheads, 13
Meridian Club, 5
The Wig and Pen, 8
TO 1, 2 AND AUSTRALIA INSTITUTE OF SPORTS
TO 3, 4 AND CANBERRA VISITORS CENTRE
N
TURNER
Haig Park
BRADDON
Masson St.
Girrahween St.
Froggatt St.
Barry Dr.
McCaughy
Northbourne Ave.
Moore St.
Mort St.
Rugby Park
Donaldson St.
Australian National Botanic Gardens
Clunies Ross St.
Daley Rd.
North Rd.
University Ave.
Cooyong St.
Currong St.
Rudd St.
Childers St.
Marcus Clarke St.
West Row
Alinga St.
East Row
Petrie St.
Ainslie Ave.
Circuit
Petrie Pl.
City Walk
Bunda St.
Entrance to Gardens
ACTON
Ellery Cres.
London
Akuna St.
Ballumbir St.
REID
Elimatta St.
Australian War Memorial
Reid Park
Fairbairn Ave.
TO BLACK MT. AND TELSTRA TOWER
Australian National University
CIVIC
VERNON CIRCLE
Binara St.
Glebe Park
Currong St.
Euree St.
Garran Rd.
ScreenSound Australia
McCoy Ct.
Gordon St.
Edinburgh
Corranderk St.
Booroondara St.
Amaroo St.
Anzac Park West
Anzac Pde.
TO NATIONAL AQUARIUM AND WILDLIFE SANCTUARY
Balmain Cres.
Liversidge St.
Footbridge
London Circuit
Allara St.
Parkes Way
Lennox
Constitution Ave.
St. John the Baptist
National Exhibition Center
Commonwealth Park
Regatta Point
Parkes Way
Captain Cook Memorial Water Jet
Blundells' Cottage
National Museum of Australia
Lake Burley Griffin
National Library
Wendouree Dr.
Russell Dr.
RUSSELL
Commonwealth Ave.
Langton St.
Parkes Pl.
National Science and Technology Centre
PARKES
National Carillon
TO AUSTRALIAN AMERICAN MEMORIAL (5m)
Flynn Dr.
National Rose Garden
King Edward Tce.
High Court
Parkes Pl.
National Gallery of Australia
Kings Park
Morshead Dr.
STIRLING PARK
Coronation Dr.
United Kingdom
Parkes Place
King George Tce.
Portrait Gallery
Old Parliament House
Canada
Forster Cr.
Queen Victoria Tce.
Federation Mall
Kings Ave.
Lake Burley Griffin
Hunter St.
Perth Ave.
South Africa
State Circle
Arkana St.
Ireland
United States
Schlick St.
Capital Circle
Blackall St.
Bowen Dr.
Turrana St.
Blackall St.
YARRALUMLA
CAPITAL HILL
Parliament House
Brisbane Ave.
BARTON
Adelaide Ave.
Grey St.
Melbourne Ave.
Sydney Ave.
Mundaring Dr.
State Circle
Telopea Park
Hobart Ave.
Jardine St.
Tench St.
Wentworth Ave.
Howitt St.
Eyre St.
FORREST
National Circuit
Canberra Ave.
Kennedy St.
Giles St.
Dominion Circuit
Leichhardt St.
Manuka Park
KINGSTON
Empire Circuit
Ovens St.
Dawes St.
Cunningham St.
Manuka Circle
Oxley Dr.
Collins Park
MANUKA
Canberra Ave.
Tasmania Circle
Captain Cook Cres.
GRIFFITH
HUME PLACE
Arthur Circle
Torres St.
Monaro Cr.
La Perouse St.
Mugga Way
0 300 yards
0 300 meters

To the north of the lake is **Vernon Circle,** marking the center of Canberra City and the southern edge of the area known as **Civic.** Civic serves as the city's social center and bus interchange. Restaurants, shops, pubs, and nightclubs particularly crowd the pedestrian mall known as **City Walk** (the area between Northbourne Ave., Akuna St., Bunda St. and London Circuit). Immediately north of Vernon Circle, Commonwealth Ave. becomes Northbourne Ave.

To the south of the lake is **State Circle** and the "official" part of the capital. Within State Circle, **Capital Hill's** huge four-pronged flagpole reaches up from the new Parliament House. One corner of the area known as **Parliamentary Triangle** encloses most of the city's museums and government-related attractions. Commonwealth Ave., Kings Ave., and Parkes Way form the three sides of the triangle.

The key to understanding the city plan is the system of roundabouts, the multiple concentric streets ("circuits"), and the wheel-spoke offshoots. If you drive, a good map is absolutely essential. Roundabouts are well marked, but signs often refer to districts rather than to streets. The railway station and an assortment of budget lodging are in **Kingston,** southeast of Capital Hill. The embassies populate **Yarralumla,** west of Capital Hill. **Dickson,** northeast of Civic via Northbourne Ave. and Antill St., and **Manuka** ("MINE-icka"), southeast of Capital Hill, have clusters of reasonably priced restaurants.

LOCAL TRANSPORTATION

The primary hub for Canberra's public transit system, **ACTION** (☎13 17 10), centers on the city bus interchange, located at the junction of East Row, Alinga St., and Mort St. Full maps and timetables for all routes are available, free of charge, at the ACTION information office, next to the Civic Library on East Row, between Alinga St. and London Circuit. Route maps are also clearly posted near the passenger shelters at the city bus interchange. Relevant timetables are posted at individual bus stops. Buses generally run M-Sa 6am-12:30am and Su 7am-8:15pm, though some routes have more limited hours.

ACTION bus fares are based on a zone system, but the airport and the majority of the city's attractions and budget accommodations fall within the central zone, so you'll probably only need the **one-zone fare** ($2.30; concessions $1.20). These are valid for a single trip; if you ask for a **transfer ticket** from the bus driver, the single ticket is good for 1hr. **Fare-saver tickets** ($19.80; concessions $9.90) are available for 10 one-zone rides. To make the most of a single day, purchase an all-zone **Shopper's Off-Peak Daily ticket** ($5.40; concessions $4.70), valid weekdays 9am-4:30pm and after 6pm, and all day weekends and public holidays. Purchase tickets on the bus or at most news-agencies.

Though considerably more expensive than an ACTION off-peak daily ticket, City Sightseeing's less logistically-complex **Canberra Tour** makes 14 stops in a red, double-decker bus, covering all major tourist attractions. The ticket is valid for 24hr. and unlimited stops. Tickets can be bought on the bus, in most hotels, or at the visitors center. (☎6257 3423 or 0500 505 012. $25 per person.) **Canberra Cabs** (☎13 22 27) covers the city and suburbs at all hours.

Thanks to a superb system of **bicycle paths,** the capital can also be covered easily on a bike. A ride along the shores of Lake Burley Griffin is an excellent way to take in Parliamentary Triangle without having to find parking. For **bike rental,** the best deal is through the **YHA** in **O'Connor**. (☎6248 9155. Open daily 7am-10pm. Full-day $25; YHA guests $6.) Closer to the city center is **Mr. Spokes Bike Hire and Cafe** on Barrine Dr. in Acton Park, near the Ferry Terminal. (☎6257 1188. Open daily 9am-6pm in summer, 9am-5pm in winter. $10 per hr.)

PRACTICAL INFORMATION

TOURIST AND FINANCIAL SERVICES

Tourist Offices: Canberra Visitors Centre, 330 Northbourne Ave. (☎6205 0044, accommodations booking 1800 100 660; www.canberratourism.com.au.), about 3km north of Vernon Circle. Take bus #30, 31, 32, 39, 50, 80. Open M-F 9am-5:30pm, Sa-Su

9am-4pm. Wheelchair accessible. Smaller volunteer-staffed **Canberra Tourism Booth,** inside Jolimont Tourist Centre, is 2 blocks from the city bus interchange. Open M-F 9am-5pm, Sa-Su 11am-3pm.

Budget Travel Office: STA Travel, 13 Garema Pl. (☎6247 8633), on the corner of City Walk. Open M-Th 9am-5pm, F 9am-7pm, Sa 10am-2pm.

Embassies and High Commissions: Unless specified, all locations are in Yarralumla. **Canada** (☎6270 4000; fax 6273 3285), on Commonwealth Ave. south of the lake. Open for consular services M-F 8:30am-12:30pm and 1-4:30pm. **Ireland,** 20 Arkana St. (☎6273 3022; fax 6273 3741). Open M-F 9:30am-12:45pm and 2-5pm. **New Zealand** (☎6270 4211; fax 6273 3194), on Commonwealth Ave., south of the lake. Open M-F 8:45am-5pm. For consular services, contact the consulate in Sydney (☎8256 2000; fax 9221 7836). **South Africa** (☎6273 2424; fax 6273 3543), on the corner of State Circle and Rhodes Pl. Open M-F 8:30am-5pm. The consular section is open M-F 8:30am-1pm. **United Kingdom** (☎6270 6666, emergency 6285 6171; fax 6270 6606), on Commonwealth Ave. Open M-F 9am-5pm. Consular services downtown, SAP building, Level 10, corner of Bunda and Akuna St. Open M-F 9am-3pm. **United States,** 1 Moonah Pl. (☎6214 5600, emergency 6214 5900). Open M-F 8am-5pm. Contact the consulate in Sydney for routine consular services (☎9373 9200).

Currency Exchange: American Express Shop 1, Centrepoint, 185 City Walk (☎6247 2333). Cardholders and travelers cheque users can have mail held for 3 weeks at no charge. Send mail (Name), Attn: Client Mail, P.O. Box 153, Civic Square ACT 2608. No fee for AmEx Traveler's Cheque transactions. Currency exchange incurs a 1% fee. Open M-F 9am-5pm, Sa 9am-noon. **Thomas Cook** (☎6247 9984), Canberra Centre shopping mall, Bunda St., corner of Petrie Plaza. Free cashing of Thomas Cook checks, flat fee of $7 on other checks and currency exchange. Open M-F 9am-5pm, Sa 9:30am-12:30pm.

LOCAL SERVICES

Library: Civic Library (☎6205 9000; www.act.gov.au/library), on East Row between Alinga St. and London Circuit. 1 of 9 branches within the ACT. Open M-Th 10am-5pm, F 10am-7pm, Sa 9:30am-5pm. See **National Library of Australia,** p. 87.

Ticket Agencies: Ticketek (☎6219 6666; www.ticketek.com), GIO building, 11 Akuna St., Civic. Tickets to sport and music events and **Royal Theater.** Open M-F 9am-5pm, Sa 9am-noon. **Canberra Ticketing** (☎6257 1077), on London Circuit, covers the **Canberra Theatre** and **Playhouse.** Open M-Sa 9am-5:30pm, later on the nights of shows.

Travel Books and Maps: Map World (☎6230 4097), inside the Jolimont Tourist Centre. Open M-F 8:30am-6pm, Sa 9am-3pm.

Public Markets: Gorman House Markets (☎0410 774 540), on Ainslie Ave. between Currong and Doonkuma St., vend crafts, clothing, and miscellany. Open Sa 10am-4pm. The **Old Bus Depot Markets,** 49 Wentworth Ave., Kingston (☎6292 8391), features many food and arts-and-crafts stalls. Open Su 10am-4pm.

EMERGENCY AND COMMUNICATIONS

Emergency: ☎000.

Police Attendance: ☎1 1444.

Police: On London Circuit opposite University Ave., Civic (☎6245 7208).

MEDIA AND PUBLICATIONS

Newspapers: The main newspaper is the *Canberra Times* ($1.10). They also put out a local newspaper, *The Chronicle*.

Entertainment: *bma* (bands music action) is Canberra's free, alternative, entertainment bi-monthly. *Good Times,* released on Thursdays in the Canberra Times, also has a list of entertainment options.

Radio: Easy Listening, 106.3FM; Mix, 104.7FM; Rock, Triple J 101.5FM; News, 1440AM; Tourist Info, 88FM.

Crisis Lines: Drug and Alcohol Crisis Line (24hr. ☎6205 4545). **Poison Info Centre** (24hr. ☎13 11 26). **Gay/Lesbian Info and Counseling Service** (☎6247 2726), daily 6-10pm, after-hours recording. **Women's Info and Referral Service** (☎6205 1076), M-F 9am-5pm.

Late-Night Pharmacy: Day and Night Chemist, 9 Sargood St. (☎6248 7050), in the O'Connor Shopping Centre. Open daily 9am-11pm. **Urgent Prescription Service** (☎6249 1919) operates after 11pm for emergencies.

Hospital/Medical Services: Canberra Hospital (☎6244 2222, emergency 6244 2611), on Yamba Dr., Garren. Follow signs to Woden southwest from Capital Hill.

Internet Access: Cheap access is not common. The **ACT Library Service** (see **Local Services,** p. 83) and the **National Library** (see **National Library of Australia,** p. 87) offer free 30min. and 1hr. sessions, but **book ahead. KC's Cafe,** 11 East Row (☎6257 5558), charges $2.50 per 15min., and $6 per hr. Open M-Sa 9am-late, Su 11am-late. **Cafe Cactus** (☎6248 0449), on Bunda St. in the Center Cinema Bldg., is $10 per hr. Open M-F 8am-8:30pm or later, Sa-Su 9:30am-late. 20% YHA discount.

Post Office: General Post Office (GPO), 53-73 Alinga St. (☎6209 1680). Open M-F 8:30am-5:30pm. **Australia Post** at Civic Square, outside Canberra Centre mall, has stamps and counter service. Open M-F 8:45am-5:15pm. **Postal Code:** 2601 (City).

ACCOMMODATIONS

HOSTELS AND DORMS

Canberra City Backpackers, 7 Akuna St., Civic (☎1800 300 488). This centrally-located, swanky new hostel-hotel puts travelers within easy reach of downtown cafes, shops, and nightlife. Multiple kitchens and common areas, rooftop BBQ, small gym, heated pool, pool tables, laundry, bike rentals ($16 per day), security cameras, in-room lockers ($10 deposit), in-room TVs with free movies. 24hr. reception. Bunks $24; singles $60; twins $70; doubles with bath $95; triples $90.

Canberra YHA Hostel, 191 Dryandra St., O'Connor (☎6248 9155; fax 6249 1731). Bus #35 travels to and from the city interchange, stopping directly out front. By car, follow Northbourne Ave. north from city center. Turn left on Macarthur Ave., go 2km, then turn right on Dryandra. Situated away from the urban jungle along the eastern edge of a Canberra Nature Park, 5km northwest of the city center, this pleasant, family-friendly hostel is impeccably clean with a wonderfully helpful staff. A great place for watching birds and meeting other travelers. Multiple kitchens, 3 daily shuttles to the city (free), TV/pool room, great movie selection, bike rental (full-day $6), small store, laundry, Internet kiosks ($2 per 20min.). Key deposit $10. Reception daily 7am-10pm. Dorms $20, under 18 $13; twins $48-56.

Victor Lodge Bed and Breakfast, 29 Dawes St., Kingston (☎ 6295 7777; www.victorlodge.com.au), 6 km south of the city center. Free pickup in Civic at Jolimont Tourist Centre by arrangement. Bus #38 or 39 from the city bus interchange stops 2 blocks away on Eyre St. Within biking distance of Parliamentary Triangle. Kitchen, TV, laundry, Internet ($1 per 7min.). Bike hire ($15 per day). All-you-can-eat continental breakfast included. Key deposit $10. Reception daily 7:30am-9:30pm. Dorms $23; singles $44, weekly $245; doubles $59. VIP.

Australian National University (☎6249 3454). Accommodation available in several residence halls. The clean and recently refurbished **Fenner Hall,** 210 Northbourne Ave. (☎6279 9000, afterhours 6279 9017; fax 6257 4926), generally has more rooms during summer and university holidays, though it's worth calling during term-time as well. If you're longing for the college dorm experience, ANU is the place. Vast common kitchen area, TV, game room, Internet access in computer lab. Reception daily 8:00am-12:30pm and 1:30-5pm. Singles $14, $95 per week; doubles $21/$144.

Kingston Hotel, 73 Canberra Ave., Kingston (☎6295 0123; fax 6295 7871), on the corner of Giles St., about 7km from Civic. Take bus #38 or 39. Canberra's least expensive pub stay. The vinyl bunk mattresses, room carpet, and shared bathrooms could use a serious upgrade, but you can't beat the price. It's worth checking out the rooms before booking. Linen $5.50. Key deposit $10. Dorms $16.50.

MOTELS AND GUESTHOUSES

Macquarie Hotel, 18 National Circuit, Barton (☎6273 2325; fax 6273 4241), on the corner of Sydney Ave., near the Parliament building and on the #35 or 36 bus line. The huge complex is full of reasonable rooms with shared facilities. Breakfast included. Book ahead, especially in Jan. Reception daily 7am-10:30pm. Singles with sink $49, singles with TV and fridge $61; twins and doubles with TV and fridge $84.

Blue and White Lodge, 524 Northbourne Ave., Downer, and **Canberran Lodge,** 528 Northbourne Ave., Downer (both ☎6248 0498; fax 6248 8277). It's hard to differentiate between the two B&Bs. Each guesthouse offers TV, fridge, and kettle in a large, clean, floral-smelling room. Some rooms have verandas. Breakfast included. Reception daily 7am-9pm. Singles $55, with bath $83; doubles $77/94.

CAMPGROUNDS

Canberra Motor Village, Kunzea St., O'Connor (☎6247 5466 or 1800 026 199; fax 6249 6138). 4km northwest of the City Center, along the eastern edge of a Canberra nature park. Take Bus #34 or 35 to Miller and Macarthur Ave. By car, follow Northbourne Ave. north from Civic, turn left on Macarthur, then right on Dryandra, and take an immediate left on Kunzea. Toilets, showers, laundry, BBQ, pool, tennis courts, store, restaurant, and playground. Key deposit $10. Reception daily 7am-10:30pm. Sites for 1 $15, with power and water $21, extra person $6. $3.30 extra on weekends and public holidays.

Canberra Carotel, Federal Hwy., Watson (☎6241 1377; fax 6241 6674). 7km north of the City Center, on the #36 bus line. By car, follow Northbourne Ave. until it becomes Federal Hwy. Swimming pool, store, playground, BBQ, toilets, showers, and laundry. Reception M-F 7am-9pm, Sa-Su 7am-8pm. Sites for 2 $14, powered $17; extra person $2.50. On-site caravans for 2 $39; extra person $4. Bungalows for 2 $55; extra person $6 (up to 5 people max). Cabins with cooking facilities for up to 3 $80. Family cabins with cooking facilities for up to 10 $115. Prices rise during public holidays.

FOOD

In a city populated by government officials, cheap food is never easy to find. Inexpensive cafes near the city bus interchange, along with the food court at Canberra Centre (☎6247 5611), a three-story mall with main entrances off either City Walk or Bunda St., between Petrie Plaza and Akuna St., provide welcome exceptions. On Bunda St., opposite the Canberra Centre, the **City Market** complex packs in fruit stands, butcher shops, and prepared food stalls. You'll also find a vast Supabarn **supermarket.** (☎6257 4055. Open M-F 8am-10pm, Sa-Su 8am-9pm.)

Asian Noodle House, 29 Woolley St., Dickson (☎6247 6380). Take bus #33, 35, or 38 to Dickson Shops. Surrounded by Japanese, Korean, and Chinese food shops, this unpretentious favorite specializes in tasty Laksa noodles, Lao cuisine, and Thai dishes $10-13). Dine in or takeaway. Vegetable mains $8. Open daily 11:30am-10pm. BYO.

Ali Baba (☎6257 2538), at the corner of Bunda St. and Garema Pl., Civic. Don't be put off just because this Lebanese eatery is part of a chain. The lamb, beef, chicken, or veggie kebabs are hot and filling ($5-6) and can be customized with an assortment of sauces. Open daily Su-Th 9am-10pm, F-Sa 24hr.

Little Saigon Restaurant (☎6230 5003), at the corner of Alinga St. and Northbourne Ave., Civic. Popular Vietnamese restaurant has traditional food at tantalizing prices. Mains $9-13. Tasty hot and sour soup $4.50. Open daily 9am-3pm and 5-10:30pm.

The Tandoor House, 39 Kennedy St., Kingston (☎6295 7318). Though you may feel a bit rushed at times, sit back and savor the flavorful Indian curries, vindaloos, masalas ($11-16), and yummy breads ($2-3). Open M-Sa noon-2:30pm, daily 5:30-11pm.

The Pancake Parlour, downstairs at 121 Alinga St., Civic (☎6247 2982). Despite its slightly multiple-franchise feel, late night munchies and early-morning cravings are easily satisfied, whether you opt for fruit pancakes ($7-10) or more standard steak and fish fare ($11-16). Daily early bird dinner specials 5-7pm. Open Su-Th 7am-10:30pm, F-Sa 7:30am-2:30am. 10% YHA discount.

SIGHTS

LOOKOUTS

A stop at one of the city's lookouts can give you a general idea of what's in store on a sightseeing tour. On a hill in Commonwealth Park at Regatta Point, on the north shore of Lake Burley Griffin, the **National Capital Exhibition** provides a panorama of Canberra with a 10min. film and displays on the planning and growth of the city. (☎6257 1068. Open daily 9am-5pm. Free. Wheelchair accessible.)

ACT

Farther back from the city's center, Mt. Ainslie and Black Mountain offer broader views of the city and are—for the energetic—within walking distance. North of Lake Burley Griffin and east of the city center, **Mt. Ainslie** rises 845m above the lake, the Parliamentary Triangle, and the Australian War Memorial, providing the classic postcard view down Anzac Pde. To reach the summit by car, turn right onto Fairbairn Ave. from the Memorial end of Anzac Pde., to Mt. Ainslie Dr. Hiking trails lead to the top from directly behind the War Memorial.

Two lookout points above the city on **Black Mountain** are a vigorous walk away. The first, on Black Mountain Dr., accessible by taking Barry Dr. to Clunies Ross St. and heading left, faces southeast and takes in the Parliamentary Triangle and Lake Burley Griffin. The second viewpoint faces north toward the surrounding countryside and the **Australian Institute of Sport.** From the peak of Black Mountain, **Telstra Tower** climbs 195m to ensure viewers an unobstructed gaze in every direction. Exhibits in the tower catalogue the history of Australian telecommunications. (☎6248 1991 or 1800 806 718. Open daily 9am-10pm. $3.30.)

PARLIAMENTARY TRIANGLE

A showpiece of grand architecture and cultural attractions, Canberra's Parliamentary Triangle is the center of the capital. The triangle is bordered by Commonwealth Ave., Kings Ave., and across the lake, Parkes Way.

PARLIAMENT HOUSE. The focal point of the triangle, Parliament House, takes the ideal of unifying architecture and landscape to a new level. The building is actually built *into* Capital Hill so that two sides jut out of the earth, leaving the grassy hilltop on its roof undisturbed and open to the public 24hr. The design intentionally places the people above Parliament. Perched on this landmark is a four-pronged stainless steel flagpole visible from nearly every part of Canberra. Inside the building, free guided tours *(every 30min., daily 9am-4pm)* give an overview of the unique features of the building and the workings of the government housed inside. Visitors can even observe both houses of Parliament in action from viewing galleries. The House of Representatives, which meets more often than the Senate, allows advance bookings. The televised **Question Time** provides some viewer-friendly acrimony. Every day when the House and the Senate are sitting *(M-Th in approximately 2-week blocks, except during recess in Jan. and July)*, the floor is opened up at 2pm for on-the-spot questioning of the Prime Minister and other ministers. *(☎6277 5399, reservations 6277 4889;* www.aph.gov.au/house. *Open daily 9am-5pm. Free. Wheelchair accessible.)*

OLD PARLIAMENT HOUSE AND THE NATIONAL PORTRAIT GALLERY. This building, aligned with the front of Parliament House, served as Australia's seat of government from 1927-88, until the current Parliament House was completed. It is now a political history museum and home to the National Portrait Gallery. *(☎6270 8222, gallery 6270 8236. Daily "Behind the Scene" tours of Old Parliament House every 45min. 9:30am-3:15pm. Daily tours of the Portrait Gallery 11:30am, 2:30pm. Open daily 9am-5pm. $2, concessions $1, families $5. Wheelchair accessible.)*

NATIONAL GALLERY OF AUSTRALIA. The third side of the Parliamentary Triangle is comprised of the four large modern buildings on Parkes Pl., just off King Edward Tce. On the southeastern end, nearest Kings Ave., the National Gallery displays an extensive Australian art collection, including paintings by famed postmodernist Arthur Boyd, Aboriginal works spanning more than 30,000 years of indigenous culture, and a good contemporary collection. Keep your eyes out for a few big-name French impressionists, too. The surrounding sculpture garden is free and open 24hr. *(☎6240 6502, info 6240 6501; www.nga.gov.au. Open daily 10am-5pm. 1hr. guided tours daily 11am and 2pm. Aboriginal art tour Th and Su 11am. Free; separate fees for special exhibits $8-15. Wheelchair accessible.)*

HIGH COURT OF AUSTRALIA. Australia's highest court is encased in a seven-story wall of seemingly impregnable glass and steel. You almost expect the justices to yell, "Help, let us out!" When court is in session, visitors may watch proceedings from public galleries in the courtrooms. *(Next door to the National Gallery. ☎6270 6811. Open M-F 9:45am-4:30pm. Free. Wheelchair accessible.)*

NATIONAL LIBRARY OF AUSTRALIA. The nation's largest library (six million volumes) is the final stop on Parkes Pl. Open for research and visitation, it houses copies of Australian publications on over 200km of shelving. The library also features alternating exhibits on Australian topics. Free **Internet** and printing. *(☎6262 1111, exhibition schedule 6262 1156; www.nla.gov.au. Free tours Tu and Th 12:30pm. Open M-Th 9am-9pm, F 9am-6pm, Sa 9am-5pm, Su 1:30-5pm. Wheelchair accessible.)*

ACT

LAKE BURLEY GRIFFIN. The last two attractions in the Parliamentary Triangle are actually located in the middle of the lake. The **Captain Cook Memorial Jet** blows a six-ton column of water to heights of up to 147m to commemorate Captain James Cook's arrival at the east coast of Australia. Might as well celebrate in style, right? The bell tower of the **National Carillon** is located on Aspen Island at the other end of the lake's central basin. A gift from Britain on Canberra's 50th birthday in 1963, the Carillon, one of the largest musical instruments in the world, is rung several times a week. *(Concert schedule www.nationalcapital.gov.au/visiting/carillon.htm.)*

OTHER GOVERNMENT BUILDINGS. West of Capital Hill, on the south side of the lake, Yarralumla is peppered with embassies of over 70 nations, displaying a multicultural melange of architecture. The Lodge, home to the Australian Prime Minister, is on the corner of Adelaide Ave. and National Circuit, but heckler's be warned—it's closed to the public. Farther down Adelaide Ave., at the Royal Australian Mint, on Denison St. in Deakin, you can watch coins being minted. Push a button to "press your own" dollar coin…for $2. *(☎6202 6819. Open M-F 9am-4pm, Sa-Su 10am-4pm; coin production M-F 9am-noon and 1-4pm. Free. Wheelchair accessible.)*

NORTHEAST

Anzac Pde. extends northeast from Parkes Way, continuing the line formed by the old and new Parliament Houses across the lake.

AUSTRALIAN WAR MEMORIAL. The popular crucifix-shaped memorial, with artifacts, photos, and depictions of wartime life by major Australian artists, makes a moving tribute. The Hall of Memory holds the tomb of an unknown Australian soldier underneath a beautiful handmade mosaic dome. *(Anzac Pde., on bus route #33 from Civic. ☎6243 4261. 1½hr. tours daily 10, 10:30, 11, 11:30am, 1, 1:30, 2pm. Open daily 10am-5pm. Free. Wheelchair accessible.)*

ST. JOHN THE BAPTIST CHURCH. This church has given services since 1845, long before the current city rose up around it. Its former schoolhouse is now a museum of pioneer life in Canberra. *(On the corner of Anzac Pde. and Constitution Ave. Parrish office ☎6248 8399; museum 6249 6839. Open daily 9am-5pm. Museum open W 10am-noon, Sa-Su 2-4pm. $1.)*

PENNY FOR YOUR THOUGHTS. No that waitress isn't stiffing your change, the 1-cent and 2-cent pieces were removed from circulation starting in 1992. Their introduction goes back to Valentine's Day 1966, when Australia moved from the British currency system to a decimal-based one. Officials were so concerned with the smooth transition between systems that they composed the "Decimal Change Over Song": In come the dollar and in come the cents / To replace the pounds and the shillings and the pence / Be prepared for change when the coins begin to mix / on the 14th of February 1966. Chorus: Clink go the coins clink clink clink / Change over day is closer than you think / Learn the value of coins and the way that they appear / And things will be much smoother when the decimal point is here.

NORTHWEST

SCREENSOUND AUSTRALIA. Formerly the **National Screen and Sound Archive,** Screensound is one of Canberra's least-known but most enjoyable attractions. The bonanza of sight-and-sound relics of Australian radio, film, and television ranges from the 1800s to today. *(On McCoy Circuit in Acton; catch bus #34 to Liversidge St. ☎6248 2000. Open M-F 9am-5pm, Sa-Su 10am-5pm. Free. Wheelchair accessible.)*

AUSTRALIAN INSTITUTE OF SPORT (AIS). After Australia left the 1976 Olympics empty-handed, the disgruntled nation took action and established the AIS as a training facility for the nation's top athletes in 1981. Tours led by resident athletes take regular humans through the world of the aerobically superhuman, with a stop at the hands-on Sportex exhibit where you can try rowing, wheelchair basketball, or golf. If you're ashamed of your performance, get to work. A pool and several tennis courts are open for your muscle-toning pleasure. *(On Leverrier Crescent just northwest of O'Connor. Take bus #80 from Civic. ☎6214 1010. Open M-F 8:30am-5pm, Sa-Su 10am-4pm. Tours M-F 10:20, 11:30am, 2:30pm; Sa-Su 10am, 11:30, 1pm, 2:30. $12, child $6, family $33. Outdoor Tennis Courts $10 per hr. Pool $4, swimcap mandatory.)*

AUSTRALIAN NATIONAL BOTANIC GARDENS. Running along the northwestern border of the campus on Clunies Ross St. at the foot of Black Mountain, the Botanic Gardens' flora includes the national collection of Australian native plants as well as a rainforest. *(Take Bus #34 to Daley Rd.; walk 20min. toward the lake along Clunies Ross Rd. ☎6250 9540. Concerts Sa-Su evenings in the summer months. Free guided walks daily 11am and 2pm. Open daily 9am-5pm. Visitors center open 9:30am-4:30pm. Free.)*

NATIONAL AQUARIUM AND WILDLIFE SANCTUARY. Unless you're a kid (or have one), you may have trouble justifying the trip from the city center. The nearly seven-hectare sanctuary for native Australian fauna does have some redeeming features koalas, dingoes, and Tasmanian devils), but it's little more than your average animal park. *From Parkes Way, heading out of the city to the west, Lady Denman Dr. branches south toward the aquarium at Scrivener Dam. (☎6287 1211. Open daily 9am-5pm. $16, concessions $12.50, child $9.50, family $46.)*

ENTERTAINMENT

Casino Canberra, 21 Binara St., can help you strike it rich, or not. The upstairs nightclub, **Déjà Vu,** allows people to relax or get down on weekends. (☎6257 7074. Club open F-Sa 9pm-late. Cover F-Sa $5. Casino open daily noon-6am.) In addition to the usual first-run cinemas, Canberra has some funky art-house alternatives, including **Electric Shadows,** on Akuna St. near City Walk. (☎6247 5060. Tickets $13.50, students $8.50; before 5pm $8.50/$7.)

Housing several venues in varying shapes and sizes, the **Canberra Theatre** on London Circuit is the best place to start looking for live entertainment. Register for the free Under 27 Club and take advantage of great savings on tickets. (☎6257 1077. Ages 18-27 tickets $25; full price $30-65.)

Canberra's calendar is packed with minor **festivals,** but there are two annual events that temporarily transform the city. For 16 days in April, **Canberra Festival** brings musical productions, a hot-air balloon show, and street parties to the captial. The last day of the festival is a public holiday, Canberra Day. Mid-September (Sept. 14-Oct.13, 2002) ushers in **The Floriade,** which paints the shores of Lake Burley Griffin with thousands of springtime blooms and relieves the city of all accommodation (book ahead). Contact the tourist office (☎6205 0044) for details.

NIGHTLIFE

Canberra's after-hours scene is surprisingly vibrant. The student population supports a solid range of bars and clubs, while relaxed licensing allows boozing to continue until 4am. Most places claim to close "late," meaning midnight on slow nights and until whenever people stop partying on busier nights. On weekend nights, just wander around Civic and follow the pounding music and scurrying clubgoers. The clientele at hot spots can usually be characterized as one of three different crowds: raging uni students, posh government officials, or unwinding defense school students. Check out the city's entertainment publications, p. 83.

ACT

The Wig and Pen (☎6248 0171), on Alinga St., 2 blocks west of the bus interchange. This cozy, laid-back pub, named for its location in the solicitors district, is the perfect place to sample some incredible, prize-winning homebrews and catch up with friends. After a few schooners ($5), you'll be primed for crazier clubs and bars. Bands (jazz, folk, blues) every night. Open M-F noon-late, Sa 2pm-late, Su 3pm-late.

Gypsy Bar, 131 City Walk (☎6247 7300). A Canberra institution. One of the few places where you'll find ripped-jeans, flannel shirts, black turtlenecks, and government suits partying in the same place. The unpretentious Gypsy books both local talent and big names, from laid-back acoustic to full-on hardcore, and pulls it off with style. Tu all-night Happy Hour and free pool. Th-Sa cover $5-15. Open Tu-F 5:00pm-late, Sa 8pm-late.

Filthy McFadden's (☎6239 5303) in the far corner of Green Sqaure at the intersection of Jardine and Eyre St., Kingston. Frequented by loyal backpackers and regulars, "Filthy's" epitomizes the Irish country pub. Pints of Guiness will set you back $6, but you can bring in pizza from the shop next door. What more can you ask for? Live music Su nights. Open daily noon-late.

Mooseheads, 105 London Circuit (☎6257 6496). A rare Canadian bar with rare Canadian paraphernalia. Especially popular with uni students. The adjacent nightclub, **The Moose Upstairs**, gyrates Th-Sa with retro dance (70s-early 90s) and Top-40 until 5am. Sa cover $5. Bottle of the bar's Canadian namesake $5. Open M-Sa 11am-late.

The Meridian Club, 34 Mort St., Braddon (☎6248 9966). A short walk north from the city bus interchange in Civic. Canberra's only exclusively gay/lesbian club. The dance floor, a large raised platform, grooves and grinds, especially on F-Sa nights. Cover F-Sa $5, students $3. Open Tu-Th 7pm-midnight, F 7pm-late, Sa 8pm-late, Su 6-10pm.

ANU Student Uni Bar (☎6249 0786), in the student union building, near the corner of North Rd. and University Ave., Acton. A popular student hangout and the cheapest pub in Canberra, hosts some of the biggest names in music. Check *bma* (see p. 83) for a comprehensive gig listing. Open M-Sa noon-late, except during uni holidays.

DAYTRIPS FROM CANBERRA

SOUTH OF CANBERRA

Bushland pushes on Canberra's borders with the promise of an easy retreat from urban refinement. The Tourist Drive 5 hits the major southern attractions on a long, full day of sightseeing. If you travel the loop in a counter-clockwise direction, the first two stops will transport you back in time to galaxies far, far away.

CANBERRA DEEP SPACE COMMUNICATIONS COMPLEX. One of the most powerful antenna centers in the world, Canberra Deep Space Communications Complex will awe novices and serious space cadets. The 70m radio dish tracks signals from an orbiting spacecraft. The visitors center, the **Canberra Space Centre,** has displays on the history of space exploration. An old Telstra phone booth now serves as the NASA hotline, a visitors' link to the latest space mission info. *(Off Paddy's River Rd., 40km southwest of Civic. ☎6201 7880; www.cdscc.nasa.gov. Open daily 9am-5pm. Free.)*

TIDBINBILLA NATURE RESERVE. Dedicated to preserving the natural gum-forest habitat of the kangaroos, wallabies, koalas, emus, and other animals that roam the area, the reserve loosely monitors its residents to better your chances of encountering them. Thirteen marked bushwalks in the park range from 30min. strolls to full-day outings. The walk to **Gibraltar rock** (3hr.) rewards not-so-easy rock climbing with stupendous views. The **Birrigai Time Trail** (3km) is an easy trail that allows bush walkers to see a 21,000-year-old rock shelter. The **Tidbinbilla Visitor Centre,** off Paddy's River Rd. a 40min. drive southwest of Civic, has info on bushwalks and ranger-led activities throughout the 5500-hectare park. *(☎6205 1233; www.act.gov.au/environ/tidbin. Park open daily 9am-6pm. $9 per car per day, full-year pass $16.50. Visitor Centre open M-F 9am-4:30pm, Sa-Su 9am-5:30pm. M-F Bushbird Feed 2:30pm; Sa-Su Koala Walk 1pm, Bushbird Feed and Wetland tour 2:30pm. Other programs offered throughout the week as staffing permits.)*

ACT

NAMADGI NATIONAL PARK. The expansive Namadgi National Park is the western border of Tidbinbilla Nature Reserve and fills almost all of the southern arm of the ACT with preserved alpine wilderness traversed by only one major paved route, the Naas/Bobayan Rd. Though the park has walking tracks for all experience levels, it is most famous for its untrammeled recesses accessible only to serious hikers. **Campsites** at Orroral River, Mt. Clear, and Honeysuckle Creek, each with parking nearby, have firewood, untreated water, and toilets. The **Namadgi Visitor Centre,** on the Naas/Bobayan Rd. 3km south of **Tharwa,** sells maps and has info about Aboriginal rock painting and camping options. *(☎6207 2900. Park open 24hr. Camping $3.30 per person. Register at Visitor Centre. Open M-F 9am-4pm, Sa-Su 9am-4:30pm.*

LANYON HOMESTEAD. Built in the 1800s, the buildings at Lanyon Homestead survey Canberra's European architectural history from the days of convict labor through the colonial era. An Aboriginal canoe tree gives evidence of earlier habitation at the same site. Lanyon's greatest draw may be the **Nolan Gallery,** which has many of Sidney Nolan's paintings of bushranger Ned Kelly (see **Glenrowan,** p. 584). *(Tharwa Dr., 30km south of Canberra. Homestead ☎6237 5136, gallery 6237 5192. Open Tu-Su 10am-4pm. Homestead buildings $6, gallery $3, both $7. Wheelchair accessible.)*

NORTH OF CANBERRA

NATIONAL DINOSAUR MUSEUM. The privately-run museum includes over 300 fossils, 10 full-sized dinosaur skeletons and three reconstructions, complete with skin and teeth. *(Barton Hwy. at the corner of Gold Creek Rd. Follow Northbourne until the turnoff to Barton Hwy. ☎6230 2655. Open daily 10am-5pm. $8.50, families $24.)*

GINNINDERRA FALLS AND GORGE. Just over the New South Wales border on the Murrumbidgee River, 20km from Civic, a privately-owned park holds the Ginninderra Falls, which spill 200m down into the Ginninderra Ravine. The park is also known for its **rock-climbing** faces. *(☎6278 4222. Open daily 10am-5pm. $4.50, children $2.50; or $10 per vehicle.)*

NEW SOUTH WALES

From a historical perspective, there's no disputing that New South Wales is Australia's premier state. It was here that British convicts lived through the first bitter years of colonization, dreaming of what might lie beyond the impassable Blue Mountains, and here that explorers first broke through the Great Dividing Range, opening the interior of the country for settlement and ensuring the stability of the colony. In the central plains and on the rich land of the Riverina, Merino wool and agricultural success provided the state with its first glimpses of prosperity. Then, in 1851, prospectors struck gold just west of the mountains, and Australia's history changed forever. No longer the desolate prison of exiled convicts, New South Wales became a place that promised a new life and a chance to strike it rich. Although the gold rush days are long gone, New South Wales has continued to grow. Today, it's the most populous state and—thanks largely to Sydney—the diverse and sophisticated center of modern Australia.

The country's biggest and flashiest city, Sydney sits midway along the coast, still basking in the glow of its Olympic moment. North and south of Sydney, sandy surfing and swimming beaches string together in an almost unbroken chain. The trip up the coast is the be-all-and-end-all of backpacker party routes, with the large coastal towns of Port Macquarie and Coffs Harbour whetting appetites for the full-on delights awaiting in the legendary counter-culture of Byron Bay. The south coast is colder but refreshingly far less crowded and every bit as beautiful. Directly west of Sydney's suburban reaches, the Blue Mountains encompass some of the state's favorite getaways and separate the coastal strip from the expansive Central West and outback regions. The New England Plateau, along the Great Dividing Range north of the wineries of the Hunter Valley, achieves an unusually lush and high-altitude setting for a cozy collection of small Australian towns and stunning national parks. Just below the carved-out enclave of the Australian Capital Territory, the Snowy Mountains offer winter skiing and superb summer hiking.

The attractions of New South Wales are as varied as the terrain. Whether it's the cosmopolitan buzz of Sydney, the challenging bushwalks of the Blue Mountains, the laid-back surf culture of Byron, or the post-apocalyptic simplicity of the outback, most visitors find plenty to write home about.

NEW SOUTH WALES HIGHLIGHTS

NAMBUCCA HEADS. Relax and soak up the rays on the peaceful beaches of Nambucca Heads or paint your own masterpiece on the V-Wall (p. 175).

BLUE MOUNTAINS. Escape urban life in the great outdoors of the Blue Mountains. Venture to the Three Sisters stone outcropping at Echo Point (p. 134).

HUNTER VALLEY. Tour the vineyards and taste the fine red and white wines of the Hunter Valley (p. 146).

JERVIS BAY. explore the underwater world of Jervis Bay (p. 203).

THREDBO. Fly down the long runs on the slopes of Thredbo (p. 212).

NIMBIN. Inhale the counterculture and wily ways of Nimbin (p. 187).

SYDNEY. 'nuff said. (p. 95).

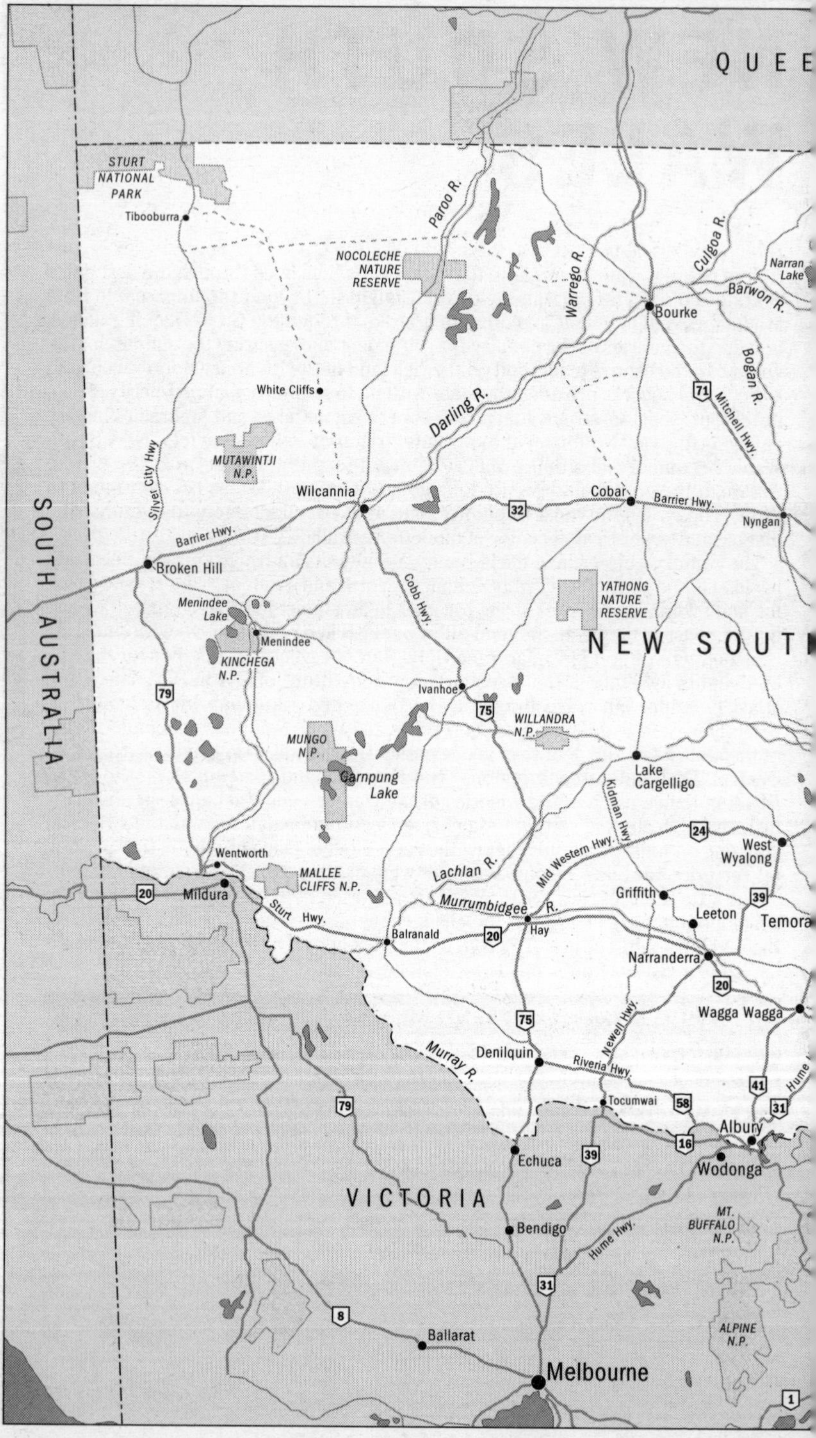

QUEE
STURT NATIONAL PARK
Tibooburra
Paroo R.
NOCOLECHE NATURE RESERVE
Warrego R.
Culgoa R.
Narran Lake
Barwon R.
Bourke
Bogan R.
White Cliffs
Darling R.
71
Mitchell Hwy.
MUTAWINTJI N.P.
Silver City Hwy
Wilcannia
Cobar
Barrier Hwy.
32
Nyngan
SOUTH AUSTRALIA
Barrier Hwy.
Broken Hill
Cobb Hwy.
YATHONG NATURE RESERVE
Menindee Lake
Menindee
KINCHEGA N.P.
NEW SOUT
Ivanhoe
79
75
WILLANDRA N.P.
MUNGO N.P.
Garnpung Lake
Lake Cargelligo
Kidman Hwy
24
West Wyalong
Mid Western Hwy.
Wentworth
Lachlan R.
MALLEE CLIFFS N.P.
20
Mildura
Griffith
39
Leeton
Temora
Murrumbidgee R.
Sturt Hwy.
Balranald
20
Hay
Narranderra
20
Wagga Wagga
75
Newell Hwy.
Denilquin
Murray R.
Riveria Hwy.
41
Hume
79
Tocumwai
58
31
Albury
16
Echuca
39
Wodonga
VICTORIA
MT. BUFFALO N.P.
Bendigo
Hume Hwy.
31
8
Ballarat
ALPINE N.P.
Melbourne
1

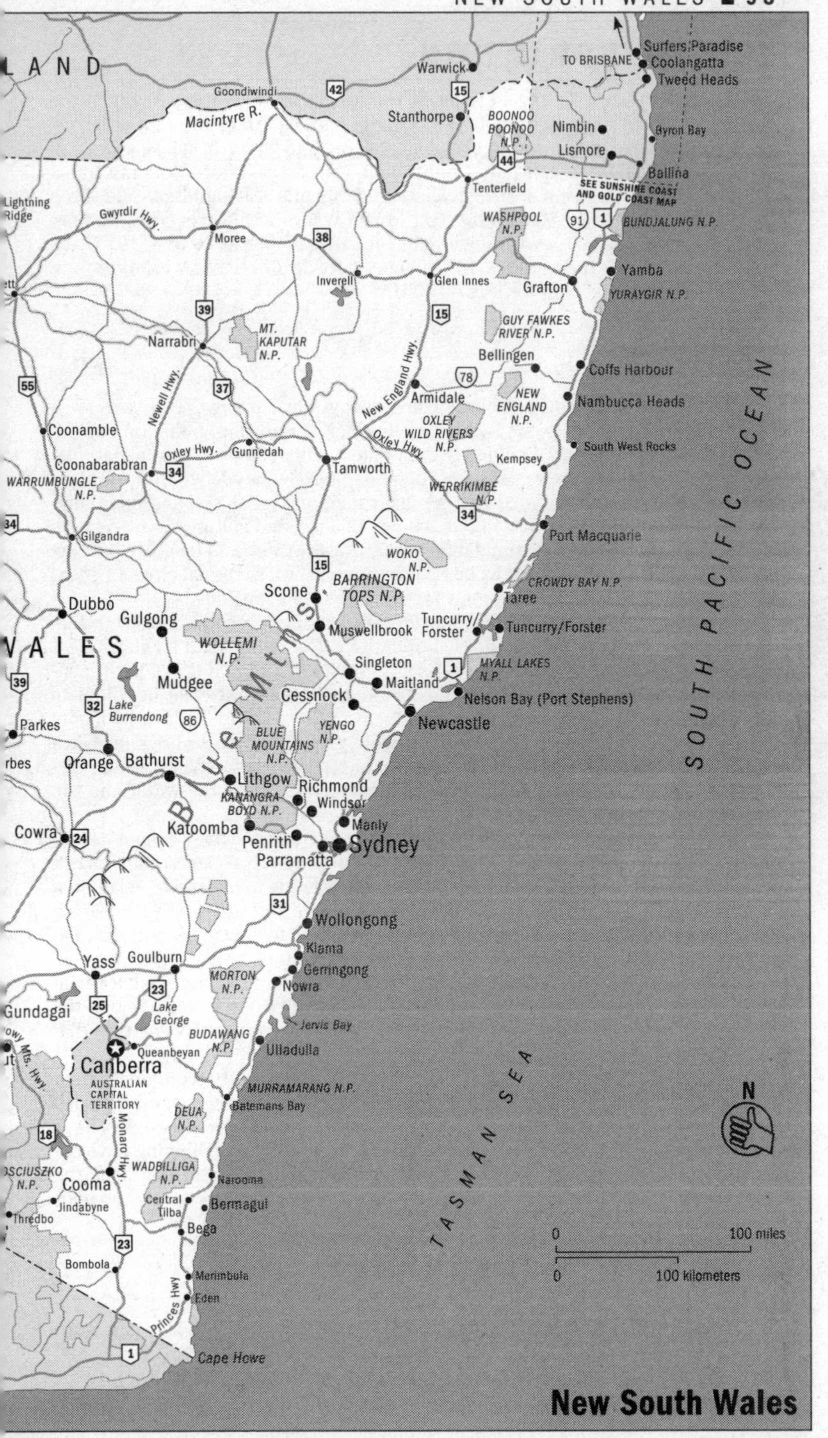
New South Wales
SOUTH PACIFIC OCEAN
TASMAN SEA
Sydney
Canberra
AUSTRALIAN CAPITAL TERRITORY
Newcastle
Wollongong
Blue Mtns.
TO BRISBANE
Surfers Paradise
Coolangatta
Tweed Heads
Byron Bay
Ballina
Lismore
Nimbin
Warwick
Stanthorpe
Goondiwindi
Macintyre R.
Tenterfield
SEE SUNSHINE COAST AND GOLD COAST MAP
BOONOO BOONOO N.P.
WASHPOOL N.P.
BUNDJALUNG N.P.
Yamba
YURAYGIR N.P.
Grafton
Glen Innes
Inverell
Moree
Gwyrdir Hwy.
Lightning Ridge
Narrabri
MT. KAPUTAR N.P.
GUY FAWKES RIVER N.P.
Bellingen
Coffs Harbour
Nambucca Heads
NEW ENGLAND N.P.
Armidale
New England Hwy.
OXLEY WILD RIVERS N.P.
Oxley Hwy.
South West Rocks
Kempsey
Newell Hwy.
Coonamble
Gunnedah
Tamworth
Coonabarabran
WARRUMBUNGLE N.P.
WERRIKIMBE N.P.
Port Macquarie
Gilgandra
WOKO N.P.
BARRINGTON TOPS N.P.
CROWDY BAY N.P.
Taree
Scone
Dubbo
Gulgong
Muswellbrook
Tuncurry/Forster
WALES
WOLLEMI N.P.
Singleton
Maitland
MYALL LAKES N.P.
Mudgee
Cessnock
Nelson Bay (Port Stephens)
Lake Burrendong
Parkes
YENGO N.P.
BLUE MOUNTAINS N.P.
Orange
Bathurst
Lithgow
Richmond
KANANGRA BOYD N.P.
Windsor
Manly
Cowra
Katoomba
Penrith
Parramatta
Klama
Gerringong
Nowra
Yass
Goulburn
MORTON N.P.
Gundagai
Lake George
Jervis Bay
BUDAWANG N.P.
Queanbeyan
Ulladulla
MURRAMARANG N.P.
Batemans Bay
Monaro Hwy.
DEUA N.P.
WADBILLIGA N.P.
Cooma
Narooma
Central Tilba
Bermagui
Jindabyne
Thredbo
Bega
Bombola
Merimbula
Eden
Princes Hwy
Cape Howe
N
0
100 miles
100 kilometers

TRANSPORTATION

New South Wales has an excellent **public transportation** system, especially in the coastal part of the state. For timetables or route info regarding bus, rail, or ferries in Sydney and throughout the state, call **CityRail** (☎13 15 00) or **Countrylink** (☎13 22 32; www.countrylink.nsw.gov.au). Countrylink, New South Wales' sole rail transport, gives a 50% discount for Australian students and ISIC-holders. The three major bus companies are **McCafferty's** (☎13 14 99; www.mccaffertys.com.au), **Greyhound Pioneer** (☎13 20 30; www.greyhound.com.au), and **Premier** (☎13 34 10). Greyhound and McCafferty's have a 10% discount for ISIC/VIP/YHA cardholders; Premier has a 20% discount for ISIC/VIP/YHA.

SYDNEY ☎02

Sometimes elegant, sometimes bizarre, and always amazing, Sydney pulses with energy and swaggers with the self-assurance that stems from being one of the world's great cities. Nearly 4 million Sydney-siders (about 20% of the total national population) make this Australia's unofficial capital. Sydney is where it all goes down, where most international visitors first touch Australian soil and find themselves in a cosmopolitan whirlwind of fashion, finance, and culture. Some Aussies find Sydney's get-go energy intimidating, preferring the more laid-back Melbourne. But for the tourist, it isn't quite as fast-paced as some international cities of equal size; this is Australia, after all, famous for its "no worries" attitude.

Still basking in the glow of its Olympic moment, Sydney is an optimistic, cutting-edge, internationally influential hotbed of activity. But beneath all its shiny newness, Sydney contains as old a history as any city in Australia. In 1788, its stupendous natural harbor, then called Port Jackson, drew the First Fleet of colonists and convicts north of their intended settlement at Botany Bay. Today, the iconic Harbour Bridge and Sydney Opera House occupy the foreshores of Sydney Cove and draw visitors to the water's edge for a few photo-framing moments, which easily become hours on sunny days when sailboats skim across the water and the sidewalk cafes buzz with chatter.

Though geographically bounded by water and mountains, Sydney cannot be culturally contained--its international presence has mixed both Western and Eastern elements into a thoroughly unique blend. The city is home to a massive Asian population that flavors a culture whose food, language, and attitude clearly draw from European heritage. Sydney is also famous as one of the most gay-friendly cities in the world; the annual Mardi Gras event attracts enormous crowds of all persuasions. The economic diversity of the city is somewhat less inspirational: a social chasm exists between the wealthy, wisteria-lined avenues of the North Shore, the bland neighborhoods of the Western suburbs, and the poverty-stricken areas that Aborigines and more recent immigrants call home.

Nonetheless, after the construction, beautification, and economic boom brought by the 2000 Olympic Games, spirits are high. Australians are notorious for their obsession with sports, and the world's greatest celebration couldn't have found a more appropriate home than multi-ethnic, athlete-worshipping environmentally conscious Sydney. Eager to serve as a springboard to the continent, the locals are glad you came; after raging at the clubs, relaxing by the water, and marvelling at the taste of Down Under history and culture, you will be too.

INTERCITY TRANSPORTATION

BY PLANE. Sydney's **Kingsford-Smith Airport,** 10km southwest of the Central Business District, serves most major international carriers. **Qantas** (☎13 13 13) and **Ansett** (☎13 13 00) cover most domestic destinations. **Luggage storage** is available ($2-3). The **New South Wales Tourism Centre,** in the international terminal, offers a

SYDNEY HIGHLIGHTS

SYDNEY HARBOUR. Mrs. Macquaries Point has grand views of the Harbour (p. 118).

DARLING HARBOUR. host to several Olympic events, this popular tourist area holds the Sydney Aquarium and Powerhouse Museum (p. 120).

BONDI BEACH. You've seen it on postcards, now see it in real life. The world-renowned Bondi Beach has been the backdrop for many surf movies (p. 100).

SYDNEY OPERA HOUSE. Defining the Sydney skyline, the Opera House is not be missed. If you're luck enough to catch a show, make sure to be on time. (p. 117).

KINGS CROSS. This is the place for nonstop partying. (p. 128).

booking service and free calls to all area youth hostels. (☎9667 6050; fax 9667 6059. Open daily from 5:30am until after the last flight lands.)

Transportation into the city is available directly outside the terminal. **Airport Express** runs to the city center (#300), Kings Cross (#350), and the northern and eastern beaches. (☎13 15 00. Daily 5:30am-11pm. $7 one-way, $12 return.) **Kingsford-Smith Transport** runs to city and inner suburb accommodations. (☎9667 3221. Every 20min. daily 5am-10pm. $7, $11 return.) A variety of independent shuttles run to the city for around $7. A **CityRail** link (☎13 15 00) at the airport runs to the city center and the outer suburbs. Many hostels offer free pickup. A **taxi** to the city center costs about $20 from the domestic terminal and $25 from the international area; the drive takes 20-45min., depending on traffic.

BY TRAIN. Countrylink (☎13 22 32) **trains** depart from the **Central Railway Station** on Eddy Ave. Branch offices at **Town Hall Station, Bondi Junction Station,** in the **Countrylink New South Wales Travel Centre** next door to Wynyard Station, and on Alfred St. at Circular Quay also sell tickets. Fares include all meals. To Perth, Adelaide, or Alice springs, holiday class is about twice as expensive as coach and includes a sleeping berth, while a luxurious first-class trip is about three times as much as coach. Return fares are generally double the price of one-way. Countrylink gives 50% ISIC discounts; all other services generally give 20% ISIC discounts. Seniors and children aged 4-16 pay half price; children under 4 ride free.

FROM SYDNEY TO:

DESTINATION	COMPANY	DURATION	TIMES	PRICE
Adelaide	Great Southern	25hr.	M, Th	$176
Alice Springs	Great Southern	45hr.	Su, W	$390
Brisbane	Countrylink	14½-15hr.	2 per day	$110
Byron Bay	Countrylink	12½hr.	2 per day	$98
Canberra	Countrylink	4hr.	3 per day	$47
Coffs Harbour	Countrylink	8hr.	3 per day	$79
Melbourne	Countrylink	10½hr.	2 per day	$110
Surfers Paradise	Countrylink	14-15hr.	2 per day	$105
Perth	Great Southern	3 days	M, Th	$459

BY BUS. Fifteen bus companies operate from the **Sydney Coach Terminal,** Central Station, on the corner of Eddy Ave. at Pitt St. (☎9281 9366. Open daily 6am-10pm.) **Luggage storage** is available ($6-9 per day). Because special rates and concessions vary, consult a travel agent for the lowest rate on any given itinerary—the folks at the Central Station coach terminal are well-informed. The two major national companies, McCafferty's (☎13 14 99; www.mccaffertys.com.au) and Greyhound Pioneer (☎13 20 30; www.greyhound.com.au), have recently merged and generally offer more frequent trips to major destinations than the smaller regional carriers, but their rates are often not the best. Be sure to shop around.

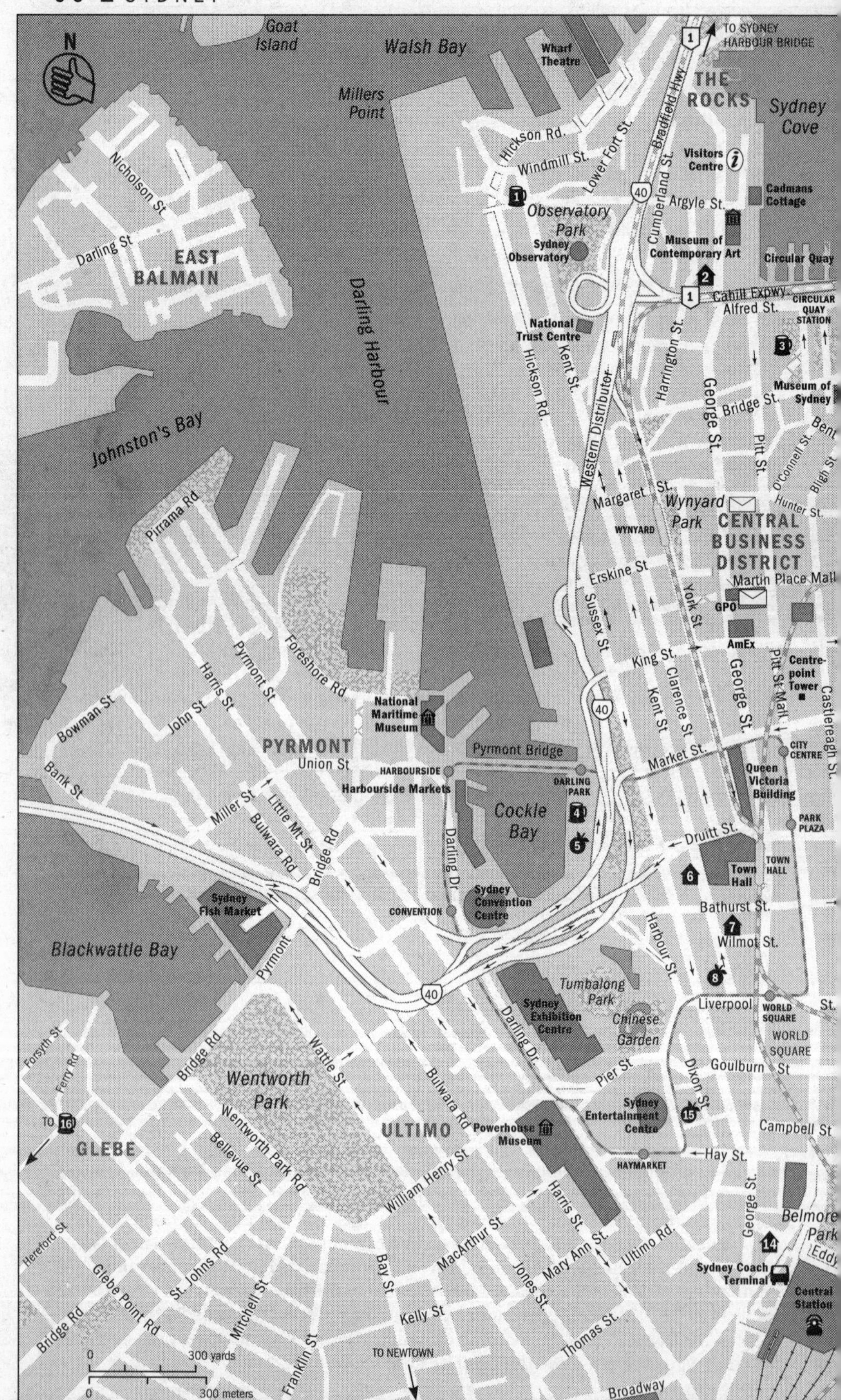
Goat Island
Walsh Bay
Wharf Theatre
TO SYDNEY HARBOUR BRIDGE
THE ROCKS
Sydney Cove
Millers Point
Hickson Rd.
Windmill St.
Lower Fort St.
Bradfield Hwy
Cumberland St.
Visitors Centre
Cadmans Cottage
Argyle St.
Observatory Park
Sydney Observatory
Museum of Contemporary Art
Circular Quay
Nicholson St
Darling St
EAST BALMAIN
Darling Harbour
Cahill Expwy.
Alfred St.
CIRCULAR QUAY STATION
National Trust Centre
Kent St.
Hickson Rd.
Harrington St.
Museum of Sydney
Western Distributor
George St.
Bridge St.
Bent
Johnston's Bay
Pitt St.
O'Connell St.
Bligh St
Hunter St.
Margaret St.
Wynyard Park
WYNYARD
CENTRAL BUSINESS DISTRICT
Pirrama Rd
Erskine St
Martin Place Mall
Sussex St
York St
GPO
AmEx
King St.
Pyrmont St
Harris St
Foreshore Rd
Clarence St
Centrepoint Tower
Pitt St Mall
Castlereagh St.
Bowman St
John St
National Maritime Museum
Kent St
George St.
PYRMONT
Pyrmont Bridge
CITY CENTRE
Market St.
Union St
Bank St
HARBOURSIDE
Harbourside Markets
DARLING PARK
Queen Victoria Building
Cockle Bay
PARK PLAZA
Miller St
Little Mt St
Bulwara Rd
Bridge Rd
Darling Dr.
Druitt St.
TOWN HALL
Town Hall
Sydney Fish Market
Sydney Convention Centre
CONVENTION
Bathurst St.
Harbour St.
Wilmot St.
Blackwattle Bay
Pyrmont
Tumbalong Park
Sydney Exhibition Centre
Chinese Garden
Liverpool
WORLD SQUARE
St.
Darling Dr.
Wattle St
Forsyth St
Ferry Rd
Bridge Rd
Wentworth Park
Bulwara Rd
Pier St
Goulburn St
Dixon St
Sydney Entertainment Centre
TO
GLEBE
Wentworth Park Rd
Bellevue St
ULTIMO
Powerhouse Museum
Campbell St
William Henry St
HAYMARKET
Hay St.
Harris St.
George St.
Belmore Park
Eddy
Hereford St
Glebe Point Rd
St. Johns Rd
Mitchell St
Bay St
MacArthur St
Jones St.
Mary Ann St.
Ultimo Rd.
Sydney Coach Terminal
Central Station
Kelly St
Thomas St.
Bridge Rd
Franklin St
TO NEWTOWN
0
300 yards
0
300 meters
Broadway

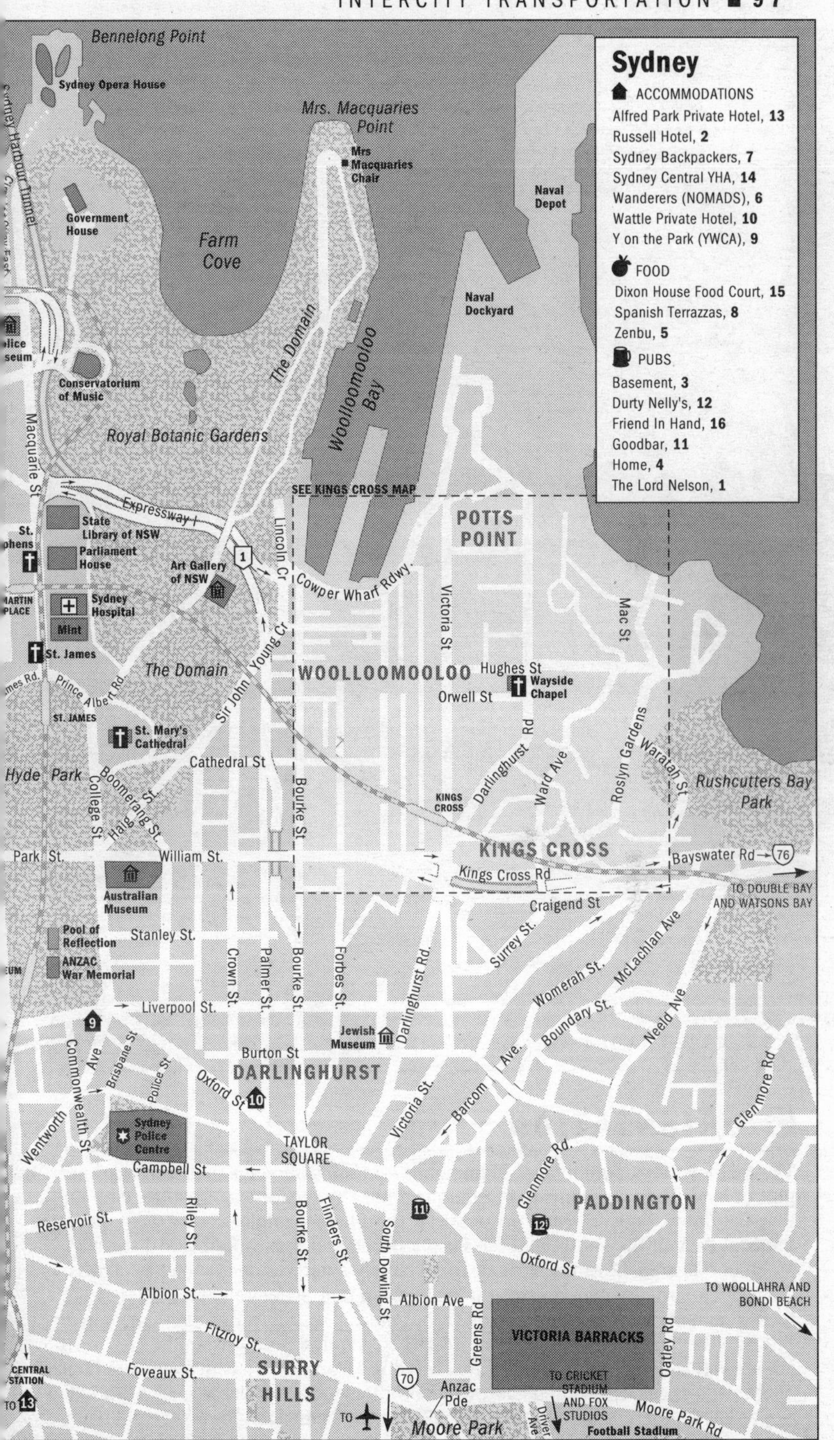
Sydney
ACCOMMODATIONS
Alfred Park Private Hotel, 13
Russell Hotel, 2
Sydney Backpackers, 7
Sydney Central YHA, 14
Wanderers (NOMADS), 6
Wattle Private Hotel, 10
Y on the Park (YWCA), 9
FOOD
Dixon House Food Court, 15
Spanish Terrazzas, 8
Zenbu, 5
PUBS
Basement, 3
Durty Nelly's, 12
Friend In Hand, 16
Goodbar, 11
Home, 4
The Lord Nelson, 1
Bennelong Point
Sydney Opera House
Mrs. Macquaries Point
Mrs Macquaries Chair
Government House
Farm Cove
Naval Depot
Naval Dockyard
Woolloomooloo Bay
The Domain
Conservatorium of Music
Royal Botanic Gardens
Macquarie St
Expressway
State Library of NSW
Parliament House
Art Gallery of NSW
Sydney Hospital
Mint
St. James
SEE KINGS CROSS MAP
POTTS POINT
Lincoln Cr
Cowper Wharf Rdwy.
Victoria St
Mac St
WOOLLOOMOOLOO
Hughes St
Orwell St
Wayside Chapel
Sir John Young Cr
Prince Albert Rd.
ST. JAMES
St. Mary's Cathedral
Cathedral St
Hyde Park
College St
Boomerang St.
Haig St.
Bourke St
KINGS CROSS
Darlinghurst Rd
Ward Ave
Roslyn Gardens
Waratah St
Rushcutters Bay Park
KINGS CROSS
Park St.
William St.
Bayswater Rd
76
Kings Cross Rd
TO DOUBLE BAY AND WATSONS BAY
Australian Museum
Craigend St
Pool of Reflection
Stanley St.
ANZAC War Memorial
Crown St.
Palmer St.
Bourke St.
Forbes St.
Darlinghurst Rd.
Surrey St.
Womerah St.
McLachlan Ave
Liverpool St.
Boundary St.
Neeld Ave
Jewish Museum
Burton St
DARLINGHURST
Commonwealth St
Ave
Brisbane St
Police St
Oxford St
Victoria St.
Barcom Ave.
Glenmore Rd
Wentworth Ave
Sydney Police Centre
TAYLOR SQUARE
Campbell St
Glenmore Rd.
PADDINGTON
Reservoir St.
Riley St.
Bourke St.
Flinders St.
South Dowling St
Oxford St
Albion St.
Albion Ave
Greens Rd
VICTORIA BARRACKS
TO WOOLLAHRA AND BONDI BEACH
Oatley Rd
Fitzroy St.
CENTRAL STATION
Foveaux St.
SURRY HILLS
70
Anzac Pde
TO CRICKET STADIUM AND FOX STUDIOS
Moore Park Rd
TO
Moore Park
Driver Ave
Football Stadium

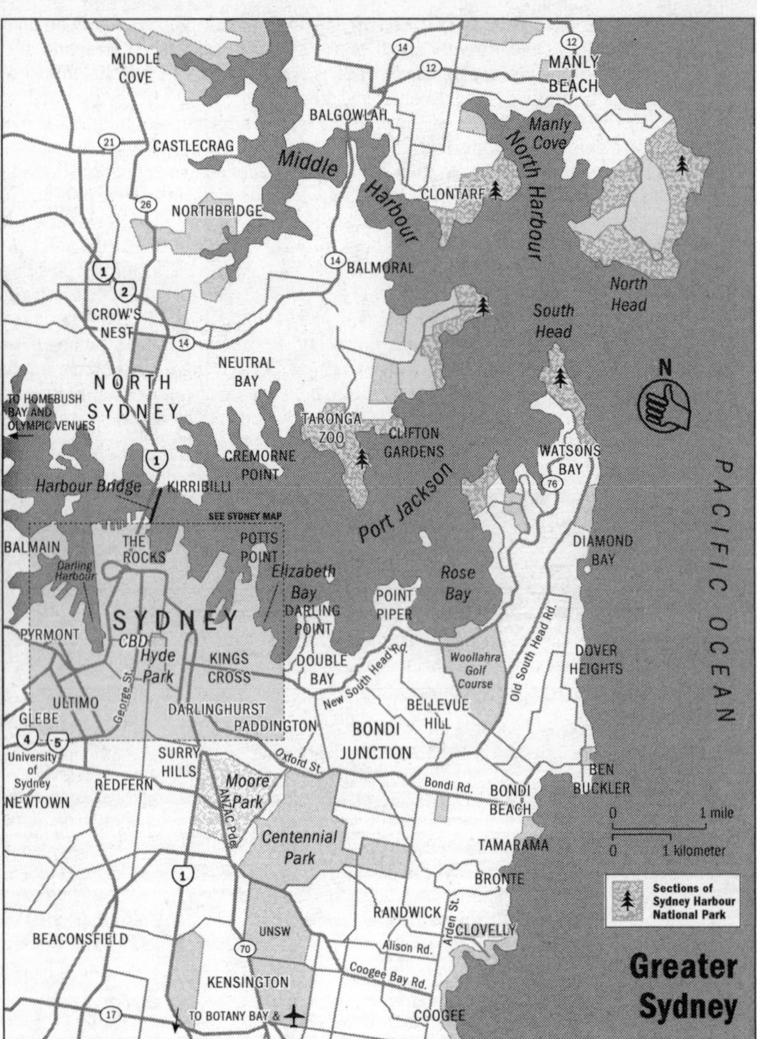

ORIENTATION

The Sydney metropolitan area is immense—Aussies all want their own car and plot of land. The city seems to be contained only by the forces of nature, with **Ku-Ring-Gai Chase National Park** to the north, the **Blue Mountains** to the west, **Royal National Park** to the south, and the **Pacific Ocean** and **Sydney Harbour** to the east. Much of this area, however, is made up of largely quiet, residential outer suburbs.

The standard city map creates the impression that Sydney's center is far larger than it actually is. In truth, the walk from Central Station to Circular Quay along Pitt St. takes only 30min., and from Kings Cross only 15min. Inside the city itself are areas that Sydney-siders call "suburbs"; don't worry, you haven't wandered out of Sydney—these are sections of town that others might call large neighborhoods or precincts. For a bird's eye view of it all, ascend **Centrepoint Tower** (see p. 119).

SYDNEY COVE AND THE CITY CENTER. Sydney's most famous sights lie on the Harbour at **Sydney Cove,** directly north of the city center. On the Cove, and at the southern end of the **Sydney Harbour Bridge** is **The Rocks,** a historic neighborhood with upscale boutiques. Drivers entering downtown Sydney from the north can enter over the **Harbour Bridge** or through the **Harbour Tunnel** which enters the city east of the Cove. (southbound toll for either $2). Though less scenic, the tunnel is a more convenient route for anyone heading into the eastern suburbs. The **Sydney Opera House** perches prominently on Bennelong Point east of the cove and north of the sprawling **Royal Botanic Gardens** and an emerald gem of a park called the **Domain** south of the Gardens. For the best views of the Harbour Bridge and Opera House, take a stroll via **Mrs. Macquaries Rd.** through the Royal Botanic Gardens to **Mrs. Macquaries Point,** the tip of the peninsula that forms the northeast corner of the Botanic Gardens; or take a ferry ride from the wharves at **Circular Quay.**

Sydney proper, or the **city center,** is bounded by Circular Quay to the north, **Central Station** to the south, **Darling Harbour** to the west, and the **Royal Botanic Gardens** and **Hyde Park** to the east. **George St.** and **Pitt St.** are major avenues that run parallel from Circular Quay straight through the heart of the city to Central Station in the south. Street numbers begin at the water and increase proceeding from The Rocks to the 800s near Central Station. Martin Place, a pedestrian mall spanning the five blocks between George and Macquarie St., is the heart of the **Central Business District (CBD).** Farther south in the CDB, the next major center of activity is **Town Hall,** located on Druitt St. between George and Kent St. In between Town Hall and the station is Sydney's rapidly growing **Chinatown,** radiating from the intersection of Hay, Sussex, and George St. This area is home to the famous weekend-discount **Paddy's Market,** also known locally as **Haymarket. Redfern,** the area directly south of Central Station, **may be unsafe at night.** The area around Central Station supports several backpacker accommodations and a number of cheap restaurants

INNER SUBURBS. Many tiny municipalities (or "neighborhoods") known as the **inner suburbs** populate the rest of Sydney's central urban area. Despite their proximity to one another, the suburbs maintain distinct characters and special attractions. Many areas overlap, and some are known by more than one name. West of the city center, **Pyrmont** covers the point of land between Darling Harbour and Blackwattle Bay. The waterside here is also called **Darling Harbour** and is serviced by the Sydney Monorail. South of Pyrmont, **Ultimo** approaches the west side of Central Station and ultimately reaches the Chinatown area. **Glebe,** southwest of Ultimo and just north of the **University of Sydney,** benefits from the presence of students in all the usual ways: casual cafes, cheap food, crowded pubs, and well-supplied bookstores. Glebe Point Rd. is the center of activity in this district and home to a number of hostels. **Newtown,** just south of the university, is a bohemian neighborhood centered around King St. with a mix of rambunctious students and eclectic gay and lesbian shop owners.

The infamous inner suburb of **Kings Cross,** east of the city center at the far end of William St., reigns as the center of Sydney backpacker culture. Lively and crowded hostels and cafes line Victoria St. north of William St., while busy nightclubs and pubs are packed in along Bayswater Rd. The bawdy strip shows and solicitors on Darlinghurst Rd. explain the neighborhood's seedy reputation. Travelers should watch all belongings while in the Cross and avoid walking alone at night. **Female backpackers on their own should probably steer clear of the area from dusk until dawn.**

Near Kings Cross, **Woolloomooloo** gets down to the business of shipping while **Potts Point** and **Elizabeth Bay** nourish Sydney's wealthier denizens. Here again, suburban borders get fuzzy; a posh Potts Point address may be across the street from your Kings Cross hostel. To the south of Kings Cross, **Victoria St.** goes chic with the city's coolest cafes lining the way to **Darlinghurst.** Along with **Surry Hills** to the south and **Paddington** to the east, Darlinghurst provides fashionable housing for young, creative types. Sydney's nightlife revolves around the outrageous clubs along **Oxford St.,** the main road through Darlinghurst, Paddington, and Woollahra to the east. Just south of the army's stately Victoria Barracks, **Moore Park** and **Centennial**

Park to its east form the city's largest swath of greenery and house Sydney's major athletic facilities, including the **Sydney Football Stadium** and **Cricket Ground.**

FAR EAST AND SOUTHERN BEACHES. Outside of these central areas, surroundings get less urban. East of Paddington, **Woollahra's** terrace houses provide a nice change of scenery. To the north, **Double Bay** and **Rose Bay** are among Sydney's most exclusive residential areas and are the location of Sydney's elegant resort shopping areas. **Bondi Junction,** south of Woollahra, is the last train stop on the eastern end of the subway system. Ten minutes east by bus or subway is the famous **Bondi Beach** (BOND-eye), model of many a surf movie and home to the majority of Sydney's celebrity types. Farther south, the beaches of **Tamarama, Clovelly,** and **Bronte** offer low-key alternatives for families and quieter sunbathers. **Coogee Beach** lies farthest south and rivals Bondi with its popular beachlife and young residents. Decide for yourself by taking the hour-long walk along the coastline between Bondi and Coogee Beaches, sampling all the beaches in between.

NORTH SHORE. The second half of Sydney's professional district fronts the **north shore** of Sydney Harbour at the other end of Harbour Bridge. **North Sydney** was originally settled by wealthy merchants and its upper-class heritage gleams through today. It's the playground of wealthy urbanites and posh business people. While tourist attractions on the north shore are essentially limited to **Taronga Park Zoo** in Mosman and the beach community of **Manly** (both accessible by ferry), the beautiful, more secluded north shore beaches are worthy escapes from the city proper. The meandering ferry rides to Manly and Taronga (see p. 121) are interesting enough in themselves to justify the trip on a pleasant day.

LOCAL TRANSPORTATION

Sydney's well-oiled public transportation machine makes for simple traveling. The **Sydney Transit Authority (STA)** is comprised of **Sydney Buses, CityRail Trains,** and **Sydney Ferries;** the network stops just about anywhere. For information or route advice on any part of the STA system, call 13 15 00. A **bus information kiosk** is at Circular Quay, on the corner of Alfred and Loftus St. (Open M-F 8am- 8pm, Sa-Su 9am-2pm). There's a **ferry kiosk** near Wharf 4, Circular Quay (open M-F 7am-6pm, Sa-Su 8am-6pm), and a **train kiosk** at Central Station (open daily 6:30am-10:30pm). Check out various passes, frequently cheaper than paying individual fares. For $13 per day, the **DayTripper** grants unlimited use of Sydney ferries, local buses, and central CityRail lines. The **TravelPass** for the four centermost zones includes unlimited seven-day access to buses, trains, and ferries for just $29.

The **Sydney Pass** includes unlimited bus, train, and ferry use within the basic TravelPass zone, return Airport Express service, access to both Explorer Buses, and passage on Sydney Harbour cruises and the higher-speed ferries to Manly and Parramatta. (3-day pass $90, ages 4-16 $45, families $225; 5-day pass $120/$60/$300; 7-day pass $140/$70/$350.)

BY BUS. Buses don't automatically stop at bus stops; hail them as you would a taxi. Fares range from $1.50 and $4.60 (children half-price, seniors $1-3, ask for student concessions). Pay when boarding. Color-coded **TravelTen** passes cover 10 trips at a significant discount and can be purchased from most news agencies ($11 for a Blue TravelTen allows for 10 trips within the city and inner suburbs). The **Bus Tripper** ($9.50) covers one day of bus travel. Most buses run between 5am and 11:30pm, but there is 24hr. service between the city center, Kings Cross, and other central locales. The STA info line (☎ 13 15 00) has schedule details.

In addition to local commuter bus service, the STA operates two sightseeing buses, the **Sydney Explorer** and the **Bondi & Bay Explorer,** that allow passengers to get on and off at major attractions along designated routes. The Sydney Explorer covers sights between the Harbour and Central Station, moving as far east as Woolloomooloo Bay and as far west as Darling Harbour, originating in Circular Quay every 18min. between 8:40am and 5:22pm. The Explorer services are expensive, but can be an excellent way to do concentrated touring. ($30 for a 1-day pass for either route, ages 4-16 $15, families $75; tickets combining both routes over two non-consecutive days are $50/$25/$125. Purchase tickets on a bus at any stop along the route.) The Bondi & Bay Explorer service visits the eastern bays and southern beaches down to Coogee, departing from Circular Quay every 30min. between 9:15am and 4:15pm. Start early to get the most bang for your buck.

BY SUBWAY AND TRAIN. Sydney's **CityRail** subway system rumbles from Bondi Junction in the east to the most distant corners of the suburban sprawl in the north, west, and south 24 hr. a day. Service is fast, frequent, and easy to navigate. CityRail's lowest one-way fare is $2.20, but most trips cost a little bit more. Return fares are double the one-way price weekdays before 9am. At all other times, the purchase of a round-trip "off-peak return" ticket gets you a sizeable discount. The combined service **TravelPass** is generally a bargain for regular subway users.

Both the **Monorail** and **Light Rail** (☎8584 5288; www.metrolightrail.com.au; www.metromonorail.com.au) provide futuristic if impractical methods of transportation. Riding above the city bustle is a nice change if you are going from one point directly to another and don't mind the slightly heftier fee. The Monorail links the City Centre with Darling Harbour and Chinatown. (Every 3-5min., M-Th 7am-10pm, F-Sa 7am-midnight, Su 8am-10pm. $3.50, seniors $2.20, under 6 free; day pass $7, families $20.) The Light Rail connects Chinatown, Darling Harbour, Star City, and Ultimo. (Every 10-15min., 6am-midnight; every 30min. midnight-6am. 24hr. $2.20-4.50, seniors/ages 4-15 $1.10-3.30; adult unlimited day pass $7, concessions $5, families $20; signal the driver from designated stopping areas.)

BY FERRY. STA green and gold **ferries** (www.sydneyferries.nsw.gov.au) provide passengers with a magnificent view of the harbour. Ferries embark from the **Circular Quay** wharves between the Opera House and the Harbour Bridge daily 5am-midnight. The **information office** (☎9207 3170) is opposite Wharf 4. Short one-way trips in the harbor cost $4.20; a **FerryTen** pass for the same area costs $26.30 and works much like the TravelTen bus pass. The fare for the high-speed JetCat to Manly is $6.60 (FerryTen pass $54.70). The STA's fastest and longest commuter ferry service is the RiverCat to Parramatta ($6.30, FerryTen $44.60). Children ages 4-16 and concession card-carriers ride all these ferries for half-price.

STA has several **Sydney Ferries Harbour Cruises:** the Morning Cruise (1hr.; daily 10am and 11:15am; $15, ages 4-16 $7.50, families $37.50); the Afternoon Cruise (2½hr.; M-F 1pm, Sa-Su 1:30pm; $22, $11, $55); and the after-dark Evening Harbour Cruise (1½hr.; M-Sa 8pm; $19, $9.50, $47.50). The Sydney Ferries **information** line has details. (☎9207 3170. Operates M-F 7am-6pm, Sa-Su 8am-6pm.)

BY CAR. The **National Royal Motorist Association (NRMA),** Level 2, 430 Forest Rd., Hurstbille, is a comprehensive driver's resource (see **Essentials,** p. 67). Anyone doing extensive driving should consider joining—benefits include roadside and accident assistance, knowledgeable staff, accurate maps, and emergency passenger transport and accommodation. (☎13 21 32. Open daily 7am-10pm. $99 first-time annual membership, $46 renewal or if a member of an international agency.)

All major **car rental** companies have desks in Kingsford-Smith Airport, and most appear again on William St. near Kings Cross. The big names include: **Avis,** 214 William St. (☎13 63 33 or 19357 2000); **Budget,** 93 William St. (☎13 27 27 or 8255 9600); **Hertz** (☎13 30 39 or 9360 6621), corner of William and Riley St.; **Thrifty,** 78 William St. (☎9331 1385 or1300 367 227); **Dollar** (☎9223 1444), on Sir John Young Crescent. All rent cars starting around $55 per day, with surcharges for 21-25 year-olds and airport pickup. Dollar is a little cheaper than the others with small, manual transmission cars starting at $40 per day ($28 per day with longer rentals) with unlimited kilometers, and automatic transmission cars for $45 per day. However, it is a smaller chain, which can make interstate travel and drop off more difficult.

In general, local and regional outfits offer much better monetary deals than the big companies, but consider the possible downsides: fewer locations translates to more difficult interstate travel and drop off. **Delta Car Rentals,** 77 William St., has small manual cars from $39 per day. (☎9380 6288 or 13 13 90; www.deltacar.com.au. Open daily 8am-5pm. Ages 21-24 $12 surcharge.) **Bayswater**

Car Rental, 180 William St. at corner of Dowling, Kings Cross (☎9360 3622), is cheap and has the lowest age limit, 20. All companies offer reduced long-term rental rates, and most offer free pickup from the airport or Central Station.

Hostel notice boards overflow with fliers for privately-owned cars, campers, and motorcycles **selling** for as little as several hundred dollars. When purchasing a car this way, it's a good idea to make sure it's registered to the seller so the registration can be transferred. For more information on car sales, see **Essentials,** p. 66. **Kings Cross Backpackers Car Market,** Level 2, Kings Cross Car Park, on the corner of Ward Ave. and Elizabeth Bay Rd., brings buyers and sellers together. They offer third party insurance for travelers—meaning that in the case of an accident that is your fault, they will pay for the other person's damages, a feature difficult to get elsewhere—and their knowledgeable staff has invaluable information on registration and other matters for car-buyers. (☎9358 5000 or 1800 808 188; www.carmarket.com.au. Open daily 9am-5pm. Weekly charge from $40. Required vehicle inspection $26.) **Travellers Auto Barn,** 177 William St., offers guaranteed buy-back agreements on cars over $3000. Minimum buy-back rates are 30-50% of purchase price, depending on the length of time you take the car. Cheaper cars are also available, but do not come with warranties and buy-back guarantees, whereas purchases over $3000 include 5000km engine warranties and free NRMA Service membership. (☎9360 1500. Open M-Sa 9am-6pm, Su 10:30am-3pm.)

BY TAXI. Taxis can be hailed from virtually any street. Initial fare is $2.25 ($1.10 surcharge with call-in request), plus $1.32 per km. Tipping is not expected, though rounding up the fare is appreciated. Some companies are: **Legion Cabs** (☎13 14 51 or 9211 2300); **RSL Cabs** (☎13 22 11 or 9698 3511); **Taxis Combined** (☎9332 8888); **St. George Cabs** (☎13 21 66); **Premiere Taxi** (☎13 10 17).

BY BICYCLE. For taking in lots of scenery at a manageable pace, cycling is hard to beat; by complementing cycling with ferries and trains, in a single day it's possible to tour the Harbour and northern and eastern beaches, or even venture out to Royal or Ku-Ring-Gai Chase National Park. **Bicycles in the City,** 722 George St., near Chinatown, hires bikes from $20 per day in-season and provides cycling maps and comprehensive information for day and longer adventure tours. (☎9280 2229. Open daily 9am-6pm.) **Inner City Cycles,** 151 Glebe Point Rd., rents bikes starting at $33 per day. (☎9660 6605. Open daily 9am-6pm, Th until 8pm.) For a coastal ride, visit **Manly Cycle Centre,** 36 Pittwater Rd., at Denison St. in Manly. (☎9977 1189. Open M-Sa 9am-6pm, Th until 7, Su 9am-5pm. $12 per hr., $18 per 2hr., full-day $25.) **Bicycle NSW,** Level 2, 209 Castlereagh St., has 10,000 members and organizes weekly rides. (☎9283 5200. Annual dues $59.)

PRACTICAL INFORMATION

TOURIST AND TRAVEL INFORMATION

Tourist Office: The **Sydney Visitors Centre,** 106 George St. (☎9255 1788 or 1800 067 676; www.sydneyvisitorcentre.com), located in the white, historic sailors' building in the Rocks. The 17min. presentation on the Rocks area is an entertaining introduction to the city's history. Friendly staff and mountains of brochures provide enough information for even the most enthusiastic traveler. Open daily 9am-6pm.

Travel Offices: The main travel office is Travellers Contact Point, but other offices can meet travellers' more specific needs.

Travellers Contact Point, Level 7, 428 George St. (☎9221 8744; fax 9221 3746; sydney@travellers.com.au), between King and Market St. Free 30min. Internet access. Mail forwarding and holding in Australia, including your own email address, $50 per year. Employment board with recruiting officers for travelers with work visas. Open M-F 9am-6pm, Sa 10am-4pm. MC/V.

Student Uni Travel, Level 8, 92 Pitt St. (☎9232 8444; www.sut.com.au), near Martin Pl. Free 15min. email and Internet access. Mail forwarding. Luggage storage $1 per day. Job agency and visa assistance. Open M-F 9am-6pm, Sa 10am-5pm. ISIC/NOMADS/VIP/YHA. MC/V.

Australian Travel Specialists, Jetty 2 and Jetty 6, Circular Quay (24hr. ☎9555 2700; fax 9555 2701), on the waterfront. Comprehensive information on trips around Sydney and beyond. Locations also at Manly Ferry Wharf, Harbourside Shopping Centre (Darling Harbour), and Centrepoint Shopping Centre. Open daily 7am-9pm.

YHA Travel Center, 422 Kent St. (☎9261 1111; www.yha.com.au), behind Town Hall, between Market and Druitt St. Open M-W, F 9am-5pm, Th 9am-6pm, Sa 10am-2pm. MC/V.

Consulates: Canada, Level 5, 111 Harrington St. (☎9364 3000). Open M-F 8:30am-4:30pm. **New Zealand,** Level 10, 55 Hunter St. (passport ☎02 9223 0222, visa 9223 0144; fax 9221 7836 or 9223 0166). **United Kingdom,** Level 16, 1 Macquarie Pl. (☎9247 7521; fax 9251 1201). Open M-F 10am-12:30pm and 1:30-4:30pm. **United States,** 59th floor, 19-29 Martin Pl., MLC Centre (☎9373 9200). Open M-F 8am-12:30pm; phones answered 8am-4:30pm.

FINANCIAL SERVICES

Banks and exchange offices are crammed on the streets of Sydney, particularly in the Central Business District **(CBD).** They are generally open M-F 9am-5pm. **ATMs** are equally ubiquitous and usually accept Cirrus, MasterCard, Plus, and Visa.

Singapore Money Exchange: 304-308 George St. (☎9223 6361), opposite Wynyard Station. 5% commission on traveler's checks. Other locations include: 401 Sussex St., Chinatown (☎9281 0663); on Eddy Ave. near Central Station, Shop #10 by the Greyhound office (☎9281 4118); in Darling Harbour's Harbourside Mall (☎9212 7124); Centrepoint Tower's Castlereagh St. level (☎9223 9222). All open daily 9am-5:30pm.

Thomas Cook: (☎1800 801 002). Several locations in the international terminal (☎9317 2100) of the airport. $7 charge on traveler's checks and currency exchanges. Open daily 5am-9:30 or 10pm. There are dozens of other offices, including 175 Pitt St. (☎9231 2877). Open M-F 8:45am-5:15pm, Sa 10am-1pm.

Money Change: On the mall at Darlinghurst Rd. and Springfield Ave., Kings Cross. 5% commission on traveler's checks and currency. Open daily 8am-11:45pm.

American Express Office: (☎1300 139 060). Dozens of locations around the city, including Level 3, 130 Pitt St. (☎9236 4200), around the corner from Martin Pl. Traveler's Cheques cashed and currency changed with no commission; $3.20 minimum or 1.1% commission to buy cheques. Mail held for card and traveler's cheque holders up to a month. Open M-F 8:30am-5pm, Sa 9am-noon.

LOCAL SERVICES

Bookstores: Dymocks Booksellers, 424-430 George St. (☎1800 688 319; www.dymocks.com.au). Open M-W 9am-6pm, Th 9am-9pm, F 9am-6pm, Sa-Su 9am-5pm. Australia's largest bookstore has franchise locations all over the city center.

Library: Sydney City Library, Town Hall House, 456 Kent St. (☎9265 9470), at the corner of Kent and Druitt St. Open M-F 8am-7pm, Sa 9am-noon. The **State Library of New South Wales** (☎9273 1414), part of the former hospital complex on Macquarie St., houses galleries and research facilities. Open M-F 9am-9pm, Sa-Su 11am-5pm.

Ticket Agencies: Ticketek (☎9266 4800; www.ticketek.com.au), has offices in retail stores and an information kiosk at 195 Elizabeth St., or you can buy online. Full-price advance booking for music, theater, sports, and selected museums. Phone lines are open for credit card purchases M-Sa 9am-9pm, Su 8am-8pm. **Ticketmaster** (☎13 61 00; www.ticketmaster7.com), covers many concert and theatrical venues. Phones answered M-Sa 9am-9pm, Su 9am-5pm.

Weather: 24hr. ☎11 96.

EMERGENCY SERVICES

Emergency: ☎000 anywhere in Australia for police, ambulance, or fire assistance.

Police: 570 George St. (☎9265 6595). Kings Cross police station, 1-15 Elizabeth Ba Rd. (☎8356 0099), on Fitzroy Gardens.

MEDIA AND PUBLICATIONS.

Newspapers: The main papers are the (more white-collar) *Sydney Morning Herald* and *The Australian* ($1.10) and (more blue-collar) *Daily Telegraph* (90¢).

Nightlife: *Streetpress, The Revolver,* or *3-D World* (www.threedworld.com.au). For gay nightlife, check out *Sx* (www.sxnews.com.au) or *Sydney Star Observer* (www.ssonet.com.au). All free. See **Nightlife,** p. 128.

Entertainment: The *Metro* section of Friday's *Sydney Morning Herald*, as well as free weeklies *Beat* and *Sydney City Hub.*

Radio: Rock, Triple J 105.7FM and Triple M 104.9FM; News, ABC 630AM; Tourist Info, 88FM.

Crisis Lines: Alcohol and Drug Information Service 24hr. ☎9361 2111. **Rape Crisis Centre** 24hr. ☎9819 6565, outside Sydney ☎1800 424 017. **HIV/AIDS Information Line** ☎9332 4000; phones answered M-F 8am-7pm, Sa 10am-6pm. **Suicide prevention** ☎9331 2000 or 1300 360 980. **Gay & Lesbian Counselling Service** ☎9207 2800 or 1800 805 379, daily 4pm-midnight.

Late-Night Pharmacy: 24hr. Prescription and Delivery Service ☎9966 8397. **Crest Hotel Pharmacy,** 60A Darlinghurst Rd., Kings Cross (☎9358 1822), opposite the rail station. Open Su-M 8:30am-midnight, Tu-Sa 8:30am-2am. **Wu's Pharmacy,** 629 George St., Chinatown (☎9211 1805). Open M-Sa 9am-9pm, Su 9am-7pm.

Medical Services: Sydney Hospital (☎9382 7111 or 9382 7009), on Macquarie St. opposite the Martin Pl. station. **Traveller's Medical and Vaccination Centre,** Level 7, 428 George St. (☎9221 7133). Consultation fee $40. Open M-F 9am-6pm, Th until 8pm, Sa 9am-1pm. **Kings Cross Travellers' Clinic,** 13 Springfield Ave. (☎9358 3066). Provides travel medical services and vaccinations. Consultation fee $40. Open M-F 9am-1pm and 2-6pm, Sa 10am-noon. **Contraceptive Services,** Level 3, 195 Macquarie St. (☎9221 1933). Open M-F 8:30am-4:30pm, Sa 8:30am-1pm.

POST AND COMMUNICATION

Internet Access: Internet cafes are as copious as pubs and McDonald's. Cheap rates abound, especially near Chinatown and Kings Cross; common charges in the city center are $3 per hr. and $4 for unlimited use, but rates fluctuate. **Global Gossip** shops are franchised across the city and offer 3min. free access. 770 George St., near Sydney Central YHA. (☎9212 1466) Internet $3.25 per hr. Open daily 9am-midnight. Other locations include: 111 Darlinghurst Rd., Kings Cross (☎9326 9777); 108 Oxford St., Darlinghurst (☎9380 4588); 14 Wentworth, Sydney City (☎9263 0400); 37 Hall Street, Bondi Beach (☎9365 4811); and 317 Glebe Point Rd. (☎9552 6966). Hours and Internet rates vary by location. They also offer postboxes and mail-forwarding ($9.95 per month) and super-cheap **international call rates** in their on-site phone booths. There are also about half a dozen competitively priced places on George St. near Chinatown and the Sydney YHA.

Directory Assistance: ☎013.

Post Office: Sydney General Post Office (GPO), 1 Martin Pl. (☎13 13 18), corner of George St. Open M-F 8:15am-5:30pm, Sa 10am-2pm. Poste Restante available at 310 George St., inside Hunter Connection across from Wynyard Station. They will hold mail for up to a month. Enter up the ramp with the "Hunter Connection" sign and go up the escalator. Open M-F 8:15am-5:30pm. Many hostels will also hold mail for up to a month. **Postal Codes:** 2000 for city center, 2001 for *Poste Restante.*

WORKING IN SYDNEY

Sydney is bursting with backpackers seeking jobs, especially young Brits taking advantage of working-holiday visa (for info on **work permits,** see p. 35). Fortunately, in economically optimistic Sydney, there is generally plenty of work available for the persistent. Those who arrive without prior arrangements report a 2-3 week or shorter lag before finding semi-permanent employment. Virtually all Sydney hostels have services to help guests find work (NOMADS Wanderers on Kent

CYBER-SYDNEY ;-)

www.cityofsydney.nsw.gov.au The homepage of Sydney. Visitor guide and information on services provided by the local government.

sydney.citysearch.com.au A comprehensive business directory, entertainment listings, shopping, restaurants, and gay/lesbian info.

www.ninemsn.com.au/sydneyguide The website for "the official guide" pamphlet to Sydney, with attractions, restaurants, etc. by region

www.sydney.com.au Sydney's sights, accommodations, and transportation.

australia.craigslist.org/syd This newcomer is a community notice board, with work, housing, and events listings.

www.eatstreetsatnight.com.au Listings of restaurants open late into the night for late-night munchies.

sydneyforchildren.com.au Information on a wide range of activities and services for children and families.

and Sydney Central YHA distribute lists of employment agencies at their employment desks and help with issues like taxes, Medicare, and visas); and travel magazines like *TNT* and *OVG* contain work advice and listings of work agencies.

It pays to start preparing before leaving home. Have a resume typed and saved on a disk; you can print it at most Internet shops. The best way to prepare for job hunting in Sydney is to do research and establish contacts before arriving. Qualified applicants in computer fields enjoy the most success in landing high-quality positions. If you don't have the opportunity to set up house before commencing your search, it is advisable *not* to list hostel numbers as contact information, or you'll look transient. Instead, use a friend, get a cellular phone, or set up a mailbox at **Global Gossip** (see **Internet,** p. 57) or **Travellers Contact Point** (☎9221 8744); both are good sources for job search ideas and allow you to receive incoming faxes. **Student Uni Travel** is another useful job agency (☎9232 8444).

On the web, **Monster** (www.monster.com.au) gives access to thousands of job listings while allowing you to post your resume for potential employers. A personalized search agent will deliver new job listings fitting your criteria. **Cowley's Job Centre** (www.cowleys.com.au) allows you to advertise yourself as well, and provides access to employment news groups and links to other employment-related packages. Newspapers are always an essential resource. The *Sydney Morning Herald* is stuffed with job classifieds on Wednesday and Saturday. *The Australian* is especially strong for computer opportunities in its Tuesday listings.

For tax info, visit the **Australian Taxation Office,** 100 Market St., GPO Box 9990, at the Centrepoint shopping plaza in the Central Business District. There you can grab the annual *TaxPack*. The helpful officers at this office report that the biggest misunderstanding for foreigners is that they believe they will be charged the 47% income tax while their tax number is being processed by immigration. In fact, travelers are given a 28-day grace period and are taxed starting at the 29% non-resident rate. However, it is essential to apply for a tax file number (after you have a work visa), and many employers will not even consider your application until you've file the paperwork. (☎13 28 61; www.ato.gov.au. Open M-F 8:30am-4:45pm.)

ACCOMMODATIONS

As the travelers' gateway to Australia, Sydney supports a thriving budget accommodation market. The first question most travelers must answer when looking for a bed in Sydney is whether or not to stay in Kings Cross. Well-located, traveler-friendly, and party-ready, Kings Cross has become an established backpacker mecca, and the high concentration of steadily improving hostels ensures that beds are almost always available. However, the omnipresence of prostitutes and go-go bars make many travelers uncomfortable. In addition, tales of theft are rampant. If you do opt to stay in the Cross, be sure you feel comfortable with your hostel's security measures before letting your valuables out of sight.

While staying in the city center brings the benefit of convenient transportation, many travelers sing the praises of more remote suburbs, as the nightlife and good-value restaurant options around the CBD are quite limited. Glebe offers the second-highest concentration of backpackers (after the Cross), but with a safer, more laid-back feel. While Bondi is Sydney's high-profile beach, the accommodations at Coogee Beach are generally nicer. The accommodations listings are generally divided by neighborhood, though there is a special section entitled **Upscale Bargains** (p. 112) for those willing to pay a little more to really live it up.

Unless stated otherwise, hostels accept major credit cards, have 24hr. access, no linen fee, and a 10am check-out. Laundry, when available, is generally $2-$2.20 per wash. Prices listed are **winter rates** and most dorm beds increase in price by a few dollars ($2-5) during peak season (Nov.-Feb.). The most expensive time to travel, by far, is during late December and April.

KINGS CROSS AND AROUND

Some accommodations in the Cross can be seedy and run-down, but plenty of clean, well-maintained rooms exist. The shabbier places have been left out of our listings. The Victoria St. locations are rather stately, as hostels go. **CityRail** runs from Martin Pl. in the city to Kings Cross Station. Various **buses** run from Circular Quay (#324, 325, 327) and Chatswood (#200) to the Cross as well. It's a 10min. walk from the east side of Hyde Park down William St. to Darlington St.—you've arrived when you reach the world's largest Coca-Cola sign.

The Pink House, 6-8 Barncleuth Sq. (☎9358 1689 or 1800 806 384; thepinkh@qd.com.au), off Ward Ave. Unlike most other Kings Cross hostels, the Pink House feels like a house–a big, fun, light-pink house. Copious group activities (daytrips, pub

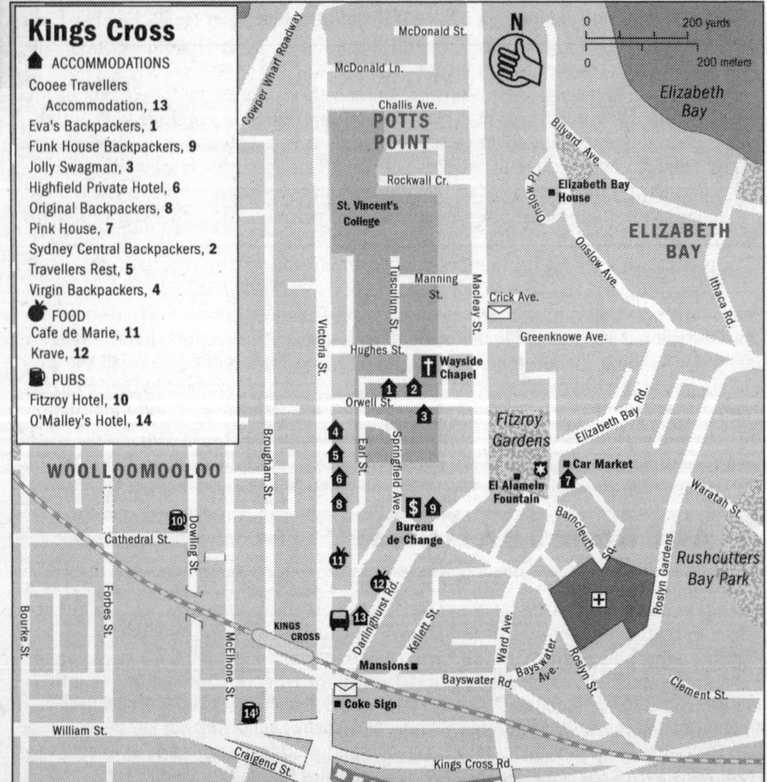

NEW SOUTH WALES

outings, skydiving, inter-hostel soccer) promote a family atmosphere as well as get you a discount. Brick kitchen opens onto garden terrace with BBQ. All rooms have TVs and couches. Luggage storage $5 per week, $15 per month. Laundry $5. Free 20min. Internet. Book ahead. Reception daily 8:30am-9pm. Dorms $17-22; twins and doubles $50; triples $63. 7th night free. VIP/YHA. Discounts for long-term stays. MC/V.

Original Backpackers, 160-162 Victoria St. (☎9356 3232; www.originalbackpackers.com.au). Wrap-around front porch, 2 kitchens, and dining area make for the most spacious hostel common area in the Cross. Cable TV, Internet ($2 per 15min.), a safe for valuables, and laundry ($4.40). Luggage storage free 1st day, $2 per day after. Every room has a TV and fridge and some boast baths, kitchens, and balconies at no extra cost. Linen $3, key deposit $20. Reception 24hr. Dorms $20, weekly $120; singles $35/$210; twins and doubles $50/$300. Discounts for long-term stays. MC/V.

Funk House Backpackers, 23 Darlinghurst Rd. (☎9358 6455 or 1800 247 600; www.funkhouse.com.au). Above Hungry Jack's; enter via Llankelly Pl., an alley off the main drag. A very young backpacker feel. Spray paint murals of Jimi Hendrix, Jim Morrison, and Ray Charles cover the doors and much of the walls. Free 15min. Internet and 3 free beers for all guests. Breakfast included with 3-day stay. All rooms have fans; doubles and twins have TV and fridge. Laundry $4. Reception daily 7am-10pm. 3- to 4-bed dorms $21, 3-day $60, weekly $120; twins $52/$150/$320. VIP.

Sydney Central Backpackers (☎9358 6600; fax 9356 3799; www.sydneycentralbackpackers.com.au), 16 Orwell St. Clean, spacious bedrooms and the cleanest baths in Kings Cross. The rooftop offers a BBQ, pool table, and gorgeous views of the city and opera house. Fridges in every room. Free pickup from airport or Central Station. Laundry $4. Key deposit $20, blanket deposit $10. Reception daily 8am-10pm. Dorm $20; twins and doubles $52. 7th night free. MC/V.

Eva's Backpackers, 6-8 Orwell St. (☎9358 2185; www.evasbackpackers.com.au). Cozy, homey feel, with tidy rooms and family management. Mesmerizing view. Daily security patrols. Free luggage storage. Laundry $6. Internet $2 per 30min. Key deposit $10. Book ahead. Reception daily 7am-2pm and 5-8pm. Bunks in 4- to 10-bed dorms $20; twins and doubles $50; triples $60. 7th night free. MC/V ($50 minimum charge).

Jolly Swagman Backpackers, 27 Orwell St. (☎9358 6400 or 1800 805 870; www.jollyswagman.com.au). Dorms get messy, but lounges and kitchens make up for it. Twins/doubles have TVs, fridges, and quilts. Offers everything: travel agency, bus trips to beaches, videos, Nintendo games, pub crawls, cafe (entrees from $6-7), and Internet ($2 per 1hr.). Free 24hr. pickup and luggage storage. Key deposit $20. Laundry $4. 24hr. reception. Check-out 9am. Dorms $20, weekly $120; doubles $52/$300. MC/V.

The Virgin Backpackers, 144 Victoria St. (☎9357 4733; fax 9357 4434). Not the latest Dirk Diggler cinema venture, but rather a swanky, tightly-knit hostel. The action-packed common room comes with jukebox, pool table, and free BBQ M and F. Internet cafe and travel desk downstairs. Continental breakfast included. Free airport or city pickup. Luggage storage $2. Laundry $4. Reception daily 8am-8pm. Dorms $20, weekly $119; twins $23/$139; doubles $49/$297. AmEx/MC/V.

Cooee Travellers Accomodation, 107-109 Darlinghurst St. (☎9331 0009 or 1800 200 793; www.cooeetravellers.com). Slightly cramped rooms and common spaces are balanced by excellent security and brand-new facilities. Internet $3 per hr. Free towels. Key deposit $30. Laundry $6. Dorm $22, with bath $25.30; twins $27.50/$29.70. MC/V.

Highfield Private Hotel, 166 Victoria St. (☎9326 9539; www.highfieldhotel.com). Ideal for less hectic, comfortable long-term stays. Pristine bathrooms, small kitchen and TV room, security-coded lock, and a safe for valuables. Linen $2.50. No laundry. Key deposit $10. Reception M-F 7:30am-9pm, Sa-Su 8am–8pm. 3-bed dorms $21, weekly $120; singles $40/$240; doubles $55/$330. MC/V.

Travellers Rest, 156 Victoria St. (☎9358 4606). This job-oriented hostel provides lists of potential employers. TV, fridge, sink, and phone in room. Laundry $2.80, key deposit $10. Check-out 9am. Reception daily 8am-noon and 4:30-6pm. Dorms $20, weekly $124; twins $45/$262; doubles $50/$288. No advance bookings or credit cards.

CITY CENTER AND NEAR CENTRAL STATION

These accommodations are conveniently located near the city center and main lines of transportation. Excluding the first three listings, nicer accommodation can generally be found in Kings Cross or Glebe.

Sydney Central YHA (☎9281 9111; fax 9281 9199; sydneycentral@yhansw.org.au), corner of Pitt St. and Rawson Pl. Visible from Central Station's Pitt St. exit. The mothership has landed. Pool, sauna, game room, employment and travel desks, TV rooms, Internet ($2 per 30min.), parking ($11 per night), multiple kitchens, arranged activities, bar and cafe, and more. Its size is both amazing and a little alienating. No sleeping bags allowed. Lockers $3, free linen, towels $1, laundry $4.40. No key deposit. 14-day max. stay. Reception 24hr. Check-in from noon. Dorms $24-29; twins $72, double with bath $80. Under 18 half-price. Non-YHA add $3. Wheelchair accessible. MC/V.

NOMADS Wanderers on Kent, 477 Kent St. (☎9267 7718 or 1800 424 444; fax 9267 7719; www.wanderersonkent.com.au), between Druitt and Bathurst St., a block from Town Hall. The best located hostel in the entire city, with short walks to Darling Harbour, the Rocks, and CBD nightlife. Swipe-card access to the elevator, rooms, and bathrooms, and the security cameras on every floor make it the most secure as well. Beautiful rooms with brand-new furniture. 320 beds and much more: tanning booth $3 per 3min., employment and travel desks, TV rooms, Internet $6 per hr., attached bar and cafe. No sleeping bags. Lockers $4-6 per day, linen deposit $20, laundry $4, key deposit $10. 28-day max. stay. Free airport shuttle with 2-night stay. Reception 24hr. Dorms $22-27.50; twins/doubles $34. NOMADS members $1 discount per night for most rooms, 7th night free. Wheelchair accessible. AmEx/MC/V.

Sydney Backpackers, 7 Wilmot St. (☎9267 7772 or 1800 887 766; fax 9267 2272 or 1800 014 411; www.sydneybackpackers.com.). Turn onto Wilmot off George St. at the Planet Hollywood restaurant. Incredibly large and clean dorms have satellite TV and fridge. Common spaces are cozy but never cramped. Rooftop BBQ, keycard room access, Internet $2 per 10min., laundry $4.40. Reception 6:30am-11pm. Dorm $25, weekly $159; double $84/$504. AmEx/DC/MC/V.

Y on the Park (YWCA), 5-11 Wentworth Ave. (☎9264 2451 or 1800 994 994; www.ywca-sydney.com.au), on the southeastern corner of Hyde Park; Wentworth Ave. is at the junction of Liverpool and Oxford St. More like barracks à la Martha Stewart—loads of carpeting, closet space, and pastels. Everything's sparkling and spacious. Women-only floor. A/C, heat, TVs, kitchen. Free short-term luggage storage. Laundry $4. Cheap Internet cafe $2 per 30min. (open daily 7am-7:30pm). Key deposit $20. Reception 24hr. Check-in from 1pm. 4-bed dorms $30; singles $70, with bath $108; twins $95/$132; doubles $85; triples $108/$142; family $118. 10% YWCA discount. Wheelchair accessible. AmEx/MC/V.

Hotel Bakpak Westend, 412 Pitt St. (☎9211 4588; www.hotelbakpak.com), near Haymarket. Balances its somewhat stark rooms with a great dining area and tons of organized activities including free yoga sessions and pub crawls. Laundry $6. Airport pickup and breakfast included. Lockers $2-5 per day. Reception 24hr. Dorms with bath $24-27, weekly $140-165, monthly $532; 'church' dorm (26 beds) $19/$133; twin with bath $69; double with bath $76-$82. MC/V.

Alfred Park Private Hotel, 207 Cleveland St. (☎9319 4031; fax 9318 1306), a 10min. walk south on Chalmers St. from Central Station, off Prince Alfred Park. Not in the best area of town. Former home of a sea captain with 14 children. All rooms available in the budget range feature TVs, fridges, fans, and armoires. Kitchen and courtyard eating area. Free pickup. Airport shuttle $6. Laundry $6. Key deposit $10. Reception daily 7:30am-11pm. Check-out 9am. Dorms $19-22, with TV, fridge, bath $27.50; singles $66, with bath $77; twins $88; doubles $99. Limited wheelchair access. MC/V.

GLEBE

To get to Glebe Point Rd, take bus #431, 432, 433, or 434 from the eastern side of George St. By car, follow George St. south towards Central Station until it feeds into Broadway, then turn right onto Glebe Point Rd. opposite Victoria Park.

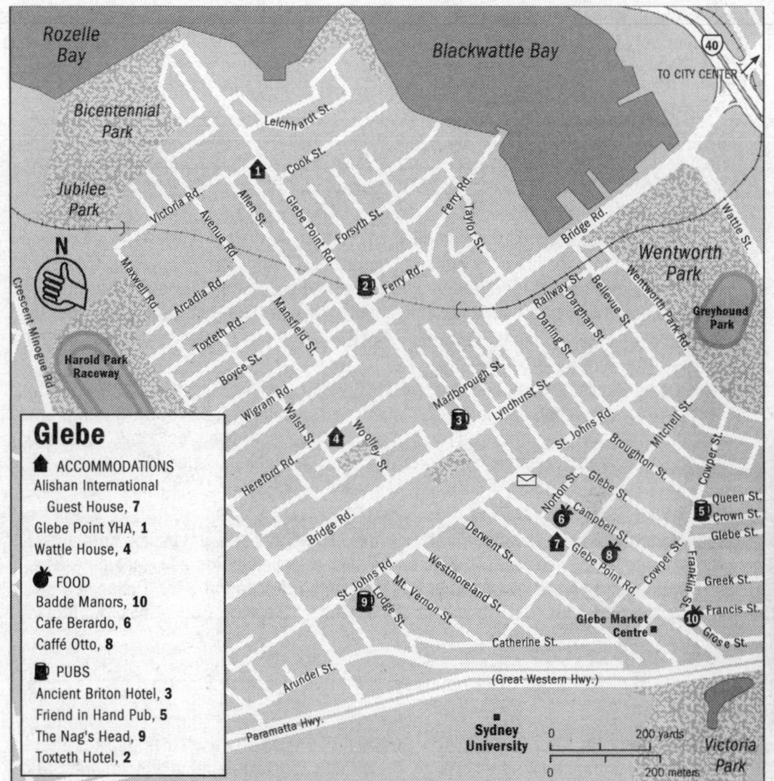

Wattle House, 44 Hereford St. (☎9552 4997; www.wattle house.com.au). A 5min. walk from Glebe Point Rd. A hostel with a B&B feel, this is Sydney's smallest—and one of its nicest—backpackers. Restored Victorian decor includes lace curtains, brick kitchen, and manicured garden. Plush bean bags fill the small TV room, where guests get acquainted over complimentary hot chocolate. Laundry $4. 2-week max. stay. Book way ahead. Reception M-F 9am-6pm, Sa-Su 10am-noon. 4-bed dorms from $25; doubles $60-70. Weekly rates available. MC/V.

Alishan International Guest House, 100 Glebe Point Rd. (☎9566 4048; www.alishan.com.au). Neat Victorian house features new rooms with TVs and fridges. The dorms are a bit less sparkling than the private rooms, but both are great values. Parking. Key deposit $10. Laundry $4. Reception daily 8am-10:30pm. Dorms $27-33; singles with bath $95; twins and doubles with bath $105; family room for 4 with bath $154, each extra person $16. Wheelchair accessible room available. AmEx/DC/MC/V.

Glebe Point YHA, 262-264 Glebe Point Rd. (☎9692 8418; fax 9660 0431; glebe@yhansw.org.au). Guests hang out on the roof for BBQs and in the subterranean lounge to play pool. Spacious kitchen and dining area. Sinks in rooms. Regular bus service to the airport and city center $10. No sleeping bags allowed. Luggage storage $2 per bag per week. Laundry $4.20. Key deposit $10. Internet $2 per 20min. Reception daily 7am-10:45pm. Dorms $22-26, weekly $150; twins and doubles $31. Non-YHA add $3.50. MC/V.

BONDI BEACH

Take bus #380, 382, or L82, which run from Circular Quay via Oxford St. or drive east along Oxford St. **CityRail** trains run to Bondi Junction, where a bus can be caught to the waterfront. Accommodations in Bondi are generally better than those in the CBD or the Cross.

Indy's Bondi Beach Backpackers, 35A Hall St. (☎9365 4900; www.indysbackpackers.com.au). 1½ blocks inland from Campbell Pde., set back from the street beyond the Commonwealth Bank. Extensive surfboard exchange program. Large screen TV, Nintendo 64, and video library. Free use of bikes, inline skates, wetsuits, and boards. Breakfast included. Laundry $4. Internet $2 per 30min. Key deposit $25. Reception daily 8am-10pm. Check-out 10am. A less social location is at 252 Campbell Pde. Book through main office. Free transfers to other locations in Surry Hills and Coogee. Large dorms $16.50-19, weekly $115.50-133; doubles at 252 Campbell Pde. $49 ($45 per night for 4-6 day stay), weekly $299. VIP. AmEx/MC/V.

The Biltmore Private Hotel, 110 Campbell Pde. (☎9130 4660; fax 9365 0195). As close as you can get to Bondi's waves without a houseboat. Comfy common room with big TV, kitchen, luggage storage, and free boogie board and scooter use. Laundry $4. Internet $2 per 20min. Key deposit $20. Reception daily 7:30am-10:30pm. Dorms $17, weekly $95; singles $36/$169; doubles $46/$249; beachfront doubles $55, in summer $300; triples $54/$285. MC/V.

Noah's Bondi Beach, 2 Campbell Pde. (☎9365 7100, reservations 1800 226 662; fax 9365 7644), up the hill on the beach's south end. It can get a bit rowdy. Rooftop balcony with BBQ and a great view. Free surf and boogie board use. Pool table, TV, $2-10 dinners in restaurant. Female-only dorm with bath available. Laundry $5. Key deposit $20. Dorms $21-24, weekly $126-144; twins and doubles $55/$350; beachside double $60/$380. VIP. AmEx/DC/V.

Bondi Beachside Inn, 152 Campbell Pde. (☎9130 5311; www.bondiinn.com.au). 7 stories of rooms over the beach; ideal for families or couples. Rooms have kitchenette, TV, balcony, and phone. No laundry. Key deposit $5. Reception 24hr. Oceanview singles and doubles $110-120, land-side $100. Wheelchair accessible. AmEx/DC/MC/V.

COOGEE BEACH

Take bus #373 or 374 from Circular Quay, #372 from Central Station, or #314 from Bondi Junction.

Surfside Backpackers, 186 Arden St. (☎9315 7888; www.surfsidebackpackers.com.au), entrance off street behind McDonald's; buzz to be let in. You couldn't ask for a better location. Balconies connecting the sunny rooms encourage socializing. The bigger dorms, especially the 16-bed dinosaur, are somewhat cramped, but that's par for the beachside hostels. Female-only dorm available. Laundry $4. Internet $2 per 30min. Key deposit $20. Reception M-F 8am-12:30pm and 5-8pm, Sa-Su 8:30am-12:30pm and 5-8pm. Check-out 9:30am. Dorms $20-23, weekly $110-140; doubles $50-52/$320. No doubles in summer. VIP. No credit cards.

Coogee Beach Wizard of Oz, 172 Coogee Bay Rd. (☎9315 7876 or 1800 013 460; www.wizardofoz.com.au), 1½ blocks from the center of the beach. Hardwood floors, fresh paint, and lots of open common space allow for relaxation and socializing with the Munchkins. Free Th BBQs in summer. Free pickup. No smoking. Laundry. Key deposit $20. Reception daily 8am-1pm and 5-8pm. Check-out 9:30am. Dorms $20, weekly $120; doubles $55/$300. VIP. MC/V.

Aegean Coogee Bay Road Backpackers, 40 Coogee Bay Rd (☎9314 5324; www.pip.com.au/aegean). A 10min. walk inland. A bit crowded, but with a relaxed communal feel. Brims with amenities: 6 full kitchens, heated outdoor pool, sauna, rooftop balcony, and BBQ. No smoking or alcohol. Luggage storage $2-3. Linen $2 in summer. Laundry. Internet $2 per 20min. Key deposit $20. Reception daily 8am-10pm, in winter 8am-noon and 5-10pm. Check-in 24hr. Dorms in winter $80, summer $120; doubles from $50-70. Wheelchair accessible. AmEx/DC/MC/V with a $3 surcharge.

MANLY

To get to Manly from Circular Quay, take the **ferry** (25min.; M-F 6am-7pm, Sa-Su 8am-7:30pm; $10.60 return) or **Jetcat** (15min; M-Sa 6am-midnight, Su 7:15am-11pm; $13.20 return, $10 when ferry is not operating). See **Local Transportation,** p. 101.

Manly Beach Resort, 6 Carlton St. (☎9977 4188; fax 9977 0524; www.manlyview.com.au). From the ferry, walk 10min. down Belgrave St., which becomes Pittwater

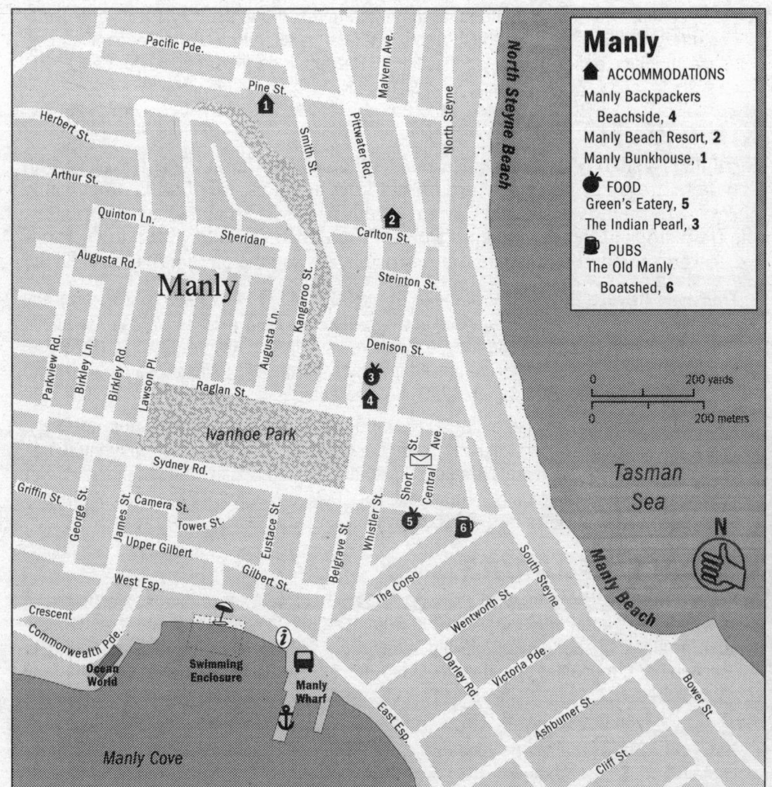

St., and turn right onto Carlton St. A nicer-than-budget accommodation that also has backpackers dorms and apartments. Free pickup from the wharf 9am-noon. Heated pool, TV room, laundry. Key deposit $20. Reception 24hr. All rooms have bath. Dorms $20; doubles $50, weekly $315. VIP. Motel rooms: singles $100; twins $115; 10% off weekly stays. Advance motel room bookings require $100 deposit. AmEx/DC/MC/V.

Manly Backpackers Beachside, 28 Raglan St. (☎9977 3411; www.manlybackpackers.com.au). From the ferry, cross the Esplanade to Belgrave St., which becomes Pittwater St., and turn right onto Raglan St. Despite the blank, narrow hallways, the hostel manages to have an open, friendly atmosphere and cozy dorms. Enormous TV room with skylights. Safe at reception; small lockers not in rooms. Free body boards and Su BBQs. Laundry $4. Key deposit $30. Max. stay 2 weeks. Reception M-F 9am-7pm, Sa-Su 9am-6pm. Dorms $22, weekly $105-147; twins and doubles $50-70. VIP. MC/V.

Manly Bunkhouse, 35 Pine St. (☎9976 0472 or 1800 657 122; www.bunkhouse.com.au). From the ferry, cross the Esplanade to Belgrave St., which becomes Pittwater St., then turn left onto Pine St. (10min.). This small and quiet hostel is one of the best-kept in Manly; each 4-bed dorm has its own kitchenette, bathroom, TV, heater, lockers, and closet space. Free wharf pickup. Key deposit $20. Dorms $20, weekly $100; twins $50/$300. Wheelchair accessible. VIP.

COLLAROY

To get to Collaroy, take bus #L90, L88, or any of the Northern Beach expresses which originate at Wynyard Station (Carrington St. side), or take the ferry to Manly and catch buses #151, 155, or 156.

Sydney Beachouse/Collaroy Beach YHA, 4 Collaroy St., Collaroy (☎9981 1177; www.sydneybeachouse.com.au). A chic contemporary house 100m from the water, with tons of activities (free didgeridoo lessons) and free surf boards, snorkeling gear, skateboards, and bikes. Buses to bush walks, national parks, and to Palm Beach. Free Luggage storage. Laundry $4. Key deposit $20. Reception daily 8am-9pm. Dorms $24-25, weekly $140-147; family rooms for 5 $104. MC/V.

KIRRIBILLI

Kirribilli is a slightly upscale, quiet, residential neighborhood. Most travelers who stay here are older and many are on working holidays. Kirribilli is most easily accessed by taking the Neutral Bay ferry from Wharf 4, Circular Quay. Alternately, the train stops at nearby Milson's Point. From Milson's Point, walk down Ennis Rd. towards the harbor, turn left onto Kirribilli St., and then left onto Carabella St.

Tremayne Private Hotel, 89 Carabella St. (☎9955 4155; fax 9922 5228), from the Neutral Bay ferry, walk up Holbrook St., turn right and take a 5min. walk up Carabella St. Rooms with balconies and fridges. Kitchen. Laundry $5. Key deposit $10. Breakfast and M-F dinner included. Reception 8am-10pm. Dorms $20; singles $170, with bath $220; twins and doubles $260/$280. No credit cards.

Glenferrie Lodge, 12A Carabella St. (☎9955 1685; fax 9929 9439), from the ferry, walk up Holbrook St., and take a left onto Carabella St. A stately house with ample balcony space and a courtyard. Breakfast included. TV hire weekly $20. Laundry $4. Key deposit $50. Reception daily 24hr. Check-out 10:30am. Dorms $25, weekly $145; singles $35/$170; doubles $55/$290. MC/V.

NEW SOUTH WALES

UPSCALE BARGAINS

Russell Hotel, 143A George St., The Rocks (☎9241 3543; www.therussell.com.au). A small, inviting hotel with exquisitely-furnished, brightly painted rooms and a rooftop garden overlooking The Rocks. Relaxing sitting room with bar is well-suited for reading or socializing. Continental breakfast included. Reception daily 6am-10pm. Check-in from 1pm. Check-out 11am. Singles $115-165, with bath $200-245; doubles $130-180/ $215-260; suite or studio $285. Extra person $15. Not wheelchair accessible.

Hotel 59, 59 Bayswater Rd., Kings Cross (☎9360 5900; www.interspace.net.au/inns/hotel59.html). A brothel less than a decade ago, Hotel 59 is still a fantastic deal for your dollar; it now offers 8 thoughtfully-arranged family rooms with TV and bath. Full breakfast included. Reception daily 7:30am-6pm. Check-out 11am. Rooms $90-135. Extra adult $15, child $10. MC/V.

Manly Lodge, 22 Victoria Pde., Manly (☎9977 8655; fax 9976 2090). Luxurious rooms with bath are a steal for families or couples. A/C, TV, VCR, and fridge; some have hot tubs and kitchens. Communal sauna, spa, gym, laundry $6. Breakfast included. Twins from $120-159; doubles $110-144; deluxe $130-168. Extra person $35, children under 10 $20. For Sa only bookings, rates increase $30. Lower weekly rates in winter.

Wattle Private Hotel, 108 Oxford St., Darlinghurst (☎9332 4118; www.wsydneyhotel.com), on the corner of Palmer St. Cozy and elegant rooms with TV and fridge, some with balcony and extensive furniture. Reception daily 8am-8pm. Singles $88; twins $110; doubles $99. Studio $350 weekly. Extra person $10. MC/V.

FOOD

Sydney's streets overflow with eateries of every flavor for any budget. Asian options, most notably Thai and Chinese cuisine, rank highly among the international selections. The Central Business District is rife with quick lunch stops for the professional masses still dreaming of three-martini lunch status. Sandwiches, meat pies, and focaccias run $2.50-6 at sandwich counters throughout these blocks. Slightly south, the feeding frenzy of **Chinatown** lurks west of Central Station, around Hay St., Little Hay St., and the Dixon St. Plaza. Just east of the center, the Oxford St. social artery runs between Surry Hills in the south (where many of the city's best **Thai** kitchens line up on Crown St.), and the (very) **Little Italy** on Stanley St., between Crown and Riley St., in Darlinghurst. Cafes in Little Italy serve excellent **coffee** and hearty hot sandwiches. Continuing east through Darlinghurst, the strip of restaurants on Oxford St. near St. Vincent's Hospital (at Victoria St.) is known for a quality variety of **Asian** and **European flavors.** Victoria St. runs north from Oxford at the hospital into **the land of high cappuccino chic** before depositing the last of its cafe class amidst the hostels of Kings Cross. In the Cross, Darlinghurst Rd. and Bayswater Rd. offer fare abiding by the local atmosphere of **late-night cheap bites** and fast-food chains.

As usual, a large student population means good, **cheap cafes** and restaurants on both Glebe Point Rd. in Glebe and Kings St. in Newtown. Blues Point Rd. on McMahons Point and Fitzroy St. in Kirribilli lead the North Shore's attempts at affordability with style, featuring several cafes well-loved by the locals. **Breakfast** is big on the beachfront drives of Manly, Bondi, and Coogee. At most coastal cafes, $6-7 buys a large cooked breakfast and an excuse to appreciate the view over the morning paper. Manly offers even less expensive food counters along the Corso. Though the neighborhoods vary in their offerings, none disappoint.

KINGS CROSS

Govinda's, 112 Darlinghurst Rd. (☎9380 5155). A unique, can't-miss restaurant and cinema. $16 covers a mostly Indian, wholly vegetarian, all-you-can-eat buffet, and a current movie in the upstairs theater, which features cushy, reclining sofas for total viewing bliss or dark room flirtation. Open daily 6-10:30pm. AmEx/MC/V.

Café de Marie, 166 Victoria St. (☎9358 2343). Squeeze into this tiny 20-seat cafe for its famous French toast ($7). Sandwiches $6-7. Open daily 9am-3pm, M-Sa 6pm-9:30pm. No credit cards.

Paper Box Thai Noodle Bar, 274 Victoria St. (☎9356 2373). Construct your own heaping pan-Asian dish by choosing noodles, sauces, soups, vegetables, and meats ($9-13). The grilled satays are a filling snack ($2.50-$3.50). Open daily noon-3:30pm and 5-10:30pm. No credit cards.

Krave, 37 Darlinghurst St. (☎9358 6436). Breakfast ($5) and pasta specials ($6.90) make this 24hr. diner an affordable stop for dinner or a post-partying recharge. Open daily. BYO. No credit cards.

Harry's Café de Wheels, Cowper Wharf Roadway, Woolloomooloo (☎9357 3074). Northeast of the Cross in a stand near the Navy shipyard. Open for a late-night post-party pastie. Meat pie and peas from $4. Open Su-Th 7am-2am, F-Sa 7am-4am.

CITY CENTER

Dixon Street Food Courts, Chinatown. The **Dixon House Food Court,** 80 Dixon St. (Downstairs, on the corner of Little Hay St.), boasts cheap Asian meals. Meals $6-10. Open daily 10:30am-8:30pm. The **Harbour Plaza Food Court,** at the corner of Dixon and Goulburn St., is more chaotic, but slightly cheaper: several restaurants offer hearty $5 meals. Open daily 10am-10pm. No credit cards.

Zenbu, 31 Wheat Rd., Darling Harbour, IMAX Complex (☎9211 9888). The menu of Japanese fusion cuisine, the "usual in an unusual way," includes tasty saki-tails ($8.50-$9) and an extensive sushi bar. Mains like the tuna with green tea noodles run $15-20, but that includes complementary 5min. head and neck massages given right at your table. Open daily 11:30am-1am, Th-Sa until 2am. AmEx/DC/MC/V.

Soup Plus, 383 George St., CBD (☎9299 7728). With a $25 cover on F-Sa nights, this smoky jazz bar is an expensive dinner option, but the value-per-dollar is unbeatable. The price covers entertainment and a 2-course dinner; entrees include *mousaka*, lasagna, and stuffed pumpkin, $5 cover M-Th from 7:30pm.

Sydney Fish Markets, Bank St., Pyrmont (☎9552 2180; www.sydneyfishmarket.com.au). Catch the light rail from Central Station or Haymarket. Where Sydney restaurants and locals get the catch of the day, including oysters (1 dozen $6.50-$10.50) and sashimi. Good fish'n'chips start around $6. Open daily 7am. AmEx/MC/V.

Blackbird Cafe, Balcony Level, Cockle Bay Wharf (☎9283 7385). Very trendy eatery with a great view of Darling Harbour. Coffee, cakes, and a wide variety of alcohol with an ambiance posh enough to justify the price. Board games, comfy leather couches, outside heaters, and books make for an unbeatable lounging atmosphere. Open daily 8am-1am. AmEx/DC/MC/V.

Spanish Terrazas, 541 Kent St. (☎9283 3046). Affordable tapas ($6-9) and paella ($32-$35 for 2) in the pricey Spanish Quarter. Wash it all down with a pitcher of sangria while you enjoy the live Latin music. Open M-Sa lunch 11:30am-3:30pm, dinner M-Th 5:30pm-10pm, F-Sa 5:30pm-midnight. AmEx/DC/MC/V.

Chinta Ria—Temple of Love, Roof Terrace, Cockle Bay Wharf (☎9264 3211). A fantastic spot for soaking in the trendy wharf neighborhood amongst stunning Malaysian decor. Yummy, if pricey, Malaysian fare from $14-20. Live music outside Tu. Open daily noon-2:30pm and 6-11pm (10:30pm on Su). No reservations. AmEx/DC/MC/V.

Mama's Kitchen, 57 Liverpool St. (☎9264 5841). Not only is there a jukebox and diner booths, but this is one of the truly inexpensive places downtown to get a filling pasta dish ($4-9). Open daily noon-11:30pm. AmEx/MC/V.

Sushi King, 396B George St. (☎9233 3272). CBD food courts are filled with sushi stands offering sizable rolls for $1.60, but this place is open later and has late-day discounts. Open 8am-8:30pm. No credit cards.

Genghis Khan, 469 Kent St. (☎9264 3863). Diners crowd around the central grill to watch the chef cook their self-selected Mongolian BBQ. 1-serve lunch $9.20, dinner $13; all-you-can-eat $15.20/$18.20. Open M-F noon-3pm, Su-W 6pm-10pm, Th-Sa 6pm-10:30pm. AmEx/DC/MC/V.

GLEBE

Glebe could be called Sydney's restaurant district.

Caffé Berardo, 119 Glebe Point Rd. (☎9518 4443; www.berardocaffe.com). The world's only distributor of a delectable Roman wood-fired 'Berardo' roast. A cozy, funky place to kick back with a cuppa. Live music and spoken word F night, Sa DJ. Open Tu-Sa 8am-6pm, Su 9:30am-5pm. No credit cards.

Pho Glebe, 97 Glebe Point Rd. (☎9660 3888). Beautiful rock pool with live goldfish and blue-tiled chairs and tables. $7.50 lunch specials and entrees from $12. Open daily 6-10:30pm, Sa-Su noon-3:30pm. No credit cards.

Badde Manors, 37 Glebe Point Rd. (☎9660 3797). World music plays in the background as the scent of freshly ground coffee permeates the air in this vegetarian cafe. Gourmet coffee, fresh sorbet, and smoothies. Tofu or Lentil burger $8.50. Open M-F 7:30am-midnight, Sa 8am-1am, Su 9am-midnight. No credit cards.

Cafe Otto, 79 Glebe Point Rd. (☎9552 1519). High-ceilinged diner with an insulated outdoor courtyard, serving everything from popular pastas ($12-18) and pizza ($12-16) to pricier meat dishes. Separate kids menu. For dessert, try the local fave: sticky date pudding ($8.50). Open Su-Th 9am-11pm, F-Sa 9am-midnight. BYO. AmEx/MC/V.

NEWTOWN

King St. bisects Newtown and provides backpacker style cheap eats, from Indian takeaways and Thai restaurants to filling breakfast deals. Newtown is a very young and bohemian place—cheap and tasty options are endless. It's the new hot place for backpackers.

Tamana's North Indian Diner, 196 King St. (☎9519 2035) with smaller location at 236 King St. It's rare to find a fast-food joint with such a faithful following. Tamana's keeps local favor with its generous curry portions for under $7 and a wide variety of dishes labeled with degrees of spiciness. Open daily 11:30am-10:30pm. No credit cards.

Simply Thai, 186 King St. (☎9565 5111). A merely typical King St. ethnic option as far as atmosphere is concerned—but the food is very cheap and very fresh. $6 lunch special. Open Th-Su noon-3pm, Su-Th 5-10pm, F-Sa 6-11pm. DC/MC/V.

Kilimanjaro African Eatery, 280 King St. (☎9557 4565). Re-creates the flavors of several African nations with meals cooked in glazed clay pots and served in a simple dark-wood setting. Lots of couscous dishes. Filling entrees from $10. Appetizers and sides $6. Open daily noon-late. BYO.

COFFEE CONFUSION Just after arriving in Australia, sleepy-eyed and weary from your travels, you stumble into a coffee lounge in great need of a nice, big cup of coffee. Only trouble is, upon ordering, you're asked what kind. "Flat white?" the barista queries, and you stare back, blankly, quite confused and a bit anxious for that dose of caffeine. Don't panic—there are a few things you should know. Perhaps most importantly, coffee drinks are all made with espresso, as opposed to the automatic-drip style brewing machines. This means that if you drink it black, it tastes quite a bit stronger. The most common drinks are: **short black** (about 60ml of espresso); **long black** (120-200ml espresso); and **flat white** (espresso with cold milk). Then there are the fancier, but more commonly known, espresso drinks: café latte (espresso, hot milk, and froth); cappuccino (espresso, hot milk, and heaps of froth); macchiato (espresso with a bit of froth); and vienna coffee (espresso, whipped cream, and powdered chocolate). Any of these drinks can be made weak, medium, or strong. And you'll get whole milk unless you ask for something different, like cream or lowfat milk (referred to as "skinny,"). Though coffee may not be Australia's specialty (to put it mildly), there are some deliciously caffeinated drinks. So go out there, hold your head high, and order yourself a flat white that's strong and skinny.

Pizza Picasso, 503 King St. (☎9557 7700). These "pizza artists" create with funky ingredients like smoked salmon, chili chicken and baby corn, and much more. Medium pizzas ($9-16) easily feed 2 people. Open M-Sa 5-10:45pm, Su 5-9:45pm. MC/V.

Happy Chef, 264 King St. (☎9550 3423). One of the best Chinese take-aways; from $6. Open M-Th 11am-10pm, F-Sa 11am-11pm, Su 11:30am-10pm. AmEx/MC/V.

DARLINGHURST AND PADDINGTON

Oxford St. addresses start at the street's origin on Hyde Park, but confusingly begin again once the street runs southeast from Darlinghurst into Paddington at the intersection with Victoria and Dowling St. Noting whether an address is in Darlinghurst or Paddington is the easiest way to locate an Oxford St. property.

Una's, 340 Victoria St. (☎9360 0885). Austrian food in a delightful wood and brick enclave. The locals have been coming here for over thirty years. Try the strawberry pancakes for a great breakfast. Vienna schnitzel ($12.50) and bratwurst ($10.90). Open daily 7:30am-10:30pm. Licensed and BYO $1.50. No credit cards.

Chocolate by the Bald Man, 447 Oxford St., Paddington (☎9357 5055). Enough chocolate to overwhelm the most diehard cacao bean fanatic, from ice cream to whole beans. Try the hot chocolate ($3.80) with a pastry or fudge ($6-10). Popular strawberry fondue plate $6.50. Open M-F 10am-6pm, Sa-Su until 6:30pm. AmEx/Mc/V.

Bill & Toni's Restaurant, 74 Stanley St. E. Sydney (☎9360 4702). Heaping 1st courses of pasta only $7.50. For the hungrier, mains including schnitzel, casseroles, and veal are $11 and a full meal is $17. Free bread and orange punch complete the feast. Open daily noon-2:30pm and 6pm-10:30pm. BYO. No credit cards.

Micky's Cafe, 268 Oxford St., Paddington (☎9361 5157). Every combination under the sun: stirfry, burgers, burritos, cheesecakes, pasta, risotto, chicken satay, and Caesar salad. Meals from $10-16. Open daily 9am-midnight, F-Sa until 1am. MC/V.

Arthur's Pizza, 260 Oxford St., Paddington (☎9331 1779). In a city with surprisingly few good pizza options, Arthur's hits the spot with gourmet options like lamb and marinated chicken. Be prepared for waits of 1hr. or more in peak hours. Pizzas from $12-20, family size $26. Open daily 5-10pm, also F-Sa noon-3pm. AmEx/MC/V.

Burgerman, 116 Surrey St., Paddington (☎9361 0268), off Victoria St., near Willam St. Also at 249 Bondi Rd. (☎9130 4888). A 70s-style American burger joint with a metallic-techno-hip identity crisis. For an Aussie treat, get a burger with beetroot ($7). Open daily noon-10pm. Licensed and BYO $4 corkage.

Green Chillies, 113-115 Oxford St., Darlinghurst (☎9361 3717). Despite the address, the entrance is around the corner on Crown St. Traditional Thai dishes with far more style than you pay for. Entrees $11-15. $6.50 takeaway lunch specials Tu-F. Open Tu-F noon-3:30pm and daily 6-10:30pm. Licensed and BYO, corkage $2 per person. MC/V.

SURRY HILLS

Uchi Lounge, 15 Brisbane St. (☎9261 3524). A reasonably-priced place for a night of self-indulgence. Japanese fusion menu with speciality items like chrysanthemum sushi and grilled eggplant parmesan. Entrees $12-16. Open M-Sa 6:30-11pm. MC/V.

Prasits Northside Thai Take Away, 395 Crown St. (☎9332 1792). Several blocks south of Oxford St., near Fitzroy St. Fresh, creative, dishes such as the flavorful green peppercorn stir-fry ($12). Tasty spring rolls ($2). Limited seating. Open Tu-Su noon-3pm and 5:30-10pm. AmEx/MC/V.

Mehrey Da Dhaba Indian Street Restaurant, 466 Cleveland St. (☎9319 6260). The Dhaba brings a tradition of inexpensive, and filling food across the ocean without losing any of the flavor. Whole tandoori chicken $9.50. Vegetarian meals from $6-10; meat dishes $10-13. *Naan* or *roti* $1.20. Open Su-Tu 5:30-11pm, W-F noon-3pm and 5:30-11pm, F noon-3pm and 5:50pm-midnight, Sa noon-midnight. BYO. No credit cards.

BONDI BEACH

Bondi Tratt, 34b Campbell Pde. (☎9365 4303). Mostly Italian with occasional mod-Oz twists. Try some kangaroo, if you dare. Hey, it's supposed to be low-fat, if chewy. Entrees from $12.50. Open daily 7am-11pm. BYO. AmEx/MC/V.

Gabby's Cafe, 94 Campbell Pde. (☎9130 3788). Gabby's has served its all-day filling breakfasts ($7) for more than 20 years. Open daily 7am-5pm. No credit cards.

Flavour of North India, 138 Campbell Pde. (☎9365 6239). Warm and ready curries $6-8. Fresh *naan* ($1.50-2) tempers the spicier options. Open daily noon-10:30pm, until 11:30pm on weekends. MC/V.

COOGEE BEACH

Coogee Bay Hotel (☎9665 0000), corner of Coogee Bay Rd. and Arden St. An entertainment complex with a full-size concert hall, 3 bars, and a restaurant. Cook your own juicy T-bone or chicken breast for $14.50, with salad and roll. $6 kids chicken nuggets or fish'n'chips. Open daily noon-3pm and 6-9:30pm, Su until 9pm. AmEx/DC/MC/V.

Barzura (☎9665 5546), at the end of Carr St. at the south end of the beach, a 2min. walk from Coogee central. Outdoor seating. Breakfast until 1pm ($8-10), modern Australian entrees $16-20. Open daily 7am-11pm. Licensed and BYO wine only (corkage $2.50 per person). AmEx/MC/V.

MANLY

Cheap cafes, takeaways, and American imperialist fast-food chains colorfully line the Corso, which connects the harbor to the Pacific, while more expensive, image-conscious cafes can be found on Steyne St. running parallel to the ocean.

Green's Eatery, 1-3 Sydney Rd. (☎9977 1904). On the pedestrian stretch of Sydney Rd. near the ocean side of the Corso. Sunny, vegetarian cafe serves amazingly hearty meals, with rice and interesting vegetable combos for $4-7. Try the chick pea casserole or the sauteed vegetables with tofu. Open daily 8am-6:30pm. No credit cards.

The Indian Pearl, 26-28 Pittwater Rd. (☎9977 2890). North of the town center. Savory curry and tandoori dishes include chicken, lamb, and beef dishes from $13. Tandoori chicken entree for just $9.90. Takeaway $2 cheaper. Open daily 5:30-11pm. BYO wine only. Free delivery. AmEx/DC/MC/V.

SIGHTS

Sydney's sights range from architectural landmarks to beaches, from museum tours to neighborhood strolls. Because of the city center's manageable size, most cultural attractions could be seen in less than a week of serious sightseeing. However, while many of Sydney's neighborhoods do not have specific "sights" per se, their attraction lies in their tasty cafes, off-beat stores, and local nooks and crannies. There's architecture to appreciate in Paddington, markets to rummage through in Glebe and Newtown, and tanned and toned beach action on Bondi and

Coogee. Find adrenaline-fixes and pulse-quickeners in **Activities** (p. 122) and the best spots for retail-therapy in **Shopping and Markets** (p. 127).

THE ROCKS AND CIRCULAR QUAY

At the base of the bridge, The Rocks is the site of the original Sydney Town settlement. Built during the lean years of the colony's founding, the area remained quite rough-and-tumble well the 1900s. In the 70s, when plans to raze the slums were revealed, a movement to preserve the historic area began. Today, The Rocks bustles with tourists wandering from charming cafes to historical storefronts. Street performers and live bands liven-up the The Rocks Market (every Sa-Su; see **Shopping,** p. 127). **Sydney Visitors Centre** and the **Rocks Walking Co.** share the white, three-story Sailors' Home at 106 George St. The former has info on local attractions and displays on the history of the Rocks, and the latter conducts informative walking tours of The Rocks. (Visitors Centre: ☎9255 1788 or 1800 067 676. Open daily 9am-6pm. Walking Co.: ☎9247 6678. 90min. tours depart M-F 10:30am, 12:30, and 2:30pm; Sa-Su 11:30am and 2pm. $16, ages 10-16 and seniors $10.70, under 10 free.)

SYDNEY OPERA HOUSE. Standing like a fleet of sailboats full of wind, the Sydney Opera House defines the city skyline. Designed by Danish architect Jørn Utzon, Sydney's pride and joy took 14 years to construct. A saga of bureaucracy and broken budgets (planned at $7 million, the building cost $102 million by the time it was finished) plagued the construction and eventually led the architect to leave the project. In 1973, Queen Elizabeth opened the building, despite strong winds, a false fire alarm, and 1400 spectator seats initially set up facing the wrong way. The Opera House has recovered from a rocky start by starring in thousands of tourist photographs daily and hosting operas, ballets, classical concerts, plays, and films; the Opera House has come to symbolize Sydney itself. *(On Bennelong Point, opposite the base of the Harbour Bridge. ☎9250 7250; www.soh.nsw.gov.au. For box office info, see* ***Entertainment,*** p. 125. *At least 1 45min. tour every hour (up to every 15min.) daily 8:30am-5pm. $15.40, concessions $10.60, family $41.45.)*

SYDNEY HARBOUR BRIDGE. Spanning the harbor, the arching steel latticework of the massive Harbour Bridge has been a visual symbol of the city since its opening in 1932. It is the best place to get a look at the Harbour and the cityscape. Pedestrians can enter the bridge walkway from a set of stairs on Cumberland St. just south of Argyle St. in The Rocks. At the bridge's southern pylon, there is an entry on the walkway which leads up to solid photo-ops. **The Harbour Bridge Museum** inside the pylon tells the baffling story of the bridge's construction. *(☎9247 7833 for more info. Open daily 10am-5pm. Admission to lookout and museum $5, child 4-12 $3, family $12.)* For high adventure, **Bridgeclimb** will take you up to the apex for a gut-wrenching view of the city and Harbour. Only mildly strenuous and hyper-safe, this has maximum bragging potential with minimum stress—though it will noticeably lighten your wallet. *(☎8274 7777. Open daily 7am-4:30pm, 3hr. climbs leave every 10min. DayClimbs M-F $125, age 12-16 $100; Sa-Su $150/$125. NightClimbs M-F $150/$125; Sa-Su $170/$150.)*

CIRCULAR QUAY. Of course it's pronounced "key." How else would you say it? Between Dawes Point and Bennelong Point is the departure point for both the city ferry system and numerous private cruise companies. The Quay becomes a lively hub of tourist activity on weekends, with street performers, souvenir shops, and easy access to many major sights. It's also a prime place for those sun-worshippers who find the concrete jungle of the CBD blocks their rays.

SYDNEY OBSERVATORY. This huge sandstone building atop Observatory Hill caters to the starry-eyed. Guided tours of the heavens (through the telescopes) take place nightly, with an earlier session during the winter season of early sunsets. In the daytime, the observatory is a museum of astronomy with displays, films, talks, and simulated skyscapes. *(On Miller's Point, a quick walk west of George St. via Argyle St. ☎9217 0485; www.phm.gov.au. Open daily 10am-5pm. Museum free. Evening Tours $10, concessions $5, families $25; book ahead. Wheelchair access via Cumberland St.)*

MUSEUM OF CONTEMPORARY ART. Injecting a little modernity into an area largely absorbed with its past, the smallish museum is a playground for an uber-hip artsy crowd. The extensive collection of Aboriginal work is worthwhile. *(140 George St. ☎9252 4033, recorded info 9241 5865; www.mca.com.au. Open daily 10am-5pm. Free guided tours M-F 11am and 2pm. Free.)*

MUSEUM OF SYDNEY. Even history has succumbed to the technology age. Located in the site of the first Government house, this new and stylish museum celebrates the city's past through films and high-tech multimedia and interactive exhibits. *(37 Phillip St., corner of Bridge St. ☎9251 5988; www.mos.nsw.gov.au. Open daily 9:30am-5pm. $7, concessions $3, families $17.)*

ROYAL BOTANIC GARDENS. All of the city center's greenery is concentrated in charmingly landscaped plants, flowers, and trees filling 30 hectares around Farm Cove. Not for the heartsick—couples shamelessly lounge everywhere. Within the gardens, attractions such as the Aboriginal plant trail and the formal rose garden are free, but the **Tropical House** greenhouses charge admission. *(Open daily 10am-4pm. $2.20, concessions $1.10, family $5.50.)* **Government House,** in the northwest corner of the Gardens, served as the home of the governor of New South Wales as recently as 1996. *(☎9931 5222. Grounds open daily 10am-4pm; house tours F-Su 10:30am-3pm every 30min. Free.)* On the eastern headland of Farm Cove, the Botanic Gardens end at **Mrs. Macquaries chair.** The chair, carved from the stone at the point, was fashioned for the wife of Governor Lachlan Macquarie and is now a classic Sydney photo-op. Daily guided walks begin at a visitors center, located in the southeast corner of the park near Art Gallery Rd. *(Gardens open sunrise to sunset. Free. Visitors Centre: ☎9231 8125. Open daily 9:30am-4:30pm. 2hr. guided walks daily 10:30am.)*

THE HARBOUR

The **Sydney Harbour National Park** preserves four harbor islands, several south shore beaches, a few green patches on the northern headlands, and North and South Head. Float around the waterways on **Captain Cook Cruises.** (☎9206 1111; www.captaincook.com.au. More than 20 departures per day from 9:30am. Departs from Circular Quay.) Guided visits to the Harbour islands themselves must be booked ahead through the **National Park Information Centre,** 110 George St., The Rocks, in **Cadman's Cottage**. (☎9247 5033. Open M-F 9am-4:30pm, Sa-Su 10am-4:30pm. Tours depart from the Cottage.) **The Heritage Tour** focuses on history (M, F-Su 12:30pm; $20, concessions $15.40). **The Water Rats** tour visits the sets of the popular TV show (M, F-Su 11:45am; $20, concessions $15.40). **The Gruesome Tales Tour** focuses on the grisly aspects of convict history (Sa 5:45pm, daylight savings 6:45pm; $24; unsuitable for children).

ISLANDS. The early colony's most troublesome convicts were once isolated on Pinchgut Island, off Mrs. Macquaries Point. The name came from the habit of punishing unruly convicts by isolating them on the exposed rock with a diet consisting of only bread and water. The island was later renamed **Fort Denison** for the fort that was built to protect the city from a feared Russian invasion. On **Goat Island,** west of the city center, near the shore at Balmain, the sandstone gunpowder station and barracks were the site of cruel punishments for the convicts who built them.

BEACHES. The park's south shore beaches—**Nielson Park, Camp Cove,** and the nude beach **Lady Jane**–are situated on Vaucluse Bay, accessible by bus #325, which runs to Watsons Bay. Popular North Shore Harbour beaches include **Balmoral Beach,** on the north side of Middle Head, a 15min. walk from Military Rd.; **Chinaman's Beach,** north of Balmoral, a 7min. walk from Spit Rd.; and **Manly Cove,** at the Manly Wharf ferry port. To get to Balmoral Beach, take bus #244 to Balmoral. To get to Manly, take a ferry or Jetcat; or bus #143 or 144 from Spit Junction. Up the coast from Manly are **Freshwater, Coogee,** and **Narrabeen**—all of which are less commercial and less crowded.

CITY CENTER AND THE DOMAIN

SYDNEY CENTREPOINT TOWER. Rising 325m above sea level (and containing four floors of shopping mall), the tower affords a stunning panoramic view of the city and surroundings. The 40-second ride to the top of Australia's highest building is steep in grade and price, so don't waste the trip on a cloudy day. When the sky is clear, views extend as far as the Blue Mountains to the west, the New South Wales central coast to the north, and Wollongong to the south. Sydney Tower Restaurants, the city's only revolving restaurants, spin on the second-highest floor. *Let's Go* does not recommend looking down from the top after eating—it could get messy. *(100 Market St. ☎9229 7444; www.sydneyskytour.com.au. Open Su-F 9am-10:30pm, Sa 9am-11:30pm. $20, concessions $16, families $55. Restaurant reservations ☎8223 3800. Buffet lunch $39.50, dinner $47.50. Fixed price menu also available.)*

TOWN HALL. Sydney's age insures that architecture in the center is far from uniformly modern. The French Renaissance-style Town Hall was built in the prosperity of the late 1800s; the building's ostentation merits at least a passing look. The wood-lined concert hall fields an 8000-pipe organ; free recitals are held periodically. *(483 George St. ☎9265 9007. Open daily 9am-5pm. Free admission. Tours with Centrepoint Touring Company ☎8223 3815.)*

QUEEN VICTORIA BUILDING. The imposing statue of Queen Victoria, visible from the north corner of Town Hall, guards the entrance to its namesake's lavish building. The Byzantine edifice was constructed in 1898 as a home for the plebeian city markets, but recent renovations have brought in ritzier shopping venues. Fortunately, a stroll in the fantastic wood and brass interior still doesn't cost a cent. *(455 George St. ☎9264 9209; www.qvb.com.au. Open M-Sa 9am-6pm, Su 11am-5pm.)*

SYDNEY HOSPITAL AND NEW SOUTH WALES PARLIAMENT HOUSE. The 1814 hospital building is a landmark of colonial architecture. In 1854, with new wealth coming in from the recent gold rush, Sydney Hospital's south wing became a branch of the Royal Mint. The central section of the building is still Sydney's main medical facility, while the **NSW Parliament House** occupies the north wing. Visitors are welcome in the building, with access to public viewing galleries during parliamentary sessions and free tours. *(Parliament faces Macquarie St. between Martin Pl. and Hunter St. ☎9230 2637. Open M-F 9:30am-4pm. Free admission. Book ahead for tours when Parliament is not in session or for Parliamentary session viewing.)*

AUSTRALIAN MUSEUM. The, um, creatively titled museum houses a unique mix of natural and cultural history. Stuffed re-creations of prehistoric Australian megafauna cast shadows over popular Aussie animals such as the koala and kangaroo. Though the science exhibits are fun for kids, the museum's treatment of the cultures of indigenous Australian peoples, both historically and as part of Australian society today, is superb for all ages. *(6 College St. On the east side of Hyde Park. ☎9320 6000; www.austmus.gov.au. Open daily 9:30am-5pm. $8, students $4, ages 5-12 $3, Aussie seniors and under 5 free, families of 4 $19. Special and temporary exhibits cost extra, up to $5.)*

HYDE PARK. Between Elizabeth and College St. at the eastern edge of the city center, Hyde Park was set aside in 1810 by Governor Lachlan Macquarie, and is still Sydney's most structured public green space, complete with fountains and stately trees. A buzzing urban oasis during the day, the park warrants some caution for those strolling at night. In the southern half, below Park St., the Art Deco-style **ANZAC Memorial** commemorates the service of the Australian and New Zealand Army Corps in WWI, as well as that of the Australians who have fought in the nation's eight other overseas conflicts. *(☎9267 7668. Open daily 9am-4:30pm, W 1pm-4:30pm only.)* On the park's east sits **St. Mary's Cathedral,** a Neo-Gothic structure. The original structure was erected in 1833, burned to the ground in 1865, and completed again in 1928. The originally-planned two Gothic towers on the southern end were constructed in 2000. An exhibit placed awkwardly in the crypt gives an informative and thoughtful account of the cathedral's place in a modern city. *(☎9220 0400. Crypt open daily 10am-4pm. $3 admission, $2 photography permit. Tours Su noon after mass, or by arrangement. Tourists not permitted during masses.)*

THE DOMAIN. Behind the buildings on Macquarie St., the unmanicured, grassy expanse of the Domain stretches east along the south edge of the Royal Botanic Gardens. Concerts fill the area during January's **Sydney Festival** (see p. 126). During the rest of the year, the park is most popular for corporate weekday lunch breaks and Sunday-morning rabble-rousing at **Speakers' Corner,** modeled after London's traditional weekly public speaking in the park.

ART GALLERY OF NEW SOUTH WALES. Sydney's major art museum's strength lies in its contemporary Australian works, Asian collections, and its extensive Aboriginal and Torres Straight Islander gallery. *(Northeast corner of the Domain, on Art Gallery Rd. ☎9225 1744; www.artgallery.nsw.gov.au. Open daily 10am-5pm. Free.)*

DARLING HARBOUR

The site of several events of the XXVII Olympiad, Darling Harbour, on the west side of the city center, is a popular tourist stop reminiscent of Disneyland with its immaculate brick walkways, trams, squealing children, and opportunities to spend money. The concentration of tourist attractions in this small area makes it a perfect outing for afternoon sightseeing and a popular spot for families. On foot, Darling Harbour is only 10min. from Town Hall Station. Follow George St. north, then turn left on Market St. to Pyrmont Bridge. Bus #888 approaches Darling Harbour from Circular Quay by way of Town Hall, and ferries run from Circular Quay to the Aquarium steps. For transport as tourist-oriented as the destination, hop on the **monorail** from Pitt St., at Park or Market St. in the CBD (see p. 101). For more info on 2000 Olympic sites, see p. 122.

SYDNEY AQUARIUM. Over 11,000 marine animals from Australia's many aquatic regions inhabit the tanks on the pier at Darling Harbour's eastern shore. If you need more evidence that Australia has the weirdest fauna on earth, stop at the mudskipper containment where these freaks of the fish world display their ability to live out of water by absorbing moisture from the air. More conventional attractions include the recently-opened Great Barrier Reef exhibit, a seal pool, and a small touching pool. The underwater Oceanariums, three plexiglass walking tunnels through huge enclosures with fish, sharks, and coral reefs, makes the pricey admission more understandable. *(Aquarium Pier. ☎9262 2300; www.sydneyaquarium.com.au. Open daily 9am-10pm, last entry 9pm. Seal sanctuary closes at sunset. $22, concessions $13, ages 3-15 $10, under 3 free, families of 5 $48. Wheelchair accessible.)*

POWERHOUSE MUSEUM. The largest museum in the southern hemisphere explores the breadth of human ingenuity through exhibits, interactive displays, and demonstrations focus on technology and applied art and science. From decorative arts to space exploration, communication to transportation advances, the museum's astounding variety makes it popular with visitors of all ages. *(500 Harris St. Just south of Darling Harbour, between Ultimo and Haymarket. ☎9217 0444. Open daily 10am-5pm. $8, students $3, ages 5-15 $2, families $18, Australian seniors and under 5 free.)*

CHINESE GARDEN. This serene garden was a bicentennial gift to New South Wales from her sister province in China, Guangdong. The delicately manicured plot in traditional southern Chinese style provides a remarkably sheltered break from the hubbub of the city. There are admission packages which include Devonshire tea or lunch from $8-14. *(On the corner of Harbour and Pier St. ☎9281 6863. Open daily 9:30am-5pm. $4.50, concessions $2, families $10, wheelchair-bound persons free.)*

NATIONAL MARITIME MUSEUM. Docked opposite the aquarium are the massive destroyer *HMAS Vampire* and submarine *HMAS Onslow*. Both were used in training exercises during the Cold War years, and are now part of the Maritime Museum. The museum provides a fascinating survey of Australia's maritime history from the times of early Aboriginal trading to the present; the exhibits on customs and smuggling are particularly interesting. More importantly, you can climb all over the submarines and battle ships. *(2 Murray St. ☎9298 3777; www.anmm.gov.au. Open daily 9:30am-5pm. Admission to museum $10, concessions $6, families $25; to both vessels and the museum $14/$7/$30. The museum is wheelchair-accessible but the ships are not.)*

INNER EAST

The suburbs just east of the city center are some of Sydney's most vibrant areas for shopping, eating, and meandering. Although Kings Cross tends to be a bit seedy, the neighborhood is not without a certain vibrance and charm. Oxford St. slides through Surry Hills, Darlinghurst, and Paddington in an endless string of cafes, boutiques, and hip homeware outlets. Sydney's large, outgoing gay community calls much of this strip home. Buses #378, 380, and 382 run the length of Oxford St., connecting the city center to the inner eastern suburbs.

FOX STUDIOS AUSTRALIA. This state-of-the-art theme park and studio only opened in Moore Park in late 1999. *The Matrix* and *Mission Impossible: II* were filmed on location here, as will the next two prequels of *Star Wars*. The park features 16 movie screens, pubs, and restaurants, not to mention a **backlot tour** with interactive exhibits on the film and TV industry. *(☎9383 4000; www.foxstudios.com.au. Backlot access $25, concession $20, ages 6-15 $15. Open daily 10am-5pm.)*

MOORE PARK. South of Paddington and east of Surry Hills, Moore Park contains the **Sydney Football Stadium** and the city's major **cricket oval** (p. 25). For a tour of the Stadium and a small museum of Aussie sports history, call **Sportspace.** *(☎9380 0383. Tours M-F 10am and 1pm during non-game days. $19, concessions $15.)*

CENTENNIAL PARK. The city's largest park abuts Moore Park's east side and stretches north to meet Oxford St. between Paddington and Woollahra. The park includes eight small lakes, a bird sanctuary, athletic fields, and cycling tracks.

SYDNEY JEWISH MUSEUM. This moving and informative museum is a remarkable exhibition of Australia's Jewish heritage and the horrors of the Holocaust. *(148 Darlinghurst Rd. at the corner of Burton St. ☎9360 7999. Open Su 11am-5pm, M-Th 10am-4pm, F 10am-2pm. $7, concessions $6, children $4, families of 4 $16.)*

NORTH SHORE

Coastal amusements at the northern beach resort of **Manly** have a tacky boardwalk feel unusual for an Australian beach. For less contrived pleasure, the **Manly to Spit Bridge** walk (9.5km; 3hr.) offers uncluttered harbor coastline, sandy beaches, national park, and bayside homes. The walk begins at the Manly Visitors Centre next to the wharf. (☎9977 1088. Open M-F 9am-5pm, Sa-Su 10am-4pm.) From the Spit Bridge, bus #144 and 143 return to Manly and run to Sydney.

TARONGA PARK ZOO. The koalas, kangaroos, and tigers at Taronga Zoo enjoy million-dollar harbor views. The impressive collection includes animals from all over Australia and the world. Admission includes an enclosed chair-lift safari ride, widely considered the best part of a visit. *(At the end of Bradley's Head Rd. in Mosman. To reach the zoo, take a 12min. ferry ride from Circular Quay, then a short jaunt on a shuttle. ☎9969 2777; www.zoo.nsw.gov.au. Open daily 9am-5pm. $22, students $15.50, ages 4-15 $12, families $56. A Zoopass, purchased at Circular Quay, covers admission, ferry, and bus transport. $25.40, children $12.70.)*

OCEAN WORLD. This aquatic playground earns rave reviews for its strange and rare specimens of tropical fish. There is a snake show three times daily, and weekends bring an extensive array of tours and presentations geared especially toward children. *(On the West Esplanade at Manly Cove. ☎9949 2644. Open daily 10am-5:30pm. $16, concessions $11, families of 5 $40. Shark feeding M, W, F 11am.)*

PLAYING WITH FIRE As with all modern Olympic Games, the Sydney 2000 games were preceded by the relay of the Olympic torch around the country. With over 10,000 torchbearers and a route in excess of 27000km, the 2000 Torch Relay was the longest in history. The lighted torch arrived in Yulara, NT, and zig-zagged across the continent for 100 days before reaching the opening ceremonies in Sydney. The route was designed to run within an hour's drive from the homes of 85% of the Australian population.

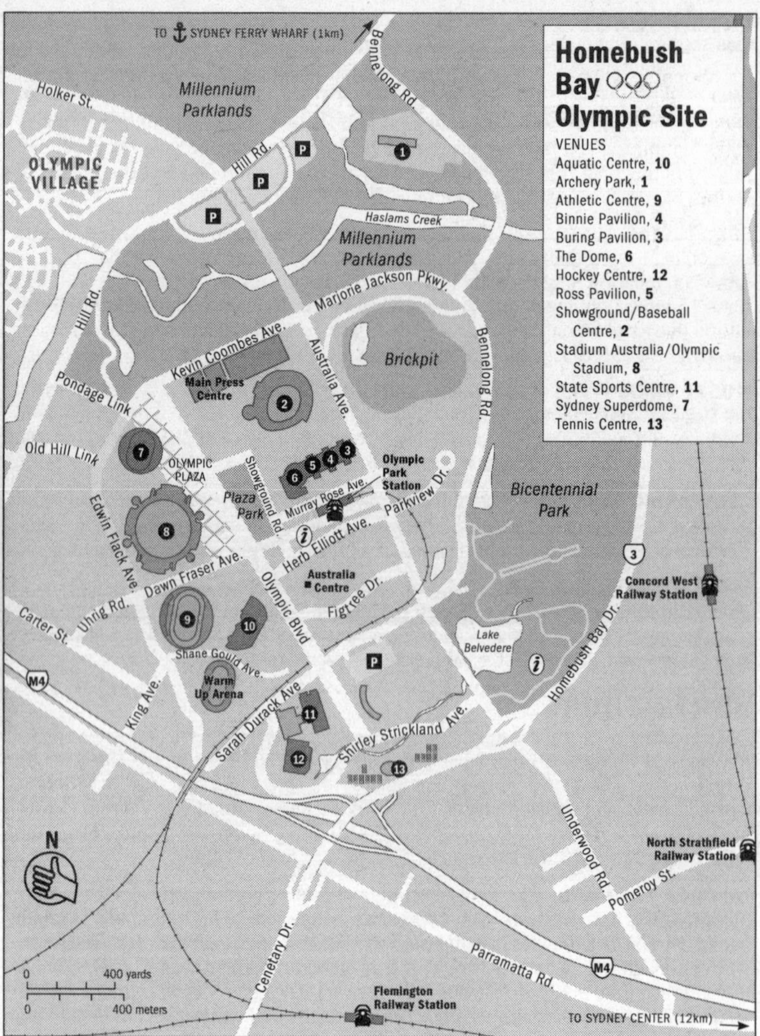

HOMEBUSH BAY OLYMPIC SITE

Australia and Greece are the only two countries that have participated in every Summer Olympics since the beginning of the modern games in 1896, and the September 2000 Games marked the second time Australia hosted the event (the first was in Melbourne, in 1956). Built to host the greatest athletes in the world and remaining as a tribute, the impressively huge Homebush Bay Olympic Site is where most events took place, 14km west of the city center along the Parramatta River. To get to Homebush Bay, take a CityRail train to the Olympic Park Station; **do not take the train to "Homebush."** Bicycles can also enter the area from near the Concord West train station and follow a pathway that carves through the surrounding wetlands of Bicentennial Park and into the heart of Homebush Bay. Contact the Homebay Bush Visitors Centre for information on tours (*☎9714 7888; www.oca.nsw.gov.au*).

OLYMPIC VILLAGE. At the Homebush Site, you can visit the largest **Olympic Stadium** to date (110,000 seats), **Stadium Australia,** as well as the other venues that hosted basketball, gymnastics, tennis, tae kwon do, volleyball, judo, hockey, wrestling, weightlifting, boxing, field hockey, and archery contests. *(Stadium open daily 9:30am-5:30pm. Tours daily every 30min. 9:30am-3:30pm.)* The **Sydney International Aquatic Centre** is open to the public for both swimming and diving. *(1 Herb Elliot Ave. ☎9752 3666. Open M-F 8am-5:30pm.)*

ACTIVITIES

NAUTICAL DIVERSIONS

Sydney's most popular pastimes are inspired by the Harbour and the coastline's natural playgrounds.

SAILING. On any sunny day, white sails can be seen clipping across the waters. **East Sail Sailing School** caters to all experience levels and offers intimate courses and trips. *(At D'Albora Marina on Rushcutters Bay. Follow William St. until it merges with Bayswater Rd., then turn left on Beach Rd. ☎9327 1166; www.eastsail.com.au. Open daily 8am-6pm. 2½hr. sailing trips depart daily at 10am; up to 12 passengers, but usually less. $86.)* **Sydney by Sail** runs introductory sailing lessons from the National Maritime Museum. *(☎9280 1110 or 0419 367 180; www.sydneybysail.com. Trips daily depending on weather and demand; 8-12 person max. 1½hr. lesson at 11am $54; 3hr. lesson at 1pm $98; book ahead.)*

DIVING. Sydney's rocky shores include several worthwhile spots for both shore and boat diving. With over 20 different dive sites, it's possible to dip in all along the coast. **ProDive** has excellent advice on local diving spots and all the gear you'll ever need. They also offer certification courses. *(City center: Level 7, 428 George St. ☎9264 6177 or 1800 820 820. Coogee: 27 Alfreda St. ☎9665 6333. Both open M-F 8:30am-5:30pm, Sa-Su 8:30am-5pm. 4-day courses from $295; trips and courses for other Australian locations can be arranged. Boats and gear for a full-day $120; gear alone $75.)*

SURFING. Surfing at **Bondi Beach** makes all the postcards, but Sydney has other beaches with equally appealing waves and smaller crowds. **Coogee** can be just as crowded as Bondi, and **Tamarama** is smaller but with trickier rips. The locals are protective of **Maroubra,** south of Coogee, and to an extent the beaches north of the Harbour. Up north, **Manly** ranks with Bondi and Coogee as a popular city beach. Farther up the coast, **Curl Curl, Dee Why, North Narrabeen, Newport Reef,** and **Palm Beach** are well worth the relative seclusion they offer. To get to the northern beaches, take bus #183, 187, 188, 189, 190, 151, or any of the northern beach expresses that originate at Wynyard Station (Carrington St. side); or take the ferry to Manly and catch bus #151, 155, or 157. The **Manly Surf School** gives surf lessons to everyone from beginners to more experienced surfers. *(At North Steyne Surf Club. ☎9977 6977; www.manlysurfschool.com. Open daily, lessons 11am-1pm. 2hr. $45, twice $80, 5-day $150; prices include wetsuit and board. Bookings essential.)* In Manly, **Aloha Surf** rents boards and wetsuits. *(44 Pittwater Rd. ☎9977 3777. Open F-W 9am-7pm, Th 9am-9pm. Short and long boards half-day $20, full-day $40; bodyboards $20.)* **Bondi Surf Co.** rents surfboards and bodyboards with wetsuits. *(72-76 Campbell Pde. ☎9365 0870. Open daily 9am-6pm 2hr. $30, full-day $60; credit card or passport required.)*

FISH AND WHALES. A number of charter boats run guided deep-sea **fishing** trips; groups get cheaper rates. **Whale watching season** is from June-July and Sept.-Oct. **Halicat** has both fishing and whale watching tours for up to 23 people running from Rose Bay and Cremorne. *(410 Elizabeth St., Surry Hills. ☎9280 3043 or 1800 679 629. Reef fishing $110. Sport fishing trips go farther out and find bigger fish $200. Trips depart 6:30am and return mid-afternoon. Whale watching 3½hr. weekend trips $85, seniors and students $75, children $55.)* **Zane Grey** offers similar rates. (*☎9565 4949. Reef fishing $100; sport fishing $160. Trips depart 7am and return mid-afternoon.)* Award-winning **Broadbill** runs a smaller operation (their boat holds six) at competitive prices from Sans Souci Wharf. *(☎9534 2378. Sport fishing $170-200. Trips depart 7am and return 5-6pm.)*

CRUISES. **Ferry cruises** are a great way to take in the harbor. In addition to those offered by Sydney Ferries (see p. 101), **Australian Travel Specialists** book a number of 1-3hr. Harbour cruises that run out of Circular Quay and Darling Harbour between 9:30am and 8pm and cost anywhere from $19-116. *(☎9555 2700.)* **Matilda Cruises** has lots of options: ferries between Darling Harbour and Circular Quay; the **Rocket Harbour Express** between Sydney Aquarium, Circular Quay, the Opera House, Taronga Zoo, and back to Darling Harbour; and sailing tours. *(Pier 26 near the Aquarium. ☎9264 7377. Harbour to Quay: $4, concessions $2. Express: $20.50, families $50. Sail from $27, seniors $22.)*

CANOES. To explore the area's inland waterways or to get a more in-depth look at the harbor coast from the seat of a canoe, call **Balmoral Marine.** *(On 2 Esplanade at Balmoral Beach. Take bus #244 or 247 toward Mosman from Wynyard Station. ☎9969 6006. Open daily 8:30am-5pm. 1hr. $10, full-day $50; deposit $10.)*

AERIAL EXPLOITS

SKYDIVING. Skydiving in Australia is cheaper than almost anywhere else. **Simply Skydive Australia** throws people out of planes from 4300 feet—with an instructor and parachute attached. *(☎9970 5037. With Sydney pickup $295.)* **Skydive Tandem** does the same from Bankstown Airport. *(☎9791 9056. $325, backpackers $275.)*

SCENIC FLIGHTS. For aerial views of Sydney without having to plummet towards it, a couple places offer scenic flights around Sydney and environs—but it'll hurt your wallet. **Sydney Air Scenic Flights** runs from the Bankstown Airport. *(☎9790 0628. Blue Mountains 1hr. $185; Sydney Harbour 1hr. $185; coastal tour 1¼hr. $340; day tours also available to Hunter Valley, Snowy Mountains, and Coffs Harbour.)* **Dakota National Air** also operates out of the Bankstown airport. *(☎9791 9900 or 1800 246 747; www.dakota-air.com. F night Sydney Harbour with champagne supper 1hr. $149; Su morning Harbour 1hr. $105; other tours available.)*

EXTRA TERRESTRIAL ADVENTURES

WALKING TOURS. Walking tours of The Rocks depart from the Visitors Centre. *(106 George St. ☎9247 6678. See p. 102.)* Additionally, Unseen Sydney conducts 1½hr. walking tours entitled *History, Convicts, and Murder most Foul* that include a complimentary drink from the historic Hero of Waterloo's cellar. *(☎9907 8057. Tu and Th-Sa 6:30pm. $19, students $15.)* The Original Sydney Walking Tours runs five different tours delving into the sensational past of The Rocks and Kings Cross. *(☎9380 2059 or 0413 139 162. $14, concessions $10.)*

SELF-GUIDED WALKS. They don't cost a cent and are a better way for the purist to enjoy Sydney's beautiful landscape. The walk from the Opera House to Mrs. Macquaries Chair through the Royal Botanic Gardens is deservedly popular, while the walk from Watson's Bay to the Gap provides equally beautiful serenity with even more isolation from the urban center. The walk from Manly to Spit Bridge is a bit rigorous and provides views and lush flora from the other side of the Harbour, while the walk from Bondi to Coogee Beach has a city beach at every valley and a breathtaking Pacific view at every peak. Which sounds more appealing?

RAW POWER. **Australian Travel Specialists** *(☎9555 2700)* book a number of chauffeured Harley-Davidson motorcycle tours, ranging from a Harbour tour *(1hr., $99)* to a mammoth tour of the Hunter Valley and Blue Mountains *(8hr., $345).*

OTHER RENTALS. Several places rent **in-line skates** or **skateboards.** In Bondi Junction, visit **Bondi Boards and Blades.** *(230 Oxford St. ☎9369 2212. Open daily 10am-6pm. $11 first hr., $5.50 per hr. afterwards, $22 per day. Group discounts.)* In Manly, try **Manly Blades.** *(49 North Steyne St. ☎9976 3833. Open M-W 9am-7pm, Th 9am-9pm, F-Sa 9am-7pm, Su 9am-6pm. $12 per hr., full-day $25, 24hr. $30. Scooters $20 per hr.)* In Paddington, try **Total Skate.** *(36 Oxford St., Woollahra, close to Centennial Park. ☎9380 6356. $10 first hr., $5 per additional hr., $30 per day.)*

RSVP: Anyone will tell you that seeing a show at the world-famous Opera House is a must-do for a Sydney tourist. Just be sure to be on time for the seating, as doors close to all comers promptly at showtime: two past Australian prime ministers will attest to that. If you're lucky, they'll let you in at a later junction, but more than one tardy tourist has missed the whole shebang by only a few minutes.

ENTERTAINMENT

PERFORMING ARTS

The iconic **Sydney Opera House** is the linchpin of Sydney's creative culture and its primary venue. With five stages (described below), the Opera House nimbly hosts a variety of the city's artistic endeavors. (Box office for all venues ☎9250 7777; www.soh.nsw.gov.au. Open M-Sa 9am-8:30pm and Su 2hr. prior to show only for ticket pick-up.) Doors close at showtime. Student rush ticket policy differs from company to company; contact each one for information.

Opera Theatre. The excellent **Opera Australia** (☎9699 1099, tickets 9319 1088; www.opera-australia.org) performs here. Reserved seats range from $83-180 and sell out fast, even though there are 1547 of them. Partial-view seats (blocking more than ¼ of the stage) start at $43. Standing room and listening-only (totally obstructed stage "view") are $33 and are available over-the-counter only at 9am the morning of the performance and are limited to 2 per person. Leftover tickets are sometimes sold 30min. before showtime on performance night as student rush tickets for $33 (ISIC required). **Australian Ballet Company** (☎1300 36 97 41; www.australianballet.com.au) and the **Sydney Dance Company** (☎9221 4811; www.sydneydance.com.au) share the same theater space. Call for ticket prices and info.

Concert Hall. The 2678-seat Concert Hall, the most majestic of the Opera House's stages, is the one-stop shop for symphony, chamber, and orchestral music performances. **Sydney Symphony Orchestra** (☎9334 4644; www.symphony.org.au) and the **Australian Chamber Orchestra** (☎9357 4111; www.aco.com.au) perform here throughout the year. Call for ticket info.

Drama Theatre. The Drama Theatre most frequently stars the **Sydney Theatre Company** (☎9250 1777; www.sydtheatreco.com/~exstce). The theatre seats 544. Advance seating from $50, student rush tickets from $15 available 30min. prior to show, standing room tickets at $25 available 1hr. prior to show.

Playhouse Theatre. A traditional round-stage forum with 398 seats. Contact the **Bell Shakespeare Company** (☎9241 2722; bellshakespeare@orangemail.com.au) for information on which of Will's classics they might be presenting.

Studio Stage. This catch-all, transformable stage seats 300 and exhibits less traditional Opera House offerings, including cabaret shows and copntemporary performances.

SPECTATOR SPORTS

Australia is a land of beer-guzzling, meatpie-gorging, obscenity-hurling mega-fans (see **Sport,** p. 25). Check out a sports match for an unforgettable lesson in social psychology, mob action, and VB-induced testosterone rituals. All events below sell tickets through **Ticketek** (☎9266 4800; www.ticketek.com.au), and are played in stadiums in Moore Park, accessible by bus #349, 373, 393, and 395.

Rugby League. The **Sydney Football Stadium** (☎9360 6601), home to the **South Sydney** and **Sydney City Side** teams, draws rowdy, fiercely-loyal fans throughout the winter season and in Sept. for the Wynfield Cup. Tickets $17-25, children's discount.

Australian Rules Football. This head-crushing, uniquely Aussie game is held at the Sydney Football Stadium. Root, root, root for the home team: the **Sydney Swans**. Tickets cost more and are harder to get than rugby tickets ($20-60).

Cricket. The games feel perpetual, the rules are maddeningly complicated, and the "athletes" are men wearing white straw hats and sweater vests. Head to the **Sydney Cricket Ground** (☎9369 6601). Tickets $10-40, depending upon the game.

CINEMAS

Sydney doesn't have a great film scene. It's American. It's Hollywood. Ticket prices are obscene. It's the same as everywhere else on this green Earth. But here, Tuesdays are **bargain day,** often half price. Prices during the rest of the week hover around $13-14, children $10-11. Call **Movieline** (☎13 27 00) for show times at all theaters. For info on the **Sydney Film Festival,** see p. 126.

Hoyts Centre, 505 George St. (☎9273 7373). The largest mainstream theater, located midway between Chinatown and the CBD.

Reading Cinemas, Level 3, Market City Mall, Chinatown (☎9280 1202). Undercuts other theaters by a buck or two and has Sunday double-features.

Govinda's, 112 Darlinghurst Rd., Darlinghurst (☎9360 7853). Reaps cult, classic, and contemporary films, and throws in an all-you-can eat buffet (see **Food,** p. 112).

Chauvel Cinema, Paddington Town Hall, Paddington (☎9361 5398). At Oxford and Oatley St. Specializes in indie, arthouse, and un-dubbed foreign films.

Panasonic IMAX Cinema, Southern Promenade, Darling Harbour (☎9281 3300). The eight-story high movie screen is the largest in the world. A different film is shown every hour. Open daily 10am-10pm.

GAMBLING

Okay, so gambling destroys marriages, depletes hard-saved nest eggs, and is a tax on people who are bad at math. But games of chance can't be all bad: public lottery revenues financed the Sydney Opera House after all. Australia, with just 1% of the world's population, fields 20% of its gaming machines (known locally as "pokies"). These video poker machines allow you to compete against a computer very effectively programmed to kick your ass. New South Wales lays claim to more than half of the continent's collection; pokies fill pub rooms across the state. But it might be the state governments that are the real gambling addicts. The New South Wales treasury takes a healthy cut from Sydney's $1.2 billion **Star City Casino,** 80 Pyrmont St., Pyrmont (☎9777 9000), in West Darling Harbour. The twinkling complex entices the punters 24hr. with lucky 7 restaurants, 7 bars, a nightclub, plastic trees, and an endless (okay, a mere 145,000 square meters) gaming room with 1,500 poker machines and 160 gaming tables. The casino can be accessed by light rail or shuttle bus to the casino or monorail to Harbourside.

FESTIVALS

Sydney-siders aren't as gung-ho as Melbournians when it comes to flaunting random festivals, but they still know how to party.

Sydney Festival, throughout Jan. (☎8248 6500; www.sydneyfestival.org.au). Features arts and entertainment events. Check the *Daily Telegraph* for details on free concerts in The Domain, street theater in The Rocks, and fireworks in Darling Harbour.

Tropfest, throughout Feb. (☎9368 0434; www.tropfest.com.au). World's largest short film festival screens in The Domain, Royal Botanic Gardens, and cafes along Victoria St.

Gay and Lesbian Mardi Gras, Feb. 8-Mar. 2, 2002 (☎9557 4332; www.mardigras.com.au). Brings the rip-roaring, no-holds-barred festivities of this huge international event. The festival climaxes on its final day with a parade attended annually by over 500,000 people and a gala party at the RAS Show Ground in Moore Park. Though the party is restricted and the guest list fills up way, way ahead of time, travelers can get on the list by becoming "International Members of Mardi Gras" well in advance. Intl. Membership $60, tickets around $110, concession $55.

Royal Agricultural Society's Easter Show, the two weeks surrounding Easter (☎9704 1111; www.eastershow.com.au). Held at the Homebush Olympic Site. The carnival atmosphere and rides make it fun even for those with no interest in farming.

Sydney Film Festival, mid-June 2002 (☎9660 3844; www.sydfilm-fest.com.au). The ornate State Theatre, 49 Market St., between George and Pitt St., and Dendy Opera Quays showcase documentaries, retrospectives, and art films from around the world. The festival tours Australia throughout the year.

City to Surf Run, Aug. 12, 2001 (☎9282 3606). Draws 50,000 contestants for a semi-serious 14km trot from Park St to Bondi Beach. Some are world-class runners; others treat the race as a lengthy pub crawl. Entries ($25) are accepted up to race day.

Manly Jazz Festival, Sept. 28-31, 2002 (☎9977 1088; www.pcn.com.au/manlyjazz). Oz's biggest jazz festival, featuring all types of national and international artists.

Bondi Beach Party, Dec. 25 each year. Bondi sets the pace for debauchery all along the coast as people from around the world gather for a foot-stomping Christmas party.

Sydney-to-Hobart Yacht Race, Dec. 26 each year. Brings the city's hungover attention (see above) back to civilized entertainment.

SHOPPING AND MARKETS

Australians, especially Sydney folk, take pride in their fashion-conscious attitudes. The **Sydney Visitors Centre** has a fantastic free booklet with information on city shopping, weekend markets, and suburban malls.

In the city center, the upscale **Queen Victoria Building** and **Centrepoint Shopping Centre** are crammed with consumers, **Harbourside** on Darling Harbour is a yuppie magnet, and **Market City** in the heart of Haymarket is a bargain shopper's haven. **Oxford St.** has some funky finds; **Glebe Point Rd.** offers alternative labels as well as standard brandnames. Newtown's **King St**. is the place to go for vintage bins and colorful boutiques. Those who can afford it should venture to **Double Bay** or **Castlereagh St.,** where designer fashion houses, jewelers, and other indulgences await. To get to Double Bay, take a ferry or buses #323, 324, or 325 from Circular Quay.

Sydney has numerous year-round weekend markets, all of which tend to specialize in arts, crafts, and souvenirs. Haggling is fun, the food is reasonably priced, and there's generally at least one cart selling fresh fruit. **Paddington Markets,** 395 Oxford St., is Sydney's best known and liveliest market, featuring entertainment, food, and a variety of crafts. (☎9331 2923; www.paddingtonmarket.com.au. Open Sa 10am-4pm.) **Paddy's Markets,** on Ultimo Rd. at Hay St, is legendary and as old as the city itself. Be sure to head up to the second level; it's not just a food court, but also home to a handful of brand name factory outlets. (☎1300 361 589; www.paddysmarkets.com.au. Open Th 10am-6pm, F-Su 9am-4:30pm, rain or shine.) **Paddy's Flemington,** run by Paddy's Markets, is off Parramatta Rd. in the Sydney Markets across from the Homebush Bay Olympic Site. (Open F 10am-4:30pm, Su 9am-4:30pm; see p. 123.) **The Rocks Market,** at the north end of George St. under the bridge, is more upmarket with antiques, jewelry, and collectibles, as well as street performers and live musicians. (Open Sa-Su 9am-5pm, rain or shine.) **Glebe Markets,** at Glebe Public School, on the corner of Glebe Point Rd. and Derby Pl., sells new and second-hand crafts. (Sa 10am-4pm, weather permitting.) The hip **Bondi Beach Market,** at Bondi Beach Public School on Campbell Pde., features locally made arts and crafts. (☎9315 8988. Open Su 10am-4pm, weather permitting.)

THE 30¢ CONE A good deal is hard to pass up, even when it's being offered by an organization gradually achieving world domination through global capitalism. And McDonald's—the American behemoth rumored to have more restaurants per capita in Australia than anywhere else in the world—offers one of the best in its 30¢ soft-serve ice cream cone. A sizeable mound of luscious vanilla ice cream can be had for a couple of those silver coins jangling in your pocket. Just 150 cones (much like 42 pints of Guinness) are said to be enough to sustain a healthy human life for a single day, and a savvy traveler can survive on considerably less.

NIGHTLIFE

Whether they're out on the town for drinks and dancing or huddling around a TV for the latest crucial sports telecast, many Sydney-siders hit the pub and club scene four or five times per week. Different neighborhoods have distinctly different scenes, and the scenes vary from night to night. Bars in **Kings Cross** attract a large, straight male crowd, which quickly spills over from the strip joints into the pubs and dance clubs. Backpackers round out the mix in this neighborhood, giving several spots an international feel. Outside Kings Cross, travelers generally congregate in pubs to avoid the high cover charges and inflated drink prices of Sydney's high-profile dance venues. **Gay Sydney** struts its stuff on Oxford St. in Darlinghurst and Paddington, where some establishments are specifically gay or lesbian and many others are mixed. Because the gay clubs provide much of the city's best dance music, flocks of young, beautiful club scenesters of all persuasions fill any extra space on their vibrant, vampy dance floors. **Taylor Square,** at the intersection of Oxford, Flinders, and Bourke St., is the heart of this district. Suits clog the bars in the **Central Business District,** and night spots in **The Rocks** tend toward the expensive. For more casual pub crawling, wander on Bourke and Flinders St. in **Surry Hills.** Large student populations in **Glebe** and **Newtown** make for a younger crowd and cheaper drinks on special nights at pubs in these areas.

Major concerts are held in the **Sydney Entertainment Centre,** Harbour St., Haymarket (☎9320 4200; www.sydentcent.com.au; box office open M-F 9am-5pm, Sa 10am-1pm); the **Hordern Pavilion,** in Moore Park; and the **Enmore Theatre,** 130 Enmore Rd., Newtown (☎9550 3666). Sydney's daily **live music** scene consists largely of local bands casting their pearls before pub crowds. The *Metro* section of the Friday *Sydney Morning Herald* and free weeklies such as *Beat* and *Sydney City Hub* contain listings for upcoming shows, along with info on art showings, movies, theater, and DJ appearances city-wide. The bible of the Sydney clubber is *3-D World* (www.threedworld.com.au), a free Tuesday publication that can be found in hostels, music stores, and trendy clothing stores. It gives the lowdown on special events for each night of the week. Look for the free *Streetpress* or *The Revolver*, which highlight the weekly hotspots for shaking your groove thang; *Drum Media* covers music. *Sx News* (www.sxnews.com.au) and *Sydney Star Observer* (www.sonet.com.au) focus on the gay community.

BARS AND PUBS

KINGS CROSS

Fitzroy Hotel, 129 Dowling St. (☎9356 3848), on the corner of Cathedral St., 3 blocks west of Victoria St. A neighborhood pub comfortably sequestered from the more hectic Cross. Upstairs is popular with backpackers for its casual atmosphere and pool tables ($2 per game). Frequent discounts through local hostels. Schooners $3.40. M $2.50 Happy Hour 5:30-7:30pm. Tu Free pool. Open M-Sa 10:30am-midnight, Su 3-10pm.

O'Malley's Hotel, 228 William St. (☎9357 2211), on the corner of Brougham St. Upscale style in a casual pub atmosphere. The row of TVs makes O'Malley's into something of an Irish sports bar, but its nightly live music (local rock bands) is the best in the Cross. Eclectic crowd proves that backpackers, business-types, and locals can indeed mix. Schooners of Toohey's $3.30. Open M-Th 11am-2am, F-Su 11am-3am.

Darlo Bar, 306 Liverpool St. (☎9331 3672), on the corner of Darlinghurst Rd. A crowd of starving actors, students, and the tragically hip come to drink beer (schooner $3.40). All ages and income brackets represented. Open M-Sa 10am-midnight, Su noon-10pm.

Bourbon and Beefsteak, 24 Darlinghurst Rd. (☎9358 1144). It's 7am, there is nowhere that you *haven't* had a drink, but you can still stomach the neon and excessive Australian flag regalia. Somehow everybody ends up here at one time or another while carousing in the Cross. Open 24hr. Breakfast all-day.

PADDINGTON

Durty Nelly's, 9-11 Glenmore Rd., Paddington (☎9360 4467), off Oxford St. at Gipps St. Sydney's best traditional Irish pub takes its Guinness very seriously; those in the know claim it's hands-down the best around (schooner $4.20). Even on weekends when it's packed, the dark wood decor and the jovial staff create a relaxing refuge from the nearby Oxford St. melee. Open M-Sa 11am-midnight, Su noon-10pm.

Grand Pacific Blue Room (☎9331 7108), corner of Oxford and S. Dowling St., Paddington. A very cool lounge bar with live acoustic performances. Shed the backpack for a night to join a young sophisticated crowd wearing tank tops and shiny pants, drinking Cosmopolitans and caipiroskas. DJs Th-Su (Th jazz/funk, F hip-hop, Sa R&B, Su hip-hop). Open Tu-W 5:30pm-1am, F-Sa until 3am, Su until 1am. F $8 cover, Sa $10 cover.

Albury Hotel, 6 Oxford St., Paddington (☎9361 6555). A classic drag venue: a bit touristy, but when you go to Rome, you see the Vatican, right? Two large rooms provide separation between the drag show entertainment and dancing, and the bar scene. Together, these halves comprise a fully functioning meat market–surely you will leave with a story to tell your friends. A mixed gay-and-straight crowd revel in the debauchery. Schooners $4.10. Shows at 10, 11pm, and the main performance at midnight. Happy Hour daily 2-8pm. Open M-Sa 2pm-2am, Su 2pm-midnight. Cover F-Sa $5.

THE ROCKS

The Lord Nelson, 19 Kent St. (☎9251 4044), on the corner of Argyle St. west of The Rocks center. Nautical flags drape from sturdy wooden beams in this colonial building. Sydney's oldest hotel and pub, first licensed in 1841 to a former convict landlord, shelters a young crowd. A very chill place for an after-work pint from one of Sydney's only micro-breweries. Try the award-winning Old Admiral (pint $6). Open daily 11am-11pm.

The Hero of Waterloo, 81 Lower Fort St. (☎9252 4553), one block off Argyle St. west of The Rocks center. Since 1845, this pub has been an Australian favorite; its underground tunnels were once used for rum smuggling. The older group of regulars has been drinking here since before you were born (so they must be very drunk by now). Live entertainment (Irish and folk music) W-Su. Open M-Sa 10am-11pm, Su 10am-10pm.

CITY CENTER

The CBD is mainly a professional crowd, but backpacker options can be found.

The Basement, 29 Reiby Pl. (☎9251 2797). Arguably the hottest live music venue in the CBD with acts ranging from jazz to rock. Schooner $5.50. Open daily noon-3pm for lunch, 7:30pm til late. Cover ranges from $10 to $50 for the most exclusive acts.

Jackson's on George, 176 George St. (☎9247 2727), near Circular Quay. 4 swanky levels–danceclub, pool bar, games, and restaurant. "Stik" drinks ($9) pack a punch with fresh fruit, ice, and spirits. F-Sa Happy Hour 5-7pm. Schooners $3.50-3.90. Open M-Th 11am-3am, F-Su til 6am. Cover F-Sa $10 after 10pm.

Scubar, 4 Rawson Pl. (☎9212 4244; www.scubar.com.au). In the YHA basement; 1min. west of Central Station. Pool competitions, big screen cable TVs, and periodic jug-and-pizza dinner deals bring backpackers over from next door in droves. Not really a place to meet Sydney-siders, but a mecca for international travelers. M $6.50 jugs of beer. Open M-F noon-late, Sa-Su 5pm-late.

Scruffy Murphy's, 43-44 Goulburn St. (☎9211 2002), on the corner of George St. It may not be the most authentic Irish pub, but it's a decent live music venue in the city center. And it's always chockers. Pub, disco dance, and terrace. Schooners $3.50. Tu $7-jugs. Open 24hr. No cover.

GLEBE

Toxteth Hotel, 345 Glebe Point Rd. (☎9660 2370), on the corner of Ferry Rd. Lively and always packed, right near most of Glebe's hostels. Schooners of VB $3.50. M, W free movies in the beautiful courtyard. Open M-Sa 11am-midnight, Su 11am-11:45pm.

Ancient Briton Hotel (☎9660 1417), corner Glebe Point Rd. and Lyndhurst St. Packed with local students by night, the AB won "coldest beer on tap" from the *Sydney Telegraph*. Schooners $3.20. Pool $1 per game. 2-for-1 cocktails Th-Sa 8pm-11pm. Happy Hour Su-W 6:30-8:30pm beer $2.30. Tu-W pool contests. Video jukebox upstairs in the funky pool lounge. Open daily 8am-midnight, Su until 10pm.

The Nag's Head Hotel, 162 St. John's St. (☎9660 1591; www.nagshead.com.au) corner of Lodge. A relaxed English-style pub with rooftop garden. Princess Diana's ex-chef whips up excellent dishes in the bistro next door. Schooner $3.40. W Uni night with $8 jugs, 3 spirits for $10. Open daily 11am-midnight.

Friend In Hand Pub, 58 Cowper St. (☎9660 2326), off Glebe Point Rd. The name is ripe for jokes, so we'll just skip to the skinny. Tu poetry competition; W legendary crab races and eating contests prove that it's possible to earnestly bet on pretty much anything; Th trivia night, promising "absolutely pathetic prizes." Somewhat tamer on weekends. Schooner $3.25. Open M-Sa 10am-midnight, Su noon-10pm.

NEWTOWN

Kuletos Cocktail Bar, 157 King St. (☎9519 6369). Deliciously fruity liqueurs go down smooth during Kuletos' M-Sa 6-7:30pm Happy Hour, with 2-for-1 drinks. Mixed drinks are normally pricey from $10, but the immense range provides mouth-watering flavors. The Toblerone, Red Corvette, and Peach Passion are the house favorites. Open M-Sa 4pm-late, Su 3-10pm; extra Happy Hour Th 9:30-10:30pm.

Marlborough Hotel, 145 King St. (☎9519 1222). The Marley is the place to be after Happy Hour at Kuletos. Tu comedy night; Th-F DJ; Sa band night. Schooner $3.30, Before 6pm $2.80. No sandals. Open M-Sa 10am-late, Su noon-midnight.

NORTH SHORE

Sydney-siders call going to the North Shore "OTB"—over the bridge.

The Old Manly Boatshed, 40 The Corso, Manly (☎9977 4443; www.manlyboatshed.com.au). A nice alternative to DJs and clubbin'. Cityslickers deem it a must-stop during a night out OTB. Live music most weeknights. M comedy. Open daily 6pm-3am.

Coogee Bay Hotel (☎9665 0000), corner of Coogee Bay Road and Arden St., Coogee Beach. Large and swanky, supplying the juice for the Coogee scene. Backpackers and UNSW students swarm to the cheap drinks. Multiple bars, beer garden, and a nightclub with no cover. Selina's Entertainment Center, in the hotel, is one of Sydney's more popular concert venues and gets international acts. Schooners $3.50. M-Sa Happy Hour 9am-6pm. Open Su-W 9am-midnight, Th-Sa 9am-3am or later.

Newport Arms Hotel (☎9997 4900), Kalinya St., Newport. A mostly family-oriented hotel with large gardens. A nice traditional-feeling pub—definitely not a raging scene. Sa Happy Hour 6-10pm. Waterfront Restaurant and bar open from M-F 10am-11pm, Sa 10am-midnight, Su 10am-10pm.

NIGHTCLUBS

Home, 101 Cockle Bay Wharf, Darling Harbour (☎9266 0600). Looks like the ruby slippers finally worked. The scene is ultra-trendy and very happening—be prepared for huge lines to get in. The cover charge is steep, but hey, it's popular. F-Sa 4 dance floors and 15 DJs have the place grinding with everything from disco to break-beat from 10pm-7am (F $20, Sa $25). Discounts for members. Absolutely 18+; photo ID required.

Imperial Hotel, 35 Erskineville Rd., Erskineville (☎9519 9899). Take a train to Erskineville, take a taxi, make the hike. The costumes at the outrageous weekend drag shows make it well worth it. The "Priscilla: The New Generation" show adds one more layer to the parody and homage surrounding Swedish super-group ABBA; scenes from *Priscilla* were filmed here. The crowd is straight, gay, lesbian, and huge by showtime. Schooners of VB $2.50. M free pool, Happy Hour 5pm-9pm. Show W-Th 12:30am, 1:30am; F-Sa 10:30pm, 11:30pm, 1:15am, and 2:15am; Su 10:30pm, 11:15pm. Th-Sa dance music until 7am. Open M-Tu 4pm-2am, W 2pm-3am, Th 4pm-6am or later, F-Sa 1pm-8am, Su 4pm-midnight. No cover.

Goodbar, 11A Oxford St., Paddington (☎9360 6019). The best hip-hop hangout in the city, and the only place to be on Th nights. The dance floor is downstairs with funky lounge chairs. Open W-Sa 9pm-3am. Cover W $10, Th $6, F $10, Sa $15.

Arq, 16 Flinders St., Taylor Sq., Darlinghurst (☎9380 8700). Ultra-trendy dance club with a mixed gay and straight crowd. Upstairs, bump to techno with buff and beautiful boys on podiums. Downstairs, an alternative crowd jams to soul and funk in the bar. Drag shows Th 12:30am, 1:45am. Open W-Th 5pm-6am, F 5pm-9am, Sa 5pm-noon, Su 5pm-9am. Cover F $15, Sa $20, Su $5.

DCM, 31-33 Oxford St., Darlinghurst (☎9267 7036 or 9267 7380; www.dcmsydney.com). Once voted the best club in the southern hemisphere by *Harper's Bazaar*, trendy twenty-somethings still "dress to impress" in order to get by the door and get their freak on. Open F-Su 10pm-late. Cover $22.

Tantra, 169 Oxford St., Darlinghurst (☎9360 6759). Nothing but good old house remixes at this local fave. Come here to dance hardcore or not at all. Open F-Su 9pm-6am. Cover F-Sa $20, Su $10.

Q-Bar, Level 2, 44 Oxford St., Darlinghurst (☎9360 1375). Entering Q-Bar is a bit like navigating into the Bat Cave–you'll need to locate the "Synergy Hair" sign, go underneath it through an unmarked corridor, and hop onto an old elevator to the party upstairs. Head-spinning, body-thumping dance floor covered in the tightly-clad. Th "Prom Nights" are the exception; rock owns the night. F "Qushi" distributes free sushi from 5-10pm. Open daily 4pm-4am or later, but the floor rarely heats up until midnight.

Gas, 477 Pitt St., Haymarket (☎9211 3088; www.gasnightclub.com.au). The place to break it down in the CBD, with hip-hop, heavy house, and a bit of disco. Open Th 10pm-5am, cover $12; F 10pm-5am, $15; Sa 10pm-6am, $20. Cover before 11pm $8-10.

Midnight Shift, 85 Oxford St., Darlinghurst (☎9360 4463). While the door policy is not strictly male-only, the "no open shoes under any circumstances" sifts out most curious women. The showy, sexual atmosphere gets deeper and dirtier as the night progresses, attracting a very mixed mob–testimony to the club's 20+ years of popularity. Draft beers $3-3.80. Open daily noon-6am or later.

DAYTRIPS FROM SYDNEY

Sydney's attractions are not just limited to the city proper. The surrounding hills and valleys contain a sampling of the greater natural beauty for which the continent is known. The small towns outside Sydney give a feel for, well, small town life that the lights of the big city often drown. If your stay in Oz is confined to Sydney, each of these daytrips at least give a flavor of the rest of the continent.

ROYAL NATIONAL PARK. Just 30km south of Sydney's city center, Royal National Park is an easy and glorious escape from city life. The national park, Australia's oldest and the world's second-oldest (after the United States's Yellowstone), consists of over 16,000 hectares of beach, heath, rainforest, swamp, and woodland. The range of activities available in the park is as diverse as the habitat—bushwalkers, birdwatchers, swimmers, and surfers all find favorite getaways in different corners of the park. Across the Princes Hwy. on the west side of the park, the smaller, often-forgotten **Heathcote National Park** contributes another 2000 hectares of heathland to the cause of travelers trying to lose themselves in green.

BOTANY BAY NATIONAL PARK. Straddling the two headlands at the entrance to Botany Bay, this national park has a unique combination of natural and cultural heritage features. It's the site of first contact between Aboriginal people and the crew of James Cook's *Endeavour* in 1770. It's also the place where the Comte de Laperouse, France's famous explorer, arrived within a week of the British First Fleet in 1788. Beneath the park's gouged sandstone cliffs, there are rich marine environments. Above them, you'll find remnants of the heathland vegetation which Banks and Solander, Cook's botanists, first studied in 1770. There's more to this place than you might think.

PARRAMATTA ☎02

In April 1788, Governor Phillip led an expedition to discover what lay upriver from the new settlement of Sydney, and Australia's second town was established as a result. Parramatta is now a suburban extension of the city, complete with a nearby theme park for daytripping Sydney-siders. The five-floor Westfield mall is said to be the largest in the Southern Hemisphere. Parramatta also maintains several buildings from the early days of colonization. Most notable is the **Old Government House** in Parramatta Park at the west end of town. Originally a cottage built by Governor Phillip in 1790, the house grew into Georgian grandeur through renovations made by Governor Macquarie between 1812 and 1818. The oldest public building in Australia, it contains the country's largest collection of pre-1855 colonial furniture. (☎9635 8149. Open M-F 10am-4pm, Sa-Su 11am-4pm. $3.30, concessions $2.20, family $8.80.) **Elizabeth Farm,** 70 Alice St., in Rosehill, east of the town center, was the home of John and Elizabeth Macarthur, founders of the Australian Merino wool industry. (☎9635 9488. Open daily 10am-5pm. $7, concessions $3, family $17.) In 1789, the colonial government made its first land grant to convict James Ruse at the site of **Experiment Farm Cottage,** 9 Ruse St. (☎9635 5655. Open Tu-F 10:30am-3:30pm, Sa-Su 11:30am-3:30pm. $5.50, concession $4, family $14.)

West of Parramatta, in Doonside, **Featherdale Wildlife Park,** 217 Kildare Rd., provides wonderful interactive animal fun that allows visitors to cuddle koalas, feed kangaroos, and see close-up the country's largest collection of native Australian animals. (☎9622 1644. Open daily 9am-5pm. $15, students $12, families $38.) The park is 40min. from Sydney by car (Reservoir Rd. exit from M4) and also accessible by bus #725 from the Blacktown train station ($5 return from Central Station). Attractions at **Wonderland Sydney** range from wombats to waterslides to roller-coasters galore. (☎9830 9100. Open daily 10am-5pm. $42.90.) Take the Wallgrove Rd. exit from the M4 or catch Busways bus #738 (return $5) from the Rooty Hill train station (from Central Station off-peak return $6).

Parramatta is 20min. from Sydney along Parramatta Rd. Before reaching Parramatta, the road becomes the M4 Tollway at Strathfield, the most direct route to the Blue Mountains. Both **trains** and **ferries** make the trip to Sydney. The one hour cruise on the sleek RiverCat pontoon (every hr. from wharf 2, $5.50), is preferable to the 30min. train ride ($3.60). **CityRail** also runs to: Blackheath ($10, concessions/children $5); Katoomba ($9.60/$4.80); Lithgow ($12.60/$6.30); Penrith ($4.20/$2.10). The **Parramatta Visitors Centre,** 346 Church St., is within the Parramatta Heritage Center. (☎9630 3703; fax 9630 3243. Open M-F 10am-5pm, Sa-Su 10am-4pm.) Parramatta's accommodation scene does not cater to budget travelers, but Sydney is close enough to allow commuting. **The Sushi Train,** 188 Church St., whirls plates of sushi around on a conveyer belt tempting customers to sample the color coded samples ($2-4.50). (☎9891 1399. Open daily 11:30am-8pm. No credit cards.)

PENRITH ☎02

The town of Penrith, 35km west of Parramatta along the Great Western Hwy. (M4 Motorway) hovers on the edge of Sydney's sphere of suburban influence at the base of the Blue Mountains. Running through the west half of town, the **Nepean River,** a wide, placid corridor, is one of Penrith's best features. The **Nepean Belle** paddlewheel riverboat makes leisurely trips through the Nepean Gorge in **Blue Mountains National Park.** (☎4733 1274. Departs Tench Reserve Park, off Tench Ave., with morning, afternoon, and dinner cruises. Shortest cruise 90min., $18.) Just 5km north of town along Castlereagh Rd., the **Sydney International Regatta Centre** and **Penrith Whitewater Stadium** served as the **Olympic** venues for all rowing and canoeing events. The landscaped grounds (open daily 9am-5pm) around the Regatta Centre's water course are good for picnicking or just frolicking in the grass. Alternatively, test your inner champion with a go at the actual Olympic whitewater course (☎4730 4333; www.penrithwhitewater.com.au. Book ahead. 90min. rafting $49.50 winter, $55 summer; guided or self. Paddling $25. Canoe or kayak instruction $66 half-day, $110 full-day. Guided 45min. stadium tour $5.50, senior $4.40, child $2.75, family $13.75). On the way back from the stadium, celebrate your bravado with a visit to the **Sun-Masamune Sake Brewery**, 29 Cassola Pl. off of Lugard St. (☎4732 2833; www.sun-masamune.com.au. Open daily 2-4pm.)

CityRail trains (ticket office at railway; open M-F 5am-9pm, Sa 5:45am-8:30pm, Su 6:45am-8:30pm) runs to: Blackheath (1½hr., 15-21 per day, $7.80); Katoomba (1hr., 15-21 per day, $5.80); Lithgow (2hr., 12-14 per day, $10); Parramatta (30min., 23-34 per day, $4.20); Sydney (1hr., 23-33 per day, $6.40). The **Penrith Valley Visitors Centre,** on Mulgoa Rd., in the carpark of the Panther's World Entertainment Complex, provides info on Penrith and the Blue Mountains. (☎4732 7671; fax 4732 7690; www.penrithvalley.com.au. Open daily 9am-4:30pm.) **Explorers Lodge,** 111 Station St., often houses herds of athletes frequenting the area and accordingly provides extra long beds, a rock climbing machine, a small gym, and laundry facilities ($5.40) to wash all those sweaty workout clothes. The young owners keep a laid-back atmosphere in this spacious and convenient house. (☎4731 3616; fax 4731 3191; redback@pnc.com.au; www.explorerslodge.com. Free linen. Reception daily 9am-9pm. Flexible check-in time. Check-out 11am. Dorms $27.50; twins and doubles Apr.-Aug. $55, Sept.-Mar $66.) **Nepean River Caravan Park,** on MacKellar St. in Emu Plains just a short drive over the river, provides inexpensive sleeping arrangements. Creature comforts include kitchen, swimming pool, games room, and TV lounge. (☎4735 4425. Reception M-F 8am-7pm, Sa-Su 8-11am and 4-7pm. Linen $10. Dorms $16.50; sites for 2 $16, powered $19.50; cabins for 2 $50, with bath $55. MC/V.)

KU-RING-GAI CHASE NATIONAL PARK

The country's second oldest national park, Ku-Ring-Gai Chase (named after a local Aboriginal group) was seven years old when the Australian colonies federated in 1901. The Park came close to serving a far more central role in the new nation's development as the site of the capital city. However, the proposal to build the city on the park land in medieval English style—as a moated fortress capital to be called **Pacivica**—was eventually passed over in favor of the plan that led to the creation of Canberra. The park, 24km north of Sydney, includes over 15,000 hectares covering most of the southern headlands of Broken Bay. Waterways leading out to the ocean carve their way through the park's sandstone rock landscape giving the park a rugged beauty. Many Sydney-siders come for the numerous Aboriginal rock engravings and the exotic wildflowers that bloom early in winter.

TRANSPORTATION. Ku-Ring-Gai Chase is split in two by access roads. **Ku-Ring-Gai Chase Rd.** from the Pacific Hwy. and **Bobbin Head Rd.** from Turramurra provide access to the southwest area of the park. From Sydney, you can reach the Bobbin Head Rd. entrance by first taking the **train** to Turramurra (35min., $3.60) and then catching bus #577 of **Shorelink Bus Company** (☎9457 8888; 15min.; M-Sa every 30min., Su every hr.; $2.90) to just outside the park gates. **Palm Beach Ferry Service** (☎9918 2747) stops at **The Basin** (8 per day, $8 return). **Palm Cruises** (☎9997 4815) runs to Bobbin Head (scenic cruise at 11am daily, $30) and Patonga (at least 1 per day, $13). Sydney Bus #L90 goes from Central Station to Palm Beach near the ferry wharf (1½hr., approx. every 30min.). The Bobbin Head section of the park has access roads with no gates, but the park is closed from sunset to sunrise.

PRACTICAL INFORMATION. The Bobbin Head area in the southwest is home to the **main visitors center,** a picnic area, lush views of the valley, and peaceful headwaters of Cowan Creek. The volunteer-run **Kalkari Visitors Centre,** on Ku-Ring-Gai Chase Rd, 4km inside the park gates, distributes free hiking maps and offers educational information on the park's wildlife. (☎9457 9853. Open daily 9am-5pm.) **Bobbin Head Information Centre,** inside the Wildlife Shop at the bottom of the hill at Bobbin Head, is the official information outlet for the park. (☎9472 8949. Open daily 10am-4pm.) Gates to West Head, Bobbin Head and Appletree Bay are locked at 8pm during daylight saving and 5.30pm outside daylight saving periods. The park entrance fee is $9.90 per car.

ACCOMMODATIONS. The only place you can camp in Ku-Ring-Gai Chase National Park is at The Basin, where you'll find toilets and showers. You can get there on foot along The Basin Track or take an hourly ferry from Palm Beach.

Campsite bookings are essential. Rates are $9 (adults) or $4.50 (children) per night from September to April and $7.50 (adults) or $4 (children) per night from May to August. A maximum of eight people can stay on each site. If you'll be leaving your car in the park while you stay at The Basin, you'll need to purchase a vehicle day pass for each day ($10). If you're arriving at The Basin by boat or ferry, landing fees will apply ($2.20, children $1.10). The **campground** at the Basin is accessible by ferry from Palm Beach or by a 3km hike on the Basin track from West Head Rd. The site has cold showers, toilets, gas BBQs, and a public phone, but all supplies, except bait and drinks, must be carried in. Bookings must be arranged through the NPWS automated reservation service. (☎9974 1011. Open 24hr. Sites for 2 $11, each additional person $2.20; holidays $15.50, $3.30.) Both the park's **hostel** and **camping area** can be reached by car from the east side of the park, but both require that you leave the car behind somewhere along West Head Rd.

If camping's not your scene, you can spend a weekend at **Towlers Bay House** (☎9974 1011). The four-bedroom house is self-contained and fully furnished and can accommodate up to eight people. Its facilities include showers, toilets, a kitchen, a barbecue and a swimming pool. The house is located at Towlers Bay, just south of The Basin (where there's a phone, picnic area, park information and a general store). It's available only on weekends, and bookings are essential. Towlers Bay House costs $500 per weekend during school holidays and $400 per weekend outside holiday periods. Possibly the most refreshing and remote hostel in the greater Sydney area, the **Pittwater YHA Hostel** enjoys lush green scenery from its lofty, terraced perch over Pittwater. Take bus #156 from Manly (1hr.), bus #E86 from Wynyard (1¼hr.), or follow Pittwater Rd to the ferry at Church Point Wharf ($6.50 return). The open, outdoorsy hostel provides a retreat without the distraction of TV or radio. Canoe hire is $9 a day or $10 for length of your stay. (☎9999 2196; fax 9997 4296. Linen $2. No laundry. Bookings required. Reception daily 8-11am and 5-8pm. Dorms $19; twins $48. Sa $25/$58. Non-YHA add $3. MC/V.)

HIKING. Ku-Ring-Gai Chase has **bushwalks** for any level of expertise. The discovery walk (20min.; wheelchair accessible) just outside the Kalkari Visitors Centre is a quick, easy way to spot a few kangaroos, emus, and some native plant life. An easily accessible bushwalk (10km) begins at the Bobbin Head Rd. entrance to the park and follows the **Sphinx-Warrimoo Track** for 6.5km to Bobbin Head. The hike can be made into a circuit by taking the Bobbin Head Track (3.5km) back to the park entrance. The bushwalk passes through mangroves, along a creek, and near an Aboriginal engraving site. The **Aboriginal Heritage Walk** (3.5km) at West Head is a moderately difficult hike which incorporates the Red Hands Cave, a shelter site, and an engraving site (access by West Head Rd.). Rock engravings in the park include mythical beings and whales up to 8km long. For the best views of the Hawkesbury River as it feeds into **Broken Bay,** proceed north along West Head Rd. until you reach a picnic lookout area.

BLUE MOUNTAINS

The motto of the Blue Mountains region, "come up for air," bespeaks the get-away-from-it-all attitude of this tourist wonderland. Although a variety of adventure activities such as abseiling (rappelling) and canyon rafting have become popular in recent years, the major attractions of the Blue Mountains remain their excellent hiking trails and lookouts. Sunlight filtering through eucalyptus oil suspended in the air gives the forest its tint. From the lookout points, the earth falls away into endless blue foliage speckled with white bark and bordered by distant sandstone cliffs. Whether you have a hankering for drenching waterfalls, serene rainforest, or jaw-dropping panoramic views, you'll find it here.

Because the so-called mountains are actually a series of canyons separated by several high plateaus, colonial explorers found impassable cliffs at the edges of the valleys instead of hills. A successful route through the mountains was not found until 1813, when the bitter white guys finally cried "uncle" and asked the

THE BLUE MOUNTAINS REGION AT A GLANCE	
AREA: Over 8079km²	**GATEWAYS:** 60km west of Sydney (M4 Motorway) to the Great Western Hwy.; Katoomba, Lithgow, Oberon.
FEATURES: Blue Mountains Nat'l Park (p. 136), Kanangra-Boyd Nat'l Park (p. 145), Wollemi Nat'l Park (p. 145).	**CAMPING:** Minimum impact camping allowed; see the parks.
HIGHLIGHTS: Camping, bushwalking, abseiling, canyoning, rafting, and more.	**FEES:** Free entry to any of the national parks.

Aboriginal community, who had lithely crossed the mountains for centuries, how to get across. Today, the mountains are the first stop on most backpacker trips west from Sydney and an easy getaway for Sydney-siders. The short trip inland, a 1½hr. drive or a 2hr. train ride, grants summertime visitors a reprieve from the oppressive heat that hangs over the coast. In winter, crisp sunny days, occasional snowfalls, and Yulefest (Christmas in July) festivities draw travelers.

TRANSPORTATION

BY CAR. The Blue Mountains are an easy 1½hr. drive west of Sydney. The M4 Motorway goes to Penrith and meets the **Great Western Hwy.,** the main route through the mountains. All service centers and attractions lie on or near this road. Alternatively, the northern route, **Bells Line of Road** (see p. 143), roams west from Windsor, northeast of Parramatta, providing a more beautiful passage.

BY TRAIN. CityRail **trains** stop throughout the Blue Mountains at most of the towns along the Great Western Hwy., offering the least expensive option for travelers who are willing to walk sizable distances from rail stations and bus stops to trailheads. Within the towns, most distances are walkable, and local bus companies cover those that aren't (for bus info, see **Katoomba,** p. 138). There is **no public transportation** to Kanangra-Boyd National Park or Wollemi National Park.

BY TOUR. There are two above-par companies running **smaller-bus tours** into the Blue Mountains from Sydney. **Wonderbus** offers a tour that includes stops at Euroka Clearing Campground, Wentworth Falls, Katoomba's Echo Point, and Blackheath's Govetts Leap. The aim is to allow time for wilderness bushwalks with the experienced driver-guide. Participants who wish to adopt a more leisurely touring pace can arrange for an overnight stay in the mountains. (☎9555 9800. Departs daily 7:30am, returns 7pm. $60.) **Wildframe Ecotours** provides similar services and offers a trip into the challenging Grand Canyon, a tremendous rainforest-filled gorge in Blackheath. (☎0500 505 056. Daytrip $72, concession $60; with 1 night at the YHA hostel in Katoomba $105; 2 nights $125.) Both companies offer other trips as well, including **spelunking** and **abseiling.**

Several companies run **large-bus tours** to the mountains from Sydney. **AAT Kings,** Jetty 6, Circular Quay, offers several options. (24hr. ☎9518 6095. Basic tour $89, concessions $84; bushwalking package with cattleman's lunch $90/$85; bushwalking with horseriding or 4WD $117/$108. Depart 8:30am, return 5:45pm. Jenolan Caves tour with 6:45pm return $109/$99. 10% YHA discount.) **Mountain Bus Co.** services a daytrip to the park's highlights and stops at the Olympic park on the way back to Sydney. (☎1800 507 071. 10hr.)

ORIENTATION

Three national parks divide the wild stretches of the region. **Blue Mountains National Park,** the largest and most accessible of the three, spans most of the Jamison Valley (south of the Great Western Hwy. between Glenbrook and Katoomba), the Megalong Valley (south of the Great Western Hwy. west of Katoomba) and the Grose Valley (north of the Great Western Hwy. and east of Blackheath). The Grose and Jamison Valleys appeal primarily to hikers, while horseback riders favor the

Megalong Valley (for more information on horse-riding, see **Blackheath**, p. 142). **Kanangra-Boyd National Park** (see p. 145), tucked between two sections of Blue Mountains National Park in the southwest reaches of the mountains, is reserved for skilled bushwalkers. The park, accessible by partially paved roads from Oberon and from Jenolan Caves, has only one 2WD road. **Wollemi National Park** (see p. 145) contains the state's largest preserved wilderness area. It's a place so unspoiled and untrafficked that a species of pine tree thought to be long extinct was found here in 1994, alive and well. Access to Wollemi, the southern edge of which abuts the north side of **Bells Line of Road,** is possible at Bilpin and at several points north of the central Blue Mountains.

The national parks of the Blue Mountains region are administered by different branches of the **National Parks and Wildlife Services (NPWS).** If you are planning to bushcamp or even to drive into these parks, contact the appropriate NPWS office (see specific park listings) a few days in advance to ensure that roads are drivable and that no bushfire bans are in place. Additionally, it is recommended that you leave a bushwalk plan filed with the appropriate NPWS office before you go.

BLUE MOUNTAINS NATIONAL PARK

The largest of the Blue Mountain region national parks, the eponymous park lies in between Kangara Boyd and Wollemi National Park to the north and south. The main gateway towns are Katoomba (p. 138) and Blackheath (p. 142), and the rest of the park lies spread around the Great Western Hwy. and Bell's Line Rd.

ALONG THE GREAT WESTERN HIGHWAY

Coming out of Sydney, the Great Western Hwy. passes Penrith, right before the entrance to the Blue Mountains National Park. It extends to Lithgow, passing several gateway town within the park.

GLENBROOK ☎02

Blue Mountain Tourism operates an office in the town of Glenbrook that serves as the gateway to the Blue Mountains region from Sydney. (☎1300 653 408; fax 4780 5729. Open M-F 9am-5pm, Sa-Su 8:30am-4:30pm.) A few kilometers south of Glenbrook you'll find the easternmost entrance to **Blue Mountains National Park,** one of eight protected areas making up the World Heritage site collectively known as the Greater Blue Mountains Area. This World Heritage status was just awarded two years ago. From the highway, take Ross St. until it dead-ends. Turn left on Burfitt Pde. (later named Bruce Rd.) and follow it to the park. (☎4787 8877; www.npws.nsw.gov.au. Car $6, cyclists and pedestrians free.)

The walking track to **Red Hands Cave** starts at the NPWS Visitors Centre and runs an easy 8km circuit through patches of open forest, leading ultimately to a gallery of **hand stencils** attributed to the Daruk Aborigines. Along the way to the cave, the trail passes **Jellybean Pool,** a popular swimming hole near the park's entrance. You can reduce the length of the hike to a mere 300m stroll (one-way) if you drive to the Red Hands carpark and begin there.

Four kilometers beyond the Bruce Rd. entrance of the park, over mostly paved roads, is the **Euroka Clearing Campground.** The site has pit toilets, BBQ plates, and pumped creek water. Kangaroos congregate close by at dawn and dusk. The park entrance is locked in the evenings (winter 6pm-8:30am; summer 7pm-8:30am), and that campers are advised to bring ample firewood, food, and drinking water. Call the NPWS in Richmond to arrange permits in advance. (☎4588 5247. Open M-F 9am-5pm. Sites $5 per adult per night, $3 per child per night.) Bushcamping is free.

At **Blaxland,** roughly 4km west of Glenbrook, Layton Ave. turns off onto a pleasant 2km detour towards **Lennox Bridge,** the **oldest bridge** on the Australian mainland. As you approach the bridge, constructed between 1832-1833, take note of the **Glenbrook Lagoon.** It's the spot where the team of Blaxland, Lawson, and Wentworth set up their first camp before tackling the mountains.

West of Blaxland (and the towns of Warrimoo, Valley Heights, and Springwood) lies **Faulconbridge,** site of the National Trust-owned **Norman Lindsay Gallery,** at 14 Norman Lindsay Crescent. The gallery displays a large collection of work by the controversial and multitalented artist who once inhabited the house. Lindsay drew intense criticism in the first half of the 20th century because of his use of female nudes as his primary subjects. Lindsay's popular children's book, *The Magic Pudding*, not featuring nudes, has been in continuous publication since 1918. To get to the gallery by car from Sydney, turn right off the Great Western Hwy. onto Grose Rd., in Falconbridge, and follow the well-posted signs for the next 9km. Public transportation to the site is limited to a taxi ride ($10-12) from the Springwood Railway Station. (☎4751 1067. Open daily 10am-4pm. $8, concessions $5.50.)

WOODFORD ☎02

Woodford, about 15km east of Katoomba on the Great Western Hwy., serves as a turn-off to a few popular campgrounds. A left off the highway onto Park Rd., a left onto Railway Pde., and a right onto Bedford Rd., leads to the **Murphys Glen Campground** (10km south of Woodford). Located within a forest of tall eucalypts, turpentines, and angophoras, the campground has pit toilets, but lacks drinking water. (No permits required. Free.) Also within Blue Mountains National Park is the **Ingar Campground.** To get there, drive west past Woodford (and the towns of Hazelbrook, Lawson, and Bullburra), turn left off the highway onto Tableland Rd., travel 2km., turn left at Queen Elizabeth Dr., and proceed 11km along an unpaved road to Ingar. The campground has pit toilets, but lacks drinking water and cooking facilities. (No permits required. Free.) Nearby, a small pond and creek make the spot popular for picnics and camping.

The town of **Wentworth Falls,** 14km beyond Woodford, is renowned for its picturesque waterfall walks and record foliage diversity (more varieties of plants exist in the Blue Mountains than in all Europe). To find the trailhead at the **Wentworth Falls Picnic Area,** turn off the Great Western Hwy. onto Falls Rd., and continue to the end of the road. From this area, several viewpoints are within easy reach. The 15min. walk to **Princes Rock** ends at a lookout with views of Wentworth Falls, Kings Tableland, and Mt. Solitary. The 30min. walk to **Rocket Point Lookout** wanders through open heathland and has views into the Jamison Valley. To find the trailhead at the **Conservation Hut,** turn off the highway at either Falls Rd. or Valley Rd., turn right onto Fletcher St., and continue straight to the parking area. Perched on the rim of the valley, the hut is both a cafe with a killer view and a Blue Mountains National Park information center. (☎4757 3827. Open daily 9am-5pm.)

For an ambitious and stunning loop hike, follow the **Valley of the Waters Track** to **Empress Lookout,** head down the metal stairs, and then turn left at the intersection with the Nature Track. Continue straight ahead and at the intersection with Wentworth Pass, follow **National Pass**. Keep the cliffs on your left. After traversing the cliff band, the path ascends a steep set of stairs up to Wentworth Falls and the Wentworth Falls Picnic Area. From the carpark, you can head back to the hut via the **Short Cut Track** (4hr. circuit) or the **Undercliff-Overcliff Track** (5-6hr. circuit). Spectacular scenery and lush hanging swamps will reward the effort.

On starry nights, visit the **Kings Tableland Observatory,** 55 Hordern Rd. A local astronomer-extraordinaire shows you constellations, globular clusters, and distant planets. (☎4757 2954. Open W-Sa 7-9:30pm. 2hr.; $10, children $8, family $28.)

LEURA ☎02

The likeable and affluent town of Leura (pop. 8500), 5km west of Wentworth Falls and adjacent to Katoomba, offers shops, cafes, and galleries along its central street, Leura Mall. As one tour guide put it, "Leura is a latte and an afternoon at antique stores, and Blackheath is a flat white and a stop-off at second hand shops." (For translation help, see **Coffee Confusion,** p. 115.) **Everglades Gardens,** 37 Everglades St., is a lush example of the floral cultivation for which the town is known. (☎4784 1938. Open Sept.-Feb. daily 10am-5pm, Mar.-Aug. 10am-4pm. $6, concessions $4.) Near the gardens, Fitzroy St. intersects Everglades St. and leads east to

Watkins Rd., which soon turns into Sublime Point Rd. and ends at the breathtaking overlook at **Sublime Point.** For travelers continuing west toward Katoomba, the 8km **Cliff Drive,** beginning at Gordon Rd. near the south end of Leura Mall, provides a scenic escape from the highway. The loop passes many lookouts and a handful of trailheads. In Katoomba, Cliff Dr. turns into Echo Point Rd. If you're up quite early in the morning, turn south off of the Great Western Hwy. down **Mt. Hay Rd.** and travel 12km to a majestic sunrise over the cliffs (the last 2km are unsealed).

KATOOMBA ☎02

The image most widely associated with the Blue Mountains is that of the Three Sisters, a trio of towering stone outcroppings jutting out into the Jamison Valley, silently holding vigil over the dark blue-green valley below. One of the most accessible places to marvel at the formation is found at Echo Point, at the south end of Katoomba. In addition to its enviable natural setting, Katoomba (pop. 9000) offers excellent hiking, climbing, and biking opportunities and a very convenient rail-accessible location. The result is an outdoor enthusiast's dream. Though Katoomba is touristy, the town retains a distinctively liberal flavor, replete with VW vans, vegetarian eateries, and dredlocked 'dos.

TRANSPORTATION

Trains: Katoomba Railway Station (☎4782 1902) is on Main St., at the north end of Katoomba St. **CityRail** trains and **Countrylink** (☎13 22 32) trains and buses run to: **Bathurst** (2hr., 1 per day, $19); **Blackheath** (13min., 17-23 per day, $3); **Dubbo** (5hr., 1 per day, $52); **Glenbrook** (50min., 18-28 per day, $5); **Lithgow** (45min., 12-15 per day, $6); **Mt. Victoria** (20min., 12-15 per day, $3); **Orange** (3hr., 1 per day, $29); **Parramatta** (1½hr., 20-29 per day, $10); **Penrith** (1hr., 19-26 per day, $6); **Sydney** (2hr., 20-29 per day, $11); **Zig Zag Railway** (45min., $5) but make sure you request this stop with the guard at the rear of the train (see p. 144). **Mountainlink** (☎4782 3333) runs to **Leura** ($2.60), **Blackheath** ($4.80), and **Mt. Victoria** ($5.30). 50% discount for concessions.

Buses: Greyhound Pioneer (☎13 20 30) runs from opposite the Gearin Hotel, 273 Great Western Hwy., to: **Adelaide** (21½hr., 1 per day, $121); **Bathurst** (2hr., 1 per day, $30); **Broken Hill** (14hr., 1 per day, $121); **Dubbo** (4¾hr., 1 per day, $53); **Lithgow** (40min., 1 per day, $15); **Orange** (3hr., 1 per day, $33); **Penrith** (40min., 1 per day, $15); **Sydney** (2½hr., 1 per day, $30).

Local and Park Transportation: Blue Mountains Bus Company (☎4782 4213) runs between **Katoomba** and **Woodford** with stops at **Katoomba Station,** near **Echo Point,** the **Edge Cinema, Leura Mall,** the **Valley of the Waters trailhead,** the **Scenic Skyway,** and **Wentworth Falls.** Fares $1.80-3; unlimited all-day pass $7.50. Regular service daily approximately 7:30am-6pm. For day-touring at your own pace, the **Blue Mountains Explorer Bus** (☎4782 1866) runs an 27-stop circuit allowing passengers to get on and off as often as they choose. $22, concessions $19, students up through high school $11. All prices include a ticket to see *The Edge* movie. Buses run daily every hr., 9:30am-5:30pm. Timetables for both services are available at the Blue Mountains Tourism Authority center on Echo Point. All pickups from the **Carrington Hotel** on Main St.

Taxis: Katoomba Leura Radio Cars (☎4782 1311) picks up 24hr. anywhere between Wentworth Falls and Mt. Victoria. Initial fare $4, plus $1.07 per km.

Automobile Clubs: NRMA (road service ☎13 11 11).

Bike Rental: Cycletech, 182 Katoomba St. (☎4782 2800). Mountain bikes half-day $27.50, full-day $49.50. Non-front suspension bikes half-day $19, full-day $27.50. Helmets, locks, and repair kits included. 10% discount for YHA and backpackers. Open M-F 9am-5:30pm, Sa 9am-5pm, Su 9am-4pm.

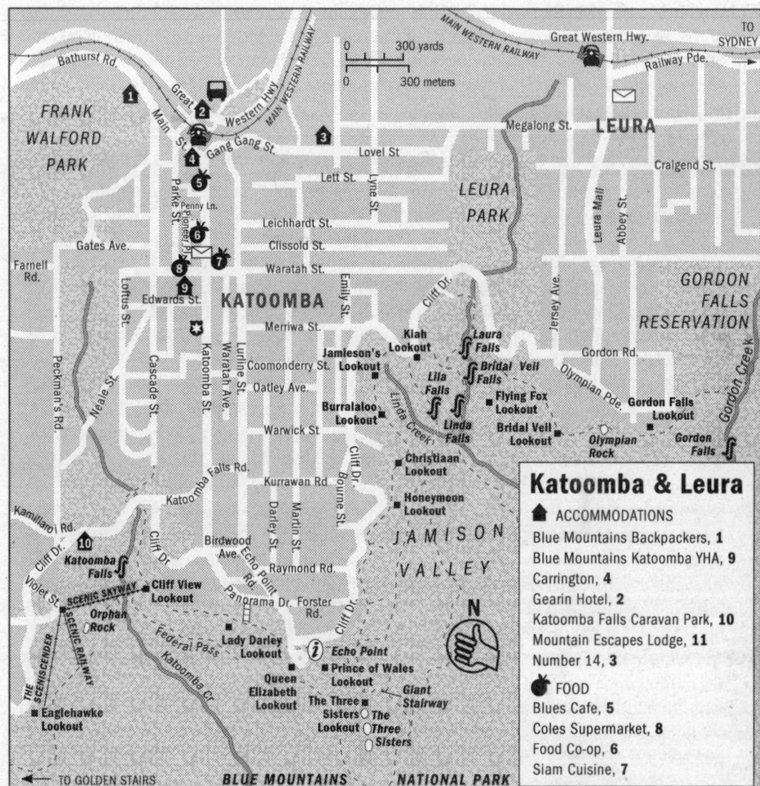

ORIENTATION AND PRACTICAL INFORMATION

Katoomba sits just south of the Great Western Hwy., 2km west of Leura and 109km from Sydney. The town's main drag, **Katoomba St.,** runs south from the Katoomba Railway Station through town toward Echo Point. Echo Point Rd. brings visitors to the Blue Mountains' most famous view, the Three Sisters.

Tourist Office: Blue Mountains Tourism (☎1300 653 408; fax 4739 6787; www.bluemountainstourism.org.au), at the end of Echo Point Rd., on Echo Point. Take Lurline St. south and veer left onto Echo Rd. when Lurline St. ends. Open daily 9am-5pm. For hiking advice from park rangers, try the NPWS Blue Mountain Heritage Center in Blackheath (see p. 142).

Hospital: Blue Mountains District Anzac Memorial Hospital (☎4780 6000), on the Great Western Hwy., 1km east of the railway station.

Internet Access: Barcode 6ix Internet Caffe, 6 Katoomba St. (☎4782 6896). Snacks and coffee available. $3 per 30min., $5 per hr. Open daily 9am-9 pm.

Post Office: Pioneer Pl. (☎4782 1005). Open M-F 9am-5pm. **Postal Code:** 2780.

ACCOMMODATIONS

Katoomba increasingly hosts larger numbers of budget travelers than anywhere else in the Blue Mountains, and this trend is coupled with diminishing options outside the town line. Although beds here are plentiful, so are the vacationers that swamp the town Nov.-Apr. and on winter weekends. Advance bookings are highly recommended, especially on school holidays and long weekends.

Number 14, 14 Lovel St. (☎4782 7104; www.bluemts.com.au/no14). A 5min. walk east of the train station via Gang Gang St. If the mix of slate and rare Baltic Pine floors, the outstanding kitchen, the sunny side-porch, and the comfortable furnishings don't convince you to stay in this small home-away-from-home, the quiet and friendly atmosphere will. No TV. Reception daily 8am-noon and 4:30-9:30pm. Single-sex dorms $20; twins and doubles $50; 1 double with bath $58.

Blue Mountains Katoomba YHA, 207 Katoomba St. (☎4782 1416; bluemountains@yhansw.org.au). A 5-10min. walk south of the train station via Katoomba St. This fully renovated Art Deco guesthouse just opened in 2001. You may initially feel like a kid in a candy store, overwhelmed by the all the amenities. Spacious kitchen, relaxed dining area, huge commons area, gas fireplace, pool table, Internet, TV/video lounge, activity-planning room, outside terrace, laundry, lockers, and ample parking. The amazingly helpful staff provides heaps of information and insights on how to best enjoy your time in the mountains. Linens included. Reception daily 7am-10pm. Dorm $16-20; double $60; double with bath $68; family room $60-80 per room.

Blue Mountains Backpackers, 190 Bathurst Rd. (☎4782 4226; fax 4782 4236; bluemountains@hotmail.com). A 5min. walk west of the train station. It's a fun, friendly, mellow accommodation aimed at a young crew. Small kitchen, dining area with TV/video, common room, and a travel desk. Free luggage storage. Bike $21 per half-day, $29 per day. Linen $1. Key deposit $10. Reception daily 9am-noon and 5-8pm. Tentsites $12, weekly $63; dorms $13-17/$91; twins and doubles $50/$294. VIP/YHA.

Mountain Escapes Lodge, 77 Darley St. (☎1800 357 577; www.bluemts.com.au/escapes). A 15min. walk from the train station and a 5min. walk to Echo Point. Colorful walls, abundant windows, and wood floors add to the homey feel of this small, gracious hostel. TV/video, kitchen, BBQ, laundry, off-street parking. Linens and continental breakfast included. Reception 24hr. Dorm $22; double with veranda $60.

Katoomba Falls Caravan Park, on Katoomba Falls Rd. (☎4782 1835), south of town via Katoomba St. Well-positioned for bushwalks and the Scenic Skyway, Sceniscender and Scenic Railway. Toilets, hot showers, indoor BBQ, laundry, children's playground. No linen. Key deposit $20. Reception daily 8am-7pm. Sites for 2 $24, families $26; powered for 2 $26.40, family $30; cabins for 2 with bath $81, each extra person $11.

FOOD AND ENTERTAINMENT

Katoomba St. is littered with cafes, takeaways, and nicer restaurants serving a variety of cuisines at all price levels. The **Blues Cafe,** 55-57 Katoomba St., prepares excellent, high-class veggie cuisine for dine-in or take-away. (☎4782 2347. Open daily 9am-5:00pm. Light meals $4-9, mains $8-13.) **Siam Cuisine,** 172 Katoomba St., has delicious, authentic Thai food. (☎4782 5671. Open Tu-Su 11:30am-2:30pm and 5:30-10pm. Lunch specials $6, mains $10-14. BYO.) One of several popular cafes clustered at the top of the hill near the train station, **Coles supermarket** is next to K-Mart on Parke St. (Open daily 6am-midnight.) The **Food Co-op,** on Hapenny Ln. off Katoomba St. (pedestrian access only), sells organic and bulk foods. (Open M-Sa 9am-5pm. 10% YHA discount.)

Katoomba's nightlife revolves around two main downtown pubs. The historic **Carrington Hotel,** 15-47 Katoomba St., oversees three separate establishments. There's a small piano bar at the hotel, a mellow watering hole at the top of Katoomba St., and a large pub with an upstairs nightclub on Main St. (☎4782 1111. DJs F-Sa. Nightclub open Th-Sa until 4am. Open daily 11am-late. Th cover $25, includes all drinks. Sa cover $5.) The **Gearin Hotel,** 273 Great Western Hwy., can get rowdy and smokey. The crowd varies in age but tends to be more alternative than other nightspots in town. On Wednesdays, the Gearin hosts a popular local band Jam Night. (☎4782 6028. Open 11am-late.)

The **Edge Maxvision Cinema,** 225 Great Western Hwy., projects *The Edge,* a 38min. film on the Blue Mountains, onto a six-story screen. The movie takes viewers to several places in the mountains that cannot be accessed by visitors, including the secret grove where the recently-discovered Wollemi pine species grows. The cinema also shows other giant-format films and recent feature films. (☎4782 8900. *The Edge:* Six shows daily 10:30, 11:20am, noon, 1:30, 2:25, and 5:30pm. $12.50, concessions $10.50, child $8. Other films: W-M $10.50, $9.50, $8; Tu $8.)

FUN WITH TRIPLETS According to Aboriginal legend, Katoomba's Three Sisters are more than just pretty rocks; they are beautiful maidens trapped since the Dreamtime (the Aboriginal time of creation) in stone pillars. Once upon a time, three exquisite sisters lived at home with their father, the Witchdoctor of their Katoomba tribe. Word of their beauty spread far and wide, reaching three brothers of the Nepean tribe, who were so enamored that they simply had to marry the mistresses. Ancestral law prohibited the women from marrying outside their tribe. Undaunted by this obstacle, the brothers attempted to capture their objects of affection by force and waged war on the Katoomba tribe. The Katoombans were no match for the mighty Nepeans; when the Witchdoctor realized this, he magically transformed his daughters into stone for protection. The sisters awaited the end of the war and their father's return. But the Witchdoctor of Katoomba fell in battle, and his daughters are still waiting at Echo Point for someone to release them from their imprisonment.

LOOKOUTS, WALKS, AND ACTIVITIES

ECHO POINT. Nearly everyone who visits Katoomba ventures out to Echo Point, at the southernmost tip of town, to take in the geologic grandeur of the **Three Sisters.** Even after sunset, strategically placed floodlights lend a surreal brilliance to these three golden dames (dusk- 10:30pm). There are numerous short trails and dramatic overlooks in the Echo Point area. If you're up for a longer, more demanding 4-5hr. circuit, descend the steep and taxing 860-step **Giant Stairway Walk** down the back of the Three Sisters and connect up with the **Federal Pass Trail.** At the trail junction, turn right and follow Federal Pass as it snakes its way through the Jamison Valley, past the picnic area at Cooks Crossing (at the base of **Katoomba Falls**) and the beautiful, free-standing pillar known as **Orphan Rock.** Just beyond Orphan Rock are two ways out of the valley. You can either hike the seemingly endless **Furber Steps** and ascend through overhanging sandstone and clay rock formations, past the spray of waterfalls, and through rainforest foliage; or you can buy a ticket to ride the harrowing, mechanized **Scenic Railway** (see below). From the top of the canyon, it's possible to return to Echo Point via the **Prince Henry Cliff Walk.**

NEW SOUTH WALES

SCENIC RAILWAY STATION. Located at the corner of Violet St. and Cliff Dr., this transportation hub offers three unique perspectives on the Blue Mountains region. The **Scenic Railway,** the **world's most steeply inclined railway,** is a tourist attraction in its own right. Originally designed for hauling unappreciative chunks of coal, its 52-degree pitch now thrills white-knuckled tourists and hikers during its seven-minute trip in or out of the Jamison Valley (one-way $5). The large, brand-new **Sceniscender** cable car smoothly travels a similar route as the railway, from cliff-top to valley floor (one-way $10). The **Scenic Skyway** is a cable gondola suspended high over the Katoomba Falls Gorge. Though you only travel out and back, the views looking down are tremendous. *(☎4782 2699; www.scenicworld.com.au. Open daily. Trips depart approximately every 10min. from 9am-4:50pm. $8.)*

NARROW NECK PLATEAU. Jutting out and separating the Jamison Valley and the Megalong Valley, the Narrow Neck Plateau offers short and long **walks,** excellent **mountain biking,** panoramic views, and spectacular **sunsets.** To reach the plateau by car, follow Cliff Dr. west out of Katoomba. Just past the Landslide Lookout, turn right onto the gravel **Glen Raphael Dr.** You can drive about 1.5km along Narrow Neck, up to a locked gate, but the next 7km is for walkers or bicyclists only. One kilometer after the Cliff Dr. turnoff is the trailhead for the **Golden Stairs.** This track runs steeply down the cliff face and intersects the Federal Pass track. To get to the Scenic Railway *(1½hr. one-way),* turn left at the bottom of the stairs. To get to **Ruined Castle** *(5-6hr. return),* a distinctive rock formation reminiscent of crumbling turrets, turn right at the bottom and follow the path to the Ruined Castle turnoff on the right. At the Ruined Castle, a short climb to the top yields views straight across the valley to distant parts of the Blue Mountains and Kanangra-Boyd National Parks. Because of the grueling ascent back up the Golden Stairs, many walkers on the return from Ruined Castle continue east, past the Golden Stairs junction, to the Scenic Railway (see above). If you do this, add another hour onto your itinerary.

TOURS. Several companies in Katoomba organize adventure trips throughout the Blue Mountains, from guided **bushwalking** to **abseiling** to **canyoning. High 'n' Wild Mountain Adventures,** 3/5 Katoomba St., can definitely keep you busy. *(☎4782 6224; www.high-n-wild.com.au. Open daily 8:30am-5:30pm. Mountain bike tours half-day from $75, full-day $130; abseiling $75/$119; year-round canyoning courses from $129; rock climbing course $129. $10 student/backpacker discount.)* The Katoomba Adventure Centre, 1 Katoomba St., offers similar packages but has recently imported the New Zealand whitewater sport known as "River Bugging" and introduced it to the narrow rivers of the region. *(☎1800 624 226. Open daily 9am-6pm. Rafting from $130, summer only.)* The **Australian School of Mountaineering,** 166 Katoomba St., inside the Paddy Pallin outdoor shop, offers both introductory and advanced technical courses. *(☎4782 2014; www.ausmtn.com.au. Open daily 8:30am-5:30pm.)* **Tread Lightly,** one of the few tour operators in Australia with national *Advanced Ecotourism* accreditation, focuses on the ecology, flora and fauna, history, and Aboriginal Culture of the Blue Mountains. *(☎4788 1229; www.treadlightly.com.au. Wilderness walks from $25; "Rocks to Rainforest" 4WD from $85; Glow worm night walk $38.50.)* **Fantastic Aussie Tours,** 283 Main St., at the top of the railway stairs, arranges a variety of coach-based excursions. *(24hr. ☎4782 1866 or 1300 300 915; www.fantastic-aussie-tours.com.au. "Blue Mountains Highlights" M-F 11:30am-3:15pm or 2-5:15pm. $44, concessions $32, family $103; Jenolan Caves daily 10:30am-5:15pm from $69/$57/$192.)*

BLACKHEATH ☎02

Behind the facade of restaurants, pubs, and upscale shops lining the highway, Blackheath is primarily a small, friendly, residential town in a great location. To the northeast lies the beautiful Grose Valley, which offers many of the area's best lookouts and most challenging walks. To the south is the Megalong Valley, a popular spot for horseback riding. Given its prime position and its easy accessibility, Blackheath is a natural choice as a Blue Mountains base, though its services are more limited than Katoomba's.

TRANSPORTATION. The Great Western Hwy. snakes 11km west and north from Katoomba to the town of Blackheath on the way to Mt. Victoria and Lithgow. Mountainlink runs **buses** from Katoomba to Mt. Victoria by way of Blackheath, and comes as close as possible to the town's major trailheads. (☎4782 3333. Service M-F 7:30am-6pm, Sa 6:30am-4:30pm; from $4.80.) CityRail **train** service connects Blackheath to: Glenbrook (1hr., 15-22 per day, $6); Katoomba (11min., 15-23 per day, $3); Lithgow (30min., 12 per day, $5); Parramatta (2hr., 15-20 per day, $10); Penrith (1¼hr., 15-20 per day, $8); Sydney (2½hr., 15-20 per day, $13). Hikers, keep in mind that Blackheath Station is 3km from the trailhead at Govetts Leap.

PRACTICAL INFORMATION. Regional tourist information falls under the auspices of **Blue Mountains Tourism,** at Echo Point, Katoomba (☎1300 653 408). Questions concerning Blue Mountains National Park, Wollemi National Park, and Kanangra-Boyd National Park are best handled by the NPWS-run **Blue Mountains Heritage Centre,** at the end of Govetts Leap Rd. Staffed by park officials who know their stuff, the centre also has exhibits, detailed trail guides for sale ($2-4), and refreshments. (☎4787 8877. Open daily 9am-4:30pm.)

ACCOMMODATIONS AND FOOD. The **New Ivanhoe Hotel,** at the corner of the Great Western Hwy. and Govetts Leap Rd., has clean, tasteful, and not-at-all-pub-like rooms. (☎4787 8158. Light breakfast included. Reception at bar Su-Th 6am-midnight, F-Sa 6am-2am. Twins and doubles $66, with bath $88.) The tent camping area at **Blackheath Caravan Park,** on Prince Edward St. off Govetts Leap Rd., lies in a tree-covered grove down a steep hill, secluded from the rest of the park. (☎4787 8101. Toilets, showers, BBQ. Key deposit $10. Reception daily 8am-7pm. Sites $9 per person, powered $12; trailers for 2 $42, each extra person $6.60.)

There are two **NPWS camping areas** accessible from Blackheath: **Perrys Lookdown,** 8km from the Great Western Hwy. at the end of the mostly unpaved Hat Hill Rd. (5 walk-in sites; 1-night stay only) and **Acacia Flat,** on the floor of the Grose Valley, a hefty 4hr. hike from Govetts Leap and a 2-3hr. hike from Perrys Lookdown. Both sites are free and lack facilities other than pit toilets. Campfires are not permitted. Water from Govetts Creek is available at Acacia Flat, but it must be treated before use. There is no reliable water source at Perrys Lookdown.

If small Blackheath is too big for you, head 7km west on the Great Western Hwy. to **Mt. Victoria,** a quiet village that serves as an alternate Blue Mountains base. It has several historic buildings, including **Manor House,** on Montgomery St., the former summer home of John Fairfax, built in 1876. The **Victoria and Albert Guesthouse,** 19 Station St., has a pool, spa, and sauna. (☎4787 1241. Reception daily 8am-8pm. B&B for 1 with shared bath Su-Th $50, for 2 $90; F-Sa $66/$100; with bath Su-Th $75/$120; F-Sa $90/$150.)

HIKES AND LOOKOUTS. Walks in the Blackheath area vary widely in length and level of difficulty. The **Fairfax Heritage Track** (30min. one-way) is wheelchair-accessible and leads to the **Govetts Leap,** one of the most magnificent lookouts in Blue Mountains National Park. From Govetts Leap, the moderate **Pulpit Rock Track** (3hr. return) follows the cliff line north for spectacular views along the way of Horseshoe Falls and a 280-degree view of the Grose Valley from the Pulpit Rock lookout. The **Cliff Top Walk** travels the other direction to **Evans Lookout** (2hr. return) past the majestic **Bridal Veil Falls,** a thin and wispy stream that takes nearly 10 seconds to tumble all the way into the valley below.

The **Grand Canyon Walking Track** (5km; 3-4hr. circuit) is undoubtedly one of the most popular hikes in all the Blue Mountains. You can start either at **Neates Glen** or **Evans Lookout.** If you need to park a car, leave it at the Grand Canyon Loop Car Park, along the Evans Lookout Rd. The circuit passes through sandstone cliffs, wet rainforest, and exposed heathland. Anthropologists speculate that the Grand Canyon was probably a route long used by Aboriginal people to gain access to the deposits of chert (often modified into cutting tools) at the base of Beauchamp Falls. Archaeological evidence suggests that Aborigines occupied the Grand Canyon from at least 12,000 years ago.

Six kilometers north of Blackheath along the Great Western Hwy. is **Hat Hill Rd.,** a mostly dirt route that bumps and bounces to an excellent lookout and a popular trailhead for the **Blue Gum Forest.** Near the end of the road, the turnoff leading to the parking area for **Anvil Rock** and the magical features of the misnamed **Wind Eroded Cave** (the feature is the result of water) is well worth the side trip. At the end of the road, the trail from **Perrys Lookdown** steeply descends 600m and leads to a forest still inhabited by parrots, cockatoos, and lyrebirds (5hr. walk).

The **scenic drive** into the **Megalong Valley** begins on Shipley Rd., across the Great Western Hwy. from Govett's Leap Rd. Cross the railroad tracks from the highway and take an immediate left onto Station St., following it until it turns right to become Shipley Rd. Megalong Rd. is a left turn from Shipley Rd., leading down to a picturesque farmland area that contrasts nicely with the surrounding wilderness. In the valley, outfitters conduct guided **trail rides** or supply horses. **Werriberri Trail Rides** is on Megalong Rd. near Werriberri Lodge. (☎4787 9171. Open daily 9am-3:30pm; reservations 7:30am-8:30pm. 30min. $19, 3hr. $57.) The **Megalong Australian Heritage Centre,** a bit farther south on Megalong Rd., has longer guided rides, unguided outings, livestock lassoing shows, and 4WD bush trips. (☎4787 8188. Open daily 8:30am-6pm. Horse rides daily 10am-4pm. 3hr. ride with lunch $82, full-day $95. Unguided: $25 for first hr., $22 each additional hr. 4WD $25 per hr.)

ALONG THE BELLS LINE OF ROAD

The difference between taking the Great Western Hwy. through the Blue Mountains and taking Bells Line of Road through the same region is similar to the difference between setting out to get drunk with a tumbler of cheap gin and doing so with a bottle of fine wine. You eventually wind up in the same place, but one route allows you to savor the experience a bit more along the way. This 87km drive between Windsor and Lithgow provides bucolic passage through the mountains, perfect if you have the luxury of time.

KURRAJONG HEIGHTS. At the top of the Heights, 16km west of Richmond, the **Kurrajong Heights Grass Ski Park** rents specially designed "grass karts" (made of little more than a steel frame, four rubber wheels, and a hand brake) that allow you to careen 450m down a mountainside regardless of the weather or season. An uphill lift ensures that visitors get the most out of their time. *(☎4567 7184. Open Sa-Su and public holidays 9am-5pm. 1hr. $11, each extra hour $6.)*

BILPIN. The town of Bilpin, 5km west of Kurrajong Heights, has several active orchards and roadside fruit stands that sell fresh-picked produce most of the year.

MT. TOMAH BOTANIC GARDEN. A couple kilometers west of Berambing, Mt. Tomah Botanic Garden is the cool-climate and high-altitude plant collection of Sydney's Royal Botanic Garden. The plants thrive on the rich volcanic soil and grow in naturalistic arrangements, with the exception of the herbs and roses in the formal terrace garden. The garden's best moments are in spring (Sept.-Oct.), when the large collection of rhododendrons and other flowers bloom, and in autumn (April -May) when the deciduous forest areas change their colors. Free tours depart the visitors center during the week. *(☎4567 2154. Open daily Mar.-Sept. 10am-4pm, Oct.-Feb. 10am-5pm. $4.40, concession $2.20, family $8.80.)*

MT. WILSON. People come from far and wide to see the formal, European-style gardens and unspoiled rainforest of the small town of Mt. Wilson, 8km north of Bells Line of Road, between Mt. Tomah and Bell. For a sample of the fern-laden rainforest, turn right onto Queens Ave. off the main road through town and proceed about 500m until you reach a park area on the left. From there, follow signs to a moderate 45min. circular walk (steep steps) that leads to the base of two small waterfalls. Three gardens in and around town stay open throughout the year: **Sefton Cottage,** on Church Ln. *(☎4756 2034; open daily 10am-6pm; $3);* **Merry Garth,** on Davies Ln., 500m from Mt. Irvine Rd. *(☎4756 2121; open daily 9am-6pm; $3);* and **Lindfield Park,** on Mt. Irvine Rd., 6km northeast of Mt. Wilson *(☎4756 2148; open daily 10am- dark; $3).*

ZIG ZAG RAILWAY. The Zig Zag Railway, 10km east of Lithgow at Clarence, is a functional train operating on a piece of the 1869 track that first made regular travel possible across the Blue Mountains and down into the Lithgow Valley. *(☎6351 4826. 1½hr. tours depart daily at 11am, 1, and 3pm. $17 return, concessions $14, ages 5-18 $8.50.)* By request, CityRail **trains** from Sydney's Central Station stop near the bottom of the track *($13).*

LITHGOW ☎02

The Great Western Hwy. and Bells Line of Road meet on the west side of the Blue Mountains at Lithgow, a medium-sized, vaguely industrial town, at the end of the Sydney's CityRail train line. The town has little charm beyond its utility for exploring nearby wilderness areas such as Wollemi National Park to the north and the Jenolan Caves and Kanangra-Boyd National Park to the south.

Grand Central Hotel, 69 Main St., is the pick of the litter with its spacious singles and TV lounge. Take a left out of the train station and walk two blocks. (☎6351 3050. Singles $23.) The **pub** and adjacent **bistro** are pleasant. (Open daily noon-2pm and 6-9pm.) The **Blue Bird Cafe,** 118 Main St., prepares huge omelets and great milkshakes. (☎6352 4211. Open daily 6:30am-7:30pm.) The Food For Less **grocery store** is on Railway Pde. (☎6352 2011. Open M-Sa 7am-10pm, Su 7am-6pm.)

Blackfellows Hands Reserve, 24km north of Lithgow, off Wolgen Rd. to Newnes, was a meeting place for Aboriginal tribes, and paintings adorn the walls of the cave. **Gardens of Stone National Park,** 30km north of Lithgow, features pagoda-like formations from millions of years of erosion. The highest lookout in the Blue Mountains (1130m) is indisputably worth the 5min. detour along the **Hassans Walls Link** drive. The spectacular granite formations of **Evans Crown Nature Reserve** (☎6354 8155), 32km west of Lithgow, is a climbers' playground.

WOLLEMI NATIONAL PARK

Covering 4875km^2, Wollemi ("WOOL-em-eye") National Park is the second largest park in New South Wales. It extends north of Blue Mountains National Park all the way to the Hunter and Goulburn River valleys. Because 2WD access is extremely limited, the park still has many pockets of undiscovered land. One such area yielded an amazing find in 1994, when scientists found a species of pine tree known previously only through the fossil record. The location of the **Wollemi Pine** grove is a closely-guarded secret.

The southernmost entrance point to the park is at Bilpin on Bells Line of Road. In this corner of the park, also accessible from Putty Rd. north of Windsor, the **Colo River** slices the landscape along the 30km Colo Gorge. The picturesque, car-accessible **camping area** at **Wheeny Creek** lies near good walking tracks and swimming holes. Entrance and campgrounds are free. Additional information is available at the **National Parks and Wildlife Service** office, 370 Windsor Rd. (☎4588 5247. Open M-F 9:30am-12:30pm and 1:30-5pm.)

Farther west, a 37km unsealed road from Lithgow takes starry-eyed observers within 1.5km of **Glow Worm Tunnel,** an abandoned railway tunnel housing hundreds of tiny bioluminescent worms. Be sure to bring a flashlight; keep in mind that what you're looking at is not a beautiful constellation but a wall plastered with shining excrement. The **Lithgow Visitors Centre,** 1 Cooerwull Rd., off the Great Western Hwy. in Lithgow, has maps and info. (☎6353 1859; fax 6353 1851. Open daily 9am-5pm.) There are no marked trails in the northern section of Wollemi National Park.

KANANGRA-BOYD NATIONAL PARK

Southwest of the Blue Mountains National Park, the 680km^2 that comprise Kanangra-Boyd National Park awe with stark wilderness punctuated by rivers and creeks, still-developing caves, and the dramatic sandstone cliffs that mark the edges of the Boyd Plateau. The park's remote location and rugged terrain attract serious bushwalkers looking for long-term solitude.

The park is nonetheless worthwhile for the casual visitors who follow its only 2WD access, the unpaved Kanangra Walls Rd., across the **Boyd Plateau** to the famous lookouts at **Kanangra Walls.** From the east via Mt. Victoria, drive to Jenolan Caves off the Great Western Hwy. (see p. 136). From there, a 5km stretch of dirt road will lead to the park and the junction with Kanangra Walls Rd. At the intersection, turn left. The Kanangra Walls car park is another 26km further. From the west, drive to the town of Oberon and follow the unpaved Jenolan Caves Rd. south to the junction with Kanangra Walls Rd. Turn right to reach the lookouts.

The **National Parks and Wildlife Service** office, 38 Ross St., Oberon (northeast of the park), has details on the park's longer tracks. Be sure to call before visiting or you may find the branch unattended. Cave exploration permits must be obtained at least four weeks in advance. (☎6336 1972. Open M-F 9am-4:30pm.)

The **Boyd River Campground,** on Kanangra Walls Rd. 6km before Kanangra Walls, has the park's only car-accessible camping. There are pit toilets and fireplaces. Bring your own wood and/or a camp stove. Potable water is available from the Boyd River though it should be treated before consumption. Park use fees apply: $6 per day per vehicle; camping $3, child $2.

Three **scenic walks** begin at the Kanangra Walls car park. **Lookout Walk** (20min. return) is a wheelchair-accessible path leading to two viewpoint. The first gazes out across the Kanangra Creek gorge towards **Mt. Cloudmaker,** and the other peers into the ravines at the head of the eight-tiered, 400m **Kanangra Falls.** The **Waterfall Walk** (20min. one-way with steep return) leads from the second lookout to the deep pool at the bottom of **Kalang Falls.** The moderate **Plateau Walk** (2-3hr.) branches from the Lookout Walk between the parking lot and the first lookout, descending briefly from the plateau before ascending to Kanangra Tops for views of Kanangra Walls. Along the way, **Dance Floor Cave** contains indented floors and other signs of old-time recreation in the park. A water container placed in the cave in 1940 catches pure, drinkable water dripping from the cave ceiling. Longer walks, like the **3-4 day hike** from Kanangra Walls to Katoomba via Mt. Stormbreaker, Mt. Cloudmaker, the Wild Dog Mountains, and the Narrow Neck Plateau, should be planned in advance with help from the Oberon NPWS.

JENOLAN CAVES

Known by the Aborigines as "Binoomea," meaning dark places, the amazing limestone and crystal formations of Jenolan ("Je-NO-lan") Caves, 46 km south of the Great Western Hwy. (on the northeastern edge of the park) from Hartley following Jenolan Caves Rd., have beguiled visitors since they were opened to the public in 1838. The caves can be reached by bus from Katoomba (see p. 138). Nine different areas within the massive cave system, overseen by the **Jenolan Caves Reserve Trust,** at the Jenolan Caves turn-off, offer **guided tours.** (☎6359 3311; www.jenolancaves.org.au. Ticket office open daily 9am-5pm, winter 9am-4:30pm. M-F 11 tours per day, Sa-Su 25; $14.50-27.50.)

Lucas Cave (1½hr., $14.50) displays a broad range of features and is generally presented as the place to start, but the large crowds can seriously detract from the experience. **Orient Cave** (1½hr., $22) and **Imperial Cave** (1hr., $14.50) both have a more tolerable flow of visitors as well as several eye-catching stalactites and stalagmites. The **Temple of Baal** (1½hr., $22) and the **River Cave** (2hr., $27.50) are also exciting options. Orient Cave and **Chifley Cave** (1hr., $14.50) are partially wheelchair accessible. **Adventure tours,** run by the Trust, take small groups of people who want to get down and dirty through some of the cave system's less accessible areas the hard way. These trips involve moderate to strenuous climbing, some crawling, and a healthy dose of darkness. Spelunkers heading into the **Plughole** (2hr., $55) must be at least 10 years old; those venturing into **Aladdin Cave** (3hr., $60.50) must be at least 12; and those exploring **Mammoth Cave** (6hr., $155) must be at least 16. The Trust also offers theme tours such as ghost tours and off-track adventures with miner's lights and overalls (2hr., from $27.50). For those not wanting to go underground, well-defined pathways amble along the surface and lead to Carlotta Arch, the Devils Coachhouse, McKeown's Valley, and the Blue Lake.

Overnight **camping** is available at Jenolan Caves. Each site has a fireplace, and the campground has a shared amenities block ($11 per site per night). Serious outdoor enthusiasts might want to head off for two to three days of hiking along the original dirt roadway that once connected Katoomba and Jenolan Caves back in the late 1800s. Today the **Six Foot Track** is a 42km trail from Jenolan Caves to Nellies Glen Rd. off the Great Western Hwy., at the west end of Katoomba.

NEW ENGLAND HIGHWAY

The New England Hwy., a lovely alternative to the traditional coastal route, exudes simple beauty and features a cooler year-round climate. This 566km stretch of road branches west from the Pacific Hwy. in Newcastle and continues along Hwy. 15 to Brisbane. The numerous, inviting country towns dotting its length are serviced by many of the area's major bus lines. The highway traverses the Hunter Valley, cruising slightly west of Maitland (but tantalizingly close to the vineyards), past Singleton's army base, and through Muswellbrook's coal mines and Scone's horse stud farms. Just beyond Tenterfield, the road begins the climb up and over the Dividing Range, from Tamworth to Armidale, and into New England proper. The national parks in New England (clustered in southern Queensland and northern New South Wales) are worth re-routing an itinerary. Unfortunately, most are only accessible by vehicle (some only by 4WD), although **Gumnuts Wilderness Adventures** (☎6775 3990) and **Waterfall Way Tours** (☎6772 2018), both based in Armidale, lead half-, full-, and multi-day trips into the surrounding natural areas. Call the Armidale Visitors Centre (☎6772 4655) for an update.

HUNTER VALLEY ☎02

Although using the words "budget travel" and "world-premier wine region" in the same sentence may arouse suspicion and seem the result of one-too-many glasses of some potent vintage, visiting the Hunter Valley without draining your bank account is easy. Over 100 wineries take advantage of the region's warm dry climate and sandy loam creek soils. Chief among the varieties produced in the area

Got ISIC?

ISIC is your passport to the world.

Accepted at over 17,000 locations worldwide.
Great benefits at home and abroad!

o apply for your International Student, Teacher or Youth Identity Card

CALL 1-800-2COUNCIL
CLICK www.counciltravel.com
VISIT your local Council Travel office

Bring this ad into your local Council Travel office and receive a free Council Travel/ISIC t-shirt! *(while supplies last)*

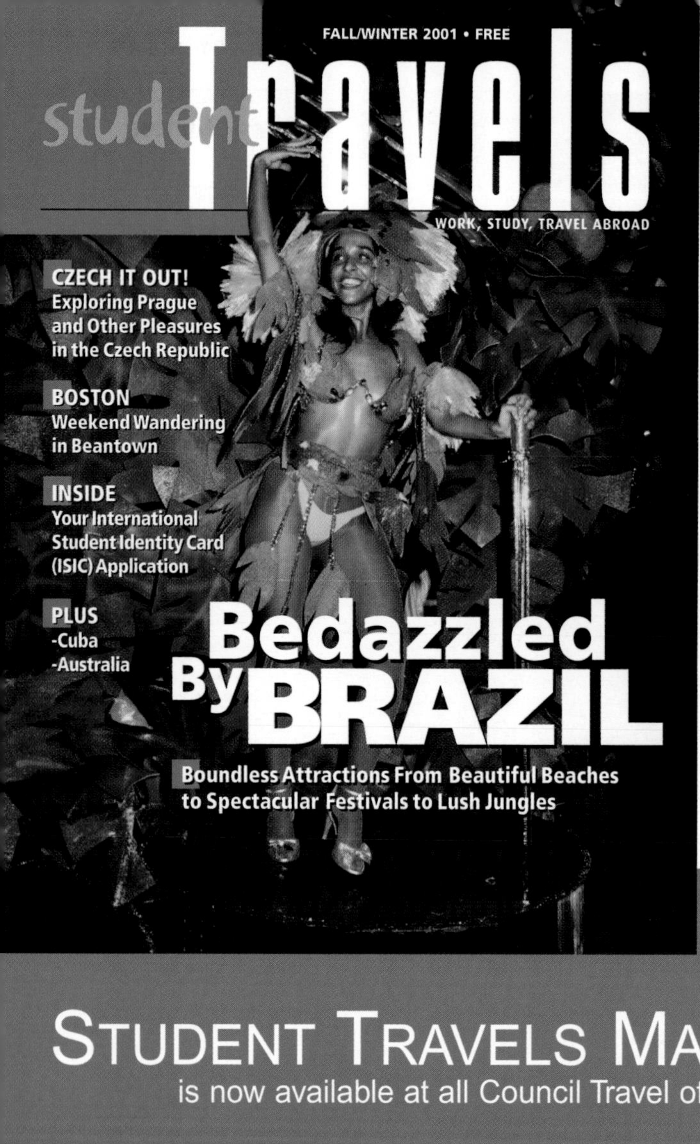

FALL/WINTER 2001 • FREE

student Travels

WORK, STUDY, TRAVEL ABROAD

CZECH IT OUT!
Exploring Prague and Other Pleasures in the Czech Republic

BOSTON
Weekend Wandering in Beantown

INSIDE
Your International Student Identity Card (ISIC) Application

PLUS
-Cuba
-Australia

Bedazzled By BRAZIL

Boundless Attractions From Beautiful Beaches to Spectacular Festivals to Lush Jungles

STOP IN FOR YOUR FREE COPY TODAY!

STUDENT TRAVELS MAGAZINE

is now available at all Council Travel offices.

This FREE magazine is the student guide to getting around the world - on a student's budget!

Find your local office at
www.counciltravel.com

1-800-2COUNCIL

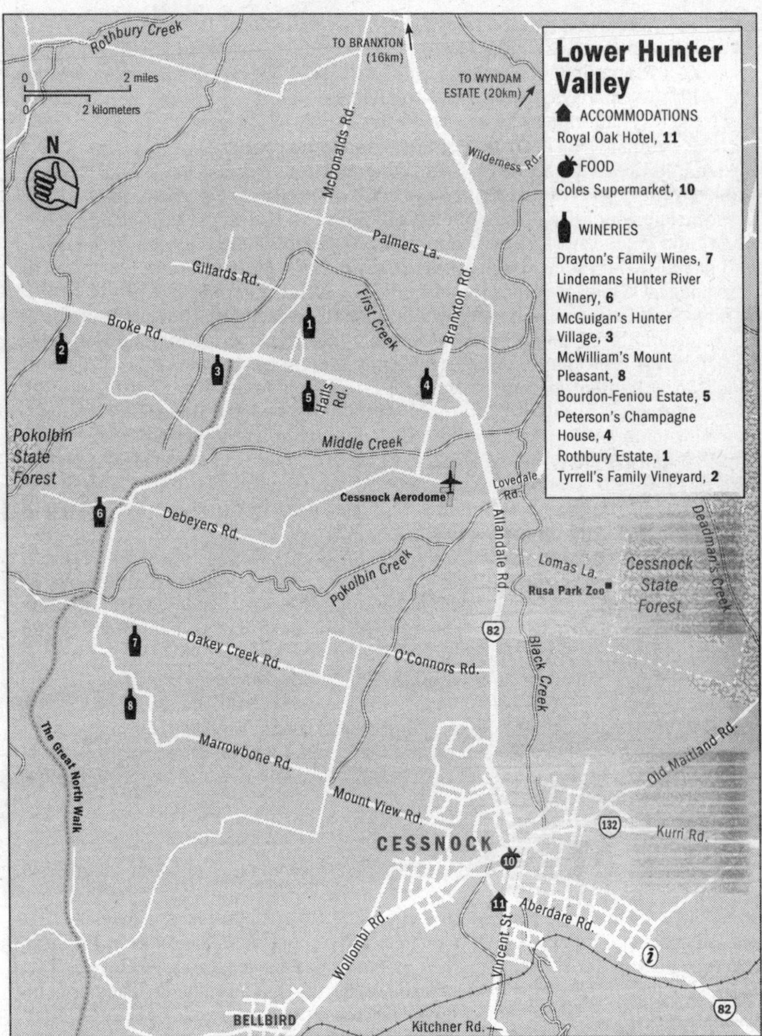

are the spicy, peppery **Shiraz** and the crisp **Semillon** with its strong citrus character. While most of the vineyards are clustered in the lower Hunter Valley northwest of **Cessnock** at the base of the Brokenback Mountains, several notable labels are situated in the upper Hunter, centered around the small town of **Denman.** Though only 8-10% of all Australian wines are made from Hunter Valley fruit, local vintages claim more than their share of national wine trophies and medals. For other Aussie wine regions, see Barossa Valley SA, p. 431; Rutherglen VIC, p. 585; Yarra Valley VIC, p. 537. For more information on vineyard touring see p. 434.

TRANSPORTATION AND TOURS

The best time to visit wine country is mid-week, when the number of people is fewer and the prices of tours and accommodations are lower. **Countrylink** (☎13 22 32) departs daily from Sydney to Scone (4½hr., $45) via Muswellbrook (3½hr., $39). **Keans Travel Express** (☎6543 4688 or 1800 043 339) departs from Bay 14 in Sydney Central Station's coach terminal (M-Sa 3pm, F 3pm and 6pm, Su 6:40pm) en route to: Cessnock (2¼hr., $27); Singleton (2¾hr., $32); Muswellbrook (3½hr., $35); Scone (3¾hr., $42). **Rover Motors,** 231 Vincent St. in Cessnock (☎4990 1699 or 1800 801 012), connects Cessnock and Newcastle, directly M-Sa (1¼hr., 4-6 per day, $10). On Sundays, take the bus to Maitland (45min., 5 per day, $7) and then catch the CityRail train to Newcastle (50min., 5 per day, $4).

Unless you have a car to get you to the individual wineries, and a responsible designated driver who can resist all the tempting free tastings, you'll need to book a tour. If you're starting in Newcastle or Maitland, the standard 10- to 20-person tour generally lasts from 9am to 5pm (or 10am-4pm if you're in Cessnock) and visits four to five wineries. The **Vineyard Shuttle Service** is cheapest, and is run by an entertaining and informative tee-totaler who lets his passengers suggest wineries rather than following a strict itinerary. (☎4991 3655. M-F $27; Sa-Su $30-35; with evening restaurant transfer add $8). **Shadows** visits both boutique and large, commercial wineries. Book ahead to arrange door-to-door transfers for Newcastle and surrounding addresses. (☎4990 7002. $35, with lunch $55.) **Hunter Vineyard Tours** (☎4991 1659) picks up from Cessnock ($38, with lunch $55) and Newcastle and Maitland ($43/$60). **Trekabout** creates a more intimate setting by limiting tours to six people. (☎4990 8277. M-F half-day $28, daily full-day $44). **Bicycle rental** is available from **Grapemobile Bicycle Hire** in Pokolbin, located at the corner of McDonalds Rd. and Palmers Ln. (☎4991 2339. Half-day $20, full-day $25). **Horse-drawn carriage tours** are available through **Paxton Brown** (☎4998 7362; from $53 with gourmet lunch) and **Pokolbin Horse Coaches** (☎4998 7305; 2hr. ride $35, with lunch $45). Alternatively, **Hertz,** 1A Aberdare Rd., is the only car rental company in Cessnock. (☎4991 2500. Open M-F 8am-5pm, Sa 8-noon.) If you're not on a tour and your Bacchanalian revelries have gotten the best of you, **Cessnock Radio Cabs** (☎4990 1111) can get you home safely.

NEW SOUTH WALES

Several tour companies offer daytrips from Sydney. **Wonderbus** runs straight to the Hunter Valley. (☎9555 9800. Departs 7:30am, returns 7:30pm. $100, with lunch $120.) **Oz Trails** caters to groups of 2-11 people. It visits the valley, but makes two extra stops—one at Lake Macquarie and the other along the Hawkesbury River—to showcase the beauty of the region. (☎9387 8390. $108, tea and lunch included.)

WINERIES

Most wineries are open for free tastings and occasional tours daily 10am-5pm (some 9:30am-4:30pm), although some of the smaller ones are only open on weekends. Of the 100-plus wineries, the largest are **McGuigan's, Lindemans, Tyrrell's, Drayton's, Rothbury Estate, Wyndham Estate,** and **McWilliams-Mount Pleasant Estate.** The smaller boutiques, such as **Ivanhoe, Pokolbin Estate, Rothvale,** and **Sobel's**, only sell the wines they produce on their private premises. They are not as glitzy but are generally more relaxed. Check with the Cessnock visitors center (see below) about free tours of individual wineries. Wine prices vary widely, but typically start around $14 per bottle.

CESSNOCK AND THE LOWER HUNTER VALLEY ☎02

The best and most popular launching point to see the vineyards is the centrally-located town of Cessnock.

MATH SURE IS HARD WITH A HANGOVER

One ton of grapes—once squished, crunched, and processed—yields roughly 1000 bottles of wine. The typical acre in the Hunter Valley yields 3.5 tons in a good year. Thus, even the smaller wineries of thirty acres can produce upwards of 70,000 bottles per vintage. The cooler climates of more southerly regions, like the Barossa Valley SA (see p. 431) and the Yarra Valley VIC (see p. 537), produce 5-6 tons per acre. The Hunter Valley is quick to claim quality over quantity. The success of the region is probably its proximity to Sydney—but the wines are still damn good.

ORIENTATION AND PRACTICAL INFORMATION. Most visitors to the Hunter stay in the lower valley, the most accessible part of the valley to Sydney and Newcastle. By car, Cessnock is approximately 2hr. from Sydney and 30km west of the Sydney-Newcastle Fwy. along Aberdare Rd. The **Cessnock Visitors Centre,** 1.2km off Vincent St. on Aberdare Rd. in Turner Park, has info on the wineries and weekly specials on accommodations and meals. The indispensable (and free) *Hunter Valley Wine Country Visitors Guide* includes area maps, a calendar of events, and info on wineries, cellar doors, attractions, restaurants, and accommodations. (☎4990 4477; www.winecountry.com.au. Open M-F 9am-5pm, Sa 9:30am-5pm, Su 9:30am-3:30pm.)

The town of **Maitland** is 30min. east of Cessnock along the Hunter River. A historic city, it once rivaled Sydney as a potential state capital. The **Visitor Information Centre** is in Ministers Park, near the junction of High St. and the New England Hwy. (☎4933 2611; www.maitland.tourism.nsw.gov.au. Open daily 9am-5pm.)

ACCOMMODATIONS AND FOOD. The **Chardonnay Sky Motel,** 210 Allandale Rd., about a 10min. drive north of town, has the best atmosphere of the accommodations options. Motel rooms are $20 cheaper if you tandem sky dive next door at NSW Skydiving Centre (see below). People are always dropping in here. (☎4991 4812; fax 4991 2259. Continental breakfast included. Backpacker heated bunks $20; spacious motel doubles with TV and bath Su-Th $65, F-Sa $99; Wheelchair accessible.) **Cessnock Caravan Park,** on O'Connors Rd. near the intersection of Allandale Rd. and about 5min. north of town, has a pool, BBQ, and one wheelchair-accessible cabin. (☎4990 5819; fax 4991 2944. Sites for 2 Su-Th $16, F-Sa $18; on-site caravans $35/$65; cabins $45/$85; special access cabin $80/$95.) **Pubstays** are also available in Cessnock. The **Caledonia Hotel** (☎4990 1212) and the **Royal Oak Hotel** (☎4990 2366) both offer basic rooms Su-Th from $45, F-Sa from $55. **Coles supermarket** is at the intersection of Cooper and Darwin St.

ACTIVITIES. The adrenaline rush and mind-boggling views (once you pry your eyes open) are well worth the cost at the **Hunter Valley Tandem Skydiving Centre,** 210 Allendale Rd. **Balloon Aloft** (☎4938 1955), **Cloud Nine** (☎9686 7777), and **Hunter Valley Ballooning** (☎1800 818 191) all have sunrise hot air balloon flights lasting roughly 1hr. ($220-245; usually includes a champagne breakfast).

WINERIES OF THE LOWER HUNTER VALLEY. The vineyards of the lower Hunter are situated along a tangle of rural roads, so the free map from the Cessnock visitors center is the best way to navigate. Even so, the entire area is well-signposted, and large billboard maps are located at the major intersections. You couldn't ask for a better starting point than **Tyrrell's** (☎4993 7000), on Broke Rd. The enigmatic, self-deprecating guides give 1hr. free tours M-Sa at 1:30pm revealing the entire wine-making process of the 142-year-old family business. The free tastings aren't skimpy, so make sure you keep in mind the other stops. **McGuigan's** (☎4998 7402), on McDonalds Rd., is an all-purpose stop. In addition to the great wines, they also have a cheese shop with free tastings. The souvenir store sells wine-related paraphernalia at tourist-inflated prices, but the on-site bakery and deli serve up affordable fudge, pies, and sandwiches to keep you going. **Wyndham Estate** (☎4938 3444), on Dalwood Rd., is the oldest winery in Australia, first planting vines in 1828. Today it has an excellent tasting room along with a huge space filled with wine casks for tables. **Petersons Champagne House** (☎4998 7881), at the corner of Broke and Branxton Rd., is the only place in New South Wales strictly devoted to the bubbly, including an interesting selection of sparkling red wines.

Of the smaller boutique wineries in the lower valley, **Rothvale** (☎4998 7290), on Deasys Rd., consistently receives high praise. Another notable boutique, **Ivanhoe** (☎4998 7325), on Marrowbone Rd., is owned and operated by a member of the distinguished wine-making Drayton family. The vineyard produces a deliciously sweet-and-fruity dessert wine. If you'd like some tips on the art of wine tasting, take a lesson at the **Hunter Valley Wine School.** The tour finishes with an evaluation of three whites and three reds. (☎4998 7777. Daily 9-11am. $25. Book ahead.)

THE UPPER HUNTER VALLEY ☎02

A few towns well northwest of Cessnock are great bases from which to explore the Upper Hunter Valley vineyards. **Singleton** (pop. 12,500), on the New England Hwy., is the home of the **world's largest sundial.**

MUSWELLBROOK. On the New England Hwy., Muswellbrook ("MUSCLE-brook") is closest to the action. The small town (pop. 10,700) has an abundance of historical buildings, many of them visible on the 4.5km Muswellbrook Heritage walk beginning at the Old Tea House on Bridge St. (New England Hwy.). The highway is also the site of a living **Vietnam Memorial,** a grove of 519 trees that represent each of the Australian casualties in the conflict. The **Tourist Office,** 87 Hill St., just off Bridge St., shares a building with the Upper Hunter Wine Centre. (☎6541 4050; fax 6541 4051; www.muswellbrook.org.au. Open daily 9:30am-5pm.) **Eatons Hotel,** 188 Bridge St., has basic rooms. (☎6543 2403. Singles $20; twins $30; doubles $30.) **Pinaroo Caravan Park** is 3km south on the New England Hwy. (☎6543 3905. Pool, laundry, BBQ, social room. Sites for 2 $12.50, powered $16.50; cabins $47-60.)

SCONE. A better choice for accommodation is in Scone, 26km north on the New England Hwy., a small but pretty town which prides itself on being the **horse capital of Australia.** The distinction is owed to the annual, week-long Scone Horse Festival in mid-May, which includes an air show featuring WWII fighter jets. The week culminates in three days of thoroughbred racing for the Scone Cup. The race course is 5min. from the town center. The **Scone Visitor Information Center** is at the corner of Kelly (New England Hwy.) and Susan St., in front of the train station. (☎6545 1526; www.horsecapital.com.au. Open daily 9am-5pm.) The peaceful **Scone YHA,** 1151 Segenhoe Rd., 8km off the highway in a converted country schoolhouse surrounded by horse stud farms, has a kitchen, BBQ, warm fireplace, and friendly hosts. (☎/fax 6545 2072. Dorms $17; twins and doubles $36; family rooms $45; non-YHA members add $3.50 per person). The **Highway Caravan Park,** 248 New England Hwy., is a place to pitch a tent and that's about it. (☎/fax 6545 1078. Sites for 2 $11, powered $16.50; caravans with bath $31-42.)

WINERIES OF THE UPPER HUNTER VALLEY. Though the Upper Hunter Valley has fewer wineries, is more spread out, and has less tourists, it has many fabulous wines. Pick up the *Vineyards of the Upper Hunter Valley* brochure with listings and a map from any area tourist centers. The well-marked trail starts off the New England Hwy. a few kilometers north of Muswellbrook. Unfortunately, no tour groups operate here, so you need your own car. All the wineries can easily be visited in one day, but be sure to keep tabs on how much wine you're drinking. **Rosemount Estate** (☎6549 6400), on Rosemount Rd., is the largest vineyard and has extraordinary varieties from a light Sauvignon Blanc to a mild Shiraz to a more peppery Cabernet Sauvignon. Since it exports 70% of its 2.5 million cases, you may be familiar with this label from home. **Arrowfield** (☎6576 4041), on Denman Rd., is also a large winery worth visiting. It prides itself on producing affordable, approachable wines. **Cruickshank Callatoota Estate,** 2656 Wybong Rd. (☎6547 8149), specializes in Cabernet Sauvignon and Cabernet Franc wines. **James Estate** (☎6547 5168), on Rylstone Rd., produces a delicious Shiraz.

TAMWORTH ☎02

Coo-ee! Welcome to country, folks. Tamworth (pop. 38,000) annually hosts the **Country Music Festival,** which brings famous crooners and hordes of people to town (Jan. 18-Jan. 27, 2002; www.countrymusic.asn.au). The country spirit is otherwise maintained by gallon-hatted city slickers and cheesy tourist attractions such as a giant golden guitar and a concrete slab with handprints of country artists.

TRANSPORTATION. The **train station,** corner of Brisbane and Marius St., has a travel center that sells all bus and train tickets. (☎6766 2357. Open M-F 8:30am-5:30pm, Sa 8:30am-noon.) **Countrylink** (☎13 22 32) runs express trains to Sydney

(6hr., 1 per day, $71.50; ISIC 50% discount). All buses run from the **coach terminal** next to the tourist information center. **Greyhound Pioneer** (☎13 20 30) and **McCafferty's** (☎13 14 99) travel to: Brisbane (9-10hr., 3 per day, $62); Coonabarabran (3hr., 1 per day, $65); Sydney (6-8hr., 1 per day, $60); 10% ISIC/VIP/YHA discount. **Kean's Travel Express** (☎6543 1322) goes to Port Macquarie (8¼hr.; M, W, F 1 per day; $64.50, ISIC $51.50) and Scone (2½hr.; Tu, Th, Su 1 per day; $27, ISIC $13.50). **Budget** (☎13 27 27) has cars from $39 per day. **Avis** (☎6760 7404) sometimes offers deals for multi-day car hire. Call **Tamworth Radio Cabs** 13 10 08 or 6766 1111.

PRACTICAL INFORMATION. Tamworth is 412km north of Sydney on the New England Hwy (which enters the town from the east and departs south) and is a convenient rest stop on a journey to Brisbane (578km). The town center lies along **Brisbane St.**, which crosses the Peel River, becoming **Bridge St.** in West Tamworth. The **information center** is at the corner of Peel and Murray St. (☎6755 4300; www.tamworth.nsw.gov.au. Open M-F 8:30am-4:35pm, Sa-Su 9am-5pm.) The **library,** 203 Marius St., has **Internet access.** (☎6755 4457. Open M-Th 10am-8pm, F 10am-6pm, Sa 9am-noon. $2.20 per 30min.)

ACCOMMODATIONS AND FOOD. Most rooms for January's Country Music Festival are gone by the previous March and numerous places will not take reservations for that week; throughout the rest of the year, beds are plentiful. The **YHA Country Backpackers,** 169 Marius St., opposite the train station, is the only hostel in town and perhaps the cleanest one in New South Wales. (☎6761 2600; fax 6761 2002; tamworthyha@optusnet.com.au. No heat. Linen and breakfast included, towels $1. Laundry $6. Free pickup from the bus station. Internet $1 per 15min. Dorms $18; doubles $42.) **Tamworth Hotel,** 147 Marius St., also opposite the train station, is the most upscale pubstay. The downstairs restaurant has breakfast deals from $6-9 (☎6766 2923, fax 6766 2847; rumbler@ozemail.com.au. Singles $30. AmEx/MC/V.) **Paradise Caravan Park,** next to the info center along the creek, has grills and a playground. (☎/fax 6766 3120; big4tam@tpgi.com.au. Linen $5.50, laundry for $4.40, $5 key deposit. Reception 7am-7pm. Sites for 2 $13.20, powered $18; budget cabins for 2 $44; cabins with A/C, kitchen, and TV $55. 7th night free off-season. MC/V.) Each end of Peel St. is marked by locally beloved cafes. The **Inland Cafe,** 407 Peel St., is slightly more cosmopolitan and chic in its decor and atmosphere. (Open M-W 7am-6pm, Th-Sa 7am-11pm, Su 9am-5pm. MC/V.) The **Old Vic Cafe,** 261 Peel St., has a bit more laid-back feel and sells its own homemade sauces and vinaigrettes. (☎6766 3435. Open M-Th 8am-6pm, F-Sa 8am-10pm, Su 9am-4pm. BYO. MC/V.) Both serve up gourmet entrees ($15) like grilled tiger prawns and goat cheese frittata to the delight of locals who pack them both at mealtime.

The Coffee Bean, Shop 18, Tamworth Arcade at 345 Peel St., takes coffee-brewing seriously; they also have a more whimsical line of pastries and cakes, as well as **Internet access.** (☎6766 3422. Open M-W, F 8am-5pm; Th 8am-7pm; Sa 8am-3pm. Internet $6.70 per 1hr. MC/V.) There are a number of Thai and Chinese eateries on the main drag. Coles **supermarket** is at 436-444 Peel St. in the KMart shopping plaza. (Open 24hr. except closed Sa noon-Su 8am, Su 8pm-M 6am. AmEx/MC/V.)

SIGHTS AND ACTIVITIES. You don't have to be a country music fan to enjoy Tamworth—you just need a high tolerance for kitsch. The turn-off for **The Golden Guitar Complex,** south of town on the New England Hwy., is marked by, predictably enough, a gaudy 12m golden guitar. Inside, a realistic "Gallery of Stars" **wax museum** dresses 22 replicas in the donated clothes of the crooning stars themselves, including Slim Dusty. In an odd juxtaposition, a large gem and mineral display shares the complex. (☎6765 2688; www.big.goldenguitar.com.au. Open daily 9am-5pm. $6, child $3 child, family $14.) The popular **Hands of Fame Cornerstone** is on the corner of the New England Hwy. and Kable Ave. This cement memorial holds the imprints of country music celebrities. Also check out **Joe Macguires' Noses of Fame,** 148 Peel St. (☎6766 2114), a 15min. walk west of town, for a more comical monument to country. For real devotees, the **Australian Country Music Foundation,** 93 Brisbane St., is an archive with a small museum display (☎6766 1577.

Open M-Sa 10am-2pm. $5.50, $3.30 concession). **The Rent,** 5 Brisbane St. shows 4-5 movies daily. (☎6766 3707. $11, $8.50 concession, $7 child.)

Bring out your inner cowboy or cowgirl at one of the **"Jackaroo and Jillaroo schools"** in the Tamworth area, with crash courses on how to ride horses, train dogs, milk cows, lasso, operate farm equipment, and muster cattle from the saddle. Certificates and help finding **jobs** are given upon completion. **Leconfield** runs a highly recommended school of this type about an hour out of Tamworth. If you're lucky, they'll even let you castrate a baby lamb the old fashioned way—with your teeth. (☎6769 4328; www.leconfield.com. 5-day course from $375 begins M. Free Tamworth pickup at the YHA.)

Parallel to Peel St., one block south along the river, is **Bicentennial Park,** a reclusive stretch of greenery, ponds, and picnic tables with a delightful bit of masonry on its rocks. (Open daily 8am-4:45pm.) The **Oxley Scenic Lookout** at the top of White St. gives a bird's-eye view of the bustling city. It also marks the start of the **Kamilaroi Walking Track** (6.2km), a scenic tour that passes by the **Endeavour Drive Marsupial Park,** past the top end of Brisbane St. with its free roaming 'roos, echidnas, and red-necked wallabies. (Open daily 8am-5pm.) A lighter **Heritage Walk** (4.7km) loops through town, starting at the corner of Kable and Brisbane St.

NEW SOUTH WALES

ENTERTAINMENT AND NIGHTLIFE. Nightlife in Tamworth is amusing. Teenagers too young to drink cruise Peel St. in their parents' cars and climb about on public landmarks making eyes at each other. Meanwhile, their older siblings fill their bellies with liquid courage. The **RSL Club,** behind Peel St. on Kable Ave., is really the only constantly country live venue. (☎6766 4661. Th-Sa 7:30pm, Su 2:30pm. Th "country music jamboree." Generally no cover.) The **Imperial Pub,** on the corner of Marius and Brisbane St., draws a mix of ages. (☎6766 2613. Live mainly rock music Th-Su.) Most pubs close around midnight.

ON THE OXLEY HIGHWAY

The New England Hwy (15) reaches a juncture at Bendemeer, 41km north of Tamworth. Here, you can head coastward along the Oxley Hwy (follow signs to Walcha), a stretch of raw and remote national parks that are nothing short of spectacular. From Armidale, follow the New England Hwy south for 22km to Uralla where a tourist route takes a shortcut directly to Walcha along the Oxley Hwy. The Oxley meets Port Macquarie at the coast, 178km east from Walcha.

ARMIDALE ☎02

The town of Armidale (pop. 25,000) has two claims to fame: it has four distinct seasons, and it has a number of self-guided historical walks. If you are on a crusade to see leaves fall or if you are a fan of power-walks, Armidale is the comfortable but common place for you. The University of New England's campus, 5km from Armidale's center, brings energy and business to a healthy number of pubs. The town is also conveniently positioned at the beginning of "Waterfall Way" (see p. 153).

Armidale's main drag is **Marsh St.** The **Visitors Centre,** 82 Marsh St., is attached to the bus terminal, next to the Pizza Hut. (☎6772 4655 or 1800 627 736; fax 6771 4486; www.new-england.org/armidale. Open M-F 9am-5pm, Sa 9am-4pm, Su 10am-4pm.) The **bus terminal,** 82 Marsh St., behind Pizza Hut, holds **McCafferty's** (☎13 14 99) and **Greyhound** (☎13 20 30). One block up Marsh St. is **Beardy St. Mall,** Armidale's cluster of shops and cafes. **New England Travel Centre,** 188 Beardy Mall, is helpful. (☎6772 1722; www.newengland.tvl.com.au. Open M-F 9am-5pm, Sa 9am-noon.) For a **taxi** call 13 10 08 or 6766 1111.

The **Pembroke Caravan Park,** 39 Waterfall Way (also known as Grafton Rd.), a 2km east of town, has an adjoining **YHA hostel.** (☎6772 6470 or 1800 355 578; fax 6772 9804; www.pembroke.com.au. Free lockers. Linen $7, $10 with blankets. Laundry $2.40, no dryers. Reception 7:30am-6pm. Check-out 10am. Sites $15; dorms $16, non-YHA $19; caravans $30-34; cabins $41-78. MC/V.) **Tattersall's Hotel,** 174 Beardy St., is a town center pubstay with bright, cozy rooms. (☎6772 2247. Breakfast included. Singles $27.50; doubles $44; $11 extra per person. MC/V.)

Following Marsh St. south, up the hill to the corner of Kentucky St., leads to the much-praised **New England Regional Art Museum.** (☎6772 5255. Open daily 10:30am-5pm. Free.) As you exit the art museum, the **Aboriginal Cultural Centre and Keeping Place** is on your right. (☎6771 1249; http://home.bluepin.net.au/acckp. Open M-F 10am-4pm. Free.) **Waterfall Way Tours,** 5 Canambe St., travels by 4WD to up to six national parks along the Waterfall Way, focusing on natural history, with some Aboriginal and European history as well. (☎6772 2018; www.waterfall-way.com.au. Half-day $50; full-day with lunch $100; overnight tours available.) **Horseback riding** and **fishing** are also popular; the visitors center has details

FROM ARMIDALE

APSLEY AND TIA GORGES. The highlights of the eastern end of **Oxley Wild Rivers National Park** (see p. 154) are the must-see waterfalls of the Apsley and Tia Gorges, which are most easily accessed from the Oxley Hwy. The larger part of the park is usually accessed from Waterfall Way, closer to Armidale (see p. 154). About 20km east of Walcha and 83km from Armidale is the turn-off for the **Apsley Gorge,** 1km off the highway. This mighty gorge will take your breath away. At the far carpark is a stairway leading part of the way into the gorge with a good view of the falls. Swimming in the pool is permitted at your own risk. Beware of sometimes-submerged boulders just in front of the falls. The 2km **Oxley Walk** (45min.) takes you around the rim of the gorge and across a bridge over the Oxley River. Camping and fresh water are available. Nineteen kilometers south of the Apsley Falls entrance is the small picnic and camping area of **Tia Falls.** A nearby walk shows off the **Tia Gorge.**

Small and unexciting, Walcha is still a useful jumping-off point for Apsley and Tia Gorges and the rest of Oxley Wild Rivers National Park. You'll find the **tourist information center** in the Old School Art Gallery on the Oxley Hwy. (6777 2713. Open daily 8am-5pm.) For basic pub stay and food, try the **Commercial Hotel,** on Churchill Ln also off the highway. (☎6777 2551. Singles $27.50.)

WERRIKIMBE NATIONAL PARK. Remoteness and poor access roads have preserved the rugged wilderness of Werrikimbe National Park. This is a camper's paradise, and many choose to stay for days and weeks, gleefully veering from the paths into the depths of temperate and subtropical rainforest, eucalypt forest, and snow gum woodlands. District Managers in Armidale (☎6776 4260; armidale@npws.gov.au) or Port Macquarie (☎6583 5518) have info on expeditions beyond the western section of the park. Look closely for the sign for Werrikimbe National Park and Moorback Rd, which appears 40km south of Walcha. The first 15km of this track isn't bad, but the twisting, climbing, and loose gravel may wear on conventional vehicles. Inside the park, the tracks crumble but remain flat and direct. You can either go left a few kilometers to Moorback Rest Area or right to Cobcroft's Rest Area. **Moorback** is set amid snow gum woodlands and by the Moorback Creek. Walks meander along the creek and deeper into the forest. Campsites at **Cobcroft** are set in open eucalypt forest with a few tree ferns for seasoning. The **Carrabeen Walk** (1hr.) passes through an adjacent warm temperate rainforest. The vivid passage crosses through gullies of Antarctic Beeches with gnarled, web-like bases that on take astounding shapes. The campsites have pit toilets and firewood.

WATERFALL WAY ☎02

Waterfall Way (Rte 78) runs east-west between Armidale and the north coast of New South Wales. Along the way, the aptly-named tourist route passes four excellent national parks with accessible campgrounds, several tiny hamlets, and the charming town of Bellingen (see p. 176). The 169km route is worth the trip, but be cautious on the sometimes steep highway. In addition to the parks below, the Ebor Falls, approximately 42km west of Dorrigo and 600m off the highway, are a killer photo-op. A 600m walk from the carpark leads to a scintillating lookout. Waterfall Way Tours (☎6772 2018) runs to the national parks (see Armidale, p. 152).

OXLEY WILD RIVERS NATIONAL PARK

Oxley is an extensive park of rough, rocky terrain with a network of gorges, campsites, bushwalks, and appropriately wild rivers. Useful pamphlets with photos and maps can help you choose a site to camp or picnic; contact the Armidale **NPWS** (☎6773 7211; fax 6771 1894; armidale@npws.nsw.gov) or **Armidale Visitors Centre** (☎1800 627 736; visit@northnet.com.au). For information on **Apsley and Tia Gorges** at the more remote eastern end of the park, see p. 153.

Dangars Gorge is an easy 22km trip from Armidale, with the 120m Dangars Falls as the centerpiece. Take Gangarsleigh Rd (Kennedy St) from Armidale for about 11km, then go left at the Perrott's War Memorial; 10km of gravel lead to the gorge. The rest area there is equipped with BBQ, firewood, and pit toilets, and is the trailhead for a series of walks ranging from the Gorge Lookout path (100m) to 10-14km half-day treks. An eroding, unofficial path from the rest area leads down to the Gorge riverbed and a deep pool, zig-zagging along a steep gradient (2hr.).

Long Point is a secluded wilderness area in an open eucalypt forest adjacent to a rare dry rainforest, a fact that has earned it World Heritage status. Dry rainforest sounds oxymoronic, but the main criterion for rainforest classification is a closed canopy forest ceiling. The turn-off for Long Point appears 40km east of Armidale along Waterfall Way. A 7km stretch of sealed track passes through Hillgrove where a left turn skips onto a dirt track that reaches the park 20km down. The attached campsite has pit toilets, picnic tables, and fresh water, and is the trailhead for the excellent **Chandler Walk** (5km, 2-2½hr.), leading through a grove of mosses, vines, and yellow-spotted Hillgrove Gums, which are found only in this area. A tremendous lookout along the walk surveys the valley and Chandler River.

The **Wollombi Falls** gorge is severe and the surrounding forest rugged and dry. Turn-off 40km east of Armidale onto a 2km bitumen road leading to the Falls. The strenuous **Chandler River Track** (5.6km; 4hr.) starts here. Alternately, a moderately strenuous 1.2km walk leads to the river, or a 700m path heads to a gorge lookout. There is a bush camping site near the entrance to the gorge area.

NEW ENGLAND NATIONAL PARK

New England National Park offers some fabulous bushwalking trails. Its densely-vegetated basalt cliffs formed from several lava flows from the Ebor volcano over 18 million years ago. The park gets chilly in summer and down-right cold in winter. Near the park entrance, 85km from Armidale and 75km from Dorrigo, is the **Thungutti Campground.** Nearby begin the Wright's Lookout Walk (2½hr.) and Cascades Walk (3½hr.). Most people skip these outskirts to head for the **Point Lookout Picnic Area,** the park's hub, with toilets, fire pits, and ample parking. Point Lookout Rd heads up to the area; about 11km is gravel, 2.5km sealed. Point Lookout marks the start of nine walks ranging from 5min. to 3½hr., all of which can be linked for nearly a full day of walking. The Point Lookout, a vertical escarpment rising 1564m from sea level, surveys dense forest often shrouded in mist. **Eagles Nest Track** (2hr.) passes straight down and along the steep cliffside. It takes some ingenuity to negotiate the rocky areas through moss-covered beeches, snow gum woodland, and water sprays that turn to icicles in winter. The difficult **Lyrebird Walk** links with the Eagles Nest Track and can be made a 2km (1hr.) route or a 7km (3½hr.) circuit.

GLEN INNES ☎02

Glen Innes (pop. 10,000), 1hr. from both Armidale and Tenterfield on the New England Hwy., has a Celtic heritage and constantly finds cause to celebrate it. A full slate of annual festivals complement the changing seasons. Glen Innes's most striking monument is a collection of vertical megalithic **Standing Stones** overlooking the town and valley, an homage to an ancient Celtic form of timekeeping. Resting solemnly on **Martins Lookout,** 1km east of the visitors center on Meade St. (Gwydir Hwy.), the Stones bear an uncanny resemblance to Stonehenge.

The main commercial street in town is **Grey St.,** parallel to and one block west of the **New England Hwy.** (called Church St. as it runs through town). The **Gwydir Hwy.,** known in town as **Meade St.** and **Ferguson St.,** runs west 65km to Inverell and east 160km to Grafton and the Pacific Hwy. **Countrylink** (☎13 22 32) runs to: Armidale (1¼hr, 1 per day, $13.20); Byron Bay (6hr., 1 per day, $13.20); Grafton City (1¾hr., 1 per day, $25.30); Sydney (9¾hr, 1 per day, $85.80); Tamworth (3½hr, 1 per day, $29.70); Tenterfield (1¼hr, 1 per day, $13.20); 50% discount with ISIC. **Greyhound** (☎13 20 30) and **McCafferty's** (☎13 14 99) send **buses** to: Armidale (1hr., 3 per day, $33); Brisbane (5hr., 2 per day, $62); Sydney (9hr., 1 per day, $68); Tenterfield (1hr., 3 per day, $26); 10% discount with ISIC/VIP/YHA. Buses stop at various local service stations; contact individual companies for specifics. Call **taxis** at 6732 1300. The **Visitors Centre,** 152 Church St., is near the intersection of the New England and Gwydir Hwy. (☎6732 2397; www.gleninnestourism.com. Open M-F 9am-5pm, Sa-Su 9am-3pm.) Grey St. is home to several banks with **ATMs, supermarkets,** pubstays, greasy eateries, and the library with **free Internet access.** (☎6732 2302. Open M-F 9:30am-5:30pm, Sa 9am-noon.)

Cheap rooms are available at the pubs on Grey St. (singles $20; twins and doubles $35). **New England Motor Lodge,** on the northern end of town at 160 Church St., has much nicer rooms and a swimming pool for a bit more coin. (☎6732 2922. Singles $78-88; doubles $83-93; family $130-150.)

TENTERFIELD AND NEARBY PARKS ☎02

It was in Tenterfield in 1889 that Sir Henry Parkes made his "one nation" speech that foresaw Australian federation. Although it clings to its history with preserved buildings and the Sir Henry Parkes Festival—a celebration of nationhood and community achievements—travelers today know Tenterfield as a base for exploring nearby parks and a stop on the way into Queensland's Southern Downs region.

TRANSPORTATION AND PRACTICAL INFORMATION. The New England Hwy. becomes **Rouse St.** in town. Greyhound and McCafferty's stop south of town near the BP and Ampol petrol stations, but **do not stop** at the town's bus station. Several of the buses barrel in late at night or early in the morning. **Greyhound** (☎13 20 30) and **McCafferty's** (☎13 14 99) **buses** run to: Armidale (2hr., 2 per day, $40); Brisbane (4-5hr., 3 per day, $51); Glen Innes (1hr., 3 per day, $26); Sydney (10-11hr., 1-per day, $68); ISIC/VIP/YHA 10% discount. **Crisp's** (☎07 4661 2566) undercuts the big companies with its daily Brisbane service (4hr., $46.50). **Kirkland's** (☎1300 367 077; www.kirklands.com.au) services Lismore (4hr., $25), with a connection to Byron Bay (1hr., $12). **Countrylink** (☎12 22 32), operating locally as **Edward's Coaches** with a **train** transfer in Armidale (2hr.), travels to Sydney (11hr., daily 6am, $90.20) via Glen Innes (1hr., $13.20) and Tamworth (5hr., $47.30.) ISIC gets you a 50% discount. **Sullivan's Newsagency** on Rouse St. books both Crisp's and Kirkland's tickets (☎6736 1242. Open M-F 7am-5:45pm, Sa 7am-12:30pm, Su 7am-10:30pm. No credit cards.) The **tourist office,** 187 Rouse St. at the corner of Rouse and Miles, keeps extensive park info. (☎6736 1074; www.tenterfield.nsw.gov.au. Open M-F 9am-5pm. Sa-Su 9am-4pm.) The **library** at the corner of Rouse and Manners has free 1hr. **Internet access** (☎6736 1454. Open M-F 10am-5pm.)

ACCOMMODATIONS AND FOOD. The **Tenterfield Lodge** is essentially a caravan park with a historic building doubling as a motel with rooms and dorms. From the tourist office turn left onto Manners St. and walk 1km to the end of the road. (☎6736 1477. Large communal kitchen and TV area. Sites for 2 $15, powered $16.50; on-site vans $30-40; dorms $18; doubles $40; cabins with bath $50.) Sellers Foodmarket, 220 Rouse St., is a convenient **supermarket.** (Open M-F 8:30am-6pm, Sa 8:30am-noon. MC/V.)

PARKS. Tenterfield lies near three national parks; a great map ($8) is available at the visitors center or the NPWS, 68 Church St, Glen Innes (☎6732 5133). **Boonoo Boonoo National Park** ("Bunner Bernoo") is 27km away; take Rouse St south, turn right on Nas St, then quickly bear left on Mt. Lindesay Rd. The next 27km to the park entrance is mostly unsealed. From the entrance, 14km of gravel leads to **Boonoo Boonoo Falls,** the park hub and overnight camping area (no water; $5). The park is dominated by eucalypts and has a few rock pools. There's a swimming hole 5km back from the falls toward the park entrance. If you can't reach Uluru (Ayers Rock), you'll have to make do with **Bald Rock National Park,** featuring the largest exposed granite rock in Australia. To reach it, head down Mt. Lindesay Rd for 29km to a gravel road that runs 5km to the park's camping area. The **Burgoona Walk** (5km) takes you to the 1277m summit, with a view of the McPherson Ranges and the Clarence River. **Girraween National Park** (see p. 324) is Queensland's extension of Bald Rock National Park, and is 9km down a paved road 11km north of Wallangara on the New England Hwy. **Woollol Woollol Aboriginal Culture Tours** runs an Aboriginal-guided trip to both Boonoo Boonoo and Bald Rock National Parks ($55, for 2 $105; book at visitors center).

NORTH COAST

Called the Holiday Coast by Sydney-siders, the sandy fantasyland of the northern New South Wales coast caters to meandering backpackers, die-hard surfers, and swarms of families. Existing somewhere between the rat-race of the big city and the permanent-vacation attitude of points north, this area offers locals easy access to both bright lights and holiday hot-spots, with a slightly slower pace of life. Newcastle and Port Macquarie draw travelers itching to sunbathe, water-ski, or hang-ten. At the other end of the spectrum, inland eco-activist centers Lismore and Bellingen thrive on highly productive agricultural land punctuated by scenic national parks and fast-flowing rivers. With virtual cult status, Byron Bay synthesizes these two distinct flavors, magnetically pulling sunburned, party-ready mobs and detaining them for a spell (or a bender) before they head for the Queensland beaches. For coverage of Tweed Heads, see **Tweed Heads and Coolangatta,** p. 312.

NEWCASTLE ☎02

Newcastle (pop. 265,000) is a city with a complex. As the world's largest coal exporter, Newcastle ships out over one and a half million tons each week, giving it a historical reputation as a smokestack-ridden industrial metropolis. But as the second-largest city in NSW, Newcastle stubbornly insists that it has balanced its industrial roots with a pleasantly livable (and visitable) environment. It isn't just talk: Newcastle offers high-adrenaline surfing, a spectacular view of the Pacific, and easy access to the nearby Hunter Valley wineries and wetland reserves.

TRANSPORTATION

Trains: Newcastle Railway Station, Wharf Rd., Queen's Wharf (☎13 15 00). **CityRail Trains** chug often to **Sydney** (3hr., at least 1 per hr. 2:45am-11:15pm, $17). The main transfer station for **CountryLink** access to the northern coast is **Broadmeadow,** a 5min. train ride on CityRail. From Broadmeadow: **Brisbane** (12hr., 2 per day, $98); **Coffs Harbour** (6-7hr., 3 per day, $57); and **Surfers Paradise** (12hr., 2 per day, $98). Luggage storage ($1.50, open daily 8am-5pm). Broadmeadow station open daily 6am-7:15pm; after hours use ticket machines. Ask for student discounts.

Buses: The bus depot butts up against the wharf side of the railway station. Several bus lines including **Greyhound** and **McCafferty's** zip to: **Sydney** (3½hr., at least 5 per day, $27); **Brisbane** (14½hr., 4 per day, $74); **Byron Bay** (10hr., 2 per day, $73); **Cairns** (42½hr., 4 per day, $247); **Coffs Harbour** (7hr., 3 per day, $52); **Port Macquarie** (4hr., 2 per day, $38); **Surfers Paradise** (12hr., 3 per day, $74); **Taree** (3hr., 3 per day, $37). **Rover Motors** (☎4990 1699) goes to **Cessnock** (1¼hr., M-F 6 per day, $10). **Port Stephens Coaches** (☎4982 2940; www.psbuses.nelsonbay.com) shuttles to **Port Stephens** daily (1hr.; M-F 11 per day, Sa-Su 4 per day; $9). Be sure to ask for backpacker/student discounts. Note: the depot has no ticket offices, so tickets should be purchased in advance from a Newcastle travel agency (the CountryLink office in the train station sells bus tickets).

Public transportation: City **buses** (☎4961 8933) run along Hunter St. every few minutes during the day, less frequently at night; some run as late as 3:30am. Tickets allow unlimited travel for 1hr. ($2.40).

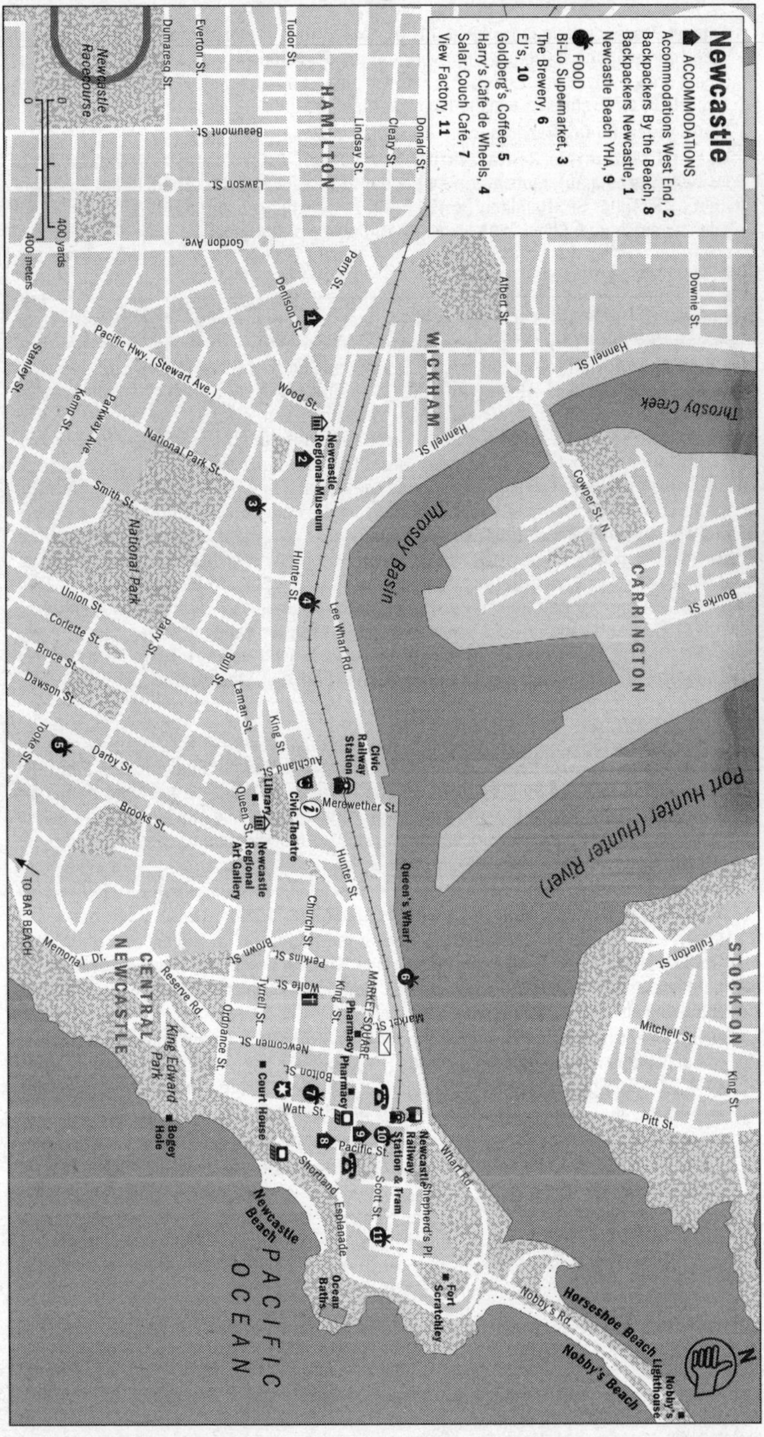

Newcastle
ACCOMMODATIONS
Accommodations West End, 2
Backpackers By the Beach, 8
Backpackers Newcastle, 1
Newcastle Beach YHA, 9
FOOD
Bi-Lo Supermarket, 3
The Brewery, 6
EJ's, 10
Goldberg's Coffee, 5
Harry's Cafe de Wheels, 4
Salar Couch Cafe, 7
View Factory, 11
HAMILTON
WICKHAM
CARRINGTON
STOCKTON
CENTRAL NEWCASTLE
Newcastle Racecourse
Throsby Creek
Throsby Basin
Port Hunter (Hunter River)
PACIFIC OCEAN
National Park
King Edward Park
Newcastle Regional Museum
Civic Railway Station
Civic Theatre
Library
Newcastle Regional Art Gallery
Queen's Wharf
MARKET SQUARE
Pharmacy
Court House
Newcastle Railway Station & Tram
Fort Scratchley
Ocean Baths
Newcastle Beach
Bogey Hole
Horseshoe Beach
Nobby's Beach
Nobby's Lighthouse
TO BAR BEACH
Hunter St.
Hannell St.
Pacific Hwy. (Stewart Ave.)
Tudor St.
Donald St.
Lindsay St.
Parry St.
Denison St.
Beaumont St.
Lawson St.
Gordon Ave.
Everton St.
Dumaresq St.
Albert St.
Downie St.
Cowper St. N.
Bourke St.
Wood St.
National Park St.
Parkway Ave.
Kemp St.
Stanley St.
Smith St.
Union St.
Corlette St.
Bruce St.
Dawson St.
Tooke St.
Darby St.
Brooks St.
Bull St.
Laman St.
King St.
Auckland St.
Queen St.
Merewether St.
Lee Wharf Rd.
Church St.
Brown St.
Perkins St.
Wolfe St.
Tyrrell St.
Newcomen St.
Bolton St.
Watt St.
Pacific St.
Market St.
Ordnance St.
Reserve Rd.
Memorial Dr.
Shortland Esplanade
Scott St.
Shepherd's Pl.
Wharf Rd.
Nobby's Rd.
Fullerton St.
Mitchell St.
Pitt St.
0 400 yards
0 400 meters
N

Ferries: Passenger ferries (☎4974 1160) depart from the tip of the wharf, just west of the train station, and cross the river north to **Stockton** (15min.). The ferry leaves at least once every 30min. (M-Sa 5:15am-midnight, Su and holidays 8:30am-10:05pm.) Tickets ($1.70, children and students 85¢) can be bought onboard.

Taxis: Newcastle Taxi Services (☎4979 3000). MC/V.

Car and Motorcycle Rental: Thrifty Car Rental, 113 Parry St. (☎4961 1141; www.thrifty.com.au), rents from $44 per day ($11 surcharge for drivers under 25). **Budget,** 107 Tudor St., Hamilton (☎4913 2727; www.budget.com.au) is a bit pricier but has no surcharge. Check both websites for online specials specific to Newcastle.

ORIENTATION

Hunter St., at the heart of the city, is Newcastle's commercial district and is (as one hostel owner put it) "not very inspirational." The mostly-pedestrian street, south of the harbor and parallel to the wharf, is overrun with chintzy stores and gangs of kids on skateboards. Unless you want to mail a letter, get cash, visit the tourist office, or bet on horses, stay away from Hunter St. and stick to the outer edges of town. On the eastern end of the main drag, atop a peninsular hill, lies **Fort Scratchley,** a number of hostels and seaside bars, the crashing waves, and the emerald-green **Foreshore Park. Queen's Wharf** runs the distance of the city, starting with the Convict Lumberyard on east Scott St., next to the train station and near the shore. Climb the **Queen's Wharf Tower** to get a 360° view of the city to the south and the harbor to the north. Follow the wharf to the western end of town, near Hamilton, and look for the perpendicular (north/south) **Darby St.** and **Beaumont St.** to find Newcastle's hip happenings. Westward Hunter St. leads to a split in the highway; the New England Hwy. heads west toward the **Hunter Valley wineries** (see p. 146) and the Pacific Hwy. climbs north up the coast. Take a ferry from Newcastle's town center to cross the river to the residential area of **Stockton.**

PRACTICAL INFORMATION

Tourist Office: 363 Hunter St. (☎4974 2999; www.newcastletourism.com). From the train station take a right onto Scott St. and continue as Scott merges onto Hunter St. Walk past Darby St. and the office will be on your left after a couple blocks (right before the Civic Theatre). Free maps of Newcastle and the MacQuarie area. Internet $3.75 per 30min. Open M-F 9am-5pm, Sa-Su 10am-2pm.

Currency Exchange: In the city center on Hunter St. (store numbers 49-101) between Watts and Newcomen, there are a number of banks and 24hr. ATMs.

Library: (☎4974 5300), on Laman St. next to the Newcastle Art Gallery at the corner of Darby and Laman, in the Newcastle Memorial Cultural Centre. **Internet access** free for non-email sites, email $2.75 per 30min. Call 4974 5340 to book ahead. Open M-F 9:30am-8pm, Sa 9:30am-2pm.

Surfing: Pacific Dreams, 7 Darby St. (☎4926 3355; www.pacificdreams.com.au), is the only place in town that rents boards (from $20 per day and $100 per week). Open M-Th 9am-5:30pm, F 9am-8pm, Sa 9am-4pm, Su 10am-3pm. Credit card and driver's license required. Also see **Backpackers by the Beach**, p. 159.

ESCAPE RUN AGROUND Newcastle was originally a colony to which the most troublesome convicts were sent—this is where the baddest of the bad ended up. In November 1800, a band of 15 men determined to escape, seized a supply ship, the *Norfolk*, pirate-style. However, the clever convicts were not able to navigate through a gale and wrecked their getaway ship on the shore of what is now Stockton. Six decided they'd learned their lesson and stayed put, but nine were only frustrated by the failure and snatched another, smaller ship from shore. Proudly sailing past Nobby's Point to freedom, they were later captured by a naval boat. Two men were hanged and the other seven were sent elsewhere for further punishment. Ironically, two of the less adventurous pirates who remained on shore after the shipwreck successfully made it to Sydney by other means.

Police: (☎000). On the corner of Church and Watt St. (☎4929 0999.)

Hospital: John Hunter Hospital (☎4921 3000), John Hunter Lookout Rd., New Lambton, accessible by 30min. bus ride (#363, 232, or 332).

Pharmacy: City Pharmacy, 53 Hunter St. (☎4929 2866). Also sells prepaid phone cards. Open M-F 8:30am-5:30pm.

Internet Access: Nomads Backpackers by the Beach has speedy computers at only $4 per 1hr. (see p. 161). **Newcastle Regional Museum,** 787 Hunter St., has 3 free terminals, although they're slow and often have a wait. Also see public **library** and **tourist office** above. For a snack while you email, try **The Last Drop,** 37 Hunter St. (☎4926 3470), an espresso bar with access ($6 per hr.) as you eat gourmet sandwiches or down your cappucino. Open M-F 8am-11pm, Sa 8am-4pm. **Salar Couch Cafe** has free access.

Post Office: Corner of Scott and Market St. Open M-F 8:30am-5pm. **Postal Code:** 2300.

ACCOMMODATIONS

With tourism (and a hankering for backpackers' business) on the rise, budget accommodations have flourished in Newcastle. Inquire about negotiable long-term rates, especially in winter. Other than the listings below, pub rooms abound (starting around $40). Remember to book ahead in summer, on weekends, and around national holidays.

Newcastle Beach (YHA), 30 Pacific St. (☎4925 3544; fax 4925 3944). Just around the corner from the breaking surf and local train station lies this crown jewel of hostels in a breezy, bricked, and retro-feeling remodeled heritage building. This hostel offers cavernous accommodations, compulsively cleaned facilities, steaming hot showers, and a common area reminiscent of a country club with a TV, pool table, and fireplaces for chilly winter months. Inexpensive winery tour for $35. Kitchen. Occasional BBQ. Internet access $2 per 20min. Free Linen. Laundry $4. Reception 7am-10:30pm. Reservations recommended a month ahead in summer. Dorms $20-22; twins and doubles $54; non-YHA members $3 extra. MC/V.

Backpackers by the Beach (NOMADS), 34-36 Hunter St. (☎4926 3472; fax 4926 5210; backbeach@nobbys.net.au). Less than a 5min. walk north of the train station, this hostel occupies its own yellow corner of Hunter and Pacific St. Modern but small dorms, with heaps of bright light, and high ceilings. All-female/male dorm rooms have single-sex bathrooms. Unbeatable access to beaches, transportation, and the wharf. A young and friendly staff makes for an easygoing atmosphere. Free surfboard loans. Free linen, kitchen, TV room, weekly BBQ. Speedy Internet $4 per 1hr. Key deposit $15. Reception 7am-11pm. Make reservations a week ahead in summer. Dorms $18; twins/doubles $46. $1 per night discount with a week's booking. Non-NOMADS/VIP/YHA members $3 extra. MC/V.

Backpackers Newcastle, 42-44 Denison St., Hamilton (☎4969 3436 or 1800 333 436; newcastlebackpackers.com). A 30min. walk west of the city center, but within drunken hollering distance of happening Beaumont St. Though the rooms are not great, the laid back, familial atmosphere in the common areas helps make up for it. Books winery tours. 2 kitchens, ping-pong table, TV area, reading room, and co-ed bathrooms. Free pickup and drop off in town. Free surf lessons. Unrestricted parking. Free linen. Laundry. Reception 8am-11pm. Dorms $17; doubles $40. VIP/YHA. MC/V.

Accommodation West End, 775 Hunter St. (☎4961 4446; fax 4961 0766). At the corner of the Pacific Hwy. with accompanying noisy traffic. A 20min. walk from the city center and another 10min. from any serious nightlife. Kitchen. Private sinks in most rooms. Free daytime pickup from Newcastle Station. Free luggage storage. Free linen. Laundry $5. Reception 24hr. Make reservations a week ahead. Dorms $25; singles $46; doubles and twins $58; 7th night free. 10% student discount. MC/V.

FOOD

Darby St. is popular for its diverse eateries. **Hunter St.** has $5-6 lunch specials, but you should stick to the Pacific Street end if you're looking for atmosphere. If you're trying to sneak a cheap dinner, go early, as many places close at 6pm.

Though a 20min. walk southwest of city center, over 80 restaurants line Hamilton's **Beaumont St.,** a popular hang-out for students, and home to tasty, cheap, and bustling restaurants. Monday through Wednesday nights in Newcastle bring dinner specials at many restaurants. Cheap food-court options can also be found at **Market Square,** in the center of a pedestrian mall on Hunter St. running from Newcomen to Perkins St., and **The Oasis,** on the corner of Beaumont and Cleary St. The huge **Bi-Lo supermarket** (☎4926 4494) in the Marketown shopping center at the corner of National Park and King St. is open 24hr.

Salar Couch Cafe, 54 Watt St. (☎4927 5329). This new Peruvian-inspired addition to the Newcastle scene combines great food with unbeatable atmosphere. Enjoy $6 lunch specials while perusing their book collection in the "boudoir", a socks-only area of comfortable floor pillows, or surfing the Net for free. Open M-Sa 11:30am-2pm, F-Sa 6pm-late (weekends are packed). No credit cards.

ej's on scott (☎4925 2330), corner of Scott and Pacific St. A block from the train station, breakfast or lunch courtesy of a professional catering company. Their gourmet deli makes $3-6 sandwiches and wraps with fixings like mango chutney and creamy camembert. Huge glass windows and a relaxed atmosphere encourage you to linger over a wide selection of coffee and teas. Open M-F 8am-6pm, Sa-Su 7:30am-6pm. MC/ V.

Goldberg's Coffee House, 137 Darby St. (☎4929 3122). Early in the evening, this place is where everybody meets up for dinner or drinks before heading out for the night. Swing in for a late cup of coffee ($3-5) or a glass of wine to scope and be seen at this Euro-style coffeehouse. Open 8am-midnight or later.

Harry's Cafe de Wheels, 672 Hunter St. (☎4926 2165). What better place to sample a famous Australian meat pie than the oldest "takeaway" joint in the nation. Follow in the footsteps of Bill Cosby, Shirley MacLaine, Pamela Anderson, and repeat customer Elton John. The "Tiger" presents brave souls with a pie smothered in mushy peas, mashed potatoes, and gravy. A quick and historic snack or light meal at only $2-4. Open daily 9am until late (ranging from 11pm-5am).

Al Gator's, 38 Hunter St. (☎4929 1386). Across the street from Bogie Hole Cafe is possibly the best bang for your lunch buck in the city. A tasty variety of sandwiches are nearly all under $4 and include a number of healthy vegetarian options. Limited outdoor seating lets you catch the sunshine while you chow down. Open Su-F 6am-4pm.

The View Factory (☎4929 4580), corner of Telford and Scott St. On the eastern part of town, with an artsy feel. Specialty salads, pastas, and lighter lunch options, including vegetarian ones. Entrees $6-18. Buy one, get one free M-Tu dinner deal. YHA discount. Open M-Sa 11am-midnight, Su 11am-6pm. AmEx/MC/V.

The Brewery Restaurant, 150 Wharf Rd. (☎4929 6333; www.qwb.com.au). On the water, this is the neighborhood drink spot. A gourmet menu with entrees from $6-20. Management hosts free BBQ, beer, and trivia contests for hostelers on advertised nights. Dress "smart." Open daily 10am-2am, W "uni night", live bands or DJ on Sa.

SIGHTS AND ACTIVITIES

Newcastle's public image problems are nothing new: the city was established in 1804 as a settlement for the most egregious of convicts and was dubbed "Sydney's Siberia." However, looking closely, one finds that this hard-luck town has a number of redeeming aspects. Its ornate **heritage buildings,** built by convicts, are the architectural highlights of the town, along with the **Cathedral** in the city center. But people don't come to Newcastle for Victorian balconies—they come for the seaside parks, the gut-wrenching crash of the sea against the rocky shore, and the hardcore surf where four-time world champ Mark Richards once cut his teeth.

NEWCASTLE'S TRAM. The famous tram offers a delightful, informative city overview and tells of the devastation from a freak earthquake in 1989. The ride is a great way to get a quick feel for the city's sights, from the historic architecture to whales breaching off the coastline. (*☎4963 7954, huntertourism.com/tram; 45min.; departs daily from Newcastle Railway Station every hour 10am-2pm. $10, children $6.50, family of 2 adults, 2 children $29.*)

THREE OF HEARTS With Australia's origins as a penal colony, it's no surprise that many historic buildings were built by convict labor. The Rose Cottage, the oldest building in Newcastle built in 1828, is made entirely of handmade bricks. But each brick, rather than a signature, has a playing card symbol. Convicts, unable to read or write, adopted a suit and number as their John Hancock and eventually even became identified by it, losing their original name.

FORT SCRATCHLEY. Climb the hill for the best view in the city. Play around on the cannons and explore the underground tunnel system for $2.50. The fort has been an inactive military site since the 1970s and now houses the Military Museum and, next door, the Maritime Museum. *(Military Museum open Sa-Su noon-4pm. Free. Maritime Museum ☎4929 2588. Open Tu-F 10am-4pm, Sa-Su noon-4pm. Free.)*

BEACHES. Newcastle's shore is lined with white sand beaches, tidal pools, and landscaped parks. At the tip of Nobby's Head peninsula is Nobby's Lighthouse, surrounded by (you guessed it) **Nobby's Beach,** a terrific surfing spot. Walking clockwise around the peninsula from Nobby's leads to a surf pavilion, then to the **Ocean Baths**, a public saltwater pool on the cliffs overlooking the surf; keep walking to find its predecessor **Bogey Hole,** a convict-built ocean bath at the edge of the manicured **King Edward Park.** Farther along, you'll see a cliff walk leading to the **Susan Gilmore nude beach;** farther still is the large **Bar Beach,** popular with surfers.

BLACKBUTT RESERVE. A 182-hectare tree sanctuary with five walking trails over 20km, and many animals along the way. There's a koala enclosure as well as kangaroo and emu reserves. If you're lucky, you can pat a koala Sa-Su 11:30am and 2:30pm. It may be stoned, but it's not stupid; definitely don't stick your finger in its mouth. Bring your own picnic food; no food is available. *(Catch bus #232 or 363 in the city center for 45min. to Lookout Rd., Cardiff Heights and follow signs down the hill. ☎4952 1449; www.ncc.nsw.gov.au. Open daily 7am-5pm, wildlife exhibits 9am-5pm. Free.)*

NEW SOUTH WALES

WETLANDS CENTRE. As well as offering sanctuary to birds and reptiles, the center offers respite to urban-weary humans with walking paths, a creek, and a swamp for canoeing. Every Sunday brings activities like wilderness wine-tastings and "Billagong" breakfasts at sunrise by canoe. *(Take the CityTrain to Sandgate, in the suburb of Shortland, and then walk 10min. on Sandgate Rd. ☎4951 6466; www.wetlands.org.au. Canoe rental $7-10 per 2hr. Bikes $6 per hr. Open M-F 9am-3pm, Sa-Su 10am-3pm. Entry fee $4.50, $9 for family—2 adults, 2 children.)*

NEWCASTLE REGIONAL MUSEUM. A somewhat haphazard collection of hands-on science exhibits and heritage displays that fills three floors. Check out the coal mine re-creation before you head up to the top level for slow **free Internet access.** *(787 Hunter St. ☎4974 1400; www.amol.org.au/newcastle. Open Tu-Su 10am-5pm. Free.)*

NEWCASTLE REGION ART GALLERY. The gallery displays Australian and international art and ceramics and hosts traveling exhibitions. However, the surrounding leafy, cloistered neighborhood may be the highlight. *(Laman St., off Darby St., behind Civic Park. ☎4974 5100. Open Tu-Su 10am-5pm. Free.)*

FESTIVALS. Surfest rides into town in late February for a two-week international surfing spectacular, drawing crowds from all of Oz. The **Newcastle Jazz Festival** plays out in late August at Club NOVA. The **King St. Fair** is a city-wide carnival in early December. **Newcastle Maritime Festival's** boat races and watersports are the last week of January.

ENTERTAINMENT AND NIGHTLIFE

The Post, a free Newcastle newspaper, publishes a guide to the next week's live music around the area each Wednesday. For info on clubs and pubs, peruse the free local guide *TE (That's Entertainment)* at the tourist office. **SJ's,** 8 Beaumont St. (☎4961 2537), is a gaming room and pub that gets swamped on weekend nights and specializes in rock bands W-Su. The **Northern Star Hotel,** 112 Beaumont

St. (☎4961 1087; www.northernstarhotel.com.au), is a popular jazz spot, while the **Kent Hotel,** 59-61 Beaumont St. (☎4961 3303), fronts more mainstream bands. Check out **ClubNOVA** (☎4926 2700; www.clubnova.com.au) at the corner of King and Union St. for regular rock concerts, or head to **Mercury Hotel,** 23 Watt St. (☎4926 1119) for the hottest dance club in town (W, F-Sa nights until 3am, cover varies $6-10). The **Clarendon Hotel,** 347 Hunter St. (☎4927 0966) offers signature cocktails for only $2.50 during its uni Happy Hours (W 9-11pm). Attracting a large backpacker and student crowd, the **Brewery** (see **Food,** p. 159) packs it in with homemade brews. If it's raining, catch a movie at the **Greater Union,** 183 King St. (☎4926 2233), or a play at the **Civic Theatre,** 375 Hunter St. (Ticketek, ☎4929 1977).

DAYTRIPS FROM NEWCASTLE

Fifteen minutes south of Newcastle is **Lake Macquarie,** one of Australia's largest coastal saltwater lakes (four times the size of Sydney Harbour) and a weekend-vacation hot spot. The shore is popular with surfers and families on holiday, with hefty waves, deep caverns at **Caves Beach,** and a mining village at **Catherine Hill Bay.** Spelunkers must go at **low tide** so as not to get trapped in the caves. Find tide tables at the **Lake Macquarie Information Center,** 72 Pacific Hwy., in the Blacksmiths. (☎4972 1172; www.lakemac.com.au. Open M-F 9am-5pm, Sa-Su 9am-4pm.)

The mountainous **Watagans National Park** separates Lake Macquarie from the Hunter River. An hour from Newcastle and the Hunter Valley, it's ideal for hikes, picnics, or camping. There are seven campsites, most with firewood, grills, toilets, and water. Call the **NPWS Hunter** office (☎4358 0400; www.npws.nsw.gov.au) for more info. Many visitors use Newcastle as a "gateway to the Hunter," or as spring-board to wine sampling at the many nearby vineyards (see p. 215).

PORT STEPHENS BAY AREA ☎02

North of Newcastle, Port Stephens is a placid, secluded bay and sleepy rural town-ships defined by blue-green water and the **Tomaree National Park.** Most of the region's activities, restaurants, and facilities are in Nelson Bay. Anna Bay and Shoal Bay offer beautiful and somewhat isolated beaches. During the summer, surfing beaches and luxury resorts draw backpackers and families alike, clogging central shopping areas with traffic. The ocean beyond the surf also attracts visi-tors of the aquatic kind: bottlenose dolphins are visible twelve months of the year in the harbor and, quite cheeky—they'll come right up to you and tag along the daily dolphin cruises. Locals say the dolphins do more people-watching than vice-versa. The whale-watching season runs from June to October as the giants head north to warmer waters to breed. On the coastal edge of the national park, aban-doned Australian-American forts are left over from WWII training camps. Port Stephens also boasts some of the most spectacular sand dunes in the country, an attraction which is growing in popularity to rival the sealife.

TRANSPORTATION

Port Stephens Buses (☎4982 2940 or 1800 045 949; www.psbuses.nelsonbay.com) run from Newcastle (1½hr.; M-F 11 per day, Sa-Su 4 per day; $9 roundtrip, $4.50 for students) to four of the townships and Sydney (3hr., 1 per day, $25). The main stop in Nelson Bay is at the **Bi-Lo** on Stockton St. **Local buses** run hourly on weekdays,

YANKS IN OZ Although Port Stephens' harbor is nearly 2½ times the size of the Sydney Harbour, it has historically enjoyed a clandestine existence. During WWII, American General Douglas MacArthur took advantage of this hidden, and very deep, body of water to train his fleets. Through the entire Pacific phase of the war, the area remained successfully out of sight of the Japanese. The American soldiers, in exchange for covert amphibious training grounds, helped the local townships build infrastructure and roads that still exist today.

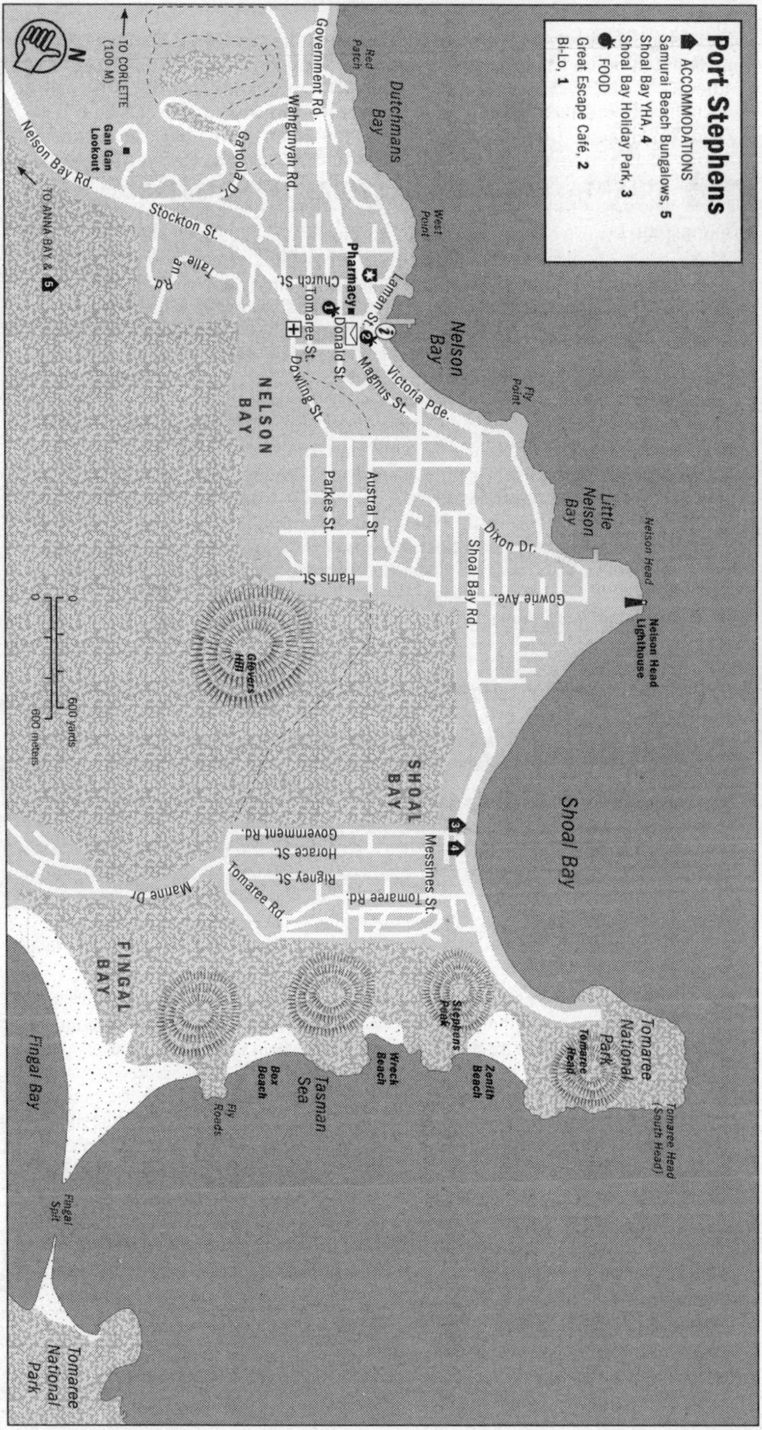

Port Stephens

ACCOMMODATIONS
Samurai Beach Bungalows, **5**
Shoal Bay YHA, **4**
Shoal Bay Holiday Park, **3**

FOOD
Great Escape Café, **2**
Bi-Lo, **1**

every 2 hours on weekends (around $3; 1 day unlimited travel $11); it may be more convenient to rent a car from Newcastle to avoid being stranded in one township or another for a few hours. The Port Stephens **Ferry** Service (☎4981 3798) makes three trips daily to **Tea Garden,** across the water from Nelson Bay (8:30am, noon, 3:30pm; $17 roundtrip; $40 family—2 adults, 2 children). For a **taxi,** call 4984 6699.

ORIENTATION AND PRACTICAL INFORMATION

Nelson Bay Rd. leads from Newcastle to four local residential townships of the Port Stephens area. The road forks onto **Gan Gan Rd.,** which leads to the seaside township of **Anna Bay,** home to **Stockton Bight,** the largest sand dune area in the southern hemisphere, and close to the popular surfing destination of **One Mile Beach,** known simply as "The Big Beach" to locals. Gan Gan and Nelson Bay Rd. rejoin en route to three other townships: **Nelson Bay** (the largest), **Shoal Bay,** and the quite rural **Fingal Bay.** The marina, shopping complex, and cafes are located on **Victoria Parade** and **Stockton St.** in Nelson Bay. The **Salamander Shopping Centre,** a 5min. bus ride west, is home to the Tomaree public **library** (☎4982 0670). **Internet access** is available in the library. (Free. Email $2.75 per 30min. Book ahead for both. Open M, W, F 10am-6pm; Tu, Th 10am-8pm; Sa 9:30am-2pm.) **Terrace Cafe** also offers Internet access in a convenient shopping arcade on Victoria Pde. overlooking the tourist office. (☎4981 0750. $2 per 15min. Open daily 8am-5pm, F-Sa 8am-9pm.) The **tourist office,** on Victoria Pde., by the wharf in Nelson Bay, arranges bookings for local attractions. (☎4981 1579; www.portstephens.org.au. Open daily.)

NEW SOUTH WALES

ACCOMMODATIONS

Winter often brings great deals, but available beds drop and prices rise in the summer. Book four to six weeks ahead on weekends, in summer, in January, and around holidays. Beware of significant price spikes on weekends in the hotel/motel market. All of the following are on the Port Stephens local bus route. Check with the tourist office for a full listing of local motels and caravan parks.

Samurai Beach Bungalows Backpackers (☎/fax 4982 1921; samurai_backpackers@nelsonbay.com). On Robert Connell Circle, reached by Frost Rd., off of Nelson Bay Rd. just outside Anna Bay. Solidly in the bush, this is a city-weary traveler's dream. There's a volleyball court, an outdoor kitchen, TV, pool table, free surfboards and boogie boards, and a campfire at night. Ask the owner about "sandboarding" the local dunes. Linen included. Bike rentals $12 per day, free use for those staying 3 or more days. Sparse 5-bunk dorms with shared bath $17; doubles with TV, bath, coffee maker and mini-kitchen from $44; family room $60. VIP. MC/V.

Shoal Bay Holiday Park (☎4981 1427 or 1800 600 200; shoal@portstephens.nsw.gov.au). On Shoal Bay Rd. on the way to Fingal Bay, within hearing distance of the ocean. New kitchen. 2 Common television areas, pool and ping-pong tables, tennis courts, trivia contests, and movie nights. Laundry $2. Reception daily 8:15am-6pm. Powered tent and caravan sites for 2 adults $18-22, additional adult $7.50. 4-person budget bungalows at $30-60, family cabins for 5 with bathroom $44-126. Discount for 7 night stay.

Shoal Bay YHA, 59-61 Shoal Bay Beachfront Rd. (☎4981 0982). In the Shoal Bay Motel, across from the beach and a 15min. walk west of the Tomaree trails. Rooms have TV, fridge, heat and A/C. The 6-bed women's dorm has an attached bathroom, as does the 6-bed men's dorm which is separated from the common room only by partitions and a curtain. Kitchen, TV lounge, sauna, BBQ. $20 key deposit includes linen rental. Laundry machines $6. Reception 7:45am-10pm. Dorms $17, twins/doubles $23; non-YHA members $23/$29; family rooms with bath$42.

FOOD

Nelson Bay—the Port Stephens hub—is the best place to find cheap food, particularly on Magnus and Donald St., both parallel to Victoria Pde. Try breakfast near the water at the **Great Escape Cafe,** 19 Stockton St., Nelson Bay (☎4984 3322), at the corner of Stockton and Victoria Pde. Upstairs from the Great Escape is the **Greek Village Restaurant** (☎4984 3388); bring along a bottle of wine and enjoy a romantic evening of Greek cuisine. Trusty supermarket **Bi-Lo** has locations on the corner of Stockton and Donald St. (☎4981 1666) and in the Salamander Shopping Center which also offers a **Woolworth's** and a number of fast-food joints.

SIGHTS AND ACTIVITIES

You've probably seen sport-utility-vehicle ads on TV and wondered if anyone really drives off-road like that. Now's your chance to find out. The fun-loving folks at Port Stephens Council (☎4980 0255) will let you buy a day pass for $5 so you and your 4WD can go play on **Stockton Bight,** the biggest sand dune in the Southern Hemisphere; passes available at the Mobil station in Anna Bay. Follow signs to Anna Bay from Nelson Bay Rd.; the Mobil is past the beach access sign. For renting or participating in more organized group-duning, try the **6 Wheeler Bushmobile Dune Adventure** and conquer the deserts for just $20 per person (☎4938 5744; www.bushmobile.com.au). Even braver? **Sand Safaris** offers a pricey but worthwhile adventure activity (☎4965 0215 or 0418 209 747; sandsafaris.com.au; 4-5 trips daily, pickup from Newcastle Airport). $99 a head gets you two hours on your very own ATV and an award-winning guided trip at 40km/h over dunes nearly 100m high. For tamer sand activities, ask about camel rides at the Nelson Bay tourist office or join **Sahara Trails** on spectacular 2hr. dune and beach horse rides and 1hr. beginners bush rides starting at $15. (☎4981 9077; www.saharatrails.com. Open daily. Bookings required.)

Whale watching and **dolphin cruises** depart five times per day in the summer (winter trips are weather-permitting). The cheapest of the lot is the large **Tamboi Queen,** which cruises the harbor for sightings of the over 150 dolphins that live there year-round. (☎4981 1959. 2-4 trips daily, 1½hr. dolphin cruise $18.) On the ocean side, try **Moonshadow cruises** (☎4984 9388) daily whale watching cruises. Book a **high speed jet boat ride** at the tourist office or call 4984 9811 (15min for $33). **Blue Water Sea Kayaking** (☎0409 408 618; www.seakayaking.com.au) offers 2hr. trips throughout the day at around $30.

For second-to-none views of the bay's rippling blue-green waters and stark headlands, and the expanse of the South Pacific horizon, it's worth making the 30min walk to the summit of **Tomaree Head** at the end of Shoal Bay. Follow Shoal Bay Rd. until it ends at the Tomaree National Park; signs direct you to the tracks. You can find opportunities for **surfing** and **nude bathing** on the Anna Bay shore; inquire at the Nelson Bay tourist office for information.

Shoal Bay Bike Hire, 63 Shoal Bay Rd., near the YHA, is a cheaper bike option. (☎4981 4121. $10 per 2hr.; $20 per day. Open daily 9am-5pm. Hours vary in winter.) **Toboggan Hill Park,** in Nelson Bay, off Salamander Way behind the Aquatic Center, is a small theme park with a 700m downhill toboggan run, a 19-hole mini golf course, indoor rock climbing, and many other diversions. (☎4984 1022; www.nelsonbay.com/toboggan. Open daily 9am-6pm, off-season 10am-4pm. $2 entry fee on weekends. All activities $4-5.)

MYALL LAKES NATIONAL PARK

If you consider yourself an ecotourist, you may well find paradise in the Myall Lakes National Park among over 10,000 hectares of lakes, 40km of beaches, walking tracks traversing coastal rainforest, heath, and paperbark swamp. With only two major vehicular access points ($6 vehicle entry fee per day), the lake area enshrouds a number of restive outdoor spots if you're willing to look for them. To find seclusion, pick up the park notes at the visitor center and explore the various ways to access the park from The Lakes Way. Most people enter via **Bulahdelah,** 83km north of Newcastle and 70km south of Taree along the Pacific Hwy., and 60km southwest of Forster by The Lakes Way. **Bulahdelah Visitor Centre** (☎4997 4981) at the corner of Pacific Hwy. and Crawford St., is the park's only "interpretive center," with comprehensive maps and information. From Bulahdelah, take

NEW SOUTH WALES

the Myall Way (Lakes Rd.), a one-lane partly-paved road with an absurd 100kph speed limit. Beware of cars, caravans, and boat tugs barreling along.

The road finishes at **Bombah Point,** a center of activity for both the Myall Lake and Bombah Broadwater. Here, the office and kiosk of **Myall Shores Ecotourism Resort** (☎4997 4495) distribute maps and some supplies. They rent canoes ($12 per hr.) and outboards ($38 per 2hr.) and also sell gasoline. The facilities within this **campground** include BBQs, laundry, a store, and a restaurant. (Campsites $17-22, powered $20-26, varying with the season.) A **toll ferry** carries vehicles over to the Mungo Brush area of the park. (5 min., every 30min., $3.) The almost-all-paved **Mungo Brush Rd.** extends 25km along the coast to the park's southern edge. The lake side of the road has various entrances to the usually-crowded Mungo Brush **campgrounds** that have toilets, BBQs, **no water,** and access to the shallow lake. (NPWS office ☎4987 3108. Sites for two $10, not including $6 daily vehicle fee. First-come first-served. Pay a ranger if one comes by, or use the honesty box.) On the other side of the park, accessible via Seal Rocks Rd. (turnoff after Bungwahl on The Lakes Way) is the secluded **Yagon** park campsite on the ocean headland.

Access points all along the road lead to the **beach.** At the northern end of Mungo Brush begins the poorly signposted **Mungo Brush Rainforest Walking Track,** a 1.5km loop through a rainforest that is unusually fertile for this stretch of coast. This track has its share of interestingly large and intimidating vegetation, and koalas snooze in the trees year round. Other tracks on this side of the ferry can be walked consecutively to make up the hardy **Mungo Track,** which will take the day if you're moving along reasonably quickly; pick up the trail map before setting out.

FORSTER AND TUNCURRY ☎02

Small they may be, but Forster and its lesser twin town Tuncurry, situated on twin isthmuses, are the height of civilization in the popular Great Lakes region—Aussie holiday spots frequently passed over by international travelers. Blessed with a temperate climate and endless stretches of empty beaches nearby, the Forster area is a nice break from the party scenes of Sydney or Byron Bay.

TRANSPORTATION AND PRACTICAL INFORMATION. From the south via the Pacific Hwy., **The Lakes Way** turn-off heads east right after Buladelah, and Forster is one hour down the road. From the north, The Lakes Way turn-off is east at Rainbow Flat, and Forster is a 15min. drive. **Great Lakes Coaches** (☎4983 1560) connects to Bluey's Beach (3-4 per day, 2 per day Sa-Su; $9) and Sydney (5½hr., 1-2 per day, $44) via Newcastle (3hr., 2-3 per day, $28). **Eggins Comfort Coaches** (☎6552 2700) goes to Taree (1hr.; 2-4 per day M-Sa, $10; 50% student and YHA discounts). The **Great Lakes Visitors Centre,** on Little St. by the wharf, is the **coach terminal** and a booking agency. Tickets can also be bought on the bus. (☎6554 8799. Open daily 9am-5pm.) **Cyberdine Internet Cafe** in the Forster Arcade off of Wharf St. charges $1.10 for 10 min. access (☎6557 5130. Open M-F 9am-5pm, Sa 9am-1pm.)

ACCOMMODATIONS AND FOOD. Do you like nice people? If not, you will after meeting the owners of the **Dolphin Lodge (YHA),** 43 Head St., who treat you to surf and boogie boards, a kitchen, and a TV lounge, all just a stone's throw from the beach and town. They make pre-arranged pickup at the bus stops in Nabiac on the Pacific Hwy., rent bikes, and have Internet access at $2 per 10 min. (☎/fax 6555 8155. $10 key deposit. Dorms $18; singles $28; doubles with bath $42.) **Smugglers Cove Holiday Village,** 45 The Lakes Way, has top notch facilities—a pool, mini-golf, a kitchen, and $5 canoe hire. (☎6554 6666. Sites $22, powered $29; winter $14, $20; economy cabins $60, with bath $75; winter $44/$55) The tourist office can provide you with a list of budget motel clones around the area.

For food, try any of the small **markets** on Wharf St., which is also home to a number of restaurants serving burgers, pizza, and Chinese food. When work gets out on Friday, **Lakes and Ocean Hotel** gets its taps running full volume. Live bands play on weekends. **Fat Ant Cafe,** 32 Wharf St. (☎6555 3444), transforms into a groovy nightclub on Friday nights at 10pm.

SIGHTS AND ACTIVITIES. **Tobwabba,** 10 Breckenridge St., means "place of clay" to the Worimi Aborigines who welcome visitors to this studio and art gallery. For those seeking souvenirs that are a little more original than the ubiquitous stuffed kangaroos and koalas, the beautiful prints and canvasses are an interesting alternative. (☎6554 5755; www.tobwabba.com.au. Open M-F 9am-5pm, Sa 10am-4pm. Another location is on Beach St. at the end of Wharf St.) At the north end of **Forster Beach,** at the end of West St. off Head St., there's a gas BBQ, a saltwater swimming pool, and the beach. For stunt skiing, seaplane flights, fishing cruises, or diving, consult the visitors center. **Biking** to the beaches of Booti Booti National park is the best way to go (at least an hour each way). Once in the park, beach after beach provide ample rest stops and the treasured **Green Cathedral** is an easy turn-off from the road. Bike hire is available from the Dolphin Lodge YHA (see above; $10 per 4hr., $16 per day; guests $8/$12). Boat and tackle rental sheds line the lake shore. Near Forster, **Eureka Trails** offers **horseriding.** (☎6554 1281. $20 per 1hr., $35 per 2hr.) **Forster's Dive School** at Fisherman's Wharf opposite the post office, runs a variety of trips, including a **swim with dolphins** cruise, which lowers passengers near the mammals on a boom net (2hr., $38), and trips to the shipwreck *S.S. Satara.* (☎6554 7478. Rates vary; two dives with equipment $127; advanced divers only for shipwreck.) **Action Divers,** 1-5 Manning St. offers slightly cheaper rates. (☎6555 4053. two dives with equipment $115.)

NEAR FORSTER

GREAT LAKES REGION

BOOTI BOOTI NATIONAL PARK. For a piece of Booti Booti, follow The Lakes Way south of Forster along the coastline of Elizabeth Bay. Wallis Lake, the forest between the road and beach, and the hinterland on the road's other side comprise **Booti Booti National Park** (NPWS Office ☎6554 0446; booti.booti@npws.nsw.gov.au). **Cape Hawke** is quite a climb by bike, but provides both a spectacular view and access to a significant part of NSW's coastal rainforest. **Tiona Park,** 30min. south of Forster, rents sites on both the lake and beach sides of the road. (☎6554 0291. Sites $18; cabins $38-67.) Tiona Park is also home to the popular **Green Cathedral** set along the lake's edge. The sheltered waters of Lake Wallis can be affordably enjoyed with **Lakeside Family Boat Hire,** off Lakes Way. (☎6554 0309. Sea buggies $5 per 1hr., paddle boats $5 per 30min., double canoes $10 per 1hr., motor boats $25 per 1hr.) A walk (1hr.) around the lake through cabbage tree palms and eucalyptus will lead you to the ocean and **Elizabeth Beach.** You can camp with less clutter at **The Ruins Camping Area** by the soft white sand of **Seven-Mile Beach** next to a mangrove forest. (BBQ, toilets, and showers; pay camping fees in slots at the entrance to The Ruins Camping Area; $17.50.) Good **surfers** should travel 1km north to **Janice's Corner.**

BLUEY'S BEACH AND PACIFIC PALMS. Approximately 20min. along The Lakes Way south of Forster, a sign appears for Bluey's Beach. The road, Boomerang Dr., passes several beaches and continues through the small town of Pacific Palms before rejoining The Lakes Way a few kilometers south. **Elizabeth's Beach** is the first turn-off on the left. Patrolled by pelicans and lifeguards, the waves usually die down in summer, making the safe surf ideal for swimmers. Farther along Boomerang Dr is **Shelly's Beach,** a calm secluded stretch with clothing-optional bathing. **Boomerang Beach,** home of myriad **surfer** dudes, is just a couple minutes farther. You can crash at **Moby Dick,** a plain caravan park with a cafe/restaurant, open from 8am-10:30pm. (☎6554 0292. Sites $17-25, powered $20-30; cabins $45-125.) From here, Boomerang Dr. loops through **Pacific Palms,** which has a small strip of shops selling junk food, sundries, and magazines. At its end is the **Info Center.** (☎6554 0123. Open daily 9am-4pm.) A bit farther on, you can camp in style at the **Oasis Caravan Park.** There's petrol, a market, and a small pool on the premises. (☎6554 0488; fax 6554 0268. Reception daily 8am-8pm, later in summer. Sites $14-18; cabins $73-125.) **Great Lakes Sea Planes** (☎6555 8771) offers scenic flights departing from Forster Marina and Pacific Palms for as low as $40 per person. Pacific Palms is also home to the 6,500 hectare **Wallingat State Forest** which adjoins the Wallis Lake system. **Whoota Whoota lookout** is spectacular with panoramic views of the endless coastline.

SANDBAR. A kilometer south of the southern end of Boomerang Dr. along The Lakes Way is the turn-off for a dirt road that takes you 2km to **Celito Beach.** The 300m boardwalk leads through dry littoral forest to a beach to drool over, whether you're a surfer or a sunbather. Take a left off on the main dirt road to the **Sandbar Caravan Park,** to reach a wilderness site on **Smith's Lake.** (☎6554 4095. Sites $10-30; cabins without bath $40-85; prices vary with season.)

SEAL ROCKS. South of Pacific Palms and Bluey's Beach, The Lakes Way turns westward to skirt **Myall Lakes National Park** on its way to rejoining the Pacific Hwy at Buladelah. Between Smith's Lake and Myall Lake, there is an easterly turn-off from The Lakes Way onto **Seal Rocks Rd.** The community of Seal Rocks has insisted that most of the road (15km) remain unpaved to protect its seclusion from tourism. Beyond this road, a narrow dirt track leads to **Boat Beach.** Swimmers, windsurfers, and fishermen share this spot. The **Seal Rocks Camping Reserve** is near Number One Beach. (☎4997 6164. Sites $12.10; vans $39.60; cabins $49-52.)

TAREE ☎02

Taree, on the Manning River off the Pacific Hwy., is a small base for nearby beaches, state parks, and forests. The many budget hotels, motels, and caravan parks outside Taree and surrounding areas make it a convenient stop on long road trips. Though northbound travelers usually push on a little farther to the welcoming arms of Port Macquarie, Taree has a growing B&B and "country retreat" industry, particularly in nearby Wingham, allowing for a more comfortable pit stop.

Taree's main street, **Victoria St.,** conveniently feeds directly to the Pacific Hwy. Most shops, food, and bus stations are on Victoria St. or the streets between Pulteney and Macquarie St. **Countrylink** (☎13 22 32), **Greyhound Pioneer** (☎13 20 30), **Premier** (☎13 34 10), **Eggins Comfort Coaches** (☎6552 2700), **Great Lakes Coaches** (☎1800 043 263), and **McCafferty's** (☎13 14 99) run **buses** to: Brisbane (10-11hr., 7 per day, $54-66); Byron Bay (7-7½hr., 6 per day, $54-65); Coffs Harbour (3-3½hr., 7 per day, $37-40); Forster (1hr.; 2-4 per day; $10, $5 YHA); Port Macquarie (1-1½hr., 6 per day, $26-35); Sydney (5-6hr., 10 per day, $44-59). The **Manning Valley Tourist Office** on the Pacific Hwy., 4km north of town, is just past the Big Oyster car dealership (☎1800 801 522 or 6552 1900. Open daily 9am-5pm).

Taree is 200km south of Coffs Harbour, 83km south of Port Macquarie, and 310km north of Sydney. **Beaches** near Taree are gorgeous and inviting, but have unexpected currents: swim only where patrolled. The closest is **Old Bar Beach** in the little village of Old Bar, a 15min. drive southeast from the town center on Old Bar Rd. **Wallabi Point,** to the south, offers great surfing and has a swimming lagoon. **Diamond Beach** and **Hallidays Point,** two well-known beaches farther south, offer **camping.** A 40min. drive to the north is **Crowdy Head,** site of a lighthouse lookout.

Accommodations are cheap and plentiful. **Exchange Hotel,** on the corner of Victoria and Manning St. offers basic but clean rooms. (☎6552 1160. Reception at bar 10am-late. Singles $20; doubles $30.) Motel after indistinguishable motel line the Old Pacific Hwy. with doubles starting at $45. **Taree Caravan Park,** near the tourist office and across from the Arlite Motor Inn, has a pool and wheelchair access. (☎6552 1751. Laundry $3. Reception daily 8am-8pm. Sites for 2 $10, powered $15; cabins for 2 $30-35, with bath $37-44. MC/V.)

FROM TAREE TO PORT MACQUARIE

CROWDY BAY NATIONAL PARK. Home to some of the area's most popular beaches, bushwalks, picnic areas, and a healthy supply of kangaroos, Crowdy Bay has something for every visitor. The park supposedly derives its name from

FREE WILLY: THE PREQUEL Long before a certain killer whale gained Hollywood fame, Taree had its own local celebrity when "Willy," a tropical whale, became stuck in the nearby Manning River. It soon faced starvation unless it could return to the open sea. As the whale's plight became known, a media frenzy descended upon Taree as local entrepreneurs flooded shops with Willy T-shirts and conservationists and government officials squabbled over how to get the animal out safely. Nets and an inflatable pontoon later returned Willy to the wild, but not before the whale achieved what one local remarked as "more for [Taree] tourism in three months than our tourism commission has done in years."

Captain Cook's passing observation that the headland was crowded with Aborigines. Coralville Rd., at Moorland on the Pacific Hwy., leads into the southern entrance of the park. Wild eastern grey kangaroos live at all three of the camping sites: **Diamond Head, Indian Head,** and **Kylie's Rest Area** (named for Australian author Kylie Tennant). There are septic toilets and cold showers at Diamond Head; all other sites have squat toilets. Whereas groups of **kangaroos** hop within feet of astounded visitors, and **whales** can be spotted off the headlands, it often takes an expert to spot more elusive **koalas** at Indian Head and Kylie's Hut. There are three reasonably tame **bushwalks** in the park which pass through delicate habitats stunted from exposure to wind and subject to harsh salt sprays. The shortest walk is along the base of the cliff of the headland, accessible from Diamond Head at low tide. The **Cliff Base Walk** passes rock pools abounding with marine life. The longer **Diamond Head Loop Track** links Diamond Head and Indian Head, while a third track goes from Kylie's Hut to the beach at Crowdy Bay. Visitors must bring their own fresh water into the park. The roads are 2WD-accessible dirt tracks. (Daily vehicle fee $6, one-time camping charge for 2 $10.)

NEW SOUTH WALES

BULGA STATE FOREST. A 50km daytrip from Taree and the site of a 99km tourist drive, the Bulga Forests are actually four separate forests: the Bulga, Doyles River, Dingo, and Knorrit. The Bulga is home to **Tirrill Creek Flora Reserve,** with walking trails, picnic areas, and the **Blue Knob Lookout,** from which even Taree is sometimes visible. **Maxwells Flat,** with toilet and BBQ facilities, has camping.

The most spectacular sight of the Bulga drive is **Ellenborough Falls,** an hour's drive from Taree. Created by a fault line 30 million years ago, it's one of the largest drops in the southern hemisphere (200m). There are multiple walking tracks, the most difficult of which leads to the bottom of the gorge. At the top of the Falls, there are picnic tables, restrooms, and a refreshment kiosk (open Sa-Su 10am-4pm). The falls can be reached without the Bulga drive, by an east-west trip through **Comboyne.** This route also gives access to the **Boorganna Nature Reserve.** Both this and the Bulga drive are along rough, unsealed roads. For more info, call the **Manning Valley Tourist Office** in Taree (see **Practical Information,** p. 168).

ALTERNATE ROUTES. A different coastal drive runs through **Crowdy Bay National Park** and **Laurieton,** rather than taking the Pacific Hwy.; the change adds negligible time. A quick drive through **Dooragan National Park** leads to the amazing lookout at **North Brother** mountain, with a panorama of the surrounding valley and bodies of water. There are also walking trails in Dooragan.

East of the Pacific Hwy. from Taree to Port Macquarie, there's another series of parks. **Middle Brother State Forest** and **Coopernook Forest Drive** are accessible from Moorland. Middle Brother, near **Kendall,** contains many trails, lookouts, the two largest blackbutt trees in the state, and the equally huge **Big Fella Gum Tree.** The Coopernook drive, 25km northeast of Taree, goes through the **Coorabakh National Park,** and **Landsdowne** and **Comboyne State Forests.** Along with walks and lookouts, there is the **Big Nellie** volcanic plug, a 20min. climb to the top, and the swimming spot of **Waitui Falls.** The NWPS office in Taree (☎6552 4097) has more info.

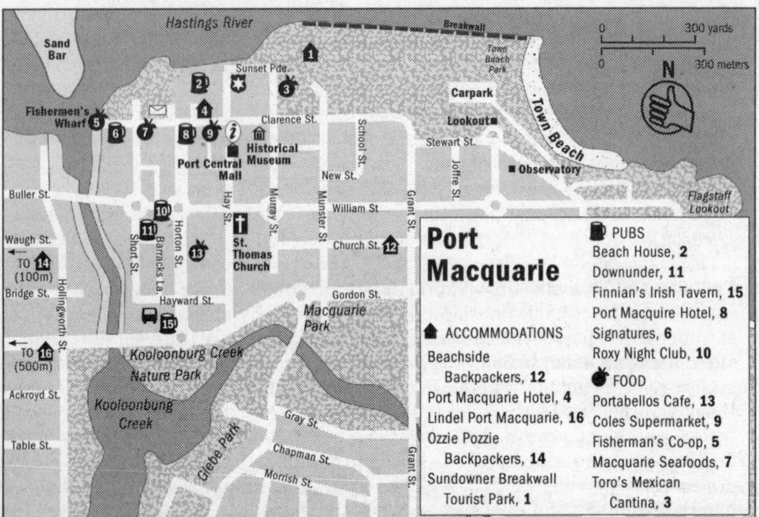

PORT MACQUARIE ☎02

Travelers with their blinders on en route to Sydney and Byron Bay make the sad mistake of bypassing Port Macquarie (pop. 40,000), once a lock-up for Sydney's worst offenders. Today, the coastal town is growing into a veritable action-sport capital. Though hard-core partiers don't dominate the town, crowds swarm to the surrounding beaches and nature reserves in the summer.

TRANSPORTATION

Major bus lines including **McCafferty's** (☎13 14 99), **Premier** (☎13 34 10), and **Greyhound** (☎13 20 30) pass through town once per day. Check to make sure your bus stops at Hayward St., and not out on the highway. **Budget** (☎13 27 27), at the corner of Gordon and Hollingsworth St; **Hertz,** 102 Gordon St. (☎6583 6599); and **Thrifty** (☎6584 2122), at the corner of Horton and Hayward St. hire **cars.**

ORIENTATION AND PRACTICAL INFORMATION

Port Macquarie's town center is bordered on the north by the Hastings River and on the west by a narrow, bridged section of Kooloonbung Creek. **Horton St.,** is the main commercial drag, and the area in the surrounding two-block radius comprises the central business district. Perpendicular to Horton St., and running along the river to the Marina, is **Clarence St.,** along which you'll find numerous restaurants and cafes. To the northwest of town, across Kooloonbung Creek, is **Settlement City,** an upmarket residential district with its own shopping center. The well-organized **Visitor Information Centre** is at the corner of Clarence and Hay St. (☎6581 8000 or 1300 303 155. Open year-round M-F 8:30am-5pm; in summer Sa-Su 9am-4pm, in winter 9am-2pm.) Other services include: the **police** (24hr. ☎6583 0199), on the corner of Hay St. and Sunset Pde.; **Internet** at the **library,** on the corner of Grant and Gordon St. (☎6581 8723; open M-F 9:30am-6pm, Sa 9am-noon; **Internet** $4 per hr., bookings essential).

ACCOMMODATIONS

Port Macquarie has a range of good budget options; most offer the seventh night free. During peak season (school holidays and Easter), when motels and caravan parks sometimes double their prices, booking ahead is essential.

Ozzie Pozzie Backpackers (NOMADS), 36 Waugh St. (☎6583 8133 or 1800 620 020; ozziepozzie@bigpond.com), off Gore St. between Buller and Bridge St. Friendly owners go beyond the call of duty creating an activities board. Bright rooms (with lockers) open onto a cozy inner courtyard with hammocks. Kitchen open 7:30-11:30am and noon-10:30pm. Daily muesli cereal for breakfast and W vegetarian chili dinner included. Free use of bikes ($50 deposit) and boogie boards. Laundry, Internet. Free pickup from bus stop. Reception daily 8am-noon and 3-8pm. Dorms from $18; twins and doubles from $46; 1 double with bath from $50. ISIC/NOMADS/VIP/YHA.

Beachside Backpackers (YHA), 40 Church St. (☎/fax 6583 5512; portmacqyha@hotmail.com). The closest hostel to the beaches and a 5min. walk from the town center. Clean, comfortable, and friendly. Free use of bikes, boogie boards, fishing rods, and lockers. Exercise bike and stairmaster keeps health nuts from causing a ruckus. W night BBQs $5. Common area has lights-out at 11pm. Free pickup from bus stop. Reception daily 8am-10pm. Dorms $18; twins $40.

Port Macquarie Hotel (☎6583 1011), at the corner of Horton and Clarence St. You certainly can't beat this location, and its Art Deco flair. Basic singles from $33, with TV and bath $55; doubles $50/$66.

Sundowner Breakwall Tourist Park, 1 Munster St. (☎6583 2755 or 1800 636 452; www.sundowner.net.au). A huge waterfront park adjacent to Town Beach and the Hastings River. Great tenting area. Pool, BBQ, convenience store, free Internet at office, tackle shop, and food stand. No linen. Book far in advance in summer. Sites $19 off-peak, $22-32 holidays and long weekends; powered $21/$24-35; 5 person cabins $49.50/$69-95; 4 person cabins with bath $65.50/$91-130; 5 person 2-bedroom ocean view cottages $104.50/$182-225. Each additional person $8.

Lindel Port Macquarie, 2 Hastings River Dr. (☎/fax 6583 1791 or 1800 688 882; lindel@midcoast.com.au), on the heavily-trafficked corner of Hastings River Dr. and Gordon St., 10min. from the town center. Modern facilities with pool, BBQ, TV room, billiards, Internet, kitchen and pickup. Free use of boogie boards, and fishing gear. Quiet time at 11pm, but kitchen and common room remain open 24hr. Key deposit $10. Dorms from $18; twins and doubles from $40. VIP.

FOOD

Clarence St. is lined with a number of affordable restaurants and cafes. The **Port Central Mall,** left of the tourist office, has a food court, a **supermarket**, and delis.

Macquarie Seafoods (☎6583 8476), at the corner of Clarence and Short St., is the best bet for fresh seafood takeaway. Fish'n'chips $5.30. Open daily 11am-8pm.

Fishermans Co-op (☎6584 7399), at the marina at the bottom of Clarence St. The catch comes in straight off the boat. Open M-F 9:30am-5:30pm, Sa-Su 9:30am-5pm.

Portabellos Cafe and BYO Restaurant, 124 Horton St. (☎6584 1171), prepares handmade dishes using regional foods. Mouth-watering sandwiches ($5-8) are available for lunch. Open Tu-Sa 10am-3pm and 6:30pm-late.

Toro's Mexican Cantina (☎6583 4340), on Murray St. between Sunset Pde. and Clarence St., serves up filling burritos and enchiladas ($12-14). Open 5pm-late. BYO.)

SIGHTS

HISTORIC BUILDINGS. The beautiful **St. Thomas Church** was built by convicts between 1824 and 1828. The jail's former superintendent is buried under one of the pews, because he feared that if he was buried in the cemetery, his body would be exhumed by vengeful convicts. *(On the corner of Hay and William St. ☎6584 1033. Open M-F 9:30am-noon and 2-4pm.)* The history of a thousand shipwrecks along the coast is kept alive in the **Port Macquarie Maritime Museum.** The outstanding collection of model ships and nautical paraphernalia is housed in the former Pilot Station, built in 1882. *(6 William St. ☎6583 1866. Open M-Sa 11am-3pm. $2.)* Take a trip back in time by visiting the **Port Macquarie Historical Museum,** an eclectic assortment of military weapons and disturbingly eerie mannequins wearing period costumes *(22 Clarence St; ☎6583 1108; open M-Sa 9:30am-4:30pm, Su 1-4:30pm. $4.50, students $3, children $2)* or **Timbertown,** a turn-of-the-century Australian town. *(Off the Oxley Hwy. southwest of Wauchope. ☎6585 2322. Open daily 9:30am-3:30pm. Free.)*

KOALAS. You're in luck if you like **koalas**—the Port Macquarie area has the biggest urban population in the country. The secret to spotting them in the wild is to look through the trees and not at individual forks in the trees. At one of Australia's few **Koala Hospitals,** there are usually four or more injured or sick koalas on site. *(On Lord St., 20min. from the town center on Lord St. ☎6584 1522. Open daily 9am-4:30pm; feedings at 8am and 3pm. Gold coin donation requested.)* At the **Billabong Koala Breeding Centre** you can pet not just koalas, but also wallabies and kangaroos. *(61 Billabong Dr., west of the intersection of the Oxley and Pacific Hwy. 10km from central Port Macquarie. ☎6585 1060. Feedings 10:30am, 1:30, 3:30pm. $9.50, backpackers $7.50, children $6.)*

BEACHES. Starting at the **Lighthouse Beach** lookout, at the end of Lighthouse Rd. south of town, follow an 8km track back to Port Macquarie to all eight area beaches. Hostels are usually willing to drop you off at the lookout. From the viewpoint, retrace your steps back up Lighthouse Rd. (5-10min.) to the sign for **Miners Beach** (a nude beach). The forest path leads to the beach and then continues up along the cliffs. North of Harry's Lookout is **Shelly Beach,** home to huge **goannas.** Next in line is **Nobby's Beach,** immediately north of Nobby's Hill (the obelisk here stands in memory of those who died swimming in the dangerous blowhole—don't even think about it). After Nobby's you'll find **Flynns Beach** (popular with surfers), **Rocky Beach,** and **Oxley Beach.** The walking track ends at **Town Beach,** a good spot for swimming, "sunbaking," and fishing. From the headlands overlooking Town Beach, you can see **North Beach,** across the inlet to the Hasting River.

PARKS. The **Sea Acres Rainforest Center,** at Miners Beach, preserves the largest, most southerly-occuring coastal rainforest in Australia. A 1.3km boardwalk circles through a portion of the 72-hectare reserve. Guided walks, led by volunteers, head out roughly every 45min. The last tour leaves at 3pm. The visitors center has a 20min. film and ecological displays. *(☎6582 3355. Open daily 9am-4:30pm. $10.)* At the end of Horton St. is one of several entrances that lead into **Kooloonbung Creek Nature Park,** a 52-hectare conservation area of peaceful bushland. Several kilometers of footpaths wind through mangroves and rainforest. At the northern tip of North Beach is **Point Plomer** and **Limeburner Creek Nature Reserve,** the site of Aboriginal artifacts and the Big Hill walking track. A vehicle ferry runs across the river from Settlement Point in Settlement City. The 16km coastal road to Point Plomer is unsealed and rough, but bikeable. **Campsites** are available at Melaleuca near Big Hill and Barries Bay at Point Plomer. The campgrounds provide toilets and cold showers. Bring drinking water. *(☎6583 8805. Sites for 2 $6, each extra person $3. Check-in daily at campground kiosk 8am-4pm. Book ahead in summer.)*

THONG TH-THONG THONG THONG Although goannas roam the sand and fruit bats flutter around at night, Shelly's Beach used to have a more famous resident wandering about. The beach was once home to Harry, the Port's legendary citizen-squatter who had camped in a small caravan on the beach since 1960. The somewhat eccentric Harry kept an autograph and souvenir book and was a delight to chat with. Sadly, Harry passed away three weeks after being recognized as the honorary mayor of his hometown. Though his footsteps may no longer cross the sand, the amiable beach bum will always be remembered. True, the remains of his famous "thong tree" still exist. But Harry has left an even greater legacy (if that's possible): the railed footpath up to Harry's Lookout. The view from the lookout is so gorgeous that it's been the site of more than 100 weddings; many locals have the pictures to prove it. Next time you wander down Shelly's Beach or up to the lookout, think of the pleasant man who once called this place home.

ACTIVITIES

BY LAND. Aussie extraordinaire Greg leads **Port Macquarie Camel Safaris.** Caravan along Lighthouse Beach and perhaps even spot a wild koala. Pickup in the camel car can be arranged. *(☎6583 7650. 20min. $15, children $10; 1hr. $28/$18. Book 1hr. tours in advance.)* **Bicycles** can be rented from **Graham Seers Cyclery.** *(In Port Marina on Park St. ☎6583 2333. $6.50per hr., $22 per day, $55 per week.)* **Macquarie Mountain Tours** visits four nearby **vineyards** for free tastings. *(☎6582 3065. Th, Sa, Su afternoons. $29.)*

ON THE SHORE. **Port Macquarie Sea Kayak** takes paddlers out in 2-person boats to play in the surf. *(☎0438 847 058. Tu, Th, Sa 10am-2pm. $35, includes BBQ lunch.)* Built in 1949, **The Pelican** is the second oldest wooden boat still in survey, operating on the Hastings River. You don't travel fast, but you cruise in style. *(Town wharf. ☎6582 3328 or 0418 652 171. 2½hr. Explorer cruise M, W, F 2pm $18, children $10; 5hr. BBQ cruise Tu, Th 10am $36/$18.)* **Port Venture** has the largest boat. *(Town wharf. ☎6583 3058. 2hr. tea and dolphin cruise Tu and Th-Su 10am and 2pm $20, backpackers $15; 4-5hr. BBQ cruise M and W 10am, from $35.)* **Waterbus Everglade Tours** offers similar trips. *(Town wharf. ☎6582 5009. 2hr. tea and dolphin spotting cruise daily 10am and 2pm $22; 3½hr. oyster farm lunch cruise Th 11am $32; 5½hr. Everglades lunch cruise Tu 9:30am $50.)*

ON THE DEEP BLUE. **Oceanic Star** runs half-day reef and game fishing charters, as well as cruises to look for whales and dolphins. *(Town wharf. ☎6584 6965. 6hr. fishing trips daily 6am $95; 2hr. wildlife cruises $50, children $35. Free pickup locally.)* **Gypsy Boat Hire** can provide many water vehicles for your recreation pleasure. *(52 Settlement Point Rd. ☎6583 2353. Fishing boats 2hr. $20; runabouts 2hr. $25; half cabin cruisers 2hr. $30; BBQ pontoon boats 2hr. $45.)* **Settlement Point Boatshed** has similar deals for similar prices, and has canoes. *(Next to Settlement Point Ferry. ☎6583 6300. Canoes $15 per 4hr.)* **Port Macquarie Dive Centre** can help you create personalized adventure weekends, whether you want to snorkel, scuba, or ski tube. *(Town wharf. ☎6583 8483; www.portdive.tsn.cc.)*

FROM THE BEACH. If you've had enough of simply looking at the crashing waves from the beach, give **Learn to Surf** a call. Level I surf coach, Debbie, will have you laughing and ripping the curl in no time. *(☎6584 4189 or 0413 282 932. Boards and wetsuits provided. M-Tu and Th-Sa. 1-1½hr. $25 per person.)*

IN THE SKY. Coastal Skydivers has one of the cheapest backpacker prices for tandem skydiving in NSW. *(☎6584 3655. 3000m jumps $290, backpackers $250.)* **High Adventure Air Park** offers a variety of tandem flights. *(☎6556 5265. 30min. hang-gliding $175, 30min. para-gliding $165; 30min motorized microlight $140.)*

NIGHTLIFE

The local watering hole is the **Port Macquarie Hotel,** on the corner of Clarence and Horton St. (☎6583 1011. M-Th and Su 10am-midnight, F-Sa 10am-2am.) Party-goers in their Saturday-best flock to the **Beach House** nightclub, on the town green just down the street from the Port Macquarie Hotel. (☎6584 5692. Open until 3am. $5 cover after 10pm.) Look for the **Roxy Night Club** on William St. between Horton and Short St. (☎6583 5466. Cover after 11pm F-Sa.) **Downunder** (☎6583 4018), on Short St., next to the Coles supermarket, has karaoke on Wednesday and rocking music on weekends. **Signatures,** 72 Clarence St. (☎6584 6144), has a daily Happy Hour from 5-6pm. **Finnian's Irish Tavern** (☎6583 4646), on the corner of Gordon and Horton St., attracts a slightly older crowd. Live bands perform on the weekends. A free entertainment guide, *Hastings Happenings*, is published on Wednesdays.

SOUTH WEST ROCKS ☎02

Because South West Rocks is *way* off the typical backpacker trail and is a tough place to get to without a car, it is often bypassed in the frenetic rush to travel up and down the coast to more mainstream destinations. Although the lack of any nightlife might be a drawback, you can easily fill your days with spectacular scuba diving, leisurely bushwalks, and quiet beaches.

PRACTICAL INFORMATION. The turn-off for South West Rocks and **Hat Head National Park,** off the Pacifc Hwy., is about 10km north of Kempsey. After crossing the Macleay River and Spencers Creek, the twisting rural route becomes Gregory St. To visit the national park and the **Cape Smoky Lighthouse,** turn right onto Arakoon Rd., drive 6km, and then turn right onto Lighthouse Rd. To find the **tourist information center** in South West Rocks, housed in the old Boatman's Cottage, drive to the end of Gregory St. and turn left on Ocean St. The volunteer staff there knows the area's trails, beaches, and history inside and out. (☎6566 7099. Open daily 10am-4pm.) **Cavanagh's Coaches** (☎6562 7800) has **buses** departing from Kempsey (30min., 2-3 per day, $8).

ACCOMMODATIONS AND FOOD. Next door to the tourist office, **Horseshoe Bay Beach Park** is just paces from a surf and swim beach. (☎6566 6370. No tent-only sites. Powered sites $28, winter $18; vans $61/$34; cabins $77/$53.) The **Seabreeze Hotel & Bay Motel,** on the corner of Livingston and Prince of Wales St., provides basic accommodation. All rooms have a private bathroom, TV, small fridge, and a toaster. (☎6566 6909. Reception at the motel office on Prince of Wales St. M-F 8am-6pm, Sa 8am-2pm, Su 8am-noon; after hours see the bottle shop next door. Singles $50-70; doubles $65-80; twin $70-85; extra person $12; rooms with balconies and ocean view more expensive.) **Arakoon State Recreation Area,** a 5-10min. drive from the town center, features **campsites** at the Trial Bay Gaol (see **Activities,** below). The sites are cheap and right next to Front Beach. (☎6566 6168. Toilets, water, coin-operated hot showers. Sites for 2 $15-22.50, powered $19.50-27.) If you're weary of multi-share hostels and less-than-thrilling pub stays, check out the **Smoky Cape Lighthouse Bed & Breakfast,** at the end of Lighthouse Rd., Arakoon. The heritage-listed, fully-restored lighthouse keeper's home is definitely a splurge, but it has two amazing queen size bedrooms and some of the best views anywhere on the coast. There are also two self-contained cottages that can sleep up to eight people. (☎6566 6301; www.smokycapelighthouse.com. 3-course breakfast included. Singles $99, doubles $154. Cottages for 2 nights $330-440, 3-7 nights $550-1,375 depending on season.) The full spectrum of food service is available in South West Rocks. Fast-food takeaways and pizza joints crowd the town center. Some of the best slow food around is served up at **Geppy's Seaside Restaurant,** at the corner of Livingstone St. and Memorial Ave. The gregarious owner, Geppy, will amaze your palate with modern Italian dishes made from the freshest ingredients. (☎6566 6196. Open daily 6pm-late. Entrees from $6.50, mains from $17.)

ACTIVITIES. The best **surfing** waves break northwest of the tourist office at **Back Beach.** If you just want to lounge about on the sand, try **Front Beach.** It edges Trial Bay, a warm-water swimming hole. To see what's under the waves, and visit Fish Rock Cave—considered one of the ten best dives in Australia—contact the **Fish Rock Dive Center,** 328 Gregory St. Though their prices are higher than elsewhere, courses range from beginners to instructor and the centre offers technical expertise in rebreathers, nitrox blending, and underwater photography. (☎6566 6614; www.fishrock.com.au. 4-5 day open water course with on-site accomodation $525; double boat-dive $80, including 2nd cylinder; full set of gear $40.) **South West Rocks Dive Centre,** Shop 5, 98 Gregory St., also takes divers out to Fish Rock Cave and offers certification classes for similar prices. (☎6566 6474. Open daily 7:30am-5pm. Book in advance.) To get to the **Trial Bay Gaol** from the visitor information centre, head south on Gregory St. and turn left on Landsborough St. At the second roundabout, follow Philip Dr. past the Lagoon View Caravan Park, and until it turns into Wilson St. At the juncture of Wilson and Caldwell St., turn left and continue to Laggers Point and the historical prison. A good spot for bushwalking is **Little Bay.** Drive to the end of Wilson St. and into the Arakoon Recreation Area. From the Overshot Dam carpark, you can follow the **Gap Beach Track** into **Hat Head**

National Park, around Little Smoky in the Cape Range, to Gap Beach (45min. one-way). From Gap Beach, it's possible to continue on to **North Smoky Beach** and the **Smoky Cape Lighthouse.** The lighthouse promontory is a great vantage point for spotting migrating humpback and southern right whales. Pick up a trail map from the park office at the Trial Bay Gaol.

NAMBUCCA HEADS ☎02

For the traveler in need of a break from relentless tourist attractions and constant activities, peaceful Nambucca Heads ("nam-BUH-kuh"; pop. 6500) provides a welcome break. Nambucca's allure is its Nambucca River, that winds lazily through lush hills on its way to the Pacific, and its dazzling beaches. The friendly residents often refer to the area as "our paradise."

TRANSPORTATION

The **railway station** is a few kilometers out of town. From Mann St., bear right at the roundabout to Railway Rd. **Countrylink** (☎13 22 32) goes to Coffs Harbour (1hr., 3 per day, $5.50). **King Bros** (☎6568 1296 or 1300 555 611) runs **buses** to Coffs Harbour (45min., 4 per day, $5), and **Joyce's** (☎6655 6330) serves Bellingen (1hr., 3 per day, $5.60). **Greyhound** (☎13 20 30), **McCafferty's** (☎13 14 99), and **Premier** (☎13 34 10) stop daily on their Sydney-Brisbane route. **Radio Cabs** (☎6568 6855) run 24hr.

ORIENTATION AND PRACTICAL INFORMATION

Driving north, the Pacific Hwy. splits off to the right and joins the multiple-personality **Riverside Dr.,** the main road in Nambucca Heads. As Riverside Dr. climbs the hill at the RSL club, it becomes **Fraser St.** At the town center, it becomes **Bowra St.** On the way back out to the Pacific Hwy., it's **Mann St.** and then **Old Coast Rd.** To get to the beaches, follow **Ridge St.** until it forks upon leaving town. **Liston St.,** to the left, leads to the **Headland** and **Surf Beach. Parkes St.,** to the right, leads to **Shelly Beach.** For general information, visit the brand-new **Nambucca Valley Visitor Information Centre,** at the intersection of the Pacific Hwy. and Riverside Dr. (☎6568 6954; fax 6568 5004; www.nambuccatourism.com. Open daily 9am-5pm.) The **bus stops** for travelers heading north and south from Nambucca Heads are also along the highway, near the information centre. Behind the northbound bus stop is a shopping center with a **supermarket** and a movie theater. Another supermarket is located on Back St., up the hill from the RSL Club. For an **Internet** fix, head for **The Bookshop and Internet Cafe** (see **Food and Entertainment,** p. 176).

ACCOMMODATIONS

Nambucca and the surrounding townships of Bowraville, Scotts Head, and Valla Beach are "chock-a-block" with accommodations situated near the beaches or along the Pacific Hwy. near the tourist office. Book ahead for summer holidays.

Beilby's Beach House, 1 Ocean St. (☎/fax 6568 6466; beilbys@midcoast.com.au). From downtown, take Ridge St. toward the beaches, turn left on Liston St. and follow the signs. This romantic guesthouse with private verandas and a large pool is ideal for families and couples. Less than a 5min. walk to the beach. Free bikes, surfboards, and boogie boards. Kitchen, Internet, laundry, off-street parking. Arrange for pickup. Breakfast included. Twins and doubles $46; double with bath $60; triple $60; queen with bath $70; double with connecting twin and bath from $77.

Nambucca Heads Backpackers, 3 Newman St. (☎6568 6360; www.midcoast.com.au/~jpilgrim), after the second speed bump on Bowra St., turn right onto Rosedale St., continue 2 long blocks to Newman St., and turn right. Free boogie boards, snorkeling gear, and bikes. 2 kitchens, common lounge, TV, laundry, and Internet. Pickup during business hours. Reception daily 7am-11pm. Dorms from $18, off-peak 3-night special $45; twins and doubles from $38; 6 person self-contained unit $50. VIP.

White Albatross Holiday Resort (☎6568 6468; www.white-albatross.com.au), at the ocean end of Wellington Dr., next to the popular V-Wall Tavern. A sprawling caravan park with a gorgeous setting near a swimming lagoon and the Nambucca River. Picnic and BBQ areas, camp kitchen, laundry, small game room, convenience store, takeaway cafe. Linen $5.50. Sites from $19; on-site vans from $27.50; flats and mobile homes from $47; service units from $80. All prices for two people; extra person $8.80.

FOOD AND ENTERTAINMENT

Bowra St. has an assortment of quick, cheap food possibilities. **The Bookshop and Internet Cafe,** on the corner of Bowra and Ridge St., is the perfect place to trade in your old books and have a delicious lunch. The cafe serves mouth-watering sandwiches ($6-9) and unusual juices ($4.50), including spinach, celery, and watermelon. (☎6568 5855. Open daily 9am-5pm. Internet $9 per hr.) The **RSL Club,** at the intersection of Nelson and Back St., has a gorgeous view of the river. (☎6568 6288. Bistro open noon-2pm and 6-8:30pm. Meals $6-11.) The **V-Wall Tavern,** at the mouth of the Nambucca River on Wellington Dr., also has unbeatable views and an active night scene, with discos on Saturdays. (☎6568 6344. Open daily 10am-midnight. Meals $7-9.) The **White Albatross Kiosk,** the holiday park's takeaway and general store, is adjacent to the tavern and has the cheapest prices of the three. (☎6568 9160. Open daily 7:30am-7:30pm. Sandwiches $3-5.) The **Golden Sands Tavern,** 31 Bowra St., serves cheap lunch specials ($6.50) and with a la carte items from $7-16. (☎6568 6000. Open daily noon-2:30pm and 6-9pm.)

SIGHTS AND ACTIVITIES

Nambucca is full of delightful and spontaneous artwork. Don't miss the **mosaic wall** in front of the police station on Bowra St., a glittering, 3-D, 60m long sea serpent scene made completely of broken crockery and a toilet. Many of the town's lampposts are painted with colorful underwater scenes. Hundreds of rocks along the breakwater **V-Wall,** named because of its shape, are painted with dates and rhyming ditties from years of tourists, honeymooners, and families. It's one of the few places where graffiti artists are welcomed and even provided with an outdoor gallery; travelers are encouraged to contribute to this creative legacy. Hostel owners typically provide paint packets. Supplies are also available at **Valley Community Arts,** in the Seascape Shopping Centre at the corner of Ridge St. and Estuary Lane. (☎6568 7645. Open M-F 9am-4pm, Sa 8:30-11:30am.)

The **Nambucca Boatshed Boathire,** 1 Wellington Dr. (☎6568 5550), and **Beachcomber Marine** (☎6568 6432), on Riverside Dr., both have a good selection of motor boats. **Got Lost Kayak Tours** can set you up with touring sea kayak. (☎6564 7346; gotlostinnambucca@hotmail.com. Half-day self-guided $44; full-day escorted tour $120 per person.) **East Coast Adventures,** 5 Mann St., has on-site **scuba** certification courses (PADI), with accommodation, and runs trips to the Solitary Islands and Fishrock Cave. (☎6569 4422. Double boat-dive with all equipment $95; Learn-to-Dive course $165, with 4 nights accommodation $219.)

There are **walks** of varying difficulty throughout the beach and bush areas of Nambucca, some of which pass by the gorgeous **Rotary, Captain Cook,** and **Lions Lookouts.** For more structured exploring, contact **Kyeewa Bushwalkers** (☎6569 5627). The group organizes walks on Wednesdays, Saturdays, and Sundays.

To get the inside edge on surfing, call the president of the **Loggerheads Malibu Board Riding Club** (☎6568 7314) or try **Surf Beach** for yourself. The 16km beach separating Nambucca Heads and **Scotts Head** to the south is also a great surfing beach.

BELLINGEN ☎02

Bellingen ("BELLIN-gin"; pop. 2350), situated 30min. from the World Heritage-listed Dorrigo National Park (see p. 178), is a laid-back town situated cozily on the banks of the Bellinger River, roughly half-way between Coffs Harbour and Nambucca Heads. Although its heyday was 50 years ago, when it was the financial and commercial center for the Coffs Harbour region, Bellingen has reinvented itself.

Reputedly having more artists per capita than anywhere down under, locals claim to live in the second-most alternative town in Australia (after Nimbin, of course).

TRANSPORTATION AND PRACTICAL INFORMATION. Running parallel to the Bellinger River, Hyde St. cuts right through the center of town. Travel east to reach Urunga and Coffs Harbour. Drive west to explore the rainforests of Dorrigo National Park and streets of Armidale. Buses stop at Hyde and Church St. **King Bros** (☎1300 555 611) services Coffs Harbour (1hr., 3 per day, $5.20), while **Joyce's** (☎6655 6330) runs to Nambucca Heads (1hr., M-F 3 per day, $5.60). **Keans** (☎1800 043 339) travels to: Coffs Harbour (45min., 1 per day, $11.50); Port Macquarie (3hr.; M, W, F 1 per; $28) via Nambucca Heads (1hr., $21); Tamworth (5hr.; Tu, Th, Su 1 per; $49) via Armidale (3hr., $26). **Traveland**, 42 Hyde St. (☎6655 2055) books seats on various bus services. Local travel is easily accomplished through **Bellingen Taxi** (☎6655 9995). As of August 2001, the permanent location of the **Bellingen Tourist Information Centre** has yet to be determined. Ask locally for an update when you arrive in town. The **library,** in the park across from the post office, has **Internet** access. (☎6655 1744. Open Tu-W 10:30am-5:30pm, Th-F 10:30am-12:30pm and 1:30-5:30pm. Book ahead. $2 per 10min.)

ACCOMMODATIONS AND FOOD. Winner of the 2001 NSW Tourism Board award for "Best Budget Accomodation," **Bellingen Backpackers (YHA),** 2 Short St., can't help but impress with its huge verandas, awesome tree-fort, and terraced sites that overlook the Bellinger River. The lounge/kitchen has oversized floor pillows, musical instruments and a small, hidden TV. Be sure to check out all the photographs, especially the upstairs "Nude Wall of Fame." The super-friendly owners and staff pick up guests from the Urunga train or bus stations and arrange group day-trips to Dorrigo National Park ($15). Bike rentals ($5), laundry and Internet are available. (☎6655 1116; belloyha@midcoast.com.au. Dorms $20; twins and doubles $46; sites for 2 $14.)

The delicious **Cool Creek Cafe,** 5 Church St., books local and national musicians. Call or check the website. (☎6655 1886; www.coolcreekcafe.com.au. Open M and Th-F 5-10pm, Sa-Su 11am-3pm and 5-10pm; during holidays and festivals daily 11am-10pm . Lunch from $7.50, dinner $13-24.) The **Lodge 241 Gallery Cafe,** 117-121 Hyde St. on the western edge of town, combines panoramic views, displays of local art, and generous portions of freshly prepared dishes. (☎6655 2470. Open Su-Th 8am-5pm, F-Sa 8am-late.) The **Natural Lifestyles and Produce Market,** held the second and fourth Saturday of every month at the **showgrounds** on Black St., specializes in eco-friendly foods and has healthy breakfast for $5. (☎6655 2924. Open 8am-1pm.)

SIGHTS AND ACTIVITIES. Even if you're not in the market for a "didg" and have no idea how to circular breathe, **Heartland Didgeridoos,** 25 Hyde St., has an outstanding collection of instruments. The owners are incredible players and offer lessons. (☎6655 9881; www.heartdidg.com. Open M-F 9am-5pm, Sa 10am-2pm. Didgeridoos from $100. $15 per 30min. lesson, $20 per hr.) Just across the Bellinger River on Hammond St., behind the Bellingen Caravan Park, is the entrance to **Bellingen Island,** a year-round home to an active colony of "flying foxes," or **fruit bats** with a 1m wingspan. A forest trail loops through the surprisingly open understory for excellent views. The **Promised Land** and the **Never Never River,** both lovely spots with BBQs and excellent, crocodile-free **swimming holes,** are easier to reach than their names imply. They are an easy 10-15km bike ride from town. Cross the Bellinger on Bridge St. and take a left at the first rotary onto Wheatley St. Continue straight until you see a sign for Gleniffer. Bear right at this sign and continue for another 6km. The route passes the humble abode of David Helfgott, the inspiration for the movie *Shine*, and the house of Serge Cockburn, the young actor from *Crocodile Dundee 3*. You'll find the Never Never behind the church in Gleniffer. To get to the Promised Land, cross the bridge and take the first right. Shy and elusive platypuses live in the Never Never—see if you can spot one.

Bellingen Canoe Adventures has rentals and tours. (☎6655 9955. $11 per hr.; $33 per 4hr; half-day tour with 3 rapids $44.) To see the sights from the top of a saddle, contact **Valery Trails** (see p. 182). **Gambaarri Tours** offers half-day local tours with an Aboriginal guide and an introduction to traditional dance and spear throwing. (☎6655 4195. $50, children $25.)

Though it may seem surprising for such a small town, Bellingen hosts several major festivals during the year. The annual **Jazz Festival** (www.bellingenjazz.holidaycoast.com.au), held Aug. 18-20, 2002, features scheduled, ticketed concerts as well as free street jams. The **Global Carnival and World Music Festival** (www.globalcarnival.com), happening Oct. 5-7, 2002, attracts a diverse group of musicians, dancers, and artists, along with enthusiastic crowds.

NEAR BELLINGEN: DORRIGO NATIONAL PARK

Dorrigo National Park, part of the World Heritage-listed "Central Eastern Rainforest Reserves," is close enough to Bellingen to set up and support a **Rainforest Centre,** complete with a cafe and newly-renovated educational and audio-visual displays. Keep your eyes open; red-necked pademelons (a miniature species of wallaby) are often hopping through the picnic area. (☎6657 2309. Open daily 9am-5pm.) Allow 35min. to drive from Bellingen (29km east) or 1hr. from Coffs Harbour (64km east). Dorrigo is lush rainforest, with sections of multi-layered canopy and wet eucalypt forest. When the rain makes things sloppy, the **leeches** have a field day. Pick them off, or buy a cream stick from the Centre that repels them. Do *not* rub them with salt, as this has a negative effect on the health of the rainforest. The 75m long **Skywalk** extends out and over the steep slope behind the Rainforest Centre up in the tree canopy, 21m above the forest floor. For a more relaxed stroll, try the **Walk with the Birds** (2.5km; 45min. return). On the **Wonga Walk** (6.6 km; 2½hr. return) you'll soak your shoes as you journey past waterfalls. Drive the well-maintained, gravel **Dome Rd.** from the Rainforest Centre to the **Never Never Picnic Area** (10km) for several hiking tracks. From the park, follow Megan Rd. to visit the spectacular **Dangar Falls** overlook. A sealed pathway leads from the viewpoint to the base of the falls if you want to go for a swim.

COFFS HARBOUR ☎02

Situated along a coastline backed by the hills of the Great Dividing Range, covered in lush banana plantations, Coffs Harbour (pop. 60,000) is a popular spot for partiers, scuba divers, and adrenaline-junkies, partly for its proximity to Solitary Islands National Marine Park. Coffs's rapid expansion in the past decade has come at the expense of its coastal charm, but four social and tight-knit hostels make it a worthwhile stop. Much of the town's tourism aims to please thrill-seekers with cash to spare, although it does have the cheapest scuba certification courses on the east coast. The entire city seems to subscribe to a play hard, party hard philosophy that even the most sedentary find hard to resist.

TRANSPORTATION

Trains: The **railway station** is at the end of Angus McLeod St. by the jetty. From High St., turn right on Camperdown St. and take your first left. **Countrylink** (☎13 22 32) goes to: **Brisbane** (6-7hr., 2 per day, $71.50); **Byron Bay** (4hr., 4 per day, $42); **Nambucca Heads** (40min., 3 per day, $5.50); **Sydney** (9hr., 3 per day, $79).

Buses: The long-distance bus stop is on Elizabeth St., near the corner of High and McLean St. **McCafferty's** (☎13 14 99), **Greyhound Pioneer** (☎13 20 30), and **Premier** (☎13 34 10) go to: **Byron Bay** (4-5hr., 3-4 per day, $44-51); **Brisbane** (7hr., 3-5 per day, $54); **Newcastle** (6½hr., 2-4 per day, $50-54); **Port Macquarie** (2½hr., 2-3 per day, $35-41); **Sydney** (8-9hr., 3-5 per day, $57-74). **King Bros** (☎1300 555 611) runs locally to **Bellingen** (1hr., 3 per day M-F, $5.20) and **Nambucca Heads** (1hr., 4 per day M-F, $5.60). **Keans** (☎1800 043 339) travels once per Tu, Th, Su to: **Armidale** (4hr., $27); **Dorrigo** (1½hr., $15); **Tamworth** (5hr., $51). Return trips once M, W, F.

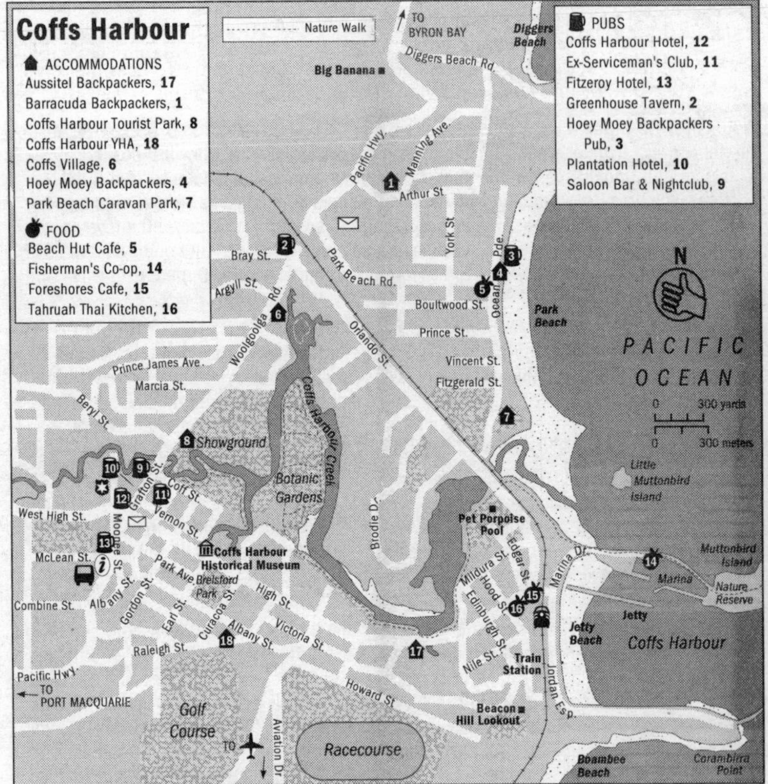

Car Rental: Coffs Harbour Rent-A-Car (☎6652 5022), at the Shell Service Station, on the corner of Pacific Hwy. and Marcia St., rents from $44 per day. **A Little Car and Truck Hire,** 32 Alison St. (☎6651 3004), rents cars from $29; 4WD from $90; 5-day minimum hire required. National companies such as **Budget** (13 27 27) and **Delta Europcar** (☎13 13 90) are also available.

ORIENTATION AND PRACTICAL INFORMATION

The Pacific Hwy., as it passes through Coffs Harbour, takes on two new names: **Grafton St.** and **Woolgoolga Rd.** Three large shopping centers divide the focus of the town: the **Palms Centre Mall** on Vernon St. in the center of town; the **Jetty Village Shopping Centre** on High St. near the water; and the **Park Beach Plaza** on the Pacific Hwy. in the northern part of town. The NPWS **Muttonbird Island Nature Reserve** is accessible by walking along the breakwater boardwalk at the end of Marina Dr.

Tourist Office: Visitor Information Centre (☎6652 1522 or 1300 369 070; www.coffstourism.com), on the corner of Elizabeth and McClean St. Open daily 9am-5pm.

Currency Exchange: ANZ bank, on the corner of Moonee and High St. Other banks with 24hr. international **ATMs** are in the Palms Centre Mall and the Park Beach Plaza.

Police: 16 Moonee St. (☎6652 0299). **Water Police** (☎6652 0257), on the wharf.

Hospital: (☎6659 1599), on Victoria St.

Post Office: (☎6652 2022), in the Palms Centre Mall; (☎6652 7499), in the Park Beach Plaza. Open M-F 8:30am-5pm, Sa 9am-noon.

Internet: Coffs Harbour City Library (☎6648 4905), on the corner of Coffs and Duke St. Free, but try to book a time-slot in advance. Open M-F 9:30am-6pm, Sa 9:30am-3pm. **Happy Planet Computers,** 13 Park Ave. (☎6651 7520). Open M-F 9am-5:30pm, Sa 9am-noon. $2 per 10min., $6 per hr., $20 per 10hr.

ACCOMMODATIONS AND CAMPING

Coffs has three central caravan parks; one near the beach and two near the town center. All caravans and hostels provide a seventh night free during off-peak.

Aussitel Backpackers, 312 High St. (☎6651 1871 or 1800 330 335; www.aussitel.com), a 20min. walk from the town center; 10min. walk from the beach. Social, clean, and wholesome. The open kitchen/lounge area includes Internet and a TV. Features include a BBQ, pinball machine, darts, heated pool, luggage storage, and laundry. Surfboards, boogie boards, wetsuits, bikes, and canoes are available. The dive centre, **East Coast Adventures** (see p. 181), operates out of the hostel and offers a great PADI certification. Quiet time after 11pm. Free pickup and drop off. Dorms $18; twins and doubles $42. NOMADS/VIP/YHA.

Barracuda Backpackers (NOMADS), 19 Arthur St. (☎6651 3514 or 1800 111 514; barracud@key.net.au), a 5min. walk from the Park Beach Plaza; 5min. walk from the beach. Each 4-bunk dorm has linen, lockers, and a small fridge. Internet, BBQ, pool, spa. Free use of didgeridoos, fishing gear, cricket bats, boogie boards, and surfboards. Courtesy 1hr. orientation tour of town by van, frequent organized activities, and rides to local sights. Dorms $20; twins $44; doubles $48, with bath $50. ISIC/VIP/YHA

Coffs Harbour YHA, 110 Albany St. (☎/fax 6652 6462; coffsyha@keynet.com.au), a 10 min. walk from the town center; 20min. walk from the beach. This laid-back 2-story feels like a beach house. A chalkboard downstairs lists local activities. Kitchen, common area, TV, Internet, laundry, and pool. Bikes available for $5 plus $15 deposit. Bus runs to the beaches twice daily (10am and 3pm) and on request to local attractions. Breakfast $3-6. Dorms $20; twins and doubles from $44; family rooms for 4-6 from $64.

Hoey Moey Backpackers (☎6651 7966 or 1800 683 322; hoey@hoeymoey.com.au), at the corner of Park Beach Rd. and Ocean Pde. A 10min. walk from the Park Beach Plaza; 2min. walk to the beach. This place is a backpackers, motel, and pub all rolled into one ("Hoey Moey" is slang for "Hotel Motel"). The lively pub has weekly bands, a beer garden, and meals starting at $5.50. Kitchen, BBQ, and TV lounge. Free bikes, surfboards, and boogie boards. All rooms have a bath, TV, and small fridge. Shuttle to town available. Reception 7am-7pm. Key deposit $10. Hostel-style dorms $18; doubles $37.50. Motel singles $36.50; doubles $43.50; each extra person $11. ISIC/VIP/YHA.

Park Beach Caravan Park, near the Surf Club on Ocean Pde., is the closest to the beach. (☎6648 4888. Sites $16, powered $18.50; on-site vans $35; cabins $44-68.) **Coffs Harbour Tourist Park,** 123 Pacific Hwy. (☎6652 1694. Sites $15.50, powered $16.50; on-site caravans $29; cabins $44.) **Coffs Village,** 215 Pacific Hwy., is in the Clog Barn complex. (☎6652 4633; fax 6651 5009. Sites $13, powered $16.50; cabins $44.) Many motels are clustered along the Pacific Hwy. and Park Beach Rd.

FOOD

Dining options are, in general, unspectacular. Across from the Jetty Village Shopping Center, on High St. near the harbour, is a row of popular restaurants. A local favorite is **Tahruah Thai Kitchen,** 366 High St. (☎6651 5992. Open daily 6-10pm. Mains from $9.) A few doors down, **Foreshores Cafe,** 394 High St., serves yummy breakfasts (from $5), as well as gourmet sandwiches. (☎6652 3127. Open daily 7:30am-3pm.) The **Fisherman's Co-op,** at the end of Marina Dr. by the breakwater boardwalk, serves hot seafood straight off the boat. (☎6652 2811. Fish counter open daily 9am-6pm; cooked counter open daily 11am-early evening.) Head for the **Beach Hut Cafe** on Ocean Pde. just down the street from the Hoey Moey Backpackers. Eggs and hotcakes are served all day. (☎6651 2773. Breakfast from $5.50. Open daily 7:30am-3pm. Dinner served Sept.-Mar. 6-9pm.) For vegetarian options, stroll on over to **Neil's Place,** 40 Moonee St. Try the lentil burger with satay sauce and salad on a multi-grain roll for $5. (☎6652 5922. Open M-F 7:30am-5pm.) The **Palms Centre Mall** and **Park Beach Plaza** each have **supermarkets,** cheap takeaways, and sit-down cafes. The Hoey Moey Hotel, Plantation Hotel, and Greenhouse Tavern (see **Nightlife,** p. 183) all have cheap pub meals.

DIVING OFF THE SOLITARY ISLANDS

Solitary Islands Marine Park stretches 70km from Coffs Harbour to the Sandon River and encompasses nearly 100,000 hectares. It is composed of at least 19 protected beaches, headlands, creeks, and rocky islands. Because of the unique mixing of warmer, tropical waters from the north and cooler, temperate waters from the south, the area has some of the most diverse marine life. Species common to the Great Barrier Reef mingle with species typically found near Tasmania. The marine park is well-respected as a top diving spot. Visibility is often better during the winter, but the water gets chilly. Luckily, you can swim with harmless gray nurse sharks year-round. Contact the **NSW Fisheries and Marine Parks Office,** 32 Marina Dr., for more info. (☎6652 3977. Open M-F 8:30am-4:30pm.)

Scuba diving certification is a requirement for independent diving. Most dive schools follow PADI protocol. A basic dive course lasts four to five days. An intro-dive, or "resort dive," does not result in any certification and usually requires an afternoon session followed by morning boat-dives. For an overview on diving, see p. 292. Coffs has two dive shops that rent equipment and run trips to the Solitary Islands. A third company offers only courses and trips.

East Coast Adventures, 312 High St. (☎6569 4422 or 1800 330 335), at the Aussitel Backpackers. This company offers a 4-day PADI course and a 4-night Aussitel dorm package for $219. No minimum amount of people required to dive. Charter double boat-dive $120, with advanced certification $95. Open daily 9am-5pm.

Jetty Dive Centre, 398 High St. (☎6651 1611). The 4-day PADI course, including all boat-dives, costs $185 for backpackers staying at any Coffs hostel, minimum 6 people required. Double boat-dive with gear from $107; single intro-dive $109, double intro-dive $137. Snorkeling charters $45. Open daily 9am-5pm.

Pacific Blue Dive Center, 40 Marina Dr. (24hr. ☎6652 2759). Courtesy pickup available. Double boat-dive with gear $105; double intro-dive $135. 4-day PADI course $165, minimum 4 people required. Open daily 7am-6pm.

SIGHTS

The Coffs Harbour **jetty,** built in 1890, was the center of a busy marine industry at the start of the 20th century. Commercial fishing boats continue to take refuge in the protected harbour but the area's emphasis has shifted in recent years to recreation. The jetty foreshore has BBQ facilities and is an easy walk from **Jetty Beach.** The breakwater boardwalk, near the marina, connects the mainland to **Muttonbird Island** (named after the wedge-tailed shearwaters that nest there), a terrific lookout for spotting **whales.** The island was sacred to the region's Aborigines, whose adolescent males would swim out to the island for several weeks of initiation into manhood. **Park Beach**, and the beach immediately north of the marina, are also popular hang-outs, but have dangerous currents. The best **surfing** is at **Diggers Beach,** north of Macauleys Headland, accessible off the Pacific Hwy. From the Big Banana, turn onto Diggers Beach Rd. and follow it to the end.

The **Botanic Gardens**, one block north at the corner of High and Hardacre St., displays colorful native and exotic plants and endangered species. (☎6648 4188. Open daily 9am-5pm. Donation.) The 4km-long **Coffs Creek Walk** connects Rotary Park, at the intersection of Gordon and Coff St. in the city center, and the Coffs Creek inlet, near Orlando St. and also has a detour to the gardens. You can make the hike a 10km circuit by following the 6km-long **Coffs Creek Habitat Walk** that edges the northern side of the creek.

At the **Pet Porpoise Pool (Oceanarium),** on Orlando St. by Coffs Creek, dolphins and seals perform tricks daily at 10:30 am and 2:15pm in the Sea Circus. (☎6652 2164. Open daily 9am-5pm. $15.50, concessions $11, backpackers $13, children $7, families $47.) For the Dr. Doolittle experience, visit the **Coffs Zoo,** 12km north of Coffs along the Pacific Hwy. past Moonee Beach, and converse with the pythons, monkeys, and koalas. (☎6656 1330. Open daily 8:30am-4pm, later during holidays. $14.50, concessions $10.50, children $7, families $36.)

The **Coffs Harbour Historical Museum,** 191 High St., documents the history of the area with a model banana plantation, the optic from South Solitary Island Lighthouse, and other displays. (☎6652 5794. Open daily 10am-4pm. $2.) The **Bunker Cartoon Gallery,** at the corner of Hogbin Dr. and Albany St. near the airport, is Australia's first and only black-and-white collection of contemporary and classic original cartoons. (☎6651 7343. Open daily 10am-4pm. $2.) Meanwhile, the **Big Banana,** on the Pacific Hwy. 4km north of town, is quintessential kitsch. Zoom around the plantation on a monorail and learn more than you need to know about banana cultivation methods ($12), try your luck at ice-skating ($12) or tobogganing (5 rides $15), or just gawk at the giant banana out front. (☎6652 4355. Open daily 9am-4pm. Admission and feelings of inadequacy free.)

ACTIVITIES

There's no shortage of activities and the field is ever-increasing. Hostels can offer good rates, but don't hesitate to call companies and ask about commission-free fun. Some companies may offer cheaper rates during the winter months.

WATER SPORTS

WHITEWATER RAFTING AND JET SKIING. The **Nymboida River,** 2hr. west of Coffs, is the most popular place to raft. The rapids, mostly grade 3 to 4 with some grade 5 sections, pass through dense rainforest. The **Goolang River,** a man-made kayaking course, is a steady grade 3. **Liquid Assets Adventure Tours,** the pioneers of sea rafting, runs unbeatable whitewater rafting on the Goolang. *(☎6658 0850. Half-day, $77. Sea kayaking 3hr., $35. Surf-rafting 3hr., $35.)* **Rapid Rafting** also plunges down the Goolang. *(☎6652 1741 or 1800 629 797. Full-day $125; half-day $80.)* Award-winning **Wildwater Adventures,** 754 Pacific Hwy. 7km south of Coffs *(☎6653 3500)*, and **WOW Rafting Professionals** *(☎6654 4066 or 1800 640 330)* lead one- and multi-day trips down the Nymboida, complete with BBQ dinner and commentary. *(Full-day $153; two-day with camping $325; 4-day with camping $560.)* **Wild Scenic Rivers** will also take you down the Nymbodia for slightly cheaper. *(☎6652 1741 or 1800 629 797. Full-day 7am-5pm $145.)* **Coffs Water Sports** offers jet skiing. *(☎0418 665 656. Single-seat jet ski 30min. $65; double-seat 30min. $85.)*

SURFING. With the sand as its chalk board, **East Coast Surf School** has a remarkable success rate with novices. Classes for advanced surfers are also available. Call to arrange pickup from hostels. *(☎6651 5515. One 2hr. group lesson $34 per person, five 2hr. group lessons $136 per person; Single 1hr. private lesson $56.)* **Coopers Surf Centres** rent equipment and has 3 store locations in Coffs. *(380 High St. (☎6652 1782); Park Beach Plaza (☎6652 5466); Palms Centre Mall (☎6652 6369). Surfboards $20, longboard $25, bodyboards $10.)*

FISHING AND WHALE WATCHING. The fishing boats **Adriatic III** *(☎6651 1277)* and **Cougar Cat 12** *(☎6651 6715)* will set you up with bait, line, and tackle. *(Half-day reef fishing $65; game fishing by appointment.)* **Whales** swim north past Coffs from June to July and again from September to November. The catamaran **Pacific Explorer** *(☎6652 7225 or 0418 663 815)* and the **Spirit of Coffs Harbour II** *(☎6650 0155)* lead whale-watching cruises. *(At the Marina. 2-2½hr. cruise $45, concessions $35.)*

OTHER ACTIVITIES

ON HORSE. Valery Trails, on Valery Rd. off the Pacific Hwy., offers 2hr. horseback rides. *(25min. south of Coffs. ☎6653 4301. Daily 10am and 2pm. $35.)* **Bushland Trail Rides,** 217 Grays Rd., Halfway Creek, off the Pacific Hwy., goes to Newfoundland State Forest. *(35min. north of Coffs. ☎6649 4487. 2hr. $35; 3½hr. $65; full-day $110.)*

ON WHEELS. 4WD Discovery Tours *(☎6651 1223 or 0419 993 965)* and **Mountain Trails 4WD Tours** *(☎6658 3333)* both offer a variety of guided trips to see rainforest, waterfalls, and glow worms. *(☎6658 3333. Half-day $55; full-day $85-88; night tour $48.)* **Bob Wallis Bicycle Centre,** at the corner of Collingwood and Orlando St., rents mountain bikes. *(☎6652 5102. Open Jan.-Sept. M-F 8:30am-5pm, Sa 8:30am-1pm; Oct.-Dec.*

also Su 9am-1pm. 24hr. $17, plus $50 deposit.) **Blue Tongue Tours** leads 8 different minibus tours. *(☎6651 8566. Bellinger Valley and Dorrigo National Park $50; South West Rocks, Smoky Cape, and Nambucca Heads $60.)*

ON ROCKS. If the outdoor elements have done a job on your body, head for the climate controlled **Coffs Rock** and give indoor rock climbing a try. *(13 GDT Seccombe Close off Orlando St. ☎6651 6688. Open W-Th 1-8pm, Sa-Su noon-5pm. $14 per visit.)*

IN THE SKY. **Coffs City Skydivers** offers tandem skydiving from 3000m. *(☎6651 1167. $299, backpackers $231; shorter dives $205. Free pickup.)*

ENTERTAINMENT AND NIGHTLIFE

Coffs nightlife, focused around Grafton St., isn't quite as pumping as the daytime scene, but finding the party crowd isn't too difficult; hostels sometimes organize nights out for their guests. Most pubs have cover bands or DJs on weekends.

The popular **Saloon Bar & Nightclub,** 76 Grafton St. (☎6658 0877), doesn't have a cover until 11pm. It's a pick-up scene lacking subtlety, but it does have frequent drink specials and money-saving three-drinks-for-$10 backpacker/student cards available at the coat check. **Hoey Moey Backpackers Pub** (☎6652 3833), on Ocean Pde., has hard rock a few nights a week. **Coffs Harbour Hotel,** at the corner of Grafton and West High St. across from the Palms Centre Mall, pours the best drink in town—$5 pints of Guinness. (☎6652 3817. W karaoke, Th-Su live bands.) Some of the cheapest drinks in town are at the state-subsidized **Ex-Serviceman's Club** (☎6652 3888), on the corner of Grafton and Vernon St. You'll need a passport or laminated driver's license to get in, so don't forget it. Friday nights are the most happening, but non-members must arrive before 10:30pm. Many people start their evenings at the club. The **Fitzroy Hotel** (☎6652 3007), on Grafton St. one block south of the Coffs Hotel, has a 24hr. license and often doesn't close until the last person leaves. The **Plantation Hotel** (☎6652 3855), on Grafton St. half a block north of the Coffs Hotel, has a relaxed sports bar and live music on weekends with an occasional cover. The **Greenhouse Tavern** (☎6651 5488), on the Pacific Hwy. across from the Park Beach Plaza, has two bars and live music weekly.

WOOLGOOLGA ☎02

On its edges, Woolgoolga is an intriguing coastal town. It is flanked to the south by a strikingly-white Indian temple, Guru Nanak Sikh Gurdwara, indicating a healthy Punjabi Sikh community, and to the north by a mini-replica of the Taj Mahal, complete with large artificial elephants in the front lawn, announcing an Indian restaurant. If you leave the Pacific Hwy. and continue to the town center, however, the novelty disappears but beautiful coastline remains. The views from the **Woolgoolga Headland** of the **Solitary Islands Marine Reserve,** an aquatic sanctuary with marine biodiversity approaching that of the Great Barrier Reef, are fantastic. Dolphin and whale sightings are common from May to October. From the headland, the surfing- and fishing-friendly **Back Beach** stretches to the south and the patrolled **Front Beach** extends to the north. To stroll in the rainforest, go to the roundabout on the Pacific Hwy. near the elephants and exit onto Pullen St. Drive 3km, veer left at the fork, and then continue another 1km until you reach a locked gate. A short walk along an old forestry road leads to a waterfall.

Ryans buses (☎6652 3201) run to Coffs Harbour (45min., 6 per day M-F, $8) and Grafton (1½hr., M-F 2 per day, $13). The **Tourist Information Centre** is at the corner of Boundary Rd. and Beach St., the main drag. (☎6654 8080. Open M-F 9:30am-4pm, Sa 9:30am-1pm, Su 11am-1:30pm.) **Internet** is available at **Access.Net,** 66 River St. (☎6654 9999. Open M-F 9am-6pm, Sa 10am-5pm. $2 per 20min.)

To sleep in the bush—or near it, anyway—turn left at the town center onto Wharf St. and drive 1km to the end of the road where you'll find the peaceful **Lakeside Holiday Park,** with direct access to the beach and a lake. (☎6654 1210. Sites for 2 $11-15.50, powered $16-22; on-site vans $24-44; cabins $40-66.) To sleep in the middle of town, look for a spot at **Sunset Caravan Park,** also right on the beach. (☎6654 1499. Site for 2 $16-23, powered $19-28; 5-person cabin $45-83.) The ornate, but weary-looking **Raj Mahal** restaurant, behind the artificial elephants, has very good food. (☎6654 1149. Open daily 5:30pm-late, and Tu-Su noon-3pm.) Though not in Woolgoolga, **Coffs Harbour Dive Centre,** (15min. north of Coffs Harbour), conducts trips to both the north and south Solitary Islands. (☎6654 2860. Double boat-dive $80, full-gear hire $33; 2hr. snorkeling $50.)

BALLINA ☎02

Technically an island, Ballina is a peaceful port and beach town 30min. south of Byron Bay. Getting around is surprisingly easy considering the extensive **network of bike paths** linking Ballina and Lennox Head. Pick up a *Bike Safe* booklet for a map from the tourism office. **Lighthouse Beach** and **Pat Morton Lookout** are two great vantage points for whale watching. The 68-hectare reserve at **Angels Beach,** in East Ballina, mixes playful dolphins, dune ecology, and ocean invertebrates. **Flat Rock,** in particular, has an incredible array of marine life occupying three distinct inter-tidal zones. Sea anemones, sea stars, octopus, and neptune's necklace are just some examples of the thriving underwater world.

TRANSPORTATION AND PRACTICAL INFORMATION. **McCafferty's** (☎13 14 99), **Greyhound Pioneer** (☎13 20 30), and **Premier** (☎13 34 10) stop in Ballina on their Sydney-Brisbane runs. The long-distance **bus stop** at the **Transit Centre** is a good 4km from town center, in a large building complex known affectionately as **The Big Prawn** for the enormous pink shrimp nailed to the roof. **Ballina Taxi Service** (☎6686 9999) will take you into town for $10-12. Regional bus companies stop in town at the Tamar St. bus zone. **Blanch's Bus Company** (☎6686 2144) travel daily to Lennox Head (20min., 7 per day, $4.60) and Byron Bay (50min., 7 per day, $7.40).

The **Visitor Information Centre,** on the eastern edge of town at the corner of Las Balsa Plaza and **River St.** (the main drag), can provide more details on area and regional activities. (☎6686 3484; balinfo@balshire.org.au. Open M-F 9am-5pm, Sa-Su 9am-4pm.) Cyber-licious **Internet** access is at the **Ballina Ice Creamery Internet Cafe,** 178 River St. (☎6686 5783. Open daily 9:30am-9pm. $6 per hr.)

ACCOMMODATIONS AND FOOD. The **Ballina Travelers Lodge (YHA),** 36-38 Tamar St., is a motel and hostel combo. Go one block up Norton St. from the tourist office, then turn left. The friendly Aussie owners keep the lodge quiet and meticulously clean. The YHA part of the complex has four basic rooms, a separate communal kitchen/TV area, a BBQ, and a laundry. The larger motel rooms have TVs and lots of amenities. There's a small pool, bikes (for a nominal fee), limited fishing gear, and free boogie boards. Courtesy pick up from the Transit Centre by arrangement. (☎6686 6737. Dorms from $18; twins and doubles $42-52; non-YHA add $3.50. Motel rooms $66-105.) The **Ballina Central Caravan Park,** 1 River St., is just north of the info center. (☎6686 2220. Open daily 7am-7pm. Sites $14.50-16.50, powered $16.50-20; cabins $35-72). **Paddy McGinty's,** 56 River St., is the local Irish pub and serves counter lunches and dinners. (☎6686 2135. Mains from $9. Open daily 11am-3pm and 6-9pm.) Delicious deli-food awaits at **Sasha's Gourmet Eatery,** in the Wigmore Arcade off River St. Takeaway selections such as pasta salads, quiches, and fancy sandwiches ($4-7) make for a perfect picnic. (☎6681 1118. Open M-F 9am-5pm, Sa 9am-1pm.) **Cafe Fresco,** 177 River St., prepares meals with Mediterranean overtones. (☎6686 2411. Mains from $8.50. Open daily 11:30am-3pm and 6-9pm.)

ACTIVITIES. **Ballina Ocean Tours** (☎6686 3999) offers 2½-3hr. dolphin and whale-watcing tours at 9am and 1pm ($45-55). Learn to surf or just perfect your technique with **Ballina & Evans Head Surf School** (☎6682 4393. Private 1½hr. lessons in Ballina $45, in Evans Head $35). **Forgotten Country**, located in Byron Bay, leads half-day to multi-day tours to nearby rainforests, waterfalls, and even an ancient shield volcano. (☎6687 7845. $55-330. 10% student discount.) **MV Bennelong** conducts cruises along the Richmond River (☎6688 8266. 2hr. $16) For self-guided exploring, **Jack Ransom Cycles,** 16 Cherry St., just off River St., rents bikes. (☎6686 3485. Half-day $10; full-day $16.50, plus $50 deposit.)

NEAR BALLINA: BUNDJALONG NATIONAL PARK

From the south, take Woodburn-Evans Head Rd. 11km east to **Evans Head,** between Broadwater and Bundjalong National Parks. There is camping at the beachside **Koinina recreation park,** on Terrace St. at the north end of Evans Head. (☎6682 4329. Sites $10, powered $12.)

At Evans Head is a little-known entrance to **Bundjalong National Park;** cross the Evans River Bridge and turn right. The road narrows into dirt track, and several turn-offs lead to rest stops and boat launches on the estuary. Continue 2km to the road's end at the **Gamma Garra Picnic Area.** Three walks begin across the footbridge next to the park and finish at an Aboriginal midden. The **Dirrawong Track** hugs the river and passes through swamp and dry littoral forest. The **Jenna Jenna Track** crosses an Aboriginal campsite, and the **Guweean** leads through a dry forest. Camping is forbidden in these sections of the park. Two kilometers south of the river is **Chinamans Beach,** a favorite among serious surfers.

LISMORE ☎02

Lismore (pop. 45,500) is a large country town. Wide, tree-bordered boulevards, brick sidewalks, and well-preserved buildings give the town the charm of a slower era, while students at nearby Southern Cross University help to sustain Lismore's cultural venues. A legacy of environmental protection follows naturally from Lismore's surroundings: three World Heritage-listed rainforests and the volcanic remains of Mt. Warning National Park. The disproportionately high number of rainbows (due to the position of local valleys), earn the area the nickname "Rainbow Region." Lismore is refreshingly normal. It's one of the few places where you can walk through the business district without feeling like a tourist target.

TRANSPORTATION

The **railway station** is on Union St., across the river. **Countrylink** (☎13 22 32) hugs the rails to Sydney (12hr., 2 per day, $98) and Brisbane (4hr., 1 per day, $33). The new **Transit Centre** (☎6621 8620) is on the corner of Molesworth and Magellan St. **Kirkland's** (☎1300 367 077) runs **buses** to: Brisbane (4½hr., 2-4 per day, $33) via Byron Bay (1hr., $12) and Surfers Paradise (3hr., $31); Murwillumbah (2hr., 2-4 per day, $17); Tenterfield (3 hr., M-F 1 per day, $25). Local operator **Marsh's** (☎6689 1220) services Nimbin (45min., M-F 3 per day; $7.50). **Greyhound Pioneer** (13 20 30) runs once a day to Brisbane (5½hr., $37) and Sydney (11½hr., $88). The best way to get around might be to rent a car. Options include **Hertz,** 49 Dawson St. (☎13 30 39), and **Thrifty,** 147 Woodlark St. (☎1300 367 227). For a **taxi,** call 13 10 08.

ORIENTATION AND PRACTICAL INFORMATION

In the hinterlands west of Ballina, Lismore lies off the Bruxner Hwy. (called **Ballina St.** in town) just east of the **Wilson** (or **Richmond**) **River.** Approaching the river from the east, Ballina St. crosses **Dawson, Keen,** and **Molesworth St.,** the busiest part of town. Perpendicular to these streets in the town center are small **Conway** and **Magellan St.,** and the main thoroughfare **Woodlark St.,** accessible from the Dawson St. roundabout and leading across the river to **Bridge St.** and **Nimbin.**

At the corner of Molesworth and Ballina St., the **Lismore Visitor Information Centre** has a small indoor tropical rainforest ($1) and a topographical map of the nearby national parks. (☎6622 0122; www.liscity.nsw.gov.au. Open M-F 9:30am-4pm, Sa-Su 10am-3pm.) Other services include: **ATMs** everywhere; **police** on Molesworth St. (☎6623 1599); **Internet** access at **Lismore Internet Services,** 172 Molesworth St. (☎6622 7766; open M-F 9am-5pm; $5.50 per hr.); **post office** on Conway St. between Molesworth and Keen St. (☎6622 1855; open M-F 8:30am-5pm). **Postal code:** 2480.

ACCOMMODATIONS

Currendina Lodge/Lismore Backpackers, 4 Ewing St. (☎6621 6118; currendi@nor.com.au), from the tourist office, go left on Ballina St., cross Keen St., and turn left on Dawson St. Ewing is the second right off Dawson. The Lodge has neat rooms, TV lounge, kitchen, and a screened-in porch. Internet and laundry. Reception daily 8am-10pm. Dorms $19, weekly $100; singles $24/$125; doubles $38/$155.

Lismore City Motor Inn, 129 Magellan St. (☎6621 4455), on the corner of Dawson St. Comfortable motel-style rooms with bath, TV, small fridge, and A/C. Pool and laundry. Reception daily 7:30am-9pm. Singles $55; twins and doubles $60; extra person $10.

Lismore Palms Caravan Park, 42 Brunswick St. (☎6621 7067), follow Dawson north and turn right onto Brunswick. Basic with kitchen and laundry. Sites $14, powered $17.

FOOD

The demand by uni students for cheap vegetarian eats has resulted in some terrifically funky cafes. The cheapest **supermarket** in town is Woolworth's on Keen St., with a back entrance on Carrington St. (Open M-Sa 7am-10pm, Su 9am-6pm.) Many pubs offer cheap lunch and dinner meals.

20,000 Cows, 58 Bridge St. (☎6622 2517). No cows are served at this vegan restaurant, with wild tablecloths pinned down with tall candlesticks and comfy sofas for lounging. Fresh pasta, Indian, and Middle Eastern food (mains $8-15). Open W-Su from 6pm.

Dr. Juice Bar, 142 Keen St. (☎6622 4440). An vegetarian/vegan student haunt. The Doctor prescribes marvelous smoothies, veggie burgers, and wildly popular apricot tofu cheesecake, all for less than $6. Open M-F 9am-6pm, Sa 10am-2pm.

Caddies Coffee, 20 Carrington St. (☎6621 7709). The indoor deck, outdoor patio, and beautiful stained glass make this a sure shot, with sandwiches, pasta, focaccia. Open M-F 8am-6pm, Sa 8am-1:30pm.

SIGHTS

Two blocks up Molesworth St. from the tourist office, and next to the fire station, is the **Lismore Regional Art Museum.** The gallery shows change regularly. (☎6622 2209. Open Tu-F 10am-4pm, Sa-Su 10:30am-2:30pm. Donation requested.) Farther along the street is the fabulous **Richmond River Historical Society,** 165 Molesworth St., in the Municipal Building. There's a natural history room with preserved baby crocs and mummified tropical birds, and a hallway with Aboriginal boomerangs. (☎6621 9993. Open M-Th 10am-4pm. $2.)

For a breath of fresh air, there are many parks nearby. **Rotary Park,** is a hoop pine and giant fig rainforest equipped with an easy boardwalk. The **Boatharbour Nature Reserve,** 6km northeast of Lismore on Bangalow Rd., sports 17 hectares of rainforest trees, the remnants of the "Big Scrub Forest." The original 75,000 hectares of lowland forest throughout northern New South Wales has been almost completely deforested. **Tucki Tucki Nature Reserve,** which doubles as a koala sanctuary, is 15min. from Lismore on Wyrallah Rd. Lismore's water supply comes from the **Rocky Creek Dam,** home to a waterfront boardwalk and a platypus lagoon.

NIGHTLIFE AND ENTERTAINMENT

Like any hard-working town, Lismore knows how to kick back and have a few. The town's nightlife centers around the hotel pubs in the town center. With **Powerhouse** nightclub and **Main St. Bar** under the same roof, the **Canberra Hotel,** 77 Molesworth St., is the main nightspot in town. The bar has live music gigs Thursday through Saturday and plenty of pool tables. (☎6622 4736. Open Th-F until 3am, Sa 4:30am.) **Mary Gilhooleys Irish Bar,** on the corner of Woodlark and Keen St. at the roundabout, has pints of Guinness for $6. (☎6622 2924. F-Sa live music. Open M-W 10am-midnight, Th-Sa 10am-1am.)

NEAR LISMORE: THE VILLAGES

Though the roads to the 10 small villages within the Lismore region are indirect and confusing, each hamlet yields some unique feature to draw visitors, if only for an afternoon. **Bexhill's** main attraction is an open-air cathedral and periodic organ recitals. **Dunoon,** near the Whian Whian State Forest, has rows of macadamia nut factories, some with free samples. Scenic **Rosebank** is particularly beautiful in late October when the jacarandas are in bloom.

The Channon, 20min. from Lismore, is home every second Sunday to the **Channon Markets,** the largest in the region, with spectacular displays of music, crafts, and homemade food. It's also the closest village to the lovely **Protestor's Falls,** named for a group of activists who, in 1979, were determined to prevent logging of the Terania Creek Forests. They arrived for a one-day demonstration and stayed for six weeks. Their efforts paid off: the tall, elegant stands of intertwined limbs were declared a national park, and the falls still empty into a shaded swimming hole.

NIMBIN ☎02

A popular day trip from Byron, Nimbin is an experience you won't forget, though as Australia's "Cannabis Capital," maybe you will. Galleries and psychedelic streetscape facades attest that the area's artistic talents are as rich as the surrounding soil. Since thousands of university students descended on Nimbin Village (pop. 700) for the 1973 Aquarius festival, Australia's answer to America's Woodstock, the community has retained an image as Australia's hippie and drug capital. While the presence of mumbling, shifty-eyed drug dealers downtown once were an immediate turn-off, recent crackdowns have begun to move activity behind discreet cafe doors for a more "civilized" approach to the abundant cannabis culture. The area's natural beauty and pure living also offer a degree of promise; more than 350 'shared communities,' some open to the public, are sheltered by the volcanic valley around the town. Residents' lives are closely intertwined with the land and its fruits, most of which are legal. Life is, well, interesting

TRANSPORTATION. The Nimbin Shuttle Bus (☎6680 9189) is the only direct public transportation to the village. It departs daily to Nimbin from **Byron Bay** at 10am, returning at 2:30pm ($22, one-way $12). For visitors who just want a glimpse of the spectacle, Byron-based tours to nearby national parks often stop in town for an hour or two; all tours are $25. **Jim's Alternative Tours** (☎6685 7720) is the most engaging with its own "psychedelic soundtrack" and witty commentary. **Mick's Bay to Bush** (☎6685 6889) and **Wayne's Nimbin Tours** (☎6687 2254, 04 1229 3686) have stops in the village as well. **Nimbin Explorer Eco-Tours** runs full-day tours of the sacred rocks, Djanbung Gardens Permaculture Centre Rainbow Power Company, and nearby rainforest including Protestors' Falls. (☎6689 1557. Tours M-F. Pickup in Ballina 9am, return 6pm.)

PRACTICAL INFORMATION. Nimbin's commercial district and center is on **Cullen St.** between the police station and the corner hotel. You'll know you're there by the vivid murals, wild storefront displays, and thin wisps of smoke. **The Nimbin Tourist Connexion,** at 80 Cullen St. near the end of the road in town, has info on national parks and Nimbin's "straight" side, and an **ISA** booking agency for buses and trains; it also has the cheapest **Internet** access in town at $3 per 1hr. (☎6689 1764. Open M-F noon-5pm, Sa-Su noon-2pm.)

ACCOMMODATIONS AND FOOD. Though many visitors to Nimbin come for just the day, the town's hostels are eager to welcome those who wish to take a few days to sample all that Nimbin has to offer. **Nimbin Backpackers at Granny's Farm** is a 10min. walk from the town center north on Cullen St. Turn left just before the bridge. The creekside lodge has two pools, showers, a large kitchen and TV room, frequent BBQs, and loose horses; platypuses frolic in the creek. Nightly outdoor fires are great icebreakers. (☎6689 1333. Laundry $4. Sites $8 per person; dorms $17; doubles $38.) **Nimbin Hotel & Backpackers,** in the center of town where

Sibley St. splits from Cullen, boasts the cheapest beds in town (☎6689 1246. Dorms $15.) For pure living, the **Rainbow Retreat,** 75 Thorburn St., is a 20min. hike from the town center and miles from anywhere else. Take a left onto Thorburn from Cullen St. just across a green stream; the hostel is up a rocky, unpaved driveway through a horse pasture. (☎6689 1262; www.skybusiness.com/rainbowretreat. Free bus from Byron M, W, F at 2pm. Tentsites $8; dorms $13; brightly colored VW $27; wagon double $33.)

Nimbin eateries are all along Cullen St. (like everything else). The **Rainbow Cafe,** 64A Cullen St, was the first alternative cafe in Nimbin, with focaccia sandwiches for $7. (☎6689 1997. Open daily 8am-5pm.) **Choices Cafe,** 45 Cullen St., grills tofu burgers and meat kebabs for $5-6 (☎6689 1698. Open 9am-4pm.) A nearby **grocery,** Nimbin Emporium, 58 Cullen St., sells health and bulk foods with a video rental shop out back. (☎6689 1205. Open M-F 8:30am-7:30pm, Sa-Su 8:30am-6:30pm.) **Bush Theatre/Picture Factory,** just outside the village center on Cullen, has put together a $12-13 movie/meal deal including wine. (☎6689 1111. F-Su, special backpackers nights Tu-W through Granny's Farm; normal movie admission $7.) The **Cave,** 81 Cullen St. behind the community center, doubles as a vegetarian cafe and groovy nightclub in summer. (☎6689 1183. Cafe open daily 9am-11:30pm.)

SIGHTS AND FESTIVALS. The mural-covered **Nimbin Museum,** on Cullen St., redefines creativity and historical interpretation. It's complete drug-induced strangeness, but at the same time ingenious (or is that redundant?). Party vans burst through the front facade, and the 3D tangle of cobwebs, clocks, psychedelic fans, and tree branches lend credence to Einstein's quotation, found in the second room: "Imagination is more important than knowledge." The rooms relate the founders' version of regional history, with proportionate coverage of all three major historical periods: the first room is about Aborigines, the second about European settlers, and the next five about the hippies. This last group is illustrated by fluorescent-lit cave rooms, melted skeletons (presumably illustrating nuclear meltdown), and marijuana legalization propaganda. (☎6689 1123. $2 donation requested.) The HEMP (Help End Marijuana Prohibition) Party (which must be one raging party) has its base at the **Hemp Embassy,** 51 Cullen St. (☎6689 1842; www.nimbinaustralia.com/hemp. Open daily 9am-6pm.) The attached Hemp Bar offers "refreshments." (☎6689 1842; hempbar.nimbinaustralyia.com.) On the first weekend of every May, crowds flock to the tiny town for the annual **Mardi Grass,** the brainchild of the Hemp Embassy. Events include the Hemp Olympics, where contestants battle it out in everything from a bong-throwing competition to a joint-rolling contest (both artistic and speed). The **Cannabis Cup** lets lucky judges test local growers' product in categories including aroma, size, and effect.

In 1973, the Australian Union of Students created the **Aquarius Festival** as a forum for a new future. An indirect outcome of the festival, and a major employer in Nimbin, is the **Rainbow Power Company,** a 10min. walk from the city center down Cullen St to Alternative Way, on the right. The building, made of mud bricks, is a remarkable achievement in solar and wind energy production; they even sell their excess generated power to the electricity grid for general consumption. (☎6689 1430; www.rpc.com.au. Open M-F 9am-5pm, Sa 9am-noon. Group tours by advance arrangement; 1hr. $2.) For a hands-on look at earth-conscious living, trek to **Djanbung Gardens Permaculture Centre,** 74 Cecil St. Take a left onto Cecil Street at the southern end of Cullen; the gardens are just after Neem Rd. A resource center offers insights (and workshops) on organic gardening, permaculture design, village and community development and more. Guided tours of the garden every Tu and Th at 10:30am. An in-depth farm tour on Sa at 11am, other times by appointment. (☎6689 1755; www.earthwise.org.au. Open Tu-Sa 10am-4pm.)

NEAR NIMBIN: NIGHTCAP NATIONAL PARK

An 8000-hectare park with the highest rainfall in the state and containing the southern rim of the 20-million-year-old **Mt. Warning** volcano crater, Nightcap has two main areas: **Mt. Nardi,** 12km out of Nimbin, and the **Terania Creek/Protestors Falls** area, 15km out of **The Channon** (20km from Nimbin). Mt. Nardi, one of the highest peaks, is accessible on sealed roads and has BBQ and picnic facilities. The viewing platform has info on the walk to nearby **Mt. Matheson** (1.5km) and the **Pholi's Walk** (2km), with a lookout to the **Tweed Valley.**

Gravel Terania Creek Rd leads to Protestor's Falls in the Terania Creek basin and to a picnic area with BBQ, toilets, wood, and shelter. **Camping** is limited to one night. The track to Protestor's Falls (1.4km return) passes **Waterfall Creek** on the way (see **The Villages,** p. 187). **Tuntable Falls** in the Tuntable Falls commune is a 120m waterfall (from the parking lot, 3-4hr. return). From Nimbin, the turn-off is 6km down Sibley St; then go another 6km. The **Nimbin Rocks,** and Aboriginal sacred site, are the other way out of town, toward Lismore. **Hanging Rock Falls** is just 25min. from Nimbin near Wadeville. The natural swimming hole is perfect for picnics and bordered by basalt columns.

BYRON BAY ☎02

The "come for a day, stay for a week" coastal malaise that infects many a wandering traveler on the Holiday Coast of Australia hits its peak in Byron Bay, one of the most popular stops on the Sydney-to-Cairns route. With Byron's excellent family and surfing beaches and refreshing lack of high rises and mass consumerism, it's not hard to see why. While Byron feeds its indignant-granola masses with palm reading, massage classes, and bead shops, it's more than just commercialized karma. The relaxed, rejuvenating coastal town with a famously "alternative" attitude is nirvana for its diverse devotees: aged hippies, dredlocked backpackers, bleached surfers, ravers, young families, sharp businessmen, and yoga gurus. Although laid-back, few are "tuned out;" a passion for environmentalism, liberalism, vegetarianism, and sunshine is manifest here.

TRANSPORTATION

Trains: Countrylink (☎13 22 32) runs to: **Brisbane** (5hr., 1 per day, $26); **Coffs Harbour** (4hr., 3 per day, $42); **Surfers Paradise** (4½hr., 1 per day, $15); **Sydney** (13hr., 2 per day, $98); 50% discount with 15-day advance purchase.

Buses: Between **Greyhound** (☎13 20 30), **McCafferty's** (☎13 14 99), **Kirkland's** (☎1300 367 077), **Blanch's Coaches** (☎6686 2144), and **Premier** (☎13 34 10), buses run to: **Ballina** (30min., 3-7 per day, $8); **Brisbane** (3-3½hr., at least 10 per day, $28-33); **Coffs Harbour** (4-5hr., 8 per day, $40-49); **Lennox Head** (20min., 3-7 per day, $5); **Lismore** (1hr., 2-4 per day, $12); **Murwillumbah** (1hr., 2-6 per day, $13); **Port Mac-**

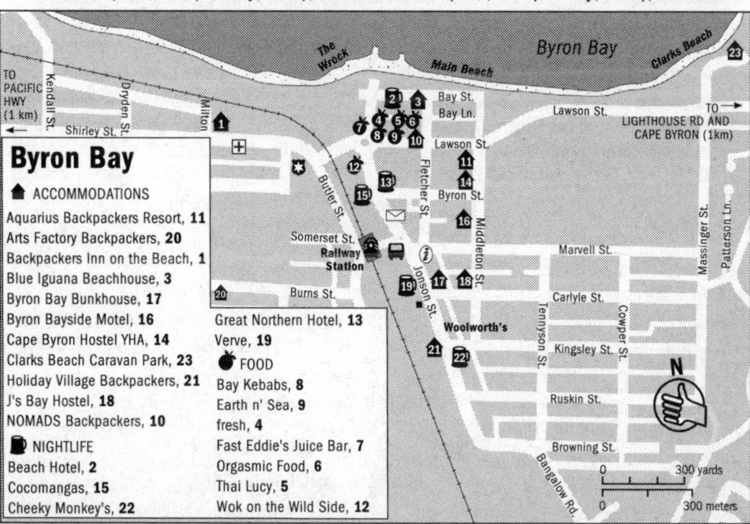

BLOODY HELL! Certain beachfront properties in Byron Bay that are currently worth millions couldn't be given away less than 20 years ago. An acre near Clarks Beach that cost only $100 in 1970, is now worth a thousand times that. Why? Well, Byron used to be the home of a whaling station that dumped truckloads of whale blood and parts into the water, transforming the bay into a shark extravaganza during the 1960s. Without tourists coming to stick their toes in the water, the town subsisted on the rather unpleasant business of pig slaughtering. All in all, Byron was a rather rough and unpleasant place. Then whaling became illegal and the piggery closed. Now, too cool for its own good, Byron is an exploding tourist destination–trying to balance its granola goodness with the bucks and backpackers that are scrambling in droves up the coast from Sydney. The lesson? Always buy cheap property on the water. Always.

quarie (6-7hr., 4 per day, $62); **Surfers Paradise** (2hr., at least 6 per day, $24-26); **Sydney** (12-13hr., 8 per day, $74-85). Buses depart from the Bus Depot in the center of town. Tickets can be purchased at **Peterpan Adventures,** see **Practical Info** p. 190.

Car Rental: Byron Odyssey Car Rental (☎1800 771 244; www.byronodyssey.com.au), at the corner of Marvel and Jonson, rents from $39 per day. **Earth Car Rentals** is at 4 Middleton St. (☎6685 7472, 6680 9708). **JetSet Travel,** at the corner of Marvell and Jonson St. offers competitive rates (☎6685 6554; bustop@lis.net.au). International chains including **Thrifty,** 67 Shirley St. (☎6685 8966; www.thrifty.com.au), and **Hertz,** 11-21 Butler (☎6685 6522), have offices in the area.

NEW SOUTH WALES

ORIENTATION AND PRACTICAL INFORMATION

Byron is not on the Pacific Hwy., but is accessible from it through nearby Bangalow. From Bangalow, **Bangalow Rd.** enters Byron Bay from the south. Turn off a roundabout onto Browning St., which leads to **Jonson St.,** the southern boundary of the city center. **Lawson St.** is to the north of town, running at times along **Main Beach.** To the east, Lawson St. becomes **Lighthouse Rd.,** running past Clarks Beach, The Pass surfing spot, Wategos Beach, the lighthouse, and the Cape Byron lookout. To the west, Lawson becomes **Shirley St.** and curves off to **Belongil Beach.** Farther west it becomes **Ewingsdale Rd.** and passes the **Arts and Industrial Estate** before reaching the Pacific Hwy.

Tourist Office: The official tourist information center is **Peterpan Adventures,** 87 Jonson St. (☎6880 8926 or 1800 252 459; www.peterpans.com). Friendly staff will book for free any number of local adventure activities. Luggage storage $5 per day. Open daily 9am-7pm. Another local information center (☎6685 8050) behind the train station has accomodation and limited activity materials.

Budget Travel: Most hostels book activities, and there are a few travel agencies in town. **Byron Bus and Backpacker Centre,** 84 Jonson St. (☎6685 5517; bustop@lis.net.au), behind the long-distance bus stop. A booking agency with no service fees. Backpack storage $5 per day. Open daily 7am-7pm.

Currency Exchange: Banks on Jonson St. are open M-Th 9:30am-4pm, F 9:30am-5pm. Other **ATMs** are across the street from the tourist office.

Taxis: Byron Bay Taxis (☎6685 5008). 24hr. wheelchair access and minibuses available.

Police: (☎6685 9499). On the corner of Butler and Shirley St.

Hospital: Byron District Hospital (☎6685 6200), Shirley St. next to the police. Open 24hr.

Internet Access: The Gossip Shop, 33 Byron St. (☎6680 9556; www.thegossipshop.com.au), is the cheapest in town at $2 per hr. Open daily 9am-7pm. **Global Gossip,** 84 Jonson St. (☎6680 9140), is open late at the bus stop. $3.95 per 1hr.. Open daily 9am-11pm. Internet cafes literally line the streets of backpacker-ready Byron Bay. Most activity booking offices also offer free Internet access with bookings.

Post Office: 61 Jonson St. Open M-F 9am-5pm. **Postal Code:** 2481.

ACCOMMODATIONS

In summer, especially around Christmas, Byron floods with thousands of tourists; everything gets packed, and some accommodation prices go up 150-200%. The best advice is to book early, but demand is so high that some hostels do not take reservations in summer. Many unlucky would-be Byron dwellers make do in Ballina (see p. 184) or Lennox Head (see p. 196).

HOSTELS

Byron has numerous hostels and the standard of quality is amazingly high, with common amenities like free shuttles from the bus station, activity booking desks, luggage storage, and pools. Most of the hostels have strict 11pm lights-out in the common room and 10am check-out.

Aquarius Backpackers Resort, 16 Lawson St. (☎6685 7663 or 1800 028 909; www.aquarius-backpack.com.au), at the corner of Middleton St., 2 blocks off Jonson St. Formerly a luxury resort, many of the spacious rooms have 2 levels, porches, and fridges; all have beautiful rosewood beds. Poolside bar with Happy Hours, fully licensed travel desk, parking, kitchen, and cafe (pancakes $6). Each night, guests get a complimentary $3 voucher for use at the on-site bar or cafe. Free boogie boards and shuttle bus. Linen $1, blanket deposit $10. Laundry $4. Key deposit $10. Internet $4 per hr. Bikes and surfboards $35 per day. Reception daily 7am-9pm. 24hr. check-in. Dorms with bath $25; doubles $55. 3 and 7 day discounts. VIP/YHA. MC/V.

Backpackers Inn on the Beach, 29 Shirley St. (☎6685 8231; www.byron-bay.com/backpackersinn). Follow Jonson St., veer left onto Lawson St., cross the railroad tracks, and continue on Shirley St. to the corner of Milton St. The only hostel in Byron with direct beach access. Large, functional, and social. Loft kitchen, volleyball, heated pool, BBQ, pool table, free bus shuttle, and Internet ($6 per 1hr). Free luggage storage, bikes, and boogie boards. Small cafe sells food like veggie burgers and chicken sandwiches for $6 and under. Reception daily 8am-8pm. Reservations 2-3 days ahead. Dorms $23; doubles from $50. Rates drop $1 nightly after 3 days, and another $1 after a week. ISIC/VIP/YHA. Wheelchair accessible.

Arts Factory Backpackers Lodge, on Skinners Shoot Rd. (☎6685 7709; www.artsfactory.com.au). Cross the railroad tracks behind the bus stop and take a right on Burns St. to Skinners Shoot Rd. Welcome to Wonderland, Alice. Sprawling 5-acre grounds with "funky abodes" ranging from teepees to island bungalows in a lake. Free daily activities include didgeridoo-making, yoga, fire-twirling, massage classes, and drum workshops. Volleyball courts, pool, sauna, laundry ($4), Internet ($4.50 per 30min), bikes ($8 per day). Surfboard and bodyboard $15 per day. Weekly talent shows and $7 BBQ. Cafe open for breakfast and lunch. Reception daily 7am-noon and 4-9pm. Dorms $16-21; weirdly wonderful options $23-26; twins and doubles $62-66; sites $14. $2 discount in winter, 3 and 5 night discounts. ISIC/VIP/YHA. MC/V.

Byron Bay Bunkhouse, 1 Carlyle St. (☎6685 8311 or 1800 241 600; www.byronbaybunkhouse.com.au). Opposite the Jonson St. Woolworth's. Crowded and loud, but with $4 dinners (tacos, pasta, etc.) that can be eaten on the beautiful, candle-lit terrace. Live entertainment and BBQ on W. Pancake breakfast included. Free linen and boogie boards. Laundry $4. Key deposit $15. Reception daily 7:30am-10pm. Dorms $19-21, weekly rates available. Wheelchair accessible. MC/V.

NOMADS Main Beach Backpackers (☎6685 8695 or 1800 150 233; fax 6685 8609), corner of Lawson and Fletcher St. Take a right on Lawson from the beach end of Jonson St. High ceilings, wood paneling, fireplace, rooftop deck, patio, saltwater pool, secured parking, and a common room with TV and pool table. Clean bedrooms have individual lockers. Pancake breakfasts, BBQ twice a week. Laundry $4. Reception daily 8am-9:30pm. Book a month ahead. Dorms from $18, weekly $105; twins and doubles $40-45. ISIC/NOMADS/VIP/YHA. Wheelchair accessible. MC/V.

J's Bay Hostel (YHA), 7 Carlyle St. (☎6685 8853 or 1800 678 195; jbay@nor.com.au). Clean, colorful, and cozy, J's has one of the best all-you-can-eat-and-drink BBQ deals,

NEW SOUTH WALES

with live music Tu and F ($6). Billiards and picnic tables in an upstairs covered pavilion, very large kitchen, heated pool, and secure parking. Family-friendly. Free use of bikes and boogie boards. Laundry $4.80. Reception daily 8am-9pm. Book a week ahead. Dorms $21-23; twins and doubles $55, with bath $65-68; separate family building $65. Non-YHA add $3. Wheelchair accessible. MC/V.

Cape Byron Hostel (YHA) (☎6685 8788 or 1800 652 627; fax 6685 8814), corner of Middleton and Byron St. From the bus stop, go 2 blocks down Byron St. and take a left on Middleton. Pinball machines, a pool table, and video games in the living room. Upstairs deck and eating area overlooks a heated pool bordered by palm trees. $10 BBQ and wine Tu and F. Free bikes and boogieboards. Family-friendly. Secured parking. Laundry $4. Internet $1 per 10min., $5 per 1hr. Reception daily 6:45am-10pm. Dorms $18-22; twins and doubles $55-65, with bath $65. Wheelchair accessible.

The Blue Iguana Beachouse, 14 Bay St. (☎6685 5298), opposite the Surf Club, on the corner of Bay and Fletcher St. True relaxation in an intimate beachhouse near the town center. Sundeck and screened front porch with couches and TV. Free surfboards and bodyboards. Off-street parking. Reception daily 9am-noon and 4-9pm. Book a week ahead. Dorms with bath $25; doubles $70. 7th night free. No credit cards.

Holiday Village Backpackers, 116 Jonson St. (☎6685 8888 or 1800 350 388; fax 6685 8777). 2 blocks from the tourist center. Small rooms surround a large courtyard usually filled with party-hardy backpackers. Picnic tables, volleyball, heated pool, spa, TV and video room. Free bikes, surfboards, and boogie boards. All-you-can-eat BBQ M and F $10. Free luggage storage. Linen $2 washing charge, $10 blanket deposit. Laundry $4.40. Internet $4 per 1hr. Reception daily 7am-9:30pm. Book 2 days ahead. Great deal for groups—they have dorm-style apartments with TV, bath, and kitchen ($25 per person). Dorms $20-23; doubles $55. Weekly discount $14. VIP.

MOTELS AND CAMPING

Byron Bayside Motel, 14 Middleton St. (☎6685 6004; fax 6685 8552). Take Byron St. from Jonson St. Great location near the town center and beaches. Large, clean rooms with beautiful furniture, full kitchen, TV, laundry, and sparkling private bathroom; many feature balconies with carefully tended flowerbeds. Secure parking garage. Off-season singles $70; doubles $75, each extra person $15. Prices increase $6 for weekends, $30 for holidays. Wheelchair accessible. AmEx/MC/V.

Clarks Beach Caravan Park (☎6685 6496; www.bshp.com.au/clarkes). Great location on Clarks Beach, off Massinger St. Well-kept sites. $10 key deposit. Lights out 9:30pm. Reception 7am-7pm. Sites for 2 $18, peak season $28-31, weekly $108/$168-217; powered sites for 2 $22/$32-35; weekly $132/$192-245; cabins with bath $75/$90-110, weekly $450/$540-770.

FOOD

Thai Lucy (☎6680 8083), on Bay Ln. in the alley opposite Hog's Breath Cafe on Jonson St. You'll have to wait to get in, but the food is fantastic. Indoor and outdoor seating. Medium range prices (entrees $12-18) but worth it for every savory bite. Takeaway available. Open daily noon-3pm and 5:30-10pm. BYO.

Earth n' Sea, 11 Lawson St. (☎6685 6029). Cheesy, doughy, comfort food. The surfer decor and the friendly banter between waiters make this long-running, family-friendly joint a great place to unwind. It caters to "pastaholics," hitting a nerve with anyone who wants to stuff their face with carbo-goodness. Try their original "Beethoven" pizza, a surprisingly delicious combo of prawns, banana, and pineapple. Pastas from $10, twenty different pizza pies from $15. Delivery available. Open daily 5:30-9pm, lunch and later hours in summer. AmEx/MC/V.

Orgasmic Food (☎6680 7778), on Bay Ln. behind the Beach Hotel . Word is spreading throughout NSW about the self-titled "best falafels in Australia" ($6). When you sample their Middle Eastern fare along with some freshly crushed sugarcane juice, you'll see why. Outdoor seating. Open 10am-late daily. No credit cards.

fresh, 7 Jonson St. (☎6685 7810). Perhaps the best people-watching spot in Byron Bay. Enjoy pricey Pacific cuisine (entrees $16-20) at this trendy hotspot while warming your heels on the heated tile floor. Open daily 8am-late.

Fast Eddie's Juice Bar, 11 Jonson St. (☎6685 8805). A misleading name, as Fast Eddie's serves up stylish and healthy full meals and iced juicy nectars. The soy-dominated menu has a wide range of veggie options, including tofu burgers ($7.50) and daily salad specials ($8-10). Ask here about upcoming concerts and parties; an informal network of local DJs circulates through. Open daily 8am-10pm.

Bay Kebabs (☎6685 5596), corner of Jonson and Lawson St. Try the traditional *doner* (lamb and beef), or the highly addictive marinated chicken ($6). $5.90 meal deal gets you a sizable "small" kebab and a drink. Open daily 10am-late.

Wok on the Wild Side, 18 Jonson St. (☎6685 6220). Choose from 5 different noodles and 9 choices of meat and vegetarian options in making your own pasta stir-fry in Malay, Chinese, or Thai sauces. Large portions at $9-12 make this a great dinner option. Open daily noon-midnight. No credit cards.

Supernatural Food (☎6685 5833), at the Arts Factory. Hare Krishna staff prepares "karma free" vegetarian dinners including Indian curries and samosas ($7.50-14.50). Candles cast flickering shadows on the lofty ceiling; long wooden tables are surrounded by stone statues, sculptures, and a splashing waterfall. Open for dinner from 6pm.

SIGHTS

Built in 1901, the **Byron Bay Lighthouse,** at the end of Lighthouse Rd., is Cape Byron's crowning glory, the most powerful lighthouse in Australia. A steadily rotating beam pierces through 40km of darkness every night. The interior is red cedar, the outside concrete. The last lighthouse keeper left in 1988, long after the lighthouse became fully automated. The keepers' cottages are still standing, however; one is a small museum and the other is available for private holiday rental. (Grounds open daily year-round 8am-5:30pm. Tours during school holidays.) A boardwalk leads to the lighthouse, a 1hr. walk passing along Main Beach to Clarks Beach and **Captain Cook Lookout.** From here, a walking circuit follows the beach to **The Pass,** and winds up a steep gradient past Wategos Beach to the **Headland Lookout,** the easternmost point in Australia and an excellent place for spotting dolphins and whales. The lighthouse is just a short distance farther; the track then heads through forest back to Captain Cook Lookout.

Byron's artistic community is flourishing; the best example is **The Cape Gallery,** 2 Lawson St., which exhibits primarily local artists and a fine pottery collection. (☎6685 7658; www.capegallery.com.au. Open daily 10am-5pm, 6pm in summer. AmEx/MC/V). The **Byron Fine Art Gallery** in the Byron Arcade at 13 Lawson St. also showcases local works (☎6680 8433; www.byronfineart.com.au. Open 10am-5pm every day except Tu.) **Gondwana Gifts,** 7-9 Byron St., has Aboriginal art and free weekly didgeridoo and fire-twirling lessons. (☎6685 8866; info@ozarts.net. Open M-F 10am-5pm, Sa 10am-4pm. AmEx/MC/V.) West of town, the **Arts and Industrial Estate,** off Ewingsdale Rd. (called Shirley Rd. in town), houses a number of stores hawking industrial glass and metals, paintings, sculptures, crafts, and factory-outlet shoes. Colin Heaney **blows glass** at 6 Acacia St. (☎6685 7044. Gallery open M-F 9am-5pm, Sa-Su 10am-4pm; glass-blowing M-Th 9am-4pm, F 9am-2:30pm.)

ACTIVITIES

Many activities have extended packages up to a week or more for those who wish to sharpen their skills beyond the first stumbling day. Nearly all have free pickup and return to and from your accomodation.

SURFING.

Boards slung over their shoulders, herds of bleach-blond surfers trudge dutifully to Byron's beaches every morning at sunrise. Surf schools entice novices by providing all equipment and soliciting through hostels; most have a stand-up guarantee. Byron has excellent surfing spots all around the bay, so no matter the wind conditions there are always good waves somewhere. Just off Main Beach, The Wreck is known for waves that break close to the beach. Working down the shore toward the lighthouse, The Pass promises long, challenging rides, but can be dangerous because of overcrowding, sharp rocks, and boats. The water off Wategos Beach, close to The Pass, is best for longer surfboards, since the waves are slow and rolling. Again, the rocks can be dangerous. Cosy Corner, on the other side of the headland from Wategos, has great northern-wind surfing. On the western side of Main Beach, southern winds bring Broken Head and Belongil Beach alive.

Byron Bay Surf School (☎1800 707 274; www.byronbaysurfschool.com). 4hr. lesson $33; 3- and 5-day courses and all-female lessons available. The original surf school in the area.

Black Dog Surfing (☎6680 9828, after hours 0412 804 970; www.byronbay.com/blackdog). Has multi-day packages. 3hr. lesson $35; 3, 5, and 10-day courses and private lessons available. Lessons can be booked through **Bay Action,** 14 Jonson St., (☎6685 7819). Surfboards full-day $22, weekly $66; wetsuits $10/$40; boogie boards $15/$45.

Style Surfing (☎6685 5634; www.byron-bay.com/byronbaystylesurfing). All-inclusive 4hr. beginner package with free pickup. The accompanying photographer captures the real you instead of the vision of grace and loveliness you think you are. $33.

KAYAKING AND RAFTING.

Ocean Kayaking Byron Bay (☎6685 7651). Half-day trips past the area's wrecks and reefs to a snorkeling site. $35.

Dolphin Kayaking (☎6685 8044). Half-day guided tour of Byron's marine life, taking guests right up to a school of local dolphins or whales in season. $35.

Wildwater Rafting (☎6653 3500). Trips on the nearby Goolang, Nymboida, and Gwydir rivers, with pickup in Byron Bay and Coffs Harbour. Starting at $70.

DIVING.

Most diving is done at **Julian Rocks Marine Park,** 2.5km off Main Beach, widely considered one of the 10 best dive sites in Australia. Julian Rocks has both warm and cold currents and is home to 500 species of fish, including the occasional grey nurse shark. Required medical clearances are $50. Dive certification courses can go up by $70-100 or more during the summer.

Sundive (☎6685 7755; fax 6685 8361), on Middleton St. next to the YHA. Has an on-site pool and offers many types of dives. Courses usually start on Tuesdays, but certification courses over two weekends are sometimes offered. 4-day PADI certification $350, winter 20% discount; intro dives $130; day dives $78; additional trips $50; snorkeling trips $45.

Byron Bay Dive Centre, 9 Marvel St. (☎6685 8333 or 1800 243 483; www.byronbaydivecentre.com.au), between Middleton and Fletcher. 4-day SSI certification courses start M and Th $450, winter $350; intro dives $135; daydives $75; additional trips $65; snorkelling $55.

OUT OF THE SKY.

Byron Air Charter (☎6684 2753 or 6684 4976). Scenic flights over Cape Byron and Mt. Warning starting at $40 per seat.

Skylimit (☎6684 3711). Offers motorized ultralight tours from $70.

Flight Zone Hanggliding School (☎6685 8768, 0408 441 742). Tandem flights $105 for half an hour, as well as multi-day courses.

Byron Airwaves (☎6629 0354 or 0408 441 742). Tandem flights $105.

Skydive Cape Byron (☎6685 5990 or 1800 666 770; www.skydive-cape-byron.com). Tandem dives directly over Cape Byron.

Skydive (☎6684 1323). Dives $229-343 depending on height.

Byron Bay Beach Club Flying Trapeze and Circus School (☎6685 8000), on Bayshore Dr., has trapeze classes and also squeezes in some tumbling, juggling, trampoline jumping, and sundry circus skills. 2hr. lesson $35, with pickup.

WHAT'S IN A NAME? The North Coast Steam Navigation Company's 2240-ton vessel *T.S.S. Wollongbar* was once the fastest ship on the east coast of Australia. It ran bi-weekly to Sydney and could hold up to 300 passengers. On May 14th, 1921, however, it became a permanent part of Byron Bay, and is now known simply as **The Wreck.** On that fateful day, the ship's captain decided to lift anchor and go to sea. Bad timing–a gale sprang up, and six waves in rapid succession knocked the ship sideways onto the shore and split its back while it was grounded. Hoping to recover some of their losses, the owners sold off whatever they could; some of the ship's furniture is on display around town. The unmoved ship has itself become a Byron landmark, with the stern still visible at low tide. Perhaps it's just an unlucky name: the next *Wollongbar* was torpedoed by a Japanese submarine during World War II.

RUBBED DOWN.

Samadhi Flotation Centre (☎6685 6905), opposite Woolworth's. Massages and great-value massage classes. Full-day intro massage classes with breakfast and lunch $50; 1hr. massage $55, backpackers $50. Open M-Sa 9am-6pm, Su 10am-6pm. Book ahead. MC/V.

Relax Haven (☎6685 8304), at the rear of Belongil Beachhouse on Childe St., 2km from town. Much smaller but offers great value. 1hr. float and 1hr. massage $40.

Vision Studios (☎0414 368 057; www.zenshiatzu.com), on Jonson St. where it turns into Browning. Full-day courses in zen shiatzu massage every Tu and Th. Open 9am-3:30pm, includes breakfast/lunch, $45.

SMOKIN' TOURS.

All tours provide shuttle service to the Channon and Bangalow Sunday markets.

Jim's Alternative Tours (☎6685 7720; www.byron-bay.com/jimstoursa). Great 9hr. trip through Minyon Falls and Nimbin, with a route along Cape Byron allowing for dolphin-spotting. Funky CD music accompanies Jim's locally infamous operation, which was named "Party Tour of the Year" by The International Party Guide. $25.

Mick's Bay to Bush Tours (☎6687 2574, 0418 662 684). Day tours through Nimbin, Minyon Falls, the Rainbow Temple, and the rainforest, including a stop at a swimming hole. $25, including chai tea and munchies.

Wayne's Nimbin Tours (☎6687 2254, 04 1229 3686). Offers a tour led by a local whose family has lived near Nimbin since 1902. $25, including beer and nuts.

Nimbin Explorer Eco Tours (☎6689 1557). Treks through the rainforest to Protesters' Falls, an area that was saved from logging, along with a stop in Nimbin and Djanbung Gardens. $25.

OTHER ACTIVITIES.

Rockhoppers (☎0500 881 881; www.rockhoppers.com.au). Runs full-day mountain bike tours, abseiling trips down a 100m waterfall. Some trips include the sunrise at Mt. Warning. Biking $69, abseiling $119, includes BBQ lunch and pickup.

Wave Rock, 1/91 Centennial Circuit at the Arts and Industrial Estate (☎6680 8777; www.byronbayclimbing.com). Anindoor rock climbing room with over 50 different climbs. A 10min. car ride from center of city. Open M-F 10am-8pm, Sa-Su 10am-6pm. $12 per 2hr. Boot rental $6. Chalk bag $3. Backpackers special with instruction and equipment $15.

Byron Bay Bicycles, 93 Jonson St. (☎6685 6067). Half-day $12, full-day $26, weekly $85.

Pegasus Park Equestrian Centre (☎6687 1446), 15min. west of Byron. Leads rides and canoe rows along Byron Creek. $35 per 1hr. ride, $55 per 2hr.

NIGHTLIFE AND ENTERTAINMENT

Byron Bay's pubs have an atmosphere that is both mellow and lively; Jimmy Buffett would be at home here. Drinks tend to run $9 per cocktail and $4 per beer.

Cheeky Monkey's (☎6685 5886), on the corner of Jonson and Kingsley St. Packed with backpackers dancing on the tables, and generally being rowdy. Dinner specials $6-7. Open daily 7pm-3am.

Beach Hotel (☎6685 6402), on Jonson St. overlooking the beach. A local favorite of slightly older drinkers, with a garden bar and huge patio. The large indoor stage often plays host to both local and nationally recognized bands. Live music W-Su; no cover.

Verve (☎6685 6170; www.vervenightclub.com), on Jonson St., in the Woolworth's parking lot. The new kid on the block, with a movie theater that converts into a stylish nightclub at 9:30. Free Internet access and a cafe offering Japanese snacks add respite from shaking your booty. Cover $3-5; no cover before 11pm. Closes at 3am.

Cocomangas, 32 Jonson St. (☎6685 8493). Has a slightly calmer and smaller dance floor and affordable drinks. Try the tasty Jam Jar, a mix of juices, gin, malibu, and triple sec for only $4.50. M 70s night; Tu R&B; W 1 free drink for the first 75 women; Th R&B and hip-hop. Cover $3-5; no cover before 10pm, midnight in winter. Closes at 3am.

Pighouse Flicks (☎6685 5828), at the Piggery on Skinners Shoot Rd. by the Arts Factory. Shows art and foreign (read: American) films three times nightly. Opens at 5pm. 4 shows Sa $10.90. Movie-and-dinner deal with nearby vegetarian restaurant $15.90.

NEAR BYRON BAY: LENNOX HEAD

Lennox Head (pop. 2300) lies between Ballina and Byron Bay. It's renowned for its excellent **surf**—it has one of the longest right-hand surf breaks in the world, and from Jun.-Aug., it's rated one of the top 10 areas in the world. Lennox is a great spill-over location if Byron gets too crowded. The highway enters the town on Tourist Rd. The town center is accessible by taking the roundabout to coastal Ballina St., which becomes Pacific Pde and runs along **Seven Mile Beach,** prime dolphin-spotting territory. **Lake Ainsworth** is at the north end of Pacific Pde. **Lennox Point,** 2km south, is an excellent but crowded surf area. Blanch's Coaches run through Lennox Head a few times daily to **Byron Bay;** the bus stop is on Ballina St. near the town center, or flag them down along Pacific Pde. (☎6686 2144. $5.)

ATMs, food stores, eateries, and the local pub are clustered within one minute's walk of each other at the southern end of Ballina St. **All Above Board,** 68 Ballina St (☎6887 7522), rents surfboards ($16.50), Malibus ($22), and body boards ($9).

The **Lennox Head Beach House,** 3 Ross St, is north of the town center, just off Pacific Pde and a short walk from Lake Ainsworth. The intimate beachouse has surfboards, boogie-boards, bicycles, and fishing rods; unlimited use of windsurfers and catamarans is just $5, and lessons are free. Aspiring gourmets can help themselves to the herb garden and dine in the open courtyard. Once a week, enjoy a massage from their "natural healing center." Bedrooms are small but tidy. (☎6687 7636. Dorms $21; doubles $42-44. Non-YHA add $2. Ask about weekly rates.) **Lake Ainsworth Caravan Park** is across Ross St next to the lake. (☎6687 7249. Sites $14, powered $16.50; cabins $33-50; peak season add $5-10.)

MURWILLUMBAH ☎02

Located in a mountain valley halfway between Byron Bay and Tweed Heads, Murwillumbah ("mur-WOOLUM-buh") is a small country town dissected by the mud-colored **Tweed River**. The town's name (often shortened by locals to "MUR-buh") has several suggested meanings, including "place of high mountain that catches sun" and "place of many possums and people." There are several national parks near Murwillumbah including **Springbrook, Lamington, Mebbin, Border Ranges, Nightcap, Mt. Jerusalem, Mooball,** and **Mt. Warning** (see **Mt. Warning and Border Ranges,** p. 197). Approaching Murwillumbah from the east on the Pacific Hwy., the ancient volcanic plug that forms Mt. Warning dominates the skyline.

Though the majority of town lies west of the Tweed River, you'll find the Pacific Hwy., the tourist office, and the **railway station** on its east bank. **Kirkland's** (☎1300 367 077) buses stop at the corner of Main and Queen St. and continue on to: Brisbane (2¼ hr., 4 per day, $22); Byron Bay (1hr., 2-4 per day, $13); Surfers Paradise (1¼ hr., 1-2 per day, $16). Northbound **Greyhound Pioneer** and **McCafferty's buses** stop at the Stafford St. BP station; southbound buses stop outside the tourist info center. In **Budd Park,** at the corner of the Pacific Hwy. and Alma St., is the **Tourist Information Centre,** in the **World Heritage Rainforest Centre.** (☎6672 1340; www.tactic.com.au. Open M-Sa 9am-4:30pm, Su 9:30am-4pm.) To find the town center, cross the Tweed River on the **Alma St.** bridge. Alma St. crosses Commercial Rd. and becomes **Wollumbin St.** A 24hr. Coles **supermarket** is in the Sunnyside Shopping Center at the end of the block. Parallel to Wollumbin St. one block north is **Main St.** (also called Murwillumbah St.), along which are a handful of eateries.

The **Mt. Warning/Murwillumbah YHA,** 1 Tumbulgum Rd., is a well-kept, colorfully-painted lodge. From the info center, cross the Alma St. bridge, turn right on Commercial St., and follow the river less than 1km. The lodge sits on the riverbank, with a fabulous deck directly facing Mt. Warning. The YHA offers free use of inner tubes and a canoe for lazing in the river. There's also a small pontoon moored to the riverbank that sports comfy hammocks and serves as a swimming platform. (☎6672 3763. Kitchen, laundry, separate TV lounge. M, W, F trips to Mt. Warning. Bike rental available. Reception daily 8-10am and 5-10pm. Dorms $21; twins and doubles, including the "penthouse," $46.) Just past the YHA, the small but excellent **Tweed River Regional Art Gallery,** 5 Tumbulgum Rd., awards the world's biggest portraiture prize, a whopping $100,000. Past prize-winners hang proudly on the walls. (☎6670 2790; www.tweed.nsw.gov.au. Open W-Su 10am-5pm. Free.)

WHIAN WHIAN AND MULLUMBIMBY ☎02

Surrounded by Nightcap National Park, the **Whian Whian State Forest** ("WHY-an WHY-an") is another rainforest and waterfall showcase, easily accessible from Dunoon, Mullumbimby, or some of the small villages around Lismore. One of the best ways to see the park is by following the **Whian Whian Forest Drive** (30km; 2hr.). Traveling roughly east-to-west, the first highlight along the drive is the view of **Minyon Falls.** A bit further along, a short detour to the right onto **Peates Mountain Rd.** leads to **Rummery Park** (200m), a popular picnic and camping spot, and **Peates Mountain Lookout** (3.5km). The lookout is a 5-10min. walk from the road. Beyond the junction with Peates Mountain Rd., the Forest Drive continues through logged areas replanted with blackbutt trees, the **Gibbergunyah Roadside Reserve** (a 40m strip of unlogged forest on either side of the road), and the **Big Scrub Flora Reserve.** The drive ends near the **Rocky Creek Dam,** a favorite family picnic stop.

The town of **Mullumbimby** ("MUH-lum-BIM-bee"; pop. 2700) is so small it doesn't even have a tourist office. It is, however, a convenient stopping place when travelling to Whian Whian as well as the **Border Ranges National Park.** Mullumbimby has a string of motels on Dalley St. The **Mullumbimby Motel,** 121 Dalley St., is popular and nicely landscaped. (☎6684 2387. Singles $48, twins and doubles $58.) **Brunswick Valley Coaches** (☎6685 1385) runs to **Brunswick Heads** (30min., 2 per day, $4.40), the transfer point for **Kirkland's** (☎1300 367 077), serving Byron Bay (30min.; 4 per day M-F; $8). Tucked in the hills, 7km beyond Mullumbimby on Monet Dr. off Coolamon Scenic Dr., is the harmonious and tranquil **Crystal Castle.** If you ever wonder what kind of aura you are radiating, here's your chance. A photograph and interpretation of your aura costs $25. (☎6684 3111. Open daily 10am-5pm.)

MT. WARNING AND BORDER RANGES

From a distance, the stoney spire of **Mt. Warning** greatly resembles a gigantic thumb extending towards the heavens. Named by Captain Cook in 1770 in an effort to warn mariners of dangerous offshore reefs, and known to the area's Aboriginal people as "Wollumbin" (meaning "fighting chief of the mountains"), **Mt. Warning National Park** today attracts hikers and geology-enthusiasts alike. Formerly a shield volcano with twice the height, most of the ancient lava flows have eroded away leaving behind an enormous bowl-shaped landform known as a caldera—the largest in the southern hemisphere. The prominent spire in the middle of the caldera represents the volcano's erosion-resistant central chamber. The summit of Mt. Warning is the first place on the continent to greet the dawn. The climb to the peak offers a fantastic 360° view of the coast and surrounding forest. The **Summit Track** (8.8km return; 4-5hr.) is moderately strenuous. The last segment of the trail is a vertical rock scramble with a necessary chain handrail. Watching the sunrise is spectacular, especially during the dry season (June-Nov.), although you'll need a flashlight for the climb. Bring your own water and keep in mind the only toilets are at the start of the walk. To reach the Summit Track from Murwillumbah, take Kyogle Rd. 12km west, turn on Mt. Warning Rd., and go about 6km to Breakfast Creek. *Let's Go* doesn't recommend **hitchhiking,** but it is a popular way to get from town to the mountain.The nearest hostel to Mt. Warning is the **Murwillumbah YHA** (see **Murwillumbah,** p. 196). The **Mount Warning Caravan Park** also makes a great base for exploring the mountain. (☎6679 5120. TV room, pool, BBQ, and a few friendly wallabies. No kitchen. Reception daily 8am-5pm. Sites for 2 $15, powered $18; 6- to 8- person vans $33; cabins $44, with bath $66.)

If you find Mt. Warning too touristed, the gorgeous **Border Ranges National Park** is an ideal getaway. It takes some work to get there, but its seclusion rewards you with the shade of a lush canopy and a great vantage point for viewing the volcano region. Take the Kyogle Rd. west from Murwillumbah for 44km; the Barker Vale turn-off leads 15km along gravel road to the park entrance. Inside the park, the road becomes the **Tweed Range Scenic Drive** (60km; 4-5hr.). The drive exits the park at **Wiangaree,** 13km from Kyogle and 66km from Murwillumbah.

The first picnic area in the park is **Bar Mountain,** with a lovely beech glade. Less than 1km farther is the even more remarkable **Blackbutts** picnic area, with striking views of Mt. Warning and the basin. If heights don't scare you, try the **Pinnacle Lookout,** another 8km north. To reach the **Forest Tops** camping area, travel 4km past the lookout, turn left at the juntion, go another 4km, and turn left again. If you turn right instead of left at this last junction, you'll wind up at the **Brindle Creek** picnic area, the departure point for the **Brindle Creek Walk** (10km return; 3-4hr.), a track that winds among rainforests and waterfalls and ends at the **Antarctic Beech** picnic area, home to 2000-year-old trees.

SOUTH COAST

Princes Hwy., south of Sydney, is the string that binds the pearls of the South Coast. All of New South Wales' undiscovered seaside treasures—towns such as Kiama and Narooma, and natural areas such as Booderee National Park—reward those who seek them out. Exploring this coast is a refreshing escape from the hectic pace of the city and other tourist-mobbed places.

WOLLONGONG ☎02

Directly down the coastline, about 80km from Sydney, Wollongong ("WOOLEN-gong") suffers from the city-versus-town identity crisis that plagues many of Australia's mid-sized cities. New South Wales' third-largest metropolitan area (pop. 230,000), Wollongong has a city center small enough to be walkable yet urban enough to be unattractive. The easy view of Port Kembla's steel, coal, and grain plants, collectively labeled "Australia's Industry World," showcases the most concentrated industrial area in the entire country. Still, it's close enough to the peaks of the Illawarra Escarpment and the waters of the Tasman Sea to allow for adrenaline-pumping activities, and some of the best surfing is within easy reach.

TRANSPORTATION. **CityRail trains** (☎13 15 00) stop at Wollongong City Station on Station St. and continue on to: **Bomaderry,** the closest stop to Nowra, (1½hr., 4-10 per day, $11); **Kiama** (45min., 11-16 per day, $7); **Sydney** (1½hr., 12-28 per day, $16). **Buses** arrive at Wollongong City Coach Terminus (☎4226 1022), on the corner of Keira and Campbell St., and run to: **Batemans Bay** (3-3¾hr., 2-3 per day, $31); **Bermagui** (6hr., 1 per day, $43); **Melbourne** (15hr., 1 per day, $66); **Narooma** (4½-5¼hr., 2-3 per day, $42); **Sydney** (1½-2hr., 1-3 per day, $12); **Ulladulla** (2¾ hr., 2-3 per day, $24). **Murrays** runs to **Canberra** (3½hr., 1 per day, $31).

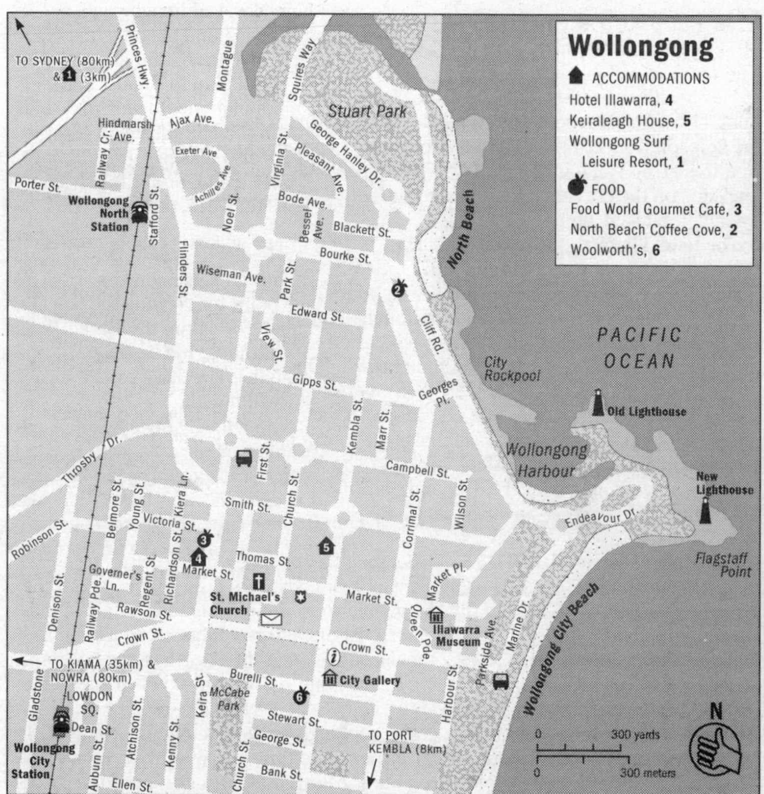

ORIENTATION AND PRACTICAL INFORMATION. The Princes Hwy. leads directly into Wollongong, becoming **Flinders St.** just north of the city center and merging into **Keira St.** downtown. The **pedestrian shopping mall** on Crown St., between Keira and Kembla St., is the city's commercial heart. **ATMs** are abundant here. **Tourism Wollongong,** 93 Crown St., is on the corner of Crown and Kembla St. (☎4227 5545 or 1800 240 737; fax 4226 6629. Open M-F 9am-5pm, Sa 9am-4pm, Su 10am-4pm). **Network Cafe,** 176 Keira St. has Internet access. (☎4228 8686. Open M-W 10am-6pm, Th 10am-10pm, F 10am-midnight, Sa 9:30am-midnight, Su 10am-5pm. $6 per 1hr.)

ACCOMODATIONS. Rooms in the **Hotel Illawarra,** on the corner of Market and Keira St., are not as swanky as the nightclub downstairs, but they're tidy and easy to crawl home to after an evening of your favorite *schooners*. Rooms get noisy on weekends due to the bar below. (☎4229 5411; fax 4229 5140. Laundry $2. Key deposit $20. Bunks $35; singles $35; doubles $70.) **Wollongong Surf Leisure Resort,** Pioneer Rd. in Fairy Meadow, is the nearest campground located 4.5km north of downtown. It is a 13min. walk from Fairy Meadow CityRail station. Inquire at Tourism Wollongong for directions. (☎4283 6999; fax 4285 1620. Laundry, pool, spa, and indoor tennis courts. Hot shower 10¢ per 5min. Key deposit $20. Bicycle hire $5 per 1hr. Reception M-Sa 8am-9pm, Su 8am-6pm. Sites for 2 $16.50, powered $20; extra person $5.50.) **Keiraleagh House,** 60 Kembla St. between Market and Smith St., is Wollongong's cheapest and friendliest option, though the house and backyard show their age. (☎4228 6765; fax 4228 6216; backpack@primus.com.au. Light breakfast included. Laundry, kitchen, TV lounge. Key deposit $10. Bunk rooms $17; singles $25; doubles $45.)

FOOD AND NIGHTLIFE. The restaurants lining Keira St., north of Market St., cover an astonishing variety of Asian cuisines with main dishes from $9-12. The most affordable and always packed **Food World Gourmet Cafe,** 148 Keira St., serves healthy and tasty Chinese dishes from $6-9. (☎4225 9655. Open Su-W 11am-8pm, Th-Sa 11:30am-9pm.) For a picnic lunch at North Beach, stop in at nearby **Coffee Cove,** on Bourke St. half a block from the ocean, and pick up a sandwich ($3-6) or a fresh fruit salad for $3. (☎4229 7876. Open daily 7am-4pm.) **Woolworth's supermarket** is on the corner of Kembla and Burelli St. (☎4228 8066. Open M-Sa 7:30am-midnight, Su 8am-10pm.)

The **Hotel Illawara** (see **Accommodations,** p. 199) draws a 20-something crowd in the early evening for cocktails and conversation. On weekends, DJs rule the dance-floor spinning music into the wee hours. (F-Sa cover $5; back room after 1am $10. Open 24hr., except Su-M midnight-11am.) Another favorite night spot, the **Bourbon Street Night Club,** 150 Kiera St., often has hundreds of party-goers lined up as early as 8pm, eager to join the in-crowd. (Open W-Sa 8pm-3am.) The **Glasshouse Tavern,** 90 Crown St. (☎4226 4305), between Kembla and Corrimal St., has recently changed into more of a tavern than a dance club, though good times still abound. Its late-night cafe is a quieter place to catch up with friends. At the alternative, student-dominated, **Oxford Tavern,** 47 Crown St., up-and-coming rock bands take the stage Wednesday, Friday, and Saturday night. (☎4228 3892. Open Su-Tu, Th 10am-11pm and W, F-Sa 10am-3am.)

SIGHTS AND ACTIVITIES. Wollongong Harbour is by far the city's best feature. The small cove, created using convict labor, shelters both sailboats and the local fishing fleet. The old lighthouse, visible from the beach, adds an air of old-time charm absent from the city's center. Visitors and residents enjoy a beautiful walking and cycling path following the harbour's edge. Just north of the harbour, surfers wait for waves at North Beach. If you want to break into the surfing scene or just refine your technique, Pines Surfriders School can help. (☎0500 824 860. Adults $38.50 per hr.; students $33; group booking, 3-person minimum, each $22.)

The **Wollongong City Gallery,** on the corner of Kembla and Burelli St., creatively displays a fabulous collection of regional, Aboriginal, and contemporary art. (☎4228 7500. Open Tu-F 10am-5pm, Sa-Su noon-4pm. Free.) **Hangdog Climbing Gym,** 130 Auburn St., offers both outdoor rock-climbing courses and 100 different indoor climbs on 40 ropes. (☎4225 8369. Open M-F 10am-9pm, Sa-Su 9am-6pm. Entry $14, harness included.)

If you're keen on exploring the heavy industry of Port Kembla, 2hr. educational tours are available at **Australia's Industry World,** Springhill Rd., Coniston. (☎4275 7023; fax 4275 7204; www.aiw.org.au. W and F 9:30am. Bookings necessary. Adults $16, family $55.) South of Port Kembla, **Lake Illawarra** draws crowds from Wollongong when the weather is good. CityRail **trains** run to Port Kembla station, located just a short walk from the lake. (10 min., 18-31 per day, $2-3.)

DAYTRIPS FROM WOLLONGONG. The winding Bulli Pass road twists inland to the Southern Fwy., 12km north of Wollongong, and leads to a magnificent panoramic view of the area. Down at sea level, Wollongong's biggest attractions await at Bulli Point (also know as Sandion Point Headland), Headland, and farther north, Austinmer Beach. Beach bums flock to Bulli or Thirroul for some of the area's best surfing. (CityRail runs from Wollongong, $2.) English writer D.H. Lawrence resided in Thirroul, between Bulli and Austinmer, for several months in 1922, and described the area in his novel *Kangaroo*. The home is privately owned and inaccessible to the public, but the beach is open for strolling and literary speculation. North of Bulli Pass, Lawrence Hargrave Dr. winds along the coast providing tantalizing glimpses of the shore below, before reaching the lookout at Bald Hill, north of Stanwell Park, perhaps the best view on this stretch of coast. It was here that Lawrence Hargrave contributed to the development of aviation by experimenting with box kites. Today, the hill continues its service as an aeronautical jumping-off point for skilled hang gliders.

The **Illawarra Escarpment** defines Wollongong's inland border. The nearest peak, **Mt. Keira,** is a short drive from town on Mt. Keira Rd. Take the #39 bus to get within 8km of Mt. Keira's peak. Bushwalking trails lead to a fantastic view from the top. In the southern suburb of Berkely, on the north shore of Lake Illawarra, **Nan Tien Temple,** the largest Buddhist Temple in the Southern Hemisphere, towers above the horizon and welcomes visitors. (☎4272 0600. Open Tu-Su 9am-5pm. Donation for entry to museum and offerings. Wheelchair accessible.) **Rutty's bus** #34 goes from the bus terminal on Marine Dr. to the temple ($3.20). The **Cockatoo Run,** a scenic mountain railway, stops at Wollongong City Station and offers day-long excursions that climb over the escarpment into the highlands and back. (☎1300 653 801. Operates W and Su most of the year. $40; children $30; family $110.)

KIAMA ☎02

Under the right conditions, when the wind is high and the waves surge from the southeast, water washing into a sea cave in Kiama ("KAI-amma") is forced noisily upward through a hole in the rocks to heights of 20-35m. Reminding visitors of a whale spouting, the oceanic "geyser" attracts onlookers from miles around. Stand well back from **Kiama's Blowhole** as a surprising blast of water could potentially knock the overzealous into the turbulent surf below the craggy cliffs. Appropriately, the word *Kiama* means "sound of the sea." Even if the wind and waves don't comply, Kiama and the surrounding area make for a worthwile coastal stop. Situated 40km south of Wollongong via the Princes Hwy., Kiama and the nearby beaches at Gerringong and Gerroa lie within a reasonable daytrip of Sydney.

TRANSPORTATION. From the **CityRail** station, on Bong Bong St. just west of Blowhole Point, **trains** (☎13 15 00) run to: Bomaderry/Nowra (30min., 10-15 per day, $4); Sydney (2hr., 12-16 per day, $13); Wollongong (45min., 13-17 per day, $5). From the Bombo Railway Station, **Premier Motor Service** (☎13 34 10) goes to: Batemans Bay (2½-3¼hr., 2-3 per day, $31); Bega (5-5½hr., 2-3 per day, $46); Bermagui (5¼hr., 1 per day, $43); Melbourne (15hr., 1 per day, $66); Narooma (4-4¼hr., 2-3 per day, $42); Nowra (40min., 2-3 per day, $13); Sydney (2½hr., 2-3 per day, $18); Ulladulla (2¼hr., 2-3 per day, $13); Wollongong (35min., 2-3 per day, $12).

PRACTICAL INFORMATION. Dotted with trees, historic buildings, and takeaways, Manning St. is the main street in town. The center of tourist life is **Blowhole Point,** down Terralong St., towards the coast. The **Visitors Centre** is on Blowhole Pt. (☎4232 3322, toll free ☎1300 654 262; fax 4226 3260. Open daily 9am-5pm.) **Internet** access is available in the Kiama Library, 7 Railway Pde. (☎4233 1133. Open M, W, Th, F 9:30am-5:30pm, Tu 9:30am-8:00pm, Sa 9:30am-2pm. $3.30 per 1hr.)

ACCOMMODATIONS AND FOOD. The **Kiama Backpackers Hostel,** 31 Bong Bong St., a few steps downhill from the CityRail Station, feels a bit like a university dormitory but manages to preserve the backpackers spirit. (☎/fax 4233 1881. TV, kitchen. Internet $5 per hr. Key deposit $10. Free use of bikes, fishing reels, and surfboards. Dorms $16; singles $21, F-Sa $23; twins and doubles $37, F-Sa $42.) Behind the Visitors Centre on Blowhole Point, the **Blowhole Point Holiday Park** reveals picturesque views of the harbour. (☎4232 2707; fax 4232 4290. Sites for 2 $20-23, peak season $25-30; simple cabins $71-76/$102.) Twelve kilometers south of Kiama, in the peaceful town of Gerringong, the **Nestor House YHA,** 28 Fern St., welcomes offers respite from the hustle and bustle of urban life. From the train station, follow the station access road away from the platform, and turn left at the first intersection. Then, follow the YHA signs for 1.5km. A short walk from beautiful Werri Beach, this collection of simple and clean rooms sits immediately behind the local Uniting Church. (☎/fax 4234 1249. Reception 4-9pm. Dorms $19.)

For a bite to eat with a view of the ocean, locals recommend the fish'n'chips ($6.50) at the **Kiama Harbour Takeaway,** located below the Blowhole Point Holiday Park, in the beige building nearest the mainland. (☎4232 1138. Open daily 10:30am-6:30pm, later during summer.) The **Coffee Table Bookshop,** 2/3 Railway Pde., serves up delicious breakfasts and an assortment of gourmet sandwiches for $7-10. (☎4233 1060. Open M-Sa 9am-5pm, Su 10am-4pm.)

SIGHTS AND ACTIVITIES. Every visitor to Kiama should give the **Blowhole** a chance to do its trick. It's an impressive show. At **Marsden Head,** at the end of Tingira Crescent, near the Endeavour Lookout, the **Little Blowhole** erupts more regularly than its highly celebrated larger sibling. It's worth the extra trip if "big brother" proves to be a disappointment. For swimming, check out either the **natural rock pool** on the northern side of Blowhole Point or the deeper rock pool, north of Kiama Harbour at Pheasant Point. To the north of Pheasant Point, experienced **surfers** brave the riptides at **Bombo Beach.** Slightly north of Bombo Beach, just around the next headland, sightseers will discover the striking rock formation known as **Cathedral Rock.** Surfers refer to this same area as the **Boneyard,** but despite the menacing nickname, it's a popular spot for catching waves. Don't be fooled, though—it's still no place for neophytes. To the south of Blowhole Point, surfers and swimmers frequent the patrolled **Surf Beach**. The next stop on a surfer's tour of the Kiama area lies 8km south at **Werri Beach** in Gerringong. For those who get tired of just idly gazing out across the ocean, Kiama Charter Service (☎4237 8496), Kiama Harbour Game and Reef Fishing Charter (☎4232 1725), and Signa Charter can send you out on the deep sea for some **sport fishing.** (☎4233 1020. 7hr. $65-70, including bait and gear.)

The **Saddleback Mountain Lookout** offers a vista that can extend from Wollongong to Jervis Bay on clear days. Follow Manning St. south until it bends inland, then proceed straight onto Saddleback Mountain Rd. at the edge of town. The steep path up the mountain is signposted from Saddleback Mountain Rd. Farther west, the **Barren Grounds Nature Reserve** is accessible by Jamberoo Mountain Rd. by way of Tourist Dr. 9 through Jamberoo. The reserve contains several moderate **hiking trails** from 2km to 19km. The area is known as the home to over 160 species of birds. Turning off Jamberoo Mountain Rd. leads nature-lovers to **Minnamurra Rainforest** (☎4236 0469) in **Budderoo National Park,** a rare tract of subtropical rainforest with two delightful bushwalks originating from the Visitors Centre. The 1.6km. **Rainforest Walk** (45min.), a looping, boardwalked track, tours the unusual plant life in the park. The longer, steeper, 2.6km walk to the **Minnamurra Falls** (2hr.) branches off from the Rainforest Walk and rewards hikers with, strangely enough, waterfalls. (Open daily 9am-5pm. Rainforest access until 3pm, waterfalls access until 4pm. $10 per car.)

NOWRA AND BOMADERRY ☎02

Every sign in the Shoalhaven directs you to Nowra. Smaller sibling Bomaderry lies immediately north, across the Shoalhaven River. Together, they are the population centers of the shire. Rock climbers come from all over for what many claim to be the best sport climbing in Australia.

TRANSPORTATION AND PRACTICAL INFORMATION. CityRail's last stop is in Bomaderry on Railway St. **Trains** (☎13 15 00) run to: Kiama (30min., 12-15 per day, $4); Sydney (2¾hr., 12-15 per day, $15); Wollongong (1½-2hr., 9 per day, $8.50). **Premier Motor Service** (☎13 34 10) runs **buses** to: Batemans Bay (1¾hr., 2-3 per day, $20); Bega (4¼hr., 2-3 per day, $35); Bermagui (4hr., 1 per day, $32); Kiama (40min., 2-3 per day, $12); Melbourne (13½hr., 1 per day, $63); Narooma (2¾hr., 2-3 per day, $30); Sydney (3-3¼hr., 2-3 per day, $18); Ulladulla (1hr., 2-3 per day, $13); Wollongong (1¼hr., 2-3 per day, $12). **Kennedy's Coaches** (☎4421 7596, 0411 232 101) services Fitzroy Falls (1hr., 1 per day, $10) and Kangaroo Valley (30min.-1hr., 2 per day, $7).

The new **Shoalhaven Visitors Centre** lies on the corner of Princes Hwy. and Pleasant Way, south of the bridge to Nowra, on the left. (☎4421 0778 or 1800 024 261; www.shoalhaven.nsw.gov.au. Open daily 9am-4:30pm.) The **National Parks and Wildlife Service,** 55 Graham St. Nowra, has info on parks in the area. (☎4423 2170; fax 4423 3122. Open M-F 8:30am-5pm). Flatearth Internet Cafe, Level 1 Nowra Mall, has **Internet access.** (☎4423 7771. Open 9am-5pm M-F. $6 per hr.)

ACCOMMODATIONS. Due to its proximity to Berry, Kangaroo Valley, and Jervis Bay, many choose to stay in Nowra when exploring the area. The historic, 1920s bungalow-style **M&M's Guesthouse,** 1A Scenic Dr., on the right just across the bridge into Nowra, transports lodgers back to a bygone era. (☎4422 8006; fax 4422 8007. Breakfast included. Laundry, TV, pool table. No kitchen. Dorms $35; doubles $50; groups of 4, $25 each.) For cheap and scenic camping sites, head for **Nowra Animal Park.** From Bomaderry, take a right on Illaroo Rd., just before the grey metal bridge to Nowra; follow McMahon's Rd. left from the roundabout, and take a left on Rockhill Rd. The owner can also direct travelers to local rock climbing sites. (☎/fax 4421 3949. Toilets and hot showers. Reception 8am-5pm. Sites $5.50 per person; powered sites $2 extra.) Separate from the campground is a rehabilitation center for wombats, koalas, and other animals, open to the public for $7.

ROCK CLIMBING AND OTHER ACTIVITIES. Most area climbers recommend **Thompson's Point,** on the southern shore of the Shoalhaven river and find PC, Grotto, and South Central to be challenging. Climbers must supply their own gear. **The Gym** (☎4421 0587), at the corner of McMahons and Illaroo Rd., offers indoor rock climbing. On weekends, the more adventurous can try flying sail planes at the Nowra Naval Air Station, Braidwood Rd. Contact the **Royal Australian Naval Gliding Association** (☎4421 1333). **Skydive Nowra** (☎0500 885 556) offers tandem skydives ($360) and freefall courses ($380). Book in advance.

NEAR COWRA

KANGAROO VALLEY

The fading Caltex petrol station in the middle of Kangaroo Valley's main thoroughfare is probably the last vestige of the original one-marsupial town. Today, Kangaroo Valley (pop. 280) has gone decidedly arts-and-crafts touristy, but the area is still remote, pleasant, and rightfully popular for B&B and camping retreats.

At the northwest end of town, the **Hampden Bridge** spans the Kangaroo River. Built in 1898, it is Australia's oldest suspension bridge. Located on the north side of the bridge, **Kangaroo Valley Safaris,** 2210 Moss Vale Rd., organizes canoe camping trips. (☎4465 1502. Open daily 8am-5pm. Rents canoes for $48 per day, kayaks for $30-55 per day, and tents $25 per day.) **Kennedy's Coaches** (☎4421 7596; 0411 232 101) goes to the park from the Kangaroo Valley post office enroute to Moss Vale (25min., 1 per day, $4); a bus does not return until the following morning.

The **Bendeela Picnic Area,** 7km outside town provides plenty of **free** camping, toilets, BBQ, and water. Reach it by driving north out of town and turning left on Bendeela Rd., following signs to the entrance. For campers looking for showers or a roof, there is **Glenmack Caravan Park** on the main road just east of town. (☎4465 1372. Reception 8am-6pm. Sites $8 per person; cabins for 2 $50-72.) At one of **Morton National Park's** entrances, 20km from Kangaroo Valley on Moss Vale Rd., **Fitzroy Falls** greets visitors. Run by the National Park Service, the **Fitzroy Falls Visitor Centre** has maps for bushwalking trails. (☎4887 7270. Open daily 9am-5:30pm.) By **car,** avoid the steep, winding Kangaroo Valley Rd. leading west from Berry and opt for the Moss Vale Rd., which leads northwest from Bomaderry, off the Princes Hwy. Check road conditions ahead of time for both routes. **Prior's** (☎1800 816 234) runs **buses** M-Sa to: Batemans Bay (2¼hr., $18); Narooma (4hr., $24); Parramatta (3hr., $19); Sydney (3½hr., $19); Ulladulla (1½hr., $13).

JERVIS BAY

Almost entirely enclosed by its northern headland, Jervis Bay is a serene body of water surrounded by the strikingly white beaches of Beecroft Peninsula. It teems with marine life and contains underwater rock formations that make for arguably the **best diving** in Australia outside of the Great Barrier Reef. To take in the bay, stop at any of the towns—Huskisson is the largest—along the shore and wander down to the water's edge even if you decide not to don a mask and fins.

Underwater, Jervis Bay is an exquisite natural meeting place for tropical marine life from the north as well as a variety of southern species not found in the Great

Barrier Reef. Divers rave about the massive archways and rock shelves; spots such as Cathedral Cave and Smuggler's Cave are perfect for **cave diving.** The Arch, Stoney Creek Reef, and the Ten Fathom Dropoff are known for **deep diving.** Steamers Beach Seal Colony is great for **open-water dives** and **snorkeling.** Despite chillier waters, visibility is best from April to early August. **Jervis Bay Sea Sports,** 47 Owen St., takes certified divers out for a day. Ask about the 4-day PADI course ($385) if you're not certified and wish to be. (☎4441 5012. Two dives $70; equipment rental $45 extra.) **Pro-Dive,** 64 Owen St. (☎4441 5255), offers similar services.

For those content to enjoy marine life from a drier vantage point, **Dolphin Watch Cruises,** 50 Owen St. (☎1800 246 010) and **Dolphin Explorer Cruises,** 62 Owen St. (☎1800 444 330), offer 3hr. whale watching trips ($40) during peak whale migrations (June-Nov.) and 2½hr. dolphin cruises ($25).

Fishermen work for their dinner at nearby Currambene Creek, and **Husky Hire-a-Boat** rents and delivers boats. (☎4441 6200. Open dawn-4:30pm. $40 per 2hr.; $55 per 3hr.; $50 deposit required.) If you just want to paddle around, **Jervis Bay Kayak Company** allows you to stretch your arms in sleek style. (☎4443 3858. Rentals $50 per day; half-day guided tours $77; full-day tours $110.) Tour cost includes transport, snack, and park user fees.

HUSKISSON. Twenty-four kilometers southeast of Nowra along the coast of Jervis Bay lies Huskisson. **Nowra Coaches** (☎4423 5244) goes to Huskisson (35min., 2-4 per day, $4-8) and Jervis Bay Village in **Booderee National Park** (1¼hr.; Tu and Fr; $9). For tourist info, visit the **Huskisson Trading Post** on the corner of Tomerong and Dent St. (☎4441 5241. Open daily 9am-5pm.) **Leisure Haven Caravan Park,** 1.5km outside of town along Currambene Creek on Woollamia Rd., provides sites with free hot showers and laundry. (☎4441 5046. Key deposit $20. Reception 8am-6pm. Sites for 2 $16-20, powered $18-28.) **The Husky Pub,** on Owen St. overlooking the Bay, is the town's pubstay. The rooms are basic. (☎4441 5001; fax 4441 6754. Bar and reception M-F 11am-10pm, Sa-Su 11am-11pm. Singles $30, doubles $55.)

BOODEREE NATIONAL PARK. On the southern end of the bay, **Booderee National Park,** which is under joint management with the Aboriginal people, has two **camping** areas: **Greenpatch** on Jervis Bay (hot showers, toilets, water; $14-17.50 per site) and **Cave Beach** near Wreck Bay to the south (cold showers, no electricity; $9-11 per site). The **Visitors Centre,** just beyond the park entry gates, accepts campsite bookings and can provide maps to the various hiking tracks. (☎4443 0977. Open daily 9am-4pm. $10 per car per day.) The **Botanic Gardens** are inside the park as well. (☎4442 1122. Open M-F 8am-4pm, Sa-Su 10am-5pm. No additional charge.) The beach at **Green Patch,** often a good place to see rainbow lorikeets and eastern gray kangaroos, is a popular **snorkeling** spot. **Murrays Beach,** staggering in its beauty, is a popular place for **swimming.**

ULLADULLA ☎02

Moving south through the Shoalhaven, the next major service center is Ulladulla ("uh-luh-DUH-luh"). The town was called Ulladulla back in 1828 because it was thought to sound like its original Aboriginal name, "Woolahderrah." Today, nearly 12,000 people call Ulladulla home. Off the coast, between Jervis Bay and Ulladulla Harbour, divers will find a fair number of shipwrecks to explore, including the famous 1870 wreck of the Walter Hood.

Premier Motor Service (☎13 34 10) **buses** stop at the Marlin Hotel (southbound) and the Traveland Travel Agency (northbound) on the way to: Batemans Bay (45min., 2-3 per day, $10); Bermagui (3hr., 1 per day, $24); Kiama (2hr., 2-3 per day, $13); Melbourne (12½hr., 1 per day, $63); Narooma (1¾hr., 2-3 per day, $19); Nowra (1hr., 2-3 per day, $13); Sydney (5hr., 2-3 per day, $26); Wollongong (3hr., 2-3 per day, $24). The **Visitors Centre** is on the Princes Hwy., in the Civic Centre (☎4455 1269. Open M-F 10am-5pm, Sa-Su 9am-5pm.) **Internet** is available there and at the adjacent **library.** (Open M-F 10am-7pm, Sa 9am-noon. $1.10 per 30min.)

The local hostel, **South Coast Backpackers,** 63 Princes Hwy. between Narrawallee and North St., is a small, friendly operation with laundry, TV, kitchen, beautiful hardwood floors, bright wall colors, off-street parking, and a great sundeck and hammock area. (☎4454 0500. Key deposit $10. Dorms $20; twins and doubles $42. VIP.) At the end of South St., **Ulladulla Tourist Park** has camping space, though the site area slopes slightly. (☎1300 733 021; fax 4455 2457. Showers, toilets, laundry, BBQs, pool, and access to a secluded beach. Reception 8am-9pm. Sites $8-14 per person; powered $11-16; cabins $44-89, peak season $100-165.)

The people at the **Ulladulla Dive Shop,** 10 Wason St., can give seasoned advice on **diving** in the area or they can take you out themselves. (☎4455 5303. Open Nov.-Apr. daily 7am-7pm; May-Oct. M-F 9am-5pm, Sa-Su 8am-5pm. Equipment $55 per day; intro dives $85.) Bushwalkers generally stop in Ulladulla on the way out to the **Pigeon House Walk.** Turn off the Princes Hwy. onto Wheelbarrow Rd. 3km south of Burrill Lake. The trailhead is located 27km farther at a picnic area. The walk, which involves some ladder climbing, is a strenuous 5km affair—allow 3hr., but the view at the top is a knock-out. The **Coomee Nulunga Cultural Track,** on Deering St. across from the Lighthouse Oval car park, combines natural beauty and Aboriginal history. The peaceful, coastal 1-2hr. walk is dotted with hand-painted garawanga daran (dream posts) that depict local plant and wildlife. Take the guided walk ($7.50), arranged by the local **Aboriginal Land Council** (☎4455 5883), to get the most out of your visit. Nearby **Lakes Burrill** and **Conjola** have nice **swimming** beaches, and **Mollymook Beach,** just north of town, is good for **surfing.** Dolphins have been known to ride the waves along with surfers.

NEW SOUTH WALES

MURRAMARANG NATIONAL PARK

With expansive views of the Pacific and tame kangaroos all over, the coastline in the Murramarang National Park makes a great detour from the highway and a superb spot to check out the 'roo beach bums who lazily congregate on **Pebbly Beach.** The shore itself is at the far end of a 15min. drive over mostly unpaved roads. A number of worthy campgrounds and caravan parks are speckled throughout the park, but tent **camping** sites are cheapest at the Pebbly Beach camping area. (☎4478 6006. Sites $11 per person includes park user fee.) At the southernmost point in the Shoalhaven half of Murramarang National Park, **Durras North** looks onto Durras Lake and a beautiful windswept ocean beach. **Durras Lake North Caravan Park,** approximately 16km south of Durras North by car, the first of several caravan parks at the end of Durras Rd., is clean and quite a kangaroo gathering place. (☎4478 6072. Reception 8:30am-9:30pm. Powered sites $16; caravan for 2 $35, each extra adult $10.)

SOUTH FROM BATEMANS BAY

Batemans Bay, 10km south of Durras Lake on the Princes Hwy., and just inland from Murramarang National Park, has some spectacular diving spots. On the way out of Shoalhaven and into the Eurobodalla shire, the larger towns center around industries like fishing and dairy farming and are less touristed. Smaller, quieter villages hidden in the countryside, such as Mogo and Central Tilba, are the most compelling reasons to follow the Princes Hwy. along the coast.

BATEMANS BAY ☎02

The town begins where the Kings Hwy. from Canberra (152km inland) meets the Princes Hwy. at the coast. Situated south of the junction at the mouth of the Clyde River, upmarket tourists visit Batemans Bay on holiday from the capital. Nevertheless, the town is suitable for budget travelers. The azure waters of Batemans and Malua Bay are so beautiful, they tempt the most hydrophobic.

TRANSPORTATION AND PRACTICAL INFORMATION. **Buses** leave from outside the Promenade Plaza on Orient St. **Premier Motor Service** (☎ 13 34 10) goes to: Bega (2½-3½hr., 2-3 per day, $21); Bermagui (2½hr., 1 per day, $17); Kiama (3hr., 2-3 per day, $20); Melbourne (12hr., 1 per day, $56); Narooma (1-1¾hr., 2-3 per day, $13); Nowra (2hr., 2-3 per day, $20); Sydney (5½hr., 2-3 per day, $33); Ulladulla (45min., 2-3 per day, $10); Wollongong (3½hr., 2-3 per day, $31). **Murrays**

TELLING A FURPHY In Australia, the expression "telling a Furphy" describes a story that has been exaggerated as it passes by word of mouth to become a tall tale. It is much like the children's game "Telephone" where the message at the end is usually very different from the original. The term dates back to the 1850s gold rush during which Furphy's Farm Water Cart was used to deliver water to farmers and miners. The carts usually brought the news along with their water delivery. By the end of the day the news was usually sensational. The story of Doc Ladmore's record find—an eight-pound hunk of the purest gold around—is the perfect example of a Furphy. While the measurement may have been true, the story alleges that he stumbled upon the nugget in his front yard. If you ask one of the locals in Mogo to direct you to the famous patch of grass, you'll be sent to a massive mine in the ground.

(☎13 22 57) goes to Canberra (2½hr., 1-2 per day, $24). The staff at **Batemans Bay Tourist Information Centre,** on Princes Hwy. at Beach Rd., gives good advice on the local beaches. (☎4472 6900; fax 4472 8822. Open daily 9am-5pm.)

ACCOMMODATIONS AND FOOD. The **Batemans Bay Backpackers (YHA),** inside a caravan park on the corner of Old Princes Hwy. and South St., off the new Princes Hwy., offers tidy facilities as well as daily trips to Pebbly Beach ($11) and Mogo ($5). The hostel rents bikes ($12 per day) and lends boogie boards. (☎4472 4972; fax 4472 4045. Laundry, kitchen, TV, pool. Call to arrange pickup from the bus stop in town. Dorms $19; twins and doubles $42; non-YHA $3.50 extra.) Small and friendly, **Beach Road Backpackers,** 92 Beach Rd., is an easy walk from town. (☎4472 3644; fax 4472 7208. Trips to Pebbly beach $15. TV, kitchen, free pickup and drop off at bus stop. Bike hire $7.50 per day. Dorms $19; doubles $40. VIP.)

SIGHTS AND ACTIVITIES. The 1880 wreck of the Lady Darling is considered the **best wreck dive** around. Other dives include the Burrawarra Wall, the Maze, and Montague Island, perfect for all levels and for snorkeling too. The **Dive Shop,** 33 Orient St., can be your link to the water world. (☎4472 9930. Single boat dive $38; double $66; full equipment hire $50-88.) The **Opal and Shell Museum,** 142 Beach Rd., owned and operated by a veteran opal miner, hosts an extensive display of opals and shells from Australia and around the world. (☎4472 7248. Open daily 10am-6pm, except Tu. Closed in August. Adults $1.50, family $3.) Buy or rent a surfboard at **Kaffir Surfboards.** (☎4472 3933. Single fin $25; 3-fin thrusters $35.)

To indulge in a spot of bushwalking, join the locals from **Batemans Bay Bushwalkers** ($2). Contact Len Tompkins (☎4472 3113) or ask the tourist office for a schedule. Traveling south on the coastal road, Malua Bay and Broulee have good **surf. U-Canoe** has canoe and kayak hire. (☎4474 3348. 1 person $35 per day, 2 people $45, 3 people $55; includes pickup and delivery.)

Further inland lies **Mogo,** 10km south of Batemans Bay, an 1850s gold rush town currently riding the craft craze. Take the tour at **Old Mogo Town,** James St. off Princes Hwy., a reconstructed 19th-century mining town, and experience the gold rush yourself. Where else can you go panning for gold, see Tasmanian death masks, and even get hitched? (☎4474 2123. Open daily 10am-4pm. $12, includes tea and biscuit, gold panning, and tour; 10% off with *Let's Go* guide.) **Mogo Zoo,** 222 Tomakin Rd., off Princes Hwy in Mogo, houses endangered animals like snow leopards, red pandas, and pythons. (☎4474 4930. Open daily 9am-5pm. $12.)

NAROOMA ☎02

With several parks and other protected natural areas nearby, the town of Narooma is a good basecamp for outdoor exploration. For instance, only 7km offshore, fur seals, crested terns, and some 10,000 pairs of fairy penguins inhabit the **Montague Island Nature Reserve.** However, since only 70 people are allowed to visit each day, the reserve is only accessible through official NPWS-sanctioned tours (3½hr.; 1-2 per day; adults $66, families $198). Book through NPWS or the Visitors Centre (see below). **Eurobodalla National Park** (☎4476 2888), a popular 2WD-accessible destination, protects a 30km. stretch of coastline, from Moruya Head in the north to Tilba Tilba Lake in the south. Featuring, among other things, lush spotted gum forest, this park has one campground at Congo ($5 per person), near the town of **Moruya.**

On Wagonga Head, off Bar Rock Rd., ocean waves and coastal winds have left one rock, known as **Australia Rock,** with a hole, amazingly enough, in the shape of Australia, minus a bit of the Cape York peninsula. The resemblance is uncanny. **Glasshouse Rocks,** another locally famous rock formation, lies at the south end of Narooma Beach. Depending on the winds, **surfers** will head out to Handkerchief, Bar, Carter's, or Josh's Beaches.

Premier Motor Service (☎13 34 10) stops in Narooma and goes to: Batemans Bay (1hr., 2-3 per day, $13); Bega (1½hr., 2-3 per day, $14); Bermagui (40min., 1 per day, $8); Kiama (4-5hr., 2-3 per day, $30); Melbourne (11hr., 1 per day, $50); Nowra (3-3½hr., 2-3 per day, $30); Sydney (6½-7½hr., 2-3 per day, $44); Ulladulla (2-2½hr., 2-3 per day, $19); Wollongong (4¾-5½hr., 2-3 per day, $42). **Murrays** (☎13 22 51) runs from Narooma Plaza to Canberra (4½hr., 1-2 per day, $36).

The **Narooma Visitors Centre,** on Princes Hwy., handles advance bookings for some campgrounds and tours. (☎4476 2881; fax 4476 1690. Open daily 9am-5pm.) The **National Parks and Wildlife Service** office is a block away on the corner of Princes Hwy. and Field St. (☎4476 2888; fax 4476 2757. Open M-F 9am-5pm.)

The **Bluewater Lodge (YHA),** 8 Princes Hwy., is clean and comfortable. The extremely knowledgeable and gracious owner has lived in the area his whole life. (☎4476 4440; naroomayha@narooma.com. Breakfast included. Laundry, kitchen, TV. Bikes and canoes $5 per day. Internet $5 per 1hr. Reception 8am-noon and 3-9pm. Dorms $19; non-YHA $22.) **Easts Riverside Holiday Park,** off the Princes Hwy. just after the bridge into town (☎4476 2046; fax 4476 3746. Reception 8am-6pm. Sites for $18-25, powered $20-30.) **Narooma Golf Club and Surfbeach Resort,** on Ballingala St. (☎4476 2275; fax 4476 2336), has fine views of the water and good facilities. (☎4476 2275; fax 4476 2336. Open 8:30am-5pm, later in summer. Sites for 2 $18-25, powered $22-30.)

CENTRAL TILBA AND TILBA TILBA ☎02

You know you're in a small town when you ask about the population, and in response a local begins counting as people pass. **Central Tilba** (pop. 70) was 80 years old and fading into the hillsides in 1974 when the National Trust took the whole village under its wing and began a process of partial restoration. Central Tilba sits 15km south of Narooma off Princes Hwy. Blink and you'll miss **Tilba Tilba** (pop. 30), a few kilometers away, literally a bend in the road. **Pam's Village Store** (☎/fax 4473 7311) marks the center of local life in Central Tilba and the start of a moderate, 11km (4hr.) walking track up **Gulaga (Mt. Dromedary).** If you're lucky, you'll catch sight of a superb lyrebird (also known as a native pheasant) with its unbelievably elegant tail feathers. The **Umbarra Aboriginal Cultural Centre,** located a few kilometers down the road to Bermagui from the Princes Hwy., features a small museum, an educational video, and activities like spear throwing and Dreaming story. The centre also provides a 4-5hr. guided tour ($50), departing at 9:30am, to secluded areas of the mountain, including explanations of local Koori culture. Call ahead for bookings. (☎4473 7232. Open M-F 9am-5pm, Sa-Su 9am-4pm. Activities Sept.-June daily 9:30am-3pm, June-Aug. M-F 9:30am-3pm; $7 per person.) Nearby, at the lower end of Tilba Tilba, in a jarring juxtaposition of cultural traditions, is the 3½ acre **Foxglove Spire Gardens,** a tranquil, English-style arrangement of flowers, shrubs, and trees. (☎4473 7375. Open daily 9am-5pm. $5.50.)

Premier Motor Services offers limited bus service to Tilba. (☎13 34 10. Call for timetable and fare.) The **Bates General Store,** just off the highway on Bates St., provides tourist info and can help you find local accommodations. (☎/fax 4473 7290. Open M-Sa 8am-5pm, Su 8:30am-5pm.) Further down Bates St. stands the award-winning **ABC Cheese Company.** Their delicious sun-dried tomato cheese won 2nd place at the 1998 World Championship Cheese Contest held in Wisconsin, USA. (☎4473 7387. Open daily 9am-5pm. Free samples.) To compliment your feasting, stop at the **Tilba Valley Winery,** 5km north of Tilba off Princes Hwy. for a ploughman's lunch ($10) or a free wine tasting. (☎4473 7308. Open M-Sa 10am-5pm, Su

THE MEELKMAN If you've been to the dairy section of an Australian grocery store, you've heard of Bega ("BEE-ga"). In the heart of dairy country, about 50km south of Cobargo, where the road from Bermagui rejoins the Princes Hwy., Bega is the town that produces Bega cheese. Several bus companies pass through Bega, making stops opposite the volunteer **Information Centre,** 91 Gipps St. (☎/fax 6492 2045. Open M-F 9am-5pm.) The Bega Co-Operative Creamery Company has been making cheese here since 1899, and the **Bega Cheese Factory and Heritage Centre,** off the Princes Hwy. northwest of town across the bridge, offers visitors a behind-glass view of the cheese-making machinery and cheese tastings. (☎6491 7777. Open daily 9am-5pm. Free entry.) At **Grenvillea Estate Winery,** a family estate on Buckajo Rd., you can sample the featured vintages until you feel courageous enough to wander up to the barn to watch the mechanized, vacuum-driven milking of the cows. (☎6492 3006. Open daily 9am-5pm. Cow milking 3pm. Free.) Twenty-two kilometers northeast of Bega, **Mimosa Rocks National Park** is 5000 hectares of protected coastal land and lagoon. The park has short walking tracks, picnic areas, and **camping** available at Aragunnu, Picnic Point, Middle Beach (trail access only), and Gillards Beach. (Narooma NPWS ☎4476 2888. Sites for 2 $6; collector at site. No drinking water at sites.)

11am-5pm. Picnic and BBQ facilities.) The only pub in Central Tilba, **The Dromedary Hotel,** on Bates St., has reasonably priced rooms with a TV lounge and laundry. Space is limited so call ahead. (☎4473 7223; fax 4473 7238. Singles $30; doubles $60.) **Farmstays** and **B&Bs** make up the rest of accommodations in the area. Though more expensive, the **Wirrina B&B,** on Blacksmith's Ln. next to ABC Cheese, pampers guests with fresh flowers, a clawfoot bathtub, gourmet breakfasts, and a stunning veranda view of the countryside. (☎/fax 4473 7279. Singles $75; doubles $95.)

SNOWY MOUNTAINS

In winter, the Snowies, Australia's highest mountains, are a wonderland for skiers and snowboarders, while the warmer months bring swarms of hikers. Kosciuszko National Park, home of Mt. Kosciuszko (2228m), Australia's highest peak, covers most of the area. The Snowy Mountains Hwy. and the Alpine Way ramble past the boulder-strewn countryside where the skiing industry is king, though compared to other mountain ranges around the world, the runs are shorter and less challenging.

Conditions on each mountain can vary wildly. Thredbo is a black diamond paradise. Perisher, despite its ominous-sounding name, will delight those willing to wander aimlessly over the Australian slopes. Snowbunnies will find unbeatable deals and easier slopes at Mt. Selwyn.

KOSCIUSZKO NATIONAL PARK

Named after the heroic Polish nationalist, Thadeus Kosciuszko ("Kaw-zee-AW-sko"), Kosciuszko National Park contains Australia's **tallest mountains,** several stunning **wilderness areas,** and all NSW **ski fields.** While the park may forever be associated with ski resorts, outdoor enthusiasts are beginning to appreciate the year-round beauty of **Yarrongobilly Caves** and the summer, wildflower-strewn alpine walks that lead to the rooftop of Australia. Numerous **hiking tracks** and **camping** areas are available throughout the park. There's an entry fee for Kosciuszko ($15 per car per 24hr.), though motorists passing through non-stop are exempt. During ski season, snow chains must be carried. The Shell stations along the Alpine Way, at Khancoban and Jindabyne, allow one-way chain rental and drop-off ($20). Trail maps, camping information, guide books, and park stickers can be obtained at the Snowy Region Visitors Centre in Jindabyne (see p. 209), the entrance station on the way to Perisher Blue (stickers only), or the **NPWS office** at the corner of Scott and Mitchell Ave. in Khancoban. (☎6076 9373. Open daily 8:30am-noon and 1-4pm.)

KOSCIUSZKO NATIONAL PARK AT A GLANCE	
AREA: 6494km²	**THE SLOPES:** Thredbo, Perisher Blue, and Mount Selwyn.
HEIGHTS: Mount Kosciusko: 2229m. Mount Selwyn: 1520m.	**GATEWAYS:** Cooma and Jindabyne.
FEATURES: Australia's tallest mountain for which the park is named, the Snowy River, Yarrongobilly Caves, Mount Selwyn.	**CAMPING:** Free, although a few privately-run sites charge various fees.
HIGHLIGHTS: Skiing some of Australia's best slopes; camping, and hiking during the warmer months.	**FEES:** $15 per day vehicle fee, though motorists passing through non-stop are exempt.

COOMA ☎02

Often considered the capital of the Snowies, Cooma links together Canberra, other coastal towns, and the mountains. Because of its peripheral location on the eastern edge of the Snowy Mountains region, Cooma is far enough away from the price-inflated snowfields to permit bargain accommodations and reasonable rental rates during the ski season—for those willing to commute.

TRANSPORTATION AND PRACTICAL INFORMATION. The main drag through Cooma is **Sharp St.**, flanked on either side by Massie St. and Commissioner St. **Buses** come through frequently during ski season, but service is severely curtailed the rest of the year. **Countrylink** (☎13 22 32) and **Greyhound Pioneer** (☎13 20 30) run to: Canberra (1½-2hr., 3-5 per day, $30); Jindabyne (50min., 3-4 per day, $20); Sydney (6hr., 3-4 per day, $66); Thredbo (1¾hr., 3-4 per day, $26). **Snowliner Coaches,** 120 Sharp St. (☎6452 1584), services Jindabyne (50min., 2 per day, $12) on school days only. See **Harvey World Travel,** 114 Sharp St., opposite the visitors center, for reservations. (☎6452 4677. Open M-F 9am-5:30pm, Sa 9am-noon.)

The **Cooma Visitors Centre,** 119 Sharp St., is in the center of town. (☎6450 1742; fax 6450 1798; cvc@snowy.net.au. Open daily mid-Oct.-May 9am-5pm; June-mid-Oct. 7am-5pm.) **Internet access** can be found at the **Visitors Centre** (see above; $5 per 30min.) or at **Percy's News Agency,** 158 Sharp St. (☎6452 2880. Open M-F 6am-6:30pm, Sa 6am-3pm, Su 6am-2pm. 30min. $3.)

ACCOMMODATIONS AND FOOD. The **Cooma Bunkhouse Backpackers,** 30 Soho St., on the corner of Commissioner St., has great year-round hostel accommodation. Every room is equipped with a private bathroom, kitchen, and TV. (☎/fax 6452 2983. Reception 7am-10pm. Heated dorms $25; singles in adjacent motel $33; doubles $45; family $60. VIP.) The re-named **Alpine Guest House** (formerly the Family Motel), 32 Massie St., offers friendly service and ski season steals. (☎6452 1414; fax 6452 5536; family@snowy.net.au. Internet $5 per hr. Reception 8am-10pm. Rooms with bath $19 per person.) On Sharp St., 1.6km west of the town center, **Snowtels Caravan Park,** provides a kitchen, laundry, and BBQ. (☎6452 1828; fax 6452 7192. Sites $15, powered $20; caravans $33-$44; cabins with bath $45-90.)

The brand-new **Organic Vibes,** 82A Sharp St., is a beacon of hope to road-weary travelers surviving on fish'n'chips and meat pies. The mother and daughter team sells organic produce, gluten and wheat-free pastas, and fresh juices. Be sure to try the dried mangoes or one of the home-made lunch specials. (☎/fax 6452 6566. Open M-F 9am-5:30pm, Sa 9am-noon.) **Mystic Phoenix,** 142 Sharp St. has inexpensive veggie and vegan entrees from $3-7. (☎6452 2499. Open M-W 7:30am-6pm, Th 7:30am-8pm, F 7:30am-9pm, Sa 7:30-3pm.) Delicious Lebanese *shish tawook* (chicken kebab) is at **Rose's Restaurant,** in Nassar's Four Mile Roadhouse, 6km west of Cooma on the Snowy Mountain Hwy. (☎6452 4512. Open until 9pm most days.) Stock up on **groceries** at Woolworth's, located on the corner of Vale and Massie St., as well as 228 Sharp St. (Open daily 7am-10pm.)

SKIING. Because the ski resorts of Thredbo, Perisher, and Mt. Selwyn lie within a 100km radius of Cooma, **rental shops** clutter the streets. Flashing signs advertising "round-the-clock" rentals are reminiscent of a casino town that depends on gambling for its livelihood. Rates are comparable to those closer to the mountains. Skis, poles, and boot rental runs about $30 the first day and $10-15 per day thereafter, and about $45 for the first day of a snowboard and boot rental. The visitors center has brochures with 10%-15% discount coupons. (See p. 212.)

SIGHTS. The **Snowy Mountains Hydro-Electric Scheme,** now **Snowy Hydro Limited,** is one of the world's greatest engineering feats of its kind, and has its administrative center in Cooma. The Scheme diverts snowmelt waters from the east of the Great Dividing Range to the west, where it irrigates the fertile but dry plains. Simultaneously, huge quantities of hydro-electric power can be generated at peak times if necessary. Carried out between 1949 and 1974, the Scheme included the construction of 16 large dams and is responsible for nearly every body of standing water in the Snowy Mountains. As with most man-made achievements, advances come at a cost. The system has put Australia's legendary **Snowy River** in serious jeopardy. With only 1% of its original volume, the mighty river has been reduced to a trickle. There are huge campaigns currently lobbying the government to restore the parched waterway to at least 30% of its original flow to keep it from running dry. The Visitor Centre is just north of town on the Monaro Hwy. (☎6453 2004; www.snowyhydro.com.au. Open M-F 8am-5pm, Sa-Su 8am-1pm. Free.)

JINDABYNE ☎02

On the scenic shores of man-made **Lake Jindabyne,** the town of Jindabyne is a logical stopping point for those who can't afford to sleep in chalets at the foot of the Thredbo chairlifts. During ski season, "Jindy" plays its part as a satellite ski town, with the corresponding services and high seasonal prices. After the ski season, bushwalkers and backpackers stop through while exploring the vast Kosciuszko National Park. The original town was flooded as part of the hydro-electric scheme (see p. 210), when the water level is low, visitors can swim to the old church.

TRANSPORTATION AND PRACTICAL INFORMATION. During the ski season, Jindabyne Coaches (☎6457 2117 or 0411 020 680) runs shuttles to the Skitube. From there it's possible to catch a train up to Perisher Blue ($13 return). Transport into Jindabyne from the northeast passes through Cooma (see p. 209). Greyhound Pioneer (☎13 20 30) operates limited service in the winter and Mushwandry Bus Service (☎6452 3802 or 1800 636 525) offers limited service in the summer. The **Snowy Region Visitors Centre,** on the Alpine Way at the east end of town, combines a NPWS office and a tourist center. (☎6450 5600; fax 6456 1249. Road conditions ☎6456 1553, snow reports 6450 5553. Open daily 8:30am-5pm.)

To get to the slopes from Jindabyne, follow the **Alpine Way.** It leads to the Skitube station (23km from town), that services **Perisher Blue** resorts, and then continues on to **Thredbo** (30km further). From Thredbo, the Alpine Way extends its sometimes treacherous path through the mountains to **Khancoban,** a full-service town on the western edge of **Kosciuszko National Park.** Cars traveling to Khancoban are required to carry **snow chains.** The **Shell station** at the Perisher/Thredbo junction, outside of Jindabyne, rents snow chains for $20, and has a drop-off program with the Shell station in Khancoban.

Jindabyne is a goldmine for **job-seekers** arriving early in the winter season, providing wages from $13 and a fun working community. For job inquiries, check the employment bulletin at the IGA supermarket. Encounters with true ski bums, who alternate seasons between the northern and southern hemispheres, are not infrequent; many have been living for years in a perpetual state of winter.

Internet access is at **Leading Edge Video,** Lakeview Plaza on Snowy River Ave. (☎6456 2665. Open Su-Th 10am-9pm, F-Sa 10am-9:30pm. $10 per hr.) or **Snowy**

Mountain Backpackers (see below; $10 per hr.). The **Jindabyne NETcafe** is in the left end of the Town Centre plaza. (☎6457 1722. Open June-Oct. daily 10am-9pm; Nov.-May M-F 10am-5pm. $12 per hr.)

ACCOMMODATIONS. Even in the height of ski madness, affordable accommodation in Jindabyne does exist, but availability may be a problem. Be sure to book well in advance. Snowy Mountain Backpackers, 7 Gippsland St., behind the Nuggets Crossing shopping plaza, combines an unbeatable location with new facilities, laundry, Internet, and kitchen. (☎6456 1500 or 1800 333 468; backpackers@snowy.net.au. Key deposit $5. Reception June-Oct. daily 8am-8pm; Nov.-May 9am-6pm. Bunks $20-30; doubles $50-120. Wheelchair accessible. VIP.) The **Jindy Inn,** 18 Clyde St., has private rooms with bathrooms, TV, and fridge. There's a well-equipped kitchen downstairs and a nice adjoining restaurant. During ski season the inn functions more as a B&B. Bookings are essential and single-night stays rare. (☎6456 1957; fax 6456 2057. Breakfast included. 24hr. reception. Bunks from $20 per person; singles $22; June-Oct. prices rise. **Jindabyne Holiday Park** is in the center of town on a choice stretch of Lake Jindabyne shoreline. (☎6456 2249; fax 6456 2302. Laundry, camp kitchen. Key deposit $20. Ski-and-boot rental $30; snowboard-and-boot $40. Sites for 2 $15, powered $18. Extra person $5. On-site caravans Oct.-June from $30, July-Aug. from $65.) The **Station Resort** is in a self-contained village located 6km south of Jindabyne, at the corner of Barry Way and Dalgety Rd. Popular destination for the cheapest lodging and the least hassle. Bars, restaurants, and bus services are all on the premises. Rooms become increasingly cheaper with a maximum of six people sharing the motel-style rooms. (☎6456 2895 or 1300 369 9090. Laundry, TV, Internet, small fridge, bath, no kitchen. Reception 24hr. During ski season, F-Sa 2-nights $421 for 2, includes 3 meals, ski hire, and 2 days skiing; 5-night Su-Th $505, includes 5 days of skiing.)

NEW SOUTH WALES

FOOD AND NIGHTLIFE. Cheap food is hard to come by in this alpine town that seems compelled to match the sky-high resort prices. Preparing a flavorful range of traditional and multi-cultural dishes, the newly-opened **Mad Az Cafe,** 8 Gippsland St., adjacent to the Snowy Mountain Backpackers, has fair prices and a relaxed, funky interior. (☎6456 1503. Open June-Oct. daily 8am-10:30pm; Nov.-May Su-W 8am-6pm, Th-Sa 8am-10:30pm. Meals $7-22.) **Wrap A Go-Go,** Lakeview Plaza on Snowy River Ave., warms up visitors with spicy Mexican meals and tasty wraps. (☎6457 1887. Open daily noon-9pm; summer closed M. Mains $10-14.) An IGA **supermarket** is in the Nuggets Crossing shopping center.

In the evenings, people relax at the **Lake Jindabyne Hotel,** on Kosciuszko Rd. in the center of town. Entertainment ranges from relaxed drinking to concerts by top-notch rock bands. On Wednesday night, LJH is the first stop for many locals. (☎6456 2203. Open M-Sa 10am-late, Su 10am-midnight. Schooners of VB $3.50.)

ACTIVITIES. The experts at **Wilderness Sports,** in Nuggets Crossing, organize cross-country skiing, back-country snowboarding, and alpine touring adventures from $100 per day in the Thredbo area. (☎6456 2966; www.backcountry.com.au. Open daily June-Oct. 8am-8pm, Nov.-May 9am-6pm.) Their **Backcountry Centre** is at the top of the Kosciuszko Express chairlift at Thredbo. (☎6457 6955. Open daily 9am-4pm. Snowshoe hire $30 per day; half-day abseiling $69; full-day Mt. Kosciuszko tour $110, with lunch.) **Paddy Pallin,** next to the Shell station at the Perisher/Thredbo junction, offers similar services as well as mountaineering courses and mountain bike and kayak rental. (☎6456 2922 or 1800 623 459. Introduction to mountaineering 4-days $680; mountain bikes $15 per hr., $48 full-day; kayaks $33 half-day, $48 full-day.) **Upper Murray White Water Rafting** organizes thrill-ride rafting down the Murray River. (☎6452 7998 or 1800 677 179. Sept.-Apr. full-day $140.)

THE MOUNTAINS

THE SKI SLOPES	PERISHER BLUE	SELWYN SNOWFIELDS	THREDBO
THE LOW-DOWN	Australia's premier resort with Perisher Valley, Blue Cow, Smiggens, and Guthega alpine villages.	Lacks the difficulty of other mountains in the park, but has 45 hectares of marked trails.	Home to Australia's longest slopes. Outdoor activities abound year-round.
FEATURES	7 peaks, 51 lifts, and over 95 trails.	Beginner runs and a few expert; draws families.	12 lifts and a majority of intermediate runs.
PRICES	$75 per day, under 14 $41; night skiing (Tu and Sa) $15/$10. 2hr. group lessons $38.	$33 per half-day, under 15 $19; full-day $46/ $23. Cross-country skiing is free.	$75 per day, under 15 $41; night skiing (Tu and Sa) is free with valid lift pass. 2hr. group lessons $40.
GATEWAYS AND ACCOMMODATIONS	Cooma and Jindabyne.	Cooma and Jindabyne.	Cooma, Jindabyne, and Thredbo Resort.

PERISHER BLUE

New South Wales's premier ski resort, Perisher Blue (☎1300 655 822; www.perisherblue.com.au), is actually four resorts in one. One lift ticket buys entry to the interconnected slopes leading down to the **Perisher Valley, Blue Cow, Smiggins,** and **Guthega** alpine villages. Surprisingly, access between the seven peaks is relatively easy. Situated above the natural snow line, with a slightly higher elevation than its competitors, Perisher offers some of the best snow around. **Zali's Run,** named after the Australian World Cup skier, is a popular intermediate slope. **Kamikaze** and **Double Trouble** will really put snowbunnies to the test.

All **lift tickets** include unlimited use of the Perisher-Blue Cow segment of the Skitube. Purchase tickets at Bullocks Flat or at the **Perisher Blue Jindabyne Ticket Office** in the Nuggets Crossing shopping center. (☎6456 1659. Open daily 7am-7pm.) **Murrays** (☎13 22 51) and **Lever Coachlines** (☎6262 3266) offer daytrip skiing and snowboarding packages from Canberra from $100. (Includes return bus, park entry, lift ticket, and equipment hire.)

Perisher is not a full-service village and has no budget accommodation or overnight parking. On busy days, the Perisher Valley day lot fills up quickly and is often entirely inaccessible due to road conditions, but the **Skitube** (☎6456 2010) is an all-weather train that makes the 8km journey into the Perisher Valley Alpine Village from **Bullocks Flat,** located along the Alpine Way. You can either start your adventures in the Village, or keep riding the skitube halfway up the mountain to the Blue Cow terminal. There, chairlifts take more advanced skiers and boarders to the blue and black runs atop **Guthega Peak** and **Mt. Blue Cow.** To get to the Skitube station at Bullocks Flat, take **Jindabyne Coaches** (☎6457 2117), which runs shuttles from **Jindabyne** (4 per day, $13 return). By **car,** drive along the Alpine Way from Jindabyne until you reach the station; there's plenty of parking. Once at the Perisher Station, follow your nose to the Bullocks Flat platform, on the lower level, to **Lil' Orbits Donuts,** where you can grab 12 cinnamon mini-donuts for $3. If donuts aren't enough, **Gingers** (☎6457 5558), on the main floor, serves up hot cheese and tomato melts ($3.20) and veggie patties ($5).

THREDBO

Thredbo was recently awarded the NSW Tourist Destination of the Decade. Though it does not have the abundance of slopes that Perisher has, it does sport the longest—5.9km. Many skiers and boarders eat, sleep, and party in nearby Cooma and Jindabyne, though an extensive resort lies at the base of its slopes.

TRANSPORTATION AND PRACTICAL INFORMATION. Thredbo-bound hitchhikers can be found standing at the roundabout just outside of Jindabyne. *Let's Go* does not recommend hitchhiking. From June to early October, **Clipper Tours** (☎9585 9400) runs **shuttles** between Thredbo and Jindabyne (4-5 per day, $25 return). **Greyhound Pioneer** (☎13 20 30) also runs June-Oct. from Cooma (1½hr., 2-3 per day, $22). During the summer, **Mushwandry Bus Services** (☎6452 3802 or 1800 636 525) runs from Cooma through Jindabyne to Thredbo. Bookings are essential; seating is limited. **Thredbo Information Centre** is at 6 Friday Dr. (☎6459 4194 or 1800 020 589; www.thredbo.com.au. Open ski season daily 8am-6pm; summer 9am-4pm.) **SKE Cafe,** in Kellar Plaza, connects skiers to the **Internet**. (☎6457 7333. $10 per hr.) Charges for ski and snowboard rentals at **Thredbo Sports,** at the base of the Kosciuszko Express chairlift, and at the east end of the village near the Friday Flat lift, are $10-20 higher than in Jindabyne or Cooma. (☎6459 4176. Skis, stocks, and boots $49; snowboard and boots, $57.)

ACCOMMODATIONS AND FOOD. With its nearest competitors charging hundreds of dollars more per night, the **Thredbo YHA Lodge,** 8 Jack Adams Path, is the best deal in town. Though less luxurious than its neighbors, the lodge has a comfortable chalet feel with ample common space, a big kitchen, and an Internet kiosk. Five minutes of morning chores are expected of guests to keep costs down. All arrangements for two-, five-, and seven-night stays must be made in advance to Thredbo Bookings, YHA NSW, GPO Box 5276, Sydney NSW 2001; or in person to the YHA Membership & Travel Centre, 422 Kent St., Sydney (☎9261 1111; fax 9261 1969; travel@yhansw.org.au). For a more impromptu visit, contact the manager at the lodge, Dean Bighall, about 1-night openings from cancellations. (☎6457 6376; fax 6457 6043; thredbo@yhansw.org.au. Reception 7-10am and 4:30-9pm. Single-night, if available, June $25; July-Oct. $46-56; Oct.-May $20. During ski season, 2-night F-Sa $112; 5-night Su-Th $231; 7-night Su-Sa $343.) Other lodges can be booked through **Thredbo Resort Centre.** (☎1800 020 589. Open daily Mar.-Aug. 9am-6pm; Sept.-Feb. 9am-5pm, though hours can vary.)

Eating on the mountain can quickly burn big holes in the pockets of your snowpants. *Let's Go* does not recommend burning big holes in the pockets of your snowpants. **Alfresco Pizzeria,** just below the Thredbo Alpine Hotel, serves pastas and pizza that will satisfy the biggest appetite. (☎6457 6327. Open daily noon-9pm. Large pies from $14). **Altitude 1380,** on Mowamba Pl., has lunches ranging from $7-11. Their coffee is famous. (☎6457 6190. Open 10am-3:30pm, until 5pm for coffee, and 6:30-9pm.) After a tiring day on the slopes, collapse at the **Schuss Ski Club,** in Palmers Lodge (☎6457 6297), for an afternoon of live entertainment. Later in the evening, after everyone catches their second wind, the Schuss bar can be so much fun that many skiers don't make it to the slopes the next day.

ACTIVITIES. For the use of hikers and ganderers, the **Kosciuszko Express** chairlift runs year-round. (All-day summer pass $21. Operates daily 8:30am-4:30pm.) Several excellent walks depart from the top of the mountain for sweeping views of Kosciuszko National Park. From the top of the chairlift, the **Mt. Kosciuszko Walk** (12km return) leads to the mountain's summit, though the easy walk to Kosciuszko Lookout (4km return) also provides sweeping views. Another option is the **Dead Horse Gap & Thredbo River Track** (10km), which ends in the Village. Free maps of all trails are available throughout Thredbo. **Snowy Mountains Climbing School** (☎0417 422 198) offers year-round diversions such as mountaineering, snowcamping, climbing, and abseiling (4 abseils $49). For more info, inquiries can also be made at **Thredbo Sports** (see p. 212).

MOUNT SELWYN

Along the Snowy Mountains Hwy., halfway between Cooma and Tumut, the **Selwyn Snowfields** offers beginner and budget skiing. (☎6454 9488; www.selwynsnow.com.au.). Primarily a family resort, Selwyn has a small number of trails, minimal amenities, and only a couple advanced runs. Elevation at the base is 1492m and the summit is only 122m higher. When natural snowfall is scarce, Mt. Selwyn relies on its 80% snowmaking coverage. **Lift tickets** are inexpensive. (Half-day valid 8:30am-12:45pm or 12:45-4:30pm $33, under 15 $19; full-day $46/23. Over 65 and under 6 are free.) Forty-five hectares of marked trails and no lift fee make **cross-country skiing** another attractive option.

Equipment hire for alpine or cross-country skis and snowboards is pretty reasonable on the mountain. (Skis half-day $22, full-day $29; snowboards $35, $44.) **Toboggans** are available for $8 per day (toboggan lift ticket $15 per 20 rides) with a 1½hr. **lift and lesson** package. ($68, under 15 $45; includes full-day lift ticket.) There is no accommodation at Mt. Selwyn, but Cooma (see p. 209) is an hour commute.

NEAR THE PARK: YARRANGOBILLY CAVES

Hidden near a valley floor in the beautiful northern scrub wilderness of the Kosciuszko National Park, the Yarrangobilly Caves attract curious visitors and hardcore spelunkers alike. The **Yarrangobilly River,** located off the Snowy Mountains Hwy. 77km south of Tumut and 109km northwest of Cooma, runs through a 12km long stretch of limestone, riddled with caves. The caves are a well-signposted 6.5km from the highway, downhill on a windy unsealed road. There is a $3 per car site fee for the Yarrangobilly Caves precinct. Only **South Glory Cave** is open for a **self-guided tour** (45min.), but you'll need a token from the visitor center to explore beyond the unusual "glory arch" entrance. (Open daily 9:30am-4:30pm. $9; children $5.50; family $22.) The remaining caves are open to **guided tours.** (Daily at 11am, 1, and 3pm; other times with advance scheduling. $11; children $8; family $33.) Tours last between 1-1½ hours. **Jillabenan Cave** is the only wheelchair-accessible cave. Its array of stalactite and stalagmite formations amid crystal-lined nooks is spectacular. **Jersey Cave** and **North Glory Cave** contain equally stellar sights. After wandering around underground, head to the surface and try a **short bushwalk** on a maintained trail, or take a load off in the 27°C **thermal pools** near the river, a 700m steep downhill walk from the carpark (free). The **NPWS Visitor Centre** at the site is an essential first stop. (☎6454 9597; fax 6454 9598. Open daily 9am-5pm).

HUME CORRIDOR ☎02

As the major route between Australia's two largest cities, the Hume Hwy. makes it possible for travelers to drive the 872km between Sydney and Melbourne in only nine to ten hours. Though the drive can easily become tedious, detours along stretches of the Old Hume Highway to various historic villages tucked away in the countryside can periodically relieve the monotony. For towns along the Hume Corridor in Victoria, see **Hume Corridor,** p. 580.

SYDNEY TO GOULBURN

As the state capital recedes in the rearview mirror, the Hume Hwy. leads into an area known as the "Cow Pastures," a name given for its use as grazing land when Sydney was just a colony. Now divided into the towns of **Liverpool, Campbelltown, Camden,** and **Narellan,** this area was the site of some of Australia's first colonial land grants, including the 1805 grant to John Macarthur, whose wildly successful investment in wool and wine is popularly considered the starting point of the nation's wealth. Spread across 410 hectares at **Mt. Annan Botanic Garden,** off the F5 freeway between Camden and Campbelltown along Tourist Drive 18, the native-plant collection of **Sydney's Royal Botanic Garden** includes flora from throughout Australia. Outside the visitors center you can look at a young specimen of the recently-discovered rare **Wollemi pine.** (☎4648 2477. Open daily Apr.-Sept. 10am-4pm; Oct.-Mar. 10am-6pm. Admission $4.40.) For a day of Australiana, **Gledswood,** on Camden Valley Way closer to Camden, entertains visitors with historic house tours and farm activities, including sheep-shearing, cow milking, and boomerang-throwing. (☎9606 5111. Open daily 10am-4pm. Tours 11am and 3:15pm, $6.50. Shearing show noon; $4, family $25.)

There's a **caravan park,** with basic facilities in the town of **Mittagong,** 40min. south of Campbelltown. (☎4871 1574. Sites for 2 $15, powered $18.) The **Lion Rampant Hotel,** is a clean and comfy pub stay. (☎4871 1090. Singles $30; doubles $40.) **Bowral,** 3km farther south, was the childhood home of legendary cricketer **Sir Donald Bradman.** The **Bradman Museum,** on Saint Jude St., documents the history of Australian cricket. (☎4862 1247. Open daily 10am-5pm. $8.)

Thirty kilometers south of Mittagong on the Hume Hwy. take the Bundanoon/Exeter exit to find Morton National Park. Several walking trails in the thick forest stretch towards the sandstone cliffs at the parks interior. At the park's edge, the town of **Bundanoon** has one lovely accommodation—the **Bundanoon YHA Hostel,** a spacious, old, Edwardian guesthouse on Railway Ave., on the north end of town. The hostel has friendly managers, a full kitchen, and a comfortable lounge. (☎4883 6010; fax 4883 7470. Reception 8-10am and 5-8:30pm. Dorms $18; twins and doubles $44; family rooms $58. Non-YHA members $3 more.) From the hostel, a short trail (1hr.) leads to the bioluminescent bliss of the **Glow Worm Glen,** best seen at night. Trails from the glen cross into the National Park. Hiking maps available at the hostel cover the entire area. CityRail **trains,** from Sydney's Central Station, stop at Bundanoon's railway station daily ($15).

GOULBURN ☎02

Settled in the early 1830s, Goulburn (pop. 22,000) has long been a regional center, once of agriculture and the judicial system, now of enterprises like the Merino wool industry. The city still has buildings that date from the 1800s. This connection between the past and the present gives Goulburn a feeling of historical continuity unusual among the towns of New South Wales.

Goulburn is on the Hume Hwy. between Yass (87km) and Sydney (195km) and 10km east of the junction with the Federal Hwy. **Countrylink** (☎13 22 32), **Fearnes Coaches** (☎1800 029 918), **Greyhound Pioneer** (☎13 20 30), **McCafferty's** (☎13 14 99), and **Murrays** (13 22 51) service area towns and major destinations such as Sydney and Canberra. **Trains** and **buses** stop either at the Goulburn Railway Station, at the intersection of Verner and Sloane St., opposite Belmore Park on Montague St., or at the Big Merino.

The **Goulburn Visitor Information Centre,** 201 Sloane St., distributes the *Self-Guided Heritage Walking Tours* guide to the city's historic buildings. (☎4823 4492; www.goulburn.nsw.gov.au; visitor@goulburn.nsw.gov.au. Open daily 9am-5pm.) **Internet access** is **Toga Tux Computers,** 203 Auburn St. (☎4822 7777. Open M-F 9am-5pm, Sa 9am-1pm. $6 per 1hr.)

The **Goulburn Gateway Service Station** (☎4821 9811), on the corner of Common St. and the Hume Hwy., next to McDonald's, has budget accommodations. The owners converted the defunct bus depot behind their petrol station complex into a small **dormitory.** The location is unusual, but the bedroom is clean and livable. (Reception 24hr. Beds $14.50.) The smattering of eateries includes the spacious **Goulburn Deli,** 140 Auburn St. It serves up fast, tasty sandwiches from $5 and melts from $6. (☎4821 8818. Open M-F 8am-5pm, Sa 8am-2pm.)

The **Goulburn Brewery** on Bungonia Rd., southeast of the city center, is open daily for visitation, but tastings and tours (45min.) happen on Sundays (11am and 3pm), or by prior arrangement. The restaurant and small bar serve lunch, dinner, and ale. Do not ask for a beer, the brewery doesn't serve any. Be sure not to miss the upstairs exhibit on Francis Greenway (1777-1837), Australia's first "Government Architect" and designer of the brewery. (☎4821 6071. Open daily 11am-5pm or later. Tours $8; tastings $1. Admission free.) **Bungonia State Park,** 35km east of Goulburn, has plenty of natural wonders and camping ($5 per night). Experienced cavers can put their skills to the test while **adventure caving** in some of the deepest caves in Australia. (☎4844 4277. Car entry fee $6 per day.)

ALBURY ☎02

Spanning the Murray River, which marks the border between New South Wales and Victoria, the Albury-Wodonga metropolitan area (pop. 90,000) belongs to both states. Right on the Hume Hwy., it breaks the transit between Sydney and Melbourne and provides an excellent base for daytrips to nearby wineries, alpine retreats, and the neighboring Riverina. The preponderance of quality budget accommodations and cheap eats makes Albury the most backpacker-friendly pitstop along the Hume. Many linger a while, especially during the summer months when the river is high and ripe for outdoor excursions.

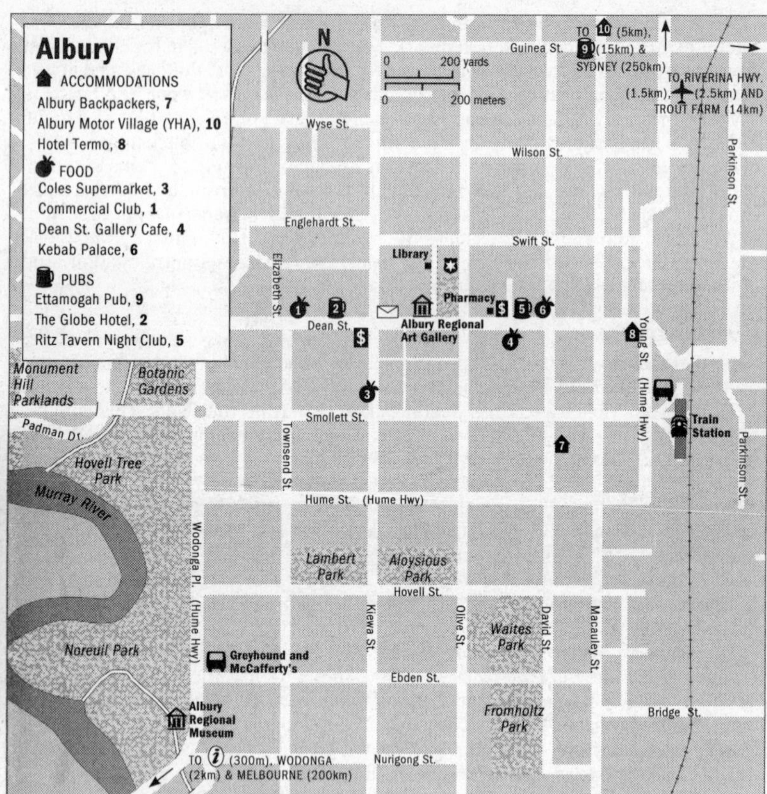

TRANSPORTATION

The impressive Albury railway station is at the eastern end of Dean St. Inside, the **Countrylink Travel Centre** books Countrylink and V/Line transport. (☎6041 9555. Open M-F 9am-5pm.) **Countrylink** (☎13 22 32) trains run to: Goulburn (5hr., 2 per day, $66); Melbourne (3hr., 2 per day, $56.10); Sydney (7½hr., 2 per day, $85.80); Wagga Wagga (1¼hr., 2 per day, $22); Wangaratta (45min., 2 per day, $12); Yass (4hr., 2 per day, $47.30). **V/Line** (☎13 61 96) services destinations in Victoria far more frequently and cheaper; they go to: Echuca (3-4hr., 1-2 per day, $37.70); Melbourne (3-3½hr., 4-6 per day, $40); Mildura (10hr.; M, W, Th, Sa mornings; $61); Wangaratta (45min., 4-6 per day, $10.80); Rutherglen (40min; M, W, Th, Sa mornings; $6.70); Swan Hill (5½-7hr., 1-2 per day, $45.50). **McCafferty's** and **Greyhound** (☎13 20 30) now run jointly from the corner of Ebden St. and Wodonga Pl. to: Adelaide (16½hr., 3 per day, $95); Brisbane (26½hr., 5 per day, $135); Canberra (5hr., 4 per day, $33); Melbourne (4½hr., 5 per day, $39); Sydney (9½hr., 5 per day, $46); Wangaratta (45min., 2 per day, $23).

ORIENTATION AND PRACTICAL INFORMATION

The **Hume Hwy.** (Hwy. 31) from Sydney enters Albury from the northeast, runs through town, and then turns sharply west to bypass Wodonga. The **Murray Valley Hwy.** (Hwy. 16) runs along the Victorian side and enters Wodonga from the southeast, running through town before uniting with the Hume Hwy. Along the river on the New South Wales side, the **Riverina Hwy.** (Hwy. 58) runs west to Corowa. Albury's main street, **Dean St.,** runs east-west from the railroad tracks and is crossed by (the easternmost) **Young St.,** Macauley, David, Olive, Kiewa, and Townsend St. **Smollett St.** runs parallel to Dean St. one block south.

Tourist Office: Gateway Visitors Information Centre (☎6041 3875 or 1800 800 743; fax 6021 0322), in the Gateway Village between Albury and Wodonga just south of the Murray on the Hume Hwy. A bus goes back and forth between Albury (Dean St.) and Wodonga (High St.), passing by the info centre every 30min. Open daily 9am-5pm. 24hr. computer information station outside.

Currency Exchange: Several banks and 24hr. **ATMs** line Dean St. Bank hours M-Th 9:30am-4pm and F 9:30am-5pm.

Police: 539-543 Olive St. (☎6023 9299), near Swift St.

Post Office: (☎6051 3633), at the corner of Dean and Kiewa St. Open M-F 9am-5pm. Poste Restante services available. **Postal Code:** 2640.

Internet Access: Albury City Library (☎6041 6633), in the city block behind the Regional Art Centre, has 2 terminals. Free for research, but email costs $2.75 per 30min. Book ahead. Open M-F 9am-7pm, Sa 9am-2pm.

ACCOMMODATIONS

Albury Backpackers, 452 David St. (☎6041 1822; www.alburybackpackers.com.au). Just south of Smollett St. Recently renovated, this comfy hostel has laundry facilities, kitchen, dining hut, and mosaic-tiled hall bath. Laid-back travelers bond through town pub crawls, varied regional daytrips, and renowned overnight canoe trips run by the affable owner (1-day Murray trip $26, 2-day $59). Linens included. Internet $5 per hr. Check-out 11am. Dorms $16; twins and doubles $36. Wheelchair accessible. VIP.

Albury Motor Village (YHA), 372 Wagga Rd., Hume Hwy (☎6040 2999; albury@motor-village.com.au). 5km north of the city center in Lavington just beyond Kaylock Rd. Greyhound and McCafferty's will drop off here; $10 cab ride from train station. Quiet, clean, and family-friendly. Pool, kitchenette, TV lounge, parking, laundry. Internet $2 per 20min. Key deposit $10. Reception 7:30am-10:30pm. Book ahead in summer. Dorms $17; powered sites for 2 $16; self-contained cabins for 2 $60-120 (all but deluxe cabins are BYO linens). AmEx/DC/MC/V.

Hotel Termo, 47 Dean St. (☎6041 3544), 1 block from the train station. Basic pub accommodations upstairs and popular nightspot. Linens and breakfast included. Singles and doubles $16.50 per person; with bath $22 per person. AmEx/DC/MC/V.

FOOD AND NIGHTLIFE

Pizza competition is fierce in Albury. The **Commercial Club,** 618 Dean St., serves a $10.10 all-you-can-eat lunch and dinner with a rich variety of vegetables, meat dishes, and surprisingly gourmet desserts. It's the best deal in town, and there's a casino downstairs, (☎6021 1133. Open daily for lunch noon-2pm, dinner 6-9pm. Sign in at the lobby desk.) **Dean St. Gallery Cafe,** 6/499 Dean St., serves popular breakfasts ($5-10), pastas and foccacias ($6-8), and some of the best coffee in town. Art-lined seating area can get crowded, especially in the mornings. (☎6041 1099. Open M-F 8am-5pm, Sa 8am-3pm.) Kebabs, souvlakis, and falafels come in all sizes ($4-7) at the **Kebab Palace,** 1/462 Dean St. (☎6041 6220. Open Su-W 10:30am-10pm, Th-Sa 10:30am-5am.) **Coles supermarket** is in the West End Plaza on Kiewa St. between Dean and Smollett St. (Open M-Sa 7am-midnight, Su 7am-8pm.)

Bars and clubs in Albury move in and out of popularity. The current hotspot is **The Globe Hotel,** just a few doors down from the Commercial Club on Dean St. Monday "Hospitality Nights" feature live cover bands and Happy Hour prices, with $2 beer and $4-5 spirits. (☎6021 2622. W Uni Nights; F-Sa DJs spin. Open Su until midnight, M and W 3am, Tu and Th 1am, F-Sa 4am.) **The Ritz Tavern,** 480 Dean St., satisfies late-night partiers with DJs until dawn. (☎6041 4484. F-Sa cover upstairs $5 after midnight. Open W 7pm-1am, Th until 4am, F-Sa until 5am.)

SIGHTS AND ACTIVITIES

On Wodonga Pl. between Smollett and Dean St., the **Albury Botanic Gardens** (☎6023 8241) have diverse arboreal displays and plenty of grassy picnic space. To take in

FOLLOW THAT MOTH Occurring on November 30 in 2002, the annual **Ngan Girra festival** is a cultural celebration held in Mungabareena Reserve near Albury. The festival celebrates the traditional confluence of several local Aboriginal groups, who gathered to follow the springtime Bogong moth migration. The moths, after being smoked out and cooked, were a high-nutrient feast. The indigenous term for this particular "meeting place" is *ngan girra*, or *kamberra*, which was only altered slightly when it was used to create the name of the Australian capital city, Canberra.

a sweeping view of the region, climb to the top of the **Monument Hill Bushlands** and gaze out on Albury-Wodonga from the base of the Deco obelisk Albury War Memorial. Walk uphill from Dean St., or follow the street up and around the back of the hill. The **Albury Regional Art Gallery,** 546 Dean St., presents a changing array of contemporary art exhibitions, including a collection of works by Australian artist Russell Drysdale. (☎6023 8187. Open M-F 10:30am-5pm, Sa-Su 10:30am-4pm. Free.)

On the Riverina Hwy. 14km east of Albury, the **Hume Weir Trout Farm** raises Rainbow Trout for commercial and recreational purposes. You can pet baby trout, catch trout (rod and bait free, fish caught cost $8.50 per kg), and sample smoked trout. (☎6026 4334. Open daily 9am-5pm. $6, students $5, children $3.50.)

DAYTRIP FROM ALBURY: ETTAMOGAH PUB

Just 15km north of Albury along the Hume Hwy., the **Ettamogah Pub** explodes in goofy fun as it caters to gawking tourists and satirizes and stereotypes all things Aussie. The late cartoonist Ken Maynard had been drawing the place for the *Australia Post* for years before someone decided to actually construct it. The amusement-park-style village is composed of eye-popping, off-kilter buildings decorated with a running stream of witticisms. The centerpiece is the hilariously constructed and fully-operational Ettamogah Pub itself, capped with a vintage Fosters beer truck on the roof, a crashed airplane next door, and business-card-slathered tree-trunk columns inside. (Pub open M-Th 9:30am-9pm, F until 11pm, Sa-Su until 10pm.) Other sights include a hollowed-out tree sealed with jail bars and dubbed Lock Up, a police "office" covered in corny cop punnery, a picnic area, and an endless supply of goofy signs and sayings. The **Ettamogah Winery** (☎6026 2394) predates the pub but is now part of the complex, and it has free tastings and wine sales. Next door is a restaurant and souvenir shop. (Open daily 9am-4pm.) There's no admission to tour the site, and signs will clearly direct you from the highway.

RIVERINA

Dry, brown, and flat, much of the Riverina's terrain looks ill-suited for farming. Heavy irrigation, however, has turned the land into fertile plains. Although not a prime sightseeing destination, the Riverina does attract budget travelers seeking seasonal farm or fruit-picking work in order to save up for more exciting destinations. Two rivers supply water to the region: the Murrumbidgee, that starts as a trickle in the Snowy Mountains, and the Murray.

WAGGA WAGGA ☎02

New South Wales' largest inland city (pop. 58,000), Wagga Wagga (typically abbreviated "WAH-guh") derives its name from the local Aboriginal tribe, for whom repetition implied plurality. "Wagga" means crow. Hence "wagga wagga" means a place of many crows. Currently, Wagga Wagga is home to Charles Sturt University, and consequently thousands of university students.

Baylis St. is the town's main thoroughfare, becoming **Fitzmaurice St.** once it crosses the bridge over Wollundry Lagoon. **Countrylink** (☎13 22 32) and **Fearnes Coaches** (☎1800 029 918) operate **bus** and **train** service to Gundagai (1hr., 1 per day,

PICKING WORK. Seasonal picking jobs abound in the Riverina year-round, although December to April is the easiest time to find work. Conditions can be tough—even the basics such as water and toilets are unusual, and pay is typically based on how much you pick, not how long you work. To find out more about seasonal work, check out **Employment National** (www.employmentnational.com.au), call the **Harvest Hotline** (toll free ☎1300 720 126), or check out the "Seasonal Work" section of the **Australian Jobsearch** website (http://jobsearch.deetya.gov.au). Riverina tourist offices keep copies of the useful *Working Holidays in the Riverina*, also available online at www.riverinatourism.com.au.

$22) and Sydney (6½-7¼hr., 3 per day, $75). **Greyhound Pioneer** (☎13 20 30) runs to: Canberra (3hr., 2 per day, $29.70); Griffith (2hr., 2 per day, $30); Gundagai (1hr., 2 per day, $23); Sydney (8¼hr., 2 per day, $40). The bus stop is located at the railway station, on the south end of Station Pl.

The **Visitor Information Centre** is on Tarcutta St. (☎6926 9621; www.tourismwaggawagga.com.au. Open daily 9am-5pm.) **Civic Video,** 21 Forsyth St., provides **Internet** access. (☎6925 8222. Open M-Sa 10am-7pm, Su 10am-4pm. $2 per 15min.) **I.T.NABYTE** (see below) also has web access ($5.50. per 1hr).

For inexpensive accommodations, try the brand-new **Wagga Wagga Guesthouse** (NOMADS), 149 Gurwood St., a popular spot with seasonal workers because of its amenities: kitchen, TV, laundry, lockers, Internet, wheelchair accessibility. (☎6931 8702. Singles $20; doubles $38; weekly rates available.) Otherwise, basic **pubstays** (singles $25) line Baylis St., as do restaurants. The awesomely funky **I.T.NABYTE** (say the name slowly), at 11 Gurwood St., serves up light vegetarian lunches ($6-8.50) that can be savored while seated inside on the leopard print sofas, or outside in the sun-filled back patio. (☎6921 8866. Open M-Th 9:30am-10pm, F-Sa 9:30am-11pm, Su 10am-10pm.) There's a Coles **supermarket** (☎6921 5377) on the corner of Baylis and Forsyth St.

At the corner of Baylis and Morrow St. you'll find the new **Civic Centre,** including the **Wagga Wagga Regional Art Gallery** (featuring local and touring exhibitions), the **National Art Glass Collection,** and the **Carnegie Print Collection.** (☎6926 9660. Gallery open Tu-Sa 10am-5pm, Su noon-4pm. Glass collection open W-Su 10am-5pm.) The attractive **Botanic Gardens,** with an entrance near the intersection of Urana and Macleay St., are arranged across nine hectares. Pathways wind pleasantly among the trees. (☎6925 4065. Open daily 7:30am-dusk. Free.) The **Wiradjuri Walking Track** meanders for 30km, covering many of the city's natural highlights. The trail runs through the Botanic Gardens, along the Murrumidgee River, past Lake Albert to many panoramic views of the region.

NEW SOUTH WALES

NARRANDERA ☎02

Downtown Narrandera ("na-RAN-dra") feels refreshingly like an intimate Anytown, Australia. This low-key transportation hub (pop. 5,000) doesn't try to trip over itself to nab tourists. About halfway between Adelaide and Sydney off the Sturt Hwy., and a day's drive from Melbourne en route to Brisbane along the Newell Hwy., Narrandera provides excellent budget beds for commuters.

The main street, **East St.,** runs north-south, one block east of Cadell St. The **Tourist Information Centre** is on Cadell St. (☎6959 1766. Open daily 9am-5pm.) There is **Internet access** at the **library,** 39-51 East St. (☎6959 2128. Open M-Tu and Th-F 10am-5:30pm, W 1-5:30pm, Sa 9:30am-noon. 20min. per $1.10.) Two blocks east of East St., **Countrylink** (☎13 22 32) **buses** run from the railyway station to Griffith (1¼hr., 1 per day, $12) and Wagga Wagga (1½hr., 1-2 per day, $8). **McCafferty's** (☎13 14 99) and **Greyhound** (☎13 20 30) run at least once daily from the Mobil Roadhouse on the Sturt Hwy., Gillenbah, to: Canberra (4¾hr., $39); Griffith (1¼hr., $20); Melbourne (6hrs., $68); Sydney (10hr, $53); Wagga Wagga (1hr., $20).

For a decent bed above the liveliest pub in town, the **Charles Sturt Hotel,** on the corner of East and Douglas St., offers nicely furnished rooms and friendly hospitality. (☎6959 2042. TV lounge, BBQ. Reception at bar 10am-late. Singles $20; doubles $25.) The **Royal Mail Hotel** is also a pubstay that's a fair deal. (☎6959 2007. Singles $15; doubles $30; family $40.)

Venice Pizza & Pasta, 116 East St., serves super-tasting—you guessed it—pastas and pizzas from $7. (☎6959 3066. Open Su-Th 5-11pm, F-Sa 5pm-late. BYO.) **Hing Wah,** 94-96 East St., has great Chinese food. (☎6959 2059. Open daily 5-9pm, and Tu-Sa noon-2pm. Mains $12-19.) Foodworks **supermarket** is at the corner of East and Bolton St. (☎6959 2388. Open M-F 8am-6:30pm, Sa 8am-2pm, Su 9am-1pm.)

Today, Narrandera is an excellent place to look for Koalas relaxing in River Red Gum trees, thanks to the **Narrandera Koala Regeneration Reserve,** established in 1972, on the southeast edge of town along the Murrumbidgee River. See the **Tourist Information Centre** for details about walking tracks and driving possibilities or contact retired resident Roy Aussell, who is happy to show visitors around the reserve (☎6959 2441. Free, though donations to support the koalas are welcomed.)

While inside the information centre, you can't miss the **world's second largest playable guitar**—Bristol, England recently reclaimed the title with one slightly larger. In an adjacent building, the **Tiger Moth Memorial** houses a WWII plane, a reminder of Narrandera's use as a training site for the Royal Australian Air Force. (Open daily 9am-5pm. Free.)

CENTRAL WEST

The cities and towns of the Central West lie between the rugged plateaus of the Blue Mountains and the stark dryness of outback New South Wales. The major route into the region from the east is the Great Western Hwy., which crosses through the Blue Mountains to Bathurst. From Bathurst, the Mitchell Hwy. heads northwest to Dubbo, Bourke, and beyond, and the Mid Western Hwy. runs southwest to Cowra and eventually Hay. Both of these roads intersect the Newell Hwy., the major route between Melbourne and Brisbane, which cuts a long path across the Central West. Most towns of the Central West, surrounded by miles of rolling agriculture, are regarded as waystations between grander destinations. Even with a short stay in this region, you'll notice an extraordinary degree of hospitality in locals who have chosen to live the less hectic life.

BATHURST ☎02

The first inland settlement, Bathurst (pop. 30,500) features wide avenues and large, ornate lampposts, suggesting it was once slated for greatness. It is an unadorned route though, on the southwest corner of town, that has brought the city notoriety. Originally built as a scenic drive in 1938, the 6km circular road up Mt. Panorama and back down doubles as a public road and the track for the annual touring car races **AMP Bathurst 1000** (for V-8 engines) and **Australian 1000 Classic** (2-litre class). In mid-November and early October, respectively, these events draw crowds of over 40,000 to this otherwise low-profile town. Largely thanks to the races and the large population of students at Charles Sturt University, Bathurst has a certain vibrance that the industrial towns of the region lack.

TRANSPORTATION AND PRACTICAL INFORMATION. Bathurst is 101km west of Katoomba on the Great Western Hwy. **Trains** and **buses** leave the **Railway Station** at the corner of Keppel and Havannah St. **Countrylink** (☎13 22 32) goes to: Cowra (1½hr.; M, W, F 2 per day, Sa 1 per day; $16.50); Dubbo (2½-3½hr., 3 per day, $33); Forbes and Parkes (3½hr., 6 per week, $29); Katoomba (2hr., 2 per day, $18.70); Lithgow (1-1¼hr., 3-7 per day, $11); Orange (1hr., 1-2 per day, $22); Parramatta and Penrith (2½-3½hr., 2 per day, $27.60-$30.80); Sydney (3½-4½hr., 2 per day, $37.40); ISIC 50% discount. **McCafferty's** (☎13 14 99) and **Greyhound** (☎13 20 30) run to: Dubbo (2½-3½hr., 3 per day, $46); Katoomba (2hr., 2 per day, $30); Lithgow (1-1¼hr., 3-7 per day, $30); Parramatta and Penrith (2½-3½hr., 2 per day, $30); Sydney (3½-4½hr., 2 per day, $30). Both have a 10% ISIC/VIP/YHA discount. The **Bathurst Visitors Centre,** 28 William St., has brochures and free maps. (☎6332 1444 or 1800 681 000; www.bathurst.nsw.gov.au. Open daily 9am-5pm.)

WALTZING MATILDA No song—not even Australia's official national anthem—is as deeply ingrained in the hearts of Aussies as *Waltzing Matilda.* The folk ballad originated in the social upheaval of the shearing disputes between unionist woolworkers and wealthy landowners during the late 19th century. Conflict erupted in September 1894 at Dagworth Station (Orange, NSW), when laborers and police fired at each other, and a shed containing 100 "jumbucks" (colloquial for sheep, derived from an Aboriginal term) with hundreds of bales of wool was burned to the ground. Banjo Paterson, a wealthy man who sided with the workers, adapted an old Scottish folk song to commemorate the event. Completed in 1895, the song still strikes a chord in the Australian psyche, recalling the tough frontier spirit of the bushmen and shearers. Its sentiments are best expressed where the swagman (the song's hero), cornered and facing certain capture at the hands of the squatter (rich landowner), chooses death rather than surrender: "But the swagman, he up and he jumped into the waterhole/Drowning himself by the Coolabah tree/And his ghost may be heard as it sings in the Billabong/'Who'll come a-waltzing Matilda with me?'"

ACCOMMODATIONS AND FOOD. Bathurst has a few pubstays downtown. **Bathurst Explorer's Hotel,** 357 Stewart St., offers luxurious rooms with TV, fridge, heat, A/C, and a $12 dinner coupon for area restaurants. (☎6331 2966 or 1800 047 907. Reception 24hr. Singles $59; twins and doubles $69, $10 per extra person. $6 weekend surcharge.) **East's Bathurst Holiday Park,** is on Sydney Rd. (the Great Western Hwy.), 4km east of town. (☎6331 8286 or 1800 669 911; fax 6332 6439. Showers, laundry, BBQ, TV room. Reception daily 8am-6pm. Sites for 2 $16, powered $18.50; cabins $50, with bath $62. MC/V.)

Ziegler's Cafe, 52 Keppel St., has a range of salads, grilled veggie dishes, and burgers. (☎6332 1565. Open M-Sa 9am-9pm, Su 10am-3pm. Dinners $12-22. BYO. AmEx/DC/MC/V.) Indulge in delicious pastries or gourmet sandwiches for $6 on the veranda at **Bernard's Bakery,** 81 George St. (☎6331 2042. Open M-F 6:30am-6pm, Sa 7am-5pm.) Coles **supermarket,** 47 William St., has a deli with sandwiches ($3) and pizza for $6.50. (☎6332 9566. Open M-Sa 6am-midnight, Su 8am-10pm.)

SIGHTS. A trip to Bathurst would be incomplete without a spin round the **Mt. Panorama circuit,** southwest on William St. until it becomes Panorama Ave. As you twist your way up and down the steep hills, you'll gain an appreciation for the pros who do it in excess of 200kph. Don't let the banner ads and tire piles seduce you; local police patrol the area frequently, looking for drivers who edge above the 60kph speed limit. The recently expanded **National Motor Racing Museum,** near the starting line, keeps the thrill of the race alive year-round. (☎6332 1872. Open daily 9am-4:30pm. $6.60, concession $5, family $15.40.) The **courthouse** on Russell St. was considered so grand when it was built in 1880 that residents of the town thought there must have been a mistake putting it in Bathurst. Rumors circulated that the building had been meant for a more prominent colony in India or Africa; the massive railings encircling the building would easily have kept elephants out. (Open M-F 9am-5pm, but hours vary when in use.) The east wing houses a **museum** with Bathurst artifacts ranging from Aboriginal weapons to penny-farthing bicycles. (Open Tu-W, Sa-Su 10am-4pm. $2, children $1, family $5.) Don't miss the **Abercrombie Caves,** 70km south of Bathurst via Trunkey Creek. The majestic Grand Arch is the largest limestone archway in the Southern Hemisphere. (☎6368 8603. Open daily 9am-4pm. $12; guided tour 2pm $14.50.).

FORBES ☎02

A feeling of timelessness and the nearby Parkes Radio Telescope, famous for its involvement with putting the first man on the moon, compensate for a lack of compelling sights. Once the stomping grounds of renowned bushranger **Ben Hall,** Forbes (pop. 8000) shows little evidence of its checkered past.

The **Newell Hwy.** runs through Forbes, with Dubbo 153km to the northeast, Orange, 93km to the east, and Cowra, 90km to the southeast. The downtown, anchored by Lachlan St., is surrounded by the flood-prone **Lake Forbes,** which looks suspiciously like a river to the untrained eye. From the old **railway station** on Union St., **Countrylink** (☎13 22 32) runs **buses** to: Dubbo (2hr., 3-4 per week, $19); Orange (2hr., 13 per week, $16.50); Parkes (30min., 1-3 per day, $5.50); Sydney (7hr., 1 per day M-Sa, $74.80); ISIC 50% discount. From the Cal-Tex 24 Roadhouse, 1km north of town on the Newell Hwy., **Greyhound Pioneer** (☎13 20 30) handles services to: Coonabarabran (5hr., 3 per day, $54) and Parkes (30min., 2 per day, $43). **Harvey World Travel,** 6 Templar St., sells all bus tickets with $5 service fee. (☎6852 2344. Open M-F 9am-5pm, Sa 9am-noon.) The old railway station on Union St. has been converted into the **Forbes Railway Arts and Tourist Centre.** (☎6852 4155; fax 6852 4433. Open daily 9am-5pm.) **Complete Insite Solutions,** on the corner of Rankin and Templar St., has **Internet.** (☎1300 303 074. Open M-F 9am-5:30pm, Sa 9am-12:30pm. $4.40 per hr.)

Pubstays in Forbes are some of the best and cheapest in the area. Everything's huge at the **Albion Hotel,** 135 Lachlan St., from the clean rooms to the men's showers that could house a town meeting. (☎6851 1881. Reception at bar. Singles $25, doubles $38.) **Apex Caravan Park,** 86 Reymond St., 2km south of the town center via Bridge and Flint St., is along the river. (☎6851 1929. Showers, laundry, BBQ. Sites for 2 $13.20, powered $16.50; cabins from $41, with bath $61.) Buy **groceries** at Woolworth's, on the corner of Rankin and Grenfell St. (☎6852 2421. Open M-Sa 7am-9pm, Su 8am-8pm.)

NEW SOUTH WALES

Back in the gold rush days when Forbes had 80,000 prospector residents, Ben Hall was reputedly head of an outlaw gang known for robbery, whippings, arson, kidnapping, and murder. Among the locals, the debate continues over whether Hall was forced into crime by injustice or whether he was a dirty-dealing bushranger at heart. The **Albion Hotel,** formerly the Cobb & Co. Stage Coach stop, offers the **Bushrangers Hall of Fame and Underground Tour.** Guided tours go through the tunnels where gold and money were transported between banks in an attempt to dodge robberies. (Open daily 10am-6pm. Admission hours flexible; inquire at bar. $5, seniors $4, children $3.) **Lachlan Vintage Village,** off Newell Hwy., recreates the 1860's gold rush with exhibits including a replica of Ben Hall's home. (☎6852 2655. Open daily 8am-5pm. $8, children $4.)

NEAR FORBES: PARKES RADIO TELESCOPE

The **64m dish,** visible from the Newell Hwy., 55km northeast of Forbes (20km north of Parkes) on the road to Dubbo, belongs to the **Parkes Radio Telescope.** The combination of low radio interference, proximity to Sydney, and expert staff puts Parkes at the forefront of research. A major contributor to astronomy since its opening in 1961, the Parkes Telescope has participated in high-profile projects including the televising of the first moon walk, portrayed in the movie *The Dish*, and the rescue of NASA's Apollo 13. Recently, the telescope has been used to seek out **hidden galaxies** in the southern skies and to understand mysterious cosmic **dark matter.** The **Visitors Discovery Centre** is a surprisingly low-tech facility with displays on the telescope. The knowledgeable staff and a 20min. film make it interesting even for non-scientists. (☎6861 1777. Open daily 8:30am-4:15pm. Free. Film $3.)

MUDGEE ☎02

A land of wine and honey cradled in the foothills of the Great Dividing Range, Mudgee (pop. 18,000, from the Aboriginal "nest in the hills") has over 20 vineyards—and not much else to offer the tourist, though locals proudly proclaim that Mudgee is "tasting better each year."

Mudgee is a 3½hr. drive from Sydney on Hwy. 86, between Lithgow (159km) and Dubbo (109km). **Countrylink** (☎13 22 32) runs 1-2 times per day to: Coonabarabran (3hr., $30.80); Lithgow (2½hr., $22); Sydney (5hr., $45.10). Countrylink gives a 50% ISIC discount. Book at Harvey World Travel, Shop 28-29, Town Centre, Church St. (☎6372 6077. Open M-F 8:30am-5:30pm, Sa 8:30am-noon.) For **taxis,** call 13 10 08.

The **Mudgee Visitors Centre,** 84 Market St., is armed with maps and advice. (☎6372 1020 or 1800 816 304; fax 6372 2853; www.mudgee-gulgong.org. Open M-F 9am-5pm, Sa 9am-3:30pm, Su 9:30am-2pm.) The **NPWS office,** 160 Church St., administers the northwest section of Wollemi National Park (☎6372 7199; mudgee@npws.nsw.gov.au. Open M-F 9am-5pm. See p. 145.) Get free **Internet access** at the public library on Market St. (☎6372 0441. Open M-F 10am-6pm, Sa 9:30am-12:30pm. Book ahead.) Mudgee Business Enterprise Centre has more terminals. (☎6372 6088. Book ahead. $2.50 per 30min., $4 per hr. Open M-F 9am-5pm.)

Pubstay accommodations are the most readily available in town. **The Woolpack Hotel,** 67 Market St., is near the visitors center; turn left and go one block down Market St. (☎6372 1908. Reception 7am-midnight at bar. Singles and doubles $20. MC/V.) The **Mudgee Riverside Caravan and Tourist Park,** 22 Short St., behind the visitors center, has showers and laundry. (☎6372 2531; rivside@winsoft.net.au. Linen $7. Washer $2, no dryer. Reception daily 8am-8pm. Check-out 10am. Sites for 2 $13, powered $17. Cabins with bath and A/C $55-66. AmEx/MC/V.)

Red Heifer Grill and Carvery, 1 Church St., inside the Lawson Park Hotel, is a great spot for good grub—grill-your-own-steak dinner ($14-17) with bottles of local wine from $10. Entrees ($10) come with all-you-can eat salad bar for only $5 extra. (☎6372 2183. Open daily 10am-10pm, lunch noon-2:30pm and dinner 6-9pm.) (☎6372 6665. Open M-Sa 8:30am-5pm. No credit cards). A Bi-Lo **supermarket** is on Church St., in the cavernous Town Centre shopping plaza next to Harvey World Travel. (Open M-Sa 7am-10pm, Su 8am-8pm.)

NEAR MUDGEE: WINERIES

Mudgee's calling cards are its victual offerings, ranging from small, communal vineyards to large, self-sufficient wineries. There are many vineyards in the area; consult the tourist office for extensive information. Travelers passing through in September will find the streets hopping with the **Mudgee Wine Festival.** If you want to do the wine-tasting circuit but also wish to avoid running afoul of stringent drink-driving laws, a number of companies offer tours. Try **Mudgee Transit Corporation** (☎6372 0091; half-day $45, full-day $60), or **Mudgee Valley Tours.** (☎6372 6766. 4hr. Su-F tour $45; full-day Sa, includes lunch, $50.) **Poet's Corner Wine Cellar,** which is a conglomeration of Craigmoor, Montrose, and Poet's Corner labels, has been making tawny Rummy Port for 70 years. To reach the winery, bike or drive 7km northwest of Mudgee on Henry Lawson Dr., then turn onto Craigmoor Rd. (☎6372 2208. Open M-Sa 10am-4:30pm, Su 10am-4pm.) **Huntington Estate Wines,** 8km from town past the airport on Cassilis Rd., has an array of reds for sample on a free self-guided tour. (☎6373 3825. Open M-F 9am-5pm, Sa 10am-5pm, Su 10am-3pm.) **Botobolar,** 89 Botobolar Rd., 16km northeast of town, is an organic winery with daily tastings. (☎6373 3840. Open M-Sa 10am-5pm, Su 10am-3pm.)

DUBBO ☎02

The hub of the Central West, Dubbo is a busy, working-man service city filled with down-to-earth Australians. It's easy to forget that just on the far side of that last roundabout is nothing but empty agricultural lands for a very, very long way. It's not quite the outback, but venture past the city limits by night, with only the stars lighting the desolate road, and you might feel like it is. Headlined by the awesome Western Plains Zoo, Dubbo's interest in luring tourists has also resulted in an impressive roster of attractions beyond the zoo.

TRANSPORTATION. **Countrylink trains** and **buses** (☎13 22 32) depart from the **railway station** on Talbragar St. to: Albury (7hr., 1 per day, $74.80); Broken Hill (8½hr., 1 per day, $85.80); Forbes (2hr.; Su, Tu, Th 1 per day; $18.70); Melbourne (10½hr., 1 per day, $97.90); Orange (2hr., 1 per day, $22); Sydney (7-11hr., 2 per day, $66); Wagga Wagga (5½hr.; Su, Tu, Th 1 per day; $47.30); ISIC 50% discount. The **Shell Station,** at the intersection of Newell and Mitchell Hwy., is the drop off point for **Greyhound Pioneer** (☎13 20 30), **Rendell Coaches** (☎6884 2411), and **McCafferty's** (☎13 14 99). They service: Adelaide (15hr., 2 per day, $108); Brisbane (11½-14hr., 3 per day, $88-103); Broken Hill (8hr., 1 per day, $108); Coonabarabran (2hr., 3 per day, $43); Melbourne (11½-13hr., 2 per day, $92-108). All give a 10% ISIC/VIP/YHA discount. All tickets can be booked at the railway station. (Open M-F 8am-

5pm, Sa-Su 8-9:30am and 10:30am-2pm.) Drop off in Dubbo frequently occurs in the wee hours of the morning as coaches ramble on to further destinations. To reach accommodations, rely on 24hr. **taxis** (☎6882 1911). **Darrell Wheeler Cycles,** 25 Bultje St., hires bicycles for $15 per day. (☎6882 9899. Open M-F 8:30am-5:30pm, Sa 8:30am-1pm.) Bike trails criss-cross town and head out to the zoo. **Thrifty** (☎6882 8899), on the corner of Talbragar and Darling, rents cars from $40 per day.

ORIENTATION AND PRACTICAL INFORMATION. Dubbo sits at the intersection of Hwy. 39 (Newell Hwy.) between Melbourne and Brisbane, and Hwy. 32 (Mitchell Hwy.), leading from Sydney and Bathurst to points west. The town's sprawling layout could make life difficult for those without a car, but major sights are in two clusters, so plan accordingly. **Talbragar St.** runs east-west, parallel to the two major highways that sandwich the town. The intersection of Talbragar and **Macquarie St.** marks the town center, with most of the action, including **banks, ATMs,** and **pharmacies,** running down Macquarie St.

The **Dubbo Visitors Centre,** on the corner of Erskine and Macquarie St., in the northwest corner of the small downtown area, has maps of biking trails and books river cruises. (☎6884 1422; www.dubbotourism.com.au. Open daily 9am-5pm.) Find **Internet** at Dubbo Regional **Library,** on the southwest corner of Macquarie and Talbragar St. ($5.50 per hr; open M-F 10am-6pm, Sa 10am-3pm, Su noon-4pm), or the Grapevine Cafe.

ACCOMMODATIONS AND FOOD. Plenty of hotels cluster around Talbragar St. in the city center with singles from $20. The cheapest beds are at the **Dubbo YHA Hostel,** 87 Brisbane St., close to the old inter-city bus station. Walk out of the visitors' center onto Erskine St., turn right and walk a block, then turn right on Brisbane St. The talking pet cockatoo adds flavor to an otherwise unglamorous place, as do nightly fire-front gatherings to watch sports on the telly. (☎/fax 6882 0922; yhadubbo@lisp.com.au. Washer $2, no dryer. Bike rental $6 per day. Reception 7:30am-10:30pm. Bunks $17; twins and doubles $34; family $45, group discounts for 3 or more. MC/V.) The upscale **Amaroo Hotel,** 83 Macquarie St., is in the center of town. (☎6882 3533. Breakfast included. Singles $55; doubles $77. MC/V.) The excellent **Dubbo City Caravan Park,** on Whylandra St. just before it becomes the Newell Hwy. northwest of the city center, has shaded sites overlooking the Macquarie River and the most beautiful bathrooms in a NSW caravan park. Kids will dig the playground and pool. (☎6882 4820; dccp@dubbo.nsw.gov.au. Bike rental $15 per day, $10 per half-day. Linen $9. Laundry $4. Reception daily 7:30am-7:30pm. Check-in 1pm. Curfew 10pm. Sites from $14, powered $18, with bath $24; caravans $28; cabins from $42, with bath $49. AmEx/DC/MC/V.)

Sandwich shops and bakeries are plentiful in the city center, but there is no real cheap restaurant. For the best coffee concoctions, seek out the **Grapevine Cafe,** 144 Brisbane St. (☎6884 7354. Lunch $8-11. Internet $2.50 per 30min. Open M-Sa 8:30am-10:30pm, Su 9am-6pm.) A food court with a cafe, Asian noodles, and a Subway is inside **Riverdale Shopping Centre** at 49 Macquarie St., as is Woolworth's **supermarket** (open M-Sa 7am-10pm, Su 8am-8pm); the movie theater attached provides a quick flick. (☎6881 8600. $12.50, concession $9.80, children $8.70. All Tu shows $7.60.) There are **local markets** at the showground on Wingewarra St. every 2nd and 4th Saturday of the month. (Open 2nd Sa 9am-1pm with crafts, produce, bric-a-brac, 4th Sa 8am-noon with fresh produce, cheese, flowers.)

SIGHTS. Dubbo's premier tourist attraction is the **Western Plains Zoo,** on Obley Rd., 4km south of the city center off the Newell Hwy. In addition to Australian native species, the zoo houses Bengal tigers, black rhinoceri, and Australia's only **African elephants;** exhibits are arranged by continent around a paved track suitable for driving or biking with BBQ/picnic areas along the way. Many of the animals wander unrestrained through loose enclosures. Don't miss the nursery for injured and orphaned animals: the sight of infant joeys snuggling together under baby blankets is priceless. On weekends and select days during school holidays, early morning zoo walks are available at 6:45am for an additional $3. (☎6882 5888; www.zoo.nsw.gov.au. Open daily 9am-5pm, last entry 3:30pm. $18, students $13, ages 4-16 $9.50. Bike rental $11 per 4hr., plus $10 deposit.) On Obley Rd. 2km past the zoo, **Dundullimal Homestead** is a National Trust-registered slab house dating from the 1840s, with a saddlery workshop and petting zoo. (☎6884 9984. Open daily 10am-5pm. $6, under 16 $3. Animal shows Tu, Th-Su 3:30pm.) In conjunction with the Homestead, **Macquarie River Cruises** offers trips on one of the biggest river boats in outback New South Wales, stopping for tea at the Homestead before a hay ride and trip down the river (2hr. cruises from $16; book through the Visitors Centre). The dough-faced animatronic models of **Old Dubbo Gaol,** on Macquarie St. between Commonwealth and State Banks, tell the bygone convicts' sad, macabre stories that proves any subject (including the hanging of eight men) can be funny if you add enough goofy talking mannequins. (☎6882 8122. Open daily 9am-5pm, last admission 4:30pm. $7, students $5.50, ages 5-18 $3.50.) Down the street, at the **Dubbo Observatory,** on Camp Rd. off Newell Hwy., you can see the three galaxies only visible in the Southern Hemisphere. (☎6885 3022. 2 shows nightly, book ahead. $13.50, families $38.50.)

If you want a taste (and smell) of the real Central West Australia, do not miss the huge **livestock markets** 4km north on the Newell Hwy. towards Gilgandra; look for the sign. Entering, watching, and mingling with the *cockies* (farmers) is free of charge; just be sure to stay in the background or you may find yourself suddenly the proud owner of $8000 worth of cattle. (Auctions M and Th cattle 8am-noon or 1pm, sheep noon-3 or 4pm; some F.)

Learn about aerodynamics, Aboriginal history, woodcraft, and flying sticks (that only come back to you with a little skill) at **Jedda Boomerangs,** on Minore Rd., White Pines. As you head southwest toward the zoo, turn right onto Minore; it's 4km down Minore Rd. The excellent and informative hourly tour culminates in burning your own design on a boomerang (costs $7 extra to take it home) and learning how to throw one so that it really comes back to you. (☎6882 3110. Open daily 10am-4pm. Free admission. Tour $5.50, children $3.30.)

Inquire at the tourist office about local wineries. There are three tours which go to the zoo and other local attractions: **White Gum Tours** (☎6884 3883), **Langley's Dubbo Day Tours** (☎6884 5333), and **Jolly Swagman Tours** (☎6884 9984).

NEW SOUTH WALES

NORTHWEST: BACK O' BOURKE

The empty stretches of northwest New South Wales are sparsely populated, difficult to reach, and largely untouched by the typical traveler. What's that you say? You're not the typical traveler? You want to explore and embrace the arid western lands—the dusty brown hills, dusty brown roads, and dusty brown cows? What deep knowledge you will have gleaned when you have stepped one toe past Bourke's city limits merely for the sake of being able to say to your typical-traveler friends Sydneyside, "Yes, I have been Back O' Bourke. I have seen desolation not unlike a nuclear winter. I know what life looks like after the road ends."

COONABARABRAN ☎02

For folks living in a tiny town in the middle of nowhere, the lifestyle of Coonabarabran ("coon-a-BAR-a-bran"; Aboriginal for "an inquisitive person"; pop. 3000) embodies all that is good about the laid-back and friendly country life. As the astronomy capital of Australia, thanks to low-levels of urban light pollution, a large number of clear night skies, and relative proximity to major urban areas (Sydney and Brisbane are only a day's drive), it draws many visitors.

TRANSPORTATION. Coonabarabran lies 159km northeast of Dubbo on the Newell Hwy. It's accessible from the northeast through Gunnedah on the Oxley Hwy., which joins the Newell and enters from the north. **Countrylink** (☎13 22 32) runs from the visitors center to Sydney (8hr.; Su-F 1 per day; $79, ISIC $40). **McCafferty's** (☎13 14 99) and **Greyhound Pioneer** (☎13 20 30) leave from the Caltex Service Station outside of town heading to: Bendigo (12½hr., 1 per day, $115); Brisbane (9-9½hr., 3 per day, $91); Dubbo (2hr., 3 per day, $43); Echuca (11hr., 1 per day, $115);

Melbourne (13-15hr., 2 per day, $115); Narrabri (1½hr., $51); Sydney (10hr., 1 per day, $121), via Dubbo; ISIC/VIP/YHA 10% discount. **Harvey World Travel,** 79 John St. (☎6842 1566) makes transport bookings with a $5 service fee. Inquire at the Visitors Centre about local car hire and bus tours of Warrumbungle National Park, 30km from town. For **Satellite Taxis** call 1800 421 113.

PRACTICAL INFORMATION. The main drag is **John St.** (the Newell Hwy.), home to several motels and crossed by **Dalgarno, Cassilis,** and **Edwards St.** Warrumbungle National Park and the observatories are both east of town. The **Coonabarabran Visitors Centre** is at the south end of town on John St. It has a display on **Australian megafauna,** including the skeleton of a 33,000-year-old giant Diprotodon, the largest marsupial ever to roam the earth. (☎6842 1441 or 1800 242 881; www.lisp.coona barabran.com.au. Open daily 9am-5pm.) Other services include: **National Parks and Wildlife Service,** 56 Cassilis St. (☎6842 1311), with info on Warrumbungle National Park; **24hr. ATMs; Internet cafe** (see **Accommodations,** below).

ACCOMMODATIONS AND FOOD. Book ahead for accommodations during school holidays. The **Imperial Hotel,** corner of John and Delgarno St., is over a pub with thin walls and floors through which to hear the cries (and crying) of pokies players downstairs. (☎6842 1023. Reception 8:30am-11pm. Check-out 9am. Singles $22; doubles $31; $12 per extra person. AmEx/MC/V.) The other two pubstays, also on John St., are smaller but similar. At the **John Oxley Caravan Park,** 1km north of town on the Oxley Hwy., the affable hosts tend a shop, playground, and gas grill. (☎6842 1635. Reception daily 8am-8pm. Linen $11. Sites for 2 $12, powered $15; on-site vans $28.50; cabins $36.50, with bath $45.) A number of **bed and breakfasts** and **farmstays** are also available in Coonabarabran and within Warumbungle. Singles start at $40. Ask at the visitors center.

The **Golden Sea Dragon Restaurant,** next to the visitors center at 8 John St., mixes a golden Buddha with instrumental Bette Midler but serves fantastic Chinese fare. (☎6842 2388. 2-course traveler's special $12. Open daily noon-2:30pm; 5pm-10pm, 11pm on weekends.) There are plenty of tidy lunch counters on John St. **Woop Woop Cafe,** 38a John St., lets you brag to friends about discovering the "hole-in-the-wall" eatery with the best coffee in town. A converted storeroom, the cafe contrasts its corrugated steel walls with paintings by local artists and a remarkably highbrow menu (sandwiches $10, salads $9). (☎6842 4755. Open Tu-Th 8am-6pm, F-Sa 8am-late, Sun 10am-6pm. BYO. MC/V). The **Jolly Cauli Coffee Shop,** 30 John St., has reasonable prices and **Internet access.** (☎6842 2021. Open M-F 8am-5pm, Sa 9am-1pm. Devonshire tea and scone $5. Internet $6 per hr. No credit cards) The IGA **supermarket** is on Dalgarno St. (Open M-W 8:30am-6pm, Th-F 8:30am-6:30pm, Sa 8:30am-4pm, Su 9am-1pm.)

SIGHTS. The highlight of Coonabarabran is the **Skywatch Night and Day Observatory,** 2km from town on the road to Warrumbungle National Park. The effusive staff guides night viewing sessions that clarify the jumbled stars (there's a planetarium for cloudy nights). The accompanying **astro mini-golf** is fun. (☎6842 3303; www.skywatch.cx. Open daily 2-5pm. Night session: Nov.-Jan. daily 9, 10pm; Feb. 9pm; Mar. 8:30, 9:30pm; April-Sept. 7, 8pm; Oct. 7:30, 8:30pm. Exhibition or golf $7.70, ages 5-16 $5.50, families $22; exhibition and nightshow $12.10/ $7.15/$33.) Australia's largest optical telescope (3.9m) resides at **Siding Spring Observatory,** 28km from Coonabarabran on the road to Warrumbungle National Park. The observatory's visitor center offers an interactive, multimedia window onto the work of the resident astronomers, though no public viewing of the night sky. You'll see groundbreaking research here but might have more laughs at Skywatch. (☎6842 6211. Special tours by arrangement. Open daily 9:30am-4pm. $5.50, concessions $3.30, family $13.20.) The **sandstone caves** within the **Pilliga Nature Reserve** were hollowed out by wind and water erosion and are tricky to locate, but the visitors center has explicit directions.

BETTER THAN A LET'S GO MAP! Things really are different Down Under. The night sky is an entirely different panorama from the world's flip-side, yielding hours of neck-crimping stargazing. The Milky Way is a clear beacon, cutting a fiery swath directly through the center of the sky, and three galaxies are visible only in the Southern Hemisphere. Whereas *Polaris*, the North Star, guided European explorers for centuries, lost travelers in Australia have a trickier task. First, find the Southern Cross (which really looks more like a kite), its four points vibrantly marked. Check out the pattern on the Australian flag to get an idea of what you're looking for. Two bright "pointer" stars guide the way from their left side, if you're having trouble. Now gauge the distance of the long axis of the cross and extend it down and to the left one, two, three times. Fix that point and drag your finger down to the skyline. That point is due south. Got it? Neither do we.

WARRUMBUNGLE NATIONAL PARK

The jagged spires and rambling peaks of the Warrumbungle Mountains, at the juncture of the lush east and the barren west, are the result of volcanic activity millions of years ago. Softer sandstone worn away under hardened lava rock has left unusual shapes slicing into the sky above the forested hills. Kangaroos and wallabies have long called the area home, while hikers, rock-climbers, and campers have more recently discovered its splendor.

A 75km **scenic drive** branches off from the Newell Hwy. 39km north of Gilgandra and runs through the park, circling back to the highway at Coonabarabran (approximately 12km unsealed). The park entry fee can be paid at the **Warrumbungle National Park Visitors Centre,** on the park road 33km west of Coonabarabran. They have $2 bushcamping and free rock-climbing permits. (☎6825 4364. Open daily 9am-4pm; outside drop-box for after hours fees. Entry $5 per car; pedestrians free.) The **NPWS** has a district office 56 Cassilis St., Coonabarabran (☎6842 1311).

Of the park's serviced **camping** areas, only four are open to individual travelers (sites for 2 $10, extra person $2). **Camp Blackman** is car-accessible and has toilets, rainwater, showers, and a pay phone (powered $15, extra person $3). **Camp Pincham** lies a short walk from the nearest carpark, while **Burbie Camp** is a 4km hike from the park road (both areas have toilets and showers). **Gunneemooroo** ("place of snakes") is reached by car on the unsealed road from **Tooraweenah** (bushcamping only). Firewood cannot be collected in the park, so bring a fuel stove. Pets are also not allowed.

The **Gurianawa Track** (1km; 15min.) runs an easy circle around the visitors center, passes fields of kangaroos, and includes views of the Siding Spring Observatory and the area's extinct volcanoes. The short walk (1km return) to **Whitegum Lookout,** 27km from Coonabarabran at the east end of the park, offers striking views of the surrounding mountains. The most popular of the park's longer walks, the hike to **Grand High Tops** (12.5km; 5-6hr.) starts at a carpark 1km south of the main park road and 500m west of the visitors center turn-off. The steep circuit through the southern half of the park passes stunning views of **Breadknife,** an imposing 90m stone tower, and turn-offs for most of the park's other major sights. The walk back via West Spiney adds 2km and provides a chance to see the eagles that often fly around **Bluff Mountain.**

NARRABRI ☎02

Equidistant from Sydney and Brisbane (560km), Narrabri ("NEHR-uh-BRYE"; meaning "forked waters"; pop. 7900) is a wheat and cotton-growing center that has two major attractions: the six-dish Australia Telescope complex and the beautifully rugged scenery of Mount Kaputar National Park.

TRANSPORTATION AND PRACTICAL INFORMATION. **Countrylink** (☎13 22 32) **trains** run to Sydney (8hr.; 1 per day; $79, ISIC $40) from the train station at the east end of Bowen St., four blocks from Maitland St. **McCafferty's** (☎13 14 99) and **Greyhound Pioneer** (☎13 20 30) **buses** depart from the corner of Bowen and

Maitland St., two blocks south of the post office for Brisbane (8hr., 2 per day, $65) and Melbourne (14½-16hr., 2 per day, $123), via Coonabarabran (1¼hr., 2 per day, $51) and Dubbo (4hr., 2 per day, $64). Both give a 10% ISIC/VIP/YHA discount. Tickets can be booked through **Harvey World Travel,** 60 Maitland St. for a $5 service fee. (☎6792 2555. Open M-F 8am-5:30pm, Sa 8:30-11:30am.) **Thrifty,** 39 Maitland St. (☎6792 3610), and **Budget**, 121 Barwan St. (☎13 27 27), rent cars.

PRACTICAL INFORMATION. The **Narrabri Visitors Centre** lies opposite Lloyd St. on the Newell Hwy. (Tibbereena St.), which veers north in town along Narrabri Creek. (☎6792 3583 or 1800 659 931; www.tournarrabri.nsw.gov.au. Open M-F 9am-5pm, Sa-Su 9am-noon.) The main drag is **Maitland St.,** which runs parallel to Tibbereena one street farther from the creek. The **library,** on the corner of Doyle and Barwan, has ridiculously cheap **Internet access.** (☎6792 3562. $2 per hr. Open M-W, F 10am-5:30pm, Th 11am-7pm, Sa 10am-noon.) The **NPWS** office, Level 1, 100 Maitland St., offers info about outdoor activities. (☎6799 1740. Open M-F 8:30am-4:30pm; enter around the corner on Dewhurst St. and go up the stairs.)

ACCOMMODATIONS AND FOOD. All seven pubs along the central three-block stretch of Maitland St. offer inexpensive accommodation, and there are a number of motels on the highway. Camping is also a great option (see **Sights,** below). A few dollars more than some of its competitors, but in the best location, the **Tourist Hotel,** 142 Maitland St., has comfortable beds in small tidy rooms with shared bathrooms. (☎6792 2312. Singles $25; doubles $40, with bath $50. MC/V.) The cheapest motel and camping are both at the **Narrabri Motel and Caravan Park,** 52 Cooma Rd., on the Newell Hwy. toward Coonabarabran. (☎6792 2593. Pool, grill, and free linen. Sites for 2 $12, powered $16; singles $45; doubles $53; cabins with bath $45-53.) Several lunch counters and bakeries are on Maitland St. **Watson's Kitchen,** 151 Maitland St., is a local fave. (☎6792 1366. Open M-F 6am-6pm, Sa 6am-1pm, Su 7am-noon. No credit cards.) Woolworth's **supermarket** is on the corner of Lloyd and Maitland St. (Open M-Sa 7am-10pm, Su 8am-8pm. AmEx/MC/V.)

NEW SOUTH WALES

SIGHTS. Signs on the Newell Hwy. heading toward Coonabarabran lead to the **Australia Telescope,** 24km west of Narrabri, a set of six large radio dishes which comprise the largest, most powerful telescope array in the Southern Hemisphere. The Visitors Centre has a helpful staff, and its videos and displays are fun and simplified to layman's terms. When the dishes aren't in use, the staff is happy to show you their innards. (☎6790 4070. Open daily 8am-4pm; staffed M-F. Free.)

East of Narrabri, the peaks of the **Nandewar Range** beckon travelers to leave the paved road behind (either by hiking or unsealed action) and scale the summit of **Mt. Kaputar,** whose views encompass one-tenth of New South Wales. The entrance to the central section of **Mount Kaputar National Park** lies 31km east of Narrabri heading south on Maitland St. and Old Gunnedah Rd. **Bark Hut Camping Area** is 14km inside the park, and **Dawsons Spring Camping Area** is 21km inside near the Mt. Kaputar summit. Both have hot showers, toilets, electricity, and BBQs (sites $3, children $2); be sure to bring your own firewood. The two cabins at Dawson's Spring are a great deal for families or groups. (4 beds, full kitchen, shower. $55 per night, 2 night min. Book well in advance at NPWS office.) The park's most famous attraction is **Sawn Rocks,** an amazing basalt rock formation, in the northern section accessible from the Newell Hwy. north of Narrabri (30min drive NE, 15min walk from the parking lot). The eerie organ-pipe geometry is best seen from down in the creek bed. There is an excellent pamphlet available from the NPWS office in Narrabri with hiking info on 13 tracks of varying difficulty, including Mt. Kaputar, Sawn Rocks, and Waa Gorge ($2.50). The roads to and within the park are mostly unsealed and unstable after rain; call the NPWS office (☎6799 1740) for updates.

BOURKE ☎07

On a blistering hot day, Bourke ("BURK") can be eerie. It's dead quiet. Haze covering the unusually wide, naked streets distorts distance. Bourke is a study in racial division of the sort that is often hidden beneath the surface of Australian society. At one end of Oxley St., the main drag, white office workers stroll past the immaculately restored Federation-style courthouse, post office, and banks. At the other end, Aboriginal kids in worn clothing loiter beside the pub, convenience store, and public housing office. That shouldn't scare you away; visiting Bourke is an educational experience in this and many other ways. An important inland port town in the 19th century, Bourke is rich with history, and today it's both a symbolic (as per the idiom "back o' Bourke") and a real gateway to the outback.

Bourke lies on the Mitchell Hwy. (Hwy. 71), 367km northwest of Dubbo and 142km south of the Queensland-NSW border. The Mitchell Hwy. becomes Anson St. through town; Richard St. branches off to the north and runs all the way to the Darling River. Oxley St. runs off Richard St. to the left, and should be avoided at night. Mitchell St. crosses Richard St. a half block from Oxley St. Buses head to Dubbo (4½hr.; M, W, F, Sa 9:15am; $56.10), connecting to Sydney ($65). Buy tickets at **Bourke Courier Service,** 34A Mitchell St. (☎6872 2092. Open M-F 9am-5pm.) Buses depart from the **Tourist Information Centre,** on Anson St., a block west of Richard St., which can also suggest farms for **year-round work.** (☎6872 1222; Tourinfo@lisp.com.au. Open Easter-Oct. daily 9am-5pm, Nov.-Easter M-Sa 9am-5pm.) The **library,** 29 Mitchell St., has **Internet access.** (☎6872 2751. Open M-Tu, Th-F 9am-5pm, W 9am-noon and 1-5pm, Sa 9:30am-12:30pm. $2.50 per hr.)

Port of Bourke Hotel, 32 Mitchell St., has large rooms with hardwood floors, shared baths, A/C, and heaters; many open onto balcony. (☎6872 2544; fax 6872 2687; pobh@bigpond.com. Singles $34; doubles $60.60; family rooms $57, with bath $83.) For a real "outback" experience, contact **Comeroo Camel Station,** Comeroo, in the red desert, where you can bushcamp, take a camel safari, or stay in cottages. You need 4WD to reach the 100,000-acre family-run station. (☎/fax 6874 7735. Breakfast and dinner included. $60 per person). A **supermarket** is at the corner of Warraweena and Darling St. (☎6872 2613. Open daily 7:30am-7:30pm daily.)

The **Back o' Bourke Exhibition Center,** 29 Oxley St., 1km north of town off North Bourke Rd., provides information on the city's history, modern-day farming, fruit growing, and recreation attractions. Paddle boats run down the river from the Kidman Caravan Park. (☎6872 1321; www.backobourke.com.au. 1hr. cruise M-Sa 9:30am and 2:30pm, Su 2:30pm. $10, children $5.)

The all-purpose guide *Back o' Bourke Mud Map Tours,* free at the tourist office, details trips just beyond the town borders or several thousand kilometers into the outback. Trips include **Mt. Oxley's** eagles, **Gundabooka National Park's** Aboriginal rock art (NPWS ☎6872 2744), and **Brewarrina's** Aboriginal cultural museum. (☎6839 2868. Open M-F 9am-5pm. $6, concession $3.) The manly **Darling River Run,** billed as "the last of the Great 4WD Adventures," is a 439km route tracing the Darling to its junction with the Murray at Wentworth and passes famous bush pubs, camping spots, and fishing holes.

BROKEN HILL ☎08

Broken Hill sits at the extreme western end of New South Wales, right on the edge of nowhere. In 1883, Charles Rasp, a German-born boundary rider, discovered that the misshapen hill known locally as the "hog's back" was in fact the biggest lode of silver-lead ore in the world. Rasp and his associates attracted thousands of people, transforming once-thought worthless scrubland into a booming expanse almost overnight. Like Victoria's Goldfield boom towns, Broken Hill's burgeoning tourism board hopes to lure visitors with the area's rich history. Local mining continues to this day, on the same giant lode of silver, zinc, and lead discovered by Rasp. However, as the last operational mine is expected to shut its shafts in 2006, the town's other markets now silently battle for the position of leading industry. At the same time, the city supports a thriving art scene that has century-old roots in miners' "naive art," attracting a broadening international renown each year. This odd conjunction of commercialism, contemporary artistry, and a history of gritty labor has imbued Broken Hill with a character unlike other towns in Australia.

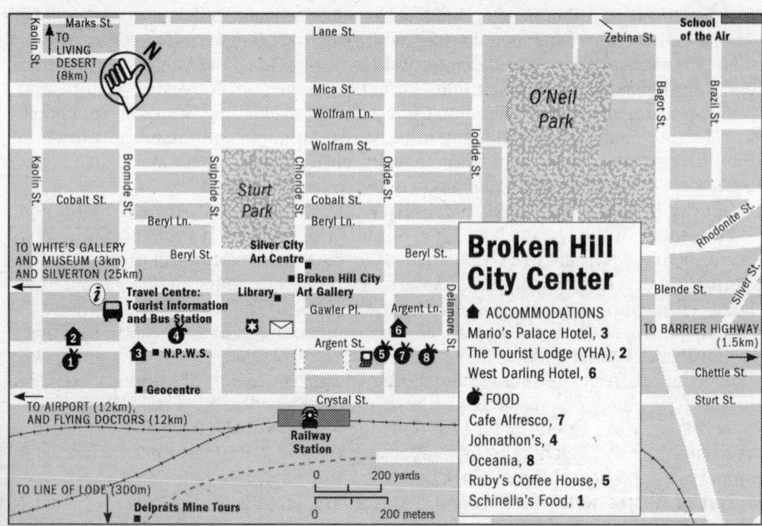

TRANSPORTATION

Trains: The train station (☎8087 1400), is on Crystal St. near the intersection with Chloride St. Great Southern (☎13 21 47) runs the *Indian-Pacific* to **Sydney** (16½hr.; W, Su 4:30pm; $117, ISIC $59) and to **Perth** (48hr.; Tu, F 9:20am; $343/$172) via **Adelaide** (6½hr., $59/$30). Great Southern also runs the *Ghan* to **Alice Springs** (27hr., Su 5:50am, $250, ISIC $30) via **Adelaide** (6¼hr.; $59/$30). Countrylink (☎13 22 32) trains go to **Sydney** (16¼hr.; daily 4am; $86, ISIC $43).

Buses: The bus depot (☎8087 2735; open M-F 9am-4pm) is in the Visitors Centre, at the corner of Blende and Bromide St. **Greyhound** (24hr. ☎13 20 30) goes to: **Adelaide** (7hr.; daily 10:30am;$75, ISIC $68); other destinations are accessible via **Dubbo** (9hr.; daily 3:35pm; $108/$97), including **Sydney** (16hr.,$121/ $109) and **Brisbane** (24hr., $211/$190). To connect with V/Line to **Melbourne** take the Tom Evans coach (☎03 5022 1415) to **Mildura** (3½hr.; M, W, F 3:45pm; $49, ISIC $40).

Local buses: Murton's Citybus runs 4 routes throughout greater Broken Hill M-F 8am-5:30pm and Sa roughly 9am-noon. Timetable available at the Visitors Centre.

Taxi: Yellow Radio Cabs (☎13 10 08).

Car Rental: Sundry around-town rentals can go as low as $58 per day. **Thrifty,** 190 Argent St. (☎8088 1928), and **Hertz** (☎8087 2719) are at the visitors center.

Bike Rental: The YHA Tourist Lodge (☎8088 2086) hires bikes for $10 per day.

ORIENTATION AND PRACTICAL INFORMATION

Rather than use the points of the compass, Broken Hill's streets are aligned with the line of lode upon which the mining city has long depended. Most shops and services congregate in the walkable rectangle bounded by **Bromide** (W), **Mica** (N), **Iodide** (E), and **Crystal** (S) St. Cutting west-to-east, one block above Crystal St., Argent St. is the main thoroughfare, with most of the food and lodging. Several outlying attractions require motorized transport (particularly **Silverton, Mutawintji National Park,** and the **Living Desert**), but rental cars are extremely expensive. Organized tours are a reasonable option for seeing the sights.

Broken Hill has adopted the phone code of South Australia (08), as well as its **time zone,** Central Standard Time (CST), 30min. behind the rest of NSW.

NAIVETÉ PAYS. While Broken Hill is notable for both its mining, with the Line of Lode as an obvious symbol, and its art, with close to 40 private galleries, the two scenes are not mutually exclusive. The modern artistic movement in the area can be traced to one man, Sam Byrne, who took up painting after a lifetime of work in the mines. Untrained and unrefined, Byrne's works gained popularity because of the stories they told, depicting memories from a childhood in the New South Wales outback and a career underground. Other miners, particularly Pro Hart and Hugh Schulz, soon followed suit, and the tradition of "naive art" in Broken Hill was born.

Tourist Office: Broken Hill Visitor Information Centre, (☎8087 6077; www.murrayoutback.org.au), on the corner of Blende and Bromide St. From the railway station, turn left onto Crystal and walk 2 blocks west, then turn right onto Bromide; the office is 2 blocks down on the left. Tune your radio to 88FM for a recorded replay of the town's history. Open daily 8:30am-5pm.

Tours: Many tour operators offer similarly priced daytrips to **Silverton** ($45-50), **Mutawintji National Park** ($125-150), the **Living Desert Sculptures** ($20-25), and multi-day outback safaris (many hundreds of dollars). Though pricey, the tours are the best option for lone risk-averse travelers and for those without their own vehicle; for groups, renting a car is more economical.

National Parks Information: New South Wales National Parks and Wildlife Service (NPWS), 183 Argent St (☎8088 5933; fax 8088 4448).

Bank: ANZ, 357 Argent St. (☎13 13 14) is right next to **Commonwealth,** 338-340 Argent St. (☎13 22 21). Both open M-Th 9:30am-4pm, F 9:30am-5pm. 24hr. **ATMs**.

Library: Broken Hill Library (☎8088 3317), on Blende St. Free **Internet access.** Open M-W 10am-8pm, Th-F 10am-6pm, Sa 10am-1pm, Su 1-5pm.

Police: 252 Argent St. (☎8087 0299).

Internet Access: Slow but free at the library (see above). A faster, cheap alternative is **pcProNET,** 387-389 Argent St. (☎8087 8686). $2.75 per 30min. Open M-F 9am-5:30pm, Sa 9am-12:30pm.

Post Office: 260 Argent St (☎8087 7071). Open M-F 9am-5pm. Poste Restante available; pickup at the window around side of building. **Postal Code:** 2880.

ACCOMMODATIONS

If everything is full, try a pubstay on Argent St. Campers have also been known to set up in the dried-up creek near the Pinnacles Mine, southwest of town.

Mario's Palace Hotel, 227 Argent St. (☎8088 1699). Visitors don't stay here for the quality of the rooms but for the sheer experience. Foyer, corridor, and lounge walls beam with waterfall murals painted by a local Aborigine. One wildly-decorated 6-person bedroom was featured in *Priscilla Queen of the Desert*. All rooms have fridge, TV, A/C, heat, and electric blankets. Key deposit $10. Singles $31, with bath $42; doubles $44, $53; *Priscilla* room $90-135. AmEx/MC/V.

The Tourist Lodge (YHA), 100 Argent St. (☎8088 2086; mcrae@pcpro.net.au). This sprawling hostel has a swimming pool to beat the desert heat. A/C and heat will cost you a little more. The tourist center and bus depot are at the back door. Kitchen with TV, common room with ping-pong table, laundry. Reception 7:30am-noon and 3-9pm. Key deposit $10. Dorms and twins $16, non-YHA $18; singles $20-28. AmEx/MC/V.

West Darling Motor Hotel, 400 Argent St. (☎8087 2691; fax 8087 1963). On the corner of Oxide St. The hotel of choice for ore magnates back in the day, now a quality budget pub accommodation. Plain, neat rooms overlooking the town center, some with fridge and veranda, all with A/C, heat, and washbasin. TV lounge, parking, and continental breakfast. Reception open when bar is: M-Sa 11am-midnight, Su 11am-10pm. Singles $28, weekly $168; twins and doubles $53/$315, with bath $60/$360; family $55-60/$330-360, with bath $66/396. AmEx/DC/MC/V.

FOOD

Broken Hill's numerous hotels, service clubs, and takeaways, most on or near Argent St., offer a fair amount of cheap chow. **Cafe Alfresco,** on the corner of Argent and Oxide St., serves up big portions of quality pasta ($10.90). The funky pizzas (from $11) are decent but depressingly small. There's sidewalk dining for those who prefer their meals, well, *al fresco*. (☎8087 5599. Open 8am-late.) The oddly-spelled **Johnathon's,** 198 Argent St., makes yummy toasted foccacias ($4.20), cheap breakfasts (under $10), and has a substantial vegetarian selection. (☎8087 8344. Open M-F 9:30am-3:30pm.) To beat the heat, try a $3.50 fruit smoothie at **Ruby's Coffee Lounge,** 393 Argent St.; banana is the biggest seller. (☎8087 1188. Open M-F 8am-4pm.) **Oceania,** 423 Argent St., has an $8 all-you-can-eat Chinese buffet. (☎8088 4539. Open Tu-F noon-2pm and daily 5-9:30pm.) **Schinella's Food and Liquor,** on Argent St. across from the YHA hostel, has a solid variety of **groceries** and booze. (Open M-Sa 8:30am-6pm, Su 9am-1pm.)

SIGHTS

DELPRAT'S MINE TOUR. Gain insight into the city's rugged history with a tour of the original Broken Hill Proprietary mine. The fantastic two-hour trip—all 130m underground—features equipment demonstrations and an insightful comparison of the mining labor system through time, with former miners-*cum*-annotative tour guides. Don your miner's hat and marvel at how they did it with only a candle 100 years ago. *(The BHP mine site is on the Broken Hill. Follow the gravel road off Iodide St. just past the train tracks; it's a mildly steep 10-15min. walk. ☎8088 1604. Tours M-F 10:30am, Sa 2pm; during school holidays, daily 10:30am and 2pm. $28, concessions $26, children $22, family $83-120; book ahead during school holidays.)*

LINE OF LODE VISITORS CENTRE. The pinnacle of Broken Hill's tourism movement, on the pinnacle of the hill itself. This shiny new complex runs daily surface tours of the South Mine as well as special night tours throughout the week. Just outside, the **Miners' Memorial,** dedicated April 21, 2001, pays homage to the hundreds of individuals who have died mining the Lode from the 1850s to the present. The center also contains a touchscreen database of the fallen miners, as well as a reasonably-priced cafe with panoramic views of the city below. *(The entire conglomerate is on Broken Hill's highest point, a 5-10min. walk past Delprat's up the hill. ☎8088 6000; www.lineoflodebrokenhill.org.au. Tours 2hr.; daily 10am and 2pm; $16.50, concessions $14.40, under 16 $8.80, families $27.50. Sunset barbecue tour F 5-8pm; $18.50/$16.50/$9.50/$38.50. Miners' Memorial $5.50/$4.40/$2.50/$15.50. Night tours $11.50-13.50. Open daily 9am-10pm. AmEx/DC/MC/V.)*

BUSHY WHITE'S MINING MUSEUM. Former-miner Bushy White teaches the history of Broken Hill mining through creative dioramas and demonstrations. Set up in White's own house, the museum offers the experience of going underground without actually going; the dedicated owner uses insightful methods of instruction to reenact the real mining experience. Over 250 of White's original mineral art works depict mining equipment and techniques as well as landscapes and random Australiana. *(1 Allendale St. Off of Brookfield Ave., about 2km west of the city center. ☎8087 2878. Tours when you show up. Open daily 9am-5pm. $4, family $10. Wheelchair accessible.)*

GEOCENTRE. Any questions you've ever had about geology, metallurgy, and mining techniques are answered in a sharp display on science of the earth. Exactly. Regardless, the real highlight is an extensive display of just plain cool rocks. *(On the corner of Bromide and Crystal St. ☎8087 6538; www.pcpro.net.au/~geocentre. Open M-F 10am-5pm, Sa-Su 1-5pm. $3.50, concessions and children $2.50, family $6.50-8.)*

ROYAL FLYING DOCTOR SERVICE. The Flying Doctors provide health care to outback residents in over 80% of Australia. A museum and brief, exciting film detail the history and workings of this noble institution. *(At the Broken Hill Airport. ☎8080 1717. Open daily 9am-noon, also M-F 1-5pm. $3.30 admission supports the RFDS.)*

SCHOOL OF THE AIR. The School of the Air provides remote education for distant schoolchildren. Visitors can observe the proceedings on weekdays but must book at the tourist office the day before and be seated by 8:20am (demerits for tardiness). The worthwhile proceedings give a real feel for the quirks of life in the bush and outback. *(On Lane St., 2 blocks east of Iodide St. $3.30, children $2.20)*

LIVING DESERT RESERVE. Impressive eclectic art has been set up in the Living Desert Reserve. In 1993, the Broken Hill Sculpture Symposium commissioned a group of local and international sculptors to create sandstone works atop a hill. The masterful pieces blend Aboriginal with modern and international influence and are best viewed at sunrise and sunset, when the light plays upon the colors. A 1½hr. walking trail from the sculpture site leads past gullies, ledges, and plenty of outback critters back to the carpark. *(Head north 8km along Kaolin St. You can drive all the way up the hill by obtaining a gate key from the tourist office for $6 with a $10 deposit, but the 15min. hike from a nearby carpark is more fun and free.)*

BROKEN HILL CITY ART GALLERY. A variety of excellent local work and a strong collection of 20th-century Australian painting constitutes this small collection. The signature piece, *Silver Tree,* is a delicately wrought arboreal centerpiece commissioned by Charles Rasp for the 1882 Melbourne Exhibition. *(Corner of Blende and Chloride St. ☎8088 5491. Open M-F 10am-5pm, Sa-Su 1-5pm. $3, concessions $2, families $6.)* Across Chloride St., the **Silver City Art Centre** houses **The Big Picture,** which is just that. Local artist Peter Andrew Anderson has created the largest canvas painting in the world at 100m long at 12m high. The work, which is hung in a circle that you actually walk into, depicts all the attractions of the Broken Hill outback. *(☎8088 6166. Gallery free; admission to The Big Picture $4.95.)*

NEAR BROKEN HILL: SILVERTON

Diminutive Silverton makes Broken Hill, 25km to the south, look like a metropolis. The 1876 discovery of silver, zinc, and lead ore at Thackaringa brought Silverton into existence. Prospectors arrived in droves, and the population peaked at around 3000 in 1885. Unfortunately for Silverton, most of the ore was gone by this point, just as Broken Hill's lode was revealing its precious potential. This combination of circumstances rendered Silverton a ghost town, home today to fewer than 60. Silverton revels in its emptiness and has been used in numerous bleak films, including the classic *Mad Max II.* But don't let concern over post-nuclear desert mutants keep you away from Silverton; it is an experience like no other.

Silverton's handful of buildings ranges from old brick ruins that have stood abandoned since the 1800s to some good art galleries specializing in outback naturalism. The **Silverton Gaol,** erected in 1889, was used infrequently after the evaporation of Silverton's population and was converted to a boys' reformatory in the 1930s. The buildings were closed in 1943 and then reopened as a museum in 1968. The former cells are packed with old-tyme geegaws, including a great array of daguerreotypes from the mining days and random assorted Australiana. (☎8088 5317. Open daily 9:30am-4:30pm. $2.50, students $1.50, under 12 50¢.) The main social activity 'round these parts is getting sloshed, making the legendary **Silverton Hotel,** (☎8088 5313) the most important building in town. Filled to the rafters with a huge diversity of beer cans and signs with naughty sayings, the hotel serves simple food and drink until 8 or 9pm. Try the hot quandong pie, made from a staple fruit in local bush tucker.

Penrose Park, just north of town, offers scandalously cheap accommodation: primitive campsites and unadorned, livable 6- to 8-person bunkhouses with kitchen, A/C, BBQ, and fridge. 8 tennis courts are free for day use, $4 at night. (☎8088 5307. Sites $4 per person or $10 per family; bunkhouses $25-35; showers $1; BYO linen.) The **Silverton Camel Farm,** on the road from Broken Hill, grants rides on the temperamental humped beasts. (☎8088 5316. $5 per 15min.; $25 per hr.; 2hr. sunset safari $50; day rides including BBQ lunch $100.)

During the Ice Age, glaciers scraped the plains 6km west of Silverton until they were as level as a freshly zambonied ice rink. After years of government deforestation, the **Mundi Mundi Plains,** are one of the largest stretches of flat plains on Earth. Looking out 400km to the horizon, you'll understand why the plains were named after the aboriginal word for "neverending."

MUNGO NATIONAL PARK

Ages ago, before the pyramids at Giza were even a sparkle in the eye of world history, hunter-gatherer communities flourished on the banks of Lake Mungo, in the extreme southwest corner of present-day New South Wales. Forty thousand years and 1600 Aboriginal generations later, life continues at **Mungo National Park,** one of the oldest continually inhabited sites in the world. Today the lake is dry (and has been for 15,000 years), and Mungo has undergone some spectacular weathering. Sand dunes on the edges of the lake bed have been sculpted into strange, otherworldly landforms by erosion, accelerated over the course of the past hundred years by settlers' unwitting introduction of harmful foreign species: grazing sheep and foraging rabbits. Known as the **Walls of China,** their erosion has revealed countless fossils and artifacts, including **Mungo Three,** a skeleton of a human male that is, at an estimated 40,000 years, the oldest remaining *Homo sapiens* relic in the world. (The skeleton was buried again in a secret location so that it wouldn't be plundered.) The colored layers of sand clearly demarcate periods of water change up to 120,000 years ago. The archaeological information uncovered here has earned the **Willandra Lakes** region status as a **World Heritage Site.**

Mungo is 110km northeast of Mildura, Victoria on the **Arumpo-Ivanhoe Rd.** Roads within and around the park are unsealed but accessible to 2WD vehicles in good weather. Road conditions can be checked with the NPWS (☎03 5021 8900). There is a $6 vehicle entry fee for the park. An excellent 70km driving tour skirts the Walls of China and encompasses all of the park's best features. The **Visitors Centre** near the park entrance has maps and displays on megafauna and Aboriginal life in the area, and collects camping and lodging fees. A nature walk (1½hr.) through the Mallee scrub begins just outside the center. The shearer's quarters next to the Visitors Centre have been converted into bare-bones bunk rooms with surprisingly clean bathrooms and showers (☎03 5021 8900. $16.50; children $5.50. Book ahead.) **Camping** is allowed near the Arumpo Rd. entrance and at Belah Camp on the driving tour. Visitors must bring drinking water. Belah observes a strict total fire ban, excepting gas BBQs; firewood must be self-supplied at the Arumpo camp. (Campsites $5.50 per person for up to 2, $2.20 per additional person up to 6; honor system, but park rangers perform spot checks.)

MEGAFAUNA TO MEGAMEN Evidence collected throughout Australia strongly suggests that the early Aborigines shared the continent with some fearsome beasts: giant mammals now termed megafauna. One of the more novel species, *Zygomaturus trilobus,* was sized like a buffalo, built much like a wombat, and possessed either a horn similar to a rhinoceros's or a short, flexible trunk. Strangest of all is *Procoptodon goliah,* a kangaroo twice as big as the largest red 'roos, which climbed trees and ate leaves. Its skull was flattened and its eyes were set forward in the head, giving it a snub-nosed, eerily humanoid visage. Unlike regular kangaroos, Goliah's arms and shoulders allowed it to manipulate objects and even reach overhead, much like the ancestors of human beings. If primates hadn't beaten out marsupials in the race toward human sentience, we might all be hopping today.

NORTHERN TERRITORY

Against the backdrop of a pastel sky, silver eucalyptus trees contort their limbs into ghost-like curves, and cockatoos squawk noisily from their branches. Sparse clumps of foliage and palm trees break the otherwise dry woodland. In the distance, the thick smoke of a bush fire bruises the horizon. Into this scene, a well-worn 4WD rumbles down an endless road toward a fiery sunset, bellowing pumpkin-colored dust behind its growling motor. The mud-caked license plate says "Northern Territory: Outback Australia." And if it's Outback Australia that you're after, you've come to the right place.

The Northern Territory stretches into the country's most extreme regions. In its 1.3 million square kilometer area, the 200,000 inhabitants could enjoy 6.5 square kilometers of land apiece. Instead, nearly 60% choose to settle in the population centers of Darwin in the tropical Top End or Alice Springs in the desert-like Red Centre. The rest scatter among three or four substantially-sized towns such as Katherine or Tennant Creek or upon the cattle stations, Aboriginal homelands, and national parks that give droplets of human life to the vast outback. The stretches between such outposts can be a day's drive, even on the main highways, giving rise to the notion that most of the NT is simply MT (empty). However, the wonderfully wide-open spaces truly reveal the Australian landscape at its best.

Thirty percent of the Territory's population is indigenous, with whites and Aborigines living together in relatively mild, if indifferent, peace. However, separatism is rampant, and most businesses and services are predominantly run and staffed by whites. Though colonization began in the 17th century, the Territory's European population was slow to grow. Only telegraph and railway construction and the gold rushes brought an influx of white Australians to this frontier land.

Today, mining and cattle-breeding remain prominent sources of income, but are quickly being equalled or surpassed by tourism. Apart from the residents of protected Aboriginal land, Territorians are anything but territorial. In fact, travelling through the NT is getting easier as the tourism infrastructure keeps building. Of the premier attractions, Kakadu and Litchfield National Park in the Top End, or Uluru and the MacDonnells in the Red Centre, are very accessible (once the vast distances between are overcome). While being a tourist in the NT is certainly more adventurous than participating in the overcrowded, overfed beach culture of the east coast, it is most rewarding (and highly recommended) to stay for longer than a whirlwind tour of the NT's greatest hits. It will take a little more time and effort to cultivate a real appreciation of the tremendous land and cultures it breeds.

As a land that stands for independence, it is not surprising that the NT has not pushed for statehood. A Territory referendum for statehood in 1998 was voted down by a substantial margin. For now, it will continue to be financially run by Canberra, but in spirit and in reality, the region grasps firmly to its political status. The spectacular sunsets and overwhelming star-scapes in the Northern Territory have a way of making governmental dictums and daily minutiae unimportant in the face of the realization that life goes on as it will.

TRANSPORTATION

The NT's vast expanses make transportation a significant issue. Darwin, Alice Springs, and Yulara (Ayers Rock Resort) are most commonly reached by air. Smaller planes often fly to smaller destinations, but the price can be daunting. There is **no train** system traversing the Territory, except from Alice heading south

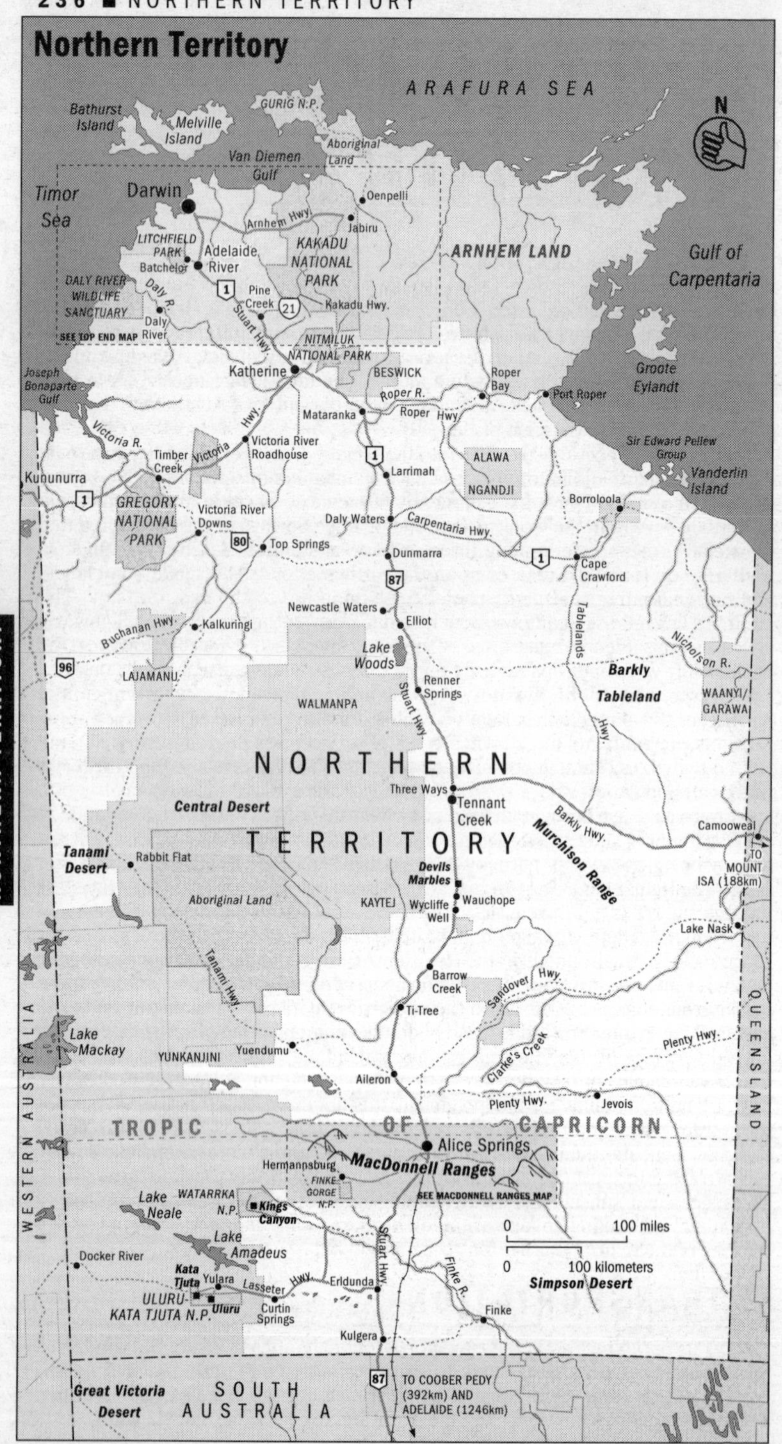
Northern Territory
ARAFURA SEA
Bathurst Island
Melville Island
GURIG N.P.
Aboriginal Land
Van Diemen Gulf
Timor Sea
Darwin
Oenpelli
Arnhem Hwy.
Jabiru
LITCHFIELD PARK
Adelaide River
Batchelor
KAKADU NATIONAL PARK
ARNHEM LAND
Gulf of Carpentaria
DALY RIVER WILDLIFE SANCTUARY
Daly R.
Daly River
Pine Creek
Kakadu Hwy.
Stuart Hwy.
SEE TOP END MAP
NITMILUK NATIONAL PARK
Katherine
BESWICK
Roper Bay
Port Roper
Groote Eylandt
Joseph Bonaparte Gulf
Roper R.
Mataranka
Roper Hwy.
Victoria R.
Victoria River Roadhouse
Timber Creek
Victoria Hwy.
Sir Edward Pellew Group
ALAWA
Larrimah
Vanderlin Island
Kununurra
NGANDJI
GREGORY NATIONAL PARK
Victoria River Downs
Borroloola
Daly Waters
Carpentaria Hwy.
Top Springs
Dunmarra
Cape Crawford
Newcastle Waters
Elliot
Tablelands Hwy.
Buchanan Hwy.
Kalkuringi
Lake Woods
Nicholson R.
LAJAMANU
Renner Springs
Barkly Tableland
WALMANPA
WAANYI/GARAWA
NORTHERN TERRITORY
Three Ways
Tennant Creek
Central Desert
Barkly Hwy.
Murchison Range
Camooweal
TO MOUNT ISA (188km)
Tanami Desert
Rabbit Flat
Devils Marbles
Aboriginal Land
KAYTEJ
Wauchope
Wycliffe Well
Lake Nash
Tanami Hwy.
Barrow Creek
Sandover Hwy.
Ti-Tree
Lake Mackay
YUNKANJINI
Yuendumu
Clarke's Creek
Plenty Hwy.
Aileron
Plenty Hwy.
Jervois
TROPIC OF CAPRICORN
Alice Springs
Hermannsburg
MacDonnell Ranges
FINKE GORGE N.P.
SEE MACDONNELL RANGES MAP
Lake Neale
WATARRKA N.P.
Kings Canyon
0 100 miles
0 100 kilometers
Lake Amadeus
Docker River
Simpson Desert
Finke R.
Kata Tjuta
Yulara
Lasseter Hwy.
Erldunda
ULURU-KATA TJUTA N.P.
Uluru
Curtin Springs
Finke
Kulgera
WESTERN AUSTRALIA
QUEENSLAND
TO COOBER PEDY (392km) AND ADELAIDE (1246km)
Great Victoria Desert
SOUTH AUSTRALIA

NORTHERN TERRITORY HIGHLIGHTS

FLORENCE FALLS. The water falls heavy and hard at Florence Falls in Litchfield National Park (sp. 261).

MUSEUM AND ART GALLERY OF THE NT. See the Aboriginal exhibitions and the infamous boat-eating croc at the Museum and Art Gallery of the NT (**P. 245**).

KING'S CANYON WALK. Don't look down on the King's Canyon Walk in Watarrka National Park (p. 280).

ULURU. The rock never disappoints (p. 284).

VALLEY OF THE WINDS. Free your mind in Valley of the Winds at Kata Tjuta (p. 286).

to Adelaide. **Greyhound** (☎13 20 30) and **McCafferty's** (☎13 14 99) buses offer extensive service to most major tourist centers but not to the farther reaches of the national parks. **Renting a car** is the best way to retain freedom and flexibility, but it's also the most expensive, and you must be at least 21. There are many national chains which have offices all over the NT; **Territory-Thrifty Car Rental** (1800 891 125) and **Budget** (☎13 27 27) are the cheapest, but limit kilometers (100km per day, each additional km $0.25-0.32), whereas **Britz** (☎1800 331 454) offers unlimited kilometers and rents 4WD to customers under 25 years of age. Each company does one-way rentals, but there is a one-way fee, usually $300-400.

The major tourist centers in the area are accessible by sealed or gravel roads. You'll only need a 4WD to venture into the bush on dirt tracks; however, this is necessary to see many of the spectacular sights of Kakadu National Park and the MacDonnell Ranges. Furthermore, if you rent a conventional vehicle, it won't be insured on unsealed or gravel roads. Rental companies determine their own restrictions, even for 4WD vehicles; explain your desired itinerary before you rent. If going to remote areas, ask for a high-clearance 4WD with two petrol tanks; trendier recreational vehicles often have 4WD but are too low to the ground to navigate many of the roads. Also, make sure the 4WD you rent is not so top-heavy that it could potentially flip over in rough terrain driving. There are many safari tours that operate in national parks and the bush for those who want the rugged experience without the hassle of renting. They usually run about $100-$130 per day. **Wilderness 4WD Adventures** (☎1800 808 288) or **Gondwana** (☎1800 242 177) are good for Top End tours, and **Wayoutback Desert Safaris** (☎8953 4304) for the Uluru area. These companies center around small groups and try to get off the beaten path. It's still best to do some research for a tour company that offers the price, length, and ruggedness that you're looking for.

If going beyond the highways, make sure to bring lots of extra water, food, emergency materials (tire, tools, rope, jack, etc.), and inform a friend, visitors center, or ranger station of your travel plans. Avoid driving at dusk and dawn, when **kangaroos** tend to loiter in the road. There are many sections of unfenced ranch land along the highways; beware of **wandering cattle.** Another risk is quite common: **road trains** (multi-part trucks) which carry supplies across the Territory. They can up to 50m long, often generating dust storms behind them. *It is especially dangerous to pass road trains; if done, take extreme caution.* When venturing onto unsealed roads, be sure to call ahead to find out **road conditions** (☎1800 246 199); they vary tremendously, especially in the Top End from May-Oct., when some tracks may be washed out entirely. For **weather reports** and forecasts, dial 8982 3826. The **Automobile Association of the Northern Territory (AANT)** (☎8941 0611) can provide assistance is affiliated with national and international services and can provide invaluable assistance (see **Essentials,** p. 67).

DISTANCES FROM DARWIN TO:	KILOMETERS	APPROX. TIME
Alice Springs	1491km	15hr.
Batchelor	98km	1¼hr.
Kakadu National Park	257km	3hr.

NORTHERN TERRITORY

DISTANCES FROM DARWIN TO:	KILOMETERS	APPROX. TIME
Katherine	314km	3½hr.
Litchfield National Park	129km	1½hr.
Pine Creek	226km	2½hr.
Tennant Creek	986km	10hr.

DISTANCES FROM ALICE SPRINGS TO:	KILOMETERS	APPROX. TIME
Darwin	1491km	15hr.
Kata Tjuta (Mt. Olga)	500km	5¼hr.
Katherine	1177km	12hr.
Tennant Creek	504km	5hr.
Uluru (Ayer's Rock)	461km	4¾hr.
Watarrka (King's Canyon)	331km	4hr.
Yulara	444km	4½hr.

THE TOP END

A lush tropical crown atop a vast interior desert, the winterless Top End enjoys perpetually warm weather; like in other extreme northern parts of Australia, seasons here are divided only into the **Wet** monsoonal season and the semi-desert-like **Dry** season. In the latter season, backpack-toting pilgrims descend on Darwin and use this oasis of civilization as a base from which to explore the region's prime natural wonders—Kakadu and Litchfield National Parks.

While very few do, brave souls who venture to the Top End during the Wet season (Nov.-May) will be rewarded with views of the region at its most dramatic. Torrential rains drench the reddish dust and spark the growth of a velvet green blanket of vegetation, and clouds of mozzies (mosquitoes) with a harsh bite. Top Enders are willing to share their vast home for half the year, but they also seem to rejoice when the rain drives out the trespassers and, once again, Mother Nature puts their fierce outback spirit to the test.

DARWIN ☎08

With tropical temperatures, never-ending nightlife, tons of travelers, and an endless supply of energy, one thing is clear: Darwin (pop. 80,000) is *hot.* Doused by rain half the year and flooded by visitors the rest, Darwin is the only city for a long, long distance. As both the capital of the rugged Northern Territory and Australia's gateway to Southeast Asia, Darwin blends the outback country style with the eclectic flair of an international community.

During the Dry, the incessant sunshine and azure beaches hypnotize mobs of midriff-baring backpackers to come to Darwin and play under the palm trees and stars, at the bars, with the didgeridoos, and with each other. However, Darwin's character has not always been so footloose and fancy-free. Darwin suffered nearly two years of intense Japanese bombing as Australia's hardest hit target in WWII. After rebuilding over the next decades, the city was decimated a second time by Cyclone Tracy on Christmas Eve, 1974. With true Territory grit, Darwin started from scratch once again, creating the convenient city center, manicured parks, and touristy outdoor mall that exist today.

The mining industry and tourism contribute to the city's current fortunes, with scores of hostels and bars accommodating backpackers. Still, visitors don't come to Darwin looking for refined, urban pleasures. They're on their way to explore the natural splendors of the Top End, including Kakadu and Litchfield National Parks, even if they may forget that for a few days while under Darwin's spell.

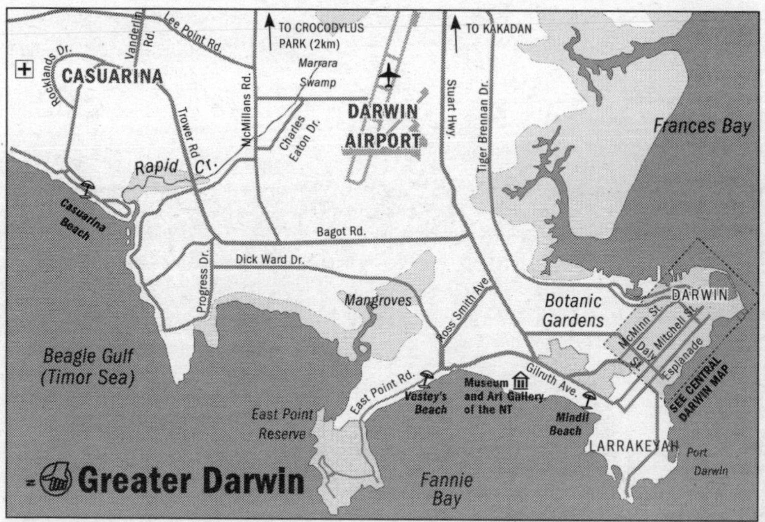

INTERCITY TRANSPORTATION

BY PLANE. Darwin International Airport (☎8920 1850) is about 10km northeast of the city center on McMillans Rd.; from Darwin city center, take a left on Bagot Rd. off the Stuart Hwy. **Qantas,** 16 Bennett St. (☎13 13 13), and **Ansett** (☎13 13 00) at the Smith St. Mall, have domestic return services to: Adelaide ($671); Alice Springs ($432); Ayers Rock ($564); Brisbane ($470); Broome ($388); Cairns ($531); Melbourne ($791); Perth ($762); Sydney ($630). Numerous airlines offer international service to Southeast Asia, Singapore, and Bali. Other airline offices include **Royal Brunei Airlines,** 22 Cavenagh St. (☎8941 0966); **Merpati Nusantara,** 6 Knuckey St. (☎8981 5229); the Territory-carrier **Airnorth** (☎8945 2866), at the airport. Travel agencies can arrange the cheapest airline tickets.

For transport between the city and the airport, the **Darwin Airport Shuttle** is your best bet. (☎8981 5066 or 1800 358 945. $7.50 one-way, $13 return.) If notified in advance, many accommodations will pay or reimburse patrons for the ride. **Taxis** (☎13 10 08) run to the airport for $18-20.

BY BUS. The **Transit Centre,** 67-69 Mitchell St., between Peel and Nuttall St., is the locus of intercity bus travel. (☎8941 0911. Open daily 6am-7:45pm.) **Greyhound** (☎13 20 30) and **McCafferty's** (☎13 14 99) run to: Adelaide (39hr., 1-2 per day, $352); Alice Springs (20hr., 2 per day, $184); Broome (24hr., 1 per day, $242); Cairns (41hr., 1 per day, $372); Katherine (4hr., 4 per day, $50); Melbourne (51hr., 1 per day, $408); Sydney via Alice Springs and Adelaide (67hr., 1 per day, $473); Tennant Creek (12hr., 3 per day, $130).

ORIENTATION

The Darwin area is situated on a peninsula, with the city center in the southeastern corner. The tree-lined **Esplanade** and the rocky **Lameroo Beach** run along the western edge of the peninsula. The center of the backpacker district is located at the Transit Centre on **Mitchell St.,** which runs parallel and one block east of the Esplanade. The **Smith St. Mall,** a pedestrian zone occupying the block between Knuckey and Bennett St., is home to a multitude of shops and services., and run perpendicular to the Esplanade at the southern end of the city. At the tip of the peninsula, just below the city center, **Stokes Hill** and the **Wharf** area hold a number of sights.

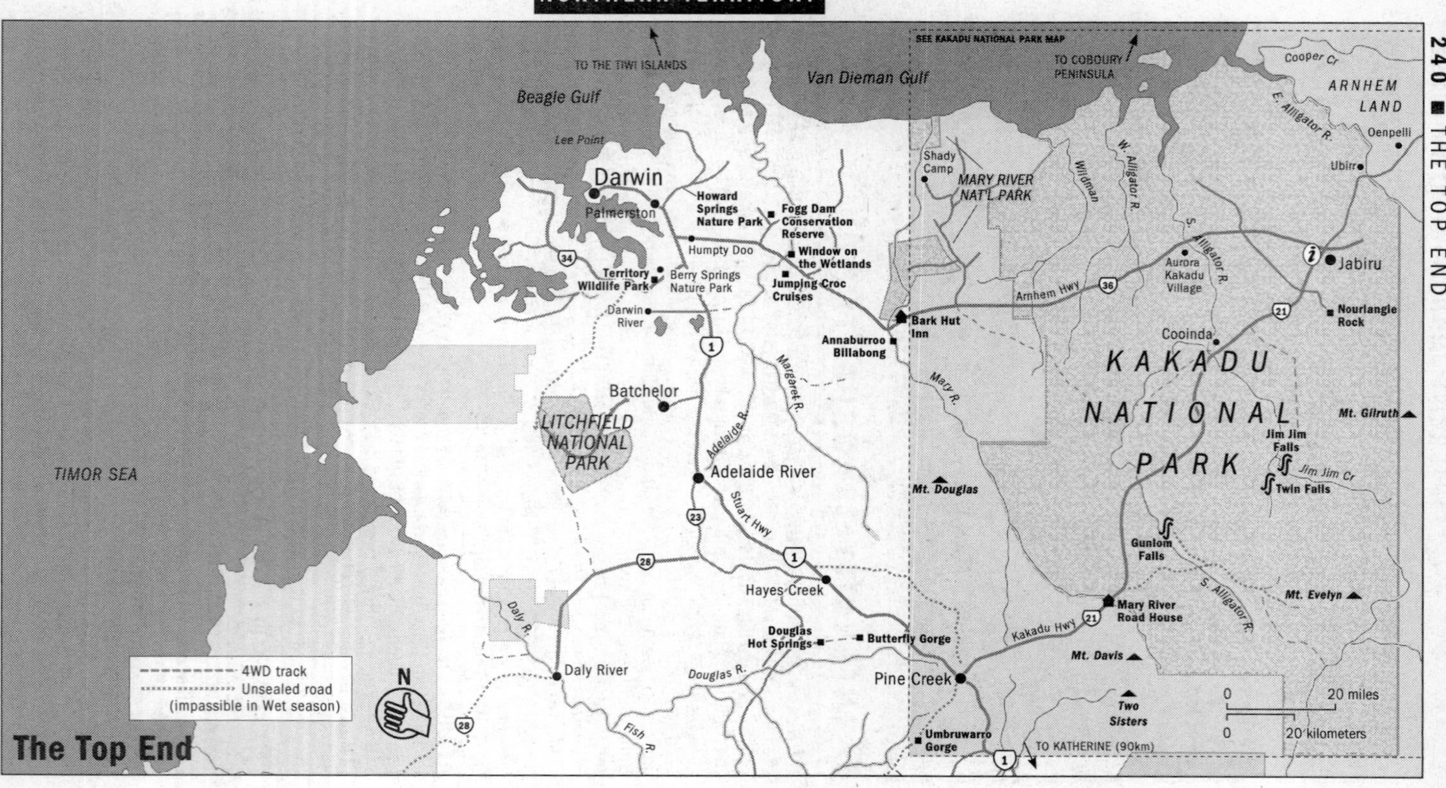
The Top End
TIMOR SEA
Beagle Gulf
Van Dieman Gulf
Lee Point
TO THE TIWI ISLANDS
TO COBOURY PENINSULA
SEE KAKADU NATIONAL PARK MAP
Darwin
Palmerston
Howard Springs Nature Park
Humpty Doo
Berry Springs Nature Park
Territory Wildlife Park
Darwin River
Fogg Dam Conservation Reserve
Window on the Wetlands
Jumping Croc Cruises
Annaburroo Billabong
Bark Hut Inn
Shady Camp
MARY RIVER NAT'L PARK
Wildman
W. Alligator R.
S. Alligator R.
E. Alligator R.
Cooper Cr
ARNHEM LAND
Oenpelli
Ubirr
Jabiru
Nourlangle Rock
Aurora Kakadu Village
Cooinda
KAKADU NATIONAL PARK
Mt. Gilruth
Jim Jim Falls
Jim Jim Cr
Twin Falls
Gunlom Falls
Mt. Evelyn
Mary River Road House
Mt. Davis
Two Sisters
Mt. Douglas
Arnhem Hwy
Kakadu Hwy
Stuart Hwy
Mary R.
Margaret R.
Adelaide R.
Adelaide River
Batchelor
LITCHFIELD NATIONAL PARK
Hayes Creek
Douglas Hot Springs
Butterfly Gorge
Douglas R.
Pine Creek
Umbruwarro Gorge
TO KATHERINE (90km)
Daly River
Daly R.
Fish R.
36
21
1
23
28
34
0
20 miles
0
20 kilometers
N
4WD track
Unsealed road (impassible in Wet season)

Moving northeast out of downtown, **Daly St.** eventually becomes the **Stuart Hwy.** and heads out to the airport. **Smith St.** continues north of the city center for 500m before converging with Gilruth Ave., which leads to the **MGM Casino, Mindil Beach,** and the **Museum and Art Gallery of the NT.** Gilruth Ave. to **East Point Rd.** eventually leads to the **East Point Reserve,** 6km from the city center.

LOCAL TRANSPORTATION

Public Transit: Darwinbus (☎8924 7666) runs to suburbs and beaches along the major thoroughfares. Terminal located between Harry Chan Ave. and Bennett St., with stops along Mitchell and Cavenagh St. Fares $1.40-2.40. **Tourcards** allow unlimited travel for a day ($5, concessions $2.50) or a week ($25, concessions $12.50).

Taxis: Darwin Radio Taxis (☎13 10 08. $1.26 per km). **Territory Shuttle** (☎8928 1155) will take you anywhere downtown for $2.

Car Rental: Cars are not necessary to see the city, but many people rent cars to explore the rest of the Top End. Rental companies abound but availability decreases in the Dry, so book ahead. Sedans generally start around $55 per day, and 4WD from $100 per day, including 100km per day and $0.23-0.33 per extra km. Damage liability can usually be reduced at an additional rate of $15-45 per day. Large chains with a wide selection include: **Avis,** 145 Stuart Hwy. (☎8981 9922); **Budget** (☎8981 9800) at the corner of Daly St. and Doctors Gully Rd.; **Hertz** (☎8941 0944) at the corner of Smith and Daly St.; **Territory Rent-a-Car,** 64 Stuart Hwy. (☎8981 4796). **Nifty,** 39 Cavenagh St. (☎8941 7090), specializes in small vehicles. For short distances, **Port** (☎8981 8441) at Fisherman's Wharf, and **Europcar,** 77 Cavenagh St. (☎13 13 90), offer rates from $39 per day and charge for each km, while unlimited km are available at Nifty, **Britz,** 44-66 Stuart Hwy. (☎8981 2081), and **Advance,** 86 Mitchell St. (☎8981 2999). The minimum age for rental is 21 at Britz and **Apollo,** 93 McMinn St. (☎8981 4796); the rest require renters to be at least 25.

Buying and Selling Used Cars: Travelers Car Market (☎0418 600 830), at Peel and Mitchell St. caters to backpackers. Sellers pay $40 per week to cram into the lot, but buyers browse for free. Cars sell fastest May-Oct. Open daily 8am-4pm. Also check bulletin boards at hostels and Internet shops. Registration requirements vary for each state. The **Auto Association of the Northern Territory (AANT)** is at 79-81 Smith St. (☎8981 3837. Open M-F 8am-5pm.) Also, see **Buying and Selling Used Cars** (p. 69).

Bike Rental: Available through most hostels ($4 per hr., $16 per day).

PRACTICAL INFORMATION

Tourist Office: Darwin Region Tourism Association (DRTA) (☎8981 4300; fax 8981 0653; info@drta.com.au), in Beagle House Building at the corner of Mitchell and Knuckey St.; also at airport. Open M-F 8:30am-5:45pm, Sa 9am-2:45pm, Su 10am-1:45pm. Main office of the **Parks & Wildlife Commission of the Northern Territory** (☎8999 5511; www.nt.gov.au/pawis) is in Palmerston near Darwin, but info can be found at the DRTA.

Travel Offices: Tours can be booked from dozens of locations on Mitchell St. and at the Smith St. Mall. **STA,** Shop T-17 in Galleria, Smith St. Mall (☎8941 2955). Sells ISIC ($16.50) and VIP ($29) cards. Open M-F 9am-5pm, Sa 9am-2pm. **Flight Centre,** 24 Cavanagh St. (☎13 16 00), guarantees to beat any quoted current airfare price. Open M-F 9am-5:30pm, Sa 9am-noon.

WHO'S FITTEST NOW? Charles Darwin was not aboard the HMS Beagle in 1839 when it sailed into the harbor that his former shipmates named in his honor. He had been down under three years previously, but disembarked near modern-day Sydney. Darwin's tour of Australia included the Blue Mountains in New South Wales, which he described as having a "desolate and untidy appearance." He wrote of the continent, "Nothing but rather sharp necessity should compel me to emigrate."

Currency Exchange: Bank South Australia, 13 Knuckey St. (☎8981 1322). Open M-Th 9:30am-4pm, F 9:30am-5pm. **ANZ Bank** (☎13 13 14), on Knuckey St. by the Smith St. Mall. Open M-Th 9:30am-4pm, F 9:30am-5pm.

American Express: Travelers World, 18 Knuckey St. (☎8981 4699). Holds mail (no packages) for 30 days for card holders or Traveler's Check holders. Address mail "ATTN: Client Mail, GPO Box 3728, Darwin NT 0801." Open M-F 8:30am-5pm, Sa 9am-noon.

Backpacking Supplies: NT General Store, 42 Cavanagh St. (☎8981 8242), at Edmunds St., has everything you need for the outdoors and a large selection of good maps. Open M-W 8:30am-5:30pm, Th-F 8:30am-6pm, Sa 8am-1pm.

Book Exchange: Read Back Book Exchange (☎8981 8885), Darwin Plaza off Smith St. Mall. Open M-F 9am-5:30pm, Sa 9am-3pm. **Dusty Jackets,** Shop 3, 29 Cavanagh St. (☎8981 6772). Open M-F 10:30am-5pm, Sa 9am-noon.

Library: Northern Territory Library (☎8999 7410), in the Parliament building at the corner of Mitchell and Bennett St. Open M-F 10am-6pm, Sa-Su 1-5pm.

Emergency: ☎000.

Police: 24 Mitchell St. (24hr. ☎8927 8888). Open M-F 8am-11pm, Sa-Su 8-11pm.

Hotlines: Crisis Line (☎1800 019 116). **NT Aids Council** (☎1800 880 899). **Sexual Assault Referral** (24hr. ☎8922 7156).

Pharmacy: Darwin Pharmacy, Shop 46, Smith St. Mall (☎8981 9202). Open M-Sa 8:30am-7pm, Su 9am-5pm.

Hospital: Royal Darwin Hospital (☎8922 8888), on Rocklands Dr. in Tiwi, Casuarina, 9km from the city center.

Internet Access: Everywhere. The cheapest option is **Didjworld Internet Shop,** 60 Smith St. (☎8981 3510), in the Harry Chan Arcade, which charges $0.09 per min. (7-10pm $0.08 per min.) Open M-Sa 9am-10pm, Su 10am-8pm. **Global Gossip,** 44 Mitchell St. (☎8942 3044). $6.95 per hr.; $3.50 per hr. from 8-9am. Open daily 8am-1am.

Post Office: General Post Office Darwin, 48 Cavenagh St. (☎13 13 18), at Edmunds St. Poste Restante held 30 days. Open M-F 8:30am-5pm, Sa 9am-noon. **Postal Code:** 0800.

MEDIA AND PUBLICATIONS.

Newspapers: *NT News* (90¢) daily; *Darwin Sun* on Wednesday.

Entertainment: *The Top End Visitors' Guide* monthly; *Arts Darwin* monthly; Entertainment section of *NT News* on Wednesday and Friday.

Radio: Rock, Triple J 103.3FM and HOT-100 101.1FM; News, ABC 105.7FM; Tourist info, 88FM.

ACCOMMODATIONS

There are plenty of hostels in Darwin. Most are clumped on Mitchell St. with plenty of pubs, takeaways, and Internet shops nearby. As you walk away from the Transit Centre on Mitchell St. out of town, the street numbers increase. Beds fill up during the Dry, so book ahead. During the Wet, you'll be rewarded for your bravery with lower prices.

Darwin City YHA, 69 Mitchell St. (☎8981 3995; darwinyha@yhant.org.au), next to the Transit Centre. Large, clean, and efficient–the king of Darwin hostels sets the standard that the rest of Darwin scrambles to imitate. International crowd and very competent staff. Large lockers in every room, A/C, pool, kitchen, dining area, sun deck, 2 TV rooms, and luggage storage ($2 per day). $5 all-you-can-eat BBQ on F. Free airport shuttle. Linen and key deposit $15. Laundry $2.20. Reception 24hr. Dorms $17; singles or doubles $39, with bath $50. Non-YHA $3-6 more.

Melaleuca Lodge, 50 Mitchell St. (☎8941 3395 or 1800 623 543; fax 8941 3368). With the patios, pool, palms, and prime location, Melaleuca is the hostel of choice for the young and hip. A/C, lockers, 2 kitchens, TV rooms, laundry. Free luggage storage, free airport pickup, free pancake breakfast. Reception 24hr. Dorms $20-22; twins $55; doubles $65. NOMADS/VIP. Wheelchair accessible.

NORTHERN TERRITORY

Chilli's Backpackers, 69A Mitchell St. (☎8941 9722 or 1800 351 313; fax 8941 9835). With a central location, sun decks, and spas, this is an exceedingly popular hostel. Airport shuttle reimbursed for 2-night stay or longer. Laundry. Pool. Key deposit $20. Reception in the Dry daily 6am-11pm, in the Wet 6am-9pm. Dorms $21; twins and doubles $50, with bath $52. NOMADS/VIP/YHA.

Salvation Army Red Shield Hostel, 49 Mitchell St. (☎8981 5994), south of Knuckey St. Great location and the best prices in town, but not for party animals: no drugs or alcohol, and no guests after 11pm. Call ahead to get on waiting list. Laundry $2. Key deposit $15. Reception daily 8:30am-4:30pm. Singles $15-18; family $22. Cash only.

Frogshollow Backpackers, 27 Lindsay St. (☎8941 2600 or 1800 068 686), at Woods St., 10min. from the Transit Centre. Patrons can enjoy exceptional facilities under cool overhanging palm trees. Airport shuttle reimbursed for 2-night stay or longer. Lockers and luggage storage, pool, spa, laundry, spacious kitchen, TV room, Internet, free breakfast. Key, linen, and cutlery deposit $20. Reception daily 6am-9pm. Dorms $20; twin and doubles $46, with bath $55. VIP/YHA.

YWCA Darwin "Banyan View Lodge," 119 Mitchell St. (☎8981 8644; fax 8981 6104). The spacious lodge offers simple, orderly rooms. Large kitchen, tiny spa, TV lounges, parking, laundry. Reception M-F 8am-6pm, Sa-Su 8am-4pm. Dorms $18; singles $38, with A/C $43; twins $48/$53; triple with bath and A/C $61.

Wilderness Lodge, 88 Mitchell St. (☎8981 8363; www.wildlodge.com.au). Smallest of the Mitchell St. hostels, Wilderness Lodge is cozy and very low-key. Free airport pickup. Free pancake breakfast. Pool, kitchen, luggage storage. Key deposit $10. Reception daily 6am-8:30pm. 4-, 6-, or 8-person dorms $20; doubles $50. NOMADS/VIP/YHA.

Globetrotters, 97 Mitchell St. (☎8981 5385; fax 8981 9096), is a partying hostel and pub in one, and madness ensues around the big-screen TV during football games. Rooms are somewhat crowded with 6-8 beds. Pool, kitchen, laundry. Key and linen deposit $20. Reception 24hr. Bunks $21; twins and doubles $58. NOMADS/VIP/YHA.

Elke's Inner City Backpackers, 112 Mitchell St. (☎8981 8399 or 1800 808 365; elkes@downunder.net.au), 10min. walk from the Transit Centre. With its laid back atmosphere, is the home of Smokey, the hostel cat. Patio, pool, spa, kitchens, TV room, laundry, Internet $6 per hr., free light brekkie. Airport shuttle reimbursed. Key deposit $10. Reception daily 6am-9pm. Dorms $22; single or twin $48; double $50.VIP/YHA.

Camping options in Darwin are limited. With harsh weather half the year and no campgrounds in central Darwin, die-hard campers need to head out of town. Camping or sleeping in cars is strictly forbidden in the Mindil Beach area. The **Shady Glen Caravan Park** is closest to the city, about 10km from central Darwin at the intersection of the Stuart Hwy. and Farrell Crescent. Patrons are treated to pool, kitchen, BBQ, laundry, and sparkling amenities. (☎8984 3330. Sites $10 per person; campervan sites $21.50 per night.)

FOOD

Darwin has a variety of options to feed the onslaught of budget travelers. The food stalls inside the Transit Centre and in the side arcades off Smith St. Mall offer hot, relatively cheap, mostly Asian cuisine. The **Mindil Beach market** (Th and Su night) offers cheap, delicious pan-Asian food in a great atmosphere ($7-8 for a full meal). The **Parap market** is smaller and more mellow, but is popular with locals seeking fresh fruit and veggies. Take bus #4 to Parap Shopping Plaza. (Open Sa 8am-2pm.) **Victoria Hotel,** 27 Smith St. Mall (☎8981 4011), has all-you-can-eat greasy lunch for $8.95., and **Sizzler,** on Mitchell St. next to the cinema, has generous buffet deals ($16.95 dinner, $13 lunch). The **Wharf Arcade,** at the end of Stokes Hill Wharf, is a popular and pricier sunset dining spot. Woolworth's **supermarket** is at the corner of Knuckey and Smith St. (Open M-Sa 6:30am-midnight, Su 8am-10pm.)

About Coffee (☎8981 2922), on Mitchell St. next to the Transit Centre. With meals of all shapes and sizes, it is about so much more than coffee. The real deal is the $11 specials; only the most massive appetites should attempt the "God Burger," which could feed a small kingdom. Open daily 8am-1am.

The Mental Lentil (☎8981 1377), in the Transit Centre. Amidst the sprawl of typical, unappealing takeaways, this is an oasis of varied vegetarian (and vegan) cuisine. Falafel roll $6.50, smoothies $3.50. Open M-F 11am-9pm, Sa 4-9pm.

Rendezvous Café, Shop 6, Star Village (☎8981 9231) at Smith St. Mall. Better Malaysian and Thai dishes than the food courts, but cheaper than the fancy Asian restaurants in town. A local crowd knows the good value and eats it up. Main dishes $8.50-13. Open M-W 9am-2:30pm, Th-F 5:30-9pm, Sa 9am-2pm and 5:30-9pm.

The J Spot Cafe, Shop 11, Vic Arcade (☎8981 4120), at the Smith St. Mall. A cool elegant atmosphere makes for a nice meal or coffee break (you'd never even know you were in a mall). Breakfast from $5, lunch $7-10. Open M-F 7am-5pm, Sa 8am-3pm.

Ben's Bakehouse, Shop 4, Anthony Plaza (☎8981 1561), at the Smith St. Mall. Tempting pies, pastries, and other sinful delights. Open M-F 6am-6:30pm, Sa-Su 6am-3pm.

Simply Foods, Star Village at the Smith St. Mall (☎8981 4765). Wholesome meals and snacks at a good price, with lots of vegetarian options. Creative sandwiches or big salads for $4-6. Open M-F 9am-3pm.

Major's (☎8941 5741), on Mitchell St. across from Transit Centre. The spot to get your greasy burgers or condoms before, during, or after a night of heavy boozing. Open 24hr.

SIGHTS

Though travelers through Darwin are often raring to hit Kakadu and Litchfield, some of Darwin's own attractions justify a diversion. Most sights are accessible by foot, bike, or a short public bus ride. The **Tour Tub,** popular with seniors, rounds up passengers at major accommodations or at the corner of Smith and Knuckey St. and herds them to 10 popular sights from Stokes Hill Wharf to East Point Reserve. (☎8981 5233. Runs daily 9am-4pm. Full-day pass $25.)

NORTHERN TERRITORY

MINDIL BEACH SUNSET MARKET. A celebration of arts, crafts, and food, the Mindil night market is where Darwin really shines. Outback goods, pottery, and clothes from Bali are on sale, while musicians and street performers vie for your attention. Grab a dinner of samosa, laksa, and fruity ice cream for about $8-10, and watch the setting sun with the rest of Darwin. *(Open May-Oct. Th 5-10pm, additionally June-Sept. Su 4-9pm.)*

THE MUSEUM AND ART GALLERY OF THE NORTHERN TERRITORY. Pressed for time in Darwin? Then this museum is the place to go. Exhibits include: a thorough introduction to Aboriginal art, a documentary film and soundbytes of Cyclone Tracy, a maritime annex, and many displays of Territorial wildlife, including "Sweetheart," a gargantuan 5m croc famous for sinking fishing boats (though he never killed anyone). Also part of the museum is the **Fannie Bay Gaol,** which served as Darwin's main jail from 1883-1979. The marked self-tour leads through eerie rooms where prisoners once slept and two were executed. *(Museum is along the shore heading toward Vestey's Beach, away from Darwin; turn left on Conacher St. off Gilruth Ave. Gaol is on the right farther up Gilruth, which becomes East Point Rd. ☎8999 8201. Open M-F 9am-5pm, Sa-Su 10am-5pm. Free. Wheelchair accessible.)*

MINDIL BEACH AND VESTEY'S BEACH. Prime locales for soaking up UV rays are north of the city, just off Gilruth Ave. Mindil Beach is on the left behind the casino, and Vestey's Beach is a just north of the museum. Box jellyfish warnings apply from Oct.-Mar., but stings have been recorded all months of the year (see p. 53). *(Heading away from downtown, take Smith St. past Daly St. and turn right onto Gilruth Ave. at the traffic circle. 30min. walk, or catch bus #4 or #6.)*

AQUASCENE. Darwin's most unusual sight lets you share an intimate moment with a warm and friendly...fish. Each high tide, you can wade into the water and hand-feed bread to an enormous horde of surprisingly large fishies—watch those fingers—or take in the scene from the concrete bleachers. Fishing punishable by $10,000 fine. *(28 Doctors Gully Rd. North off Daly St. ☎8981 7837. Call ahead for the feeding schedule or check "Darwin and the Top End Today" guide. $5, under 15 $3.30.)*

BI-SEXUAL BARRAMUNDI The premier fish of Top End, the illustrious barramundi, is served on almost every street corner in Darwin. Though it tastes quite bland, the curious biological development of the barramundi is anything but conventional. While the mature male spawns around age 3, the same creature shifts gears from male to female at age 6 or 7. The female barramundi, having undergone a complete sex transformation, can carry millions of eggs and can grow over a meter long. Just food for thought, to accompany your next beer-battered barra burger.

PARK IT. The area around Darwin is full of tranquil parks, perfect relief from the city streets, and they are all free. Just north of Daly St., the shaded paths of the **Botanic Gardens** wind through a series of Australian ecosystems: rainforest, mangroves, and dunes. The gardens are old enough to have survived cyclones in 1897, 1937, and 1974. *(Entrances on Geranium St. off the Stuart Hwy., and just past Mindil Beach on the opposite side of Gilruth Ave. Wheelchair accessible.)* The **East Point Reserve** occupies the peninsula to the north of Mindil and Vestey's Beach, and draws city-loathers with an coastline, picnic areas, and predator-free swimming in Lake Alexander. Wallabies are often spotted, especially in the evening. *(Access from East Point Rd. A 45min. bike ride from city. No bus service.)* Soothing walking trails, picnic areas, and inspirational views of Darwin Harbour lie in wait at the under appreciated **Charles Darwin National Park.** *(Bennett St. eastbound becomes Tiger Brennan Dr. Follow this for 5km to the park entrance on the right. ☎8947 2305. Open daily 7am-7pm.)*

CROCODYLUS PARK. This research and education center holds lions, rheas, iguanas, and other assorted critters in addition to the featured reptiles. Sure, you might encounter crocs in the wild, but they probably won't let you hold them and pose for a picture. *(Take Local bus #5, then walk 10min. ☎8947 2510. Open daily 9am-5pm. Feedings and tours 10am, noon, 2pm. $19.50, concessions $16, ages 4-15 $10. Shuttle available from city at ☎8941 5358. $27, concessions $23, ages 4-15 $16, prices include park entry.)*

WWII OIL STORAGE TANKS. Enormous underground tunnels, originally constructed to hold oil, now host ghostly-lit yet rather mundane WWII photos. ("Here's the 144th Australian Airborne taking a well-deserved break. Here they're building a latrine.") Still, wandering the spooky setting is fun. *(Along Darwin Harbour, on Kitchener Dr. Open Apr.-Oct. daily 9am-5pm; Nov.-Mar. Tu-F 10am-2pm. $4.50.)*

OTHER MUSEUMS AND EXHIBITS. At the **East Point Military Museum,** photos and a video display the decimation caused by the Japanese bombing on Darwin harbour in 1942. *(East Point Rd. at East Point Reserve. It's a 7min. drive or 45min. bike ride from downtown. ☎8981 9702. Open daily 9:30am-5pm. $9, seniors $8, children $4.50, families $25.)* The **Australian Aviation Heritage Centre's** collection of old aircraft is crowned by an old American B-52 bomber. (*10km from Darwin on the Stuart Hwy., served by buses #5 and #8. ☎8947 2145. Open daily 9am-5pm. $11, students $7.50, children $6, families $28.)* To learn more about Darwin's underappreciated reef system, visit **Indo Pacific Marine.** A pool containing a fascinating ecosystem that is self-sustained (no feeding, no filters) is the main attraction here. *(On Stokes Hill Wharf. ☎8981 1294. Open in the Dry daily 9am-5pm; in the Wet M-Sa 9am-1pm, Su 10am-5pm. $14, concessions $12.60, under 14 $5, families $33. Free talks every 30min.)*

ACTIVITIES

Darwin, at least in the Dry, has sunny skies and blue waters. **Scuba diving** is popular; certified divers can explore sunken vessels in the harbor. While Darwin's waters teem with box jellyfish during the Wet, divers are usually safe farther from shore. To get out, try **Cullen Bay Dive** (☎8981 3049. $35, $75 with full gear; certification course approx. $400). **Biking** is a convenient way to explore Darwin. A 45min. bike path extends from Darwin City to East Point Reserve (see p. 246).

Darwin also has a choice of gravity-defying adventures. At **The Rock** on Doctor's Gully Rd. next to Aquascene (see above), climbing connoisseurs can tackle an impressive variety of wall climbs, and overhangs in the bowels of the old tanker. (☎8941 0747. Open daily 12:30-8:30pm. Unlimited-length sessions $10; harness rental $3; boot rental $5.) The wild at heart can go **sky diving** from 10,000 ft. with **Pete's Parachuting** (☎1800 641 114; tandem $289). **Parasailing** with **Odyssey Adventures** provides breathtaking aerial views for breathtaking prices. Sunset flights run June-Sept.; book ahead. (☎0418 891 998. Single $65; tandem $60.)

SCARY THINGS IN THE WATER, PART I. Australia's coastal regions and some inland waters contain two types of crocodiles: the freshwater crocodile, *Crocodylus johnstoni,* and the saltwater crocodile, *Crocodylus porosus,* which can live in fresh or salt water. It is easy to distinguish between "freshies" and "salties." Salties are significantly larger than freshies and have rounded snouts, whereas freshies have narrow snouts. Avoid wild mangroves when bushwalking; saltwater crocodiles hide there. When you see a sign about freshies, it will probably refer to minimum risk and warn you merely to be cautious, since freshies nip only when provoked. When you see a sign about salties, it will most likely refer to death or danger and tell you to stay out–salties eat humans. Freshies have to mind the distinction, because salties eat freshies, too. That's why many areas inhabited by salties don't have freshies. Or swimmers. (see p. 380)

ENTERTAINMENT AND FESTIVALS

You can quickly blow your bus fare at the 24hr. **MGM Grand Casino** (☎1800 891 118). Feel slightly better about your value proposition at the **Darwin Cinema Centre,** 76 Mitchell St., which shows recent mainstream flicks. (☎8981 3111. $13, students $9.50.) For something original, the infinitely more interesting **Deckchair Cinema** shows offbeat, artsy films (many foreign) under the stars in a sunken amphitheater. Heading away from Darwin Harbor on Bennett St., turn right on McMinn and left on Frances Bay Dr.; the cinema is 100m down on the right. Walking takes 20min., but go in groups or call the shuttle. (☎8981 0700. Dry season only. W-Su 7:30pm, additional shows F-Sa around 9:30pm. $11, concessions $9.)

Darwin has several venues for **theater.** The **Darwin Entertainment Centre,** 93 Mitchell St., between Peel and Daly St., with an imposing coral facade, hosts the noteworthy events. Call the box office for same-day 50% discounts and free shows. (☎8981 1222. Open M-F 10am-5:30pm.) The **Botanic Gardens Amphitheatre** has open-air theater in the midst of the lush gardens. **Brown's Mart,** 12 Smith St. (☎8981 5222), near Bennett St., features productions in one of Darwin's oldest buildings.

Darwin celebrates the Dry with a number of festivals. The **Darwin Beer Can Regatta,** held off Mindil Beach in early August, is decidedly not dry. Teams of devout beer-chuggers use their empties to construct vessels fit for America's Cup competition and race them across the harbor. The **Darwin Cup Carnival** begins in July and ends with Cup Day in August (along with the Territory's Picnic Day). On the second Sunday of June (June 9, 2002), the Greek population of Darwin stages the **Glenti Festival,** a musical and culinary event, on the Esplanade. Ask the tourist office for an **Australian Football League (AFL)** schedule; March holds several important competitions. When the Dry draws near its close in mid-August, Darwin goes for broke with the 17-day **Festival of Darwin,** and then awaits the rain.

NIGHTLIFE

Darwin has a *big* bar scene. People go out every night, and they go out late. The late-night booze scene extends all over the city center, catering primarily to backpackers and tourists looking to party hearty on their holiday. Pubs and clubs advertise heavily with posters and brochures, hoping to grab the attention of good-looking, scantily-clad backpackers making the rounds. The genuine flavor of local Darwin might be difficult to locate, because everyone is quickly swept away by the crazed vibe in the air. The distinction between pub and club blurs, as most pubs have a dance floor of varying crowdedness.

Lost Arc, 89 Mitchell St. (☎8942 3300). The most reliable party in town is found with the *beautiful* crowd at this funky joint. Extraordinary people-watching from the plush sidewalk couches. Tu-Th and Su live music. Open M-Th and Su 4pm-2am, F-Sa 4pm-4am. Next door, **Discovery** breaks it down on weekends with theme nights ranging from retro to dance. Cover $6-8. Open F-Sa 9pm-4am.

Lizards Outdoor Bar and Grill, (☎8981 6511), at the corner of Mitchell and Daly St. The spacious outdoor beer garden adorned with lush palm trees gives Lizards the best night-time ambiance in town. Half-pints from $2.50. Th-Su live music, F great Latin band. Open M-F 3pm-2am, Sa-Su 11am-2am.

Shenannigans, 69 Mitchell St. (☎8981 2100). A loud and happy bar, always crowded with a boisterous, primarily male crowd, Shenannigans draws locals and backpackers with live music. M karaoke. Tu Trivia night. Happy Hour F 4:30-6:30pm. Open M-Sa 10am-2am, Su noon-2am.

The Victoria Hotel, 27 Smith St. Mall (☎8981 4011). The lines out the door welcome you to the most sexually charged outback-meets-blitzed-backpacker scene. Travelers elbow their way into a dense crowd of Territorians. **Settlers** pub downstairs serves beer in a rough and rustic atmosphere. Live music every night. Open M-F 10am-4am, Sa 11am-4am, Su noon-4am. Upstairs, **Banjo's** dancing and pool tables draw backpackers. Open M-F 11am-4am, Sa-Su 7pm-4am.

Nirvana, (☎8981 2025), on Smith St. near Peary. Technically not a bar, this upscale Southeast Asian restaurant hosts quality musical entertainment for the price of a drink and some munchies. Tu open jam session. Th-Sa jazz. Open Tu-Sa 9am-2am.

Throb, 64 Smith St. (☎8942 3435). Darwin's only gay and lesbian nightclub is not as raunchy as its name might suggest; the assorted crowd is stylish and chill. Funky pool tables and friendly staff. Sa drag shows at midnight. Open Th-Su 4pm "til late."

Squires, 3 Edmund St. (☎8981 9761), off Smith St. behind Woolworth's. Away from the backpacking hordes, locals know the place to go for a no-frills beer and a game of pool. W and F 5-7pm "Topless waitstaff"—leave the kids at home. Th $3 stubbies. Happy Hour M-F 12:30-1:30pm and 5-6pm. Open daily 11am-4am. Next door is **Time,** Darwin's original dance club. Cover $6-10. Open Th-Sa 10pm-4am.

OFF THE COAST: THE TIWI ISLANDS

In the Timor Sea, 80km north of Darwin, lie the Tiwi Islands, **Melville** and **Bathurst.** Melville is Australia's second biggest island, ranking behind only Tasmania. Together, the Tiwis represent 8000km^2 of Aboriginal-owned tropics. The main attractions are remoteness, contemporary Aboriginal communities, and relaxing beaches. The only way to see the islands is through **Tiwi Tours.** (☎8924 1115. Day-trip $298, child $268; 2-day camping $564/$493.)

ARNHEM HIGHWAY: THE TOP END WETLANDS

Intersecting the Stuart Hwy. 33km southeast of Darwin, the **Arnhem Hwy.** glides for 120km through the **Adelaide** and **Mary River Wetlands** before hitting **Kakadu National Park.** During the Dry, these wetlands are a lush sanctuary for birds and crocs; during the Wet, much of the area floods. The **Fogg Dam Conservation Reserve,** 25km east of the junction of the Stuart and Arnhem Hwy. and 10km north on an access road, is a breathtaking spot to view the winged inhabitants of the area. No patience or binoculars is needed: cormorants, herons, storks, egrets, and ibises fill the air with bird-song. The **Window on the Wetlands Visitor Centre** is another 4km east on the Arnhem Hwy., located on one of the three hills that represent the Turtle Dreaming for the Limilngan-Wulna people. (☎8988 8188. Open daily 7:30am-7:30pm.)

Jumping **crocodiles,** Batman! Three kilometers east of the Wetlands Visitor Centre on the Arnhem Hwy. is one of the Top End's overdone tourist experience. Giving new meaning to takeaway cuisine, boat attendants dangle chunks of raw pork over the water and pester saltwater crocs until they give up and "jump" for the bait. The crocs' athleticism is impressive, but the whole spectacle is slick and slightly disturbing. If you are up for it, try the **Adventure Cruises NT.** (☎8988 4547. Daily 9, 11am, 1, 3pm. $22, family $55.) **Adelaide River Queen** offers the same spectacle. (☎8988 8144. 1½hr.; daily May-Aug. 9, 11am, 1, 3pm; Sept.-Apr. 9, 11am, 2:30pm. $31, children $18. Wheelchair accessible.)

The last stop on the way to Kakadu, only 45km from the park border, is **Bark Hut Inn and Caravan Park,** offering hot meals, baked goodies, and simple accommodations with A/C and shared facilities. (☎8978 8988. Open daily 6am-11pm. Sites for 2 $13.50, powered $20; singles $35; doubles $50.)

KAKADU NATIONAL PARK

This World Heritage site is awesome in its size and in its wonders. When the Aboriginal spirit Warramurrungundji set out on her daunting task to create much of the Kakadu region, she had an immense vision. At 19,804 square kilometers, Australia's largest national park contains six distinct ecosystems, four river systems, abundant wildlife, and dozens of Aboriginal outstations and sacred sites where Aboriginal lifestyle and ceremony are still vibrantly practiced and protected. If you came to the Territory to get off the beaten track, to see an untainted piece of Australia, Kakadu is the place.

From the burnt-cinnamon earth of the Dry to the raging waterfalls of the Wet, the ever-changing Kakadu presents a surreal cross between the tropics and the desert. Quiet in the eastern stone cliffs and noisy with birds in the wetlands and low-lying woodlands, Kakadu's music is equally dichotomous. The grassy savanna woodlands filled with eucalyptus trees comprise 60% of the park and support a variety of wildlife. Monsoon forests spot the park, and hills and ridges undulate throughout the southern region giving way to the rugged stone country that juts out of the park's eastern border. Floodplains and billabongs surround Kakadu's four river systems and present a serene expanse of silver and green, while tidal flats and coast in the north offer some of the most diverse flora and fauna.

Intimately intertwined with this awe-inspiring landscape is the living legacy of the Aboriginal community that resides in Kakadu. Aboriginal people have inhabited this land for an estimated 50,000 years and have left the treasure of the world's largest, and possibly oldest, collection of rock art upon the stone escarpments. Today's Aboriginal population in Kakadu has dwindled from its original 2000, recorded when Europeans first came to Australia, to 300. Those remaining live largely in the outlying bush, inaccessible to visitors, but some live in the relative civilization of Jabiru. The number of clans has likewise decreased from 20 to 12, and of the dozen languages once spoken here, only three remain active. Gagudju, a language spoken here a century ago, lives on in the park's name.

Aboriginal people are active in the management and conservation of the park, and about 30% of the employees in Kakadu are of Aboriginal descent. Half of Kakadu is still owned by its traditional Aboriginal owners, who leased their land to the Australian National Parks and Wildlife Service in 1978. The other half is owned by the commonwealth and is under Aboriginal claim. Cultural sensitivity is a primary goal throughout the park, and the most sacred Aboriginal dreaming sights remain off-limits to visitors.

KAKADU AT A GLANCE

AREA: 19, 804km²

FEATURES: Stone country, floodplains of the Alligator River System, township of Jaribu, Jim Jim and Twin Falls.

HIGHLIGHTS: Galleries of Aboriginal rock art, walks through grasslands and to sunset lookout points, river boat cruises, 4WD treks to waterfalls and plunge pools.

GATEWAYS: Darwin (see p. 238), Pine Creek (see p. 259).

CAMPING: Ranging from free bush camping to commercial campgrounds (see p. 253).

FEES: $16.25 park entrance fee. Fees are required for Yellow Water River Cruise, Guluyambi East Alligator Cruise, and day tours of Jim Jim and Twin Falls.

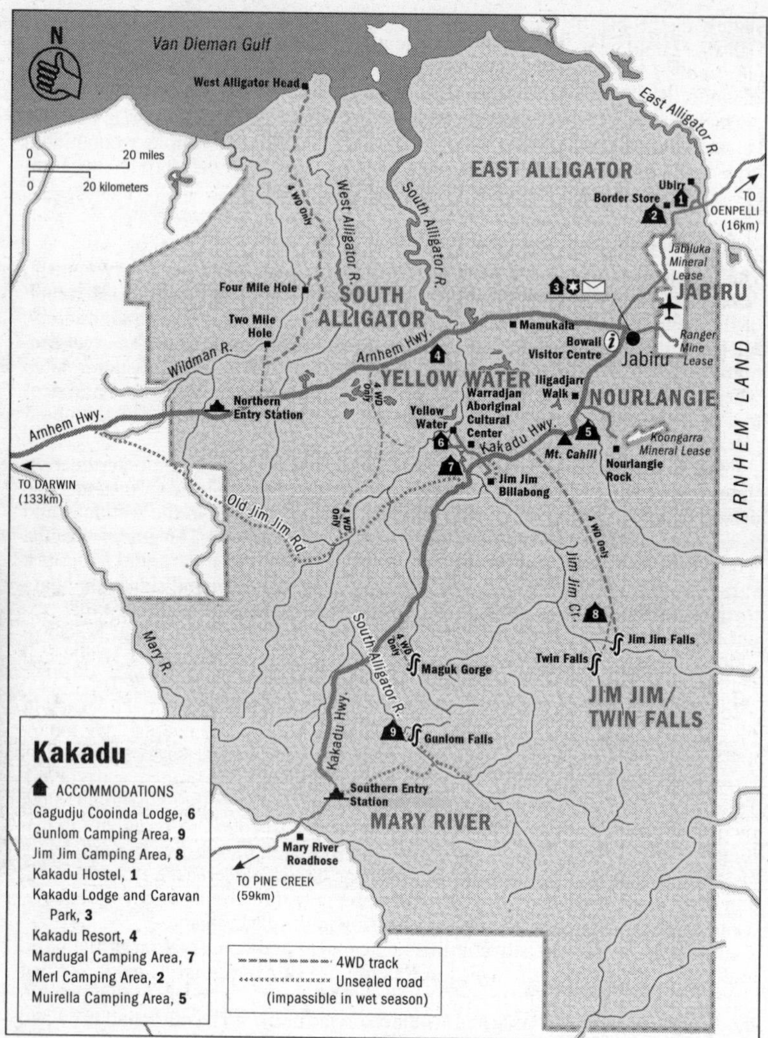

ORIENTATION

Kakadu National Park is roughly rectangular. The two entries into the park are the **Arnhem Hwy.** in the north, which runs east-west, and the **Kakadu Hwy.** in the south, which runs northeast-southwest. These two fully paved roads converge in the park's northeastern interior near the township of **Jabiru** ("JAB-ber-roo"). They remain open year-round, except during the most severe floods in the Wet.

Kakadu is divided into seven regions. The **South Alligator Region** is east of Kakadu's north gate, 120km east of the junction between the Arnhem and Stuart Hwy. It is marked by the flood plains that sprawl around the mighty South Alligator River and includes the Kakadu Resort, 77km from the park entrance. After another 39km, the Arnhem Hwy. enters the **East Alligator Region** and arrives at Ubirr Rd., the 36km turn-off to **Ubirr,** a rock art site and lookout. The Kakadu Hostel and Border Store are near Ubirr.

WHEN TO GO. Locals say they have a hard time describing Wet Kakadu to Dry season visitors, and vice versa. For most travelers, **the Dry,** from April to October, is the most convenient and comfortable season to visit. Dry highs average 30°C (86°F), lows 17°C (59°F), and the humidity is low. It can get cold at night; travelers should carry an extra layer and repellent to ward off commando mosquitoes. During the Dry, almost all roads are open except for a few unpaved ones early in the season. Check at the Bowali Visitor Centre for road openings (see **Practical Information,** p. 252). Most camping, accommodations, and attractions operate in the Dry.

The Wet dramatically alters the landscape of Kakadu with its monsoon rains and floods. Locals insist that the Wet is the most beautiful time of the year, as the land teems with green foliage and flowers. Still, the oppressive humidity, heat–35°C (95°F) highs and 25°C (77°F) lows–and bugs make much of the park harder to enjoy. The famous falls, particularly Jim Jim and Twin, are at their most powerful but can only be seen from the air. One plus of the Wet–boat cruises are up and running, as the Ubirr drive becomes a river (see **East Alligator** sights, p. 255).

The junction of the Arnhem and Kakadu Hwy. is about 1km past Ubirr Rd. in the **Jabiru Region.** Just 2km from this junction, tidy **Jabiru** (pop. 2000) is the primary town in Kakadu, with the Kakadu Lodge and Caravan Park, post office, and a grocery store. The **Bowali Visitor Centre** is 5km from Jabiru on the Kakadu Hwy.

The remaining four regions are accessed from the Kakadu Hwy. The turn-off for the **Nourlangie Region** is 21km from Jabiru; a 12km paved road leads to Nourlangie Rock. The turn-off for the **Jim Jim/Twin Falls Region** is 20km farther on the Kakadu Hwy. This 4WD-only road (impassable in the Wet) runs 60km to the Jim Jim Falls and camping area, and 10km more to Twin Falls. The **Yellow Water Region** is much easier to reach (just 9km farther down the highway). The Warradjan Aboriginal Cultural Centre and Gadgudju Cooinda Lodge are located in the Yellow Water area. The south gate of Kakadu is 99km farther on the Kakadu Hwy. through the **Mary River Region; Pine Creek** is an additional 59km farther. Several reader-friendly maps, like the *Visitor Guide and Map* booklet, come with park entry permits.

TRANSPORTATION

Armed with the *Kakadu National Park Visitor Guide and Map,* the most ideal way to do Kakadu is in your own car. A 4WD is most convenient and will allow for a more personal and (literally) off-the-beaten-path experience. However, renting a 4WD is expensive and rental companies might not even allow access to certain sights even if the roads are open; check with them before you book. A 2WD will get you to the top tourist destinations in the Dry, except Jim Jim and Twin Falls.

Flights: The Jabiru Airport (☎8979 2411), 6.5km east of Jabiru on the Arnhem Hwy, is the base for aerial tours of Kakadu. **Kakadu Air** offers bird's-eye **scenic flights** of Kakadu ($75 per 30min., $125 per hr.). Flights during the Wet are popular since many roads close. Courtesy shuttles run between the airport and Jabiru.

Car Rental: Territory Rent-a-Car (☎0418 85 86 01), has a desk in the Gagudja Croc Hotel on Flinders St., Jabiru. Small sedans from $93.50 per day, 100km. **4WD unavailable.** Many people rent cars out of Darwin (see p. 239).

Hitchhiking: Kakadu has some extremely desolate roads, so hitching often becomes walking, and is strongly discouraged. However, people have been known to occasionally wait at the head of 4WD access roads to catch a ride to more remote sites. *Let's Go* does not recommend hitchhiking.

TOURS

One economical way of getting to the park and its sites without a vehicle is a day tour from Darwin with **Greyhound Pioneer,** which can be expanded to three or more days. The conductors double as knowledgeable, witty tour guides, and although the visit compresses the sights without exploring the rugged, remote gems, it does give a memorable dose of Kakadu. You have the option of connecting with tours of the rivers and Jim Jim/Twin Falls. (☎13 20 30. $84, not including park entry fee.)

If you're looking for a more rugged outback experience and have extra time and money, plenty of **tour companies** offer packages. Almost all 4WD operations work out of Darwin. Some rely on lodge accommodations, others camp under the stars, but all encourage more than two to three days to really see the park. **Wilderness 4WD Adventures** specializes in tours with biology-trained guides geared toward fit nature lovers. (☎1800 808 288. 3-5 days, $425-645.) **Northern Territories Adventure Tours** also offers 4WD safaris. (☎1300 654 604. Camping 2-5 days, $320-675; 3-day "safari in style" includes indoor accommodation, $750.) **Gondwana Adventure Tours and Expeditions** gets kudos for super cheap prices. (☎1800 242 177. 3-day $369, 4-day $429.) All these tours involve a lot of hiking and hot sun. **AAT Kings** offers slightly less rugged tours of Kakadu in a coach. (☎8941 3844. 1-3 days, $147-495.)

PRACTICAL INFORMATION

Tourist Information: The **Bowali Visitor Centre** (☎8938 1120; fax 8938 1123), 2km west of Jabiru on the Kakadu Hwy., is an excellent source of information and a site unto itself. During the Dry, rangers give free daily talks and guided walks at different sites in the park. Open daily 8am-5pm. Wheelchair accessible. Reach the **Park Manager** at P.O. Box 71, Jabiru NT 0886.

Travel Agency: Jabiru Tourist Centre, Jabiru Plaza (☎8979 2548). Open M-F 9:30am-5pm, Sa-Su 9:30am-12:30pm and 3:30-4:30pm. Tours can also be booked from hotels.

Ranger Stations: Ranger stations can relay information to the police and clinic from more remote areas, but the stations are only open to the public sporadically (daily 8am-4pm, but often called away). **South Alligator Ranger Station** (☎8979 0194), 40km west of Bowali Centre near Aurora Kakadu Village; **East Alligator Ranger Station** (☎8979 2291), 40km north of Bowali Centre on the Ubirr Rd.; **Jim Jim Ranger Station** (☎8979 2038), down a 2.5km road that turns off the Kakadu Hwy., 45km south of Bowali; **Mary River Ranger Station** (☎8975 4578), 1km from the south entry station.

Auto Services: Diesel and unleaded **fuel stations** are at the Aurora Kakadu Village, Jabiru, Cooinda, the Border Store near Ubirr, and the Mary River Roadhouse at the south entrance. Jabiru's Mobil Station (☎8979 2001) has **auto repair.** Open daily 7am-8pm.

Potable Water: At Bowali, Jabiru, Cooinda, and Aurora Kakadu Village. *Rangers recommend boiling water from any other source, including the campgrounds listed below.*

Banks: Westpac Bank, Jabiru Plaza (☎8979 2432), has currency exchange and a 24hr. **ATM.** Open M-Th 9:30am-4pm, F 9:30am-5pm. Cooinda Lodge has **EFTPOS** only.

Police: Jabiru Police, 10 Tasman Crescent (**Emergency** ☎000 or 8979 2122), across the street from Jabiru Plaza at the end of Flinders St.

Health Clinic: Jabiru Community Health Clinic, Jabiru Plaza (24hr. ☎8979 2018). Open M-Tu, Th-F 8am-noon and 1-4pm; W 9am-noon and 1-2:30pm.

Swimming: You'll need a cool dip here to wash away the dust and soothe the mozzie bites. The only 100% safe places to swim in Kakadu are the lodge pools and the mighty Olympic size **Jabiru Pool.** (☎8979 2127. Open daily 9am-7pm. $2.) People have been known to **swim at their own risk** at Gubara, Jim Jim and Twin Falls, Maguk, Gunlom, Yurmikmik, Gimbat, and Jarrangbarnmi, although freshies do live in these places and **salties** occasionally enter the area. Check at Bowali for reports of saltie sightings.

Internet Access: Library, Jabiru Plaza (☎8979 2097). Open Tu-W 10am-4pm, Th noon-6pm, Sa 10am-2pm. $5.50 per 30min.

Post Office: Jabiru Plaza (☎8979 2727). Open M-F 9am-5:30pm year round; Sa 9am-noon, in the Dry; Sa 9am-2pm, Su 9am-noon, in the Wet. **Postal code:** 0886.

IS IT WET HERE OR IS IT JUST ME? It's all just "Wet" or "Dry" to most Top End residents, but Aborigines, long acquainted with wildly diverse climatic patterns, break the year into six seasons. **Gunumeleng,** from mid-October to late-December, is the "whisper of the Wet," which comes in the form of drenching afternoon thundershowers punctuated by the greatest frequency of lightning strikes on the planet (an average of 10,000 per month Nov.-Jan.). Landscape browned by the Dry turns green again amid high temperatures and oppressive humidity. From January to March, the "real" Wet season—**Gudjewg**—brings monsoon rains with enormous amounts of water, peaked humidity, and green land with gushing waterfalls. While the ubiquitous spear grass shoots up 3m; the animals that live on the ground can get trapped in the swollen waterways. April comes, and with it **Banggerreng,** the "knock 'em down" storm season where the first glimpses of sunny skies peek through the clouds. The beginning of dry times is the cool **Yegge,** May to mid-June, when the wetlands begin to recede, leaving fields of water lilies in their wake. The coldest weather comes in **Wurrgeng,** from mid-June to mid-August. With no rains to replenish the floodplains, the land dries out and turns brown. This season slips into **Gurrung,** full of heat but little water, the end of which is signaled in October by the return of the thunderclouds of Gunumeleng.

ACCOMMODATIONS

Commercial accommodations in Kakadu are not ideal for the budget traveler. Options are limited, motel rooms are expensive, and the budget dorms leave much to be desired. Still, advance reservations are strongly recommended in the Dry.

Kakadu Lodge and Caravan Park, Jabiru (☎8979 2422; fax 8979 2254). While lacking in personality, it has an abundance of comfort. A/C, linen, towels, swimming pool, laundry, bistro. Reception daily 7:30am-7:30pm. Bistro open daily 6-9pm. Campsites with access to amenities $10 per person, powered for 2 $25; 5-person cabins with kitchen and bath $192; lodge rooms $121. Wheelchair accessible.

Gagudju Lodge Cooinda (YHA), Cooinda (☎8979 0145; fax 8979 0148), in the Yellow River Region. Pricey motel rooms, crowded campgrounds, and budget rooms in a cul-de-sac of trailers. Shared bath, fridge, laundry, and coin-op BBQ. Reception daily 6am-11pm. Takeaway and buffet open daily 6-9:30am, 11:30am-2:30pm and 6-9pm. Sites $10 per person, powered $13; budget single $25, non-YHA $30.50; budget double $63; motel rooms $198.

Kakadu Hostel (☎8979 2232), 2km south of Ubirr, in the East Alligator Region. This hostel is more than just worn around the edges. It has thin walls and no locks on the dorms. But it is laid-back, close to Ubirr, and cheap. Above-ground pool, laundry, kitchen. Dorms have A/C; twins and doubles have fans. All beds $22.

Kakadu Resort (☎8979 0166), in the South Alligator Region, closest to the northern entrance of the park. Swimming pool. Reception daily 6:30am-10pm. Powered and unpowered sites $7.50; twins and doubles $185.

CAMPING

Camping is one of the best and cheapest ways to enjoy the outdoors in Kakadu. The park runs four large first-come, first-serve campgrounds with **showers and toilets** ($5.40, under 16 free; collected on site in the Dry, at Bowali in the Wet). **Merl Campground,** 4km from Ubirr in the East Alligator Region, has spacious and shady lots made somewhat private by vegetation. In the Dry, ferocious swarms of mozzies make this campground inhospitable (some say uninhabitable). Check about Wet-season access. The quiet **Muirella Park Campground** is located down a 6km gravel track from the Kakadu Hwy. in the Nourlangie Region; the turn-off is

30km from Jabiru. **Mardugal Campground,** 2km south of Cooinda turn-off on the Kakadu Hwy., is well placed near Yellow Water and the road to Jim Jim and Twin Falls. The relatively mozzie-free **Gunlom Campground** sits 11km from the southern entrance of the park in the Mary River Region, and 37km down a gravel road. The park also has free camping areas, in all regions, for those who want to rough it. Check the *Visitor Guide* for locations. These areas offer only the most basic facilities (outhouses) or none at all, but are generally uncrowded (Jim Jim and Twin Falls being the exceptions). Travelers should bring plenty of water.

FOOD

Kakadu is known for the game in the bush, not on the plate. Dining options, and groceries outside Jabiru, are sparse and expensive; bringing food is recommended. The **Jabiru Cafe** in the shopping plaza has reasonably priced fare that provides a welcome respite from cereal and Vegemite sandwiches. (Open M-F 8:30am-4pm, Sa 9am-1pm, Su 10am-2pm.) The **supermarket** is in Jabiru plaza. (Open M-F 9am-5:30pm, Sa 9am-3pm, Su 10am-2pm; in the Dry Sa 9am-5pm.) Simple groceries can also be bought for big bucks at the **Border Store** in Ubirr. (Open daily 8:30am-5:30pm.) The Border Store also has a popular BBQ that features barra, buffalo, and croc burgers (all around $7). There is a bistro open in the evenings at the **Kakadu Lodge** in Jabiru (open daily 6-9pm). The **Gagudju Lodge Cooinda** has takeaway and an expensive but filling buffet meals (dinner $13.50) three times a day (open daily 6-9:30am, 11:30am-2:30pm and 6-9pm).

SIGHTS AND HIKES

A natural and cultural wonderland, Kakadu offers a variety of well-established sights for nature lovers and history buffs. Walks and hikes range in difficulty levels to suit all visitors. The main sights are viewed from short, relatively tame walking trails; a few are wheelchair accessible. The optional climbs to the lookout points at Ubirr and Nourlangie are steeper. A number of excellent, longer walks reward the fit and adventurous who choose to venture farther out into the bush.

All sights and walks are open during the Dry; many are subject to closure during the Wet. The park brochure is a good supplement for descriptions and directions; *Kakadu By Foot* ($3) in the Bowali Visitor Centre gives detailed descriptions of the walks. Bring lots of water (at least 1L for every hour of walking), insect repellent, sunscreen, and sturdy shoes. Snakes and spiders live in these areas—long trousers and thick socks will help protect against bites. **Salties** are also common, so never swim or wade in water sources and stay away from the water's edge.

For experienced hikers, unmarked and **overnight bushwalks** are the most genuine way to see Kakadu without the crowds. These routes generally follow the creek lines and gorges along the escarpment. Routes and campsites on unmarked walks

BURN, BABY, BURN! During the Dry, the horizon frequently billows with the purple-gray smoke of bush fires. Don't panic: Aborigines have been using controlled bush burning for thousands of years for a variety of reasons such as hunting, communication, ceremony, and horticulture. Under the guidance of Aboriginal people, Kakadu National Park continues to widely and successfully use bush fires for fire management. Burning is done in small patches during the Wet and early Dry season in order to prevent the build-up of thick undergrowth which could provide fuel for devastating late Dry season fires. Although Aboriginal people used to light bush fires by hand, this method has been replaced by high-tech satellite imagery and plane-dropped fire bombs. Meanwhile, some bush fires are still caused naturally by lightening late in the Dry, and these are the most dangerous. Seeing a bush fire up close is an eerie experience, especially at night. Bright orange tongues of flame devour the bases of trees and plants, generating a thick, organic odor and a distinct crackling sound.

must be approved. For overnight camping permits and route plan approval, contact the Bowali Visitor Centre by phone, mail, or in person (see **Practical Information,** p. 252). Permits are free but require one week for processing. The Bowali Visitor Centre also sells topographic maps of Kakadu ($8).

REGION	MAJOR SIGHTS	ACCOMMODATION	SERVICES
South Alligator	Mamukala wetlands	Kakadu Resort	Food and fuel at Kakadu Resort
East Alligator	Ubirr, Guluyambi river cruise	Kakadu Resort	Food and fuel at Kakadu Resort
Jabiru	Bowali Visitor Centre, Iligadjarr walk	Kakadu Lodge and Caravan Park	Food and fuel in Jabiru
Nourlangie	Nourlangie	none	none
Yellow River	Warradjan Aboriginal Cultural Centre, Yellow Water cruise	Gagudju Cooinda Lodge	Food and fuel at Cooinda
Jim Jim/Twin Falls	Jim Jim/Twin Falls	none	none
Mary River	Gunlom	none	Food and fuel at Mary River house (just outside the park)

SOUTH ALLIGATOR REGION. **Mamukala Wetlands** is a floodplain and bird-watching area off the Arnhem Hwy., 8km east of the South Alligator River crossing and 1km down an access road. A 100m wheelchair-accessible path leads to a lookout where patient ornithologists can observe snowy egrets and Jabiru storks hunting for food. In late August and September, the plain comes to life as 25,000 *bamurru* (magpie geese) descend upon it. The birdhide and 3km circular trail are lackluster, though. During the driest of the Dry, an 80km 4WD track 1km east of the northern entry station extends out to **Van Diemen's Gulf** (no swimming; the sea here is full of the usual culprits). **West Alligator Campsite** is great for wildlife viewing at the coast. Check at the Bowali Visitor Centre for all road conditions.

EAST ALLIGATOR REGION. The gem of this region is **Ubirr,** a collection of sandstone outliers on which Aboriginal ancestors created rock-art thousands of years ago (see **Ancient Graffiti**, p. 256). A wheelchair accessible circuit *(1km, 1hr.)* passes significant sights such as the **Namarrgarn Sisters,** which tells the story of the appearance of crocodiles, and the **Main Gallery,** which displays several different layers of rock art. A steep, rocky climb *(250m, 30min.)* leads to the top of Ubirr, with a spectacular view of the distant stone escarpment and the emerald floodplains. Sunsets on top of Ubirr are magical, but be prepared to share the experience with chattering tourists. (Open daily Apr.-Nov. 8:30am-sunset, Dec.-Mar. 2pm-sunset.) Four free art site talks are given daily during the Dry; check at Bowali for the schedule.

The **Guluyambi River Cruise** is Kakadu's best boat tour. While the sunbathing salties on the banks of the East Alligator might try to steal the show, it is the wonderful Aboriginal-guided demonstration of local culture, bush tucker, and hunting tools that is most memorable. The boat sizes are smaller and more intimate than the Yellow River Cruise, and patrons get to view the shores of Arnhem land up close (without a permit). The tour runs from the upstream boat ramp. *(☎1800 089 113. 1¾hr. Departs daily May-Nov. 9, 11am, 1, 3pm; call in the Wet. $30, child $15.)* The highly recommended **Bardedjilidji Sandstone Walk** *(2½km; 2hr.)* covers much of the same territory on land through weathered sandstone pillars, arches, and caves; some of the sandstone cliffs are believed to have been formed over 1.5 billion years ago. From the base of the formations, tree roots extending 20m down the jagged cliffs to the ground are visible. The second half of the walk passes a small billabong and river. The trailhead is near the upstream boat ramp.

JABIRU REGION. The **Bowali Visitor Centre** is a good place to start a tour of the park, but most sights here are man-made. A captivating eight-screen slide-show displays the stunning visual beauty of the park; don't get caught up in the virtual because the real is right outside. The **Iligadjarr Walk** *(3.8km; 2hr.)*, leaving from the

ANCIENT GRAFFITI Over 5000 sites of Aboriginal rock art have been noted in Kakadu, most on the escarpment wall, and an estimated 10,000 sites remain undiscovered. The age of the art is difficult to determine, partly because pictures dating back thousands of years sit side-by-side with paintings done in the 1980s. Certain works have been "repainted" by descendants who are familiar enough with the old stories to "retell" them by the brush. Some recovered paintings date to 50,000 years ago, a few depicting extinct animals. Corresponding to the climatic changes that affected prehistoric Aborigines, there are three general styles identified in the rock art. The pre-estuarine period (50,000-8000 BC) corresponds to a wooded Kakadu with an overall uniform style suggesting a small regional population. The estuarine period (8000-2000 BC), during the bountiful hunting era when the ocean was rising, shows previously unknown animals in an "X-ray" art style, which depicts the insides as well as outlines of animals. Booming wildlife meant growing communities, reflected in a rise in artistic diversity. In the freshwater period (2000 BC-present), Aborigines captured an even greater variety of species with more complex X ray images, eventually adding their own renditions of the first contact with the white colonists.

Malabanjbanjdju or Burdulba camping areas, is Kakadu's unappreciated sunset spot. Wide-ranging grassy floodplains, flocks of snow-white egrets, the sky aflame, the Arnhemland Escarpment in the distance, and *not another soul within sight*: this is Kakadu. Far to the east, past the airport, the **Ranger Uranium Mine** is the most active such mine in Kakadu. *(☎ 1800 089 113. Ground tours depart daily from Jabiru Airport. 1½hr., 10:30am and 1pm., $20. Reservations essential.)*

NOURLANGIE REGION. The principal pull of this part of the park is **Nourlangie** itself, a huge rock outlier used as a shelter and art studio by earlier Aborigines. A wheelchair-accessible walking track (1.5km) passes the Main Gallery and ascends to a tame lookout. Many mystical images are painted on the walls of Nourlangie, including Nabulwinj-bulwinj, a dangerous spirit who eats females after striking them with a yam. **Anbangbang** rock shelter, formed by a gargantuan boulder leaning perilously over a narrow walkway, steals the show from the artwork. The farthest point on the loop is **Gunwarrdehwarrde Lookout,** a craggy climb with a view of the distant escarpment, where Aborigines believe Lightning Man Namarrgon lives. Three art site talks are given daily in the Dry for free.

Some of the secondary walks in the Nourlangie Region allow appreciation of the main site from a distance. The **Nawurlandja Lookout** *(600m, 40min.)* and **Mirrai Lookout** *(1.8km; 1½hr.)* are short, steep climbs that provide the best photo opportunities. **Anbangbang Billabong** *(2.5km,1hr.),* close to Nourlangie Rock, is an easy walk circling the water with delicate lilies and jagged cliffs—but be prepared to share your walk with every bus tourist (accessible only in the Dry). The **Barrk Sandstone Bushwalk** *(12km, 6-8hr.),* one of the longest and most dramatic established walks in the park, branches off from the lookout walk and makes a loop past the sandstone cliffs of the Nourlangie region. Impressive views of surrounding lowlands, many ecosystems, rock art, and an untouristed, quiet atmosphere make it perfect for the curious and fit traveler.

JIM JIM/TWIN FALLS REGION. Perhaps the most beloved and most elusive sights in the park lie deep in this region. The opening day of the 4WD-only access road in the Dry, eagerly awaited by tourists and tour guides alike, can be frustratingly uncertain. **Jim Jim Falls,** 60km up a tough road, cascades 150m down into a deep, clear green pool. Shy Jim Jim is not visible for much of the year—by June or July its waters have decreased to a hesitant trickle; in the Wet, the falls rush with roaring intensity. However, the same rain that causes the awesome spectacle also prevent road access to it; the only way to see the falls during the Wet is by air. There is a lookout 200m from the carpark. A boulder-ridden walk (1km) leads to the plunge pool, which remains quite cold for much of the Dry due to lack of direct sunlight. For the most capable hikers, the stunning **Barrk Marlam walk** *(3km, 4-6hr.)* branches off the path to Jim Jim. It's a rugged one-way, straight up and across the escarpment, but the enjoyable exertion of the climb is dwarfed by the jaw-dropping, eye-bugging views of the gorge from the top.

Over the river (you must have a decent 4WD and a snorkel is recommended, for this crossing) and 10km through the woods is **Twin Falls.** They are spectacular—two roaring cataracts down a steep cliff—but you'll have to earn the view; it is a 400m walk and a 500m swim up a narrow gorge to get there (you might want to equip yourself with a flotation device and a waterproof camera). Both Jim Jim and Twin are home to freshies, which tend not to bother people, although an occasional saltie makes its way into the pools. **Swim at your own risk.**

For those who lack a 4WD, tours to Jim Jim and Twin falls depart daily from Jabiru and Cooinda. Try **Katch Kakadu Tours** *(☎8979 3315; $126.50, child $99);* **Lord's Kakadu** *(☎8979 2970; $125);* **Kakadu Gorge and Waterfall Tours** *(☎8979 0145; $130; same tour leaves Cooinda for $125).*

YELLOW WATER REGION. Yellow Water, part of Jim Jim Creek, is the most popular billabong in Kakadu—not to swim in, but to cruise past meters-long crocodiles sunning themselves on the banks or floating ominously on the surface of the water. It is also famous for its less-threatening wildlife, visible on a circular walk *(1.5km)*—Jabiru storks, pied geese, and ducks pretend not to notice the clanking noise of the metal walkway. There's also a wheelchair-accessible platform to view the billabong. Still, the most popular way to do Yellow Water is on a **Yellow Water cruise,** where knowledgeable guides point out the variety of birds and the occasional croc. The sunrise cruise is the most breathtaking, but in the end, viewing Kakadu from a powerboat is a bit like watching a videotape, so skip the hand-holding and get out on the trail! *(☎1800 553 888. In the Dry, 1½hr. and 2hr. tours each depart 3 per day; $33, $38. In the Wet, 1½hr. tours, 6 per day 7am-5pm, $33.)*

Far more enlightening is the **Warradjan Aboriginal Cultural Centre,** 1km from the Cooinda Lodge, which shows visitors Kakadu's Aboriginal history. The exhibit is refreshing after being assaulted by disconnected Aboriginal trivia on the trail. Built in the shape of a *warradjan* (turtle), the center contains fantastic displays of Aboriginal culture, ranging from tools and rock art to biographies of significant local figures. Especially poignant are the exhibit's directness, willingness to criticize the effects of tourism, and discussion of current tension between the communities of Kakadu. It concludes with moving statements by local Aborigines on the future of their land and community. *(☎8979 0051. Open daily Sept.-June 9am-5pm, July-Aug. 7:30am-6pm. Free.)*

MARY RIVER REGION. This is the land where the rivers begin. In the headwaters of the South Alligator River, a series of falls called **Gunlom** flow rapidly from December to May, but cease almost completely in the Dry. A wheelchair-accessible footbridge leads to the plunge pool, and a steep walk *(1km, 1hr.)* travels to the top of the falls and a series of enchanting smaller pools. Gunlom is the only escarpment cascade that conventional 2WD vehicles can reach in the dry season via the Gunlom Rd., a stone's throw from Kakadu's southern entry gate.

The secondary sights in the region are more challenging for both your car and your legs. **Maguk,** or **Barramundi Falls,** is a smaller cascade; the 4WD turn-off is located 32km north of the Gunlom turn-off on the Kakadu Hwy. It flows during both seasons and is reached via a 12km road and then a hike *(2km, 1-2hr.)* through monsoon forest. The **Yurmikmik Walking Tracks** pass Wet-season waterfalls. The trailhead is 21km down the Gunlom Rd off the Kakadu Hwy. There are three different circular day tracks *(2km, 45min.; 5km, 2hr.; 7.5km, 4hr.)* and two longer tracks which require overnight permits (see **Practical Information,** p. 258). The 11km walk features a series of waterfalls and the 13.5km walk features plunge pools during the Wet. Both of these longer walks are difficult, unmarked, and require good navigation and preparation. Near the Yurmikmik walks lies **Jarrangbarnmi,** one of the *djang andjamun* areas that bring catastrophic consequences if entered. This

KAKADU DREAMING Aborigines believe that Kakadu, like the rest of the world, was created during the Dreaming, or Creation Time, when the acts and deeds of powerful ancestral beings shaped the land. There are three categories of land in Aboriginal culture: ceremonial sites, *djang* (Dreaming), and *djang andjamun* (Sacred Dreaming). The ceremonial sites are now used for burials, rites of passage, and other events. At *djang* sites, a creator passed through, took shape, or entered or exited the Earth, leaving the site safe to visit. *Djang andjamun* sites, however, where the ancestor still lingers, are considered spiritual hazard zones, such as the 2000 square kilometer "Sickness Country" in the southern part of Kakadu. Laws prohibit entry to the latter group of sites. One of the primary Creation Ancestors in Kakadu is Warramurrungundji, or "Mother of the Earth." She traveled to Kakadu with her husband from the islands to the northeast. Upon arriving, she sent out her spirit children, teaching them various languages and how to hunt and gather, while she herself created river systems, billabongs, and wildlife. Her work completed, she sat down and became a rock. Similar stories involving the acts of ancestral spirits describe the creation of other features. A triangular rock at Nourlangie, for instance, is the stolen feather of a powerful spirit. Because the features of the land are linked to the ancestors, the land is not an inherited possession, but a sacred site.

series of pools on **Koolpin Creek** is home to **Bula** and **Bolung,** two Creation Ancestors. Visitor numbers are restricted, and no one can enter the area without a permit and entry key, organized by the southern entry station *(☎8975 4859).*

ARNHEM LAND

Take the expansive wilderness, serenity, and the cultural spirit found in Kakadu, multiply it by ten, and you still won't be able to do justice to Arnhem Land's grandeur. Sprawling across the entire northeastern region of the Top End, and several times the size of Kakadu, this Aboriginal homeland was established in 1931. It remains largely uninhabited, save for four or five small settlements and about 100 Aboriginal outstations. The area's inland borders are cut square, but the endless coastline takes an untamed, jagged path from the Cobourg Peninsula in the west (location of Gurig National Park) to the Gove Peninsula in the east. Arnhem Land also includes the Groote and Elcho islands off-shore. The natural and cultural treasures here are incredible—but be aware that there are Aborigines who welcome tourism and its revenues, and there are also those who would prefer to see their lands free from the swarms of outsiders.

PRACTICAL INFORMATION. Venturing into Arnhem Land is a serious matter. There are very few roads (those that do exist are erratically navigable only in the Dry), and there are virtually no signs and services. Moreover, Arnhem Land is off-limits by law to non-Aborigines, so a permit is required to enter.

Permits for entering Arnhem Land depend on where you want to go. The **Northern Land Council** in Jabiru issues permits for three locations close to Kakadu. (☎8979 2410; fax 8979 2650. Open M-F 8am-4:30pm.) A permit for **Injaluk** ($13.20 per person) can be issued on the spot but might take up to an hour to process. Permits for **Sandy Creek** and **Wunyu Beach** ($77 per person) take longer to process; apply in advance. To venture to the secluded beaches and wildlife of **Gurig National Park** on the Cooburg Peninsula, contact the Parks and Wildlife Commission of the Northern Territory. (☎8979 0244. $211 per vehicle with 5 adults for 7 nights.) For permits to other sections of Arnhem Land, contact Darwin's Northern Land Council (☎8920 5100 or 1800 645 299; fax 8445 2633.)

The road into Arnhem Land from Ubirr crosses a tidal river **(Cahills Crossing).** It is very important to check with the Northern Land Council about tidal information before driving or you might find your car tipped over in the saltie-ridden East Alligator River. Driving into Arnhem Land, and especially beyond Injalak, should not be taken lightly. People occasionally have breakdowns or get mired in mud or sand, so it's wise to go with at least one other person. Bring a shovel, a kangaroo jack (higher than a normal jack), two spare tires, rope, and plenty of water.

SIGHTS AND ACTIVITIES. The **Injalak** ("IN-yaluk") **Arts & Crafts Association** is located in Oenpelli (Gunbalanya), a short 16km dirt-road drive from Ubirr. The association has artists working on-site who create exquisite pieces such as pandanus baskets, limited edition bark and paper paintings, screen printed textiles, and didgeridoos. The works are distributed to art galleries around the world, but visitors can purchase pieces on-site. (☎8979 0190. Open M-F 8am-5pm, Sa 8am-noon.) Injalak also sponsors **Aboriginal-guided tours** through a local rock art gallery whose breadth and isolation put Ubirr and Nourlangie to shame—there are no crowds or roped-off galleries here. (2hr. tours $60; max. 6 people. Book ahead.)

Much more remote than Injalak are Sandy Creek and Wunyu Beach. **Sandy Creek,** on Arnhem's north shore, is popular for excellent barramundi, salmon, and tuna fishing. Ideally, anglers should have a boat, though people do fish from the shore. The drive to Sandy Creek (3hr.) is 4WD only. Also on the northern shore is **Wunyu Beach,** a long, virtually untouched, and often windy beach that is ideal for relaxing and strolling. Sunbathers and would-be swimmers beware—the water (and Sandy Creek as well) is teeming with **salties.** The drive to Wunyu takes at least 2½hr. on a 4WD road. Neither Sandy Creek nor Wunyu Beach have facilities, though people do camp at their own risk. Campers must bring their own water, food, and shelter. Stopping on the road to Injalak, Sandy Creek, and Wunyu is prohibited.

TOURS. For those seeking experienced guides and drivers, tours might be the best way to reach Arnhem Land. Multi-day tours with flights from Darwin run several thousands of dollars; 4WD daytrips from Kakadu are much cheaper. Departing from Jabiru and Cooinda are **Outback NT Touring** (☎1800 089 113; $160, child $128) and **Lord's Kakadu and Arnhemland Safaris** (☎8979 2422. $165, child $100).

STUART HIGHWAY: DARWIN TO KATHERINE

The Stuart Hwy. connects Darwin to Adelaide, SA, drawing a divide in the middle of the continent across red, dry desert terrain. The first stretch from Darwin to Katherine is 314km long and contains a number of pleasant stops along the way.

Only 25km south of Darwin is the turn-off for **Howard Springs Nature Park.** Once used as a WWII rest and recreation military camp but now popular among local civilians, the springs offer swimming (with barramundi and turtles) and a short 30min. nature hike. (☎8983 1001. Open daily 8am-8pm. Free.) About 10km farther south on the Stuart Hwy. is the turn-off for **Cox Peninsula Rd.,** which leads 11km west to **Territory Wildlife Park.** A cross between a large zoo and *Jurassic Park*, the park encompasses 400 hectares of various habitats and is a top-notch Top End experience. Visitors can enjoy direct contact with all sorts of marsupials, an enclosed tunnel aquarium, the Birds of Prey presentation, a reptile pavilion, and a house for nocturnal critters. Oh yes, emus, too. (☎8988 7200. Open daily 8:30am-6pm, last admission at 4pm. $18, concessions $9, families $40.) **Darwin Day Tours** runs a half-day tour to the park. (☎8924 1124. Daily 7:30am-1:30pm. $45, concessions $42, child $41; includes entrance fee.) After animal gazing, relax the muscles 1km down the road at **Berry Springs Nature Park** with picnic spots and lukewarm soaking grounds. (Open daily 8am-6:30pm. Free.)

Eighty kilometers south of Darwin and 7km down an access road lies **Lake Bennett Resort,** an upscale lodge next to a stunning lake. The accommodations are expensive, but all activities are open to day visitors. Swim, canoe ($15 per hr., $40 per day), fish, or play golf before watching the sunset. Guest rooms include fridge, A/C, and TV, with shared bath and kitchen facilities. The staff will meet bus travelers at the Stuart Hwy. (☎8976 0960. Sites $10 per person; caravan site $20, powered $25. Dorm $25; twin $168; triple $190. NOMADS.) The turn-off for **Batchelor** and **Litchfield National Park** (see p. 260) is 6km south of the resort.

Between the fuel stops at Adelaide River and Hayes Creek, and 200km from Darwin, **Tjuwaliyn (Douglas) Hot Springs,** is a worthwhile stop. The last 7km of the access road to the springs is gravel, but tame enough for all cars in the Dry. Be forewarned that at certain spots, the springs live up to its "hot" name; though downstream has cooler currents. Camping is available ($3.50, child $1, family $8). **Pine Creek** (see p. 259) is the final stop on the route, only 9km from Katherine.

LITCHFIELD NATIONAL PARK

Although shadowed in size and popularity by Kakadu, Litchfield National Park, established in 1986, has natural wonders second to none. Its spring-fed falls and close proximity to Darwin are a popular daytrip because its widespread paved access renders the sights more accessible (and therefore more crowded) than its big sibling. Staying for more than the day and visiting with a 4WD allows you to explore the more isolated waterfalls, chiseled gorges, rock formations, and bush land plateaus that give Litchfield unique charm.

LITCHFIELD AT A GLANCE	
AREA: 1460km^2. **CLIMATES:** Monsoonal, with distinct Wet (Nov.-Apr.) and Dry (May-Oct.) seasons. **FEATURES:** The Tabletop Range, Reynolds River. **HIGHLIGHTS:** Waterfall after spectacular waterfall, the rigorous 4WD trek to the Lost City and beyond.	**GATEWAYS:** Batchelor, Darwin (p. 238). **CAMPING:** Buley Rockhole, Florence Falls, Surprise Creek Falls, Tjaynera (Sandy Creek) Falls (4WD only), Wangi Falls, and Walker Creek. **FEES:** Entry free.

TRANSPORTATION AND ORIENTATION. Tours from Darwin to Litchfield abound, some combined with Kakadu. The most economical option is a **Greyhound** bus daytrip that hits all of the sites accessible by sealed roads. (☎8941 5872; $75.) **Darwin Day Tours** runs a similar tour. (☎8924 1124; $104, child $75; with lunch.)

The park is located 100km southwest of Darwin. The main entrance (paved access) is reached from the Stuart Hwy. through the township of **Batchelor** (pop. 350), which has food and camping. The Stuart Hwy. turn-off is 90km south of Darwin. From there it is 10km to Batchelor and another 18km to the park entrance. At that point, the **Litchfield Park Rd.** winds its way east through the park, connecting all the sights and access roads. The most popular points of interest are **Florence Falls** (42km from Batchelor) and **Wangi Falls** (68km from Batchelor). The more secluded sights are along a **4WD track** that starts between Florence and Wangi and stretches south along the Reynolds River. Beyond Wangi, the road continues north out of the park and provides an unsealed route back to Darwin (115km). Litchfield Park Rd. is open most of the year to all vehicles; the 4WD tracks close in the Wet.

PRACTICAL INFORMATION. There is no ranger station, but information is available through the **Parks and Wildlife Commission of the Northern Territory** in Darwin (☎8999 5511). Entry is free, and detailed maps ($5.50) are available at the Batchelor Store. Call 8976 0282 for **road conditions,** especially during the Wet. The nearest **post office** is in Batchelor. (☎8976 0020. Open M-F 9am-5pm, Sa 9am-noon.) **Petrol** is available next door at the Batchelor Store.

CAMPING AND ACCOMMODATIONS. Spending a night in Litchfield is highly recommended, if only for the superb stargazing. Camping in the park generally costs $6.60 per person (children $3.30, family $15.40) for basic unpowered sites with showers and toilets. The **Wangi Falls** campground fills up early in the day and can be uncomfortably crowded; more serene options lie near **Florence Falls** and **Buley Rockhole.** Visitors with a 4WD have extra choices at Florence Falls and **Tjaynera (Sandy Creek) Falls.** Barebones facilities (toilets and tap water) exist at **Surprise Creek Falls** and **Walker Creek** for a reduced fee ($3.30 per person, children $1.65, family $7.70). Caravan camping is allowed only at Wangi Falls, and generators are not permitted.

The better options for caravans lie outside the park. **Litchfield Tourist & Van Park** is only 4km from the park border on the way to Batchelor and nearby fishing on the banks of the Finnis River. (☎8976 0070. Sites $7, powered for 2 $16.50, family $25; cabins for 2 $55; overnight vans for 4 $45.) Just a bit further down the road is the family-run **Banyan Tree Caravan Park.** (☎8976 0030. Sites $5.50, powered for 2 $16.50.) The beautifully manicured **Jungle Drum Bungalows,** next door to the Butterfly Farm in Batchelor, have Balinese decor and a relaxing atmosphere. (☎8976 0555. Dorms $22; cabin single $66, double $88.)

FOOD. If you didn't remember to pack a lunch, there is a food kiosk at **Wangi Falls.** (Open daily 9am-5pm.) In Batchelor, the **Butterfly Cafe Restaurant** has hearty home-cooked meals; check out the **Bird and Butterfly Sanctuary** while you are on the premises. (☎8976 0199. Cafe open daily 8:30am-4pm and 6-11pm. Sanctuary open daily 9am-4pm; $6, child $3, and free tea or coffee.) Basic **groceries** are available at the **Batchelor Store.** (☎8976 0045. Open M-F 7am-7pm, Sa-Su 7:30am-7pm.)

SIGHTS AND SHORT WALKS. Impressive waterfalls at Litchfield are among the main attractions. At **Wangi** ("WONG-gye"), two dramatic falls plunge into a large, clear pool. Safe swimming and good snorkeling, a kiosk serving obligatory meat pies, and all of suburban Darwin dragging eskies behind them, combine to make Wangi more of a public beach than anything else. The walking trail (45min. return) to the top of the falls is nondescript. The equally dramatic **Florence Falls** makes visitors exert some effort to reach the pool, but the ability to explore the area from several vantage points is much more satisfying. The car park is near the lookout point above the falls; to reach the plunge pool at the bottom you can either take the staircase or the scenic 15min. walk that meanders along with the creek. A walk (3.2km) through lush monsoon forest connects Florence Falls with **Buley Rockhole,** featuring a number of soothing swimming spots. At **Tolmer Falls,** a short distance from Florence Falls southwest on the main road, there is another steep fall plunging from a sandstone gorge. Swimming is not allowed due to the gentle ecosystem that is home to ghost bats, but a commanding view awaits from the lookout deck. Next door is **Tjaetaba Falls,** accessible via a 4WD track and a fairly steep but rewarding walk through monsoon forests and eucalyptus woodlands. Tjaetaba is a sacred Aboriginal site; swimming is not permitted. Also worth seeing are the **magnetic termite mounds** (see p. 663), located on Litchfield Park Rd. about 20km from Batchelor. These mounds range in age from 50 to 100 years old, and are aligned so that their broad backs face east-to-west, in order to soak in the softer sunlight of the morning and evening.

For those with 4WD, **The Lost City** is 10.5km down an access road 40km past the park entrance. Visitors can wander among the haunting natural arrangement of sandstone towers. Early morning is especially spellbinding, with the structures shrouded in hazy mist and the place to yourself. **Tjaynera Falls** (Sandy Creek Falls) lies about 7km off Litchfield Park Rd on a 4WD-track. A mild trail (1.7km) leads to the plunge pool, matching Wangi's beauty without the noisy crowds. For real seclusion, continue 20km farther on the same track to **Surprise Creek Falls.** During the 1hr. drive, the landscape alternates between thick forest and grasslands, dotted with ghostly cathedral termite mounds. The falls are typically deserted and make one of the best sunset spots in the Top End.

DIDGERIDOO 101 So, you want to buy a "didge." According to traditional folklore of the Yolngu Aborigines of northern Australia, the didgeridoo has been around since the beginning of time; though rock paintings tell scientists that they have existed for the past 20,000-50,000 years. Traditionally used in the *corroboree* dance ceremonies, the didge playing has recently been taken up by modern musicians and beginners alike solely for musical purpose. The didgeridoo itself is made from a eucalyptus tree naturally hollowed out by termites. Once cut, the bark is shaved from the outside and the mouthpiece is dipped in bee's wax. In the Aboriginal tradition, painted didges are only played in formal ceremonies honoring birth, marriage, or death, but their beauty and higher prices make them ubiquitous in tourist shops. Each didge has a unique sound, which depends on its length, diameter, bore-width, twists in the chamber, and the chamber wall texture created by the former termite inhabitants. Most stores allow wandering shoppers to have a go at their selection of didgeridoos, and many will package and send them home.

PINE CREEK ☎08

The tiny town of Pine Creek (pop. 650) sits at the junction of the Stuart and Kakadu Hwy. It provides a convenient base for nearby Kakadu, and **Copperfield Dam,** 6km southwest of town off the Stuart Hwy., is a pleasant spot for picnicking and swimming. Another 22km on the same turn-off is **Umbrawarra Gorge,** a favorite with locals and rumored to be better than its Katherine sister. The only remnant of Pine Creek's gold-mining glory days of the 1870s can be found at **Gun Alley Gold Mining,** 159 Gun Alley, where visitors can pan for gold and take home their findings. (☎8976 1221. Follow the "gold panning" signs. Open in the Dry daily 8:30am-3pm, in the Wet by appointment. $5.50.)

On the main street (named Main Tce.), the **Diggers Rest Motel** has well-kept cabins with kitchen, bath, TV, and A/C, and doubles as a **tourist centre.** (☎8976 1442. Reception daily 8am-8pm. Singles $65; doubles $75; for 3-5 people $85.) Next door is the general store doubling as a **bus depot** at **Ah Toys.** (☎8976 1202. Open M-F 9am-5:30pm, Sa 9am-12:30pm.) **Greyhound/McCafferty's** runs to Darwin (3hr., 3 per day, $37) and Katherine (1hr., 3 per day, $18). Around the corner on Moule St., the **post office** doubles as a **bank**. (☎8976 1220. Open M-F 9am-noon and 1-5pm.) The adjacent **Mayse's Cafe** not only serves good meals for $6-9 but (you guessed it) doubles as an **Internet** cafe. (☎8976 1241. Open daily 7am-8pm. Internet $2.50 per 15min., $8 per hr.) The casual and congenial **Kakadu Gateway Caravan Park** has a multitude of accommodation choices available, BBQ, kitchen, TV room, and free laundry. (☎8976 1166. Sites $8, powered $18; singles $35; budget double $40, double $55, budget twin $65; family $70; swag room with no beds $8 per person.)

KATHERINE ☎08

The only stoplight along the 1500km of the Stuart Hwy. between Darwin and Alice Springs is found in the rough-and-tumble town of Katherine (pop. 11,000). With a turbulent history of destructive floods (the most recent in 1998) and subsequent rejuvenation, Katherine remains edgy. Noisy conflict along the main street is not unusual (especially at night). Tourism is the primary industry here, staffed by both the Aboriginal Jawoyn and Dagoman inhabitants and the white population. While it can be a refreshing blast of civilization after the wilderness of the Kimberley or the outback down south, tourists are not here to see the town. Katherine is more of a stopover for those on their way Nitmiluk, Kakadu, Darwin, or Alice Springs. In the end, it reminds one of the good and the bad that come with cities, and encourages travelers to "head bush" once again.

TRANSPORTATION

Greyhound/McCafferty's buses (☎1800 089 103) stop at the **Transit Centre** on Katherine Tce. Both companies run to: **Darwin** (4hr., 4 per day, $48); **Alice Springs** (15hr., 2 per day, $162); **Broome** (19hr., 1 per day, $204); **Townsville** (29.5hr., 1 per day, $262). Local car rental places are **Territory Rent-a-Car,** 6 Katherine Tce. (☎8971 3183), in the Transit Centre; **Hertz,** 392 Katherine Tce (☎8971 1111); **Delta** (☎13 13 90), at Knotts Crossing Resort.

ORIENTATION AND PRACTICAL INFORMATION

Katherine marks the intersection of three main roads. The **Stuart Hwy.** becomes **Katherine Tce.** in town; most shops and services are here. The **Victoria Hwy.** leaves from the northern side of town, past the hot springs and heading eventually to the Kimberley. Finally, **Giles St.** heads east from the middle of town, reaching **Nitmiluk National Park** (29km). The **Transit Centre** and the Woolworth's shopping mall are on the southern end of Katherine Tce., near **Lindsay St.** Parallel to Katherine Tce. to the east, **First** through **Fourth Street** support various tourist accommodations.

Katherine Region Tourist Association, on the corner of Lindsay St. and Katherine Tce. (across from the Transit Centre) is more impartial than the travel desk in the Transit Centre. (☎8972 2650; fax 8972 2969. Open in the Dry M-F 8:30am-6pm, Sa-Su 10am-3pm; in the Wet M-F 9am-5pm, Sa-Su 10am-3pm.) **Westpac, Commonwealth,** and **ANZ banks** and 24hr. **ATMs** are on Katherine Tce. (All open M-Th 9:30am-4pm and F 9:30am-5pm.) The **police** (☎8972 0111) are 2.5km south of town on the Stuart Hwy., and the **hospital** (☎8973 9211) is on Giles St. (Gorge Rd)., 3km from Katherine Tce. Email and Aboriginal art is at the **Didj Shop Internet Cafe,** on Giles a block west of Katherine Tce. (☎8972 2485. Open Apr.-Oct. M-F 10am-10pm, Sa 11am-7pm, Su 10am-3pm; Nov.-Mar. M-F 10am-7pm, Sa 11am-7pm, Su 10am-3pm. $7 per hr. 15min. free with coffee purchase.) The **post office** is on the corner of Katherine Tce. and Giles St (open M-F 9am-5pm). **Postal code:** 0850.

ACCOMMODATIONS

Kookaburra Backpackers (☎8971 0257), on the corner of Lindsay and 3rd St. This hostel boasts not only an ideal layout (every group of 4 or 8 guests shares a clean bathroom, refrigerator, outdoor picnic table, and fully-stocked kitchenette) but also extremely friendly employees and guests. Free transport to and from Transit Centre (3 blocks), pool, and organized BBQs. Laundry $3. Key deposit $10. Runs a 3-day camping tour through Kakadu from Katherine to Darwin ($350, includes meals and camping equipment). Reception daily 7:30am-2:30pm and 4-8pm. Book ahead in the Dry. Dorms $16; twins with TV and fridge $45; light brekkie included. NOMADS/VIP/YHA.

Victoria Lodge, 21 Victoria Hwy (☎1800 808 875). A 10min. walk from Katherine Tce. A great deal at a deluxe hostel. Sparkling refurbished rooms share common areas with leather couches, microwave, bathroom, spacious kitchenette, and TV. Free transport to Transit Centre. Dorms $15; singles $35; twins $45; doubles $50. YHA.

Palm Court Backpackers (☎8792 2239), on the corner of 3rd and Giles St. Comfortable and mellow. Rooms with fridge and toilet. Kitchen, pool, BBQ. Free transport to and from Transit Centre. Laundry $3. Key deposit $10. Bikes $10 per day. Reception daily 6:30am-2pm, 4-8pm. Dorms $15; twins and doubles $42-45. NOMADS/VIP/YHA.

Camping is available along the Victoria Hwy. The **Red Gum Caravan Park** (☎8972 2239) is 1km from town (a 10-minute walk). Laundry, pool, and BBQ. (Sites $13.50, for 2 $18, powered for 2 $20; cabin $60, $12 each extra person). The **Riverview Caravan Park and Motel** (☎8972 1011) has a pool and spa, and is located at the hot springs. Laundry, BBQs. (Sites for 2 $16, powered $19; singles $20; doubles and twins $25; budget cabins for 2 $50.)

FOOD

A giant Woolworth's **supermarket** is across from the Transit Centre, on Katherine Tce. (☎8972 3055. Open daily 7am-10pm.)

Bucking Bull Burger Bar (☎8972 1734), Shop 1 on Katherine Tce. A local's favorite, this is the spot to enjoy some authentic country cookin'. Extraordinary mango smoothies $2.50. Backpackers breakfast special $5.90. Open daily 5am-5pm.

Mekhong Thai Cafe & Takeaway (☎8972 3170), on the corner of Katherine Tce. and the Victoria Hwy. One of the tastier options in town. Indoor and outdoor seating, and a large vegetarian menu. Mains $9-$16. Open M-F 6pm-10pm.

Starvin' Pizza and Cafe, 32 Katherine Tce. (☎8972 3633), just north of Giles. The good ol' reliable pizza joint, where you can fill up on hearty Italian pizza ($9.80-$15.90). Open M-Sa 9am-10pm, Su 11am-10pm.

Tommo's Bakery, 14 2nd St. (☎8971 1155), on the corner of Giles St. This large, humble bakery is the place to grab a sandwich (from $2.70), pastry ($2), or iced coffee ($2). Open M-F 5am-5pm, Sa 5am-1pm.

SIGHTS AND ACTIVITIES

Two kilometers along the Victoria Hwy. from Katherine Tce., **hot springs** bubble along the Katherine River—though "not hot, but warmer than I might expect" might be a better description. Popular with tourists of all ages, the springs have swimming, toilets, and wheelchair access along Croker St. Shopping for local didgeridoos should begin at **Coco's Place,** 21 First St. (☎8971 2889), across from the cinema. Coco knows his stuff and will demonstrate circular breathing for you, but expect to pay more for his expert lessons. Make your own didgeridoo (and keep it) with **Whoop Whoop** overnight trips. (☎8972 2941. F-Sa. $220.) The local extension of **School of the Air** (see p. 276) is on Giles St. 1.5km from Katherine Tce., broadcasting lessons to rural schoolchildren. (☎8972 1833. Classes Mar-Dec. M-F 9, 10, 11am, 1, 2pm. $5.) From May-Oct., evening **river cruises** provide wildlife spotting and lively dinner around a campfire. **Far Out Adventures** cruises the Katherine River and has BBQ-style meals with BYO. (☎8972 2552. $45, includes pickup.) **Travel North** runs a **crocodile night** along the Johnstone River that includes wine and stew. (☎1800 089 103. $40; $49, includes pickup.)

NIGHTLIFE

Action can be found most nights around the pool tables of **Kirby's Sports Bar** in the Katherine Hotel/Motel, on the corner of Katherine Tce. and Giles St. (Open Su-W 11:30am-11:30pm, Th 11:30am-12:30am, F-Sa 11:30am-1:30am.) A more mellow atmosphere can be found at the **Last Chance Saloon** at the Crossways Motel, on the corner of Katherine Tce. and the Victoria Hwy. (☎8971 0422. Open late.) On the weekends, dancing fiends let loose until the wee hours at **Rio** nightclub, on Katherine Tce. just south of the Victoria Hwy. (Open F-Sa 10pm-4am.)

NITMILUK NATIONAL PARK (KATHERINE GORGE)

Nitmiluk National Park provides water and land activities in a setting as dramatic and striking as its bigger cousins, Kakadu and Litchfield. Composed of a sandstone plateau sliced by rivers and tributaries, Nitmuluk is popular with tourists who have come to admire the rocky cliffs rising from the river, the thick growth of plants in the monsoon forest, and the 168 species of birds decorating the skies.

Since 1989, the park has been owned by the local Jawoyn Aborigines, who leased its management for 99 years to the Northern Territory Government. Aboriginal livelihood remains a significant presence in the park, and the 450 recorded galleries of rock art dispersed throughout the region are physical reminders of the strong presence of the Jawoyn people. The name "Nitmiluk" is part of a Jawoyn Dreaming story in which **Nabilil** the dragon names the gorge after hearing the "Nit! Nit! Nitnit!" song of the cicada. It was the death of Nabilil that sent water gushing forth to create the Katherine River. Other important figures of the Nitmiluk Dreamtime include **Bula,** the original creator of the landscape who resides underground in the "Sickness Country" to the north of Katherine, and **Bolung,** the rainbow serpent who inhabits the second Gorge and threatens destruction if disturbed. Further information regarding the Jawoyn Dreamings in the park is available at the Visitor Centre.

NITMILUK AT A GLANCE

AREA: 292,008 hectares.

FEATURES: Katherine River and 13 gorges, Edith Falls, and the Seventeen Mile Creek.

HIGHLIGHTS: Paddling a canoe down the river, hiking up the cliffs and through shady gorges.

GATEWAYS: Katherine (p. 262).

CAMPING: Permanent campgrounds near the Visitor Centre and at Edith Falls, and registered overnight bush camping.

FEES: Entry free.

ORIENTATION AND PRACTICAL INFORMATION

The 13 gorges on the Katherine River form the centerpiece of Nitmiluk. They primary base to see the gorges is the **Nitmiluk Tourist Centre,** located at the end of the sealed Gorge Rd. 30km east of Katherine; the **Southern Walks** and water activities are found here. The second entrance to the park is reached 40km north of Katherine on the Stuart Hwy., where a 20km access road leads to **Edith Falls,** a campground, and a few short hikes. The long **Jatbula Trail** extends all the way from the Tourist Centre to Edith Falls.

Buses: Travel North (☎1800 089 103) runs buses from all accommodations in Katherine to the Tourist Centre. 25min., 4 per day, $18 return. Book ahead.

Tourist Info: Nitmiluk Visitor Centre (☎8972 1886), provides hiking information and camping permits (staffed daily 7am-7pm). A tourist desk in the gift shop takes care of canoe rental, helicopter tours and boat cruises, and reception for the campground (Open daily 7am-7pm). There is an exhibit on the Jawoyn and natural history of the park, as well as a **bistro** (☎8972 3150) that serves burgers for $6-7 and Thai chicken salad for $9.65. Open daily 8am-8:30pm, Happy Hour 5-6:30pm. Contact the **Parks and Wildlife Commission** in Katherine for more info on Katherine Gorge. (☎8972 1886; fax 8971 0702; PO Box 344, Katherine NT 0851.)

Climate is most comfortable for visitors is from May-Sept., after the seasonal storms and before the humidity builds up. In the Wet months sections of the Katherine river flood and make some activities unavailable. However, locals praise the stunning greenery of the Wet before the foliage turns a dreary brown.

Tours: Nitmiluk Tours offers **helicopter flights**. Booked at the Visitor Centre (☎8972 1253). 3 Gorges $55, 8 Gorges $82.50, 13 Gorges $137.50. Free **ranger-guided activities** are scheduled regularly during the Dry. Slide shows M and Th 7:30pm, campfire talks W 7:30pm.

CAMPING

A shady **caravan park** is available near the Visitor Centre, with toilets, showers, laundry, phones, and BBQ facilities. Register at the Visitor Centre. (Sites $8 per person, powered $12.) A second permanent **campground** next to Edith Falls allows tents and reasonably-sized caravans, and has showers, BBQ, a food kiosk, and a picnic area, but no powered sites ($5 per person). Plenty of beautiful pools and waterfalls cool the grounds. The lower pool, a short walk from the carpark, is a huge, crystal-clear plunge pool with a waterfall.

Overnight camping in the depths of the park is permitted (register at the center; $3.30 per person per night; $50 deposit, $20 if only going as far as Crystal Falls from Nitmiluk Centre). Areas, with toilets and (usually) a water source, are located along the Jatbula Trail and at the 4th, 5th, and 8th gorges in the Southern Walks area. Fires are permitted along the Jatbula, but not in Southern Walks.

NITMILUK BY WATER

From May to September, quiet waters allow for canoeing, boating, and walking. **Nitmiluk Tours** (☎8972 1253) does all rentals for water activities, which can be booked at most accommodations in Katherine or at the Visitor Centre. **Canoeing** is justifiably the most popular; it allows you to travel at your own pace and provides great views without racking up the expense of a boat cruise. Paddling on the cooler water is also more comfortable than hiking—temperatures here are sizzling year-round. If traveling alone, it's a good idea to find a partner since paddling is only half the battle of the gorge tour—dragging the canoe across rocky portages is the other. No more than 75 canoes are permitted in the gorge at a time; book ahead. (Single canoes half-day $28, full-day $39, overnight $78; doubles $42, $58, $116. Half and full-day canoes require $20 cash deposit. Overnight canoes require $3.30 permit and $60 cash deposit.) Another popular aquatic activity is **swimming,** but keep in mind that you may be sharing the bath with freshwater crocs. Many people like to swim near the boathouse and at deep plunge pools at the end of some hikes. A **boat cruise** lets visitors zoom along the gorges in flat, shaded motor vessels; at the end of each gorge, passengers transfer to a new boat on the next gorge. The crowded arrangement makes it hard to enjoy the natural solitude of the area and destroys any chance of moving at one's own pace. (2hr.; departs from the boat jetty; 4 per day in the Dry; $34, children $13.50.) Daily "adventure" and "safari" tours combine boating and hiking. (4hr.; departs 9am; $49. 8hr. $85.)

NITMILUK BY LAND

Walking tracks in the park fall in all difficulty levels and range from 2.5km to 66km. The abundant flora, fauna, and rocky outcroppings provide a different view from canoeing, but it is often 10°C hotter on the trail than it is near the water, and the sun can be brutal. The Southern Walks are usually open during the Wet; the Jatbula Trail is not. **For all overnight walks, register with the rangers before setting out.** Semi-detailed topographic maps are $7.50 at the Visitor Centre.

SOUTHERN WALKS. The main trail of the Southern Walks starts at the Visitor Centre and parallels the gorge at a 1.5km separation. Each individual side trail branches off and heads directly for the gorge. Much of the main trail hiking is through unremarkable surroundings; it the scenery on the short side trails that provide the vistas of the gorges. The **Lookout Loop** (3.7km return, 2hr., moderate) is a steep climb up the side of the gorge, with excellent views of the river and 17-Mile Valley. The **Windolf** walk (8.4km, 3½hr., moderate) has views of the lower gorge and occasional Aboriginal art, passes the panoramic **Pat's Lookout,** and ends at a gorgeous plunge pool. The **Butterfly Gorge** walk (12km, 4½hr., difficult) provides a good overview of the region, with woodlands and rock formations giving way to a dense, tranquil monsoon forest in a side gorge that does, in fact, possess an unusually large population of butterflies. The walk ends at a deep swimming spot. **Lily Ponds** trail (20km, 6½hr., difficult) covers even longer distances and more treacherous terrain, but rewards with a sheltered pool in the third gorge. The Southern Walks region has two overnight walks—**Eighth Gorge** and **Jawoyn Valley**—each a difficult 30-40km. The Jawoyn Valley loop holds galleries of Aboriginal art.

At the opposite end of the Jatbula Trail (below), two short walks leave from the Edith Falls carpark. The **Sweetwater Pool** walk (9km, 4hr., moderate) leads to a waterhole and good camping. The **Leliyn Trail** (5.2km, 3hr., easy) leads to the smaller but equally amazing upper pools.

JATBULA TRAIL. The popular Jatbula Trail is a 66km, 5-day, one-way-only sojourn between Nitmiluk Centre and Edith Falls. There are eight 1-4 day segments between the center and Edith Falls, through rainforest pockets, an Aboriginal amphitheater, and waterfalls. The only day walk portion of the Jatbula Trail is the Northern Rockhole walk (16km, 4hr., moderate), which leaves the Tourist Centre, winds through a valley, and ends at a rock face and waterhole.

VICTORIA HIGHWAY: KATHERINE TO KUNUNURRA

From downtown Katherine, the "Vic" careens westward 512km to Kununurra, WA (see p. 666). There isn't much in between, save two service areas and some stunning scenery. Two hundred kilometers west of Katherine, the **Victoria River Roadhouse** has petrol, a restaurant, and quiet campsites with breathtaking views of the nearby escarpment. (☎8975 0744. Sites for 2 $12, powered $17.50; budget rooms $35; motel rooms from $60.) A few Victoria River **cruises** leave from the Roadhouse (Daily 9am, 4pm. Boat cruise 1½hr., $35. Fishing cruise 2½hr., $50.) The highway passes through **Gregory National Park** (Timber Creek Ranger Station. ☎8975 0888.) The Territory's second-largest national park (after Kakadu) features 2WD-accessible bushwalks and lookouts over Victoria River Gorge, as well as rugged 4WD tracks through the isolated surroundings. **Timber Creek,** a rowdy roadside town, is another 90km west of Victoria River. The **Wayside Inn** has a small restaurant and accommodations. (☎8975 0722. Sites for 2 $11, powered $17; single $36.60; double $57.50.) River cruises can be booked next door at **Max's Victoria River Boat Tours** (☎8975 0850. $55 per 4hr.). At the 468km mark, **Keep River National Park** is home to Aboriginal rock art sites and a few bushwalks. Camping is permitted at two sites (15 and 28km down a gravel road); jokes about "keep"-ing the river clean are strictly forbidden throughout the park. Finally, about 480km west of Katherine (but less than 40km from Kununurra) is the border crossing into WA. There are strict quarantines against fruits, veggies, honey, and plant material. Also be aware that Western Australia clocks are 1½hr. behind the Territory's.

DOWN THE TRACK

Heading south down the Stuart Hwy. from Darwin, the lush vegetation and cinnamon earth of the Top End give way to short grasses, resilient shrubs, and a deep, barren red that stretches for miles, broken only by occasional rock formations. On the stretch between Katherine and Alice Springs, you'll never feel like you're close to anything—just drive and gape at the expanse.

STUART HIGHWAY: KATHERINE TO TENNANT CREEK

There are 672 long kilometers between Katherine and Tennant Creek. for those driving the trek, take the proper precautions (see **Transportation,** p. 235). Twenty-seven kilometers south of Katherine is the 200km turn-off to an unsung gem, **Cutta Cutta Caves Nature Park** (☎8972 1940). Meaning "starry starry," the name refers to the delicate calcite crystals that grow within the dark, temperate passages. The cave extends 720m through an underground labyrinth of limestone columns and jagged ceilings, although visitors can only venture through the first 250m (the depths get too cold and reach 99% humidity). **Tours,** the only way to see the cave, are led by fun, knowledgeable guides, and proceed through five impressive chambers. (1hr. Depart daily year-round 9, 10, 11am, 1, 2, and 3pm, except during floods in the Wet. $10.) "Cultural Adventures" are offered at the Aboriginal owned and operated tours of **Manyallaluk,** 100km southeast of Katherine (50km on the Stuart Hwy., and a 50km access road). The name refers to the Frog Dreaming. (☎8975 4727 or 1800 644 727. Operates Mar.-Dec. On-site 1-day tours $99, child $60.50. From Katherine 1-day tours $132/$71.50; 2-day $450/200.)

Another 106km south on the Stuart is the township of **Mataranka,** renowned for Elsey National Park and the thermal pool near Mataranka Homestead. **Elsey National Park** (13,840 hectares) features the emerald Roper River, perfect for canoeing, swimming, or fishing. To reach the park, continue 2km south past "downtown" Mataranka and take a left onto Homestead Rd. The turn-off for Elsey

YUMMY? Along the eternal stretches of road in the Northern Territory, good food can be harder to find than fuel. The staples of a roadhouse hot-food counter are guaranteed to be either deep-fat-fried or else crammed full of hearty mystery-meat. As you browse the array of suspicious Sausage Rolls and Kidney Pies that have been waiting for hours under a heat-lamp, notice the dazzling number of combinations of parts of a cow that you can find in a pie crust. Plan accordingly and bring your own snacks, or you will end up having a Wing Ding. And eating it, too.

is 4km down this road. Another 11km farther on is picture-perfect **Jalmurark campground,** where visitors can hike to the pristine pools at **Mataranka Falls** (4km) or rent a canoe and relax along the Roper River. (Canoe shop open daily in the Dry 8am-7pm. Single canoes $5 per hr., $25 per day; doubles $7/$35.) The campground has private sites with showers and toilets ($6.60, child $3.30).

Another 3km past the Elsey turn-off on Homestead Rd is **Mataranka Homestead resort** and its crowded sapphire **thermal pool. Greyhound** and **McCafferty's buses** between Katherine and Tennant Creek all stop at the Homestead (times vary) which holds a general store, takeaway eatery (daily 7am-8pm), restaurant (daily 6:30-8:30pm), and bar with live entertainment most nights (daily 7:30pm-late). You can also embark on a **free tour** of the historic homestead (departs daily in the Dry at 11:30am), or rent a canoe. **Camping** includes showers, laundry, and kitchen facilities at a budget lodge. (☎8975 4544 or 1800 754 544. Dorm $17; budget double $36; motel double $75. Sites $8, powered for 2 $20; cabins for 2 $93.)

From Mataranka to Tennant Creek, there are several fuel stops and roadhouses: **Larrimah** (☎8975 9932); **Daly Waters** (☎8975 9925); **Elliot** (☎8969 2025); **Renner Springs** (☎8964 4505); **Three Ways** (☎8962 2744).

TENNANT CREEK ☎08

The dusty outback town of Tennant Creek (pop. 35,000) is not your ordinary fuel stop, but the self-proclaimed "Golden Heart" of the NT. Located 988km south of Darwin on the Stuart Hwy., the town is a rugged blip of modern development amid an expanse of bush and Aboriginal land. Stemming from Australia's last great goldrush in the 1930s, which drew fortune-seekers to the surrounding Barkly region, Tennant Creek made its place on the map. Even with a prosperous $4 billion output of gold since the 1960s, Tennant Creek is very much a town that watches the road trains and travelers go by. No one seems to stay for long (except the locals), but Devil's Marbles, mining history, and the regional artistic flavor of the Warumungu Aborigines all make the pause more engaging.

TRANSPORTATION

Buses: The **Transit Centre** (☎8962 1070) is on Paterson St., near the intersection with Stuart St., at the north end of town. Open M-F 7am-6pm and 9:30-11pm, Sa 8am-1pm, later when buses arrive. Greyhound and McCafferty's **buses** run to: **Alice Springs** (5-6hr., 2 per day, $101); **Darwin** (13hr., 2 per day, $130); **Katherine** (8-9hr., 2 per day, $83); **Mt. Isa** (7½hr., 1 per day, $97). **Townsville** (20hr., 1 per day, $193).

Auto Club: AANT (☎8962 2468; after hours 8962 3126), on Irvine St. in Wyatt Motors.

Bicycle Rental: Bridgestone Tyre, 52b Paterson St. (☎8962 2361), on the corner of Davidson St. Half-day $5, full-day $10. Open M-F 8am-5pm.

ORIENTATION AND PRACTICAL INFORMATION

The Stuart Hwy., called **Paterson St.** in town, runs from north to south. Intersecting Paterson are, from the north, **Stuart St.** (not to be confused with the Stuart Hwy.), **Davidson St.,** then **Peko Rd.** on the left side of Paterson, and **Windley St.** on the right. Continuing south is **Memorial Dr.** to the right.

Tourist Office: Tennant Creek Regional Tourist Association (☎8962 3388; fax 8962 2509), 1.5km up Peko Rd., provides info and tours. Open May-Sept. daily 9am-5pm, Oct.-Apr. M-F 9am-5pm, Sa 9am-noon.

Currency Exchange: ANZ Bank (☎13 13 14), on Paterson St. between Davidson and Stuart St. **Westpac Bank** (☎8962 2801), at the corner of Paterson St. and Peko Rd. Both open M-Th 9:30am-4pm, F 9:30am-5pm, with 24hr. **ATMs.**

Police: (☎8962 4444), on Paterson St. near Windley St.

Hospital: Tennant Creek Hospital (☎8962 4399, after hours 8962 4232, ambulance 8962 1900), on Schmidt St. Take a left turn at the end of Memorial Dr.

Pharmacy: Amcal Chemist (☎8962 2616), across from the Transit Centre. Open M-F 9am-5:30pm, Sa 9am-12:30pm.

Internet Access: At the **public library,** on Peko Rd. (☎8962 2401). $2.20 per 30min. Open M-F 10am-6pm, Sa 10am-noon. Also at **Switch** (☎8962 3124), on Paterson just north of the Transit Centre. $2 per 20min. Open M-F 8:30am-10pm, Sa 8:30am-8pm.

Post Office (☎8962 2196), at the corner of Paterson St. and Memorial Dr. Open M-F 9am-5pm. **Postal Code:** 0861.

ACCOMMODATIONS

Campers will be taken care of at the Outback Caravan Park (☎8962 2459), 300m from Paterson on Peko Rd. The desolate surroundings melt away with the shady sites, manicured grass, and fantastic swimming pool. Kitchen, BBQ, laundry and friendly staff. (Sites $8; powered for 2 $20; deluxe cabins with bath $48-$68)

Safari Backpackers YHA, 12 Davidson St. (☎8962 2207), west of Paterson St. Small, clean, and comfortable. Shared bath, kitchen, laundry, and lounge. Reception daily 7am-9pm. Dorms $14; twins and doubles $36. YHA.

Tourist's Rest Hostel (☎8962 2719), on Leichardt St. Walk south on Paterson and turn right on Windley St. Friendly and spacious, with an aviary and funny lawn decor. Kitchen, pool, TV, and laundry. Daytrips to Devil's Marbles $55, with 1-night's stay $66.60. Reception 24hr. Dorms $17; twins and doubles $39. NOMADS/VIP/YHA.

FOOD

Paterson St. is lined with takeaway snack bars and restaurants. **Rocky's** provides tasty pizza in a no-frills setting. (☎8962 2049. Open daily 4-11pm. Large pizzas $10-18.) **Bullwinkle's** does not exist. **Top of Town Cafe,** just north of the Transit Centre has cheap veggie burgers and a sandwich bar. (☎8962 1311. Open M-W and Sa-Su 8am-7pm, Th-F 8am-10pm.) **Margo Miles Steakhouse,** across the street from the Transit Centre has fancy Italian dishes and, of course, plenty of steak for around $15. (☎8962 1311. Open M-F noon-2pm and 6pm-9pm, Sa-Su 6pm-9pm.) **Mr. Perry's Ice Cream,** on Patterson St. south of Memorial Dr., actually has good Chinese takeaway. (☎8962 2995. Open M-Sa 8am-5:30pm, Su 10am-3pm.) Adjacent is the **Tennant Food Barn,** which offers the cheap **groceries.** (☎8962 2296. Open M-W and F-Sa 8:30am-6pm, Th 8:30am-6:30pm, Su 9am-6pm.)

SIGHTS AND ACTIVITIES

Simply put, there ain't much to do in Tennant Creek. **Battery Hill** houses a working gold stamp battery (for crushing ore and extracting gold) and an underground gold mine replica. Each has history-heavy tours running twice daily. (☎8962 3388. $13, children $6.50.) History buffs can visit the **Tennant Creek Telegraph Station Historical Reserve,** 10km north of Tennant Creek, on the Stuart Hwy. Built in 1872, the station was integral to the overland telegraph project. There is a self-guided tour through the building. (Ranger-led talks May-Oct. F 10am-2pm.) The **Parks and Wildlife Commission** (☎8962 4599) manages the station as well as the nearby proposed **Daven-**

port Range National Park (4WD only). For a pleasant cycling trip, the **Ted Ryko Bike Trail** leaves from the north end of town and runs for 5km to the **Mary Ann Recreational Dam,** passing the **Honeymoon Ranges.** About 3km east of Paterson St. on Peko Rd. lies the **Bill Allen Lookout,** with impressive views of the entire Tennant Creek area. Man-made beauty is closer to town at the Aboriginal **Jurnkurakurr Mural,** on the corner of Paterson and Windley St.

STUART HIGHWAY: TENNANT CREEK TO ALICE SPRINGS

Geologists say it was wind erosion. Aborigines credit the Rainbow Serpent. Whatever the cause, the rock formations known as the **Devil's Marbles** are baffling. Located just off the Stuart Hwy., 80km from Tennant Creek, the giant 7m-thick granite boulders balance precariously on one another, providing visitors with opportunities for short climbs and some intriguing photographs. Two tours run from Tennant Creek and include a BBQ back in town. Devil's Marbles Tours emphasizes geological and cultural appreciation. (☎0418 891 711. Departs daily 10:30am; $55. Sunrise tours depart M, F 5am; $65.) **Garyo's** is more action-packed, staging numerous photo-ops on, in between, and around the rocks. (☎8962 2024. Daily tour 11am-5pm; $50.) **Camping** at the Marbles is basic. (Pit toilets, BBQ, no water. $3.30, child $1.65.) The closest town to Devil's Marbles is **Wauchope,** 9km south, which has petrol, food, and accommodations. (☎8964 1963. Sites $5, powered $14.50; motel singles $30; doubles with bath $70.) Small towns farther along the highway have roadhouses that provide basic services including petrol, food, and accommodation: **Wycliffe Well** (☎8964 1966), rumored to receive frequent UFO visits; **Barrow Creek** (☎8956 9753); **Ti Tree** (☎8956 9741); **Aileron** (☎8956 9703).

THE RED CENTRE

The dry, desolate outback at the center of Australia takes its name from the color of the oxidized dust that stretches to the edge of the horizon. To many travelers and Australians, the Red Centre represents the essence of the continent, where flat land perpetually bakes under a scalding sun. The gnarled vegetation is weedy and sparse, and the wildlife is locked in a constant struggle for survival with the unforgiving climate, with unbearable bush flies and exhausting heat in the summer, and with freezing nights in the winter. Out of this stark landscape, at the geographic center of the continent, rises Uluru (Ayers Rock), a celebrated symbol of the land down under and the largest rock in the world.

Alice Springs is the outback's unofficial capital and the gateway to the desert beyond. The region's natural wonders include the MacDonnell Ranges, Watarrka (Kings Canyon), Uluru, and Kata Tjuta, all of which do their best to disrupt the red monotony of central Australia. These monuments have magnetic appeal, and tourists are attracted like little iron filings. Prepare to brave endless distances and remote disasters to experience the "real" outback.

ALICE SPRINGS ☎08

The only city of any size for a long, long way in any direction, and inhabited by only 27,000 souls itself, Alice Springs is a desert outpost in the heart of the continent. Connected to the world by endless tracks, Alice springs to life next to the waterless Todd River and impressive natural backdrop. Sandstone hills of the MacDonnell Ranges loom large over every street corner, constant reminders that this is the outback. Wilderness dominates here, and the town's lights can't hold a candle to the sparkling night sky of desert country.

Many travelers use Alice to explore the Red Centre, but the city works hard to be independently attractive. It's a relatively young town, only growing rapidly after 1929 when the Old Ghan Railway to Adelaide was completed. Today, tourism surpasses the mining and cattle industries, and a plethora of attractions can easily fill up a three- or four-day visit (and quickly empty your wallet). While downtown Alice might be teeming with tourist shops that focus on Aboriginal

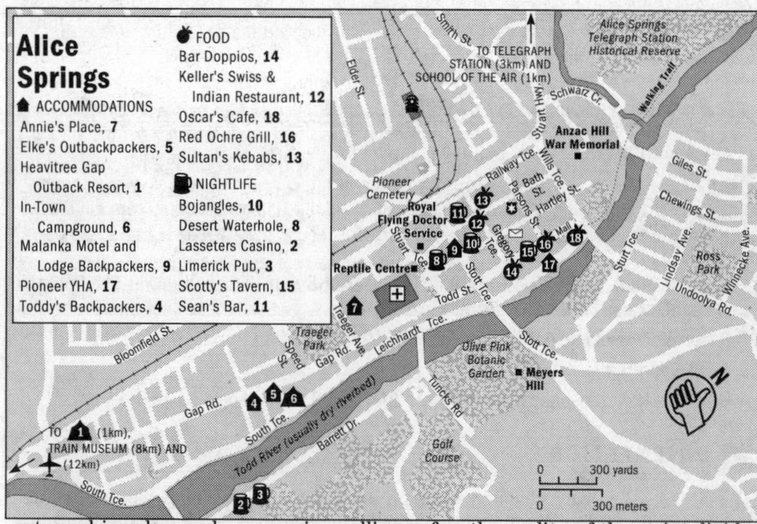

art, opal jewelry, and cappuccino-selling cafes, the reality of the strict divide between Aborigines and the white population is alarmingly strident; nowhere else in Australia is the racial divide so apparent. As white life beats on about the concrete streets of Alice, Aborigines dwell in small circles from dawn till dusk along the Todd River, still speaking in soft hushes of their native language. The scene in Alice is a reminder of Australia's harsh past and current struggle.

TRANSPORTATION

Airplanes: Alice Springs Airport (☎8951 1211), 20km south of the city on the Stuart Hwy. Provides domestic service, tourist info, currency exchange, and car rental agencies. **Qantas** (☎13 13 13) and **Ansett** (☎13 13 00) fly to: **Adelaide** (2hr., 2 per day, $350); **Brisbane** (4½hr., 2 per day, $520); **Cairns** (3½hr., 1 per day, $400); **Darwin** (2hr., 3 per day, $330); **Melbourne** (3hr., 2-4 per day, $460); **Perth** (3½hr., 2 per day, $450); **Sydney** (3½hr., 2 per day, $470); **Yulara** (45min., 3 per day, $160).

Trains: Alice Railway Station is a 20min. walk away from central Alice. From George St., take a left on Larapinta Dr. which turns into the Stuart Hwy. and runs into Alice. The ***Ghan*** runs to: **Adelaide** (20hr., Tu and F, $197); **Melbourne** (33hr., Tu, $292); **Sydney** (46hr., F, $390). The tourist office and Traveland make reservations, or call 13 21 47.

Buses: Greyhound and **McCafferty's** (☎8952 7888) run from the bus station at the corner of Gregory and Railway Tce. Service to: **Adelaide** (19-20hr., 1-2 per day, $168); **Cairns** (33hr., 1 per day, $343); **Darwin** (18-20hr., 2 per day, $184) via **Tennant Creek** (5-6hr., 2 per day, $101) **Sydney** (45hr., 1 per day, $289); **Townsville** (28hr., 1 per day, $294). They also provide: 2-day Ayer's Rock and Olga's tour ($250); 3-day Ayer's Rock, Olga's, King's Canyon tour ($279). 10% discount fares with ISIC/VIP/YHA.

Public Transportation: ASBus (☎8950 0500) is the infrequent public bus system, with routes to the outskirts of town. Runs M-F from about 8 or 9am to 6pm, on Sa only in the morning, and Su not at all. Fare $1.40-$2.40.

Taxis: Alice Springs Taxis (☎8952 1877), queue on Gregory Tce. just east of Todd Mall.

Car Rental: Territory-Thrifty (☎8952 9999), corner of Hartley St. and Stott Tce. Has cars from $85 per day, 4WD from $115 per day. Open daily 8am-5:30pm. **Hertz,** 76 Hartley St. (☎8952 2644), near Stott Tce., from $73 per day. Both companies have airport locations open M-F 8am-5pm, Sa-Su 8am-1pm. **Britz** (☎8952 8814), corner of Stuart Hwy. and Power St. rents 4WD with unlimited kilometers to those under 25, from $142 per day. Open daily 8am-5pm. Local rental companies, which are often cheaper, include: **Advance,** 9 Railway Tce. (☎8953 3700); **Appollo,** 3 Larapinta Dr. (☎8952

SIGNS OF THE TIMES You may notice that many restaurants throughout the Territory have signs outside demanding "No Thongs. No Singlets. Neat and Clean Dress," or something similar. In Alice Springs, the more subtle read simply "Dress Regulations Apply," but some signs go so far as urging those not following these strictures to "Bugger Off." Many see this as simply an attempt to take the edge off the outback harshness, similar to an American maxim "No Shirt, No Shoes, No Service." But others see in it a thinly-veiled racism, an effort to keep Aborigines, who are perceived as dressing much more shabbily, out of establishments. Shop owners will denigratingly point to a competitor who, with no dress regulations, "has *that* kind of crowd."

7255); **Maui,** (☎8952 8049), on the corner of Stuart Hwy. and Power St.; **Outback Auto Rentals,** 78 Todd St. (☎8953 5333).

Roadside Assistance: AANT (24hr. ☎8952 1087).

Road Conditions: ☎1800 246 199.

Bike Rental: At most hostels. At **Pioneer YHA,** $9.90 per half-day, $16.50 per day.

ORIENTATION

The Stuart Hwy. runs through Alice on its way from Darwin (1486km) to Adelaide (1570km). The **MacDonnel Ranges** form a natural border at the southern side of town, and the break between the east-west ranges, called **Heavitree Gap,** allows both the Stuart Hwy. and the **Todd River** to pass through. The major routes to the outlying areas are along **Larapinta Dr.,** which curves from town to the West MacDonnells, and **Ross Hwy.,** which heads to the East MacDonnells south of the gap. Downtown, the major north-south streets are (from west to east) the Stuart Hwy., Railway Tce., Bath St., Hartley St., Todd St., and Leichhardt Tce.; the major east-west streets are (from north to south) Wills Tce., Parsons St., Gregory Tce., Stott Tce., and Stuart Tce. Todd St. becomes the pedestrian-only **Todd Mall** between Wills and Gregory Tce., while the two indoor malls are **Alice Plaza** (Todd Mall at Parsons St) and **Yeperenye Plaza** (Hartley St. north of Gregory Tce.).

PRACTICAL INFORMATION

Tourist Office: Central Australian Tourism Industry Association (☎8952 5800; fax 8953 0295), on Gregory Tce. at the end of Todd Mall. Books transportation, tours, and accommodations, sells road and Larapinta Trail maps, and has National Park info. Grab their free excellent city map (yellow). Open M-F 8:30am-5:30pm, Sa-Su 9am-4pm.

Budget Travel: Traveland (☎8952 7186), on Todd Mall. Open M-F 8:30am-5pm, Sa 9am-noon. **Flight Centre** (☎8953 4081), on Todd Mall, guarantees lowest airfares. Open M-F 9am-5:30pm, Sa 9:30am-12:30pm.

Tours: Many, many tours operate out of Alice Springs to Uluru. **Wayoutback** is a highly recommended company that offers off-the-beaten-path 4WD tours of Uluru-Kata Tjuta and King Canyon, with lots of walking and bush camping. (☎8953 4304. 3-day tour $420, 5-day $665; VIP/YHA $15 discount.) **Northern Territory Adventure Tours** also offers popular tours from Alice. (☎1300 654 604. 2-day $217, 3-day $395, 5-day $625.) **Greyhound/McCafferty's** (☎8952 7888) has many discounts.

Currency Exchange: National Australia (☎8952 1611), and **ANZ** (☎8952 1144), are in Todd Mall, along with **ATMs.** Both open M-Th 9:30am-4pm, F 9:30am-5pm.

Library: Next to the tourist office (☎8950 0555). Open M-Tu, Th 10am-6pm, W and F 10am-5pm, Sa 9am-1pm, Su 1-5pm.

Emergency: ☎000. **Crisis Line** ☎1800 019 116.

Police: (☎8951 8888), on Parsons St, at the corner of Bath St.

Pharmacy: Amcal Chemist (☎8953 0089), in Alice Plaza on the Todd Mall at Parsons St. Open daily 8:30am-7:30pm.

Hospital: Alice Springs Hospital (☎8951 7777, emergency 8951 7529, ambulance 8952 2200), on Gap Rd. south of Stuart Tce.

Internet Access: At the **library** ($6 per hr.). Book ahead. The other best deal is **Internet Outpost,** on Gap Rd. next to Melanka Backpackers. $7 per hr. Open daily 10am-11pm.

Post Office: GPO, on Hartley St. south of Parsons St. (☎8952 1020; fax 8953 4049). Open M-F 9am-5pm. **Postal Code:** 0870.

ACCOMMODATIONS AND CAMPING

The hostels of Alice are concentrated on or near Todd St. and Gap Rd. All listings have air-conditioned rooms, a pool, and $2 laundry; all recommend booking in advance; most have bike rental from $12-15 per day; *everybody* (hostelers, Internet cafes owners, the little girl drinking from the water fountain) will be happy to book tours (and collect a handsome commission).

Annie's Place, 4 Traegger Ave. (☎1800 359 089; fax 8952 8280). 3 long blocks south of Todd Mall and 1 block west of Todd St. Daily courtesy shuttles to bus stations. Annie and crew have gone the extra mile with great rooms (all with TV) and fun, friendly bohemian atmosphere. The kitchen has beautiful stone-work walls and there's an in-house cafe. Inquire about their unique tours to Ulura and the Olga's. Internet $5 per hr. Reception daily 5:30am-8pm. 4-or 6-bed dorms $16; doubles $45.

Elke's Outbackpackers, 39 Gap Rd. (☎1800 633 354; fax 8952 8143), at Baedem St., 1km south of Todd Mall. Elke's compensates for its distance from town by providing several free shuttles daily. The efficient, professional folks here have converted a motel into a well-serviced and popular hostel. Each outstanding dorm room has its own bath, kitchenette, TV, and balcony. Reception daily 5am-8:30pm. 8-bed dorms $18; twins and doubles $50; motel rooms $75; light breakfast included. VIP/YHA.

Pioneer YHA (☎8952 8855; fax 8952 4144), on the corner of Parsons and Leichardt St. 1 block off Todd Mall. By far, the most central location in town. What was originally a deckchair cinema is now a comfortable yet impersonal hostel. Coral-colored rooms, large 24hr., free safe and luggage storage. Key and linen deposit $20. Reception daily 7:30am-8:30pm. 6-to 16-bed $18; 4-bed $20. YHA. Wheelchair accessible.

Melanka Lodge Backpackers, 94 Todd St. (☎8952 4744; fax 8952 4587). Reminiscent of a university dorm, complete with the party atmosphere and crowded rooms, Melanka's lures tourists with a loaded snack bar, sofa-strewn TV room, and their very own nightclub draws the backpacker crowd. Just remember you came here to party. Free airport pickup; airport drop off $10. Reception daily 5am-8:15pm. 3- to 8-bed dorms $16; singles $42; twins and doubles $42. VIP.

Toddy's Backpackers, 41 Gap Rd. (☎8952 1322; fax 8952 1767), next door to Elke's. Courtesy bus meets most flights and buses. Reception daily 6am-8:30pm. Dorms $12-17; singles, doubles, and twins with sink and fridge $40; motel doubles with bath, TV and fridge $52; light breakfast included. NOMADS.

Melanka Motel, 94 Todd St. (☎8952 2233; fax 8952 2890). This mirror-image to the Melanka Backpackers is better-kept, fancier, and more expensive. Large bathrooms, fridge, TV with free in-house movies, free tea and coffee. Reception daily 7am-9pm. Singles $83; twins and doubles $88; family rooms $99.

The closest **camping** option to town is at the aptly-named **In-Town Campground,** on the corner of Breadon and Todd St., near Elke's. (☎8952 6687. Sites $8.) Caravans have to head to the **Stuart Caravan Park,** 2km west of town on Larapinth Dr. (☎8952 2547. Reception daily 8am-8pm. Sites $10, powered $18.) At **Heavitree Gap Outback Resort,** you will find a motel, bistro, and grazing wallabies. Take the Stuart Hwy. for 3km and make a left on Palm Circuit. (☎8950 4444. Reception daily 7am-9pm. Sites for 2 $16.40, powered $18.40.)

FOOD

The good news is the quality of food in Alice soars above that of the rest of the NT. Unfortunately, the prices soar even higher. If you've got the money to spare, there are a handful of overpriced outdoor cafes on Todd Mall near Gregory Tce. Otherwise, there's a McDonald's, Hungry Jacks, KFC, and Pizza Hut—you can't miss their neon signs. **International Travellers Cafe,** in Annie's Place (see **Accommodations,** above), has excellent $7 dinners ($5 for Annie's guests), including vegetarian stir-fry and lasagna, while **Toddy's** has all-you-can-gorge carnivorous mediocrity nightly at 7pm for $7.50. Coles **supermarket** (open 24hr.) is on Bath St. at Gregory Tce., and **Woolworth's** is in the Yeperenye Plaza. (Open M-Sa 7am-midnight, Su 7am-10pm.)

Bar Doppios, Fan Arcade (☎8952 6525), at the Gregory Tce. end of Todd Mall. The town's most happening coffee shop serves extraordinary food at a good price. Australian with a twist, Middle Eastern, and Southeast Asian fare (mains $9-$10). Vegetarian friendly. BYO. Open M-Th 7:30am-5pm, F-Sa 7:30am-5pm, 6-10pm, Su 10am-4pm.

Keller's Swiss and Indian Restaurant (☎8952 3188), on Gregory Tce. east of Hartley St. Switzerland and India are exact opposites in geography, climate, political temperament, spelling, and cuisine, making for a titillating combination in one restaurant. *And* the food is really good and vegetarian-friendly. Spaetzle with mushroom-gruyere cream sauce or delicate vegetable curry $13.50. Open daily 5:30pm-late.

Sultan's Kebabs, 52 Hartley St. (☎8953 3322). With the feel of a Middle Eastern fun house, Sultan's is Turkish and delightful. Kebabs (with veggie options) from $6. Pizzas from $8. Sweet, sweet sutlac $4. Open M-Sa 11am-late, Su 5pm-late. F-Su belly dancers at 8pm.

Red Ochre Grill, Todd Mall (☎8952 9614), near Parsons St. Where esteemed 5-star hotel guests sample what a top-notch chef can do with regional ingredients. Aboriginal artwork and didgeridoo music round out the atmosphere for a memorable but pricey meal. This might be your only chance to eat Wallaby Mignon $23. Smoked chicken with sun-dried tomatoes and native pasta ($16) is also delicious. Open daily 6:30am-10:30pm.

Oscar's Cafe, Todd Mall (☎8953 0930). Swank, sophisticated, and proud of it, Oscar's spoils weary travelers with zesty Italian meals in a spacious, well-lit room with window walls. Mains $16-23. Open daily 9am-10pm.

SIGHTS

Many sights are located near Todd Mall. Covering Alice's more distant sights is difficult without a vehicle. The **Alice Wanderer** shuttle service circles hourly past the major tourist sights in the Alice area. (☎8952 2211 or 1800 669 111. Runs 9am-4pm, departing from the southern end of Todd Mall; no reservations required. All-day ticket $25.) The vigorous may prefer to hire a bike.

CITY CENTER

ANZAC HILL. The best place to view a postcard sunset is atop Anzac Hill, which offers a panorama of the MacDonnell Ranges that seems out of place for a city backdrop. *(Walk to Wills Tce. between Bath and Hartley St.; a metal arch marks the start of the easy 10min. "Lions Walk" from the base to the obelisk at the top. Vehicle access is around the corner on the Stuart Hwy.)*

REPTILE CENTRE. Wallet-friendly and truly hands-on fun (leavened with a little fear) is all yours at this home to snakes, lizards and joining the family in 2002, a saltie. Come, let a python slither all over you. *(9 Stuart Tce. On the corner of Bath St. ☎8952 8900. Open daily 9am-5pm. Feedings 11am, 1, 3pm. $7, children $4.)*

ALICE SPRINGS CULTURAL PRECINCT. One admission fee gets you into seven different sights, but the central attraction here is **Museum of Central Australia** and its displays on dinosaurs and the Big Bang. The precinct also has several galleries of art and crafts, an aviation museum, and a memorial cemetery. *(2km west of town on Larapinta Dr. ☎8952 5800. Open daily 10am-5pm. $7, concession $4, family $18.)*

ABORIGINAL ARTS AND CULTURE CENTRE. Owned and operated by Arrernte, the Centre holds the "Didgeridoo University," where you can graduate with a 1hr. degree in Didgeridoo Playing. Cap and gown extra. There's also a museum and tiny art gallery. *(86 Todd St. ☎8952 3408. Open M-F 9am-5pm, Sa-Su 8am-4pm. Degree $11.)*

OLIVE PINK BOTANICAL GARDEN. The desert scrub is hardly a "garden," but it's not a bad place for a picnic. Skip the walking trails and plant displays and head for the excellent lookout over the city. *(On the opposite bank of the Todd River, 2km from Todd Mall, is Tuncks Rd.; the garden is down on the left. ☎8952 2154. Garden open daily 10am-6pm. Visitor centre open daily 10am-4pm. Admission by donation.)*

NATIONAL PIONEER WOMEN'S HALL OF FAME. In this frontier land of masculine bravado, this is a refreshing site that provides biographical sketches of over a hundred pioneer women. *(In the Old Courthouse on Parson St. at the corner of Hartley St. ☎8952 9006. Open Feb.-Nov. daily 10am-2pm. $2.20.)*

OUTSIDE THE CITY CENTER

ALICE SPRINGS TELEGRAPH STATION HISTORICAL RESERVE. Numerous walking paths with beautiful wildflowers meander along the riverside, through the surrounding desert hills where wallabies can be seen in the morning and late afternoon, and up to a superb lookout. The Reserve is the original location of Alice Springs, and an unremarkable handful of 19th-century buildings remain. *(4.5km north of town on the Stuart Hwy. with a marked turn-off; or walk 4km (45min.) from downtown along the pleasant path that parallels the Todd River. ☎8952 3993. Park open daily 8am-9pm. Buildings open 8am-5pm. $6, concessions $4.95, child $3.30.)*

DESERT PARK. "No, the desert is not a desolate wasteland but a vibrant habitat, full of life!" is the recurring theme here. To prove it to you, they've got kangaroos, emus, and a nocturnal house. The not-to-be-missed **Birds of Prey** show is one of the only attractions in Alice guaranteed to evoke audible "oohs" and "ahhs." *(Desert Park transfers runs a shuttle every 1½hr. 7:30am-6pm from most accommodations to the park. Call for pick-up ☎8952 4667. $30, concession $20; includes admission. Park ☎8951 8788. Open daily 7:30am-6pm. Bird's of Prey show 10am, 1:15, 3:30pm. Entry $18, concessions $9.)*

FRONTIER CAMEL FARM. Alice Springs considers itself the camel capital of Australia, and the Camel Farm keeps the dream alive with camel rides. *(3km beyond where Palm Circuit crosses a traffic circle and emerges as the Ross Hwy. Open daily 9am-5pm. 1½hr. rides daily 10:30am-noon, Apr.-Oct. also 1-2:30pm. $6, children $3, families $12.)*

TRAIN MUSEUM AND TRANSPORT HALL OF FAME. The Old Ghan Train and Museum and the adjacent Road Transport Hall of Fame may be 10km from the city, but are still two of Alice's definitive sights. The museum highlights the trials of the enormous locomotive project, while the Hall of Fame is a spacious warehouse with a collection of vehicles from memory lane and many dashing pictures of handsome road trains to make your heart beat fast. Wait, that's just the gas fumes. *(Accessible by Norris Bell Ave. off the Stuart Hwy. Train Museum ☎8955 5047. $5.50, concessions $4.40. Hall of Fame ☎8952 7161. $5/$2.50. Both open daily 9am-5pm.)*

CHATEAU HORNSBY. It's a trek to get out here, but there's something to be said for sipping wine at the only vineyard in the Northern Territory. *(10km south of Alice on the Stuart Hwy., turn left on Colonel Rose Dr. for 4km, then left on Petrick. ☎8955 5133. Open for tasting Mar.-Dec. daily 10am-5pm. Free.)*

ENTERTAINMENT AND NIGHTLIFE

The *Alice Spring News* (free at the library) has a "Dive Into Live" section listing upcoming events. The 500-seat **Araluen Centre,** on Larapinta Dr., presents artsy, independent flicks every Sunday, as well as live theatre and concerts. (☎8951 1122. Box office open daily 10am-5pm. $11, concessions $8.80.) The popular **Sounds of Starlight Theatre** is in the Todd St. Mall a few doors down from Parsons St. Led by one fine didgeridoo player, the performance has a natural beauty that

THE WORLD'S LARGEST CLASSROOM It's Monday morning, and 140 children ages 4-13 are standing thousands of kilometers apart, yet singing their national anthem together. Forget virtual schools—the technology that carries these kids' lessons is nothing more complex than short-wave radios. The **School of the Air** is central Australia's educational answer to its vast geography and isolated families spread out on remote cattle stations, roadhouses, and Aboriginal lands. The program, stationed in a dozen outback towns, brings children in contact with each other and their Alice-based teachers for three to four hours each week. Their makeshift classrooms are sheds, trailers, or rooms in homes. A parent or appointed instructor supplements their education with an additional five to six hours of weekly schooling. The closest student to Alice is 80km away; the farthest is 1000km. Founded in 1951, the Alice School is the oldest of its kind, though Australia now has 16. It covers 1.3 million km² of land, and has been dubbed "the largest classroom in the world." And it turns cutting class from an art form into a walk in the park. *(Coming from Alice, before the turn-off to the Reserve, a sign on the Stuart Hwy. points down Head St. ☎8951 6834. Open M-Sa 8:30am-4:30pm, Su 1:30-4:30pm. $3.50, concessions $2.50.)*

unfortunately gets swept away by the overbearing synthesizer and cheap lighting tricks. (☎8952 0826. Open Apr.-Nov. Tu-Sa 7:30pm. $16.50, YHA $13, children $11.)

Toasty taverns (and not debaucherous dance clubs) are the staple of after hours Alice. It all starts and ends at **Bojangles,** 80 Todd St. south of Gregory Tce., which is everything you could ask for in a saloon: peanut shells on the floor, animal hides on the wall, a honky-tonk piano in the corner, and a generous helping of outback cowboys. (☎8952 2873. Open daily 11:30am-3am. Su Blues Jam 3pm-late.) A few doors down at the Melanka Lodge, the dance floor of the **Desert Waterhole** typically draws the young backpackers. (☎8952 7131. Happy Hour 5-7pm, $7.50 jugs. M, W, F, Su live music 8pm. Open daily 5pm-late.) The popular and friendly **Sean's Bar,** 51 Bath St., is your best bet for a pint ($6.60) of Guinness. (☎8952 1858. Open daily 6pm-late.) In the Todd St. Mall, the relaxed **Scotty's Tavern** is an established local's favorite. (Open Su-Th 11am-midnight, F-Sa 11am-1am.) Across the Todd River and a $10 cab ride from town is **Lasseter's Hotel Casino,** the setting of the climax of *Priscilla, Queen of the Desert.* (☎8950 7777. Open Su-Th 10am-3am, F-Sa 10am-4am.) The adjacent **Limerick Pub** is an upscale joint ready to take any money that you haven't gambled away. (Open Su-Th 4pm-3am, F-Sa 4pm-4am.)

FESTIVALS AND EVENTS

Heritage Week is a NT celebration held in late April featuring historical reenactments and displays. Around the same time, a month-long horse racing festival, the lavish **Alice Springs Cup Carnival,** entertains at the Pioneer Race Park and culminates on the first Monday in May with **Bangtail Muster** parade. On the Queen's Birthday Weekend in early June, the plucky cars and motorcycles of the **Finke Desert Race** traverse 240km of roadless dusty desert from Alice to the town of Finke in the south. The not-so-traditional **Camel Cup Carnival** (including a Miss Camel Cup Competition) race is held the first Saturday in July, followed the next Saturday by the more traditional, agriculture-focused **Alice Springs Show.** The **Alice Springs Rodeo** and the **Harts Range Annual Races** are both held in August. Early October brings the definitive Alice Springs festival, the **Henley-on-Todd Regatta.** A good-natured mockery of the dry river, the race is in bottomless "boats" propelled Flintstones-style—by foot. The race is subject to cancellation: the river flowed in 1993. The **Corkwood Festival** (late Nov.) is a folk event featuring craft booths during the day and energetic bush dancing at night.

THE MACDONNELL RANGES

To the north of the Uluru-Kata Tjuta and Watarrka area lie central Australia's mountains. The MacDonnell Ranges roll west to east across the horizon, creating pockets of interesting geological formations and wildlife that break the otherwise endless desert surrounding. From a distance, the green shrub that covers its undulating ridges appears like a soft blanket of grass, but up close, Australia's rusty orange earth and rock, prickly ground-cover, and glowing white-ghost gums keep the range rugged. The MacDonnell's pastel colors have inspired painters and photographers, and numerous walking tracks cajole visitors to take a closer look.

THE MACDONNELLS AT A GLANCE	
LENGTH: 460km. **FEATURES:** West MacDonnell Nat'l Park along Namatjira Dr., Finke Gorge Nat'l Park off Larapinta Dr., several nature parks to the east, and Alice Springs (at Heavitree Gap) in the middle. **GATEWAYS:** Alice Springs (see p. 270).	**HIGHLIGHTS:** Camping, walking, and swimming, and stunning scenery. **CAMPING:** Throughout; they are described under each sight listing. **FEES:** A small fee is charged only at Stanley Chasm (p. 277) and the Hermannsburg Historical Precinct (p. 277).

WEST MACDONNELLS

AAT Kings Tours, *does a Larapinta-Namatjira loop in two days, by bus. (☎8952 1700. Departs W, Sa 8:30am. $270, child $218.)* ***Palm Valley Tours*** *makes a daily 4WD trek from Alice to Finke Gorge National Park. (☎8952 0022 or 1800 000 629. Open daily 7am-4:30pm. Pick-up and drop-off from Alice accommodation. $85.)*

More popular than their eastern counterparts, the sculpted gorges and waterholes of the West MacDonnells shelter vestiges of the bygone rainforest era and hardcore 4WD enthusiasts who know that this is where the good stuff is. **Larapinta Drive** heads out of Alice past the tame beginnings of the West MacDonnells, and **Namatjira Drive** veers off into deeper territory. A fulfilling loop can be made by continuing on Larapinta Drive, which passes by **Finke Gorge National Park** and connects with the western end of Namatjira Drive via **Tylers Pass.** If you're willing to brave rough, unsealed roads, hop on board.

Another way to see the West Macdonnells is to take the **Larapinta Trail,** an enormous, nearly-complete hiking trail that starts at the Telegraph Station in Alice and will extend 220km west to **Mt. Razorback.** The trail connects the main attractions and is usually hiked in two- to four-day pieces from one gorge to another. Before attempting the long hikes, seek info from the **Park and Wildlife Commission** in Alice. (☎8951 8211; fax 8951 8258; P.O. Box 1046, Alice Springs NT 0871.) The voluntary **registration** is a good idea—a $50 deposit is refundable as long as the Parks and Wildlife Commission (☎1300 650 730) doesn't end up sending out a search and rescue mission for you. Pick up the flyer *Bushwalks* from the Tourist Office in Alice for a list of hikes—mostly on the Trail—organized by a small informal group (they only ask a contribution to vehicle costs).

LARAPINTA DRIVE

All distances listed after sights and are from Alice Springs.

JOHN FLYNN MEMORIAL GRAVE. *7km.* Here lies the minister who brought the Royal Flying Doctor Service to the outback. The massive boulder atop the grave was taken from the Devil's Marbles (see p. 270), near Tennant Creek.

SIMPSON'S GAP. *17km.* Erosion from millions of years of floods created this striking opening in the mountain ridges. *(Open daily 5am-8pm. Free.)*

STANLEY CHASM. *50km.* When the sun shines directly into this 80m-high fissure at midday, the walls glow orange and the crowds gather to ogle. It took 100 million years to form, but a visit will only take 30min. That is, unless you are willing to wade a rockhole and scramble across rocky terrain, to the deserted second chasm. *(☎8956 7440. $5.50, concessions $4.50.)*

HERMANNSBURG HISTORICAL PRECINCT. *126km.* A collection of old broken-down houses from the early Lutheran mission is found here, as well as a gallery saluting Aboriginal artist Albert Namatjira. Hermannsberg has petrol, groceries,

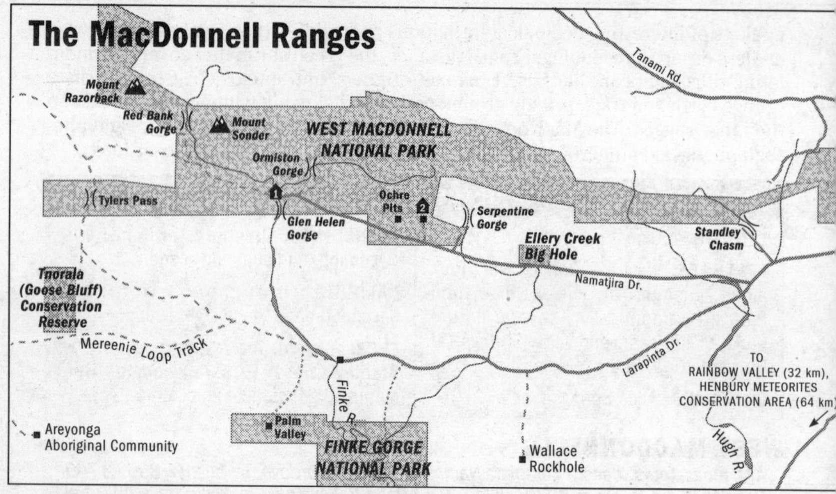

and a service station, where you can obtain a **Mereenie Tour Pass** for the 4WD track to Kings Canyon, p. 280. *(☎8956 7402. open daily, Mar.-Nov. 9am-4pm, Dec.-Feb. 10am-4pm. $4.50, child $3. Gallery $3.50.)*

FINKE GORGE NATIONAL PARK. *146km.* This 460km² park contains the Finke River, reputedly the oldest river on the planet; some stretches date back 350 million years. The park's main attraction is **Palm Valley,** home to the extremely rare Red Cabbage Palm. The unique pockets of plant life, combined with the ancient riverbed, create a timeless air in which bird watching is effortless and dinosaur-spotting would hardly surprise. Two worthwhile walks are: the **Mpulungkinya Walk** (5km; 2hr.), which traipses among the thickest growth of palms; the **Arankaia Walk** (2km; 1hr.) turns back half-way and climbs the valley rim for a pleasant lookout. It is important to keep to the marked trail when on these walks to avoid further human damage to the delicate palm seedlings. Near the campground, the **Kalaranga Lookout** (1.5km; 45min.) quickly surmounts some steep crags to bring 360° vistas of the park. *(The park is accessed through the 21km 4WD-only road that follows the path of the mostly dry Finke River, off Larapinta Dr. A full-facilities* ***campground*** *is 16km into the park. Sites $6.60, child $3.30, family $15.40.)*

NORTHERN TERRITORY

NAMATJIRA DRIVE

All distances are listed after sights and are from Alice Springs.

ELLERY CREEK BIG HOLE. *96km.* The 18m-deep pool in a creek through a mountain gap makes up for a very cool dip. The nearby **Dolemite Walk** traverses lush forest through spinifex, surrounded by striking views. *(Camping with basic facilities. Caravans permitted. Sites $3.30, child $1.65, family $7.70.)*

SERPENTINE GORGE. *102km.* An easy walk (1hr.) leads to a slim and seductive gorge, while a shorter but steeper trail ascends to another amazing lookout. *(Free, isolated bush camping is available at the unremarkable ruins of Serpentine Chalet, 6km down the highway and 3km on a rough unsealed road.)*

OCHRE PITS. *108km.* A 10min. stroll leads to the swirly walls of ochre, still used by Aborigines as a palette for ceremonial paint.

ORMISTON GORGE. *130km.* Welcome to the MacDonnells happy meal. The spellbinding gorge was named by Peter Warburton, who thought the area looked a lot like his own Glen Ormiston back in Scotland. He's right, except for the gorge's dry vegetation, sand dunes, and steep orange cliffs. A 10min. walk leads to some of the cold pools of the gorge (some 14m deep); head instead for the excellent longer hikes. The **Ghost Gun Lookout** (1½hr.) climbs the side of the gorge for a most

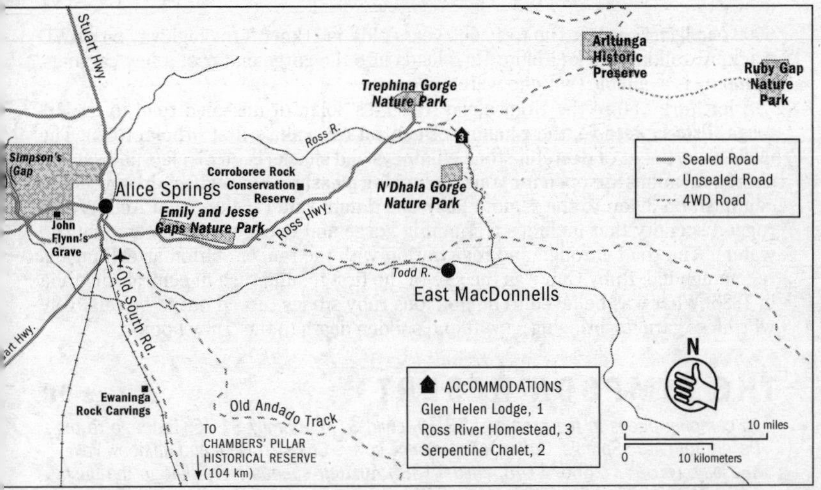

impressive lookout. Late afternoon is the best, when the orange walls are well-lit and rock wallabies come out to play. The **Pound Walk** (7km; 3-4hr.) is less popular and therefore more peaceful, offering some great vistas of the surrounding hills, before approaching the gorge from the back. *(Camping available with showers. Caravans permitted. Sites $6.60, child $3.30, family $15.40.)*

GLEN HELEN GORGE. *132km.* The **Glen Helen Lodge,** with petrol, snacks, and accommodations, is the main draw here. The gorge itself is only a 10min. walk from the parking lot. *(☎8956 7495. Camping sites $9, powered for 2 $22; dorms from $19. Helicopter flights of the region $35-$180.)*

REDBANK GORGE. *156km.* The narrow slit through the mountains shades a series of chilly pools. *(Two campgrounds with basic facilities. $3.30, child $1.65, family $7.70.)*

GOSSE BLUFF. *187km.* You can view the site of the ancient comet crater up close from the 11km 4WD track, or take in the whole picture from the **West MacDonnell Lookout,** a turn-off near the north end of Tyler Pass.

NORTHERN TERRITORY

EAST MACDONNELLS

*All camping prices in this area are: $3.30, child $1.65, family $7.70. Tours offer daytrips to the area from Alice—**Roving Outback Tours** (☎8953 4694; departs 7:45am, 9½hr., $120) and **Alice Experience** (☎1800 803 174; departs 6am; 6hr.; $89, child $62).*

Just beyond Heavitree Gap south of Alice, **Palm Circuit** branches off the Stuart Hwy. and heads east. After a few kilometers, it becomes the **Ross Hwy.** and plunges into the East MacDonnells. The East Macs are less thrilling geologically than their western counterparts, but are also less crowded and see less tour buses.

The **Emily and Jessie Gaps,** 10km east of Alice on the Ross Hwy., are important sacred sites in the Aboriginal Dreaming. **Trephina Gorge Nature Park,** is 59km east (plus 7km of access road). Trephina Gorge features the **Trephina Gorge Walk** (1hr.), an enjoyable trek along the gorge rim and riverbed; the **Panorama Walk** (1hr.), an uneventful affair except for the incredible lookout. John Hayes Rockhole, 4km down a 4WD track, is home to the stunning **Chain of Ponds Walk** (1½hr.), a sojourn past a great lookout on the rim and through a picture-perfect series of ponds on the gorge floor. Camping with pit toilets and BBQs is available near both gorges.

The Ross Hwy. continues another 29km east toward the **Ross River Homestead** (☎8956 9711), one of the most popular destinations in the East MacDonnells, offering hands-on outback activities such as camel-riding, bushwalking, and boomerang-throwing, and catering to an older crowd looking for a more sheltered "outback" experience. **N'Dhala Gorge** (80km from Alice), the site of an estimated

6000 **Aboriginal carvings** (up to 10,000 years old), is 11km off the highway on a 4WD track. A walking track (1.5km; 1hr.) leads into the gorge and past a few carvings. Camping is available (with no water).

A left fork before the Homestead traverses 36km of unsealed road to the **Arltunga Historic Reserve,** the remains of central Australia's first official town. The usual assortment of decrepit stone chimneys and shacks is on display, and several short gold mines are open for your spelunking pleasure. Four-wheel-drive vehicles can push on 39km to the remote **Ruby Gap Nature Park** (154km from Alice), with rugged scenery that includes a stunning gorge and excellent bush camping (no water). The road is rough and registration with the ranger station at Arltunga is recommended. Ruby Gap was the site of the first mining rush in central Australia in 1886. What was believed to be precious ruby stones turned out to be relatively worthless garnets, bringing a swift and sudden death to the "ruby boom."

THE SIMPSON DESERT ☎08

All camping prices in the area are: $3.30, child $1.65, family $1.75. Tours go to the Desert from Alice Springs. ***Outback Experience*** *covers Chamber Pillar and Rainbow Valley in a day. (☎8953 2666. $148, child $138.)* ***Austour*** *spends more time in the bush. (☎1800 335 009. 3-day $665, child $540.)*

South of Alice, the Stuart Hwy. passes Heavitree Gap and Palm Circuit. On the road to the airport, the unsealed and isolated **Old South Rd.** veers right toward the **Simpson Desert.** Stock up on supplies before heading down it. Charles Sturt first explored this part of the Simpson in 1845, so bent on conquering the outback that many of his men died from complications caused by the desert's harsh conditions.

The first worthwhile spot is the **Ewaninga Rock Carvings,** 39km south of Alice. The weathered markings are a sacred site for Aborigines, but a pleasant 30min. stroll allows respectful visitors to view the carvings. The Aboriginal community of **Maryvale Station,** 62km more along the Old South Rd., marks the 4WD-only turn to **Chambers Pillar Historical Reserve** (4hr. one-way). This sandstone formation was a landmark for early travelers and their carved initials (a practice now subject to high fines). The trek is more hard-core than stupendous, but sunsets at the rock are masterpieces of color. (No water or facilities.)

NORTHERN TERRITORY

Rainbow Valley is a jagged, U-shaped ridge standing in the desert like a Hollywood backdrop 22km east of the Stuart Hwy. on a sandy unmarked 4WD track (97km from Alice). The valley is most famous for its winter sunsets, when the red-orange-yellow-bleach white formation is illuminated at the ideal angle, but the dynamic changes of the sand dunes and occasional lake are fascinating year-round. (Toilets and BBQ, but no water.) Another 51km down the Stuart, the unsealed **Ernest Giles Rd.** veers west toward Watarrka; 11km past the turn-off and 4km north on an access road lie the **Henbury Meteorite Craters.** This circular ridge of mountains is the remnant of a 4000-year-old meteorite impact site. Basic camping ($3.30) and a self-guided walk (20min.) are available. The Museum of Central Australia's meteorite exhibit, in Alice, makes this site much more meaningful (see p. 270). Heading farther south, all that lies along the Stuart Hwy. until Coober Pedy, SA are over-priced roadhouses, rising from endless miles of spiky spinifex shrub.

WATARRKA NATIONAL PARK (KINGS CANYON)

Watarrka National Park contains the wayward tourist mecca of Kings Canyon, cutting deep, sunburned grooves in a section of the George Gill Mountains. The canyon's knife-sliced, concave walls shelter waterholes that sustain tropical greenery. Erosion is visible across the canyon, especially in the eccentric domes atop both sides of the precipice. The weathered humps act as natural staircases to the fantastic views atop. Scattered on the flat canyon roof, the domes create an intimidating maze dubbed the Lost City. Watarrka grows more popular every year.

TRANSPORTATION. There are **three different ways** to drive to Kings Canyon from Alice Springs. First, the fully-paved route—the Stuart Hwy.—runs 202km south to the roadhouse settlement of **Erldunda,** at its junction with the Lasseter Hwy. Travelers changing buses here may end up spending the night. (☎8956 0984. Sites for 2 $16, powered $21; motel single $72; double $86.) From the junction, take the Lasseter Hwy. west 110km and turn right on Luritja Rd., which goes north 163km to the Kings Canyon park entrance. Second, vehicles with 4WD can take a "shortcut" along Ernest Giles Rd., a 100km stretch of unpaved road that begins 132km south of Alice off the Stuart Hwy. The road is rough and can take 4hr., so the Stuart Hwy. may be faster. Ernest Giles meets Luritja Rd. 100km south of the park entrance. Check local road conditions before attempting this road. Third, it's also possible to reach Kings Canyon from Alice Springs via Hermannsburg in the West MacDonnells. Take Larapinta Dr. to the scenic but corrugated 4WD-only **Mereenie Loop Rd.** (200km) which passes through Aboriginal land. There are no accommodations or camping allowed on the Mereenie, so plan to do the drive within one day. A $2.20 pass is required and can be obtained in Hermannsburg at Larapinta Service Station, Glen Helen Lodge, or Kings Canyon Resort, or at the Visitor Centre in Alice.

Most tours to Kings Canyon are included in Uluru-Kata Tjuta multi-day packages (see p. 272) coming out of Alice Springs. **Austour** runs a long (17hr.) daytrip from Alice. (☎1800 335 009. $180, children $150.)

ACCOMMODATIONS AND FOOD. The **Kings Canyon Resort** (☎8956 7442; fax 8956 7410), 7km up the road from the canyon turn-off, is the beginning and the end of civilization in Watarrka. The resort has the **Desert Oaks Cafe** (open 5:30am-10am and 11am-2pm), and a **grocery store** in the **fuel station** (open daily 7am-7pm). **Outback BBQ** (open daily 6-9pm) offers cook-your-own from $16, while **George Gill Bar** provides musical entertainment. (Open daily 11am-late.) Rooms at the resort have A/C, heat, TV, fridge, and share a bath and kitchen. Comfortable, grassy **campsites** have flush toilets, showers, and a pool. The compact, tourist-bus-ridden resort's major drawback is the expense. (Reception daily 6:30am-9:30pm. Book ahead. Sites for 2 $26, powered $29; 4-bed dorms $42, YHA $38; twin $97; quad $163.) Camping is also available at **Kings Creek Station,** just outside the park's eastern entrance. It's a more low-key outpost with a friendly staff, and you just can't beat the prices at the **Camel Safaris,** which start at $5 for a five-minute ride. (☎8956 7474. Sites $10.50, child $6, family $33; powered add $2.50; cabin single $45, includes hot breakfast.) No camping is allowed in the National Park.

NORTHERN TERRITORY

HIKING. The park has three well-marked paths. An easy walk (2.6km; 1hr.) follows **Kings Creek** along the bottom of the canyon. Cut loose with the challenging **Kings Canyon Walk** (6km; 3hr.), scaling the rocky, steep slope around the top of the canyon, much of the Lost City, and the exhilarating rail-less edge. The view is astounding; on a clear day, you can see Uluru. A side track (20min.) descends into the **Garden of Eden,** a waterhole shaded by palm trees and the narrow canyon walls. Water and hiking footwear are essential; there's an outhouse and an info display at the parking lot, but no other facilities at the trailhead. The long canyon walk has three emergency call boxes. The wheelchair-accessible **Kathleen Springs Walk** (2.6km; 1.5hr.) winds through sandstone valleys to a rockhole sacred to local Aborigines. The access road is 20km south of the Canyon turnoff. The **Sunset Viewing** picnic area with water, toilets, and BBQ is 1km before the main parking lot, but is not as good as the resort's **Sunset Viewing Boardwalk,** with all-encompassing views of the George Gill Range.

YULARA (AYERS ROCK RESORT) ☎08

Between the rock and a dry place stands the well-sculpted, immaculate community of Yulara. The municipal name shelters the employees of Ayers Rock Resort from the fact that they live on a tourist farm resembling a child's gameboard. The single road that loops through all parts of the resort curves in an effort to avoid looking preplanned, and the town's facilities are carefully landscaped in an effort to blend into the outback. However, Yulara's monopoly on the tourist market is not as well disguised; be prepared for hefty mark-ups on food and more than a bit extra for prime real estate just 19km down the street from the world's largest monolith. This place is ideal if you want to forget that you're in the outback. If not, glance at the distant rocks to remember where you are and why you came here.

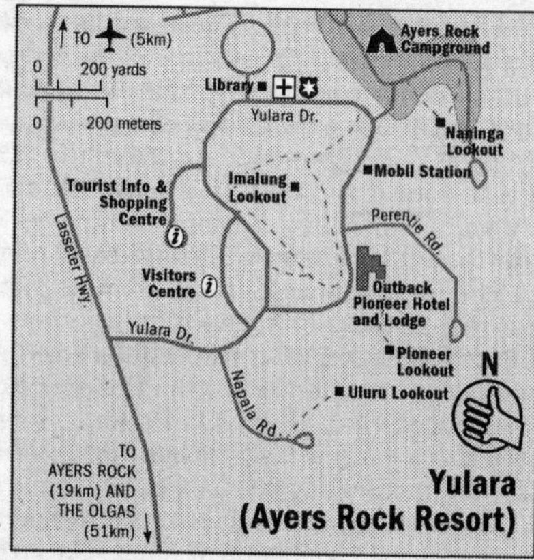

TRANSPORTATION. **Connellan Airport** lies 5km north of town. **Airnorth, Qantas** (☎13 13 13), and **Ansett** (☎13 13 00) fly to: Adelaide ($607); Alice Springs ($168); Brisbane ($651); Cairns ($552); Darwin ($559); Melbourne ($647); Perth ($564); Sydney ($597). A free airport shuttle run by AAT Kings meets all flights and picks up from all accommodations. **Greyhound/McCafferty's** buses depart for Alice Springs daily from the Outback Pioneer Hotel (6hr., 12:30pm, $74). Ayers Rock Resort runs a free village shuttle around the resort loop (every 15min., daily 10:30am-12:30am). **Territory Rent-a-Car** (☎8956 2030), **Hertz** (☎8956 2244), and **Avis** (☎8956 2266) have offices at the airport or at the **Tourist Information Centre** (☎8957 7324). Most backpackers come to Yulara on camping tours out of Alice Springs, which can be combined various stops to other sites (see p. 272).

A handful of walks around town lead to six different lookout points, all with impressive views of the usual suspects. To get to Uluru and Kata Tjuta from the resort, you'll need a vehicle. **Uluru Express** (☎8956 2152) offers the most flexible transportation to Uluru ($30, child $15), Kata Tjuta ($45, child $25). **Anangu Tours** is owned by Aborigines who can share some insider knowledge; book through the Cultural Centre. (☎8956 2123. 2hr. tours $47; children $24; families $142.) **Greyhound Pioneer** does a sunset run to Uluru from the resort (4hr., departs 3pm, $62) and also runs to Kata Tjuta (5½hr., departs 6am, $40). Book ahead. If you've got the dough and desire, you can also get there on a **Harley-Davidson motorcycle** (☎8955 5288. Passenger tours from $55; self-drive from $324 for 5hr. plus $2000 deposit.)

PRACTICAL INFORMATION. The **Tourist Information Centre,** in the main town square shopping center, has general info, a list of daily outdoors conditions, and several tour agencies. (☎8957 7324. Open daily 8:30am-8:30pm; service desks maintain shorter, variable hours.) The so-called **Visitors Centre,** with a grand set of stairs rising from the road near the entrance to the village, is actually little more than a gift shop and museum with a smattering of town info. (☎8957 7377. Open daily 8:30am-7pm.) **Fuel** is available at the Mobil station. (☎8956 2229. Open daily 7am-9pm.) The **library** has the cheapest **Internet** access. (☎8956 2351. Open M-F 10:30am-1:15pm and 2-5pm, Sa-Su 1-4pm; $10 per hr.); the resort charges $9 per 30min. Other services include: **police** (☎8956 2166); a 24-hour **medical centre** (☎8956 2286; clinic open M-F 9am-noon and 2-5pm, Sa-Su 10-11am); **ANZ bank** with 24hr. **ATM** in the shopping center (open M-Th 9:30am-4pm, F 9:30am-5pm); the **post office** (☎8956 2288; open M-F 9am-6pm, Sa-Su 10am-2pm). **Postal code:** 0872.

ACCOMMODATIONS. The resort offers little choice when it comes to accommodations for the budget traveler. For all lodge reservations call ☎1300 139 889. The **Outback Pioneer Lodge,** on Yulara Dr., has a rather impersonal YHA hostel with barracks-type dorms. Don't get it confused with the hotel portion of the resort, or you might end up booking a more expensive room. (☎8967 7888. Free luggage storage. Reception daily 4am-11pm. 20-bed dorms with no door locks $32, YHA $26-29;

4-bed dorms $40/$34-$37.) The **Resort Campground** corners the market on camping, since it is not allowed elsewhere in the national park. Campers have access to a swimming pool, communal kitchen, laundry, hot showers, and BBQ. (☎8956 2055. Sites $12.10, child $5.50, family $35; powered for 2 $28.60, child $5.50, family $39.) Beyond camping or dorm rooms, the next price range at Yulara is from $132-146 for twin/double rooms at the **Outback Pioneer Hotel** or cabins at the Campground. Free but less conveniently located camping is available 100km east of Yulara at **Curtin Springs,** or, unofficially, at the basic rest stops along the way—or in your car. (☎8956 2906. Powered sites $11; showers $1; rooms from $45.)

FOOD. The **Outback Pioneer Hotel** has a run-of-the-mill **snack bar** with $6.95 burgers. (Open daily 8am-9pm.) Their nightly BBQ, with live entertainment (from 6-9pm) ranges from beef or veggie burgers to emu sausages ($14-24). It's also the only place to buy takeaway **liquor.** Most food in the area is overpriced; **Gecko Cafe** in the shopping center has creative wood-oven pizzas at $18-25. (Open daily 10am-10pm.) The shopping center has a **Takeaway** counter (open 7am-8:30pm); an **ice creamery** (open daily 11am-7pm); a **supermarket** (open daily 8:30am-9pm).

ULURU-KATA TJUTA NAT'L PARK

Out of the flat, scrub-brush landscape of the Red Centre, where tumbleweed and dust funnels provide the only visible movement, Uluru (Ayers Rock) and Kata Tjuta (the Olgas) hulk like hibernating animals. These shockingly gigantic rock formations, with their smooth ridges and pocket-like caves, break not only the horizon but also the banks of many eager tourists who gather for their once-in-a-lifetime glimpse of "sunset at Uluru." They descend upon the desert from all corners of the globe; it is no secret that this is the premier sight of central Australia, and, some might say, the continent. As the largest single rock in the world, fiery-orange Uluru warrants the hype. Nearby Kata Tjuta, a cluster of rounded hump-like mini-Ulurus, are less touristed but no less astounding and humbling.

These natural wonders are a centerpiece for the local Anangu Aborigines, who, for 22,000 years, have revered Uluru as a sacred site of the Dreaming. Since Uluru's European discovery in 1872 by Ernest Giles, the area has also become one of Australia's primary tourist meccas. A sense of indigenous loss off-set by industry gain is still present. Today, the park is managed jointly by the National Park Service and Anangu residents, and a strong effort is made to incorporate geologic

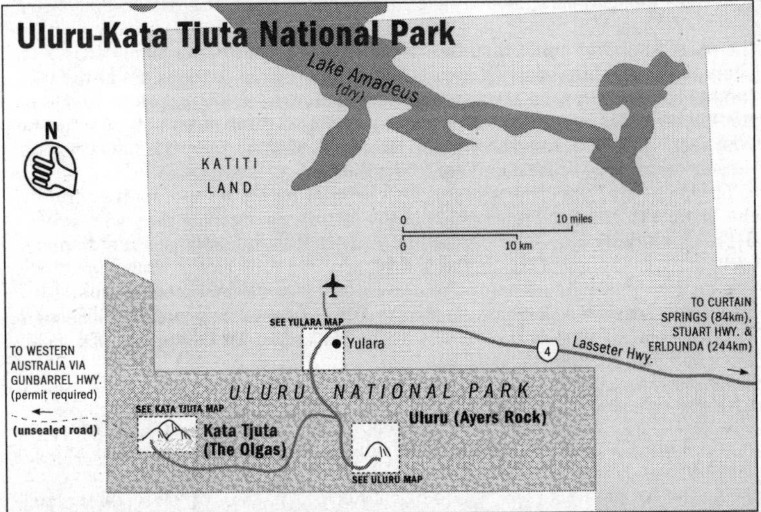

and cultural information. Many think of Uluru-Kata Tjuta as the symbol of the outback. With the natural splendor, cultural significance, and contemporary balancing-act between indigenous livelihood and visitor needs, it just might be. But the hard-earned solitude that lends the outback its true flavor is missing in this highly-marketed area. Still, Uluru and Kata Tjuta are so stunning that a visit is definitely worth it, even for travelers bent on keeping to the backroads.

The typical Uluru tourist routine includes little more than a hurried climb and a few sunset or sunrise snapshots of the rock. Hold on one second though! While Uluru might be considered "The Rock," a trip to the area is not complete without learning about the meaning of Uluru to the Aborigines who have called the Red Centre their home for 60,000 years. Take a walk around the base of the rock, where aged indigenous paintings can be found, take a peak at the informative Cultural Centre, and *definitely* explore the skyscraping Olgas—you have not visited Yulara if you miss these sites.

ULURU AND KATA TJUTA AT A GLANCE

AREA: 1325km^2

ULURU: 348m in height, 3.1km in length, 1.9km in width, 9.4km around.

KATA TJUTA: Mt. Olga, it's tallest peak, is 546m.

GATEWAYS: Many travelers come from Alice Springs (4.5hrs away) or Yulara.

HIGHLIGHTS: The colors of Uluru at sunset and sundown, the Valley of the Winds, walks through Kata Tjuta.

CAMPING: No camping is allowed within the National Park. There is a commercial campground at Yulara.

FEES: 3-day entry pass $16.25.

TRANSPORTATION. To get to Uluru-Kata Tjuta by road, travel on the Stuart Hwy. to **Erlunda,** which lies 202km south of Alice Springs and 483km north of Coober Pedy, then drive 264km west on the **Lasseter Hwy.** Long before reaching Uluru, you'll see **Mt. Connor,** a big mesa in the distance. This tricky imitation, often mistaken for Ayers Rock, has its own viewing area right off the highway.

PRACTICAL INFORMATION. The Uluru-Kata Tjuta National Park **entrance station** (☎8956 2252) lies 5km past the Yulara resort village, where all visitors must purchase a three-day pass ($16.25). Uluru is 14km ahead, and 4km farther is the turn-off to Kata Tjuta (42km). These roads are all paved. (Park open daily hour-before-sunrise to hour-after-sunset, i.e. Dec.-Feb. 5am-9pm; Mar. 5:30am-8:30pm; Apr. 6am-8pm; May 6am-7:30pm; June-July 6:30am-7:30pm; Aug. 6am-7:30pm; Sept. 5:30am-7:30pm; Oct. 5am-8pm; Nov. 5am-8:30pm.) **No camping** is permitted within the park. There are toilet facilities at the Cultural Centre, the main carpark at Uluru, and the sunset-viewing area at Kata Tjuta. Picnic facilities are at the Cultural Centre and the Kata Tjuta sunset-viewing area. As in the rest of the Red Centre, the **bush flies** can be unbearable from Dec.-Apr. Bring mesh netting to cover your face. In case of **emergency,** radio alarms throughout the park can contact a ranger; or call 8956 3138 (daily 7am-5:30pm).

The **Uluru-Kata Tjuta Cultural Centre,** 1km before Uluru, is an informative effort by the Anangu to enlighten tourists about the history surrounding the rock. (☎8956 3138. Open daily Nov.-Mar. 7am-6pm; Apr.-Oct. 7am-5:30pm.) Free displays include explanations of the mythical origins of the rock and of Anangu culture. The center, built with all-natural materials in the Aboriginal mode, contains an information desk, a snack bar, the **Maruka Arts and Crafts** shop (☎8956 2558; open daily 8:30am-5:30pm), and ceramics at the **Walkatjara Art Centre.** (☎8956 2537. Open M-F 9am-5:30pm, Sa-Su 9:30am-2pm.)

ULURU (AYERS ROCK)

The Uluru-hype is big, and Uluru is even bigger. The rock is actually only the exposed tip of a giant slab that extends down 5-6km. Eons of geological activity have tilted and eroded once-horizontal sedimentary layers into vertical grooves on the surface of the rock (see "A Geological Recipe," p. 285). Up close, meter-long grooves become gorges, and the smooth rock walls reveal a rough, scaly exterior.

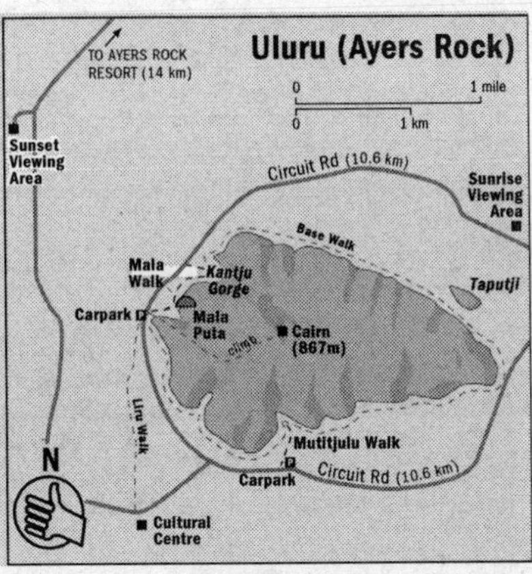

The strategically situated **sunset-viewing area,** 5km from the rock, is the place to hear the nightly oohs and aahs of awestruck travelers, punctuated by the clicking shutters and useless flashes of hundreds of cameras. The road continues on a **paved loop** around the rock. The **main carpark** and toilets are just to the left along the loop. A **sunrise-viewing area** lies on the opposite side of the rock.

The Anangu prefer that people not climb because of the spiritual significance the rock represents as the Mala Dreaming track. It is a good idea to visit the **Cultural Centre** and understand Anangu motivations before deciding one way or the other. Aside from respecting cultural tractions, realize that this the climb is no joke. It is a difficult hike, even for the young and able-bodied (notice the plaques at the base that memorialize those who have died—33 total deaths in the past 20 years). A fixed chain helps with the brutal initial uphill, the steepest part of the climb (you will need this the most on the way down). The climb requires rugged footwear and plenty of water: visitors should avoid climbing in the middle of the day or if they have medical conditions or loosely attached hairpieces. The park restricts climbing during extreme heat. The summit affords a panorama of the Red Centre's expanse, broken by Kata Tjuta and Mt. Connor.

Several more humbling vantage-points allow visitors to enjoy the rock while obeying Anangu preferences. An ambitious **circuit walk** (9.4km; 3-4hr.) traces the base of the rock and promises at least moments of solitude with Uluru. The **Mala Walk** (2km; 1hr.) is a segment of this circuit which leads from the main parking lot past magnificent walls and a "stone wave" to **Kantju Gorge.** There is a free ranger-guided Mala Walk offering a look at Uluru from an Aboriginal perspective; meet the ranger at the **Mala Walk** sign at the base of Uluru, near the main parking lot (1½hr.; daily Oct.-Apr. 8am, May-Sept. 10am; free). A smaller parking lot to the right from the loop entrance serves the **Mutitjulu Walk** (1km, 45min.), which leads to the waterhole home of the watersnake Wanampi. Both the Mala and Mutitjulu walks are wheelchair accessible. Grab *An Insight Into Uluru* ($1) at the Cultural Centre for an expanded self-guided tour of these two walks.

A GEOLOGICAL RECIPE One of the most unique concoctions out of Mother Nature's cookbook. Allow at least 550 million years for preparation time. **Ingredients:** Arkose, a feldspar-rich sandstone (for Uluru) and conglomerate, a collection of rocks from pebbles to boulders cemented together by sand and mud (for Kata Tjuta). **Instructions:** Start by depositing the arkose and conglomerate on the alluvial fans of ancient mountain ranges (550 million years ago). Cover with a shallow sea and compress with thick layers of sediment, cementing the deposits into solid rock (500 million years ago). Fold and fracture the entire region, turning the horizontal Uluru arkose almost 90°(where it will remain), and the Kata Tjuta conglomerate between 15°-20° (400-300 million years ago). Slowly erode the rocks from the surface for about 300 million years. Finally, shift the climate from wet swampland to arid desert (500,000 years ago) and garnish with sand dunes between the two formations. **Yields:** One pair of world-class geological wonders. Not bad for a first try.

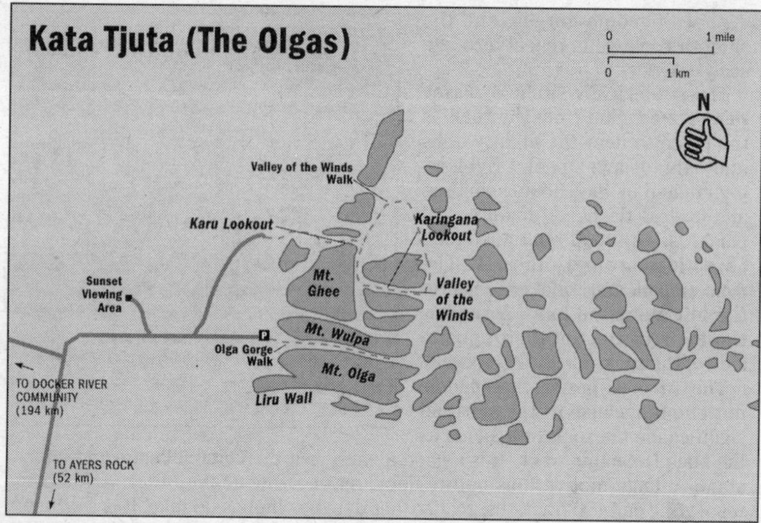

KATA TJUTA (THE OLGAS)

Perhaps more beautiful than the Rock are the 36 undulating domes scattered over an area several times the size of Uluru. Kata Tjuta ("many heads") is the second conspicuous rock formation in the Red Centre, and it seems as though Uluru might just be a ploy to keep tourists away from this less-touted treasure that provides an amazing perspective from each angle. The giant rocks sit like eggs on the horizon, and yet, up close, you look like a mere ant in comparison to the steep valleys of red rock through which you can walk.

The 44km road to Kata Tjuta leaves the main road 4km after the park entrance station. The **Dune Viewing Area,** 25km down the road, is at the end of a wheelchair-accessible walk (300m) allowing relaxing and all-encompassing views of Kata Tjuta. This also is an underappreciated sunrise spot. The **sunset-viewing area** (toilets available) is just short of the starting points for the two walks. The **Olga Gorge walk** (2.6km; 1hr.) is an easy path between a pair of the most daunting domes. The dome on the right is **Mt. Olga** (546m), the highest peak in the range. The amazing winding **Valley of the Winds walk** (7.4km; 3hr.) traces a majestic circuit through the outer wall of domes and into the inner sanctuary.

QUEENSLAND

If the variety of the continent's natural attractions could be condensed into one state, the result would look something like Queensland, Australia's deliciously layered natural paradise. Queensland changes, east to west, from reef islands to sandy shores, from hinterland rainforest to the glowing red outback. At the base of this fantasyland sits the capital city of Brisbane, a diverse and manageable urban break from the surf and sun, located in the southeast tip of the state. Moving north, Queensland's coastal side crawls with backpackers year-round—with the same faces popping up in every town, the journey often feels like a never-ending party. The downside for those on this heavily-touristed route is that real Aussie culture can be masked by the young crowd that has flooded its shores. Moving from one hot-spot to another can be mind-numbing as you wade through a never-ending swamp of brochures, billboards, and tourist packages.

The enjoyment of a Queensland visit will endlessly multiply the more you get off this beaten track. Those willing to temporarily trade sandals for hiking boots can explore the rainforest-drenched far north and the jewel-bedecked outback, where history, like tourism, proceeds at a koala's pace. Inland, you'll encounter charming country towns, pockets of thriving Aboriginal culture, and plenty of history—all without a hint of the rampant tourism of the coast. In Queensland, appreciating Oz at its extremes can be as simple as driving toward Cape Tribulation and watching the rainforest practically tumble into the pounding ocean.

TRANSPORTATION

The Queensland coast as far north as Cairns, along with the far north and its interior, is comprehensively serviced by public transportation. Don't underestimate the distances involved; even within the state, many people choose to fly if they want to get from Brisbane to Cairns quickly. If you've got the time for a leisurely trip, though, taking a bus up the coast allows you to stop at innumerable spots along the way. The major bus lines are **Greyhound** (☎13 20 30) and **McCafferty's** (☎13 14 99), and the train line is **Queensland Rail** (☎13 22 32). If you have a few friends to chip in for costs or if you're traveling with a family, **renting a car** provides the most convenience and freedom to wander off the beaten track. All the major car rental establishments are here, plus dozens of cheaper local ones. To tackle the area from Cooktown north through Cape York as well as some of the desert roads, you'll need **4WD.** This is pricey; it's also tough to find an automatic transmission 4WD (try **Allcar Rentals** in Port Douglas, ☎4099 4123). Roads in the tropics are especially harrowing, and often impassible, during and immediately following the **wet season** (Nov.-Apr.). It's best to call ahead for **road conditions** (☎3361 2406).

The central office of the **Royal Automobile Club of Queensland (RACQ)** is at 300 St. Paul's Tce., Fortitude Valley, Brisbane. With affiliations worldwide, RACQ has excellent maps, car buying or selling information, and technical services. (☎3361 2444, for statewide roadside service call 13 11 11. Open M-F 8:30am-5:30pm. 1-year membership $67, overseas transfer free.) For more info, see **On the Road,** p. 67.

THE GREAT BARRIER REEF

The Great Barrier Reef, one of the world's greatest living wonders, stretches for 2300km from just offshore of Bundaberg to Papua New Guinea, encompassing hundreds of islands and cays and thousands of smaller coral reefs. This marine wonderland is easily accessible from the Queensland coast, but when, where, and how to explore it involve complicated and important decisions. Many people who don't plan sufficiently end up paying a lot for bad visibility or a mediocre dive site. It's important to first familiarize yourself with the types of reef and the life forms

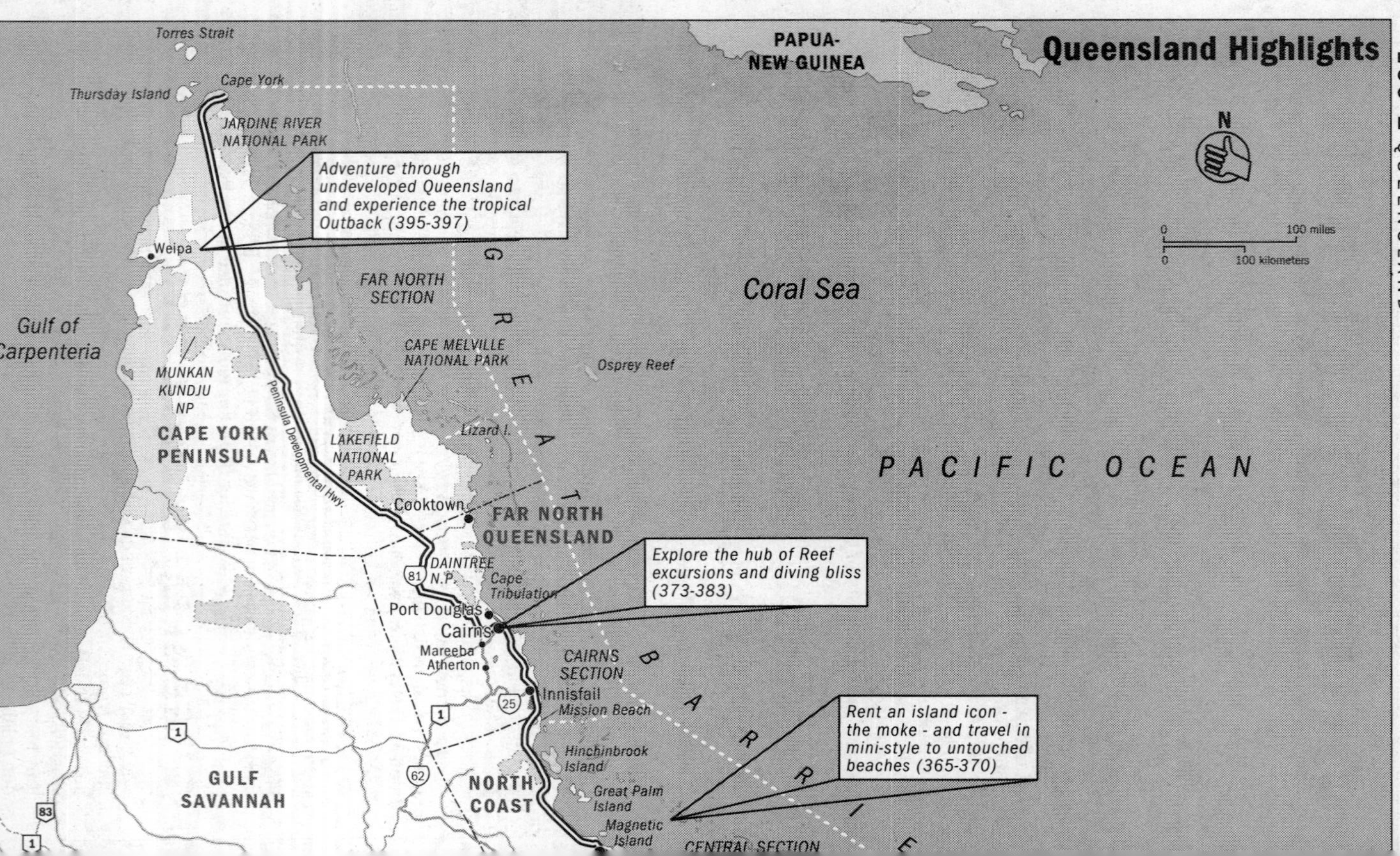
Queensland Highlights
N
0 100 miles
0 100 kilometers
PAPUA-
NEW GUINEA
Coral Sea
P A C I F I C O C E A N
Torres Strait
Thursday Island
Cape York
JARDINE RIVER NATIONAL PARK
Weipa
Gulf of Carpenteria
Adventure through undeveloped Queensland and experience the tropical Outback (395-397)
FAR NORTH SECTION
CAPE MELVILLE NATIONAL PARK
G R E A T B A R R I E
Osprey Reef
Lizard I.
Peninsula Developmental Hwy.
MUNKAN KUNDJU NP
CAPE YORK PENINSULA
LAKEFIELD NATIONAL PARK
Cooktown
FAR NORTH QUEENSLAND
DAINTREE N.P.
Cape Tribulation
Port Douglas
Cairns
Mareeba
Atherton
Explore the hub of Reef excursions and diving bliss (373-383)
CAIRNS SECTION
Innisfail
Mission Beach
Hinchinbrook Island
Great Palm Island
Magnetic Island
CENTRAL SECTION
Rent an island icon - the moke - and travel in mini-style to untouched beaches (365-370)
NORTH COAST
GULF SAVANNAH
81
25
1
62
83

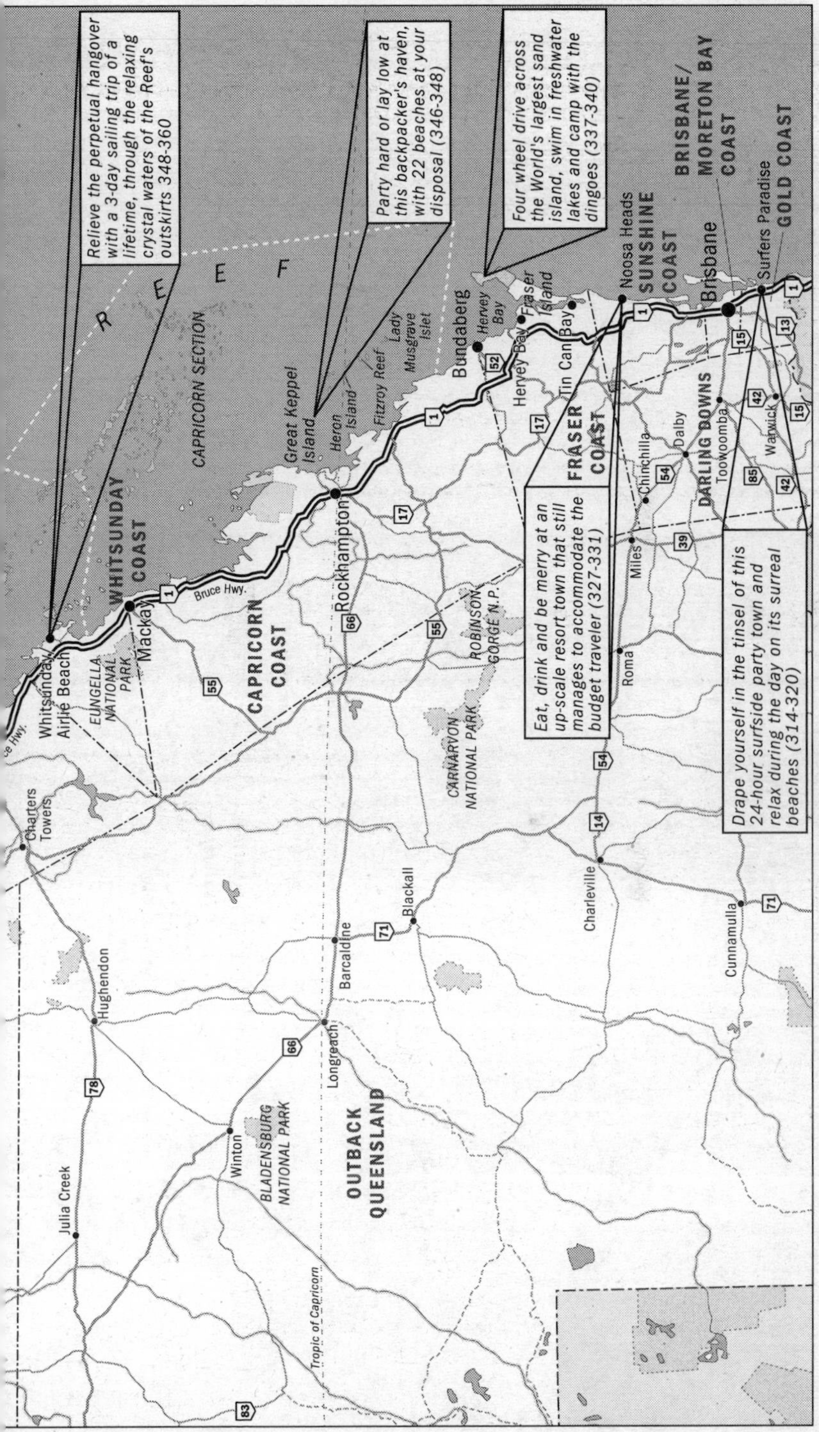

Relieve the perpetual hangover with a 3-day sailing trip of a lifetime, through the relaxing crystal waters of the Reef's outskirts 348-360

Party hard or lay low at this backpacker's haven, with 22 beaches at your disposal (346-348)

Four wheel drive across the World's largest sand island, swim in freshwater lakes and camp with the dingoes (337-340)

Eat, drink and be merry at an up-scale resort town that still manages to accommodate the budget traveler (327-331)

Drape yourself in the tinsel of this 24-hour surfside party town and relax during the day on its surreal beaches (314-320)

Charters Towers
Julia Creek
Hughendon
Whitsunday/Airlie Beach
EUNGELLA NATIONAL PARK
WHITSUNDAY COAST
Mackay
REEF
CAPRICORN SECTION
Bruce Hwy.
Winton
BLADENSBURG NATIONAL PARK
CAPRICORN COAST
Great Keppel Island
Tropic of Capricorn
Longreach
Barcaldine
Rockhampton
Heron Island
OUTBACK QUEENSLAND
Fitzroy Reef
Lady Musgrave Islet
Blackall
CARNARVON NATIONAL PARK
ROBINSON GORGE N.P.
Bundaberg
Hervey Bay
Fraser Island
Tin Can Bay
FRASER COAST
Charleville
Roma
Miles
Chinchilla
Noosa Heads
SUNSHINE COAST
Dalby
DARLING DOWNS
Toowoomba
Brisbane
BRISBANE/MORETON BAY COAST
Cunnamulla
Warwick
Surfers Paradise
GOLD COAST

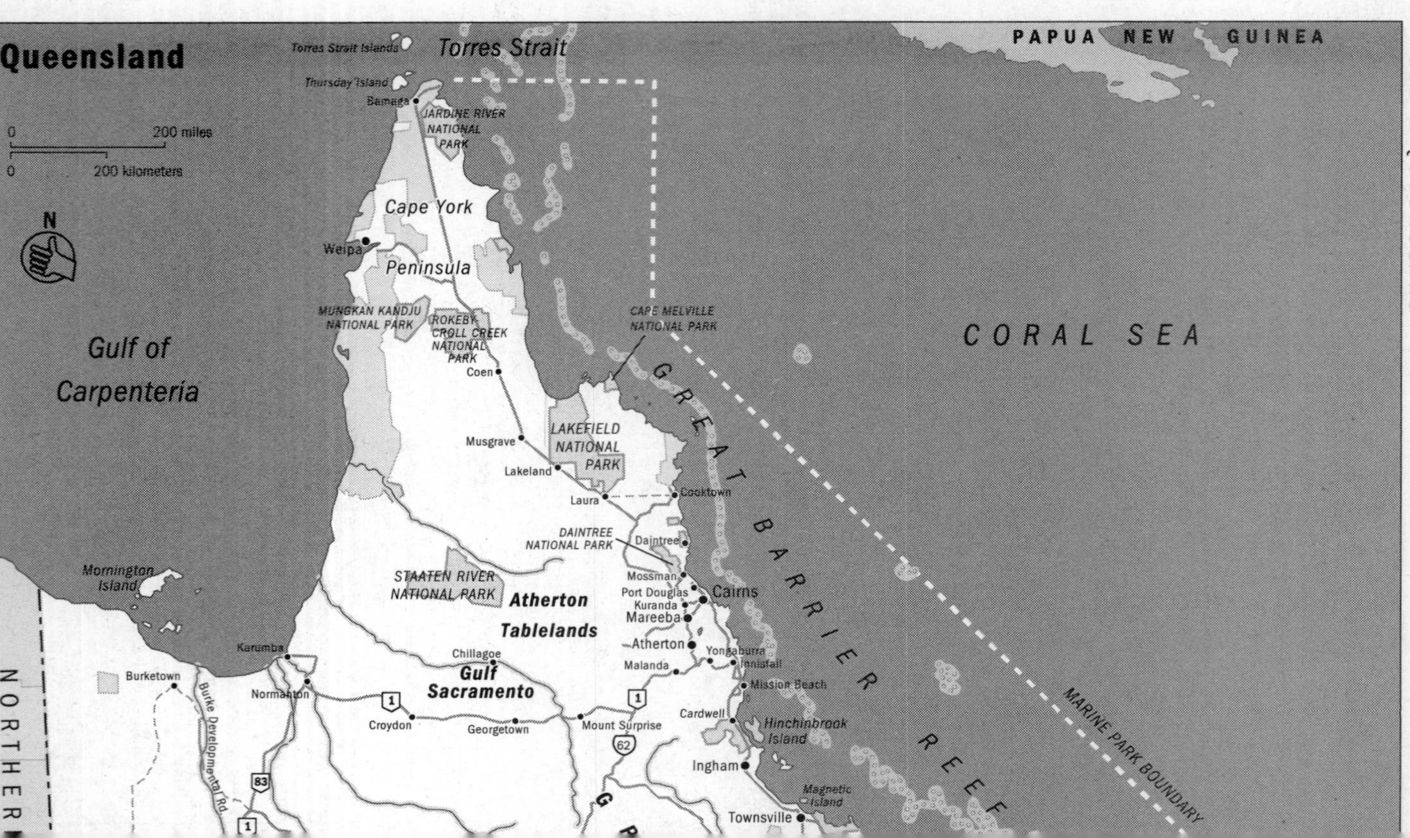
Queensland
0
200 miles
0
200 kilometers
N
Gulf of Carpenteria
Torres Strait Islands
Torres Strait
Thursday Island
Bamaga
JARDINE RIVER NATIONAL PARK
PAPUA NEW GUINEA
Cape York
Weipa
Peninsula
MUNGKAN KANDJU NATIONAL PARK
ROKEBY CROLL CREEK NATIONAL PARK
Coen
CAPE MELVILLE NATIONAL PARK
CORAL SEA
GREAT BARRIER REEF
MARINE PARK BOUNDARY
LAKEFIELD NATIONAL PARK
Musgrave
Lakeland
Laura
Cooktown
DAINTREE NATIONAL PARK
Daintree
Mornington Island
STAATEN RIVER NATIONAL PARK
Atherton Tablelands
Mossman
Port Douglas
Kuranda
Mareeba
Cairns
Atherton
Yongaburra
Innisfail
Malanda
Mission Beach
Karumba
Chillagoe
Gulf Sacramento
Burketown
Normanton
Burke Developmental Rd.
1
Croydon
Georgetown
Mount Surprise
62
Cardwell
Hinchinbrook Island
Ingham
Magnetic Island
Townsville
83
NORTHER

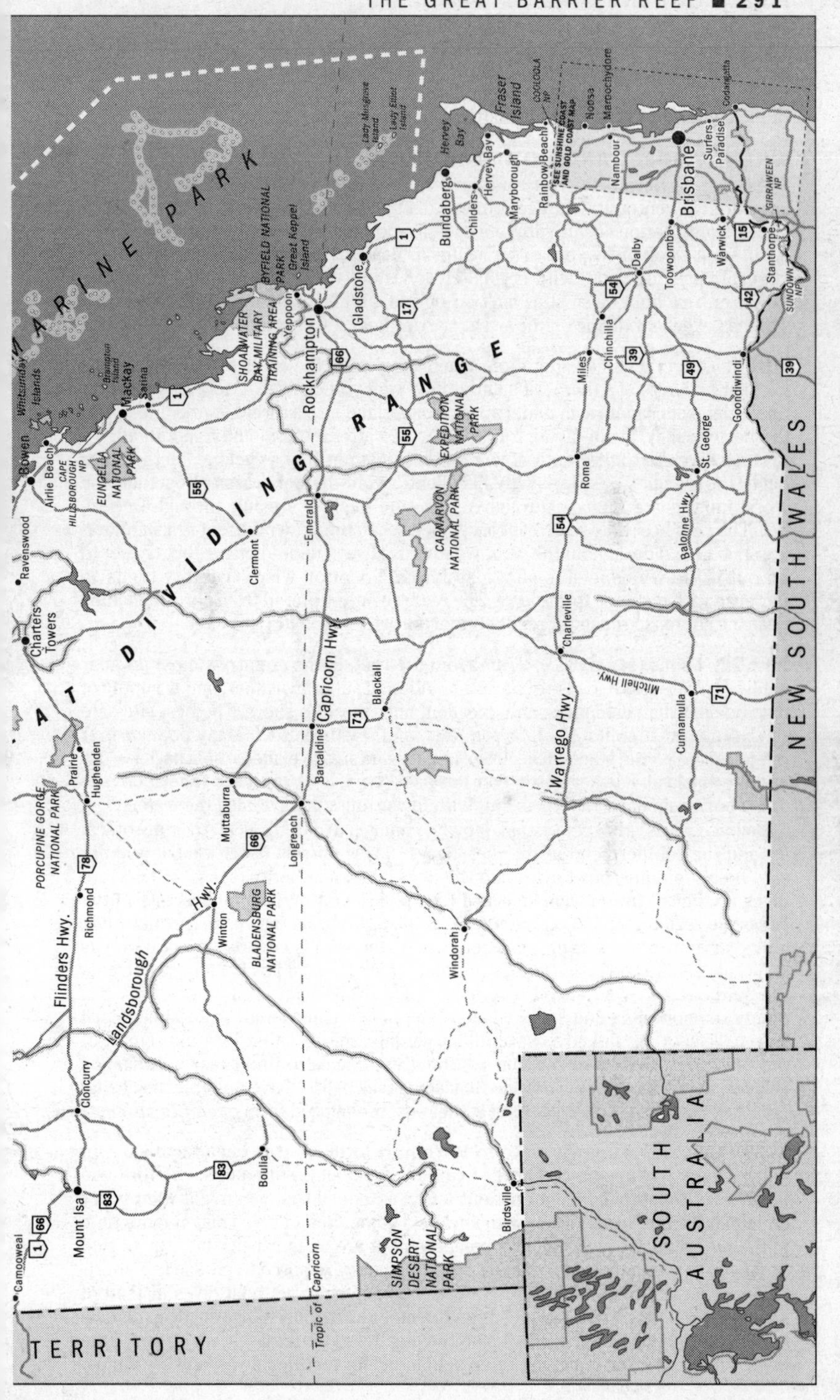
MARINE PARK
GREAT DIVIDING RANGE
TERRITORY
SOUTH AUSTRALIA
NEW SOUTH WALES
Tropic of Capricorn
Whitsunday Islands
Bowen
Airlie Beach
CAPE HILLSBOROUGH NP
EUNGELLA NATIONAL PARK
Brampton Island
Mackay
Sarina
SHOALWATER BAY MILITARY TRAINING AREA
BYFIELD NATIONAL PARK
Great Keppel Island
Yeppoon
Rockhampton
Gladstone
Lady Musgrave Island
Lady Elliot Island
Bundaberg
Hervey Bay
Childers
Maryborough
Fraser Island
COOLOOLA NP
Rainbow Beach
SEE SUNSHINE COAST AND GOLD COAST MAP
Noosa
Maroochydore
Nambour
Brisbane
Surfers Paradise
Coolangatta
Toowoomba
Warwick
GIRRAWEEN NP
Stanthorpe
SUNDOWN NP
Dalby
Chinchilla
Miles
Goondiwindi
St. George
Balonne Hwy.
Roma
EXPEDITION NATIONAL PARK
CARNARVON NATIONAL PARK
Emerald
Clermont
Ravenswood
Charters Towers
Charleville
Mitchell Hwy.
Cunnamulla
Warrego Hwy.
Capricorn Hwy.
Blackall
Barcaldine
Longreach
Muttaburra
Hughenden
Prairie
PORCUPINE GORGE NATIONAL PARK
Richmond
Flinders Hwy.
Landsborough Hwy.
Winton
BLADENSBURG NATIONAL PARK
Windorah
Cloncurry
Mount Isa
Camooweal
Boulia
Birdsville
SIMPSON DESERT NATIONAL PARK
1
66
83
78
55
17
54
39
49
42
15
71

you'll see (for an overview see **Marine Life,** p. 30). *Let's Go* describes individual diving and snorkeling sites and operators throughout the book, but before making a choice, take some time to get a general sense of the options. With care and a touch of luck, your experience will be magical.

WHEN, WHERE, AND HOW TO DIVE

The Great Barrier Reef is vast, and furthermore, many of Australia's very best dive sites aren't even on it—they're at more distant, smaller reefs in the **Coral Sea.** If you're a very serious diver with lots of time and money, you may want to invest in a trip for a week or two out to such sites as **Osprey, Flinders, Lihou,** or **Marion Reef,** superbly pristine spots with crystal-clear visibility. For most budget travelers, however, reaching these sites isn't an option, and it fortunately isn't necessary. There is excellent diving on the Great Barrier Reef if you plan it well.

WHEN. One crucial consideration: when comparing the quality of dive sites, it's not just about what's there—it's about how well you can see it, too. Bad weather or silt deposits can turn an underwater wonderland into a turbid, murky mess. For the best **visibility,** avoid diving for a day or two after a storm and a month after a cyclone if you're to the south of where it hit. Just north of a cyclone, on the other hand, the visibility is surprisingly excellent. Avoid the **wet season** altogether; the worst months are January through March, and the best are July through December. The very best time to dive is November, when the spawning reef is a shimmering spectacle. Throughout the year, weather is always unpredictable, but try not to go out if the windspeed is above 20 knots. Location-wise, visibility tends to increase with distance from shore. The reef recently suffered from coral bleaching near the shore, so the outer reef definitely provides better diving sites.

WHERE. Cairns (see p. 373), 27km from the reef, is the country's most popular gateway to the reef because of its combination of superb weather, ample supply of dive-boats, urban amenities, and excellent sites close to shore. The best sites are the Norman Reef, Milin Reef, Saxon Reef, and Hastings Reef. Many popular tour operators go to the somewhat closer and less impressive sites of **Michaelmas Cay** and **Green Island.** Farther north, **Port Douglas** (see p. 387) and **Cape Tribulation** (see p. 391) offer similarly rich reefs, but with fewer tourists traversing the waters.

Below Cairns, the ecosystem slowly changes from tropical to subtropical around the southern end of the reef. **Beaver Cay** is **Mission Beach's** most popular site, home to numerous turtles and the occasional manta ray (see p. 369). Shore dives are cheap from **Magnetic Island** (see p. 365), but by far the best site in the **Townsville** region is found on the wreck of the **S.S.Yongala** (see p. 364) which sank one year before the *Titanic* disaster. Today, the ship is covered in coral polyps and other sealife and is the world's premier wreck site, but its challenging currents are suitable for experienced divers only. The **Whitsunday** area (see p. 357) has plenty of snorkeling and some island diving; most trips depart from **Airlie Beach** (see p. 353) or are linked to several-day sailing cruises. Other locations south of the reef offer far less to see, but can be great places to find **cheap certification courses; Hervey Bay** (see p. 334) and **Bundaberg** (see p. 340) have possibly the cheapest PADI courses in the state. **PADI** is the most recognized form of certification.

HOW. Australia is a great place to learn how to dive—it is cheap and safe. In Queensland, you need a **certification card** to go on all certified dives. Before you begin a certification course or set out for an extended trip, you might want to try an **introductory** or **"resort" dive,** with a trained guide. Resort dives may require time in the pool, and are always more expensive, but are an indispensable way to find out if you're willing to spend the big time and money required to pursue this sport.

If you decide to do a PADI open water course, try to get boat dives instead of shore dives. If you do an Advanced Open Water course, insist that the deep dive be to 30m and no shallower, and choose the electives you want—don't just take the ones offered. **Medical exams** are often demanded for certified dives, and are almost always necessary for certification courses. Such "dive medicals" cost about $50 and are generally cheapest in diving hotspots like Airlie Beach and Cairns.

Once you are choosing a dive operator, think about some questions: How long do you want to dive—a day-trip or a multi-day trip? How big of a boat do you want? For personal dive instruction and a group atmosphere, smaller boats may be the way to go. Finally, are you going with other divers or with friends who may prefer other water activities? If you are already certified, don't assume you're an expert—be honest with dive operators about your experience and ask questions.

ALTERNATIVES TO DIVING

Diving is the ideal way to get an up-close view of the reef, but it's expensive, requires bulky, complicated equipment, and often requires time-consuming, costly training. By contrast, if you can swim, try **snorkeling.** Renting a mask and fins can be as cheap as $10 per day, and just a little more for a wetsuit. Gear is sometimes free with sailing trips or even hostel stays. Good snorkeling is often available just off the shore of islands or beaches; you can grab your gear and swim unguided. When wearing fins, be extremely aware of where you are flapping—if you hit the coral you may kill it, erasing hundreds of years of growth. Better yet, snorkel with your natural ten-toed flippers. **Reef walking** is an archaic and very destructive way to see coral; it can result in broken ankles, ruined coral, and dead creatures. If you don't want to get wet at all, an even tamer choice is to view the reef through one of the **glass-bottom boats** cruising from islands or beach towns.

BRISBANE ☎07

Commonly unexplored (and unappreciated) by those on the coastal pilgrimage, Brisbane (pop. 1,500,000) spreads around its central river with a wide spectrum of interests and attractions. Contrasting riverside to hillside, parkland to high-rise, alterna-chic to yuppie, and classy to seedy, Brisbane today is neither glamorous nor industrial—but practical, clean, and full of youthful energy.

The Brisbane River lends an easygoing grace to the city through which it weaves. River transportation is simple and pleasant—hulking ferries and slim kayaks glide between Chinatown and the South Bank Parklands, between investment banks in the Central Business District and the trendy West End. The sunny, warm climate has attracted artistic emigrés, eager to shed winter jumpers and rev up the city's cultural institutions. Always a good bet for temporary employment, Brisbane only recently earned a reputation as a tourist destination. Today, visitors to Brisbane enjoy not only the serene waterfront and peaceful parklands, but corner cafes, rocking nightclubs, and heaps of live local music.

INTERCITY TRANSPORTATION

BY PLANE. **Brisbane International Airport,** 17km (25min.) northwest of the city, has luggage storage ($4-10 per day) and is served by 23 airlines, including **Qantas,** 247 Adelaide St. (☎13 13 13) and **Ansett,** 63 Adelaide St. (☎13 13 00). Both open M-F 8:30am-5pm. The **Travellers Information Service** is located on level 2 of the international terminal, 3km from the domestic terminal aboard the $2.70 Coachtrans bus. (☎3406 3190. Open 5am until last flight of the night.) The **Roma Street Transit Centre** in town has info and books accommodations on level 3 (see below).

SkyTrans, on level 3 of the Transit Centre, runs a daily **shuttle bus** between the airport and Transit Centre. (☎3236 1000. Every 30min. 5am-8:45pm, last bus to city 10:45pm. $9, return $15, same day return $12; children $5.) A trip to one of the major hotels costs $11. A **taxi** between the airport and downtown costs about $20. Privately-owned, **Airtrain** recently began direct service to the airport, making connections to both Brisbane's Queensland Rail in the city (22min., 4 per hr., $9) and the Gold Coast (1½hr.; 2 per hr.; $20, includes bus transfers). Timetable available from QR's Transinfo (☎13 12 30).

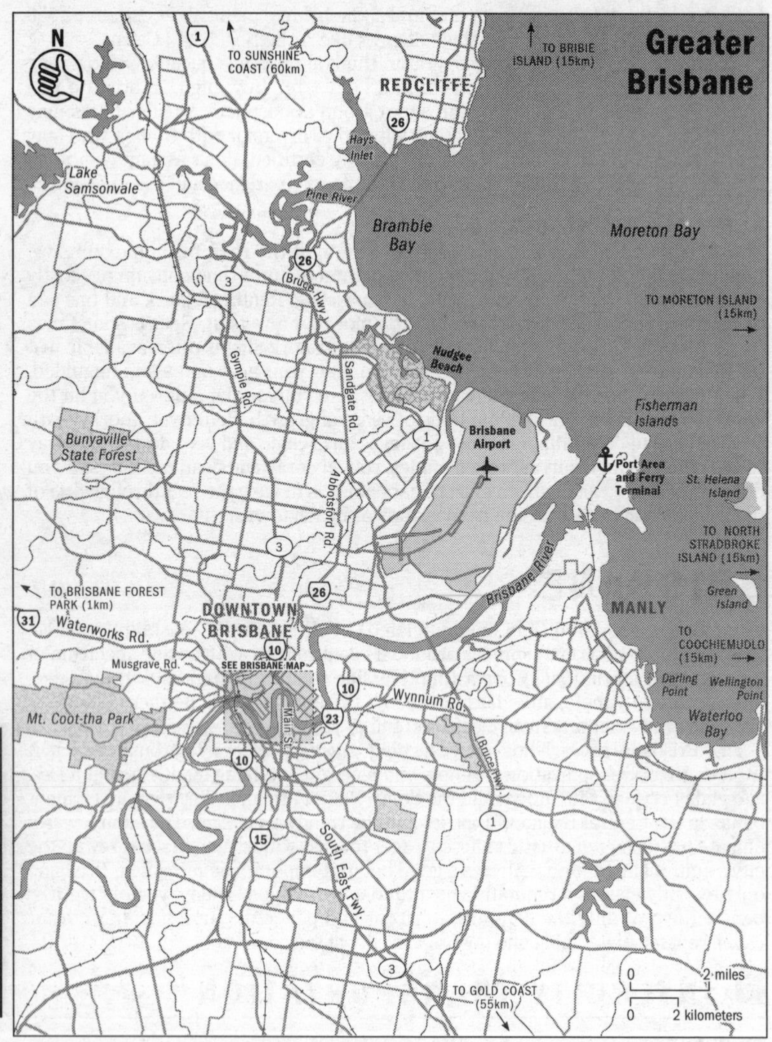

BY TRAIN. The **Roma Street Transit Centre,** 500m west of the city center, is Brisbane's main intercity bus and train terminal. (☎3236 2020. Open daily 4:30am-midnight.) **Lockers** ($5 per day) are on level 1 and 3, and showers are on level 2. **Queensland Rail** (☎3235 2222; bookings ☎13 22 32; reservations for packages including air and accommodations ☎1800 627 655) has offices at Central Station on the corner of Ann and Edward St., diagonally opposite the Palace Backpackers, and on level 1 of the Transit Centre. Travel times can vary considerably depending on the train. The snazzy new Tilt Train is the fastest way to travel; it runs north along the coast from Brisbane to Rockhampton (book ahead). Trains run to: Bundaberg (4¼-7½hr., 2-3 per day, $51.70); Cairns (32hr., 4 per week, $162.80); Gladstone (6-9¾hr., 2-3 per day, $72.60); Mackay (18hr., 6 per week, $119.90); Maryborough West (3½-6¼hr., 2-3 per day, $45.10; connecting bus to Hervey Bay); Prosperine (19½hr., 6 per week, $125.40; connecting bus to Airlie Beach); Rockhampton (7-11½hr., 2-3 per day, $81.40); Sydney (16hr., 1 per day, $110); Townsville (24hr., 6 per week, $141.90). Concessions travel for half-price.

For long travel itineraries, Queensland Rail's **Sunshine Rail Pass** is good for a given number of travel days within a six-month span on any Queensland service and unlimited travel on **Citytrain,** the intracity network. Passes available at the Queensland Rail booth at Roma Street Transit Centre or Central Station. (14-day $291.50, 21-day $327.70, 30-day $423.50; students and children half-price. Book ahead.) There are many other passes available to overseas travelers.

BY BUS. McCafferty's Greyhound (☎13 14 99) covers destinations along the east coast and offers 10% concessions for ISIC/VIP/YHA, and 20% for seniors and children. Adults receive 5% discount on return fares. Some routes are more frequently serviced Oct.-Mar. **Kirklands Coaches** (☎(1300) 36 70 77) and **Premier Coach Service** grant 25% concessions for ISIC/YHA, and 50% for children aged 14-3. Coachtrans (☎13 12 30, ☎3236 1901) and **Suncoast Pacific** (☎3236 1901) also service the Queensland coast. See table, p. 299.

ORIENTATION

The Brisbane River meanders through the city, creating easily identifiable landmarks. The city's heart is cradled in the bottom of a sideways S-curve, connected to South Bank by the **Victoria Bridge.** The **Transit Centre** is on Roma St.; a left turn out of the building and a 5min. walk southeast down Roma St. crosses **Turbot St.,** and leads to the corner of Albert and Ann St. and the grassy **King George Square** (a front lawn for the grand **City Hall**). Adelaide St. runs along the farther side of the square, and one block over the **Queen St. Mall** runs parallel; it's a popular open-air pedestrian thoroughfare lined with shops and cafes, which was recently refurbished for $25 million and the center of Brisbane proper. Underneath the mall and the adjoining **Myer Centre** shopping complex is the **Queen Street Bus Station.**

If you know the Royal British family, you'll have no problem memorizing the streets of the city; continuing south from Queen St., the parallel east-west streets are **Elizabeth, Charlotte, Mary, Margaret and Alice St.**, which is bordered by the **Botanic Gardens.** Intersecting these streets north-south, from the river, the major streets are **William, George, Albert, Edward, and Creek St.**

Brisbane's neighborhoods radiate out from the city center. A right turn out of Roma St. (the commonly-used term for the Transit Centre) leads to **Petrie Tce.** and **Paddington,** both most easily reached by passing under the railway bridge and taking the first left up the hill. North of Boundary St. is **Spring Hill,** bordered to the west by **Victoria Park** and 15min. from the Queen St. Mall up steep Edward St. A 15min. walk down Ann St., the nightclub-heavy **Fortitude Valley** offers an alternative scene but contains some slightly seedy areas—use caution if walking alone at night. Fortitude Valley is also home to the small and authentic **Chinatown,** which has served as the film location for several Jackie Chan flicks. Down Brunswick St., at the intersection with Hardcourt St., officially begins **New Farm,** with its free art galleries and cafes. South of the river, the Victoria Bridge footpath turns into Melbourne St. and heads into **South Brisbane,** crossing Boundary St. six blocks later into the heart of the **West End. South Bank** is to the east of the southern end of the bridge; further along the riverside, **Kangaroo Point** forms a peninsula into the River.

LOCAL TRANSPORTATION

BY TRAIN. Citytrain, Queensland Rail's intracity train network, has three major stations. The main transit center is at **Roma St.; Central Station** is at Ann and Edward St; the final station is at **Brunswick St.** One-zone journeys in the city area cost $1.80. One-day unlimited travel is $8.60. (Trains run M-Th 4:19am-12:09am, F 5am-2am, Sa 6am-1am, Su 6am-11pm. All return trips are free Sa-Su.)

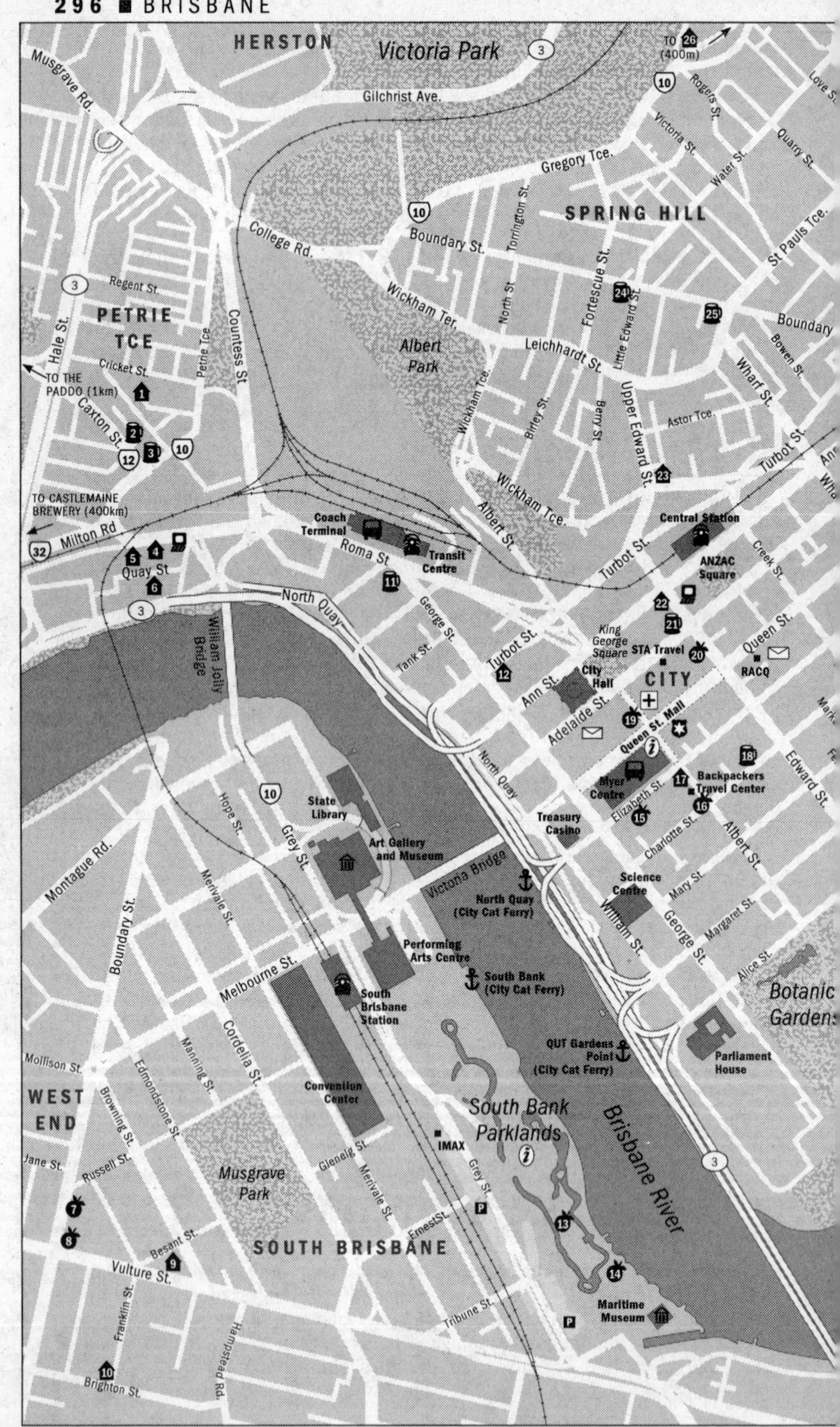
HERSTON
Victoria Park
SPRING HILL
PETRIE TCE
CITY
WEST END
SOUTH BRISBANE
Albert Park
Botanic Gardens
South Bank Parklands
Musgrave Park
Brisbane River
TO THE PADDO (1km)
TO CASTLEMAINE BREWERY (400km)
Coach Terminal
Transit Centre
Central Station
ANZAC Square
King George Square
STA Travel
City Hall
RACQ
Queen St. Mall
Myer Centre
Backpackers Travel Center
Treasury Casino
Science Centre
Parliament House
State Library
Art Gallery and Museum
Performing Arts Centre
South Brisbane Station
Convention Center
North Quay (City Cat Ferry)
South Bank (City Cat Ferry)
QUT Gardens Point (City Cat Ferry)
IMAX
Maritime Museum
Victoria Bridge
William Jolly Bridge
Musgrave Rd.
Gilchrist Ave.
Gregory Tce.
College Rd.
Boundary St.
Wickham Ter.
Leichhardt St.
Upper Edward St.
Turbot St.
Roma St
North Quay
George St.
Ann St.
Adelaide St.
Queen St.
Elizabeth St.
Charlotte St.
Mary St.
Margaret St.
Alice St.
Albert St.
Edward St.
William St.
Milton Rd
Quay St
Caxton St.
Cricket St.
Regent St.
Hale St.
Countess St
Petrie Tce
Montague Rd.
Boundary St.
Grey St.
Hope St.
Merivale St.
Melbourne St.
Cordelia St.
Manning St.
Edmondstone St.
Mollison St.
Browning St.
Russell St.
Jane St.
Vulture St.
Besant St.
Franklin St.
Brighton St.
Hampstead Rd.
Tribune St.
Ernest St.
Glenelg St.
Rogers St.
Victoria St.
Water St.
Quarry St.
St Pauls Tce.
Love St.
Torrington St.
North St.
Fortescue St.
Little Edward St.
Bowen St.
Wharf St.
Astor Tce.
Birley St.
Berry St.
Wickham Tce.
Albert St.
Creek St.
Tank St.
TO 26 (400m)

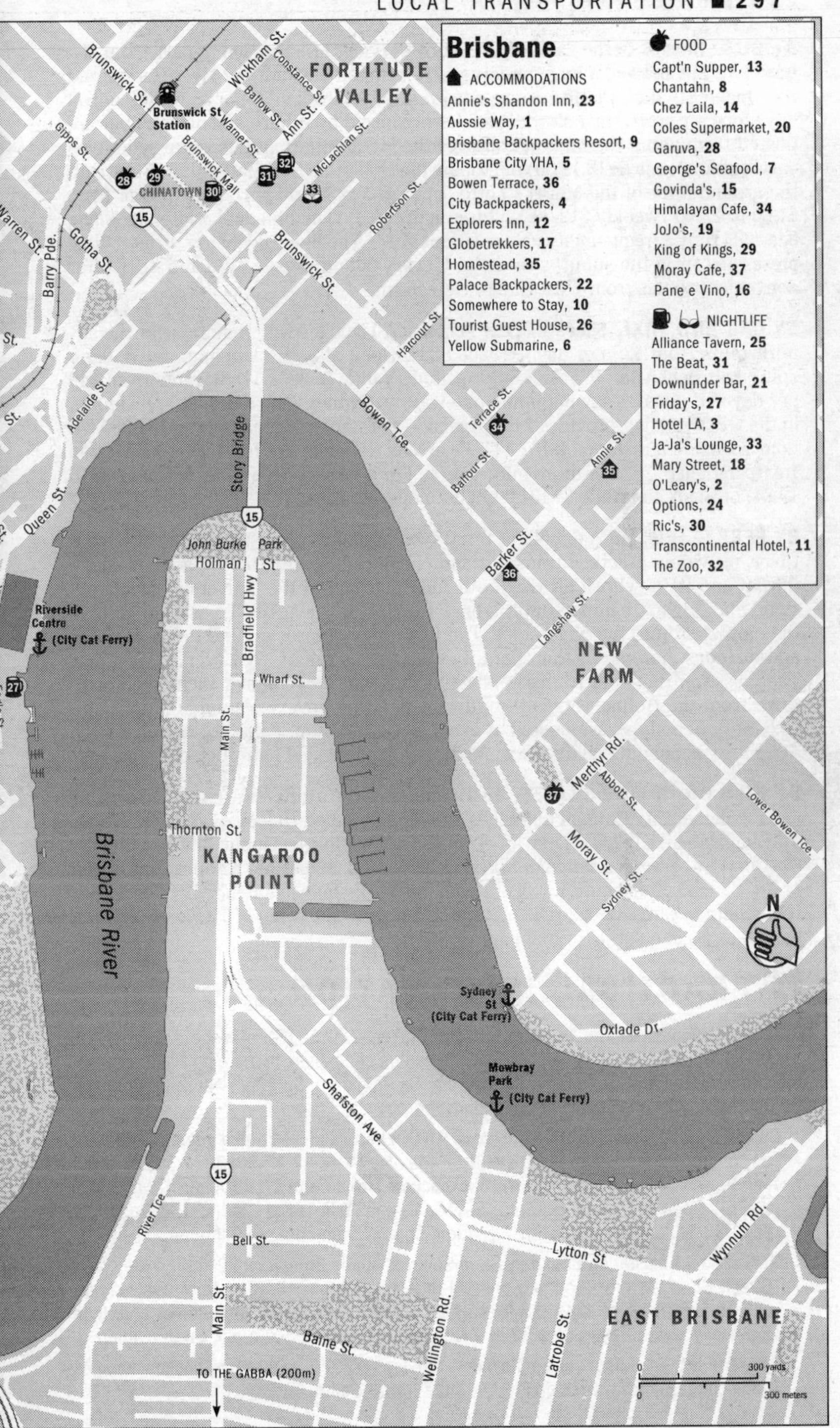
Brisbane
ACCOMMODATIONS
Annie's Shandon Inn, 23
Aussie Way, 1
Brisbane Backpackers Resort, 9
Brisbane City YHA, 5
Bowen Terrace, 36
City Backpackers, 4
Explorers Inn, 12
Globetrekkers, 17
Homestead, 35
Palace Backpackers, 22
Somewhere to Stay, 10
Tourist Guest House, 26
Yellow Submarine, 6
FOOD
Capt'n Supper, 13
Chantahn, 8
Chez Laila, 14
Coles Supermarket, 20
Garuva, 28
George's Seafood, 7
Govinda's, 15
Himalayan Cafe, 34
JoJo's, 19
King of Kings, 29
Moray Cafe, 37
Pane e Vino, 16
NIGHTLIFE
Alliance Tavern, 25
The Beat, 31
Downunder Bar, 21
Friday's, 27
Hotel LA, 3
Ja-Ja's Lounge, 33
Mary Street, 18
O'Leary's, 2
Options, 24
Ric's, 30
Transcontinental Hotel, 11
The Zoo, 32
FORTITUDE VALLEY
Brunswick St Station
CHINATOWN
Brunswick St.
Wickham St.
Constance St.
Ballow St.
Warner St.
Ann St.
McLachlan St.
Brunswick Mall
Gipps St.
Robertson St.
Warren St.
Barry Pde.
Gotha St.
Harcourt St.
Adelaide St.
Bowen Tce.
Terrace St.
Balfour St.
Annie St.
Story Bridge
Queen St.
John Burke Park
Holman St
Barker St.
Riverside Centre
(City Cat Ferry)
Bradfield Hwy
Wharf St.
Langshaw St.
NEW FARM
Main St.
Merthyr Rd.
Abbott St.
Lower Bowen Tce.
Thornton St.
KANGAROO POINT
Moray St.
Sydney St.
Brisbane River
N
Sydney St (City Cat Ferry)
Oxlade Dr.
Mowbray Park (City Cat Ferry)
Shafston Ave.
River Tce
Bell St.
Lytton St
Wynnum Rd.
EAST BRISBANE
Baine St.
Wellington Rd.
Latrobe St.
TO THE GABBA (200m)
300 yards
300 meters

BY BUS. Citybus is the "all-stops" major service. Most buses depart from the **Queen St. Bus Station,** a huge underground terminal beneath the Myer Center and the Queen St. Mall. Platforms are named after Australian animals, while central city stops are sorted by color. Schedules organized by suburb and bus number are posted throughout the city and all over the Mall. Suburban bus route schedules vary; call **TransInfo** (☎13 12 30) or stop by the Queen St. Bus Station Info Centre on the ground floor of the Meyer Centre (open M-F 8:30am-5pm). Fares range from $1.60 to $3.60 (weekly $12-30; children half-price). The blue and white **City Circle bus** #333 runs a frequent city center circuit (70¢). The blue and yellow striped **Cityxpress** runs from the suburbs to the city every 30min. Buses #190 and #191 offer convenient routes from West End to New Farm.

BY CAR AND TAXI. ShoeString Car Rentals, 360 Nudgee Rd., Hendra, near the airport, rents from $29 per day. (☎3268 3334. Open M-Sa 7:30am-5pm, Su 7:30am-2pm.) **Letz Rent-A-Car,** 925 Ann St., Fortitude Valley (☎3852 1188), rents from $48 per day and does 21-day minimum one-ways to Sydney. The **RACQ,** 261 Queen St., in the GPO building provides 24hr. roadside assistance to members (☎131 905 24-hour roadside assistance ☎131 111. Overseas transfers are free). See **Queensland Transporation,** p. 287, for more information. For a **taxi,** try **Yellow Cab Company** (☎13 19 24) or **Black and White** (☎131 008); both operate 24hr.

BY FERRY. Brisbane's excellent ferry system makes good use of the Brisbane River, providing practical transport and cheap sightseeing tours. The new, sleek **CityCat** and its newborn **KittyKat** both run upstream to the University of Queensland and downstream to Bretts Wharf. North Quay near the Treasury Casino is the closest stop to the city center. The **City Ferry** operates around the city center and includes more stops than the City Cat (ferries run at least every 20-30min.). The **Crossriver** runs four routes connecting Brisbane's two banks, including downtown from the Holman St. to the Edward St. stops (every 15min. M-Su 5:30am-10:30pm). Schedules are posted at every dock and stop. Fares for all ferries are $1.80-3.80, depending on distance; Australian students get half-price concessions.

BY BIKE OR IN-LINE SKATES. In Brisbane City alone there are 350km of cycling paths; City Council publishes a pamphlet called *Brisbane Bicycle Maps.* You can also bike to sights like Mt. Coot-tha or Stradbroke Island. **Brisbane Bicycle,** 87 Albert St., carries a range of bikes. (☎3229 2433. $9 per hr., $20 per 24hr. Open M-Th, Sa 8:30am-5:30pm, F 8:30am-8pm, Su 10am-4pm.) **Skatebiz,** 101 Albert St., rents in-line skates. (☎3220 0157. 2hr. $11, 24hr. $27.50. Open M-Th 9am-5:30pm, F 9am-9pm, Sa 9am-4pm, Su 10am-4pm.)

PRACTICAL INFORMATION

Tourist Office: Brisbane Tourism Info Booth, (☎3229 5918) is in the middle of the Queen St. Mall, but they can only provide info on companies that are part of their association. Open M-Th 9am-5pm, F 9am-8pm, Sa 9am-4pm, Su 10am-4pm. The *Brisbane Tourism* guide is available at most tourist booths.

Budget Travel Offices: Flight Centre (☎13 16 00) has 11 offices and a guarantee to beat any quoted current price. **STA Travel,** 111 Adelaide St. (☎13 17 76, 3221 3722). Open M-F 9am-5:30pm, Sa 9am-3pm). **Backpackers Travel Centre,** 138 Albert St. (☎3221 2225). Open M-Th 9am-5:45pm, Sa 10am-4pm. **YHA Travel Centre,** 154 Roma St. (☎3236 1680). Open M-Tu, Th, F 8:30am-5pm, W 9am-5pm, Sa 9am-3pm.

Banks: Banks cluster on Boundary St. in South Brisbane Brunswick St. in the Valley, and Queen St. in the city. Most are open M-Th 9:30am-4pm, F 9:30am-5pm. Typically no charge for cash exchange, $5 for traveler's checks. **ATMs** are ubiquitous. **American Express,** 131 Elizabeth St. (☎3229 2729), is open M-F 9am-5:30pm, Sa 9am-noon.

Employment: Backpackers Employment Service (☎3236 4899; www.backpackersaustralia.com.au), has a desk on level 3 of the Transit Centre.

FROM BRISBANE TO:

DESTINATION	COMPANY	DURATION	PER DAY	PRICE
Adelaide	McCafferty's	30½hr.	1	$211
Airlie Beach	McCafferty's	18¼hr.	6	$137
	Premier	18¼hr.	1	$114
Bundaberg	McCafferty's	6-7½hr.	4	$55
	Premier	6-7¾hr.	7	$40
Byron Bay	Kirkland's	3½hr.	4 M-F, 2 Sa-Su	$24
	McCafferty's	3½hr.	7	$34
	Premier	3½hr.	4 M-F, 2 Sa-Su	$28
Cairns	McCafferty's	25-30hr.	7	$182
	Premier	25-30hr.	1	$165
Coolangatta	Kirkland's	2¼hr.	4 M-F, 2 Sa-Su	$14.50
	McCafferty's	2¼hr.	7	$17
	Premier	2¼hr.	3	$15
Hervey Bay	McCafferty's	5hr.	10	$41
	Premier	5hr.	1	$30
Lismore	Kirkland's	4½hr.	4 M-F, 2 Sa-Su	$33
	McCafferty's	4½hr.	1	$37
	Premier	4½hr.	3	$40
Mackay	McCafferty's	15-16hr.	7	$121
	Premier	15-16hr.	1	$101
Maroochydore	McCafferty's	2hr.	3	$18
	Premier	2hr.	1	$17
	Suncoast	2hr	9 M-F, 7 Sa-Su	$20.80
Melbourne	McCafferty's	24-28½hr.	2	$164
Mission Beach	McCafferty's	26hr.	4	$117
	Premier	26hr.	1	$156
Mooloolooba	Premier	2-3hr.	1	$17
	Suncoast	2-3hr.	9 M-F, 7 Sa-Su	$20.80
Noosa	McCafferty's	2-3hr.	6	$20
	Premier	2-3hr.	1	$17
	Suncoast	2-3hr.	9 M-F, 7 Sa-Su	$24
Rockhampton	McCafferty's	10½-14¼hr.	9	$79
	Premier	10-14hr.	1	$70
Surfers Paradise	Kirkland's	1¼-1½hr.	4 M-F, 2 Sa-Su	$14.50
	McCafferty's	1¼-1½hr.	8	$17
	Premier	1¼-1½hr.	3	$13
Sydney	McCafferty's	16-19hr.	6	$89
	Premier	16-19hr.	3	$76
Toowoomba	McCafferty's	2hr.	12	$19.50

Backpacking and Camping Equipment: Equipment stores line Albert St. between **Globetrekker,** 142 Albert St. (☎3221 4476). Open M-F 9am-6pm, Sa 9am-4:30pm, Su 10:30am-4:30pm. **Mountain Designs Australia,** 105 Albert St. (☎3221 6756). Open M-Th 9am-5pm, F 9am-9pm, Sa 9am-5pm, Su 10am-4:30pm. YHA discounts.

Bookstores: The Queen St. Mall area has many bookstores. **Bent Books** 205a Boundary St. (☎3846 5004; www.bentbooks.com.au) in the West End, has a broad collection of secondhand and new books.

Library: The **State Library** (☎3840 7666), in South Bank. Open M-Th 10am-8pm, F-Su 10am-5pm. Call ☎3840 7785 to book **free** 1hr. **Internet access.** The **John Oxley Library** (☎3840 7880) on level 4, is devoted to Queensland research and history, and holds historical exhibitions. Open Su-F 10am-5pm.

Public Markets: South Bank Markets (see **Sights,** p. 302). **Brunswick Markets,** Brunswick St., Fortitude Valley, is a hippie scene of second-hand items, clothes, and toys. Sa 9am-3pm. **Riverside Markets,** Eagle St. (☎0414 88 80 41), Su 8am-4pm.

Used Cars: Backpacker's Car Connection (☎3392 0137).

Emergency: ☎000. **Police,** ☎3364 6464.

Hospital: Travellers Medical Service, level 1, 245 Albert St. (☎3211 3611). Open M-F 7:30am-7pm, Sa 9am-5pm, Su 10am-4pm. **Brisbane Sexual Health Clinic,** 484 Adelaide St. (☎3227 8666, 3227 7091), offers **free testing.** Open M-Tu, F 9am-5pm, W 8am-noon, Th 9am-noon and night appointments.

Internet: Library (see above). Cheap in the Valley. **Central,** 269 Edward St. (☎3211 2966), across from the Palace. $2 per hr., $10 per week. Open daily 7am-late. **Emailplus,** 328 Upper Roma St. (☎3236 0433). $4.40 per hr. Open daily 9am-late. **Cafe Scene** (☎3216 1624), corner of Brunswick and Ann St. $3.30 per 30min.

Post Office: GPO, 261 Queen St. (☎3405 1434; Poste Restante 3405 1448). Half a block from the end of the mall. Open M-F 7am-6pm. Poste Restante until 5pm. For weekend mail, try level 2, Wintergarden Center (☎3405 1380). Open M-F 8:30am-5:30pm, Sa 9am-4pm, Su 10:30am-4pm. **Postal Code:** 4000; GPO code: 4001.

MEDIA AND PUBLICATIONS

Newspaper: *The Courier-Mail* (88¢).

Nightlife: *Time Off* and *Rave* Magazines (free). For info on gay and lesbian nightlife, check out *BrotherSister.*

Radio: Rock, Triple J 107.7FM or Triple M 104.5FM; News, 936AM; Tourist Info, 88FM.

ACCOMMODATIONS

Accommodations are clustered in four main areas of the city: the city center; South Brisbane and West End, near the riverside parklands, cultural and performance venues, and colorful Boundary St.; Fortitude Valley and New Farm, with cafes, art galleries, street festivals, and a funky night pulse; the Petrie Terrace area, close to the Transit Centre and Caxton St. party scene. Most of the accommodations listed have courtesy pickup/drop-off. Unless otherwise noted, check-out is 10am and key deposits are $10. Linen and cutlery are usually free with a deposit.

CITY CENTER

Palace Backpackers (☎3211 2433 or 1800 676 340), on the corner of Ann and Edward St. The former Salvation Army headquarters, this 7-level building is a backpacker landmark. The amazingly efficient staff checks in only backpackers up to the 350 person capacity. Near-nightly after-hour parties make for noisy halls. 3-story veranda, big kitchen, rockin' backpackers pub (see **Nightlife,** p. 306), Internet, roof-deck, and cafe (meals $3-8). Laundry. Reception 24hr. 7-9-bed dorms $17, weekly $112; 5-6 bed dorm $19; 4-bed dorms $20; singles $33; twins $48; doubles $45. VIP.

Explorers Inns, 63 Turbot St. (☎3211 3488 or 1800 623 288; explorer@powerup.com.au), on the corner of George St. Pleasant budget hotel with an affordable restaurant. Compact rooms have bath and TV. Nonsmoking. Reception M-F 24hr., Sa-Su until 10pm. Singles, doubles, twins $75; triples and quads $97.

Annie's Shandon Inn, 405 Upper Edward St., Spring Hill (☎3831 8684; fax 3831 3073). Like Grandma's house, complete with family snapshots, cozy beds, and pastels. Cold breakfast included. Kitchenette. Laundry $1.60. Reception 7am-9pm. Check-out 9am. Singles $44, with bath $55; twins and doubles $55/$66.

FORTITUDE VALLEY AND NEW FARM

Globetrekkers, 35 Balfour St., New Farm (☎3358 1251; www.globetrekkers.net.au), between Brunswick St. and Bowen Tce. Friendly, small 100-year-old house with lots of character. Pool. Unlimited Internet $2. Laundry. Women's Dorm. $18, weekly $98; singles $33, with bath $38; twins and doubles $40, with bath $44. Park your campervan in back and have access to the facilities for $10 per person. Reception 9am-9pm. Cash only. Book ahead. ISIC/NOMADS/VIP/YHA.

Bowen Terrace, 365 Bowen Tce., New Farm (☎3254 0458), on the corner of Barker St, which is off Brunswick St. Warm, welcoming colonial house. Only 16 beds, but worth trying to secure a room. Lounge, small kitchen, new game room, and large deck. Motel-like rooms with TV, fridge, and coffee machines. Singles $27.50; twins $36.30; doubles $44, with bath $52. Cash and travelers checks only.

Homestead, 57 Annie St., New Farm (☎/fax 3254 1609 or 1800 658 344). Giant murals and rooms with names like "Babes in the Woods" or "Great Expectations." Social atmosphere on quiet street. Free bus to airport, Transit Centre, and city. Planned trips, kitchen, garden, a shamrock-shaped pool, and free bike use. Key deposit $10. Reception daily 7am-7pm. Dorms $17; singles $35; twins and doubles $42. VIP/YHA.

Tourist Guest House, 555 Gregory Tce., Fortitude Valley (☎3252 4171 or 1800 800 589; tourist_guest_house@yahoo.com.au). Colonial style B&B with front porch. Traditional B&B rooms with TV, sink, and fridge. Dorm $20; singles $45, with bath $55; twins and doubles $55/$65; triples $65/$80.

PETRIE TERRACE

Yellow Submarine, 66 Quay St. (☎3211 3424). Painted bright yellow, this little house has a lot of character despite slightly tired rooms. Ken cooks at least one free dinner a week. Outdoor TV lounge and a new pool. Book ahead. Reception 7am-10pm. 6-bed dorms $18, weekly $100; 3-bed dorms $20/$105; doubles/twins $44/$250.

City Backpackers, 380 Upper Roma St (☎3211 3221 or 1800 062 572). 400m from the Transit Centre, next to YHA. Completely renovated with enormous kitchen and rooftop dining with fantastic views. Clean, comfortable rooms. Irish pub, **The Fiddler's Elbow,** has live music W and Su. Kitchen, Internet $2 per 35min. Laundry $2. Dorms $18; singles $35; twins and doubles $44. VIP/YHA.

Aussie Way, 34 Cricket St. (☎3369 0711). Pleasant 1872 colonial home offers a quiet escape from raucous Caxton St. Pool, Internet, TV lounge. Dorms $19; single $35; twins and doubles $44; twins weekly $105. ISIC/NOMADS/VIP/YHA. Cash only.

Brisbane City YHA, 392 Upper Roma St. (☎3236 1004; fax 3236 1947). Private, clean, and low-key, with a friendly staff. Perfect for couples or friends, not for socialites. Cafe reading loft. 6-bed dorms $17.50; 3-bed dorms $18.50; twins $44; doubles $48, with bath $66. Non-YHA add $3.50.

SOUTH BRISBANE

Somewhere to Stay, 45 Brighton Rd. (☎3844 6093 or 1800 812 398; reception@somewheretostay.com.au), on the corner of Franklin St. Large rooms with bath, some have gorgeous views. Pool, big kitchen, garden, and free bus to city. Internet $5 per hr. Check-out 9:30am. Reception 7am-10pm. 4-bed dorms $14-18; singles $23-28; doubles $35-51. NOMADS/VIP/YHA.

Brisbane Backpackers Resort, 110 Vulture St. (☎3844 9956 or 1800 626 452; fax 3844 9295), near the corner of Boundary St. Large rooms with bath, TV, fridge, some with balcony. Tennis court, swimming pool, spa, Internet, nightly movies, and cafe. Reception 24hr. Check-out 9:30am. 6-bed dorms $19, weekly $114; 4-bed dorms $20/$120; singles, twins, doubles $52/$325. Cheaper, basic accommodation in their building across the street $14 per person. ISIC/VIP/YHA.

FOOD

The West End has small, trendy sidewalk cafes and Mediterranean-style restaurants, particularly along Boundary St. and Hardgrave Rd. Chinatown in Fortitude Valley has lots of cheap Asian food, while trendier New Farm has more expensive eateries. The city center has a variety of options. Coles Express **supermarket** at the corner of Queen and Edward St. (Open M-Th, Sa 6am-9pm, F 6am-10pm, Su 9am-7pm.) For ice cream, try **Cold Rock,** with locations around Brisbane.

CITY CENTER

Govinda's Vegetarian Restaurant, upstairs at 99 Elizabeth St. (☎3210 0255). Hare Krishna owners only serve 1 meal per day (except F), but it's a $7 all-you-can-eat extravaganza with free entertainment. Juice bar mixes $2 lassies. Su $3 feast with chanting and dancing. Open M-Sa 11:30am-2:30pm, F also 5:30-8:30pm, Su 5-7pm.

Pane e Vino (☎3220 0044), corner of Charlotte and Albert St. As its name suggests this hip coffee bar also serves great panini ($9.90) and is blessed with a large selection of wine. Open daily 7:30am-late.

JoJo's (☎3221 2113), corner of Queen St. Mall and Albert St. Perched between chaotic Queen St. Mall and majestic skyscrapers, JoJo's attracts travelers, students, and businessmen to its three counters: grille, Thai, and Italian. Dishes are cooked to order for $10-27. Daily specials. Open M-F 9:30am-11:30pm, Sa-Su 11am-11:30pm.

WEST END AND SOUTH BANK

George's Seafood, 150 Boundary St. (☎3844 4100). A tiny seafood shop that will grill, batter, or crumb any fillet for $1 extra. Unbeatable deal: crumbed wild Barramundi fillet for $5.50. Open M-F 9:30am-7:30pm, Sa 8:30am-7:30pm, Su 10:30am-7:30pm.

Hwongs, 83A Mollison St. (☎3844 6701). Vegetarian options abound on Hwong's crowded menu of Vietnamese and Chinese favorites. Friendly service. Open daily 11am-3pm, 5pm-10pm; closed Su lunch.

Chantahn, 150 Boundary St. (☎3844 8808). This small cafe offers a Mediterranean menu of primarily Greek cuisine. Early bird dinner $5. Belly dancing and plate smashing F-Sa nights. BYO. Open daily 8am-2pm, 5pm-late.

Chez Laila, South Bank Parklands on the boardwalk (☎3846 3402). A Lebanese restaurant where "people eat to live longer." Outdoor deck overlooking the river and city skyline. The best Lebanese falafel for miles ($8). Open daily 8am-late.

Capt'n Snapper (☎3846 4036). Parklands off Tribune St. Delicious fresh seafood, steak, and a well-stocked all-you-can-eat salad bar. Open daily 11am-late.

NEW FARM

Himalayan Cafe, 640-642 Brunswick St. (☎3358 4015). Tibetan and Nepalese delicacies in an unnaturally oxygen-rich environment and warm atmosphere. The back room seats patrons on cushions. Diced goat, lightly spiced, cooked with pumpkin and potato $12. Vegetarian options. Open Tu-Su 5:30-10:30pm. Lunch F-Su 11am-3pm.

Moray Cafe (☎3254 1342), corner of Moray and Merthyr Rd. Quiet location near the river. Attitude without pretense. Hip, popular, half-outdoor cafe with bright colors, good music, and international, veggie-friendly fare. Best Caesar salad in Queensland, hands down ($13.50). Licensed. Kitchen closes at 10pm. Open daily 8:30am-late.

FORTITUDE VALLEY

Garuva, 174 Wickham St. (☎3216 0124). A fantastic dining experience. Enter via a narrow passage through several doors in rooms decorated with overhanging trees and full-length mirrors. Once in, sit on a cushioned rug as a white curtain is drawn around you. Meals from six nations, sweet potato and bean curry to shark $12.50. Book ahead. Open F noon-2pm, M-Sa 6pm-11pm.

Veg Out, 320 Brunswick St. (☎3852 2668). Mix and match veggie and vegan meals on the mall. Licensed. Open M-Th 8am-7pm, F-Sa 8am-midnight, Su 9am-5pm. Cash only.

King of Kings, 175 Wickham St. (☎3852 1889). Halfway between Brunswick St. and Chinatown. Waiters constantly bring trolleys filled with a variety of tasty yum cha dishes not even Superman could resist. Big plates cost $3, but the dishes are all designed to be shared. Open M-F 9:30am-3pm, Sa-Su 8:30am-3pm. Also open for dinner.

SIGHTS

CITY TOURS. One of the best deals is **City Sights,** an 1½hr. bus tour of cultural and historical attractions. Jump on and off the circuit bus and get unlimited access on public bus and ferry networks. Tickets can be purchased on the bus, from any customer service center, or at most tourist offices. *(Tours leave every 45min. daily 9am-3:45pm. $20, concessions $15.)* For a tour of the Brisbane River, the large **River Queen** paddlewheel boat departs daily from the Eagle St. Pier, with factual commentary of passing sights and accordion music. *(☎3221 1300. 1½hr. Lunch cruise $22, with buffet $35. Buffet dinner cruise $49-55. Book ahead.)* **Brisbane City Trips** offers several different city and river trips, including half-day *($42)* city highlight tours, an afternoon float upstream to Lone Pine Koala Sanctuary and Mt. Coot-tha *($46)*, or a night tour of Brisbane for $40. *(☎3830 4455. Children 40% off, concessions 10%.)*

CASTLEMAINE BREWERY. The womb of XXXX, self-proclaimed "Queensland's beer," is 5min. from Caxton St on Milton Rd. The 45min. walking tour ends (and your day really begins) with you, an hour, and four tall ones. Meet at the Castlemaine Sports Club, at the crest of Heusser Tce. behind the brewery. *(☎3361 7597. M-W 11am, 1:30, and 4pm; occasionally W 7:30pm. $7, W 7:30pm with BBQ $15. Book ahead.)*

CARLTON BREWHOUSE. Thirty minutes south of Brisbane are the brewers of VB, Foster's, and Carlton. The tour may be slightly dry, but the four beers at the end sure aren't. *(In Yatala. CoachTrans buses depart daily to the Gold Coast from Roma St. 9:15, 11:15am. ☎3826 5858. Tours 10am, noon, and 2pm. $7.50, concessions $5. Book ahead.)*

CITY HALL. Opened in 1930, it earned the epithet "Million Pound Town Hall" for its outrageous building cost. The recently restored **clock tower,** a landmark of the city skyline, stands 92m high with an **observation deck.** The **Brisbane City Gallery** inside hosts remarkable changing exhibits. *(☎3403 4048. Deck open M-F 10am-3pm, Sa 10am-2:30pm. Art Gallery open daily 10am-5pm. Free.)*

QUEENSLAND CULTURAL CENTRE. On the south side of Victoria Bridge, the Centre contains many of Brisbane's major artistic venues, including the art gallery, museum, performing arts complex, state library, and theater company. The **Queensland Art Gallery** has over 10,000 works, primarily Australian and Aboriginal. *(☎3840 7303. Open daily 10am-5pm. Free guided tours M-F 11am, 1, 2pm; Sa 11am, 2, 3pm; Su 11am, 1, 3pm. Free admission; special exhibitions $12.)* The **Queensland Museum** has dinosaur skeletons, whale models, and live samples of the largest species of cockroach. *(☎3840 7555. Open daily 9:30am-5pm. Free admission; special exhibitions $8-11.)*

POWERHOUSE CENTRE FOR LIVE ARTS. New Farm Park's Powerhouse is an alternative arts venue, housing performances, dining, and galleries. *(119 Lamington St., New Farm Park. ☎3358 8600; www.brisbanepowerhouse.org.)*

SCIENCENTRE. With over 170 hands-on exhibits, Sciencentre offers plenty for kids to play with and gives parents a sacred respite. *(110 George St. Between Mary and Charlotte St. ☎3220 0166. Open daily 10am-5pm. $8, concessions $6.)*

PARKS AND GARDENS

SOUTH BANK PARKLANDS. Built on the former World Expo '88 site, South Bank offers splendid views of the city, tree-lined and cafe-dotted boulevards, weekly markets, and a reminder of the relaxed Brizzy way. The **man-made lagoon**—with real sand beach, shallow and deep ends, and gorgeous night lighting—is ingenious. it reflects the young, laid-back attitude of Brizzy. *(Lifeguard on duty 9am-6pm.)* There's also a well-stocked **Maritime Museum** with wrecks and models. *(At the old South Brisbane Dry Dock, south end of the parklands. ☎3844 5361. Open daily 9:30am-4:30pm. Last entry 3:45pm. $5.50, concessions $4.40, kids $2.80, families $13.80.)* On the weekends, the park center houses a **crafts village** with crafts, psychics, clothes, and massages. *(Open F 5-10pm by lantern-light, Sa 11am-5pm, Su 9am-5pm.)* The Parklands also organizes free events, including car shows, fireworks, and weight lifting championships. The **Visitor Information Centre** is toward the Victoria Bridge end of the park, near the Tribune St entrance. *(Just across the river by Victoria Bridge. Accessible by foot, bus—orange B stop on Grey St, CityTrain—South Brisbane or Vulture St. Stations, or ferry—terminal stop South Bank. ☎3867 2051; www.south-bank.net.au. Open daily 9am-6pm, except F 9am-10pm. Although there are no official gates, South Bank is "open" 5am to midnight.)*

BOTANIC GARDENS. Visitors here stroll among palm groves, camellia gardens, and lily ponds. If you search hard, you can see large lizards strolling the ground as well. *(10min. walk from the city center. City Circle bus #333 stops at Albert or George St., near the entrance on Alice St. Free tours depart the rotunda near the Albert St. entrance.* ☎ *3403 0666. Open 24hr. Tours M-Sa 11am and 1pm.)*

MT. COOT-THA PARK BOTANIC GARDENS. Mt. Coot-tha: the other botanic garden. It includes a Japanese Garden, botanical library, tropical dome, lots of Scrub Turkey, and plenty of picnicking green. The park also has Queensland's first **Planetarium.** *(☎3403 2578. 45min. programs W-F 3:30 and 7:30pm, Sa 1:30, 3:30, and 7:30pm, Su 1:30 and 3:30pm. $10, concessions $8.50, children $6, families $28; free exhibit in the foyer.)* Hop back on the #471 bus to reach the **Mt. Coot-tha summit,** with a view of greater Brisbane that's spectacular at night. The casual Kuta Cafe (meals under $12) and the fancier and expensive Mt. Coot-tha Summit Restaurant (mains $25) both have panoramic views. *(☎3369 9922. Cafe open Su-Th 7am-11pm, F-Sa 7am-midnight.)* To walk back to the gardens, find the JC Slaughter Falls track from the summit, with an optional Aboriginal Art loop. At the bottom of the trail, exit the carpark to the right, and follow the road for 5min. *(7km from the city center. From Town Hall, bus #471 takes 12min. to the gardens, 20min. to the summit; 1 per hr. Gardens ☎3403 2535. Tours M-Sa 11am and 1pm from the information centre. Open daily Apr.-Aug. 8am-5pm; Sept.-Mar. 8am-5:30pm; gates close at 4pm.)*

BRISBANE FOREST PARK. You can picnic, camp, birdwatch, cycle, ride horses, and hike on the 28,500 hectares of The Gap. The *Information Guide* describes a number of walks and has an invaluable map. The park includes the Walkabout Creek Wildlife Center, a small wildlife center inhabited by wallabies, native birds, and various water creatures. *(60 Mt. Nebo Rd. Take the #385 bus from Albert St. ☎3300 4855. Open Su-F 9am-4:30pm, Sa 10am-4:30pm. $3.50, concessions $2.50.)*

WILDLIFE

QUEENSLAND

AUSTRALIA ZOO. The crocs get fed everyday at 1:30pm—a spectacle you won't forget, especially if crocodile hunter Steve Irwin is there. Cuddle a python, feed a kangaroo, and patiently follow the world's oldest Galapagos tortoise. *(In Beerwah. Catch the 7:50am "Crocodile Train" from the Transit Centre, and the zoo's bus will meet you at Beerwah; call ahead to arrange other bus pickups. ☎5494 1134; www.crocodilehunter.com. $16.50, concessions $13.50, child $8.50. Open 8:30am-4pm.)*

ALMA PARK ZOO. The zoo has walk-through kangaroo and deer enclosures, koalas, monkeys, and water buffalo, and allows feeding of some of the friendlier animals. Twenty acres of gardens with BBQs make it an ideal picnic spot. *(Alma Rd., Dakabin. 30min. north of Brisbane. Take the Caboolture train line to Dakabin—departs Roma St. several times daily. A courtesy bus will meet you. ☎3204 6566; www.almapark zoo.com.au. Open daily 9am-5pm. Hold a koala at noon and 2:30pm. $18.50, concessions $10.)*

LONE PINE KOALA SANCTUARY. The world's largest koala sanctuary has around 130 koalas, including 21-year-old Sarah, the oldest koala in the world. Emus, Tasmanian devils, raucous laughing kookaburras, and lots of hand-feedable 'roos try to raise the average activity level. Check out the wall of fame in the restaurant, where every famous entertainer imaginable has been photographed with one of the Pine's koalas. *(Take bus #430 from the Koala platform in the Myer Centre 7:30am-5pm, or take the Wildlife Cruise 19km upstream on the Brisbane River to the sanctuary. Cruise ☎3221 0300. Return $22, concession $18, children $12. Departs North Quay at 10am; free pickup from city accommodation. Sanctuary ☎3378 1366. $14.50, concessions $12, children $9.50.)*

AUSTRALIAN WOOLSHED. Sheep are the focus, but clever sheep dogs steal the show. Help out by feeding the baby farmyard animals or milking the cows. *(Samford Rd., Ferny Hills. 800m from the Ferny Grove railway station, 30min. north of Brisbane. ☎3872 1100; www.auswoolshed.com.au. $15.70, concessions $11.50, children $10.50.)*

ACTIVITIES

ROCK CLIMBING AND SKYDIVING. Join **Outdoor Pursuit** at Kangaroo cliffs, past Southbank towards the Peninsula, for **rock climbing** or **abseiling** every other Su 8:30am. *(☎3391 8776. $39. Book ahead.)* Think you need some practice first? Try **indoor climbing.** *(224 Barry Pde, Fortitude Valley. ☎3216 0492. $20.* A little higher up, **Brisbane Skydiving Centre** will show you the city at 200km per hr. from 12,500ft. *(☎1800 061 555. $220, including free pickup.)*

WATER ACTIVITIES. Brisbane has many waterways that are perfect for **canoeing.** Written guides to the popular **Oxley Creek** and **Boondall Wetlands** are available from libraries or tourist offices. For rentals, try **Goodtime Surf and Sail.** *(29 Ipswich Rd, Woolloongabba. ☎3391 8588. Canoes from $27.90 per day; kayaks from $20. Deposit $55. Open M-F 8:30am-5:30pm, Sa 8:30am-4pm, Su 10am-3pm.)* **ProDive** goes to the area's reefs and wrecks. *(☎3368 3766. Day trip 2 dives $118, gear $45. Gear and pickup included.)*

BUSHWALKING. **Rob's Rainforest Explorer Day Tours** takes you through Mt. Glorious and Samford Valley (M, Th; in **Brisbane Forest Park,** see above), Glasshouse Mountains and Kondalilla Falls (Tu, F; see p. 334), the Green Mountains of Lamington National Park (W; see p. 320), or on Saturday to Springbrook National Parks, see p. 321. *(☎3357 7061 or 0409 496 607. $58, including transport.)*

ENTERTAINMENT AND FESTIVALS

Brisbane has seemingly continuous festivals and diverse theater, arts, and music. Call the **Queensland Cultural Centre** (☎3840 7444) for a current schedule and info on discounts. The **Performing Arts Complex,** just across Victoria Bridge in South Brisbane, is composed of four theaters: the **Concert Hall** hosts symphony and chamber orchestras; the 2000-seat **Lyric Theatre** sponsors drama, musicals, ballet, and opera; the 850-seat **Optus Playhouse** shows drama; the 315-seat **Cremorne Theater** stages intimate productions—the theaters are gorgeous and reason enough to go. (☎136 246. $5 tours M-F noon from the ticket sales foyer. Book ahead.)

The **Queensland Conservatorium** (enquiries ☎3875 6264) presents university-affiliated and professional concerts. **Opera Queensland** (☎3875 3030) produces three productions a year. For contemporary Australian theater, **La Boite,** 57 Hale St., Petrie Tce. (☎3010 2600) offers six plays a year. The **Queensland Ballet** (☎3846 5266), the oldest dance group in the country, is renowned for its neoclassical style. The **Queensland Theatre Company** offers eight shows annually. (☎3840 7000. $20-45.) For tickets for all above theatres, call 136 246.

Escape the mainstream with Sunday afternoon jazz at **Jazzy Cat,** 56 Mollison St. (☎3846 2544; www.jazzycat.com.au. Su 1:30-4:30pm.) **The Bombshelter,** 200 Main St., Kangaroo Point (☎3391 2266), features great acts Sunday as well, 3-7pm.

The former state treasury building at the meeting of Queen, Elizabeth, and George St. continues to exploit money—but now for "fun"—in the enormous **Treasury Casino,** a Brisbane landmark with five restaurants, seven bars, over 100 gaming tables, and more than 1000 gaming machines. (☎3306 8888. Open 24hr.)

The **Entertainment Centre** (☎3265 8111), on Melaleuca Dr. in Boondall, is Brisbane's largest indoor complex for sports, concerts, and special events. By Citytrain, take the Shorncliffe line to Boondall Station (27min., departs at least every 30min.). The **"Gabba,"** Vulture and Stanley St., Woolloongabba (☎3292 3100 for cricket, 3335 1777 for footy), is Queensland's major **cricket** and **football** stadium. Take the bus to the station on the corner of Main and Stanley St. ($2.60) or the train to Vulture St. Tickets are available from Ticketmaster (☎13 61 22).

The **Brisbane River Festival** (☎3846 7444) celebrates spring the first week of September. The **Brisbane International Film Festival** (☎3220 0444; www.biff.com.au) is held annually the last week in July and the first week in August, with alternative and retrospective releases. The **Valley Fiesta** (☎3252 5999), in mid-July, features street festivals, local bands, and dance performances. Most exciting of all, the **Australia Day Cockroach Races** will be run on Jan. 26, 2002 at the Storybridge Hotel, 196 Main St., Kangaroo Point (☎3391 2266). Root your favorite bug on!

NIGHTLIFE

Brisbane nights roll by in sweaty nightclubs, noisy pubs, and smoky jazz lounges. Fortitude Valley is home to Brisbane's most exciting nighttime scene, with alternative bars and dance clubs, live music, and several gay establishments. Weekends are huge and weeknights sparse on Caxton St. in Petrie Terrace, with a decidedly more mainstream set. The city center is a big draw for backpackers, with its many Irish Pubs, drink specials, and rocking Thursday nights.

Be glad you don't have to keep track of the myriad live performances in Brisbane—the Wednesday or Saturday editions of the *Courier-Mail*, as well as free entertainment guides such as *Rave*, *Time Off*, *Scene*, and *BrotherSister* (a guide to gay and lesbian entertainment and clubs) all take care of this task. They are all at the record store **Rocking Horse,** 101 Adelaide St., and many local nightclubs.

CITY CENTER AND RIVERSIDE

Mary Street, 138 Mary St. (☎3221 1511). User-friendly but packed. 5 scenes, 1 cover ($7): squeeze your way past a young crowd to the grunge stage, pool room, acoustic den, beer garden, or stylish lounge. Open Th-Sa 5pm-5am.

Victory Hotel, 127 Edward St., corner of Charlotte St. (☎3221 0444). This classic Aussie pub, featuring a beer garden, heaps of bars, and a nightclub, might be the busiest in all Queensland. W-Su live bands. Th 2 for 1 drinks. W-Su Happy Hour 7pm-9pm. Open M-Tu 10am-10pm, W 10am-1am, Th-Sa 10am-3am, Su 11am-3am.

Downunder Bar, under the Palace Backpackers (☎3211 9277). Whether you like it or not, it's Brizzy's backpacker central. Have your hostel key or student card ready (only backpackers and students are welcome) and your international mojo working. Dinners $8. Food served noon-2:30pm and 6-9pm. Dance every day until 3am.

Friday's, 123 Eagle St., Riverside Centre (☎3832 2122). A young crowd gets classy at this giant riverfront hangout. The maze of rooms offers eclectic entertainment–dance music, modern tunes, and live music. Th-Su live bands; Th $1.50 drinks 8pm-midnight. Th $6 cover, Sa $8. Open Su-M 10:30am-late, Tu-Sa 10am-5am.

QUEENSLAND

FORTITUDE VALLEY

The Empire Hotel, 339 Brunswick St. (☎3852 1216), corner of Ann St. The true one-stop party venue in town. **The Empire,** downstairs, supplies a hard techno beat and sci-fi decor. Open daily until 5am. **The Wonder Bar,** upstairs, satisfies a late-nighter of any breed. To the left, comfy couches and alternative tunes; to the right, fresh and funky chemical beats. Open M-F 10am-5am. Sa noon-5am. Su 5pm-3am. Cover $7.

Ja-Ja's Lounge, 29 Mclachlan St. (☎3852 1199). Cruisy new club complete with comfy couches, cinema, and beautiful split level hardwood dance floor. Complete with luscious lounges in the loos. Open Tu-Th and Su 9pm-5am, F-Sa 5pm-5am.

Ric's, 323 Brunswick St. Mall (☎3854 1772). Acoustically and electronically eclectic: this hip hangout with outdoor seating, live music, and an upstairs techno bar is always packed. Sa-Su live bands. Open Su-Th 11am-1am, Sa-Su 11am-5am.

The Zoo, 711 Ann St. (☎3354 1381). A converted warehouse flowing with alternative and indie bands. Cover $5-20. Open W-Su 8:30pm-2am. Cash only.

The Beat, 677 Ann St. (☎3852 2661). Other clubs come and go, but the Beat goes on, turning 23 this year. The techno beat is straightforward, but the scene is anything but. Th dollar drinks till midnight. Shows daily. Cover $6.

Hotel Wickham, 308 Wickham St. (☎3852 1301). A gay and lesbian pub that turns into big dance party on weekend nights. Open Su-Th 10am-3am, F-Sa 10am-5am.

PETRIE TERRACE

The Paddo, 186 Given Tce. (☎3369 0044). Restaurant **Fibber McGees** has fantastic deals. M $5 steaks; Tu, Th 2-for-1. F-Sa bands. **Saloon Bar** next door has live music Th-Sa and as many cowboy hats as specials. Open Su-Th noon-2am, F-Sa noon-3am.

THAT'S WHAT IT'S ALL ABOUT? Pokies. What are they and why can't you seem to escape from their shadows? Pokies machines turn Australia into one big Casino. Whether it be in the smallest bush hamlet or the largest city, every pub and sports club on this continent has a room full of these machines. They patiently wait to take hard-earned gold coins and more from patrons, who also wait usually just as patiently, though in vain, for the big payoff. Methinks the money's wasted better on VB.

Hotel LA, 68 Petrie Tce. (☎3368 2560). On the corner of Caxton St. A tad upscale with plenty of social climbers, but the only place with a weekday crowd. Tu and Th 2-for-1 on drinks and meals 6pm-10pm. Open daily 7am-5am.

O'Leary's, 25 Caxton St. (☎3368 1933). This sleek English pub offers a log fire for the winter and a beer garden for the summer. Open Su-Th 5pm-midnight, F-Sa 5pm-2am.

Transcontinental Hotel, 482 George St. (☎3236 1366). The Trans spills deals including 2 for 1 pots and spirits on Tu. Open M-Tu 9am-midnight, W and Su 9am-3am, Th-Sa 9am-4am. Smart/Casual dress.

SPRING HILL

Alliance Tavern, 320 Boundary St. (☎3832 7355). On the corner of Boundary and Leichhardt St. A standard Aussie pub with pool tables and DJs spinning Top-40 dance music. Bar open daily 8am-2am, nightclub W-Su 9pm-2am. Nightly drink specials.

Options, 18 Little Edward St. (☎3831 4214). A mixed scene with dance floors and live entertainment; particularly good F-Sa. F-Sa cover after 10pm. Open F-Sa 8pm-5am.

MORETON BAY AND ISLANDS

With the Gold Coast to the south and the Sunshine Coast to the north, one would think, following the coastal logic (e=m (sea)^2), that Moreton Bay would be filled with travelers. Instead, Brisbane, inexplicably built inland, draws most journeyers away from one of the most spectacular areas in the world. Don't let this happen to you. The forest of masts on Manly's marina promises smooth sailing. Here, at the mouth of the Brisbane River, a comfortable culture thrives in perpetual slow-motion. Across the bay, North Stradbroke Island offers wonderful diving, surfing, whale watching, and swimming. Although this area lacks pre-packaged fun, the natural beauty of Moreton Bay is worth self-motivating.

NORTH STRADBROKE ISLAND ☎07

A fierce cyclone in 1896 cleanly split the land mass once called Stradbroke Island (20km south of Brisbane). While South Stradbroke (see p. 319) has remained relatively uninhabited, its northern neighbor, separated by a 200m channel, is now home to 3000 people. With miles of sandy white surf beaches, famous blue inland lakes, and excellent dive sites, "Straddie" is an ideal step off the beaten path.

TRANSPORTATION. Despite its apparent isolation, North Stradbroke can be easily reached from Brisbane by public transportation. Take **Citytrain** to Cleveland (usually every 30min., $3.70). From Cleveland, the courtesy bus **"Bessie"** runs from the train station to meet the **Stradbroke Flyer** ferry, which departs for One Mile Jetty in Dunwich. (☎3286 1964. 30min., 8-9 per day, 6:30am-6:30pm. Return $12.) Alternately, **Stradbroke Ferries** provides a bus (80¢) to its **Water Taxi** service. (☎3286 2666. 30min.; 10-12 per day, 6am-6pm; return $11, students $10.) Take the Vehicular Ferry only if you have a car. (1hr.; 11-14 per day; return $84 for the car and as many people as can fit in it. Book ahead.) **Island Transport Services** also serves a vehicular ferry. (☎3829 0008. $82 per car.) The **North Stradbroke Island Bus Service** runs between Point Lookout, Amity, and Dunwich. (☎3409 7151. 14 per day; M-Su 7:15am-7pm. Return $8.60.) Most **car rental** companies on the mainland will not rent vehicles to Stradbroke travelers due to salt corrosion, though a few will rent 4WD vehicles.

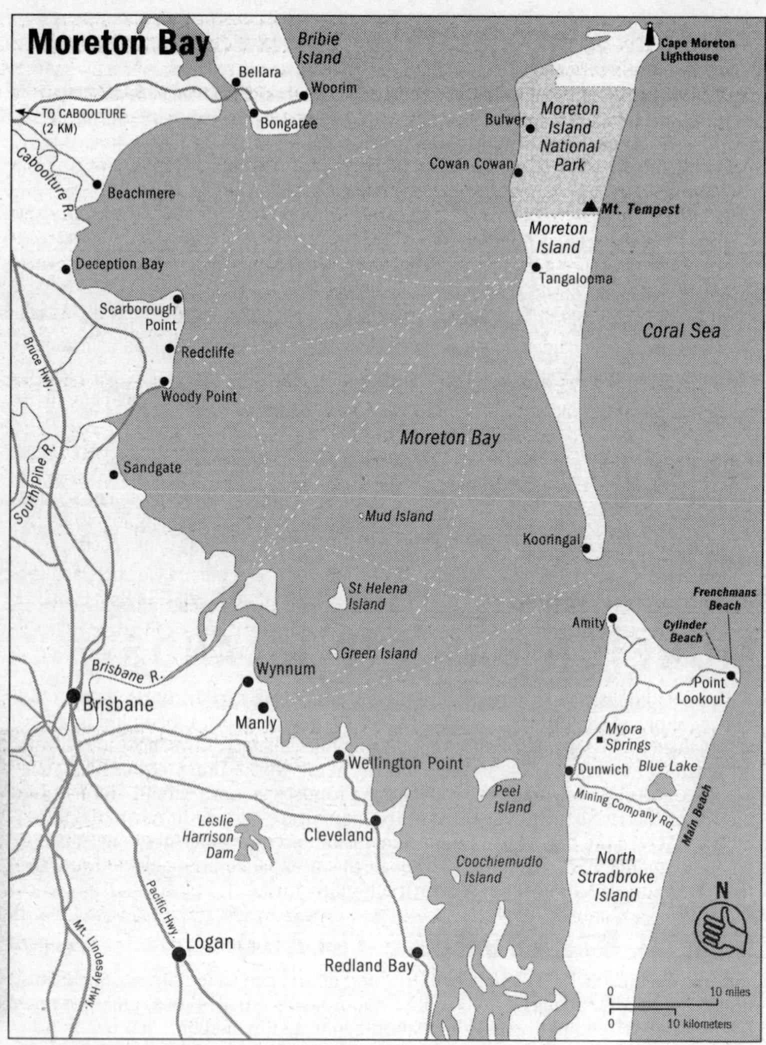

ORIENTATION AND PRACTICAL INFORMATION. North Stradbroke Island has three distinct townships: residential **Dunwich,** the ferry drop off point; **Amity Point,** north of Dunwich, with calm beaches and great fishing; **Point Lookout,** 22km northeast of Dunwich, with most accommodations. **East Coast Rd.** is the main road connecting Dunwich and Point Lookout; its name changes to Mooloomba Rd. near the end. The middle of the island consists of lakes, swamps, national park land, and habitat reserves, while sadly much of the southern end consists of sand mining operations. The **tourist office** books tours and manages the campgrounds; it's the yellow building at the base of the Dunwich green. (☎3409 9555; fax 3409 9789. Open M-F 8:30am-5pm, Sa-Su 8:30am-3pm.) Although there's **no bank** on the island, there is an **ATM** in Dunwich. **Internet** is available at the two hostels. **Police:** ☎3409 9020. **Hospital:** ☎3409 9059.

ACCOMMODATIONS. Two hostels in Point Lookout and seven **campsites,** two in Dunwich, two in Amity, and three in Point Lookout, serve the island. Camping is permitted on the rest of the island at least 11km from the causeway (shore camping permit $3.80; site $6 per person per night, powered $9.50). Make bookings through the tourist office.

North Stradbroke Island Guesthouse, soon-to-be **Stadbroke Island Backpackers** on the left of the entrance to the Point Lookout area and close to Home Beach, has $8 transportation from Brisbane and an attached dive center. (☎3409 8888. Key deposit $10. Dorms $20; doubles $48. VIP/YHA.) **The Stradbroke Island Hostel,** 76 Mooloomba Rd, is halfway between the Guesthouse and the end of Point Lookout, on the left just past Endeavor Rd. It has a relaxed atmosphere and a funky common room where guests gather. (☎3409 8679; straddiehostel@hotmail.com. Dorms $16, weekly $84; doubles $38/$210.) **Stradbroke Island Tourist Park,** on the road to Point Lookout, is close to the beach. (☎3409 8127; fax 3409 8566; ladbrooke@ecn.net.au. Reception 8am-5pm, Su 8am-3pm. Prices up considerably during peak. Sites for 2 $13.20; powered $17.60; cabins for 2 $55, for 7 $88.

FOOD AND ENTERTAINMENT. Most food is in Point Lookout, clustered in the **Lookout Shopping Village** and **Centre Point Shopping Centre.** At the top of the hill towards Point Lookout, **Straddie Hotel Pub** (☎3409 8188) has a brasserie with mains for around $19 and specials for less. With outdoor pool tables and a bar, it's the local hangout and gets packed on weekends. (Food served 7:30-9:30am, noon-2pm, 6-8pm.) For **groceries,** try Bob's 727 Foodmarket in Centrepoint Shopping Village, Point Lookout. (☎3409 8271. Open 7am-9pm.) Food on the island is not cheap, so bringing food is a good idea.

SIGHTS AND ACTIVITIES. The island is known for its **scuba diving. Stradbroke Island Scuba Center,** below the Guesthouse, has daily trips to 15 sites. (☎3409 8888. Single dive $80; double $116; 4-day PADI $350; snorkeling $44, including boat trip and gear.) **Stradbroke Island Tours** (☎3409 8051) will show you the island highlights in half a day for only $30. **Straddie Adventures** offers popular adventure tours. (☎3409 8414 or 0417 741 963 www.straddieadventures.com.au. Sandboarding $25; sea kayaking and snorkeling $35; half-day 4WD tour $55. VIP.)

The easiest and cheapest thing to do on North Stradbroke Island is walk—miles of unspoiled beaches and seemingly unexplored bush will keep a spirited traveler busy for days. Heading toward the end of Point Lookout on the left is a "Beach Access" sign for **Frenchman's Beach,** a convenient starting point for any beach walk. Farther up, near the RSL Club, lies the entrance to the **Gorge Walk,** a 15min. stroll past rocky headlands and gorges, white sand beaches, and blue waters. This obligatory walk is famous for **whale-watching** June-Sept. and dolphins, turtles, and manta rays year-round. The Gorge Walk also passes the **Blowhole,** where crashing waves are channeled up a narrow gorge and transformed into fountains of spray. The swimming **lagoon,** 4.5km along the beach, is a lovely day hike or picnic spot. **Main Beach** stretches 32km, drawing **surfers** with some of Queensland's best waves during early summer's northerly winds. **Cylinder Beach,** which runs in front of the Stradbroke Hotel, is more family-oriented, but good breaks can be found.

On hot summer days, **Myora Springs,** 4km along East Coast Rd. from Dunwich toward Point Lookout, is a refreshing place to cool off. The aptly named **Blue Lake** is a lovely freshwater spot that's part of **Blue Lake National Park.** Drive 8km along Tazi Rd. from Dunwich and follow the signs (regular cars must stop 2.7km away and walk the rest, while 4WD vehicles can drive almost all the way, following a sand track). To tour the beaches with your own 4WD, buy an access permit from the tourist office or at most campsites ($7 for 48hr., $12 per week).

MANLY ☎07

Manly is a content harborside village where there seem to be more boats than people. A quick trip from Brisbane and near most ferry services, Manly is the perfect accommodations base for exploring the nearby islands as well as a quiet space to return to after a day fishing, sailing, or scuba diving. The main street leads to a jam-packed small craft harbor where you don't have to be the manliest to anchor.

TRANSPORTATION AND PRACTICAL INFORMATION. From Brisbane, take Citytrain to the Manly stop on the Cleveland line (35-40min. from Roma St., 5am-11:54pm; at least every 30min. daily; $2.60). The **Tourist Information Centre,** 43A Cambridge Pde., is across from the Manly Hotel. (☎3348 3524. Open daily 10am-3pm.) There is **Internet** at Go Video, 11 Cambridge Pde. (☎3396 0554. $2.50 per hr. Open daily 10am-9pm.

ACCOMMODATIONS AND FOOD. **Moreton Bay Lodge,** 45 Cambridge Pde., has the best backpacker-style lodging on the Bay. It's a quiet, friendly spot with spacious rooms, TV, kitchen, spotless bathrooms, and helpful owners. (☎3396 3020. Airport and train pickup. Free bike use. Key deposit $20. Dorms $14, weekly $91; singles $30, with bath $35; doubles $40/$50; triples $50/$60. VIP.) A neat symmetry divides the hostel from the casual but lovely **Bay Window Cafe and Bar,** where guests get a 10% discount. **Manly Hotel,** 54 Cambridge Pde., is a newly remodeled favorite of businessmen. The hotel has a bar and a restaurant that serves three meals daily. (☎3249 5999; fax 3893 1248. W karaoke; F bands. Singles $38.50-$77; doubles $49.50-$88.) A **grocery** store is in the Shopping Centre (☎3396 1980. Open M-Sa 7am-7:30pm, Su 7am-7pm.)

SIGHTS AND ACTIVITIES. A brisk 20min. walk along the Esplanade from the harbor leads to the center of a nearby town, **Wynnum by the Bay.** Strolling farther, past the end of the harborwalk and through the soccer fields, leads to the **Wynnum Mangrove Boardwalk,** a 500m walk guided by informative signs. The mangroves grow in dense concentration, and it's possible to see clearly their pneumatophores (specialized "breathing roots") protruding through the mud in small clumps. On the Esplanade in Wynnum is a huge **tidal pool** perfect for a dip. Parks with changing rooms and BBQs run along the Esplanade.

If sailing floats your boat, book a trip on **Solo,** a famous Australian ocean racing yacht. A daytrip includes fast sailing around Moreton Bay, lunch, snorkeling, swimming, and either a stop at Peel Island for its isolated beaches and water-tubing, or on Moreton Island for sand tobogganing. Solo also offers a moonlight sail from 6-11pm, including a full dinner. (☎3348 6100. Th, Sa-Su. Daytrip $85. Moonlight $75. NOMADS/VIP discounts.) **Manly Eco Cruises** offers 50min. tours around Moreton Bay from Manly. (☎3396 9400. Sa-Su 11am, noon, 1, 2, 3pm. $13, students $11.) For free sailing, show up at the **Royal Queensland Yacht Club** for the friendly **WAGS** (Wednesday Afternoon Gentleman's Sailing) races; the winner gets a bottle of rum. Yacht owners are always looking for temporary crew; if you are a beginner, they may teach you. (☎3396 8666. W noon. Women welcome.)

MORETON ISLAND ☎07

Moreton, not usually considered a tourist destination, is a haven for the adventurous. The **Tangalooma Wrecks,** 14 old dredges sunk between 1964 and 1984, are a great diving or snorkeling destination. The striking **Big Sandhills** provide an ideal opportunity for sandboarding. Around the headland is a walking track with whale sightings and outstanding panoramas including, the **Cape Moreton lighthouse.** Hiking trails lead to the top of **Mt. Tempest,** the world's highest sand mountain.

Civilization on the island is centered around the **Tangalooma Resort** (☎1300 652 250), which offers day cruises with 9am pickup from Brisbane's Roma St. Transit Centre; return departs the resort at 3:30pm ($35, children $18, family of 4, $90). The resort operates tours of the island, the most popular being the Blue Lagoon ($32) and a desert tour ($16) which features sand tobogganing. **Gibren Expeditions** gives two- and three-day 4WD camping tours of the island that are nothing short of spectacular.(☎1300 559 355. 2-day tour $189, 3-day $289, add $20 for the ferry.) **Dolphin Wild Island Cruises** sends a power catamaran from the mainland for a daytrip full of wrecks, dolphins, and sand tobogganing. (☎5497 5628. $89, children $44. Half-day Feb.-Aug. $45, $29.) Charter the 10-person **Moreton Island Taxi Service** 4WD or join them for a full-day tour of the island's highlights. (☎3408 2661. Charter around $80 roundtrip to the lighthouse. Tour F-M. $79, concessions $60.)

OTHER ISLANDS IN MORETON BAY

Moreton Bay is dotted with more than 300 islands perfect for daytripping. Cheap accommodation other than camping is sparse, but a day is plenty to sample the islands' offerings: pristine beaches, snorkeling, and an occasional whale sighting.

COOCHIEMUDLO ISLAND. A popular getaway for locals, Coochiemudlo entices with shops, restaurants, and occasional crafts markets. **Coochiemudlo Island Ferry Service** runs a vehicular ferry from Victoria Point Jetty. (☎3820 7227. 12 per day. Return $33, pedestrians $2, children $1.) **Bay Islands Taxi Service** also services Coochie from Victoria Point (☎3409 1145. $2, kids $1). The **Coochie Bus Service** offers a 30min. tour of the island. (☎0427 113 686. $5.50, children $2.)

BRIBIE ISLAND. At the northern end of Moreton Bay, Bribie is the only island accessible by car. From Brisbane, go 45km north to Caboolture, then 19km east. The **tourist office** is just over the bridge from the mainland. (☎3408 9026. Open M-F 9am-4pm, Sa-Su 9am-noon.) Bribie is separated from the mainland by **Pumicestone Passage,** a marine park teeming with mangroves, more than 350 species of birds, sea cows, turtles, and dolphins. Vehicles give easy access to great fishing on the mainland side of the channel and surfing on the east.

ST. HELENA ISLAND. Formerly the Alcatraz of Australia, St. Helena now perhaps offers less options to get ashore. In its glory days, it was the first prison in Queensland and the only commercially viable prison in the world. The only way to visit the island is with the **Cat-o'-Nine-Tails** vessel, which offers day and night tours to the island—actors put on a show of St. Helena's colorful past and turn tourists into prisoners. Cruises run from **Manly.** (☎3396 3994. $59, concessions $52, children $32. Night tour $65. Evening "ghost tour" is not for children.)

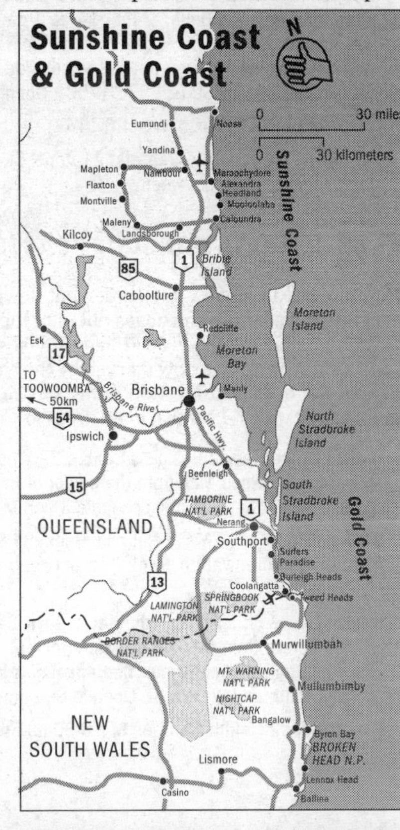

GOLD COAST

Gorgeous beaches, thumping nightclubs, excellent theme parks, and plenty of accommodations make the Gold Coast Australia's premier holiday destination. The region's permanent population of 390,000 triples to 1.2 million every summer as Australian and foreign tourists flock to the sun, sand, and parties. The term "Gold Coast" has a few possible origins: tourist officials say it's for the stretches of golden sand beaches, but cynics point to high rises and tacky tinsel glitter primarily found in Surfers Paradise. Around Surfers, natural attractions abound—to the south, outstanding point breaks have created some of the world's best surfing beaches and to the north South Stradbroke Island offers a peaceful escape from the bustling coast. A trip to the "Green behind the Gold," the less-touristed but rewarding Gold Coast Hinterland, will complement time spent on the coast.

COOLANGATTA AND TWEED HEADS ☎07

Evidently, the name Surfer's Paradise is taken. However, the outstanding point breaks off the twin towns Coolangatta, QLD and Tweed Heads, NSW have created some of the best surfing in Australia, if not the world. With three surfing beaches and a huge variety of conditions on any given day, this area is the true surfer's paradise. Summer brings a young crowd of surfers and backpackers as well as families on holiday, but anyway you cut it, the atmosphere is always relaxed. With less neon, fewer skyscrapers, and better breaks and beaches, Coolie and Tweed Heads is the perfect place for a break from the up-tempo Gold Coast scene. As locals like to say, they're close enough to Surfer's and far enough away. The Tweed-Coolangatta border is only really marked by discrepancies in daylight savings time, most notably at New Year's Eve, when eager partygoers and champagne lovers run across the street and ring in the new year twice.

TRANSPORTATION

Buses: Coach Trans (☎13 12 30), runs to **Brisbane** (2¼hr., about every hr. 5:15am-4pm, $15) via **Surfer's Paradise** (45min., $4). Greyhound, McCafferty's, and Pioneer Motor Services all stop in town on their service to **Brisbane** (2hr., 8 per day, $12-24) and **Sydney** (15hr., 10 per day, $71). Suncoast Pacific's (☎5531 6000) runs to **Noosa** (4¾hr. daily 3:15pm, $30) via **Maroochy** (4hr.). Kirklands runs 2-4 buses per day to **Brisbane** (1½hr., $13) and **Byron Bay** (1½hr., $15). Surfside buslines (☎13 12 30) runs the best **public transportation** within the Gold Coast. Routes 1 and 1A run from Kingscliff NSW up to Paradise Point, including, of course, a stop at Surfer's Paradise (45min., every 10-60min., 24hr., $4); a 1-day unlimited travel pass is $10, or buy sector tickets. Connections will get you to Gold Coast theme parks, and if you buy your admission ticket from the driver, the bus ride is free. Purchase tickets at **Golden Gateway Travel,** 29 Bay St. (☎5536 1700). Open M-F 7:30am-5:30pm, Sa 7:30am-3pm.

Taxi: Tweed Heads Taxis (☎5536 1144).

Car Rental: Tweed Auto Rentals, 21 Appel St., Kirra (☎5536 8000 or 1800 819 051). Rentals from $140 per week.

QUEENSLAND

ORIENTATION AND PRACTICAL INFORMATION

The state border divides the settlement down the length of **Dixon St.** which bends right into **Boundary St.** and heads out onto the rounded peninsula. At the end of the peninsula is the infamous **Point Danger,** whose cliffs were responsible for Captain Cook's shipwreck. It is now marked by the world's first laser lighthouse and a 270° view of the ocean. At the **Twin Towns Service Club,** Boundary St. meets **Griffith St.** and **Wharf St.,** the respective main drags of Coolangatta and Tweed Heads

Tourist Office: Tweed Business Center, 39 Wharf St. (☎5536 4244 or 1800 674 414). Towards the Tweed Mall from the corner of Bay and Wharf St. Their free *Tweed-Coolangatta Visitors Guide* is indispensable. Open M-F 9am-5pm.

Banks: Find 24hr. **ATMs** at National Bank, 84-88 Griffith St., at the corner of Warner St., and at Commonwealth Bank in the Tweed Mall. Both Open M-Th 9:30am-4pm, F 9:30am-5pm.

Internet Access: Food and the net at **Java Bay Internet Cafe,** 69 Wharf St. (☎5599 3232) across from the Tweeds Mall. Open M, W, F 8am-6pm, Tu and Th 8am-5:30pm, Sa 9am-3pm. $5 per 30min. **Coolangatta Internet Cafe** (☎5599 2001) is on the corner of Griffith and Warner St. Open M-Sa 9am-7pm, Su noon-4pm. $4 per 30min.

Post Office: 2 Griffith St. Open M-F 8:30am-5pm. **Postal code:** 2485.

ACCOMMODATIONS

There are plenty of beds here, but true budget accommodation is limited; make sure to book in advance in the high season.

Sunset Strip Budget Resort, 199 Boundary St. (☎5599 5517; www.sunsetstrip.com). Close to town and the best breaks, the Sunset Strip has excellent facilities including an enormous kitchen, pool, and lounge areas. Guests of all ages intermingle happily. Large, yet incredibly cozy and personal. Th night $6 BBQ in summer. Reception 7am-11pm. Singles $35; twins, doubles, triples $22.50 per person; quads $20 per person.

Coolangatta YHA, 230 Coolangatta Rd., Billinga (☎5536 7644), near the airport, 3km north of Coolie; look for the huge murals. Features kitchen, laundry, game room, BBQ, TV lounge, pool, Internet access ($2 per 20min.), bikes with surfboard racks, daily drop off and pickup at the town center, and the best waves. Courtesy pickup from bus stop with advance notice. Breakfast included. Dorms $20, $110 per week including 5 dinners; singles $35; doubles $44. Non-YHA members $3 more.

Kirra Beach Hotel (☎5536 3311), on the corner of Miles St. and Marine Pde. It may be around Kirra Point from Coolangatta, but its clean, bright rooms are a stone's throw from some of the world's most perfect barrel waves. Singles $33; doubles $44-55.

Kirra Beach Tourist Park, Charlotte St., Kirra (☎5581 7744). As you come in to town from the north, stay straight on Coolangatta Rd.; Charlotte St. is the first on the right. Great facilities, laundry, pool, TV room, jungle gym for the kids. Linen $6.50. Office open 7:30am-7pm. Sites for 2 $17-24; spacious cabin for 4 $70, peak $100.

FOOD AND NIGHTLIFE

Little Malaya Restaurant, 52 Marine Pde, has a tasty menu, which includes many vegetarian options for around $10. (☎5536 2690. Open noon-2pm and 5:30-10pm. AmEx/DC/MC/V.) The **Rainbow Bay Surf Club,** 2 Snapper Rocks, has an incredible view overlooking Rainbow Bay. Family oriented and packed in the summer, they serve lunch ($6.50-10), dinner ($12), and drinks. (☎36 37 36. Open 11:30am-2pm, 5:30-8pm.) Cruise over to **Portuguese Hot Chicks,** 91 Griffith near Warner St., for a late night chicken burger ($3.50) and chips. No promise of hot, Portuguese women. (☎5536 6597. M-W 10am-9pm, Th 10am-10pm, F 10am-late, Sa 8am-late, Su 8am-9pm.) Coles 24hr. **supermarket** is in Tweeds Mall on Wharf St. and there is a 24hr. convenience store on Griffith St.

The pink, spaceship-like **Twin Towns Service Club** (☎5536 2277) at Griffith and Wharf St. has tons of slot machines, cheap food and booze, live entertainment and free Monday night movies. For a younger crowd and a longer night, head to **Calypso,** at 97 Griffith St., with its video wall, plush seating, and live music Th-Su. Free cocktails for girls, Th 6-8pm and Su 4-6pm (☎5599 2677. Open daily 10am-12:30am.) Dance at the **Balcony Beach Club** on Marine Pde. with its chic nightclub feel. (Open Th-Su 8pm-3am.) Downstairs, the **Coolangatta Hotel** has live music Tu-Su, with karaoke Sunday afternoons and cover bands the rest of the week. (Open Sa-Th 9am-midnight, F 9am-2am.)

If you yearn for more, try **The Sands** on McLean St., which features bands F-Sa. (☎5536 3066. Open late.) If that's still not enough action, **Surfer's** is a quick bus away on Surfside buslines (45min.; runs 24hr.; $4; see **Orientation and Practical Information,** p. 312). Disco and bowling combine in a medley of flying pins, driving beats and stylish shoes at **Cosmic Rock 'n' Bowl** F-Sa evenings at the Coolangatta-Tweed **Tenpin** (☎5536 1606), across from the Tweed Mall.

SIGHTS AND ACTIVITIES

Tweed Heads-Coolangatta's greatest attractions are the beaches that line its perimeter. **Rainbow Bay** and **Coolangatta Beach,** off of Marine Pde, have the safest swimming on the Gold Coast and are thus family-oriented. **Flagstaff** and **Duranbah Beaches** lie to the southeast; the latter is famous among surfers for its fast waves. The three point breaks, **Kirra, Snapper Rocks,** and **Greenmount,** are some of the best in the world. Surfers are welcoming and surf shops are on every corner. **Kirra Surf,** located where Coolangatta Rd. meets Musgrave St., is a landmark surfshop in the area. You can find board rentals at **Pipedreams** on Griffith St. (Open M-Sa 9am-5pm, Su 10am-3pm.) For a surfing lesson, call Dennis at **Walkin' on Water**. He'll provide all equipment and get you standing in no time. (☎5534 1886; www.walkinonwater.com. Lessons from $25.)

The walkway that begins to the left of Point Danger, facing the ocean, and continuing to Greenmount, is beautiful with lush greenery on one side, and sand and sea on the other. You'll trip over kangaroos, emus, and gorgeous exotic birds at the fabulous **Currumbin Wildlife Sanctuary,** 7km north along the Pacific Hwy., a Surfside bus stop. See the lorikeet feedings (daily 8am and 4pm), but be sure to duck. (☎5534 1266. Open daily 8am-5pm.) For another pretty view, walk up to the **lookout** on Razorback, via Wharf and Florence St., to view Mt. Warning and some of the world's most special sub-tropical rainforests.

Tweed Endeavor Cruises leads terrific river and rainforest cruises on a 150-person double-decker vessel. The 1½hr. tour is fairly uneventful, but the 4½hr. tour is very worthwhile. (☎5536 8800. 1½hr. cruise W and Su $24, concessions $22, kids $12. 4½hr. with BBQ lunch M, W, F-Su $49, concessions $46. 4½hr. with seafood lunch Tu and Th $58/$54.)

SURFERS PARADISE ☎07

Though Adam and Eve might have packed up and left, today's partygoers pluck the proverbial apple of this Eden night after long, dance-filled night. Surfers, partyers, and families may have replaced Adam and Eve, and concrete and neon may have covered the Garden, but in Surfers Paradise, there's still plenty of bare skin, no hint of embarrassment, and the apple is near-impossible to resist. Narrow urban strips, packed with storefronts, cafes, and other amusements, hug miles of gorgeous beachside. Though towering hotels shade the very beaches that caused their creation, Surfers Paradise is on nearly every backpacker's itinerary. Why? They come for the thundering nightlife, techno clubs throbbing until 5am, and post-pub street stumbling that follows. When they wake up, all is calm, the beach is just as beautiful as the day before, and life is good. Then—repeat. Don't be put off though by the party atmosphere—Surfers also serves as a convenient base for nearby theme parks, the lush Hinterland, and unspoiled South Stradbroke Island.

TRANSPORTATION

Buses: The **Transit Centre** is at the corner of Beach Rd. and Ferny Ave., 1 block west of Paradise Centre. All the major bus companies and a few regional companies service Surfers Paradise, including Premier Motor Service (☎13 34 10), Travel Coach (formerly McCaffertys/Greyhound; ☎13 14 99), and Kirklands (☎1300 367 077; best for Byron Bay and NSW coast). Service to: **Brisbane** (1½-2hr.; every 45min. 4:40am-11:25pm; $14.50-17); **Byron Bay** (1½-2hr., $26-27); **Cairns** (30hr., $190); **Sydney** (14-15hr., $85). Lockers are available 6am-8:30pm (12hr. $4-8).

Local Buses: Surfside (☎13 12 30 or 5574 5111), the local 24hr. bus company, runs frequently to numerous roadside stops on the Gold Coast Hwy., as well as the Pacific Fair Mall, the theme parks, and Southport. Prices vary, but are inexpensive. **Gold Coast Tourist Shuttle** (☎5574 5111) offers transport to all theme parks with pickup and drop off from local accommodations and unlimited travel on Surfside's service (1-day Gold pass $15, concessions $8; 1-week $43/$22). With the purchase of a theme park ticket from a Surfside driver you receive free return transport to the park and free unlimited travel for the rest of the day. **Gold Coast Get Around** (☎5506 9744) provides a similar service, with transport to all theme parks and most local destinations (7-day pass $65, children $30, family with up to 3 children $130).

Taxis: Regent Taxis (☎13 10 08 or 5588 1289). For those not in a hurry, **peddle cabs** are often found on the corner of Cavill Ave. and Gold Coast Hwy.

Car Rental: Red Back Rentals, in the Transit Centre, offers reliable rental packages, as well as **bicycles.** (☎5592 1655. Open daily 8am-5pm.) **Thrifty** (☎5538 6511), on the corner of Enderley Ave. and Gold Coast Hwy., rents from $39.

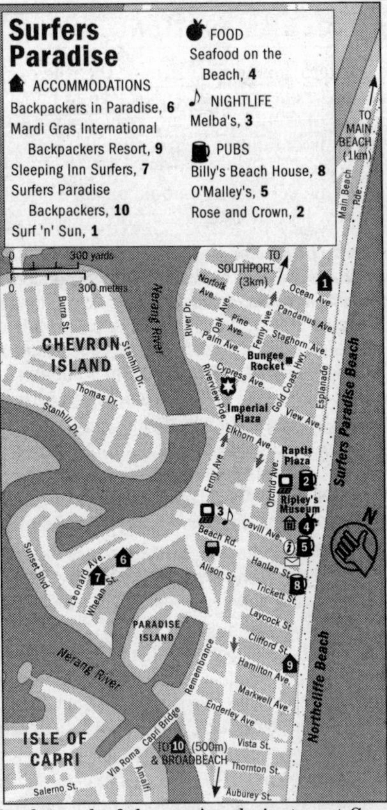

ORIENTATION

That maps of Surfers are long and thin, reflecting the fact that all the action is squeezed into a strip many kilometers long and just a few blocks wide between the Pacific Ocean and the **Nerang River.** Three main avenues run parallel to the shore: the **Esplanade,** which skirts the beach; the southbound **Gold Coast Hwy.,** a block over; **Ferny Ave.,** the northbound Gold Coast Hwy., one more block inland. Surfers centers on **Cavill Mall,** a pedestrian street lined with restaurants, cafes, bars, souvenir shops, and the Paradise Centre. Cavill Mall runs perpendicular to the Esplanade, which continues north past **Main Beach** to the **Marina** and the **Spit,** the end of the peninsula just past Seaworld. To the south is **Broadbeach,** home to the enormous Conrad Hotel Jupiter Casino and the monolithic **Pacific Fair Mall.**

PRACTICAL INFORMATION

Tourist Offices: Gold Coast Tourism Bureau (☎5538 4419; fax 5570 3259) is the main tourist office, located in a green kiosk on Cavill Mall. Pick up a map and the listings booklet *Wot's On* or *Point Out.* Open M-F 8:30am-5:30pm, Sa 9am-5pm, Su 9am-3:30pm. The **Backpackers Information Centre** (☎5592 2911 or 1800 359 830; fax 5538 1282) is located in the transit center. Open daily 8:30am-6pm. After hours, info and a direct phone to hostels are still available.

Banks: Westpac, corner of Cavill Ave. and Gold Coast Hwy., has a 24hr. **ATM.** Bank open M-Th 9:30am-4pm, F 9:30am-5pm.

Police: 68 Ferny Ave. (☎5570 7888), opposite the Cypress Ave. carpark. There's also a substation on the corner of Cavill Mall and the Esplanade (☎5531 5540).

Medical Services: Gold Coast Medical Transport (☎13 12 33). **Surfers Pardise Day Night Surgery,** Galleria Mall, on the highway (☎5592 2299). Open daily 7am-10pm.

Internet Access: Magic TV, 50 Cavill Ave. (☎5527 6522), on the corner of Ferny Ave. $4.95 per hr. Open daily 10am-10pm. **Email Centre,** 51 Orchid (☎5538 7500). $4 per hr. Most hostels also have connections. Open daily 8:30am-midnight.

Post Office: Main branch is inside the Paradise Centre, on Cavill Mall. Open M-F 8:30am-5:30pm, Sa 9am-noon. **Postal code:** 4217.

ACCOMMODATIONS

In Surfers, hostel staff assume the role of camp counselors, each night leading the troops to cheap meals and the good party scene. Nightclubs provide hostels with plenty of freebies, so any traveler with party intentions should opt for hostel accommodations to help reduce the sucking sound of the Surfer's money vacuum. If you didn't come to party, seek quieter digs at highway hostels. Summer and Easter are peak seasons—book ahead. All hostels have free pickup, 10am check-out, $10 key deposit, laundry and TV rooms.

Surfers Paradise Backpackers Resort, 2837 Gold Coast Hwy. (☎5592 4677 or 1800 282 800; www.surfersparadisebackpackers.com.au). A 15min. walk south along the highway to the corner of Wharf Rd. in front of the Parkroyal Hotel and 150m to beach. Free courtesy bus. Spotless, happy and family-run, "The Resort" also has outstanding facilities: big kitchen bar, gym, tennis court, pool, free laundry, dorms with private bath. Free board use. Bicycle rental $5. Sauna (45min. $4). Internet $1.50 per 15min. Reception daily 7:30am-7pm. Dorms $21; units $25-29 per person. VIP/YHA.

Trekkers, 22 White St., Southport (☎5591 5616 or 1800 100 004). 3km north of city center; call for free pick-up. 10min. to beach. Guests feel they are an integral part of this beautiful, comfortable, and social hostel. Spotless rooms, most with private bath, all doubles have TV. Free courtesy bus. Salt water pool, free board and bike use. W BBQ night. Reception daily 7:30am-8pm. Dorms $18; doubles $46. ISIC/VIP/YHA.

Mardi Gras International Backpackers Resort, 28 Hamilton Ave. (☎5592 5888 or 1800 801 230). A short walk to the beach. Clean, small dorms with balcony, TV, and private bath. Beer garden, carpark, gym, kitchen. Reception daily 7:30am-midnight. Dorms $20; doubles $50.

Aquarius, 44 Queen St., Southport (☎5527 1300 or 1800 229 955). Call for courtesy bus or, from Surfers, follow the Gold Coast Hwy. over the bridge and take your first left. Clean rooms, glow worm trips, Internet, pool, spa, and garden. Reception daily 7:30am-9:30pm. Dorms $17; doubles $44. ISIC/VIP/YHA.

Sleeping Inn Surfers, 26 Whelan St. (☎5592 4455 or 1800 817 832; www.sleepinginn.com.au). A 10min. walk from the Transit Centre across Ferny Ave. Self-contained units have kitchens and living rooms with TV. Mellow atmosphere. Reception daily 7am-9pm. Dorms $16; singles $30; doubles $38; apartments $48-150. ISIC/VIP/YHA.

Surf 'n Sun, 3323 Gold Coast Hwy. (☎5592 2363 or 1800 678 194). Corner of Ocean Ave., close to beach. Famous for its party atmosphere, and proximity to the beach. Private bathrooms, courtesy bus, pool. Reception 7:30am-11pm. Dorms $21, $112 weekly; doubles $50. VIP/YHA.

Backpackers in Paradise, 40 Whelan St. (☎5538 4344 or 1800 268 621). Two blocks down Whelan St. off Ferny Ave. Closest to the city center and the cheapest rates in town, though rooms are a bit tired. Large pool and lounge with giant TV. Hostel bistro serves $5 breakfasts and dinners. Reception daily 8am-7pm. 12-bed dorm $15; 8- and 4-bed dorms with bath $17; doubles $44. NOMADS/VIP.

British Arms, 70 Sea World Dr. (☎5571 1776 or 1800 680 268; www.britisharms.com.au) on the way to the Spit. Close to Main Beach with nice rooms and a great pub separate. Reception 8am-9pm. Dorms $21; doubles $50. VIP/YHA.

Cheers, 8 Pine Ave. (☎5531 6539 or 1800 636 539), just off Ferny Ave. The largest hostel in Surfers. Rooms are basic, but the bar and beer garden are gorgeous. Pool, jacuzzi, free Internet. Reception daily 8am-10:30pm. Dorms $21. VIP/YHA.

FOOD

Heaps of inexpensive bistros, 24hr. cafes, fast food joints, and Asian restaurants cluster around Cavill Mall. Tedder Ave. near Main Beach is lined with bistros, bakeries, classy cafes, and Ferraris. Towards the Spit, at **Peter's Fish Market,** 120 Sea World Dr., opt for the best fish'n'chips in town ($5.50), or try your luck cooking

QUEENSLAND

WHAT A WHOPPER Throughout Australia, the yellow and red signs for the fast food joint "Hungry Jack's" provoke a mental double-take. Haven't I seen that logo before? Once inside, the mystery deepens. Whoppers? Chicken tenders? My god, they've ripped off Burger King! Hey, Sherlock, it *isn't* a big BK imposter. Burger King is well aware of Hungry Jack's—it's theirs. Before Burger King expanded to Oz, some enterprising fellow went to the Australian patent office and got the rights to the name "Burger King," thinking the big boys in the States would pay him off to use the name in Australia. The fast food intelligentsia was not duped, however. Simply changing the name to Hungry Jack's, Burger King set up shop in Australia with the same logo, food, and promotions. And don't even think about it, McDonald's is already here...

their fresh raw seafood. (☎5591 7747. Open daily 9am-8pm.) **Seaway Cafe** has snacks to satisfy those who trek to the end of the spit. (☎5591 6970. Open daily 8am-5pm.) A Woolworth's **supermarket** is located in the basement of the Paradise Centre. (Open M-F 8am-9pm, Sa 8:30am-5:30pm, Su 10:30am-4pm.)

Golden Ring Chinese Restaurant (☎5592 5900), in the alley next to Hungry Jack's, on the corner of Cavill, across from the beach. Locals rave about the honey chicken ($6). Open 10:30am-2am.

Seafood on the Beach, 4 The Esplanade (☎5527 5736). Lures you from the water for $7 fish'n'chips. Open daily 6am-9pm.

Hard Rock Cafe (☎5539 9377), on the corner of Cavill Ave. and Gold Coast Hwy. All glitzy places need one. Open daily 8am-late.

Hook and Chook, 15 Tedder Ave. (☎5532 0097). Baits patrons with $3-5 sandwich and burger takeaways. Open M-Sa 7:30am-8pm, Su 8:30am-8pm.

Anglers Arms, 50 Queen St.,Southport (☎5532 1677). Children's fish'n'chips whose size is quite mature. Open M-W and F-Su 10am-10pm, Th 10am-midnight.

BEACHES, SURFING, AND WATER SPORTS

The beach stretches unbroken 25km from the quiet **Main Beach** on the Spit peninsula all the way south to Coolangatta's Snapper Rocks. Surfers Paradise is a bit of a misnomer, however. The outstanding beach breaks are great for beginners, but the best surfing is to the south. Surfing conditions vary considerably, especially as sand shifts to alter the breaks. Local surfers sometimes drive up and down the coast looking for the best break. Since weather conditions significantly alter an area's quality and level of danger, beginners and experienced surfers alike should ask around first. For more detailed info, hang ten to www.coastalwatch.com or listen to 90.9 Sea FM's surf reports. For your own safety always swim between the flags, even though the beaches are patrolled by Surf Life Savers.

The most popular beach among boardless beachgoers is **Surfers North.** Near the end of Staghorn Ave. and just north of Surfers Paradise, it's the most central hangout off the Paradise Centre Mall and the recipient of blaring music from the local radio station during the summer. Further south is **Broadbeach,** then **Kurrawa,** near the Pacific Fair Shopping Center. **Burleigh Heads** has a popular surfing area, though it can be mobbed and often has dangerous breaks.

For equipment, try the **Surfers Beach Clubhouse** kiosk on the beach end of Cavill Mall. (☎5526 7077. Longboards $15 per hr., $25 per 3hr., $40 per day. Wet suits $5 with a board. Short boards, in-line skates, or boogie boards $15 per hr., $20 per 3hr., $30 per day. Bag storage $5. Open summer 8am-5pm, winter 9am-4:30pm.) Their surf school will get you standing for $45, $35 for those in local backpacker accommodation. **Gold Coast Kayaking** runs excellent sea kayaking tours from the Spit to South Stradbroke Island, where you go for a bushwalk to the surf beach. (☎0419 7332 02. Leaves 8:30am. $30 including pickup.) **Cable Ski World** (☎5537 6300), on Oxley Dr. in Runaway Bay, offers waterskiing ($30), and bungee jumping ($69); buy their Gold Card for $5 and get a 25% discount; closed in winter.

SIGHTS AND ACTIVITIES

Ripley's Believe It or Not museum, in Raptis Plaza on Cavill Mall, a worldly collection of mind-boggling facts, people, and feats, is well worth a visit, especially on a rainy day. (☎5592 0040. Open daily 9am-11pm; $11.50, backpackers $10, children $8, family discount.) For more traditional art, visit the **Gold Coast Arts Gallery,** 135 Bundall Rd, 3km from the city center. (☎5581 6567. Open M-F 10am-5pm, Sa-Su 11am-5pm. Free.) **The Gold Coast Marathon** (☎5527 1363) will stream down the flat coast 7 July 2002. Mid-October means **Honda Indy 300** (www.indy.com.au), a four day extravaganza of races highlighted by the Indy event, which follows a track around Surfers and down the Esplanade. Crowds pack the streets and hang out of highrises. Airshows, street parties, and fireworks complement the races. Hotels and hostels get booked months ahead.

THEME PARKS AND THRILL RIDES

Tickets to all parks can be bought at reduced prices from the tourist info booth on Cavill Mall. Surfside, Coachtrans, and Gold Coast Tourist Shuttle provide **transportation** to all parks. Because of the high prices and long lines, arrive early to get the most out of the park. **Dreamworld, Wet n' Wild, Seaworld,** and **Movie World** distribute brochures and pamphlets everywhere.

DREAMWORLD: The much trumpeted "Tower of Terror" is the tallest and fastest ride in the world, shooting forward at up to 160kph, then straight up 38 stories, and straight down again. *(In Coomera, a 25min. drive from Surfers. ☎5588 1111 or 1800 073 300; www.dreamworld.com.au. Open daily 9:30am-5pm. $52, concessions and children ages 4-13 $32; $48, $30 at info booth.)*

WET 'N' WILD. On hot summer days, the whitewater flumes of this water park will cool you down, while in the winter, the slides and pools are heated. *(☎5573 2255; www.wetnwild.com.au. Open daily from 10am; closing times vary. $31, children $20; $28, $18 if purchased at info booth on Cavill Ave.)*

SEAWORLD. Lots of fish, dolphins, sharks, seals, some sad-looking pigeons, a few rides, and a hilarious sea lion show are all on display on the Spit, north of Surfers. A new polar bear exhibit brings the Arctic to Oz. *(On Seaworld Dr. ☎5588 2205; www.seaworld.com.au. Open daily 10am-5pm. $52, concessions and children ages 4-13 $33; $48/$30 at info booth. Swimming with dolphins $105, arrive early in the morning to reserve; must be over 14.)*

MOVIE WORLD. This Warner Brothers park offers the 6min. *Wild Wild West* ride that climaxes in a 70kph, 20m drop into water; a new Pokemon Island Adventure for the young; a *Lethal Weapon* roller coaster that suspends passengers from the rail. *(A 25min. drive north of Surfers, on the Pacific Hwy. ☎5573 8485;www.movieworld.com.au. Open daily 9:30am-5:30pm. $52, concessions $33; $48, $32 at info booth.)*

OTHER SPILLS AND CHILLS. Indulge James Bond fantasies at the **Australian Shooting Academy** where first-timers can bust some caps under safe, supervised conditions. *(Upstairs in the Paradise Centre, beside Tenpin Bowling. ☎5527 5100. Open daily 10am-10pm; must be 18 with a picture ID or bring a legal guardian. $70-115.)* There's **indoor rock climbing** (☎5526 2007) for $8 in the Mark Shopping Centre on Orchid Ave; lessons available. Several **thrill rides,** including various forms of **bungee jumping** and **virtual reality** rides, share a small plot on the corner of the Gold Coast Hwy. and Palm Ave. *(Most open daily 10am-10pm. Thrills $5-75.)* The highlight is **Bungee Rocket,** a small, two-person compartment that propels occupants 150 ft. up in 1 second with 5.5Gs. *(On the corner of Palm Ave. and Gold Coast Hwy. ☎5570 2700. $30.)*

PARKING IN PARADISE Everyone knows that there is nothing more irritating than returning to your car only to find that the village parking patrol has ticketed you for mistakenly misjudging the two hours that the meter had given you (Unless your car has rolled into the bushes, that is.) No need to fear in Surfers though. For over 35 years beautiful betties decked in nothing more than a golden bikini have travelled the streets of Surfers placing coins in meters on the verge of expiring. So if you return to your car and find a car from the Meter Maids, know that they've saved you from paying a parking fine. Check them out in the mini Meter Maid Museum, upstairs in the Paradise Center.

ENTERTAINMENT AND NIGHTLIFE

Aside from partying and drinking, the main nighttime activity in Surfers seems to be getting the best deals on partying and drinking. Most of the hostels provide free passes and cheap meal tickets for several clubs. The majority of clubs are on Orchid Ave., known as the "Avenue," and are open until 5am; it seems that people don't get tired in Paradise. **Bring your passport,** as some clubs won't accept other forms of ID. The Gold Coast Backpackers Association organizes events every night, the highlights being Tuesday "70s" night and the infamous **club crawl** (☎1800 359 830. W and Sa 9:30pm. Get tickets from participating hostels for around $16, includes entry to clubs, a free drink at the three clubs, a photo, and a t-shirt.) High rollers try their luck at **Conrad Jupiters Casino** (☎5592 1133, box office ☎1800 074 144). For details on the Surfers nightly events go to www.emugigs.com.

Rose and Crown (☎5531 5425), Raptis Plaza on Cavill Ave. Popular with many crowds, dance and Top-40 play in one room, and talented live bands perform in the other. Drink specials and prizes. Open Tu-W 8pm-3am, Th-Sa 8pm-5am Su 8pm-2am. Cover $6.

Cocktails and Dreams, The Mark, Orchid Ave. (☎5592 1955). Make like Tom and Cruise to this constantly packed club. Popular with backpackers and more. Organizes events with the hostels, such as Tu 70s night, W and Sa Club Crawl. Downstairs, **The Party** plays an alternative songlist. Open F, Sa 8pm-5am, Su-Th 9pm-5am. Cover $5.

Sugar Shack, 20 Orchid Ave. (☎5538 7600). Fun, casual dance hall which grooves to the classic hits from every era. Open 11:30am-5am. Cover $3.

The Drink, 4 Orchid Ave. (☎5570 6155). Euro, stylish, and busy. Open Tu-Su 8pm-5:30am. Cover after 10pm $5.

O'Malley's, 1 Cavill Ave. (☎5570 4075). Packed pub with balcony view over the Mall and The Esplanade. Live music every night. Open Su-Th noon-midnight, F-Sa noon-2am.

Billy's Beach House (☎5531 5666), corner of The Esplanade and Hanlan St. Pool tables, lots of dance space, and plenty of bar. Th $2 stubbies. Su 4:30pm, free BBQ w/ drink purchase. Happy Hour 8-10pm. Live music Th-Su. Open 10am-5am. Sa cover $5.

M.P., or the **Meeting Place,** Forum Arcade (☎5526 2337). Connects 26 Orchid Ave. to 3171 Gold Coast Hwy. Surfers' only gay club. Open late. Open Tu-Su 9pm-late.

Melba's, 46 Cavill Ave. (☎5538 7411). A restaurant turned classy nightclub by dark. Melba's avoids Orchid Ave's meat market feel. Grooves to mainstream and techno. Happy Hour 4-10pm Restaurant open daily 9am-3am. Club open 8pm-5am, W-Th and Sa-Su 7pm-5am, F 5pm-5am. Cover $8.

DAYTRIP FROM SURFERS: SOUTH STRADBROKE

Separated from the Spit by a thin channel, South Straddie is the Gold Coast's hidden gem and a must for any traveler to the area. Largely undeveloped and home to friendly free-roaming wallabies, the long, narrow island (22km by 3km) is blessed with quiet river beaches on the west side and gorgeous empty surf beaches with breathtaking white sand dunes on the east side. The main activity center is the **South Stradbroke Island Resort,** which has pools, spas, sauna, watersports, tennis courts, restaurants, and a virtual monopoly on non-camping accommodation. Individual cabins have TV and fridge. (☎5577 3311 or 1800 074 125. $90 per person.)

The island also offers camping options with toilets, showers, and BBQ. **Tippler's camping area** is just 300m from the resort. (☎5577 2849. Sites for 2 $12, $13 peak.) **Ferries** run from Gate C, Runaway Bay Marina, 247 Bayview St., Runaway Bay, off the Gold Coast Hwy. past Southport. Return from Surfers Paradise transit center to Runaway Bay is $5, but free for those staying at the resort; either way it's cheaper than the bus. (☎5577 3311. 20min.; depart Runaway daily 7 and 10:30am, return 2:30 and 5pm; return $25.)

GOLD COAST HINTERLAND

Unbelievably, within an hour or so from the bustling coast, you can be bushwalking through lush, subtropical rainforest, enjoying spectacular views, and strolling through laid-back towns. The Hinterland makes a perfect escape from the glitz of the coast; a little exploration will undoubtedly complete your visit to the region.

Travel by car offers the most flexible and wallet-friendly means to see the Hinterland. An easy one-day drive along **Pacific Hwy. 1** from the Gold Coast starts at **Murwillumbah,** then passes **Nerang,** the **Natural Bridge,** descends into the valley, ascends to **Springbrook,** and finally returns to the Coast via **Mudgeeraba.** Along the way, you will see turn-offs for Lamington National Park, Mt. Tambourine, Springbrook National Park, and Mt. Cougal National Park. For more info, contact Queensland National Parks (☎5544 0634).

Alternatively, buses and tours can get you almost anywhere in the Hinterland. **Mountain Coach Company** has a bus tour to O'Reilly's in Lamington National Park via Mt. Tamborine from Coolangatta, Burleigh, and Surfers. (☎5524 4249. $39, children $22, family of 4 $114; including pickup.) **Scenic Hinterland Day Tours** offers a trip to Springbrook and Natural Bridge, including Purlingbrook Falls, a 1000 year old forest, and subtropical rainforests. (☎5531 5536. $37.90, concessions $34.90, child under 12 $25.90, family of 4 $114.85.) **All State Scenic Tours** accesses Lamington National Park from Brisbane, leaving the transit centre Su-F at 9:30am and returning at 3pm. (☎3003 0700. Return $44 Children 4-16 $33.) Some hostels offer tours to Lamington National Park or to see the glowworms at the Natural Bridge.

LAMINGTON NATIONAL PARK

The 200 square kilometers of Lamington National Park are split into two sections: **Green Mountains/O'Reilly's** and **Binna Burra.** The park's 160km of well-trod paths lead to spectacular waterfalls, clear springs, subtropical rainforest, and the NSW border ridge, with magnificent views of Mt. Warning's ancient volcanic crater.

GREEN MOUNTAINS. Green Mountains/O'Reilly's can only be accessed via Canungra along a switchback road, off the Pacific Hwy. The information centre books camping for O'Reilly's and for Green Mountain campsites accessed only by walking trails. (☎5544 0634. Open M, W, Th 9-11am and 1-3:30pm; Tu, F 1-3:30pm. $3.50 per night.) From O'Reilly's, the Toolona Creek circuit (17km; 5-6 hr. return) will take you past numerous waterfalls on its way to stunning panoramas. Python Rock is another popular route, leading to the Morans Falls.

BINNA BURRA. To get to Binna Burra, follow the signs for Beechmont and Binna Burra from Nerang. The **Binna Burra Mountain Lodge,** Binna Burra Rd., Beechmont (☎5533 3622), operates a daily bus service to the coast. (Return $22, children $11, and has camping for $10 per person.) The lodge has very pricey lodging ($159, with private bath $189), as well as camping facilities. (Site $10-30; powered extra $3.50; 2-bed safari tent $40, 4-bed $60.) The **information center** at the lodge also has bush camping permits, groceries, and maps of the different hiking circuits. (☎5533 3584.

Open daily 1-3:30pm. Permit $3.85.) **Ship's Stern circuit** (19km return) has unique rainforest species, giant trees, waterfalls, and views of its lush valleys.

TAMBORINE MOUNTAIN

Tamborine, a 600m-high plateau, contains nine small national parks of subtropical rainforest. Beautiful waterfalls and native wildlife make this a hiker's paradise. Fresh, cool air, views of the coast and inland mountains, and an attractive town are all just a short drive from the coast. To get to the park, exit the **Pacific Hwy. 1** at Oxenford and follow the steep, twisting **Oxenford-Tamborine Rd.;** use low gear. Near the highway exit, check out the **Russel Hinze Park,** a swamp and island refuge for various water birds. Approaching the plateau, the road changes its name to MacDonnell Rd., without warning. Turn right onto Long Rd., right at the roundabout, and left at Geissman Dr. to reach the **Tamborine Natural History Information Centre,** in Doughty Park. (☎5545 3200. Open daily 10:30am-3:30pm.)

The town of **Mt. Tamborine** offers Devonshire tea houses, B&Bs, and pottery shops. It's just an hour's drive from Brisbane or the Gold Coast, which translates into a constant flow of visitors. Luckily, most visitors don't venture far beyond town, so if you set out on the trails, you'll enjoy relative solitude. For budget travelers, Tamborine is better as a daytrip, because beds are pricey. The **Joalah National Park** circuit (2.3km; 1hr.) offers subtropical rainforest and the picture-perfect Curtis Falls, but no vistas. The track begins on Eagle Heights Rd., either from the carpark off Dapsang St. or the shops near Geissmann Dr. The **Witches Falls Walking Track** (2.7km; 50min.) runs along the western side of the plateau. This path is stunning at points, but there is more backyard than rainforest at the beginning. During the Dry (winter) the raging falls turn into a leaky faucet. Head north on Tamborine Mountain Rd. to and follow signs to reach **Cedar Creek Falls** a stellar hike (4km) in the national park of the same name.

SPRINGBROOK NATIONAL PARK

Continuing on the PAcific Hwy., a turn off for Springbrook Rd., leads to the unattended **Info Centre** in the old schoolhouse, which has color maps of the many walks, lookouts, and camping and picnic areas. (Ranger ☎5533 5147. Open 8am-4pm.) Farther on Springbrook Rd., the Canyon Lookout leads to the **Twin Falls Circuit** (4km) and the fabulous, day-long **Warrie Circuit** (15km). The Warrie track leads through rock wedge caves and behind, around, and under countless waterfalls.

The first accommodation to catch the sun, **Springbrook Mountain Lodge YHA,** 317 Repeater Station Rd., is a small hostel at the top of Springbrook Rd., near the Best of All Lookout. (☎5533 5366. Advance notice $18 roundtrip bus from Gold Coast. Book ahead. Dorms $23; twins and doubles $26; family cabin $88, $132 weekend.) At the Springbrook Homestead (☎5533 5200) on Springbrook Rd., you'll find the only public **observatory** in Southeast Queensland. Call ahead.

To reach the Natural Bridge, look for signs after the Springbrook-Mudgeeraba Rd. for Natural Bridge via Muwillumbah-Nerang Rd., heading back towards the Gold Coast. The **Natural Bridge,** Springbrook's most popular sight, is about 1km from the carpark at the turn-off, 3km north of the NSW border. The arch is a gorgeous cavern where a waterfall tumbles through a hole in the hardened lava that was opened by the drill-like force of heavy boulders and swirling water. At night, the cavern comes alive with bats and **glowworms.**

WILL THE REAL SLIM SHADY PLEASE STAND UP

Throughout the Hinterland one can find a scarce Australian species known as the lyrebird. Capable of copying up to twenty different sounds that they hear in their environment, the lyrebird originally imitated sounds of other birds and animals. Now, as testament to their invaded habitat, the birds are known to make the sounds of chainsaws, rewinding cameras and car horns—proof that you can teach an old bird new tricks. Hopefully, no one will bring a mobile phone into their home.

CRIMSON CRAZINESS The Reds are more than communists in Queensland. In fact, they are the state's rugby union team. But do not confuse the Reds with the Marroons, the state's rugby *league* team. Rugby union is the mode of rugby played in the World Cup. Rugby league features less men on the field and is only played in Australia and Britain. The Marroons battle the Blues, New South Wales' rugby league team, every year in a three game series known as the State of Origin. These three games are arguably the most significant yearly athletic event in OZ and the atmosphere at the games and in the pubs of Queensland and New South Wales is nothing short of electric as the Blues and Marroons battle to preserve the honor of their state.

MT. COUGAL NATIONAL PARK

Just 30min. from the Gold Coast and tucked away in the town of Currumbin are three natural pools with cliff jumps. Signs from the Pacific Hwy. between Burleigh Heads (just south of Surfers) and Coolangatta lead there via **Currumbin Creek Rd. Currumbin Rock Pool,** a deep freshwater pool with short cliff dives and smaller pools for lounging above and beneath short falls, is 10min. down the road. Another 6km along Currumbin Creek Rd. is **Mt. Cougal National Park** (☎5532 3032), a rugged part of Springbrook National Park in the Currumbin Creek headwaters. A 200m walk to **Cougal Cascades** takes you into the rainforest to a **natural water slide,** where cool water cascades over smoothed rocks. Not much further along the same path is another natural pool with a much higher jump than those at the Currumbin Rock Pool. Only very daring folks attempt these slides and jumps; **use caution** and common sense at all of these risky attractions, and obey posted warnings.

SOUTHERN AND DARLING DOWNS

West of the Great Dividing Range lie the hills and valleys of the Southern Downs, and the towns of Toowoomba, Warwick, and Stanthorpe. Toowoomba's carefully crafted greenery is only beginning to draw tourists, but the rich agriculture, rustic beauty, and quiet, small town feeling of Warwick and Stanthorpe draws backpackers for seasonal work. For those coming to the Downs with time to spare, Giraween and Sundown National Parks please visitors with their wildflower displays (Sept.-Mar.), granite outcroppings, and spectacular views. Stanthorpe is also the center of Queensland's only wine region, the Granite Belt.

TOOWOOMBA ☎07

With over 150 parks and gardens, many connected by bike and walking paths, Toowoomba has outgrown its name, which is derived from an Aboriginal word meaning "swamp." Using the "Garden City" as a more appropriate alias, Toowoomba consists of a formidable commercial center that fades into a seemingly endless suburbia, backed by breathtaking views of the Dividing Range.

McCafferty's buses leave from 28-30 Neil St. (☎4690 9888). **Buses** run to: Brisbane (2hr.; Su-F 13 per day 5:30am-6pm, Sa 11 per day; $19.50); Melbourne (22hr., 2 per day, $156); Sydney (15hr., departs daily 9pm, $76). For northern destinations, connect in Brisbane. The **Tourist Information Center,** 476 Ruthven St., has Internet access. (Open T-F 10am-5pm, Sa 10am-2pm. $4.40 per 30min.)

For a truly pleasant stay, **Mrs. Bee's Bed & Breakfast,** at 11 Bouton Tce., will pick you up at the bus station, whisking you away to a whitewashed room at the top of the hill.(☎9639 1659; www.interbed.com.au/mrsbees. Continental breakfast included. Family friendly. Dorms $22, with YHA $20; singles $30/$25; family of 5 $60. Wheelchair accessible. MC/V.) For inexpensive lodgings close to town and the bus station, the **pubs** around Russell and Ruthven St are the way to go.

Most of Toowoomba's restaurants, bars, and cafes are around Margaret St., also (appropriately) known as "Eat Street." **The Spotted Cow,** at the corner of Campbell and Ruthven St., has great food and rocks at night with one-man cover bands. (☎4639 3264; www.spotted-cow.com. Open Su-Th 11am-late, F and S 11am-3am.)

The **Carnival of Flowers** (☎4632 4877; www.carnivalofflowers.com.au) is Toowoomba's biggest draw. Held for a week in September, Sept. 22-31, 2002, the carnival features a parade, flower shows, and the exhibition of prize-winning private gardens for the public. In the "Garden City," you'll also find **Ju Raku En,** Australia's most traditional and **largest Japanese Garden,** on the University of Southern Queensland campus. (Open daily 7am-dusk.) **Queen's Park Gardens** on Lindsay St. are another floral highlight, especially during spring and summer.

STANTHORPE ☎07

As the commercial center for the Granite Belt, Stanthorpe (pop. 5000) offers a pleasant escape from the city. Its cool, crisp climate in winter and location in the heart of Queensland's best wine country have made it a year-round destination for many Brisbane residents, while its abundant fruit-picking opportunities attract flocks of backpackers in the summer months. The town is an ideal base for visiting the renowned local wineries, exploring the granite formations and wildflowers of the surrounding national parks (Sundown, Girraween, Boonoo Boonoo, and Bald Rock), or enjoying a romantic getaway into the beautiful countryside.

PRACTICAL INFORMATION. Coming in from Warwick off the New England Hwy., Stanthorpe's main street, **High St.,** turns into **Maryland St.** as it bends south in the center of town. The **tourist office,** 28 Leslie Pde., sits by the bridge at Quart Pot Creek. (☎4681 2057; fax 4681 1200. Open M-F 9am-5pm, Sa-Su 9am-4pm.) The **bus station,** 57 Maryland St. (☎4681 1434), is inside the Mobil petrol station. **Crisps** and **McCafferty's buses** run to: Brisbane (3½hr., $29); Toowoomba (2hr., $22); Warwick (45min., 2 per day, $15.50).

ACCOMMODATIONS AND FOOD. The cheapest and most central accommodation options are in the pub hotels clustered on Maryland St. The rooms are clean and have sinks; most also have a TV lounge upstairs and a fireplace room and bar downstairs. The **Country Club Hotel,** 26 Maryland St. (☎4681 1033), has singles for $35, weekly $95. The **Central Hotel** has clean, basic rooms, a very friendly staff, and the cheapest weekly rates in town. (Singles $25, weekly $80.)

If you're looking for work in the orchards or just a relaxing place to stay, try the friendly family run **Elphick Lodge,** north of town on Rd. by the Big Apple Mobil Station (Dorm $17, $120 per week, transport to farms and town included). **Top of the Town Caravan Park,** 10 High St., is 15min. north of the town center. (☎4681 4888. Reception 7am-6pm. Campsites $10, for 2 $16.50; caravans for 2 $37; cabin with kitchen, bath, and TV $50.) Alternative accommodations are available on "host farms," small cattle stations, but you'll need a car to reach them. Most cost $30-40 per person. **Callemondah,** 58km west of Stanthorpe on Texas Rd., charges $33 per night to stay on the sheep and cattle station. (☎4685 6162. Book ahead.)

Coffee and lunch shops are mostly located along the main road. **Il Cavallino,** 130 High St., is an Italian trattoria with exquisite, carefully crafted dishes. Using the Ferrari horse as an emblem, and a racecar-themed decor to match, its higher prices ($10-25) are made worthwhile by its leap in quality and atmosphere. (☎4681

PIES IN THE BACK OF YOUR HEAD Australia's common magpie birds are well known to attack humans that venture anywhere near their nests during the spring breeding season. Many Aussies have felt the sting of a swooping beak, often when riding their bicycles or taking a stroll in the park—they like to peck out the eyes of invaders to their nesting area. Children take cover during school recess, sometimes having to run for cover inside. Magpies don't attack, however, when one is looking at them. So, to avoid attack, some cautious natives wear ice cream containers on their heads with eyes painted on the back. You decide whether it is more humiliating to be attacked by an bird or wear an ice cream container on your head.

QUEENSLAND

1556. Open Tu-Su. 5:30pm-late.) Reward yourself after a long weeks work at **Anna's Restaurant** (☎4681 1265 www.annas.com.au), on the corner of O'Mara Tce. and Wallangarra Rd., just past the tourist office, a model of outback elegance with weekend italian buffets. (F $22.50, Sa $27.50 Book ahead.) A Woolworth's **supermarket** is on the corner of High and Lock St. (Open M-F 8am-9pm, Sa 8am-5pm.)

WINERIES. The famous Granite Belt wineries line either side of the New England Hwy. just south (and a little north) of Stanthorpe. Unfortunately, the wineries can't be reached by public transportation or on foot. Tours provide for a joyful day and a late-afternoon nap. The tourist office has lists of all the local winery tours, but **The Grape Escape,** led by jolly Chris Pascoe, is the best. (☎4681 4761; www.grapeescape.com.au. From $60, including pickup, drop off, and lunch. Book ahead.) If you're driving (and wishing you weren't), the way to the wineries is well-marked; most are close to the highway. **Ballandean Estate Wines** (☎4684 1226) is Queensland's oldest family operated winery and gives tours at 11am, 1, and 3pm. **Golden Grove Estate** (☎4684 1291), just across the road, offers a different taste.

SIGHTS. For a view of the town and more, walk 30min. up to the **scenic lookout** on Mt. Marlay. From Woolworth's, follow the signs up Lock St. Stanthorpe's gem is the fascinating **Historical Museum,** 15min. up High St. from the town center, near the showgrounds. It's a delightful cornucopia of historical oddities: fruit fly catchers, ancient heating devices, and even a handmade TV. (☎4681 1711. Open W-F 10am-4pm, Sa 1-4pm, Su 9am-1pm. $3, children $1.) The more classic **Stanthorpe Regional Art Gallery** is in the same building as the library, across from the Civic Center on Lock St. (☎4681 1874. Open M-F 10am-4pm, Sa 1-4pm, Su 10am-1pm. Free.)

The 1872 discovery of tin in **Quart Pot Creek** marked the beginning of years of mining around Stanthorpe. Today, amateurs can try fossicking (digging for gems); a license is required. **Blue Topaz Caravan Park** in Severnlea, 7km south of Stanthorpe, supplies licenses. (☎4683 5279. $5.10, families $7.20.) Strike gold at **Thanes Creek Fossicking Area,** 40km west of Warwick (☎3237 1435).

Stanthorpe has two major festivals: the largest is the Apple and Grape Harvest Festival (☎4681 4111; www.appleandgrape.org; Feb. 22-Mar. 3, 2002) an extravaganza with a gala ball, rodeo, wine fiesta, and museum exhibition (held every even numbered year). The **Granite Belt Spring Wine Festival,** celebrating the release of the new vintage, is held at the wineries during the first three weekends in October. The winter months are devoted to the **Brass Monkey season,** a general and ongoing Downs-wide wine-and-dine celebration of the area's (and particularly Stanthorpe's) position as the coldest winter region in Queensland, featuring traditional Christmas dinners every weekend.

NEAR STANTHORPE: NATIONAL PARKS

In addition to the parks listed below, two New South Wales national parks, **Bald Rock** and **Boonoo Boonoo,** are easily accessible from Stanthorpe. None of the National Parks can be reached by public transportation; you need a car to see the splendor of the parks.

GIRRAWEEN NATIONAL PARK. Girraween is a popular destination for bushwalkers, birdwatchers, campers, and picnickers. To get there, drive 26km south on the New England Hwy., turn left at the sign, then drive 9km on a sealed road. Massive granite boulders, which seem precariously balanced on top of each other, are interspersed among eucalypt forests, lyre birds, and Queensland's only wombat population. A spectacular, but somewhat perilous, 1½hr. return hike takes you to the granite **Pyramid,** which offers a breathtakingly expansive view including the famous **Balancing Rock,** and **Bald Rock**, Australia's second largest rock, just across the border in NSW. The **Castle Rock** track (1½hr. return) is a more moderate climb to a spectacular 360° view from this high summit. The hike to the **Granite Arch** (25min. return) is even more mellow. In the spring, **wildflowers** sprout from the bases of rocks, hence the park's name—girraween is the Aboriginal name for "place of flowers." The **Visitor Center,** at the southern end of Bald Rock Creek, is usually open seven days a week; the rangers daringly post the day's hours on an erasable board. Nearby, there are picnic, swimming, and rock-climbing areas. Camping is available in designated areas with hot showers, toilets, and barbecue grills. (☎4684 5157. $4 per person, families $15. Self-register upon arrival, but book in advance for Easter and Christmas.)

SUNDOWN NATIONAL PARK. Sundown offers rugged terrain, spectacular gorges, high peaks, and panoramic views, as well as swimming holes, fishing, and canoeing in a primitive area. To get there, drive 75km along Texas Rd. north from Stanthorpe and turn left at the signs for Glenlyon. For a longer route with wider roads, take the New England Hwy. south to Tenterfield (40km) and turn right onto the Bruxner Hwy. The 16,000-hectare park has very different geology than neighboring parks, with a mix of sedimentary and igneous rocks that has produced sharp ridges. The **Severn River** cuts the park in two. As there are no graded walking tracks, areas of interest can be reached by following the river and side creeks. The **Permanent Waterhole** is a beautiful large waterhole on a major bend in the river, a 20min. hike upstream along the west bank. The **Split-Rock** and **Double Falls** are well worth the 3-4hr. return hike up **McAllisters Creek.** Cross the river east into the creek, being careful not to get sidetracked by the old 4WD track. Camping is accessible by 2WD vehicles and hikers on the western side of the river. Access from Ballandean to the east is strictly 4WD. Campsites have pit toilets, fireplaces, and BBQ. ($3.50 per person, families $14.)

SUNSHINE AND FRASER COASTS

And the beach just keeps on coming. See surf and sun, bikes and boards, surfers and sophisticates—or see no one at all. With stretches just as beautiful as the Gold Coast, minus the touristy droves, hype, and neon, the Sunshine Coast is a slightly warmer vacationland with 300 days of sunshine per year. Beaches envelope developed resort towns, and waters greet those eager to partake in aquatic pleasures. The largest of the islands that dot Queensland's coastal waters, sandy Fraser Island, reclines paradoxically under a cover of rainforest growing right out of sand. Its legendary dunes and freshwater lakes are frequented by a parade of package tours and bold independent travelers. Farther north, fruit-picking is popular and a bevy of workers' hostels have sprung up to meet the demand.

MAROOCHY ☎07

Maroochy is the general name for an area of coast encompassing the towns of **Maroochydore, Alexandra Heads, and Mooloolaba** (north to south). Die-hard surfers fill the beaches, and their stereotypically laid-back attitudes permeate the region. Maroochydore is the urban center, heavily oriented toward small industry, and located where the Maroochy River flows into the ocean. About 1km south, Alexandra Heads is best known for great surfing and a safe family beach. Another 2km south, Mooloolaba is lined by beachfront esplanades with nightclubs and an aquarium. Maroochy is a popular base for fruit-picking work, with lychee and ginger season from Feb. to Mar., strawberries from June to Oct., and tomatoes from Nov. to Feb. Average pay is about $11 per hour, and most hostels help find work.

TRANSPORTATION. Suncoast Pacific, Premier, and **McCafferty's** all stop at the Suncoast Pacific terminal in the Scotlyn Shopping Center on First Ave. off Aerodrome Rd., Maroochydore. McCafferty's and Premier run to: Airlie Beach (16hr., 1 per day, $131); Brisbane (2hr., 4 per day, $18); Bundaberg (5¾hr., 1 per day, $42); Cairns (26hr., 1 per day, $179); Hervey Bay (3¾-4¼hr., 3 per day, $28); Mackay (14½hr., 1 per day, $118); Noosa (30min., 3 per day, $12); Rockhampton (10hr., 1 per day, $77). Suncoast Pacific goes to Brisbane (2hr., 7 per day, $21) and the Gold

Coast (3hr., 1 per day, $33.30). The local blue **Sunshine Coast Sunbus** operates hail and ride, connecting the three towns. (☎13 12 30 or 5492 8700. Fares $1.90-8.80.) Service #1 and #1A run from the Sunshine Plaza, down Cotton Tree Pde. and the Alexandra Headlands to the Mooloolaba Esplanade (at least every 30min. to Noosa, $5). Service #2 will take you from the Sunshine Plaza to Nambour.

ORIENTATION AND PRACTICAL INFORMATION. Aerodrome Rd. is the main commercial strip in Maroochydore. **Alexandra Pde.** runs from the end of Cotton Tree Pde., past Alexandra Heads, all the way to Mooloolaba, turning into Mooloolaba Esplanade near the end. **The Wharf,** home to many restaurants and shops, is on the right off Parkyn Pde., which is a quick left off the Mooloolaba Esplanade after it bends around by the Surf Club. The **tourist office** (☎5479 1566) is on Sixth Ave. just off Aerodrome Rd. Other services include: **taxi** (☎131 008; about $10 from Maroochydore to Mooloolaba); **Internet** at Infoconnect, 11 Ocean St., Maroochydore (☎5475 8555; $4.50 per 30min.); **post offices** at 22 King St. Cotton Tree, 1/32 Brisbane Rd., Mooloolaba, and 10 Ocean St., Maroochydore. (All open M-F 9am-5pm.) **Postal Code:** 4557, 4558.

ACCOMMODATIONS. Most hostels in Maroochy arrange fruit-picking work. **Palace Backpackers at Mooloolaba,** 75 Brisbane Rd., sports a colorful modern building and is close to the nightlife. Bunk dorms have kitchens on each level. Spacious doubles with bath and dorms with TV are in a separate, brightly-colored, motel-like building. Daily buses go to the good surf breaks. (☎5444 3399 or 1800 020 120. Dorms $22; doubles with bath $55. VIP.) **Suncoast Backpackers Lodge,** 50 Parker St., parallel to Aerodrome Dr., Maroochydore, is small, friendly, and clean, with a common space, kitchen, pool table, and continuous tunes. (☎5443 7544. Courtesy pickup and drop off in Mooloolaba. Key deposit $10. Reception daily 8:30am-1pm and 5-8pm. Dorms $18, weekly $108; twins and doubles $40, $120. VIP.) **Maroochydore YHA Backpackers,** 24 Schirmann Dr., is just over the river, a few blocks off Bradman Ave.; take Sunbus #1 or call for pickup. Eight-bed dorms have cement floors but the pool, gardens, enormous kitchen, large common areas, and afternoon trips to the hinterland, Australia Zoo, and beyond ensure you'll only use your room for sleeping. (☎5443 3151. Laundry $2. Reception daily 7:45am-1pm and 5-7pm. Dorms $18; singles $34-40; twins and doubles $40.) **Maroochy Shire Council** operates caravan parks in Cotton Tree (☎5443 1253), on Alexander Pde. (☎5443 7917), in Maroochydore (☎5443 1167), and Mooloolaba (☎5444 1201).

FOOD AND NIGHTLIFE. Maroochy has many good Thai restaurants, but the best is **Som Tam Thai,** on the corner of Fifth Ave. and Aerodrome Rd. (☎5479 1700. Open daily 5-10pm. Mains around $13.) **Krishna's Cafe,** Shop 2/7 First Ave., Maroochydore, has all-you-can-eat vegetarian meals (lunch $6.50, dinner $8; open M-F 11:30am-2:30pm, F, Su 5:30-8pm). Pick a pot and paint it **at Hard Clay Cafe,** Shop 2/20 Brisbane Rd., Mooloolaba. It also has great breakfast and gourmet sandwiches for under $5. (☎5444 2144. Open daily 8:30am-5pm.) **Mandolin Seafoods,** 174 Alexander Pde. has cheap, fresh seafood cooked to order. (☎5478 0777. Open M-Th 11am-7:30pm, F-Su 11am-8pm.) Coles **supermarket** is in Sunshine Plaza. (Open M-F 8am-9pm, Sa 8am-5:30pm, Su 10:30am-4pm.)

Mooloolaba comes alive after dark. **Friday's on the Wharf,** on the River Esp., is modern, but the old weatherboard sheds from the bar retain some of that old coastal Queensland character. (☎5444 8383. Tu Uni night. Restaurant open daily noon-3pm and 5:30-9pm; nightclub open late Tu, F, Sa.) The walls of **O'Malley's,** 109 The Esplanade, seem to sing: "come ant dance wyt me in Irlaunde." With no less than 17 beers on tap, you'll be dancing in no time. The bistro serves $9-12 Irish fare. (☎5452 6344. Open noon-2pm, 6-8pm. Bar open 10am-late. Live music daily.) **Secrets 2000,** 89 The Esplanade, knows the recipe for a busy nightclub: 13 TV screens, three bars, a DJ, and a dance floor. A NOMADS/VIP/YHA card will get you free entry and a free drink. (☎5478 3422. Open Tu-Su until 3am.)

ACTIVITIES. Being in Maroochy means spending time near the water. **Bad Company,** 6-8 Aerodrome Rd, Maroochydore, is a surf shop across the street from a good strip of beach. (☎5443 2457. Open M-F 9am-5pm. Short boards and body boards half-day $15; longboards half-day $25.) **Maroochydore Beach** offers good beach breaks for shortboard riders. **Alexandra Headlands** can have rips, large swells, and big crowds. If you'd rather ride the pavement hit up, **Skate Biz,** 150 Alexandra Pde., offers in-line skates, bikes, skateboards, and scooters. (☎5443 6111. Open daily 9am-5pm. half-day$7.50, full-day $22.) At **Underwater World,** on the Wharf, the largest oceanarium in the Southern Hemisphere, you can get a kiss from an eccentric seal (11am, 1, 3:30, 5pm) or glide through a wrap-around clear aquarium on a moving walkway. Sharks, giant rays, and 250kg Moreton Bay gropers swim inches overhead. (☎5444 8488; www.underwaterworld.com.au. Open daily 9am-6pm, last entry 5pm. $21.50, concessions $14, children $11.) If you're up for it, you can **dive with the sharks.** (Operated by Scuba World. 30min.; certified divers $95, tank and wetsuit only $82.50; non-certified, including scuba lesson $110; double dive on the Sunshine Coast reefs $109.)

Crew in sailing races at the **Mooloolaba Yacht Club** (☎5444 1355), near the end of Parkyn Pde., noon Wednesday and Sunday. Spots aren't guaranteed, but sign up for the "funsail" and bring a six-pack for the skipper.

NOOSA ☎07

Upper-class couples, pensioners, Australian families, and backpackers all come to Noosa in roughly equal numbers to enjoy the gorgeous beaches (Main Beach is great for surfing newcomers), glitzy shopping areas, outdoor dining, and lush, tropical greenery. Some criticize Noosa for catering to upscale vacationers with carefully crafted trendiness, but the area manages to draw backpackers in droves anyway, with high quality and fairly accommodating prices to the budget traveler. The cultures intermingle without friction during the day, but stick to their own at night. Weary, hungover backpackers may find welcome relief from the foam and tinsel of the Gold Coast, with activities to suit every whim and bush and rustic inland towns just around the corner. Cooloola National Park, just north of Noosa, is a wilderness ripe for 4WD-ing, hiking, canoeing, and camping.

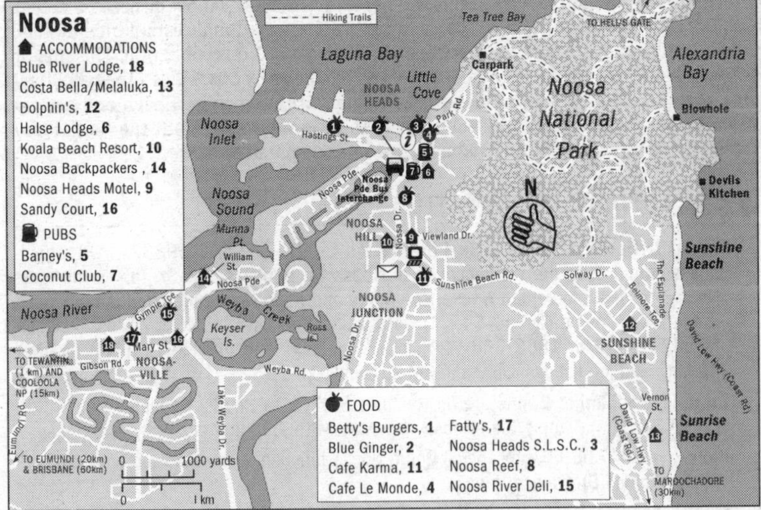

TRANSPORTATION

Buses: McCafferty's (☎13 14 99) and **Premier** run to: Airlie Beach (15hr., 2 per day, $130); Brisbane (3hr., 5 per day, $20); Bundaberg (5hr., 1 per day, $38); Cairns (25hr., 2 per day, $177); Hervey Bay (2¼-3½hr., 5 per day, $19); Mackay (13hr., 2 per day, $117); Maroochydore (30min., 4 per day, $9); Rockhampton (8½-9½hr., 2 per day, $75). **Suncoast Pacific** (☎5449 9966) goes to: Brisbane (2hr., 7 per day, $24); Gold Coast (3hr., 1 per day, $33.30); Hervey Bay (4hr., 1 per day, $22); Tin Can Bay (2hr., 1-2 per day, $16).

Public Transportation: Sunshine Coast Sunbus (☎13 12 30 or 5492 8700), offers frequent hail-and-ride service around Noosa. **Service #1** to Maroochydore, Mooloolaba, and Caloundra. **Service #10** to Noosa Junction, Noosa Heads, Tewantin, Sunshine Beach, and Sunrise Beach. **Service #12** to Eumundi and Cooroy. Fares $1.90-8.80; buses run approximately 6am-9pm, later on weekends.

Taxis: Suncoast Cabs (☎13 10 08) provides 24hr. service.

Car Rental: Henry's, 13 Noosa Dr. (☎5447 3777), has cars and bicycles. **Thrifty** (☎136 139) offers 4WD rentals for Fraser Island, and an esky free of charge. **Noosa Sunrover Rentals,** Noosa Harbour, Tewantin (☎5449 7833), specializes in 4WDs.

ORIENTATION

The Noosa area can be a bit confusing to navigate because its distinguishing features all have irritatingly similar names. The three main communities are Noosa Heads, Noosa Junction, and Noosaville; Noosa National Park is also a prime attraction. These areas are connected by Noosa Drive and Noosa Parade, and are located along the Noosa River, which runs into Noosa Sound and Noosa Inlet. Seriously…this isn't something to joke about. **Noosa Heads** is the main tourist area, and activity revolves around the sidewalk-chic **Hastings St.,** one block north of the **Noosa Parade Bus Interchange.** Many trendy shops, restaurants, upscale hotels, and Main Beach line the street; the entrance to **Noosa National Park** is at its end.

A 15min. stroll down Hastings St. to the wooden sidewalk ramp leads to the heart of **Noosa Junction,** Noosa's business center. The **post office, supermarket,** and a string of **banks** all lie within 5min. of each other. **Noosaville** is 3km southwest of Noosa Heads (30min. walk), and is the departure point for most cruises to Fraser Island. Its main street, **Gympie Tce.,** is filled with international restaurants, motels, and boat hires. The **Sunshine Beach** area is 3km east of Noosa Junction. The cluster of beachfront hostels here are best reached by car or by bus, since the walk along the busy David Low Way takes at least 30min. Both Sunshine Beach and nearby **Sunrise Beach** (just try to tell them apart) are popular spots, but the total 40km stretch of sand leaves ample room for bathers to spread out.

PRACTICAL INFORMATION

Tourist Office: Tourism Noosa Information Centre (☎5447 4988; www.tourism-noosa.com.au), at the T intersection of Noosa Dr. and Hastings St. This is the most Noosa-focused info center. *Noosa: The Guide* and *Hello Noosa* are good introductions to the town. Open daily 9am-5pm. **Travel Bugs,** 9 Sunshine Beach Rd., Noosa Junction (☎5474 8530 or 1800 666 720), does bookings and provides Internet ($3 per 30min.) and job listings. Open daily M-Su 8am-10pm.

Currency Exchange: Banks are on Hastings St., Noosa Heads; Sunshine Beach Rd., Noosa Junction; Gympie Tce., Noosaville. Open M-Th 9:30am-4pm, F 9:30am-5pm.

Police: (☎5447 5888), on Langura Court, Noosa Junction; also at the corner of Hastings St. and Noosa Dr., Noosa Heads.

Medical Services: Noosa Hospital, 111 Goodchap St., Noosaville (☎5445 9200).

Internet Access: The cheapest Internet is available (to non-guests as well) at **Koala Beach Resort** ($1 per 15min.). Also at: **Travel Bugs** (see **Tourist Office,** above).

Post Office: 91-93 Noosa Rd., Noosa Junction (☎5447 3280; fax 5447 5160). Open M-F 9am-5pm, Sa 9am-12:30pm. **Postal Code:** 4567.

ACCOMMODATIONS

Lodging in Noosa comes in three general categories: hostels, motels or hotels, and "holiday units," which are sometimes private homes. Intense competition for budget travelers makes for low hostel prices and perks such as cheap meals, courtesy shuttle service, surfboards, and on-site bars. With Noosa's increasing popularity, there aren't always enough budget beds to go around and during Christmas and school vacations, rates can double; be sure to book ahead. Motel and hotel rooms can top $200 on Hastings St., but are much cheaper without a beachfront view. Families may find it cheaper to rent units or homes; **Accom Noosa** (☎5447 3444 or 1800 072 078; www.accomnoosa.com.au) can help find affordable, longer stays. Camping is not allowed in Noosa National Park, but it is possible in **Cooloola National Park** (see p. 332).

NOOSA HEADS

Halse Lodge (YHA), 2 Halse Ln. (☎5447 3377 or 1800 242 567; www.halselodge.com.au), up the hill across Noosa Dr. from the Noosa Pde. bus interchange. This stately house built in 1880 attracts a mellow crowd, though the thin walls make the mornings not so mellow; ask to be in the annex. Large common areas. A tiny bar is festive until the 11pm common space lockdown. Laundry $2. Reception daily 7am-8pm. Dorms $22; twins and doubles $49. Prices rise slightly at peak times.

Koala Beach Resort, 44 Noosa Dr. (☎5447 3355 or 1800 357 457; www.koala-backpackers.com). A 10min. walk from the bus interchange; take a right onto Noosa Dr. and follow it over the hill. Popular with a young, hard-partying crowd. Laundry, pool, volleyball court, small basement kitchen, and outdoor eating area. Internet $1 per 15min. Reception daily 7:30am-8pm. Dorms with bath $20; twins and doubles $45. VIP.

Noosa Heads Motel, 2 Viewland Dr. (☎5449 2873), on the corner of Noosa Dr., just up the hill from the Noosa Junction rotary. Just minutes away from the action, but a beautiful jungle-like lot makes it feel hidden in the wilderness. Clean units with bath, double beds, kitchen, TV, and covered parking. Downstairs units $69; upstairs units $79; add $10 for each additional person up to 4.

SUNSHINE BEACH AND SUNRISE BEACH

Although these hostels are removed from the Noosa action (25min. walk from the Junction), they are close to the beach. By car, they're off the David Low Hwy.

Costa Bella/Melaluka, 7 Selene St. (☎5447 3663 or 1800 003 663; www.melaluka.com.au). Take the highway to Sunrise Beach; left turn at Vernon St. and make 2 quick rights down the hill. Although it may lack the communal hostel atmosphere, you'll have to pick your jaw off the floor after seeing the new, spacious Costa Bella units, which are self-contained with ocean views and patios. The other 2 buildings also offer fully equipped units. 2 pools, BBQ, Internet. Laundry in each unit. Frequent 5min. courtesy van to town. Reception M-F 8am-8pm, Sa-Su 9am-7pm. Old buildings $22 or $24 per person; Costa Bella $26 per person.

Dolphins, 14 Duke St. (☎5447 2100 or 1800 454 456; www.dolphinsbeachresort.com). Energy and friendliness make this a choice Noosa spot, close to the beach and shops. Self-contained units have cable TV, kitchen, and bathroom. Don't get tangled up in the web of hammocks next to the all fun outdoor common area. Internet, table tennis. Dorms $20; twins and doubles $55. NOMADS/VIP/YHA.

NOOSAVILLE

Most of the travelers who stay in this less glamorous part of town prefer the serenity of the Noosa River to the beaches, which are a 30min. walk away.

A MOVING LOCAL LANDMARK Betty, of Betty's Burgers, had to leave her Hastings St. shop after 20 years of serving Noosa. The city responded by buying her a caravan from which to serve her legendary $1 burgers. The lesson of this experience was not lost on Betty, whose burgers are now $1.70. Follow your nose to the end of Hastings St., away from the national park, turn right at the roundabout, and head toward the beach to the caravan. Open daily 8am-4pm.

Noosa Backpackers Resort, 11 Williams St. (☎5449 8151 or 1800 626 673). Located on a side street 2min. from the river, 25min. from Main Beach. Courtesy van, weekly movie nights, and daily theme dinners ($6-7.50). Discounts offered on their Trailblazers tour of Fraser Island. Game room, cable TV, swimming pool, Internet. Reception daily 8am-9pm. 4-bed dorms $19; doubles $42, with bath $50. VIP.

Blue River Lodge, 181 Gympie Tce. (☎5449 7564), directly across from Noosa River. Spotless units with 2 bedrooms, but 1 will remain locked unless you pay $10 for each guest beyond 2. Pickup available. Laundry. Units $60. 7th night free.

Sandy Court, 30 James St. (☎5449 7225). A half-hostel complex 2min. from the river. Units are motel rooms with 3-4 bunks installed, which translates into spacious kitchens, TV lounges, and bath. Parking, laundry, Internet $6 per hr. Free pickup. Check-out 9:30am. Reception 6:30am-8pm. Dorms $20; twins and doubles $45.

FOOD

With over 140 restaurants in Noosa, more than 30 of which are on Hastings St., you can be sure to find some great, reasonably priced food. The three main food clusters are Noosa Hill and Junction; Hastings St., Noosa Heads; Gympie Tce., Noosaville. The surf clubs are a great place for a cheap meal or a sunset beer; try **Noosa Heads Surf Life Saving Club,** 69 Hastings St. (☎5447 2355). Backpackers, however, tend to eat at hostels, most of which offer meals for $7 or less. **Franklin's supermarket** is off Sunshine Beach Rd. in Noosa Fair Shopping Centre, Noosa Junction. (Open M-F 8am-9pm, Sa 8am-5:30pm, Su 10:30am-4pm.)

Fatty's, 4 Thomas St., Noosaville (☎5474 4399). Stuff your face with great pizza and pasta while watching wipeouts on the big screen. Fat Hour (5-6:30pm) is fatter than your average Happy Hour. Open daily 5pm-midnight, lunch F-M 11am-2pm.

Blue Ginger, 30 Hastings St., Noosa Heads (☎5447 3211). Bright and classy, serves gourmet Thai food. BYO. Yum Cha F-Su 11:30am-2pm. Dinner daily 5pm-late.

Café Le Monde, 52 Hastings St., Noosa Heads (☎5449 2366; fax 5449 2108). A local favorite and breakfast gathering place for local surfer celebs. The express lunch baguettes are great ($7 for a foot-long; available 11am-5pm). Live music 5 nights a week. Open daily 7am-midnight.

Noosa River Deli, 255 Gympie Tce., Noosaville (☎5474 0404). A pleasant riverside spot for lunch. Sandwiches from $5. Light meals $8.50-9.50. Open daily 8am-4pm.

Café Karma, 16 Sunshine Beach Rd., Noosa Junction (☎5474 8588). Gourmet sandwiches ($6-8.50) in a nice setting. Open M-Sa 7am-5pm, Su 7am-3pm.

Noosa Reef, Noosa Dr. (☎5447 4477), on the hill between Hastings St. and the Junction. Modern and airy, with a family atmosphere. The cafe deck has great views of the town. Parents can send their kids to the adjoining video/play room for a $8 meal while they enjoy pizza, steaks, and fish'n'chips for $8-19.

SIGHTS AND ACTIVITIES

NOOSA NATIONAL PARK. Noosa National Park (☎5447 3243), is a 454-hectare area of tropical vegetation, coastal walking paths, and rare wildlife, which bills itself as the most visited park in Australia with over one million visitors per year. A lovely, koala-strewn path (1.4km) through the woods from the Noosa information booth on Hastings St. will land you at the entrance; or follow Hastings St, take a left on Park Dr. and follow the boardwalk. The park is ideal for walking and jogging, though you should take caution at night. The tourist office provides maps of five interconnected paths, ranging from 1 to 4.2km. The coastal track, which offers elevated views of the ocean and ends at exhilarating **Hell's Gates,** is gorgeous at sunrise, and offers many places to **surf** if you walk your board in. Beautiful stretches of **beaches** are on **Alexandria Bay** on the eastern side of the park, accessible primarily from **Sunshine Beach.** Water and toilets are available, but camping is prohibited. **Little Cove,** hidden discretely between Hastings St. and the national park, a 5min. walk from the shops, is a charming and secluded beach.

SURFING. With warm water temperatures and a strong surfing community, the Sunshine Coast is a great place to surf. The best season is November to March, as the waves in winter tend to be fickle. Noosa is a wave mecca of five right-hand points, with the bonus of a beautiful backdrop. **First Point** is great for longboarders, while **Little Cove** suits beginners. The best waves are perhaps **National Park** and **Tea Tree,** with long lines and barrel sections, but unfortunately this is not a secret we are divulging—in good conditions it can get extremely crowded. For isolation, try **Double Island Point** to the north in Cooloola, but watch out for rips. On the other side of Noosa National Park, try **Sunshine Beach,** with varying conditions, but so much surf there's almost always a good break somewhere.

Learn to Surf, with a world champion Merrick Davis, guarantees you'll be standing by the end of one lesson. *(☎0418 787 577. Book ahead. $30 per 2hr.)* For boards, try **Noosa Longboards,** Shop 4/64 Hastings St., Noosa Head. *(☎5474 2828; body boards $10 per 4hr., $15 per day; shortboards $15/$25; longboards $25/$40. Open M-F 9:30am-5:30pm, Sa 9:30am-5pm, Su 10am-5pm.)* **Impact Surf,** Shop 1-7 Sunshine Beach Rd., Noosa Junction. *(☎5474 9198; body boards $10 per 4hr.; surfboards $25. Open M-F 9:30am-5:30pm, Sa 9:30am-5pm, Su 10am-5pm.)*

OTHER ACTIVITIES. Kitesurf lets you try out your water wings as kite and surfboard join forces for an exhilarating new sport. *(☎5455 6677 2hr. lesson $75.)* **Clip Clop Horse Treks** lets you splash through lakes and trot through bush around Lake Weyba for a day. *(☎5449 1254. $150.)* **Aussie Sea Kayak Company** runs sea kayaking tours in the waterways around the Sunshine Coast. *(☎5477 5335. 2hr. sunset tour with champagne $40, half-day $60, full day includes lunch $105.)* Tandem skydive over the coast with **Sunshine Skydivers,** one of the least expensive operators in the state. *(☎0500 522 533. 12,000 ft. $245, backpackers $209; 14,000 ft. $319/$259.)* Cruise around the Great Sandy National Park using thermals and natural lift while **paragliding.** *(☎5445 7466. 40m instructional tandem flight $80, full-day lesson $130; full certification courses offered.)* Noosa is also a great departure point for **Great Sandy National Park** (for other options, see **Cooloola National Park,** p. 332, and **Fraser Island,** p. 337).

QUEENSLAND

ENTERTAINMENT AND NIGHTLIFE

Barney's, on Noosa Dr. near Hastings St., has an unpretentious surfing mood perfect for a relaxing beer. Get a "huge" beer for $8—you won't mind taking your time. (☎5447 4544. Happy Hour 4-6pm. Open 10:30am-midnight.) **The Koala Bar,** 44 Noosa Dr., in the hostel, is backpacker-central with pool tables, DJ, and nightly specials to spice up the evening, which ends abruptly at the stroke of midnight. The **Coconut Club,** next to Barney's near Hastings St., known as "The Nut," has dancing in a faux tropical setting. (Open W-Su; $5 cover F-Sa.) Noosa's slightly upscale night spot, **Rolling Rock,** Upper Level, Bay Village on Hastings St., Noosa Heads, is packed with the tragically hip. Th guest DJs rock the house; Su features live local bands. (☎5447 2255. Open 9pm-3am every night, but door closes at 1:30am. Cover $6 after 10pm W-Su. M $3 drinks. Cash only.) **Reef Bar** (☎5447 4477) is underneath the Noosa Reef restaurant on Noosa Dr. This nightspot offers pool tables, sports channels, and accomplished drinkers.

COOLOOLA NAT'L PARK

Extending 50km north of Noosa up to Rainbow Beach is the sandy, white coast and 64,000 hectares of forest of Cooloola National Park. Together with Fraser Island, Cooloola forms the Great Sandy Region, the largest sand mass in the world. Intrepid explorers and Sunday strollers alike will enjoy this wilderness area. The beaches are generally uncrowded, but in summer months and holidays there's a thick blanket of tents and picnickers on the sands.

TRANSPORTATION. **Rainbow Beach** approaches the park at its northernmost tip. The 2min. **Noosa Northshore Ferry** (☎5447 1321) leaves from across from Moorindil St. in **Tewantin** for the park ($4.50 per vehicle). **Rainbow 4WD Hire,** 9 Karoonda Crescent, Rainbow Beach (☎5486 3555), rents 4WDs from $110 per day. **Noosa's Cooloola/Everglades Cruises** picks up along the Sunshine Coast for its full-day Everglades BBQ cruise. They also offer a two-in-one safari which includes a tour of Cooloola beach. (☎5449 9177 or 1800 657 666. M and W-F. Everglades $62, children $40; 2-in-1 $95, $62.) **Polleys Coaches** tours Tin Can Bay ($9) and Rainbow Beach ($11.50) from **Gympie.** (☎5482 9455. Departs M-F 6am and 1:30pm.)

PRACTICAL INFORMATION. Cooloola National Park stretches 50km along the coast from Noosa in the south to Rainbow Beach in the north. The road from Tewantin, northwest of Noosa, accesses the park and the western side of Lake Cootharaba. Information on the park is available from **Cooloola Shire Council,** 242 Mary St., Gympie (☎5482 1911); **Rainbow Beach Tourist Information Centre**, 8 Rainbow Beach Rd., Rainbow Beach (☎5486 3227); **Queensland Parks and Wildlife** office in Rainbow Beach (☎5486 3160); Noosa tourism offices.

ACCOMMODATIONS. Hidden in the bush, but only 20min. from Noosa, **Gagaju** is a stress-free escape on the border of Cooloola National Park and Noosa River. It's as eco-friendly, welcoming, and in touch with nature as a place could be. Dorm accommodation is in 10- to 14-bed bush bunkhouses—it's like camp, but much better. (☎5474 3522 or 1300 302 271. Free pickup from Noosa. Running water and laundry. Sites $11 per person; dorms $18. Canoe trips: half-day $22, full-day $32, 2-day $79, 3-day $99.) **The Rocks Backpackers Resort,** 3 Spectrum St., Rainbow Beach, is a clean, modern hostel, that organizes cheap Fraser 4WD trips. (☎5486 3711. Dorms $18; doubles $38-48.) **Camping** is permitted at 14 sites in the park. (Permits $4 per person, payable at the self-registration stations.)

QUEENSLAND

SIGHTS. The Cooloola National Park forests hold many natural wonders: rainforests growing from pure sand, winding waterways shaded by mangroves, and characteristic Aussie critters like kangaroos and ground parrots. Even the plants are unusual: endangered *boroniakeysii* (pink-flowered shrubs) mingle with thin, stubborn stalks of blackbutt, and melaluka "tea trees" dye the river a deep black. One of the best ways to enjoy the park is to canoe or motor up to **Lake Cootharaba,** Queensland's largest natural lake, and the **Everglades,** where the dark water creates mirror images of the dense riverbanks lined with sedges. As in any wilderness area, keep **safety** in mind and watch out for the wildlife. Sharks in the river system occasionally approach the shore, and swim alongside the stingrays, catfish, and jellyfish in the ocean. Use caution when swimming in inland lakes.

The beach in Cooloola is famous for its natural beauty. Extending from Rainbow Beach to Double Island Point are the 200m-high cliffs of the **Coloured Sands.** When the weathering of iron-rich minerals in the dune soils formed the cliffs, they were stained in a complex range of tones and hues; rain intensifies the colors. Aboriginal legend speaks of Rainbow, a representative of the gods, who was killed in an attempt to save a beautiful maiden, as he crashed to the ground; his colors permeated the sand. **Carlo Sandblow,** near Rainbow Beach, has great views on both sides. Captain Cook named **Double Island Point** in 1770, when he believed the point was actually islands. The **lighthouse** at the point offers 360° views of the coastline.

SUNSHINE COAST HINTERLAND

Just inland of the Sunshine Coast lies a veritable smorgasbord of tourist delights: stunning national parks, roadside crafts markets, and kitschy tourist traps. The hinterland is inaccessible via public transportation, but can be reached by driving or a tour. **Storeyline Tours** offers several options including a tour of Montville, Blackall Range, and Glasshouse Mountains, or a morning trip to the Eumundi Markets. (☎5474 1500. Montville-Glasshouse M half-day $34, concessions $32, children $17; full day $48/$46/$25. Markets W and Sa $12, children $5.) **Noosa Hinterland Tours** hits the same regions. (☎5474 3366. Montville-Glasshouse M-F full-day $50, children $20; markets $12/$9.) **Off Beat Rainforest Tours** accesses exclusive rainforest for eco-guided walks in Conondale National Park. (☎5473 5135; www.offbeattours.com.au. $115, children $75.)

POMONA. Pomona, north of Eumundi, is home to the **Majestic Theatre,** the oldest silent movie theater in Australia. *(☎5485 2330. Th evening 8:30 wine, movie, and supper $9, children $7. Annual movie festival in early Sept.)*

EUMUNDI MARKETS. Some hostels in Noosa provide shuttle service to the famous **Eumundi Markets,** a bustling collection of just about anything from sweets to sheets and soaps to boats. Get there early for the good stuff. *(20min. south of Noosa Heads. Open Sa 7am-2pm.)* A kinder, gentler "upmarket market" appears on Wednesday. *(For more info, contact Eumundi Historical Association ☎5442 8581).*

YANDINA. In the town of Yandina, just south of Eumundi, is the **Ginger Factory,** 50 Pioneer Rd., where the zest on your sushi and the bite in your ale most likely originate. The factory is the largest ginger processing plant in the southern hemisphere. If that doesn't impress you, neither will the factory, though the huge vats of multi-colored ginger in different stages of processes are worth a free peak. *(☎5446 7096. Open daily 9am-5pm.)* Across the street is **Nutworks,** with free multi-flavored macadamia nut tastings. Just off the Bruce Hwy., on the Nambour connection, is a big pineapple and **Big Pineapple Plantation,** a working fruit and nut plantation, with small rides and shows. *(☎5442 1333. Open daily 9am-5pm.)*

BLACKALL RANGE. The sheer Blackall Range escarpment rises from the plains to cradle green pastures and rainforests, sprinkled with the old country villages of Mapleton, Flaxton, Montville, and Maleny. Once known for its hippie appeal, Montville now has a couple blocks of antiques, galleries, crafts, teahouses, and a cuckoo clock shop. *(From Noosa follow the Bruce Hwy. south to Nambour and then turn toward the Blackall Range. The Montville Information Centre is on Main St. ☎5478 5544.)*

KONDALILLA AND MAPLETON FALLS. Kondalilla and Mapleton Falls National Parks, both on the road north of Montville, have pleasant trails and picnic areas. The 80m Kondalilla Falls (Aboriginal for "rushing water") are especially gorgeous. Although the Picnic Creek walk (1.2km) will technically get you to the lookout and rock pool, the best views of the rushing waters are sprinkled along the Kondalilla Falls circuit track (2.7km) that begins at the lookout. The Wompoo circuit (1.3km) at Mapleton Falls, located just past Mapleton on the Obi Obi Rd., winds its rainforested way to an excellent lookout, though the carpark lookout gives a better view of the falls. *(Ranger ☎5494 3983.)*

A RUNNING BET In a Pomona pub in 1957, a bet was made that no one could run up Mt. Cooroora (439m) in less than an hour. In just 40min., Bruce Samuels won himself 40 pounds. The challenge has since become an annual race to be crowned King of the Mountain. The record stands at under 25min. to climb this extremely steep 1.5km path with its loose stones, slippery spots, and caution signs. Most run the race in about 2hr. and then immediately proceed to the pub.

QUEENSLAND

GLASSHOUSE MOUNTAINS. The Glasshouse Mountains rise abruptly from the rolling farmlands south of Landsborough. According to Aboriginal legend, this group of 13 volcanic peaks represents the father Tibrogargan, the pregnant mother Beerwah, and their many children. This distinct landscape was formed by gradual weathering since the last activity 20 million years ago. Walking access is limited, but experienced climbers can ascend Mt. Beerwah and Mt. Tibrogargan. *(Signs are posted off the Bruce Hwy.)*

HERVEY BAY ☎07

For many travelers, Hervey Bay ("HAR-vee") is little more than a pause before heading to Fraser Island. Since most backpackers stay here for a few nights while in transit to Fraser, it makes for one of the craziest backpacking party atmospheres on the coast. The whale-watching season (Aug.-Oct.) also draws crowds and stands as one of the bay's touristy draws.

TRANSPORTATION

Trains: A shuttle bus links Hervey Bay to **Maryborough Coach Terminal,** on Lennox St., Maryborough ($4.40), leaving Hervey Bay 30min. before trains leave Maryborough. **Tilt Train** (☎13 22 32) departs Maryborough to: **Brisbane** (4½hr., 1-2 per day, $45.10); **Bundaberg** (1hr., 1-2 per day, $18.70); **Rockhampton** (4¾hr., 1-2 per day, $52).

Buses: Bay Central Coach Terminal, Bay Central Shopping Center, Pialba (☎4124 4000). Open M-F 6am-5:30pm, Sa-Su 6am-1pm. **McCafferty's** (☎13 14 99) runs to: **Airlie Beach** (13hr., 4 per day, $84-123); **Brisbane** (5-6hr., 8 per day, $30-41); **Bundaberg** (2hr., 3 per day, $11-25); **Cairns** (23hr., 5 per day, $155-168); **Mackay** (11hr., 5 per day, $71-108); **Maroochydore** (4hr., 3 per day, $28); **Noosa** (3½hr., 4 per day, $18-24); **Rockhampton** (6-6½hr., 5 per day, $30-69). **Premier** also run to these destinations at considerably cheaper prices, but only run one bus a day.

ORIENTATION AND PRACTICAL INFORMATION

QUEENSLAND

Hervey Bay is actually a clump of suburbs facing north toward the Bay. Named from west to east the suburbs are: **Port Vernon, Pialba, Scarness, Torquay,** and **Urangan.** Most of the action is along **The Esplanade** at the water's edge, where takeaway shops and tour booking agencies seem to repeat endlessly. The harbor extends all the way down the Esplanade and then around to Pulgul St., and is a superb place to pick up cheap seafood fresh from the trawlers.

Tourist Office: There are countless booking agents on The Esplanade. The two offices staffed by volunteers are true information centers offering unbiased advice. **Bay Central Tourist Information Center,** Bay Central Shopping Center, Pialba (☎4124 8244; fax 4128 1122), next to the coach terminal. Open M-F 9am-5pm.

Currency Exchange: National Bank, 415 The Esplanade (☎13 22 65), has an **ATM.** $5 fee to change traveler's checks. **ANZ** (☎4125 5371) changes traveler's checks ($7) and cash ($5). Both open M-Th 9:30am-4pm, F 9:30am-5pm.

Emergency: ☎000.

Police: (24hr. ☎4128 5333), on the corner of Queens and Torquay Rd.

Hospital: Hervey Bay Hospital, Nissen St., Pialba (☎4120 6666).

Taxi: Hervey Bay Taxi (☎13 10 08).

Bicycle Hire: Rayz Pushbike Hire (☎0417 644 814), offers free delivery and pickup. $12 per day; tandems $24. Open 7am-5pm.

Camping Gear: Torquay Disposals and Camping, 424 The Esplanade (☎4125 6511). Open M-F 8:30am-5pm, Sa 8:30am-4pm, Su 8:30am-noon.

Internet Access: 346 The Esplanade, Scarness (☎4124 2289). 5¢ per min. or $3 per hr. Open M-Sa 8:30am-10pm, Su 9:30am-10pm.

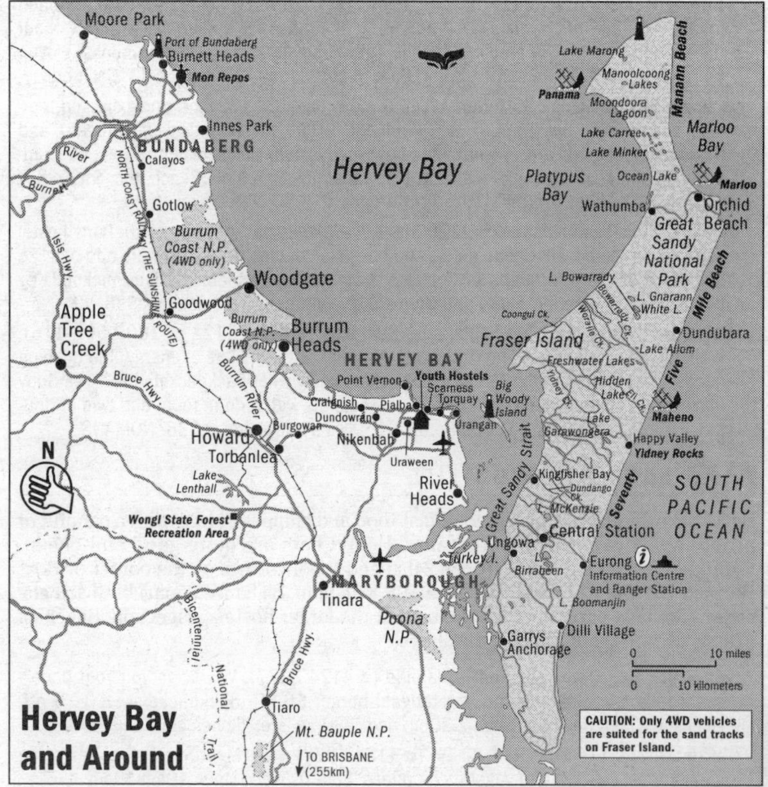

Post Office: 414 The Esplanade, Torquay (☎4125 1101) and 564 The Esplanade, Urangan (☎4128 9280). Both open M-F 8:30am-5pm. Another at Bay Central Shopping Centre (☎4125 9126), across from bus terminal in Pialban, is also open Sa 8:30-11:30am. **Postal Code:** 4655.

ACCOMMODATIONS

Hostel courtesy buses line up like pigs at a trough to meet incoming buses at the Bay Central Coach Terminal. Most hostels run Fraser 4WD safaris. While you can book a safari that is not based at your accommodation, you can often get free nights when booking tours through respective hostels.

Colonial Backpackers YHA (☎4125 1844 or 1800 818 280), corner of Pulgul and Boat Harbour Dr., Urangan. Rustic, relaxing, relentlessly spotless, but removed from the center of town. A licensed in-house restaurant sprawls onto the pool deck area, whipping up tasty meals for $5-13. Free pickup and drop-off. Laundry $2. Key deposit $10. Reception 6:45am-9:30pm. Dorms $18-19.50; twins and doubles $45-52; log cabins $23-26 per person; villas $25-39 per person.

The Woolshed, 181 Torquay Rd., Scarness (☎4124 0677). 5min. from the beach and shops. This unique smaller hostel has an outdoor setting featuring waterfalls, ponds, and gardens. Chickens have the run of the backyard and rooms have character. Co-ed bathrooms with great showers. Kitchen and BBQ area. Laundry. Check-out 10am. Reception daily 6:30am-at least 8pm. Dorms $17; doubles, twins $40.

QUEENSLAND

Friendly Hostel, 182 Torquay Rd., Scarness (☎4124 4107). The owners are indeed friendly, if a bit firm; partiers need not apply. The place feels more like a B&B without the second B; cable TV, reading libraries, fully supplied kitchen, and no bunks. Pickup on request. Laundry. Reception 8am-10pm. 3-bed dorms $17; twins $40. Cash only.

Beaches Backpackers, 195 Torquay Tce., Torquay (☎4124 1322). A pool-centered, partying hostel. 24hr. bar (Happy Hour 3-4pm and 7-8pm, table-dancing encouraged), and a budget bistro (7-11am, 6-9pm). Mega-package includes Fraser Island safari, Whitsunday sail, and a smattering of nights at their other hostel in Airlie Beach from $530. Key deposit $10. Reception daily 7am-7pm. Dorms $16.50. VIP.

Koala's, 408 The Esplanade (☎4125 3601; www.koala-backpackers.com). Party hostel across from the beach. Cheap meals and bar which bumps till late. Beware add-ons like linen hire $1.50 and heaps of deposits, from cutlery to blankets. Free pickup. Key deposit $10. Reception 7am-7pm. Dorms $15, with bath $18; doubles $38. VIP.

Smuggler's Rest, 369 The Esplanade, Scarness (☎4128 2122 or 1800 502 115). Walk the planks (or down The Esplanade) to great rates and lots of energy. The building needs some work, but the former backpackers know what backpackers like. Free Sony Playstation, first-run videos $2. Self-contained units with a dorm room and twin or double. Reception daily 8am-10pm. Dorms $15; twins and doubles $38. NOMADS.

FOOD AND NIGHTLIFE

Hervey Bay has the usual spread of fast-food and chippers, along with a handful of prohibitively expensive restaurants. Hostel eats are quite good and cheap. Express, 414 The Esplanade (open 24hr) and Woolworth's, on the corner of Boat Harbour Dr. and Elizabeth St. (open M-F 8am-9pm, Sa 8am-5:30pm) both sell **groceries.** The best party bets are the bars at the larger hostels, especially Beaches, Fraser Escapes, and Koalas (see above).

The Black Dog Cafe, 381 The Esplanade (☎4124 3177). Will serve you your bone—sushi rolls $4.50-6, outstanding teriyaki burger $6.20. Backpackers get 10% off. Licensed. Open daily 10:30am-2:30pm and 5:30pm-late; kitchen closes at 9:30pm.

Curried Away, 174 Boat Harbour Dr. (☎4124 1577), near Main St,. Pialba, has some great curries ($9-12) and vegetarian options. Free Delivery. Open 10am-10pm.

China World, 402 The Esplanade (☎4125 1233), on the corner of Tavistock St. Has an $11 all-you-can-eat dinner buffet. Open M-F 11am-2pm and 5:30-9pm.

Dolly's, 406 The Esplanade (☎4125 5633), is a local bar with live music, free pool (7-9pm), and $6 jugs (9-10pm). Courtesy bus available. Open daily 9pm-3am.

QUEENSLAND

ACTIVITIES

WHALE WATCHING. Weighing up to 40 tons, the equivalent of 11 elephants or 600 people, the humpback whale stops in Hervey Bay on its migration back to Antarctica after giving birth in the warmer waters up north. The whales assemble in Platypus Bay, 50km from Urangan Harbour, where sightings are undeniably dramatic. Whale watching is big business from August to November. Fourteen boats in Hervey Bay form the whale-watching fleet: most offer guaranteed whale sightings during the season or your next trip is free. The flagship vessel is the *Spirit of Hervey Bay*, built for whale watching, underwater viewing, and a whale-listening hydrophone. *(☎4125 5131 or 1800 642 544. Departs Great Sandy Straits Marina 8:30am and 1:30pm for a half-day cruise. $79, children $44.)* *M.V. Princess II* offers an affordable full-day, small-boat experience. This tour is more personalized, though it lacks the glitz of the big, fancy vessels. *(☎4124 0400. BBQ lunch included. Full-day $65, children $35.)* *Quick Cat* offers a half-day, small-boat experience. *(☎1800 671 977. Departs Great Sandy Straits Marina 8am and 1pm for a half-day cruise $66, children $44.)*

Every year, the return of the humpback whales is celebrated with the aptly-named **Whale Festival,** held for two weeks in August. It features an Electric Light Parade in which locals carry desk lamps up and down the streets. *(☎4124 9609.)*

DIVING. Divers Mecca may be the best place on the coast to do a PADI Open Water certification course. This course is one of the cheapest in Australia and it includes four boat dives, not shore dives. *(403 The Esplanade. ☎4125 1626 or 1800 351 626. Courtesy pickups. Open daily 9am-5pm; courses begin M and Th. Intro dive $80, PADI certification $169, Advanced Open Water $242.)*

OTHER ACTIVITIES. Splash Safaris explores the waters off Fraser Island, stopping on deserted beaches and snorkeling among coral reefs. You get more out of the full-day tour to the tip of Big Woody Island. *(☎0500 555 580; www.splashsafaris.virtualave.net. Half-day $59, full-day $69.)* **Torquay Beach Hire** offers beach activities. *(The Esplanade, Torquay Beach. ☎4125 5528. Waterskiing $25, big banana $9, catamaran $25.)* **Skydive Hervey Bay** includes a scenic flight over Fraser Island. *(☎4124 8248. 10,000ft $219; 14,000ft $308.)* **Humpback Camel Safari** offers 2hr. rides. *(Toogoom, 15min. from Hervey Bay. ☎4128 0055. Pickup available. $38.50.)*

FRASER ISLAND ☎07

Fraser Island, the world's largest sand island and a World-Heritage-listed national park, attracts 350,000 visitors every year. Backpackers up and down the coast can't stop talking about the island—an untrammeled wilderness scarred only by a 4WD track. It's a must-stop on the trek up (or down) the coast. This is the ideal destination for any outdoorsman: 4WDer, bushwalker, or fisherman. Although a sand island, it is covered with dense rainforest and punctuated by over 200 lakes. The winds perpetually resculpt the island's topography, but its unique natural beauty is a constant.

TRANSPORTATION

BY BOAT

Fraser Island Vehicular Ferry Services runs ferries from several locations (return fare: $16.50 walk-on; vehicles $82, $5.50 for each person in addition to the driver)

- **Fraser Venture** (☎4125 4444), the most convenient for independent 4WDers, from Riverheads to Wanggoolba Creek; 30min.; daily 9, 10:15am, 3:30pm; Sa also 7am.
- **Fraser Dawn** (☎4125 4444), from Urangan Boat Harbor to Moon Point; 60min.; 8:30am, 3:30pm.
- **Kingfisher** (☎4125 5511), from Riverheads to Kingfisher. 45min.; 7:15, 11am, 2:30pm.
- **Rainbow Venture** (☎5486 3154), on the southern tip, connects Inskip Point near Rainbow Beach (see p. 332) to Hook Point. 15min.; continuously 7am-4:30pm; walk-on $5; vehicles $30, includes passengers.

BY PLANE

Air Fraser Island (☎4125 3600) offers one-way or same-day trips ($50) and an overnight trip, including 4WD hire, return flight, and camping equipment ($190). They also offer a scenic flight over Fraser (30min., $165).

GUIDED TOURS

A structured, safe, and hassle-free way to see the island is on a tour, assuming you're willing to forego the freedom of a personal 4WD and outdoor camping. Tour options are plentiful, but forget daytrips—you'll need at least two days to see the island. The prices are higher than the hostel self-guided specials, but once you've factored in food, permits, and petrol, the tours are a good deal, especially for those traveling alone.

Fraser Experience Tours (☎1800 606 422). Offers personal, fun, informative tours with a maximum of 14 in a group. 2-day $165; 3-day $250, with Tin Can Bay and Rainbow Beach, $270.

Trailblazers Tours (☎5474 1235 or 1800 626 673). Operates a 3-day tour through Noosa Backpackers Resort. This is the best guided safari package available for a younger crowd, mixing guiding and camping, including Cooloola National Park's Coloured Sands. Departs M, W, Sa; $229.

Sand Island Safari's (☎1800 246 911). More expensive outfit, running 3-day tours with a maximum of 16 people. Departs T, W, F, Sa; $290.

Kingfisher Bay Wilderness Adventure Tours (☎4120 3333 or 1800 072 555; www.kingfisherbay.com). The most expensive, but very well run, with accommodation at the spacious Wilderness Lodge. 2-day overnight $198; 3-day overnight $270; quad share, twin share extra.

Fraser Island Top Tours (☎4125 3933 or 1800 063 933; www.fraserisland-tours.com.au). Offers accommodation in Fraser Island Retreat, Happy Valley. Day-tour $82, children $49. Wilderness Safari leaves M, Tu, Th, Sa; Northern Adventure leaves Su, W, F; both 2 days $170. 3-day safari departs T and F $299, children $229 and stays at the Cathedral Beach Resort.

Fraser Venture Tours (☎4125 4444 or 1800 249 122). Attracts a younger set to their daytrips and 2-3 day safaris with accommodation at Eurong Beach Resort. Day-tour $82; 2-day safari $170; 3-day safari $280.

Stefanie Yacht Charters (☎4125 4200 or 1800 650 776). Sails with 11 guests for 2 days and 2 nights, accommodation and food included. Departs Su, Tu, Th, but varies with demand. $295.

PRACTICAL INFORMATION

Tourist Office: For information, contact the **Hervey Bay tourist offices** (p. 334), or **Fraser Coast Tourism Board,** Maryborough (☎4122 3444 or 1800 444 155).

Permits: If you're going over in a car, you'll need a **vehicle permit** ($30, valid for a month; includes map and island details). **Camping permits** ($4 per person per night) are good for all campgrounds except the privately run Cathedral Beach Resort and Dilli Village, both on the east shore. With the permit comes a packet identifying allowed camping areas; some have curfews. Both permits are available from: **Hervey Bay City Council,** 77 Tavistock St., Torquay (☎4197 4444; open M-F 8:15-5pm); **Marina Kiosk,** Buccaneer Ave., Urangan (☎4128 9800; open daily 6am-6pm); **Hervey Bay Tourism and Development Office** (☎4124 2912 or 1800 811 728; www.herveybaytourism.com.au), corner of Uraween and Maryborough-Hervey Rd. Camping permits can also be picked up in the convenience store.

General supplies: Stock up at Eurong Beach Resort, Fraser Island Retreat at Happy Valley, Kingfisher Bay Resort, Cathedral Beach Resort, or Orchid Beach.

Telephones: Central Station, Dundubara, Waddy Point, Indian Head, Yidney Rocks and the resorts.

Showers: Cold showers are available at all campgrounds except Lake Allom. Coin-operated hot showers are available at Central Station, Waddy Point, Dundubara.

Air ambulance: Nambour QAS ☎5441 1333 or dial 000.

Tow Truck: ☎4127 9188 (Eurong) or 4127 9167 (Yidney Rocks).

ACCOMMODATIONS

Accommodation is included in the guided tour packages, but if you are arranging your trip independently, there are heaps of options. **Cathedral Beach Resort and Camping Park** has camping sites. (☎4127 9177. Sites for 2 $22; for 4 $31.) **Eurong Beach Resort** offers motel units. (☎4127 9122. Twins $88, each additional person $6.) **Fraser Island Retreat** (☎4127 9144) has individual lodges for $53-150 per person. The upscale **Kingfisher Bay Resort** (☎1800 072 555) is well hidden in the bush on the western side of the island, offering four-person self-contained cabins for $250 and shared accommodations in the wilderness lodge from $33 per person. There are seven main **camping** areas on the island, but camping is also allowed on designated beaches, including **Eastern Beach** (see **Practical Information,** above).

D-I-N-G-O ... And Dingo was his name-O. Don't get these wild creatures mixed up with any farmer's dog by petting or feeding dingoes. About 160 dingoes roam Fraser Island, and they are some of the purest dingo's around as they have rarely interbred with domesticated dogs. By feeding the dingoes, visitors to Fraser have helped make the dogs more aggressive and less fearful of humans and now dingoes routinely steal food from the campsites of unthinking city slickers. And remember, as the Queensland Parks and Wildlife Service say, "BE DINGO SMART."

THE LAY OF THE LAND

INLAND. Lake McKenzie is the most popular of the freshwater lakes, with white sands, shady pine trees, and water in various shades of perfect blues. **Lake Wabby** is at the eastern base of the steep Hammerstone Sandblow, which gradually encroaches this perched lake. Some visitors enjoy sliding down into the lake, but the trip is fast (the drier the sand, the faster) and you hit the water hard—a bad combo for your spine. Walking across the dune feels like crossing a vast desert, perfect for practicing your Lawrence of Arabia impersonation; in fact, Fraser and nearby Cooloola National Park combined have more sand than the Sahara. The southernmost lake, **Boomanjin,** is, like many others, lined with fallen leaves from the overhanging swamp paperbarks and tea trees, which give it tea-colored (but not flavored) water. It's the largest lake on Fraser, and the largest perched lake in the world. There are also a number of freshwater creeks good for swimming, especially **Eli Creek. Wanggoolba Creek** is a silent beauty, muffled by its sandy bottom; the only babbling you'll here is from other tourists or conversations between the eel and catfish inhabitants.

THE EASTERN BEACH. There is a *lot* of beach on Fraser Island, and most of it looks the same, bordered by raging surf and low-lying trees announcing the tentative start of island vegetation. The Eastern Beach is perfect for 4WDing, but be careful (see **Driving on Fraser,** p. 339). **Don't swim in the ocean,** as tiger sharks and riptides are real dangers. Heading north from Eurong, patches of rocks decorate the beach. There are short bypasses at **Poyungan Rocks** and **Yidney Rocks** and a longer route around the **Indian Head** promontory, where one can spot ospreys and whales (in season on calm days). Almost at the top of passable beachland, a collection of shallow tide pools called **The Champagne Pools** make prime swimming holes at low tide. Be careful at the pools as the rocks are slippery and incoming waves can cause serious injury by crashing over the rocks that dam the pools. Other attractions along the beach are the **Coloured Sands,** or **Cathedrals,** massive sand formations of countless shades, and the **Maheno shipwreck,** the remains of a massive cruise liner that washed ashore in a storm in the early part of the century.

HIKING. Hiking can be cheaper and more rewarding than 4WDing, and is the safest way to access the **Western Beach,** a soft white silica paradise. Consider trying a smaller chunk of the island near Central Station *(ranger station ☎4127 9191)* like **Lake McKenzie,** and **Lake Wabby** before attempting a more ambitious itinerary off the beaten track. If hiking really interests you, contact Phil at **Mango Hostel,** 110 Torquay Rd. *(☎4124 2832)*, for information about setting up itineraries.

DRIVING ON FRASER.

Driving on Fraser is only possible in a 4WD vehicle or a well-equipped motorcycle. Speed limits are established on the island: 35km per hr. on inland roads and 80km per hr. on the Eastern Beach. Don't rush—you can't. The one-laned roads are pure, soft sand; getting stuck is not out of the ordinary (have shovels handy). Allow at least 30min. to travel 10km on inland roads. The beaches themselves are registered national highways—all normal traffic rules apply, the roads are even patrolled by Breathalyzer and speedgun-wielding policemen. Larger vehicles will occasionally stay on the right, however; in any case, always use your blinker. Beware the tides; don't drive two hours each side of high tide.

SELF-DRIVE WITH HOSTELS. Extremely popular with backpackers, these three-day and two-night unguided group 4WD tours bring back stories, dirty clothes, and lots of sand. Unlike in guided tours, participants camp out at night. Hostel self-drive safaris usually cost about $130, plus the hidden costs of fuel (about $5-10 per person), insurance *(around $15-20)*, food and booze *($15-20 per person)*. Usually the group must buy insurance or leave a bond of about $500. Packages include 4WD hire, ferry passes, camping permits, access fees, camping equipment, and full preparatory briefing. Usually, the hostel hosts an afternoon meeting on the day before departure, a 4WD briefing the morning of, and a pre-departure supermarket run. To drive on the safari, you must be over 21 years old, but anyone can ride.

The type of partying you'll get with a group is usually related to the aura at the particular hostel: YHA attracts quieter groups, while Beaches, Koalas and Fraser Escapes party hard. *Let's Go* does not recommend Fraser Escape 4x4 Safaris because they top-load their vehicles, making them less stable.

RENT YOUR OWN 4WD. For folks who want the thrill of hurtling down a beach independently, several companies rent 4WDs at comparable costs: 4-seater $130; 5-6 seater $150-160, 8-11 seater $150-170. **Aussie Trax** also offer older model Land Rover ex-military vehicles *($115; seats 6)*. Hire companies also offer camping kits for $10-14 per person per day. Some good operators include: **Bay 4WD Centre,** 54 Boat Harbour Dr. *(☎4128 2981)*; **Aussie Trax,** 56 Boat Harbour Dr. *(☎4124 4433 or 1800 062 275)*; **Safari,** 55 Old Maryborough Rd. *(☎4124 4244 or 1800 689 819)*. All of these companies pickup locally. It's worth asking whether a rental agency belongs to the **Fraser Coast 4WD Hire Association,** the local watchdog. Hostels can also arrange 4WD hire.

BUT ALL THE COOL KIDS ARE DOING IT... Although beach driving can be a lot of fun, reckless driving can lead to disaster. The most serious danger is creek cuts in the beach; test the depth of a creek before attempting to cross. Don't cross if the water is higher than your knees–instead, wait for the tide to go down. Also, don't drive at night when it is difficult to see and other drivers are more likely to be drunk and foolhardy. Location is also important; you're tempting fate by driving on the eastern beaches south of Dilli Village and Ungowa, north of the Ngkala Rocks, or on the west side north by Moon Point.

BUNDABERG ☎07

Bundaberg is not high on the list of Australia's choice idling spots; most visitors get coffee at the bus terminal, stretch their legs, and hop back on board. However, it is the hottest spot to put in a few weeks on the vegetable-picking circuit and a great, cheap place to learn to dive. In the fields backpackers seeking to beef up their bank accounts mix with seasoned life-long workers. At the end of the day it's all about kicking the dirt off your work boots, occasionally splurging on Bundaberg's famous rum, and saving energy for another day in the fields. Some last a day, others months. Despite Bundy's dearth of activities—or because of it—the survivors enjoy some of the purest camaraderie on the coast.

TRANSPORTATION

Trains: The train station is at the corner of Bourbong and McLean St. Ticket office open M-F 4-5am, 7:45am-5pm. Sa 8:45am-1pm and Su 2-4:15pm. **Tilt Trains** (☎132 232) depart for **Brisbane** (1-2 per day, $51.70); **Maryborough** (1-2 per day, $18.70), with bus connections to **Hervey Bay** ($23.10); **Rockhampton** ($47.30).

Buses: The Coach terminal is on Targo St. To get to town from the station, turn right and pass the roundabout and McDonald's to Bourbong St. **McCafferty's** and **Premier** (1 per day) run to: **Airlie Beach** (11hr., 3 per day, $73-93); **Brisbane** (7-7½hr., 8 per day,

$41-46); **Cairns** (19-20hr., 7 per day, $132-125); **Hervey Bay** (1¾hr., 7 per day, $11-20); **Mackay** (8½hr., 7 per day, $61-79); **Maroochydore** (5½hr., 1 per day, $28-42); **Noosa** (5hr., 2 per day, $28-38); **Rockhampton** (4-4¾hr., 7 per day, $21-45).

Local Bus Transport: Duffy's City Buses (☎4151 4226). Route #4 passes near the Bundaberg rum distillery on the way to Bargara (4 per day). Route #5 also passes the distillery on its way to Burnett Heads (3-5 per day). **Stewart & Sons** (☎4153 2646) connects Bundaberg with Innes Park, Elliott Heads, and Moore Park.

Taxi: ☎4151 2345.

PRACTICAL INFORMATION

Tourist Office: City Council Visitors Centre, 188 Bourbong St. (☎4153 9289; fax 4151 2527; www.bundaberg.qld.gov.au). Open M-F 8:30am-4:45pm, Sa-Su 10am-1pm. **Tourist Information Centre,** 271 Bourbong St. (☎4152 2333; www.sunzine.net/bundaberg). Open daily 9am-5pm.

Police: 258 Bourbong St. (☎4153 9111).

Hospital: Bundaberg Base (24hr. ☎4152 1222), on Bourbong St. near Tallon Bridge.

Internet: The Cosy Corner, on Barolin St., opposite the post office. $1.10 per 15min. Open M and Th 8am-7:30pm, Tu-W 8am-9:30pm, Sa 8am-5pm, Su 11am-5pm.

Post Office: (☎4131 4451), on the corner of Bourbong and Barolin St. Open M-F 8:30am-5pm, Sa 8:30am-midnight. **Postal Code:** 4670.

ACCOMMODATIONS

The better hostels in town help find jobs (usually within a day of beginning your search), provide free transport to and from work, have strict alcohol policies, and are equipped with walk-in fridges. For those on a looser budget, or just in town for the night, motels are down Bourbong St.; the farther from town, the cheaper. Those not working should consider the beachside backpackers in Bargara.

Bundaberg Backpackers and Travellers Lodge, 2 Crofton St. (☎4152 2080; fax 4151 3355), across from the bus terminal at the corner of Targo and Crofton St. The Hilton of hostels, this no-nonsense, air-conditioned haven is by far the picker's and 'packer's pick of the litter. Free pickup at train station. Laundry. Key deposit $20. Reception daily 8am-8pm. Check-out 10am. Dorms $20, weekly $130. VIP/YHA.

Workers and Diving Hostel, 64 Barolin St (☎4151 6097). From the bus station call for a ride, or walk across the street, down Crofton St., and take a left onto Barolin St. (10min.). Friendly place, still serious about their picking, but 15min. from town. TV lounge, small kitchen. Reception daily 8am-noon and 3-7pm. Dorms $17, weekly $107; self-contained units $18/$110. NOMADS.

QUEENSLAND

WORKING IN BUNDY. Experienced workers will tell you that the first few days are the hardest. If you can bear through three or four days of a sore back though, picking work can be rewarding, especially to the wallet. The wage is generally $10 per hr., after taxes. Under contract work, getting paid for how much you pick can reel in even more. Usually, you need to pay for a week of accommodation at a hostel before they'll find work for you. Most of the year (except Dec.-Jan.), work can be found within a day or so, and the farm will teach you what to do—anyone (with proper work authorization, see p.73) can do it. The job involves a fair amount of luck—weather, farmers, personality, what you're picking; generally, snowpeas and avocados are good, and mangos and chilies are bad, but some people will swear by the latter. Most workers stay 3-4 weeks, seeking to beef up their bank accounts.

OUTSIDE TOWN

Iluka Forest Retreat, 127 Logan Rd., Innes Park (☎4159 3230 or 1800 657 005). For those not working, another great budget option is close by. Hidden in the bush between fields of sugarcane and the Woongarra Marine Park's reef. Spread out cabins make for few people and lots of wildlife. Great for couples. Free snorkel gear and pickup in Bundaberg. Reception 7am-7pm. Dorms, doubles, and family rooms all $15 per person.

Kelly's Beach Resort (YHA), 6 Trevor's Rd., Bargara (☎4154 7200 or 1800 246 141; fax 4154 7300; www.kellysbeachresort.com.au). A beautiful budget resort on Bargara beach. Self-contained villas, pool, tennis court, sauna, eco-tours, 24hr. laundry, pickup from Bundaberg. Key deposit $10. Dorms $22; doubles $55. 7th night free.

FOOD

Bundaberg has a few good spots to fill up your tummy and to absorb all that rum. **Numero Uno,** 167A Bourbong St., has great pizzas and pasta specials. (☎4151 3666. Open M-Sa 11:30am-2pm and 5pm-late, Su 5pm-late.) **Zulu's at the Queenslander Hotel,** 61 Targo St. (☎4152 4691), has cheap meals ($6-14) and $8 jugs of beer.

SIGHTS AND ACTIVITIES

Diving in Bundaberg is rock-bottom cheap. **Salty's,** 208 Bourbong St., offers a four-day PADI course in an on-site heated saltwater pool with shore dives to the Coral Coast's volcanic rock fringing reef. (☎4151 6422 or 1800 625 476; www.saltys.net. Open M-F 8am-5pm, Sa 8am-noon, Su 8-10am. 4-day classes start M, Th $169. 2 boat dives on the artificial reef $100. 2 shore dives $45, 2 reef dives $215.) **Bundaberg Aqua Scuba,** 66 Targo St. (☎4153 5761), across from the bus terminal, offers two shore dives for $45 and a $164 PADI open water course, including four shore dives. Also organizes cheap accommodation for those in courses. Call both places to organize dive trips to Lady Musgrave or Lady Eliot Islands.

Love it or hate it, Bundaberg **Rum** is Australia's best selling spirit. Distillery tours are popular but disappointing—much is on video and only one drink comes with the price. Duffy's buses, routes #4 and #5, stop near the distillery. (☎4150 8684; www.bundabergrum.com.au. Tours on the hour M-F 10am-3pm, Sa-Su 10am-2pm. $7.70; some hostels arrange free transportation.)

Celebrating the start of the turtle nesting season, the week-long Coral Coast Turtle Festival, held in November, features a carnival, shows, markets and parades, marking the official start of the turtle rookery season. **Mon Repos** (15km from the city center) hosts the largest loggerhead turtle rookery in the South Pacific. Access to the beach is limited during the season, but guided walks operate from the visitor center. (☎4159 1652. Open daily Nov.-Mar.)

HOSTEL FIRE. Located 53km south of Bundaberg, Childers struggles to come to terms with the tragic Palace Backpackers fire that killed 15 international backpackers in June 2000.

CAPRICORN COAST

Stretching from the Fraser Coast to the Whitsundays, so-called for its position on the Tropic of Capricorn, this stretch of coastal tropics is one paradise after another. The Bruce Hwy. worms its way north through sugarcane fields and along the tropical coast, where some oceanside towns and island getaways have been shaped into backpacker havens. Other towns, such as Mackay, still grimace at the sight of sandals and an unwashed t-shirt, but lie in proximity to such isolated spots as the Eungella National Park. The isolated park rewards its few intrepid visitors with tumbling waterfalls and elusive platypuses. Off-shore getaways, like Great Keppel Island, almost within sight of Rockhampton's shore, lack roads entirely and thrives on its twenty-two quiet beaches.

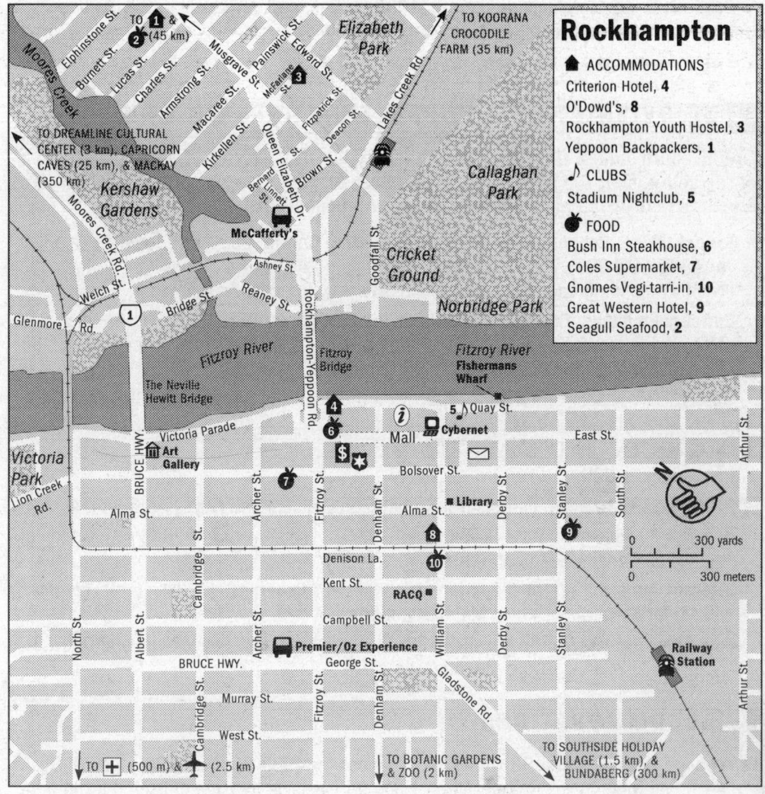

ROCKHAMPTON ☎07

Australia's self-proclaimed "beef capital," Rockhampton is ruled by the human minority (pop. 60,000) while the cattle majority (pop. 3.5 million) bide their time for revolt. Straddling the Tropic of Capricorn, this Great Barrier Beef is a gateway to Great Keppel Island and the small seaside town of Yeppoon. Many inexplicably stately buildings loom over chain stores and shops on the town's meticulously laid out grid of streets. For the most part Rocky is a serious, very conservative town, with its share of hair salons and saddle shops. However, a few interesting cultural activities stir this country town, providing a day's worth of entertainment.

TRANSPORTATION

Train Station: At the end of Murray St. From the city center, go south (away from the river) on any street, then turn left on Murray St. Lockers $2. The high-speed **Tilt Train** goes to **Brisbane** (7hr., daily 7:40am, $57-174). Taxi into town about $9.

Buses: McCafferty's terminal (☎4927 2844) is behind KFC on Linnet St., off Queen Elizabeth Dr., which becomes Fitzroy St. on the other side of the bridge. Lockers $2-4. **Premier's** terminal (☎4921 1890) is on the south side of Rockhampton, on George St. between Fitzroy and Archer St. Both have services to: **Airlie Beach** (6hr., 5 per day, $44-70); **Brisbane** (12hr., 5 per day, $70-79); **Bundaberg** (4hr., 5 per day, $30-54); **Cairns** (17hr., 6 per day, $109-122); **Hervey Bay** (6hr., 4 per day, $40-69); **Mackay** (4hr., 6 per day, $31-50; **Maroochydore** via **Noosa** (10hr., 3 per day, $59-75). For information on transport to **Great Keppel Island,** see p. 346.

Public Bus: Capricorn Sunbus (☎4936 1002) covers most corners of the city, with a sliding fare scale (usually $2-4).

Taxi: ☎13 10 08.

ORIENTATION AND PRACTICAL INFORMATION

On the south side of the **Fitzroy River,** the city has a flawless grid design, with most of the action near the river's edge along **Quay St. East St.** runs parallel to Quay and houses a pedestrian mall between **Fitzroy** and **Denham St.**

Tourist Office: Rockhampton Tourist Information Centre, 208 Quay St. (☎4922 5339 or 1800 805 865). The in-house, constantly updated *Rovin' Round Rocky Region* is helpful and comprehensive. Open M-F 8:30am-4:30pm, Sa-Su 9am-4pm.

Currency Exchange: Commonwealth Bank, 74 East St. (☎4922 1733), in the mall and **ANZ,** 214 Bolsover St. (☎4931 7764) both exchange traveler's checks for a $7 fee, $5 for cash. Open M-Th 9:30am-4pm, F 9:30am-5pm.

Library: 69 Williams St. (☎4936 8265), on the corner of Alma St. Free **Internet** terminals. Book ahead for a 30min. session. Open M, Tu, F 9:15am-5:30pm, W 1-8pm, Th 9:15am-8pm, Sa-Su 9:15am-4:30pm.

Emergency: ☎000.

Police: (☎4932 1500), on Bolsover St. between Denham and Fitzroy St. Open 24hr.

Hospital: Rockhampton Base Hospital (☎4920 6211, emergency 4920 6270). On top of the hill on Canning St., near North St.

Internet Access: Free at the library or connect at **Cybernet,** 12 William St. (☎4927 3633) for $5 per hour. Open M-F 8:30am-5pm.

Post Office: (☎4927 6566; fax 4927 6802). On East St. between William and Derby St. Open M-F 8:30am-5:30pm. **Postal Code:** 4700.

ACCOMMODATIONS

Yeppoon Backpackers, 30 Queen St., Yeppoon (☎4939 8080 or 1800 636 828). A great gateway to explore Great Keppel and a beachside treasure in itself. Pickup from Rockhampton (daily 6pm) or take the Young's bus from Rockhampton for $7.30 (6 per day). Runs trips to Cooberrie, Koorana, 4WD Fire Rocks, and "Serenade" boat trips. Pool, spa. Reception 7:30am-8:30pm. 4-bed dorms $18, doubles $38. VIP/YHA.

Rockhampton Youth Hostel (YHA), 60 MacFarlane St. (☎4927 5288; fax 4922 6040). From the McCafferty's terminal, take a left on Queen Elizabeth Dr. and a right on MacFarlane St. Kitchen, TV room. Free pickup. Packages include 1 night in Rocky, 2 on Great Keppel, with return ferry ticket and shuttle $96. Key deposit $10. Reception 7am-noon and 5-10pm. Dorms $20, with YHA $16.50; twins and doubles $47, $40.

Criterion Hotel, 150 Quay St. (☎4922 1225; fax 4922 1226), just south of the Fitzroy bridge on the river. Grand, picturesque, and plenty of framed pictures showing off the building's colorful past. Bar, 2 restaurants, and rooms with bath. Reception 7am-midnight. Singles $29-48; twins $45-53; doubles $40-53. triples $63; quads $73.

O'Dowd's, 100 William St. (☎4927 0344), corner of Denison St. A gorgeous new Irish pub in town. Rooms are squeaky clean and comfortable. Common room has a TV and fridge. Laundry $2. Key deposit $10. Singles $28; twins $40; family room $60.

Southside Holiday Village (☎4927 3013), south of city center on Bruce Hwy. Well-kept tourist park with pool and courtesy bus. Laundry. Reception 6am-11pm. Sites $15 per 2; powered sites for 2 $21; on-site vans $33; budget cabins $36.

FOOD

Beef: it's what's for dinner in Rocky. Buy your own at Coles **supermarket** in City Centre Plaza on Fitzroy and Bolsover St. (open M-F 8am-9pm, Sa 8am-5pm), and cook it on the free BBQs along the river.

OLYMPIC DREAMS You've heard of the breakfast of champions; now meet the beds of champions. At the end of the Sydney Olympics, the beds from the Olympic village had to go as the village was made into condominiums. Where did these Olympian beds go? You could be sleeping in one tonight. Hostels from around Australia bought the beds, which have a muted chrome frames and electric blue plastic headboards. Though you might never win gold, you can still sleep like a champion.

Great Western Hotel, 39 Stanley St. (☎4922 1862). The best steakhouse in town with a rodeo arena out in the back. The rump melts in your mouth for $17. W practice rodeo rides 7:30pm; F bull rides. Hosts weekly events including rodeos, meat-cutting, and indoor campdrafts. Cover $8-10.

Gnomes Vegi-tarri-in, 104 William St. (☎4927 4713), near the intersection with Denison St. The ultimate in vegetarian hideaway: candle-lit tables, small waterfall out back, 2 dozen varieties of tea ($3 a pot), and delicious dishes from an entirely vegetarian menu. Mains $11. Open Tu-Th 10am-10pm, F-Sa 10am-11pm.

Bush Inn Steakhouse, 150 Quay St. (☎4922 1225), in the Criterion Hotel. A great place to chew some of Rocky's finest for $11-23. W-Sa live rock and roll.

Seagulls Seafood, (☎4939 2233), Anzac Pde., Yeppoon. Swoop on in for what locals call the best fish'n'chips on the Capricorn Coast.

SIGHTS AND ACTIVITIES

BOTANIC GARDENS AND ZOO. No need to choose—here you can sample native and exotic flora and fauna in one swift stroke. The gardens remain a highlight of Rockhampton's sights along with the zoo which has an enormous geodesic dome aviary, chimpanzees, and the usual line-up: 'roos, crocs, cassowaries, dingoes, free roaming peacocks, wombats, and koalas. There are feedings at 3pm. *(10min. ride from the city on Sunbus route #4A; departs from the arcade carpark on Bolsover St. between Denham and Williams St. $2.85 one-way, usually runs 5min. past the hour, about every hour. Zoo ☎4936 8000. Open daily 8am-5pm. Gardens ☎4936 8254. Open daily 6am-6pm. Both free.)*

DREAMTIME CULTURAL CENTRE. The Dreamtime Cultural Centre provides a humble but elegant perspective on the indigenous peoples of Australia and the Torres Strait Islands. The center is set in a park with a meandering trail highlighting different medicinal plants of the area. Get boomerang instructions and a didgeridoo demonstration at the end of the tour. *(5min. north of Rockhampton by car, on the corner of Yeppoon Rd. and the Bruce Hwy. Sunbus #10 runs from Rocky. ☎4936 1655. Open M-F 10am-3:30pm. Tours regularly 10:30am-1pm. $12, concessions $10, children $5.50.)*

CAVING. The **Capricorn Caves** are ancient limestone caves that feature the **cathedral** with its incredible natural acoustics and a natural light spectacle during summer solstice (mid-December-mid January). There are both 1hr. and day tours of the caves. Included in the price is an opportunity to take a self-guided tour through a "dry rainforest." The caverns also host **Wild Caving Adventure Tours,** which allow you to spend 3hr. rock-climbing, being sardined in 12cm wide tunnels, and squeezing through Fat Man's Misery. *(23km from Rockhampton. ☎4934 2883; www.capricorncaves.com.au. Open daily 9am-4pm. Admission and basic 1hr. tour $13, children $6.50. Day tour $33. Adventure tour $45. Book at least 24hr. ahead; call for transportation services.)*

HIKING. With its shadowy presence over Rockhampton, **Mt. Archer** stands at 604m, with vast views of the city and the surrounding landscape. From the summit you can hike back to the base on the walking track (11km; 4-5hr.) to German St., then take German St. to Moores Creek Rd. to Musgrave St. into the city. Standing above rainforests and eucalypts, the lookout also offers a unique perspective on the layout of the city.

FARM STAY. Myella Farm Stay offers an all inclusive farmstay on 10.5km² for 17 people with activities such as horse and motorbike riding, 4WD tours, cow milking, and, of course, campfires. *(125km southwest of Rockhampton. Free pickup from Dululu, which is on a McCafferty's route. ☎4998 1290. 3-days, 2-night $210 including buffet meals.)* **Namoi Hills Cattle Station** offers a farmstay on 130km² of land, a la carte didgeridoo making tours, sapphire mining, and overnight horse rides and camp outs. *(160km west of Rockhampton in Dingo. ☎4998 1290; www.namoihills.com. 1st night package $38.50 including meals, subsequent nights $17.60.)*

CARNARVON GORGE NAT'L PARK. This rugged national park is rich with Aboriginal rock art, deep pools, and soaring sandstone cliffs. The gorges, however, are the main attraction. Camping facilities are available. Winter is the best time to visit, but be aware that at night temperatures fall below freezing. *(500km southwest of Rockhampton and Gladstone on Bruce Hwy. For info, contact the ranger ☎4984 4505.)*

NIGHTLIFE AND ENTERTAINMENT

The nightlife in Rocky doesn't pack the same punch as Balboa. Still, the sports-themed **Stadium Night Club,** on the corner of Quay and William St., where 20 TVs ensure you won't miss a moment of the action, also bumps with Top-40 dancing late into the night. (☎4927 6996. Open W-Su 8pm-5am. F-Sa $5 cover after 11pm.) The **Criterion Hotel,** 150 Quay St. stands as an early meeting place. (☎4922 1225. Open M-Tu 10am-midnight, W-Th 10am-2am, F-Sa 10am-3am, Su 11am-midnight.) For a pint of Guinness ($6), live rock music (Th-Sa nights), and some Irish grub ($7-10), good laddies and lassies hit **O'Dowd's,** 100 Williams St. On Friday nights join the Guinness club and drink as much as you can for $25. (☎4927 0344. Open M-Sa 8am-2am, Su 8am-midnight.)

GREAT KEPPEL ISLAND ☎07

A trip to Great Keppel is like winning an instant vacation: it's a high-flying resort escape that miraculously falls within your budget. The largely untouched island is surrounded by unbelievably clear waters, 22 beaches with fine snorkeling right off-shore, and a brilliant night sky streaked by shooting stars. While budget accommodations abound, the island's posh resort doesn't mind the odd backpacker crashing its nightlife or taking its catamaran out for a lazy afternoon. For many visitors, it's enough to curl up on any of the beaches and seize a taste of paradise.

TRANSPORTATION

Young's Coaches' Route #20 runs to both ferries from the corner of Denham and Bolsover St., Rockhampton. (☎4922 3813. 5-11 per day; $7.30.) **Rothery's Coaches,** offers accommodation pickups or meets at the Tourist Services' ferry. (☎4933 6744. 8, 10:30am, 1:30pm; $15.40 return, children $8). Before arranging your own transport to Great Keppel Island, consider the **packages** offered by some of the hostels (see **Accommodations,** below). If you choose independent transport, to get to the island you will need a ferry (30min. from Rosslyn Bay) and to get to the ferry you will need a bus (40min. from Rockhampton). **The Freedom Flyer** leaves from Keppel Bay Marina, Rosslyn Bay. (☎4933 6244. 9, 11am, 3pm. $29 return, students $22, children $15.) They also run various day cruises starting at $49. **Keppel Tourist Services** runs a ferry to the island, leaving from the Great Keppel Island Transit Centre, Rosslyn Bay, to Rockhampton. (☎4933 6744 or 1800 356 744. Daily 7:30, 9:15, 11:30am, 3:30pm, F 6pm as well; $30 return, concession $22 children $15.)

For drivers, free, though unsecured, parking is available outside the ferry terminals. Safer is **Great Keppel Island Security Car Park** (☎4933 6670), on the Scenic Hwy, which offers a courtesy bus to the harbor ($6.50 per day, covered $8).

The ferries let passengers out on the main beach. Parallel to the beach is the island's main (and only) drag, the **Yellow Brick Road** (we are in Oz, but the road's dark brown) that runs the entire commercial strip of Great Keppel, a 5min. stroll.

ACCOMMODATIONS

When considering accommodations, look at the big picture—most accommodations on the island offer packages including bus and ferry transfers and rooms on the mainland that manage to ease the price and trouble of arranging transfers yourself. Camping is not allowed on Great Keppel but is increasingly possible on nearby Keppel Group islands. For package information, try **Yeppoon Backpackers** or **Rockhampton YHA** (see Accommodations, p. 344).

Great Keppel Island Holiday Village (☎4939 8655 or 1800 180 235; www.gkiholiday village.com.au). A friendly, relaxed throw-back to the way the island used to be. Free use of snorkel gear and 4WD drop-offs in the middle of the island every other day for hikers, and motorized canoe trips. Also organizes camping packages on nearby Middle Island $30. BBQ. Check-out 10am. Reception daily 8:30am-5:30pm. Dorms $24; tents with a wooden double bed $50. Cabins for with shower 2 $90; each extra person up to 4 $15.

Great Keppel Island Village YHA (☎4933 6744). Currently being run by Keppel Haven and affiliated with the Rockhampton YHA. Out back, a path-connected, plant-surrounded smattering of "safari tents" sits cozily. Reception daily 7am-1pm, 3-5pm; check-in at ferry. Dorms $20.60; twins and doubles $46.

Keppel Haven (☎4939 2050 or 1800 356 744). "Safari tents" make a tent village, while bunkhouses and cabins provide more comfortable, expensive stays. Very few showers and toilets in tent village. Watch out for hidden costs in tent village, like linen $6, $12 double, plus a $20 deposit. Pay BBQ. Key deposit $10. Reception daily 7am-5:30pm. 3- or 4-share $17.50; singles $27.50; twins and doubles $40. 4-person bunkhouses with linen $100. Self-contained cabins $120.

FOOD AND NIGHTLIFE

With a grand total of eleven establishments on the island, Great Keppel has what might be generously termed limited offerings. You're best off buying food on the mainland. **Island Pizza** (☎4939 4699) serves pleasant somewhat pricy pizza. (W-Su 12:30-2pm and 6-9pm.) The **Wreck Bar** is on the beach, where the only things wrecked are the patrons. (F-Su cover bands. Open daily noon-2am.)

ACTIVITIES

The resort's **Wreckreation Centre** makes bookings for non-guests, and posts a list of daily activities. (☎4939 5044. Open daily 8am-5pm.) Great Keppel has 22 beaches marking its 27km circumference, while all of "civilization" is within an 8min. stroll. **Monkey Beach,** a mere 30min. jaunt south of the hostels, has the best and most accessible **snorkeling. Long Beach,** a 35min. walk past the airstrip, exists in splendid isolation. Hike to **Mt. Wyndham** for unparalleled views of your paradise. Other walks go to the **Old Homestead** and the **lighthouse.** *Keppel Haven's Track Map* is helpful for bush walks (50¢ at the Keppel Tourist Services ferry terminal on the mainland, or $1.50 on the island).

To traverse the inviting water with a bit of speed or sport, visit the fellas at the Resort's **watersports area,** off the Yellow Brick Rd., just before the resort. They offer everything from high-speed banana rides ($10) to catamaran/windsurfer hire ($15 per hr.) to waterskiing ($20) to parasailing (one of the last companies that gives the thrill of beach takeoffs and landings; $55). (Open 9am-4:30pm.) The **Beach Shed** (☎4925 0624) at Keppel Haven, has jet skis ($30 per 10min.), jet ski tours (1hr. including snorkeling $40), snorkel gear ($10), and kayaks ($10 per hr.). The **Dive Shop** (☎4939 5022), up the beach, offers dive trips for the certified ($77, $55 with own gear) and the uninitiated ($99); tag along and snorkel for $33. **Sea kayaking,** run by Geoff at Island Backpackers, is another adventurous way to spend the afternoon. Geoff also offers a cheaper canoe and snorkel adventure (sea kayaking/snorkeling trip including lunch $35, for GKI Holiday Village guests $30).

For the even more adventurous, **Tandem Skydive** has beach landings. (8000ft. $275, 12,000ft. $375.) The catamaran **Euphoria** offers a 3hr. sail and snorkel trip ($35, children $25), as well as a sunset cruise. ($39, children $25. Book at resort.) For a slower pace, hop on a dromedary and enjoy **camel riding** on the beach ($35 per 30 min. or $50 for 1hr. sunset ride).

NEAR GREAT KEPPEL ISLAND: THE KEPPEL GROUP

The isolated and largely deserted islands in the Keppel Group provide the possibilities to play Gilligan (with a planned return, of course). The coconut-infested **Pumpkin Island** offers beautiful vegetation, coral, and white beaches. And it can all be yours—well, nearly yours, I mean who would play the professor, the movie star, Mary Anne…A maximum of 28 people on the island choose between one of the five cabins for up to 6 people. The island has toilet, showers, BBQ, drinking water, and plenty of deserted beaches. (☎4939 4413 or 4939 2431. Cabins $130 per night.) For transport, call Keppel Bay Marina (☎4933 6244) or a water-taxi (☎4933 6133), but it's not cheap—$260-300 roundtrip on a boat that can carry 6-10 people. **Middle Island, Humpy Island,** and **North Keppel** also offer camping.

WHITSUNDAY COAST

Stretching from Mackay to the small town of Bowen, right above Airlie Beach, the well-deserved claim-to-fame of this coastal stretch are the Whitsunday Islands. Any passerby must experience the islands by spending a few relaxing days sailing on the clear waters, exploring the world underneath the water, and visiting secluded patches land made of nothing but white sand amidst those waters. Accessed by Airlie Beach, near Proserpine, the Whitsundays characterize this tropical stretch, that both draws a crowd, but manages to make every visitor to feel the solitude of outback Queensland.

MACKAY ☎07

Emerging out of miles and miles of sugarcane, Mackay ("MICK-eye") serves as a convenient gateway to the hidden treasures of the rainforested national parks inland and the isolated islands offshore, letting its travelers seek something different. The Finch Hatton Gorge, Eungella ("Yun-guh-lah"), and Cape Hillsborough

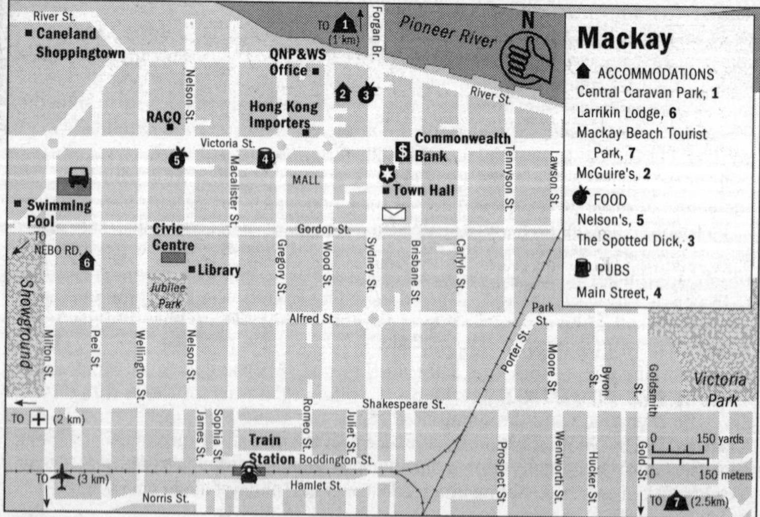

National Parks reveal a breath-taking beauty too often overlooked. While controlled cane fires glow on the night horizon, the moderate heat of the city's nightlife makes it a reasonable spot to spend an evening, before you take a stroll through the city's gardens or strike out for the wilderness.

TRANSPORTATION

Trains: The train station (☎4952 7418) is about 5km south of town on Connors Rd., off Nebo Rd. No public transport, but a taxi costs about $10 and some hostels offer free pickup. Purchase tickets in town at any travel agency. Lockers $2-4.

Buses: Mackay Bus Terminal (☎4951 3088) is on Milton St. between Gordon and Victoria St. **McCafferty's** and **Premier** (1 per day to all destinations) run to: **Airlie Beach** (1¾-2hr., 5 per day, $18-33); **Brisbane** (14hr., 6 per day, $101-121); **Bundaberg** (8¼-9¾hr., 3 per day, $51-93); **Cairns** (9½-12hr., 6 per day, $88-97); **Hervey Bay** (10¾hr., 4 per day, $74-108); **Maroochydore** via **Noosa** (12hr., 3 per day, $90-117); **Rockhampton** (4¼hr., 6 per day, $31-50).

Taxis: Mackay Taxi (24hr. ☎13 10 08).

Car Rental: Avis (☎13 63 33 or 4951 1266) is located at the airport. **U-Drive** (☎4957 5606 or 1800 670 110) offers courtesy pickup. **Thrifty** (☎4957 3677 or 1800 818 050) is at 3 Mangrove Rd.

ORIENTATION AND PRACTICAL INFORMATION

Mackay's city center rests on the southern bank of the Pioneer River. **River St.** runs along the waterfront, and the town's main drag, **Victoria St.,** is the next parallel street to the south. Plenty of nightlife and restaurants line **Sydney** and **Wood St.,** which are perpendicular to Victoria St. The **Bruce Hwy.** comes into the west side of town, and the exit leads to **Gordon St.,** parallel to and just south of Victoria St.

Tourist Office: Mackay Tourism Office, 320 Nebo Rd. (☎4952 2677; www.mackayregion.com). At the southwestern corner of the city in an incredibly inconvenient location if you don't have a car. Open M-F 8:30am-5pm, Sa-Su 9am-4pm.

National Parks Office, 2 Wood St. (☎4944 7800). National park info, videos on the reef, and permits for the Cumberland Islands and other national park camping ($3.85 per person per night). Open M-F 8:30am-5pm.

Currency Exchange: Commonwealth Bank, 63 Victoria St. (☎4953 5559). Traveler's check and cash exchange $5 fee. Open M-Th 9:30am-4pm, F 9:30am-5pm.

Library: (☎4968 4516) next to the Civic Centre on Gordon St. Open M, W, F 9am-5pm, Tu 10am-6pm, Th 10am-8pm, Sa 9am-3pm.

Emergency: ☎000.

Police: 57 Sydney St. (24hr. ☎4968 3444), between Victoria and Gordon St.

Hospital: Mackay Base Hospital (24hr. ☎4968 6000). Follow Gordon St. west to the Bruce Hwy., turn right at Bridge St.; it's on the left before the bridge.

Internet: Hong Kong Importers, Bazzar Arcade, 128 Victoria St (☎4953 3188). $5 per hr. Open M-F 8am-5:15pm, Sa-Su 9am-2pm.

Post Office: 69 Sydney St. (☎131 318). Between Victoria and Gordon St. Open M-Th 8am-4:30pm, F 8am-5:30pm. **Postal Code:** 4740.

ACCOMMODATIONS

Larrikin Lodge (YHA), 32 Peel St. (☎4951 3728; larrikin@mackay.net.au), 200m from the bus terminal. Small kitchen/TV area breeds a friendly atmosphere at Mackay's only true hostel. Laundry $2. Reception 7-10am and 5-10pm. Dorms $17.50; twins $41; family room $61. Cash only.

McGuire's, 17 Wood St. (☎4957 7464). Cheapest beds, beer, and lunch in town. Rooms are clean, twins are spacious, but large dorm holds row upon row of beds. 4-bed dorm is best. Dorms $15, 2 nights $20; singles $25, weekly $125; twins $40/$180.

Mackay Beach Tourist Park, 8 Petrie St., Illawong Beach (☎4957 4021 or 1800 645 111), 3km south of the city center. Pool patrolled by wandering peacocks. Reception 7am-7pm. Sites for 2 $15.40, powered $21; cabins for 2 $47.30.

Central Caravan Park (☎4957 6141), on Malcomson St. Just over the Forgan Bridge, near the city center. Pool, laundry, and kitchen. Reception 7am-7pm. Sites for 2 $13, powered $16; cabin doubles $28; Villa doubles with A/C and bath $40.

FOOD AND NIGHTLIFE

Cheap fresh seafood cooked to your liking (crumbed, battered, or grilled) makes **Nelson's,** 171 Victoria St., a favorite of locals and travelers alike. (☎4953 5453. Open Su-Th 10am-7:30pm, F-Sa 10am-8pm.) **The Spotted Dick,** 2 Sydney St., is not the local herpes clinic; in fact, its wacky decor and crazy cuisine make it one of Mackay's best eateries. Meals run $8-18, and most of the wood-fired pizzas cost less than $10. (☎4957 2368. Th-Su house band; W "krazy karaoke." Happy hour M-F 4:30-6:30pm. Open Su-Th 10am-late, F-Sa 10am-2am. Kitchen open daily noon-2pm and 6-8:30pm.) The Victoria Street Markets are open Sunday from 9am-12:30pm. A Woolworth's **supermarket** is in the Caneland Shopping Centre. (Open M-F 8am-9pm, Sa 8am-5pm.)

The cream of Mackay's **nightlife** crop is **Main Street,** on the corner of Victoria and Gregory St, the biggest club in town where DJ-hosted party madness rages around pool tables and two bars. (☎4957 7737. Open Th-Su 8pm-3am. F-Sa cover $5.) Cruise to **McGuire's,** 17 Wood St. (☎4957 7464), for their cheap jugs of Toohey's New ($6) and live entertainment W-Su. Break on through to the other side at **Doors,** 85 Victoria St., where drink specials, a big screen with not-so-subliminal messages like "take home someone ugly tonite," and a great dance pit make for a sweaty night of drunken fun. (☎4957 7737. Open Th-Su 8pm-3:30am. Cover $3 F-Sa.)

SIGHTS AND ACTIVITIES

While most of Mackay's attractions lie in its surroundings, the town manages a few sights of interest. Pick up *A Heritage Walk in Mackay* free from the tourist office to guide you to the historical and cultural hot spots. Don't miss **Queen's Park,** on Goldsmith St., where the lovely **Orchid Gardens** overflow with delectable flowers. To see the town is style, hop on a **Harley Trike** with Frank, who's beard is nearly as big as his Mackay loyalty. (☎0409 540 261. $25.)

Mackay Adventure Divers offers the best way to daytrip around the islands south of the Whitsundays. Snorkel or dive on Cumberland, Scawfell, and the Llewellyn Wreck. Spend your surface interval on a deserted beach. (☎4953 1431. Full-day cruise with 2 dives $135.) A few hours with **Reef Flight** and you'll see isolated Bushy Reef from above in a seaplane, from below while snorkeling in its adjacent suspended lagoon, and with your eyes closed while relaxing on the coral beach. (☎4953 0220. 35min. flight and 2½hr. on the island. $224.)

DAYTRIPS FROM MACKAY: CARLISLE ISLAND

Just like Heron Island to the south, Brampton Island is no longer accessible to day-trippers, campers, or anyone not willing to spend $130 per person per night. Fortunately, you can slide by the island's resort and find solitude and isolation on nearby Carlisle Island. This island, fringed by coral, is monitored by the National Parks office in Mackay, which arranges **camping** permits ($4 per person per night). Carlisle has a toilet, BBQ, and lots of shady trees. If the guests-only boat transfer to Brampton Island P&O Resort (☎4951 4499) is not full, you may be able to grab a spot ($25 each way), and arrange a $10 boat transfer to Carlisle.

ON THE ROAD

MACKAY TO EUNGELLA

The road to Eungella heads out from the south side of Mackay, along the Bruce Hwy., to the west. At a four-way intersection with a rail crossing, turn right onto the Peak Downs Hwy. and follow it to a junction with Eungella Rd. The road leads through the endless sugarcane fields of Pioneer Valley, sometimes ablaze at sunset when unchanging winds make the best time for controlled burning.

After passing the town of Marian on Eungella Rd., the **Illawong Sanctuary,** is 4km after the bridge, in **Mirani.** Ogle at the peculiar ice cream-eating emu. (☎4959 1777. Open daily 9:30am-5pm. $11, children $5.50. Croc feeding 2:15pm. Day trip from Mackay including city tour, sapphire fossicking, and hot meal. $50.) Farther along Eungella Rd., in **Pinnacle,** is **The Pinnacle Hotel,** where stopping for Wendy's famous homemade pies is a must. (☎4958 5207. Open 9am-11pm. Pie $3.50.)

FINCH HATTON GORGE

After the Pinnacle Hotel is a well-marked turn-off to beautiful **Finch Hatton Gorge** (10km from Eungella Rd.). Contact the ranger (☎4958 4552) for the latest on trail conditions, as the narrow road dips through several creeks that are often too full to cross from January to March. Walking trail maps are available for free at the QPWS office in Mackay. Don't miss the hike up to **Wheel of Fire Falls** (4.2km, 1hr.), where rushing rapids cascade down the rocky riverbed with the rainforest as backdrop. The side track to **Araluen Falls** (400m) winds past two tree trunks remarkably intertwined like licorice strands, and ends at a zig-zag waterfall pouring into a deep, gorgeous pool. Aboriginal legend has it that those who swim nude in the pool will be blessed with healthy children, but you'll likely argue frozen children, due to the cold temperatures. In either case, for the sake of tradition, get there early on a summer morn to take a proud paddle for progeny.

On the dirt road to Finch Hatton Gorge is the idyllic **Platypus Bush Camp,** with open-air huts and sites that afford great views and sounds of the adjacent creek area burgeoning with platypuses, fireflies, and fruit bats. The camp features an open-air kitchen, a gently rocking porch swing, a rainforest-walled shower, a creekside hot tub built out of rock, and an amazing cast of characters, human and otherwise. The Honeymoon Hut offers platypus viewings from bed and a crisp stream running by your doorstep. Call Wazza to arrange a pickup. (☎4958 3204. Dorm bunks $15; doubles $45; camping $5 per person; bring your own food.)

QUEENSLAND

EUNGELLA NATIONAL PARK

Following Eungella Rd., 84km west of Mackay, is the 52,000-hectare Eungella National Park, a range of steep rainforest-covered slopes and deep misty valleys. The cheapest way to see the park is by car, as there is **no public transportation**. Be careful on the road to Eungella, as it climbs 800m in 3km; take the turns slowly.

If you lack transport, two companies run daytrip bush safaris that may be the best way to see the park unless you're a botany whiz. **Jungle Johno's Bush, Beach, and Beyond Tours** is led by farmer-cum-tour-guide Wayne, who is deeply knowledgeable in topics from horticulture to folklore. He'll also take you to the Finch Hatton Gorge and Broken River. (☎4959 1822. $75, concessions $69, children $45.) Col Adamson's **Reeforest Adventure Tours** offers tours to the Park and Gorge. (☎4953 1000. $85, pensioners, YHA or VIP $79.50, children $52.50.)

What you can see from hilltop views or on any of the nine walking trails is gorgeous. The mountains trap clouds, resulting in high precipitation, and serve as natural barriers between this park and other swaths of rainforest in Queensland. Red cedars, palms, and giant ferns coat many slopes, and platypuses splash in the water at the bottom of the ravines. Over the years, Eungella has seen a dramatic change of focus—it has been prospected for gold, planted with sugar cane, logged, grazed for dairying, and in 1941 declared a national park.

Just outside the entrance to the park, the **Eungella Chalet,** surrounded by Eungella's green mountains, overlooks the vast Pioneer Valley, where clouds can settle into a puffy river; sunrises are other-worldly. Venturing onto the hang glider's ramp next to the pool, where the Australian championships were once held, feels like toeing a diving board over the edge of the earth. The licensed restaurant serves breakfast (7-9am), lunch (noon-2pm; $6-13), and dinner (6-8:30pm; $15-25). Mountain bike hire costs $12 per half-day. Backpackers rates are offered on weekdays. (☎4958 4509; fax 4958 4503. Singles $28; twin shares $22; twins and doubles $50; motel suites $72; 1-bedroom cabin $88. MC/V.) Near the chalet, **The Hideaway Cafe,** a delightful restaurant with yet another amazing view, serves vegetarian options and gourmet burgers for $5-8. (☎4958 4533. Open daily 8am-4pm.)

Five kilometers along the hilltop pastures, meadows, and fields from the Chalet, you'll cross **Broken River,** with excellent platypus-spotting, a picnic area, a campground with toilets and hot showers ($4 per person), and a ranger station (☎4958 4552; open daily 8-9am and 3:30-4:30pm). Nine walking trails depart from trailheads between the chalet and Broken River. The short **Rainforest Discovery Walk** (1km), from Broken River picnic area, is a self-guided track.

CAPE HILLSBOROUGH NATIONAL PARK

Heading inland from Eungella, about 20km north on the Bruce Hwy. is the right-hand turn-off to Cape Hillsborough National Park, where rugged, pine-covered mountains tumble into the bright blue Coral Sea. Rocky outcrops protrude through the tropical rainforest, where kangaroos and scrub turkeys roam.

The brand-new, well-built, must-see **Diversity Trail** (1.2km) is an aptly named jaunt with a boardwalk through many species of mangroves, an area of open woodland with many straight, dowel-like grasstrees (which Aborigines used for spears), and a massive pile of seashells (a midden) under a rock where Aborigines broke open the catch-of-the-day. Signs are posted at the park's entrance.

The fairly steep **Andrews Point Track** (2.6km) begins in sheltered rainforest before exposing onto the ridge with six lookouts. At low tide the rocky beaches of **Wedge Island** becomes accessible for intrepid explorers, but there are no official tracks on the island. The **Beachcomber Cove Track** (1.6km) provides great views from the ridge, ending at a stunning cove. For more info on the tracks, pick up the *Cape Hillsborough Visitor Information Sheet* at the ranger station or resort.

The road to the Cape ends at the **Cape Hillsborough Holiday Resort,** with a pool, and open BBQ. (☎4959 0152; www.capehillsboroughresort.com.au. Sites $9, for 2 $11; cabins $44; beach huts $55; motel rooms $66. All prices except sites increase $11 for one-night stays on the weekend and during holiday periods.)

Adjacent to Cape Hillsborough is one of the best northern beaches, **Smalley's Beach,** on a short unsealed road. Its **campsite** has toilets, water, and the beach as its front yard, but no showers ($4 per person; self-register at the campsite). Another camping option in the area is the **Haliday Hide-away,** a new budget spot next to the ocean. Follow the signs off of the Cape Hillsborough road. (☎4959 0367. Sites $10, powered $12; cabins $30.)

ABBREVIATE TILL YOU DROP Hearing a bit too many unfamiliar words ending in "y" sounds? The words aren't new, just part of the relentless repertoire of Aussie abreviations. Australians refer to objects, places, and even meals as though they were special friends needing nicknames. Sunglasses are "sunnies," BBQs "barbies," and wind or track pants "trackies." Rockhampton is "Rocky," Tasmania "Tazzie," and Brisbane "Brizzy." Bundaberg Rum is "Bundy" Rum. The morning meal is "brekkie" and snacks are "nibblies." Feel free to make up your own, as many "Aussies" do. You don't have to have a "uni" education to do so.

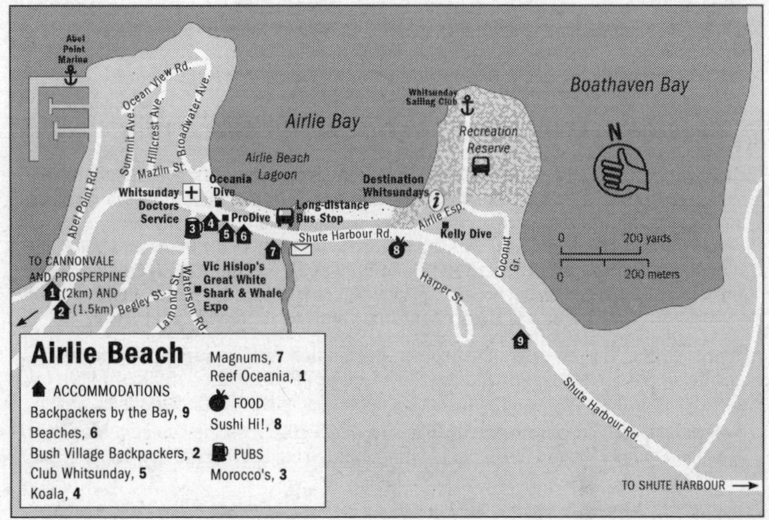

AIRLIE BEACH ☎07

Walking down the street of Airlie Beach ("AIR-lee"; pop. 3700) means being bombarded by advertisements. Airlie was once nothing but mudflats until a developer's proposal was turned down by the Shire Council in nearby Bowen and he moved his project to the oceanside. Equipped with truckloads of Bowen sand, he put the "Beach" in Airlie. The spot was an upscale tourist destination until a pilot strike in the 1980s stalled Queensland's tourism for a year and a half. The resorts became budget in a bid for survival, and backpackers flocked to them. The overwhelming array of activities offered on the nearby waters of the Whitsunday Islands and the Great Barrier Reef has turned the town into the biggest backpacker draw between Brisbane and Cairns. A new $8 million waterfront lagoon was completed in 2001, makes Airlie even more attractive with year-round outdoor fun, but the blue harbor and beckoning islands are the roots of its popularity.

TRANSPORTATION

Trains: The rail station is in Prosperine. **Whitsunday Transit** (☎4946 1800) picks up arriving train passengers and runs down Shute Harbour Rd., stopping in the center of Airlie and at some accommodations. If departing via the train station, you can call Whitsunday Transit 24hr. in advance to be picked up from your accommodation and taken to the train station.

Buses: Travel offices and most hostel desks book transport. **McCafferty's** (☎13 14 99) drops off in the center of town within walking distance of most hostels; accommodations offer courtesy pickups. **Buses** run daily to: **Brisbane** (18hr., 6 per day, $107); **Bowen** (1¼hr., 5 per day, $25); **Bundaberg** (12hr., 3 per day, $110); **Cairns** (10hr., 5 per day, $79); **Gladstone** (9hr., 5 per day, $97); **Hervey Bay** (13hr., 4 per day, $123); **Mackay** (2hr., 6 per day, $33); **Maroochydore** (16hr., 3 per day, $130); **Mission Beach** (8hr., 3 per day, $79); **Noosa** (15hr., 3 per day, $130); **Rockhampton** (7hr., 6 per day, $70); **Townsville** (4hr., 5 per day, $47).

Local Transportation: Whitsunday Transit (☎4946 1800), runs between Cannonvale and Shute Harbour daily 6am-6:40pm, at least every 30min., stopping in front of Oceania

Dive. A 10-trip ticket is $19. From Airlie Beach to Shute Harbour $4.10. Night service 7-11pm Th-Sa. **Whitsunday Taxi** (☎13 10 08), serves the whole area.

Scooter Rental: Whitsunday Moke and Scooter Hire, Cannonvale (☎4948 0700), offers free pickup/drop off. Scooters $18 per hr., bikes $10 per 5hr. Open daily 8am-6pm.

ORIENTATION AND PRACTICAL INFORMATION

Airlie Beach's layout is simple enough. Its main street, **Shute Harbour Rd.,** is where most of the hostels and restaurants are located. Picnic tables line the parallel Beach Walk. Sunbathers laze on the newly created beach or on the grass around the new **Airlie Lagoon** off of Shute Harbour Rd. on the end closer to **Abel Point Marina.** To get to the marina, turn right on Shingley Dr. on the way to **Cannonvale,** a suburb of Airlie Beach along the Prosperine-Shute Harbour Rd. **Shute Harbour** is an 8km drive from Airlie Beach along Shute Harbour Rd. in the other direction.

Tourist Office: One on every street corner. **Destination Whitsundays** is upstairs on the corner of Shute Harbour Rd. and the Esplanade (☎4948 0999 or 1800 644 563; fax 4948 0111; dw@mcs.net.au). Internet $4 per hr. Open daily 7:30am-8:30pm.

National and Marine Parks Authority Office: (☎4946 7022), on the corner of Mandalay St. and Shute Harbor Rd., 2km out of town toward Shute Harbour. Info on camping and national parks. Open M-F 9am-5pm, Sa 9am-1pm.

Currency Exchange: Commonwealth Bank (☎4946 7433), charges a flat $10 fee for traveler's checks and foreign exchange. Open M-Th 9:30am-4pm, F 9:30am-5pm. There's an **ANZ Bank ATM** next to the post office.

Police: Altman Ave, Cannonvale (☎4948 8888). Open 24hr.

Medical Services: Whitsunday Medical Centre, 400 Shute Harbour Rd. (24hr. ☎4946 6275). Open M-F 7:30am-5:30pm, Sa 9am-1pm. Dive medicals $35. **Whitsunday Doctors Service** (☎4946 6241), on the corner of Shute Harbour Rd. and Broadwater Ave. Open M-F 8am-6pm, Sa 11am-1pm, Su 10am-noon. Dive medicals $33.

Internet Access: Everywhere. Expect to pay $4 per hr. There is a **Global Gossip** at 257 Shute Harbour Rd. (☎4946 6488. $3.95 per hr.)

Post Office: (☎4946 6515; fax 4946 7241), in a shopping plaza bordered by McDonald's and Magnum's next to McDonald's on Shute Harbour Rd. Open M-F 9am-5pm, Sa 9am-12:30pm. **Postal Code:** 4802.

ACCOMMODATIONS

Airlie's cornucopia of budget establishments can barely keep pace with backpacker demand, so book ahead. Check into deals if booking tours through your hostel. Check-out is 10am and key deposit $10, unless otherwise indicated. The nearby Whitsunday Islands offer cheap **camping,** but space is limited (see p. 357).

Backpackers by the Bay, 12 Hermitage Dr. (☎/fax 4946 7267 or 1800 646 994), 650m from town toward Shute Harbour. 4-bed bunk-style rooms, chill atmosphere, and amenities galore. BBQ, laundry, pool, game room, Internet, free nightly activities, and a sweet view of the bay. Free pickup and bus to town. Reception daily 7am-7:30pm. Dorms $20; twins and doubles $48. YHA/VIP.

Club Whitsunday (☎4948 1511 or 1800 678 755; fax 4948 1611), on Shute Harbour Rd. A friendly hostel where you don't have to compromise location for comfort. Smallish 4-bed dorm rooms with walk-throughs to doubles share bathrooms. Fan, A/C, and TV. Hot breakfast (cook your own eggs) and luggage storage included. Kitchen and laundry. Internet $4 per hr. Dorms $18, doubles $47.

Bush Village Backpackers Resort, 2 St. Martins Rd., Cannonvale (☎4946 6177 or 1800 809 256; fax 4946 7227), 1.5km out of town. The ultimate in cleanliness and goodwill. Cabins with kitchens and modern bath, line a driveway that leads to the pool, porch, TV lounge, video library. Continental breakfast included. Reception daily 7am-7pm. Dorms $20, non-members $22; doubles $42/$49.)

Beaches, 356-62 Shute Harbour Rd. (☎4946 6244 or 1800 636 630; www.beaches.com.au). Dorms are in former motel rooms with balcony, kitchenette, bath, TV, and fan. Secured parking, laundry, game room, spacious kitchen, Internet. Free night with overnight tour or dive course booking. Reception daily 7am-8pm. Dorms $18; doubles and twins $40-45. VIP. Credit cards accepted.

Magnums, 366 Shute Harbour Rd. (☎1800 624 634; fax 4946 5980; accom-whi@tpgi.com.au). The biggest party scene in Airlie with an open air bar and bistro and a happening nightclub. All rooms have a kitchen, bath, and balcony or porch. Reception daily 6am-10pm. Dorms $12, with dinner at Mama's Boy $15.

Reef Oceania, 147 Shute Harbour Rd., Cannonvale (☎4946 6137 or 1800 800 795; fax 4946 6846; info@reeforesort.com), 3km from town. Comfort cedes to conviviality at Reef Oceania. Pool, volleyball court, free afternoon movies, ping-pong, BBQ, bistro, and bar. Free pickup from bus stop, and free hourly bus service to and from town. Reception 24hr. Limited storage ($6 per 12hr.). Cabins for 6 start at $5.50 per person, with bath, kitchen, and TV $15.

Koala (☎4946 6001 or 1800 800 421; fax 4946 6761; whitwand@whitsunday.net.au), on Shute Harbour Rd. This edition of the famed chain pulls in a party-primed posse with a tiki-torch Polynesian flavor. 6-bed huts have a small kitchen, bath, and satellite TV. Pool, volleyball court, laundry, and Internet. Meal discounts next door at Morocco's. The only campsite in town. Reception daily 7am-8pm. Dorms $16-18; twins and doubles $46-50; camping $10, $5 for each extra person. VIP.

FOOD AND NIGHTLIFE

With the exception of a few cafes, practically all of Airlie's restaurants double as bars and clubs after 9pm. If you stay around, you'll undoubtedly be treated to entertainment—often a cheeky contest involving various states of nudity. Look for discount flyers around town. As for simple nourishment, there is a Five Star **supermarket** located next to the bus terminal. (Open daily 8:30am-6:30pm.) The Bi-Lo Supermarket, located in the Whitsunday Shopping Center in Cannonvale, has cheaper **groceries.** (Open M-F 8:30am-9pm, Sa 8:30am-5pm.)

Sushi Hi!, 390 Shute Harbour Rd. (☎4948 0400). The only place for fresh fish in town, their massive seafood rolls will fill your belly without emptying your pocket ($6 for half rolls). Marinated beef, chicken, or fish sandwiches are $6.75 per foot. Healthy smoothies ($3.50-5.50) will keep you buff for the beach. Open daily 10am-9pm.

Beaches, 356-62 Shute Harbour Rd. (☎4946 6244). An ever jam-packed backpacker mecca. Dinner at long, communal, wooden tables for $8-15. Get a free drink if you grab a coupon on the street and show up by about 5pm. Party games start daily around 9:30pm and are followed by dancing until midnight.

Magnums, 366 Shute Harbour Rd. (☎4946 6266). The wildest joint in town features M night foam parties ($12). Live guitar music plays outside, but in the club there is Top 40 music and nightly games, from cane toad racing to wet T-shirt contests. Open Su-Th 8pm-2am, F-Sa 8pm-5am.

Morocco's (☎4946 6446), next to Koala on Shute Harbour Rd. Tamer than Beaches, with slightly more upscale decor and some outdoor tables. Inside, videos play on huge big-screen monitors. Meals cost $10-17, but you can sometimes pick up a $4 discount on the street. Open daily 7-10am and 4:30pm-2am.

Tricks, 352 Shute Harbour Rd. (☎4946 6465). This place almost always manages to whip up a lively dance party. Open daily until 5am. No cover.

SIGHTS AND ACTIVITIES

The best thing to do in Airlie Beach is visit the Whitsunday Islands or dive the Great Barrier Reef, but there is no shortage of other activities.

BY LAND. Conway National Park is a few kilometers east of Airlie Beach. A self-guided **walk** lasts just over an hour and passes wrinkled fig trees, mucky mangrove swamps, and a few rare bottle trees. On the way, stop at the **QPWS** for a detailed leaflet. *(QPWS ☎4746 7022. Open M-F 8am-5pm, Sa 9am-1pm.)* **Fawlty Tours** has a daily rainforest excursion that features a look at Cedar Creek Falls. *(☎4948 0999. $42.)*

BY SEA. Reel it in with **M.V. Jillian;** troll for mackerel, cobia, and tuna, and then enjoy lunch on board. *(☎4948 0999. Daytrips depart Abel Point 8:30am and return around 5:30pm. $99.)* If you're looking for a longer fishing trip to the outer reef in pursuit of the lions of the fishing world, the beautiful **Marlin Blue** (*☎4946 5044)* has a very experienced captain. Come eye-to-eye with sea turtles and glide underneath the shadows of sea eagles as you explore the islands under your own steam. **Salty Dog Sea Kayaking Tours** gives guided day-trips to the islands and superb snorkeling spots, including meals and smokos. *(☎4946 1388 or 0419 544 841. 1-day $80, 2-day $235, longer trips by arrangement; rental $40 per day.)* **Ocean Rafting** offers daytrips on a raft that tops 65km per hr. Trips include a chance to dive and tan on the beach, as well as either visiting Aboriginal caves or taking rainforest walks. *(☎4946 6848; www.ozadventures.com. $66, children $39; lunch $10 extra.)* Cruise 300 ft. above Airlie with **Whitsunday Parasail.** After, you can enjoy the resort pool free of charge. *(On the jetty near Coral Sea Resort. ☎4948 0000. $45, with jet skis $55.)*

DANGER ZONE. Hand feed kangaroos, ducks, and emus—and watch the handlers carefully feed the crocs—at **Barefoot Bushmans Wildlife Park.** The area also features pythons, cassowaries, koalas, and a giant waterslide. *(Lot 2, Shute Harbour Rd., Cannonvale. ☎4946 1480. Open daily 9am-4:30pm. $19.80, children $9.90, families $52.80.)* One of Australia's most bizarre sights, the **Vic Hislop's Great White Shark & Whale Expo** is a shrine to the owner's unflagging efforts to document, with clippings, photos, and movies, the "dangers of sharks" and battle against these "monsters." A great white shark sits frozen in a block of ice for your viewing pleasure. *(13 Waterson Rd. ☎4946 6928. Open daily 9am-6pm. $15.)*

 DIVING

The scuba scene is hot in the Whitsunday area. Dolphins, turtles, manta rays, and even small reef sharks prowl these waters. The most popular site for overnight trips are on the outer reefs that lie just beyond the major island groups, including the Bait, Hardy, and Hook Reefs. Occasionally, boats will venture to the Black or Elizabeth Reefs. Mantaray Bay is the best spot nearby. Reasonable prices can be found year-round. All trips incur an extra $5 per day Reef Tax.

Reef Jet (☎4946 5366; www.reefjet.com.au). This fast boat takes you and 40 other passengers to Bait Reef, a good location for both beginners and advanced divers. The trip departs Abel Marina at 8:30am, returning 4:30pm, $110. 2 certified dives $171; intro dives $66, 2nd $33.

FantaSea Cruises (☎4946 5111; fax 4946 5520). Their *Reefworld* catamaran whisks you to the **Reefworld Pontoon** with its underwater observatory. Includes courtesy bus, lunch and snorkelling. Departs Shute Harbour and Hamilton Island daily ($141, concessions $116, children $71, family package $320).

Kelly Dive, 1 The Esplanade (☎4946 6122; www.kellydive.com.au). 3-day, 3-night trips on either a sailing catamran or dive boat. Small groups of 20 or 21 people. The *M.V. Sea Reef* departs 6:30pm M and Th ($490) with 10 dives. The *Pacific Star* catamaran departs W and Sa ($450 share cabins, $495 private cabins) and includes 6 dives.

Oceania Dive, 257 Shute Harbour Rd. (☎4946 6032; www.oceaniadive.com.au). The brand new 27m boat *Oceania*, the premier dive boat in Airlie Beach, departs Tu and F for a 3-day, 3-night trip to Elizabeth and Kangaroo Reefs. The boat carries 30 passengers. Advanced courses available. Up to 10 certified dives $500. 5-day course $535.

Pro Dive, 344 Shute Harbour Rd. (☎4948 1888 or 1800 075 035; www.prodivewhitsundays.com). Runs an all-inclusive 3-day, 3-night trip on *Ocean Pro.* Certified $477; snorkelers $360. PADI 6-day courses $685 with advanced certification, 5-day open-water course $499, 4-day course with two daytrips to the reef $385.

BOWEN ☎07

One of Queensland's best kept secrets, Bowen lies just 40min. north of Airlie on the Bruce Hwy. Its gorgeous beaches make the town a strong alternative to Bundaberg (see p. 340) as a place to make some cash. Several hostels will arrange $10.45 per hour (pre-tax) jobs at local farms during picking season (May-Nov.). For more info on working in Australia, see p. 76. Bowen is a stop on every McCafferty's and Greyhound bus. **Bowen Tourism** is at 42 Williams St. (☎4786 4494; fax 4786 4499. Open daily 9am-5pm.)

Horseshoe Bay is the town's biggest attraction. To get there, follow Soldiers Rd. out of town, take a right onto Horseshoe Bay Rd., and follow it to the end. Although it is sometimes crowded by a large elderly population, the small inlet is the perfect place to spend an afternoon. **Murray Bay** is a less frequented and beautiful beach. Turn right off Horseshoe Bay Rd. onto unsealed Murray Bay Rd. The road ends about a 10min. walk from the beach. **Queens Bay** is met directly in the middle by Soldiers Rd. At the far right tip of Queens Bay is **Grays Bay,** with calm water and good **fishing. Bowen Bus Service** runs to the beaches from the library on the corner of Herbert and William St. (☎4786 4414. M-F 3 per day, Sa 2 per day. $2.)

Trinity's is a hostel out of the center of town, on the corner of Soldiers and Horseshoe Bay Rd. It offers a bus to town, laundry, and Internet. (☎4786 4199. $16, weekly $105.) For those not working, the **Horseshoe Bay Resort** is a terrific option. (☎4786 2564; fax 4786 3460. Sites for 2 $14, powered $18; on-site vans $27.50; cabins $45, with A/C and TV $45, with A/C, TV, and bath $60; motel-style units $60.)

WHITSUNDAY ISLANDS

Some rising majestically from the sea, wooded and christened with creeks and waterfalls, others barely poking a tip above water, the Whitsundays are a collection of 74 islands just off the coast of Queensland. Whitsunday Island is the largest and most appealing to campers and hikers, and it's home to the deservedly famous Whitehaven Beach. Other backpacker favorites include Hook Island, with its choice snorkeling spots and Aboriginal cave painting, Day Dream Island, Long Island, and the Molle Island Group, of which South Molle is the best. More creative names include Dead Dog Island and Plum Pudding Island. At the posh resorts on Hayman, Hamilton, and Lindeman Islands many guests arrive by private helicopter, but the islands can make decent daytrips for backpackers, too.

TRANSPORTATION

Blues Ferries (aka FantaSea; ☎4946 5111), departing Shute Harbour, is one of the only companies to run direct transfers to the islands. Schedules are available at almost any booking office or hostel. Between three and eight ferries leave the harbor daily to: Long Island ($25 return); South Molle ($22 return); Hamilton ($42 return). A **Discover Pass** will get you to all three in a day ($52). **Island Camping Connection** drops campers off at any of the islands, and has camping equipment for hire. (☎4946 5255. Minimum of 2 campers, $45 per person.) Of course, the multiple-island daytrip is an option, though you'll have more time on a motorboat than on the islands. **Whitsunday All Over** ferries passengers to Daydream Island, Long Island or South Molle. (☎4946 6900. Long Island $24 return, South Molle $21; trips to both islands include lunch $40.) **Reef Express** runs daily from Abel Point Marina to Hook and Whitsunday Island in a **glass-bottom boat.** (☎4946 4447. $76.) **The Whitsunday Dreamer** chugs along to Long and South Molle Islands. (☎4946 6665. Departs Shute Harbor 9:30am; $59.)

Air Whitsunday Seaplanes flies over the islands. (☎4946 9111. 3hr. reef sight-seeing $190; 3hr. snorkelling at the reef $225; 4hr. Reef and Whitehaven.) You can also fly to Hayman Island for $180 to spend the day. **Helireef** runs 10 to 35min. scenic flights. (☎4946 9102. $65-179; trips to Reefworld $170.) Helireef also flies from Hamilton to the outer reef for the day ($329).

THE ISLANDS

The island group is rich with cheap camping options. There are 21 campsites on 17 different islands, but before embarking, you must get a permit from **QPWS** at the **Marine Parks Authority,** on the corner of Shute Harbor and Mandalay Rd., Airlie Beach. (☎4946 7022. Open M-F 9am-5pm, Sa 9am-1pm. Permits $3.85 per night. Walk-in applications are welcome, but book ahead for smaller campgrounds.)

WHITSUNDAY ISLAND. The principal draw of the Whitsunday Islands is the famed **Whitehaven Beach,** a 6km-long slip of white along the western part of the beach that resembles the foam on a cappuccino. Sand as pure as talcum powder lies softly at the bottom of ever-clear tidal pools. Behind the beach, a forest clings tenuously to the sand. Across the bay is another beach with the bonus of soft coral framed dramatically by the baby-bottom-white sand. The campsite at Whitehaven Beach has recently re-opened, and has toilets, picnic tables and shelter (limit 60 people peak, 24 people off-peak). On the other side of the island is **Cid Harbour,** a common mooring site for the 2-night boat trips. Cid Harbor houses three **campgrounds.** The largest is **Dungong Beach** (limit 36 people), which has toilets, drinking water, sheltered picnic areas, and a walking track (1km; 40min.) that leads to the second campground, **Sawmill Beach** (limit 24 people). The same amenities are provided here, but remember to take a water supply if you're camping farther south at **Joe's Beach** (limit 12 people). There is excellent **snorkeling** in the shallow waters not far from Joe's beach.

HOOK ISLAND. The beaches on Hook have beautiful stretches of coral just offshore, literally a stone's throw from **Chalkies Beach** and **Blue Pearl Bay.** *Let's Go* does not recommend throwing stones at beautiful stretches of coral. On the south side of the island lies **Nara Inlet,** a popular spot for overnight boat trips. About 20min. up the grueling path is a cave shelter used by the sea-faring Ngalandji Aboriginals, bordered on both sides by middens (piles of shells). The rare paintings inside date back to 1000 BC and may have given rise to the popular Australian myth that a boatload of exiled Egyptians washed ashore ages ago and left hieroglyphic-like traces in various corners of Queensland. Although the story is unsubstantiated, it is true that at least one glyph in the cave is a good match for "king" in Hieroglyphic Luwian, spoken in ancient Troy. **Maureens Cove** (limit 36 people), on Hook's northern coast, is a popular anchorage and has camping. Also on the island is **Steen's Beach** campground (limit 12 people), a good sea kayaking site. **Hook Island Wilderness Resort,** just east of Matilday Bay, is the best bargain resort in the islands with a range of activities from snorkelling ($10 one day rental) to fish and goanna feeding. Remember to bring a towel, kitchen utensils and sleeping bag or blanket. (☎4946 9380; fax 4946 9470. Transfers $36. Camping $14.30, two nights $25, children $7.70 extra; hut-style dorms $22; beach-front cabin with bath for up to six people $110. Credit cards acepted.) There is an underwater reef observatory at the end of the jetty (check with resort for opening hours, $8). Transfers to the island depart daily from Shute Harbor at 9am on the Prosail Dive boat.

SOUTH MOLLE ISLAND. South Molle offers some of the best **bushwalking** in Queensland. The trek (6km return; 1½hr.) from the resort to **Spion Kop,** an enormous rock precipice, is a must. Adventurous hikers scramble up the rocks for an absolutely astounding 360° view of the Whitsundays. **Sandy Beach** (limit 36 people) has over 15km of hiking trails. The trip to the island's resort is 5km through the grasslands. Another 1km will take you to Balancing Rock. Many 2-night sailing excursions moor offshore and guests come ashore to bushwalk or use the pool at the **South Molle Island Resort.** (☎4946 9433 or 1800 075 080; fax 4946 9580. Meals and nightly entertainment included. 3-share rooms $125 per person. Cheaper standby rates are often available.) The island's water activities facility has catamarans ($10 per hr.) and jet skiing ($50 per 15min; open daily 8am-4:30pm).

DAYDREAM ISLAND. Part of the Molle group, the resort here is the island. Formerly West Molle island, the original resort owners realized that the name **Daydream Island Resort** was so much more attractive. The resort re-opened under new management in September 2001.

HAMILTON ISLAND. The mini-metropolis of the Whitsundays, the **Hamilton Island Resort** has high-rise hotels, a main-drag replete with **ATM, general store,** and 14 different restaurants. Golf buggies whisk well-heeled guests from beachfront to marina in minutes. (☎4946 9999; fax 4946 8888. Transfer included. $69 per person for twin or double bungalows with bath.) The endlessly dough-consuming activities on the island will leave you breathless and spent. **Jono's Beach Hire** at the resort rents catamarans ($30 per hr.), windsurfers ($20 per hr.), and snorkel gear ($12). Soar across a valley on the **Wire Flyer,** a hang glider attached to a 325m long cable. Follow the signs posted around the island to find its hilltop location. (☎4946 8780. $35, children $25.) **FantaSea** will take you for the day. (☎4946 5111. $55 including lunch; children $27.50.)

LONG ISLAND. Only a short journey from Airlie Beach, Long Island has one campground at **Sandy Bay** (limit 12 people) and a budget resort called **Club Crocodile.** The resort's special includes a twin-share room, meals, use of the pool and spa, and bushwalking. Its launch departs regularly from Shute Harbour. (☎4946 9400 or 1800 075 125. Transfers $30 on **Blue Ferries.** Garden rooms $135 per person per night, kids $55.)

OTHER ISLANDS. On **North Molle Island** lies the mammoth Cackatoo Beach Campground (limit 48 people), fully equipped with facilities, and seasonal water supply. Other fully equipped campsites include **Gloucester Island's** Bona Bay (limit 36 people), Northern Spit (limit 24 people, no water) on **Henning Island,** the small-secluded sites (limit 12 people) at **Thomas Island,** and **Armit Island** (limit 12 people. Basic grounds with simple bush camping sites and a 12-person limit are Shute Harbour (views of Shute Harbour are actually concealed by **Repair Island**) on **Tancred Island,** Burning Point and Neck Bay on **Shaw Island, Saddleback Island,** Western Beach on **South Repulse Island,** and the four-person sites on **Olden Island, Planton Island,** and **Denmon Island.**

Finally, Boat Port (limit 12 people) on **Lindeman Island** has some terrific walks. The **Mount Odefield walk** (3.6km) goes from the Airstrip Hut to the summit. The **Loop walk** (6.3km) begins in the same spot but runs along the headlands to the northern beaches. The easiest track goes to **Coconut Beach** (5.2km).

SAILING THE ISLANDS

Traveling the Whitsundays without sailing the islands is like going to Paris without seeing the Eiffel Tower. A sailing safari is one of the most popular activities in Queensland, but it's also one of the most expensive. There are four classes of boats at play: the uninspiring **motor-powered**—this includes boats that have sails but nonetheless motor everywhere; the stately **tallships,** with rigging of yesteryear and the elegance of age; the **cruising yachts,** which offer more comfort, and with smaller numbers may give you the most actual sailing time; the proper **racing yachts,** called **maxis,** which are usually well past their racing prime, generally more expensive, and popular with partiers. Travel agents may try to push the maxis (which give higher commissions), with a valid case that these boats will get you to locations faster and thereby give you more time in each place. Then again, the powerboats will get you there even faster, so choose the balance of sail-time vs. location-time that suits you best. During the low seasons (Oct.-Nov. and Feb.-Mar.), when discounts can be found, all sailing trips are usually booked solid a few days ahead of time; unless you **book ahead,** your boat may be decided for you, or you may miss out altogether.

Ask how much time is actually spent on the safari. Many boats offer "three-day, two-night" trips that leave at midday and come back 48hr. later. When the options are overwhelming, try asking a few more questions. How many passengers does the boat take? Is it primarily a dive boat with a generator that will be running all night filling the tanks (and keeping you awake)? How much sailing is done? Is snorkel gear included? Do you want to sleep at sea, or a trip that has you sleeping on one of the island resorts? Take a late afternoon stroll down to Abel Point Marina and take a look at some of the boats (around 4 or 5pm). Talk to some of the skippers and take a gander at the cabin you'll call home for three days. Boats supply plenty of food and sell soft drinks and water at a slight mark-up. Finally, keep in mind that it can get chilly and wet out on the waves. Boats usually provide waterproof weather jackets, but quick-dry shorts are also a good idea.

Prosail (☎4946 5433). Most Prosail 3-day, 2-night trips offer an additional day on *On the Edge* for 50% off. Package deals: 2 days of sailing $155; cruise family rate $213. 3-day trips on 1 of 4 maxis, including the *Matador,* the world's largest maxi, $470-$520. 3-day, 2-night trips on cruising yachts take 12 guests and 2 crew, $470.

Southern Cross (☎4946 4999 or 1800 675 790). *Siska,* 80ft., offers the most comfort. *Southern Cross,* a former America's Cup finalist, holds 14 guests. *The Card* takes 20 guests. All 3-day, 2-night $359. *Solway Lass*, a gorgeous 127ft. built in 1902, holds 32 guests. 3-day, 3-night: twins/doubles $399, 4-bed $379. 6-day, 6-night: $739, $689.

Tallarook (☎4946 5299). This fleet has received accolades from backpackers. 48hr. trips on the *Tallarook V:* $249 including dive; each additional dive $30, certified $25 On *Freedom*: day and night snorkeling and 1 intro or certified dive $239; each additional dive $30, certified $25. 3-day, 2-night trips on the *Great Eagle:* 12 guests $340 and the *Stargazer*: 10 guests $310. All depart Abel Point.

Providence V (☎1800 655 346). 3-day, 2-night trips on a replica of a Gloucester Schooner, the original America's Cup boat. Diving can be arranged. Departs Abel Point Marina varying days 9:30am, returns third day at 4:30pm. $341.

Summertime (☎4948 0999). 48hr. trip on a 60 ft. timber ketch. Extensive bushwalks at anchor sites. Departs Abel Point Marina W, F, Su 1pm; returns W, F, Su noon. $249.

DO IT YOURSELF

Reasonably experienced sailors and boaters with a small group might consider chartering a yacht, catamaran, or power cruiser with **Queensland Yacht Charters** (☎1800 075 013). The boats come fully equipped and accesorized; sailing boats include fuel, power boats don't. Not including the hefty $770-1100 bond, rates range from $366 per night for yachts, and $325 per night for power boats, which, when divided amongst a group, often beats the cost of a cruise.

DIVING

Ninety-five percent of diving in this area departs from Airlie Beach (see p. 356). Boats normally venture to Bait, Hook, or Hardy reefs, just beyond the largest island group. The pristine Manta Ray Bay, off Hook Island, is limited by 2hr. mooring rules. A couple of trips depart from island resorts, but, departing the mainland at one of the two harbors is the best deal. If you are dead set on the full resort experience, a trip to Hardy Reef departs **South Molle Island Resort** daily at 8:30am on **Reefjet** and returns at 5:30pm. (☎4946 9433. $165, families $368, min. 3 people.)

NORTH COAST OF QUEENSLAND

The northern Queensland coast sits at the junction of the tropical far north, the rugged frontier of the outback, and the modern cities of the southern coastline. Tall green fields and smoking mills represent the region's greatest agricultural asset, sugar cane. Sunny Townsville is the economic and residential center. Off its shores, Magnetic Island offers solitude and koalas in the wild. Between the island

and Mission Beach, white beaches glow next to crystalline water, across which the Great Barrier Reef beckons. The inland territory hides swaths of rainforest populated by birds, bugs, and bouncing 'roos, and between it all, the civilization that clings to the coast wrests its existence from the unrelenting wild.

TOWNSVILLE ☎07

Townsville is a forest of greenery from which the red rock of Castle Hill rises up to tower over the topaz blue of the Coral Sea. Discover what other tourists and backpackers have blundered past on their pilgrimages north: Townsville is so much more than northern Queensland's unofficial capital. It is a city of beaches, cafes, palm-lined promenades, and sunken wrecks. The place is steeped in genuine laid-back Aussie atmosphere—a welcome respite from the frenetic Queensland coastal trek. On the weekends, locals toss shrimp on the barbie on the Strand, a 2.2km beachfront park with a bike path, children's water playgrounds, and roman-

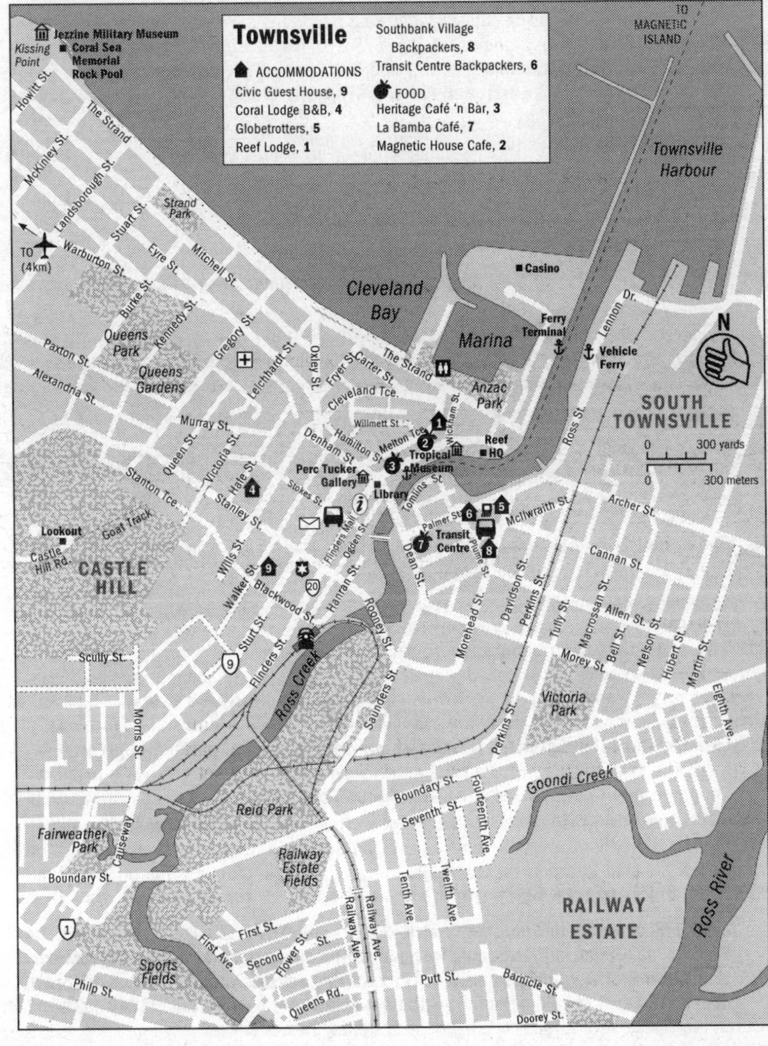

tic cupolas. Others sunbathe, inline skate, or just relax and look hip in one of the Southbank's trendy cafes. Only the excitement of the off-shore attractions could lure one away from the city leisure. The rewards of diving the world-renowned wreck of the S.S. Yongala or koala-spotting on Magnetic Island, however, make it well worth the effort. Travelers return from treasure-seeking expeditions to a city with a sophisticated nightlife dominated by wine-drinkers and music-lovers.

TRANSPORTATION

Airplanes: The **airport** (☎4727 3211) is west of town. **Qantas** flies direct daily to: **Brisbane** (1¾hr.; 5 per day; $253); **Cairns** (1hr.; 5 per day; $229); **Mackay** (1hr.; 3 per day; $253). An **airport shuttle bus** (☎4775 5544) meets all major flights and runs to town daily 5:30am-9pm. One-way $7, return $11. To drive from the airport to town, take John Melton Black Dr., which becomes Bundock St. Bear right onto Warburton St. and again onto Eyre St. From Eyre St., go left on Denham St. to the town center.

Trains: The **train station** (☎4772 8288, reservations 13 22 32) is at the corner of Flinders and Blackwood St. The *Inlander* train departs W and Su at 6pm for: **Charters Towers** (3hr., $19.80); **Cloncurry** (16hr., $78.10); **Hughenden** (8hr., $45.10); **Mt. Isa** (20½hr., $95.70); **Richmond** (10¾hr., $56.10). The *Spirit of the Tropics* leaves W and Su at 4pm heading to: **Brisbane** (24hr., $141.90); **Bowen** (5½hr., $33); **Mackay** (7½hr., $53.90); **Rockhampton** (13hr., $93.50). The **Queensland Rail Travel Centre** (☎4772 8358) is to the right of the station. Open M 7:15am-5pm, Tu and F 6am-5pm, W 7:15am-6pm, Th 8:30am-5pm, Sa 1-4:30pm, Su 7:15-10:45am.

Buses: The **Transit Centre** is on the corner of Palmer and Plume St., a 5min. walk from the city center. Open daily 6am-8:30pm. **McCafferty's** (☎13 14 99; open daily 5:30am-11pm) and **Greyhound** (☎13 20 30) run to: **Airlie Beach** (4hr., 6 per day, $47); **Brisbane** (20hr., 6 per day, $150); **Cairns** (4hr., 6 per day, $49); **Cardwell** (2¼hr., 6 per day, $32); **Charters Towers** (2hr., 2 per day, $24); **Cloncurry** (10hr., 2 per day, $97); **Hughenden** (4hr., 2 per day, $49); **Ingham** (1½hr., 6 per day, $25); **Innisfail** (4¼hr., 6 per day, $45); **Mackay** (5hr., 6 per day, $64); **Mission Beach** (3½hr., 4 per day, $45); **Mt. Isa** (12hr., 2 per day, $108); **Richmond** (5hr., 2 per day, $62); **Rockhampton** (9hr., 6 per day, $98). Phew.

Public Transportation: Sunbus (☎4725 8482; www.sunbus.com.au) has its main terminus in the center of Flinders Mall. Most tickets $3-4. 24hr. bus passes $10.

Car Rental: Townsville Car Rentals, 12 Palmer St. (☎4772 1093; fax 4721 3678). $44 per day, with 100km limited mileage. **Independent Rentals,** 25 Yeatman St., Hyde Park (☎4721 4766). $44 per day, 150km.

Bike Rental: Street Dreams, 30 Palmer St. (4771 6477). Rents bikes for $10 per day, or $15 for 24hr. (Open daily 9am-6pm.)

Automobile Club: RACQ, 635 Sturt St. (24hr. ☎4721 4888). Open M-F 8am-5pm, Sa 8am-noon.

Taxis: Taxi Townsville (24hr. ☎4713 1008).

ORIENTATION AND PRACTICAL INFORMATION

Although Townsville is a large city with a complicated lay-out, the downtown area is thankfully easy to negotiate. Buses pull into the Transit Centre on **Palmer St.,** which is also where most hostels are located. From there, it's only a 10min. walk over the **Ross River** bridge and up Dean St. to the open-air **Flinders Mall.** The beach and many nice restaurants are set along **The Strand,** a street that runs along the ocean for several kilometers. **Castle Hill** looms to the east, accessible both by road and a relatively steep walking trail.

Tourist office: Visitor Information Centre (☎4721 3660), is the big circular kiosk in the Flinders Mall. Open M-F 9am-5pm, Sa-Su 9am-1pm. **Marine Parks and QPWS Information Centre,** at Reef HQ complex (☎4721 2399), answers marine and national park questions. Open M-F 9am-5pm, Sa-Su 10am-4pm.

Currency Exchange: Bank of Queensland, 16 Stokes St. (☎4772 1799), up from Flinders Mall on the left, often has the best rates with the shortest lines. $5 commission. Open M-Th 9:30am-4pm, F 9:30am-5pm.

ATM: Machines are in Flinders Mall for both Cirrus and Plus transactions.

Police: Corner of Stanley and Sturt St. (☎4759 9777).

Hospital: General Hospital, at Douglas, access via Yolanda Dr. roundabout on University Dr. at Annandale. (☎4781 9211, emergency ☎4781 9753).

Internet Access: Internet Den, 265 Flinders Mall (☎4721 4500). $5.50 per hr. Open daily 8am-10pm. Free at the **library** across the mall. Book ahead. Open M-F 9:30am-5pm, Sa-Su 9am-noon.

Post Office: General Post Office, Post Office Plaza on Sturt St. between Stanley and Stokes St. (☎4760 2021). Open M-Sa 8:30am-5:30pm, Su 9am-12:30pm. Poste Restante open M-F 9:30am-4:30pm. **Postal code:** 4810.

ACCOMMODATIONS

As a transportation hub, Townsville's hostels cater to the weary traveler. There are some gems to choose from. Linen is usually free; expect a $10 key deposit.

Civic Guest House, 262 Walker St. (4771 5381 or 1800 646 619; www.backpackersinn.com). Hands-down the best hostel in town with free F night BBQs and well-made beds. Free courtesy bus. Internet $5 per hr. Kitchen, laundry, TV lounge. Reception 8am-8pm. 4- and 6-bed dorms $19; singles $38; doubles $42. Also available with bath. VIP. Credit cards accepted.

Globetrotters, 45 Palmer St. (☎4771 3242; globe@ultra.net.au), just east of the Transit Centre. Dorms with unbunked beds. Laundry, pool, BBQ, TV, tropical garden. Reception daily 6:30am-6:30pm. Dorms $18; twins $42, with A/C $44; triple with bath $57. VIP.

Reef Lodge, 4 Wickham St. (☎4721 1112; fax 4721 1405), off Flinders St. E. Small rooms have fridges. Free pickup from Transit Centre. Laundry, BBQ, kitchen. Reception daily 8am-10pm. Dorms $14; doubles $36; motel rooms $49.

Downtown Motel, 121 Flinders St. East (4771 5000; www.aussiebackpacker.com.au). Check-out 9am. Some dorms with bath. Dorms $14.30-17.50; doubles $27.50; motel twins or doubles $55.

Transit Centre Backpackers (☎4721 2322 or 1800 628 836; www.tcbackpacker.com.au). Surprisingly quiet for its location near the bus terminal location, though it's perfect when your backpack's too heavy to carry. Free storage. Laundry, kitchen (plates $5 deposit), TV room. Reception daily 5:30am-11pm. Dorms $15; twins and doubles $40; family rooms $65 with bath. VIP. Credit cards accepted.

Southbank Village Backpackers, 35 McIlwraith St. (☎4771 5849), across from the bus terminal. Go left out of the terminal and walk through the BP petrol station. This hostel is comprised of 7 stilt houses which show their age. Laundry, kitchen. Reception daily 8am-8pm. Dorms $13; singles $17; twins and doubles $30. No credit cards.

Coral Lodge B&B, 32 Hale St. (☎4771 5512 or 1800 614 613; fax 4721 6461), from Flinders Mall, follow Stokes St. for 4 blocks, turn left on Hale; it's on the left. One of only two B&Bs in town, this one is clean, friendly and comfortable. All rooms have A/C, TV, and fridge. Singles $50, $45 without breakfast; twins and doubles $60. Self-contained singles $65; twins and doubles $75.

FOOD

Most of the city's restaurants are along The Strand and Flinders St. E. Flinders Mall hosts the **Cotters Market,** with fruit, vegetables, and crafts Su 8:30am-2pm. **Woolworth's supermarket,** 126-150 Sturt St., is between Stanley and Stoke St. (Open M-F 8am-9pm, Sa 8am-5pm, Su 8:30am-1pm.)

Zolli's, 113 Flinders St. (☎4721 2222). You'll believe you've died and gone to the Mediterranean as you listen to Italian music, imbibe red wine, and dine on truly authentic Sicilian cuisine. Splendid mussel pasta $8.50, pizza $6-15.50. Stroll as fast as you can to this trattoria, with its friendly, impeccable service. Open daily 5pm-late.

La Bamba Cafe, 3B Palmer St. (☎4771 6322), near the corner of Dean St. Bright, colorful walls are filled with local art. A popular Southbank breakfast spot, Parisian croissants $4.50. Baguettes $7.50-8.20. Open daily 8am-2pm, M-Sa also 6pm-late.

Magnetic House Cafe, 145b Flinders St. E. (☎4771 2172). Sporting walls decorated with customers' tablecloth art, this friendly cafe has culinary daring to match. Breakfast from $6. Open M-Sa 11:30am-3:30pm and 6:30pm-late, Su 10am-3:30pm.

Heritage Cafe 'n' Bar, 137 Flinders St. East (☎4771 2799). A bohemian coffeehouse vibe, with delicious pasta dishes for $10-13.50. Greek salad $12.50. Th bucket of prawns and a XXXX beer or glass of wine for $9.50. Open M-Th 4pm-late, F-Su 5pm-late.

DIVING

Kelso Reef, Townsville's closest access to the Great Barrier Reef, is home to over 400 kinds of coral and schools of tropical fish. These sites on the outer reef are fairly well preserved, but call ahead to dive companies because high winds can obscure visibility. Townsville's best dive site isn't on the reef—in 1911, the **S. S. Yongala** went down in the tropical waters off the coast of Townsville. The still-intact shipwreck is considered one of the world's best wreck sites and one of Australia's best dives, but it requires advanced certification or a professional guide.

Sun City Watersports/Adrenalin Dive, 121 Flinders St. (☎4771 6527 or 1800 242 600). A small operation that offers the only daytrip to the Yongala wreck. The boat is functional and nothing more, but the company offers some of the best guided dives in Northern Queensland. The company also makes daytrips to the reef. Yongala trip W, F, Su; $179, with gear $199. Reef trips from $120.

Reef and Island Tours, 4 The Strand (☎4721 3555 or 1800 079 797; www.reefislandtours.com.au). Specializes in daytrips to Kelso Reef on a hi-speed catamaran, with snorkeling, fishing, or diving. $132, diving $105 for 2 intro dives, $60 for 2 certified dives. Ask about backpacker specials ($94) and student concessions.

ProDive, Reef HQ Complex Flinders St. (☎4721 1760), offers a 5-day open water course including dives on the Yongala ($495) and 3-day, 2-night cruise to the Yongala for $435 aboard the *Pacific Adventure*. Daytrips to the reef $122, with 2 certified dives or 1 intro dive $159. Open daily 9am-5pm.

Blue Adrenalin, Flinders Mall (☎4721 3001; fax 4771 2707), is a backpacker-targeted outfit. They charter the *MV Alita* for their 2 and 3 day trips to the Yongala. Departs F $375, departs Tu $475. They also offer 4 and 5 day open water courses.

SIGHTS

Although Townsville isn't known for its sights, it has about as many interesting museums and worthwhile attractions as anywhere else in the North.

REEFHQ. The center features the world's first indoor coral reef—a 2.5 million liter aquarium that scientists have rigged to work like a reef in the ocean. Tours and shows almost every hour, including a visit to the sea turtle research facility. *(2-68 Flinders St. ☎4750 0800. Open daily 9am-5pm. $16, children $7, families $38.)*

MUSEUM OF TROPICAL QUEENSLAND. If you can't get to the Yongala, visit the next best thing: the relics of the *HMS Pandora*, displayed in this flashy new museum, complete with interactive cannon-firing. Great for kids. *(78-102 Flinders St. ☎4726 0606. Open daily 9am-5pm. $9, $6.50 concessions, $5 children, $24 families.)*

OMNIMAX THEATER. Bigger than the IMAX, it shows films on the hour between 10am and 4pm. Check with the theater for current flicks. *(In the Great Barrier Reef complex on Flinders St. East. ☎4721 1481. $12, concessions $10, family $31.)*

BILLABONG SANCTUARY. Kangaroos wander this sprawling wildlife park. Several daily presentations allow you to get up-close and personal with wombats, pythons, and more. *(17km south of Townsville. ☎4478 8344; www.billabongsanctuary.com.au. Open daily 8am-5pm. $20, students and seniors $15, children $10, families $47.)*

ACTIVITIES

Most of Townsville's tourists just take a walk along The Strand looking for excitement, but adventures are only a phone call away. **Right Training,** 53 Cheyne St., Pimlico (☎4725 4571), offers a 3hr. abseiling and rock climbing combo for $87. **Castle Hill** has some challenging **walking paths** that lead to spectacular views of Townsville. Bring water and sturdy hiking boots as the paths can be steep, slippery, and long. **Coral Sea Skydivers,** 14 Plume St., leads tandem jumps daily, as well as 2- and 5-day certification courses for solo jumps. (☎4772 4889; www.coral seaskydivers.com.au. Book ahead. Tandem $240-340.) **Detour Coaches** has tours all over the city, and to the Billabong Sanctuary for $32. (☎4728 5344. M-F 12:45-4:15pm.) **White Water Rafting: Raging Thunder Adventures** takes the rapids on Tu, Th, and Su. (☎4030 7990; www.ragingthunder.com.au. Rafting $145; kayaking $128.)

NIGHTLIFE

Appropriately called **The Bank,** 166-173 Flinders St. E., this bank-turned-nightclub has constant promotions knocking down drink prices. (☎4771 6148. F basic spirits $1 until 1am. Open Tu-Sa 10pm-5am. Cover $5. Smart dress.) **Mad Cow,** 129 Flinders St. E., features less drinking, live music downstairs Su, and no strict dress code. More tavern than nightclub, three pool tables contribute to the calm-as-a-cow atmosphere. (☎4771 5727. W "Cowioki" nights. Open M-Th 8pm-3am, F-Su 8pm-5am. No cover.) A favorite hangout for young locals is **Bullwinkle's Bar & Cabaret,** 108 Flinders St. (☎4771 5647. Live bands Su nights and drink specials on most nights. Open daily Tu-Sa 8pm-5am, M 9pm-5am, Su 7pm-5am. Cover $5, students free.) Test your connoisseur skills at **Portraits Wine Bar,** 151 Flinders St. E., for wine-tasting occurs the first Tu of every month for $8. There are complimentary cheese platters from 5pm on Fridays. (☎4771 3335. Open M-Sa.) The **Exchange Hotel,** 151 Flinders St. E., specializes in beer; on Tu and Th schooners are $2, and pots are only $1.50 during Happy Hour, which occurs three times a day at 9am-noon, 3-6pm and 9pm-midnight. (☎4771 3335. Open M-Sa 9am-3am, Su 9am-noon.)

MAGNETIC ISLAND ☎07

When laid-back Townsville natives need a vacation, they don't go very far; Magnetic Island is only a ferry ride away. The island's beaches are wide and inviting, and pockets of eucalyptus trees are dotted with wild koalas. The 20km coast on the island's east side is the only inhabited area; most of the island is national park. On less crowded beaches, or when young children aren't around, people bath in the buff. Understandably, backpackers flock here in huge numbers. But even in the peak season, with the Australian school holiday crowd mixed in, there still seems to be plenty of room to stretch out in solitude.

TRANSPORTATION

The quickest way to get to Maggie Island is with **Sunferries Magnetic Island,** 168-192 Flinders St. E. (☎4771 3855). **Ferries** depart daily from Flinders St. (30min., 11 per day, $15.70 return) and the Breakwater terminal on Sir Leslie Thieses Dr. (20min., 14 per day, $15.70 return). If you have wheels, the only way to get them across the water is on Capricorn Barge Company's **Magnetic Island Car Ferry,** located down Palmer St. You, your car, and up to five friends can chug to the island for $115 return. (☎4772 5422. 1hr.; M-F 6 per day, Sa 3 per day, Su 4 per day. Book ahead.)

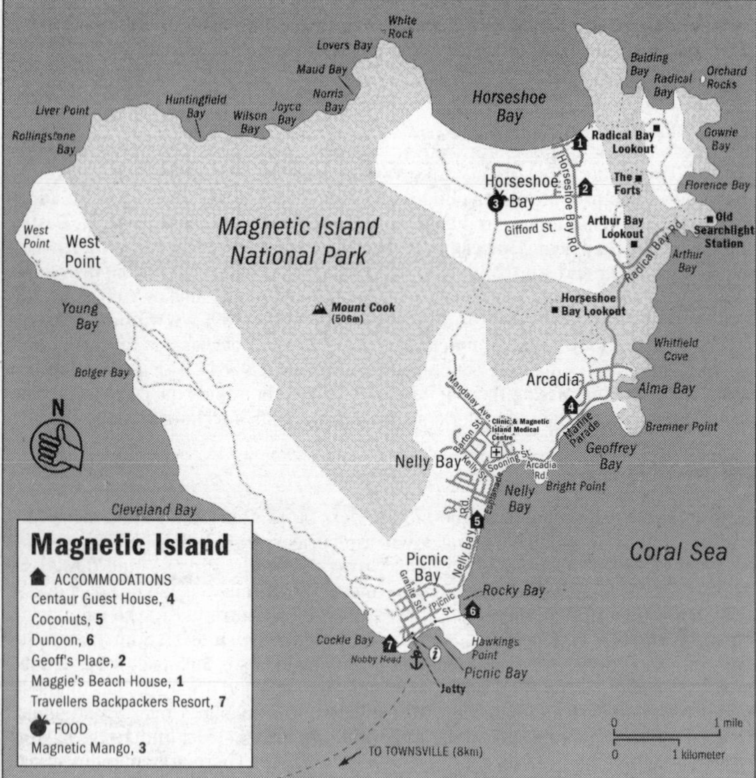

There are less than 20km of sealed roads on the island, and the bus system does a fine job of covering all of them. **Magnetic Island Buses** (☎4778 5130) roughly run every 50min; stops are marked by blue signs. Tickets are sold on the bus ($1.90-4.30), but the better deal is a one-day ($11) unlimited pass, available from the bus driver. Buses operate M-Th 5:25am-8:50pm, F-Sa until 11:50pm, Su 6:50am-8:50pm. Renting a "moke" (an open-air, golf-cart-like auto) is super-popular. Try **Moke Magnetic,** in the Picnic Bay Mall, $44 per day plus 44¢ per km, which includes petrol costs. With not much ground to cover, it turns out to be a rather inexpensive and fun jaunt. (☎4778 5377. Open daily 8am-5pm. $100 deposit or credit card.)

ORIENTATION

The island is roughly triangular in shape, and almost all accommodations, restaurants, and activities are located along the east coast. Instead of having one town that serves as the island center, civilization is spread out. The ferry lands in **Picnic Bay,** the southernmost town on the island and its culinary hub. The main road heads north towards **Nelly Bay,** only a 20min. walk away and home to the island's grocery store. Continuing north, **Arcadia** is the next cove of civilization, a 15min. bus ride from the ferry, on the shores of **Geoffrey** and **Alma Bays. Horseshoe Bay,** a 30min. bus ride from the ferry, is the island's northernmost populated area and the watersports center. From Picnic Bay you can also head west on an unpaved road (no mokes allowed) to **West Point,** a popular sunset spot.

PRACTICAL INFORMATION

Tourist Office: Information Centre (☎4778 5155; fax 4778 5158), next to jetty in Picnic Bay. Open M-F 8am-4:30pm, Sa-Su 8am-1pm.

Travel Office: Magnetic Travel, 55 Sooning St. (☎4778 5343), in the shopping plaza at Nelly Bay. Open M-F 8:30am-5:30pm.

Currency Exchange: There are **no banks** or **ATMs** on Magnetic Island. The info center does credit card cash withdrawals, charging $2 per $100 withdrawn. The **post office** is also the local agent for Commonwealth Bank.

Police: (24hr. ☎4778 5270), on the corner of Granite and Picnic St., Picnic Bay. Open M 8:30am-noon, W and F 8:30am-2pm.

Medical Center: The **Magnetic Island Medical Centre,** 68 Sooning St., Nelly Bay (24hr. ☎4778 5614), does diving medical exams for $60. Open M-F 11:30am-5:30pm, Sa 9:30am-1:30pm, Su 11am-1:30pm.

Taxi: Magnetic Island Taxis (☎13 10 08) charges about $18 to cross the island.

Internet Access: Courtyard Mall Cyber Cafe, shop 2 Courtyard Mall, The Esplanade, Picnic Bay (☎4778 5407). $6 per hr. Open daily 8:30am-5:30pm. Terminals are also available in most hostels and at the **Tourist Information Centre** for $5 per hr.

Post Office: Picnic Bay Arcade, The Esplanade (☎4778 5118; fax 4778 5944). Open M-F 8:30am-5pm, Sa 9-11am. **Postal code:** 4819.

ACCOMMODATIONS

Although most hostels offer regular courtesy buses, it can still be inconvenient to move around the island. Consider location when choosing your hostel. Camping is prohibited in the national park, but two hostels (Geoff's Place and Coconuts) have campground facilities. Standard key deposit is $5-10 and all accept credit cards.

Centaur Guest House, 27 Marine Pde., Alma Bay (☎4778 5668 or 1800 655 680; www.bpf.com.au). The best dorms on the island and believed to be the oldest hostel in Australia. Free activities include wine-and-cheese night (Sa) and pancake and ice cream night (Th). Internet $5 per hr. After hours check-in available. Reception daily 7am-8pm. Dorms $18; singles $33; twins and doubles $39; 5th night free. VIP/YHA.

Dunoon (☎4778 5161; www.dunoon.au.com), corner of The Esplanade and Granite St., Picnic Bay. A good deal for groups–sparkling beachfront cottages with kitchen, bath, dining area, and TV. Laundry, pool, BBQ, and children's area. Book ahead. Reception daily 7:30am-5:30pm. $108 for two, additional adults $15, children $7.50.

Maggie's Beach House, 1 Pacific Dr., Horseshoe Bay (☎4778 5144 or 1800 001 544; www.maggiesbeachhouse.com.au), across the street from the beach, behind the Horseshoe Bay bus stop. Competes with Geoff's Place as party-central for Horseshoe Bay with a nightly Happy Hour 5-6pm. Nightly mixers include toga and rugby parties. Cafe, laundry, Internet. Reception daily 8am-8pm. Dorms $21; doubles $75. VIP.

Travellers Backpackers Resort, 1 The Esplanade, Picnic Bay (☎4778 5166 or 1800 000 290; travellers@ultra.net.au), right in front of the pier. Motel converted into a giant hostel with 4 bars and Maggie's only public nightclub. Kitchen, pool, Internet, and giant resident crocodile Rin Tin Tin. Meals from $4. Reception daily 7:30am-midnight. Dorms with bath $12-20; twins and doubles $50. VIP/YHA.

Geoff's Place, 40 Horseshoe Bay Rd. (☎4778 5577; www.geoffsplace.com.au). A hostel with a campground atmosphere (enhanced by the large camper population), dorms are in basic wooden huts 5min. from the beach. Geoff's club has guests jamming on the weekend nights. Laundry, pool, Internet, bar, and bistro. Reception daily 8am-8pm. Sites $9, powered $14.50; dorms $19.50; doubles $44. VIP/YHA.

Coconuts, Nelly Bay Rd. (☎4778 5777 or 1800 065 696; www.bakpakgroup.com). This newcomer boasts being Australia's only hostel actually on the beach. Dorms in basic A-frames with few amenities. Bar (Happy Hour 6-7pm and 9-10pm), bistro (meals from $6.50), laundry, Internet. 8-bed dorms $16-18; doubles $60; sites $8.

FOOD AND NIGHTLIFE

Magnetic Island is known for relaxation, not gourmet cuisine. The center of gastronomical gravity is the rather pricey **Picnic Bay.** Magnetic Island **Supermarket,** 55 Sooning St., Nelly Bay, is the largest on the island. (Open M-F 8:30am-7pm, Sa 8:30am-5:30pm, Su 9am-2pm.) If you'd like to head out for a night on the town, you really have only one option. **The Shed,** a bar and nightclub in Travellers Backpackers, has DJ dance tunes F-Su. (Open 10pm-3am. No cover.)

Nelly Bay Bakery Cafe, 53 Sooning St., Nelly Bay (☎4758 1400). An extensive menu of baked goods and pizzas for $10-20. Open Su-Th 8am-9pm, F-Sa 8am-11pm.

Possum's Cafe, 55 Sooning St., Nelly Bay (☎4778 5409). Besides delectable sandwiches ($3-4) and seafood boxes ($9), they also have all day breakfast ($6-10.50). Open M-Th 8am-5pm, F-Sa 8am-7pm, Su 8am-3pm.

The Bakery, 22 McCabe St., Arcadia (☎4778 5800). Always stocked with freshly made patisserie delights. Open M-Sa 7am-4pm, Su 7am-3pm.

Michael's On Magnetic, 5 Bright Ave., Arcadia (☎4778 5645). Coffees like hazelnut and caramel $3. Pastas $8-15. Open daily 7:30-10am, 11:30am-2:30pm, and 5-9pm.

Magnetic Mango (☎4778 5018), at the end of Apjohn St., Horseshoe Bay. This sprawling mango plantation run by friendly owners and local celebrities Rina and Gary, serves fresh mango juice and smoothies for $3, mango cake special $6, and sandwiches $5.50-10.50. Any purchase from the kitchen gives you free access to the plantation—complete with goats, goldmine, and mini-golf course. Open Sa-Th 10am-sunset.

DIVING

Magnetic Island offers some of the most inexpensive dive opportunities in all of Queensland. A plethora of small wrecks and reefs provide endless exploration.

Pleasure Dives, Arcadia Marine Pde. (☎4778 5788). Incredible deals on PADI certification classes from the shore (3 days, $179). 4-day courses with one day on the outer reef ($279), as well as intro dives ($65) and certified dives ($39). Advanced courses to the Yongala wreck $349, to the reef $279. Open daily 8:30am-5pm.

Magnetic Island Dive Centre (☎4758 1399), first arcade of Picnic Bay Mall. Free pickup and drop off from any island accommodation. 3- or 4-day PADI island certification classes $175; mixed island and reef course $275. With dives on the *Yongala* 4- or 5-day courses $410, with advanced certification $495. Certified dives $40, for 2 $60; the company can provide your buddy. Resort dives $60. They also rent snorkelling gear; $10 per day includes mask, snorkel, and fins.

Reef and Island Tours (☎4778 5155; www.reefislandtours.com.au), in the tourist office at Picnic Bay. The largest company with the most expensive trips. Outer reef snorkeling daytrip $132 to Kelso Reef. 2 intro dives $105 extra; 2 certified dives $60 extra.

ACTIVITIES

TOURS. Indulge the child within and careen around Magnetic Island with **Tropicana Tours.** On an 4hr. afternoon tour, pile into a 10-seat Jeep Wrangler, cruise to the Beach Boys, feed lorikeets, see beaches, and finish with a plastic cup of wine at sunset. *(2/26 Picnic St. ☎4758 1800; www.tropicanatours.com.au. $82.50; more mild morning version $49.50; the big kahuna all-day tour including lunch $125.)* **Sunbird Tours** is a more nature-conscious way of touring Maggie. Visit mangroves, see birds, and learn about ecology with Deborah, the company's owner and a former environmental educator. *(☎4778 5177. 3hr. $30.)*

GREAT OUTDOORS. The Magnetic Island National Park has several fabulous walking tracks. The popular **Forts Walk** (4km; 1½hr.) virtually guarantees koala spotting. It's best to go from 4-6pm, when the critters are just waking up. Another option is to take the island path (8km; 3hr.) that leads from Picnic Bay through wetlands and mangroves to West Point. Make sure you bring water and sturdy shoes. **Bluey's Horseshoe Ranch** will take you riding bareback along the sand beach of Horseshoe Bay. *(38 Gifford St., Horseshoe Bay. ☎4778 5109. 2hr. $55; half-day $80.)*

WATER ACTIVITIES. Magnetic Island Sea Kayaks departs daily at 8:15am and returns about noon. *(93 Horseshoe Bay Rd., Horseshoe Bay. ☎4778 5254. $35, including a light tropical breakfast.)* Of course, you can always forgo quiet environmentalism and circumnavigate the island on a roaring jet-ski with **Adrenalin Jet Ski Tours.** *(☎4778 5533. $115 half-day tour departs Horseshoe Bay 10am, returns 1pm.)*

OTHER ACTIVITIES. At **Magnetic Island Mini Golf,** 18 holes of putt-putt can be followed by pool, ping pong, air hockey, and more. *(27 Sooning St., Nelly Bay. ☎4758 1066. Golf $4.50, children $3. Open Su-F 9am-5pm, Sa 9am-late. Ask about package deals with other amusements.)* Visit koalas, wombats, emus, and talking cockatoos at the **Koala Park Oasis.** *(Pacific Dr., Horseshoe Bay. ☎4778 5260. Open daily 9am-5pm. $10, children $4.)*

CARDWELL ☎07

A small village between Mission Beach and Townsville, Cardwell brushes up against an appealing beach, perfect for admiring, but not for a dip—salties from the bordering mangrove forests frequent the beach and boat launch. In the middle of several large farming communities, Cardwell is an ideal stop for work.

Cardwell Air Charters, 131 Bruce Hwy. (☎4066 8468.), runs scenic flights over **Hinchinbrook Island** (40min. $80) and the **Undara Lava Tubes** (half day $215), as well as a special 45 min. flight over the location of Survivor II for $95. In nearby **Ingham** (53km south) roars the towering **Wallaman Falls.** At 305m, it's Australia's **largest single-drop waterfall,** and most impressive during the Wet. For some safe and scenic swimming nearby, try **5-Mile Swimming Hole,** a local favorite only, you guessed it, 5 miles (8km) south of town off the Bruce Hwy.

Most of the establishments in town are along Cardwell's patch of the Bruce Hwy., locally known as **Victoria St.** The "transit centre" is just a swath of bitumen in the center of town called Brasenose St. **McCafferty's** and **Greyhound** run to Townsville (2hr., 7 per day, $32) and Cairns (3¼hr., 7 per day, $26).

The YHA-affiliated **Kookaburra Holiday Park and Hinchinbrook Hostel,** 175 Victoria St., is by far the best hostel in town. Friendly and immaculate, it offers free pickup from the bus stop, free bikes to pedal around town, kitchen, pool, and Internet. (☎4066 8648; fax 4066 8910; www.hitchinbrookholiday.com.au. Reception daily 8am-6pm. Sites for 2 $16.50; dorms $16.50; twins $35; doubles $40; motel doubles $61; villas sleeping 1-4 people $88.) If your holiday in Cardwell is a working one, the managers of **Cardwell Backpackers Hostel,** 178 Bowen St., behind Muddie's restaurant, arrange **fruit-picking work** ($10-13 per hr.) for guests and bus them over ($3 for bus). Privacy here is sacrificed for a communal atmosphere; guests sleep in a 12-bed dorm enclosed by a partition. (☎4066 8014. Kitchen, TV room, laundry. Dorms $12; cubicles $14; doubles $30.) The **Hitchinbrook Hop,** 186 Victoria St., has brightly-colored rooms housing well-made-up un-bunked beds. (☎4066 8671. Small kitchen, laundry, cafe, Internet. 2- or 4- bed dorms $12.)

Annie's Kitchen, 107 Victoria St., makes a mean burger for $4-6 and a huge milkshake for $3.50. (☎4066 8818. Open daily 6am-8pm.) The 5-Star **supermarket,** 198 Victoria St., offers a good selection for a small town. (Open daily 6am-8pm.)

HINCHINBROOK ISLAND ☎07

Across the Hinchinbrook Channel, just 4km from Cardwell, is Hinchinbrook Island and the untrammeled wilderness of its national park, where granite peaks loom above mangrove swamps. A trip to Hinchinbrook is a virtually human-free addition to the Queensland experience. The famous **Thorsborne Trail** (32km; 3-7 days) is the most popular hike on the island, but a limit of 40 people are allowed on the trail at one time. Book at least two or three months in advance, 12 months for specific dates during peak summer months.

Hinchinbrook Island Ferries, 131 Bruce Hwy., offers day-tours of the island including walks to some of its pristine beaches. One-way tickets are useful if you have a camping permit and want to walk the length of the island. (☎4066 8270 or 1800 777 021. $59, day-tour or return $85. Transfers available from Mission Beach and Cardwell.) **Hinchinbrook Wilderness Safaris** will pick you up at George Point and bring you back to Lucinda, south of Cardwell. (☎4777 8307. $45.)

Daytrips to the island don't require bookings, but overnight camping trips will not happen spontaneously. Get a permit in advance, read up on various trail options, and piece together a terrific camping trip (camping permits $4 per night). The folks at the QPWS, located at the **Rainforest and Reef Centre,** 142 Victoria St., Cardwell, on the north side of town near the jetty, are eager to help.

MISSION BEACH ☎07

Rapidly becoming a major backpacker destination, this nearly continuous stretch of beach is only 1½ hours from Cairns, yet remote and peaceful enough to be a veritable utopia for those seeking rest during their northern trek. Mission Beach is staggeringly beautiful; the most popular activity is simply sitting on the sand and soaking up the rays. Venturing off the beach towel, the untouched corals and sand cays of the reefs off Mission Beach make it one of the best diving spots on the Great Barrier Reef. On land, the high concentration of cassowaries mean local rainforest walks are often thrilling.

TRANSPORTATION

Greyhound and **McCafferty's** stop in Mission Beach several times daily. Both run to Cairns (2¼hr., 4 per day, $16) and Townsville (3¼hr., 4 per day, $45). Once you arrive in town, a hostel courtesy bus will take you to your accommodation. You can also use these buses during your stay, but at night you'll need to use the $3 **Mission Beach Bus Service** (☎4068 7400), which runs about once per hour between 9am-10pm except M and Tu when service stops at 5:50pm (most tickets $3, day-ticket $10). **Island Coast Travel,** in the Homestead Centre at Mission Beach, is a bus and rail ticket agent. (☎4068 7187. Open M-F 9am-5pm, Sa 9am-noon.)

ORIENTATION AND PRACTICAL INFORMATION

The region known as Mission Beach is actually a group of four communities strung along 14km of waterfront property. From north to south, these towns are: **Bigil Bay, Mission Beach, Wongaling Beach,** and **South Mission Beach.** The main streets are **Porter's Promenade,** which runs through Mission Beach proper, and **Cassowary Drive,** which runs through Wongaling. A popular landmark is the **frighteningly large cassowary,** a statue set in the center of Wongaling Beach. Just off the coast are the **Family Islands,** including the daytrip destination **Dunk Island.**

You'll find the area tourist office in the **Wet Tropics Information Centre** on Porters Promenade, just north of the Mission Beach town. (☎4068 7099; fax 4068 7066. Open M-Sa 9am-5pm, Su 9am-4pm.) Next door, you'll find another valuable resource—the **Community for Coastal and Cassowary Conservation,** which stocks a wealth of books about the region. (☎4068 7197. Open daily 10am-5pm.)

Mission Beach services include: the **Mission Beach Bus and Coach** (☎4068 7400); the **police** (☎4068 8422), 500m past said frighteningly large cassowary at the corner of Webb Rd. and Cassowary Dr. in Wongaling Beach; **Beverley's,** Shop 15, Hub Shopping Centre, where foreign currency and traveler's checks can be exchanged for no fee (☎4068 7365; open daily 9am-5pm). There are also **ATMs** at the supermarket in Mission Beach and the Mission Beach Resort.

ACCOMMODATIONS

All hostels offer free pickup at the bus station and courtesy buses to Mission Beach four times daily, accept credit cards, and do tour bookings. Even with the courtesy buses, chances are, you'll be spending a lot of time in and about your hostel, so stock up on food, and make yourself comfortable.

The Sanctuary, Holt Rd., Bingil Bay (☎4088 6064 or 1800 777 012; www.sanctuaryatmission.com). The most remote accommodation in Mission Beach is also its best. A beautiful hardwood treehouse overlooking the ocean is headquarters for 14 rooms set in the rainforest, where the only thing between you and the resident cassowaries is the screens protecting you from the mozzies. Cafe serves superb dinners $14-17. Internet, yoga classes, massages ($55), kitchen, pool, and 18 hectares of rainforest to explore. All this, and a bed in a twin room is only $23 per night; doubles $49.50.

The Treehouse, Bingil Bay Rd., Bingil Bay (☎4068 7137; fax 4068 7028). A YHA-affiliate perched on a hill, not a tree. BBQ, pool, laundry, tiny grocery store, and comfy reading space. Community spirit is encouraged by communal showers and rooms clustered around common area where music (guests' choice) plays until 11pm. Kitchen, laundry, pool. Linen provided. Tuesday night BBQs $6. Reception 6:30am-8:30pm. Dorms $19; twins and doubles $46. Sites $12 per person per night.

Scotty's Mission Beach House, 167 Reid Rd. (☎4068 8676; scottys@znet.net.au), at the end of Webb St., off Cassowary Dr. Free evening drinks and a pool that permits topless bathing definitely make Scotty's the partygoer's hostel. Laundry, TV room, kitchen, and Internet. Reception daily 7:30am-7pm. 16-bed dorms $18; 4-bed dorms with bath $21; twins and doubles $35, with bath $45. VIP.

Mission Beach Backpackers Lodge, 28 Wongaling Beach Rd. (☎4068 8317; fax 4068 8616; mblodge@znet.net.au), from Cassowary Dr., turn onto Wongaling Beach Rd. at the aforementioned frightening large cassowary; the hostel is on your left. It's a 2-story house with spacious rooms, pool, laundry, and Internet. Reception daily 8am-12:30pm and 1:30-8pm. Dorms $18; twins $37; doubles $39-48. VIP.

FOOD

Most restaurants are concentrated at the village green along Porter's Promenade. If you're looking for **supermarket** staples, check Cut-Price in Mission Beach or Foodstore in Wongaling Beach (both open daily 8am-7pm).

Toba, 37 Porter's Promenade. (☎4068 7852), at the Village Green. Serves a variety of Southeast Asian cuisine including Indonesian fried noodles, and Vietnamese and Japanese specialties. Mains $10.50-18. All furniture is authentic, and herbs are grown in the backyard. Open daily 6pm-midnight.

The Shrubbery Tavern, 44 Marine Promenade. (☎4068 7803). 1 of the town's 3 licensed bars, this tavern on the water specializes in "Greekish" cuisine (mains $12-17), and sinfully delicious banana pudding ($6.90). The eggs are from "happy chickens" and the greens are grown locally. Happy Hour 4:30-6pm. Closed Tu.

Piccolo Paradise (☎4068 7008), David St. on the Village Green. This cafe offers pasta, pizza, and a selection of espresso and juices ($3.30). Open daily 8am-9:30pm.

Port O'Call Cafe (☎4068 7390), at the corner of Campbell St. and Porter's Promenade. With a hearty $7 breakfast, or smaller $5 version, you can't go wrong at this sunny, friendly cafe. Open daily 8am-4pm.

SIGHTS AND ACTIVITIES

DIVING. Mission Beach Dive Charters is the only PADI dive center in town. In addition to a range of scuba courses, it arranges trips to the *Lady Bowen*, a 105-year-old shipwreck discovered in 1997. It also makes outer reef day trips, which include two dives. *(☎4068 7277. 4-day open water certification $395; shipwreck and outer reef both $136; gear hire $30 extra.)* **QuickCat** also makes trips to the reef via Dunk Island and directly to the reef. *(☎4068 8432. Transport $140, reef direct Su and W $80; 2 certified dives $55, 1 intro dive $60.)*

HIKING. Several beautiful **walking tracks** are in the area. *Walking Tracks in the Mission Beach Area*, a 25¢ pamphlet available at hostels and the tourist center describes several walks in the **Licuala State Forest.** The **Rainforest Circuit Walk** (1.3km; 30min.) is a 15m jaunt under the canopy of Licuala Fan Palms. Start at the carpark of the Tully-Mission Beach Rd. **Licuala Walking Track** (7.8km; 3hr.) stretches north through coastal lowland rainforest to the El Arish-Mission Beach Rd. **The Cutten Brothers Walk** (1.5km; 30min.) snakes through mangroves between Alexander Dr. and Clump Point jetty. For longer walks, the **Bicton Hill Track** (4km; starts 3km past the Wet Tropics Info Centre) and the **Kennedy Track** (7km; 4hr.) feature mangrove views, beach, and of course, loads of rainforest.

OTHER ACTIVITIES. Bush 'n' Beach offers short horseback riding lessons and trotting on the beach. *(☎4068 7893; bushnbeach@znet.net.au. 1½hr. trip $49.50; half-day $88, including brunch.)* **Jump the Beach** offers tandem skydiving several times daily. *(☎1800 638 005. 8000 ft. $228.)*

DAYTRIP FROM MISSION BEACH: DUNK ISLAND

Family Islands, just off shore are perhaps the best and shortest excursion from Mission Beach, and the perfect backdrop for a beach party or evening luau. Dunk Island, a.k.a. the "father island," lies just off-shore. The largest of the nuclear grouping, **Papa Dunk** is the only day-tripper destination. Nearby **Bedarra,** also known as "the mother," is uninhabited except for a hoity-toity resort. The "twins" are close together and slightly farther out. The smaller land masses at the fringe of the group are the brothers, sisters, and the triplets. Big family.

There are two boats that service Dunk Island. Those looking to maximize time on the island should opt for the **Dunk Island Express Water Taxi,** Banfield Pde., near Scotty's on Wongaling Beach. (☎4068 8310. 10min., 5 per day, $24 return.) For lollygaggers wishing to prolong their cruise over to the island, check out **Dunk Island Ferry & Cruises,** which departs from Clump Point Jetty, 1km north of the village green. (☎4068 7211. 30-45min, daily 8:45am and 10:30am, $26 return.) **Coral Sea Kayaking** has daytrips to Dunk including lunch, environmental interpretation, and snorkeling gear. (☎4068 9154. $80; shorter morning and afternoon trips $45.)

The **Dunk Island Resort** (☎4068 8199) monopolizes all island activities. If the room rates ($170 per person and up) seem prohibitive, don't despair. Just steps from the jetty are some of the most well-equipped campsites in North Queensland (permits $3.85 per person per night). At few other campsites can you take a hot shower, and the beach doesn't get any better than this. This isn't a well-kept secret, however, and it's small—book about a week in advance during the high season. **Dunk Island Watersports** (☎4068 8199) issues **camping permits** and rents a slew of water toys: paddle skis ($15 per hr.), sailboards ($20 per hr.), snorkel gear ($15 per hr.), and catamarans ($25 per hr.). The only place to eat on the island, besides the resort's fancy restaurant (resort guests only, please), is **BB's on the Beach,** next door to Watersports which serves good barramundi spring rolls ($7.50), as well as lunch and snack food (☎4068 8199; open daily 11am-7pm); but it's cheaper to bring your own. The main attractions on Dunk, aside from the postcard beaches, are the **walking tracks.** The local favorite is the walk circumscribing most of the island (10km; 2-3hr.), which combines Dunk history with diverse landscapes and a trip to the island's highest point. An easier option is the coastal hike (1km; 1hr.) up to **Muggy Muggy Beach** from the dock.

PARONELLA PARK

Just a little west of nowhere between Cairns and Mission Beach hides the Moorish castle of Paronella Park (☎4065 3225). In the 1930s, when Spaniard José Paronella built the main thoroughfare of Paronella, crowds could enjoy its surrounds. In the 1960s, this enchanting parkways diverted from what is now the Bruce Hwy., slipping from tourist itineraries. Recently winning Queensland's highest tourism award in 2001. The park has been discovered by the entertainment industry and has served as the backdrop for three movies, eight TV shows, a music video, and an international magazine photo shoot. Enthusiastic park guides give tours of the grounds and then leave you to explore on your own.

Unfortunately, this place is almost inaccessible via public transportation. If driving, look for signs along the Bruce Hwy. for Paronella Park (the South Johnstone exit is the fastest). If you're not tying the knot or gawking at the handmade architecture, take some time to stroll down Kauri Ave. or feed the fish and eels in the teeming waterfall pool from the ruins of the castle's grand staircase. The **ticket cottage** at the entrance provides a list of the park's horticultural highlights and some history. (Open daily 9am-5pm. Tours 40min., every 30min. $13, children $6.50.) An adjacent **caravan park** blends into its surroundings. Caravan park guests get 24hr. access to the grounds, including a guided night walk. (Sites $14, powered $16.)

INNISFAIL ☎07

North of Mission Beach en route to Cairns, lies the town of Innisfail. Offering few tourist attractions, the Johnstone River and beautiful beaches make it pleasant pit stop. Those who stay are drawn to its year-round labor market for fruit-pickers.

Just north of Innisfail, the road to the **Atherton Tablelands** (see p. 383) branches inland toward **Millaa Millaa.** The **railway station** is off the Bruce Hwy. west of town, and the **bus stop** is on Edith St. **McCafferty's** and **Greyhound** run daily to Cairns (1¼hr., 7 per day, $16) and Townsville (3½hr., 7 per day, $45). The **Information Centre,** at the corner of Bruch Hwy. and Lannercost St., books tours. (☎4061 7422. Open M-F 9am-5pm, Sa-Su 10am-3pm.)

The Codge Lodge, 63 Rankin St., near the corner of Grace St., is billed as a sport-fishing resort, but non-fishing types need not shy away. Convenient to the town center, the lodge is hands-down the best budget accommodation in town, providing a kitchen and pool. (☎4061 8055; fax 4061 8155. Book ahead during the Dry. Reception daily 24hr. Dorms $20; singles $22; doubles $44.)

FAR NORTH QUEENSLAND

The northeast corner of the continent, from Cairns north into Australia's last great frontier, is nothing short of heaven for rugged backpackers and outdoor adventurers. The Great Barrier Reef snakes close to shore here, luring divers with boat trips and visits to the spectacular corals on the reef. Vast swaths of tropical rainforest press up close to the Coral Sea by the craggy mountains of the Great Dividing Range. The rich variety of wildlife and untouched landscape prove that the Far North's greatest attraction is its natural beauty.

Cairns now caters to travelers with city comforts, but the more remote parts of this land remain untamed wilderness. The Captain Cook Hwy. leads modern-day trailblazers north into the rainforest, which becomes incredibly dense around Cape Tribulation. Wilder yet is the Cape York peninsula, starting beyond Cooktown and stretching to the Torres Strait, which separates the Gulf of Carpentaria from the Coral Sea and Australia from Papua New Guinea. The most formidable of Australian roads dares travelers to make the harrowing journey to the tip.

CAIRNS ☎07

The last sizeable city at the corner of the great tropical outback, Cairns is both the northern terminus of the backpacker route and the premier gateway to snorkeling and scuba diving on the Great Barrier Reef. Neon signs and tourist attractions bombard travelers with colors rivaled only by the flamboyant creatures of the underwater world off-shore. While tidal mudflats preclude traditional beach activities, bars, nightclubs and cafes provide plenty of diversions for travelers between forays off the coast. The atmosphere of Cairns ("cans") is friendly, laid-back, and very touristy. More of a big town than a small city, backpackers use Cairns as a home base for launching skydiving trips, scuba vacations, bungy jumps, and white-water adventures, only resting in town long enough to book their next adventure or recover from their latest night out. In addition to this herd of budget travelers, the city also caters to Asian luxury tourists. Often you will find store signs printed in both English and Japanese.

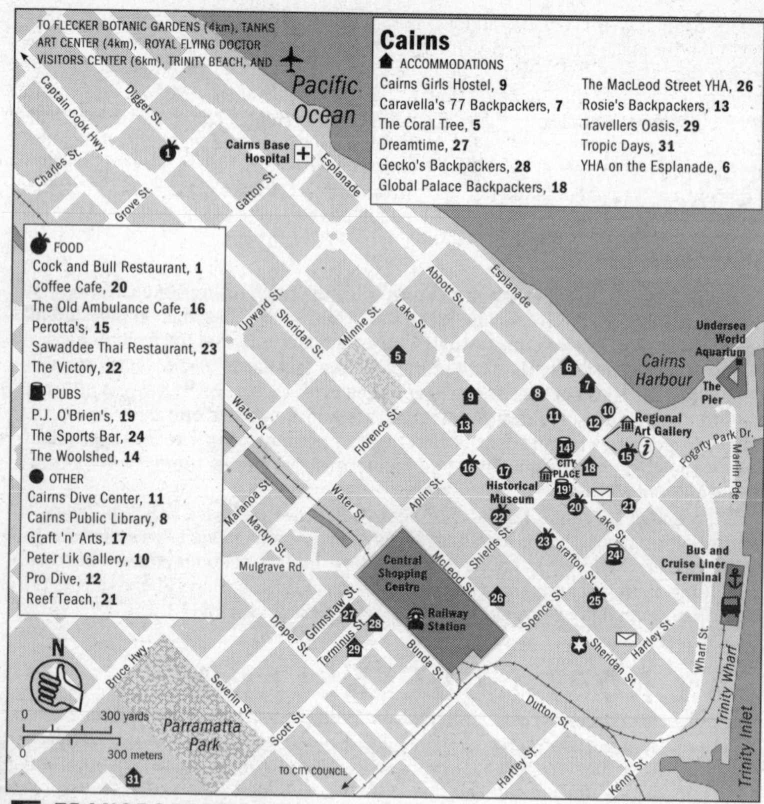

TRANSPORTATION

Flights: The **airport** (☎4052 9744) is 6km north of Cairns on Captain Cook Hwy. Follow the signs. Domestic carriers **Qantas** (☎13 13 13) and **Ansett** (☎13 13 00) have daily flights to: **Adelaide** (5-8hr., 5-7 per day, $661); **Brisbane** (2hr., 9 per day, $408); **Canberra** (5hr., 10-13 per day, $628); **Darwin** (2-5hr., 6 per day, $474); **Hobart** (6-10hr., 6-7 per day, $716); **Melbourne** (5hr., 9 per day, $683); **Perth** (5-10hr., 6-9 per day, $716); **Sydney** (3hr., 7-8 per day, $606). Smaller **Flight West Airlines** (☎13 23 92) has domestic flights and also flies to **Papua New Guinea.** Most hostels run a free shuttle bus airport pick-up service, just call from the terminal. However, to get back, you'll have to book ahead and pay $7 for **Airport Shuttle** (☎4048 8355). Buses also run to town from just outside the terminal ($4.50). 24hr. **taxis** to town are about $13.

Trains: The train station is wedged between Bunda St. and the Cairns Central shopping mall on McLeod St. From The Esplanade, walk west on Spence St. It's on the right. Luggage lockers $2 per day. **Travel Centre Office** (☎4036 9341, 24hr. bookings 13 22 32) sells tickets. 10% YHA discount for long-distance trips. Open M-F 9am-5pm, Sa 7:30am-noon, with early hours M, Tu, Th 7:30-8am. The **East Coast Discover Pass** ($347.50) covers rail from Cairns to **Sydney** and is good for 6 months. (See also **By Train,** p. 64.) Trains run to **Brisbane** (31-32hr.; M-Tu, Th, Sa 8am; $159.50). The scenic railway to **Kuranda** departs twice daily Su-F and Sa 8:30am. (☎4031 3636 for bookings. $29.60, student, pensioner and family discounts available.)

Buses: The bus station is at Trinity Wharf, on Wharf St. Open daily 6:15am-1am. Leave luggage in lockers ($6-11 per day) or with Coral Coaches ($2 per item). Open daily

5:30am-6:30pm. **Coral Coaches** (☎4031 7577) goes to: **Cape Tribulation** (4hr., 2 per day, $37); **Cooktown** (Inland: 5½hr., W and F-Sa 1 per day, $58; Coastal: 8hr.; June-Oct. Tu, Sa and Th; $64); **Karumba** (11½hr., M and W-Th 1 per day, $150); **Port Douglas** (1¼hr., 8 per day, $22). **McCafferty's** (☎13 14 99) and **Greyhound** (☎13 20 30) have 10% ISIC/VIP/YHA discounts and run to: **Brisbane** (28hr.; 5 per day; $173); **Cardwell** (3hr., 5 per day, $25); **Ingham** (3½hr., 5 per day, $33); **Innisfail** (1¼hr., 5 per day, $16); **Mission Beach** (2¼hr., 2 per day, $16); **Rockhampton** (15hr., 5 per day, $116); **Townsville** (6hr., 5 per day, $47).

Ferries: Quicksilver (☎4099 5500) departs from The Pier at the Floreat Jetty to **Port Douglas** (1½hr.; 1 per day; $22, return $32).

Local Transportation: Sunbus (☎4057 7411) depot on Lake St. in City Place. Fares $1-6; unlimited day pass $9, for central Cairns $5, families $21. Buses go south into Cairns' suburbs and as far north as Palm Cove.

Taxis: Black and White (24hr. ☎13 10 08 or 4051 5333).

Car Rental: Billabong, 132 Sheridan St. (☎4051 4299; www.billabongrentals.com.au). 2WD from $44 per day, 4WD from $134. Open M-F 8am-6pm, Sa 8am-noon. **All Day Car Rentals,** 151 Lake St. and 60 Abbott St. (24hr. ☎4031 3348). 2WD from $42 per day, 4WD from $59 per day on sealed roads, $75 unsealed. For trips far afield: **National,** 135 Abbott St. (☎4051 4600). Weekly rentals start at $45 per day, 4WD $145. Open M-F 7:30am-6pm, Sa-Su 8am-5pm; **Avis**, 135 Lake St. (☎4051 5911). Weekly rentals start at $43.25 per day, 4WD $160.

Automobile Club: Royal Automobile Club of Queensland (RACQ), 138 McLeod St. (24hr. ☎4051 6543). Open daily 7:30am-5:30pm.

Bike Rental: SkyDive Cairns, 59 Sheridan (☎4031 5466). A great way to get around the long, flat streets of Cairns. $15 per day, $200 deposit.

ORIENTATION

Cairns is tucked between the rainforested hills on the west, a harbor on the east, and mangrove swamps on the north and the south. In this modern city, the streets are straight and intersect at right angles, so navigation is easy. **The Esplanade,** with its many hostels, runs along the waterfront. At the street's southern end is the **The Pier,** which supports the pricey Pier Marketplace. Farther south, the Esplanade becomes **Wharf St.** and runs past the **Trinity Wharf** and the **Transit Centre.**

Shields St. runs perpendicular to The Esplanade to **City Place,** a pedestrian mall with an open-air concert space. From this intersection, **Lake St.** runs parallel to the Esplanade. Continuing away from the water, Shields St. also intersects **Grafton St.** and **Sheridan St.** (called Cook Hwy. north of the city). The **Cairns Railway Station** is on **McLeod St.** in front of the mega-mall.

PRACTICAL INFORMATION

TOURIST AND FINANCIAL SERVICES

Tourist Offices: Traveller's Contact Point Cairns, 13 Shields St. (☎4041 4677; fax 4041 1338; cairns@travellers.com.au). Services include mail forwarding and job listings. **Internet** $1.50 per 30min, $2.50 per hr. Open M-Sa 8am-8pm. **Tropical Tourism North Queensland,** 51 Esplanade (☎4051 3588; fax 4051 0127), near The Pier. From the train station, turn left onto Spence St., then take a left onto the Esplanade; 100m down on your left. From the bus station, head right on Wharf St., which will curve and become The Esplanade; the office is on your left, between Spence and Shields St. Open daily 8:30am-5:30pm. **City Council,** 119-145 Spence St. (24hr. ☎4044 3044; www.cityofcairns.qld.gov.au), south of Cairns Central. Free *Community Service Guide,* loaded with information and maps. Open M-F 8am-5pm.

National Parks Office: The Queensland Parks and Wildlife Service (QPWS), 10 McLeod St. (☎4046 6601; fax 4046 6604). The *Australian Guide to National Parks* is helpful, but pricey. You can pick up free information about parks in the surrounding area. Open M-F 8:30am-4:30pm.

Budget Travel: Flight Centre, 24 Spence St. (☎4052 1077, 24hr. info 1300 307 735), guarantees to beat any quoted price. Open M-F 8:45am-5pm, Sa 9am-noon. **STA Travel** has two local branches: 9 Shields St. (☎4031 4199; fax 4031 6384; open M-F 9am-6pm, Sa 10am-2pm) and shop 39 in Cairns Central Shopping Centre (☎4031 8398; open M-W and F 9am-5:30pm, Th 9am-7pm, Sa 9am-3pm).

Money: The best **currency exchange** rates are found at **Caravella's 77** hostel, 77 Esplanade (☎4051 2159; see p. 377). The **American Express Office,** 79-87 Abbott St., 2nd fl. (☎ 4031 0353), at Orchid Plaza, has $8 minimum charge for currency exchange under AUS$800, 2% commission thereafter. Open M-F 8:30am-5pm, Sa 9am-noon. **Thomas Cook,** 59-63 Esplanade (☎4041 1000; fax 4041 2550), exchanges currency for a $7 flat fee. Open daily 9am-8pm. **ATMs** at most banks accept Cirrus/MC/V.

Library: Cairns City Public Library, 151 Abbott St. (☎4044 3720). Open M 10am-6pm, Tu-F 10am-7pm, Sa 10am-4pm. **Internet** $3 per hr.

Ticket Agencies: TicketLink in the **Cairns Civic Theatre,** corner of Florence and Sheraton St. (☎4031 9555; fax 4031 3102). Call for ticket prices and show listings.

MEDIA AND PUBLICATIONS
Newspapers: *Cairns Post* (88¢).
Nightlife: *Barfly* (free), available in hostels, stores, restaurants.
Music: Rock, Hot 103.5; news 846am.

EMERGENCY AND COMMUNICATIONS

Police: (☎4030 7000, emergency 000; fax 4030 7144) on Sheridan St., between Spence and Hartley St. Open 24hr.

Hotlines: Alcohol and Drug Information (☎1800 177 833). **Lifeline** (☎13 11 14).

Pharmacy: Chemmart Pharmacy, shop 10/85 Esplanade (☎4051 9011). Open daily 9am-10pm. Gives advice to travelers continuing to Asia.

Hospital: Cairns Base Hospital (☎4050 6250), on Esplanade beyond the last couple of hostels (Bel-Air and Caravellers 149). 24hr. emergency department. More central is the **24hr. Medical Centre** (☎4052 1119) on the corner of Florence and Grafton St.

Internet Access: Internet access is everywhere in Cairns. **The Call Station,** 123 Abbott St. (☎4052 1542). Open daily 8am-11:30pm. $3 per hr. before noon. Also, **Cairns City Public Library** (see above) and **Traveller's Contact Point Cairns** (see above).

Post Office: Cairns General Post Office (GPO), 13 Grafton St. (☎4031 4303; fax 4051 3871), on the corner of Hartley St. Open M-F 8:30am-5pm. **Postal code:** 4870.

ACCOMMODATIONS

Though geographically small, Cairns is second only to Sydney as a backpacker's destination, and it's studded with dozens of budget hostels. Most are clustered along the Esplanade, but many others are located in the center of town near Cairns Central. Regardless of location, most hostels have a pool, a large kitchen, and coin operated laundry facilities. Choose carefully; most will offer you free airport pick-up, lower rates, and free or discounted meals at a local bar. Travelers who visit during the Dry can also play in the inter-hostel soccer games. Many hostels offer discounts in the off season (roughly Oct.-May).

HOSTELS

Dreamtime, 4 Terminus St. (☎4031 6753; fax 4031 6566), just off Bunda St. behind Cairns Central, a 15min. walk from the Esplanade. Daily shuttles to Pier and bus station. With only 27 beds and 3-4 bed dorms, proprietors Steve and Kathy create a cozy and sociable atmosphere by disallowing TV and greeting guests with fresh towels and good cheer. Pool, BBQ, kitchen. Book ahead. Reception 7:30am-noon and 4-8pm. Dorms $18; twins and doubles (some with fridge) $40.

Tropic Days, 26-28 Bunting St., (☎4041 1521; www.tropicdays.com.au), behind the Showgrounds, north off Scott St.; a 20min. walk west from downtown. Owners, and round-the-world travelers, Gabriel and Kathy have made a home away from home for backpackers. Jungle-themed paintings adorn walls amid a neatly tended tropical garden surrounding a sparkling pool. M BBQ. Free shuttle to City Centre. Bike hire and TV lounge. Camping $11; 3-bed dorms $18; doubles $42.

Cairns Girls Hostel, 147 Lake St. (☎4051 2767; fax 4051 2016), between Florence and Aplin St. A true gem in the morass of accommodations in the city centre, this **women-only hostel** has provided a safe haven for over 30 years. No noise after 9pm, but no curfew. 3 kitchens, 3 bathrooms, 2 lounges, and TV. Reception 7am-9:30pm. Rates on a sliding scale: $16 for the 1st night, $13 by the 4th; weekly $90.

Gecko's Backpackers, 187 Bunda St. (☎4031 1344 or 1800 011 344; fax 4051 5150). Clean, bright rooms, all with new mattresses. Friendly and helpful staff make this small backpackers seem more like a second home. Internet $2 per 20min. Reception 7am-noon and 4-8pm. 3- or 4-bed dorms $18; singles $25; doubles $40.

Travellers Oasis, 8 Scott St. (☎1800 621 353; travoasis@travoasis.com.au). 1 of the bigger operations on this side of town, Travellers Oasis has 3 main buildings around a courtyard, garden and pool. Management has chosen not to buy a TV because they'd rather have guests talking to each other. Coffee and tea included. Sa night BBQ. Reception 7am-noon and 4-8pm. 3- and 4-person dorms $18; singles $33; doubles $40.

Caravella's 77, 77 Esplanade (☎4051 2159; www.caravella.com.au), between Aplin and Shields St., 10min. from the bus station. Internet access, movies, pool table. Tour bookings. Key deposit $10. Some rooms have baths and some have A/C; ask about them when you book. Flash your *Let's Go* and ask about a $5 discount on your 1st night's stay. Dorms $20; twins and doubles $43. VIP.

The McLeod Street YHA, 20-24 McLeod St. (☎4051 0772; fax 4031 3158), right across from the train station. Rest assured that your aches and pains from your heroic endeavors on the road will be as well treated as theirs were in 2000. It has the feel of a motel more than a hostel, with open-air hallways surrounding a pool. Clean, simple dorms $19, with A/C $19; twins and doubles $46; family rooms $60. Non-YHA $3.50 extra.

YHA on the Esplanade, 93 Esplanade (☎4031 1919; fax 4031 4381; esplanade@yhaqld.org), near the corner of Aplin St., extremely close to nightclubs and cheap restaurants. A no-frills place to crash. Laundry, kitchen, TV, storage. Reception 7am-10pm. Check-out 10am. Dorms $19; twins and doubles $44-46.

Global Palace (☎4031 7921 or 1800 819 024; fax 4031 3231), corner of Lake & Shields St. This brand new hostel is what you'd imagine life in a reality TV show might be like. Rooftop pool, a cinema-screen TV, kitchen with balcony dining, pool tables, tour booking and Internet. Key and cutlery deposit both $20. The only catch is the price, $23 for 3-4 bed dorms with new mattresses (no bunks); $50 doubles or twins. VIP.

Rosie's Backpacker's, 136 Grafton St. (☎4041 0249; fax 4041 0252). A smaller newcomer, this motel-turned backpackers isn't as slick as some of the others, but what it lacks in style, it makes up for in friendliness and intimacy. Pool, TV, Internet, car and bike hire. Check-out 10am. Dorms with bathrooms and kitchens $17; doubles $36.

QUEENSLAND

FOOD

Cairns bubbles with good eats, from all-night kebab and pizza stalls on the Esplanade to upscale restaurants that specialize in seafood. For basic **groceries,** try Bi-lo Mega Fresh, Coles in Cairns Central (open M-F 8am-9pm, Sa 8am-5:30pm, Su 10:30am-4pm), or Woolworth's, near the Esplanade, on Abbott St. between Shields and Spence St. (☎4051 2015; open M-F 8am-9pm, Sa 8am-5:30pm, Su 10:30am-4pm).

Coffee Cafe, 87 Lake St. (☎4041 1899). Offers scones, jam, and a pot o' tea for $6 within earshot of the open-air concert hall. Sit outside and enjoy your breakfast all day long. Oh yeah, you can get lunch ($4-9.50) while you check your email. Open M-Sa 7am-9pm, Su 8am-9pm.

The Old Ambulance Cafe and Bistro, 135 Grafton St. (☎4051 0511). Far better than normal fare but at normal price; eat an inventive dinner (entrees $12-16.50), a fancifully presented cake ($4.50), and refresh yourself with guava juice ($3.30). Lunch until 2pm, dinner after 6pm. Open M 7am-7pm, Tu-Th 7am-10:30pm, F-Sa 7am-11:30pm.

Perrotta's at the Gallery (☎4031 5899), corner of Abbot and Shields St. A mod-looking cafe; stop in early for a pre-gallery breakfast ($4-9.50) or post-painting dinner ($20-25). Open 8:30am-10pm.

The Victory, 62 Shields St. (☎4051 1883). A trendy, intimate dinner setting where tablecloths double as crayon canvases, Victory is one of the few places in Cairns you can find fine cuisine at a reasonable price. Soup ($6.50) is delicious, and mains ($12-20) are artfully presented in gigantic portions. F Live music. Open 11:30am-late.

Cock and Bull, 6 Grove St. (☎4031 1160). From the city center it's about a 10min walk down Sheridan St.; turn right on Grove, on the corner of Grove and Digger. A big barn-like place with a serve-yourself ideology. Locals and hungry tourists frequent this establishment for its vast portions of good olde english cuisine, in all its blandness. Pokies and bar. Lunch $5-10, dinner $10-14 for mains. Open daily 8am-3am. MC/V.

Sawaddee Thai Restaurant, 89 Grafton St. (☎4031-7993). A small hideaway with authentically spicy Thai food at inexpensive prices. The Pad Thai ($11.50-13.50) is light and tangy, and there's plenty of it. Takeaway, BYO. Open M-F for lunch, daily for dinner.

SIGHTS

TANKS ART CENTRE. A trio of WWII deisel tanks have been transformed into a massive art exhibition space. The best local art is on display here, and each show lasts three weeks. The last Sunday of every month June-Nov., Tanks hosts Market Day, a free bazaar with live music and plenty of pottery, crafts, and herbs for sale. *(46 Collins Ave. Accessible from Sunbus #1B. $2. ☎4032 2349. Open daily 11am-4pm.)*

PETER LIK GALLERY. You've probably already bought at least 10 of his postcards—now see his pictures in life-size form. Lik is quickly becoming recognized as one of Australia's best photographers and his popular prints of Australian wildlife are showcased in this modern gallery. Worth a 5min. walk around. *(4 Shields St. ☎4031 8177; www.peterlik.com. Open 9am-10pm. Free.)*

CAIRNS REGIONAL ART GALLERY. The exhibits are ever-changing, often featuring the work of Australian artists and international artists working in Australia. The building is beautiful, stop in to get away from the crowded streets. *(Corner of Abbott and Shields St. ☎4031 6865. Open M-Sa 10am-3pm. $4.)*

UNDERSEA WORLD AQUARIUM. Houses a small but captivating presentation of the reef's brilliantly colored sea life. Make sure you have time for the shark feedings at 10am, noon, 1:30, and 3pm; if you book ahead, you can even dive with the sharks for 30min. After you sign the insurance waiver, of course. *(In the Pier Marketplace, near the wharves. ☎4041 1777. Open daily 8am-8pm. $12.50, children $7, families $30, 20% discount for students and pensioners. Shark diving 3:30-8pm $85.)*

FLECKER BOTANIC GARDENS. The gardens include fern and orchid houses, a Gondwanan (evolutionary flora track) garden, a meandering boardwalk, and a trail that crosses fresh and saltwater lakes. *(Hop on the Sunbus from City Place, #1B ($2.30), or drive north on Sheridan St. and take a left onto Collins Ave. ☎4044 3398. Guided walks M-F 1pm. Open M-F 7:30am-5:30pm, Sa-Su 8:30am-5:30pm. Free.)*

MOUNT WHITFIELD ENVIRONMENTAL PARK. The last bit of rainforest in the Cairns area. The park's shorter Red Arrow circuit takes about 1hr., while the more rugged Blue Arrow circuit is a 5hr. return trek up and around Mt. Whitfield. Don't stay after dark because finding a cab or a bus back into Cairns might be difficult. *(Wedged between the Tanks Art Centre and the Botanic Gardens on Collins Ave.)*

ADVENTURE ACTIVITIES

Cairns is mostly a tourist town because it's warm in the winter and it's an easy gateway to the Great Barrier Reef. At night, travelers stay in town and drink at the local pubs, but during the day they're outside the city-limits enjoying ghastly thrills, bumps, and spills for reasonable prices. Most companies pickup and drop off free of charge and can be booked from your hostel.

CYCLING. Ride with **Bandicoot Bicycle Tours** for an amazing day of cycling, wildlife-spotting, swimming, and relaxation in the tablelands above Cairns. Enjoy rides (3-7km) between trips to waterfalls, giant fig trees, and swimming holes. If you're tired, just catch a lift with the support vehicle. Lunch, morning and afternoon tea are included and feature a vegetarian-friendly BBQ and tropical fruit. *(☎4055 0155; www.bandicootbikes.com. Trips M, W, F departing 8am, returning 6:30pm. $98.)*

BUNGY JUMPING. AJ Hackett is a wild New Zealander—ask him about bungy jumping the Eiffel Tower (and then getting arrested for it). Or just sign up for one of his (legal) Australian jumps. Night bungy on request. *(☎4057 7188 or 1800 622 888; bungy@austarnet.com.au. Open daily 9am-5:30pm. $109.)*

FISHING. Cast for your own bait and then tow the line with **Fishing The Tropics.** They run their 6m boat in the Cairns estuary and the Daintree River. *(☎4057 8289. Half-day $75, full-day $140.)* **VIP Fishing & Game Boat Services** offers similar packages, along with others that feature fly fishing for black marlin June through December. *(☎4031 4355. Half-day $75, full-day $140, marlin trip price from $450.)*

HORSEBACK RIDING. Get on horseback in the outback at **Springmount Station,** a family-owned and operated working farm where kangaroos blaze across the plains teeming with birds, and your trusty steed splashes across rocky brooks. Hearty tea and damper, BBQ lunch will keep you nourished. *(☎4093 4493; springmountainstation.com. Full day $110, half day $88.)* If, like many guests, you don't want to leave, try a 2-day farmstay *($220)* or camp under the Southern Cross *(departs Tu, $242).*

HOT AIR BALLOONING. Ever wanted to ride beneath a big balloon shaped like a koala? Now's your chance. **Hot Air Cairns** will take you up, up, and away. Departs 5am and returns 10am. Packages with skyrail, rafting, and others available. *(☎4039 2900; www.hotair.com.au. $13 per 30min. $210 per hr.)*

PARASAILING. Cruise 300ft. above Trinity Inlet with **North Queensland Water-Sports.** Jet skiing and bumper tubing available. *(☎4045 2735. $50, tandem $90.)*

SKYDIVING. What goes up must come down, and these two companies let you fall in style. Jump tandem with an instructor from 8000ft., or learn to jump solo with **Skydive Cairns.** *(☎4031 5466. $228, more for higher.)* Or, for the only beach landing around, try **Skydive Mission Beach.** *(☎1800 638 005. $228, transport included.)*

WHITEWATER RAFTING. Three companies offer basically the same deal—a day of rafting that's wild but tame enough for beginners. **R n' R Rafting** has several options including multi-day and family packages. The longer your trip, the rougher your rapids. *(☎4051 7777. Half-day $83, full-day $145, and 2-day $250.)* Or check out **Raging Thunder Adventures** *(24hr. reservations ☎4030 7990. Half-day $79, full-day $13).* **Foaming Fury** has half-day rides ($77) and full-day rides including a rainforest walk ($118).

BEACH. Cairns doesn't really have a beach—it has a mudflat. However, **Trinity Beach** is nearby with nice white sand and plenty of private cove areas that keep it from feeling inundated with sunbathers. A bit further north, **Palm Cove** is a beautiful beach lined with cafes and upscale resorts. Play vacationing princess for a day here, lounging in the sun in your shades. *(Sunbus #1, 1A, 1B and 2X run to beaches from the depot in City Place. M-F every 30min., Sa-Su every hr.)*

SCARY THINGS IN THE WATER, PART II. Box jellyfish are serious business–a single jellyfish may have enough poison to kill three adults, and its sting usually proves deadly. Mistakenly called the Portuguese Man-O-War, it is notable for its four sided box-like shape. From each corner dangles a group of clear tentacles which can reach 3-4m long. These terrifying weapons can kill victims within three minutes. If you feel tempted to swim in the wet season waters, treatment for a stung victim should involve 1) preventing drowning, 2) dousing the tentacles in vinegar (never alcohol!) to de-activate them, 3) removing the tentacles, 4) resuscitating the victim, and 5) calling a DOCTOR!!! But, in the end, only abstinence is guaranteed to make the heart beat longer. They're out and about between October and May in coastal waters north of Great Keppel Island and around the placid waters of the Top End. Always ask locals about them before swimming. Some beaches install jellyfish-proof nets, and some diving establishments sell jellyfish-proof wetsuits, but stay out of the water if you are at all in doubt about your safety. (See p. 247)

DIVING AND SNORKELING

By far the most popular way to see Cairns is through goggles. Every day, thousands of tourists and locals suit up with masks, fins, and snorkels to slide beneath the ocean surface and glimpse the Great Barrier Reef. **Reef Teach,** 14 Spence St., has a 2hr. lecture by Paddy Colwell, a marine biologist who doubles as a comic. In his own passionate and entertaining way, Colwell teaches about the history of the reef, its biodiversity, and how to avoid harming the reef and yourself. Reef Teach is terrific even for advanced divers. (☎/fax 4031 779; www.reefteach.com.au. M-Sa at 6:15pm. $13 admission includes tea, coffee, and snack.)

As the main gateway to the reef, Cairns is studded with an overwhelming number of dive shops and snorkeling outfits. Knowing which one to choose can be tricky and even a little daunting when you're bombarded with brochures and booking agents. So think about some questions: How long do you want to dive—a day-trip or a multi-day trip? How big of a boat do you want? For personal dive instruction and a group atmosphere, smaller boats may be the way to go. Finally, are you going with other divers or with friends who may prefer other water activities? Unless you're all diving, you won't want a dive trip—maybe a cruise with diving options such as **Passions of Paradise** or **Great Adventures**.

In order to dive in Australia (or anywhere in the world), you have to have an open-water certification, a driver's license for the water. The only way to get this certification is to spend about 4 days and at least $300 in scuba school, where you learn about scuba equipment and diving techniques. However, **introductory dives** offer a taste of scuba diving *without* going to scuba school. For a fee, dive companies will give you a 1hr. crash course in diving basics, and then they'll take you out on a real-life—guided and supervised—scuba dive. These are great opportunities for people who are only going to be on the reef for a short time. But keep in mind you can only (legally) do a few of these before you have to go to school. Also, intro dives usually aren't on the best dive sites, and of course, they're slightly more risky than having all the training. But if they're your only option, they're worth a shot—if only because everyone should see this natural wonder underwater at least once.

DIVING DAYTRIPS

The Falla, located in The Pier (☎4031 3488; www.fallacruises.com). A swanky, restored pearl lugger boat (a.k.a. sailboat) is chartered by a small crew; with a maximum of 35 passengers. The divemasters will take novices out for a day on Upolo Reef. Leaves at 9am and returns about 6pm. The base price is $69, including lunch (children $35, families $190). First intro dive $50, second $30. First certified dive $40, second $20.

Passions of Paradise (☎4050 0676). Offers full day cruises to Paradise Reef and Upolo Cay. This boat has a young, vibrant spirit; spontaneous conga dancing is not an unknown occurrence on the deck. Face-painting and chocolate cake keep the youngsters happy even at the end of the day. The high-speed catamaran can take between 60 and 70 passengers on the 10hr. trip. Departs 8am. Base price for snorkeling, lunch, and transport is $70. Add $55 for an intro dive or 2 certified dives.

Great Adventures, 1 Wharf St. (☎4041 9944 or 1800 079 080; www.greatadventures.com.au). More expensive, but with good reason. For $144, they will speed you and 400 other passengers out to a humongous floating pontoon on the edge of the reef. There, you can do an intro dive for $94 or a certified dive for $66. You can snorkel or ride in a semi-submersible free of charge. Departs daily at 10:30am, returns 5:30pm. Ask about dive courses taken at the luxurious Green Island Resort.

MULTI-DAY TRIPS AND SCUBA SCHOOLS

Pro-Dive (☎4031 5255; www.prodive-cairns.com.au), on the corner of Abbott and Shields St. Their most popular trip is the 5-day learn-to-dive course. Although the price tag may seem hefty at $630, it includes all diving, equipment, 2 nights accommodation and 5 additional dives. If you're on a tight budget, they also offer a 3 day learn-to-dive trip on Fitroy Island Dive for $325. This trip includes housing on the island and with only 8 people taking the course with you, camaraderie is routine. Open daily 8:30am-9pm.

Cairns Dive Centre, 121 Abbott St. (☎4051 0294 or 1800 642 591; www.cairnsdive.com.au). Generally the least expensive to the outer reef, with a "floating hotel" catamaran for its flagship and a smaller boat for daytrips. Their 5-day live-aboard, learn to dive course is $550, a 4-day budget course is $297.

Tusa Dive, corner of Shields St. and the Esplanade (☎4031 1248; www.tusadive.com). The first two days of their four-day PADI courses ($572) are run in the classroom by ProDive instructors, but the two day-trips to the outer reef are on the speedy new Tusa boats which hold a maximum of 28 passengers. A diver's dive company, Tusa is more expensive than others, but is ideal for those who don't want the live-aboard experience, but still want to get to the outer reef with experts. 2-day Nitrox certification courses $435. Open 7:30am-9:30pm daily.

Down Under Dive, 287 Draper St. (24 hr. ☎4052 8300; www.downunderdive.com.au). A 2-masted clipper ship with a hot tub takes 2-day (or longer) trips, starting at $210 for snorkelers and $290 for certified divers. The company also offers diver training for those on a budget. A 4-day course starts at $280 for two days of pool training and two days on Hastings and Saxon Reefs. Open daily 7am-5pm.

NIGHTLIFE

Despite its widespread and well-deserved reputation as a haven for backpackers, the Cairns nightclub scene is still a few paces behind that of other cities. The plus—if you get your hand stamped before 10pm, these parties are all free. And your hostel will usually give you a free meal voucher for one of the clubs, too. For the latest local word, pick up a copy of *Barfly* (free), found all around town.

Ultimate Party is a Cairns pub crawl held every Saturday night. It's sort of like a giant mixer for the twenty-something tourists. Pay $45 for entry into five bars and clubs, two all-you-can eat meals, a shot in each one, entertainment, transport, a photo, and a t-shirt. At the end of the night walk, if you're able, pick up a book of vouchers for tattoos, adventure trips, and, of course, more alcohol. Call 4041 0332 if you want to sign up, or look for an Ultimate Party t-shirt on the street.

The Woolshed, 24 Shields St. (☎4031 6304 for free shuttle bus until 10pm). A rowdy all-night party for travelers. Backpackers come here to dance on the tables, drink beer, and enter the M night Mr. and Ms. Backpacker contests. Practically every hostel in town offers meal vouchers for this place. M and W Happy Hour 9:30-11:30pm. $6 pitchers, $3 basics. Cover Su-Th $5, F $6, Sa free before 10pm. Open nightly 6-9:30pm for meals, club open until 5am. Downstairs is the **Bassment,** which plays dance music until 5am Th-Sa. Free until midnight.

P.J. O'Brien's (☎4031 5333). In City Place at the corner of Shields and Lake St. Here it's St. Patrick's Day every day. With tables made from beer barrels, authentic Irish memorabilia, and quotes from Yeats in the murals, this place almost looks like an Emerald Isle museum. Pints of Guinness ($5.50) and tasty food (meals $12-18) make P.J.'s the next biggest hot spot in town. Live bands 6 nights a week, Happy Hour F 5-7pm ($4 Guinness). Neat dress required.

The Sports Bar, 33 Spence St., (☎4041 2503) is rapidly rising in popularity with its vouchers for $1 and heavily discounted meals. With billiards and multiple television sets broadcasting all sports all the time, you can stay and enjoy your dinner, or your pint, without missing the big game. Open M-F 11am-5am, Sa-Su 6pm-5am.

Tropos (☎4031 2530), on the corner of Lake and Spence St. The club plays techno, and the dance floor is a stage where the baby groovers perfect their thang. This is everyone's last stop before bed at the end (or beginning) of the night. You can't miss it—the whirling spotlight can be seen across the street. Neat dress required. W retro night. Open until 5am. Cover $5.50, free before midnight.

Johnno's Blues Bar (☎4051 8770), at the corner of Abbott and Aplin St. Red-hot jazz, cool blues, and a dash of rock 'n' roll plays 7 days a week in this rough-around-the-edges club. Th Johno and his Blues Band get the people out on the dance floor. The crowd is a mix of backpackers and locals. Free entry most nights.

1936 (☎4030 8888), the Reef Casino on Abbott St. Resembling a Parisian hotspot, this upscale nightclub has a higher standard of dress and patronage than Tropos. Expect fewer people, better dancing, and a slightly older, more sophisticated crowd. On Th get 3 drinks for $5, schooners regularly $2.80. Open Th-Sa until 3am, $5 cover.

nu-trix, 53 Spence St. (☎4051 8223), between Grafton and McLeod St. Hard to miss its rainbow-colored marquis. A gay bar and dance club with no dress code. Shows F and Sa nights when cover is $5. Open W-Th and Su 9:30pm-late, F-Sa 9:30pm-5am.

DAYTRIPS FROM CAIRNS

TJAPUKAI. Just north of Cairns and off the Cook Hwy. in neighboring **Smithfield** is the national coup of Aboriginal cultural parks: **Tjapukai.** Pronounced "JAB-a-guy," this is the most wholly rewarding, intelligently presented, and culturally fair presentation of Aboriginal myths, customs, and history in all of Queensland. It has been showered with all kinds of awards, including the 1999 Gold Award from the Pacific Asia Travel Association for the best cultural attraction in the world. Give this experience at least half a day. Learn how to throw boomerangs and spears, see a cultural dance show, view a film on Aboriginal history, and more. (☎4042 9999; www.tjapukai.com.au. Open daily 9am-5pm. $27, children $13.50. Transfers to and from Cairns and the Northern Beaches for $17 round-trip.)

ZOOS. Farther along the Cook Hwy. heading north, a pair of roadside attractions offer diversion from the coastal trek. An outback experience for the family, **Hartley's Creek Crocodile Farm** is 40km north of Cairns. The farm has hundreds of crocs, as well as kangaroos, koalas and cassowaries. Keepers taunt a croc until it eats a hand-fed chicken in the heart-pounding "crocodile attack show" at 3pm. (☎4055 3576; www.hartleyscreek.com. Open daily 8:30am-5pm. $18, children $9, families $45; includes 3-day complimentary return.) Transportation is available from Cairns on **Hartley's Express** (☎4038 2992) for $35 including admission to the farm. The larger **Wild World: The Tropical Zoo,** near Palm Cove on the Cook Hwy. 20min. north of Cairns, lets you get up close and personal with kangaroos and wallabies. There's a comprehensive reptile house, a koala colony, and public crocodile feedings. (☎4055 3669. Open daily 8:30am-5pm. $22, children $11.)

THE GREAT UNDERWATER ORGY The last thing those immobile little corals seem to be interested in is sex. But every year, for three days in November, the reef turns into a bacchanalian lovefest as coral release sperm and eggs into the water. Using the moon for synchronization, all the corals in the reef release their gametes at once so as to maximize the chance of fertilization. At night, it seems to be snowing upside-down in the ocean, as the baby-juice floats to the surface. After fertilization, miniature jellyfish-like creatures swim about until they find a hard rock to stick themselves to. These grow to become the luminous coral creatures of the Great Barrier Reef. Needless to say, this oceanic orgy is an amazing time to dive (if you don't mind being covered with coral lovestuff). To get the full voyeuristic experience, contact marine biologist Paddy Colwell (☎4031 7794; see also **Reef Teach**) for one of his one day underwater naturalist courses.

NEAR CAIRNS

GREEN ISLAND

Diminutive Green Island (technically a coral cay; see p. 30) barely pushes above the water surface; its perimeter can be walked in 15min. Though dominated by the luxury resort in the center, a short boardwalk through the rainforest and a beach path access nature. The more adventurous can forge a trail through the dense rainforest (if you walk long enough, you'll always end up back at the resort).

The cheapest and quickest way to the island is with **Great Adventures,** which offers a 45min. ferry. Extras include diving (intro dive or 2 certified dives $94), and a choice of snorkel equipment or a ride in a dinky glass-bottom boat for $11 each. (☎4044 9944 or 1800 079 080. Departs Cairns daily 8:30, 10:30am, 1pm; leaves Green Island at noon, 2:30, or 4:30pm. $46, children $23, families $115.) If you plan on doing any snorkelling or diving, **Big Cat Green Island Reef Cruises** is a better deal. For $52 you get the island for a day, plus the glass bottom boat tour or snorkelling gear. (☎4051 0444. Departs Cairns 9am. Children $29, family $138.) The sailboat **Ocean Free** specializes in trips to the island. Travelers aboard the schooner get the chance to dive and explore. (☎4041 1118. Open 9am-5:30pm. Depart Cairns daily 9am. $70, $55 children. Intro dive $55, for 2 $85; certified dive $40/$60.)

The real highlight of Green Island is **Marineland Melanesia,** 250m northeast of the resort left of the jetty, a combination gallery, aquarium, and croc farm. Come at 10:30am or 1:45pm to watch a live feeding of Cassius, the world's **largest crocodile** in captivity. That's 18ft. of pure power, man. You can also hold yearling crocodiles or tour the primitive art collection. (☎4051 4032. Open daily 9:15am-4:15pm. $9, children $4.) Just off the end of the jetty is the **Marine Observatory,** from which you can observe bits of the coral reef from 1.5m below the surface ($3). The resort has a nice pool surrounded by a couple of boutiques and small cafes (open daily 9:20am-4pm), and the **dive shop** rents snorkeling gear ($11 per day, guided snorkelling trips $15). Instructors outfit day-trippers and take them on an intro dive ($94, certified $66). **Michaelmas Cay,** just north of the island on the outer reef, has good diving and is the site of a natural bird sanctuary. Unfortunately, accommodation at the **Green Island Resort** (☎4031 3300) runs about $455 per person.

FITZROY ISLAND

Fitzroy Island is much larger than Green Island, and is generally a better choice for the budget traveler. There are affordable beds, though most people only go for a day. **Sunlover Cruises** does the trip to the island or a combination of the island and Moore Reef. (☎4050 1333. Both cruises depart 9:30am, return 5pm. $36, children $18, families $90. Combo: $14, children $7, families $36.) If a cruise sounds too easy, try traveling to Fitzroy Island via **sea kayak** with **Raging Thunder Adventures,** which now owns the resort on the island. A high-speed catamaran takes you most of the way, followed by 3hr. of reef kayaking, snorkeling, and lunch. An overnight package includes bunk accommodations at the Fitzroy Island Resort and two days of kayaking. (☎4030 790. Daytrip $110. Overnight $135.) You can also get to the island via the Fitzroy Island Flyer which leaves from Cairns and the island. (3 times daily. $36, children $18, family $90.) Once there, you can rent kayaks ($10 per day), fishing lines ($20), sailing catamarans ($20 per hr.), and aqua bikes ($10 per hr.). Raging Thunder Adventures is seeking to transform the resort into a backpacker's get-away with party nights Friday and Saturday and shared accommodation. Fitzroy can still be an island paradise if you can ignore the Top 40 hits playing at the bar and pool-side. As a budget alternative to Green Island, its coral beaches and lush rainforest are still pristine—only noise pollution disrupts the tropical scenery. (☎4051 9588, 24hr. reservation 1800 079 080. Shared bunks $31; private bunks for 1-3 people $116, 4 people $124; beach cabins $250 per family.) The resort has a **Pool Bar** which serves meals ($5-15) from 9am to 5pm. The **Raging Thunder Beach Bar** serves dinner 6-8:30pm ($12-22). Breakfast is served between 8 and 10am at the **Flare Grill** (continental $10, cooked $9.50-12).

The resort's **dive shop** offers introductory diving and snorkel gear at bargain rates. (Intro dive $65, certified $50. Snorkel gear $12. Open daily 9:30am-4pm.) Snorkel and dive trips leave at 10:30am, 12:30, and 2:30pm. To keep busy, try a walk to the **lighthouse** (5km return) starting at a clearing adjacent to the **Reefarm,** a prawn breeding farm 1km north of the resort. There are a couple good 500m walks through the rainforest on the northern end of the island as well. Just past the Restaurant, the **Secret Garden track** cuts west into the island while **Nudey Beach track** continues along the coast. The Secret Garden track is easy and has informative nature placards. The Nudey Beach track, a bit more challenging, is made of huge stone slabs leading to boulders at the shore and a (occasionally) nude beach.

ATHERTON TABLELANDS

Although much of northern Queensland is picturesque, nothing quite compares to the Atherton Tablelands. Rolling hills meet unspoiled rainforest, the perfect venue for spotting wildlife and rushing waterfalls. Take a break from the coastal confusion of Cairns and spend some unharried days at the top of the world. Traveling northeast on the Kennedy Hwy., you'll find the farming village Mareeba and touristy Kuranda. Opting for a southern route via the Gilles Hwy., you'll encounter the residential township of Atherton, charming Yungaburra, and Malanda. Bring a sweater in the winter; at an elevation of 1000m, you'll forget you're in the tropics.

The mountainous, lakeside roads give drivers both a mild challenge and rewarding panoramas. Although driving provides the fullest experience, the Tablelands are accessible without a car. **White Car Coaches,** 8 McCowaghie St., Atherton (4091 1855), services Cairns ($7.40) and Atherton ($16.80). The **Skyrail Rainforest Cableway,** a 7.5km gondola, lifts you up above the rainforest canopy into Kuranda village. A 1½hr. round trip originates in Carovonica Lakes, 10min. northwest of Cairns. (24hr. ☎4038 1555. $30, children $15. Open daily 8am-5pm.) The **Kuranda Scenic Railway** runs an antique train ride from downtown Cairns to Kuranda. Chock-full of camera-toting tourists, this bumpy journey comes with relentless, inflection-free commentary. (☎4031 3636. From Cairns Su-F 8:30 and 9:30am, Sa 8:30am; to Cairns Su-F 2 and 3:30pm, Sa 3:30pm. One-way $29.60, children $15, concessions $19.50, families $74.20.)

KURANDA ☎07

The gateway to the Tablelands, many travelers get no further than this mountain town. Its river cruises, street performers and famous markets draw sightseers from Cairns by train, bus or gondola. When the town shuts down after the last train leaves in the afternoon, you, the intrepid traveller, are left to wander its historical streets without the crowds. In the morning, the hustle and bustle begins again when the **original markets** (open W-Su) and **Heritage Markets** (open daily 8:30am-3pm) transform the cozy village into a bazaar of arts, crafts, and clothing.

Birdworld, in the Heritage Markets, has over 50 Australian squawkers as well as 23 "exotic species," including the elusive canary and pigeon. (☎4093 9188. Open daily 9am-4pm; $11, children $4; combination ticket with the Butterfly Sanctuary $19, children $6.50.) The **Australian Butterfly Sanctuary,** 8 Rob Vievers Dr., next door to the Heritage Markets, bills itself as Australia's largest butterfly enclosure. (☎4093 7575. Tours on demand. Open daily 10am-4pm. $12, children $5.) **River Cruise and Rainforest Tours,** on the Barron River just off Arara St., offers 45min. guided riverboat rides. (☎4093 7476. $12, children $6, families $30.)

If you're looking to stay overnight, **Kuranda Backpacker's Hostel** (a.k.a. "Mrs. Miller's"), 6 Arara St., is across the street to the left of the train station on the corner of Arara and Barang St. The historic building, first a wedding present from the timber mill owner to his daughter in 1907, then an army post and Methodist retreat, can be your spacious resting place for a night. With its cast iron beds and pressed metal ceilings, you'll feel like you're taking a trip back in time. In the mornings, the proprietor feeds over 50 rainbow lorikeets. Amenities include a kitchen, pool, bike rental, tropical garden, laundry, and free pickup from Cairns. (☎4093 7355. Reception 8am-6pm. Dorms $16; twins and doubles $38. VIP/YHA.) **Kuranda Bottom Pub Hotel,** on the corner of Coondoo and Arara St. just across the street from Skyrail, sports a garden bar restaurant, a pool, and tidy rooms with bath, fridge and TV. (☎4093 7206. $5 key deposit. Reception M-Sa 10am-10pm, Su 10am-4pm. Singles $44; doubles $55; each extra adult $11, child $5.50.)

Locals love **Frog's,** 11 Coondoo St, with its spacious porch stretching out back, unless you want to eat out front and watch the shoppers on the main drag. (☎4093 7405. Sandwiches $6.50; gourmet pizzas $12. Open daily 9:30am-4pm. Many places will serve you devonshire tea, but only the **Honey House,** at the entrance to the original **Kuranda Markets** has its sweets made right on the premises. There is a hive of bees in the store producing Kuranda honey. (☎4093 7261. Open 8am-5pm daily.)

LAKE TINAROO AND DANBULLA FOREST

Saturated with crater lakes and sprinkled with waterfalls, the volcanic soil of the central Tablelands sprouts bizarre forest along the shores of the **Tinaroo, Barrine,** and **Eacham Lakes.** Unsealed **Danbulla Forest Dr.** circles Lake Tinaroo. The free *Danbulla State Forest* visitor's guide, available from the **QPWS Forest Management,** 83 Main St., Atherton (☎4091 1844), lists sights along the 40min. loop. Contact the **QPWS Eacham District Office** (☎4095 3786) at Lake Eacham for information on walking paths around the lakes. The paved 3km Lake Circuit Track around Lake Eacham in Crater National Park has muskrat-kangaroos and giant iguanas.

Camping in the thick of the forests is the best way to get personal with the Tablelands. There are several state forest campgrounds around Lake Tinaroo ($3.85 per person per night, toilets available). The campgrounds are described in the visitor's guide to Danbulla; call the **QPWS** with any questions. **Note:** There is no camping in any of the national parks, only the state forest areas.

YUNGABURRA TO MALANDA ☎07

Tiny Yungaburra (pop. 400; pubs 1) is at the heart of the Tablelands with Lake Tinaroo and the Danbulla forest to the north, waterfalls to the south, Lakes Eacham and Barrine to the southeast, and the volcanic hills of the **Seven Sisters** to the west. The town is handsome, untouched by commercial tourism, yet warm to all visitors. Yungaburra hosts the biggest **markets** in the north on the fourth Saturday of each month. Homemade crafts, fresh produce, and even goats can be bartered at these authentic events. From Cairns, take the Gillies Hwy. west about 60km.

Just off the west side of Yungaburra is the **Curtain Fig Tree,** a monstrous strangler fig forming an eerie curtain in the middle of the rainforest. Pick your gaping jaw off the ground and check out the 50m tall, 500 year-old **Cathedral Fig Tree** on the east stretch of the Dunbulla Forest Dr. The best place to spot a **platypus** is at the Atherton Shire Council Pumping Station. From Yungaburra, head past the bridge and turn right onto Picnic Crossing Rd. (the road sign is actually 10m ahead of the turn-off). Follow the 2nd right-hand turn. You'll find a concrete picnic table for a late-afternoon snack and platypus families near the bend in the river.

Yungaburra's youth hostel, **On the Wallaby,** is utterly superb. The common area feels like a mountain hut with rough-edged wood furnishings and a wood-burning stove. The bathrooms and showers are sided with stone and wood, and the bunk rooms are clean and fresh. Enjoy BBQ ($6), kitchen, garden, and laundry. Guests can join tour activities (canoeing and biking) on an individual basis. Platypus spotting trips are free. (☎4095 2031. Bike rental $10 half-day, $15 per day. Reception 8am-1pm and 4-8pm. Sites $10 per person, $15 for 2 people; dorms $20; twins and doubles $45. Cairns transfers $20.) One kilometer south of Lake Eacham is the **Lake Eacham Caravan Park** with showers, laundry, and a small general store. The price includes admission to a garden and petting zoo. (☎4095 3730. Reception 7am-7pm. Sites for 2 $10, powered sites $15.40; cabins $49.50.) **Curtain Fig Motel,** 16 Gillies Hwy. in the center of town, has sparkling rooms. (☎4095 3168. Reception 7:30am-8:30pm. Doubles $77; each extra person $15.)

The **Gem Gallery and Coffee Shop,** 44 Eacham Rd., serves breakfast for under $2. Croissant with jam is $1.50, and tea is $0.50. They also have cheap opals and free opal-cutting and gold-working demonstrations, not to mention free **Internet** for customers. (☎4095 3455. Open daily 8am-late.) **Nick's Bella Vista Restaurant,** 33 Gilles Hwy., is a Swiss chalet restaurant caught in the tropics. Swiss-Italian meals run $10-27 and there's live music F-Sa. Ask to see their wine list. (☎4095 3330. Open F-Tu 11am-3:30pm and Th-Tu 6-11pm.) **Yungaburra Market** on Eacham St. is the local **supermarket.** (☎4095 2177. Open daily 6:30am-7pm.)

Only a short distance form Yungaburra, friendly and hospitable **Malanda** is a town founded in 1911 around the timber industry. Nowadays, residents guard the remaining rainforest and magnificent waterfalls and rare tree kangaroos. About 25km south of Malanda and beyond Millaa Millaa, the **waterfall circuit** leads past a series of spectacular swimming holes. From the north a sign points to the falls. Catch the loop from the south by looking for the "Tourist Drive" sign. **Millaa Millaa Falls** is the perfect waterfall: a straight, even curtain with rocks at the bottom and a bit of green on either side. **Zillie Falls** starts off as a sedate creek at the top of the falls; a rocky, slippery-when-wet path through the adjacent rainforest leads to the roaring drop where the cascading **Ellinjaa Falls** look like liquid fireworks. For more information about the falls surrounding Malanda, or on the area's geography and history, the **Malanda Falls Visitor Center** is just past **Malanda Falls** on the way out of town towards Atherton. (☎4096 6957. Open 10am-4pm daily. Adults $2.)

The **Peeramon Hotel** on Peeramon Rd., is in (surprise) **Peeramon** between Yungaburra and Malanda. From Atherton, take the first paved road on the right after leaving Yungaburra; from Cairns it's the first paved left after the Lake Eacham exit off the Gillies Hwy. A lady's **ghost**, victim of a double-murder in the hotel, still floats about the place: a photo above the piano captures her, mid-air and luminescent in a group picture on the front steps. (☎4096 5873. Reception daily 10am-late. Singles in the hotel $20, in the dongers out back $20; doubles $40.) The little-known **Platypus Forest Lodge,** 12 Topaz Rd., 6km east of the town center off Lake Barrine Rd., is a stellar B&B that's perfect for nature buffs. The owners run an immaculate lodge complete with sauna, hot tub, canoes, wood-burning stove, and loads of hospitality. Out back, platypuses, turtles, possums, and tree kangaroos inhabit a swath of rainforest. (☎/fax 4096 5926. Singles $45; doubles $55.)

The Malanda Hotel-Motel, on the corner of English and James St., is still owned by the English family who bought the town in 1911 in government auction. The streets are named for family members and the hotel is the largest timber structure in Australia. (☎4096 5101. Open 10am-midnight. Rooms $22 per person; families $55. Motel singles $33; twins and doubles $55; families $66.) The **Malanda Freshmart** is at 2/11 English St. (Open M-W 8:15am-6pm, Th until 8pm, Sa-Su until 2pm.)

At night, check out Australia's oldest movie theater, the **Majestic Theatre** at Eachem Pl. For showtimes, call the 24hr information line at 4096 5726, or go to www.majestictheatre.com.au. (Adults $8, children and pensioners $5.)

NEAR THE TABLELANDS: CHILLAGOE

Situated almost 200km west of Mareeba, the drive is half the experience on a day-trip to this old mining town. The road is mostly paved up to Dimbulah, but the last 30km into Chillagoe is bumpy dirt; 4WD is highly recommended. Lush pastoral scenes dissolve into landscapes of rust-colored dirt. Wild cattle meander along, and termite mounds of all sizes dot the landscape like cemetery headstones. When you think you're lost in the middle of nowhere, take heart—you're close to Chillagoe. The **Savannahlander train** from Cairns stops in nearby Almaden (5½hr., departs Cairns W 6:30am, $45; return service on Sa.) from which a bus goes into town. The main draw is a system of **caves.** Tours run out of **Queensland National Parks and Wildlife Service** office on the corner of Queen and Cathedral St. (☎4094 7163. Open M-F 8:30am-5pm, Sa-Su 8:30am-3:30pm. $5.50-8.25 depending on the cave.)

Chillagoe Caves Lodge, 7 King St., has a restaurant. (☎4094 7106. No laundry, kitchen. Budget with shared bathroom $33; motel rooms with bath $55.) The **Post Office Hotel,** on Queen St., offers new, fully decorated rooms. (☎4094 7119. Beds with A/C $16, with fan $11. MC/V.) Pick up **groceries** at the Chillagoe General Store, 11 Queen St. (☎4094 7100. Open M-F 7am-6pm, Sa 7:30am-4pm, Su 10am-2pm.)

PORT DOUGLAS ☎07

Port Douglas is a sleepy enclave bordered by rain forest. Without the tourists, it might be nothing more than a collection of quiet vacation homes. But with the burgeoning tourism industry, the dry season brings nature-lovers and marine enthusiasts. Snorkel and scuba trips take travelers to the pristine outer reaches of the Great Barrier Reef and up the coast to the rainforests of Daintree National Park. Many visitors forgo these trips simply to soak up the rays on Four Mile Beach.

TRANSPORTATION

Buses: Coral Coaches (☎4099 5351; fax 4099 4235), at the Marina Mirage, runs daily to: the **airport** (1¼hr., 10 per day, $27); **Cairns** (1½hr.; 10 per day; $22, same day return $39, open return $39.50); **Daintree Ferry** ($20, return $36); **Mossman** (30min.; 10 per day; $8, return $14). Buses run to **Cooktown** via the coast road (during the Dry Tu, Th, Sa 1 per day; $52) and via the inland road (W, F, Su 1 per day; $58). **Sun Palm Coaches** (☎4099 4992) run between the **Rainforest Habitat** and town, stopping at the major resorts and hostels on the way. ($3.50 one-way, $5 return.)

Ferries: Quicksilver (☎4099 5500) leaves Port Douglas from the Marina Mirage daily at 5:15pm for **Cairns** (1½hr., $22). Departs Cairns for **Port Douglas** 8am (same-day return $32).

Taxis: Port Douglas Taxis, 45 Warner St. (☎4099 5345). **24hr.**

Car Rental: Crocodile Car Rentals, #2 50 Macrossan St. (☎4099 5555), specializes in **4WD** (from $120 per day). **Allcar Rentals,** 21 Warner St. (☎4099 4123), rents 4WD from $95 a day. Both rental agencies offer **automatic 4WD.**

Bike Rental: Port Douglas Bike Hire, 40 Macrossan St. (☎4099 5799). Half-day $10, full-day $14, weekly $59. All bikes are mountain bikes and rental includes helmets. Open daily 9am-5pm.

Road Report: (☎4033 6711; www.racq.com.au), with all road conditions and closings.

ORIENTATION AND PRACTICAL INFORMATION

Port Douglas Rd. branches off of Hwy. 1 (Captain Cook Hwy.), 70km north of Cairns and launches out onto the Port Douglas peninsula. Side streets lead to **Four Mile Beach** to the east and to **Marina Mirage** to the west. The town lies on the northern tip of the peninsula where Port Douglas Rd. turns into Davidson St. and then intersects the main drag, **Macrossan St.**

Tourist Office: Port Douglas Tourist Information Centre, 23 Macrossan St. (☎4099 5599; fax 4099 5070), between Grant and Wharf St. This office (like all others in Port Douglas) is privately owned. Open daily 8am-7pm.

Banks: All banks open M-Th 9:30am-4pm, F 9:30am-5pm. **ANZ,** 36 Macrossan St. (☎13 13 14), exchanges currency for a $5 commission and has an **ATM.** No fee for cashing AmEx Traveler's Checks. If headed north, keep in mind that ATMs may be few and far between.

Medical Services: Port Village Medical Centre, Shop 17 in Port Village Centre on Macrossan St. (24hr. ☎4099 5043). Office open M-F 8am-6pm, Sa-Su 9am-noon. The nearest **hospital** (☎4098 2444) is in Mossman, on Hospital St.

Police: (24hr. ☎4099 5220), at Macrossan and Wharf St. Open M-Th 8am-2:30pm.

Internet: Mega Byte Internet Cafe, 48 Macrossan St. (☎4099 5568). $6 per hr. Open daily 9am-10pm.

Post Office: 5 Owen St. (☎4099 5210; fax 4099 4584). On the corner of Macrossan and Owen St., up the hill. Open M-F 9am-5pm, Sa 9am-noon. **Postal Code:** 4871.

ACCOMMODATIONS

Port O'Call Lodge (YHA), 7 Craven Close (☎4099 5422 or 1800 892 800; fax 4099 5495; www.portocall.com.au). Take a left off Port Douglas Rd. onto Port St. as you come into town. This incredibly comfortable, motel-like hostel has laundry, a pool, kitchen, bike rental, and Internet. Free shuttle bus to Cairns (departs M, W, Sa 8:30am; call for a 10am lift north from Cairns). The bistro serves dinner daily (meals $7.50-10.50; 6-9pm) and swings during Happy Hour (5-7pm). Free lockers. Reception 7:30am-7:30pm. Check-out 9:30am. 4-bed dorm with bath $19.50, non-YHA member $21; deluxe motel rooms are $45, during the Dry $95. VIP, NOMADS.

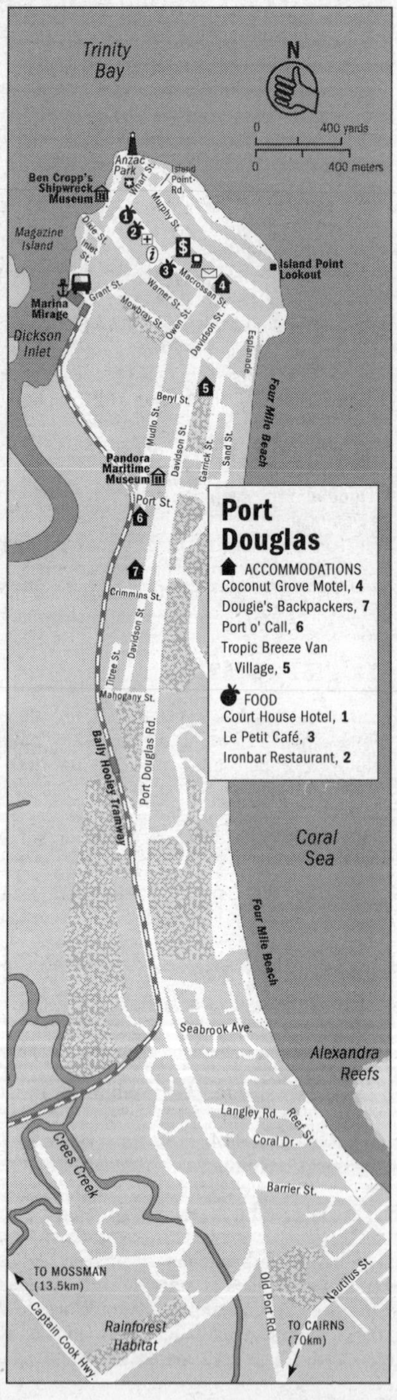

Dougie's Backpackers (☎4099 6200 or 1800 996 200; fax 4099 6047). Laundry, Internet, kitchen, TV, pool, and bike rental ($1 per hour). 15min walk from town center. Free bus to Cairns M, W, Sat 8:30am. Free pick up in Cairns between 10:30 and 11am. In-house bar open 4pm-midnight ($3 beer, $3.50 spirits). Dorms $22; doubles $60. 30 sites; $12 for 1, $20 for 2. $70 per week for one. NOMADS/VIP/YHA.

Tropic Breeze Van Village, 24 Davidson St. (☎4099 5299). Just 100m from the beach. Reception 8am-7pm. Sites for 2 $17, powered $18, extra person $5; cabins for 2 $63.50.

Coconut Grove Motel, 58 Macrossan St. (☎4099 5124; fax 4099 5144; cocogrove@cyberworld.net). Centrally located but not as well-tended as the other hostels. Laundry, kitchen, BBQ area, TV and 2 pools. Reception 8am-7pm. 6 bed dorm with bath $20; motel rooms with TV, A/C, and fridge from $85. AmEx/MC/V.

FOOD AND ENTERTAINMENT

Ironbar Restaurant, 5 Macrossan St. (☎4099 4776), is a family-friendly restaurant catering to the resort crowd. Join local entrepreneur Clancy for cane toad races every Tuesday and Thursday at 8 and 9:15pm ($3, children free). Choose your own amphibian; the winner (human, not toad) gets a free drink. The kitchen offers huge kangaroo burgers, skewered crocodile, and barbecued prawns for $4-27. (☎4099 4776; fax 4099 4959. Open M-F 11am-2am, Sa-Su 8am-2am.) Also keep in mind **Le Petit Café,** 31 Macrossan St., with homemade ice cream, sweets and treats. (☎4099 4287. Open daily 7am-6pm, later during the Dry.) The **Cactus Bar** (☎4099 5213) in the center of town is right next door to the restaurant **Lime,** 38 Macrossan St. Both are hip and happening. **Cactus** is a fashionable place for an after dinner drink (beer $4.50-6.50, mixed drinks $5.50-6.50). **Court House Hotel,** on the corner of Macrossan and Wharf St., is the liveliest joint in town. Locals flock here for the live music Wednesday to Monday nights. The owner is an American expatriate who says Port Douglas offers "the best blues this side of Chicago." (☎4099 5181; fax 4049 6249. Stubbies $3, counter meals up to $12.) **Central Hotel,** 9 Macrossan St., in the center of town, is a primarily local bar with live, local bands Tuesday to Friday nights. The bar also broadcasts all national sporting events and runs a local jackpot every Monday night. (☎4099 5271; fax 4099 4112; kimbuls@internet-north.com.au. Stubbies $4. Open daily until midnight.) **Coles Supermarket** is in Port Village Shopping Centre on Macrossan St. between Wharf and Grant St. (Open M-F 8am-9pm, Sa 8am-5:30pm, Su 10:30am-4pm.)

SIGHTS AND ACTIVITIES

The Rainforest Habitat has eight acres, three enclosures, and over 1000 animals without cages or any discernible fear of people. Mingle with the cockatoos and parrots, tickle a fruit bat's tummy, or scratch a wallaroo behind the ears. Buy a package of feed for the animals, $2. Early risers can also enjoy 'Breakfast with the Birds,' a full buffet in the aviary 8-11am for an additional $4 adults, $7 children. There is a restaurant (sandwiches $5-7) and souvenir shop also on premises. (☎4099 3235; www.rainforesthabitat.com.au. Open daily 8am-5:30pm; last entry 4:30pm. $20, children $10. 10% discount for students. Wheelchair accessible.) **Sun Palm Coaches** (☎4099 4992) departs Port Douglas depot hourly, $5 return.)

At the east end of Macrossan St., **Four Mile Beach** is almost always quiet. This gorgeous stretch attracts an array of locals, topless backpackers, and swanky resort-types. Remember to swim between the flags. (Lifeguard on duty M-Sa 9:30am-5pm.) **Extra Action Watersports** (☎4099 3175 or 0412 346 303) is just north of Marina Mirage. Steve, the owner and self-defined 'action man,' can set you up with any number of heart-stopping adventures. **Parasailing** lasts 20min. (Solo $120, couple $85 each; 2hr long family packages $275.)

Visitors can **snorkel** independently or with several private outfits, most of which depart from Marina Mirage. **Sail Away-Low Isles,** 23 Macrossan St., fits snorkeling, riding in a glass-bottom boat, and **'boom netting'** into one day. Departs daily at 8:45am. (☎4099 5799; www.reefandrainforest.com.au. 7hr. $99, children $59, families $270; call for booking.) **Wavelength** also offers daily snorkeling trips. Eight-hour ventures to the outer reef depart at 8:30am. (☎4099 5031. $123, children $83.)

Port Douglas is an excellent destination for **scuba divers.** Portions of the Great Barrier Reef lie just off Four Mile Beach and offer a plethora of marine life. When selecting a dive or snorkel shop, ask plenty of questions. Knowing boat capacity, dive difficulty, and site destinations ahead of time is important.

Quicksilver Diver (☎4087 2100; www.quicksilver-cruises.com). In the Marina Mirage. The biggest operation in town, Quicksilver picks up divers at Cairns before continuing up to Port Douglas. Ride a high-speed catamaran to the outer reef and spend the day on a pontoon enjoying submersible rides, snorkeling, and lunch buffet. $150, children $77.50. Special snorkeling tours with a marine biologist, additional $31. Introductory dive, additional $107; certified dive, additional $67. All equipment included. Catamaran departs daily at 10am.

Poseidon Outer Reef Cruises, 34 Macrossan St. (☎4099 4772; www.poseidoncruises.com.au). This one-boat operation operates dive courses in conjunction with Discover Dive, at The Links Health Club (☎4099 1192; www.discoverdive.com.au). A five-star, PADI dive center specializing in small group training. 4-day open water course $520, PADI referrals $225 per day on Poseidon. Advanced, Rescue and Divemaster courses also available. A brand new boat takes groups of 50 to the reef daily. Departs 8:30am and returns 4pm. Open daily 9am-6pm.

Haba Dive (☎4099 5254), in the Marina Mirage. Offers two dives on each of their daily trips. Groups of 40 depart at 8:30am with free pickup and lunch. Intro dives $180; certified dives $160, with equipment $190. Snorkeling $120, children $75.

DAYTRIP FROM PORT DOUGLAS: MOSSMAN GORGE

Disgorge yourself from the activity of Port Douglas life at gorgeous **Mossman Gorge.** Part of the **Daintree National Park,** the valley is riddled with hiking paths originating from the visitors' parking lot (follow signs). The shorter paths to the Mossman River are quite easy, but the 2km circuit track in the thick of the rainforest is more challenging. Be prepared to hop over small creeks (and an occasional small lizard). On any of the trails you'll feel engulfed by the magnificent green canopy.

Coral Coaches runs to **Mossman** (30min.; 10 per day; $8, return $14). If driving, take Hwy. 1 north from the junction to Port Douglas for about 20km. Follow the signs for Mossman Gorge and turn left across from the Mossman State High School. Drive about 4km to Kuku Yalanji, 1km more to the carpark at the gorge.

If you want to learn the secrets of the rainforest, spend an hour with an Aboriginal guide from **Kuku-Yalanji Dreamtime Walks,** on the road to the gorge. The tour covers traditional medicines and bush tucker, and includes tea and damper. (☎4098 2595. Tours M-F 10am, noon, 2pm. $16.50, students $12. Bookings essential.) The Aboriginal-owned operation also has a visitor center and shop. (Open M-F 9am-4pm with toilets and a picnic table.)

DAINTREE ☎07

Daintree is an excellent gateway to the rougher frontier land of the north. Kingfishers, kookaburras, and friendly faces abound in this tiny forest village of 120 residents. The town's main economic assets are the estuarine crocodiles (or salties) that live in the Daintree River: boatloads of camera-toting croc-seekers pass through the village daily. Beware that the town's exit off Coast Hwy. can flood; call 4033 6711 or one of the local restaurants for road conditions.

If you're not visiting on an all-inclusive tour package from Port Douglas or Cairns, you can book a river tour at the **Daintree General Store** (☎4098 6416)—which also serves as the town watering hole and post office. Most river excursions are similar, varying primarily in length (from 1-2½hr.). Prices range from $17 to

$28; children travel for less. Check out **Daintree Wildlife Safari** (☎4098 6125 or 4098 6146) or **Daintree River and Reef Cruise Centre** (☎4098 6115). **Chris Dahlberg** runs excellent morning bird-spotting tours from the Daintree jetty. (☎4098 7997. 2hr.; $35. Bookings essential.)

The **Red Mill House** is reason enough to visit Daintree. A TV room, swimming pool, and BBQ are just some of the extras that convince many guests to stay longer than they originally planned at this lovely B&B. The morning meal is made of fruit from the tropical garden in the backyard. The older part of the house has one single ($40), one double ($66), and one triple ($99) with bathroom facilities and a spa. The newer section offers four queen-size rooms with bath for $88. (☎/fax 4098 6233; www.redmillhouse.com.au. MC/V.) **Daintree River View Caravan Park,** smack in the middle of town, rents sites. Enquire at Jacana's Restaurant across the road. (Sites $12, powered $15.)

NEAR DAINTREE: WONGA BEACH

Halfway between Mossman and Daintree is the small seaside hamlet of Wonga Beach (pop. 700). Tucked away in this unassuming village lies **Redbacks,** 17 Oasis Dr., a juggernaut backpacker oasis. Sparkling new rooms and facilities are coupled with a seemingly endless supply of on-site activities including tennis, volleyball, gym, nightclub, beach and large pool. Laundry, Internet, kitchen, and convenience store are also on site. **Coral Coaches** from Cairns drops at the door, or follow signs off the Captain Cook Hwy. (☎4098 7871 or 1800 087 086; fax 4098 7520. Reception 6am-8pm. Dorms $18-20; doubles $70.)

CAPE TRIBULATION ☎07

About 15km north of the Daintree River, 'Cape Trib' is in the heart of **Daintree National Park** and is more of a landmark than a township. When locals talk about it, they're usually referring to a large general area served by Cape Tribulation Rd., which runs north past Cow Bay, Alexandra Bay, Thornton Peak, and the Cape. Travelers continuing up the coast from Daintree will use the **Daintree Ferry,** which shuttles across the river from 6am-midnight. (Walk-on passengers $1, cars $8.) The utterly fantastic road from Daintree to Cape Tribulation is anything but what its name would suggest. The rainforest crashes down on the ocean surf, and every forest inch is teeming with wildlife. Conservationists and capitalists are locked in a heated struggle over the future of these forests. The former vie to prevent the Cape from obtaining electricity, but tourist-minded businesses see modernization as the way to open the wilderness to travelers. Everyone involved can at least agree the lands of Cape Tribulation are some of Queensland's most beautiful.

TRANSPORTATION AND PRACTICAL INFORMATION. Because of the distances between locales, moving around is somewhat difficult unless you have a car. However, the two main hostels provide shuttles to various sights and offer a number of adventures on their own premises. **Coral Coaches** stops in **Cow Bay.** (Cairns ☎4031 7577, Port Douglas ☎4099 5351. Departs Cairns 7am, 3:30pm; Port Douglas 8:00am, 5pm. $24.) There is no official information center in Cape Tribulation. The **Queensland Parks and Wildlife Service (QPWS) ranger station** has public info, but the hours are extremely limited. (☎4098 0052. Open M-F 9:30-11:30am.) Two other sources of info are the Daintree Rainforest Environmental Centre and the Bat House (see **Sights and Activities,** p. 389).

ACCOMMODATIONS. **Crocodylus Village** is on Buchanan Creek Rd., east off Cape Tribulation Rd. Take a right after the Daintree Environmental Center if heading north from Daintree Ferry. Coral Coaches (☎4098 2600) runs there from Cairns for $32, and the hostel offers a complimentary bus to the beach four times a day. This hostel is a backpacker oasis organically entwined with the rain forest, with several open-air cabins scattered around a large wooden patio. (☎4098 9166; fax 4098 9131; www.queensland-holidays.com.au. Laundry, pool, horseback riding, sunrise paddle trek in a hybrid kayak/canoe, guided bushwalk. Reception 7:30am-

11:30pm. Book ahead. Cabin rooms $20, $18 YHA; hut for 2 with bath $65, each extra person $10, each child 5-15 $5, children under 5 free. YHA.) More appropriately called "PK's Jungle Party," **PK's Jungle Village** is about 400m after the "Welcome to Cape Tribulation" sign. The nightly entertainment pales in comparison to the weekly theme parties, usually four-keggers. If you miss the first daily Happy Hour, don't worry—there's another. (☎4098 0040; fax 4098 0006. Volleyball, horseback riding, guided bushwalking, and bike rental (half-day $12, full day $20). Laundry, kitchen, bar, and pool. Reception 7:30am-7pm. Check-out 9:30am. Dorms $24; doubles $65; triples $82; quads $104. VIP.) **Cape Trib Beach House** is a rain forest camping ground converted into a rain forest cabin resort. Relax on their pristine beach with forest dragons and butterflies. (☎4098 0030. Laundry, bar, restaurant, pool, Internet. 4 and 6-bed dorm $25-32; family-style cabins for 4 with A/C $89-99; beach front cabins with queen beds $109.)

There are also two accommodations on the way to Cape Tribulation from Daintree. The **Daintree Manor,** 27 Forest Creek Rd., just north of the river, offers breathtaking views, 24hr. power, beautiful handmade furniture, and a TV lounge with good reception. (☎/fax 4090 7041. Rooms from $85.) **Cow Bay Hotel Motel** is on the right side of the road as you drive up the coast towards the Daintree Environmental Center. (☎4098 9011. Reception 7am-10pm; 10am check-out. 6 motel rooms with TV, A/C, and bath. $66 for two people, $5 extra per person. MC/V.)

FOOD. **Palm Forest Walk Cafe** is a new restaurant catering to the backpacker set. The reasonable menu has an emphasis on middle eastern food. (☎4098 9119. Mains $10-15, entrees $8-14. Lunch menu $5-14. Open in season 10am-midnight W-Su for dinner, 10am-5pm Th-Sun otherwise.) Take a 15-20min walk around the palm forest boardwalk out back as an after-dinner digestive. **Lync Haven** is the most amusing eating establishment with its wildlife sanctuary full of orphaned 'roos to pet and feed. The menu includes burgers ($5-7) and sandwiches ($3.50-4); the veggie-friendly dinner menu (everything under $12) is expansive. (☎4098 9155. Open daily 7am-7pm.) **Rainforest Village** sells groceries and petrol, and has a phone and a post box. (☎4098 9015. Open 7am-7pm.) The last fuel sign is slightly misleading; fuel is only a short distance away in Cape Tribulation (see Wujal Wujal, p. 393).

SIGHTS AND ACTIVITIES. All attractions on Cape Tribulation revolve around the wet tropics. **The Daintree Rainforest Environmental Centre,** just before Cow Bay off Cape Tribulation Rd., is a popular stop-off, but a free walk along the brand-new 700m **Jidaboe** boardwalk just 200m down the road might prove just as rewarding. A 23m tower allows visitors to view the rainforest from above the canopy. The ticket price includes a guided walk on the rainforest boardwalk (40min.), wet tropic movies, and reference library. (☎/fax 4098 9171. Open daily 8:30am-5pm. Children $5.50, adults, $11; families $27.50; $8.80 for those lodging in the area.) A less extensive source of forest info is the **Bathouse,** opposite PK's on the west side of the highway. The all-volunteer staff will be happy to take your picture with their giant flying fox, Rex. (☎4098 0063; www.austrop.org.au. $2 donation.) Just down the road from the Bathouse is **Dubijee** ("doob-i-gee"), a visitor area with a spectacular 1.2km boardwalk through a variety of coastal forests and mangroves, a must for all visitors. Further south is the **Maardja** ("mar-ja") boardwalk through old growth rainforest, and eerily beautiful mangrove forest, home to numerous species of birds, including the threatened cassowary.

Cape Tribulation Wilderness Cruises explores the mangroves in search of crocodiles. (☎4098 9052. 3hr. $30; bookings essential.) They also offer creek walks, night cruises and package deals. **Rum Runner** is one of the several tours based out of Cairns that runs daily trips to the reef off the Cape. (☎4098 9249 or 0500 509 249. Free bus to beach from all local resorts, snorkeling equipment included. First certified dive $89; two certified dives $149. Intro dives $60.)

The popular two-day, one-night trip to **Snapper Island** is available at the Crocodylus Village through **Tropical Sea Kayaks** (☎4098 9166) for $179. This excursion features reef walking, snorkeling, beach camping, and fully prepared meals, including all equipment. **Wundu Trail Rides,** between Lync Haven and the Rainforest Village, leads horseback tours of the coral coast. Long pants and covered shoes are recommended for this excursion through the Daintree Tea Plantation. (☎4098 9156. Departs twice daily. 3hr. guided rides $55, 10% discount for groups of seven or more, minimum age 10 years.)

ROUTES TO COOKTOWN

There are two routes from Cape Tribulation to Cooktown—one inland, one coastal. The Bloomfield Track is the coastal ro—, well, track. It beats through 150km of bush as it swerves and dips, hugging the sides of precipitously steep mountains. When it's in bad condition, the Bloomfield Track is impassable. When it's in "good" condition, the road is about as much fun as can legally be had in a 4WD. Views of the rainforest and the coastline are amazing, and fording the rivers can be exciting. The trek takes about 5hr. with lots of veering, jagging, bumping, straying, dancing—whatever is necessary—to avoid large potholes and fallen trees. Call ahead for road conditions and bring lots of cash, as most places don't take credit. If you'd rather not be the one clutching the steering wheel, **Coral Coaches** (☎4098 2600) departs from Port Douglas three times a week.

The inland route to Cooktown is not as exciting as the coastal track, but it's mostly paved. The Brahma cattle that roam the road on certain sections, especially in the late afternoon, can pose a threat to drivers. Better road conditions allow focus to be less on the next pothole and more on the fantastic views.

BLOOMFIELD TRACK. On the southern section of the track lies **Wujal Wujal,** a tiny Aboriginal community with a **convenience store** and a basic **service station** (☎4060 8101; open M-Th 8am-4:30pm, F 8am-noon; service station F 8-11:30am). Off the road are the **Bloomfield Falls,** a terrific place to relax after the hard ride, but watch out for those feisty crocs.

Between Wujal Wujal and Cooktown, the mountains pull back from the coast as you drive on a dirt road through the dry savannah. North of the bridge to Wujal Wujal, the road is much less treacherous. Along the way, there are occasional general stores and small-town hotels. **Bloomfield Cabins and Camping** serves lunch and dinner ($5-15) as well as having rooms from $49 for two people. (☎4060 8207; www.bloomfieldscabins.com.)

The final stretch of road before Cooktown leads to the **Lion's Den Hotel,** where records of countless wayfarers are scrawled over the walls inside. (☎4060 3911. Open daily 8am-whenever everyone leaves. Beer $3.50, pub grub $12 a plate. Campsites with showers $5 per person. **Pay phone** in front.)

INLAND TO COOKTOWN. There are a handful of interesting stop-offs on this route through the farm and grasslands of the Far North. The prettiest, **Mt. Molloy,** is a 10min. drive (27km) southwest of Mossman on the Peninsula Developmental Rd. The **Mt. Molloy National Hotel** is a large, aged building built in 1901. The rooms are a bit dusty, but homey with comfy beds and a pub downstairs. (☎4094 1133; fax 4094 1045. Reception at pub 10am-midnight. Meals $9-15, special $6. Beds $30 single, $50 double.) The **Mt. Molloy General Store** combines a small grocery and convenience store with standard takeaway (burgers from $5). A **picnic area** with hiking information and public restrooms is 500m from the hotel.

Mt. Carbine lies 28km north. Once a prosperous mining town, it is now three roadside buildings. The **Mt. Carbine Roadhouse** has petrol, food, and backpacker lodging, and Brahma bulls outside. (☎4094 3043. Meals $7-12. Open daily 7am-7pm. Singles $15, doubles $25, $5 extra person.)

Continuing north, the road begins to literally cut through the hills, with walls of stone outcroppings flanking the pavement. **Palmer River Roadhouse,** 110km north of Mt. Molloy, decorated with various murals tracing the area's gold mining history, offers the standard Far North pub fare. (☎4060 2020. Open daily 7am-10pm. Sites $5.50, powered caravan sites $12.50. No credit cards; **EFTPOS** accepted.)

Farther north, the bitumen gives way to a gravelly, snaky descent through the hills with beautiful views of the landscape. The **Lakeland Downs Roadhouse** marks the end of the pavement for the Peninsula Developmental Rd. and the last pit stop and service station before Cooktown, 82km away. (☎4060 2188. Burgers from $5.)

COOKTOWN ☎07

In the winter, the south winds sweep through Cooktown's dusty streets, bringing with it the travellers who have abandoned the monotony of packaged tours and pre-paid holidays. Many find themselves staying longer than they planned, captivated by the life in a town where the bars close when the last patron leaves and shoes are an infrequent sight. Though Europeans arrived here in 1770 when Captain Cook's ship, the *Endeavor*, was grounded on the Great Barrier Reef, civilization still hasn't reached Cooktown. And the town residents want to keep it that way. The discovery of gold a century later at nearby Palmer's field turned the sleepy town into a port metropolis with thousands of residents. When the gold ran out, almost everyone picked up their stakes and sojourned to the southern goldfields. The tenacity of the 1600 who remain today has created a history-rich, eccentric community, full of small-town friendliness.

TRANSPORTATION

Buses: Coral Coach (☎4098 2600) has service between Cooktown and Cairns. Endeavour Farms Trading Post (see **Food,** p. 395) is the local ticketing agent. To **Cairns** by inland route (5hr.; W, F, Su 2:30pm; $58) via **Lakeland** (1¼hr.); **Cape Tribulation** (4¼hr.); **Cow Bay** (4¾hr.); **Kurada** (4¾hr.); **Mareeba** (4¼hr.); **Mossman** (6hr.); **Mt. Carbine** (3¼hr.); **Mt. Molloy** (3½hr.); **Port Douglas** (6½hr.) or by coastal route (7½hr.; Tu, Th, Sa 11:30am; $64) via **Lion's Den** (30min.).

Car Rental: The aptly named **Cooktown Car Hire** (☎4069 5694) is one of the only options this far north. It has **4WD** starting at $90.

Taxis: Cooktown Taxis (☎4069 5387). Service from 6:30am to when the pubs close.

Automobile Club: RACQ, Cape York Tyres (☎4069 5233), at the corner of Charlotte and Furneaux St. 24hr. towing. Open M-F 7am-7pm, Sa-Su 7:30am-6pm.

Service: AMPOL Station (☎4069 5354). At the corner of Hope and Howard St. Open 24hr. a day. AmEx/EFTPOS.

QUEENSLAND

ORIENTATION AND PRACTICAL INFORMATION

The Cooktown Development Rd. becomes **Hope St.** as it runs north toward **Grassy Hill.** Two blocks to the west, **Charlotte St.** holds most of Cooktown's shops and services. It's crossed by several streets, including Boundary, Howard, Hogg, and Walker. At the far-north end of town, Charlotte St. runs along the water, curves eastward, and becomes **Webber Esplanade.**

Tourist Office: Cooktown Travel Centre (☎4069 5446 or 4069 6022; fax 4069 6023; cooktowntravel@bigpond.com), on Charlotte St. next to Anzac Park. Open M-F 8:30am-5:30pm, Sa 8:30am-noon.

Currency Exchange: Westpac (☎4069 6960), on Charlotte St., between Green and Furneaux St., has an ATM but no currency exchange. Open M-F 9am-4:30pm.

Police: (☎4069 5320), across from the wharf on Charlotte St. Staffed M-F 8am-4pm; after hours, use intercom at the office door.

Medical Center: Cooktown Hospital (☎4069 5433), on the corner of Ida St. and the Cooktown Developmental Rd., on the way out of town heading south.

Internet: Cooktown Computer Stuff (4069 6010; fax 4069 5177), on Charlotte at Green St. Open M-Su 9am-5pm $6 per hr., minimum $2 charge.

Post Office: (☎4069 5347; fax 4069 5323), on Charlotte St., across from the Sovereign Hotel. Open M-F 9am-5pm. **Postal Code:** 4871.

ACCOMMODATIONS AND FOOD

Pam's Place, at the corner of Charlotte and Boundary St., is the backpacker hub of Cooktown. Perks include a large kitchen, linen, laundry facilities, bar, pool table, swimming pool, garden and morning shuttles to the bus station and airport. (☎4069 5166; fax 4069 5964. Key deposit $10. Bike rentals. Dorms $17.50; singles $36; doubles $46. Sites $8. YHA. MC/V 3.5% surcharge. EFTPOS $1 charge per transaction.) **Seagren's Inn,** 12 Charlotte St., is a historic 1880 heritage building with restaurant and accommodations. (☎4069 5357. $20 for bed in 6-bed dorm, $40 double, $90 for a family room that sleeps 7.) **Hillcrest Bed and Breakfast** is a pleasant B&B with a sunny garden and veranda at the base of Grassy Hill on Hope St. (☎4069 5305; fax 4069 5893; www.cooktowninfo.com. Pool and restaurant. Laundry. $50 double, $5-10 extra person. 3 Motel units with TV, A/C, and bath $65. Continental breakfast 7-9am, $7. MC/V.) **Alamanda Inn,** across from the Ampol station on the corner of Hope and Howard St., offers tidy guest house rooms in a flower-filled setting. (☎/fax 4069 5203. All rooms have A/C, fridge, TV, and sink. Singles rooms $40; doubles $50; self-contained family units $75. MC/ V.)

For a quick tasty treat, visit the **Endeavour Farms Trading Post** on Charlotte St. between Hogg and Walker St. Barbara, the owner, enjoys helping travelers find their way. (☎4069 5723. Open daily 8:30am-7:30pm.) You can buy groceries at the **Cooktown Progressive Supermarket** on Charlotte St. (☎4069 5633. Open 8am-6pm M-Sa, Th 8am-7pm, Su 10am-3pm.)

SIGHTS

The newly opened **James Cook Historical Museum,** on Helen St. at Furneaux St. is the crown jewel of a town obsessed with the landing of Captain Cook. This former Catholic convent built in 1889 has been expanded and renovated to house relics from Captain Cook's voyage, including the anchor and cannon he jettisoned here. (☎4069 5386. Open 9:30am-4pm daily. $7, child discounts.) The **Cooktown Cemetery,** on McIvor River-Cooktown Rd., is full of legends. Its highly segregated plots are divided into sections for white, Aboriginal, and Jewish residents. The Chinese Shrine lies at the farthest left-hand corner of the cemetery, where 30,000 slaves and their possessions were buried. Fact sheets about the cemetery can be found at any local accommodation. Twenty years ago, the city brought the **Botanic Gardens,** off Walker St., back to life after having been left to decay after the gold rush. The locals swim at **Finch Bay**, reached by following Walker St. to its end. The walking path leading to the bay branches into the trail to secluded **Cherry Tree Bay.** The trail from Cherry Tree Bay to the lookout is not well-marked at the beach, and its challenging vertical inclines are unsuitable for small children. Along the road leading to the **lighthouse** is an excellent **lookout** over Cooktown, from the lighthouse you can see the ocean and reef. During the Queen's Birthday weekend, the **Cooktown Discovery Festival**, features reenactments of Capt. Cook's landing, truck-pulling and pie-eating competitions among other entertainments.

CAPE YORK ☎07

One of the last vestiges of the great Australian frontier, Cape York consists of rugged, intense landscape and narrow mountain roads—a journey that's a challenge and a risk. There are three ways to see Cape York: by traveling with a professional guide, by reading about it in a book, or by going with your friends—if y'all have a 4WD, some wilderness experience, an emergency cell phone, and a thirst for adventure. Seriously, this trek is not for the light-hearted, and it wouldn't make a good holiday weekend. (Depending on road conditions, the trip up and back could take you up to 2 weeks.) But those who do make an attempt, or who drive even part of the southern route, are rewarded with gorgeous sunsets, lush savannahs, packs of wild hogs, inquisitive kangaroos, silver-crested cockatoos, and much more. Cape York is nature in its pristine form, for better and for worse. It's spectacular, but also isolated from the services civilization can offer.

THE BASE OF THE CAPE

Even if you haven't the time, the money, or the stamina for the full journey up the Cape, you can get an exciting sample of wilderness within a reasonable distance of Cooktown. A good two- to three-day trip runs north 62km of Lakeland along the **Peninsula Developmental Rd.** to the famed Aboriginal rock art of Split Rock, the outpost town of Laura, the truckstop at Musgrave (2hr. north, entrance to the **Lakefield National Park**), and then east along the rugged **Lakefield Rd.** and **Battle Camp Track** to complete the circuit. Four-wheel-drive is adamantly recommended for the first two-thirds of the journey and imperative for the final leg. Up here the Dry chokes the land with dust, and the Wet floods it Noah-style. If you travel on Battle Camp Rd., you'll have to ford at least three rivers and graze crater-sized pot holes.

Just like the roads, Cape York natives are tough as nails. There's close to nothing in these towns, so don't go looking for the Holiday Inn. **Laura** (pop. 100) has the **Quickan Hotel** (☎4060 3255; open daily 10am-midnight; pub grub $15; beds $28; tents $5). Limited supplies may be purchased next door to the pub at **The Ampol Station Laura** (☎4060 3238; open daily 7:30am-6:30pm). Pick up a map, petrol, groceries, or a cheap sandwich ($4.50) at the **Laura Cafe.** (☎4060 3230. Open daily 7am-9:30pm.) The **Ang-gnarra Visitors Centre**, across from the Laura Cafe, has a practically tree-less **Caravan Park** with a pool, laundry, and not quite sparkling bathrooms. (☎4060 3214. $5, powered $6.) Laura's one must-see—and it is amazing—is **Split Rock,** a series of ancient Aboriginal art sites. (15min. tour $5; 3hr. tour $10.) Bring a hat, sunscreen, hiking shoes, and water. The **Ang-gnarra Aboriginal Corporation** (☎4060 3200) offers tours.

An hour southwest of Laura (50km, 4WD only), the Aboriginal run **Jowalbinna Bush Camp** also offers tours. (☎4060 3236; fax 4051 4888. Camping sites $8 per person per night; cabins $60; permanent tents $80. Half-day tour of rock art sites $75, full-day $100; meals included.) Call the **Adventure Company** (☎4051 4777) to book cabins, meals, and tours. (Breakfast $11, lunch $14, dinner $25.) The first pitstop north of Laura on the Peninsula Developmental Rd. is about 70km away. It's the **Hann River Road House**, run by Bushy and his sister Sue. Pitch your tent here and fill up on gas or a tasty burger. (☎4060 3242. $6, caravan $10, rooms $18.)

On the Peninsula Development Rd., 138km north of Laura, lies **Musgrave** (pop. 2), marked by the **Musgrave Roadhouse** (☎4060 3229; open 7:30am-10pm), **Musgrave Roadhouse Pub,** and **Musgrave Roadhouse Lodge** (sites $5; singles $30; doubles $485). Don't blink or you'll miss it altogether. Tiny or not, Musgrave is the perfect juncture for exploring **Lakefield National Park.** This region of mango-lined floodlands—Queensland's second largest national park—features forests, plains, lagoons, and rivers. You can strike its heart by traveling back towards Cooktown along the **Battle Camp Track,** named after a battle between miners and Aboriginals during the gold rush, though perhaps it should be named after your own battle with the elements. During the wet season, the track is submerged in water, but in the Dry, Lakefield is transformed into a bird sanctuary extravaganza. Crocodiles, feral pigs, and wallaroos are also commonly spotted critters—keep that in mind when you drive through its three rivers. After entering the Battle Camp Track, north of Musgrave, travel east along the clearly-marked track past Lowlake. Bring some emergency supplies, and be prepared for a long trip. It could take you 7hr. or more to drive that route. Also be aware that locals avoid the route, so you may be alone for quite a while if something goes wrong.

Camping in these areas is by permit only ($3.85), which can be obtained on the spot at any of the three stations. The ranger station is located in the middle of the park, 112km from Musgrave. (☎/fax 4060 3271. Open daily 9am-5pm.) Camping in the southern half of the park requires a permit for the New Laura Ranger Station, while the Lakefield base requires a northern camping permit.

COEN

☎07

North of Musgrave, Peninsula Developmental Rd. swerves up and down. The frequent dips are often filled with small, impromptu creeks, which can grow to rivers during the Wet. After 109km, the road reaches **Coen** (pop. 300 on a busy day). There's not much to do here; most visitors just stop in on their way to the top.

Everything is found on Regent St. The **Ambrust General Store** offers groceries, petrol, pay phone, camping (☎4060 1134. Store open daily 7:30am-6pm.) Many establishments here do not operate, or only to a limited degree, during the Wet. The office for the **QPWS** has info packets on nearby parks and campgrounds.

Homestead Guest House, filled with memorabilia of a gold rush era, is a bit of a time capsule. (☎4060 1157; fax 4060 1158. Reception 7am-9pm. Laundry, kitchen. Single $38.50; twins and family rooms $27.50 per person. No credit cards.) The pub and social center of Coen is the **Exchange Hotel,** with beer, pool table, and pay phone. (☎4060 1133; fax 4060 1180. Reception 10am-10pm. Hotel singles $38.50; doubles $49.50. Motel singles $50; doubles $66.)

NORTH OF COEN

Another 65km north along the Peninsula Developmental Rd., a track of red earth and white sand filled with dips (read: miniature rivers cutting through the road) at every turn, leads to the **Archer River Roadhouse.** This place is a nexus of travelers venturing to and from the Tip and is a welcome reminder that yes, life exists somewhere along these lonesome roads. The kitchen serves the usual fare of beer, burgers (including the famous Archer Burger), and full meals ($16). Three-bed units and one double are modern, clean, and well-maintained. A pretty campground is also available. (☎/fax 4060 3266. Reception 7am-10pm. Singles $38.50; doubles $55.) Parts of the nearby **Archer River** dries up in the Dry. Camping is popular from June to September. Northeast of the Archer River, **Iron Range National Park** (128km to the Ranger Station), is the largest area of tropical lowland rainforest in Australia, filled with cuscus, parrots, butterflies, and the northern native cat.

Beyond the Archer River, the Peninsula Developmental Rd. bears west to the bauxite-mining town of **Weipa,** but if you're not into fishing or bauxite ore, you'll probably be bored to pieces in Weipa. **Telegraph Rd.** forks off to the north toward the **Jardine River National Park** and the town of **Bamaga** at the very tip of the Cape. If you're headed to the Jardine River, then you must be itchin' to get to the tip.

THE TREK TO THE TIP

North of the Archer River, the Cape's jungle becomes more wild, its heat hotter, its rough tracks rougher, and its wet season wetter. The trip all the way to the Torres Strait that separates Australia from Papua New Guinea is only for the hardest-of-the-hard-core, born-for-the-bush traveler. And what's to do there? Walk a kilometer from the northernmost campground, stick your toe in the water, write your name in the sand, turn around and head back to civilization. Unless you own a car, you can't get to the northernmost point without spending some cash and rental companies rarely insure cars traveling to the Cape. **Britz Rental,** 411 Sheridan St., Cairns, has a four-day minimum for 4WDs or campers going to the top of the peninsula. (☎1800 331 454. In the Dry, 4WD from $194 a day, campers from $231, not including insurance. Open daily 8am-4:30pm.)

Tour packages are often the only option. Departing from Cairns, retired bombardiers air-drop mail over the Cape on **Cape York Air** (☎4035 9399); pilots will let passengers accompany them on their daily runs ($235.95-471.90; Tu and Sa tours to the Cape $670). If you can scramble up as far as the Jardine River, **John Charlton's Cape York Boat Adventure** can show you the rest for a very reasonable fare. (☎4069 3302. Full-day trips start at $99.) Visiting the Cape is a battle, whether it's against crocs (unlikely) or wallet shock (almost certain). Still, the victory is oh-so-sweet.

CENTRAL AND WESTERN QUEENSLAND

Queensland's interior is unforgiving—water is scarce and constant threats such as locusts have hardened farmers. There are no "cowboys" here: the correct title for a greenhorn is "jackeroo" (or "jilleroo," as the gender may be). From the third year, workers are called stationhands, and the name "jackeroo" becomes a hard strike against pride. While outback towns can be unkind or indifferent to outsiders, the people living here maintain an ethic of trust. A fierce pride in the isolated lands they inhabit is often conveyed in a surprising, peculiar sort of fierce friendliness. Folks look you in the eye, and if they don't like what they see, you'll know it.

Queensland's vast interior is traversed by a few highways, unsealed in patches. Generally in better shape than north-south roads, there are several east-west routes: the **Warrego Hwy.** (54) goes west from Brisbane eventually reaching the Mitchell Hwy.; the **Capricorn** and **Landsborough Hwy.** (66), from Rockhampton to the Gemfields, Barcaldine, and Mt. Isa; the **Flinders Hwy.** (78), from Townsville through Charters Towers and Hughenden to Mt. Isa; the **Gulf Development Rd.** (1), including part of the **Kennedy Hwy.,** from the Atherton Tablelands outside Cairns through the Gulf Savannah to Normanton. Connecting them all, the so-called **Matilda Hwy.,** the major north-south road, actually encompasses fragments of the Mitchell, Landsborough, and Capricorn Hwy. and the Burke Developmental Rd.

CAPRICORN AND LANDSBOROUGH HWY.

The road west from Rockhampton cuts a diagonal through Queensland's Gemfields. Rte. 66 is called the Capricorn Hwy. until its junction with the Matilda Hwy. in Barcaldine when it becomes the Landsborough Hwy., which passes through Longreach and Winton and meets the Flinders Hwy. two hours east of Mt. Isa.

FROM THE GEMFIELDS TO LONGREACH

GEMFIELDS

Wanna be a millionaire? You might try digging in the dirt in Queensland's Gemfields. Fossicking in this area draws thousands of tourists each year. The income is hardly steady, but it can be lucrative. An unemployed couple recently uncovered a gem worth a million dollars, and a 14-year-old matched that a few years back.

The folks at **Namoi Hills Cattle Station** will take you to the Gemfields for a day of sapphire satisfaction guaranteed. (If you don't find a jewelry quality sapphire, they'll refund your money. $154.) The ranch itself alternates between being a quiet cattle station and a typical backpacker's bonanza replete with drinking, table-dancing and other such bonding activities. This dramatic transformation takes place every other day when the Oz Experience buses pull into camp. (☎4935 9277; fax 4935 9234. Make-your-own didgeridoo day $159.50. Beds $18, including dinner, continental breakfast, and a tour featuring didgeridoo playing, whip cracking, and boomerang throwing $38.50.)

Emerald, where no emerald has ever been found, is an affluent town (pop. 10,000) and a major agricultural center for grain, cotton, and mandarin oranges. A convenient stop on McCafferty's (☎4982 2755) route to Mt. Isa, the town is a stepping-off point for the Gemfields. Stop at the **Central Highlands Visitor Information Centre,** in the center of town on Clermont St. before venturing into the Gemfields. During the second week of August, the Gemfields come to Emerald for the annual **Gemfest.** (☎4982 4142. Open M-Sa 9am-5pm, Su 10am-2pm.) The new **Central Inn,** 90 Clermont St., has clean rooms with TV. (☎4982 0800. Breakfast included. Singles $39; doubles $49.) There's a Coles **Supermarket** on the corner of Clermont and Opal St. in the Market Plaza. (☎4982 3622. Open M-F 8am-9pm, Sa 8am-5pm.) The Emerald Public **library**, 44 Borilla St., has free **Internet.** (☎4982 8347. Open M noon-5:30pm, Tu and Th 10am-5:30pm, W 10am-8pm, F 10am-5pm, Sa 9am-noon.)

Forty kilometers west of Emerald, **Anakie** lies in the prime fossicking region. This village holds the last **petrol** station for 125km, and **The Big Sapphire Info Centre,** 1 Anakie Rd. (☎4985 4525. Open daily 8am-6pm.) If you need some reviving, you can buy tea and cake here for $3. Most tourists drive 10-18km further north to **Sapphire** or **Rubyvale,** where you can stop along the road to sort through pre-dug buckets of dirt ($5.50 per bucket). The **Rubyvale Caravan Park** is on Main St. and has a small heated pool. (☎4985 4118. Reception 7am-8pm. Sites $11, powered $15; cabins for 2 $45. Credit cards accepted.)

BARCALDINE

Along the Capricorn Hwy., you'll pass through Barcaldine ("bar-CALLED-in"), at the junction with the Longreach Hwy. McCafferty's **buses** stop at the **BP station** on the corner of Oak and Box St. (☎4651 1333. Open daily 6:30am-9pm.) The **Artesian Hotel,** 85 Oak St., has mostly iron-bar four-poster beds. (☎4651 1691. Reception 10am-noon. Single $10; double $15; family rooms $20.) There is an IGA **Supermarket** at 179 Oak St. (☎4651 2207. Open M-F 8am-6pm, Sa 8am-1pm.)

LONGREACH ☎07

The micropolis of Longreach (pop. 4500) is the largest town in the Central West. With its own Pastoral College and School of Distance Education, Longreach acts as the public service and educational center for the area. Visitors might forget they're in the outback when they walk down **Eagle St.,** crowded with cafes, shops, and plenty of pubs and jukeboxes to keep the town hopping.

The town's biggest attraction is not actually in town: the **Australian Stockman's Hall of Fame and Outback Heritage Centre** is a massive, multi-media museum off the Landsborough Hwy. (☎4658 2166; www.outbackheritage.com.au. Open daily 9am-5pm. $19.80, children 8-16 $9.50, children under 8 free.) Near the airport is the **Qantas Founders Outback Museum,** housed in the original 1921 Qantas headquarters, with an introductory film and a full-scale model of the first Qantas plane. (☎4658 3737. Open daily 9am-5pm. $7.70, concessions $5.50.)

McCafferty's buses depart from **Longreach Outback Travel,** 115A Eagle St., with daily service to Brisbane (daily at 4:10pm; one way $102, concessions $82) and two weekly services to Rockhampton for $65. (☎4658 1776. Open M-F 8:30am-5pm, Sa 8:30am-noon and 3:30-4:30pm, Su 10:30-11:15am and 3:30-4:30pm.) The **Information Centre** is at Qantas Park on Eagle St. (☎4658 3555; www.longreach.qld.gov.au. Open M-F 9am-5pm, Sa-Su 9am-1pm.) Free **Internet** is at the library, 96 Eagle St. (☎4658 4104. Open Tu and Th 9:30am-1pm, W and F 12:30-5pm, Sa 9am-noon.)

The cheapest place to stay is in the **Royal Hotel,** 111 Eagle St., but keep in mind that the pub downstairs hosts a disco from 9pm-2am every F and Sa. (☎4658 2118. Reception Su-Th 10am-11pm, F-Sa 10am-2am. Dorms $11; singles $22; self-contained single units $55; doubles $66.) The **Longreach Caravan Park** is a bit quieter, located on 180 Ibis St. at the corner of Owl St. (☎4658 1770. Reception daily 7am-10:30pm. Sites $14.30, powered $16.50. Self-contained cabin $49.50, with shared toilets $27.50.) The IGA Cornett Supermarket on the corner of Eagle and Swan St. is a well-stocked **grocery** store (☎4658 1260. Open M-W 8am-6:30pm, Th-F 8am-8pm, Sa 8am-4pm.)

THE FLINDERS HIGHWAY

A long, lonely route, Flinders Highway is primarily a straight shot from Townsville to Mt. Isa, though it passes through quite a few small outback towns along the way. Ravenswood and Charters Towers are only a daytrip away from the coast, yet remote enough to offer a taste of the outback. As you head further west, towns only get smaller, marked only by a lower speed limit, general store, and petrol pump. Most traffic heads straight to Mt. Isa, a bleak industrial outpost that serves as a gateway to the Northern Territory.

UP YOUR BILLABONG! Winton and Kynuna duke it out over the matter of *Waltzing Matilda*. Winton's North Gregory Hotel was the site of Banjo Patterson's first performance of Australia's unofficial national anthem, but truckstop Kynuna (163km northwest) is much closer to the actual billabong in the song, and *they've* got the original music score. Kynuna may be the real deal, but Winton's the site of the brand-new **Waltzing Matilda Centre,** 50 Elderslie St. With statues, holograms, and an underwater "ghost," it is probably the only center in the world dedicated to one song. (☎4657 1466. www.mathildacentre.com.au. Open daily 8:30am-5pm. $14. Cafe open daily 9am-4pm.) Winton's collection of eccentrics have also left their mark. **Arno's Wall,** behind the North Gregory Hotel, is a 70m stretch of home implements, motorcycles, and other flotsam and jetsam set into the concrete. A one-man crusade against the historical inaccuracies in Winton, Richard Magoffin performs his own history of *Waltzing Matilda* at his **Swagman Hall of Fame** in Kyuna. (☎4746 8401. Book ahead. Open daily 8am-10pm. Show daily 7:30pm, $15. Donation required.) On the outskirts of town, **Matilda Country Tourist Park,** 43 Chirnside St., is a haven for bush poets and travelers, with free pickup from the train and bus stations. (☎4657 1607. Reception daily 7am-8pm. Sites for 2 $12, powered $16; cabins from $60. MC/V.)

CHARTERS TOWER ☎07

South of the Atherton Tablelands, the land dries out and old outback towns begin to punctuate a barren landscape. Once nicknamed "The World" for its cosmopolitan flair, Charters Towers, 1½hr. west of Townsville, was the hub of Queensland, but only traces of its glory days remain.

TRANSPORTATION AND PRACTICAL INFORMATION. The **Queensland Rail Station** (☎13 22 32) is on Enterprise Rd. on the east side of town. **Trains** go to Townsville (3hr.; Tu and Sa 10:02am; $19.80) and Mt. Isa (17hr.; Su and W 9:03pm; $95.70). Greyhound, McCafferty's, and Douglas **buses** depart from the corner of Gill and Church St. to Townsville (1¾hr., daily, $22.) Book tickets at **Traveland,** 13 Gill St. (☎4787 2622; fax 4787 7570. Open M-F 8am-5pm, Sa 9am-noon.)

The center of Charters Towers is created by the simple T intersection of Mossman and Gill St., known as the Historic City Centre. Government offices and "The World" theater run along Mosman St., while most shops, restaurants, and banks descend down Gill St. The **tourist office,** 74 Mosman St. is at the top of Gill St. (☎4752 0314; www.charterstowers.qld.gov.au. Open daily 9am-5pm.) There are several **banks** with **ATMs** strung along Gill St. and **RACQ** (☎4787 2000) agents at Gold City Wreckers, 21 Dundee Ln. The **library** is in the Old Bank. (Open M, W, F 10am-1pm and 1:45-4:45pm; Tu and Th 1:45-4:45pm; Sa 9:30am-noon.) **Internet** is at Charters Towers Computers (open M-F 9am-4pm and Sa 9am-noon; $3.85 per 30min.) and at the library ($5 per hr).

ACCOMMODATIONS, FOOD, AND NIGHTLIFE. The **York Street Bed and Breakfast,** 58 York St., is a friendly place to stay, but a 15min. walk from the center of town. (☎4787 1028. Lodge rooms $27.50 with continental breakfast; rooms in house $45-60 with cooked breakfast.) For something cheaper, try the **Waverly Hotel** at the end of Mossman St. (☎4787 2591. Singles $22; twins $33.) **Charters Towers Caravan Park,** 37 Mount Leyshon Rd., is a 20min. walk south of town. (☎/fax 4787 7944 or 1800 357 944. Reception 7am-7pm. BBQ Tu and Th nights. Sites for 2 $11, powered $16.50; caravans with A/C and bath $27.50; cabins $44.)

The **Stock Exchange Cafe,** 76 Mosman St., serves somewhat makeshift yet tasty cuisine including quiche, burgers, or lasagna for less than $6. (☎4787 7954. Open M-Th 8:30am-5pm, F-Sa 8:30am-8pm, Su 9am-4pm.) Woolworth's, on Gill St., has **groceries.** (☎4787 3411. Open M-F 8am-9pm, Sa 8am-5pm.) Nightlife in Charters Towers is confined to two nightclubs: **Regent Club 96 Bar,** 69 Gill St. (☎4787 2600; open F-Sa until 3am); **Pegasus Night Club,** 33 Gill St., in the White Horse Tavern plays a techno/retro mix (☎4787 1064; open F-Sa 10pm-3am). The **World Theatre,** 82-90 Mosman St., features concerts, ballets, operas, and plays. (Ticket office ☎4787 8472. Open M-F 10am-1:30pm, Sa 10am-noon.) Two **cinemas** play mostly American films. (Shows W-Su nights. $9, W $6.)

SIGHTS AND ACTIVITIES. The big attraction in town is the largest **gold-producing mine** in all of Queensland. Tours are booked through the tourist office (W $13). **Gold Nugget Scenic Tours** runs a 2½hr. sight-seeing tour around town, departing the tourist office M-F at 9:30am. (☎4787 4115. $22, concessions $20.) You can also take a trip to the **Venus Battery** where the gold from the surrounding mines was refined. (☎4787 2374. Open 9am-3pm daily. Guided tours 10am and 2pm. $4.40.) The **Zara Clarke Museum** at the corner of Gill and Mary St. has an authoritative display of Charters Towers memorabilia including an old fire wagon and an iron lung. (Open daily 10am-3pm. $4.40). Two cattle stations nearby hire backpackers for a couple of weeks and offer "City Slicker" holiday packages: **Bluff Downs** is a rough-and-ready real working cattle station—mud, blood, and billabongs included. This one is for those seeking the authentic outback. (☎4770 4084. Campers $20 per 2 people per day powered, $18 unpowered; dorm $20, with meals $55). **Plain Creek** probably better suits the tenderfoot (☎4983 5228).

FROM PENTLAND TO RICHMOND

PENTLAND. About halfway between Charters Towers and Hughendon, Pentland, (pop. 300), is a good place to stay when the sun is setting and the 'roos are on the road. There is a **General Store** with **post office** (☎4788 1130; M-F open 9am-7pm, Sa 10am-noon, Su 5-7pm), a **Shell Service Station** (☎4788 1254; M-F open 7am-7pm, Sa-Su 7am-6pm) and a couple cheap places to stay. The **Pentland Caravan Park** (☎4788 1148) has sites ($11), powered caravan sites ($13.20), and cabins ($60). There are also single ($27.50) and double ($38.50) rooms. The park has a swimming pool and convenience store. The **Pentland Hotel** serves food and their spotless rooms have TV, fridge and bath. (☎4788 1106. Singles $50, twins and doubles $60.)

PRAIRIE. After a few hours, the road runs through Prairie, (pop. 60). The only town marker is an old Cobb & Co. stagecoach stop established 1894, the very venerable and pause-worthy **Prairie Hotel.** The young management is redoing this old outback resting place, and has added a menu transplanted from the coast. The hotel has two rooms, a new motel unit, and camp sites. (☎4741 5121. Sites $11; powered $16.50; singles $22; doubles $38.50. Motel singles $49.50; doubles $60.50.)

HUGHENDEN. Hughenden (HYU-enden) marks the eastern edge of Queensland's marine dinosaur territory: stop into the **Visitor Information Centre,** 37 Gray St., to see the **Muttaburrasaurus skeleton** they've got stashed in the back. (☎4741 1021. Open daily 9am-5pm. $2.) The **library,** on the corner of Gray and National St., has **Internet** access. (Open M-F 10:30am-1pm and 2-5pm, Sa 9-11:45am. $2.20 per hr.) Budget accommodation in Hughenden is limited to the ambitiously-named **Grand Hotel,** 25 Gray St. (☎4741 1588; singles $15; twins and doubles $35; shared rooms $12), and the **Allan Terry Caravan Park.** The caravan site is neatly kept, with swimming pool, laundry and kitchen. (☎4741 1190. Reception M-F 6am-9pm. Sites for 2 $10, powered $14; cabins $60.) New and immaculate rooms are a bit more expensive across the street at **Wright's Motel**, 20 Gray St. (☎4741 1677. Singles $41.80; doubles

THE DINOSAUR OUTBACK It's hard to imagine the dry, dusty outback as the home of giant marine reptiles, but 100 million years ago much of central Queensland (and some parts of New South Wales and South Australia) was a huge inland sea. This area, called the Great Artesian Basin, has yielded some incredible fossils, including the 12.8m Kronosaurus, the Ichthyosaurs, and squid-like ammonites. Fossils are still being discovered today around Hughenden and Richmond.

$49.50.) There is a Five-Star **Supermarket** on the corner of Resolution and Moran St., north of the Caravan Park. (Open M-F 8:30am-5pm, Sa 8:30-11:30am.) Once here, take heart, you're only 113km from the next outback outpost: Richmond. **Porcupine Gorge,** a beautiful natural valley, is 63km north of town. **Adventure Wildlife and Bush Treks** operates from the caravan park, and has full-day trips to the Gorge ($45, $65 if you eat their food) and camping trips to the White Mountains and Mt. Emu Goldfields ($50 to tag-along with your own vehicle).

RICHMOND. West of Hughenden along the Flinders Hwy., Richmond packs an impressive paleological punch. **Kronosaurus Korner,** 93 Goldrin St., is both the regional **Visitor Information Centre** and the **Richmond Marine Fossil Museum**, housing the bones of local cretaceous creatures. (☎4741 3429. Open daily 8:30am-4:45pm. $8.) **Internet** is at the **library**, 78 Goldring St. across from the Visitor Centre. The brand new **Moon Rock Cafe,** across from the information counter, cooks up veggie-friendly sandwiches ($3-3.50). The **Richmond Caravan Park** on your way into town from Hughendon before the Visitor Centre is of exceptional value with A/C, shared bathrooms, and kitchen. (☎4741 3772. Key deposit $10. Sites $11, powered $14; twin share bunk house $33; cabins $50.) The **Mud Hut Motel,** 72 Goldring St., has pub rooms with A/C and TV, as well as dorms in the back. (☎/fax 4741 3223. Singles $45; doubles $55; dongas $20-25.) There is a BuyRite **supermarket** on Goldring St. (Open M-F 7:30am-5pm, Sa 7:30am-12:30pm, Su 7:30am-noon.)

MOUNT ISA ☎07

When the subject of Mount Isa comes up, backpackers' conversations sober up and casual laughter dwindles. This is the city where hitchhikers on their way to the Northern Territory break down and buy a bus ticket. Honeymooning couples have been known to sell their campervans in the Isa and head to the airport. No matter what your next destination is, from Mt. Isa you've got one hell of a long trip ahead of you. Here the motel is king, and two- and three-trailer road trains crowd the roadhouses on the outskirts of town. Besides the "permanent residents"—the copper, silver, zinc, and lead miners—there are only three types of people who come here: first, road train drivers, those unforgiving warriors of the bitumen brigade; second, graziers (farmers) from outlying areas who need to stock up on food and supplies; third, you, the traveler, stopping at the biggest urban outpost on the endless haul from the Queensland coast to the tropical Top End or to the Red Centre. So take a deep breath, try not to choke, and get ready to cross the desert.

QUEENSLAND

TRANSPORTATION. The **Train Station** (☎4744 1203) is on Station St. near Miles End next to the mines. From town, take Isa St. west over the bridge until it ends; the station is on the right. (Open M and F 11:15am-6pm, T-Th 8am-3:30pm.) The *Inlander* train departs 6pm Monday and Friday to: Charters Towers (16hr.); Hughenden (11¼hr.); Richmond (9¼hr.); Townsville (19hr.) via Cloncurry (3½hr.). **McCafferty's** and **Greyhound,** 27-29 Barkly Hwy., at Campbell's Tours and Travel. From town, take Grace St. west over the river until it ends and the terminal is on your right. (☎4743 2006. Open M-F 6am-7:45pm, Sa 6-9:30am and 5:30-7:45pm. 10% ISIC/YHA discounts.) **Buses** run to: Alice Springs ($188); Brisbane ($137); Cairns ($150); Charters Towers ($97); Darwin ($216); Richmond ($52); Rockhampton ($196); Townsville ($103). Call **United Cab** at 13 10 08 anytime. **RACQ** is at 13 Simpson St. (☎4743 2542, after hours 0417 714 162.)

ORIENTATION AND PRACTICAL INFORMATION. The city center is a manageable four-by-four grid, bounded by **Isa St.** to the north, **West St.** to the west, **Mary St.** to the south, and **Simpson St.** to the east. The **Barkly Hwy.** enters from Northern Territory and runs parallel to the **Leichhardt River** until the bridge at **Miles End,** then turns left over the water into the city center on **Grace St.** From Cloncurry in the east, the Flinders Hwy. becomes **Marion St.,** which forks in two after the Riversleigh Interpretive Center at KMart Place. The right fork becomes Grace St., the left continues on as Marion St.

Traveland, 27-29 Barkly Hwy., next to the McCafferty's terminal, is a budget travel office. (☎4743 3399; fax 4743 7376. Open M-F 8:30am-5:30pm, Sa 8:30am-1pm.) The **Riversleigh Interpretive Centre,** Centenary Park, Marion St., books mine ($17.60 for a surface tour, $60 to go underground, advance bookings essential) and heritage city tours ($25.30). Admission to the **Fossil Display** is $9, children $5, pensioners $6, families $24. (☎4749 1555; fax 4743 6296. Open M-F 8:30am-4:30pm, Sa-Su 9am-2pm.) Other services include: **Commonwealth Bank** at 23 Miles St. (☎4743 5033. Traveler's checks or cash exchange fee $5. Open M-Th 9:30am-4pm, F 9:30am-5pm.) The **Guardian Pharmacy,** 14/16 West St. (☎4743 2038) is open daily 8am-8pm. **Mt. Isa Base Hospital** is at 30 Camooweal St. (☎4744 4444). The **police,** 7 Isa St., are at the corner of Miles St. (☎4743 1111. Open 24hr.) **Internet** at the **library,** 23 West St., is the best deal in town. (☎4744 4256. $2 per hr. Open M-Th 10am-6pm, F 10am-5pm.) There's a **post office** on the corner of Camooweal and Isa St. (☎4743 2454; open M-F 8:30am-5pm) and also in Mt. Isa Square opposite KMart Place. (Open M-F 8:45am-5:15pm, Sa 9am-11:45am.) **Postal code:** 4825.

ACCOMMODATIONS AND FOOD. **Traveller's Haven,** at the corner of Pamela and Spence St., is the only hostel in town, so you'll have to make do with free pickup, a nice pool and a feeling of camaraderie with everyone else staying here. (☎4743 0313. Linen $2. Key deposit $5. Reception daily 6:30am-1pm and 5-7pm. Dorms $17; singles $30; twins and doubles $40. VIP. EFTPOS/MC/V.) **Boyd's Hotel,** 16-20 West St., near the corner of Marion St., is one of the cheapest hotels in Mt. Isa. The serviceable rooms have A/C and sinks. (☎4743 3000. Rooms $30, with bath is recommended $35.) **Mt. Isa Van Park,** 112 Marian St., is clean and well-tended with lots of long-term residents. (☎4743 3252; fax 4743 3100. Check-out 10am. Reception daily 7:30am-6:30pm. Sites $13.50, powered $16.50; brand-new self-contained cabins with TV, A/C, kitchen and bathroom for 2 $55, $5.50 for extra adults, $2.50 per child.) You'll get the best value for money at the newly renovated **Central Point Motel,** 6 Marian St., which is also the most centrally located accommodation listed. (☎4743 0666; fax 4743 0611. TV, A/C, bath and kitchenette in room, and salt-water pool. Singles $66; doubles $77. AmEx/EFTPOS.)

Fast food is king in the Isa; watch locals queue up in the drive-throughs for fun. The **Buffalo Club,** on the corner of Grace and Simpson St., offers a $9.50 all-you-can-eat lunch buffet. Look decent: collared shirt yay, sandals nay. (☎4743 2365. Open daily 8am-2am.) The **Miner's Hut Cafe,** 31 Miles St., makes mean meat-free meals. (☎4743 1555. Open M-F 8am-5pm, Sa 8am-2pm.) Coles **Supermarket** is in KMart Centre, on Marian St. (☎4743 6007. Open M-Sa 8am-9pm.)

SIGHTS. Mt. Isa's excitement lies mostly underground, where most of its workforce toils in 12hr. shifts. You can take a 4hr. **Underground Mine Tour** into the belly of the beast. Put on the suit and hat and enter the winding labyrinth of tunnels. Book through the Riversleigh Centre as far ahead as possible. (☎4749 1555. 2 per day M-F; $60.) If you weren't savvy enough to book ahead, you can see the (fabricated) inside of a mine shaft at the **Frank Aston Underground Museum,** on Shackleton St., off Marion St. across from KMart. The museum's mining display occupies a hollowed-out hill, from the top of which you can see the city in its entirety (and it's a small hill). There are also surface mine tours available through the Riversleigh Centre, as well as Aboriginal tours of the area also booked there. (☎4749 0610. Open daily 9am-4pm. $6, children $1.) Australia's biggest **rodeo** comes to Mt. Isa in August, along with the world's greatest rodeo legends. If you're lucky enough to be passing through then, stay to try your luck at winning the big money steer-riding or bronc-busting.

THE GULF SAVANNAH

The area between the Atherton Tablelands and the Gulf of Carpentaria along the **Gulf Developmental Rd.,** the Gulf region revels in remoteness, welcoming the wayward visitor with respectful indifference. This is the outback's outback. The Gulf's

TAIL FROM THE ROAD Two blokes driving along the endless, dusty outback roads hit and knocked a kangaroo unconscious. Feeling sorry for the critter, they carried it back into the car. Starving for some kind of entertainment in the vast nothing of the outback, the two decided to dress up the kangaroo and put a Yankees jacket on the sleeping marsupial. When it finally woke up, the kangaroo panicked, flailing about the car with its powerful legs. The two 'roo-snatchers got so beat up they had to be hospitalized. They couldn't pay for the medical fees, though—the jacket-wearing kangaroo had pocketed the wallet and credit cards and hopped away.

few tourist attractions include historic "nowhere-to-nowhere" trains, gorges, and lava tubes. The Gulf can be an escapist fantasy or a city slicker's nightmare. The sea can be reached by Karumba Point Rd. off the Gulf Developmental Rd., 4km before **Karumba** (pop. 600) and 72km northwest of **Normaton.**

The Dry (Apr.-Oct.) is the time to visit, though even then the road conditions can be bad. Road reports are issued by the **Gulf Savannah Tourism,** 74 Abbott St. (☎4051 4658; www.gulf-savannah.com.au; open M-F 8:30am-5pm.) in Cairns, as well as in local info centers and RACQs. The most common route through the region is the **Gulf Developmental Rd.,** linking Cairns to Normanton, where it joins the desolate north-south **Burke Developmental Rd.** These are primarily single-lane, cattle-strewn, kangaroo-enticing sealed roads. Conventional vehicles are fine on most roads during the Dry, but caravans should avoid those which are unsealed. If you want to brave the Wet, 4WD is essential. *Never drive the Ootann Rd. connecting Mt. Surprise and Chillagoe or anywhere along the Mt. Isa-Riversleigh-Lawn Hill National Park route without 4WD.*

ROUTE 1 FROM CAIRNS: THE EASTERN GULF

Lying between the Atherton Tablelands and the Carpentaria Coast along Rte. 1, **Georgetown** (pop. 350) and **Mt. Surprise** (pop. 65) make for decent stopovers. The towns, along with nearby **Einasleigh** and **Forsayth,** are part of the **Etheridge Goldfield** and popular with amateur fossickers. The *Savannahlander* **train** connects Mt. Surprise and Forsayth, via Einasleigh. (☎1800 620 324. 6¼hr.; departs Mt. Surprise Th 12:15am, departs Forsayth F 7:45am. $40, concessions $20.)

The eastern Gulf's most awesome attraction is a 40min. drive from Mt. Surprise. The **Undara Volcano** erupted 190,000 years ago, creating 69 **lava tubes** in the middle of dense rainforest, with caverns averaging 10m high and 15m wide. **Undara Experience** visits nine of them. (☎4097 1411. 2hr. tour $33; daily 8, 10:30am, 1, 3:30pm. Half-day tours $63; daily 8:30am, 1pm.) At Undara, you can camp ($5 per person) or stay in the tent village ($16 per person; linen $6).

QUEENSLAND

NORMANTON AND CROYDON. **Normanton** (pop. 1200) is the largest town in the Gulf; two-thirds of its population is Aboriginal. The town is as much a relic as its famous *Gulflander* train, 20 Matilda St. (☎4745 1391), in the station on Matilda St. next to the **info centre** (open in the Dry daily 7am-6pm). There's a Westpac **bank** with an **ATM** at the corner of Landsborough and Little Brown St. Normanton's **Brolga Palms Motel** and **National Hotel** are both connected to the **Purple Pub** on the corner of Landsborough and Brown St. (☎4745 1009. Hotel singles $28; doubles $40; motel singles $63; doubles $73.)

The population of **Croydon** increases by nearly 20% when the *Gulflander* pulls in. The **Croydon Club Hotel** is the last of the 122 pubs that once catered to gold-miners. (☎4745 6184. Open daily 10am-10pm. Singles $35; doubles $45; motel singles $40; doubles $55.) **Croydon Caravan Park** is on the corner of Brown and Aldridge St. (☎4745 6238. Sites for 2 $10, powered $15.)

SOUTH AUSTRALIA

Prophets of the Australian backpacking scene are known to wander the deserts of the land, telling all who listen: "There is only one South Australia, and Adelaide is its capital." Amazingly, this message has been heeded by a relatively small number of pilgrims. The majority of travelers and tourists to the land down under bypass the chosen land and race from Melbourne to Uluru via requisite stop-overs in Adelaide and Coober Pedy. But for those who take the time to learn and love this state, with its fly-specked, harsh, but beautiful Outback north, the lovely coasts of the Eyre and Fleurieu Peninsulas, and Adelaide, the world's biggest country town, a new truth about the east coast will become evident: the best thing about Queensland's touristy beaches is the road toward South Australia.

The prophets go on: "And then God created the heavens and the Earth." Highway 87, which connects Coober Pedy with Port Augusta to the south and Alice Springs to the north, will remind the most forgetful of city slickers where exactly humanity stands on the scale of things: the stars up above join together in the glowing white choir of the Milky Way, and the harshest, driest, most sun-scorched country this side of the SA-WA border will either capture your heart and imagination, or send you scrambling for the next bus to someplace wetter.

The ancient Flinders Ranges, a portfolio of spectacular sculpting by five billion years of geological processes, is known more generally for wildlife than for nightlife (if one discounts all the nocturnal animals roaming the bush), but in nearby Parachilna the backpacker gods handed down one hell of a good time.

When relating the powers of the South Australian landscape: "And He turned water into wine." Here, in the driest state in the driest continent on earth, the population chants this mantra: save water, drink wine. Although Coopers' line of beers might be the homebrew, a good chunk of the state's economy rests on the fine vintages produced throughout the state: the Barossa and Clare valleys east-northeast of Adelaide, the McLaren Vale and Fleurieu Peninsula region to the south of the capital, and the Coonawarra region between Naracoorte and Mount Gambier, down southeast by Victoria, all provide a more refined way to get bloody pissed.

South Australia's long coastline offers everything: sheltered bays for swimming; beaches exposed to the great Southern Ocean where the waves roll in high and mighty, ready to be caught by anyone with the willingness and a board; large populations of seals, sea lions, and steel-blue fairy penguins; on-site locations from the filming of *Jaws;* great fishing from any angle; a breezy respite from the oft-raging inferno further inland..

SOUTH AUSTRALIA HIGHLIGHTS

EYRE PENINSULA. Find yourself on the deserted, cliff-fringed beaches of the Eyre Peninsula (p. 453), or lose yourself in the nearby outback (p. 449).

NARACOORTE CAVES. There's spectacular spelunking in the bat-populated formations of the Naracoorte Caves (p. 441).

FLINDERS RANGES. Gain a new perspective on time and space in the ancient, gently folding mountains of Flinders Ranges (p. 444).

SUMMER ARTS FEST. Summer outdoor film (p. 415), and one of the world's best and most eclectic music festivals, WOMADelaide (p. 418), both in the lushly decadent Botanic Gardens of Adelaide (p. 415).

COOBER PEDY. Chill out in the underground hostels of Coober Pedy (p. 451).

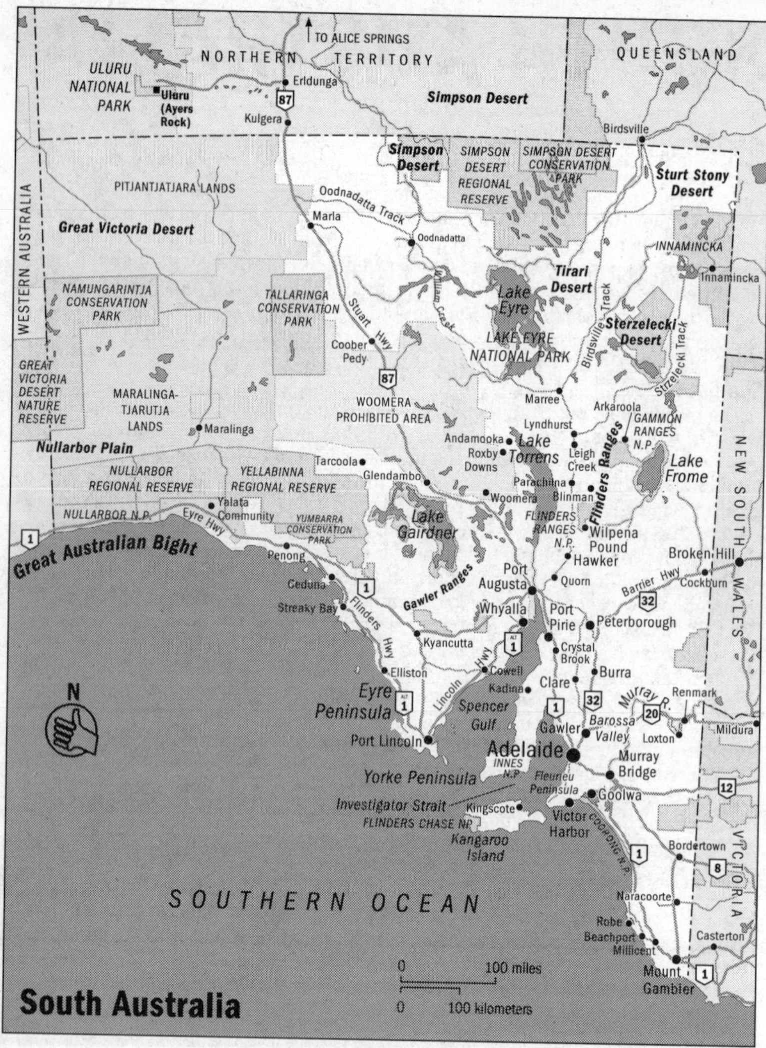

TRANSPORTATION

If you don't have a car, the most practical way to see most of South Australia's attractions is by bus. Greyhound Pioneer (☎ 13 20 30) runs between Adelaide and Melbourne, Sydney, Alice Springs, and Perth, stopping over at a few destinations in between. McCafferty's (☎ 1800 076 211) is another major bus company. Premier Stateliner (☎ 8415 5555) services smaller towns throughout South Australia. Three major train lines run through South Australia: the *Overland* to Melbourne, the *Indian Pacific* to Perth, and the *Legendary Ghan* to Alice Springs, all with various stops along the way. For more train information, see p. 409.

Major **car rental** companies with branches in SA include **Hertz** (☎ 13 30 39), **Avis** (Adelaide ☎ 8410 5727), and **Thrifty** (☎ 1300 367 277). Local outfits, often with lower prices, are listed throughout this chapter. A conventional vehicle is fine for wine and beach country, but 4WD is strongly recommended for forays into the outback. Another good option, often more practical for those traveling alone or going to out-of-the-way places, is to book a **tour.** Many choose the jump-on, jump-off flexibility of backpacker buses like the youthful **Oz Experience** (☎1300 30 00 28) or the twenty-something favorite, **Wayward Bus** (☎8232 6646); plenty of local organizations run excellent trips. Most hostels have ample tour advice and can book for guests, often at a discount. Still the greatest way to see the state is to buy a used car or 4WD upon arrival, and sell it when leaving the country—this provides the ultimate in freedom and flexibility.

ADELAIDE ☎08

To the Kaurna people, the area's first residents, the Adelaide region was known as "Tandanya," the place of the red kangaroo. For more than a million current residents, it's a green, civilized city that's a welcome break from the desertland in the north. For many backpackers though, this is a spot to get drunk, catch some rays, and then, after a week or so, hop on a bus to Alice Springs.

The first completely planned city in Australia is centered around a one-mile-square grid, separated from the suburbs, where the large majority of the population lives by vast green parklands. Residents take pride in the graceful colonial buildings, and flourishing arts scene, while enjoying a big-city lifestyle.

Adelaide appreciates the good life, plain and simple. With more restaurants per capita than any other city in Australia, the city can satisfy any palate at any budget, and then wash it all down with some of the world's best wines. The city's cultural attractions, headed by the Adelaide Festival of Arts, includes a symphony and chamber orchestra, numerous small experimental theaters, and world-class galleries and museums. For a more raucous pace, the nightclubs along Hindley St., the pubs in the city center, and the cafes on Rundle St. fit the hedonistic bill. If you have to play tourist or can only stay briefly in Adelaide, then the must-see sights and must-do museums are manageable in a few days.

INTERCITY TRANSPORTATION

BY PLANE. The **Adelaide Airport,** 7km west of the city center, services domestic and international carriers in separate terminals. A taxi ride to the city runs $11-15, but most hostels in the city or Glenelg offer free pickup with advance booking. Failing that, the cheapest way is the **Transit Regency Airport-to-City Bus,** which picks up and drops off near city accommodations. (☎8381 5311. M-F every 30min.; Sa-Su every hr. 4am-11pm. $6.60, return $11; children $2.20. Book ahead for travel to the airport.) Catch the bus at the domestic terminal directly in front of the currency exchange, or to the left as you exit the international terminal. A slightly cheaper option is the TransAdelaide **public bus #278** ($1.60), but the stop is a 15min. walk away from the terminal, at the gate to the airport.

Be sure to mention that you're an international traveler when booking domestic flights; on one-way fares it can make a big difference in price. **Qantas** (☎13 13 13), oversees **ASA** (Airlines of South Australia; ☎8682 5688 or 1800 018 234), servicing the Eyre Peninsula and **O'Conner** servicing Mt. Gambier. **Ansett** (☎13 13 00) controls **Kendall Airlines,** the biggest local carrier, with flights to: Ceduna ($310); Coober Pedy ($360); Kangaroo Island ($540); Mt. Gambier ($196). Seventeen and under receive a 25% discount, seniors 40%. **Emu Airways** (☎8234 3711 or 1800 182 343) services Kangaroo Island ($90).

BY TRAIN. Train travel is usually pricier than bus travel, but consider spending 34 hours on a bus. All interstate or long distance country trains use the **Keswick Interstate Rail Passenger Terminal** (☎13 21 47) in Keswick, a suburb 2km southwest of Adelaide's Central Business District. Only suburban commuter trains use the **Adelaide Railway Station** (☎8218 2277) on North Tce. The Transit Regency Airport-to-City Bus brings rail passengers to and from the Keswick Station. (☎8381 5311.

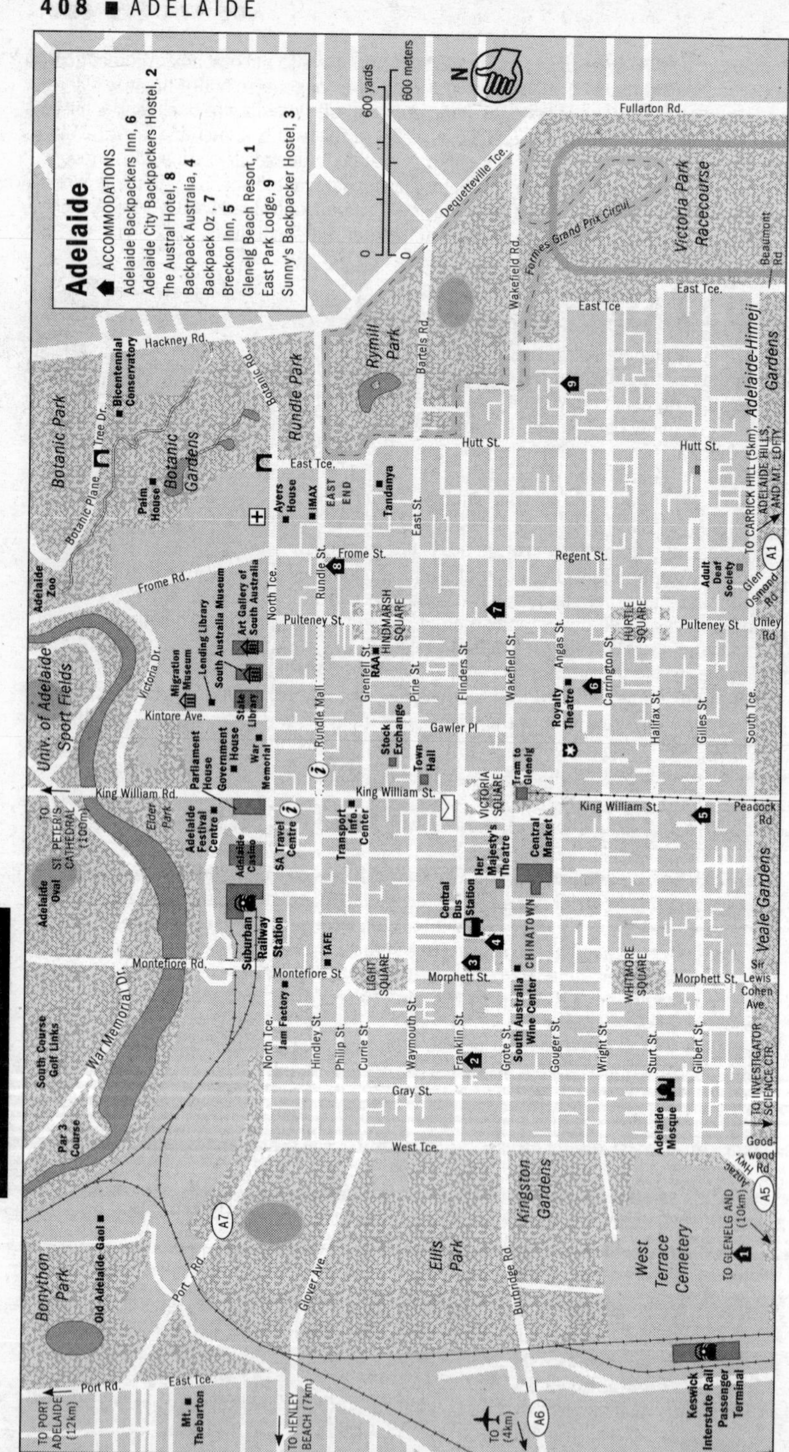

SOUTH AUSTRALIA

$3.30, children $1.10, adult return $5.50.) Book ahead for travel to the station. The Keswick terminal has car parking.

The privately-owned **Australian Rail Travel Centre,** 18-20 Grenfell St., lets you buy tickets downtown without making the trek to the Keswick terminal. (☎8231 4366; fax 8231 5771. Open M-F 8:30am-5:30pm, Sa 9am-1pm.) The **Overland** services Melbourne (12-13½ hr.; departs M, Th, F, Su 9am; $57, students $40, children $33). The **Ghan** runs to Alice Springs (19hr., departs M and Th 3pm, $197/$99/$89). The **Indian Pacific** runs to Perth (39hr., departs Tu and F 6pm, $248/$198/$124). The Indian Pacific and Ghan both connect Adelaide with Sydney (24-25hr.; departs W and Su 7:45am, Sa 8:40am; $176, students $88, children $79). All three trains offer a 10% YHA discount. Confirm times in advance. Also, international students with an ISIC card qualify for student rates; try **YHA Travel,** 135 Waymouth St. (☎8414 3000).

BY BUS. Adelaide has two central bus stations that are identical looking and adjacent to each other on Franklin St. **Greyhound** (☎13 20 30) and **McCafferty's** (☎13 14 99) are at 101 Franklin St., while **V-Line** and **Premier Stateliner** pull into 111 Franklin St. National bus companies provide regular service to and from Adelaide at prices that generally beat rail and air travel. Greyhound Pioneer and McCafferty's handle most interstate traffic, with prices within a few dollars of each other. Greyhound runs to: Alice Springs (20hr., 1 per day, $147); Brisbane (29hr., 2 per day, $174); Darwin (14hr., 1 per day, $305); Melbourne (10hr., 2 per day, $49); Perth (34hr., 1 per day, $225); Sydney (22hr., 3 per day, $104); Yulara/Ayers Rock (20hr., 1 per day, $147); several destinations in between. Within South Australia, **Premier Stateliner** (☎8415 5555) is the main carrier. The free *State Guide*, available at the tourist office and many hostels, is indispensable for planning area travel.

ORIENTATION

Surrounded by parklands, downtown Adelaide is only one square mile, bordered by North, East, South, and West Terraces. The city is bisected north-south by **King William St.;** streets running east-west change names when crossing King William St.

Keswick, with the railway station, is about 2km southwest of the central grid, while the airport and the beach suburb of **Glenelg** are southwest. Northwest of the CBD, on the Port River, is the suburb of **Port Adelaide.** The **Adelaide Hills,** including Cleland Conservation Park and Mt. Lofty lookout are east of the city. Although Adelaide is a relatively peaceful city, the parklands are unsafe at night, especially near the River Torrens and in the southwest corner of the city. **Hindley St.** also demands an extra degree of caution at night.

LOCAL TRANSPORTATION

BY PUBLIC TRANSPORTATION. Adelaide is serviced by public buses, trains, and one lone tram that make up an integrated public transport system called **TransAdelaide,** which runs two free bus services around the city: **Beeline** and **City Loop.** These yellow buses are easily identified, fully wheelchair accessible, and clearly labeled "Free Ride." Beeline runs in the city center, from the railway station on North Tce. down King William St. to Victoria Sq and back (every 5min. M-Th 7:40am-6pm, F 7:40am-9pm; every 15min. Sa 8:30am-5:20pm). City Loop, true to its name, runs both directions around a loop that covers the north half of the city, including stops at North, East, and West Tce. as well as most major tourist attractions, Central Market, and near the bus station. (Every 15min. M-Th 8:30am-6pm, F 8:30am-9pm; every 30min. Sa 8:30am-5pm.)

To roam farther, you need to tackle the mass of bus and train routes that comprise TransAdelaide's suburban system. Luckily, an info line (☎8210 1000, staffed daily 7am-8pm) will supply you with travel info. The **Passenger Transport Information Centre,** at the corner of King William and Currie St., also has route schedules. (☎ 8210 1000. Open M-Sa 8am-6pm, Su 10:30am-5:30pm.)

Single **tickets** to anywhere on bus, train, or tram are good on any service (including return trip) for 2hr. and can be purchased from bus drivers, tram conductors, and train vending machines (single trip M-F 9am-3pm $1.70; all other times $2.90). You must **validate** single or daytrip tickets each time you enter a new bus, train, or tram. Daytrip tickets ($5.60) allow one-day of unlimited travel on any service and can be purchased when boarding buses or trams, but must be bought beforehand for trains. An option for those staying longer is the Multitrip ticket, which you must buy at a newsagent, post office, or the Passenger Transport Info Centre prior to boarding. It's good for ten single rides ($19.50, off-peak $10.90).

The best way to get to **Glenelg** and the beach is to take the old, wood-panelled trams ($2.90, M-F from 9am-3pm $1.70) from Victoria Sq. to Moseley Sq. (30min.; every 15-20min. M-F 6am-midnight, Sa 7:30am-midnight, Su 8:50am-midnight). Although it's much cheaper to explore on your own, for a fully guided tour of the area, **Adelaide Explorer** does a city-to-Glenelg hop-on, hop-off tour that takes 3hr. Pick up the small bus, decorated like a tram, anywhere on the route or join at 38 King William St. daily at 9, 10:30am, noon, 1:30, or 3pm. (☎8364 1933. $25 per day, concessions $24, ages 6-14 $15, families $55; second day $7.)

BY CAR. Hertz, 233 Morphett St. (☎13 30 39); **Budget** (☎13 27 27), corner of North Tce. and Frome St.; **Avis,** 136 North Tce (☎8410 5727), have counters at the airport and in town. **Thrifty** (☎8211 8788 or 1300 367 227) is affiliated with **Caudell's Explorer Self-Drive,** Hindley St. (☎8410 5552), which offers cars from $50, and 4WD from $69-100 per day. **Bush Bashers,** 175 Hart St., Glanville (☎8242 3033), has 4WD hire from $100 with 200km, or from $120 with unlimited km (minimum age 25).

If you're under 25, it's much cheaper to hire from a smaller agency. These companies are scattered around the suburbs, but will generally pickup and drop off in town. The Adelaide-based **Smile Rent-a-Car,** 163 Richmond Rd., southwest of town, has excellent rates, no age surcharge for drivers under 25, unlimited kilometers, and friendly service. (☎8234 0655 or 1800 624 424. Small manual or automatic from $35-45, plus $10 per day for insurance.) **No Frills Car Rental** is what its name suggests, but it has no age limit and cars from $22 per day. (☎8341 2727. New cars from $38.50; 2-day min.; $10 flat-rate insurance required.) **Excel Rent-a-Car** has good rates and can arrange one-way rentals for no extra cost, but has a higher insurance deductible for the under-25s. (☎8324 1666. New cars from $40 per day.)

For campervans or motorhomes, **Britz,** 376 Burbridge Rd., Brooklyn Park (☎8234 4701 or 1800 331 454), has two- to six-berth vans (from $126 per day) and one-way rental with unlimited kilometers to all major cities in Australia. Also ask about relocation deals, where you pay as little as $1 per day, plus petrol costs. **Skippy Camper Rentals,** 1297 South Rd., St Mary's (☎8296 2999), has regular campervan rentals (minimum hire 5 days, one-way available) as well as some used camper vans and 4WDs for sale with buy-back schemes available.

BY TAXI. Des's (☎13 10 08), **Diamond** (☎13 24 48), **Yellow** (☎13 22 27), **Adelaide Independent** (☎13 22 11), **Suburban Taxis** (☎13 10 08), and **Access Cabs** (☎1300 360 940) all provide service. Access Cabs is wheelchair-accessible. Cabs are easy to find, and a 15min. ride is usually around $12.

BY BICYCLE. Many city streets have designated cycling lanes. The 40km **Linear Park Bike and Walking Track** provides the biking, jogging, or rollerblading enthusiast with beachside breezes and river views in the beautiful Adelaide foothills. Further information is available at bike shops, including **Elder Park Mountain Bike Hire.** (Behind the Festival Centre. ☎8223 6271. Open M-F 9:15am-5pm, Sa-Su 9:15am-6pm; $16-20 per day, family rates available); **Linear Park Mountain Bike Hire** (☎8223 6953. $23 per day, 20% backpacker discount). Some hostels also rent bikes.

PRACTICAL INFORMATION

TOURIST AND FINANCIAL SERVICES

Tourist Office: South Australian Travel Centre, 18 King William St. (☎1300 655 276; fax 8308 2249; www.southaustralia.com), has well-informed staff. Open M-F 8:30am-5pm, Sa-Su 9am-2pm. **Glenelg Tourist Information Centre,** Foreshore (by the jetty) Glenelg (☎8294 5833). Open M-F 9am-5pm; Sa-Su 10am-4pm.

National Parks Information: Department for Environment, Heritage and Aboriginal Affairs Information Centre, 77 Grenfell St. (☎8204 1910; fax 8204 1919). **Flinders Ranges and Outback Visitor Centre,** 142 Gawler Pl. (☎1800 633 060). Open M-F 8:30am-5:30pm, Sa-Su 10am-4pm.

Travel Agencies: YHA Travel, 135 Waymouth St. (☎8414 3000; fax 8414 3014; travel@yhasa.org.au). Open M-F 9am-6pm, Sa 9am-noon. The knowledgeable staff at **Bunnik Travel,** 122 Pirie St. (☎8359 2295, fax 8359 2305; www.bunnik-travel.com.au.), specialize in Asian and international travel. Open M-Sa 9am-5pm.

Employment: Centrelink, 55 Currie St. (☎9231 9444) or 12 Durham St., Glenelg (☎8202 6700). Valid working visa required. *Advertisers* has classifieds on W and Sa.

Passports and Visas: U.K. Consulate (☎8212 7280). Anyone seeking extensions ($170) to Australian visas should bring proof of funds (e.g. bank statement) and apply at the **Department of Immigration and Ethnic Affairs,** 4th fl. of the Commonwealth Centre, 55 Currie St. (☎13 18 81). Open M-Tu and Th-F 9am-4pm, W 9am-3pm.

Banks: Generally open M-Th 9:30am-4pm, F 9:30am-5pm. **ATMs** all around the city.

Currency Exchange: Almost any time, if you're dressed nicely, at **Adelaide Casino,** North Tce. and Railway Tce., in the same building as the train station. Passport or driver's license required. Open Su-Th 10am-4am, F-Sa 10am-6am. **American Express,** 113 Rundle Mall. Open M-F 8:30am-5:30pm, Sa 9am-noon. **Thomas Cook,** 4 Rundle Mall. Open M-Th 9am-5pm, F 9am-7pm, Sa 10am-4pm, Su 10am-2pm.

LOCAL SERVICES

Bookstores: Europa Bookstore, 238 Rundle St. (☎8223 2289), has both new and secondhand. Open M-Th 10am-6pm, F 10am-9pm, Sa-Su noon-5pm. **Twin Plaza Book Exchange** (☎8223 6309), on Twin St., off Rundle Mall had cheap second-hand books. Open M-Th 9am-5pm, F 9am-7:30pm, Sa 9am-12:30pm. Bookstores line both Rundle St. and Rundle Mall, and some avant-garde (and X-rated) are on Hindley St.

Libraries: State Library of South Australia, North Tce. at the corner of Kintore Ave. (☎8207 7248). Book ahead, by phone or in person, for free 30min. **Internet,** or wait for free 15min. slots. Open M-W, F 9:30am-8pm; Th 9:30am-5pm; Sa-Su noon-5pm. Just around the corner on Kintore St., the **Lending Library of Adelaide** (☎8203 7203) has free 30min. and 1hr. slots with fewer patrons. Open M-F 10am-5pm, Sa-Su 1-5pm.

Ticket Agency: Most cultural and sporting events are booked through **BASS** (☎13 12 46; www.bass.sa.net.au). $2.75 service charge per ticket. Open M-Sa 9am-8pm.

MEDIA AND PUBLICATIONS

Newspapers: *The Advertiser* (90¢).

Nightlife: "The Guide" in the Thursday *Advertiser. Rip it Up* and *db* on the alternative club scene (free). For gay nightlife, try *Gay Times* (free).

Radio: Rock, 107.1FM; News, ABC 831AM; Tourist Info, 88.1FM.

EMERGENCY AND COMMUNICATIONS

Emergency: ☎000.

Women's Hotline: (☎8308 0596 or 1800 188 158; www.wis.sa.gov.au). Open M-F 8am-6pm, Sa 9am-5pm.

Interpreter Services: ☎13 14 50. Free.

Pharmacy: Midnight Pharmacy (☎8231 6339), 11 West Tce. Open M-Sa 7am-midnight, Su 9am-midnight.

Medical Assistance: Royal Adelaide Hospital, North Tce. (☎8222 4000).

Internet Access: See **libraries** (see p. 411). There's also free email at the **Enigma Leisure Lounge and Bar** (see p. 418), if you buy a beer or coffee. Most hostels have kiosks. **Ngapartji,** 211 Rundle St. (☎8232 0839). $5 per 30min., or wait in line for 2 free computers on the street. Open M-Th 8:30am-7pm, F 8:30am-10pm, Sa 10am-10pm, Su noon-7pm. **Talking Cents,** 53 Hindley St. (☎8212 1266). Cheap international calls and faxes. Internet $8 per hr. Open daily 8am-9pm.

Post Office: General Post Office, 141 King William St. (☎8216 2222), at the corner of King William and Franklin St. Open M-F 8am-6pm, Sa 8:30am-noon. Poste Restante can be picked up M-F 7am-5:30pm, Su 9am-1pm. **Postal Code:** 5000.

ACCOMMODATIONS

CITY CENTER

Unless otherwise noted, all listed hostels have 24hr. access, kitchen, laundry facilities, free linen, $10 key deposit, 10am check-out, free luggage storage, and helpful tour and bus booking facilities. All take Mastercard and Visa, though some have minimum charge requirements. Adelaide hostels are rarely full in winter, but it's wise to call a day or two ahead in summer, and a week ahead during festivals. Adelaide has few budget hotel options that are not also pubs, so be prepared for the occasional sound of a pokie machine ringing through your head.

Adelaide Central YHA, 135 Waymouth St. (☎8223 6007). The best backpackers in town, despite the sometimes sterile atmosphere. The 3-floor complex, opened in Dec. 2000, is air-conditioned and clean, with individual reading lights by each bunk. Friendly staff, kitchen, TV, pool tables, and smoking room. Close to the best pubs. Around 250 beds. Book ahead in summer. Internet $1 per 10min. No lockout, no curfew. Check-out 9:30am. Dorms $18.50, non-members $22; doubles $46, with bath $66.

Backpack Oz, 144 Wakefield St. (☎8223 3551 or 1800 633 307), on the corner of Pulteney St. The closest to the action of Rundle St., this 50-bed hostel has a sociable staff. The building was a pub 120 years ago, and is still true to its roots–guests can buy a $2 beer or $1 soft drink whenever the office is open. A/C in all rooms, and sweets on the pillows. Free pickup. Free dinner, usually BBQ, on W. Internet $4 per hr. Reception 6am-10pm. Dorms $17.50; singles $37; twins and doubles $45. 7th night free.

Breckon Inn, 11 Gilbert St. (☎8211 8985; www.breckoninn.com.au), behind the Brecknock Inn. This quiet hostel is a little removed from the action but modern and clean, with a friendly staff. Laundry, work board, TV lounge, free breakfast. 6-bed $17.60; 4-bed $19; singles $33; doubles $48. NOMADS. Wheelchair accessible.

Adelaide City Backpackers Hostel, 239 Franklin St. (☎8212 2668; fax 8212 7974), a few blocks east of the bus station. Plain, sterile, and no-frills dig. Now imagine the opposite, add a courtyard, put chandeliers, paisley carpet, stained glass, and 50 beds into a historic restored home, and call it a hostel. A/C or fans in rooms. Free pickup from bus, train, and plane. Free brekkie and nightly dessert. Su BBQ $3.50-5. Bar. Dorms $18; twins and doubles $48; family rooms available. ISIC/VIP/YHA.

Adelaide Backpacker's Inn, 112 Carrington St. (☎8223 6635 or 1800 247 725; fax 8232 5464; abackinn@tne.net.au), a 10min. walk from Victoria Sq, with 2 buildings opposite each other. Free nightly deserts are never rationed, in 2000 alone the hostel management baked 4000 pies. Free pickup and drop off. Internet $2 per 15min. Huge brekkie, with everything from fry-ups to fruit, $4. Great Su night BBQ $5. Reception 6am-8pm. Dorms $18; singles $33; twins and doubles $48. 7th night free.

Backpack Australia, 128 Grote St. (☎8231 0639 or 1800 804 133; fax 8410 5881). As you leave the bus station, turn your back to the Cannon St. Hostel, walk down the alley half a block and take a right on Grote St. A *Simpsons*-bedecked hangout space and cheap beer hint that this a fun place to be. Cheap meals at pub. Clothesline and

BBQ facilities on rooftop patio. 39 beds and just a few showers, so be prepared to get up early. Rooftop camping $9 per person; dorms $16; doubles $35.

Sunny's Backpacker Hostel, 139 Franklin St. (☎8231 2430 or 1800 225 725 (BAK PAK); fax 8231 0131). Next to the bus station. Small, friendly hostel with 48 beds in crowded bunk rooms, clean communal bathrooms, and a outdoor patio. Female dorm has separate bathroom facilities. Kitchen, pool table, TV lounge. Internet access $2.50 per 30min. Free pancake breakfast (8-9am). Reception M-F 6am-9pm, Sa-Su 6am-12:30pm and 5-8pm. Dorms $18, twins $37, doubles $41; students $2 off. VIP/YHA.

East Park Lodge, 341 Angas St. (☎8223 1228; eastpark@dove.com.au), a 20min. walk from Rundle St. Diverse clientele enjoys airy, newly renovated rooms. Fantastic night-time view of Adelaide Hills and the city. Only pool in town. Create your own didgeridoo for $50. Bike and some auto and motorbike hire. Free pickup. Reception 7am-8pm. Check-out 9:30am. Dorms $16; singles $30; twins and doubles $42. VIP.

The Moors Brecknock, 401 King William St. (☎8231 5467). Above a sleepy Irish pub in the quiet part of town south of the main action, the Moors Brecknock has comfy, clean rooms with fluffy comforters. Rooms have A/C. Free breakfast. Shared bathrooms. Singles $40; doubles $55; extra person $15.

The Austral Hotel, 205 Rundle St. (☎8223 4660). Above a hip pub, which makes it easy to stumble home. Spacious rooms are less well-decorated than the pub downstairs. Slightly more expensive than a hostel, but you get a fantastic location, privacy, and lot of fun. Singles $35; twins and doubles $55; one room with 4 single beds $75.

GLENELG

Visitors preferring the sun over the city might consider basing themselves in Glenelg, a tram ride from Victoria Sq. in the city. Glenelg is relaxing, beachy, and easily accessible to the city, airport, coast, and Adelaide's outlying attractions.

Glenelg Beach Resort, 1 Moseley St. (☎8376 0007 or 1800 066 422; www.glenelgbeachresort.com.au). 1 block from the shore on your right as you walk up Jetty Rd. away from the beach. This full-blown backpackers complex won numerous awards in 1998, 1999, and 2000 for best budget accommodation. Licensed, with a lively bar. Pool tables, small stage for local bands, pleasant common area with videos, and game room. Quiet time is the rule upstairs after 10pm. Rooms are high-ceilinged and clean. Free mountain bikes, free tours Th of the wine valleys; Tu of Adelaide. Pickup and drop off at airport, bus, and train. Internet $2 per 10min. Dorms $18-20, in winter $17-18; singles $50/$40; doubles $60/$50; family rooms $100/$90. VIP.

FOOD

Adelaide claims to have more restaurants per capita than any other city in the country; like much in this city, though, the cost of a chic meal is far lower than its east coast counterpart. **Gouger St.,** in the city center near Victoria Sq., offers a wide range of good, inexpensive ethnic cuisine. **Rundle St.,** in the northeast section of the city, caters to the young hipster set, as students forgo lectures in nearby Adelaide University in favor of strong cups of espresso. Clusters of restaurants can also be found on the upscale **Hutt St.** in southeast Adelaide and North Adelaide's equally upscale **O'Connell St.** The flashy but cheap **Hindley St.,** across King William St. from **Rundle St.,** is the best spot for 24hr. food. **Jetty Rd.** in the beachside suburb of Glenelg also bursts with cafés and ice cream shops. Supermarkets dot the city, particularly on Rundle Mall, Hindley St, and Victoria Sq. Coles **supermarket,** next to Central Market on Grote St., is very near Victoria Sq. (Open M-Th midnight-6pm, F midnight-9pm, Sa midnight-5pm, Su 11am-5pm). In Glenelg, Coles is down Nile St. just off Jetty Rd.

For a real Aussie experience, late-night snackers have visited the "Pie Carts" outside the Adelaide Train Station on North Tce. since 1915. The infamous pie floater—an Aussie meat pie swimming in a thick pea soup and topped with tomato sauce—is a South Australian original, and potentially habit forming.

GOUGER STREET

Gouger St. ("GOO-jer"), a popular spot for sidewalk dining, houses the **Central Market,** with stall after stall of every imaginable edible and free samples to boot. For the most riotous, colorful experience, stop by on F evenings or Sa mornings. (Open Tu and Th 7am-5:30pm, F 7am-9pm, and Sa 7am-3pm.) Open throughout the weekdays, most Gouger St. restaurants are open for lunch on weekends only when the business crowd is around.

Noodles, 119 Gouger St. (☎8231 8177). Serves exactly that: noodles in every shape, form, and color for just $7.20. Comes with generous servings of chicken, beef, seafood, or veggies for a few dollars more. BYO. Open M 5:30pm-late, Tu-F 11:30am-3pm and 5:30pm-late, Sa-Su 5:30pm-late.

Gaucho's, 91 Gouger St. (☎8231 2299). Outstanding Argentinian food in a setting best for those trying to impress their companion. Try the chili-laced oysters *del diabolo* ($12). Open M-F 11:30am-2pm and 5:30-10:30pm, Sa-Su 5:30-10:30pm.

Cafe Fusilli, 68-72 Gouger St. (☎8221 6884). While masquerading as a standard Italian cafe by night, by day Fusilli is a budget traveler's dream. Huge bowls of home-made spaghetti with melt-in-the-mouth garlic bread are just $5. Open daily 10am-7:30pm.

Matsuri, 167 Gouger St. (☎8231 3494). Meaning "festival" in Japanese, Matsuri lives up to its name from a rock garden to a shoes-off rule. Adelaide's best sushi restaurant does come at a price, though. 6-piece packs $3-10. Noodle dishes $7-9. Open M 5:30pm-late, W-Th 5:30pm-late, F noon-2pm and 5:30pm-late, Sa-Su 5:30pm-late.

RUNDLE STREET

Rundle St., one block south of North Tce., flows neatly east from Rundle Mall. It is *the* place to be in Adelaide, day or night, and offers an incredible range of restaurants, cafes, pubs, and holes-in-the-wall.

Amalfi, 29 Frome St. (☎8223 1948), between Rundle St. and North Tce. The plain brick exterior barely hints at the excellent Italian food and fine service inside. This "Pizzeria Ristorante" sneaks onto upscale gourmet dining lists with relatively budget prices. Pasta dishes $12-15. Meat mains $14-19. For many locals, it's all about the pizza (small $10-12, large $15-18). Finish it off with divine tiramisu. Open M-Th 11:30am-3pm and 5:30-11pm, F 11:30am-3pm and 5:30pm-midnight, Sa 5:30-midnight.

Ruby's Cafe, 225b Rundle St. (☎8224 0365). Creative, quality comfort food (most small dishes $9-13, large $13-16) served on chrome tables. Breakfast served all day Su (9am-5pm), with Bloody Marys ($5) topping the menu. Open M-Sa 6:30pm-late, Su 9am-5pm and 6:30pm-late.

Vego and Love'n It!, 240 Rundle St. (☎8223 7411). Just past Mindfield Bookstore, hidden up a set of stairs on the first floor. Large portions of deliciously concocted vegan and vegetarian meals ($6.50-10) make this an extremely popular daytime eating spot. Tofu ice cream $1.50. Juices $2. Open M-F 10am-5pm.

Al Fresco, 260 Rundle St. (☎8223 4589). An Adelaide people-watching landmark and popular at any time of the day or well into the night, Al Fresco serves a tempting range of Italian cakes, focaccia, dynamite coffee, and the best *gelato* in the city (small $2.75). Pick up a light meal in minutes or linger over a latte for hours. Open daily 6:30am- "hmm...maybe 2 or 3am."

THE BEST OF THE REST

The rest of the city is a melange of cafes, pubs, and posh restaurants. Many downtown pubs offer cheap meals.

The Gilbert Place Pancake House (☎8211 7912). Off King William St., between Currie and Hindley St. Turn into the alley called Gilbert Place and walk to the end. In a city that shuts down early, a sign reading "this door will never close" (literally) is a welcome sight for hungry eyes. Fanciful $7-9 creations (Jamaican Banana, Ham

Steak and Pineapple, Bavarian Apple) and Tu $5 all-you-can-eat specials make this place stand out. 24hr.

Quiet Waters BYO, 75 Hindley St. (☎8231 3637). Large range of vegetarian dishes for those disgruntled with a largely meat-eating state. Open daily noon-2pm and 5:30-9pm.

Lizard Lounge, 172a Hutt St. (☎8237 0210). This small cafe and its exciting menu are a mouthful of the utmost fun. Coffee, tea, and hot chocolate are not cheap ($4-6) but you're paying for atmosphere. Liqueur coffees ($6.50) are killer. Light snacks and mind-boggling desserts ($6-9) add to the revelry. Open M-Sa 7pm-late.

SIGHTS

It's easy to spend a day indulging cultural cravings without tiring your legs or opening your wallet. Adelaide's sights and museums are all located along (or just off) North Tce., the city's cultural boulevard, and almost all free.

TANDANYA—NATIONAL ABORIGINAL CULTURAL INSTITUTE. The first major Aboriginal multi-arts complex in Australia and a good place to begin your education in Australian indigenous culture—the museum is nothing short of fascinating. The gift shop stocks a broad range of Aboriginal arts and crafts. *(253 Grenfell St. At the corner of East Tce. on the city loop bus route. ☎8224 3200. Open daily 10am-5pm. $4, concessions $3. Guided tours and talks by appointment. Didgeridoo performances M-Th and Sa-Su at noon; Torres Straights Islander dance F noon.)*

SOUTH AUSTRALIAN MUSEUM. This gracious building, committed to educating visitors for free, holds huge whale skeletons, native Australian animal displays, rocks and minerals, and even an Egyptian mummy. It is renowned for having the largest collection of Aboriginal artifacts in the world. *(Next to the State Library, North Tce. ☎8207 7500, tour info 8293 5666. Open daily 10am-5pm. Free. Free tours of the main body of the museum W 2pm, Sa-Su 2 and 3pm. Tours of the Aboriginal Culture Gallery daily 11:30am, 12:30, and 1:30pm; $10, concessions $7. Wheelchair accessible.)*

ART GALLERY OF SOUTH AUSTRALIA. This gallery showcases Australian, Asian, and European prints, paintings, sculpture, and decorative arts, as well as lots of Southeast Asian ceramics. The collection of Australian art, arranged chronologically by room and ending with a fine 20th-century collection, is especially impressive. There is a charge for the eclectic temporary exhibitions in the basement. *(North Tce near Pulteney St. ☎8207 7000; www.artgallery.sa.gov.au. Open daily 10am-5pm. Free. Free tours: 1hr.; M-F 11am and 1pm, Sa-Su 11am and 3pm. Wheelchair accessible.)*

MIGRATION MUSEUM. Combining history, biography, and oral storytelling to explain patterns of immigration that have shaped South Australian society, the museum's graphic stories and photographs make for an excellent, if somewhat sobering, visit. *(82 Kintore Ave. Off North Tce., behind the state library. ☎8207 7580. Open M-F 10am-5pm, Sa-Su 1-5pm. Free, donations welcome. 1hr. tour $4.50; book in advance.)*

ADELAIDE BOTANIC GARDENS. Acres of beautifully landscaped grounds surround heritage buildings, a small lake with black swans, and meandering walkways. The grounds are lush and peaceful, and contain the **Australian Arboretum** and the **Yarrabee Art Gallery. The Bicentennial Conservatory,** the largest glasshouse in the Southern Hemisphere, and the neighboring rose gardens, are the only sections with an entrance fee. Inside the conservatory, the computer-controlled atmosphere simulates a tropical rainforest, complete with misty rain. *(North Tce. ☎8228 2311. Gardens open M-F 8am, Sa-Su 9am, close at sunset. Museum of Economic Botany open M-Th 11am-3pm, Su noon-4pm. Free. Conservatory open daily 10am-4pm; $3, concessions $1.50. Free garden tours leave from the restaurant-kiosk Tu, F, and Su 10:30am.)*

THE BRADMAN COLLECTION. Those expecting a small art gallery will be surprised by the true nature of Don Bradman's fame. Room after room of willow bats, leather balls, and medals galore pay homage to Australia's unofficial national religion—cricket—and one of its greatest figures. *(State Library, North Tce., near Kintore Ave. ☎8207 7200. Open M-F 10am-5pm, Sa-Su noon-5pm. $3, concessions $2.)*

ADELAIDE ZOO. Now home to more than 1300 animals, the more than 100-year old zoo still has some Victorian buildings, and some of the animal enclosures look as though Queen Victoria herself could have visited them. The Southeast Asian rainforest, the sea lions, and the children's feeding area zoo are some of the most popular exhibits. *(Frome Rd. Less than 2km north of the city in the northern Parkland area, and a 15min. walk from North Tce. through the Botanic Gardens or down Frome Rd. Popeye boats from the Festival Centre also run to and from the zoo in summer. ☎8267 3255. Open daily 9:30am-5pm. $13, concessions $11, children $8. Guided tours daily 11am and 2pm.)*

ADELAIDE GAOL. The jail was opened in 1841 and closed for prisoners in 1988. Forty-nine prisoners were executed here, but the displays focus on the plight of female inmates and the daily activities of a prisoner—smoking, mostly. *(18 Gaol Rd., Thebarton. A moderate walk just northeast of the city or 5min. ride to Stop 1 on bus #151, 153, 286 or 287 from North Tce. ☎8231 4062. Open M-F 11am-4pm. $8, concessions $5.50, children $4.50. Guided tours Su 11am-3:30pm.)*

ADELAIDE-HIMEJI GARDEN. This garden offers a good look into the art of the Japanese garden, and begins to explain the deep religious and spiritual significance of horticulture to the Japanese. *(South Tce., east of Pulteney Rd. ☎8203 7483. Open daily 8am to 1hr. before sunset.)*

ST. PETER'S CATHEDRAL. The mother of all churches in this city of churches. Built between 1869 and 1904, this Anglican cathedral towers over North Adelaide and swings the "heaviest and finest" bells in the Southern Hemisphere. *(King William St. North of the city; a 10min. walk from North Tce. up over the river and past the cricket oval. ☎8267 4551. Open daily 9am-4pm. Free. Tours W 11am and Su 3pm. Services daily at 8:30am and Su 8, 10:30am, and 7pm.)*

CARRICK HILL. This Tudor mansion houses a private art collection surrounded by almost 40 hectares of beautifully tended English gardens and native bush. Summer evening outdoor theater here is delightful, though a taxi is the only return transport. *(46 Carrick Hill Dr., Springfield. A 10min. drive from the city center, at the southern end of Fullarton Rd.; or 25min. by bus #171 from King William St. Get off at stop #16 and walk 500m to the main gates on the left. ☎8379 3886. Open W-Su 10am-5pm. $8, concessions $6.)*

HAIGH'S CHOCOLATES VISITORS CENTRE. Australia's oldest chocolate maker, Haigh's has been churning since 1915. Known as the original creator of the hugely popular chocolate Easter Bilby, an effort to displace the tyrannical Easter Bunny (the bilby, a type of bandicoot, is a native endangered species; the rabbit is an introduced pest). Without being on a tour, you can't see much. *(154 Greenhill Rd. One block south of South Tce. and just east of Pulteney Rd. ☎8271 3770. Book ahead Open M-F 8:30am-5:30pm, Sa 9:30am-4:45pm. Free guided tours with tastings M-Sa 1:30 and 2:30pm.)*

ACTIVITIES

To appreciate the full range of outdoor activities available, travelers should visit the numerous outdoor goods stores on Rundle St.

MOUNTAIN BIKING. Rolling On Mountain Bike Tours has guided day tours around Adelaide, its forests and vineyards, or the Barossa Valley. It's a good choice even for those without much riding experience—trails are fairly flat and there's a backup vehicle if you get tired. *(☎8358 2401. $79-99.* *Also see **By Bicycle,** p. 410.)*

SNOW AND ICE. At **Mt. Thebarton,** you can ski, snowboard, sled, or skate year-round on South Australia's only real "Permasnow." OK, it's all indoors and the ski run is actually a 150m bunny hill. But where else can you ski for $9? Friday and Saturday nights are "Fridge nights" with DJs and lights. *(23 East Tce., Thebarton. 5min. by bus #151, 153, 286 or 287 to stop 2 from North Tce.; or a 15min. walk from the northwest of the city. ☎8352 7977. Open M noon-4pm, Tu and Th 10am-4pm, W and F 10am-4pm and 7:30-10pm, Sa-Su 12:30-4pm and 7:30-10pm. Skiing or boarding $9 per hr.; equipment $5.50-10. Skating $8.50; skates $2.25.)*

ABSEILING, ROCK CLIMBING, AND SPELUNKING. Rock Solid Adventure offers abseiling, rock climbing, and a two-night caving trip to Naracoorte Conservation Park. *(☎8322 8975. Abseiling and rock-climbing 4hr. $64 or 5hr. $71; spelunking $210.)*

DIVING. Glenelg Scuba Diving runs daily boat dives to Adelaide's wrecks and reefs, and offers a four-day PADI certification class. *(☎8294 7744. Dives from $33; equipment rental available. 4-5 day PADI class $295-345.)*

SKYDIVING. S. A. Skydiving is pleased to help you with a tandem jump out of a plane, free fall for 40sec., and a fleetly float to earth. They also offer a full-day solo jump course, just for out-of-towners. *(☎8272 7888. Tandem $285, solo $385.)*

SWIMMING. The **Adelaide Aquatic Centre,** Jeffcott Rd., North Adelaide, is a huge, indoor complex with a 50m pool, a diving and water polo area, and small, shallow pools surrounded by potted trees. *(30min. walk from North Tce. up King William St.; or take bus #231, 233, 235, or 237 from Victoria Sq., or from stop Z3 in front of the Festival Centre on King William St. ☎8344 4411. Pools open daily 5am-10pm; gym M-F 6am-10pm, Sa 6am-6pm, Su 9am-5pm. $4.95, concessions $3.50. Gym fees $8.40, concessions $5.20)*

SPECTATOR SPORTS. International and interstate cricket (Oct.-Mar.); Australian Rules Football (mostly on Sa); soccer, rugby and rugby union (Apr.-Sept.) are played at the **Adelaide Oval.** "Cricket's Greatest Batsman," the late Sir Donald Bradman, is key to the 2½hr. tour and to the South Australian psyche. *(Just north of the city along King William Rd. ☎8300 3800. Tours Tu, Th at 10am, Su at 2pm, except on match days. $5. Museum open Tu, Th 10am-1pm. $2. Tickets and schedules at any BASS outlet, ☎13 12 46.)*

BEACHIN' IT. Don't miss the beach suburb of **Glenelg,** with its lovely swimming beach and cafe culture. **Inline skates** can be hired at the main Glenelg beach on summer weekends, and there's often free outdoor entertainment. During the summer, the smooth sand of Glenelg's Holdfast Bay is also a great spot to try your hand at **beach volleyball** or **parasailing.** *(☎0411 19 16 53; from $45 per person.)*

ENTERTAINMENT

A two-minute walk north on King William St. from its intersection with North Tce. at Parliament House will bring you to the huge, white **Adelaide Festival Centre** (☎8216 8600). Situated on the Torrens River, this is the focus of Adelaide's cultural life, with a performance on most nights. Throughout the summer and particularly on weekend afternoons, a few outdoor theater events and concerts are free and open to the public. Pick up a calendar of events from inside the Festival Centre complex or call BASS (☎13 12 46). The **State Opera of South Australia** (☎8226 4790; www.saopera.sa.gov.au), the **Adelaide Symphony Orchestra** (☎8343 4111), and the **State Theatre Company of South Australia** (☎8231 5151; www.statetheatre.sa.com.au) all perform at the Festival Centre; it's also the place for big-name traveling musicals and theater performances. Student rush tickets are sometimes available. **Elder Hall,** North Tce., part of the University of Adelaide, has concerts of early music, as well as some chamber performances by the Adelaide Symphony. (☎8303 5925. Lunch hr. concerts F 1:10-2pm; $2.)

Adelaide's most accessible **alternative cinemas,** both on Rundle St., are the **Palace Eastend** (☎8232 3434) and **NOVA** (☎8223 6333). **Mercury Cinema,** 13 Morphett St. (☎8410 0979; www.mrc.org.au), just off Hindley St., has super-artsy fare. Tuesday night is usually discount night at movie theaters across Australia. The four-story-tall **IMAX Theatre,** in Vaughan Pl. off the east end of Rundle St., has in-your-face movies on the hour. (☎8227 0075; www.imax.com.au. Open daily 10am-10pm. 2-D movies $14.50, concessions $11.50, children $9.50; 3-D movies a dollar more.) Mid-December through mid-February brings **Cinema in the Botanic Gardens,** outdoor showings of popular and classic movies. (7:30pm; $13, concessions $10, children $8.50. Tickets at gate or through BASS ☎13 12 46.)

FESTIVALS

WOMADelaide, an enormously successful **WO**rld **M**usic **A**rt and **D**ance festival, will celebrate its 10th anniversary in mid-February 2002. **Arts Project Australia** runs the two-day show in Botanic Park, with dozens of acts from dozens of countries and workshops on six stages, while a "global village" sells international food and crafts. All walks of life come to enjoy this can't miss festival. If you're planning on visiting Adelaide at this time, make sure to book lodging well in advance. (☎8271 9905. Weekend tickets $115, students and concessions $95; daily ticket prices from $45.) **The Feast** (late Oct. to mid-Nov.) is Adelaide's annual lesbian and gay festival, with three weeks of masquerades, parties, and concerts (☎8231 2155).

A biennial event next occurring Mar. 1-10, 2002, the **Adelaide Festival of Arts** (☎8216 4444; www.adelaidefestival.org.au) is considered one of the world's best arts festivals. This year's multi-media exploration, guided by Peter Sellars, focuses on truth and reconciliation, cultural diversity and environmental sustainability. Overlapping with the Adelaide Festival, the **Adelaide Fringe Festival** (☎8100 2000) features artists out of the mainstream.

NIGHTLIFE

In this "family" city, most areas shut down promptly after dinner. If you know where to look, however, Adelaide maintains a thriving nightlife into the wee hours. The **East End,** which, very roughly, includes Rundle St. east of the mall, Pulteney St., and Pirie St., is the center of Adelaide's "pretty" scene. Bouncers here are very mindful of the **dress code** for dance clubs, and enforce it unflinchingly. The cafe scene dominates this area, as uni students and others drink schooners and smoke cigarettes on the sidewalk. **Hindley St.** is home to many X-rated venues and the like, as well as numerous fly-by-night dance clubs. However, Rundle Mall itself, next to Hindley St., is quiet at night. For nightlife info, see **Media and Publications,** p. 411.

PUBS

Grace Emily, 232 Waymouth St. (☎8231 5500). The chillest bar in Adelaide, for the moment, is not on Rundle or Hindley, but here on Waymouth St. Decor is 1950s viewed through a kaleidoscope. Live music happens several times per week, there are no pokies, and everyone is laid-back. Open daily 4pm-late.

The Cumberland, 205 Waymouth St. (☎8231 3577). One of two great bars in an otherwise sleepy district, the Grace Emily's closest neighbor is no less hip but attracts a glossier crowd. Leafy, intimate beer garden, sofa-crash room, black-clad bouncers, and beautiful people. Open daily 5pm-2am.

Austral, 205 Rundle St. (☎8223 4660). Known affectionately by locals as the "Nostril," this bar draws a young crowd. Live bands in the beer garden every F and Sa. Encourages the fine art of DJ-ing by hosting one every night Su-Th. If there's nothing happening here, there's probably nothing happening in town. Open daily until "oh, 1 or 2ish."

P.J. O'Brien's, 14 East Tce. (☎8232 5111). Adelaide's resident Irish pub, P.J.'s vast interior is packed weekend nights with a young-20s crowd. Plenty of backpackers but plenty of Adelaide natives too. Located near Rundle St., right in Adelaide's nexus of nighttime activity. Open daily noon-late.

Edinburgh Castle, 233 Currie St. (☎8410 1211). Owned by a gay couple with a mainly gay male clientele. Open M-Th 11am-midnight, F-Sa 11am-1am, Su 2pm-midnight.

NIGHTCLUBS

Enigma Leisure Lounge and Bar, 173 Hindley St. (☎8212 2313). Hip, intimate multifunctional hangout is a cafe by day and a bar/club by night. Downstairs, purple-lit leather couches and free Internet terminals in addition to the usual complement of pool table and dart board. Upstairs at the club, W is drag night and Th is reggae. Fluffiest toilet paper a budget traveler will see in Adelaide. Open M-Tu 11:30am-5pm, W-Th 11:30am-5pm and 8pm-late, F 11:30am-late, Sa 8pm-late. Cover for club $6-8.

Cargo Club, 213 Hindley St. (☎8231 2327). One of Adelaide's funkier clubs and a strong holdout from recycled Top-40 tunes. Live music ranges from jazz to African and draws a crowd that can't decide whether it is trendy or alternative. DJ with dance music on W. Doors open at 10pm. Cover around $8.

Heaven II, 7 West Tce. (☎8211 8533). This bright purple building at the corner of North and West Tce. provides a celestial vision of sorts, if your idea of the afterlife is a hedonistic mix of alcohol, dance music, lycra, and nubile 20-somethings. Features DJs, local bands, and internationally renowned acts. Once a month Heaven floods with soap suds during the foam party. Heaven's gates open between 8-10pm W-Su. There's almost always a line F-Sa and St. Peter can be moody. Cover usually $7-10.

The Planet, 77 Pirie St. (☎8359 2797). If you've come to the land down undah looking for tainted love or karma chameleons, tell your hostelmates to wake you up before they go, go to "Greed," this club's hugely popular Friday tribute to the 80s. W is "Planet Disco," complete with 70s outfits, and Sa means house music and tightly packed, writhing young bodies. An upstairs viewing area can be a welcome escape. Cover $6-9.

Disco, 69 Light Sq. (☎8212 6969). Promises only one thing: to groove all year long. Open F 10pm-late, Sa 10pm-7am, Su 10pm-late. Cover $8.

DAYTRIPS FROM ADELAIDE

PORT ADELAIDE. Port Adelaide makes the perfect Sunday daytrip. **Fisherman's Wharf** (☎8341 2040), Lighthouse Sq, Commercial Rd. is the place to be Sundays 8am-5pm and Mondays 9am-5pm. At this large indoor market you can get anything from CDs to seafood. Also on Sundays, $2 **river cruises** (1¾hr.)—with occasional dolphin sightings—depart from the wharf. To reach Port Adelaide take bus #151 or 153 from North Tce. opposite Parliament house, and get off at stop #40 (about 30min.). Alternatively, the Outer Harbor railway line links the port and the North Tce. railway station (20min., every 30min. M-F 9am-midnight). The wharf is a short walk from Port Adelaide Railway Station or from bus stop #40.

SOUTHERN BEACHES. The beaches on the western Fleurieu Peninsula, with high cliffs, occasional dolphin sightings, miles of clean sand, prime sunsets, and few people, should not be missed. Closest to Adelaide, **Christies Beach** has a park and many small shops along Beach Rd. For **snorkelers** or **divers,** the **Port Noarlunga Aquatic Reserve** is a shallow reef accessible from the end of the jetty. South again, **Seaford** has a walking and biking track along the cliffs. At the swimming beach **Moana,** cars can park close to the water. **Maslin Beach,** directly west of McLaren Vale, was Australia's first "unclad" beach and still hosts the **Nude Olympics** one day each January. Farthest south, **Aldinga Beach** is convenient to Willunga. To hit the beaches via public transportation, take the Noarlunga line **train** from Adelaide Railway Station (North Tce.) to Noarlunga. Transfer to **bus** #741 at the Noarlunga Interchange for **Maslin, Christies,** or **Moana Beach.** For **Port Noarlunga,** take bus #741, 742, or 745. Full-day ticket $5.60 for both train and bus or $2.90 for each.

NEAR ADELAIDE

ADELAIDE HILLS

In a state where much of the terrain is unfriendly at best, the Adelaide Hills region provides a haven of lush greenery. Created by one of the few natural water catchment areas, the Hills are protected by the government and therefore remain a rural playground only 15min. from Adelaide, unsullied by suburbanization. The area has become renowned for conservation efforts such as those in Warrawong Sanctuary. Huge expanses of national park surround Mt. Lofty, broken up by wineries, orchards, conservation lands, and picturesque hamlets from a gentler, slower past.

Despite their seclusion, the various points of interest in the Hills are easy to travel between. Much of the Adelaide Hills is a 15-40min. drive east from the Adelaide city center, along Hwy. 1. The Hills are accessible by public transportation ($1.70). Call the public transport **info line** (☎8210 1000) for and timetables. Most buses are considered part of the Adelaide system and charge the same fares (see p. 409). Bus #163 and 163F, leaving from Grenfell St., are the two main routes to the Hills; #165, 165F, 166, 166F, and 823 will also get you there. **Gray Line** runs a "taste of the Adelaide Hills" **tour** on Tu and Sa 9:30am-5:30pm. (☎8374 1270 or 1800 634 724. $49.) The **Adelaide Hills Visitor Information Centre** is at 41 Main St., Hahndorf. (☎8388 1185 or 1800 353 323; www.visitadelaidehills.com. Open daily 9am-5pm.)

MOUNT LOFTY. The biggest attraction in the Adelaide Hills is Mt. Lofty, visited by 500,000 people annually and part of Cleland Conservation Park. Take the South Eastern Fwy. out of the city, exit at Crafers, and follow the signs (20-25min.). The summit has spectacular views of the city, especially at night, and an **Info Centre** with extensive info about hikes in the surrounding Cleland Conservation Park. (☎8370 1054. Open daily 9am-5pm.) **Mt. Lofty Botanic Gardens** is about 30min. from Adelaide and accessible by public transport. (☎8228 2311. Open M-F 9am-4pm, Sa-Su 10am-5pm.) The limited-access **Mt. Lofty YHA,** 20km from Adelaide, is an easy choice for an overnight in the Adelaide Hills, especially for those seeking seclusion. The 16-bed stone cottage was built in 1880 (and rebuilt after the 1983 bushfires), right in Cleland Conservation Park, on the Heysen Trail and near walking trails. It's an excellent getaway, especially in summer. (Pick up the key from the rangers at the conservation park. ☎8231 5583, afterhours 8223 6007. Beds $16.50.)

STIRLING. Stirling is the first town off the highway from Adelaide. Endowed with a backpackers, a vast **supermarket,** and many pleasant **cafes,** it could be a good spot to stop overnight. The **Mount Lofty Railway Station**, 2 Sturt Valley Rd., has comfy beds in an 1883 railway building. Breakfast and linen included. (☎8339 7400; www.mlrs.com.au. Free Internet. Dorms $20; singles $35; doubles $45-50.) Stirling hosts the area's library, with free **Internet** access. (☎8408 0420. Open Tu-W and F 10am-6pm, Th 1-8pm, Sa 9am-2pm.)

ALDGATE. Less touristed than Hahndorf and more secluded than Stirling, Aldgate is one of the best towns to use as a base for exploring the Hills, mainly because it's the closest town to the Warrawong Sanctuary. Buses #163, 163F and TL9 run through here from Adelaide. The town also has one of the best budget accommodations you'll find in South Australia at **Geoff and Hazel's,** 19 Kingsland Rd. The tiny, eco-friendly hotel, set among dappled trees, is the perfect antidote to crowded hostels. The stellar owners will happily guide you (or perhaps even drive you) around the Hills, and it's the closest budget accommodation to the Warrawong Sanctuary. Balcony, cosy lounge room and kitchen, log fire, hammocks, and friendly chickens are all here. (☎8339 8360. Internet $2 per hr. Breakfast and linen included. Book ahead. Singles $45; doubles $55.) The town has a good locals pub, the **Aldgate Pump Hotel,** and a **supermarket.** (Open M-F 7:30am-6pm, Sa 8am-6pm.)

WARRAWONG SANCTUARY AND CLELAND PARK. The Adelaide Hills area has recently become famous for its conservation efforts, thanks largely to one man who recreated Australia's pre-colonization habitat at the **Warrawong Sanctuary,** Stock Road, Mylor. Over 15 years ago, one-time professor John Wamsley decided to build an elaborate fence to keep out cats, foxes, and other feral animals introduced to the Australian continent by European immigrants. Now all manner of native Australian species, virtually extinct elsewhere, flourish here: bettongs, wallabies, rainbow parrots, and short-nosed bandicoots all call this place home. Wamsley's unorthodox methods of conservation have been quite controversial, but wildly successful, leading to a public floating of the company on the stockmarket, and the development of several further locations across the country. Wamsley eventually aims to return 1% of Australia's land to the original habitat. (☎8370 9197; www.warrawong.com. Admission only by guided walks at dusk or dawn; $19.50, children $13. Cabins and restaurant on site.) The nearby **Cleland Conserva-**

tion Park (☎8339 2444) is a more traditional wildlife sanctuary; inside you can pet the fuzzy koalas all day at the **Wildlife Park.** (Open daily 9:30am-5pm. $8, concessions $6.) Also within the park, **Aboriginal Cultural Guided Tours** take place on Yurridla Trail. (☎8339 2769. W and Su 11am and 1:30pm.) The closest accommodation to Cleland, **Fuzzies Farm,** Colonial Dr., Norton Summit, offers a glimpse of post-industrial society in a co-op environment. (☎8390 1111. 1 week minimum stay. Rates include meals. Book ahead. $88 per week, plus chores.)

HAHNDORF. The most touristed village in Adelaide Hills was originally settled by German Lutherans in 1839, fleeing persecution from the King of Prussia. Most businesses in town are stretched out along Main St., including the area's **Visitor Information Centre** (see **Practical Information,** p. 411) and **post office,** 73 Main St. Just east of town, find **The Cedars: Hans Heysen House,** Heysen Rd., which was the home of Australian landscape watercolor artist Hans Heysen (1877-1963) and has been preserved in its original state. (☎8388 7277. Open M-F, Su. $5. 3 tours per day.) Masterpieces of the future are in progress at the **Hahndorf Academy,** 68 Main St. The academy includes an art gallery (both contemporary and historical), German migration museum, and a studio; much of Heysen's own stunning collection, stolen in 1995, is now back on show. (☎8388 7250. Open M-Sa 10am-5pm, Su noon-5pm.) The **Bamberg Cafe,** 81 Main St., stands out among the plethora of German eateries. (☎8388 1797. Open W-Su noon-9pm.)

FLEURIEU PENINSULA

The Fleurieu Peninsula ("FLOOR-ee-oh") stretches southeast from Adelaide, encompassing rolling hills and sweeping valleys. The peninsula holds the luscious vineyards of McLaren Vale, miles of coastline that include some of the best beaches of South Australia, as well as perfect seaside towns like Port Elliot. Those with cars will be entranced by the beautiful drives around these quiet hills.

TOURS OF THE FLEURIEU

Bee-init Tours operates a popular tour from Adelaide, with stops at two wineries in McLaren Vale, a train ride, and an evening Granite Island Little Penguin tour. (☎8332 1401. Aug.-June M, Th, and Sa 2:30pm. $48, children $31.) **Camel Winery Tours,** based in McLaren Flat, offers a one-day winery safari on camelback with up to seven winery visits and lunch included. (☎8383 0488. Starts at 10:30am. $80.) **Just Cruisin Chauffeur Car** (☎8383 0529) provides the opportunity to tour the peninsula in a 1962 Cadillac Fleetwood, highlighting wineries, nature, galleries, or the history of the region. The **Glenelg Beach Resort** (see p. 413) has fun, weekly tours from Adelaide to McLaren Vale.

MCLAREN VALE ☎08

Just 45min. (37km) south of Adelaide, the idyllic, sleepy set of vineyards in McLaren Vale (pop. 2000) sit in the grassy inland knolls of the Fleurieu Peninsula. The town is comprised of over 45 wineries—the majority of which are still family-owned, operate cellar door sales, and process world-class wines.

Premier Stateliner (☎8415 5555) comes through town from the Adelaide central **bus station** (45min., 1-3 per day, $6). Getting around without a car in McLaren Vale may be a problem. A better option is a tour of the Fleurieu out of Adelaide (see above). The best way to get to McLaren Vale is with a group of friends, a car, and a **designated driver.** The Australian police take drink driving seriously; it is not uncommon to find Random Breath Testing Units (known as Breathos) on main roads to and from wine regions. To get to McLaren, drive out of Adelaide on **Main South Rd.** Follow Hwy. A13 off of Main South Rd. on to Victor Harbor Rd., and bear left onto Main Rd., McLaren Vale's main drag. **McLaren Vale and Fleurieu Visitor Centre,** on the left and impossible to miss, offers a map of the wineries and a small bistro. (☎8323 9944; fax 8323 9949. Open daily 10am-5pm.) The road from the visitor centre south to **Willunga** is laden with wineries at every turn. **McLaren Flat,** on Kangarilla Rd., 3km east of McLaren Vale, is the center of the wine-producing area.

The majority of accommodations are old-world B&Bs at new world prices; most budget travelers just make the area a daytrip from Adelaide. There are options, however, for the intrepid traveler willing to venture a few minutes away from McLaren Vale. In **Willunga,** down Willunga or Victor Harbor Rd. from McLaren Vale, the **Willunga Hotel,** on High St., offers clean, classic pub-hotel rooms in a building dating from 1868 and generous two-course counter meals for $18. (☎8556 2135. Breakfast included. $30 per person.) Of the peninsula's many caravan parks, the **McLaren Vale Lakeside Caravan Park,** Field St., is most conveniently located for wine tasting trips. Amenities include a swimming pool, spa, and tennis courts situated in an absolutely gorgeous setting. (☎8323 9255. Sites $14, powered $17.50; vans with bath from $40.)

Most wineries have picnic grounds and some offer tables in idyllic settings. Every square centimeter of wall at **McLaren Vale Bakery** (☎8323 7476), McLaren Vale Mallon Main Rd., is plastered with awards and newspaper clippings extolling the bakery's fabulous pies. The Wine Pie, Lamb Piquant Pie, and Chicken Champagne Pie are just some of the national winners. The **Flowers Field Cafe,** on Main Rd. on the way to Willunga, marked by an enormous, painted set of pansies, has cheap comfort food and a relaxing environment. (Open Tu-Su 9:30am-5pm.)

NEAR MCLAREN VALE: WINERIES

McLaren Vale is the best-known wine area in South Australia after the Barossa Valley. The majority of the 45 wineries are small and family-owned, with notable exceptions including **Hardy's, Andrew Garret, Middlebrook,** and **Seaview.** Pick up a map from the Visitor Centre and let your taste buds take the lead. For more information on vineyard touring see p. 434.

Wirra Wirra Vineyards (☎8323 8414), on McMurtrie Rd. When you see the fence made from giant tree trunks you'll know you've arrived; once you've tasted the "Church Block Red," you won't want to leave. Open M-Sa 10am-5pm, Su 11am-5pm.

Hamilton Fine Wines (☎8523 8211), on Main Rd. One of the biggest producers in the McLaren region, run by a family dynasty. The airy cellar door is on the road toward Willunga. Open M-F 10am-5pm, Sa-Su 11am-5pm.

Dennis of McLaren Vale (☎8323 8665), on Kangarilla Rd. Fancy a drop of hot spiced mead, the oldest alcoholic beverage in recorded history? Made from fermented honey and scented with cloves. Open M-F 10am-5pm, Sa-Su 11am-5pm.

Marienberg Wines, 2 Chalk Hill Rd. (☎8323 9666). Ursula Pridham, Australia's first female winemaker, founded this winery in 1966. Open daily 10am-5pm.

Hardy's Tintara (☎8323 9185), on Main Rd. When the first vines were planted here in 1838, the vintner probably never imagined that more than 160 years later, this would be the largest winery in the area. Reds, whites, sparkling wines, ports, and brandy are all made here. Self-guided winery tours are available. Open daily 10am-5pm.

COORONG NATIONAL PARK

As the Murray River hits the sea, huge piles of clean sand have piled up along the coast and created the narrow Younghusband Peninsula, which shelters the shallow lagoon system of Coorong National Park. The rich estuarine environment is home to the largest permanent breeding colony of Australian pelicans, along with more than 230 other species of water birds. The park is listed in international environmental agreements as being of world significance, and was even named in *Outdoor* magazine's list of Australia's top ten beaches. The small, idyllic beach towns of Goolwa, Middleton, and Port Elliot are at the top of the peninsula.

TRANSPORTATION. Premier Stateliner (☎8415 5555) runs from Adelaide to Goolwa via McLaren Vale, Victor Harbor, Port Elliot, and Middleton (2hr., 1-3 per day, $14). For Goolwa **taxis,** call 8552 8222. The **Signal Point (River Murray) Interpretive Centre,** on The Wharf in Goolwa, has tourist info on the town and the district. (☎8555 3488. Open daily 9am-5pm.)

ACCOMMODATIONS. Permits are required for **camping** in the Coorong and are available at **Signal Point Interpretive Centre,** halfway down the peninsula. Otherwise, the nearby beach town of Port Elliot provides the best options for budget accommodation. **Arnella by the Sea (YHA),** 28 North Tce., can sleep up to 20 people in beautiful, early Australian-style rooms in a historic building. They also coordinate boat tours of the park. (☎8554 3611 or 1800 066 297; narnu@bigpond.com. Reception daily 8am-noon and 4-8pm. Dorms $20, non-members $22; singles $30/$33; twins and doubles $50/$55; family rooms $60/$66.) In Port Elliot, between Victor Harbor and Goolwa, **Port Elliot Caravan and Tourist Park** is poised right on the gorgeous beach of Horseshoe Bay. (☎8554 2134; fax 8554 3454. Sites for 2 $15, powered $17.50, powered beachfront sites $20.50; cabins for 2 with bath $52.50.)

ACTIVITIES. While primarily comprised of wetlands and waterways, the National Park includes almost 46,000 hectares of **sand dunes.** The dunes of the **Younghusband Peninsula** shelter a series of lagoons more than 100km long. For a budget snack, dig into the sand at the ocean's edge to find **cockles,** which can be pried open and eaten raw. Several tours highlighting the area's birdlife operate from Goolwa, including **Coorong Cruises.** (☎8555 1133; peternjo@esc.net.au. Departs 8:50am, returns 5pm. $75, children $45.) **The Spirit of the Coorong** has more ecologically-minded tours with the option of a pick-up in Adelaide. (☎8555 2203 or 1800 442 203. Half-day $53.50, children $37; full-day $70/$46.) **The Coorong Experience** is an overnight tour accommodating special interests in bushwalking, photography, or Aboriginal culture. (☎8555 2222. Maximum 8 people.)

Much of the Princes Highway is accessible by 2WD, but with a 4WD there are points to cross over to the peninsula itself. As you head south, **Parnka Point,** just west of Magrath Flat, has spectacular views of the lagoon. **Jacks Point,** 24km further south, provides a shelter and binoculars to observe the pelicans nest on islands in the lagoon. Stock up on gas and snacks at the hamlet of **Salt Creek.** In summer 4WDs can pass over at the **Tea Tree Crossing,** just south of Salt Creek. Get supplies in utilitarian **Kingston SE** at the southern tip of the park.

The hands-on **Signal Point (River Murray) Interpretive Centre,** on The Wharf in Goolwa, provides fascinating insights into the Aboriginal history and environment of the Murray River Basin, which encompasses about a third of Australia's land. The Murray River provides South Australia with about 75% of its water supply, and is currently battling with the pollution. (☎8555 3488. $5.50, concessions $4.40, children $2.75. Open daily 9am-5pm, last entrance 4pm.)

VICTOR HARBOR ☎08

Sheltered from the immense Southern Ocean by the sands of Encounter Bay, the seaside town of Victor Harbor (pop. 4600) is neither totally asleep nor wide awake, but it is completely on the beaten track. As the summer residence of South Australia's colonial governors, tourists have been streaming there ever since. Victor Harbor is now both an almost-painfully romantic seaside spot and a decent base for surfing in Encounter Bay. Besides the little penguin colony on nearby Granite Island, the main draw is its summer temperature, which can be as much as 10°C cooler than steamy Adelaide. From May to October, southern right whales swimming next to the shore capture the attention of tourists' cameras.

TRANSPORTATION. By **bus,** Premier Stateliner runs from Adelaide via McLaren Vale to and from Stuart St. in Victor Harbor. (☎8415 5555. 1½-2hr., 1-3 per day, $14.) **Sealink,** the service from Victor Harbor to Kangaroo Island, can be booked through **Traveland** (☎8552 8434), on Ocean St., and **Travelworld** (☎8552 1200), in the Harbor Mall on Ocean St. Other car services include: **Peninsular Taxi Group** (☎8552 2622); **RAA** (☎13 11 11 or 0427 527 033); **Victor Rent-a-Car,** 66 Ocean St. (☎8552 1033; 25+; from $66 per day).

ORIENTATION AND PRACTICAL INFORMATION. Victor Harbor is 85km south of Adelaide on the Main South Rd. The town is fairly easy to navigate. Flinders Pde. runs along the ocean beneath the shade of massive fir trees; the main commercial drag, Ocean St., runs one block behind, becoming Hindmarsh St. in the eastern of two roundabouts in city center. Victoria St. is the main street on the western side of the city, and leads to the highway toward Cape Jervis. The **tourist Information Centre,** near the causeway to Granite Island, is at the foot of Flinders Pde. (☎8552 5738 or 8552 7000; fax 8552 5476. Open daily 9am-5pm.) Other services include: **ATMs** on Ocean St.; **police,** on Torrens St. (☎8552 2088); **hospital,** on Bay Rd. (☎8552 1066). The **library,** 10 Coral St. just off Ocean St., has free **Internet.** (Open Tu-Th 10am-5:30pm, F 10am-6pm, Sa 10am-1pm.)

ACCOMMODATIONS AND FOOD. **The Anchorage,** on the corner of Coral St. and Flinders Pde., a few blocks east of the main green, occupies two buildings right next to the ocean. One houses the backpackers, and the other the hotel, with comfortable budget guest rooms, and the hip, ship-shaped cafe/bar. (☎8552 5970; victor@anchorage.mtx.net. Key deposit $10. 4- to 6-bed dorms $17; singles $40; doubles $65-70.) The 100-year-old **Grosvener Junction Hotel,** 40 Ocean St., has simple, pleasant rooms at backpacker rates. The bar is a fun place, although perhaps too excited about greyhound racing for non-gamblers. (☎8552 1011. TV lounge and fridge, but no cooking facilities. Continental breakfast included. Backpacker singles $22; singles $30; doubles $55.) Sitting Brando-esquely on the waterfront, **Victor Harbor Beach Front Caravan Park,** 114 Victoria St., is on the west side of the city, immediately before the bridge into Encounter Bay. (☎8552 1111; fax 8552 8307. Laundry, BBQ. Key deposit $10. Book ahead in summer. Sites for 2 $16, powered $18, each extra person $4.50; cabins for 2 $47, each extra person $5.50.)

There are places to eat scattered up and down Ocean St., and there's a vast Woolworth's **supermarket** a block away on Torrens Ln. The **Original Victor Harbor Fish Shop,** 20 Ocean St., offers fish'n'chips ($7-13) and burgers for $6-9. (☎8552 1273. Open Su-Th 9am-7:30pm, F-Sa 9am-8:30pm.) **Ocean Chinese,** on Ocean St., has popular takeaway meals for $7-15. (☎8552-3994. Open Th-Tu 1pm-late.)

SIGHTS AND ACTIVITIES. Little Penguins win top billing on **Granite Island.** Entry is free if you take the 10min. stroll from the causeway entrance, but you can also take a horse-drawn tram that's been trekking back and forth for more than 100 years. (May-Sept. daily 10am-3:20pm, Oct.-Apr. 10am-4pm. $5 return, concessions $3. Evening run for the penguins, $6 return.) The area around the head of the causeway on the mainland is a kiddie wonderland, with go-carts, fairy floss, minigolf, and more. The island's **Penguin Interpretive Centre** is open 30min. before the guided penguin walks, which start daily at dusk on the island side of the bridge. (☎8552 7555. $10, concessions $7, children $5.) There is an easy, free walking trail (30-40min.) on Granite Island which affords excellent views of the mainland and the sea, but you can really only see the penguins if you take the tour.

Near the causeway entrance, the **South Australian Whale Centre,** 2 Railway Tce., is a must for anyone interested in marine mammals. (☎8552 5644. Open daily 10am-5pm. $4.50, concessions $3.50, children $2.) For the latest **whale-sighting** info, call the center's hotline (☎1900 931 223; 75¢ per min.) or stop by the museum, where they have organized tours. To see koalas, wetland birds, and dingoes, visit **Urimbirra Wildlife Park,** 5km from Victor Harbor down the road toward Adelaide. (☎8554 6554. Open daily 9am-6pm. Koalas at 11am, 2, 4pm; croc feeding 1:30pm. $8.)

Try your hand at **parasailing** through **Odyssey Adventures,** on the Victor Harbor-Granite Island causeway. (☎8553 1294. $50, groups of 5 or more $45 per person.) Between Victor Harbor and Goolwa, Middleton has good **surf** beaches and Port Elliot has a beautiful, though crowded, beach called **Horseshoe Bay,** plus good **surfing** at **Boomer Beach** on the western edge of town. Port Elliot also has one of the few remaining **drive-in movie theaters** in Australia, with recent releases every F and Sa night. (☎8554 2168. $13 per carload.)

WHATCHAMACALLIT Although much of Australia was claimed on the dubious (and now-repudiated) doctrine of *terra nullus*, Kangaroo Island actually *was* empty of human inhabitants when Flinders and his men arrived in 1802. Eventually, however, evidence of Aboriginal occupation did surface, although none had lived here for thousands of years. The island was avoided because, in the Dreamings of the Kaurna people of the region around Adelaide, it was the gateway to the afterlife and the Isle of the Dead. Therefore all the place names were given by Europeans; one town, American River, actually owes its name to a bunch of seafaring Seppos, who paused there in the early 19th century.

CAPE JERVIS ☎08

Cape Jervis is the jumping-off point for the **Kangaroo Island ferry,** the **Heysen Trail,** and exploration of the entire Fleurieu peninsula. **Cape Jervis Station** looks straight out of a home-decorating magazine, with intricately carved chairs and a tennis court. Once solely a sheep station, the establishment, which includes the old homestead, still has the odd fleeced beast roaming around the several hundred acres. There's a variety of accommodation options, from the decked-out train car called the 'Orient Express' to the backpacker set-up in the cottage-like Shearers' Quarters. Wally, the affable owner, can help organize horseback riding and fishing trips. The **Sealink** bus picks up and drops off at the gate, and guests are entitled to free ferry transfers. (☎8598 0288; fax 8598 0278. Sites $14, powered $17; dorm $20. Singles from $45; doubles from $65, both include breakfast.) For those with transportation and the desire to camp in a breathtaking spot, **Deep Creek Conservation Park,** 13km from Cape Jervis on the road to Victor Harbor, provides campgrounds with limited facilities ($13 per car) and bush camping ($6 per car). This park features seacoast views of the Backstairs Passage and Kangaroo Island, bushwalking, wildlife, and relative solitude. **Blowhole Beach,** a steep 3km from Cobbler Hill picnic area, and **Deep Creek Cover,** 6.4km from Tapanappa Campground, are spectacular walks that cross the Heysen Trail. Visit the **Park Headquarters** (☎8598 0263), by the entrance to the park for maps, info, and permits.

KANGAROO ISLAND ☎08

Queensland shows off the Great Barrier Reef, Victoria flaunts the Great Ocean Rd., the Northern Territory struts Kakadu, and South Australia retorts with Kangaroo Island (KI)—which means that sometimes the words "touristy" and "bourgeois" don't even begin to describe it. It's expensive to get there and to get around, but this place gets a lot of east-coast backpackers, fresh from Sydney and Melbourne, who quite likely are still uncertain what a koala, kangaroo, or goanna looks like. The folks coming from Perth are less common, having already seen (and possibly run over) quite a few of the animals along the way. More sleepy than wild, Kangaroo Island (pop. 4100), Australia's third-largest island after Tasmania and Melville in the NT, does wake up long enough to showcase some of Australia's natural flora and fauna. The island has 21 national and local conservation parks, including the sprawling Flinders Chase National Park. Here you can see (and perhaps trip over) kangaroos, passive koalas, and much-hyped little penguins; stroll among a colony of Australian sea lions; watch New Zealand fur seals wave-surf; climb over and through awesome geological formations.

For visitors going to Seal Bay, Kelly Caves, and Flinders Chase, it's worth picking up an **Island Parks Pass.** Good for one year, it allows unlimited access and lighthouse tours. (Available at any of the locations and the visitors center. $28, children $22, families $77.) Although the park service runs the penguin tours in both big towns, these are not covered by the pass ($7, concessions $5.50, families $20).

TRANSPORTATION

Kangaroo Island is accessible by airplane and ferry, but once on the island there is **no public transportation.** Visitors seeking freedom to do and see as they please need to bring a car over on the ferry (return $142) or rent a car ($80-120 per day), bearing in mind that many roads are unsealed. Everyone else will just have to sign up for a tour ($160-250, usually including coach, ferry, and accommodation).

BY AIR. Specials on flights from Adelaide (30min.) can rival or even better the ferry's cost. Two airlines depart from Adelaide's airport, each two to four times per day, and land at **Kingscote Airport,** 13km from the town of Kingscote at Cygnet River. Another option is **Kendell Airlines,** 61 Dauncey St., Kingscote. (☎13 13 00 or 8231 9567. Open daily 8:30am-5pm. $50-85 one-way on "seasonal saver" or "saver" fares with no advance notice; from $78 one-way if purchased 7 days in advance.) Kendell passengers enjoy a 10% discount at **Budget. Emu Airlines** is not as earthbound as its flightless namesake. (☎8234 3711 or 1800 182 353. $90 one-away, or $84 with a 2-week advance purchase.) Sealink's **airport shuttle** service that runs on the island between the airport and Kingscote. (☎8553 2390. $10.)

BY FERRY AND COACH. Kangaroo Island Sealink has the monopoly on transport to and around the island. They run a **ferry** between Cape Jervis and Penneshaw. (Reservations ☎13 13 01. Open daily 8am-7:30pm. 45min.; 2-5 per day; one-way $32, cars $69.) **Sealink** (☎13 13 01) offers connecting **coach** service between Adelaide and the Cape Jervis ferry dock from Adelaide's central **bus station,** 101 Franklin St. (1¾hr.; 2 per day; one-way $16, return including ferry $96). Sealink also runs **coach** service on the island to and from the **ferry terminal** in Penneshaw. This can be used as a limited form of transportation to and from Kingscote or American River, even if you're not taking the ferry. Book ahead for Sealink coaches that leave Kingscote (7am and 5:30pm), arriving in Penneshaw (1hr.) via American River (30min.). Two per day leave Penneshaw (10am and 7pm) and arrive in Kingscote (1hr., $11) via American River (30min., $8).

BY CAR. A vehicle is indispensable to those who want to explore Kangaroo Island's remote sights or want to hike in its national parks. The islanders are beginning to win their campaign to get more paved roads, so a 4WD is only a plus, not a necessity. All rental companies offer free shuttles between the airport and Kingscote, and some companies also have a ferry pick-up option. **Budget,** based in Kingscote, offers Penneshaw ferry drop-off and pick-up and rents to those 21+. (☎8553 3133. From $79 per day.) You have to be 25+ to rent from Hertz-affiliate **Kangaroo Island Rental Cars,** on the corner of Franklin St. and Telegraph Rd., Kingscote, which has a counter at the airport. They also arrange competitive fly-drive packages. (☎8553 2390 or 1800 088 296. Full-day with 200km for small manual $83, for 4WD $137.50.) **Penneshaw Car Rentals** rents small, late model cars with A/C and caters to those 21+. (☎8593 0023 or 1800 686 620. Half-day with 100km $60, full-day with 240km $80; upgrade to unlimited km for $20 more.)

TOURS. Without a car, joining a tour is your only option for experiencing the island's top attractions. To see the best sights and wildlife, be sure your tour includes **Seal Bay** and **Flinders Chase National Park** (home of **Remarkable Rocks** and **Admiral's Arch**). Tours are enjoyable and informative, but usually include just one long day of touring (as in 10hr.) and may rush through the island's natural attractions. If you only have one day to pack it all in, **Kangaroo Island Adventures** (☎8231 1744) joins with **Sealink** (☎13 13 01) to cart travelers to the big sights for $159, leaving Adelaide at 6:45am and returning around 10:30pm. Flying, though more expensive, will give more precious hours on the island. **Kangaroo Island Ferry Connections** offers a day tour with pickup and drop off in Penneshaw, American River, and Kingscote, all the big sights, morning tea and lunch, and a backpacker friendly price. (☎8553 1233 or 1800 018 484. $78; children $55.) For sleeping under the stars, **CampWild Adventures** offers a two-day 4WD camping trip. (☎1800 444 321. Departs winter Tu, Th, and Sa; summer daily. $260 including coach, private ferry with dolphin watching, and park entrance. Maximum 10 people.)

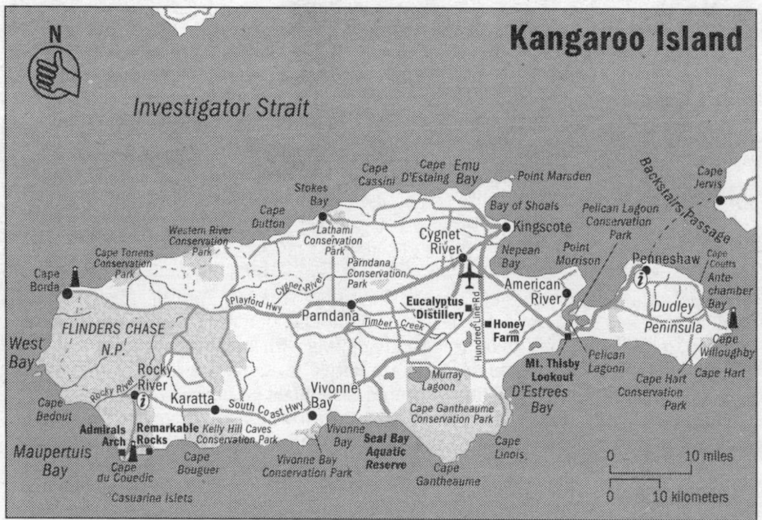

BY BIKE OR CAMEL. **Penneshaw Youth Hostel** and **Kangaroo Island Central Backpackers,** Kingscote, both rent bikes by the day (around $20). **Rent-a-bike KI,** 1 Commercial St., Kingscote, rents single and tandem bikes. (☎8553 2349. $6.50 per hr., $11 per half-day.) You could also try **Country Cottage,** Centenary Ave., Kingscote. (☎8553 2148. Mountain bikes $15 per day.) Finally, if you've always wanted to camp out with your own personal camel, call **Kangaroo Island Camel Safaris.** They offer all-inclusive trips for two or more nights exploring Dudley Peninsula. (☎8553 1147. From $98 per person per night.)

CAMPING

There are four camping sites in Flinders Chase National Park, which are convenient for hiking (see p. 447). But the most beautiful bush camping on the island is outside of Flinders, in **Cape Gantheaume Conservation Park** on D'Estrees Bay. It's a long way from Flinders Chase National Park and the road is rough, but it has a gorgeous ocean view. No facilities are available. Permits are available for $6 at Murray Lagoon ranger station (☎8553 8233), or the Gateway Information Centre (☎8553 1185), just outside Penneshaw on the road to Kingscote. Similarly basic facilities can be found closer to the road to Flinders at **Murray Lagoon;** permits also $6, from the ranger station (☎8553 8233).

Six caravan parks are scattered around the island, as well as eight other camping grounds. **Western KI Caravan Park,** on the South Coast Rd. just 3km from the Flinders Chase entrance, has lots of wildlife, a shower block, powered sites, laundry, and BBQs. (☎8559 7201. Book ahead. On-site vans $35.) Basic camping grounds with toilets but no showers are at **American River, Browns Beach, Vivonne Bay,** and **Western River** among others. Purchase camping permits ($3.50 per site per night) at the Gateway Information Centre (☎8553 1185) just outside Penneshaw.

WILDLIFE

Kangaroo Island is one of the best places in the country to see Australia's native fauna in the wild. **Kangaroos** and **wallabies** are omnipresent, especially at dusk in the western half of the island. For **koalas,** head to the **Rocky River Visitors Centre** in Flinders Chase National Park (see p. 430). Three kilometers before the entrance to Flinders Chase NP, the **Western KI Caravan Park** (☎8559 7201) on South Coast Rd. welcomes koala-spotters, and the owners are very knowledgeable on the subject of these furry little critters that live amongst the caravans. It takes luck to spot a

SOUTH AUSTRALIA

WILDFIRE! Kangaroo Island, like many of South Australia's rural areas, treats the possibility of wildfire very seriously. **Fire Ban Season** is designated from the start of December to the end of April, the driest months of the year. During this time there are a series of restrictions on camping fires: the fire must be contained in a barbeque, cooker, or fireplace, and cannot be bigger than one square meter in area. You must stay with the fire while it is alight. On particularly dry days the Country Fire Service might call for a **Total Fire Ban,** in which case only gas or electric stoves or barbeques can be used. On Total Fire Ban days walking trails are often closed as well. Never toss cigarettes or matches from cars. For more information on fire bans, call the CFS hotline 1300 362 361.

platypus, although any river in Flinders Chase has promise. Your best bet is hiking the **Black Swamp Trail,** which leaves from behind the Flinders Chase visitors center at dusk (it's 45min. along an unused road hopping with kangaroos and wallabies at night). Neither koalas nor platypuses are native to Kangaroo Island—they were introduced in the 1920s when it was feared they might go extinct on the mainland.

Penguin nesting colonies are conveniently near towns: a larger group is in Penneshaw, but they can be seen in Kingscote as well. Australian **sea lions** waddle around at Seal Bay, and fun-loving New Zealand **fur seals** are the featured attraction at Admiral's Arch in Flinders Chase. **Echidnas,** nocturnal, burrowing, egg-laying mammals, are often spotted on the Breakneck River trail, also in Flinders Chase. Emus wander near the visitors centre at Flinders Chase. Other birds, including the beautiful crimson rosella, are everywhere—try the short trails around Kelly Caves for good watching. Murray Lagoon in the southeast of the island offers some of the best waterfowl viewing. If all else fails, head for **Parndana Wildlife Park,** 3km west of Parndana on the Playford Hwy., with koalas, 'roos, emus, an indoor aviary, and even a five-legged sheep not related to Dolly. (☎8559 6050. Open daily 9am-5pm. $5, children $2.)

SIGHTS AND ACTIVITIES

For general information about the national parks on the island try **National Parks and Wildlife South Australia,** 39 Dauncey St., Kingscote (☎8553 2381; fax 8553 2531). Consider the weather when planning a trip to KI. In summer, although it may be hot inland, it will rarely be anything but moderate on the coast; always bring a wind-proof jacket and a wool sweater, especially for the night-time penguin viewings. This far south, there is only an average of 4½hr. of full sunshine in winter.

SEAL BAY CONSERVATION PARK. Arguably Kangaroo Island's finest natural attraction, **Seal Bay Conservation Park** allows visitors to stroll (with a guide only) through one of the few remaining colonies of Australian sea lions. The park is on the island's southern coast, 60km along a sealed road from Kingscote. A **visitors center** offers general info, toilets, and a few snacks. You can hike along the boardwalk, which brings you within viewing range of the sea lions, but to get onto the beach, guided **tours** (45min.) are the only option. Visiting the park between 11am and 1:30pm means more company than just pinnipeds—most tour buses arrive then; in summer, the people on the beach occasionally outnumber the animals. More expensive, and requiring bookings, **sunset tours** reveal what happens in a seal colony when the sun goes down... *(☎8553 4207. Open daily Feb.-Nov. 9am-4:15pm; Dec.-Jan. 9am-7pm. Boardwalk $6.50, concessions $5, families $18. Tours every 30-45min. $10/$7/$25. Sunset tours $20/$12/$50.)*

LITTLE SAHARA. Just a short drive from Seal Bay, a jumbo pile of hot, white sand once reminded someone of Africa, so it became known as **Little Sahara.** Surprisingly large dunes are here for the climbing and worth a stop. In the summer, try to avoid midday—this is the Sahara, after all. *(From Seal Bay, when you get back to South Coast Rd., turn left. After about 5km, take the first road left; if you cross the small bridge, you've just missed it. The road into the carpark is about a 5min. drive from the main road, but the last stretch is in rough shape; be extra careful if your car is riding low.)*

VIVONNE BAY. Vivonne Bay, shortly after Seal Bay and Little Sahara on the South Coast Rd., hosts one of the few gas stations and general stores on the western part of the island. It also houses the **Kangaroo Island Outdoor Education Field Study Centre,** which organizes opportunities for groups of tourists, both children and adults, to learn about the wildlife they are among. *(☎8559 4232; www.vivonnebay.outdoored.com.au. Classes 2 days-3 weeks, accommodation provided.)*

CAVING. The **Kelly Hill Caves,** on South Coast Rd. about halfway between Vivonne Bay and the Flinders Chase Visitors Centre, are the main attraction of **Kelly Hill Conservation Park.** The largest cave area is accessible on a 40min. guided tour. Translucent stalactites and stalagmites and petrified tree roots please visitors almost as much as the natural air-conditioning on hot summer days. **Adventure Caving tours** require advance booking. *(☎8559 7231. Open daily May-Aug. 10am-3pm; Sept.-Apr. 10am-4pm. Tours 10, 11am, noon, 1:30, 2:30, 3:30, 4:30pm. $7, concessions $5.50, families $20. Adventure $22.50-33.50, concessions $12-17, families $58.50-86.50.)*

SURFING. Kangaroo Island also provides opportunities for the board-toting to hit the **surf.** Visit the Kangaroo Island Gateway tourist information centre for the *Surfing Guide*, which details four southern beaches **(Hanson Bay, Vivonne Bay, D'Estress Bay, and Pennington Bay)** and one northern beach **(Stokes Bay).** The water off the island is pretty cool all year; surfers need a full-length wet-suit.

PENNESHAW ☎08

The town of Penneshaw (pop. 250) on Kangaroo Island's northeast coast serves as the primary ferry arrival point from Cape Jervis on the mainland. A quick stroll up North Tce. from the ferry jetty leads to the pub, petrol station, and a few small restaurants; small Nat Turner St. connects North Tce. to the post office and to Middle Tce. The **Kangaroo Island Gateway Visitors Centre,** 1km down the road toward Kingscote from Penneshaw's ferry terminus, serves as the information centre for the whole island, with a cornucopia of maps, camping permits, and a list of tours. (☎8553 1185; fax 8553 1255. Open M-F 9am-5pm, Sa-Su 10am-4pm.)

Penneshaw's main attraction, besides the ferry, is its colony of little **penguins.** Each night after sunset, the 30cm penguins waddle back to their burrows along the coastline. The **Penguin Interpretive Centre** is just east of the ferry dock, off Middle Tce. There's a lighted wooden boardwalk here with public access. Guided tours are worth the money, though, if the penguins are few and far between. (Tours including penguin center admission nightly at 8:30 and 9:30pm; in winter 7:30 and 8:30pm. $5, children $3.50.) To the left as one faces the ferry dock, a several-hundred-meter trail provides interpretive displays of the area's geology.

Kangaroo Island YHA, 33 Middle Tce., offers roomy, colorful six-bed rooms with stove, refrigerator, and bath. (☎8553 1233; fax 8553 1190. Linen $3. Reception M-F 9am-6pm, Sa-Su 9am-1pm. Dorms $13; twins and doubles $34; family rooms $50. Non-YHA $3 extra.) **Penneshaw Youth Hostel,** 43 North Tce., has simple, functional accommodations, with kitchen, TV lounge, and a small courtyard. The hostel rents mountain bikes and runs diving tours. (☎8553 1284; fax 8553 1295; adv.host@king.on.net. Reception 7:45am-7:30pm. 8-bed dorms $16; twins or doubles $38. Diving $66. VIP.)

Both hostels have cheap restaurants attached. **Penneshaw Pizza** is next to the YHA. (☎8553 1110. Open daily from 4:30pm until at least 9pm.) The **Blue Dolphin Cafe** is in the Penneshaw Youth Hostel building and offers cheap fish'n'chips and burgers, eat-in or takeaway. (☎8553 1284. Open for lunch and dinner.) Welcome Mart, Middle Tce., has **groceries.** (Open M-F 8:30am-6pm, Sa-Su 9:30am-4pm.)

KINGSCOTE ☎08

Kingscote (pop. 1500) is Kangaroo Island's largest town and was the first European settlement in South Australia. Although everyone comes to KI for points further west, Kingscote contains a beautiful beach, not so much for swimming as walking, an ocean swimming pool, and historical testimony to the spot where settlers began South Australia's first official town. More practically, the pleasant streets of this tiny town hold the island's only ATM, Internet, and supermarket.

ORIENTATION AND PRACTICAL INFORMATION. The Esplanade runs along the water and becomes Kingscote Tce. and then Chapman Tce. moving south. Most of the shops and services are one block in from the beach on **Dauncey St.,** which is intersected by Telegraph Rd., Commercial St., Murray St., and Drew St. Services include: **tourist info** at the **Kingscote Gift Shop,** 78 Dauncey St. (☎8553 2165; open M-F 8:30am-6pm, Sa-Su 8:30am-5:30pm); **National Parks and Wildlife Office,** 39 Dauncey St. (☎8553 2381; fax 8553 2531); an **ATM** at Bank SA, Dauncey St.; **police** (☎8553 2018 or 1144); **RAA** (☎8553 2162); **hospital** (☎8553 4200) for the entire island; **free Internet** at the library, 41 Dauncey St. opposite Bank SA (open M 1-5pm, Tu-F 9:30am-5pm); **post office** on Dauncey St. (☎8553 2122; open M-F 9am-5pm, Sa 9-11:30am). **Postal code**: 5223.

ACCOMMODATIONS. Ellson's Seaview, on Chapman Tce. across from the ocean swimming pool, has large rooms in the guest house that share a clean communal bathroom and are cheaper than those in the main motel. Ask for a sea view. The restaurant does no-nonsense meals that are better—and cheaper—than those at the local pub. (☎8553 2030; www.seaview.net.au. Internet access $6 per 30min., tea and coffee included. Reception 8am-8:30pm. Singles $46; twins and doubles $58, each extra person $10.) **Kangaroo Island Central Backpackers,** 19 Murray St., is four short blocks from the coast. The budget-conscious who don't mind spartan, but clean quarters and a run-down backyard can take advantage of the cheapest beds in town. Reception is next door at the second-hand shop M-F; on weekends a sign posted in the window informs guests of the necessary procedures. (☎8553 2787 or 8553 2787. Dorms $20; twins and doubles $45; family room for 4 $65.)

FOOD. Roger's Deli and Cafe, 76 Dauncey St., is attached to the news agency, and offers a typical range of pies and hamburgers for $2-5, as well as more interesting Asian cuisine for $10-15. (☎8553 2053. Open M-W 8am-5:30pm, Th-Sa 8am-7:30pm, Su 8am-2pm.) **Blue Gum Cafe,** across the street from Roger's, serves up snazzy pancakes with ice cream and maple syrup for $5.50 and $4-7 lunch sandwiches in a cheery setting. (☎8553 2089. Open M-F 7:30am-5:30pm, Sa 7:30am-12:30pm.) **A.M. Pizza** (☎8553 3228), at the south end of Dauncey St., opens at 5pm daily. A Foodland **supermarket** is on the corner of Commercial and Osmond St. (Open M-F 9am-5:30pm, Sa 9am-12:30pm.)

SIGHTS. At dusk, the rocky coast north of the ocean pool and past the jetty awakens with penguin activity. Guided **tours** of the **penguin burrows** depart twice nightly from the front of the Ozone Hotel, at the corner of Chapman Tce. and Commercial St. (☎8553 1185. Winter 7:30 and 8:30pm; summer 9 and 9:40pm. $7, children $5.50, families $20.) **Pelicans** take center stage at the jetty at 5pm, when a feeding brings them together to jostle for fish. Check time details at the KI Marine Center, a yellow tin building near the jetty. (☎8553 3112; $2 donation requested.)

North of town on the Esplanade, a beautiful beach winds 1km toward **Reeves Point Historical Site,** where the first official settlers in South Australia first put down roots—especially when they started planting mulberry trees. The beach here is unspoiled and untraveled, allowing visitors to watch pelicans and black swans forage for food, scramble down an ancient jetty where boats once loaded basalt for paving roads, and inspect tram tracks from yesteryear. The tallest hill at the point, **Flafstaff Hill,** provides a great view of the bay and the town. **Fishing** is popular with locals, and for anyone hoping to be outdoors and miss some of the tourists—well, put it this way; the tourists aren't here.

FLINDERS CHASE NATIONAL PARK

Occupying the western end of the island and 17% of its total area, the rocks and animals of Flinders Chase are the highlight of the island. The best attractions are clustered 15-20km south of Rocky River along Boxer Dr. The easternmost sight, on Kirkpatrick Point, is Remarkable Rocks. The rocks, a type of stone unlike those which comprise the cliffs all along the coast of the island, would draw your attention even if it weren't for the work of the grotesque hand of 750 million years of erosion by ice, wind, and water. Just over 105km from Kingscote (much along a dirt track), the Flinders Chase **Visitors Centre** is located at Rocky River, along the South Coast Rd. (☎8559 7235; fax 8559 7268. Open daily Sept.-May 9am-5pm; June-Aug. 10am-5pm. One-day park entry costs $13 per car.)

Five kilometers west of Remarkable Rocks, **Cape du Couedic** houses a red-capped sandstone lighthouse. Three lightkeepers lived here with their families early this century, totally cut-off from the rest of the world. Four times a year, a steamer brought food, newspapers, and schoolwork, which the families hoisted up the cliffs. Just south of the lighthouse, a footpath winds to the edge of Cape du Couedic and then to the limestone cave of **Admiral's Arch.** More common than the Australian sea lions, a few thousand New Zealand **fur seals** call this area home.

Flinders Chase National Park has **four camping sites,** all non-powered with toilet facilities. The **Rocky River site,** near the visitors centre, offers convenience and the only showers, but the sites are in a dirt clearing. Tent campers may prefer to drive 13km into the park to the nicer surrounds of nine cheaper sites at **Snake Lagoon.** The two other sites are in the less frequented northern section of the park. Permits are available for all sites at Rocky River Visitors Centre. (☎8559 7235. Book ahead. Caravans not allowed. Rocky River site $15; all other sites $6. Extra $13 park fee for cars.) You can also rent a rustic **cabin** at one of Flinders Chase's three lighthouse stations, but nobody's going to hoist you food. (Book ahead with Flinders Chase NPWS ☎8859 7235. Linen $12. Adults $12-33, children $6.50. Minimum charge: Cape du Couedic $90, Cape Borda and Cape Willoughby $60.)

Numerous short **hikes** and excellent 2- to 7-day coastline treks are available for bushwalkers on Kangaroo Island. All hikers should pick up the *Walking Trails in Kangaroo Island Parks* brochure from any visitors centre. **Breakneck River Trail** (6km; 2hr.) in Flinders Chase National Park, is a hidden treasure. It is a fairly easy, almost entirely flat, well-marked hike through a progression of plant communities, and ending at a small beach with huge waves. Look for echidnas and rare, glossy, black cockatoos. The trailhead is on West Bay Rd., 13km from the visitors centre. The **Rocky River Mouth Trail** (3.3km; 1½hr.) is shorter than Breakneck River Trail but is more demanding and consists of more interesting terrain. This is a fun trail, which runs along the Rocky River and is good for spotting wildflowers in the spring. The trailhead, with toilets and campsites, is at Snake Lagoon on West Bay Rd., 9km from the Visitors Centre.

CENTRAL WINE REGIONS

Wine is South Australia, and South Australia is wine, and nowhere more so than 70km northeast of Adelaide in the famous Barossa Valley. Grapes from the Barossa and its more rural neighbor, the Eden Valley produce some of Australia's best wines. The Clare Valley, 45min. north of Barossa, is a contender in the same game, filled with smaller, more specialized wineries. Some of the vines in the area have been growing since the 1840s, when the first German settlers planted their cuttings from Europe and prayed they would thrive. More than 150 years later, there's no doubt those prayers have been answered many times over. Sip, swill, gulp, or guzzle; this stuff is liquid joy no matter how you polish it off. For other major wine regions, see Hunter Valley, p. 146; Rutherglen, p. 585; Yarra, p. 537.

BAROSSA VALLEY ☎08

Perhaps Australia's most well-known wine region, the Barossa Valley lives up to its reputation, with wines to suit all palates and budgets. Most of Australia's largest wine companies are based here, along with plenty of renowned family operations. Barossa has a strong German heritage but does not flaunt it. Many residents are descendants of the original settlers—Lutherans who fled religious persecution in Prussia in 1842. The area retains a German sense of orderliness; the grid-like street system that separates the wineries was designed by Colonel Light, the same man who laid out Adelaide's precise streets.

TRANSPORTATION

For wine sojourns to the Barossa, a car affords the greatest flexibility, a tour leaves the details and driving to others, and a bicycle makes for an enjoyable day if the weather (and your sense of balance) remain fine; even your own two feet can bring a day of good tasting. Hiring a car in Adelaide is strongly recommended for those bent on doing a serious wine tour, as many wineries are in out-of-the-way places. Follow Scenic Route 4 for a simultaneously breathtaking and breathalyzer-inducing drive. Driving parties always should keep a designated driver absolutely alcohol-free and mock the poor, sober bastard mercilessly. Barossa Valley's police are diligent and unforgiving when it comes to *drink driving.*

Buses: Barossa Adelaide Passenger Service (☎8564 3022; after hours 8564 0325) runs from **Adelaide** (1-3 per day) to: **Angaston** ($12); **Nuriootpa** ($11); **Tanunda** ($10). Children and seniors half-price. No reservation required.

Taxi: Barossa Valley Taxi (☎8563 3600), Tanunda. Book early. About $13 from Nuriootpa to Tanunda.

Automobile Clubs: Royal Automobile Association in Gawler (☎8522 2478), Tanunda (☎0500 832 123), and Williamstown (☎8524 6268).

Bike Rental: Mountain bikes at **Barossa Bunkhaus Traveller's Hostel** (☎8562 2260), Nuriootpa ($2 per hr.; $10 per day, guests $8) or **Tanunda Caravan and Tourist Park** (☎8563 2784), Tanunda ($6 per hr., $10 per half-day, $15 per day).

ORIENTATION AND PRACTICAL INFORMATION

The Barossa Valley is a triangle made up of three main towns, Nuriootpa, Tununda, and Angaston, and a few surrounding hamlets. Approaching from Adelaide via **Gawler,** the first hamlet is **Lyndoch** (LIN-dock; pop. 1000). After Lyndoch, the **Barossa Valley Hwy.** enters the main town of **Tanunda** (pop. 4000), 70km northeast of Adelaide where the highway's name changes to **Murray St.** It then continues on to **Nuriootpa** ("noor-ee-OOT-pah"; pop. 3500) and proceeds east to **Angaston** (pop. 2700) as **Nuriootpa Rd.** If you bypass **Gawler** and take the **Stuart Hwy. (A20)** from Adelaide, the road enters the Barossa from the north at Nuriootpa.

The **Barossa Visitor Information Centre,** 66-68 Murray St., is in Tanunda. (☎1800 812 662; www.barossa-region.org. Open M-F 9am-5pm, Sa-Su 10am-4pm.) It is home to the excellent **Wine Centre** (see p. 432). The banks in the valley all have **ATMs.** The Nuriootpa Library, on Murray St. on the south edge of town, has free **Internet** access. (Open M-W and F 9am-5pm, Th 9am-6pm, Sa 9am-noon.)

SOUTH AUSTRALIA

ACCOMMODATIONS

Barossa Bunkhaus Traveller's Hostel (☎8562 2260), on the Barossa Valley Way, just south of Nuriootpa. SA's first hostel was opened by wonderful owner Jan., 17 years ago, and is still run with the same warm welcome. Intimate, impeccably clean, and set in a vineyard. You can practically reach out and touch the grapes from your bedroom window. The Adelaide bus (see **Transportation,** p. 432) will drop you at the door on request. TV, fireplace, excellent kitchen, pool, and bike rental. Book ahead in high tourist season. 12 beds. Dorms $15; doubles $44-50.

Tanunda Caravan and Tourist Park (☎8563 2784; www.tanpark.mtx.net), just south of Tanunda on Barossa Valley Way. Convenient location. BBQ, kiosk, laundry. Sites $14, powered $17; basic on-site 6-person vans $35; cabins from $45-75.

Sandy Creek YHA, in Sandy Creek Conservation Park, 2km from Lyndoch. You must get the key from the YHA, 38 Stuart St., Adelaide (☎8231 5583). Pre-booking is essential. This limited-access hostel has 8 bunks in a stone farmhouse. $17, under 18 $12.

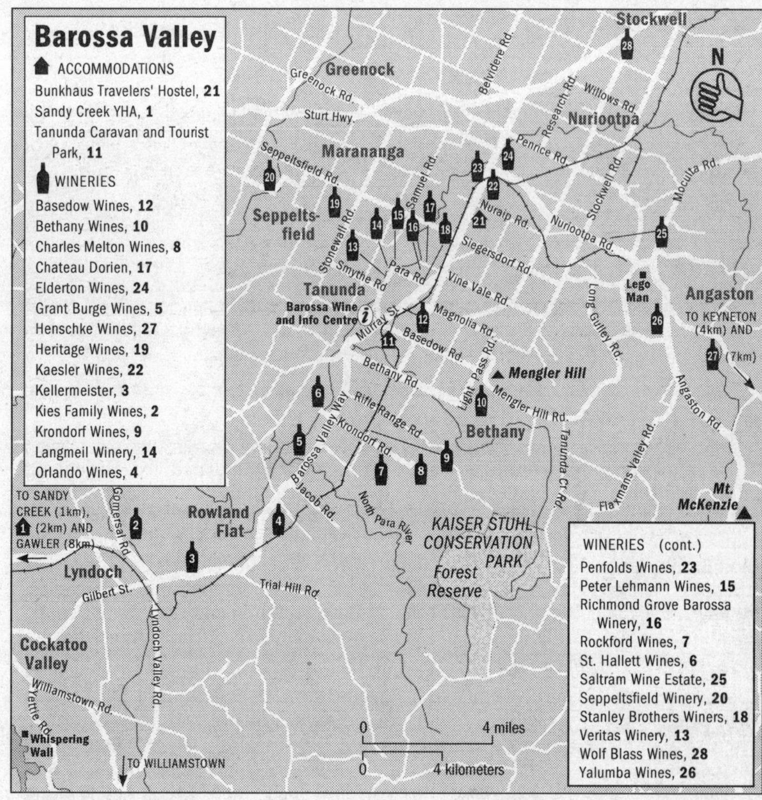

The Barossa Brauhaus, 41 Murray Rd., Angaston (☎8564 2014). The best deal of the area's generally pricey pub-hotels. Singles $25, doubles $55.

FOOD

The Barossa is not just about wine—food is also a high priority. As befits the typical crowd drawn to a wine-tasting, though, the food tends to be both high-quality and high-priced. The main streets of Tununda, Nurioopta, and Angaston are littered with yuppie joints from casual luncheries to elegant dinner spots. Don't be put off by the atmosphere; weekly and daily specials abound. Many of the wineries have lunch rooms or bistros, notably St. Halletts (see p. 435), that let you sample their produce while overlooking the younger cousins still on the vine.

The **Siegersdorf Restaurant,** inside the Top of the Valley Motel on Nurioopta's main street, has three course lunches for $12 and dinners for $15, including local specialities such as kangaroo. (Open daily noon-8pm.) Possibly the only Thai restaurant for miles around, **Shangri-La,** 51 Barossa Valley Way, is Nurioopta's other consistently-budget option, with main courses from $9-11.50. (☎8562 3559. Open M-Sa 11:30am-8pm.) Tanunda's resident German chef goes Italian at **La Buona Vita,** 89 Murray St., with $10 pizzas and $7-8 light meals. (☎8563 2527. Open noon-late.) The **Angaston Hotel,** 59 Murray Rd., has elaborate lunch specials such as poached salmon for $7.50. (☎8564 2428. Open daily noon-10pm.) If you're after something lighter and non-alcoholic, **Schaedel Haus,** 47 Murray St. in Nurioopta, is the best of the area's tea rooms. (☎8562 4394. Open 9am-4:30pm.)

A QUICK WINE PRIMER Wine tasting, like anything else, has its own vocabulary. Australia's, and the Barossa's, most famous red grape varieties are Shiraz (often called Syrah outside Australia) and Cabernet Sauvignon. Riesling, Semillon Blanc, and Sauvignon Blanc are Barossa's best-known whites. Sparkling wines are simply the ones with bubbles (Champagne is the most famous kind of sparking wine, but only sparkling wine produced in the Champagne region of France has earned the right to be called Champagne). Fortified wines are sweeter wines with added alcohol, often called dessert wines in North America and liqueur wines in Europe. Port, sherry, and vermouth are some of the most well-known fortifieds. Dry is the opposite of sweet. Crisp means the wine has an acidity, roughly the opposite of smooth or soft. In general, taste white before red, dry before sweet, and sparkling before fortified. Aroma, a word usually used with younger wines, is the same as bouquet (used with older wines)—they both mean simply "what the stuff smells like." You needn't use any of these words, though; the important question is whether or not you like what you're tasting. Cheers!

WINERIES OF THE BAROSSA VALLEY

The complete tour of over 40 wineries requires Bacchanalian spirit, Herculean effort, and Gargantuan ability to hold your liquor. Tanunda's visitor center has a full list. Most people "only" visit four to six in a day, and that is plenty for a nice buzz—each winery has free tastings, with basically no obligation to purchase, though the atmosphere differs significantly from the pub. Grapes are harvested from late February into April or early May. This is when tastings and finding **picking jobs** (check at cellar doors or with Jan at Barossa Bunkhaus Traveller's Hostel) are abundant. Most wineries in Barossa are open daily from 10am to 4 or 5pm.

WHETTING THE PALATE. If you don't understand what all the fuss over wine is about (and even if you do), start your Barossa visit with an hour at **The Barossa Wine Centre,** 66-68 Murray St., Tanunda, in the same building as the tourist office. The exhibits make the craft of wine-making and the etiquette of wine-tasting accessible to novices, while connoisseurs can peruse the in-depth displays and filmed discussions with area winemakers. (☎8563 0600. Open M-F 9am-4pm, Sa-Su 10am-3:30pm. $2.50.) Two wineries offer tours of their production facilities: **Seppeltsfield,** on Tourist Route 4 in Seppeltsfield (M-F 11am, 1, 2, 3pm; Sa-Su 11:30am, 1:30, 2:30pm; $5, children $2) and **Yaldara,** Gomersal Rd., Lyndoch (☎8524 0239; tours daily 10:15, 10:45am, 1:15, 2:15, 3:15pm; $5). The tours take about 35min. and are well worth the price. **Wolf Blass Wines,** 97 Sturt Hwy., Nuriootpa, also has a small wine heritage museum near its tasting rooms. (☎8562 1955. Open M-F 9:15am-5pm, Sa-Su 10am-5pm. Free.)

STUMBLING AROUND. If you're exploring on foot, four wineries just north of Tanunda are connected by a Wine Path (foot or cycle only) through the vineyards. On the left side of Barossa Valley Way as you head north out of Tanunda you'll find the first, the small **Stanley Brothers Winery** with pottery and jams also for sale at the cellar door and a picnic area. (☎8563 3375. Open M-F 9:30am-5pm, Sa-Su 11am-5pm.) Not far away on Para Rd., **Richmond Grove Winery,** on the banks of the small Para River, specializes in Rieslings and has picnic areas among the gum trees. (☎8563 2204. Open M-F 10am-5pm, Sa-Su 10:30am-4:30pm.) Down Para Rd. and down the Wine Path, **Peter Lehmann Wines** is a larger operation, buying grapes from about 200 growers and crushing more than 10,000 tons of grapes every year. (☎8563 2500. Open M-F 9:30am-5pm, Sa-Su 10:30am-4:30pm.) The last winery on the wine trail, **Langmeil Winery,** at the corner of Para and Langmeil Rd., has a good tasting range in a cellar door dating from the 1840s. (☎8563 2595. Open daily 11am-4:30pm.) Though not part of the Wine Path, the **Chatteau Dorrien,** at the corner of Seppeltfield Rd. and Barossa Valley Way, is only a few hundred yards north of the Stanley Brothers Winery. Those who appreciate the sweeter things in life will love their specialty honey mead wines. (☎8562 2850. Open daily 10am-5pm.)

Some traveling tips: don't be tempted to buy a wine because it's won an award. The efficient tourism industry has created enough competitions that virtually every winery has been recognized for some "outstanding" achievement. Find your own taste. Many a so-called expert's sobriquet is mere snobbery. Let your own palette be your guide and don't shy away from individuality. Finally, the narrow roads, high-speed traffic, and random police search points and breathalyzers don't mix well with wine. Be smart: choose a designated driver, or hop on one of the inexpensive, informative day tours.

RIDING SHOTGUN WITH THE DESIGNATED DRIVER. For those not confined to walking distance, the options seem endless.

Rockford Wines (☎8563 2720), on Krondorf Rd. east of Tanunda. Not to be missed, the friendly folks at the Rockford cater to small groups with copious tastings. The sweet Fraginard is divine. Their coopers also enlighten visitors on the role of the barrel in winemaking. Open M-Sa 11am-5pm.

St. Hallett Wines (☎8563 2319), on St. Hallett's Rd., Tanunda. Since 1944, St. Hallett has made every drop of their wine exclusively from Barossa or Eden Valley fruit. Premium red table wines, especially Shirazes, are the specialty. Open daily 9am-5pm. Coopers at the **keg factory** (☎8563 3012) across the road welcome visitors to watch them practice their craft, shaping the huge oak barrels that are as much a part of the best wines as the grapes. Same opening hours as cellar door.

Saltram Wine Estate (☎8564 3355), on the Nuriootpa-Angaston Rd., just outside Angaston. Smooth, fruity, and fabulously decadent—Saltram's Semillon is the stuff from which dreams are made. This winery has been working on their reds, whites, and ports since 1859. Open M-F 9am-5pm, Sa-Su 10am-5pm. Bistro open daily 11:30am-3pm.

Bethany Wines (☎8563 2086), on Bethany Rd., between Tanunda and Nuriootpa. High above the rest of the valley with a panoramic vista and lovely picnic areas. The family still uses the old gravity feed method. Open M-Sa 10am-5pm, Su 1-5pm.

Orlando Wines (☎8521 3140), at Rowland Flat. Some 250,000 people each year pay respects at this cellar door. It has built a reputation around its **Jacob's Creek** wine, Australia's largest wine export brand. One out of every five branded bottles that leaves the country bears the Jacob's Creek label. Open M-F 10am-5pm, Sa-Su 10am-4pm.

Henschke Wines (☎8564 8223), on the main road in Keyneton. Don't be put off by this winery being out of the way; it's one of the most highly regarded by the locals. Open M-F 9am-4:30pm, Sa 9am-noon.

TAKIN' THE TOUR BUS. Groovy Grape Getaways is the most popular backpackers tour to the Barossa, running from Adelaide and Glenelg daily, with free hostel pickup. The tour stops at the big rocking horse in Adelaide Hills (p. 419), the Whispering Wall, 4 wineries, the Seppelts production tour, and includes a BBQ. (☎8395 4422. $46.) If you're more serious about wine, or less than thrilled about spending a day drinking with 22-year-olds, **Prime Mini Tours** runs a small, enjoyable tour which includes a visit to Adelaide Hills's big rocking horse, the Whispering Wall, and Angas Park Dried Fruits, a gourmet lunch, and stops at four wineries. (☎8293 4900. $48-55. Free pickup.) If you're staying in the Barossa, **Valley Tours** has the least expensive full-day winery and sights tour. (☎8563 3587. $47 including lunch, with pickup and return to Barossa Valley accommodations.) **Barossa Getabout Tours** goes farther afield, with a minimum of eight persons and good group rates. (☎8524 6468. W, F, Sa; including lunch and transfers in the valley $42.)

SIGHTS AND ENTERTAINMENT

Designated drivers, take heart: not every attraction in the Barossa requires drinking. **Mengler Hill Lookout,** on Mengler Hill Rd. outside Tanunda, on Tourist Route 4, is definitely worth a stop to see the rows of vines stretching in every direction. The road linking Williamstown and Sandy Creek passes **Barossa Reservoir,** with its

THE LEGO MAN In 1993 ex-rail commissioner Tom Lucieer opened a museum of Danish plastic bricks—a collection worth nearly $100,000. Included is the original Lego toy, which is made of wood and is transported daily by two policeman in an armored car to a local bank for overnight keeping. Her Majesty the Queen has already visited the collection and is scheduled to return; maybe she needs to learn you can't hold on, but must lego. This man is in with the Lego company; several of his original designs are slated to be produced commercially, and he gets the new sets before the stores do, including many working Lego trains built as models of famous trains worldwide. So, if the kids (or the inner child) are bored by wineries, bring them to Angaston to see the Lego Man. (☎8564 2714. 37 Jubilee Ave., off Schilling St. in Angaston. Open daily 10am-5pm. $2.)

famous curved **Whispering Wall,** where murmured confidences can be heard meters away. Apparently, the only other walls like this are in Europe. Though it's hard to imagine South Australia before wine, the **Kaiser Stuhl Conservation Park,** 2km southeast of Tanunda, demonstrates what the Barossa looked like before the vines.

As if you needed an excuse to drink, festivals abound. During the **Barossa Classic Gourmet Festival** in late August and most of September, wineries invite chefs and accompany their liquid wares with gourmet feasts. Every October, the **Barossa International Music Festival** (☎8359 2994) celebrates the arrival of spring.

CLARE ☎08

Between Adelaide and the South Australian outback, Clare (pop. 4000) and its neighbor, Burra, constitute the final outposts of civilization before the Flinders Ranges and the back of beyond. The Clare Valley, running north from Auburn up to Clare along the Main North Rd, hosts some 20-odd vineyards in a group that's more compact and exclusive than those of their southern cousin the Barossa Valley. The higher altitude here (about 340m) means a respite from some of the lowland heat associated with the Yorke Peninsula, and the weather allows soaring pine and fur trees to point skyward over the golden-brown terrain—golden-brown, that is, except for those lush carpets of vineyard green.

TRANSPORTATION. If driving from Adelaide (136km south of Clare), take Main North Rd. through Elizabeth and onto the Gawler bypass, then turn left at the exit to Tarlee. Main North Rd. runs through the town and passes most of the wineries before reaching Clare. On the road from Auburn to Clare, signs pointing to "Historic Mintaro" lead to an absolutely spectacular 12km drive. **Mid North Passenger Service** runs a once-daily bus to and from Adelaide (☎8826 2346; $19; no service Sa), and once in Clare you can rent bikes or take private bus tours of the Valley.

PRACTICAL INFORMATION. In Clare itself, Old North Rd. runs one block east of Main North Rd., the highway on which visitors enter from Auburn. The **Clare Valley Tourist Information Centre,** 229 Main North Rd. in the town hall, stocks free winery and town maps. (☎8842 2131. Open M-Sa 9am-5pm, Su 10am-4pm.) Services include: **police station** (☎8842 2711); **RAA** (☎8842 2172, ☎8842 3105); **hospital** (☎8842 2500), on Farrell Flat Rd., the main road to Burra, north of the town center; a **clinic** on 41 Old North Rd. (☎8842 2100, afterhours 8842 2773). Free **Internet** access is available at the **Clare Library,** 33 Old North Rd. (open Tu, W, F 10am-6pm, Th 10am-8pm, Sa 10am-noon). Thanks be to Mercury, Roman god of merchants, commerce, and bankers, all the banks in town have **ATMs.** The **post office,** 253 Main North Rd., is open M-F 9 am-5pm. **Postal code:** 5453.

ACCOMMODATIONS. Located in Clare near the bus stop, clean rooms and low prices make **Taminga Hotel,** 302 Main North Rd., a good choice for those without their own transport. (☎8842 2808. Singles $22; doubles $33.) Slightly nicer, the **Clare Hotel,** 244 Main North Rd., has motel rooms with attached baths. (☎8842 2816. Singles $19, with bath $50; doubles with bath $55). The award-winning **Clare**

Caravan Park, 3km south of town on Main North Rd., has a lake, pool, and laundry. (☎8842 2724; fax 8842 3447. Reception 8am-7pm. Sites $14 per person, powered $17.80; self-contained cabins for two $43-49.)

Martindale Hall, east of historic Mintaro, about 20min. from Clare by car, was featured in the film *Picnic at Hanging Rock.* The Georgian mansion is now an upscale B&B. Self-guided tours are available. The beautiful road toward Mintaro is south of Clare; follow the signs reading "Martindale Hall" on the Clare-Burra road. (☎8843 9088. Open M-F 11am-4pm, Sa-Su noon-4pm. $5.50, concessions $3.80, kids $1.10.) While in Mintaro it's worth a stop at the **Mintaro Wines,** Leashingham Rd., a small family winery. (☎8843 9046. Open M-F 9am-4:30pm, Sa 10am-5pm.)

FOOD. Clare, like many larger Australian road-side towns, offers a selection of bakeries and cafes, but heartier feed comes from a counter meal in a pub hotel or the Chaff Mill Country Kitchen (see below). **Price's Traditional Bakery,** 269 Main North Rd., north of the post office, has been churning out pies, pastries, and sausage rolls for more than a century; try the $1.50 honey log with fresh cream. (☎8842 2473. Open M-F 8am-5pm, Sa 9am-1:30pm.) The staff of the friendly **Chaff Mill Country Kitchen,** 308 Main North Rd., cooks breakfast, lunch ($6-16), and dinner ($16-22) of the steak and pasta persuasion. (☎8842 3055. Open M, W-Su 10am-9pm. Closed M lunch, all day Tu.) The **Clare Hotel,** 244 Main North Rd. (☎8842 2816), reigns in the counter meal battle, offering $6-7 daily lunch specials in an airy pub environment. Clare Foodland, 47 Old North Rd., sells **groceries.** (☎8842 2416. Open M-Sa 8am-7pm, Su 9am-7pm.)

WINERIES OF CLARE VALLEY. The Clare Valley is the northernmost wine production area in South Australia, cooler than the much larger Barossa Valley. Around 28 wineries operate here, though not all have cellar doors. If a winery has tastings, however, the folks at the Clare tourist office know; pick up a guide to the valley from them before you set out. Most are small family operations, and only five Clare wineries crush more than 500 tons of grapes per year. An old railway line, parallel to Main North Rd., has been converted into the 27km scenic **Riesling Trail,** named after the most famous style of wine from the region. The trail runs between Clare and Auburn and is suitable for walking and biking (one-way 2hr. by bike). Convenient car parks in Clare, Sevenhill, Watervale, and Auburn allow for walkers to take shorter journeys. The trail passes farms and vineyards, as well a few wineries, including Sevenhill Cellars. Bikes can be hired in Clare from **Clare Valley Cycle Hire,** 32 Victoria Rd. (☎8842 2782), lodged in a private house opposite the elementary school. The tourist office in Clare also has information on many bus tours of the valley including **Clare Valley Tours** (☎0418 832 812); these tend to be comprehensive but fairly pricey.

Sevenhill Cellars, College Rd., Sevenhill, (☎8843 4222), 6km south of Clare. Made since 1851 by and for the brothers of adjoining St. Aloysius church, this is the only religious winery in Australia. Seven Jesuit brothers have continued the 150-year tradition of wine-making. Check out the ancient wine cellars. Sacramental wine, sold tax-exempt only for religious purposes, is 33% of the output. Fine reds (including St. Ignatius), whites (including St. Aloysius), and fortified wines may be purchased, and the brothers heartily encourage tasting first. Open M-F 9am-4:30pm, Sa 10am-4pm.

Taylors Wines (☎8849 2008), off Mintaro Rd. just north of Auburn, 25km south of Clare. The largest winery in the Clare Valley, and the largest estate on one site in Australia, is housed in an enormous castle-lookalike. All wines are made only from grapes grown on the estate, and all are bottled here. Family-owned, they've won many awards with their lovely, cool whites and hearty reds. Their cabernet sauvignon is particularly excellent. Open M-F 9am-5pm, Sa 10am-5pm, Su 10am-4pm.

Leasingham Wines, 7 Dominic St., Clare (☎8842 2785). Perennial medal-winner and venerable Clare institution. The appeal is rounded out by a lovely setting, friendly service, and small wine-making museum. Riesling was developed here, but the winery is now pushing ahead with reds. Open M-F 8:30am-5pm, Sa-Su 10am-4pm.

BURRA

☎08

The rest of this region may draw tourists with wines and vines, but Burra's tourist economy depends on mines. The historic mining town, 30min. (40km) northeast of Clare and 156km north of Adelaide on the main route to Sydney via Broken Hill, plays up its copper roots for tourists. Seeing it today, it's hard to believe that Burra (pop. 2100) was the largest inland town in Australia in 1851, with almost 5000 people. While the town is not exactly a thrill a minute, it has latched onto historical tourism with tenacity and deserves its reputation as a state heritage area with surprisingly fascinating exhibits.

PRACTICAL INFORMATION. The town is centered around a creek. The highway spits cars right into **Market Square,** south of the creek, at the intersection of Market and Commercial St. The **post office** is on Market Sq. next to the IGA supermarket. The **Burra Visitor Centre,** 2 Market Sq., books copper and gold mining tours and Clare Valley winery tours. (☎8892 2154; fax 8892 2555. Open daily 9am-5pm. Most are half-day tours, $28-35.) Free **Internet** access is on offer at the community library, inside the school at the end of Bridge Tce., north of the creek. (Open M, W, F 9am-5pm; Tu, Th 9am-8pm).

ACCOMMODATIONS AND FOOD. In the 1840s, when many miners lived in mud dugouts along the banks of Burra Creek, the South Australian Mining Association built the **Paxton Square Cottages,** on Kingston St., just over the small bridge visible from Market Sq. The 32 cottages have stone floors, kitchens, fireplaces, and bath—a whole cottage for the price of a single! (☎8892 2622; fax 8892 2508. Linen $5.50. $29 per person, each extra person $12.) The 154-year-old **Burra Hotel** is in the town center. (☎8892 2389. Counter meals served M-Sa noon-2pm and 6-8pm. Singles $27.50; doubles $44.)

During the day, or for a light lunch, the **Burra Country Pantry** (☎8892 2400) in Market Square offers warm breads and delectable Cornish pasties ($1.50-2) or whole meals ($5-6.50). For budget dinners, you're limited to counter meals at any of the handful of hotels. At the **Commercial Hotel** (☎8892 2010), $3.75 will get you soup and a fresh roll, $4.50 a small pizza, or $6 a generous, tasty counter meal. Market Square has a small IGA **supermarket.** (Open M-F 8:45am-5:30pm, Sa 8:45-11am.)

SIGHTS. If you have a car and want to see the town's mining history, buy the **Burra Passport** at the tourist office, which includes all details for a self-guided driving tour of the area. ($11, concessions $9; with both museum entrances $20, $18.) The best part of the Passport is the key, which you can use to get into the old **Redruth Gaol** (a police lockup), the spooky **Unicorn Brewery Cellars** (the archaeological remains of an old township), and miners' dugouts. The museums have friendly staff who provide necessary background if you've gone this far in life without a detailed knowledge of the history of copper mining. **Morphett's Enginehouse Museum,** on the site of Burra Mine, details the mechanical aspects of the mine and the pumps that brought 15 million liters of water out of the ground each day. (☎8892 2154. Open M-F 11am-1pm, Sa-Su 11am-2pm. $4.50.) The **Burra Mine,** known as the **Monster Mine,** was the world's largest copper mine in the 1870s and saved the state from bankruptcy. The museum's highlight is the chance to climb through the adit, a small underground retimbered tunnel. The **Bon Accord Mining Museum** focuses on the social history of the mines by telling the stories of individual miners. (☎8892 2056. Open M-F 12:30-2:30pm, Sa-Su 12:30-3:30pm. $4.50.)

For those tired of copper, **Mongolata Gold Mine,** 23km east of Burra, offers a guided tour of the old government battery and of the mine underground. (☎8892 2233. $10, kids $5. Book ahead by phone or at the Burra office three doors down from the Visitor Center.) **Burra Trail Rides** (☎8892 2627), Basin Farm, 3km northeast of Burra off the road to Morgan, has horse rides starting at $15 per hr. and stock driving rides for 1-3 days, with meals and camping gear supplied. All skill levels easily accommodated. Call ahead or book at the Burra Visitor Centre.

SOUTHEAST OF MURRAY RIVER

The majestic Murray River winds west from the Great Dividing Range, fed by a watershed that spans most of New South Wales and portions of Victoria. The largest waterway in Australia, it slices through the southeast corner of South Australia and empties into the Southern Ocean. Fruit, especially wine grapes, flourishes along the irrigated river basin, while the Coorong, a 145km stretch of coastal lagoons, supports over 240 species of birdlife. The towns near the Victoria border can be associated with geographic regions within that state. The area around Naracoorte is an extension of the agricultural Wimmera district (see p. 441) and Mt. Gambier continues the themes of Victoria's southwest coast.

DRIVING THE PRINCES HIGHWAY

The road from Tailem Bend south toward Mt. Gambier runs along the Coorong, providing excellent access to both the wetlands of the coast and the fishing, swimming, and surfing beaches farther to the south.

MENINIGIE. Meninigie, at the northern end of the Princes Hwy., is the last town for 146km before Kingston SE, at the junction of Hwy. 1 and Alt. 1, the inland and coastal highways respectively. Public bathrooms on the foreshore provide a spot for bathers to change, so even those just cruising through the area can take a dip at the beach. There is a gas station at the southern end of the town. Probably most useful to travelers is the office of the **National Parks and Wildlife Service,** 34 Princes Hwy. (☎8575 1200), where one can pick up the magazine called *The Tattler*, covering the southeastern coastal parks from Goolwa to the Victoria border.

ROBE. Robe, 190km south of Meninigie, is a sleepy little beach town with Victorian buildings and good surf. There is **tourist information** at the **Robe Institute and Library,** on Mundy Tce. (☎8768 2465. Open M-F 9am-5pm, Sa-Su 10am-1pm.) For **RAA,** call 0427 714 204. Robe's **YHA Hostel** is for members only, and is part of the **Robe Long Beach Tourist Park,** about 1km from the main town. Anyone can rent a cabin, though. (☎8768 2237. Linen $5.50. Dorms $23; cabins from $36.60.) Foodland **grocery** store is on Main Rd. (☎8768 2263. Open daily 7:30am-7:30pm.)

MOUNT GAMBIER ☎08

In an obsidian palace deep beneath Mount Gambier's famed Blue Lake, a disgruntled deity lives in permanent exile. The Lake King originally lived with his fellow gods in divine bliss, but betrayed them during a conflict long since forgotten, and was banished. The lake's mercurial hues reflect his shifting moods; it's a shimmering sapphire during summer, but fades to slate gray in colder months.

For historical and cultural precision, it should be noted that *Let's Go* completely made up this story. Still, it's as good an explanation as any for the Blue Lake's biannual mysteriously shifting color, a phenomenon which continues to baffle scientists. The lake is Mount Gambier's big draw, but the town's caves and lively downtown filled with cafes and pubs are worth a spin, too. Plus, as the largest town in the area (pop. 21,000), Mount Gambier makes a good base for exploring nearby wineries or the caves of Naracoorte.

TRANSPORTATION AND PRACTICAL INFORMATION. V/Line buses stop at the Shell Blue Lake service station, 100 Commercial St. W., and run to Adelaide (6hr., 2 per day, $46.90) and Melbourne (7hr., 2 per day, $50) via the Victorian cities of Heywood, Portland, Port Fairy, Warrnambool, and Geelong.

The town's commercial area lies around the intersection of Bay and Commercial St., and extends back to James and Helen St. Here are the **pharmacies, markets, 24hr. ATMs,** and **banks.** The **Visitor Information Centre,** Jubilee Hwy. E., is easy to spot, because it's part of the **Lady Nelson Centre** (see **Sights,** p. 440), a huge landlocked ship. (Both centres ☎1800 087 187. Open daily 9am-5pm.) Services include: **Library,** in the Civic Centre, has free **Internet** (☎8721 2540; open M, W, F 9am-6pm; Tu 9am-5pm; Th 9am-8pm; Sa 9-11:30am); **police,** on Bay Rd. (☎8735 1020); **post office,** 30 Helen St. (Open M-F 9am-5pm.) **Postal code:** 5290.

ACCOMMODATIONS. **The Jail,** off Margaret St., promises a unique hosteling experience. As the name suggests, this place is a recently converted prison, "decriminalized" in 1995. The four- or six-share rooms are very comfortable, and the alcohol now flows freely in the behind-bars bar, but the owners are committed to retaining some of the penitentiary charm. Provision of brekkie is based on good behavior. (☎8723 0032 or 1800 626 844. Internet $2 per 15min. Dorms $19.70-20.70; doubles $42.60.) The reformed can head for the **Blue Lake Motel,** 1 Kennedy Ave.—turn left off Jubilee Hwy. W., 750m east of the Lady Nelson Centre. The congenial owners provide clean rooms with bath with four bunks each, as well as well-priced motel rooms. (☎8725 5211 or 1800 088 291. Linen $2. Dorms $14; singles $44; doubles 52.) Two of downtown's pub hotels also have some backpacker bunks, but only sparse kitchens. The **South Australia Hotel,** 78 Commercial St. E. (☎8725 2404), has dorm beds with linen provided for $20. The **Commercial Hotel,** 110 Commercial St. W., offers a similar deal, and it's 100m from the bus station. (☎8725 3006. Dorms $15.) **Blue Lake City Caravan Park,** on Bay Rd. up by the lake, is a veritable Disneyland of caravan parks. It's spotless, with facilities that include a pool, tennis and basketball courts, an 18-hole golf course, and spacious outdoor cooking facilities. (☎8725 9856. Sites $15, powered $18; caravans from $59.)

FOOD AND ENTERTAINMENT. The Central Business District is packed with chip shops and takeaway joints, supermarkets and green grocers. Mt. Gambier's hip **Jonties Cafe,** 13 Commercial St. E., opposite the courthouse, is an excellent spot to while away the day. The vibe is chill and the gourmet food reasonably priced at under $12 for dinner. They offer unique gourmet cooking classes, so even the traveler passing through has a chance to brush up on skills. (☎8723 9499. Open M-Sa 9:30am-11pm, Sa-Su 10am-3pm.) The informal **Caffé Belgiorno,** in the Oatmill Complex, 7 Percy St., has an airy balcony and enormous portions of Mediterranean risotto and pasta for $7-11. (☎8725 4455. Open Su-Th 11am-9pm, F-Sa 11am-10pm.) For carnivorous cravings, the **Longhorn Chargrill,** Percy St., serves up slabs of red meat (burgers from $6.50, steaks from $13) with a distinctly American flavor. (☎8724 8441. Open Tu-Su noon-2pm and 5:30-9:30pm.) The **Pepper Pot Cafe,** 41 Commercial Rd. E., across the street from the town hall, serves a scrumptious breakfast for $8. (☎8724 9220. Open M-F 8:45am-4:45pm, Sa-Su 8:45am-1:30pm.)

Pubs congregate in the town center. The **Mount Gambier Hotel,** 2 Commercial St. W., has high wooden ceilings, pool tables, video games, and live bands and dancing Th-Sa. (☎8725 0611. Open daily until midnight.) **Gambier City Bowling,** on Commercial St. W., offers a weekend special of two games of ten pin, hot dog, and a drink for $10. (☎8723 2442. Open M-Sa 10am-late, Su 11am-late. $7-10, children $6.) The **Oatmill Cinema,** Percy St., shows classics and new releases. (Toll-call ☎1902 241 060; $0.85 per min. $12.50, concessions $10.) The **Sir Robert Helpmann Theatre** (☎8723 8741), in the Civic Centre on Wallace Tce., houses an experimental company as well as some touring shows in a 528-seat, ultramodern auditorium.

SIGHTS. Bay Rd. goes south through town to passing views of **Blue Lake** and its resident demons, or whatever makes it change color. The lake itself fills the crater of a volcano that erupted 4000-5000 years ago, and holds 8 billion gallons of water, which are used to supply the town's thirsty gullets and flush toilets. You can only get to the lake's surface by a 45min. tour that goes down to the pumping station in a glass lift. (☎8723 1199. Daily tours on the hr. Nov.-Jan. 9am-5pm, Feb.-May 9am-2pm, June-Aug. 9am-noon, Sept.-Oct. 9am-2pm. $5.50, children $2.)

Just south of the Blue Lake, by the entrance to the Blue Lake City Caravan Park, a clearly marked road leads up to absolutely beautiful walking tracks that access Mt. Gambier, the Devil's Teacup, and the now-dry Leg of Mutton Lake—the butterflies, crickets, and grasshoppers outnumber the flies a million to one. The 2.3km walk to the top of the mountain is best attempted in the morning.

Lt. James Grant was the first European to sight Mt. Gambier as he sailed on the brig *Lady Nelson* in 1800. A replica of this historic ship on Jubilee Hwy. E. graces the **Lady Nelson Centre,** highlighting the area's history and geological phenomena. (☎1800 087 187. Open daily 9am-5pm. $7.70, concessions $6.60, children $3.30.)

Back in town center, there are two caves. The **Cave Gardens,** at Bay Rd. and Watson Tce., the town's original water source, is the centerpiece of the town square park, with roses and trickling waterfalls (always open, lit at night, free). The flooded **Engelbrecht Cave,** on Jubilee Hwy. W. between Victoria Tce. and Ehret St., is a popular spot for adequately trained **cave divers.** Two of the cave's chambers are open for viewing. (☎ 8725 5493. Open daily 11am-3pm. Tours on the hr. $5.50, concessions $2.50.) A third nifty hole in the ground on Jubilee Hwy. E. known as the **Umpherston Sinkhole** is carpeted with trees, ivy, and flowers, has BBQ and picnic facilities, and is dramatically lit at night (always open, free).

NARACOORTE ☎08

The best part of Naracoorte is underground. The small town, roughly 125km west of Horsham, VIC, on the Wimmera Hwy., and 100km north of Mt. Gambier along the Riddoch Hwy., would be a good deal more anonymous if it weren't for the residents' cleanliness (the town was Australia's tidiest five times in the 1990s, but hasn't been so squeaky clean this century) and a nearby network of eerily gorgeous caves, recently designated a World Heritage site.

PRACTICAL INFORMATION. Almost everything in this small town is on one of two streets, **Commercial St.** and **Smith St.,** running parallel on either side of the village green. **The Sheeps Back Wool Museum and Tourist Information Centre,** northwest of the town center on MacDonnell Rd., has info and a museum. (☎8762 1518 or 1800 244 421. Open daily 9am-4pm. Museum $5.) Services include: **ATMs** and banks in CBD; Foodland **supermarket,** 63 Ormerod St. (open M-F 8:30am-8pm, Sa 8:30am-5pm, Su 9:30am-5pm); public **library** with free **Internet** (open M 10am-5pm; Tu, W, F 9:30am-5pm; Th 10am-8pm; Sa 8:30am-noon); **police,** 56 Smith St. (☎8762 0466), in a mural-bedecked building; **hospital** (☎8762 8100), at Jenkins Tce.; **post office,** 23 Ormerod St. (Open M-F 9am-5pm.) **Postal code:** 5271

ACCOMMODATIONS AND FOOD. Naracoorte Backpackers, 4 Jones St., is mostly a workers' hostel but has standard dorm beds for those stopping over as well. (☎8762 3835; www.nctebackpackers.mtx.net. Internet $2 per hr. Dorms $17; weekly $100.) Two hotels face each other across Naracoorte's central green. The **Kincraig Hotel,** 168 Smith St., offers hotel rooms with sinks. (☎8762 2200. Singles $27.50; doubles $44.) Its doppelganger, the **Naracoorte Hotel-Motel,** 73 Ormerod St., has the better restaurant, but similar accommodation. (☎8762 2400. Singles $27; doubles $47.) **Camping** is available both at Bool Lagoon and at Naracoorte Caves Conservation Park (NCCP). Get **permits** at the Conservation Park ticket office or the permit kiosk (open daily 10am-3pm) at Bool Lagoon. Questions should be directed to NCCP. (☎8762 2340. Laundry, BBQ, showers, and toilets. $17 per car.) Tucked away on Rivoli Ln. off Smith St., the **Blue Wattle** has gourmet meals at down-to-earth prices—mains around $12. (☎8762 3565. Open Th-Sa 5pm-late.)

SIGHTS. Twelve kilometers south of town is the **Naracoorte Caves Conservation Park,** a well-marked 4km west off the Riddoch Hwy. The Wonambi Fossil Centre is next to the carpark, with a wealth of information on one of only two fossil sites in Australia deemed important enough to merit World Heritage protection. (☎8762 2340. Open daily 9am-5pm.) One of the younger caves in the park, the Alexandra Cave features five chambers full of delicate calcite stalagmites, stalactites, straws, and flowstone. Blanche Cave lacks these delicate decorations, but has immense columns and windows caused by a partial collapse of the roof. Back in the 1850s, the local landlord used the cave for lavish parties, and the furniture remains inside. The most famous of the caves, the Victoria Fossil Cave, discovered in 1969, contains the remains of nearly 100 different species of Pleistocene fauna from 10,000 to two million years ago. So far nearly 4km of this cave has been explored, but it's thought to be much bigger. Buried under silt after dying in the cave, the animals' fossils provide important clues to how the Australian marsupial megafauna were affected by the arrival of humans. Infrared bat-cameras have been installed in Bat Cave to allow tourists to view the 300,000 resident bats without disturbing their breeding grounds. Wet Cave isn't quite as spectacular as the others, but it's the only cave you can see without a guide. Excellent tours are available daily 9:30am-4pm, on the following routes: Wonambi Fossil Centre and Wet Cave (self-guided); Alexandra Cave and Wet Cave; Bat Centre and Blanche Cave; Victoria Fossil Cave. (Tickets from the Wonambi Fossil Centre. 1 tour $9, concessions $7, children $5.50; 2 tours $16/ $12/$9; 3 tours $22/$16/$13; 4 tours for the cave-aholic $28/$22/$17.) The rangers insist you wear closed-toed shoes. Bring a sweater as the temperature is a constant 17°C. Adventure caving trips are available for both novices and advanced spelunkers. Book ahead via the Park's head office. Back in town, refresh yourself at the free, glittering **swimming lake** (northeast of the central green).

YORKE PENINSULA

On Yorke, sandy flats punctuate rolling farmland, and sheer cliffs, looming over the hinterland, storm into the sea. What isn't farmed is covered in scrub forest. The northern half of the Yorke primarily features copper-mining history, centered on the Copper Triangle. After Copper went bust in the 1920s, historical tourism, fishing—both recreational and industrial—became increasingly important. Visitors should take heed: in the summer a northern wind that is hotter than hell sweeps the peninsula and the air drips with swarms of Beelzebub's flies. Refuge is on hand at beach towns like Wallaroo, or the real highlight of the region, the spectacular Innes National Park, where your jaw will fall slack at the sight of the mind-blowing ocean views, electrifying surfing beaches, and gorgeous camping.

THE COPPER TRIANGLE ☎08

With Wallaroo's glittering beaches at its apex, the towns of Kadina, Wallaroo, and Moonta are collectively known as the Copper Triangle (or Coast). This trio of mining towns sprung up as a result of discoveries of large copper deposits found in the 1860s. After a worldwide copper glut in the 1920s, the largest mines closed, and now the towns revolve around enormous grain silos. All three gaily celebrate the Cornish heritage of the Yorke Peninsula during Kernewek Lowender, the world's largest Cornish festival (May 12-15, 2002). Though they may be triplets, these towns are not identical. Wallaroo is the only one located on the ocean (the area's biggest draw being the beach). Kadina is the most cosmopolitan (which isn't saying much), and Moonta plays its Cornish and mining heritage to the hilt.

TRANSPORTATION AND PRACTICAL INFORMATION. Premier Stateliner runs **buses** to and from Adelaide via Port Wakefield to all three towns. (☎8415 5555. Buses depart from and return to Adelaide twice per day M-F, and once per day Sa-Su. $18, ages 5-15 $9.) The **Moonta Station Visitor Centre,** on Kadina Rd. in the old railway station, serves the whole Copper Triangle (☎8825 1891. Open daily 9am-5pm.) A 2min. walk from the center of town, the **Kadina Community Library,** 1a Doswell Tce., offers free **Internet** access on three terminals, though you have to sign up in advance at busy times. (☎8821 0444. Open M 9:30am-1:30pm, Tu, W, F 9:30am-5:30pm, Th 9:30am-8pm, Sa 9:30am-11:30am.) Kadina is proud to host some of the peninsula's only **ATMs,** and also provides the area's **RAA** services (☎8821 1111; mobile 0418 859 070).

ACCOMMODATIONS. Basic pub accommodations are easy to find. Kadina has the **Wombat Hotel,** 19 Taylor St. (☎8821 1108. Singles $25, doubles $40, including light breakfast.) In Moonta, the **Cornwall Hotel,** 18 Ryan St., opposite the post office, has affordable rooms and cheap counter meals. (☎8825 2304. Singles $20, doubles $40; most rooms with balcony, some with kitchens.) For freedom from pubs, refuge can be found at the beautiful **Sonbern Lodge Motel,** 18 John Tce., Wallaroo. The pool table and velvet chairs look as though they would be layered in the dust of ages, if only they weren't so clean. The Sonbern also stocks plenty of tourist information. (☎8823 2291; fax 8823 3355. Singles $26, with bath $46; doubles $40/57. Most with balcony.)

FOOD. The Yorke Peninsula is famous for its Cornish cuisine, especially the pasty (about $1.50), but only Moonta is bold enough to claim the moniker, "Australia's Little Cornwall." Of the sit-down restaurants in the Copper Triangle, **Skinner's Fish Cafe,** on Jetty Rd., Wallaroo, is easily the best. Fresh seafood is served (entrees $14-24) in a dining room overlooking the jetty or outside in a leafy garden. Downstairs is an inexpensive take-away counter. (☎8823 3455. Take-away counter open daily 10am-9pm. Dining room open daily noon-2pm and 6-9pm.) **Price's Bakery,** on Owen Tce. in Wallaroo, offers what everybody at the beach wants: a clean store with good sweets ($1.50), ice creams, pasties ($1.60), sandwiches ($2-3), sparklers, and cigarettes. (☎8823 2223. Open M-F and Su 8:30am-5:30pm, Sa 8:30am-4pm.) Moonta's impeccably kept **Cornish Kitchen,** 8 Ellen St., serves up Little Cornwall's best pasties (1.60-2) and even gives old Cornwall a run for its money. (☎8825 3030. Open daily 10am-3:30pm.) Wallaroo's supermarket, **Foodland,** is conveniently located on the corner of Hughes and Hamilton St. (Open M-W and F 7:30am-6pm, Th 7:30am-8pm, Sa-Su 8am-6pm.)

SIGHTS. The deepest attraction is the **Wheal Hughes Copper Mine**, on the Wallaroo road at the outskirts of Moonta. Tours venture underground to explore the workings of this real-life mine. Reasonable fitness and a pair of socks required; boots and (heavy) helmet provided. Purchase tickets at the Moonta Visitor Centre by 12:30pm, then get yourself to the mine. (1½hr. Departs 1pm. $13.20; children $6.60, no children under six; seniors $11.) For something a bit more eccentric and entertaining, head to the multi-award-winning **Banking and Currency Museum,** 3 Graves St., in Kadina. Take a tour through this tribute to tender. Money lines everything, from the walls to the doors. The museum also has over 2500 money boxes on display. (☎8821 2906; fax 8821 2901. Open July-May Su-Th 10am-4:30pm. $3, children $1.) Wallaroo offers an overview of the area's history at the **Heritage and Nautical Museum** (corner of Emu and Jetty Rd.), not to mention George the Giant Squid. (☎8823 3015. Open W 10:30am-4pm, Sa-Su 2-4pm.)

INNES NATIONAL PARK

Stunningly gorgeous Innes National Park, on the southwest tip of the peninsula, is the real attraction of the Yorke. It's primarily known as a fantastic spot for surfing, diving, snorkeling, whale watching, and fishing, but there's plenty of room for folks just driving in to picnic and take in the views. 9141 hectares were set aside as national park land in 1970 to encourage the re-population of the rare Great Western Whipbird. Visitors may not catch sight of these rather shy creatures (which make a grating "happy-birthday-to-you" call), but the sculptured headlands and crashing waves justify the drive from up north.

The Yorke Peninsula Passenger Service (☎1800 625 099) runs **buses** daily from **Adelaide** to **Yorketown** for $28.40. However, buses go no farther than **Warooka,** west of Yorketown, and Stenhouse Bay is more than 50km farther, requiring a car for any measure of flexibility in exploring the park. A daypass costs $6 per vehicle (fee waived if camping) and can be purchased from the Visitor Centre or from any of the self-registration stations near the entrance to the park. The park's main road, 26km long, is sealed and suitable for conventional vehicles; although the side roads to beaches and overlooks are not sealed, many with 2WD cars still drive on them. The park only can be entered or exited from the westernmost point.

The park entrance, trading post, and **National Park Visitor Centre** (☎8854 3200) make up the entirety of the local metropolis, **Stenhouse Bay.** The **Innes Park Trading Post** (☎8854 4066), just inside the park entrance, has food, a bar, and information on fishing hot-spots and which park areas are safe for swimming and surfing. The Trading Post also rents rooms in a building at the park entrance ($12 per person), fills SCUBA tanks, and sells unleaded gas at regular prices.

"Beds" in the southern tip of the peninsula are usually sleeping bags, best used in the park itself. No bookings are required for **sites** in the park; self-register at the office just inside the entrance for camping in designated areas. Sites at **Pondalowie Bay** have water and toilets ($15 per vehicle). All other camping areas cost $6 per vehicle. Several **lodges** and **huts** provide shelter within the park; contact the Visitor Centre for bookings. Some have solar-powered lighting, full kitchens, and flush toilets. Others just have four walls. The lodges sleep four to 12 people. ($22-65 per person; booking and payment due two weeks prior to arrival.) The nearest hostel accommodation is about 100km from the park, in Port Vincent on the eastern coast of the peninsula. The **Tuckerway Hostel,** 14 Lime Kiln Rd., provides a simple but clean place to lay your head. The large 52-bed facility is more often used by school groups than by individuals, but the price can't be beat. (☎/fax 8853 7285. No linen. Dorms $10, under 18 $7. YHA. Definitely call ahead.) You can also find the standard pub accommodations in Warooka, about 50km away.

FLINDERS RANGES

With soft, worn-down mountain ranges instead of huge, craggy peaks, you can see that Flinders is ancient country. Geologically speaking, it's one of the three oldest mountain formations in the world. The main road (Hwy. 47) drifts between kangaroo-filled flatlands, sagebrush-covered hills; dirt-tracks (4WD-only) can take you through some beautiful gorges. Flinders is most popular from April to October, when the nights are chilly and the days sunny. It's hot, hot, hot in summer, but for drivers with A/C or hikers with a hard-core mentality it's still worth the trip. The Ranges begin at the northern end of the Gulf of St. Vincent and continue 400km into South Australia's vast northern outback, ending near Mt. Hopeless (which is a pretty accurate description of the terrain out there). The Ranges are divided into three sections--southern, central, and northern--with a National Park in each.

GUIDED TOURS

Travelers looking to tour Flinders can jump on multiple-day trips in Adelaide or get themselves to the local hotspot, Quorn (see p. 446), and take more individualized, often shorter tours from there. Many tours heading from Adelaide to Alice Springs stops at Flinders. One of the best operations is **Wallaby Tracks Adventure Tours,** run by the Andu Lodge in Quorn, with pick-up in Port Augusta or Adelaide. Their knowledgeable guides take backpackers into central Flinders, including bush camping and stops at Wilpena Pound, Aboriginal art sites, and Bunyeroo Gorge. (☎8648 6655 or 1800 639 933. 2-3 days $199-299.) The specialized **Quorn Flinders Ranges Eco-Tours,** 2 Railway Tce. (☎8648 6016), offers 4WD tours into Dutchman Stern Conservation Park (half-day $44) and northern Flinders tours (5 days). Self-drive tours are also available; inquire at Quorn's **Mill Motel,** 2 Railway Tce. (☎8648 6016), or at the Visitor Centre. The old, steam-powered **Pichi Richi Railway,** Railway Tce., travels through the Flinders Apr.-Oct., on the route of the Old Ghan. (☎/fax 8658 1109. Quorn-Woolshed Flat 2½hr., $28; Quorn-Saltia 3½hr., $36.)

Adelaide Sightseeing offers the marathon one-day return jaunt to Wilpena Pound. (☎8231 4144; $156.) **Wayward Bus,** 237 Hutt St., Adelaide, has an eight-day South Aussie Outback tour covering the Flinders and Coober Pedy. Travelers bus to Coober Pedy, then travel to the William Creek Pub and back south through the Flinders and the wine valleys. (☎8232 6646. $730, including meals and accommodation.) **Outback 'n' Coastal 4WD Adventures** has three-day Flinders camping trips with a maximum of seven passengers. (☎0417 856 712; $330.)

PORT AUGUSTA ☎08

Port Augusta (pop. 14, 800) promotes itself as the "Crossroads of Australia." There is an element of truth to this; travelers who stop here are almost all road-weary and on their way to somewhere else. The **Wadlata Outback Centre,** 41 Flinders Tce., has an excellent hands-on display of the stories, culture, and land of the outback. (☎8642 4511. Open M-F 9am-5:30pm, Sa-Su 10am-4pm. $8.25, concessions $4.95.) The fascinating **Arid Lands Botanic Gardens,** 400m north of town off the Stuart Hwy., offer bushwalking trails with labeled plants. (☎8641 1049. Open M-F 9am-5pm, Sa-Su 10am-4pm. Free.)

Port Augusta Backpackers, 17 Trent Rd., is not fancy but is ridiculously cheap, with free email, free pickup, and free breakfast. (☎8641 1063. Dorms $11.) The **Bluefox Lodge,** at Trent Rd. and Hwy 1., offers free bus-station pickup, seasonal vegetables, Internet ($2 per 15min.) and provides amusing tours of the Flinders ranges. (☎8641 2960. Beds $15; A/C $5 extra.) **Port Augusta Holiday Park (Big 4),** Stokes Tce. off Stuart Hwy., is over the bridge north of downtown and has a pool. (☎8642 2974. Dorms $13; sites for 2 $18, powered $19; on-site vans for 2 $59.) **Hot Pepper Cafe,** 34 Commercial Rd., has sandwiches, coffee, and the chicest atmosphere in town. (☎8642 2549. Open M-W 9:30am-5pm, Th 9:30am-6pm, F 9:30am-5:30pm, Sa 9:30am-noon.) Coles **supermarket** is on the corner of Jervois and Maryatt St. (☎8641 1700. Open daily 6am-midnight.)

Stateliner (☎8642 5055) runs **buses** to: Adelaide (4hr., 3-5 per day, $34.80); Whyalla (1hr., 2-5 per day, $14); Wilpena Pound (2hr.; Su, W, F; $30.50) via Quorn (35min.). The bus station is opposite the library on Mackay St. The *Ghan* and *Indian Pacific* **trains** depart from off of Stirling Rd. to Alice Springs (15hr.; M and Th 7pm; $168, concessions $82) and Perth (33hr.; Tu and F 10:50pm; $260, concessions $123). Contact **Harvey World Travel,** 91 Commercial Rd. (☎8642 6699), or call 13 22 32 to book. **Budget,** 16 Young St. (☎8642 6040), rents vehicles.

The highway becomes **Victoria Pde.** in the city. The city center focuses around **Commercial Rd.,** with **post office, banks,** and **ATMs.** Services include: **Tourist Information Office,** 41 Flinders Tce., in the same building as Wadlata Outback Centre (☎8641 0793; open M-F 9am-5:30pm, Sa-Su 10am-4pm); **National Parks and Wildlife Service,** 9 Mackay St. (☎8548 5300); the **library,** on the corner of Mackay and Marryatt St., with free **Internet** (☎8641 9151; open M and F 9am-6pm, Tu and W 9am-8pm, Th 9am-9pm, Sa 10am-1pm, and Su 2-5pm).

SOUTHERN FLINDERS

MT. REMARKABLE NATIONAL PARK

Between Adelaide and Port Augusta, near the industrial town of Port Pirie, Mt. Remarkable National Park (15,632 hectares) is the pride of the southern Flinders Range. The terrain rolls more gently and is lusher than the continuations of the Flinders farther north, perfect for laid-back bushwalking and camping. **Mt. Remarkable** can be approached on a 4hr. return hike from a trail starting 3km north of **Melrose** (24km south of Wilmington), along Main North Rd. The **Alligator Gorge** trail (1.2km; 1hr. return) has the best scenery on the eastern side of the park. Alligator Gorge is accessible at Wilmington, on Main North Rd. between Clare and Port Augusta; or by the cross-park trail (26km; 10hr.), starting from Mambray Creek.

The **park headquarters** is on the western side of the park at Mambray Creek, 45km north of Port Pirie, directly off Hwy. 1 on a road lined with magnificent eucalypts. There is a pay station with trail maps, a 54-site campground, and access to bushwalks through canyons or over ridges. (☎8634 7068. Park fees $6 per vehicle, $14 per vehicle to camp; bushcamping $4 per person.) Bush camping is prohibited during South Australia's fire ban season, from Nov. 1 to Apr. 30. **National Parks and Wildlife** (☎8634 7068) in Port Augusta has more details.

The hamlet of **Melrose,** on the eastern side of the park 20km south of Wilmington, makes a good base for hikes in Mt. Remarkable. Local mogul Joe runs the **Melrose Caravan Park.** (☎8666 2060. Sites $4-9 per person; vans from $39; backpacker accommodation $13.) **Bluey Blundstone's Blacksmith Shop** offers coffee and light meals; there's also a pricey B&B attached. (☎8666 2017. Open M and W-F 11am-4pm, Sa-Su 10am-5pm.) Despite being the oldest licensed bar in the Flinders, the **North Star Hotel** has caught up with the modern age and offers free Internet access to all customers. They also offer the standard pub-hotel amenities of rooms, cheap meals, and endless stubbies. (☎8666 2110. Rooms $45-60.)

CENTRAL FLINDERS

The most famous attractions of the Flinders, including the vast amphitheater-like Wilpena Pound, are in the central part of the range. To reach Quorn, Hawker, Rawnsley Park, or Wilpena Pound via public transport, take **Stateliner** connecting through Port Augusta. (Adelaide ☎8415 5555; Port Augusta ☎8642 5055. Departs Adelaide and Port Augusta W, F, Su.) If you have a Greyhound Pioneer bus pass, Stateliner fares into the Flinders are half-price. Stateliner service to Port Augusta via Hawker and Quorn leaves Wilpena Pound (Th-F, Su). Connections to Adelaide are available from all three buses. Wilpena Pound marks the end of regular public transport into the Flinders. Many private tours (p. 444) offer the cheapest and most flexible ways to reach the Central Flinders without a car.

QUORN ☎08

Smack in the middle of the Flinders Ranges, Quorn (pop. 1400) is the outback town from the movies. Its historical streets and hilly backdrop have appeared in at least nine films, including the WWII epic *Gallipoli*. The friendly pubs and country hospitality are completely devoid of any saccharine edge; the community creates a simple, relaxing atmosphere in which to take in the beauty of the Flinders Ranges.

TRANSPORTATION AND PRACTICAL INFORMATION. Quorn lies 40km northeast of Port Augusta and Hwy. 1, and 340km north of Adelaide, on Hwy. 47. **Stateliner** runs from Adelaide to Quorn Port Augusta. (☎8415 5555. 1 per day Su, W, F; $46.) **Andu Lodge** (☎1800 639 933; see below) offers the cheapest and most flexible travel service; they will pickup or drop off, by arrangement, in Port Augusta, Wilpena Pound, Devil's Peak, and Dutchman's Stern. **Railway Tce.** is the main street. The volunteer-staffed **Flinders Ranges Visitor Information Centre,** 3 Seventh St. (☎/fax 8648 6419), is open M-F 9am-5pm. There are **no ATMs** in the Flinders, but if in desperate need of cash some service stations will give cash advances through **EFTPOS.** Services include: **National Australia Bank,** Railway Tce., (open M-Tu, Th-F noon-4pm); **police** (☎8648 6060); **Northern Roads Conditions Hotline** (☎1300 361 033); a sparsely-stocked IGA **grocery store,** on Seventh St. (open M-F 8am-6pm, Sa 9am-4:30pm, Su 9am-2:30pm); **Internet access**, at the **library,** West Tce. (☎8648 6101; open M 8:30am-4pm, Tu and F 8:30am-6pm, W-Th 8:30am-5pm, Sa 10am-noon); **post office**, 21 Railway Tce. **Post code:** 5433.

ACCOMMODATIONS AND FOOD. **Andu Lodge,** 12 First St., is an excellent base for a Flinders holiday. Short-term staff are sometimes hired in exchange for accommodation, breakfasts, and a free Flinders trip. The main building was originally one of the first bush hospitals. They have clean rooms, a kitchen, a Western movie collection, Internet, and bike hire. (☎/fax 8648 6898 or 1800 639 933. Dorms $18; singles $28; twins and doubles $46; families $65.) The **Transcontinental Hotel,** Railway Tce., is the best backpacking option of Quorn's four pub-hotels. The bar below is a great place to chill out and meet locals. (☎8648 6076; fax 8648 6155. Singles $32; doubles $54. Ask about "backpacker specials.") There is camping (unpowered tents only) in **Warren Gorge,** a beautiful spot owned by the town; check openings at the Visitor Centre (see **Practical Information,** p. 446). The **Hawker**

SOUTH AUSTRALIA

Hotel Motel, on the north of Quorn, has firm beds, clean bathrooms, and A/C in most hotel rooms. (☎8648 4102. Singles $33; twins and doubles from $44.)

The **Quandong Cafe and Bakery,** 31 First St., has wholesome food and doubles as a pleasant art gallery. (☎8648 6155. Open daily 9:30am-4:30pm.) Though you'd never expect it by looking at Quorn, the town houses a tasty Thai takeaway (dishes $5.50-9) inside the **Buckaringa Better Buy Market,** an emporium for everything from bulk candy to desk chairs. (☎8648 6381. Open daily 9am-8pm.) For sit-down meals, the **Criterion Hotel,** Railway Tce., offers the cheapest specials in town ($6) with unlimited visits to the salad bar. (Open daily noon-1:45pm and 6-8pm.)

HIKING. With the base of the hike only 9km from town, Quorn has one of the most rewarding easier hikes in the area: the **Devil's Peak** hike (2hr. return) affords stunning 360-degree views across the Flinders region. Hikers who climb **Dutchman's Stern,** a bluff 10km north of Quorn, are rewarded with views of **Spencer Gulf.** Two main walks include a ridgetop hike (8.2km; 4hr. return) and a loop walk (10.5km; 5hr.). **Mt. Brown Conservation Park,** 16km south of town on Richmond Valley Rd., contains the usually dry **Waukerie Falls** and **Mt. Brown**. (Open May-Sept.)

WILPENA POUND AND FLINDERS RANGES NATIONAL PARK

Wilpena Pound is the stuff of legends. The Pound, 450km north of Adelaide (4-5hr. drive), looks like a huge crater, but is actually a syncline (geological downfold) outlined in quartzite. It is the best-known rock formation in the state. The surrounding national park offers spectacular views, challenging hikes, and a glimpse into Aboriginal and geological history. This is some of the best scenery in South Australia, immortalized in many of Hans Heysen's landscapes.

TRANSPORTATION AND PRACTICAL INFORMATION. Most of the tours through the Flinders stop by Wilpena Pound. You can also take the **Stateliner** bus (☎8415 5555) from Adelaide (7hr., $61) or from Port Augusta ($30.50), but be aware that camping is the only budget accommodation once in the Pound. In an **emergency,** contact park headquarters in Wilpena Pound (☎8648 4244, afterhours 8648 4248), police in Hawker (☎8648 4028), or the ranger on duty (☎8648 0049) who can connect you to medical or fire services.

The helpful **Wilpena Visitor Centre** serves as the headquarters for the national park, and is the place to get general park and hiking info, buy day-passes ($6), and register to camp. There's a general store just behind the Centre which lets you stock up on food, drink, and has camping equipment. (☎8648 0048. Both open daily 8am-6pm.) You can also use the self-registration station at the entrance to the park on the Hawker-Blinman Rd.

ACCOMMODATION. Camping in the park at designated sites costs $6 per night per vehicle, including the park entrance fee. A few sites have toilets and water, but most just have dirt. For a shower, hit the refurbished Wilpena Campground. (Sites for 2 $16, powered $22, each extra person $4. Check-in at the Visitor Centre.) The privately-owned **Wilpena Pound Resort** (☎8648 0004 or 1800 805 802; fax 8648 0028) also operates a general store, petrol station, restaurant, bar, campground, and up-scale motel with singles from $92, doubles from $99. If you're there in the summer, check for backpacker specials. Bar meals are tasty and cheaper ($9-15) than the restaurant ones. (Meals daily 6:30-8:30pm.)

HIKING. To explore **Wilpena Pound,** you must sweat or spend a bit, since no cars are allowed into the Pound itself. For any walk, advise the ranger of your plans and your expected time of return by signing into the logbook by the Visitor Centre. The helpful brochure, *Bushwalking in the Flinders Ranges National Park,* is available at the Visitor Centre. Almost all the hikes leave from the Visitor Centre and follow the same path for the first 2km or so. This early stretch along the creek is shady, flat, and filled with 'roos, parrots, butterflies, and wildflowers.

Check out the burnt-out tree on the right side of the trail that is the spitting image of the Statue of Liberty. After the trail starts climbing a bit, it crosses a creek and then leads to a cabin called **Hill's Homestead** (toilets available).

A short, somewhat steep walk up **Wangarra Hill** behind the homestead leads to the lower (5min.) and upper (20min.) lookouts over the Pound. A shuttle **bus service** from the visitors center to the Pound cuts 2km off the trip each way, leaving you about 800m from Hill's Homestead, and making it a 90min. excursion up to Wangarra and back (2-3 per day; $3 return). Visitors should leave pets at home: the park is full of traps set to kill foxes, based on a chemical produced by Australian plants, harmless to native animals, but lethal to foxes and dogs. A high-intensity scrambling climb for serious hikers is the rocky trail to **St. Mary's Peak** (11.8km return direct route, 5hr.; 16.8km circuit returning via Wilpena Pound, 7hr.).

Many visitors consider the **drive** through the park's gorges, with their colored walls and geological structures, more beautiful than the walk into the Pound itself, with the drive through **Bunyeroo Gorge** to **Brachina Gorge** as the highlight. The turn-off for the gorges is 4km north of the Wilpena junction on the road toward Blinman. These roads are usually accessible to 2WD and 4WD, but it's always a good idea to ask at the visitor center first (see **Flinders Highway,** p. 456). The best way to see the majestic beauty of the Pound is to take a **flight.** A handful of companies offer rides in four- to six-seater planes, including **Air Wilpena** (☎8648 0004; $80 per 30min.). Discounts for small groups or for backpackers are easy to arrange.

NEAR FLINDERS RANGES NATIONAL PARK

RAWNSLEY PARK STATION

Rawnsley Park Station (cabins ☎8648 0030, caravans 8648 0008), south of the park off the road between Wilpena and Hawker, offers horseback riding (minimum 2 people; 1hr. $30 per person, 2hr. $40, half-day $70, full-day $100), sheep shearing, scenic flights, 4WD tours (half-day $55; full-day $85 includes lunch), and mountain bike hire ($5 per hr., half-day $15, full-day $25). The station also runs a group-only 48-bed bunkhouse and has a caravan park.

PARACHILNA

Just north of the park, 89km north of Hawker on Hwy. 83, Parachilna is a tiny blip of a town well worth knowing about. The **Prairie Hotel** has both luxury and budget accommodation in the same complex. Film crews shooting movies or 4WD commercials (the Flinders provide the perfect terrain for showing off that cornering power) often stay in the luxury section (singles from $110). Backpackers enjoy the sparkling pool, newly-renovated kitchen/bar area with Internet, and air-conditioned rooms, but the bathrooms are very basic. The hotel's scrumptious **restaurant** does wonderful things with outback meat, offering a delicious emu burger ($10) and a feral grill ('roo, camel, venison, goat; backpacker special $12). The scene in the bar can get rambunctious, and is open until the crowd decides to leave. (☎8648 4895; ab@flinders.outback.on.net. Food noon-8:30pm. Dorms with linen $20; cabins with kitchens from $55.)

SOUTH AUSTRALIA

BLINMAN POOLS

The hostel at **Angorichina,** halfway along the unsealed, rocky road between Parachilna and Blinman, has **dorms, cabins, campsites,** and a **general store** with fuel and tire repair. (☎8648 4842. Store open M-Sa 8:30am-6:30pm, Su 9:30am-noon and 4-6:30pm. Sites $6, 2 person powered $15; dorms $13; cabins $30-65.) From the carpark, a 4hr. return hike to the spring-fed **Blinman Pools** is one of the Flinders' most beautiful hikes. **Blinman,** at the northern edge of Flinders Ranges National Park, is not an exciting town (pop. 20), but it has the necessary amenities. The short walk (20-30min.) to the **war monument** at the highest point in town is worthwhile. The 360° view over purple mountain ranges is one of the best.

NORTHERN FLINDERS

Adventurous travelers with strong legs for hiking, a strong car for driving, and a strong psyche for dealing with isolation will find much challenge and beauty in the rugged, remote terrain that stretches north toward the central deserts. To cover the couple hundred kilometers between Flinders Range National Park and Gammon Ranges National Park, drivers can either come up through Wilpena and Blinman (see p. 448) or stick to the highway from Hawker and follow the pavement as far as Copley. The stops described here are along that highway.

LEIGH CREEK ☎08

After Coober Pedy, Leigh Creek is the largest town in the state north of Port Augusta. The town, 22km south of the coalfield, was entirely pre-planned and built by the **Electricity Trust of South Australia (ETSA)** between 1979 and 1984. Therefore the town, worlds apart from every other South Australian outback town, is neatly arranged and feels vaguely like your grandmother's retirement community. About 2000 people lived here a few years ago, but now just 600 call it home because the coal mining operation, the town's lifeblood, is waning. The **visitor information office** can help you with questions. (☎8675 4316. Open M-F 9am-5pm; closed during school holidays.) The landscaped downtown area has a **pub, supermarket, cafeteria, police** (☎8675 2004), **library, theater,** and a small **hospital** (☎8675 2018). **Internet** is free at the school library. (Open M, W-Th 8:30am-4:30pm; Tu, F 8:30am-4:30pm and 7-9pm; Sa 9am-noon.) **Leigh Creek South Motors** has fuel, tires, showers, and toilets. (☎8675 2016. Open M-Sa 8am-8pm, Su 9am-8pm.) Book ahead for coal mine tours (☎8675 4316). The **hotel** in town isn't cheap. (☎8675 2025. Singles $70.) The **Open Cut Cafe,** in the town center, has light meals. (☎8675 2050. Open M-Th and Sa 8am-6pm, F 8am-8pm, Su 10am-4pm.) Leigh Creek is near the Oodnadatta Track (see p. 453).

COPLEY ☎08

Copley, 6km north of Leigh Creek, is 267 sealed kilometers northeast of Port Augusta, and 130 unsealed kilometers west of Arkaroola. **Cookes Outback Motors** (☎8675 2618) has 24hr. RAA towing, tires, and car batteries. **Copley Caravan Park** (☎8675 2288) has caravan and sites ($5 per person) as well as cabins and on-site vans for two ($40-45). The **hotel** has a busy, friendly pub. (☎8675 2635. Singles $37; twins $47.) **Tulloch's Bush Bakery and Quandong Cafe** is a gourmet aberration with quandong pie ($3; the quandong is a shiny red outback stone fruit like a peach) and unusual meat pies like kangaroo and claret. (☎8675 2683. Open daily 8:30am-4:30pm; closed Feb.)

GAMMON RANGES NATIONAL PARK

This is where Australia gets serious. The 128,228 hectares of the Gammons are more craggy, more exotic, more stunning, and more isolated than the southern Flinders and possibly than anything you've ever seen. The Gammons can only be explored on unsealed 4WD tracks and wilderness experience is advisable. Check in at the **National Parks and Wildlife Service** headquarters in Balcanoona, where the friendly rangers can give advice on bush camping and bushwalking. (☎8648 4829. Park fee $6 per vehicle per night.) Less experienced nature-lovers can camp at **Italowie Camp** or **Weetootla Gorge** and hike in the edges of the park.

OUTBACK SOUTH AUSTRALIA

North and west of the Flinders, the Australian outback surpasses legend and becomes dirt real. Much of the sparsely populated outback beyond the salt flats of Lake Torrens and Lake Eyre is encompassed by the Desert Parks area. The famous Oodnadatta Track, a favorite for 4WD TV commercials, is a rough 4WD circuit carving through this area, taking in Oodnadatta and William

Creek. The **Stuart Hwy.**, which slices the continent in half from Port Augusta up to Darwin, is the quickest, and, in most cases, the only option to Coober Pedy, Uluru, and Alice Springs. Visitors should prepare themselves mentally for the 45°C (113°F) that you'll find even in what little shade exists. If you do stop, you'll be blessed with phenomenal views of the salt flats, remnants of dry lakes that only have water in them at wintertime and not even always then, and silence—except in the summer and autumn, when thousands of bush flies make their presence felt.

DRIVE CAREFULLY. The area off the Stuart Hwy. is not for the casual tourist. With most roads unsealed, a 4WD is essential. Though arid, this area is subject to flash flooding, and is especially dangerous to drive in the summer. Talk to national park officials to plan your trip and immediately before setting out, check road conditions, updated daily, on the Northern Road Conditions Hotline (☎1300 361 033). Carry plenty of water for long drives (both for drinking and for your car), and take at least 2 spare tires. Check in with officials, and notify friends or family before and after undertaking a journey. If your car does break down on a remote road, do not panic and do not start walking—people die every year when they make this mistake. Follow the Golden Rule: stay with the car; it provides shade and can be spotted more easily by search parties.

STUART HIGHWAY: ADELAIDE TO COOBER PEDY

Welcome to the outback. As the Stuart Hwy. winds its way north and west toward the opal capital of the world, there is little to see other than the harsh reality of the bright red, arid terrain. It doubles as pasture land, as many of the homesteads do not have fences by the road, allowing sheep and cattle to roam. So keep alert.

PORT AUGUSTA. Any trip from Adelaide to Outback South Australia will probably pass through Port Augusta, the "Crossroads of Australia" (see p. 445).

PIMBA. **Spud's Roadhouse** (☎8673 7473), in Pimba, is open 24hr., hosts a hotel and a bar, and is the local **RAA** access point. One should keep in mind that from Pimba, the petrol just gets more and more expensive, hitting $1.15 per liter up in Coober Pedy; at the same time, distances are big, so top off at every opportunity.

WOOMERA. Originally designated a 'secret' town by the British military, Woomera was created in 1947 as the unofficial capital of the Woomera Restricted Area. The pre-planned village sits at the edge of the Area, the largest military test site in the world, known affectionately as "the range" by the locals. The Stuart Hwy. passes through the range on the way to Coober Pedy; you'll see signs prohibiting you from leaving the highway at this point. Joint European and Australian forces created the village, the location of which wasn't revealed on maps until the 1960s, and now there's an American military presence as well. Reassuringly, the base is currently geared more toward satellite launching than bomb testing. With a history like this, it's not surprising that the **Woomera Heritage Centre,** Dewrang Ave. in the middle of town, provides more than the usual array of Dreaming stories and nature displays. The outside is crowded with rockets and planes, and the well-designed museum professionally details the nuclear bombs, radio astronomy, and families of Woomera's unusual past. (☎8673 7042. Open daily 9am-5pm. $3.)

GLENDAMBO. Glendambo, 270km southeast of Coober Pedy, is the last stop before the mining town, so all drivers should check the petrol level and fill up. The BP here runs both the (expensive) motel and the backpacker accommodation (☎8672 1030. Budget motel singles $81, dorm beds $15.40 with only 12 beds available). About 100km north of Glendambo, the highway doubles as an emergency landing strip for the Royal Flying Doctor Service.

FORE! Budget travelers, take heart: *Let's Go* has found a golf course within your price range. And this is no ordinary course: players never have to worry about replacing divots, they never hit trees, they needn't drive little carts, they never land in the rough—and water hazards are nowhere in sight. Impossible? Nope. Welcome to golf in the outback, where land is cheap, water precious, and grass non-existent. The desolate ground may be hard, flat, almost treeless, and bone-dry, but that hasn't stopped Coober Pedy from installing an 18-hole course. There's not a scrap of fairway or tinge of bright green in sight, and so the greens fee is quite literal: $10 gets you a small square of green astroturf. Carry it around and set it down whenever it's time to take a whack at the ball. Regular cars are allowed on the course, though golfers must give right-of-way to cars when the fairway doubles as the road. Smart golfers use fluorescent orange golf balls both for visibility and because bearded dragons on the course mistake the white balls for their own eggs and steal them. Plaid pants remain optional.

COOBER PEDY ☎08

Many towns in Australia have landmarks, beaches, or events that attract tourists; in Coober Pedy, the town itself is the attraction. This remote outpost halfway on the long, dry haul between Alice Springs and Adelaide gets 150,000 tourists each year, partly because there's nowhere else to stop, and partly because the town is utterly unlike anywhere else on earth. More than half of the 3500 residents live underground in homes almost invisible from the outside, except for the occasional ventilator shaft and TV antenna sticking out of a hillside. Homes, churches, shops, even hostels, are carved out of the earth to escape the extreme temperatures, which can reach 50°C (122°F) in the summer and plunge on winter nights. More than 45 nationalities are represented, with many immigrants from southern and eastern Europe. Men outnumber women five to one (in the early days, it was 400 to one), and nearly everybody in town has some connection to opals—eighty percent of the world's opal supply is pulled from the ground in the region. This is a mining town; it's not unusual to see trucks drive through town with big "EXPLOSIVES" signs, indicating homemade fertilizer-and-diesel-fuel bombs. But no worries; this is a fun town in which to spend more time than one originally intended.

TRANSPORTATION. **Greyhound Pioneer** (☎13 20 30) and **McCafferty's** (☎13 14 99) run to Coober Pedy from Adelaide and Alice Springs. Virtually every tour between Adelaide and Alice stops off in Coober Pedy. The Stuart Hwy., running north-south across the country, goes straight through Coober Pedy. If you want to tour around while here, compare **Budget** (☎8672 5333; from $88 per day for 4WD) and **Thrifty** (☎8672 5688; 4WD not necessarily available; 2WD $99 per day), at the Desert Cave Hotel. For a **taxis** call 0408 893 473.

DON'T WALK BACKWARD! Outside town boundaries, 1.5 million **abandoned mine shafts** make the danger of carelessly stepping backward and plummeting to your death very real. Signs around town, though co-opted by the tourist industry, are no joke: do not explore opal fields by yourself. Techniques of mining make it difficult to fill in the holes, so they are left open and uncovered.

ORIENTATION AND PRACTICAL INFORMATION. Coober Pedy is 685km south of Alice Springs (6-8hr.), 730km southeast of Uluru, 538km north of Port Augusta, and 846km north of Adelaide (8-10hr.). The turn-off from the Stuart Hwy. leads into **Hutchison St.,** the main street and location of virtually every establishment, including two **backpacker hostels,** an **ATM** at Westpac Bank, and the **post office** (☎8672 5062) in the miners' store. The **Tourist Information Centre** (☎8672 5298 or 1800 637 076; open M-F 9am-5pm), is also on Hutchison St., but most people start at the unofficial tourist office, **Underground Books,** next to the Desert Cave

THE MYSTERY MAN OF MARREE One would think that the creation of the world's largest work of art would have gained much publicity. However, an anonymous fax to a local pub simply entitled "tourist attraction" tipped the world off to the awesome and curious spectacle that lay quietly in the South Australian outback: a well-crafted 4km outline of an Aboriginal hunter carved into a plateau 60km northwest of Marree, the only artwork visible from outer space. Many clues, satellite photos, and years later, the tools of inscription, artist(s), and meaning of the giant figure—known as the Marree Man—are still unknown. Controversy ensues as the world continues to scratch its head, wondering when or if the artist will step forward.

Hotel just off Hutchison St., which serves as the booking agent for tours. (☎8672 5558. Open M-Sa 8:30am-5:30pm, Su 10am-4pm.) Other services include: **police** (☎8672 5056); **RAA** (☎8672 5230), at Desert Traders. **Hospital:** (☎8672 5009); free **Internet** at the school **library,** Paxton Rd. (turn off Hutchison St. at Underground Books and follow the signs; ☎8672 5077; open M-F 8:30am-5pm, Sa-Su 1-5pm).

ACCOMMODATIONS AND FOOD. **Radeka's Backpacker's Inn,** at Hutchison and Oliver St., has bus pickup and drop off. This maze of underground "caves" is clean and comfortable. There are no doors to close, putting privacy at a minimum. (☎8672 5223. Kitchen, pool table, Internet, TV room, and the cheapest bar in town. Dorms $17; doubles $47. VIP/YHA.) The much smaller **Joe's Backpacker's** is across from Radeka's. If the owners look familiar, perhaps you saw them in *Priscilla, Queen of the Desert* carting a kangaroo carcass across the outback. The owners, far more friendly than they appear in the film, will happily show you to the two underground dugouts, each with small bedrooms and its own kitchen, TV lounge, and bathroom. (☎8672 5163; fax 8672 5821. Kitchen, TV lounge. Dorms $16.50-17.50. VIP/YHA) **Riba's Underground Camping** is on William Creek Rd., outside of town. Coming from Port Augusta, turn off 4km before Hutchison St. (☎8672 5614. Above-ground sites $5 per person, with power $7; subterranean sites $8.) Visitors interested in underground **homestays** should call Annie (☎8672 5541).

Run by an immigrant Sicilian family, **John's Pizza Bar,** Hutchison St., serves the best pizza ($6-9.50), laden with toppings. (☎8672 5561. Open daily 10am-10pm.) **Trace's Restaurant,** at the top of Hutchison St., is a disco-bedecked Greek restaurant with backpacker specials for $8. (☎8672 5147. Open daily 4pm-late.) The IGA **supermarket** is on Hutchison St. (Open M-Sa 8:30am-7pm, Su 9am-7pm.)

TOURS AND SIGHTS. More than almost anywhere in Australia, joining an organized tour is worthwhile. **Radeka's Desert Breakaways Tours** is a very good choice, popular with backpackers. The tour includes many humorous stops around town and the opal fields, a trip out to the Breakaways, and a chance to noodle for your own opals. The stop at Crocodile Harry's home, the womanizer who was supposedly the inspiration for Crocodile Dundee, may make some women uncomfortable. (☎8672 5233. 3½hr.; $28.) To get away from herds of bus-backpackers, jump on local boy **Marshy's Discovery Tour.** The 4hr. tour visits mines, the golf course, the dingo fence (see graybox p. 454), the Breakaways, and the Serbian underground church, among others. There's also a 2hr. town-only tour for those short on time. (☎8672 5464; or book through Underground Books 8672 5558. $14-28 per person.) **Riba's Evening Mine Tours** takes guests down into a mine for a 1½hr. tour. (☎8672 5614. Daily 7:30pm. $12.) For an unforgettable look at the outback, join the mail carrier on the 12hr. **Mail Run.** (☎1800 069 911 or at Underground Books ☎8672 5558. Departs M and Th 9am. $90. Book ahead.)

The town's **underground churches** are usually open to visitors. In some, miners have etched religious symbols and beautiful statues into the walls. Outside town, **The Breakaways** are a set of flat-topped mesas rising out of the flatness. Explore the 70km return loop (2hr. drive), over the aptly named **Moon Plain.** At the Breakaways, you can still see tracks where the *Mad Max III* cars raced, and drive along the road where the drag queen in *Priscilla* rode on the roof, arms outstretched, gown trailing in the wind. The community **pool,** Paxton St., gives relief from the oppressive heat. (Open 8:30am-6pm during the school year. $3, children $2.)

OPAL SHOPPING. Coober Pedy glints in the sunlight with the number of opal pushers on every corner. But not all are quality; like any gem, some opals are far more valuable than others. Decent opals will give off multiple colors other than the base color as you turn it in the light. The greater the intensity of these secondary colors, the better the opal. As all men know, size doesn't necessarily matter, and smaller opals are often of better quality. When buying, choose an opal store that's particularly well-lit; dim stores may be hiding faults in the stones. **Umoona Opal Mine,** on Hutchison St., with a broad collection, is the oldest and best opal store in town. (☎8672 5288. Open daily 8am-7pm.) If you don't find anything there to your fancy, try the store next door in the **Desert Cave Hotel.**

OFF THE STUART HIGHWAY: OODNADATTA TRACK

The Oodnadatta Track, one of the most famous outback tracks in Australia, runs 619km from Marree, north of Leigh Creek in the Flinders, through William Creek and Oodnadatta to Marla, 235km north of Coober Pedy on the Stuart Hwy. The outback doesn't get any more authentic. The road is unsealed, suitable for **4WD only,** and can be impassable after rain. Every spark of civilization is worth a stop.

East of Coober Pedy, at **William Creek** (technically on Anna Creek cattle station, which is the world's largest cattle station—almost half the size of Tasmania) airplanes can land and taxi right to the town's only substantial building, the gathering place for everyone from cattle stations far and wide: the **William Creek Pub** (☎8670 7880). Covered with signs and bedecked with bras, the lively interior mocks every fragment of political correctness that might find its way out here. The public phone outside the pub was supposedly the most expensive telephone ever installed in the Southern Hemisphere. The phone's next to a parking meter that someone dragged up from Adelaide; it's tough to find a spot for your car around here. Inexpensive accommodation and camping are also available.

Oodnadatta is a sad-looking town, but it has precious amenities, including **car repair facilities.** Check road conditions with the **police** (☎8670 7805). The **Transcontinental Hotel** (☎8670 7804) has cheap rooms, and the **Pink Roadhouse** is the place to fuel your car and yourself. The huge Oodna Burger for $7 is the local special.

EYRE PENINSULA

It's a good bet that most international tourists this far west in South Australia are bound for or coming from Western Australia. The tourist folks on the Eyre know this, and they market the peninsula as "Australia's Best Detour" and merely suggest travelers add 295km to their itineraries and pop down for a breath of fresh Eyre. Not a bad idea, for the west coast of the Eyre in particular harbors breathtakingly unspoiled cliffs and beaches. In the driest state on the driest continent on earth, the Eyre Peninsula provides a welcome belt of coves with pounding, fish-filled surf—all uncrowded and removed from anything resembling urban bustle.

TRANSPORTATION

Premier Stateliner (Adelaide ☎8415 5555, Ceduna ☎ 8625 2279, Port Lincoln ☎8682 1734, Whyalla ☎8645 9911) is the only public **bus** carrier on the Eyre with frequent service, though Greyhound stops in **Ceduna** on the way to **Perth.** Stateliner runs between Adelaide and **Whyalla** (M-Th and Sa-Su 5 per day, F 6 per day; $39.60). Buses also leave Adelaide bound for **Port Lincoln,** stopping in towns along the eastern coast (depart Adelaide M-F 2 per day, Su 1 per day; depart Port Lincoln daily 2 per day). Stateliner runs an overnight bus from Adelaide to **Ceduna** via **Streaky Bay** (depart Adelaide Su-F 1 per day; depart Ceduna daily 1 per day).

THE GREAT DOG FENCE Meryl Streep's woeful cries of "the dingo ate my baby" would have been cut short if only she had lived south of the longest fence in the world. Stretching for 5600km from Queensland through the northwest corner of New South Wales and over to Penong, SA at the beginning of the Nullabor Plain, the Great Dog Fence delineates "dingo country," keeping the wild dogs firmly in the north. The fence, completed in 1940, is mostly 6-foot-high wire matting, but around bigger cities is electrified as well. "Sheep country," to the south, is separated from "cattle country," to the north: dingoes will attack and kill cattle but not sheep. Though more than twice as long as the Great Wall of China, each part of the fence is regularly maintained by full-time dog fencers dotted along the route. Occasionally, though, the dingoes break through, panicked cries of "the fence is down" ring through the local towns, and soon mangled sheep carcasses dot the landscape.

By car, traversing the Eyre Peninsula means diverging from the inland Hwy.1 (Eyre Hwy.), which runs 468km straight across the top of the peninsula from Whyalla to Ceduna. The highlights of the Eyre are found on a triangular, coastal route via the Lincoln Hwy. and Flinders Hwy. (Alternate Hwy. 1), which takes 763km to connect the same two towns.

WHYALLA ☎08

Whyalla? Why indeed. Upon entering South Australia's second largest town, you'll be forced to wonder why these 24,000 people have set up home here. Though you may expect a promising city based on the layer upon layer of suburbia, those layers peel back to reveal a downtown of empty shopfronts due to its slumping mining economy. Whyalla is surrounded on three sides by a scrub desert and on the fourth by a decaying industrial harbor which prevents tourist access to the bay. It's passable, but little will induce you to linger, unless fishing is your fancy.

PRACTICAL INFORMATION. The **Whyalla Tourist Centre** is on the left-hand side of Hwy. 1 (Lincoln Hwy.), north of the city and next to a stranded corvette. (☎8645 7900. Open M-F 9am-5pm, Sa 9am-4pm, Su 10am-4pm.) **Westland Shopping Centre,** on the corner of McDouall Stuart Ave. and Nicolson Ave., has two **supermarkets** and a food court. If you're driving in on Alt. A-1, take the B-100 exit and follow signs to the city center. **ATMs** abound on Forsyth St. in city center.

ACCOMMODATIONS AND FOOD. There aren't many enticing options in Whyalla, but the pub-hotels are passable if you don't look too closely. The rooms at the 1920s-style **Hotel Bayview,** on Forsyth St., have A/C, TV, and fridges but are otherwise of uneven quality; be persistent in seeking out a decent one. (☎8645 8544. Singles $33; twins and doubles $66.) Down the street, the marginally clean **Whyalla Foreshore Caravan Park,** Broadbent Tce., is 2km from the post office and very near the beach. It might be the best option around. (☎8645 7474; fax 8644 2846. Sites $12, powered $16; on-site vans for 2 $28; cabins for 2 $44-53.)

For food, the **Plaza Eatery,** 7 Forsyth St., has all-day greasy breakfast (open M-F 7:30am-5pm, Sa 8am-2pm). Otherwise, there are few dining options downtown.

SIGHTS. North of the city, the **Whyalla Maritime Museum** shares the tourist information complex and tours the *HMAS Whyalla*, designed by Corvette. The first ship built in the Whyalla Shipyard, it is now the "largest permanently landlocked ship" in Australia, 2km from the nearest shore. It's one way to earn a superlative. (☎8645 7900. Open daily 10am-4pm. $6.60, children $3.30. Tours at 11am, noon, 1, 2, and 3pm. Allow 1½hr. for visit.) The **Whyalla Conservation Park,** 10km north of the Whyalla info center on Hwy. 1, offers a good chance to see the flora and fauna of these arid lands. (☎8645 1704. Open 30min. before dawn to 30min. after sunset.) The town of Whyalla, Aboriginal for "place of the water," would like guests to know that this is a good place to fish and boat.

ALTERNATE HIGHWAY 1: WHYALLA TO PORT LINCOLN

As Alt. Hwy. 1 speeds along the west coast, the gently undulating road hosts a few dots of civilization tucked away in gentle seaside breaks from the monotonously rolling plains. At least, they provide petrol stations; at most, **Cowell, Arno Bay, Port Neill,** and **Tumby Bay** are all quiet seaside towns in which to crash for a night. All four towns have pub hotels (singles around $30; twins and doubles $40) and caravan parks. **Cowell,** 111km south of Whyalla, offers one of the safest and best fishing areas in South Australia at its **Franklin Harbour,** as well as a thriving oyster industry and Australia's only commercial jade mining. The **Cowell Bakery** doubles up as the tourist info office (☎8629 2034; open M-W 8:30am-7:30pm, Th 8:30am-8pm, F-Sa 8:30am-8:30pm, Su 9:30am-8:30pm). The livelier of the town's two quiet hotels is the **Franklin Harbour Hotel,** closest to the bay. (☎8629 2015. Includes breakfast. Singles $27.50, doubles $38.50.) Considering its much larger neighbor, Port Lincoln, has no backpacker accommodation at all, it's somewhat surprising that the tiny fishing town **Tumby Bay,** 50km north, offers backpackers two different options. **Tumby Bayside Holiday Units** has dorms with a well-equipped kitchen, BBQ, TV, and laundry. (☎8688 2087. Around $15.) The pub in town, the **Seabreeze Hotel,** also has dorms and greater access to the pokie machines. (☎8688 2362. $15. NOMADS.)

PORT LINCOLN ☎08

At the southern tip of the Eyre Peninsula, breezy and tacky Port Lincoln lords over Boston Bay, the second-largest natural harbor in the world—more than three times the size of Sydney Harbour. Port Lincoln (pop. 13,000) was to be the state capital, but inadequate fresh water destined today's politicians for Adelaide instead. So instead of parliaments, Port Lincoln is graced with public toilets called the "Loo-vre." By statistical twist, there are more millionaires per capita in Port Lincoln than in any other South Australian town; the accompanying tone, however, is more glitz than glamor. Aquaculture capital, the town ships out the largest tonnage of commercial fish in Australia, as well as huge amounts of grain. Port Lincoln is a frequent port-of-call for vacationers, both as a stopover en route to the more remote attractions of the Eyre Peninsula, and as a decent destination itself.

PRACTICAL INFORMATION. Tourist destinations in Port Lincoln are generally close enough to walk comfortably. The main drag is **Tasman Tce.** (which becomes London St.), along the water, with the major hotels, pubs, cafes, and tourist shops. A few blocks inland, **Liverpool St.** provides some shopping, a small movie theater, and restaurants. The **Visitor Information Centre,** 66 Tasman Tce. (☎8683 3544), is open daily from 9am to 5pm. Other services include: **ATMs** at Tasman Tce. and Liverpool St.; **police** (☎8688 3020); **hospital** (☎8683 2200); **taxis** (☎13 10 08); **post office** at 68 Tasman Tce. The **library,** in the Spencer Institute of TAFE building, just off Tasman Tce. has free 1hr. **Internet** sessions. (☎8688 3622. Open M-Tu and Th-F 8:30am-5pm, W 8:30am-8pm, Su 1-5pm.)

ACCOMMODATIONS AND FOOD. **The Pier Hotel** (☎8682 1322), at the center of Tasman Tce., incorporates stunning ocean views with show-biz decor. Most rooms have bath. (Singles $25; twins and doubles $35; weekly rates $100, $130.) **Kirton Point Caravan Park,** at the end of London St. (Tasman Tce.), has a lovely setting 3km from the town center. (☎8682 2537. Sites $7 per person; cabins from $22.) There are **supermarkets** on Liverpool St. For a sit-down meal, a pleasant break from the showy beachfront strip is the **Cafe del Giorno,** 80 Tasman Tce., with light meals for $8-12. (☎8683 0577. Open M-Sa 10am-6pm.)

SIGHTS AND ENTERTAINMENT. Port Lincoln is home to South Australia's magnificent four-day **Tunarama Festival,** on the Australia Day long weekend in

SOUTH AUSTRALIA

late January. The festival features a rodeo and beauty contest, but fish take the day in the highly competitive tuna-tossing contest. (☎8682 1055. Jan 25-27, 2002.) The cute, little **Port Lincoln Railway Museum** is at the eastern end of Tasman Tce. (☎8682 4550; open W, Sa, Su 2-4pm; free). At the **Glen-Forest Animal Park,** 15km from Port Lincoln, you can get hands-on with dingoes, kangaroos, wombats, and camels. (☎8683 3544. Open daily 10am-5pm. $8, children $6.) Six kilometers north of Port Lincoln on Lincoln Hwy., **Boston Bay Wines** turns out first-rate whites and reds. (☎8684 3600. Tastings and sales Sa-Su 11:30am-4:30pm.)

A daytrip from Port Lincoln allows time to take in the gorgeous sea views of **Lincoln National Park,** about 20km south of town. If birds come here all the way from Siberia on their summer migrations, you know it's gotta be good. The southern tip of the park is sheltered, almost untouched wilderness named **Memory Cove.** Access is limited to 15 4WD vehicles per day. (Park entrance fee $6 per vehicle.) At the bottom of the Eyre and 32km southwest of Port Lincoln, **Whaler's Way** (☎8685 6016) is a 14km scenic tourist drive. Interpretive signs give details on the superb coastal scenery, cliff lookouts, and ancient rock caves. For entry or camping permits at either of these places, pick up an entry pass and key from the **Port Lincoln Visitor Information Centre.** For more info, contact **National Parks and Wildlife,** 75 Liverpool St., Port Lincoln. (☎8688 3111. Open M-F 8:45am-5pm.)

FLINDERS HIGHWAY: PORT LINCOLN TO CEDUNA

The Hwy. 1 (Flinders Hwy.) heads northwest from Port Lincoln to the remote outpost of Ceduna. This road is largely more of the same rolling, mallee-scrubbed land, but various species of reptiles slither and crawl across the road and one can never be sure when a kangaroo will bound by. A mere 47km from Lincoln toward Ceduna, you'll find the lazy town of **Coffin Bay,** the center of the state's oyster industry. Tourist info is available from **Beachcomber Agencies** on the Esplanade. (☎8685 4057. Open daily 8am-7:30pm; in winter 8am-6:30pm.) The Port Lincoln tourist center is more convenient for those planning day trips out of Ceduna.

Coffin Bay National Park is 17km west of the main highway. This peninsular park is a remote beach heaven; surfers, picnickers, and pelicans coexist peacefully among the dunes, estuaries, and bays. ($6 per vehicle per day.) Most areas are accessible only with 4WD, except **Yangie Bay** (15km from the entrance) and **Point Avoid** (which is much better than it sounds; 18km from the entrance). Bush camping permits and maps are available at the park entrance. **National Parks and Wildlife Service** (☎8688 3111), in Port Lincoln, has further info.

Mt. Dutton Bay Woolshed, 52km northwest of Port Lincoln and 22km southeast of a tiny town called Coulta, doubles as a hostel and woolshed museum rolled into one. The historic building with backpackers in the back and museum in the front is right on a beautiful waterfront in one of the most peaceful spots around. As many as 1200 sheep were once kept here, but today the owners keep 36 backpackers instead, and fatten them up with warm servings of pumpkin soup. From Route Alt. 1, follow signs to Broccaburra or Dutton along a dirt road toward the coast. (☎/fax 8685 4031. Museum open M-Sa 10am-5pm; admission by donation. Dorms $15. Book ahead.) About 25km north of Port Kenny along the Flinders Hwy (watch for a sign), turn toward the coast and drive about 40km to **Point Labatt Conservation Park and Aquatic Reserve,** where Australia's only mainland sea lion colony lounges near the cliffs. Beautiful **Streaky Bay,** the last town before Alt. 1 rejoins Hwy. 1, offers a peaceful bayside stop before the heat of the mainland and the looming Nullarbor hits like a blast. The **Streaky Bay Community Motel-Hotel,** Alfred Tce., on the water has a expensive rooms, but a few basic hotel rooms without bath are available at bargain prices. (☎8626 1008. Singles $22; doubles $33.)

CEDUNA ☎08

At the far west corner of the triangular Eyre circuit, the Flinders Hwy (Alt. Hwy 1) meets up with the more direct and dull Hwy. 1 (Eyre Hwy.) and rolls into Ceduna, civilization's last watering hole before the arid westward trek across the Nullarbor Plain toward Perth. People here don't ask what brought you to town; they ask which way you're heading. The **ATMs** in town are the **last ATMs** for 1300km (assuming you is headed for Western Australia). Ceduna provides the basic beds, beans, and booze, plus a few nice beaches to sit down and rest. **Decres Bay,** 12km from town within the **Wittelbee Conservation Park,** is a good swimming beach, and a little farther on is **Laura Bay,** with more of the same. Get maps and directions from the tourist office or follow the signs heading southeast from town.

Stateliner (Ceduna ☎8625 2279, Adelaide ☎8415 5555, Port Augusta ☎8642 5055) runs **buses** daily to Ceduna via Port Augusta, and Greyhound Pioneer (☎13 20 30) also passes through en route to Perth. The Eyre Hwy. becomes **Poynton St.,** briefly, as it passes through the center of town. It intersects Kuhlmann St., which itself becomes McKenzie St. as you head toward Adelaide. **Ceduna Gateway Tourist Centre,** 58 Poynton St., is laden with info on fishing and outback tours, and has email access. (☎8625 2780. Open M-F 9am-5:30pm, Sa 9-11:30am.) **ATMs** are at **ANZ Bank,** 27 Poynton St. and at **Bank SA,** 10 McKenzie St.

Ceduna Greenacres Backpackers, 12 Kuhlmann St., on the right fork as you come into town from the east, is marked with a red sign, half-hidden by trees. It has muraled concrete walls, metal bunks in small rooms, an airy courtyard, and a free home-cooked dinner. Ask owner Vaughn about the **Point Brown Swimming Hole.** (☎/fax 8625 3811; mobile 0427 811 241. Dorms $16.50; twins and doubles $33.) **The Foreshore Hotel Motel,** on O'Loughlin Tce. along the waterfront, has hotel rooms that are much less expensive than their standard motel versions. (☎8625 2008. Singles $25; doubles $29.) The **Airport Caravan Park** (☎8625 24160), on the way into town as you approach from Port Augusta, has two-person sites for $12, with power for $14, and budget cabins sleeping up to six for $27.50.

Foodland **supermarket,** Poynton St., sells groceries right in the bustle of downtown. (☎8625 3212. Open M-W 8:30am-5:30pm, Th-F 8:30am-7pm, Sa 8:30am-6pm.) **Bill's Chicken Shop,** Poynton St., serves the town's best fried chicken, fresh fish, and deli sides. (☎8625 2880. Open daily 9am-9pm.)

HIGHWAY 1: FROM CEDUNA TO PORT AUGUSTA

For those coming from the Nullarbor, the stretch of Hwy.1 running from Ceduna to Port Augusta will seem like a tropical rainforest. The scrub-covered plains of the northern Eyre Peninsula will give the lush tropics of the wet-season Northern Territory a run for their money. And with the increase in vegetation comes an increase in population. Having said that, if **Wirrulla, Poochera,** and **Minnipa,** 92km, 140km, and about 170km respectively from Ceduna, were lumped together to form a mega-town in the Northern Eyre peninsula, it would still only have one horse in it. Grin and bear it; after all, one never knows when a giant Galah is waiting in the distance. People driving straight through at 110km per hour (or *substantially* above, although *Let's Go* does not recommend such behavior) should be able to make the trip in 4.5hr. There are gas stations every 100km or so across this stretch of road; though, more competitive prices make it cheaper to fill up in Port Augusta or Ceduna before setting out. Places to stay on this stretch of road are limited to a few down-at-heel pokie hotels. Those hopelessly attached to the **Internet** should breathe easy; Wudinna (about 250km from Ceduna) has an Internet cafe on the west side of town in the Wudinna Telecentre. (Open M-F 9am-5pm. $5 per 30min.)

At one of two area tourist information joints in **Kimba,** a strange creature looms in front. Cemented on top of its little hill, **Big Galah**, a huge, pink bird motionlessly celebrates the half-way point across Australia and keeps a watchful eye on all the traversers of the Eyre Hwy. The tourist center (☎8627 2112) is open daily 8am-5pm, although the Big Galah never sleeps.

CROSSING THE NULLARBOR

Explorer Edward John Eyre minced no words describing the Nullarbor Plain, calling it "a hideous anomaly, a blot on the face of Nature, the sort of place one gets into in bad dreams." They named the highway after him anyway. Welcome to the Nullarbor—a treeless plain that could contain England, the Netherlands, Belgium, and Switzerland, with 7000 square kilometers to spare. Robert Frost has no idea what it means to say that there are miles to go before you sleep. **Greyhound bus** drivers do, however, making this grueling desert haul with just a few driver changes. (☎12 20 30. Ceduna–Perth 23hr., $226. Adelaide–Perth 36hr., $226).

The Eyre Hwy. is smooth, black bitumen all the way, finally completed in 1976 after construction began during World War II. The Ninety Mile Straight (146.6km), from Caiguna, WA to Balladonia, WA, is the longest straight stretch of highway in the country. The road is traveled fairly heavily compared with the empty roads up north; it's rarely more than 100km between roadhouses with fuel, but repair facilities are few and far between. This is a road train route, so all drivers should brace for the turbulence from passing 25m trucks. Bring along bottled water, warm clothing, and blankets. Drivers should make sure their cars are equipped with a jack, spares, coolant, and oil, and should have a mechanic check the vehicle. Each of the **roadhouses** along the way has **EFTPOS** and major credit card facilities, almost all have a caravan park and camping sites, and most have cheap accommodation. The **RAA automobile association** is at 13 11 11. **Yalata Medical Service** (☎8625 6237) is the best bet for medical service on the Nullarbor. **Police** are at Penong (☎8625 1006) and Ceduna (☎8628 7020); the Penong police can refer you to **medical service** on the Nullarbor. There are quarantine checkpoints at Norseman for Westbound travellers and Ceduna for Eastbound travellers. For details of roadhouses and scenic detours, pick up the free brochure *Australia's Great Road Journey: The Nullarbor* at the tourist office in Ceduna if coming from the east, or at the Norseman tourist office if coming from the west. **Commemorative crossing certificates** (now there's something for the mantle) are free at either office after completing the journey, unless you'd rather forget the whole experience.

Nullarbor Traveller is a backpacker-oriented camping trip that runs from Perth to Adelaide. Travelers snorkel, whale watch, explore caves, and camp under the stars. For those with cash and time, this is quite the way to cross old man Eyre's personal hell. (☎8364 0407; www.southaustralia.com/nullarbor. 7 nights, $693.)

EYRE HIGHWAY: CEDUNA TO BORDER VILLAGE

After leaving Ceduna on the long road west, hundreds of windmills and wheat silos signal the approach of **Penong,** 73km west of Ceduna, and its **hotel** (☎8625 1050; singles $33, doubles $44). Penong also has a service station (open M-Tu and Th-F 7am-10pm, W and Sa 24hr., Su 7am-midnight). Paul Gravelle's **surfboard factory** waits in Penong for the interested. At **Cactus Beach,** 21km south of Penong along a well-maintained gravel road, you can watch territorially-proud, top-caliber surfers maneuver along Castles, Cactus, and Caves, the names of the famous breaks at one of Australia's best surfing beaches. Beginners enjoy the sandy bottom at **Shelly Beach,** east of Point Sinclair. Down the main road, 78km west of Penong, backpacker accommodation is available at the all-encompassing **Nundroo Hotel Motel Inn.** (☎8625 6120. Reception open 8am-9pm. $14.50 per person.)

Yalata Roadhouse, 51km west of **Nundroo,** is a decent camping spot. (☎8625 6986. Open 7am-10pm, in winter 7am-9pm. Sites $5 per person, with power $10.) A permit is required to enter the township of **Yalata** itself, home to an Anangu community (pop. 500), 200m north of Hwy. 1. The **Head of Bight,** 78km west of Yalata, has stunning views with sand dunes to the right, sheer cliffs to the left, and blue ocean right in front. Between May and October, the view gets even better, when 60 to 100 **Southern Right Whales** breed, calve, and nurse here before returning to feed in sub-Antarctic waters for the summer. Whale watching **permits** ($8) are required and available from Yalata Roadhouse or mid-July-Oct from the **White Well Ranger Sta-**

tion (☎8625 6201) on the road south to Head of Bight. Call ahead for hours. By the time you reach the fuel stop at Nullarbor, 94km west of Yalata, you're officially on the treeless plain. There's accommodation at the **Nullarbor Hotel Motel.** (☎8625 6271. Reception 7am-10:30pm. Singles $17, doubles $28.) As the booklet says for Nullarbor, "You are now standing on one of the largest, flattest, and most enigmatic lumps of limestone on the planet." It's that good.

Gorgeous coastal lookouts line the Nullarbor, just a few hundred meters off the main road. The **Bunda Cliffs** (50km) plummet 90m straight down into the Southern Ocean. The cliffs start at Twin Rocks at Head of Bight and extend 200km to just east of Border Village. There's cheap accommodation at **Border Village**, 188km west of Nullarbor, as well as a huge fiberglass kangaroo named Rooey II. (☎9039 3474. Singles $21, doubles $41.) This is also the **agricultural roadblock** before entering WA (it's at Ceduna if you're going east), where any fruit, vegetables, honey, and plant material will be confiscated to stop the spread of the fruit fly. Check with the agriculture department for restricted items. (☎9311 5333 in WA, ☎8269 4500 in SA.)

As you enter Western Australia, it's 13km from Border Village to the roadhouses of **Eucla** (open 6am-10:30pm; pool available), 66km to **Caiguna** (open 24hr.), 79km to **Mundrabilla** (open 7am-10:30pm), 93km to **Cocklebiddy** (open 7am-7pm), 182km to **Balladonia** (open 6am-10pm), 194km to **Madura** (open 6:30am-8pm; swimming pool available), and 193km to **Norseman** (open 24hr.), the official end of the Nullarbor Plain.

TASMANIA

With Australia lying empty in a far corner of the Empire, Britain seemed to have a perfect solution for its 18th-century prison overflow problem. Parliament members happily sent their rabble across the oceans, washed their hands, and went to tea. But lawlessness was still a huge problem in the new colony, and penal officials in New South Wales decided to ship the troublemakers away once again. Australia was already at the end of the earth, but Tasmania was at the end of Australia. The British considered the wild little island, then known as Van Diemen's Land, the worst punishment available, reserved for the most heartless criminals.

Silly Poms. What was thought to be an inhospitable, weatherbeaten rock was in fact the lushest corner of the continent. Still, the penal settlements in the gorgeous areas near Hobart and Strahan were brutal indeed. Furthermore, the native Aboriginal populations were decimated by the new colony through invasion and outright genocide. During this century, Tasmania has turned from blood red to leafy green. An upsurge of conservation efforts, centralized social policies, and liberal activism mark today's political scene. The struggle against the proposed Franklin-Gordon dam in the early 1980s foreshadowed Tassie's involvement in the Australian conservation movement. Though Tasmania has historically had a politically and socially conservative government, their Green party has been represented in the state's governing coalition twice in the past decade.

Only 3% of the visitors to Australia make it down under down under, but Tassie is well worth the time and money spent getting there. A third of the state is under government conservation, mostly under the name Tasmanian Wilderness World Heritage Area, which includes one of the last great temperate rainforests on the globe. Bushwalkers from around the planet come to Tasmania's mountainous interior to explore the Overland Track, one of the premier hiking trails in the Southern Hemisphere. The uninhabited west coast bears the brunt of the Southern Ocean's fury, but the storms rarely push past the mountains, so the east coast and midlands are pleasant year-round. Tiny holiday villages filled with prosperous fishing fleets and vacationing families speckle the shore. In the southeast, the capital city of Hobart, Australia's second-oldest city, welcomes yachts from Sydney every December in a glorious and internationally famous turnout. Rolling farmland stretches north from Hobart to Launceston, Tasmania's second city and northern hub. But perhaps most spectacular about this magical island is its amazing natural diversity, its uncanny ability to house so many different species and environments in such a small space. In fact, some of Tassie's best known species can only be found within its borders, such as the slow-growing Huon pine, which can live for millennia, and the Tasmanian devil, a mysterious, scavenging marsupial. Many travelers try to see the island in just a few days, but once they lose themselves in the wilderness and history of Australia's secret stow-away, they may never be able to get enough of Tasmania.

TASMANIA HIGHLIGHTS

TASMAN PENINSULA. Thank God you're not a convict on the Tasman Peninsula. The ruins of convict-built buildings are Tasmania's biggest tourist attraction (p. 470).

GORDON DAM. Visit the controversial Gordon Dam, center of much environmental debate. It alone could power Hobart's electricity usage (p. 477).

OVERLAND TRACK. Get into the bush on the world-famous Overland Track (p. 480).

CADBURY CHOCOLATE FACTORY. Sample all of the delicious treats at the Cadbury Chocolate Factory in Hobart. Mmmm, chocolate (p. 469).

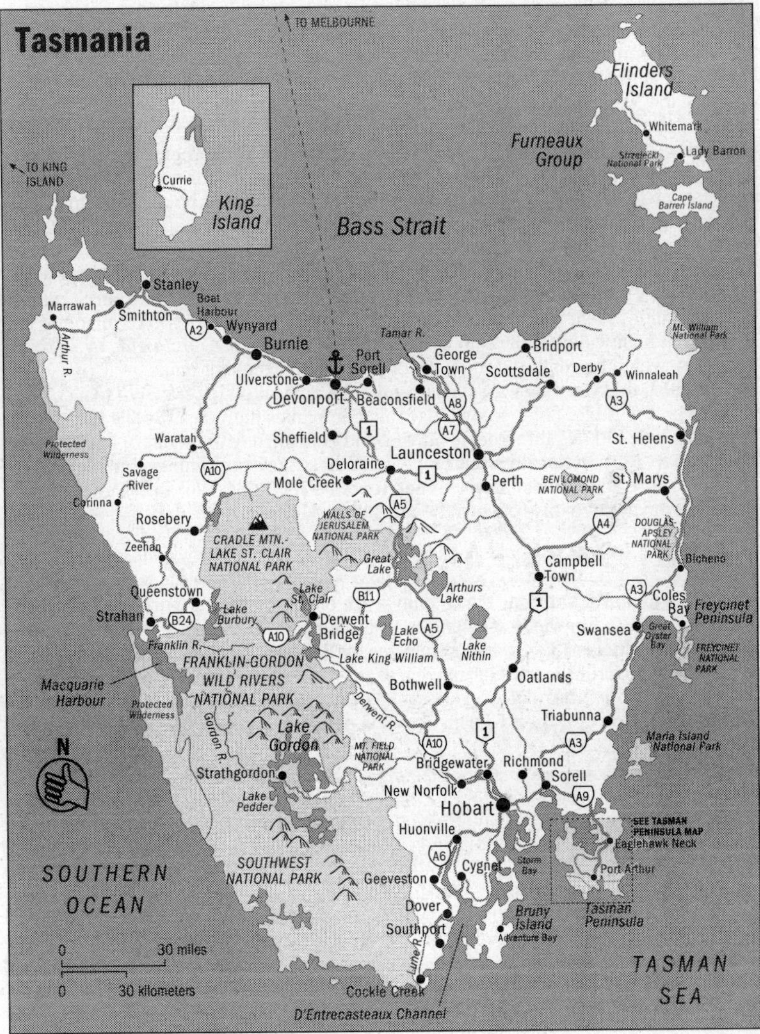

TRANSPORTATION

Tasmania has three principal gateways: Hobart (by air), Devonport (by *Spirit of Tasmania* overnight ferry or air), and Launceston (by air or to its George Town port by *DevilCat* ferry). The state then comfortably divides into south, northwest, and northeast zones as the respective domains of the gateway cities. Getting around on a budget is a bit of a challenge. There is no rail network, and the main bus lines—**Redline** and **TWT's TassieLink**—are expensive, limited, and infrequent. TassieLink offers "Explorer Passes," which are worth the investment when using their buses as a touring service (valid 7-days within any 10-day period $150, 21-days within 30-days $250). On the bright side, there are residents in every corner—including many hostel managers—who are keen to fill the void, offering reasonably priced shuttles and tours on a call-and-request basis. Seek local recommendations and information boards.

With a companion or two to share expenses, renting a **car** is more popular here than on the mainland. The gateway cities have small companies offering cheaper, older cars. Visitors unaccustomed to Tasmania's narrow, winding roads should drive with added caution. Explicitly check with the rental company on their policy regarding travel on unsealed roads (some prohibit it altogether, others increase the liability excess). Four-wheel-drive vehicles, necessary for winter travel and a portion of Tassie's back roads, come with better insurance policies on unsealed roads. Though not recommended by *Let's Go*, **hitchhiking** is relatively popular, but often means sticking to the main roads.

Biking is a satisfying alternative, especially on the more accessible east coast. *Bicycling Tasmania*, by Terry and Beedham, is trustworthy; the three major gateway cities have rental outfits catering to cycle touring. If you're planning on extensive bushwalking, pick up a copy of *100 Walks in Tasmania*, by Tyrone Thomas, which has detailed track descriptions and excellent maps.

Tours also make seeing Tassie easy and enjoyable, allowing travel to places otherwise inaccessible. Some knowledgeable companies include: **Devil's Playground Ecotours** (☎6343 1787; info@devilsplayground.com.au; day tours out of Launceston and Hobart $80); **Bottom Bits Bus** (☎1800 777 103; info@bottombus.com; day tours from Hobart $69); **Under Down Under Tours** (☎1800 064 726; info@underdownunder.com.au; two-day tours to the northwest $199).

NATIONAL PARKS

All of Tasmania's National Parks charge an entrance fee. A 24hr. pass is $3.30 (vehicles $9.90). For those planning to visit many parks, there's a two-month pass for $13.20 (vehicles $33) or an annual pass for $19.80 (vehicles $46.20). Passes are available at most of the park entrances, or from any of the Parks & Wildlife Service offices. For more information, contact the head office in Hobart, 134 Macquarie St. (☎6233 6191), or visit their website at www.parks.tas.gov.au.

HOBART ☎03

This capital city rests at the mouth of the Derwent River, shielded from the great southern ocean by a scatter of islands and breakwaters at the foot of Mt. Wellington. Founded on February 21, 1804, Australia's second oldest city, and since its days as a penal colony, Hobart's fortunes have mirrored Tasmania's success. Mining wealth helped establish the city, but as a small fish in the federated Australian pond, Hobart has never grown large or complex. Hobart's social strata is like most other cities, yet it remains largely defined by its combination of strong-willed environmental activists and relaxed setting. Hobartians, however, unite in enjoying a slower pace of life than their mainland counterparts, and they seem to like it that way. Almost all of Tassie's travelers take at least a short stop in Hobart, receiving a dose of urbanity before heading out into the great beyond.

INTERCITY TRANSPORTATION

Air and road are the only ways in and out of Hobart. Plan ahead, because buses do not run frequently. Many visitors travel by hitchhiking, although *Let's Go* does not recommend hitchhiking.

BY PLANE. **Hobart Airport** is 18km east of Hobart on Hwy. A3. International flights must make connections on the mainland. **Ansett Australia/Kendell** (☎13 13 00) and **Qantas** (☎13 13 13) fly to Melbourne at least ten times per day ($85-200) and Sydney at least twice per day ($158-308). New discount airline **Impulse** (☎13 13 81) provides even cheaper deals on the Internet (www.impulseairlines.com.au) from Melbourne; Ansett (www.ansett.com.au) and Qantas (www.qantas.com.au) also have regular Internet sales. International travelers can get better deals; bring your passport and international ticket. **Redline Airporter Bus** (☎0419 382 240) shuttles between the airport and lodgings ($8, return $15).

BY BUS. The most helpful thing to do is pick up timetables for Redline and TWT's TassieLink services from Hobart's main **bus depot,** 199 Collins St.

Redline Coaches (☎1300 360 000, line open daily 6am-9pm) runs buses to: **Bicheno** (4¾hr., M-F 1 per day, $36.10); **Coles Bay turn-off** (4½hr., M-F 1 per day, $34.70); **Devonport** (4½-5hr., 2 per day, $38.10); **Launceston** (2½hr., 2-7 per day, $22.40) via **Oatlands** (1¼hr., 2-7 per day, $12.50); **St. Helens** (3½-7hr., Su-F 1 per day, $36.60); **St. Marys** via Launceston (3-6½hr., Su-F 1 per day, $33.80); **Swansea** (4hr., M-F 1 per day, $30.30). 20% student and VIP/YHA discount.

TassieLink (☎1300 300 520) runs buses to: **Bicheno** (3hr.; W, F, Su (and M in summer) 1 per day; $24.20); **Coles Bay turn-off** (2¾hr.; W, F, Su 1 per day; $23.50); **Lake St. Clair** (3½-4hr.; Tu, Th, Su 1 per day; $35.50); **New Norfolk** (40min.; Tu, Th, F, Su 1 per day; $5.10); **Queenstown** (5hr.; Tu, Th, F, Su 1 per day; $44.70); **Sorell** (30min., 1 per day, $4.90); **St. Helens** (4¾hr.; F, Su 1 per day; $35.20); **Strahan** (6-8hr.; Tu, Th, F, Su 1 per day; $51.70); **Swansea** (2hr., M-F 1 per day, $19.70); **Triabunna** (1¾hr., M-F 1 per day, $13.90). In summer (Dec. 1-Apr. 16) daily service (usually W) and destinations increase: **Cockle Creek** (3½hr.; M, W, F 1 per day; $51.60); **Lune River** (2½hr.; M, W, F 1 per day; $22.90); **Mt. Field National Park** (1½hr., M-Sa 1 per day, $23.50); **Scotts Peak** (3¼hr.; Tu, Th, Sa 1 per day; $58.10); **Southwest hiking trails (Timbs Track, Mt. Anne, Red Tape)** (2-3hr.; Tu, Th, Sa 1 per day; $55).

Hobart Coaches, 21 Murray St. (☎6233 4232), runs to **Cygnet** (1hr., M-F 5:15pm, $8) and **Kettering** (45min., M-F 4 per day, $6.50).

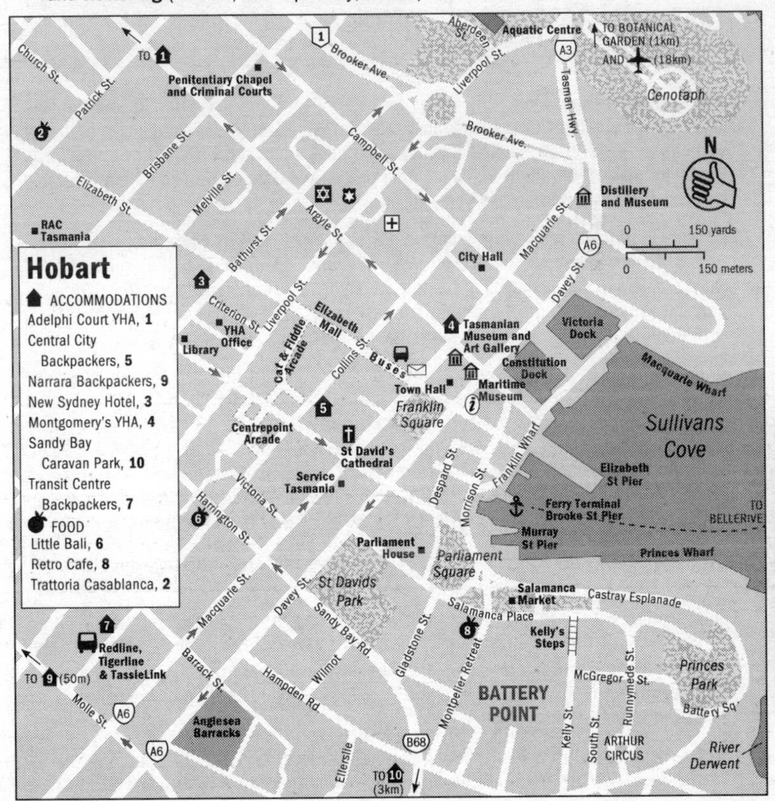

TASMANIA

ORIENTATION

Most tourist attractions and services are in the compact downtown west of the wharves of Sullivan's Cove. South of the Cove lies **Battery Point,** one of the oldest sections of the city, choked with antique shops and cottages. The northern border of Battery Point is defined by **Salamanca Place,** a row of old Georgian warehouses that have been renovated as shops and restaurants. **Franklin Wharf,** adjacent to Salamanca Place, is the departure point for the many harbor cruises. Hobart is backed by the **Wellington Range,** which affords fine views from the imposing **Mt. Wellington,** dominant on the western skyline, and the smaller **Mt. Nelson** to the south. The city proper can easily be navigated on foot, while public buses run to the outer reaches of the suburbs.

Beyond the **Queen's Domain** north of downtown, the **Tasman Bridge** spans the Derwent River. There, the Tasman Hwy. (A3) heads east and connects to A9 and the Tasman Peninsula. **Brooker Ave.** leads north up the Derwent Valley, becoming Hwy. 1 to Launceston, and connecting to A10 for points west. **Davey St.** leaves downtown as A6, heading southward toward the Huon Valley and Bruny Island.

LOCAL TRANSPORTATION

Ferries and Cruises: The best deal around is **Captain Fell's Historic Ferries** (☎6223 5893). 2½hr. dinner cruise departs Franklin Wharf nightly 6pm, $25. **Roche O'May Ferries** (☎6223 1914) sails from Brooke St. Pier to the Wrest Point Casino. Departs daily 10:30am, noon, 1:30, 3pm. $13. The **Lady Nelson** (☎6234 3348) gives less commercial river cruises of a more historical nature. 1½hr. tour departs Elizabeth St. Pier in summer Sa-Su 11am, 1, 3pm; in winter Sa-Su noon and 2pm. $5.

Local Transportation: Metro **city buses** (☎13 22 01) run through Hobart and the suburbs daily 6am-midnight. Purchase tickets on-board; $1.30-3 depending on number of sections traveled. "Day Rover" tickets ($3.40) allow unlimited travel all day after 9am. **The Metro Shop,** 9 Elizabeth St., in a corner of the Post Office, has a complete timetable for 50¢. Open M-F 8:30am-5:15pm.

By Tour: Good if you're short on time are day tours organized by **Tigerline** (☎1300 653 633) or **Experience Tasmania** (☎6234 3336). Both offer pickup and an array of combination tours to the highlights of the Hobart region. 2hr. to full-day tours $22-105; min. 4 passengers. Book through the tourist office (☎6230 8233), with a hostel reception, or direct with the company. For regional tours see **Transportation,** p. 461.

Car Rental: Car rental agencies are everywhere in Hobart. Off-season rates run as low as $17 per day. The following companies rent to ages 21-24. **Autorent Hertz,** 122 Harrington St. (☎6237 1111), rents top-end cars from $40-50 per day. For YHA discount, call ☎13 30 39 and quote Discount Program number 317961. **Thrifty,** 11-17 Argyle St. (☎6234 1341, airport 6248 5678), from $46. **Range** and **RentABug,** 136 Harrington St. and 105 Murray St. (☎6231 0678), from $28, including minibuses and campervans. **Selective Car Rentals,** 132 Argyle St. (☎6234 3311), from $25.

Automobile Club: RACT (☎6232 6300), corner of Murray and Patrick St. Open M-F 8:45am-5pm. 24hr. roadside help (☎13 11 11), insurance queries (☎13 27 22).

Bikes: Hobart Bike and Roller Blade Hire (☎6274 1205), just past the Cenotaph on the cycleway at the Regatta Ground, hires road and mountain bikes, tandems, and roller blades from $7 per hr. Long-term hire also available from $100 per week and $200 per month. Open Sept.-Dec. and Feb.-May Sa-Su 10am-5pm; open Jan. daily 10am-5pm; closed June-Aug.

Taxis: City Cabs (24hr. ☎13 10 08). City to airport $26-30.

PRACTICAL INFORMATION

TOURIST AND FINANCIAL SERVICES

Tourist Office: Hobart Tasmanian Travel and Information Centre, 20 Davey St. (☎6230 8233), at Elizabeth St. books accommodation and cars ($2.20 fee), as well as tours and walks (no fee). Open M-F 8:30am-5:15pm, Sa-Su 9am-4pm (winter Su 9am-1pm).

Budget Travel Office: YHA's Tasmanian Headquarters, 2nd floor, 28 Criterion St. (☎6234 9617). Travel insurance, passport photos, tickets, and travel advice, in addition to YHA memberships and hostel bookings. Open M-F 9am-5pm.

Tasmanian Parks and Wildlife Service: 134 Macquarie St. (☎6233 6191; www.parks.tas.gov.au), in the Service Tasmania Bldg. Open M-F 9am-5pm.

Forestry Tasmania: 79 Melville St. (☎6233 8203). Open M-F 8:30am-5:30pm.

Currency Exchange: Mobs of banks, most with **ATMs,** crowd in and around Elizabeth St. Mall. Most banks have a $5-10 fee. **Thomas Cook,** 40 Murray St. (☎6234 2699), charges $7 or 2% of traveler's checks. Open M-F 9am-5pm.

LOCAL SERVICES

Bookstores: **Fullers Bookshop,** 140 Collins St. (☎6224 2488). Classy selection and wonderful upstairs cafe. Open M-F 9am-5:30pm, Sa 9am-4pm, Su 10am-4pm. **Hobart Bookshop,** 22 Salamanca Sq. (☎6223 1803). Richly stocked shelves of new and second-hand books. Open M-F 9am-6pm, Sa-Su 10am-5pm.

Library: 91 Murray St. (☎6233 7529), at Bathurst St. Reference library open Feb.-Nov. M-Tu 9:30am-6pm, W-F 9:30am-9pm, Sa 9:30am-2:30pm; Dec.-Jan. M-Th 9:30am-6pm, F 9:30am-9pm, Sa 9:30am-12:30pm. Provides **Internet** $5.50 per 30min.

Market: Salamanca Market at Salamanca Pl. Open Sa 8am-3pm. See **Sights,** p. 467.

Laundromat: Most hostels have pay washers. **Machine Laundry/Cafe** (see p. 467).

Outdoor Equipment: Gear stores cluster along Elizabeth St. near Liverpool St. **Snowgum,** 104 Elizabeth St. (☎6234 7877), sells equipment and climbing and kayaking gear. They also rent sleeping bags, packs, and tents ($40 per week, $50 deposit) and kayaks ($95/$300). Open M-F 9am-5:30pm, Sa 9:30am-2pm.

Fishing Equipment: Get info and fishing tackle ($25.50 per day) at **Bridges Bros.,** 142 Elizabeth St. (☎6234 3791). Open M-Th 9am-5:30pm, F 9am-6pm, Sa 9am-1pm. *Angling Code for Inland Fisheries,* available at the tourist office, outlines all regulations.

MEDIA AND PUBLICATIONS

Newspaper: *The Mercury.*

Entertainment: *The Mercury* includes Gig Guide on Thursday and EG on Friday.

Radio: Rock, Triple J 92.9FM; News, ABC 729AM; Tourist Info, 88FM.

EMERGENCY AND COMMUNICATIONS

Emergency: ☎000.

Police: 37-43 Liverpool St. (☎6230 2111). **Lost and found,** ☎6230 2277.

Hospital: Royal Hobart Hospital, 48 Liverpool St. (☎6222 8308).

Pharmacy: Corby's Everyday Pharmacy, 170 Macquarie St. (☎6223 3044). Open daily 8am-10pm.

Hotlines: Crisis Watchline (24hr. ☎13 11 14). **AIDS Hotline** (☎1800 005 900). Staffed M-F 9am-5pm. **Alcohol and Drugs Hotline** (24hr. ☎1800 811 994).

Internet and Fax: Service Tasmania, 134 Macquarie St. (☎1300 135 513). Has 6 **free terminals.** 30min. limit. Open M-F 8:15am-5pm. Also try **Drifters Internet Cafe** (see p. 467) and the **library** (see **Local Services,** above).

Post Office: 9 Elizabeth St. (☎6236 3577; fax 6234 9387), at Macquarie St. The post office from which, in 1912, Roald Amundsen sent the telegram announcing he'd reached the South Pole. Open M-F 8am-5:45pm. **Postal Code:** 7000.

ACCOMMODATIONS

During the December summer festival, book well ahead.

Narrara Backpackers, 88 Goulburn St. (☎6231 3191), turn left off Harrington St. Offering spotless accommodation with a cozy atmosphere, this 3-story house proves the newest place is sometimes the best. Off-street parking. Laundry. Internet $2 per 10min. Reception daily 8am-10pm. Dorms $16; twins $36; doubles $40.

Central City Backpackers, 138 Collins St. (☎6224 2404 or 1800 811 507; www.centralbackpackers.com.au), on the 2nd floor through the Imperial Arcade. A large hostel with a kitchen, common areas, and a great location. Downstairs lounge has pool table, TV, and a bar (pints $3-4; open Nov.-Apr. nightly 6pm-late). Sleepsheet $1, full linen $2. Laundry. Internet $2 per 10min. Key deposit $5. Reception daily 8am-10pm. 6-bed dorms $18; 4-bed dorms $20; singles $34; twins and doubles $44. Cash only. VIP.

Transit Centre Backpackers, 199 Collins St. (☎/fax 6231 2400; LizK@telstra.easymail.com.au), above the bus terminal. Bright, spacious common area. Friendly proprietors live on-site. Fireplace, heaters, extra doonas for the winter chill, TV, kitchen, laundry, pool table. Free storage. No alcohol permitted on premises; coffee and tea included. Reception daily 8am-11pm. Dorms $17.

New Sydney Hotel, 87 Bathurst St. (☎6234 4516). Rooms and bathrooms are well-maintained despite their age. TV and kitchen. Downstairs music shuts down by midnight. Internet $2 per 10min. Key deposit $10. 7-night max. stay. Dorms $16; doubles $35.

Adelphi Court YHA, 17 Stoke St., New Town (☎6228 4829), take a Metro bus from Argyle St. to stop 8A opposite the hostel, or a bus from Elizabeth St. to stop 13. Adelphi is the pricey mothership of the Tasmania YHA fleet. Large common area with booking office, grocery kiosk, wash basins in rooms, laundry. Continental breakfast $4.50. Internet $6 per 30min. Key deposit $10. Reception daily 7:30-10:30am and 4-9pm. Dorms $20; singles $47; twins $53. Non-YHA add $3.50.

Montgomery's YHA, 9 Argyle St. (☎6231 2600; montys@southcom.com.au). Located downtown. Kitchen with TV but no real common room. Laundry. Phones in rooms, baggage storage, and tour bookings. Reception daily 8am-9pm; after-hours go to the pub next door. Dorms $20 for first night, $18 thereafter; non-YHA $21 per night.

Sandy Bay Caravan Park, 1 Peel St. (☎6225 1264), 3km from the city center off Nelson St., which runs into Sandy Bay Rd. across from the casino. The Busy Bee bus services the casino M-F 8am-6pm every 10min. Coin-op stove 20¢. Bedding $4. Reception Su-W 8:30am-6pm, Th-Sa 8:30am-7pm. Sites $8 per person; powered $17; on-site caravans for 2 $40; self-contained cabins for 2 $60, each extra person $8.

FOOD

Hobart has just the international cuisine the two-minute noodle weary have been craving. Restaurants downtown serve meals from every pocket of Asia, while the pubs and grills at Salamanca Place serve lunch and dinner once brekkie is finished at the cafes. The best part of town for dining is Elizabeth St. in North Hobart, where decent restaurants of a great variety of cuisines—from Turkish to Mexican to Vietnamese—cluster. For traditional local fare, the ultimate Tassie tucker is abalone or salmon with a Cascade beer. **Purity,** 69 King St., Sandy Bay (☎6211 6611) or 189 Campbell St., North Hobart (☎6234 8077), is an inexpensive **supermarket.** (Both open M-W, Sa 8am-6pm, Th-F 8am-9pm.) Get organic and bulk foods at **Eumarrah Wholefoods,** 45 Goulburn St. (☎6234 3229. Open M-F 9am-6pm, Sa 9am-2pm.) The Saturday **Salamanca Market** has deals on local produce, sauces, spreads, honey, and cheese. (Open Sa 8am-3pm.)

Retro Cafe, 33 Salamanca Pl. (☎6223 3073), on the corner of Montpelier Retreat. Regulars enjoy fine food and excellent coffee. There's great people-watching at the Salamanca Market on Sa. It can be hard to get a seat, but their all-day brekkie bagel ($10) is worth the scramble. Open M-Sa 8am-6pm, Su 8:30am-6pm.

Trattoria Casablanca, 213 Elizabeth St. (☎6234 9900). Recently renovated, this classy Italian restaurant has black-and-white photos from its namesake movie on the walls. Pastas in 15 varieties ($8.90-11) and pizzas ($8.80-20.90). Open Su-M and W-Th 5:15-11:30pm, F-Sa 5:15pm-1am.

Mures Fish Centre, Victoria Dock (☎6231 2121). A complete seafood complex. The sea-level **Bistro** serves the masses the town's best fish'n'chips ($7.50). Order and pay at the counter, then wait to be called. Separate, licensed beverage counter. Open daily 11am-9pm. The **Upper Deck** has fine dining lunches (noon-2:30pm) and winter dinner specials (6-10pm; both from $14.50). To starboard, **Orizuru** (☎6231 1790) makes fresh sushi (lunches $12; entrees $6-10; mains $16-24). Open M-Sa noon-2:30pm and 6-9:30pm. **Polar Parlour** has ice cream and desserts. Open daily 8am-9pm.

A Taste of Asia, 358 Elizabeth St., North Hobart (☎6236 9191). A favorite with locals. Quirky Asian-inspired cuisine, from sushi to stir-fry. The large take-away plates ($10) are a great deal. Open M-Th noon-8pm, F noon-9pm, Sa 4:30-9pm.

Drifters Internet Cafe, Shop 9, 33 Salamanca Pl., The Galleria (☎6224 6286). Good homemade soups ($5), foccacias ($5.50-7), and cappucino ($2.50). Even better are the 'zines, great music, and Internet access. ($2 per 10min., $9 per hr.). Open M-Th and Sa 10am-6pm, F 10am-8pm, Su 11am-6pm.

Little Bali, 84a Harrington St. (☎6234 3426). Tiny orange dining room, bright with wicker lamp-shades and flying animals. Good, quick Indonesian meals (small $6, large $8.20; 50¢ table surcharge). Open M-F 11:30am-3pm and 5-9pm, Sa-Su 5-9pm.

Vanny's, 181 Liverpool St. (☎6234 1457). Great Cambodian food–satay $4.40-6.60, curry (including vegetarian) $5.80-8.20. Open M-F 11:30am-3pm and M-Sa 3-9:30pm.

Machine Laundry/Cafe, 12 Salamanca Sq. (☎6224 9922), behind Salamanca Pl.; enter through Kennedy Ln. or Wooby's Ln. A funky new approach to laundry combines Italianate fare ($6-10), breakfast until 3pm ($7-10), and desserts ($6) with washing machines ($5 each for wash and dry). Open daily 8am-6pm.

Steve's Kebab House, 127 Liverpool St. (☎6231 6000). International kebabs are a specialty: Yankee-doodles with mustard and sauce, Aussie kebabs with a fried egg and sauce, and tasty vegetarian falafel. Everything is $6.80 or less. Open M 10am-9pm, Tu-Th 10am-10pm, F 10am-3pm, Sa 11am-3pm, Su 11am-9pm.

SIGHTS

Hobart is brimming with interesting convict history. The excellent free brochures *Hobart's Historic Places*, *Sullivan's Cove Walk*, and *Women's History Walk*, available from the tourist office, provide information and orientation.

DOWNTOWN

TASMANIAN MUSEUM AND ART GALLERY. Fine displays explore Tasmania's early convict history, unique ecology, and artistic heritage. The colonial-era art section is strong, while the mega-fauna models include a 10-foot kangaroo! *(40 Macquarie St., near the corner of Argyle St. ☎6211 4177. Open daily 10am-5pm. Free. Guided tours leave from the bookstore W-Su 2:30pm; tours can also be arranged.)*

PENITENTIARY CHAPEL AND CRIMINAL COURTS. One of the oldest, best-preserved buildings in Tasmania. The complex is an excellent example of Georgian ecclesiastical architecture; inside are the court rooms and gallows of the grim 1830s. *(6 Brisbane St. Enter on Campbell St. ☎6231 0911. Tours available M-F 10, 11:30am, 1, 2:30pm. $7.70, concessions $5.50. Ghost tours ☎0417 361 392. Daily 8pm. $7. Book ahead.)*

MARITIME MUSEUM. This facility highlights Tassie maritime heritage, with a focus on local shipping and whaling. Gunwales with model boats, ancient photographs, scrimshaw, and other crusty relics can be found throughout. Accounts of more recent catastrophic shipwrecks make for some riveting reading. *(16 Argyle St., in the Carnegie Building on the corner of Davey St. ☎6234 1427. Open daily 10am-5pm. $6.60.)*

CYCLEWAY. Along the western bank of the Derwent River is a bicycle path with views of Mt. Wellington, the Regatta Grounds, the Tasman Bridge, Government House, the Queen's Domain, the Royal Botanical Gardens, and the shipyards in Hobart. *(The tourist office has a brochure with maps.)*

OTHER SIGHTS DOWNTOWN. At Sullivan's Cove, the **Elizabeth, Brooke,** and **Murray St. Piers** harbor most of Hobart's large vessels. Look for the Antarctic Research Expedition's giant orange icebreaker, *Aurora Australis,* sometimes docked at Macquarie Wharf on the Cove's north side. **Constitution** and **Victoria Docks** are thronged with popular fishmongers and marine restaurants. Several companies run **harbor cruises** from this area (see **Ferries and Cruises,** p. 464).

THE MOUNTAINS

MT. WELLINGTON. Several kilometers west of Hobart, Mt. Wellington (1270m) is a must-see. The top is extremely windy, cold, and often snowy. On a clear day, you can see the peaks of half the state, all clearly marked on signs in the observation shelter. The summit is also home to a huge telecommunications tower that can become crowded with vehicle visitors, but surrounding walking tracks are spectacular. The road to the top closes occasionally due to snow and ice. **Fern Tree,** on the lower foothills of the mountain, is a lovely picnic area with walking tracks up the slope. *(Take the #48 or 49 Fern Tree bus to stop 27, at the base of the mountain. Getting to the top without a car may involve shelling out some dough for a narrated van trip up the road. Mt. Wellington Shuttle Bus Service $19.80 return; ☎0417 341 804 for bookings (min. 2 people). Experience Tasmania tours $20, concessions $17. Observation shelter open daily 8am-6pm. For track details, get the Mt. Wellington Walk Map from the tourist office $4.)*

MT. NELSON. South of central Hobart, the mountain offers views of Hobart and the Derwent estuary. A signal station at the top, part of the chain that connected Port Arthur to the capital, also has a restaurant. *(Take the #57 or 58 Mt. Nelson bus to its terminus. Road to the top open daily 9am-9pm. Restaurant open daily 9:30am-4:30pm.)*

SALAMANCA PLACE AND BATTERY POINT

SALAMANCA PLACE. This row of beautiful Georgian warehouses contains trendy galleries, restaurants, and shops of the much-celebrated Salamanca Market. Busy all day, the outdoor market offers a wonderfully chaotic diversity of crafts, produce, performers, and good times. *(Open Sa 8am-3pm.)*

ANTARCTIC ADVENTURE. This pleasant discovery center-*cum*-amusement park combines facts, fun, and 20min. planetarium shows of the Southern Hemisphere's starry sky. The most popular exhibit, the Blizzard, simulates downhill speed skiing. *(2 Salamanca Sq. ☎6220 8220 or 1800 350 028; www.antarctic.com.au. Open daily 10am-5pm. $16, concessions $13, under 14 $8, families $40. Planetarium show Su-F 11:30am, 1:30, 3:30pm; Sa every hour 11am-4pm.)*

BATTERY POINT. Salamanca Place butts up against the lovely historic neighborhood of Battery Point, where many of Hobart's convict-era buildings have been preserved. The Battery Point National Trust leads tours through the village, or you can do a self-guided tour by referring to walking brochures available from the tourist office. *(Tours depart Franklin Sq. Wishing Well Sa 9:30am. 2½hr. $10, children $2.50.)*

PRINCES PARK. On the edge of Battery Point, just behind the Esplanade, this lovely green space on a hill offers views of blue, blue water through the trees. The park was once the site of Mulgrave Battery, Battery Point's oldest building, and once a signal station relaying messages as far away as Port Arthur.

NORTH AND SOUTH

CADBURY CHOCOLATE FACTORY. One of Hobart's most popular attractions, Cadbury provides tours showing all stages of the chocolate process—most importantly, there are free tasting every step of the way. *(In Claremont, north of Hobart and the Derwent River. Take the Claremont service #37, 38, or 39 to the factory. ☎6249 0333 or 1800 627 367. Tours M-F 9, 9:30, 10:30am, 1pm. 1hr. $11, concessions $7.50, children $5.50. Advanced booking required. No tours Sept.)*

CASCADE BREWERY. This is the place for those who prefer death by beer rather than chocolate. Built in 1832 by a Mr. Degraves, who drew up the plans while in prison for debt default, it's the oldest brewery in Australia, producing 800 stubbies per minute. *(131 Cascade Rd. Take the Claremont service #43, 44, 46, or 49 to stop 17. ☎6221 8300. Tours M-F 9:30am and 1pm. 2hr. $8.25, concessions $5.50, children $1.65. Free beer at the end. Bookings essential.)*

BONORONG WILDLIFE PARK. See, hear, pet, and feed the beasts that roam the island's wilderness. Tasmanian devils, koalas, quolls, wombats, and injured birds live in enclosures, while 'roos and their joeys bounce independently, emus chuckle, and peacocks strut their stuff. Every visitor gets a bag of kangaroo feed. Most of the animals were orphaned or injured and will eventually be returned to the wild. *(North of Hobart in Brighton. Metro bus X1 from Hobart to Glenorchy Interchange connects with #125 or 126 to Brighton. Total journey about 1½hr. From Brighton it's a 30min. walk. By car, it's a 25min. drive north on Hwy.1; follow the signs in Brighton. ☎6268 1184. Open daily 9am-5pm. $10, children $5.)*

HISTORIC FEMALE FACTORY AND ISLAND PRODUCE TASMANIA FUDGE FACTORY. Once the Hobart jail and a factory for women and children in the 1820s, the site is now home to building ruins, memorial gardens, and fine confectioners. The poignant tours split their time between the historic site ("lest we forget") and today's small, handmade production of fudge and truffles. Um, did someone say non-sequitur? Free samples. *(16 Degraves St., South Hobart, near the Cascade Brewery. Take bus #43, 44, 46, 47, or 49 bus from Franklin Sq. to stop 16, cross onto McRobies Rd., and walk right onto Degraves St. ☎6223 3233. Shop and gardens open M-F 8am-4pm. Tours M-F at 10:30am. 1¼hr. $6.60, concessions $5.50, children $3.30. Book a day ahead.)*

ROYAL TASMANIAN BOTANICAL GARDENS. With 13 hectares and 6000 species, this is the largest public collection of Tasmanian plants in the world, and the largest collection of conifers in the Southern Hemisphere. Founded in 1818, they are also the second oldest gardens in Australia. The wildly popular Al Fresco Theatre runs an outdoor play in January, and "Shakespeare in the Garden" in February. *(North of the city, near the Tasman Bridge. Take any bus, including the MetroCity Explorer, that's headed to the eastern shore to stop 4 before the bridge; or take the X3-G express to Bridgewater, which stops at the main gate. Or walk 25min. from the city to Queen's Domain past Government House. ☎6234 6299. Open daily Oct.-Mar. 8am-6:30pm, Apr. 8am-5:30pm, May-Aug. 8am-5pm, Sept. 8am-5:30pm. Free. Outdoor Theatre $22, concessions $11.)*

ENTERTAINMENT

Check out the entertainment listings in the "EG" insert of Friday's *Age* newspaper. The arthouse cinema is the **State,** 375 Elizabeth St., in North Hobart, with indie films in glamorous facilities. (☎6234 6318. $11, concessions $7.50; W $7.) The **Theatre Royal,** 29 Campbell St., the oldest theater in Australia, produces reliably good shows. (☎6233 2299. Box office open M-F 9am-5pm, Sa 9:30am-1pm. $22-42.) The more experimental **Peacock Theatre,** 77 Salamanca Pl., is in the Salamanca Arts Centre. (☎6234 8414. $3.50-15). The **Tasmanian Symphony Orchestra,** 1 Davey St., in the Federation Concert Hall at the Hotel Grand Chancellor, is over 50 years old but still holds performances every few weeks. (☎1800 001 190. Box office open M-F 9:30am-4:30pm, Sa concert days, and all concert nights. $35-49, concessions $20.) The **Wrest Point Hotel,** 410 Sandy Bay Rd., at Nelson Rd., is the oldest casino in Australia. The emphasis is on pokies and other electronic games; there are few real gaming tables. (☎6225 0112. Tables open Su-Th 2pm-2am, F-Sa 2pm-3am.)

NIGHTLIFE

Hobart is often mocked for its lukewarm nightlife, and while this isn't the place to find a world-class club scene, there are definitely places to party. Once again, Salamanca Place draws the masses.

The New Sydney Hotel, 87 Bathurst St. (☎6234 4516). An extremely popular Irish pub where margaritas (a dubious Irish tradition) are the most popular beverage ($9.50). Tu-Su live music, mainly cover bands. No cover (except Sa $3). Open M noon-10pm, Tu noon-midnight, W-F 11:30am-midnight, Sa 1pm-midnight, Su 4-9pm.

Syrup and **Round Midnight,** 39 Salamanca Pl. (☎6223 2491). Packed late nights on weekends. **Syrup,** on the 1st floor, is a mellow lounge-bar with nibbly food and live DJs that morphs into a club at midnight. **Round Midnight,** on the 2nd floor, hosts live bands and guest DJs. F-Sa cover $4-7. Both open 6pm to the wee hours.

Club Surreal, 86 Sandy Bay Rd. (☎6223 3655), at the corner of St. George's, upstairs from St. Ives Hotel. Surreal Saturday nights are jam-packed with an 18+ crowd wanting to boogie. Huge video screens, TVs on the floor, and techno and disco dance floors connected with a slippery slide. Club cover W $4, F-Sa $8. Pub open Su-Tu 4-10pm, W 4pm-3am, Th 4pm-midnight, F-Sa 4pm-3am. Open W, F, Sa 10:30pm-4:30am.

THE SOUTH

Anchored by the capital city of Hobart, Australia's southern end grew from convict populations, matured under British colonialism, and now thrives as an arena of humble communities and outdoor wonders. Ninety minutes east of Hobart lie the Tasman Peninsula and historic Port Arthur, the most significant—and commercialized—testament to Tassie's colonial history; to the west lies the entrance to the vast expanse of the Southwest National Park in the Tasmanian Wilderness World Heritage Area. In between, amid the hop vines of the Derwent Valley and the apple orchards of the D'Entrecasteaux Channel, are the homes of people who know they've found the good life. Wandering through groves of Huon pines or trekking with camels along Bruny's beaches, you're bound to feel the same.

TASMAN PENINSULA AND PORT ARTHUR ☎03

Pinched to almost nothing, narrow **Eaglehawk Neck** connects the Tasman Peninsula to the rest of the island. Tourist buses now funnel through the very place where guard dogs once ravaged would-be escaped convicts. Initially known as the "Black Line," military units once dumped Aborigines and repeat offenders over the peninsula's steep cliffs and narrow neck, into rumored shark-infested waters. From 1830 to 1877, 12,000 convicts were shipped to **Port Arthur's** cruel colonies for offenses ranging from petty thievery and "skulking without permission" to murder. The inmates were put to work, and Port Arthur eventually became a settlement that exported timber and leather. The ruins of the many convict-built sandstone buildings are Tasmania's most popular tourist attraction, drawing 250,000 visitors annually. If Port Arthur's commercialism is too much, try the surrounding area where you can escape the crowds. The Tasman coastline, now a National Park, is particularly astounding; well-beaten walkways and open tracks provide some of the most phenomenal views in Tassie.

TRANSPORTATION. There is no real Port Arthur town, just services to the site. **TassieLink** (☎1300 300 520) is the only **bus** company servicing the tourist attraction, departing the depot in Hobart M-Sa 4pm for the YHA and Port Arthur Motor Inn (2¼hr.; $14.90). Buses depart Port Arthur M-F 6am, holidays 7am, Sa 1pm. Book at the YHA.

A 1hr. drive north, the town of Sorell is the main stop en route to the Suncoast (via the A3). **Redline** (☎1300 360 000) **buses** run to Hobart (50min.; M-F 5-8 per day, Sa 2 per day; $4). TassieLink runs up the East Coast (W, F, Su morning; also M in summer) to: Bicheno (2½hr., $18.40); Coles Bay (2½hr., $17.40); St. Helens (3¾hr., F and Su only, $28.90); Swansea (2hr., $13.40); Triabunna (1hr., $8.40).

PRACTICAL INFORMATION. By the Eaglehawk Neck Historic Site on the A9, the **Officers Mess** has basic **groceries,** takeaway, and an **information centre.** (☎6250 3722. Open daily 8am-8pm; winter Su-Th 9am-6:30pm, F-Sa 9am-7:30pm.) In Sorell, the **Westpac bank,** with **24hr. ATM,** is at 36 Cole St. at the junction of A3 and A9. (Open M-Th 9:30am-4pm, F 9:30am-5pm.) There's a **post office** on 19 Gordon St., in Sorell. (☎6265 2579; open M-F 9am-5pm.) **Postal code:** 7172.

ACCOMMODATIONS. The **Seaview Lodge Host Farm,** 732 Nubeena Back Rd., Koonya has a fairy-tale, hilltop location on 90 acres of land. **Tassie Experience & Eco Tours** runs out of the farm. TassieLink drops passengers off in Koonya 30min. before arriving in Port Arthur; free pickup available from Koonya or Port Arthur. From A9 in Taranna, follow B37 9km to Nubeena Back Rd., and then 1½km up to the farm. (☎6250 2766; www.tassie.net.au/~seaview. Linen $5. Laundry $2. Bike hire $15. Dorms $12-15; twins and doubles $30.) **Eaglehawk Neck Backpackers,** 94 Old Jetty Rd., 1km from the Neck, offers two self-contained beach huts. (☎6250 3248. Bike and canoe hire. Dorms $14. Hut for 2 Apr.-Nov. $40. Limited sites $6 per person.) The **Port Arthur YHA,** on Champ St., first left past the entrance to the historic site, sits mere meters from the ruins and has a resident ghost named Alice. (☎6250 2311. Reception daily 8:30-10am and 5-10pm. Dorms $17, non-YHA $20.) The **Port Arthur Garden Point Caravan Park,** is left off A9 1km before the historic site. (☎6250 2340. Dorms $14; sites for 2 $14, powered $16; cabins $60-80.)

SIGHTS. The prison, lunatic asylum, hospital, and church of **Port Arthur Historic Site** are a visible reminder of Australia's convict heritage. The downstairs museum area provides the most historical information, while the short **walking tours** of the grounds provide minimal insight. Buy admission tickets and Ghost Tour tickets from the YHA or front desk of the visitor complex. (☎1800 659 101; www.portarthur.org.au. Open daily 8:30am-8pm, but most buildings close at 5pm; allow 4hr. to explore. $18, concessions $14.40, children $9; after 4:30pm $9.) A 20min. harbor cruise passing by the **Isle of the Dead,** the colony's cemetery, and **Point Puer,** the convict boys' colony, is included in the price of admission; book at the visitor complex. Cruises that actually land on the Isle of the Dead cost an extra $8. The overwhelmingly popular **Historic Ghost Tour** runs nightly (times vary)—spooky stories, creepy shadows, and minimal history (90min., $14).

RECENT HISTORY

On Sunday, April 28, 1996, a gunman killed 35 people in Port Arthur historic site and township. The shock to Tasmania and Australia still lingers; the violence triggered gun law reform. Information on the murders is available in any Tasmanian bookstore and in a free booklet of the court transcription available at the visitors' desk. Be considerate of the Port Arthur community by not asking staff and shopkeepers about the incident.

AROUND THE TASMAN PENINSULA

Much of the Peninsula's coastline makes up **Tasman National Park,** which is lined by cliff-top **hiking trails.** Peter and Shirley Storey's handy *Tasman Tracks*, available at tourist shops on the peninsula, details about 50 walks and has good maps. One of the region's most intriguing sights is the **Tessellated Pavement,** just before Eaglehawk Neck. The natural platform of sedimentary rock has grooves hatched across the surface from unequal erosion, giving it the appearance of tile. The carpark is 500m up Pirates Bay Dr., and it's an easy 15min. return walk to the beach.

Continuing on A9 just past Eaglehawk Neck is C338 which leads to the **Devils Kitchen** and **Tasman Arch** carparks. Both cliffside sights are easy 10-15min. return walks. Continue along the moderate gravel track to **Patersons Arch** (15min.) and **Waterfall Bay** (45min.), where it links up with the steep **Tasman Trail** to the **falls** (1¼hr.) and **Waterfall Bluff** (1½hr.). Walking from Devils Kitchen to **Fortescue Bay** can be a breathtaking 8hr. or overnight walk. Basic **camping** is available with drinking water, showers, and toilets (sites $10; park fees apply). The Fortescue **ranger**

> **BECOME THE ANIMAL** On May 17, 1832, Port Arthur escapee George "Billy" Hunt tried to cross Eaglehawk Neck, which was protected by guard stations and savage dogs. He attempted to disguise himself by donning a kangaroo skin and hopping through the blockade. The guards bought the act—and started shooting at him; kangaroo meat was an important supplement to their rations. Hunt threw off the skin, crying "Don't shoot! It's only me, Billy Hunt!"

has details (☎6250 2433). To get to Waterfall Bay by car, take the first right off C338 and follow 4km to the cul-de-sac; for Fortescue Bay follow a 12km signposted, unsealed road east off A9, south of the B37 Taranna junction.

From Fortescue Bay, the Tasman Trail leads to **Cape Hauy** (4hr.). Starting with a deep descent from the campground, this very difficult trek passes by the spectacular **Monument,** featuring the dolorite spires of **The Candlestick, The Needle,** and **The Lanterns,** popular among ambitious **rock climbers.** The 3-day return trip to **Cape Pillar** is wicked awesome. Camping is available at **Lime Bay** with pit toilets and spring-fed water ($3). Check with the park office for updates, including summer ranger activities. **Parks and Wildlife** (☎6250 3497) is on A9 before the Devil Park.

The **Tasmanian Devil Park Wildlife Rescue Centre,** in Taranna, houses devils, 'roos, and wallabies, all feedable and touchable—well, not the devils. (☎6250 3230. Open daily 9am-5pm. $11, children $5.50, families $29.50.) Next door, **World Tiger Snake Centre,** has over 1000 snakes. Did you know a female tiger snake can store sperm in her body for up to 2 years? Imagine getting that call—"It ain't mine!" (Open daily 9am-5pm. Summer $8, children $4, families $19; winter $5, $2, $10.)

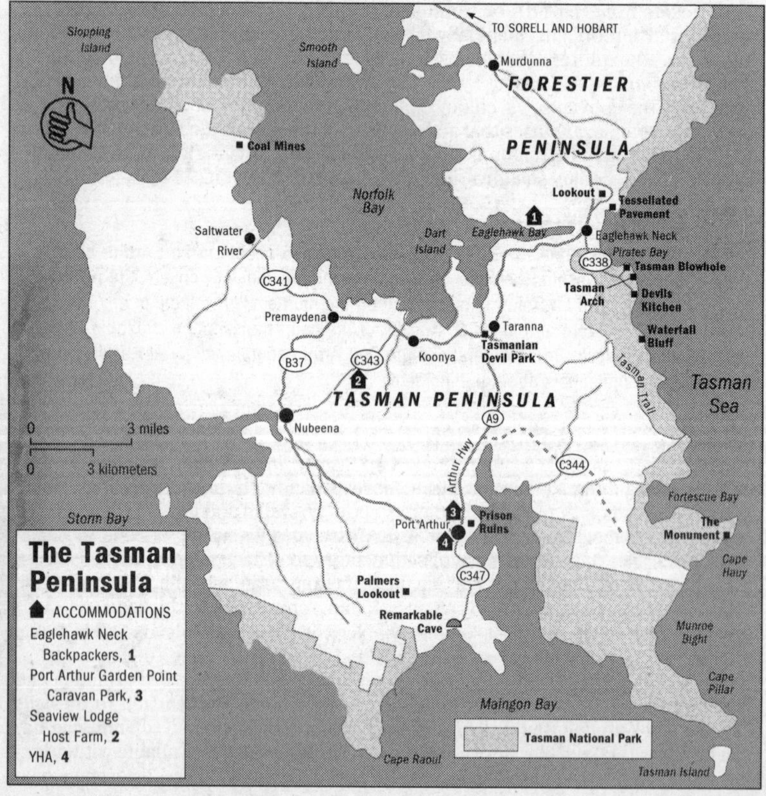

D'ENTRECASTEAUX CHANNEL

The channels, islands, and caves south of Hobart were first charted by Frenchman Bruni d'Entrecasteaux in 1792, more than a decade before the first English settlement in the area. The Huon River flows gently through the valley, feeding fertile soil in a cool climate perfect for berries, pears, and apples. The pastoral land between the river and the D'Entrecasteaux Channel teems with antique shops and vineyards. The small town of Cygnet acts as a base for exploring the area, while Bruny Island offers an adventurous escape into wild. South of the Huon River, Geeveston and the Lune River area are launchpads to the southwest. The widely circulated *Southern Tasmania's Waterways and Wilderness* is a useful navigational aid for the entire region.

CYGNET AND THE HUON VALLEY ☎03

Near the mouth of the Nicholls Rivulet on Port Cygnet 60km southwest of Hobart, The friendly, artsy community of Cygnet hosts seasonal fruit pickers and year-round travelers en route to the Huon Valley. Several testaments to the region's fruit trade lie on A6 to Huonville from Hobart. **Doran's Jam Factory** has been churning out fruit preserves since 1834. Their spiced apple butter is the local favorite; savor it with scones in their tea room. (☎6266 4377. Open daily 10am-4pm. Free self-guided tours and samplings.) Down the road, **The Huon Apple and Heritage Museum,** in Grove, is filled with paraphernalia from the apple industry. The 90-year-old peeling machine is the core of the exhibit, and you're invited to eat the remains. From March to June, 500 varieties of apples are on display. (☎6266 4345. Open Sept.-May daily 9am-5pm, June and Aug. daily 10am-4pm. $4.) This region of Tasmania is locally known for its cool-climate wines, many of which are available at the **Hartzview Vineyard and Wine Centre,** 10km east of Cygnet near Gardners Bay (via B68 and C626). In addition to its own pinot noir and fruit wines, Hartzview sells those of smaller area vineyards without cellar-door sales of their own. (☎6295 1623. Open daily 9am-5pm. Tastings $2, refunded on purchase.)

6km southwest of Cygnet (look for the sign where B68 meets C627), the **Talune Wildlife Park** is one of the very few in Australia to house the elusive platypus. Of course, loads of kangaroos, wombats, quolls, koalas, and devils frequent the premises, as well. (☎6295 1775. Open daily 9:30am-5pm. $10, children $3.50.)**Hobart Coaches,** leaves from 21 Murray St., in Hobart for the Cygnet carpark. (☎6233 4232. 1hr., M-F 5:15pm, $8.) **Mary St.** holds **Trust Bank** (☎6295 1682; open M-F 9am-noon and 1-5pm); the **library** (☎6295 1800; open Tu 10am-2pm, Th 10am-5pm, F 3-8pm), with **Internet** (30min. $5); and **post office** (open M-F 9am-5pm). **Postal code:** 7112.

The **Balfes Hill Huon Valley YHA & Backpackers,** 4 Sandhill Rd., Cradoc, 4.5km north of Cygnet, is a great place. The older building caters to eager workers willing to pick berries or prune orchards November to May. The hostel managers will help find employment and provide transportation ($10 per week or $1 per trip). The new building has comfortable bunks, clean bathrooms, kitchen, video lounge, ping-pong, billiards, laundry, and a phone. Phone ahead for pickup from the bus stop. (☎6295 1551. Dorms $15; twins $30, with bath $36; family rooms with bath $50. Non-YHA add $3.) Three **pubs** and the **Red Velvet Lounge** along Mary St. provide the only options for eating out. The Red Velvet Lounge, 87 Mary St., is part art gallery, part wholefoods store, and part cafe. (☎6295 0466. Open daily 9am-6pm.) Of the three **supermarkets,** Value-Plus is open longest (open daily 7:30am-9:30pm).

BRUNY ISLAND ☎03

Bruny was the first bit of land Abel Tasman glimpsed when he "discovered" Tasmania in 1642. Since then, Captain Cook and his understudy Captain Bligh (of *Mutiny Onboard H.M.S. Bounty* fame) both visited the island and believed it to be part of the mainland—they were proven wrong when d'Entrecasteaux sailed through the channel in 1792. Bruny once bustled with a great whaling industry, but timber and agriculture reign today. North Bruny is home to 1000-year-old frayed-looking trees called "blackboys," while South Bruny houses most of the island's 500 locals and tourists. The island captivates its visitors—families and adventurers alike—with dramatic coastal scenery, remnants of an exploratory past, and plenty of space to bushwalk, bike, paddle, and swim.

TRANSPORTATION. **Ferries** (☎6273 6725) run roughly every hour between Kettering and Bruny (15min.; M-Sa 6:50am-6:30pm, F 6:50am-7:30pm, Su 8am-6:30pm; return fare for cars $21, motorcycles $13, bicycles $5, pedestrians free). **Hobart Coaches** leaves 21 Murray St. in Hobart for the ferry terminal. (☎6234 4077. 45min., M-F 4 per day, $6.) The Lumeah YHA also offers the **Little Island Bus Service,** with pickup and drop off at Hobart Transit Centre on Collins St. or out to Bruny. (☎6293 1265. M, W, F; $35 return, ferry trip included. By booking only.) The island has no public transportation, Lumeah YHA rents **bicycles** (see below).

PRACTICAL INFORMATION. The **Visitor Centre** is across the channel in **Kettering** by the ferry terminal. (☎6267 4494 or 1800 676 740. Open daily 9am-5pm). The **Adventure Bay General Store,** 712 Adventure Bay Rd., has **petrol, EFTPOS,** and **groceries.** (Open daily 7:30am-9pm.) The Bruny Island **Online Access Centre,** at the Bruny Island District School in Alonnah, has **Internet,** scanning, and fax service. (☎6293 2036. Open Tu 2-5:30pm, W 9am-noon, 1-4pm, and 6-9pm, Th 1-4:30pm, F 1-4pm and 6-9pm, Sa 1-4pm. $5 per 30min.) The **post office** is at the **Alonnah General Store,** just off B66 in Alonnah. (Open daily 7:30am-7pm.) **Postal code:** 7150.

ACCOMMODATIONS AND FOOD. South Bruny's **Lumeah YHA,** in Adventure Bay, offers spacious dorms, huge common areas, a brick fireplace, laundry, and BBQ. They loan fishing gear, run day tours ($65), evening penguin viewing ($22), provide bus service, and arrange boat trips (1½hr., $50) or camel treks (30min., $15; 2½hr. with tea $45). Book ahead for ferry pickup ($10), massages (1hr., $40), or meals. (☎6293 1265; lumeah@tassie.net.au. Bike and kayak hire. Linen $2. Closed June-Aug. Sites $10; dorms $17; doubles $42; family rooms $56.) The **Adventure Bay Holiday Villages,** at the end of the road in Adventure Bay, are all decorated with bleached whale bones. (☎6293 1270. Coin-op showers. Laundry. Sites for 2 $12, powered $15; on-site vans for 2 $35; cabins for 2 $50.) At the start of the Penguin Island and Grass Point tracks, many of the island's protected lands offer free camping. **Cloudy Bay** on the southern part of the island and **Jetty Beach** near the lighthouse require national park passes. These, along with **Neck Beach,** on the south end of the isthmus between North and South Bruny offer primitive sites with pit toilets, no water, and no firewood. Contact the ranger at the **Labillardiere State Reserve** (☎6298 3229) for more info.

The **Hothouse Cafe,** 46 Adventure Bay Rd., 6km north of Adventure Bay, is a sheltered outdoor café with fantastic food, perfected by a panoramic view of the sea. (☎6293 1131. Open daily 10am-7:30pm. Gardens and Gumtree maze $3.)

SIGHTS AND ACTIVITIES. The **Bligh Museum,** 880 Adventure Bay Rd., contains fascinating old maps, marine photos, and memorabilia relating to the explorers who landed here, including Cook, Bligh, Flinders, and d'Entrecasteaux. (☎6293 1117. Open M-Sa 10am-4pm. $4.) The **Cape Bruny Lighthouse,** built by convicts between 1836 and 1838, is 30km southwest of Adventure Bay. (☎6298 3114. Open daily 10am-4pm. Tours by arrangement $10, children $2.) Near the lighthouse, hike down the hills and through the coastal heath and coves of the **Labillardiere Reserve** (7hr.). From Sept.-Feb., fairy penguins and muttonbirds roost on the Neck of the island. Parks and Wildlife runs free nightly tours from the Neck at dusk during the summer. The island is also a haven for rare white wallabies, diverse birdlife, dolphins, seals, and migrating southern right whales. **Cloudy Bay** has some of the best surf in Tasmania. **Jetty Beach** offers more sheltered waters suitable for kids. The **Pine Log Bight Track** (7hr.) from Cloudy Bay beach to Tasman Head is mostly a 4WD track but includes some steep climbs with fantastic views. Heading south from Adventure Bay, turn right onto Lockleys Rd. for 2.5km, then right again onto Resolution Rd. to the Mavista Picnic Area, where you can walk to **Mavista Creek** (20min.). The easy walk continues up to **Mavista Falls** (2hr.).

FAR SOUTH: GEEVESTON AND GATEWAYS TO WILDERNESS

Below Huonville, A6 roams south along the d'Entrecasteaux Channel. About 25km down, **Geeveston** teeters on the edge of the southwest wilderness. In the last Ice Age, Aborigines lived in the area's caves. Much of the region is now protected in the Hartz Mountains and Southwest National Parks, part of the Tasmanian Wilderness World Heritage Area. **TassieLink** (☎1300 300 520) **buses** run from Hobart to: Cockle Creek (3½hr.; Dec.-mid-Apr. M, W, F; $51.60); Dover (2hr., 3-4 per day M-F, $14.90); Geeveston (1¼hr.; M-F 4-5 per day, Sa-Su 1 per day; $11.20); Lune River (2½hr.; Dec.-Apr. M, W, F; $22.90).

The Geeveston **Visitor Information** is in the **Forest & Heritage Centre** on Church St. (☎6297 1836. Open daily 10am-4:30pm. Museum $5. **Internet** $2 per 30min.) Church St. has several **supermarkets** (open Su-Th 8:30am-6:30pm, F 8:30am-7:30pm); and a **post office** that's also a **bank** (☎6297 1102; open daily 9am-8pm). **Postal code:** 7116.

The **Geeveston Forest House,** at the end of Church St., has free laundry. (☎6297 1102. Singles and doubles $14.) **Lune River YHA,** 40km south of Geeveston, is "Australia's most southerly" hostel. (☎6298 3163; luneriver@trump.net.au. Pickup from Dover $5; bike hire $15 per day; canoes $10 per half-day; glow worm caves tour $30. Dorms $12.) The region has many **camping** options, with free sites at the **Tahune Forest Reserve,** 27km west of Geeveston; **Hastings Forest,** 13km west of Dover; and **Cockle Creek,** 25km south of Lune River. All are off of unsealed roads and offer pit toilets and drinking water. Cockle Creek also has a phone.

Even if you're not camping, follow the unsealed **Arve Road Forest Drive** from Geeveston to the Huon River to see native Huon pines, which take 500 years to mature and can live up to 2500 years. The easy **Huon Pines Loop Trail** (20min.) starts at the carpark past the Tahune Forest Reserve campground. Nearby, take the Arve Loop Rd. to the **"Big Tree,"** an 87m, unbelievably wide swamp gum (or mountain ash). About 10km northwest of Lune River are the **Hastings Caves,** dripping with dolomite formations. (☎6298 3209. Summer tours every hr. 10am-6pm, in winter 11am-4pm. $12, concessions $10; includes entry to the thermal springs.) The Lune River area is also known for fresh and saltwater fishing. The carpark past the free camping area in **Cockle Creek** marks the end of Australia's most southerly road. An easy walk (4hr. return) from the campground goes to South Cape Bay, the closest you can get to **Australia's southernmost tip** and neighboring Antarctica. The campground is also the endpoint of **South Coast Track** (85km). Most people hiking the full track fly into **Melaleuca** and walk back out 6-9 days later. Some combine it with the **Port Davey Track,** extending it another five days. For info on flights, which run about $100 per person one-way, contact **Par-Avion Wilderness Tours** (☎6248 5390), at the Cambridge Airport, 20km from Hobart, or **Tasair Wilderness Flights** (☎6248 5088). The area west of Cockle Creek is part of the **Southwest National Park.** Park passes are available from the Geeveston Forest and Heritage Centre.

DERWENT VALLEY AND THE SOUTHWEST

Flowing from Lake St. Clair, high in the mountain forests and down to Storm bay, the River Derwent marks the boundary between Tasmania's agricultural midlands and its wild southwest. Stretching expansively to the Southern Ocean, Southwest National Park includes the vast hydroelectric Lakes Gordon and Pedder, sites of great environmental debates and consternation. Ridgeline after ridgeline of rocky peaks roll into the southern shores of this quiet Tassie valley.

NEW NORFOLK ☎03

A misty valley enfolds the small town of New Norfolk, 25km northwest of Hobart on the Derwent. The climate is perfect for growing hops—regional cultivators harvest up to 45 tons per day. **Oast House,** on the Lyell Hwy. before town, was once used to dry the harvest; now it's New Norfolk's most hopping tourist attraction with a museum, gallery, and cafe. (☎6261 1030. Open Sept.-Dec. W-Su 9:30am-5pm, Jan.-May daily 9:30am-5pm. $4.) Eleven kilometers west of New Norfolk, the **Salmon Ponds** and **Museum of Trout Fishing** constitute the oldest trout hatchery in the Southern Hemisphere. (☎6261 1614. Open daily 9am-5pm. $5.)

TassieLink (☎1300 300 520) runs **buses** to: Hobart (40min.; 1 per day Dec.-Apr.; Tu, Th, F, Su mid-Apr.-Nov.; $5.10); Lake St. Clair (2½hr.; Dec.-mid-Apr. 1 per day; mid-Apr.-Dec. Tu, Th, Su; $26); Queenstown (4½hr.; Tu, Th, F, Su 1 per day; W in summer; $39.60). **Hobart Coaches** (☎6233 4232) runs from Hobart to Circle St. in New Norfolk (50min.; M-F 6 per day, Sa 3 per day; $5.10.) The **Derwent Valley Information Centre** is on Circle St. (☎6261 0700. Open M-F 8:15am-5pm.) Inside the **police station,** 14 Bathurst St., is **free Internet access.** (Open M-F 9am-5pm.) The **Bush Inn Hotel,** 49-51 Montagu St., north on the Lyell Hwy., includes full breakfast. (☎6261 2256. Singles $30; twins and doubles $50.) The **New Norfolk Esplanade Caravan Park,** on the river bank, has coin-op showers and laundry. (☎6261 1268. Key deposit $5. Crowded sites for 2 $10, powered $14.) Purity **supermarket** is on Charles St. (Open M-W, Sa 8am-6pm, Th-F 8am-9pm.)

MT. FIELD NATIONAL PARK

At Mt. Field, Tasmania's first national park and a good hour from Hobart, summer visitors enjoy bushwalks and waterfalls, while winter visitors head for the slopes to downhill and cross-country ski. No bus company services the park or its ski fields during the winter. **TassieLink** (☎1300 300 520) runs **buses** Dec.-mid-Apr. to: Hobart (1½hr., M-Sa 1 per day, $23.50); Lake St. Clair via Gretna (3hr., M-Sa 1 per day, $30); Scott's Peak (1¾hr.; Tu, Th, Sa mornings; $34.60). Tour companies lead trips from **Hobart. Bottom Bits Bus** offers well-led, full-day tours during the summer. (☎1800 777 103. $69.) **Closer to Nature** offers more expensive full-day tours year-round. (☎6288 1477. $100). Rangers lead free walks, slide shows, and nighttime wildlife-watching trips during the summer. Maps and park passes are available at the entrance station. Continue 100m up the road to the **park shop** (☎6288 1526) for more park info, takeaway food, and souvenirs. The **Mt. Field Information Line** (☎6288 1319) has a recording on ski and road conditions.

The National Park Office administers three basic six-person **cabins** near Lake Dobson with mattresses, a wood heater, firewood, and cold water. (☎6288 1149. Book ahead. $10 per person.) The park shop also runs a **campground** near the park entrance. The self-register campsites are equipped with showers, bathrooms, BBQ, and laundry. Its grounds fill with pademelons, and the creek is home to platypi. (Sites $7 per person, powered $10.) Past the park on B61 (Gordon River Rd.), **Mt. Field YHA** provides basic beds. (☎6288 1369. Dorms $17. Linen $1. Laundry.) Food options are scarce; some get **groceries** in New Norfolk. In a pinch, the **pub** across from the YHA has counter meals (daily 6:30-7:30pm). West 12km in Maydena, Harry's **mini-market** closes at 9pm.

The park can be divided into two distinct areas. The lower slopes near the park entrance have picnic and BBQ facilities, a park shop, and easy walks to a trio of waterfalls and the tallest flowering plant in the world. **Russell Falls,** a paved walk (10min.) from the carpark through wet eucalypt forest, has long been the favorite destination. It's definitely worth continuing up along the steep gravel road to **Lake Dobson** (16km) through eucalypts, mixed forest, subalpine woodland, and alpine mosaic. The upper slopes offer a network of extended bushwalks amid glassy highland lakes. The easy **Pandani Grove Nature Walk** (1hr.) circles Lake Dobson and introduces unusual wildlife: pineapple grass, bright red scoparia, the endemic conifers, the pencil King Billy pines, and platypi.

Though snow cover varies, skiers come to walk back in time, travelling up the slope by tow or making their own tracks in the backcountry. Without 4WD, Lake Dobson Road can only be accessed with 2WD and chains (the ski fields are a 40min. walk past the carpark). The ski kiosk rents skis and lift tickets.

SOUTHWEST NATIONAL PARK AND THE GORDON RIVER DAM

B61 Hwy., better known as **Gordon River Rd.,** continues through Maydena, winding 86km through the rugged mountains of Southwest National Park. The road passes through the settlement of **Strathgordon** (pop. 15), 12km before its abrupt end at the Gordon River Dam (about 1½hr.). **TassieLink** (☎1300 300 520) runs summer service between Hobart and Scotts Peak (3¼hr.; 1 per day Tu, Th, Sa; $58.10) via Timbs Track (2hr., $55), Mt. Anne (2¾hr., $55), and Red Tape Track (3hr., $55). The park is largely inaccessible by road, stretching south to Melaleuca and Cockle Creek between which runs the **South Coast Track** (see p. 475). The construction of the Gordon River Dam system brought condemnation from international environmental activists, who argued that the dams would destroy the region's wild beauty. Regardless, the dams were built, and today the power station is the largest in Tasmania—it alone could support Hobart's power usage.

Carved out of the Tasmanian Wilderness World Heritage Area, the unnatural Lakes Gordon and Pedder are captivating. **Hydro's Visitor Centre,** on a ledge above the dam, has brochures on the dam's construction and history. Take 196 steps down to the top of the dam. Tours go through the 1km access tunnel into the power station and provide some pro-power fodder for the conservation debate. (☎6280 1134. Open daily Nov.-Apr. 10am-5pm, May-Oct. 11am-3pm. Tours 1hr. Nov.-Apr. daily 10am, 2pm; May-Oct. 11am; $5.) **Lake Pedder** can be viewed from both the main road and the entirely unsealed **Scotts Peak Rd.** This difficult road forks off the Gordon River Rd. 28km into the park at Frodshams Pass, ending 36km later at the Huon Campground. Just 2.5km into Scotts Peak Rd. is the short and sweet **Creepy Crawly Nature Trail** (20min.). Longer walks go from Timbs Track to the **Florentine River** (4hr. easy rainforest walk), the **Eliza Plateau** (6hr.; difficult ridge climb to Mt. Eliza), and Lake Judd (8hr. unmarked track with difficult river crossings). Picnic and camp sites at the **Huon Campground** grant easy access to the **Arthur Plains** and **Port Davey** walking tracks. Other sites are at **Edgar Dam,** 8km before the end of Scotts Peak Rd., and **Teds Beach,** east of Strathgordon. Strathgordon's **Lake Pedder Motor Inn** is the only other park accommodation. (☎6280 1166. Singles $60-80; twins and doubles $70-90.) **Trout fishing** is plentiful on Lake Gordon and Lake Pedder from August to April (license required). For park info, contact the entrance station (☎6288 2258), or rangers at Mt. Field (☎6288 1141).

THE WESTERN WILDERNESS

From windy Strahan, to the deep glaciers of Lake St. Clair and the slopes of Cradle Mountain, the scenic splendor of Tasmania's west sits amidst highland pine forests. In the wilderness, millennia-old Huon pines share the forest with deciduous beeches that come ablaze in autumn as well as bellied parrots, quolls, devils, wombats, echidnas, 'roos, and wallabies.

As one of the world's great temperate wildernesses, it also is one of its last. Most of the land became protected in 1982 by the UNESCO Tasmanian Wilderness World Heritage Area, though logging and mining still threaten the areas just outside the national park. While the area's well-trammeled trails justifiably attract plenty of visitors, most of the west is entirely unspoiled by human contact; lush rainforest, forbidding crags, windswept moors, and swirling rivers have been left almost as they were when explorers first came to the region. Aborigines native to Tasmania, however, lived here for some 30,000 years. Today, the cultural sites are being returned to their rightful owners, and life goes on noticeably unchanged.

CRADLE MOUNTAIN ☎03

If you haven't seen a picture of mystic Cradle Mountain rising above quiet Dove Lake, you must not be in Tasmania. The mountain is Tassie's most iconic landmark, visited by hundreds of thousands of wilderness lovers every year. The area is a complex glacial fabric of creeks and crags that shelter the state's unique jew-

MARSUPIALS FROM HELL It doesn't spin around faster than you can see it, and it's rarely seen in convict stripes. Still, the Tasmanian devil is a remarkable creature. These marsupials are rarely more than 45cm high and aren't built for speed, being far more adept at climbing than at running. Their jet-black coats are often marked with white bands or spots, but the jaw is the most striking feature, full of jagged teeth and usually open wide. The powerful jaws can crush bones up to 7.5cm in diameter and allow the devil to eat almost anything. Devils are entirely carnivorous, hunting small mammals as well as scavenging carrion. Once common throughout Australia, they were driven off the mainland by dingoes; however, they thrive in Tasmania to the point of being considered a pest in some areas. While devils' attacks on humans are limited to the occasional theft of souls, they do sometimes kill farm animals. They are also extremely noisy, particularly when feeding, and are very irritating when they take up residence under people's houses. Despite their abundance, you won't often see the nocturnal, secretive critters in the wild; your best hope for spotting one is a wildlife park.

els: sweet-sapped cider-gum woodlands, rainforest of King Billy and celery-top pine, and carpets of cushion plants. Species—long thought to be extinct—such as freshwater crayfish, mountain shrimp, and velvet worm have been found alive and kicking around Cradle Mountain. Naturalist Gustav Weindorfer called Cradle Mountain the place "where there is no time and nothing matters."

TRANSPORTATION. **Maxwell's Coach and Taxi Service** (☎6492 1431) makes frequent, unscheduled runs between the campground, the Visitors Centre ($2), Dove Lake ($8), and offers 24hr. service to the northwest (see **Lake St. Clair,** p. 479; book ahead). **TassieLink** (☎1300 300 520) departs once daily Dec. to mid-Apr. and on Tu, Th, Sa the rest of the year from **Cradle Mountain Visitor Centre** and the **Campground** to: Devonport (1½hr., $28); Launceston (3½hr., $43.60); Strahan (3¾hr., $28).

PRACTICAL INFORMATION. **Cradle Mountain-Lake St. Clair National Park** is the northernmost end of the **Tasmanian Wilderness World Heritage Area.** It is a 1½hr. drive south from Devonport on B19 and B14 and then west on C132 to the park entrance. From the west, follow A10 from Queenstown for 2hr to C132 into the park. There is no direct road through the Cradle Mountain-Lake St Clair National Park. Visitors may most easily reach Lake St Clair via the Cradle Link Road (C132) and the Muchison and Lyell Highways (A10). Park fees apply ($9.90 daily fee per vehicle; up to 8 people). The **Visitor Centre,** just past the park entrance off of C132, features displays with helpful layouts of the walking tracks and a public telephone. (☎6492 1133. Open daily 8am-5:30pm, winter 8am-5pm.) A 7.5km gravel road runs south from the visitors centre to **Waldheim** and **Dove Lake.**

ACCOMMODATIONS AND FOOD. In peak season, accommodations fill up fast, so book ahead. On the entrance road, 2km outside the park, the **Cradle Mountain Tourist Park** provides sites, basic Alpine huts (intended for campers when it's raining), bunk rooms, self-contained cabins, and heaps of amenities. There's an unequipped cooking shelter with BBQ and a kitchen for hostelers. (☎6492 1395; cradle@cosycabins.com. Reception daily 8am-8pm. Sites $6-10 per person, powered $10-12; 3-bed Alpine huts $12-16; bunks $17-23; cabins for 2 $70-80. VIP/YHA.) The Visitor Centre runs the eight **Waldheim Cabins,** 5.5km inside the park. The Overland Track begins right outside. Heating, basic kitchen, showers, composting toilets, and limited generated power for lighting are provided. (☎6492 1110. Bunk cabins from $70-80 for up to 3; each extra person $10-19; fit 8.) **Bring your own food**—there is no produce at Cradle Mountain. The **Cradle Mountain Lodge General Store,** right outside the park, sells basic supplies at inflated prices. (Open M-F 9am-5pm, Sa-Su noon-4pm, extended summer hours.)

HIKING. Cradle Valley is the northern trailhead for the **Overland Track,** Tasmania's most prominent walk, traversing the length of the Cradle Mountain-Lake St. Clair National Park (see **Overland Track,** p. 480). The Cradle Mountain area has a web of tracks. The free park brochure map is of little use for all but the **Dove Lake Circuit** (2hr.), the most popular and environmentally friendly walk—a beautiful, mostly boardwalked, lakeside track through old-growth forest. The map for sale at the Visitor Centre ($4) is good for all other day hikes. The first stage of the **Overland Track** and its side tracks offer more arduous climbs: the hike up to **Marions Lookout** (1223m) begins along the Dove Lake track, continues steeply to the summit, and returns via Wombat Pool and Lake Lilla (2-3hr.); the ascent of Cradle Mountain (1545m) is a difficult hike from Waldheim or Dove Lake past Marions Lookout, involving some boulder-climbing toward the summit (6hr.). Registration is advised for any walks longer than 2hr. According to statistics, it rains 275 days a year, is cloudless on only 32, and can snow at any time—dress accordingly. Tracks around the Visitor Centre and the Cradle Mountain Lodge include a rainforest walk and **Pencil Pine Falls** (10min.). The lodge organizes a number of **activities:** walking tours (2½-3hr., $17), canoe trips (2½hr., $38), fly fishing (2½hr., $40), horse-riding (1hr., $31), abseiling (3hr., $35), and bike hire (half-day $15; full-day $20; deposit $200).

LAKE ST. CLAIR ☎03

Half of the headline act of the **Cradle Mountain-Lake St. Clair National Park,** Lake St. Clair is Australia's deepest lake as well as the source of the River Derwent. Its Aboriginal name is Leeawuleena ("sleeping water"), a serene juxtaposition of mountain, wood, and water. The lake anchors the southern end of the famous **Overland Track** (see p. 480), with Cradle Mountain at its northern terminus. There are also a number of day hikes and a few family-friendly nature trails near the lake.

Lake cruises with commentary run the length of the lake from the Cynthia Bay jetty (daily at 9am, 12:30, and 3pm, in summer also at 10am, winter 2pm; stopping at Echo Point $15, and Narcissus Bay $20). A return cruise is also available (book ahead at the tourist office; 1½hr.; $25, children $20). **Walking tracks** radiate from **Watersmeet,** 20min. from Cynthia Bay. **Woodlands Nature Walk** and **Platypus Bay Trail** make an easy, enjoyable loop through the woods to the water (1½-2hr.). Longer hikes head west to the sub-alpine forests of **Forgotten** and **Shadow Lakes** (3-4hr.) alongside waratah (flowering Nov.-Dec.); over the ridge, you can tackle steep, weather-beaten **Mt. Rufus** (7hr. return). If you take the ferry out in the morning, the lakeside hike to Cynthia Bay from Narcissus Bay amid rainforest, tea-tree, and buttongrass takes 5hr.; it's 3hr. from Echo Point.

TassieLink (☎1300 300 520) **buses** depart from **Derwent Bridge Wilderness Hotel** and the Visitors Centre for: Hobart (2¾hr.; summer daily, winter Tu, Th, F, Su; $35.50); Launceston (direct 3hr.; in summer M, W, F, Su; $53.70; with connections 7½hr.; year-round on Tu, Th; $74); Queenstown (1½hr., Tu, Th, F, Su, in summer also W; $21.30) via Cradle Mountain (4½hr., $42.30), Devonport (6hr., $58.40), and Launceston (7½hr.,$74). **Maxwell's Coach and Taxi Service** (☎6492 1431) operates a small, **24hr. charter service** in the Cradle Mountain-Lake St. Clair region to: Derwent Bridge (10min., $6); Frenchman's Cap (30min., $15); Hobart (3hr., $65); Queenstown (1¾hr., $35). The **Visitors Centre** is at **Cynthia Bay,** at the southern end of the lake, accessible via a 5km access road that leaves the Lyell Hwy. just west of Derwent Bridge. **Register** for any extended walks, especially the Overland Track. (☎6289 1172. Open daily 8am-5pm; late Dec.-Feb. 8am-7pm). Next door, **Lakeside St. Clair** is a privately owned tourist info center, restaurant, and booking agency. (☎6289 1137. Open daily 9am-8pm. Fishing gear $15 per day; canoe $30 per 2hr.)

The park has **free camping** sites within the entrance with walking access only and pit toilets. The closest camping is a 10min. walk from Cynthia Bay toward Watersmeet; other sites are located at **Shadow Lake, Echo Point,** and **Narcissus Bay. Lakeside St. Clair** has several accommodations just outside the park entrance with coin-op showers, a pay phone, and a kitchen with a wood-fire stove. (Sites $6 per person, powered for 2 $12; doona $5; electrically-heated backpacker bunks $25.) Opposite the Lake St. Clair access road on the Lyell Hwy. is the barn-sized **Derwent Bridge Wilderness Hotel.** Backpacker rooms are in the cramped, modular units detached from the main hotel building. (☎6289 1144. Singles and doubles $22.50.) The hotel serves plain meals at reasonable prices. (Open noon-2pm and 6-8pm.)

COLD KILLS. Many people come to Tasmania to hike the endless, untamed wilderness. Make no mistake: Tasmania's wilderness is still wild and can kill you. The greatest hazard in the wilderness is the unruly weather that can shift from zephyr to gale in a heartbeat. Even in the warmer months, carry heavy and waterproof clothing to prevent hypothermia, a lowering of the body's core temperature that can be fatal (it can snow, even blizzard, in summer). Dehydration is also a common cause of hypothermia, so take care to stay hydrated. The way to avoid hypothermia is preparation: plan your trip wisely. Do not attempt bushwalks without the proper equipment and experience. Ask about the expected conditions. Wear wool or fiber pile clothing, including gloves and a hat. Wet cotton, especially denim, is deadly. For more info on treating hypothermia, see **Essentials,** p. 43. The Parks and Wildlife Service can advise on gear.

THE OVERLAND TRACK

Connecting **Cradle Mountain** and **Lake St. Clair** through 80km of World Heritage wilderness, the Overland Track is Australia's most famous trail. Every year, approximately 8000 folks attempt the track, most taking 5-8 days to complete it. Purists contend that the track has become a congested highway, but its grandeur cannot be denied. The ascent of the state's tallest peak, **Mt. Ossa** (1617m), makes a good daytrip. The weather is fickle and will undoubtedly soak a portion of your journey.

The heavy traffic is having a disastrous impact on the path's fragile alpine ecosystems, so practicing minimum-impact bushwalking is crucial. Stay on the track, spread out when there is no track, walk on rocks, wear lightweight walking boots, rotate campsites, and use fuel stoves only. An *Essential Bushwalking Guide* is available at the normal brochure kiosks. The track huts fill easily, so hikers must carry **tents.** If you are planning to walk the track, write to request an information kit at **Parks and Wildlife Service.** (☎6492 1133; fax 6492 1120. Cradle Mountain Visitor Centre, P.O. Box 20, Sheffield TAS 7306.) A copy of the **Overland Track Map and Notes** ($9) is essential. The track itself can be undertaken from either the Cradle Mountain end (see p. 477) or Lake St. Clair (see p. 479), but most opt for Cradle Mountain and the slight downhill advantage of heading toward Lake St. Clair. The national park permit costs $13.20.

STRAHAN ☎03

The only community of any size on the entire west coast, Strahan is Tasmania's ecotourism capital, serving as a gateway to Franklin-Gordon Wild Rivers National Park and to all the glories of the southwest wilderness. Little more than a sleepy fishing village for most of the 20th century, Strahan vaulted into prominence when environmental protestors sailed from the town's wharf, situated on Macquarie Harbour, to successfully blockade the construction of dams on the Franklin and lower Gordon Rivers in the early 1980s. Since then, environmental appreciation is on the rise and tourists come by the boatloads and planeloads to experience the reverberations of a good cause.

TRANSPORTATION. **TassieLink** (☎1300 300 520) **buses** through Queenstown (45min., $7) to: Devonport (5½-7hr., $41.10); Hobart (5¼-6½hr.; Tu, Th, F, Su, Dec. to Mid-Apr. also W; $51.70) via Lake St. Clair (4hr.; $28.30); Launceston (7hr.; Tu, Th, Sa; $49) via Cradle Mt. (3½-4½hr.; Tu, Th, Sa, Dec. to mid-Apr. also M; $59.70).

NO WAY OUT From 1822 until 1833, Sarah Island was the feared penal colony for repeat offenders. Prisoners bound for Sarah Island, near the harbor's southern end, abandoned hope upon seeing the inability to escape by land or by sea. One of the darkest pits in the British penal system, its convicts were forced to wade chest-deep in the harbor's freezing water pushing giant Huon pine logs. The lucky ones got to stay on shore and build ships. In January 1834, the last ten convict shipwrights seized the last vessel and sailed it 10,000 miles right across the Southern Ocean to freedom in Patagonia. Few others escaped, or even tried; the handful who did perished in the wilderness (or in one case, turned to cannibalism). Today, all of Sarah Island's buildings have been reduced to sign-posted ruins, which tell of its harrowing past.

PRACTICAL INFORMATION. The **Strahan Visitor Centre,** on the Esplanade, is run by a theater company, an unlikely but tremendously successful association. Sailing into its ninth year and still going strong, the local play *The Ship That Never Was*, humorously explores the last great escape from Sarah Island's penal settlement. There's also a terrific exhibit, **West Coast Deflections,** on Aboriginal and settler life, featuring fine artwork and reconstructions of their dwellings. (☎6471 7622. Open daily Nov.-Apr. 10am-7pm; May-Oct. 10am-6pm. Shows daily at 5:30pm, Jan. also 8:30pm. $11, concessions $8.25. Exhibit $3.30/$2.20.) The **Parks and Wildlife Office,** in the historic customs house on the Esplanade, sells passes to national parks. (☎6471 7122. Open M-F 9am-noon and 1-5pm.) The customs house also has **Internet** access. (☎6471 7788. Open M-Th 2-7pm, F 11am-2pm, Su 1-5pm. $5 per 30min.) The **police** (☎6471 8000) are on Beach St. The **post office** is at the Customs House. (Open M-F 9am-5:30pm.) **Postal code:** 7468.

ACCOMMODATIONS AND FOOD. The **Strahan YHA,** 43 Harvey St., has kitchens and a resident platypus. From the Strahan wharf, with your back to the water, go left along the Esplanade; as it goes inland, it becomes Bay St. and then Innes St. Take a right onto Andrew St. and the first right onto Harvey St.; the hostel is right before the hill. (☎6471 7255; strahancentral@trump.net.au. Minimal reception hours daily 4-8pm. Dorms $18; twins $40.) The **Strahan Caravan Tourist Park** is on the corner of Andrew and Innes St. near the hostel. (☎6471 7239. Reception daily 8am-7pm. Sites for 2 $14, powered $18; on-site vans for 2 $45; cabins with bath $60-75.) **Strahan Central** is a posh cafe and crafts store on the corner of Herald St. and the Esplanade. (☎6471 7612. Open M-Th 8:30am-8pm, F 8:30am-4:30pm, Sa 10am-8pm, Su 10am-7:30pm. Meals $7-13.) A Rite-Way **supermarket** is also at the far end of the Esplanade. (Open daily 7:15am-7:30pm.)

SIGHTS AND ACTIVITIES. The track to **Hogarth Falls** (40min. return) a few hundred meters from central Strahan, is rampant with wildlife. Accessed through **People's Park,** the track follows **Botanical Creek,** home to aquatic critters, including the elusive platypus. North of town at the end of Harvey Rd., **Ocean Beach** stretches from Macquarie Head in the south to Trial Harbour over 30km north. It's the longest beach in Tasmania with brooding surf and windy dunes; **swimming is unsafe.** In late Sept., thousands of **mutton-birds** descend on the beach after flying 15,000km from their Arctic summer homes and go about laying their *one* egg of the season. Observe from the wooden platform to reduce erosion.

Strahan is at the northern end of fully protected Macquarie Harbour, one of Australia's largest natural harbors, at 100km^2. The placid, tannin-stained waters become choppy only at Hell's Gates—the narrow and dangerous strait where the harbor meets the Southern Ocean.

World Heritage Cruises, on the Esplanade, runs the least expensive trips through the harbor and up the Gordon River (south of Sarah Island), including passage through Hell's Gate and into the tempestuous Southern Ocean, a 1hr. guided tour of Sarah Island, and 30min. at Heritage Landing up-river to admire a 2,000 year-old Huon pine. (☎6471 7174. 5½hr.; departs daily 9am; $47, children $21;

YHA discount; smorgasbord $9.) Cruising is not the only way to reach the wilderness. **West Coast Yacht Charters,** on the Esplanade, offers trips to **Sir John Falls, Heritage Landing,** and other sites. (☎6471 7422. 1 night $140; 2 nights $360.) **Wilderness Air** seaplanes expensively fly to Sir John Falls, but venture far beyond cruise-accessible territory. (☎6471 7280. 1½hr., $125.) Paddle the river yourself in a kayak or canoe from **Hells Gates Wilderness Tours** (☎6471 7576), on Risby Cove.

South of Strahan (12km) on Lowanna Rd., lies the **Teepookana Forest Reserve,** a victim of Queenstown mining. The forest viewing tower explains Huon pine logging (3hr. moderate return walk from **Iron Bridge**). Because the reconstructed Railway (see Queenstown, below) will go through the forest, logistics about access have not been clarified. Contact the visitor centre for more info, or try **Forestry Tasmania,** on the Esplanade. (☎6471 7176. Open M-F 9am-noon and 1-5pm.)

QUEENSTOWN ☎03

In 1883, Mick and Bill McDonough, also mysteriously known as the Cooney Brothers, discovered a large outcropping of copper, later termed the Iron Blow (they initially thought they'd struck iron). The Blow was first mined in hope of finding gold, though each ton of rock yielded just two ounces of the precious metal. The **Mount Lyell Gold Mining Company** formed in 1888, but redirected its efforts toward copper in 1891, only after millions of pounds of copper had already slipped away. The company built a smelter to process the copper ore on-site, wreaking environmental havoc. Nearly every large tree in the surrounding hills was felled to feed the smelter, while the young growth was killed by the thick yellow sulphur haze released during the pyritic processing, and the exposed topsoil was washed into the Queen River by heavy rainfall. The town (pop. 2200 and falling) currently resembles a lunar wasteland in the midst of dense vegetation.

The **Mt. Lyell Mine** still chugs along, with tours exploring the working areas. All tours leave from the office at 1 Driffield St. Daily surface tours visit the old open-cut mines, the working copper mine, and other sites. (☎6471 2388. Book ahead. 1hr.; daily Sept.-May 9:15am and 4:30pm, June-Oct. 9:15am and 4pm; $12. Underground tours 2½hr., $50.) The old Iron Blow open-cut mine, just off the Lyell Hwy. near **Gomanston,** offers views of surrounding barren hills and of the water-filled crater. The **Queenstown Scenic Chairlift,** 7 Penghana Rd., and the viewing platform at the top provide a heightened perspective. (☎6471 2338. Open daily morning-sunset. $7, children $5.) The **ABT Wilderness Railway Restoration Project,** a restored railway will, once completed, leave from Queenstown Station on Driffield St. and go to Strahan. Call 6471 1700 for completion details and current destinations.

The thin road to Queenstown snakes above steep ravines (allow 45min. to Strahan). **TassieLink** (☎1300 300 520) runs to: Hobart (4¾hr.; Tu, Th, F, Su, Dec. to mid-Apr. also W; $44.70) via Lake St. Clair (2hr., $21.30); Launceston (5-6hr.; Tu, Th, Sa, Dec. to mid-Apr. also M; $52.70) via Cradle Mt. (2½hr., $21) and Devonport (4-5hr., $37.10); Strahan (45min.; Dec. to mid-Apr. 1 per day, mid-Apr. to Nov. Tu, Th-Su; $7). The **Mt. Lyell Mine Office** has info (see below). **Parks and Wildlife** (☎6471 2511) is represented by **Centrelink/Service Tasmania,** 34 Orr St., next to the post office. (☎1300 366 773. Open M-F 9am-5pm. Free **Internet.**) **Trust Bank,** at Orr and Sticht St., has no-fee currency change. (Open M-F 9am-5pm.) The **police** (☎6471 3020) are at 2 Sticht St. The **post office** is at 32 Orr St. (Open M-F 9am-5pm.) **Postal code:** 7467.

The **Empire Hotel,** 2 Orr St., retains some of the glory of its heyday as a miners' pub. (☎6471 1699. Meals $10-15. Singles $20; twins and doubles $35, with bath $45.) **Queenstown Cabin and Tourist Park,** 17 Grafton St., is across the river, 2km from town center. (☎6471 1332. Sites $8, extra person $4; powered $10/$5; backpacker beds $22/$5; on-site caravans $40/$5; self-contained cabins for 2 $62/$7.)

FRANKLIN-GORDON WILD RIVERS NATIONAL PARK

After the completion of the Gordon River Dam project in the early 1970s, Hydro Tasmania proposed a new dam along the lower Gordon, just below its intersection with the Franklin. This proposal set off years of river blockades, and over 1200 civilian arrests. Conservationists were successful in the early 1980s in scuttling the scheme, and the National Park became part of the new **Tasmanian Wilderness World Heritage Area.** On its way from Strahan to Hobart, the **Lyell Hwy.** (A10) runs between Queenstown and Derwent Bridge through the park, which is otherwise roadless for kilometers to the north and south. To use any of the Park's facilities, purchase a National Parks Pass ($3.30 per person, $9.90 per vehicle per day up to 8 people), and *Wild Way*, which lists the points of interest along the Lyell Hwy.

Three walks in particular stand out. The 10min. **Nelson Falls Nature Trail,** hidden in wet rainforest 25km east of Queenstown, leads to a lovely cataract. **Donaghys Hill Lookout,** 50km east of Queenstown, should not be missed. The 40min. return track holds mind-blowing views of the Franklin River Valley and **Frenchman's Cap** (1443m), its principal peak (3- to 5-day return hike to the top). The **Franklin River Nature Trail,** 60km east of Queenstown, is a well-maintained 20min. circuit through rainforest. Between Queenstown and Nelson Falls, **Lake Burbury** has swimming, boating, trout fishing, and camping surrounded by mountains (camping $5; no showers or laundry). Between Nelson Falls and Donaghys Hill, the **Collingwood River** also has some basic **camping** with fireplaces and picnic facilities (free). Roadside lookouts at **Surprise Valley** and **King William Saddle** (67km and 70km east of Queenstown, respectively) offer views of the eastern side of the wilderness area. The saddle marks a major divide of Tasmania. To the east lie dry plains and highlands, while to the west a 2.5m annual rainfall flows into the Franklin-Gordon rivers, through wet rainforest, and out to Macquarie Harbour.

THE NORTHWEST

The ferry brings most Tasmanian visitors to the Northwest first, and after time on the Overland Track and the Franklin River, many have a hard time leaving. World Heritage wilderness is the big draw in the Northwest, punctuated by seaports on the northwest coast and mining towns on the western highways. As an Aboriginal homeland, a fierce wilderness, an ecotourism jackpot, a mining motherlode, and a land of colonial convict myth-memory, the Northwest sees the currents that dominate Tasmania's identity play out their drama in the starkest relief.

DEVONPORT ☎03

Many people arrive in Tasmania through Devonport, which is a bit of a shock, its grim waterfront dominated by a cluster of huge gray silos. The city is a gateway to the rest of the state and there are grand views north of the downtown area.

TRANSPORTATION. The **airport** is 6km east of the city center on the Bass Hwy. Ansett-affiliated **Kendell** (☎13 13 00) and Qantas-affiliated **Southern** (☎13 13 13) operate flights to Melbourne (1hr., 4 per day, $120-225). **Fox Coaches** shuttle meets all flights and delivers passengers to town. (☎0418 142 692. $5.) The **ferry** *Spirit of Tasmania* departs Melbourne (13-14½hr.; M 7:30pm, W and F 6pm; $131-158, cars $40-55, bikes $21-27); the return departs Devonport (Tu and Th 6pm, Sa 4pm). Dinner, breakfast, and accommodation are provided. Book ahead at the Visitors Centre or dial 13 20 10. A free **shuttle** goes to the town center. **Redline Coaches,** 9 Edward St. (☎1300 360 000, line open daily 6am-9pm), runs daily buses to: Hobart (4½-5hr., 2 per day, $38.10); Launceston (1½hr., 2-5 per day, $15.70); Stanley (2-2½hr., 1-2 per day, $18); Wynward (1½hr., 1-2 per day, $11.40) via Burnie (1hr., 2-6 per day, $8). **TassieLink** (☎1300 300 520) buses leave the Visitor Centre to: **Cradle Mountain Visitor Centre** (1½hr., Dec.-mid-Apr. 1 per day, $28); Strahan (6hr., $44.10) via Queenstown (5hr.; Tu, Th, Sa (M summer); $37.10). Major car rental companies have counters at the airport and ferry terminals, including **Hertz** (☎6424 1013; open daily 8am-6pm; also at 26 Oldaker St.) and **Thrifty,** across from the ferry at the Esplanade (☎6427 9119; open daily 8am-5:30pm; $50-55 per day; age 21-24 $15 surcharge). Smaller firms are often cheaper; try **Advance,** at the airport and 11 Esplanade (☎6427 0888; open daily 9am-5pm) or **RentABug,** 5 Murray St. (☎6427 9034; open M-F 8:30am-5:30pm, Sa 8:30am-noon).

ORIENTATION. The port of Devonport is the mouth of the **Mersey River,** and the ferry terminal is on its eastern bank. Devonport is bounded to the west by the **Don River** and to the south by the **Bass Hwy.** (Hwy. 1), which has the only bridge across the Mersey. The city center lies on the western bank, with **Formby St.** at the river's edge, the **Rooke St. Mall** one block inland, each intersected by **Best St.** and **Stewart St.** running away from the river; most of the essentials lie within a block of these four streets. North of this square, Formby St. leads to **Mersey Bluff** and **Bluff Beach** at the western head of the river. The Bass Hwy. heads west to Burnie (46km) and southeast to Launceston (97km) and Hobart (300km). Drive to **Cradle Mountain** through Spreyton and Sheffield on B14 (1½hr.).

PRACTICAL INFORMATION. Tourist Information: Tasmanian Travel and Visitor Information Centre, 92 Formby Rd., is around the corner from McDonald's and books accommodations and transport. (☎6424 4466. Open daily 9am-5pm. Travel Centre only M-F.) **The Backpackers' Barn,** 10-12 Edward St., has info on bushwalking. (☎6424 3628; www.tasweb.com.au/backpack/index.htm. Lockers $1 per day, $5 per week. Equipment sale or hire. Sites $7 per day, sleeping bags and packs $5 per day. Open M-F 9am-6pm, Sa 9am-noon.)

ACCOMMODATIONS. Formby Rd. Hostel, 16 Formby Rd., is a ½km south of the city center. This brick Victorian house features roomy common spaces, a clean kitchen, and excellent company. (☎6423 6563. Linen $3. Laundry. Free bike use. Reception open whenever necessary. Dorms $14; doubles $35. Cash only.) **Tasman House Backpackers,** 169 Steele St. Take Mersey Link bus #20 from Rooke St. to stop 173, across from the hostel. Or, from Formby Rd. on the river, go west along Steele St., past the sign and then around the block to reach the entrance—left on Lovett St. and a quick left on Tasman St. (☎6423 2335; fax 6423 2340. Free city center pickup; $3 ferry shuttle. Free storage. Laundry. Internet $5 per hr. Reception daily 8am-10pm. Dorms $11; twins $13; doubles $29, with bath $36. VIP.) **Tasman Bush Tours** operates out of the house, with day-trips from $53, and 6-day Overland Track trips from $690. **Molly Malone's Irish Pub,** 34 Best St., is closest to the city center. Rooms have sink and heater. The ownstairs pub's weekend live music carries upstairs. (☎6424 1898. No laundry or parking. Key deposit $10. 4-night max. Check-in at the pub. Dorms $14; singles $30; doubles $50.) **Mersey Bluff Caravan Park,** Bluff Rd., on Mersey Bluff beach. (☎6424 8655. Sites $7.15 per person, powered for 2 $16.50; on-site caravans $44; cabins $55.)

FOOD AND ENTERTAINMENT. The **Rooke St. Mall** overflows with standard chippers and fast food. Coles **supermarket** is on Formby and Best St. (Open M-W and Sa 8am-6pm, Th-F 8am-9pm.) **The Kitchen Chimes,** 2A Stewart St., makes you feel right at home. (☎6424 1129. Open M-F 8:30am-5pm.) **Renusha's Indian Restaurant,** 153 Rooke St., near the corner of Oldaker St., will spice up your diet. (☎6424 2293. Takeaway $11-13.50; eat-in $15-18.50 with $15 minimum charge. Open M-Th 5:30-9:30pm, F-Sa 5:30-11pm, Su 5:30-8:30pm.) **Spurs,** 18-22 King St., has a country-western American theme, video games, and pool tables that attract a young crowd. (☎6424 7851. F-Sa live music. Open W-F, Su 4pm-1:30am; Sa 5pm-1:30am.)**Warehouse,** next to Spurs, is a dance club. (Open F-Sa 10:30pm-3am. Cover $5-6.)

SIGHTS. Tiagarra Aboriginal Cultural Centre and Museum, a 30min. walk from the city center to Mersey Bluff near the lighthouse, is an interpretive center that explores 40,000 years of Tasmanian Aboriginal history. The shop sells mainland Aboriginal art and instruments. (☎6424 8250. Open daily 9am-5pm. $3.30, kids $2.20.) A 15min. walk around the bluffs leads to controversial **rock engravings**—a few have been stolen, and some skeptics say wind and rain are the true artisans. From the lighthouse, the shimmering, blue Bass Strait and surrounding red-orange cliffs are gorgeous. The **Devonport Maritime Museum,** on Gloucester Ave. off Bluff Rd., preserves local history with old photographs, model boats, and an archive of family history. (☎6424 8250. Open Apr.-Sept. Tu-Su 10am-4pm, Oct.-Mar. Tu-Su

10am-4:30pm. $3, children $1, families $6.60.) An old-fashioned **steam train** runs to Coles Beach from the museum at Don River Railway, on Forth Rd. (☎6424 6335. 30min. return. Departs daily on the hr. 10am-4pm; $7, children $4, family $18.)

FROM DEVONPORT

The **Leven Canyon Reserve,** about 60km southwest of the city near Nietta, has a lookout with stunning views of Leven Gorge. To get there, take the Bass Hwy. west, then B15 south to Nietta, then C128 to the Canyon. A bit to the north of the canyon via C125 lie the **Gunns Plains Caves,** with a creek that houses platypi and freshwater crayfish in addition to the underground wonders. (☎6429 1388. Tours daily on the hour 10am-4pm. $8, children $4.)

The **Aspestos Range National Park,** including Bakers Beach, is a small coastal heathland reserve 40km east of Devonport, popular for swimming, fishing, walking tracks, and abundant wildlife. The park is accessible by car only via three gravel roads. From Devonport take C740, which heads north from B71 between Devonport and Exeter. Register to camp at **Springlawn,** just past the park entrance. (Ranger ☎6428 6277. Park fees apply.) Sites have flush toilets, BBQ, tables, water, and a public telephone. Two more scenic camping areas are 3km farther down the road on the beach by **Griffiths Point** and **Bakers Point,** and have pit toilets, fireplaces, tables, and water. (Sites $4, family $10; firewood included.) The easy **Springlawn Nature Walk** (45min.) passes through scrub and lagoons past wallabies and pademelons (their smaller relatives). The track continues up to **Archers Knob** for a view of the surrounding hills and coastline (2hr. return; moderate).

DELORAINE AND SURROUNDS ☎03

In the foothills of the Great Western Tiers, huddled in the agricultural Meander Valley between Devonport and Launceston, Deloraine functions as a perfect base for exploring the World Heritage wilderness to the southwest.

TRANSPORTATION AND PRACTICAL INFORMATION. Redline (☎1300 360 000) **buses** run out of Cashworks, 29 W. Church St. (☎6362 2143), with daily service to: Burnie (1¾hr., $16); Devonport (1½hr., $11); Launceston (45min., $8). **Deloraine Visitor Information Centre,** 98 Emu Bay Rd., doubles as the folk museum. (☎6362 3471. Open M-F 9:30am-4pm, Sa 1-3:30pm, Su 2-4pm. $2.) Services include: **Trust Bank,** 24 Emu Bay Rd. (☎13 18 28; open M-F 9am-5pm); **library,** 2 Emu Bay Rd., with **Internet** (☎6362 2770; open M-Th 11am-1pm and 2-5pm, F 11am-1pm and 2-7pm; $5 per 30min.); **police** (☎6362 4004), on Westbury Pl.; the **post office** at 10 Emu Bay Rd. (☎6362 2156; open M-F 9am-5pm). **Postal code:** 7304.

ACCOMMODATIONS AND FOOD. The **Deloraine Highview Lodge YHA,** 8 Blake St., is the best hostel around, with breathtaking views of Quamby Bluff and the Great Western Tiers, comfy bunks, and lively Scottish proprietors who can arrange tours. Go up Emu Bay Rd., turn right on Beefeater St. and left on Blake St. (☎6362 2996. Bike rental $15. Reception 8-10am and 5-10pm. Dorms $14, non-YHA $17.) The **Apex Caravan Park,** on West Pde., has river sites and showers. (☎6362 2345. Sites for 2 $12, powered $15.) A **supermarket** is at 58 Emu Bay Rd. (Open M-W and Sa 8am-6pm, Th-F 8am-9pm.)

PARKS. A 1½hr. drive southwest from Deloraine lies an awe-inspiring section of the **Walls of Jerusalem National Park.** A hike to the top of Mt. Jerusalem gives an amazing 360° view (8hr. return). Less trafficked than Cradle Mountain, the park contains the same craggy bluffs, vales, and ridges, with stretches of green mosses and lakes. The mostly duckboarded track begins from a carpark with a pit toilet off the Mersey Forest Rd. (C171). The first hour is a steep walk to the park's border and down into the Walls. From there, it's relatively level except for inclines through the gates of the Walls. A compass, a $9 park map, and overnight equipment are required even for dayhikes because of the highly variable weather. The Walls are not to be taken casually; rangers recommend it only for experienced hikers. Park fees apply and you must call ahead (☎6363 5182).

About 35km west of Deloraine off B12, **Mole Creek Karst National Park** (☎6363 5182), is home to two spectacular caves. Huge **Marakoopa Cave** features a glow-worm chamber. **King Solomon's Cave** is much smaller with fewer steps and more colorful formations. Temperatures in the caves can be a chilling 9° Celsius. Park fees do not apply, but NPWS runs tours for a fee ($8; both caves $12). The **Westbury Maze and Tea Room,** 10 Bass Hwy., between Deloraine and Launceston, has a challenging and disorienting hedge maze. (☎6393 1840. Open Oct.-June daily 10am-6pm. $4, children $3, families $14). **Ashgrove Farm Cheese** is 18km north of Deloraine on the Bass Hwy. in Elizabeth Town. Learn everything you ever wanted to know about cheese—that probably won't be much. Then eat your heart out with free cheese tastings. (☎6369 1105. Open daily 9am-5pm.)

THE NORTHWEST COAST: ALONG THE A2

West of Devonport, Bass Hwy. 1 and A2 Hwy. trace the northern coast of Tasmania. Bass Hwy. passes through Ulverstone and Burnie before reaching the junction where A2 continues northwest and A10 branches south toward Queenstown, Zeehan, and Strahan. If driving, the scenic coastal route through Penguin is worth the minor diversion. From Burnie, A2 continues past Wynyard (18km) and Rocky Cape National Park (30km) to Smithton (74km) and nearby Stanley (66km).

BURNIE. The area's major transport hub is Burnie, a declining paper mill town. **Redline,** 117 Wilson St. (☎1300 360 000), connects Burnie to: Boat Harbour (30min., M-F 1-2 per day, $5); Deloraine (1½hr., 2-6per day, $16); Devonport (45min., 2-6 per day, $8.40); Launceston (2¼hr., 2-5 per day, $21.10); Stanley (1½hr., 1-2 per day M-F, $12); Wynyard (20min., M-F 1-2 per day, $3). The **Tasmanian Travel and Information Centre** is in the Civic Centre complex. (☎6434 6111. Open M-F 9am-5pm, Sa 10am-1pm.) An **ANZ Bank** with an **ATM** is on the corner of Wilson and Cattley St. (Open M-Th 9:30am-4pm, F 9:30am-5pm.) The only budget accommodation is the **Treasure Island Caravan Park,** 253 Bass Hwy., 4km away in Cooee, with an indoor pool. (☎6431 1925. Sites $10, powered $12; dorms with kitchen $14; caravans $35; cabins $55.) Burnie's most savory sight is the **Lactos Cheese factory,** on Old Surrey Rd. (☎6431 2566. Open for free tastings M-F 9am-5pm, Sa-Su 10am-4pm.)

ROCKY CAPE NATIONAL PARK. Staying true to its name, Rocky Cape National Park (☎6458 1100) features a mountainous coastline, rare flora, and **Aboriginal cave sites.** The two ends of the park are accessible by separate access roads. The 9km eastern access road turns off A2 12km west of Wynyard and leads to walking tracks and **Sisters Beach.** The 4km western access road, 18km further down A2, ends at a lighthouse and great views of Table Cape and the Nut (see **Stanley,** below). Aboriginal caves can be accessed from both entrances via short walking tracks; the **Coastal Route** track traverses the length of the park (11km; 3hr.). There is no visitors center nor any other amenities, but the shops near both entrances stock park brochures. The small park is geared toward day use; the low-growing vegetation is still recovering from a severe (campfire-started) bushfire several years ago and offers little protection from the sun during extended walks.

STANLEY. In the far northwest of the state, Stanley is built at the base of the **Nut,** a huge volcanic plateau first seen by British Matthew Flinders in December 1798. Flinders described it as a "cliffy round lump in form resembling a Christmas cake," Aborigines referred to it as Moo-Nut-Re-ker. Tidy and quiet, Stanley's **Church St.** is lined with flowers, tea rooms, craft shops, a **newsagency** with **limited groceries** (open M-F 7:30am-8:30pm, Sa 8am-9pm, Su 8am-8:30pm), and a **post office** (open M-F 9am-12:30pm and 1:30-5pm; **postal code:** 7331). Most people spend their time fishing, swimming, and **seal** and **penguin spotting.** But the big attraction for daytrips is a steep but short (10-15min.) plod up to the top of the Nut and then a leisurely walk (45min.) around. A **chairlift** goes up (open summer daily 9:30am-5:30pm, winter 10am-4pm; $6 return, children $4), and the **Nut buggy tour** carts people around the top ($5; closed in winter). The town also houses the **Highfield Historic Site,** marking the settlement that instigated development in the northwest. From the bottom of Church St., follow the scenic route 3km to the site. (☎6458 1100. Open Oct.-Apr. daily 10am-4pm; May-Sept. Sa-Su 10am-2pm. $2-5.) The **Stanley Caravan Park and YHA** is on the waterfront at Wharf Rd., tucked under the Nut. (☎6458 1266. Reception daily 8am-8pm. Sites for 2 $15, powered $18; dorms $17; twins and doubles $38.) **Peggs Beach Coastal Reserve,** 16km west of Stanley, offers primitive, secluded **camping** along the Black River with pit toilets and no amenities (sites $3).

THE NORTHEAST

Tasmania's northeast is blessed with a sunny disposition. Folks here grow up listening to Melbourne radio, drinking Boag's beer, and disdaining the political antics of the South. The pleasant coastline is dotted by quiet fishing and port towns that make suitable summer holiday spots for families with young children. Both sides of the Tamar ("TAY-mer") River are home to vineyards and fruit farms.

LAUNCESTON ☎03

Built where the North and South Esk rivers join to form the Tamar, Launceston ("LON-seh-ston") is Tasmania's second-largest city and Australia's third-oldest, founded in 1805. The intense historic rivalry between Hobart and Launceston manifests itself most clearly in beer loyalty: Boag's is the ale of choice in the north, Cascade in the south. Though this university town continues to grow, over the hills steeple-tops still rise above the town's many red and green roofs, vigilantly guarding Launceston's character, vitality, and old-world Victorian charm.

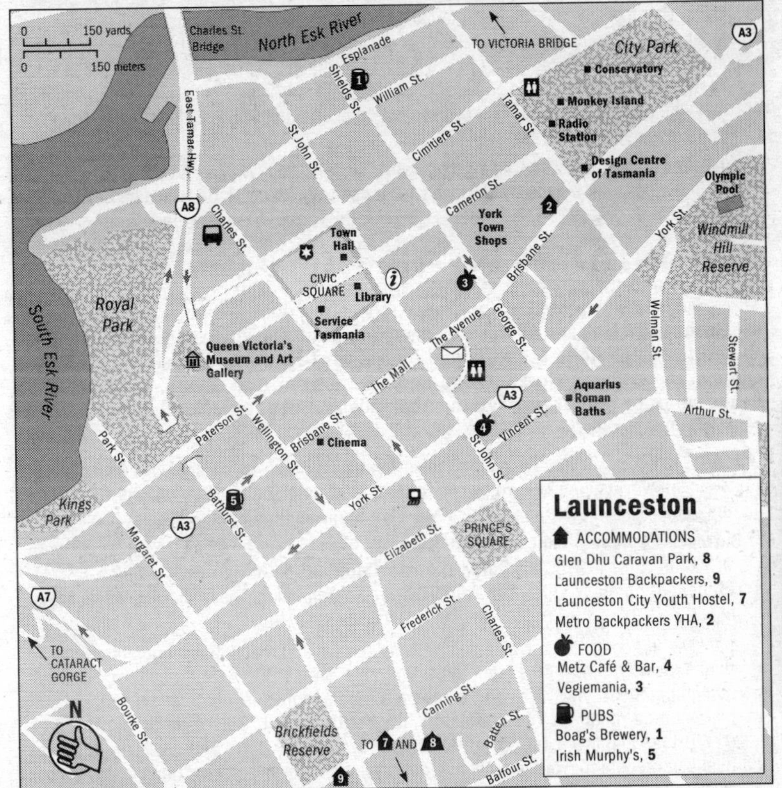

TASMANIA

TRANSPORTATION

Flights: Launceston Airport, south of Launceston on Hwy. 1 to B41. Ansett-affiliated **Kendell** (☎13 13 00) and Qantas-affiliated **Southern** (☎13 13 13) fly to **Melbourne** ($210, return $250). Tasmanian Shuttle Bus Services, 101 George St., provides airport **shuttles** that meet flights and will pickup from accommodations. (☎6331 2009. $10.)

Buses: The **Redline coaches** terminal is at 18 Charles St. (☎6336 1444; reservations 1300 360 000 daily 6am-9pm). Their buses run to: **Bicheno** (2¾hr., M-F 1 per day, $25); **Burnie** (2½-3hr., 2-5 per day, $21.10); **Deloraine** (45min., 2-5 per day, $8); **Devonport** (1½hr., 2-5 per day, $15.70); **George Town** (45min.; M-F 2-3 per day; $8.20, $10 from Melbourne ferry); **Hobart** (2½hr., 2-7 per day, $22.40); **Oatlands** (1¼hr., 2-7 per day, $16.30); **St. Helens** (2¾hr., Su-F 1 per day, $22.10); **St. Mary's** (2hr., Su-F 1 per day, $17.90). **TassieLink** buses (☎1300 300 520) leave from Gateway Travel Centre to: **Cradle Mountain Visitor Centre** (3½hr., Dec.-mid-Apr. 1 per day, $43-60); **Lake St. Clair** (3hr., 4 per week, $53.70); **Strahan** (8hr., $59.70) via **Queenstown** (7hr.; Tu, Th, Sa and M in summer; $52.70).

Public Transportation: Metro (☎13 22 01) buses run daily 7am-7pm. Fares $1-3.

Taxis: Taxi Combined (☎6331 5555 or 13 10 08). Fare to airport $18-21.

Car Rental: Budget (☎6391 8566), at the airport, from $40 per day. Ages 21-24 $18 surcharge. **Economy,** 27 William St. (☎6334 3299), from $31, rents to ages 17+.

Automobile Club: RAC Tasmania (☎6335 5633, 24hr. 13 11 11), at the corner of York and George St. Open M-F 8:45am-5pm.

Tours: Devil's Playground Ecotours (☎6343 1787; www.devilsplayground.com.au) offers day tours, with excellent guides, lunch, and all entry fees included. Among the most popular tours are Cradle Mountain (W and Su, $80); Waterfalls, Caves, and Wildlife (F, $80); and horse riding in the high country (Th, $120). For wild adventures, try **Tasmanian Expeditions,** 110 George St. (☎6334 3477 or 1800 030 230). Half-day rock-climbing/abseiling $75; 2-day cycling and canoeing $352; 3-day Cradle Mountain and Freycinet National Parks $473.

Bike Rental: Launceston City Youth Hostel, 36 Thistle St. W., (☎6344 9779), rents for $18 per day. **Rik Sloane Cycles,** 10-14 Paterson St. (☎6331 9414), rents 21-speeds for $22 per day, $92.40 per week. Open M-F 8:30am-5:30pm, Sa 9am-2pm.

ORIENTATION AND PRACTICAL INFORMATION

The town is best explored by foot, since most attractions are within four blocks of the **Brisbane St. Mall** and all the streets are one-way. The city center is bounded on the north by the **North Esk River** and on the west by the **South Esk,** which flows through the Cataract Gorge. From here, A8 runs north to George Town; Hwy. 1 heads south to Hobart through the Midlands and west to Deloraine and Devonport; A3 snakes east to St. Helens and the east coast.

Tourist Office: Gateway Tasmania Travel Centre (☎6331 4844, bookings 6331 3679; www.gatewaytas.com.au), corner of St. John and Paterson St. 1hr. walking tours from the center M-F 9:45am, $11. Open M-F 9am-5pm, Sa 9am-3pm, Su 9am-noon.

Currency Exchange: Commonwealth Bank, 97 Brisbane St. (☎6337 4432). Open M-Th 9:30am-4pm, F 9:30am-5pm. **Thomas Cook,** 85B George St. (☎6334 6304), exchanges currency. Open M-F 9am-5:15pm, Sa 9am-noon. The mall has several **ATMs.**

Hiking Equipment: Allgoods, 71-79 York St. (☎6331 3644), at St. John St. Huge, inexpensive and comprehensive, including army surplus and maps. Basic equipment hire at their **Tent City** annex, 60 Elizabeth St. Open M-F 9am-5:30pm, Sa 9am-4pm. For quality equipment at good rates and excellent advice and instruction on all things outdoors in Tasmania, head for **Launceston City Youth Hostel,** 36 Thistle St. W. (☎6344 9779; tasequiphire@email.com). Experienced manager Doug Snare will be happy to help you prepare for your journey and outfit you right down to socks. Tents from $20 per week, boots from $20 per week, stoves from $7 per week.

Bookstore: Birchalls, 118-120 Brisbane St. (☎6331 3011). Australia's oldest bookshop. Open M-Th 8:30am-6pm, F 8:30am-9pm, Sa 8:30am-5pm, Su 10am-4pm. **All Booked Up,** 81 Brisbane St. (☎6334 7066). Excellent selection, especially of literature and Australiana. Open M-F 8:45am-5:30pm, Sa 9am-4pm, Su 11am-3pm.

Library: 1 Civic Sq. (☎6336 2625). Open M-Th 9:30am-6pm, F 9:30am-8pm, Sa 9:30am-12:30pm.

Police: (☎6336 3701), on Cimitiere St. Enter through Civic Square.

Pharmacy: Centre Pharmacy, 84 Brisbane St. (☎6331 7777). Open daily 8:30am-10pm.

Hospital: Launceston General (☎6348 7111), on Charles St.

Internet: Service Tasmania (☎1300 366 773), in Henty House, Civic Sq., has 3 free terminals. Open M-F 8:15am-4:45pm. **Cyber King,** 113 George St. (☎0417 393 540). $5 per 30min., students $4; during student Happy Hour M-F 3-6pm $2.50 per 30min. Open M-Sa 9am-8pm, Su 10am-8pm. Also, see **Library,** above. $2.50 per 15min.

Post Office: 107 Brisbane St. (☎6331 9477). Open M-F 9am-5:30pm, Sa 9:30am-1pm. **Postal Code:** 7250.

ACCOMMODATIONS

Metro Backpackers YHA, 16 Brisbane St. (☎6334 4505 or 0401 666 436; www.backpackersmetro.com.au). Swanky new addition to the hostel scene in the town center. Wall-to-wall carpeting, comfy lounge with satellite TV, large kitchen and balcony with BBQ, off-street parking, and laundry. Internet $2 per 10min. Info center twice as good as the official one. Many tours. Ask manager Mark about his flags. Linen $3. Bike rental $20 per day. Reception daily 7:30am-10pm. Dorms $16, non-YHA members $19; themed doubles and twins $40/$45; family room $70/$75.

Launceston City Youth Hostel, 36 Thistle St. W. (☎/fax 6344 9779), opposite the Coats Patons building at Glen Dhu St. Turn right onto Howick from Wellington St., then left onto Glen Dhu St.; or take Metro #24 from Allgoods to stop 8. Large, spacious building with clean beds. Coin-op shower (10¢), free linen, security lockers, midnight quiet time. No co-ed dorms. Bike and hiking equipment rental (see **Hiking Equipment,** p. 488). Dorms $15, standby $14, $36 for 3 nights; singles $20; families $36.

Launceston Backpackers, 103 Canning St. (☎6334 2327; www.launcestonbackpackers.com.au), across from Brickfields Reserve, off Bathurst St., about a 7min. walk from the city center. Large kitchen, free long-term storage, laundry, Internet $2 for 10min. Key deposit $10 in summer. Check-out 10am. Female-only dorms on request. Reception daily 8am-10pm. 4- to 6-bed dorms $15.50; twins $35; doubles $37.

Glen Dhu Treasure Island Caravan Park, 94 Glen Dhu St. (☎6344 2600), 2km from downtown. Follow directions to City Youth Hostel. Lots of noise from neighboring Hwy. 1. BBQ, showers, laundry, outdoor campers' kitchen with kettle, hot plate, and toaster-oven. Sites for 2 $15, powered $17; caravans $38; cabins $63.

FOOD

Coles **supermarket** is at 198 Charles St. (☎6334 5744. Open M-W and Sa 8am-6pm, Th-F 8am-9pm.) Organic **Wholefoods Launceston,** is at 54 Frederick St. (☎6331 7682. Open M-F 10am-6pm, Sa 9am-5pm, Su 11am-5pm.)

Elaia, 238-240 Charles St. (☎6331 3307), 2 blocks south of Princes Sq. Great Mediterranean decor and classy food. Great focaccia ($10.40). Busy F-Sa for dinner. Mains $11.50-19.20. Open M-Sa 9am-late, Su 10am-5pm.

Vegiemania, 64 George St. (☎6331 2535). Tasmania's first vegetarian and vegan restaurant. Omelette $8, curry from $11.20. M-F noon-2pm $6 lunch special. Open M-F noon-2pm and 5pm-late, Sa-Su 5pm-late.

The Metz Cafe and Bar, 119 St. John St. (☎6331 7277), corner of York St. Upscale pizza pub and wine bar attract a mixed crowd of young business folk, couples, students, and travelers. $10 backpacker coupon special for an individual gourmet pizza and a schooner. Open daily 8am-midnight.

Saloon Bar, 191 Charles St. (☎6331 7355), in Hotel Tasmania. It's hard to find more for your money. Heaping plates of roast or mixed veggies for $5. Burgers for $7. Porterhouse steak $12. W and Sa live music; cover $3. Kitchen open daily noon-9pm; bar open Su-Tu noon-midnight, Th noon-1am, W and F-Sa noon-4:30am.

SIGHTS AND ACTIVITIES

The most spectacular sight in Launceston is the handiwork of the South Esk River—the **Cataract Gorge Reserve.** A 20min. walk from Paterson St. toward Kings Bridge, it's not exactly pristine wilderness—the First Basin of the gorge has been popular since the town's settlement and now hosts peacocks, an exotic tree garden, a restaurant, and a free swimming pool. Walking tracks run on either side of the river from King's Bridge; the one on the north side is easy, while the one on the south climbs to the gorge's rim for excellent views of the cataracts. The **Band Rotunda,** on the First Basin's north side (cross the Basin on the swinging Alexandra Suspension Bridge), and the **Duck Reach Power Station** at the far end of the gorge, provide info on the gorge. (☎6337 1288. Rotunda open M-F 9am-4pm, Sa-Su 9am-4:30pm. Power station daily dawn-dusk.)

For sightseeing from an aerial perspective, **Cable Hang Gliding,** in the Trevallyn State Recreation Area, sails above the Trevallyn Dam Quarry beyond the Gorge's Second Basin and the Duck Reach Power Station. (☎0419 311 198. Open Dec.-Apr. daily 10am-5pm, May-Nov. Sa-Su 10am-4pm. $10.) The less dramatic chairlift runs across the First Basin. (☎6331 8367. Open Sept.-May daily 9am-4:30pm, June-Aug. Sa-Su 9am-4:30pm. $6.60, children $4.40.)

The **Queen Victoria Museum and Art Gallery,** on the corner of Cameron and Wellington St., houses an impressive local and natural history display focusing on Tasmania's wildlife. The central foyer explains mining, mineralogy, and metallurgy. The upstairs gallery offers a brief but sweet peek of Tasmanian sculpture, paintings, ceramics, and textile art. The Planetarium is part of the complex. (☎6323 3777. Open M-Sa 10am-5pm, Su 2-5pm. Free. Planetarium shows Tu-F 3pm; Sa 2 and 3pm. $3.30, children $2.20, families $7.70. No children under 5 admitted.)

Launceston is blessed with an abundant supply of parks all around town. The **City Park,** at Tamar and Brisbane St., harbors a war memorial, botanical conservatory, and an enclosure teeming with **Japanese macaque monkeys.** (Open Mar.-Sept. M-F 8:30am-4:30pm, Sa-Su 9am-4:30pm; Oct.-Mar. closes 5:30pm.)

ENTERTAINMENT

Many downtown pubs have live music on weekends; the best and most popular is **Irish Murphy's,** 211 Brisbane St., two blocks from the mall. Rest your drinks on barrels of beer while groovin' to live music. (☎6331 4440. Happy Hour daily 9:30-10pm and F-Su 4-6pm. W-Su live music. Open daily noon-3am. F-Sa cover $3.) The hip **Cucina Simpatica** cafe, 57 Frederick St., by the Brickfields Reserve, hosts live jazz on some Su afternoons. (☎6334 3177. Open daily 10am-10pm.) For more pampered relaxation, the **Aquarius Roman Baths,** 127-133 George St., has an indoor frigidarium (cold bath), tepidarium (warm bath), caldarium (hot bath), and rubarium (heat lamps) in the style of ancient Rome—unfortunately, there are no vomitoriums. (☎6331 2255. Open M-F 8:30am-9pm, Sa-Su 9am-6pm. $20, doubles $33.) For an illuminating overview of the beer-brewing process, not to mention the free samples afterward, take the **Boag's Brewery** tour, 21 Shields St. (☎6331 9311. Open M-Th 2:30pm. Tours 1-1½hr. Free.)

DAYTRIPS FROM LAUNCESTON: GEORGE TOWN

North along A8 (50km), on the east side of the cove where the Tamar River meets the Bass Strait, lies George Town. Once considered the capital of the north, George Town now acts more as an historical center and Launceston's port. It does, however, lay claim to the title of the oldest *town* in Australia and the third oldest settlement. Now, mellow and quiet, it affords visitors serene views across the river and—if you're lucky—of glorious, pink sunsets over the western hills.

The town's seafaring history has been preserved in the **Pilot Station & Maritime Museum** in **Low Head,** 5km north of the town. Established in 1805, this convict-built estate is the oldest continuously operating facility of its kind in Australia, with displays on artifacts like **beer bottles** salvaged from shipwrecks. (☎6382 1143. Open daily 8am-8pm. $3.) The road ends at the **Low Head Lighthouse** (☎6382 1211) with great views of the peninsula and the *DevilCat.* **Fairy penguins** and seals use some of the beaches around George Town and Low Head as nesting places during the spring. **Fairy Penguin Twilight Tours** leads nightly tours one hour before sunset. (☎0418 361 860. No tours May-June. $7, children $3.) **Seal & Sea Adventure Tours** offers seal-watching tours of the Hebe Reef and Tenth Island. (☎6382 3452 or 0419 357 028. 3-4hr; 3 or more people $75 each with $200 min. charge, family of 4 $230.)

The **DevilCat ferry** (☎13 20 10) departs Christmas to mid-April weather-depending to George Town from Melbourne (6hr.; M, Th, Sa 8:30am; $145-175 one-way, concessions $125-145, cars $40-55, APEX return $250); and from George Town to Melbourne (Tu, F, Su 2pm). **Riverline buses** (☎6382 1484) leave from Pinos Hardware, 21 Elizabeth St.; the Shell Station, 32-36 Main Rd.; the ferry terminal to Launceston (45min.; M-F 2-3 per day; $8.20, $10 from *DevilCat*) and on to Hobart (2½hr., $27). The **Visitor Centre** is a hut on the road entering town from the south. (☎6382 1700. Open daily Aug.-Sept. 10am-2pm, Oct.-July 10am-4pm.) There's a **supermarket** at 8 Bathurst St. (Open M-W and Sa 8am-6pm, Th-F 8am-9pm.) The **Online Access Centre,** next to the **library,** in Regent Sq., has **Internet.** (☎6382 1356. Open M-F 9am-1am, Sa-Su noon-1am. $5 per 30min.) **Banks,** the **police station** (☎6382 4040), and the **post office** (open M-F 9am-5pm) cluster on Macquarie St. **Postal code:** 7253.

George Town itself doesn't warrant more than a day's visit, but, if you must stay, give the delightful **Traveller's Lodge (YHA),** 4 Elizabeth St., a try. Turn left at the third roundabout. The super-cozy lodge doubles as the Heritage Cable Cottage with the oldest tree in George Town in the backyard. (☎6382 3261. Check-out 11am. Sites $10. Bunks $18, non-YHA add $3.50; doubles $50.)

THE A3 EAST FROM LAUNCESTON

The road from Launceston weaves 165km east to St. Helens and the Suncoast.

SCOTTSDALE. Scottsdale is the first major service center out from Launceston. **Redline buses** leave from Roses Newsagency, 12 King St. (☎6352 2413), to Launceston (1¼-2¼hr.; M-F 2 per day, Su 1 per day except Jan.; $10.60) and Winnaleah (1½hr., M-F 1 per day, $7.90). If spending the night, try **Bellows Backpackers & Budget Accommodation,** 65 King St., a comfy retreat one block off the main road. (☎6352 2263. Reception daily 7:30am-9:30pm. 4-bed dorms $18; twins and doubles $45.) Friendly managers run the town's **Tourist Info Centre** and **Pepper Bush Peak 4WD Tours.** Themed tours cater to backpackers with specials like Platypus Wildlife—a 4hr. evening tour, mountain-top BBQ, accommodation, and brekkie for $70.

MT. VICTORIA FOREST RESERVE. The Reserve is 45min. past Scottsdale. From A3, follow signs south to Ringarooma and continue 15km on mostly unsealed roads to the carpark. The strikingly thin single-drop **Ralph Falls,** reckoned to be the tallest in Tassie, is a 10min. walk from the carpark, and Cashs Gorge lies 30min. beyond. The tough hike up Mt. Victoria passes a melange of ecosystems and a panorama of the whole Northeast from Ben Lomond to Flinders Island.

DERBY. Derby is a historic tin-mining town. The quirky **tourist centre/butcher shop** (☎6354 2364; open daily 5am-5pm) and the painted fish rock are on the north side of A3 heading east, past the second bridge. Derby's big draw is the **Tin Mine Centre** with a tea room, museum, reconstructed mining village, and the opportunity to pan for miniscule gemstones. (☎6354 2262. Open Sept.-June daily 9am-5pm; July-Aug. 10am-4pm. $4, children $1.50, families $10.)

WINNALEAH. The tiny town of Winnaleah is 2km off A3. **Redline** (☎1300 360 000) **buses** run from **Four Square Store** on Main St. to Derby (15min., M-F 2pm, $3) via Launceston (2¾hr., $16.90). **Suncoast Coach Service** (☎6376 1753), otherwise known as the mail bus, connects to St. Helens (1hr., M-F 12:30pm, $4). Six kilometers on a side road from town, the **Merlinkei Farm Winnaleah YHA,** 524 Racecourse Rd., is the only hostel before St. Helens, and doubles as a dairy farm—guests are welcome to try their hand at milking. Pickup from town available. (☎6354 2152; mervync@vision.net.au. Bunks $12, non-YHA add $3.)

CLOSER TO ST. HELENS. **Blue Lake** is in South Mt. Cameron on B82 as you approach **Gladstone** and **Mt. William National Park,** about 12km northeast off A3. An inadvertent product of mining, Blue Lake's unearthly shade of aquamarine is due to the mineral composition of the soil. The **Weldborough Pass Scenic Reserve,** just beyond Weldborough, offers a rainforest walk guided by "Grandma Myrtle" right by the highway. The 15min. circuit weaves beneath huge tree-ferns and myrtle beeches. About 30min. west of St. Helens, in the middle of a pasture in Pyengana just off A3, **Pub in the Paddock–St. Columba Falls Hotel** recalls a time before pubs had to be Irish, Western, or have pokies to attract customers. Slops, the beer-drinking pig, draws droves. (☎6373 6121. Open daily 11am-late. Meals served noon-2pm and 6-8pm. Singles $25; doubles $35.) Nearby, the 90m cascading **St. Columba Falls** unleashes 42,000L per minute. To get there, drive 10min. beyond the pub on an unsealed road ending at a carpark and a 10min. walk to the falls.

BRIDPORT

☎03

Bridport lies along the sheltered beach of **Anderson's Bay** at the estuarine mouth of the **Brid River.** With few sights, Bridport lends itself to relaxing on the beach and enjoying the estuary: birds to spot, oysters to dig, and beach cricket to play.

TRANSPORTATION AND INFORMATION. Everything in town is on Main St. including the **Bridport 2000 Plus Visitor Centre** (open daily 10am-4pm) and the **library** (☎6356 0258; open M and W 10am-1pm, Tu and F 3-7pm, Th 10am-1pm and 4-8pm, Sa 9am-1pm) with **Internet.** Bridport has **no bank,** and the nearest **ATM** is in nearby **Scottsdale.** Tubby's **supermarket** has **EFTPOS** and a **post office** desk (open daily 7am-7pm; post office open M-F 9am-5pm). **Postal code:** 7262.

The **Redline** (☎1300 360 000) **bus** from Launceston to Scottsdale (1¼hr.; M-F 2 per day, Su 1 per day except Jan.; $10.60), connects with **Stan's Coach Service** to Bridport. (☎6356 1662. 30min., M-F 2 per day, $3.)

ACCOMMODATIONS AND FOOD. The **Bridport Seaside Lodge YHA,** 47 Main St., is a budget traveler's dream. There's a large kitchen, tidy rooms, free canoes, and a veranda with expansive views of the estuary beach. (☎6356 1585. Canoe hire $15 per day. Dorms $19; doubles $42-45.) **Bridport Caravan Park,** on Bentley St., has close-quarter, wooded sites along the beach. (☎6356 1227. Sites $12, powered $15.) Bridport has the standard takeaway joints, but the real find for cheap and tasty eats—if you can stomach it—is **Springfield Fisheries,** the fish slaughterhouse, on Main St. just before crossing the bridge into Bridport. Brave past the bloody fish guts to buy hot smoked and then frozen vacuum-sealed trout. (☎6356 1104. Open daily 8am-4pm. $2 each.)

SIGHTS. A 30min. shoreline stroll north from the Main St. bridge past the old pier takes you to the **Mermaids Pool** swimming hole. Extend the walk past **wildflowers** in the spring by heading down Main St., turning right just past Walter St., and looping back around along the coast (2½hr.). Another walk to **East Sandy Point** grants great views and leads to huge dunes (1½hr. return). To get to the start of the track, follow Main St., which turns into Sandy Points Rd., and park at the gateway where the road becomes a rough 4WD track.

By car, the 77km drive from Launceston to Bridport passes the **vineyards** of the **Tamar Valley:** take A8 to B81 near Rocherlea, and then B83 to B82 in Pipers River. The **Delamere Vineyard,** 4238 Bridport Rd. is open for tastings daily 10am-5pm; $2. About 2km off B82 is **Pipers Brook Vineyard,** 1216 Pipers Brook Rd., which offers daily tours. (Open for free tastings daily 10am-5pm; tours 11am and 2pm.)

MT. WILLIAM NATIONAL PARK

More of a hill than a mountain, Mt. William overlooks a quiet stretch of coast in the sunny northeast corner, east of Bridport. The gentle 180m peak has views of the **Furneaux Islands** (see below), which once provided a bridge between Tassie and the mainland. The major reason to visit Mt. William is to safari among marsupials. Wallabies are everywhere, and echidnas pop up in the daytime. At dusk, chest-high Forester kangaroos are in motion, as well as smaller pademelons, wombats, and chazzwazzers. After dark—with a good flashlight—spot brushtail possums, spotted-tail quolls, and Tasmanian devils. Eagle-eyed visitors might even glimpse the rare New Holland mouse.

Mt. William is a relatively isolated national park with no facilities. **Drinking water** is essential to bring. In an emergency, call the **ranger** (☎6357 2108) at the north entrance. No buses run to the park, but **Terry's Bus Service** (☎6357 2193) meets **Redline** coaches in Derby and goes to Gladstone (1½hr., M-F 12:30pm, $2), about 20km southwest of the park entrance. From St. Helens, the drive takes about 1½hr. The gravel access roads are a bumpy ride even at slow speeds. The turn-off is signposted from Gladstone, and the popular north entrance is by the hamlet of **Poole;** the south entrance is by **Ansons Bay.** Both ends of the park offer ample coastal **camping** (free), hiking, and beach walks. Park fees apply. The northern access road leads to **Forester Kangaroo Dr.,** past the turn-off for **Stumpy's Bay** and its camping areas, and on to the trailhead for the **Mt. William walk** (1hr., moderate).

FLINDERS ISLAND ☎03

The largest of the Furneaux Group islands, approximately 60km northeast of Tasmania, is exceedingly remote, unpopulated, and blessed with a preponderance of natural beauty. It caters to the enterprising, adventuresome outdoor enthusiast. Getting to the island can be challenging. **Island Airlines** runs flights out of **Launceston.** (☎1800 818 826. 40min., 1-4 per day, $172 return.) **Sinclair Air Charter** will take up to 5 passengers from Bridport. (☎6359 3641. $250 one-way min. charge.) Southern Shipping can carry up to 12 passengers on their **cargo freight** from Bridport to Lady Barron. (☎6356 1752. 8hr.; M evening, Tu morning; $70 return, children $40.) Even though Flinders is a Tasmanian municipality, rental companies generally forbid long ferry vehicle transport. **Ann Campbell's Cars** (☎6359 2168), **Bowman & Lees Car Hire** (☎6359 2388), and **Flinders Island Lodge Furneaux Car Rentals** (☎6359 3521) rent cars on the island. **No bike hire** is available on the island. The island has fantastic **camping;** otherwise, budget stays are in the two major townships. **Nunamina Hostel** overlooks the sound in Lady Barron. (☎6359 3617. Twins $20.) **Interstate Hotel** is in Whitemark. (☎6359 2114. Singles $18.)

At 756m, Mt. Strzelecki in **Strzelecki National Park** (☎6359 2217) is the highest point on the island, from which you can see the other 54 Furneaux Islands, and, if you're lucky, Wilson's Promontory in Victoria. A manageable walk (3km, 5hr.) traverses fern gullies and craggy outcrops. Park fees apply.

THE SUNCOAST

Tasmania's east coast is the island's softer side, where the weather and even the people are mild. With a mountainous interior this side of Tassie is sheltered from the storms that pound the west. Agriculture and holiday tourism, when summer travelers come for fishing, swimming, and loafing in the sun, sustain the towns.

SAINT HELENS ☎03

St. Helens, off A3 just south of Mt. William National Park (see above), is the largest and northernmost of the east coast vacation villages. Getting the treasures some 15km northeast of town requires a car and the ability to handle weaving gravel roads. **Humbug Point,** via Binalong Bay Rd., offers great walks and views, while **St. Helens Point,** via St. Helens Point Rd., has free camping with pit toilets, decent fishing, and good surf at

Beerbarrel Beach. North of Humbug Point, the **Bay of Fires Coastal Reserve,** so-called for the red rocks that Capt. Tobias Furneaux mistook for fire, has long beaches and basic campsites. The access road ends at the privately-owned **Gardens** and **Margery's Corner. Leda Falls** (1½hr. drive) is opened to the public at Cerise Brook on Medea Cove Rd.

Redline (☎6376 1182) **buses** sell tickets at the newsagency at Quail and Cecilia St. and run to: Hobart (4-5hr., Su-F 1 per day, $36.60); Launceston (2½hr., Su-F 1 per day Su-F, $22.10); St. Mary's (40min., Su-F 1 per day, $5). **TassieLink** (☎1300 300 520) runs to: Hobart (4½hr., F and Su 1 per day, $35.20) via Bicheno (1hr., $9.50), the highway turn-off for Coles Bay (1¼hr., $10.80), and Swansea (1¾hr., $13.20). The **St. Helens Travel Centre,** 20 Cecilia St., makes TassieLink bookings. (☎6376 1329. Open M-F 9am-5pm, Sa 9am-noon.) **St. Helens History Room,** 59 Cecilia St., offers local history and **tourist information.** (☎6376 1744. Open M-F 9am-4pm, Sa 9am-1pm; history room $2.) A **24hr. ATM** is at **Trust Bank,** 18 Cecilia St. **Service Tasmania,** 23 Quail St., has 30min. **free Internet.** (Open M-F 8:30am-4:30pm.) The **post office** is at 46 Cecilia St. (☎6376 1255. Open M-F 9am-5pm.) **Postal code:** 7216.

The **St. Helens YHA,** 5 Cameron St., off Quail St., has basic facilities. (☎6376 1661. Reception daily 8-10am and 5-10pm. Dorms $16, non-YHA add $3.) The standard **St. Helens Caravan Park** is 1.5km from the town center on Penelope St., just off the Tasman Hwy. on the southeast side of the bridge. (☎6376 1290. Sites for 2 $12-14, powered $16-18, with bath $20-22; on-site caravans $30-40; cabins $45-70.) Wok on to the **Wok Stop,** 57a Cecilia St. Dishes in all spices and sizes are $4-11. (☎6376 2665. Open M-F 11:30am-3pm and 4:30-8:30pm, Sa-Su 5-8:30pm.) TAS **supermarket** is at 33 Cecilia St. (☎6376 1117. Open daily 7:30am-7pm.)

BICHENO ☎03

The spectacular 75km drive south from St. Helens along A3 traces the coastline's sand dunes and granite peaks to the small town of Bicheno ("BEE-shen-oh"). With postcard penguins and national parks (Freycinet and Douglas-Apsley) an easy day-trip, its own rocky shoreline, and a neighborly community, Bicheno is an enchanting town you won't want to leave. It's hard to avoid beach activities while enjoying the 3km coastal track that begins at the bottom of Weily Ave., left off Burgess St. The walk leads past the blowhole, the marine reef around Governor Island, and numerous nooks for swimming, snorkelling, and diving.

Redline buses leave from the Four-Square Store on Burgess St. (open M-Sa 8am-6:30pm, Su 8am-6pm) and run to the Coles Bay turn-off (10min., M-F 1 per day, $5), continuing to Swansea (35min., $8), with connections to Hobart (5hr., $36.10) and Launceston (2¾hr., 1 per day Su-F, $22). **TassieLink** (☎1300 300 520) runs **buses** to: the Coles Bay turn-off (5min.; M, W, F, Su 1 per day; $2.30); Hobart (3hr.; W, F, Su 1 per day; $24.20); St. Helens (1hr., F and Su 1 per day, $9.50); Swansea (40min.; W, F, Su 1 per day; $5.10); Triabunna (1½hr.;W, F, Su 1 per day; $10.50); Launceston (2½hr.; W, F, Su 1 per day; $22.60). **Bicheno Coach Service** (☎6257 0293) runs to Coles Bay (40min.; M-Sa 1-4 per day; $7.50) and **Freycinet National Park** (50min., $8), making Redline and TassieLink connections from the Coles Bay turn-off. The **Tourist Information Centre** (☎6375 1333) is a hut in the town center. It books nightly **penguin-spotting** tours year-round (1hr., $15), fishing trips (3hr., $75), hires mountain bikes ($20 per day), and sells surf gear and boogie boards. The **Online Access Centre** is on Burgess St. near the Primary School. (☎6375 1892. Open M-W 9am-noon and 5-8pm, Th 9am-noon and 6-9pm, F 9am-noon and 3-8pm, Sa 10am-noon, Su 10am-noon and 1-3pm. $5 per 30min.) The Value-Plus **supermarket** (open daily 7:30am-6pm) and the **post office** (with limited **banking** services; open M-F 9am-5pm), are at the A3 elbow in the town center. **Postal code:** 7215.

The **Bicheno Hostel,** 11 Morrison St., lies off A3 behind a little white church near the post office. Guests get 10% off penguin tours, comfortable bunks, coastal views from the kitchen, and access to a free washer. (☎6375 1651. Dorms $15.) **Bicheno YHA** is 3km north of the town center on A3. Though it has cramped bunks and old furniture, this classic bungalow, 50m from the sea, gets points for character. At night, you can often see the penguins return to their burrows. (☎6375 1293. Dorms $15, non-YHA add $3.) Both **pubs** in town have counter meals.

DOUGLAS-APSLEY NATIONAL PARK

Douglas-Apsley lacks the poster appeal of a coast, mountain, or rainforest, but it's the last significant dry eucalypt forest in Tasmania. Its 1989 elevation to national park status marked the greening of Tassie politics. No roads lead through the park.

The **Apsley waterhole** is a deep pool in the middle of the slow Apsley River, 10min. from the southern carpark. A loop to the **Apsley River Gorge** (3hr.) follows a track from the north side of the waterhole uphill and back down into the gorge, returning on an undefined track downstream along the river. The return trip includes moderate climbing, rock scrambling, and river crossings, so only attempt it when the river is low and the rocks are dry. A **lookout** on the upper banks of the right-side of the river marks the waterhole. The 3-day **Leeaberra Track,** running from north to south to prevent the spread of root-rot fungus, goes the length of the park. It requires experience, a map, and a compass. Signs along the **lookout walk** introduce the park's tree species, such as the blue gum, black wattle, and native cherry—springtime brings beautiful wildflowers. An unusual number of creatures lurk in the park, such as the endangered Tasmanian bettong and southern grayling fish.

The popular southern end of the park (Apsley River), is a 15min. drive from **Bicheno,** the nearest service center—the park has no telephones or drinking water. The obscure southern access road leaves A3 5km north of Bicheno, heading west along 7km of gravel road. The northern access road from St. Marys, mostly along the **MG logging road,** is even harder to find. There is no bus service to the park, but the Bicheno Coach Service can charter a **minibus** from Bicheno. (☎6257 0293. To southern entrance: 2 people $30 return, $15 each extra person; northern entrance: 1-4 people $50 return, 5-12 people $100 return.) Free **campsites** with pit toilets are near the carparks, and others are 50m from the Apsley waterhole. The nearest **rangers** (☎6375 1236) are in Bicheno. Park fees apply.

COLES BAY ☎03

The tiny township of Coles Bay is the service center for **Freycinet National Park.** Its sunny shelter in the lap of **Great Oyster Bay** satisfies many summer vacationers, while its remote location (27km south on C302 off A3 between Bicheno and Swansea) ensures elevated prices. **TassieLink** (☎1300 300 520) and **Redline** (☎1300 360 000) **buses** run as close as the turn-off for Coles Bay on A3 south to Hobart (3-5hr., Su-F 1 per day, $23.50-34.70) and north to Launceston (2½hr., Su-F 1 per day, $22); from the turn-off, take **Bicheno Coaches** (☎6257 0293) to town (30min.; M-Sa 1-3 per day; $6.30, return $12) or the park (40min., $7.50, return $14). The **supermarket,** on Garnet Ave., offers limited **banking** and **petrol** and houses the **tourist information office,** a **coffee shop,** and the **post office.** (☎6257 0383. Open daily in summer 8am-9pm, winter 8am-6:30pm.)

The **YHA-affiliated Iluka Holiday Centre** is at the western end of the Esplanade. The interior may be sparsely decorated, but it's just a hop, skip, and jump away from the beach. (☎6257 0115 or 1800 786 512; iluka@trump.net.au. Reception daily 8am-6pm. Dorms $15, non-YHA add $3; twins and doubles $46. Sites $15, powered $17; on-site vans for 2 $42.) **Freycinet Backpackers** is part of the **Coles Bay Caravan Park,** 3km north of town off the Coles Bay main road, or an easy 30min. walk round Muir's Beach. They offer a great kitchen, free laundry, and a return bus voucher to walking tracks. (☎6257 0100. Book 3 months ahead during peak summer season and holidays. Linen $4. Reception daily 8am-9:30pm. Sites for 2 $12, powered $14; twin-share dorms $15 per person 1st night, $12 each extra night.)

FREYCINET NATIONAL PARK

Show us a promotional brochure of Tasmania without a picture of **Wineglass Bay,** and we'll show you an episode of the Simpsons where Maggie talks. Well, there is that one episode—but you get the point. Freycinet National Park ("FRAY-sin-nay") is home to the photogenic bay, **Great Oyster Bay,** and the stately red granite **Hazards.** This popular vacation spot is just a 3hr. drive from both Hobart and Launceston.

Bicheno Coaches stops in Coles Bay enroute to the park's tracks. (☎6257 0293. Departs M-F morning, Sa-Su and return service by bookings only. $3.80, return $6.) They also offer service between Coles Bay, the Coles Bay turn-off (30min., $6.30) and Bicheno (40min., $7.50); at the turn-off, you can connect with TassieLink and Redline services to other destinations (see **Coles Bay,** p. 495). An hour's walk away, Coles Bay is the service center for Freycinet, but for information, stop at the **visitors kiosk,** near the park entrance. (☎6257 0107. Hours vary.) **Campsites** with wood, water, and basic toilets are available (sites $5, powered $6). Register and pay at the kiosk; park fees apply.

At an outdoor theatre past the kiosk, rangers offer free programs, such as nocturnal walks and Aboriginal land use (Dec.-Jan. 3 per day). A few kilometers down, just past the Freycinet Lodge, there's a turn-off on an unsealed road for **Sleepy Bay** (1.8km) and **Cape Tourville Lighthouse** (6.4km). It's an easy 20min. return walk to the Bay, good for **swimming** and **snorkeling;** the Lighthouse sits atop a cliff with amazing views of the coast. **Honeymoon Bay,** popular for **snorkeling,** and **Richardson's Beach,** popular for **swimming,** are also on the main road. All major walking tracks begin at the carpark at the end of the road. Bring your own fresh water on day hikes. The **Wineglass Bay Lookout** walk (1-2hr.) is the classic choice. Fairly steep, the trail climbs up through the red-granite Hazards and opens onto a fabulous view of the bay and Freycinet peninsular mountains. An equally-pleasant alternative is a half-day loop by **Wineglass Bay** and **Hazards Beach** (11km). The **Mt. Amos** track is taxing, but has spectacular views (3hr.). A moderate 33km hike around the whole peninsula takes two to three days. The long stretch of white-sanded **Friendly Beaches** can be accessed via the 4.5km unsealed Friendly Beaches Rd., 18km north of Coles Bay. There are **free campsites** at **Isaacs Point** (with pit toilets) and **Ridge Camp**. Neither has fresh water.

SWANSEA ☎03

Swansea is a calm bayside town, 45km southwest of Bicheno and 135km northeast of Hobart. Most visitors enjoy a relaxing holiday on the coast while taking in the local history. The Council Chambers and Community Centre are timber buildings from 1860, and the Morris General Store has been run by the same family since 1838. Swansea's most interactive historical attraction is the **Mill Complex,** made-up of the **Black Wattle Bark Mill,** the only **bark crusher** in Australia; the **Yesteryear Museum,** chronicling the ecology and changing technology of Swansea from settlement to 1960; and the **Wine and Wool Centre** (☎6257 8382; open daily 9am-5pm; $5).

Redline (☎6257 8118) and **TassieLink** (☎1300 300 520) run **buses** to: Bicheno (40min., Su-F 1-2 per day, $5.10-8); Coles Bay turn-off (30min., Su-F 1-2 per day, $7); Hobart (2-4hr., Su-F 1-3 per day, $19.70-30.30); Launceston (2hr., 1-2 per day Su-F, $22-24); St. Helens (2hr., F and Su 1 per day, $13.20); Triabunna (45min., Su-F 1-2 per day, $5.80). The **Swansea Bark Mill Complex,** 96 Tasman Hwy., operates as the **tourist centre.** (☎6257 8382. Open daily 9am-5pm.) A **supermarket** is on **Franklin St.** (Open M-F 9am-5:30pm, Sa-Su 9am-4:30pm.) The **police** (☎6257 8044) are one block back on Noyes St. The **Online Access Centre** is in the Community Centre on Franklin St. (☎6257 8806. Open M 9am-1pm, Tu 4-8pm, W 9am-3pm, Th 10am-2pm, F 6-9pm, Sa 10am-2pm. $5 per 30min.)

The **Swansea YHA,** 5 Franklin St., includes a well-equipped kitchen, a piano in the common room, metal bunks, and laundry. (☎6257 8367. Reception daily 8-11am and 5-10pm. Dorms $16, non-YHA add $3). The **Swansea-Kenmore Cabin and Tourist Park,** 2 Bridge St., at the south end of town, has a spa-sauna (for 2 $7), doves and parrots, swimming pool, kitchen, and laundry. (☎6257 8148. Limited sites for 2 $11-14, powered $14-17; on-site caravans $30-40; cabins $50-60.)

TRIABUNNA ☎03

On **Prosser Bay,** 50km southwest of Swansea and 87km northeast of Hobart, Triabunna ("try-a-BUN-na") is a tiny town in which to stock up on food before heading to Maria Island. **TassieLink** (☎(1300) 30 05 20) runs to: Hobart (1½hr., Su-F 1-2 per day, $13.90);

Sorell (1hr.; W, F, Su 1 per day; $8.40); St. Helens (2½hr., F and Su 1 per day, $20.40); Swansea (45min., Su-F 1-2 per day, $5.80). They also connect to the **Eastcoaster Island Ferry** in **Orford** (5min.). The **tourist information centre,** at the Esplanade, has **Internet.** (☎6257 4090. Open daily 9am-4pm. $2 per 5min. Booking essential.) Managers Don and Fran renovated **Udda Backpackers (YHA),** 12 Spencer St., bringing hospitality with home-baked cookies. Follow Vicary St. toward the fire station, turn left after the bridge onto a gravel road, then left onto Spencer St.; signs point the way. (☎6257 3439. Free Maria Island ferry pickup. Dorms $14; twins $28; doubles $34.) **Triabunna Caravan Park** is at 6 Vicary St. (☎6257 3575. Sites $10, powered $12; on-site vans for 2 $25.) Value-Plus **supermarket** is at Charles and Vicary St. (Open daily 8am-6pm.)

MARIA ISLAND NATIONAL PARK

Maria ("muh-RYE-uh") Island has housed penal colonies, cement industries, whalers, and farmers. Today, the island national park is almost devoid of civilization, preserved for its historical and biological significance. The ruins of the settlement at **Darlington**—along with abundant wildlife, natural beauty, and isolation—are a main attraction. Walks wander through the **Darlington Township** ruins (1½hr.), over the textured sandstone of the **Painted Cliffs** (2hr.; best done at low tide; check schedule at visitor centre) to the rock-scramble up **Bishop and Clerk** (4hr.). To reach Maria, the **Eastcoaster Express catamaran** departs Eastcoaster Resort, 5km between both Triabunna and Orford. (☎6257 1589. 30min.; late-Dec. to Apr. 9, 10:30am, 1, 3:30pm; daytrip $18, overnight $21. Bikes and kayaks $3.) Take the turn for Louisville Pt./Maria Island Ferry off A3. Brochures about the park are available at the tourist office in Triabunna; the ferry has detailed descriptions of walking tracks. On the island itself, there are no shops or facilities save a **visitor centre,** with maps and brochures, and a **ranger station** (☎6257 1420) with a telephone. Park fees apply. To get beyond the Darlington ferry wharf, walk or bring a mountain bike. The old Darlington prison has been resurrected into six-bed **units,** each with a table, chairs, and fireplace; book ahead with the ranger. (Shared toilets, sinks, and hot showers. Beds $8, children $4, entire unit $20.) The island has three **campsites: Darlington,** with ample grassy space (sites $4, families $10); **French's Farm,** 11km south down the main gravel road, with an empty weatherproof farmhouse, pit toilet, and rainwater tanks; and **Encampment Cove,** 3km down a side road near French's Farm with a small bunkhouse and pit toilet.

CENTRAL EAST

From Launceston to Hobart, the convict-built Heritage Hwy. runs through the agricultural midlands, one of the few reasonably flat parts of Tasmania. Land of colonial sandstone architecture set amidst golden fields, central Tassie offers little of the scenic grandeur so readily available just about everywhere else on the island.

THE MIDLANDS ☎03

The fertile hills between Hobart and Launceston were once garrison towns keeping watch over the colony's convicts. The spirit of the midlands is captured by the small town of **Oatlands,** a bit closer to Hobart than Launceston. There are no oats anywhere near the place, but lore says that Governor Macquarie was nostalgic for Scotland when he gave the town its name. A walk down High St. takes you past 87 old sandstone stores, cottages, and government buildings that have been recycled as antique galleries or cafes.

Redline (☎1300 360 000) runs to: Hobart (1¼hr., 2-7 per day, $12.50); Launceston (1½hr., 2-7 per day, $16.30); Ross (25min., by booking only, $8). The **Tourism Centre** is at 77 High St. (☎6254 1212; $1-2 donation requested for library **Internet** access.) The **Oatlands YHA,** 9 Wellington St., is one of the midlands' gems. (☎6254 1320. Reception daily 8:30-9:30am and 5-8:30pm. Dorms $15.) Don't miss the nightly **Ghost Tour,** from Callington Mill. (☎6254 1135. 2hr.; departs summer 8 and 9pm; $8.) A **post office** is on High St. (Open M-F 9am-1pm and 2-5pm.) **Postal code:** 7120.

SPORTIN' WOOD Aborigines crossed over to Tasmania from mainland Australia during the last Ice Age 30,000 years ago. When the ice caps melted, the isthmus connecting Tasmania to the continent flooded with water, isolating the colonists. For 30 millennia, Tasmanian Aboriginal culture thrived. Tasmanians pursued a semi-nomadic existence, following seasonal food supplies within a well-established home range. Fire was used to drive game out of the bush onto the spears of waiting hunters, and the periodic burning of vegetation shaped the terrain. Although stones were used as tools, the Aborigines used no stone-tipped weapons or implements. Instead, spears were fashioned entirely from wood, hardened in fire and sharpened with stone tools. The result was a highly effective weapon that could be thrown with deadly force at a range of 60m. Analysis has revealed that these ancient Aboriginal spears had a weight distribution and aerodynamics similar to today's javelins.

BEN LOMOND NATIONAL PARK

Tasmania's premier **ski resort** and largest Alpine area, **Ben Lomond National Park** (☎6336 5312) is about 50km southeast of Launceston. The lifts are nothing to brag about, the slopes (1300m at peak) are easier than those on the mainland, and there's less snow. Still, if you're in Tassie and you need to ski, this is where to go. During the summer, regular park fees apply; during the winter, entry costs $12 per car. To reach the park, follow A3 3km east out of Launceston, then take Blessington Rd. (C401) 40km to Ben Lomand Rd. and the park entrance. From here, a steep 18km unsealed access road leads up to the ski village; rent chains at the base ($15, fitting $5). **TassieLink** runs a **charter service** from Launceston. (☎1300 300 520. 12-seater $400.) **Ski rental** costs $40 per day. (☎6372 2574. Snowboards $50, with equipment $80, deposit $100.) Lift tickets run $20-30, students $10-15; beginner packages are available from $75. Plateau walks are suitable in spring and summer for wildflower photo-ops and views from **Jacobs Ladder Lookout.** The **Creek Inn,** at the top of the access road, plays host all year. (☎6372 2444. Dorms $20.) There is **free camping** with drinking water, 1km outside the park entrance.

VICTORIA

Victoria may be mainland Australia's smallest state, but it's blessed with far more than its share of fantastic cultural, natural, and historical attractions. Its environment runs the gamut from the dry and empty western plains of the Mallee to the inviting wineries along the fertile banks of the Murray River, from the ski resorts of the Victorian Alps to the forested parks of the Gippsland coast. Nowhere else in Australia is so much ecological diversity only a daytrip away. The capital of the state and the cultural center of the nation, sleek and sophisticated Melbourne overflows with eclectic ethnic neighborhoods, seaside strips, and student haunts. With acres of verdant gardens, countless artspaces, and a vibrant never-tiring atmosphere, it's no wonder that many Aussies claim that the best-kept secret about Australia is Melbourne.

Victoria's most distinctive attractions are found on the coast. West of Melbourne, the breathtaking Great Ocean Road winds its way along the roaring ocean. Hand-cut between 1919 and 1931 from the limestone cliffs, the road passes surfing beaches, coastal getaways, temperate rainforests, and geological wonders, including the Twelve Apostles rock formations, which poke precariously from the sea like jagged fingers. East of the capital, the coastline unfolds past Phillip Island's penguin colony and the beach resorts on Mornington Peninsula, heading into Gippsland. Here, crashing waves collide with granite outcroppings to form the sandy beaches at the edge of majestic Wilsons Promontory National Park. East Gippsland's beaches slowly give way to stony, sandy bird-filled tidal estuaries.

Most of Victoria's interior is remarkable less for its natural grandeur than for its historical significance. The mountainous exceptions are the ranges of the Grampians National Park, whose mammoth beauty evokes awe to humbled onlookers. North of the Grampians, the river-wrought lands of the Wimmera and the scraggly plains of the Mallee don't overwhelm at first sight, but the subtleties of the bush have their own delicate, small-scale beauty. Victoria's historical heart beats to the drum of the mid-19th century gold rush, which flooded central Victoria with seekers of reward. When the ore waned, a host of dusty country towns were left in its wake, today preserved in tourist-oriented nostalgia—the Goldfields and the Murray River towns in north and Central Victoria live fondly in a fascinating past of mangled miners and rugged riverboats. In his wanderings throughout the Hume corridor, legendary bushranger Ned Kelly had a plan to stick it to the man. Today, this area is a fertile land of small-scale wineries cast pale by Australia's ski mecca, the High Country. The 20th century has brought extensive agricultural and commercial development, including several massive hydroelectric public works projects that continue to impact the state's ecosystems. Still, Victoria's physical beauty remains, tempered by a refined sensibility and cosmopolitan flair that add a touch of class and culture to Australia's down-to-earth grit.

Like most visitors' experiences, this chapter begins with Melbourne. It then moves clockwise through the spokes of the Victorian wheel, starting with the area south of Melbourne and continuing through the Great Ocean Road, Victorian Outback, Goldfields, Murray River, Hume Corridor, High Country, and Gippsland. Within each region, towns are ordered moving outward from the center.

TRANSPORTATION

Getting around Victoria is a breeze, thanks to the very complete, super-efficient system of intrastate trains and buses of **V/Line** (☎13 61 96; www.vlinepassenger.com.au), which runs an information center at its main terminal in Melbourne's Spencer Street Station. V/Line has a few interstate options, but more complete national service is offered by the conglomerate **Travel Coach,** comprised of **McCafferty's Bus Lines** (☎13 14 99; www.mccaffertys.com.au) and **Greyhound Pioneer** (☎13 20 30; www.greyhound.com.au). Renting a car allows considerably more freedom, and Victoria's highway system is the most extensive and easily navigable in the country. To cut down on occasionally prohibitive rental costs, check ride-share boards at any hostel. The **Royal Automobile Club of Victoria (RACV),** 360 Bourke St. between William and Queen St., Melbourne (☎13 19 55 or 9703 6363; emergency roadside assistance 13 11 11; www.racv.com.au), has great maps and sells short-term traveler's insurance. Members of automobile clubs in other countries may already have reciprocal membership. To join in Victoria, the basic RACV Roadside Care package (including 4 free service calls per year and limited free towing) costs $50, plus a $30 first-time-joiner's fee for those over 21 (see p. 67).

VICTORIA HIGHLIGHTS

TWELVE APOSTLES. Play unabashed tourist at the spectacular Twelve Apostles rock formations in the Port Campbell National Park (p. 549).

THE LEDGE. Abseil 60m down The Ledge in Grampians National Park (p. 560).

MALLEEFOWL. See the endangered Malleefowl at Little Desert National Park (p. 562).

RUTHERGLEN WINERIES. Pamper your palate with free tastings at Rutherglen Wineries (p. 585).

TAGGERTY. Experience a living phenomenon at a self-run, eco-friendly farm (p. 581).

LIGHTHOUSE. Watch a simple Sunrise at Wilsons Promontory's lighthouse (p. 594).

MELBOURNE

☎03

Melburnians themselves are likely to tell you that there are countless reasons why this metropolis deserves the oft-touted designation as the planet's most liveable city. It's also a great place to visit. Even as the capital of Victoria and Australia's second-largest city, Melbourne gets a bad rap as a travel destination because it lacks a singular icon like Sydney's Opera House or the Northern Territory's Uluru (Ayers Rock). But rather than any single sight the city blends cosmopolitan sights, sounds, artistry and an energy that is likely to catch any lingering visitor. If you resist falling prey to the "a city is just a city" mentality, you will easily fall under Melbourne's spell and relish in all it has to offer. Both ultramodern skyscrapers and ornate neogothic edifices line its wide streets, and the rumble of the green-and-gold trams accompany the roar of thousands of sport fanatics at the Melbourne Cricket Grounds (MCG). You might spend one hour window-shopping at Southbank's chic boutiques, and the next comparing fruit amid the bustling clamor of the Queen Victoria Market, or strolling through an expansive city garden. Students enjoying late-night caffeine sessions in smoky Fitzroy cafes coexist with clubhoppers raging until 6am in South Yarra and Prahran. Sprawling over 6200 square kilometers and home to over three million denizens, Melbourne needs to be savored, not just seen.

It all began rather inauspiciously in 1825, when John Batman sailed a skiff up the Yarra, got stuck on a sandbank, then justified his blunder by claiming that he had found the "place for a village." Then named Batmania (Gotham City was already taken), the diminutive burg underwent a phenomenal growth spurt at the onset of the Victorian Gold Rush three decades later. "Marvelous Melbourne" celebrated its coming-of-age in 1880 by hosting the World Exhibition, which attracted over a million people. When the Victorian economy crashed in the 1890s following a series of bank failures, Melbourne's infrastructure collapsed, and its fetid open sewers earned it the nickname "Marvelous Smellbourne." By the early part of the 19th century though, things other than the sewage were up and running again, and Melbourne posed a legitimate challenge to Sydney for the honor of being named Australia's capital. While the Canberra compromise ultimately deprived both metropoli of this status, Melbourne was more than happy to serve as temporary home to the government until the Parliament House was completed. The city's 20th-century apex was the 1956 Olympic Games, which brought Melbourne's love for sport to an international audience.

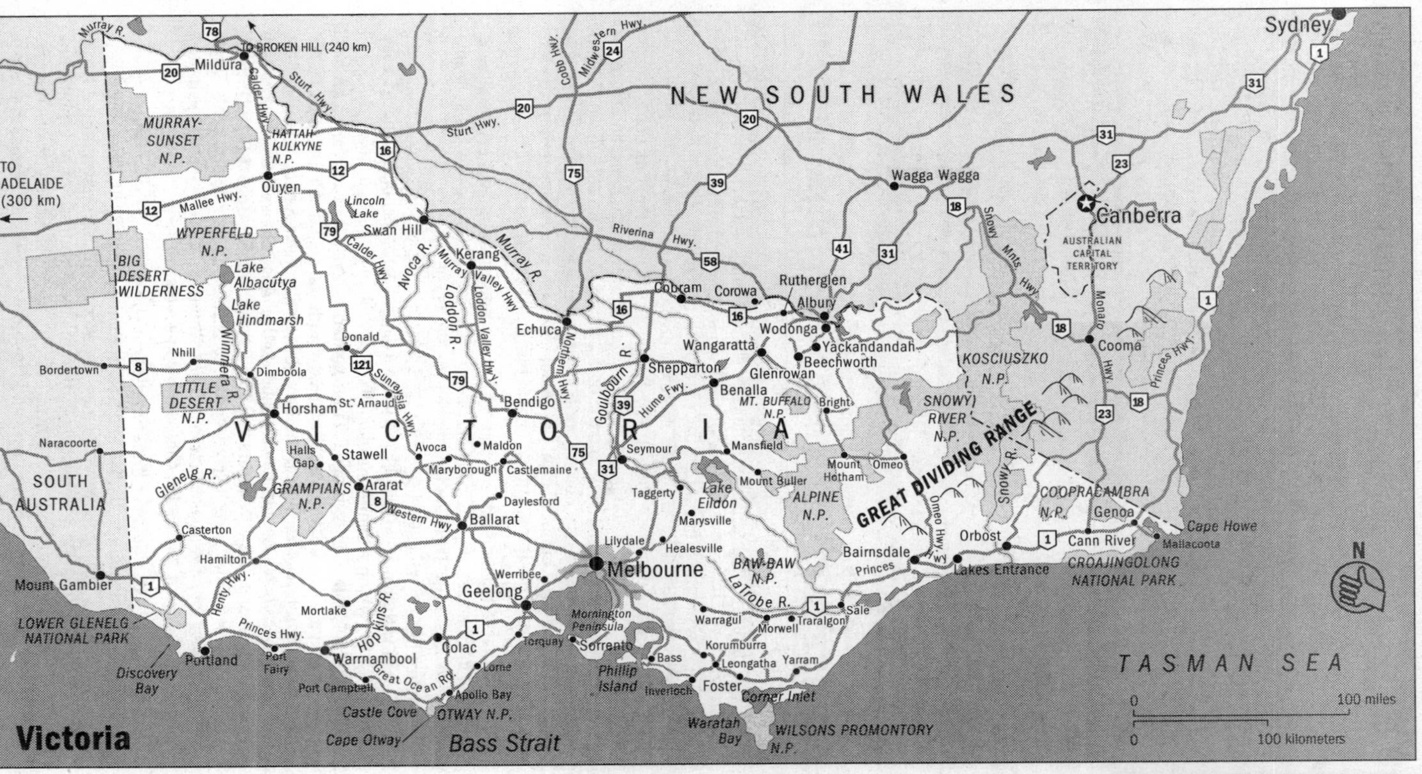
Victoria
NEW SOUTH WALES
VICTORIA
SOUTH AUSTRALIA
TASMAN SEA
Bass Strait
Sydney
Canberra
AUSTRALIAN CAPITAL TERRITORY
Melbourne
Wagga Wagga
Cooma
Monaro Hwy.
Princes Hwy.
Snowy Mnts. Hwy
KOSCIUSZKO N.P.
SNOWY RIVER N.P.
GREAT DIVIDING RANGE
Snowy R.
COOPRACAMBRA N.P.
CROAJINGOLONG NATIONAL PARK
Cape Howe
Mallacoota
Genoa
Cann River
Orbost
Lakes Entrance
Omeo Hwy.
Omeo
Bairnsdale
Princes Hwy
Sale
Traralgon
Morwell
Yarram
Corner Inlet
WILSONS PROMONTORY N.P.
Waratah Bay
Foster
Leongatha
Korumburra
Inverloch
Bass
Phillip Island
Sorrento
Mornington Peninsula
Warragul
LaTrobe R.
BAW-BAW N.P.
ALPINE N.P.
Mount Hotham
Mount Buller
Bright
MT. BUFFALO N.P.
Mansfield
Lake Eildon
Marysville
Healesville
Lilydale
Taggerty
Seymour
Hume Fwy.
Goulbourn R.
Shepparton
Benalla
Glenrowan
Wangaratta
Beechworth
Yackandandah
Wodonga
Albury
Rutherglen
Corowa
Cobram
Riverina Hwy.
Echuca
Northern Hwy.
Murray R.
Murray Valley Hwy
Kerang
Loddon Valley Hwy.
Loddon R.
Bendigo
Castlemaine
Maldon
Daylesford
Maryborough
Avoca
Avoca R.
Ballarat
Western Hwy
Geelong
Werribee
Torquay
Lorne
Apollo Bay
OTWAY N.P.
Cape Otway
Castle Cove
Great Ocean Rd
Colac
Hopkins R.
Warrnambool
Port Campbell
Mortlake
Port Fairy
Princes Hwy.
Portland
Discovery Bay
LOWER GLENELG NATIONAL PARK
Henty Hwy.
Hamilton
Casterton
Glenelg R.
Mount Gambier
Naracoorte
Bordertown
Nhill
LITTLE DESERT N.P.
Wimmera R.
Dimboola
Horsham
Halls Gap
GRAMPIANS N.P.
Stawell
Ararat
St. Arnaud
Sunraysia Hwy.
Donald
Calder Hwy.
Swan Hill
Lincoln Lake
Lake Hindmarsh
Lake Albacutya
WYPERFELD N.P.
BIG DESERT WILDERNESS
Mallee Hwy.
Ouyen
HATTAH KULKYNE N.P.
MURRAY-SUNSET N.P.
Mildura
Murray R.
Sturt Hwy.
Cobb Hwy.
Midwestern Hwy.
TO BROKEN HILL (240 km)
TO ADELAIDE (300 km)
N
0 100 miles
0 100 kilometers

The subsequent years have seen even more population growth and an increasingly international flavor; most of the recent immigrants hail from China, Southeast Asia, Italy, and Greece (Melbourne has the world's third-largest Greek population after Athens and Thessaloniki). Today, Melbourne's various neighborhoods—the frenetic Central City, alterna-funky Fitzroy, Italianate Carlton, mellow St. Kilda, chic South Yarra, and more—invite exploration and lie within minutes of each other via tram. The weather is temperate, though beware of frequent rainstorms; most of the time, it's great for beach-going or walking along the Yarra at night. With picturesque waterfronts, numerous parks, famous sporting events, and a world-class cultural scene, Melbourne coaxes visitors to relax and enjoy all the attractions of a large city with less of the tourist hype.

MELBOURNE HIGHLIGHTS

AUSSIE RULES. Catch a games of Aussie Rules Football at the MCG, Melbourne's sports obsession (p. 523).

QUEEN VICTORIA MARKET. Get great bargains in the Queen Victoria Market (p. 524).

ASTOR THEATRE. Experience the old-school grandeur and Art Deco elegance of the Astor Theatre (p. 529).

MOOMBA FESTIVAL. Partake in the unbridled pandemonium of Moomba (p. 531).

SOUTH YARRA AND FITZROY. Party like a rock star in upscale South Yarra and chiller Fitzroy (p. 531).

INTERCITY TRANSPORTATION

BY PLANE. Boomerang-shaped **Tullamarine International Airport** is 22km northwest of Melbourne and has three terminals. The international terminal houses several outfits and sits in the middle of the two domestic terminals, Qantas and Ansett. Visit www.melair.com.au for extensive information on all airport services. **Skybus** (☎9335 2811) provides ground transport to Melbourne's city center. It stops at the Spencer St. bus and train station downtown. The bus departs from the station for the airport at a quarter past and a quarter to the hour, and from the airport to the station on the hour and the half-hour. ($12, return $20). Free connection to and from major city hotels; book in advance. **Taxis** to the city center cost roughly $35 and take about 25min. **Car rental** companies are clustered to the left, when exiting from the international arrival terminal (see **By Car**, p. 509).

International terminal: Houses 25 airlines and all international arrivals and departures. Qantas international (☎13 12 11) operates on the first floor, alongside Ansett international (☎13 14 14). **Travelers Information** (☎9297 1805; fax 9297 1051), directly in front of arriving international passengers as they exit, books same-day accommodations, provides maps and brochures, and has a useful backpacker bulletin board. **Lockers** ($6-9 per day) are located on either end of the international terminal.

Domestic terminals: Qantas (☎13 13 13; www.qantas.com.au) heads the left terminal and Ansett (☎13 13 00; www.ansett.com.au) heads the right. Each flies to all Australian capitals at least once a day, and they have similar fares. Return fares with three weeks advance purchase include: **Adelaide** ($400); **Alice Springs** ($649); **Brisbane** ($363); **Cairns** ($702); **Canberra** ($286); **Darwin** ($649); **Hobart** ($198); **Perth** ($363); **Sydney** ($202). Each company also runs phone or website-only deals. **Virgin Blue** (☎13 67 89; www.virginblue.com.au) has started to provide domestic service to a few cities and tends to have the cheapest one-way fares.

BY BUS AND TRAIN. Spencer Street Station, at the intersection of Spencer and Bourke St., is the main intercity **bus** and **train station.** (☎9619 2340. Open daily 6am-10pm.) **V/Line** (☎13 61 96; www.vlinepassenger.com.au), offers unlimited travel passes within Victoria for seven days ($75) to overseas tourists only. Countrylink (☎13 22 32; www.countrylink.nsw.gov.au) covers multiple-day passes to destinations in NSW, as well as to Melbourne and Brisbane (see Local Transportation, p.

509); Great Southern (☎13 21 47; www.gsr.com.au) has destinations across Australia. The **Melbourne Transit Centre,** 58 Franklin St., (☎9639 0634; open daily 6am-10:30pm) near Elizabeth St., is the hub of Travel Coach Australia, a bus conglomerate that comprises both McCafferty's (☎13 14 99) and Greyhound Pioneer (☎13 20 30). They are listed in the chart below (see p. 509) as **Travel Coach.**

ORIENTATION

The heart of one of the world's largest urban sprawls, Melbourne's lively, dense core comprises a geometrically precise city center surrounded by a slew of distinctive suburbs. The city center alone could take up the whole of an abbreviated visit, but the surrounding neighborhoods are where the true spirit of Melbourne lives. For those keen to conquer the entire polis, the irreplaceable *Melway* guide has detailed street directories of Melbourne and surrounds; pick it up in any bookstore (around $40), or photocopy the desired pages from the library.

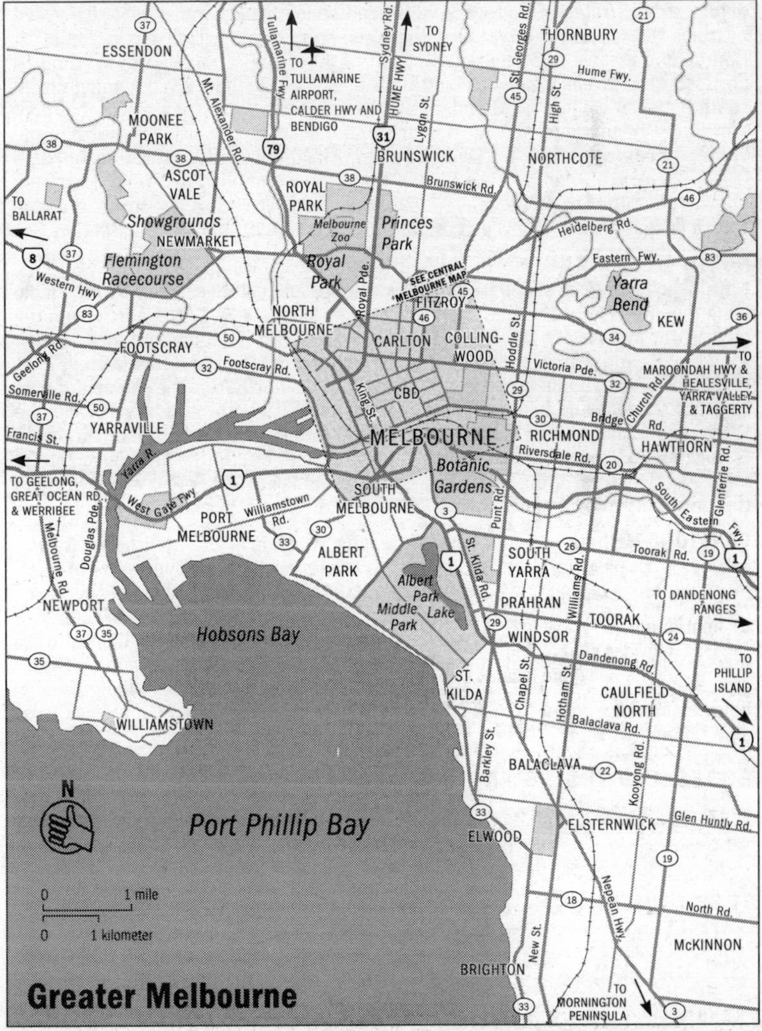

CITY CENTER. The city center, also known as the Central Business District (CBD), is composed of a well-arranged rectangular grid of streets bordered by **Spencer St.** on the west, **La Trobe St.** on the north, **Spring St.** on the east, and **Flinders St.** (which borders the Yarra River) on the south. Five major streets run east to west: La Trobe (the northernmost), Lonsdale, Bourke, Collins, and Flinders. To the north of all but La Trobe are "little" streets—roads named after their southern superior (for example, Little Collins St. is just north of Collins St.; and Flinders Ln. is just north of Flinders St.). Nine streets cross this grid running north to south: Spencer (the westernmost), King, William, Queen, Elizabeth, Swanston, Russell, Exhibition, and Spring. **Spencer St.** runs by the primary bus and train depot, bridges the Yarra River to South Melbourne, and carries trams #12, 75, 95, 96, and 109. Directly in the middle, **Elizabeth St.** carries major northbound tram lines (#19, 57, 59, and 68). One block east, **Swanston St.** also has north-south trams (#1, 3, 5, 6, 8, 16, 22, 25, 64, 67, and 72). On the east end, **Spring St.** borders Parliament and the Treasury and Carlton Gardens.

The eastern half of the city contains most restaurants and sights. **Bourke St. Mall** (a pedestrian stretch of Bourke St. between Elizabeth and Swanston St., traversed by trams #86, 95, and 96) swarms with people every day; the giant screen "alt.tv" at Bourke and Swanston St. marks the heart of the city. Both **Hardware Ln.** (running north-south between Londsdale and Bourke St.) and **DeGraves St.** (running north-south between Collins and Flinders St.) are alley-like pedestrian walks that contain shops, restaurants, and cafes with outdoor seating. The area just north of the city center bordered by La Trobe, Queen, Elizabeth, and Victoria St. borders Queen Victoria Market and is a hive of budget accommodations, while East Melbourne contains **Fitzroy Gardens** (p. 523) and Victoria's sporting shrine, the **Melbourne Cricket Ground** (p. 523. Accessible by trams #48, 70, and 75 from Flinders St.)

NORTH MELBOURNE. North Melbourne is a pleasant mix of bungalows, flats, refurbished residences, and neighborhood shops and eateries, all easily reachable from the city center. Forming its eastern edge, **Elizabeth St.** heads north from the city center and passes the **Queen Victoria Market** with its abundant, inexpensive food stocks and wares; travel west along Victoria St. (traversed by tram #57) to find loads of cool budget eateries. William St. heads north from the city center past **Flagstaff Gardens** and becomes **Peel St.** Peel and Elizabeth St. intersect near the University of Melbourne where Elizabeth continues northwest under the name **Flemington Rd.** (along which trams #55 and 59 continue), to the **Melbourne Zoo** (p. 525). At this intersection, Peel St. becomes **Royal Pde.** (tram #19), which borders the University and becomes **Sydney Rd.** to the northern suburb of Brunswick.

CARLTON. Melbourne's unofficial "Little Italy," Carlton begins at **Nicholson St.** and extends west past the Carlton Gardens, to the **University of Melbourne.** Its primary thoroughfare is **Lygon St.,** where upmarket Italian bistros, somewhat cheaper *gelaterias* and *pasticcerias*, and a smattering of ethnic and eclectic foods cater to a crowd of old Mediterranean types and college students. Public transportation does not go along Lygon St. in Carlton. To get there, either take a tram up Swanston St. (#1, 3, 5, 6, 8, 16, 22, 25, 64, 67, or 72) and then walk east along Queensberry or Faraday St., or take #96 from Bourke St. up Nicholson St. and walk west along Faraday St.

BUSES AND TRAINS FROM MELBOURNE TO:

DESTINATION	COMPANY	DURATION	TIMES	PRICE
Adelaide	Travel Coach V/Line	9-10hr. 10½hr.	3 per day 1 per day	$54 $57
Albury	V/Line	3½hr.	4-6 per day	$42.90
Alice Springs	Travel Coach Great Southern	28hr. 36hr.	1 per day 1 per week	$214 $292
Ararat	V/Line	3hr.	3-5 per day	$29.70
Ballarat	V/Line	1½hr.	7-12 per day	$15.20
Bendigo	V/Line	2hr.	5-11per day	$22.90

DESTINATION	COMPANY	DURATION	TIMES	PRICE
Bright	V/Line	4½hr.	1 per day	$42.90
Brisbane	Travel Coach Countrylink	27hr. 35hr.	3 per day 1 per day	$156 $177.10
Brisbane (via Sydney)	Travel Coach	30hr.	4 per day	$144
Cairns	Travel Coach Countrylink	56hr. 70hr.	2 per day 4 per week	$329 $339.90
Canberra	V/Line Travel Coach	8½hr. 8hr.	1 per day 2 per day	$55 $56
Castlemaine	V/Line	1½hr.	5-11 per day	$16.70
Darwin	Travel Coach	50hr.	1 per day	$389
Echuca	V/Line	3½-4hr.	2-9 per day	$29.70
Geelong	V/Line	1hr.	11-26 per day	$9.50
Mildura	V/Line	9½hr.	1 per week	$59.20
Perth	Travel Coach Great Southern	42½hr. 60hr.	1 per day 2 per week	$280 $340
Sydney	Travel Coach Countrylink	11-15hr. 11hr.	4 per day 2 per day	$59 $110
Yulara (Ayers Rock)	Travel Coach	25hr.	1 per day	$285

FITZROY. Fitzroy, Melbourne's bohemian district, is a shopping mecca for those looking for new or used clothing, music or books, or some of the best cafe and restaurant societies. While it's packed with style and populated with "ferals" (Australians' term for the nose-ring crowd), Fitzroy is blessedly low on attitude, and its establishments house a healthy mix of freaks, families, and everyone in between. Tram #11 runs the length of **Brunswick St.,** the main artery of Fitzroy. **Smith St.** makes the boundary between Fitzroy and its eastern neighbor, **Collingwood,** and is home to a number of fine eateries and factory outlet stores. Just east of Smith are a handful of **gay bars** (and a fair number of straight ones too). The blocks of **Johnston St.** between Brunswick and Nicholson St. in Fitzroy form the smallish Latin Quarter, with stores, restaurants, tapas bars, and dance clubs.

SOUTH MELBOURNE. The Yarra divides Melbourne into the more working-class suburbs of the north and the fancier ones to the south. South Melbourne, west of St. Kilda Rd. and stretching south from the West Gate Freeway to **Albert Park,** is an exception. More blue-collar than adjacent communities, this neighborhood has some quality restaurants and nightspots along its main drag, Cecil St. It's also a quick walk to the park, the **Royal Botanic Gardens** (p. 526), the city center, or the **beach** at Port Phillip Bay. Take tram #96 or 12 from Spencer St.

West of South Melbourne along Port Phillip Bay are three of Melbourne's quietest, most posh suburbs. Station Pier marks the division between Port Melbourne, the more commercial side of the area, and the more urbane Albert Park, an upscale residential neighborhood with stately seaside bungalows; ferries to **Tasmania** depart from Station Pier at the terminus of tram #109. Bay St. (City Rd. near the CBD) marks the division between Port Melbourne and more urbane Albert Park, an upscale residential neighborhood with stately bungalows along the seaside.

SOUTH YARRA AND PRAHRAN. South Yarra and Prahran ("pruh-RAN") span the area enclosed by the Yarra to the north, St. Kilda Rd. to the west, Dandenong Rd. to the south, and William St. to the east. The focus of Melbourne's gay community, **Commercial Rd.** runs east-west, separating South Yarra from its southern neighbor Prahran. The district's main street is **Chapel St.;** the section of the boulevard that lies in South Yarra is the commercial incarnation of the fancy suburbs south of the river. On sunny Sundays, the beautiful people come here to shop for Prada and Versace and then snipe about the catty salesgirls while sitting in sleek, pricey sidewalk bistros. Don't let the snots rub off on you; good deals abound in Melbourne. Seek out Chapel St., where it gets a little

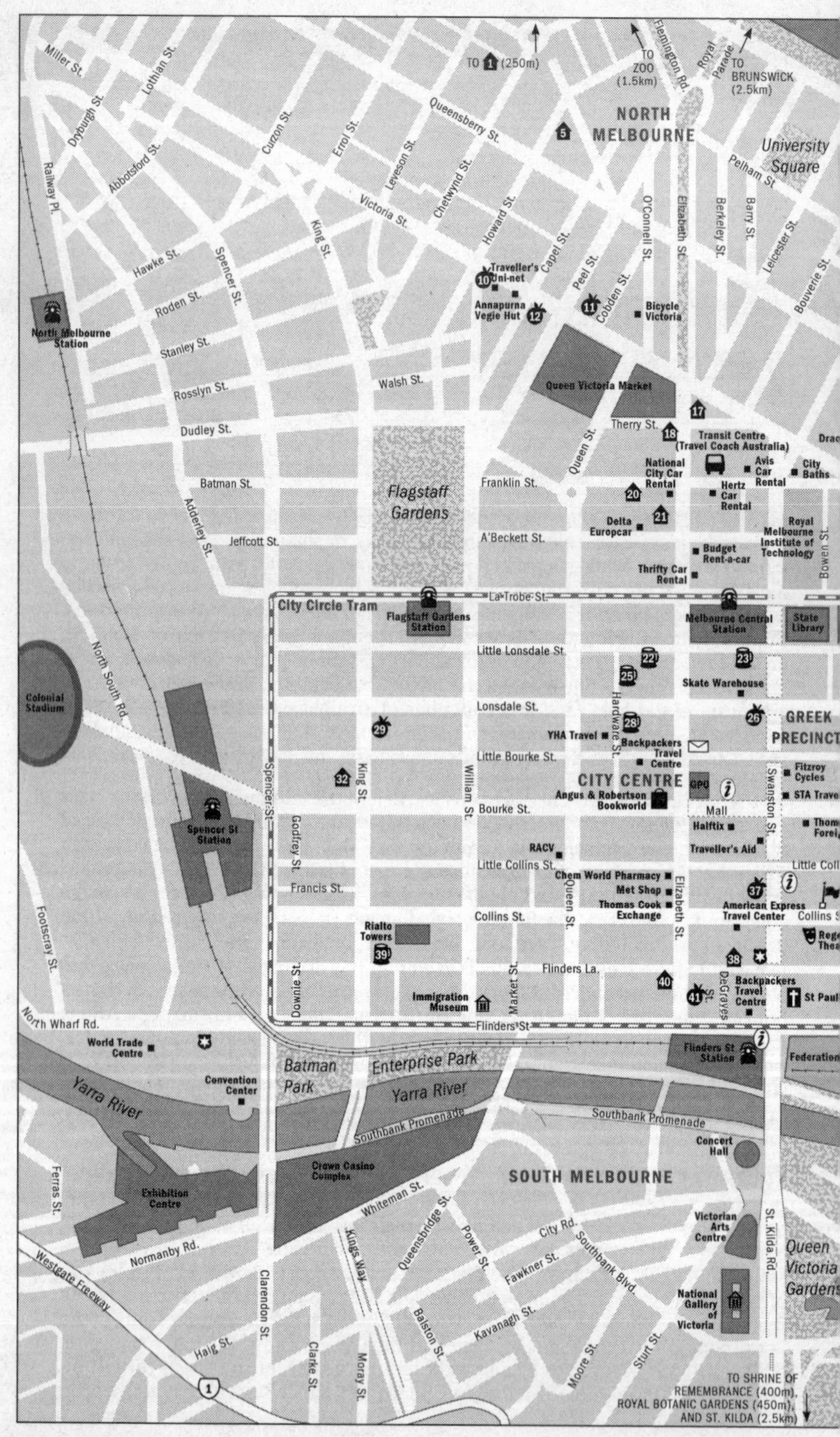

TO (250m)
TO ZOO (1.5km)
TO BRUNSWICK (2.5km)
NORTH MELBOURNE
University Square
Miller St.
Lothian St.
Dryburgh St.
Abbotsford St.
Railway Pl.
Curzon St.
Errol St.
Leveson St.
Queensberry St.
Flemington Rd.
Royal Parade
Pelham St.
Chetwynd St.
Victoria St.
King St.
Howard St.
O'Connell St.
Elizabeth St.
Berkeley St.
Barry St.
Leicester St.
Bouverie St.
Hawke St.
Spencer St.
Capel St.
Peel St.
Cobden St.
Traveller's Uni-net
Annapurna Vegie Hut
Bicycle Victoria
Roden St.
Stanley St.
North Melbourne Station
Rosslyn St.
Walsh St.
Queen Victoria Market
Dudley St.
Therry St.
Transit Centre (Travel Coach Australia)
Queen St.
National City Car Rental
Avis Car Rental
City Baths
Batman St.
Franklin St.
Hertz Car Rental
Flagstaff Gardens
Adderley St.
Delta Europcar
Royal Melbourne Institute of Technology
Jeffcott St.
A'Beckett St.
Budget Rent-a-car
Thrifty Car Rental
Bowen St.
La Trobe St.
City Circle Tram
Flagstaff Gardens Station
Melbourne Central Station
State Library
Little Lonsdale St.
North South Rd.
Colonial Stadium
Skate Warehouse
Lonsdale St.
Hardware St.
GREEK PRECINCT
YHA Travel
Backpackers Travel Centre
Little Bourke St.
CITY CENTRE
Spencer St.
King St.
William St.
GPO
Fitzroy Cycles
STA Travel
Angus & Robertson Bookworld
Swanston St.
Spencer St Station
Bourke St.
Mall
Godfrey St.
Halftix
Traveller's Aid
RACV
Little Collins St.
Chem World Pharmacy
Met Shop
Thomas Cook Exchange
Francis St.
Footscray St.
American Express Travel Center
Collins St.
Rialto Towers
Flinders La.
Market St.
Downie St.
DeGraves St.
Backpackers Travel Centre
Immigration Museum
St Paul
North Wharf Rd.
Flinders St.
World Trade Centre
Flinders St Station
Federation
Batman Park
Enterprise Park
Yarra River
Convention Center
Southbank Promenade
Concert Hall
Crown Casino Complex
SOUTH MELBOURNE
Ferras St.
Exhibition Centre
Whiteman St.
Queensbridge St.
Victorian Arts Centre
St. Kilda Rd.
Queen Victoria Gardens
Normanby Rd.
Kings Way
Power St.
City Rd.
Fawkner St.
Southbank Blvd.
Westgate Freeway
Clarendon St.
Balston St.
Kavanagh St.
National Gallery of Victoria
Haig St.
Clarke St.
Moray St.
Moore St.
Sturt St.
TO SHRINE OF REMEMBRANCE (400m), ROYAL BOTANIC GARDENS (450m), AND ST. KILDA (2.5km)

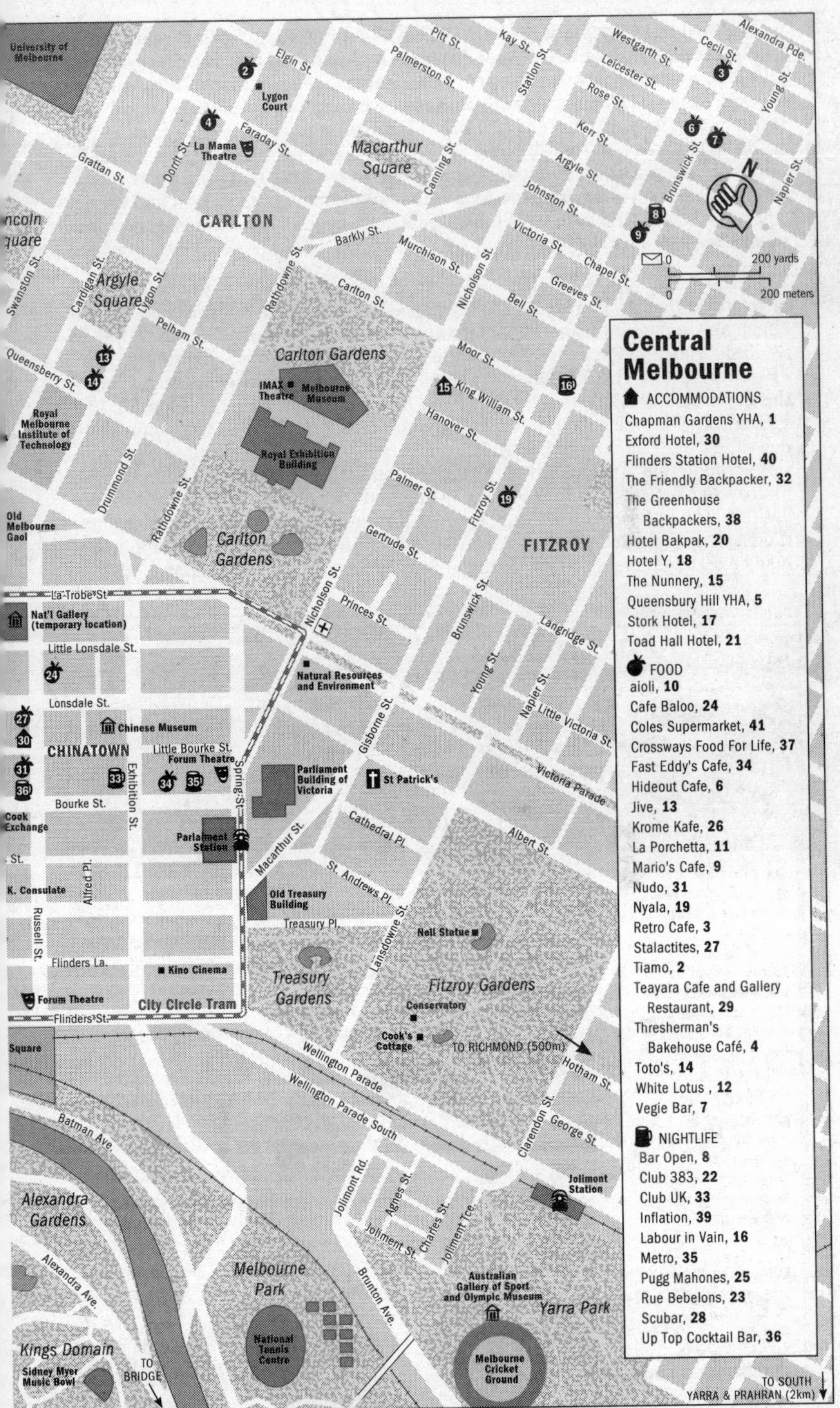

Central Melbourne

ACCOMMODATIONS

Chapman Gardens YHA, **1**
Exford Hotel, **30**
Flinders Station Hotel, **40**
The Friendly Backpacker, **32**
The Greenhouse Backpackers, **38**
Hotel Bakpak, **20**
Hotel Y, **18**
The Nunnery, **15**
Queensbury Hill YHA, **5**
Stork Hotel, **17**
Toad Hall Hotel, **21**

FOOD

aioli, **10**
Cafe Baloo, **24**
Coles Supermarket, **41**
Crossways Food For Life, **37**
Fast Eddy's Cafe, **34**
Hideout Cafe, **6**
Jive, **13**
Krome Kafe, **26**
La Porchetta, **11**
Mario's Cafe, **9**
Nudo, **31**
Nyala, **19**
Retro Cafe, **3**
Stalactites, **27**
Tiamo, **2**
Teayara Cafe and Gallery Restaurant, **29**
Thresherman's Bakehouse Café, **4**
Toto's, **14**
White Lotus , **12**
Vegie Bar, **7**

NIGHTLIFE

Bar Open, **8**
Club 383, **22**
Club UK, **33**
Inflation, **39**
Labour in Vain, **16**
Metro, **35**
Pugg Mahones, **25**
Rue Bebelons, **23**
Scubar, **28**
Up Top Cocktail Bar, **36**

more down-to-earth south of Commercial Rd. in Prahran, closer in spirit to St. Kilda. **Greville St.** branches west from Chapel and is a den for second-hand clothing, record stores, and bizarre restaurants. Trams #78 and 79 run slowly along Chapel St. By tram from Flinders St. Station, #8 travels below the Botanic Gardens, then along Toorak Rd. to its intersection with Chapel St., while #5 and #64 head south along St. Kilda Rd., and then go east along Dandenong Rd. to Chapel. The quickest way to get to the area from the central city, though, is to hop a **Sandringham Line** train from Flinders St. Station and take it to South Yarra, Prahran, or Windsor Stations, each of which lies only a few blocks west of Chapel St.

ST. KILDA. Though it's a bit removed to the southeast of the city center (and officially in the city of **Port Phillip,** see p. 538), St. Kilda is a budget hotspot with cheap accommodations and popular eateries. Trams #12 and 96 bring people to St. Kilda from Spencer St. Station, while #16 runs from Flinders St. Station. Tram #16 travels along **St. Kilda Rd.,** and passes Melbourne's two largest green spaces, the **Royal Botanic Gardens** via **Albert Park.** At **St. Kilda Junction,** St. Kilda Rd. and Fitzroy St. intersect; from here, Fitzroy curves south towards the waterfront, becoming the Esplanade. **Barkly St.** runs south from the junction on the other side, completing a triangle with Fitzroy St. and the Esplanade. The junction of Fitzroy and Barkly St. is **Grey St.,** and is the focus of St. Kilda's budget accommodations. The last street that branches south from Fitzroy St. before it turns into the Esplanade is **Acland St.,** the southern end of which is one of Melbourne's many excellent cafe districts, distinguished by its old-time cake shops.

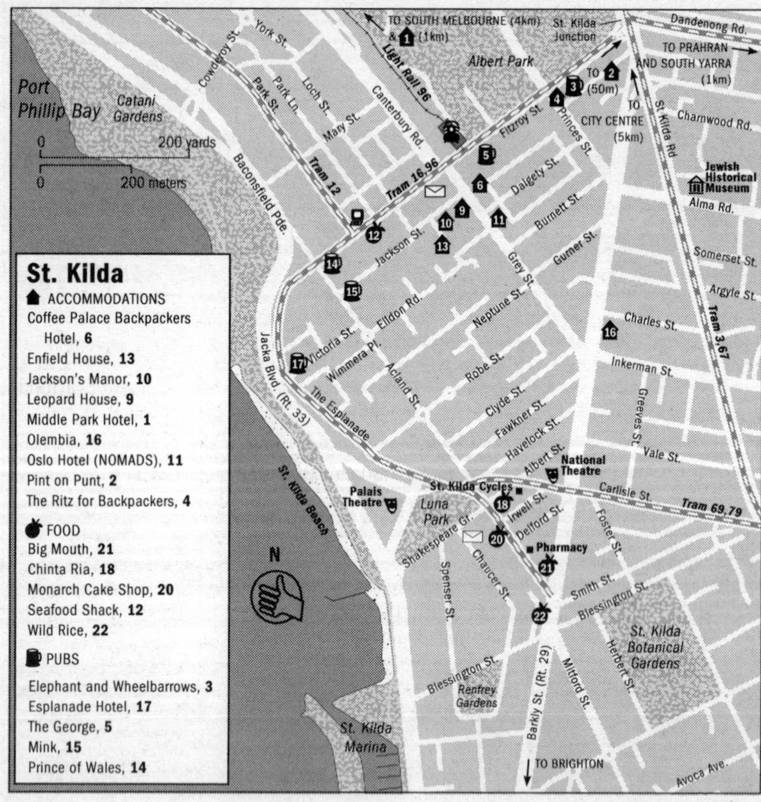

LOCAL TRANSPORTATION

PUBLIC TRANSPORTATION. Melbourne's superb public transportation system, the **Met,** comprises light-rail trains, buses, and trams. (☎13 16 38; www.victrip.com.au. Open daily 7am-9pm for inquiries.) **Tram** routes criss-cross the metropolitan area and are the most useful for navigating the city and its proximate outskirts. Weekdays they run every 3-12 min., nights and weekends every 20min. or longer; services operate M-Sa 5am-midnight, Su 8am-11pm. You don't actually have to show your pass to ride trams—but if an inspector decides to make a spot check and you're without a valid ticket, expect a $100 fine.

For those honest riders, the entire network comprises three Met zones, though you'll stay in Zone 1 unless you travel out to a distant suburb. Tickets are sold at stations, on board trams and buses (coins only), and at the **Met Shop,** 103 Elizabeth St. near Collins St. (Open M-F 8:30am- 4:55pm, Sa 9am-1pm.) **Tickets** within Zone 1 can be used on any of the three types of transportation, and are valid for unlimited travel for a 2hr. period ($2.60), a day ($5), a week ($21.70), a month ($81.30), or a year ($875). **Concession** rates are roughly half-price; you qualify if you are under 15 years old, or have a valid Australian university ID (ISIC cards or international university IDs not accepted) or pensioner card. Only two-hour tickets can be purchased from coin-operated machines on board trams and buses; if you're going to be in town for a while, the long-term passes save a lot of time, money, and hassle. If you purchase your ticket anywhere but on a tram itself, you must validate it by putting it in any of the electronic green boxes on the tram; otherwise, even if you have a ticket, you can be fined for not doing this. These instances are rare, but right now the government is in the midst of privatizing the Met; commercial interests may be more rigorous than government laxness. For more info and route maps, grab the free Met *Fares and Travel Guide* from any station.

The burgundy-and-gold **City Circle Tram** circumnavigates the **Central Business District (CBD),** provides running commentary on the city's sights and history, and is **free** (runs every 10min., Su-W 10am-6pm, Th-Sa until 9:30pm). The bus and **light-rail train** systems are mostly for commuters going to residential areas or distant suburbs, and you can't board without a valid Metcard. There are train stops at **Melbourne Central, Flagstaff Gardens, Parliament,** and **Spencer St.,** though the main rail hub is the beautiful banana-colored **Flinders St. Station** at the southern foot of Swanston St., identifiable by its big clock.

BY CAR. The usual national car rental chains mostly have offices in the Melbourne city center and at the airport, but it's cheaper to rent in the city, as the airport offices generally include a 9% airport tax. They tend to rent only to people over age 25, though some accept renters aged 21-24 with a **surcharge** (listed after price). Prices for all fluctuate frequently due to seasons and specials. National agencies include:

Atlas (☎9663 6233, airport 9335 1945; www.atlasrent.com.au). In Melbourne Transit Centre. Open M-F 7:30am-6pm, Sa-Su 7:30am-2:30pm. From $53.80 per day, $11.

Avis, 20-24 Franklin St. (☎9663 6366, airport 9338 1800). Open M-Th 7:30am-6:30pm, F 7:30am-7pm, Sa-Su 8am-5pm. From $60, $25.

Budget, 398 Elizabeth St. (☎9203 4846, airport 9241 6366), corner of A'Beckett St. Open M-Th 8am-6:30pm, F 8am-7pm, Sa-Su 8am-5pm. From $55, $16.50.

Delta Europcar, 101 A'Beckett St. (☎9600 9025; www.deltaeuropcar.com.au). Open M-F 7:30am-6pm, Sa-Su 8am-5pm. From $40 per day, $12.

National Car Rental (☎9348 9449), on the corner of Franklin and Elizabeth St., is owned by **Delta** and carries the same rates. They both offer YHA and VIP discounts and claim they will match any competitor's price. Open M-Th 7:30am-6pm, F 7:30am-6:30pm, Sa 8am-5pm.

Hertz, 97 Franklin St. (☎9663 6244, airport ☎9338 4044). Open M-Th 7:30am-6pm, F 7:30am-7pm, Sa 7:30am-5pm, Su 8am-5pm. From $56, $15.

Thrifty, 390 Elizabeth St. (☎8661 6000, airport ☎1300 367 227). Open M-Th 7:30am-6pm, F 7:30am-6:30pm, Sa-Su 8am-5pm. From $65, $15.

Backpacker Car Rental, 103 Railway Ave., Werribee (☎9731 0700). Charges $137.50 per week for the Melbourne metro area, but provides a better all-Victoria rate at $192.50 per week, which includes unlimited kilometers, insurance, and RACV roadside assistance; drivers must be at least 23 years old.

The **Royal Automobile Association of Victoria (RACV)** (☎13 13 29) on the corner of Little Collins and Queen St., and second location at 360 Bourke St. (☎13 19 55) is a comprehensive driving resource with good maps for sale. Members receive emergency roadside assistance. It's common for backpackers to join forces and buy or rent a used car. A good but out-of-the-way option for long-term rental is **Car Connection** (☎5473 4469; www.carconnection.com.au; open M-F 9am-5pm) near Castlemaine, 120km northwest of Melbourne. They offer a station wagon for up to six months for $1950 plus a $750 insurance charge, and full camping equipment for two for $250. Because they're a bit out of town, they also provide free pickup from Melbourne airport or any city hostel, as well as free first-night accommodation in Castlemaine. What a deal.

There are also tons of **bargain agencies** with names like **Rent-a-Bomb** (☎13 15 53; www.rentabomb.com.au), with 11 offices in the Melbourne area, that are only half-joking about the quality of their cars. The deals can run as cheap as $12 per day, but weigh the savings against the potential costs of breaking down in the middle of nowhere. For information on driving in Australia, see **On The Road,** p. 67.

BY TAXI. If you're out after the Met stops running at midnight, you'll have to take a taxi—that is, if you aren't going home with that sexy random from the club. All companies have a $2.80 base charge plus $1.31 per km. There's a $1 surcharge when you arrange cab pickup by phone and if you ride between midnight and 6am. The misnamed **Silver Top** (☎13 10 08) and **Black Cabs** (☎13 22 27) are both yellow.

BY BICYCLE. An extensive **bike trail** runs along the Yarra, and others loop through Albert Park and Middle Park, along the Port Phillip beaches, and around North Melbourne's gardens. Southern Melbourne's flat bayside roads make for low-impact, scenic cycling. **St. Kilda Cycles,** 11 Carlisle St., has good rates. (☎9534 3074. Open M-F 9am-6pm, Sa 9am-5pm, Su 10am-4pm. $15 per half-day, $20 per day.) Or try **Fitzroy Cycles,** 224 Swanston St. (☎9639 3511. Open M-F 9am-6pm, Sa 9:30am-5pm. $9 per hr., $35 per day.) Rates include helmets and locks. Many hostels rent bikes for little or no charge. **Bicycle Victoria (BV),** 19 O'Connell St. (☎9328 3000 or 1800 639 634; www.bv.com.au), provides insurance for members (yearly membership $63, concessions $57, families $78-88) and free info for non-members (see **Getting Around Victoria,** p. 499).

PRACTICAL INFORMATION

TOURIST AND FINANCIAL SERVICES

Tourist Offices: Melbourne Visitor Information Centre, Melbourne Town Hall (☎9658 9658, 24hr. 13 28 42; www.melbourne.org). On the corner of Little Collins and Swanston St., but slated to move to Federation Square, across from Flinders St. Station at the corner of Flinders St. and St. Kilda Rd. in late 2001. Open M-F 9am-6pm, Sa-Su 9am-5pm. Along with maps and brochures of both Melbourne and Victoria, the office provides a **Melbourne Greeter Service** that gives **free** 2-4hr. tours of the city tailored to your personal interests. Tours offered in 25 languages. Arrange by filling out a brief application at least 3 working days in advance (click "Greeters" at www.melbourne.vic.gov). Info booths at **Bourke St. Mall** and **Flinders St. Station** offer help. Open M-F 9am-5pm, Sa 10am-4pm, Su 11am-4pm.

Travel Offices: AUSRES (Australian Reservation Services) books tours, accommodations, and transportation throughout Victoria. Current office in Town Hall (☎9650 7721; www.ausres.com.au), but possibly moving to Federation Square in late 2001.

Disabled and Elderly Travelers Information: Travellers Aid, 2nd fl., 169 Swanston St. (☎9654 7690; fax 9654 1926). Also at Spencer St. Station (☎9670 2873). Both open M-F 8am-5pm. Will meet and assist elderly and disabled travelers on trains and buses M-F 7:30am-7:30pm, Sa-Su 7:30am-11:30am. Arrange ahead.

Gay and Lesbian Information: The ALSO Foundation, 35 Cato St., Prahran (☎9510 5569; www.also.org.au). Gay and lesbian helpline (☎9510 5488 or 1800 631 493).

Outdoors Information: Natural Resources and Environment (NRE), 8 Nicholson St., on the corner of Victoria Pde., East Melbourne (☎9637 8325, hotline 13 61 86; www.nre.vic.gov.au). Maps and info on licenses. Open M-F 8:30am-5:30pm. Also call **Parks Victoria** (☎13 19 63; www.parks.vic.gov.au) for all state and national park info.

Budget Travel: YHA Victoria, 83-85 Hardware Ln. (☎9670 9611; www.yha.com.au). Provides a full listing of YHA hostels and a booking service. YHA member international booking surcharge $5, domestic surcharge $2 after first 2. Non-YHA member domestic surcharge $2, no non-member international booking. Attached budget travel agency. Open M-F 9am-5:30pm, Sa 10am-1pm. **STA Travel's Victorian Headquarters,** 260 Hoddle St., off Johnston St. in Fitzroy, and *all* over Melbourne and its surrounds, including 208 Swanston St. (☎9639 0599). Open M-F 9am-6pm, Sa 10am-4pm. **Backpackers World,** 167 Franklin St. (☎9329 1990), in Hotel Bakpak. Open M-F 8am-9pm, Sa-Su 9am-8pm. Also at 35 Elizabeth St. (☎9620 2300). Open M-F 9am-6pm, Sa 11am-5pm. **Backpackers Travel Centre,** Shop 1, 250 Flinders St. (☎9654 8477; www.backpackerstravel.net.au). Open M-F 9am-6pm, Sa 10am-4pm. Also at 377 Little Bourke St. (☎9642 1811). Open M-F 9am-5:30pm, Sa 10am-3pm.

Consulates: Canada, Level 1, 123 Camberwell Rd., East Hawthorne (☎9811 9999). Open M-F 8:30am-5:15pm. **Great Britain,** Level 17, 90 Collins St. (☎9650 4155). Open M-F 9am-4:30pm. **United States,** Level 6, 553 St. Kilda Rd. (☎9526 5900). Open M-F 8:30am-noon and 1-4:30pm.

Currency Exchange: All banks will exchange money during regular operating hours. Open M-Th 9:30am-4pm, F 9:30am-5pm. **American Express** (see below) exchanges all travelers checks free of commission. **Thomas Cook Foreign Exchange,** 261 Bourke St. (☎9654 4222), near Swanston St. has a $7 commission on checks and cash. Open M-F 9am-5pm, Sa 9am-2pm, Su 11am-3pm. Several banks have offices at the airport. ANZ, Commonwealth Bank, Westpac and National Bank **ATMs** accept AmEx, Cirrus, MC, Plus, V. 24hr. outlets adorn the entire city.

American Express Travel Services, 233 Collins St. (☎9633 6318). Buys all travelers checks (no charge); min. $8 or 2% fee on cash exchanges. Poste Restante for AmEx card or traveler's check holders. Wire transfers. Open M-F 9am-5pm, Sa 9am-noon.

LOCAL SERVICES

Bookstores: Angus & Robertson Bookworld (☎9670 8861; www.angusrobertson.com.au) on the corner of Elizabeth and Bourke St. is huge and has frequent blowout sales. Open M-Th 9am-6pm, F 9am-8pm, Sa 9am-6pm, Su 10am-5pm.

Library: State Library of Victoria, 328 Swanston St. (☎9669 9888), on the corner of La Trobe St. Open M-Th 10am-9pm, F-Su 10am-6pm.

Ticket Agencies: Ticketek (☎13 28 49 or 1800 062 849; www.ticketek.com.au), and **Ticketmaster** (☎13 61 00; www.ticketmaster7.com.au), for sports, performances, and other events. Handling fee for phone booking. Both open daily 9am-9pm. **Halftix,** a booth on Bourke St. Mall opposite Myer Department Store, sells half-price tickets on performance day (Su performances sold Sa); often sells out by 2pm. Cash only; no phone orders. Open M 10am-2pm, Tu-Th 11am-6pm, F 11am-6:30pm, Sa 10am-2pm.

Employment Assistance: Most *Let's Go* accommodations listed have employment bulletin boards; some help find temp jobs free of charge. **WorldWide Workers** (☎9328 8560), in the lobby of **Hotel Bakpak** (see **Accommodations,** p. 514), charges $40 to join but provides free Internet access, discounted beer and travel, and access to top jobs. Open M-F 1-5pm. Melbourne's biggest daily paper, *The Age,* has extensive classifieds on Sa and can be accessed online at www.theage.com.au.

EMERGENCY AND COMMUNICATIONS

MEDIA AND PUBLICATIONS

Newspapers: The main newspapers are *The Age* ($1.10) and *The Herald Sun* (99¢) for local coverage and *The Australian* ($1.10) for national news.

Nightlife: *InPress* and *Beat* (www.beat.com.au), released on Wednesday (free). For gay news and nightlife, check out *MCV* (by subscription, but found in most gay establishments) and *B.News* (free, released every other Th).

Entertainment: *Age*'s Entertainment Guide and *Herald Sun*'s Gig Guide, found in Friday's paper.

Radio: Alternative, Triple R 102.7FM; Rock, Triple J 107.5FM and Triple M 105.1FM; News, 1026AM; Tourist Info, 88FM.

Emergency: ☎000.

Police: 637 Flinders St. (☎9247 6666), and 226 Flinders Ln. (☎9650 7077).

Crisis Lines: Victims Referral and Assistance Hotline (☎9603 9797). **Centre Against Sexual Assault** (☎9344 2210). **Lifeline Counseling Service** (☎13 11 14). **Poison Information Service** (☎13 11 26). **Coast Guard Search and Rescue** (☎9598 7003).

Helpful numbers: Directory assistance ☎12 23, international ☎12 25; collect calls ☎1800 REVERSE (1800 738 3773); translation and interpretation ☎13 14 50.

Pharmacy: Many along Elizabeth St., including **ChemWorld** (☎9670 9370), on the corner of Elizabeth and Little Collins St. Open M-W 7:30am-6pm, Th 7:30am-6:30pm, F 7:30am-8pm, Sa 9am-5pm, Su 11am-5pm.

Hospital: St. Vincent's Hospital, 41 Victoria Pde., Fitzroy (☎9288 2211). Take any tram east along Bourke St to stop #9. **Royal Melbourne Hospital,** Grattan St., Parkville (☎9342 7000). Take tram #19 from Elizabeth St. to stop #16.

Internet Access: There are 8 free terminals at the **State Library** (see p. 511); sign up in advance for 30min. sessions. The library's email terminals are for Australian citizens and residents only (including foreigners with a work visa or Australian student ID). In the city itself, prices tend to hover around 15¢ per minute. A major exception is **Traveller's Uni-Net Stop,** 211 Victoria St. (☎9326 4418), one block west of Vic Market, offering 8¢ per min., or $4.40 per hr. Open daily 9am-midnight. Another good deal is **Backpacker's World,** 167 Franklin St. (☎9329 1990), in Hotel Bakpak. $6 per hr.; prepaid Happy Hours $3.50 per hr. Open M-F 8am-9pm, Sa-Su 9am-8pm. St. Kilda's backpacker trades keep competitive pricing of about 7¢ per minute; multitudes of Internet shops line Fitzroy St.

Post Office: GPO (☎9203 3076; fax 9203 3040) on the corner of Elizabeth and Bourke St. Mall. Fax and Poste Restante services. Open M-F 8:15am-5:30pm, Sa 10am-1pm. **Postal Code:** 3000. The **Melbourne Airport** has a post office with full fax, photocopy, and Poste Restante services. (☎9338 3865. Open M-F 9am-5pm, Sa-Su 10am-4pm. **Postal Code:** 3045.)

GETTIN' IT ONLINE IN MELBOURNE ;-)

www.visitvictoria.com Comprehensive government web site with tons of info on food, nightlife, accommodations, and events in Melbourne and all of Victoria. Events searchable by type, town, and date.

http://melbourne.citysearch.com.au An eating and drinking guide, up-to-date entertainment listings, and a comprehensive business directory.

http://melbourne.sidewalk.com.au The latest entertainment options, restaurant listings, shopping guides, and gay and lesbian information.

ACCOMMODATIONS

Melbourne's tourist industry supports numerous budget accommodations to host its backpacker population. The two biggest hostel hives are **St. Kilda** and the area just **north of the city center** enclosed by La Trobe, Queen, Elizabeth and Victoria St. The mostly YHA-affiliated hostels in **North Melbourne** tend to be quieter and more sedate, popular with at least as many school groups and elderly travelers as 20-something backpackers, while the accommodations in the **city center** are as boisterous as they are conveniently located. **South Yarra** and **Prahran** lie farther afield but are preferred by those who enjoy the proximity to these districts' shopping and nightlife. The St. Kilda options, generally make up for what they lack in cleanliness with an unquenchable thirst to party.

Availability drops during the **high season** (roughly Nov.-Feb.) and most accommodations raise their prices a tad ($2-4). The more popular hostels tend to be booked solid during these periods (and are also in demand during school holidays, from June-Aug.), so be sure to book far in advance. During summer holiday, you can usually find accommodation at universities. **Melbourne University** (Ormond College, ☎9344 1121) offers B&B accommodation Jan.-Feb. and again in July. (Students $50 per night; non-students $55 per night; longer than 5 days $45/$50; dinner $10.) **Monash University** (Halls of Residence, ☎9905 6200) provides rooms for $30 per night from mid-Nov. to late Jan. Farther north of the city, in Bundoora, **LaTrobe University** (☎9479 1357) also offers accommodation at two of its colleges in basic dorm rooms with hallway bathroom, laundry, and kitchen on most floors. **Chisholm College** caters toward backpackers. (☎9479 2875; singles $16.50, weekly $105; doubles $26/$166; available mid-Nov. to early Feb.) **Menzies College** is a cheaper option, only if you have a full-time student ID. (☎9479 1071; singles $11-12; mid-Nov. to late Jan.) Take bus #350 (45min.) or #250 (1hr.) from Flinders St. Station.

Unless noted otherwise, all accommodations have a common room with TV, hall baths, 24hr. access, luggage storage, a guest kitchen, laundry machines ($2-3 wash, $1-2 dry), free linens, and no chore requirements. An increasingly popular form of deposit is an international passport in lieu of cash. You can generally get your passport back for the evening should you need it for ID purposes (many bars and clubs do not take student IDs or drivers' licenses).

CITY CENTER

The Greenhouse Backpacker, 228 Flinders Ln. (☎9639 6400; www.ron.com.au). Near Swanston St. Reception is on the 6th Floor. Most rooms have 4 beds with spring mattresses, large lockers, sparkling bathrooms, cable TV, communal dining room, industrial-size kitchen, and roof garden. Helpful staff offers regional tours, job advice, and travel services. Pub crawl every Th night in coordination with The Friendly (see below) Free Internet 30min. per day. Coffee, tea, and first-morning brekkie included. Dorms $24; singles $50; doubles $66. Cheaper weekly rates. Wheelchair accessible.

The Friendly Backpacker, 197 King St. (☎9670 1111 or 1800 671 115; fax 9670 9911; friendlybpacker@optusnet.com.au). 1 block east of Spencer St. Station at the corner of Little Bourke St. Not the mega-hostel like its brother the Greenhouse, but smaller and friendlier. Hallway lounges on each of 4 floors encourage interaction; cable TV and TV/VCR with movie collection encourage loafing. Weekly in-house and on-the-town activities. Heat and A/C, free Internet 30min. per day, coffee and tea, and first-morning brekkie included. Key deposit $10. Check-out 10am. Book 1 week in advance Oct.-May. Free pickup from bus station, Tassie ferry, and around town. Dorms $20, weekly $126; Oct.-Mar. $22/$140. Wheelchair accessible.

Flinders Station Hotel Backpackers, 35 Elizabeth St. (☎9620 5100; www.flinders-backpackers.com.au). 1 block north of Flinders St. Station, on the corner of Flinders Ln. The hotel is just as active as its city surroundings. Job assistance, Internet, large kitchen with gigantic walk-in refrigerator, and 24hr. supermarket across the street. The slightly seedy "Joint" bar upstairs hops until 3am nightly. Passport or driver's license key deposit. Check-out 11am. No heat or A/C, but rooms retain heat in the winter. 2-bed dorms $22, weekly $346; 3 or 4-bed dorms $17/$109; twins and doubles $55/$346; doubles with bath $64/$399. Prices may fluctuate Aug.-May. $10-12 discount and free jug of beer on weekly payment. Wheelchair accessible.

Exford Hotel, 199 Russell St. (☎9663 2697; www.exfordhotel.com.au). At the corner of Little Bourke St., in Chinatown. Basic pub accommodations, but the multicolored walls and panelling give the Exford a bright and happy feel. Some rooms offer up-and-close views of the Chinatown gates. Pub downstairs draws locals and travelers until 3am nightly. Internet $2 per 30min. No heat or A/C. Lockers in rooms. Passport or driver's license key deposit. Check-out 11am. Dorms 8-bed $17; 4-bed $18; 2-bed $22; twins and doubles $49; prices rise Oct.-May.

JUST NORTH OF THE CITY CENTER

Walk uphill on Elizabeth St. past La Trobe St. or take tram #19, 55, 57, or 59 to some of the nicest budget accommodations in town.

Hotel Bakpak, 167 Franklin St. (☎9329 7525 or 1800 645 200; www.bakpak.com/hotelbakpak), between Elizabeth and Queen St. This cavernous 6-level facility can sleep up to 650 and has established itself as a pulsing, party-hearty nerve center for Melbourne's backpacker scene. Bathrooms can be a mystifying trek from far-away rooms, and paper-thin walls may compromise privacy (or sleep), but no one beats Bakpak's cornucopia of amenities, including a budget travel agency, free airport pickup, employment service, basement "Roo Bar," cafe, Internet $6 per hr., small movie theater, and unique "Cabana style" showers. Roo Bar parties with daily Happy Hours that offer amazingly cheap drinks and provide a great way to meet fellow travelers. No smoking. Breakfast included. 10- to 16-bed barrack $18; smaller dorms $20-22; singles $45; twins and doubles $50. VIP.

Stork Hotel, 504 Elizabeth St. (☎9663 6237; www.storkhotel.com). At the corner of Therry St., adjacent to the QVM. Brimming with character, this historic building combines history with art for an entertaining home-away-from-home. All rooms are designed thematically; ask for the Great Ocean Road room, the Foster's Lager room, or, yes, even the Ned Kelly room (see **Old Melbourne Gaol,** p. 524). Ground-floor pub attracts a quirky mix of locals and travelers and hosts live music featuring area artists nightly (no cover). Sunny cafe attached makes cheap meals with fresh market produce. Towel and soap included. 5-bed dorm $25; singles $48; twins and doubles $58.

Toad Hall, 441 Elizabeth St. (☎9600 9010; www.toadhall-hotel.com.au), between A'Beckett and Franklin St. A classier, more reserved place, several cuts above the frenetic backpacker scene, Toad Hall combines the intimacy of a B&B with the conveniences and attentive staff of a large inn. Airy kitchen, plant-filled patio, quiet reading room, and basement den with cable TV, VCR, and stereo. Shared bathrooms; larger dorms have bath. Cushy quilt included. Laundry facilities and off-street parking. Heat in private rooms and larger dorms. Key deposit $20. Reception daily 7am-10pm. Check-out 10am. Dorms $20 in winter, $25 in summer; singles, twins, and doubles $60, with bath $90. Bookings advised. VIP/YHA. MC/V.

Hotel Y, 489 Elizabeth St. (☎9329 5188 or 1800 249 124; www.travel-ys.com). Between Therry and Franklin St., less than a block from the Transit Center. The Y has the feel of a luxury hotel with stellar rooms with bath, snazzy lobby, and the sleek Café Y. Internet $2 per 30 min. Coffee, tea, TV, phone, soap, and shampoo in every room. The roof garden and hallway picture-windows offer high-rise views of the city below. Budget singles $80, deluxe with A/C $90; twins and doubles $98/$120; triples $109/$131. YMCA/YWCA 10% discount. Book several weeks ahead. Credit card to confirm booking.

NORTH MELBOURNE

Residential North Melbourne is quieter and more relaxed than the city center. Though its accommodations are quite a hike from downtown, it's accessible by tram #57 and 59 from Elizabeth St. and tram #55 from William St.

Queensberry Hill YHA, 78 Howard St. (☎9329 8599; queensberryhill@yhavic.org.au). Take tram #55 north from William St. to stop 11 on Queensberry St., then go 2 blocks west to Howard St. Fairly institutional but unquestionably functional, this YHA is a congregation of services beyond simple shelter from the storm. Free parking and bike hire, passes to the city baths, rooftop patio with BBQ, licensed bistro, travel agency, huge kitchen, pool tables, Internet $4 per hr. Currency exchange $2 fee. 2-week max. stay. Dorms $20-22; singles $55; doubles with bath $78; family rooms $85. Extra $3.50 for non-YHA. Book ahead in summer. Wheelchair accessible.

Chapman Gardens YHA Hostel, 76 Chapman St. (☎9328 3595; chapman@yhavic.org.au). Take tram #57 north to stop 18, turn right onto Chapman St., and the hostel is on the left. As a newly-designated ECO-hostel, the C-Gardens uses solar heating, recycles everything from clothing to food waste, and raises their own worms to fertilize the backyard herb gardens. Small but cozy rooms in a quiet, residential neighborhood, with a gazebo out back. Free parking, bike hire, and passes to the city baths. Breakfast $5. Luggage storage $2. Key deposit $10. Reception daily 7:30am-12:30pm and 2-10pm. 3-,4-, and 5-bed dorms $21; dorm twins $22; singles $40; doubles $50. Extra $3.50 for non-YHA. 7th night free May-Nov. Book ahead.

FITZROY

The Nunnery, 116 Nicholson St. (☎9419 8637 or 1800 032 635; www.bakpak.com/nunnery). Stop 13 on tram #96, at the northeast corner of Carlton Gardens. Housed in the former convent of the Daughters of Mercy, this heavenly hostel has large dorms, halls that are snazzily decorated with an incongruous mix of religious paraphernalia and New Age psychedelia, a breezy wooden deck with BBQ, and rooms with balconies overlooking the Gardens. The attached "guest house" is considerably quieter, with upscale "boutique" rooms featuring classy wicker furniture and fireplaces. Towel and soap included. Free soup W night, wine-and-cheese F night, and pancakes Su brekkie. Internet $2 per 30min. Key deposit $20 or passport. Check-out 9:30am. Reception 8am-8pm. Dorms: 3-bed $25, weekly $165; 10-12 bed $20/$315; 6-8 bed $22/$144; 4-bed $24/$158. Singles $50/$315; bunk twins $55-60/$380; twins and doubles $60-70/$450; triples $85/$560. Boutique double $85, family $90. VIP.

MIDDLE PARK

Middle Park Hotel, 102 Canterbury Rd. (☎9690 1882; www.middleparkhotel.com). Across from the Middle Park stop on trams #95 and 96. 1km from St. Kilda, under 400m from the beach. Quality budget accommodation in a restored 1890s building with high ceilings, clean rooms, and spacious hallway showers. Plans include installation of a glass microbrewery so that patrons can watch their beer being born on the spot. Job placement assistance. No heating, though thick doonas are provided. Towel and M-F breakfast included. Key deposit $10. Reception M-F 7:30am-5pm, Sa 9am-1pm; arrange ahead for after-hours or Su check-in. 4-to 6-bed dorms $18.70, weekly $107.80; singles $38.50/$214.50; doubles $55/$275.

SOUTH YARRA AND PRAHRAN

Chapel St. Backpackers (NOMADS), 22 Chapel St., Prahran (☎9533 6855; www.csbackpackers.com.au). Just north of Dandenong Rd. across from Windsor train station, on tram routes #78 and 79. One of the best places in town, just a stumble from both Melbourne's best nightlife and St. Kilda. Staff is super-friendly and guests are social, often teaming up to hit the local hotspots. Dorms and doubles all have refreshingly clean bathrooms. Heat and A/C. Breakfast included. Internet $6 per hr. Key deposit $20. Check-out 10:30am. 6-bed dorms $19, weekly $126; 4-bed dorms $22/$147; twins $48/$322; doubles $65/$448. Prices rise slightly in the summer.

Claremont B&B, 189 Toorak Rd., South Yarra (☎9826 8000 or 1800 818 851; www.hotelclaremont.com). One block east of the South Yarra train station, on tram route #8. The only budget stay in one of the poshest sections of Melbourne. A beautifully refurbished 1886 building, it retains much of its Victorian charm while still providing all the modern amenities. Clean, bright rooms with hardwood floors, wrought-iron

THE HOUSE OF BAD TASTE. If you drive down Canterbury Rd. from St. Kilda toward the city centre, be prepared for a double-take. Along the right side of the road, amidst scores of standard modern homes, there stands a monstrous creation: a house with a completely flat front covered in shiny laser- blue paneling. If your eyes aren't too sore, take a closer look. Yep, that's Pamela Anderson's face imprinted across the entire two-floor facade. You gotta wonder if the neighbors enjoy watching the owner drive his car out of the busty blonde's mouth every morning. Ouch.

beds, heaters, ceiling fans, and TVs. Small but spotless hall baths. Breakfast included. Internet $6 per hr. Singles $56; doubles/twin $68; additional person $10; peak season $10 surcharge. $12 per day discount for weekly payments. Reservations essential.

Lord's Lodge, 204 Punt Rd., Prahran (☎9510 5658; fax 9533 6663). Take tram #3, 5, 6, 16, 64, or 67 south on St. Kilda Rd to stop 26 and walk east 2 blocks along Moubray St. A bit removed from both Prahran and St. Kilda, but a short walk to several tram stops as well as Albert Park and Commercial Rd. This reasonably clean dig attracts seasoned travelers of all types. All rooms have heaters, lockers, and fridges, except for the one tiny single dubbed the "dog's box." Three private bungalows out back also have TV. Coffee and tea included. Cheap Internet and fax. Reception M-Sa 8:30-11:30am and 5-6pm, Su 8:30-11:30am. 4-to 8-bed dorms $18, weekly $115; dog's box $25; doubles and bungalows $45, in summer $55.

ST. KILDA

St. Kilda is **backpacker heaven,** with dirt-cheap and often unkempt, grungy hostels—but hey, you get what you pay for. The hostels, centered around Grey St., largely mirror the precinct's fun-loving, gritty flavor. Though removed from the city center, it's easily accessible by tram (stop 133 on lines #16 and 96). The beach, restaurants, and lively nightlife of St. Kilda are in easy reach. If you're coming in March, book way ahead to avoid the hassle of the Grand Prix crowd (see p. 530).

Olembia, 96 Barkly St. (☎9537 1412; www.olembia.com.au). Tucked behind a small canopy near the intersection with Grey St. You'll never believe you're in a hostel. Gorgeous living room with sofas and fireplace, glass doors, and a loving feline named Alexander the Great. Ornate, high-ceilinged heated rooms with comfy mattresses are impeccably clean, as are the bathrooms. Sincere and friendly staff will point you to all the best places in town. Was home ever this good? Free parking. Bike hire $12 per day. 1 week max. stay. Key deposit $10. Reception 7am-1pm and 5-8pm. 3- to 4-bed dorms $24; singles $46; twins and doubles with box-springs $68. Book ahead in summer.

Jackson's Manor, 53 Jackson St. (☎9534 1877; www.jacksonsmanor.com.au). The one-time home of a rich English architect (Mr. Jackson), this little gem attracts a quieter crowd. It is well-heated and impeccably clean throughout, with comfortable rooms and a spacious living area featuring plants, stained glass windows, and a large oriental rug. Amenities include a furnished kitchen, ping pong and foosball room, Internet $4 per hr. Job and travel assistance. The proximity of the other Grey St. backpackers, but without all the grunge. Free parking. 4-bed dorms $22, 6-to 8-bed $20; twins and doubles $30. $12-14 discount for weekly stays.

Pint on Punt (NOMADS), 42 Punt Rd. (☎9510 4273 or 1800 737 378; admin@pintonpunt.com.au). Just north of St. Kilda Junction, on the corner of Peel St. Take tram #3, 5, 16, 64, or 67 from Flinders St. Station. New and clean, the Pint has large rooms with new mattresses. Free continental breakfast, and 30% discount offered on pub meals downstairs. Open mic W nights and live music Th-Su, but rooms generally stay quiet. Free pickup from city or airport; arrange ahead. Internet $1 per 15min. Key deposit $10. Check-in at reception 7am-noon or at the bar until 1am. Bar open M-Sa noon-1am, Su till 11pm. 4- to 6-bed dorms $17-22; singles $35; twins and doubles $45. 7th night free. NOMADS/VIP/YHA.

Enfield House, 2 Enfield St. (☎1800 302 121; infoenfield@bakpakgroup.com). Take tram #16 or 96 to stop 30 by Fitzroy and Grey St. Walk half a block down Grey St. turn right on Jackson St., then left onto Enfield St. Same owners as **Hotel Bakpak** downtown, but much more mellow. Front living room hosts M movie nights on a funky old-time projector. Circus-colored heated rooms and shared bathrooms are clean. Job assistance. Free continental breakfast M-F, pancakes Sa-Su. Reception daily 8am-8pm, closed Sa-Su 1-5pm. 4-to 8-bed dorms $19-20; singles $40; twins and doubles $50; triples $62. 7th night free. Prices rise $2-3 in summer. Book ahead in summer.

Coffee Palace Backpackers Hotel, 24 Grey St. (☎9534 5283 or 1800 654 098; www.backpackerscentre.com). 1 block off Fitzroy St. Really popular, but only with those who enjoy a party atmosphere. Plenty of amenities, from travel and employment services to a games room, to free pickup from bus station or airport. Hallway walls are notable for their impressive artwork but not for their soundproofing. Morning pancakes included. Internet $5 per hr. Key deposit passport. 4-6-bed dorms $17-18, with bath $20; twins and doubles $44. Prices rise in summer. VIP.

The Ritz for Backpackers, 169 Fitzroy St. (☎9525 3501 or 1800 670 364). Tram #16 lets off at stop 132 out front. Just above the **Elephant and Wheelbarrow** (see p. 534), the Ritz is friendly and active. Group activities inspire close bonds between staff and guests; ask to see the "book of communal love" if you want proof, or you have some stories of your own to share. Rooms are fairly sparse, but the 10-bed apartment suite upstairs has a couch, kitchen, and large windows with a view of Albert Park. Deposit for doona. Free morning pancakes. Key deposit passport or license. Check-out 9:30am. Internet $5 per hr. Reception 6am-10pm. Limited positions available to work in exchange for accommodation. Dorms $18-20; twins and doubles $44-48; apartment suite $21. Prices rise in summer. VIP.

Leopard House, 27 Grey St. (☎9534 1200). An old brick building on the corner of Jackson St. Basic bunk accommodations, the larger dorms with bath. Front patio area is a raucous social center on summer evenings. Key deposit passport or license. Limited car parking. 24hr. check-in. Check-out 9:30am. All dorms $15 winter, $20 summer.

Oslo Hotel, 38 Grey St. (☎9525 4498 or 1800 501 752; www.oslohotel.com.au). Sparse and somewhat grungy accommodation offers large backpacker dorm with bath, TV lounge suitable for groups on extended stays. Some of the better doubles have TV, fridge, toaster, and balcony access. 3 fully-furnished townhouses out back are considerably nicer but require a 2-month minimum stay. Key deposit $10. Internet $1 per 15min. Free pick up from bus station. Reception 9am-midnight. Dorms $18; doubles $55; townhouses $270 per week upon negotiation only.

FOOD

Of the Australian cities known for great food, Melbourne has perhaps the most diversity, taking its cuisine from the multicultural makeup. Explore steamy Chinatown holes-in-the-wall, Fitzroy *café couture*, Carlton's Italian cuisine, South Yarra's sidewalk bistros, or St. Kilda's mix of backpacker-targeted and upscale eateries. Multicultural influences give rise to interesting hybrids, with Chinese restaurants serving french fries, sushi, and cappuccino. The city's restaurants constitute a scene in and of themselves; on most nights, Melburnians pack into their favorite eateries until closing time (which is often whenever the proprietors feel like shutting the doors). Enjoy.

CITY CENTER

Amid the fast-paced urban jungle of Melbourne's CBD lurk what seem like a million fantastic eateries, hidden away in labyrinthine corridors or diminutive crannies between high-rise buildings. Many are Asian, including Chinese, Japanese, Indian, Nepalese, Sri Lankan, Malaysian, Indonesian, and Vietnamese. Neon-pulsing **Chinatown** fills the stretch of Little Bourke St. hemmed in by colorful red gates between Swanston and Exhibition St. Blink and you'll miss the **Greek Precinct,** on Lonsdale St. between Swanston and Russell St. It's only a half dozen or so pricey Hellenic restaurants and taverns, but serves god-like baklava. Many of the coolest cafes, most with a European air, call the CBD home as well; they often lurk in narrow brick pathways (such as the Block Arcade, between Collins and Little Collins St.) that snake through the city. For those do-it-yourself folks, a Coles 24-hr. **supermarket** hides amidst the bustle of Elizabeth St. just north of Flinders St. Above all, the city center rewards the adventurous gourmet; wander around with only your nose and palate as a guide and you're sure to find a culinary treasure.

Cafée Baloo, 260 Russell St. (☎9663 3226), between Little Lonsdale and Lonsdale St. A great bargain, mixing South Asian fare with pasta and sandwiches in an environs that attain just the right balance of dark and trendy with laid-back and friendly. Heaping portions of tasty curry and pasta with or without meat, all around $6-10. 50¢ table charge per person; no alcohol. Open M-F noon-10pm, Sa-Su 4-10pm.

Crossways Food For Life, 123 Swanston St. (☎9650 2939). Across from Town Hall. Satisfy your spirit and your stomach. All-you-can-eat vegetarian specials including rice, vegetable, dessert, and lassi only $5.50 ($3.80 concessions); a copy of "On the way to Krishna" and the "Bhagavad-gita" on every table. This lunch-only hole-in-the-wall attracts an eclectic crowd, from backpackers to businessmen. Its narrow door is difficult to spot, though the periodic Hare Krishna chanters outside help point the way to both food and enlightenment. Open M-Sa 11:30am-2:30pm.

Teayara Cafe and Gallery Restaurant, 230 King St. (☎9600 2777). Between Little Bourke and Londsdale St. Opened in May 2001, this classy new dive offers quality pastas ($5.50), coffee and cake specials ($4), and a gradual integration of Indonesian fare. Upstairs seating amongst authentic Indonesian paintings, masks, and furniture provides a romantic and exotic setting. Fully licensed and BYO. Open M-Sa 7am-late.

Krome Kafe, 273 Swanston St (☎9663 8199). Dark and laid-back, the Krome is all style. Breakfast is served all day, and there's an extensive cocktail selection. Live entertainment F night. Open Su-Th 8am-11pm, F-Sa 8am-1am. MC/V.

Nudo, 181 Russell St. (☎9639 8998), between Bourke and Little Bourke St. Not much on atmosphere (think bustling and orange), but for $5-10 you get a huge platter of stir fried noodles, rice, or noodle soups with your choice of meat. BYO. Open Su-Th 11am-11pm, F-Sa 11am-1am.

Stalactites, 177-183 Little Lonsdale St. (☎9663 3316). On the corner of Russell St. Somewhat pricey like most of its Greek Precinct counterparts, but a bit less upscale. Teeming with local Greeks, along with the background bazooki music. The $11 appetizer sampler gives a taste of nearly every little dip, snack, and meat the Mediterranean has to offer. $6 souvlaki and gyros. Cheap take-away menu. Licensed and BYO. Open 24hr. AmEx/DC/MC/V.

Fast Eddy's Cafe, 32 Bourke St. (☎9662 3551). A fave-rave with the late-night crowd for its 24hr. greasy breakfast and burgers.

NORTH MELBOURNE

The Queen Victoria Market (**QVM;** see p. 524) serves as the focal point of culinary North Melbourne. In fact, much of the city congregates here, where you can get all the fresh ingredients you need to cook up an inexpensive fabulous dinner. The surrounding area is home to some fine eateries as well. From the city, take any tram north on William or Elizabeth St.

La Porchetta, 302-308 Victoria St. (☎9326 9884), across from the QVM. Hundreds of tantalizing wood-fired pizzas (small $4.80, medium $6.10, large $7.20) of excellent quality at unbeatable prices. Takeaway available. Fully licensed and BYO wine only. Open M-Th 11am-midnight, F-Sa 11am-1am.

The White Lotus, 185 Victoria St. (☎9326 6040). 1 block west of QVM. Entirely vegan menu attempts to guide the "way to heaven," following the Buddhist tenets of Tien Tao. All meals prepared without meat, animal products, or even onions and garlic. Carnivores will be placated–nay, amazed–by the excellent imitation meat dishes, like mock abalone made from soy and wheat gluten or the spicy Mongolian "beef." Meals $8-14. Dine-in or take-away. BYO. Open Th-F noon-2:30pm, daily 5:30-11pm.

Vic Marketplace (☎9320 5822). In the QVM. The food court has excellent budget fare, mostly made from fresh goods sold next door. **Vic Fish** serves a $6.50 fish'n'chips lunch packet. **Afghan** purveys middle eastern breads, kabobs, falafel, and dips (4-7). The **Consciousness Café** has healthy salads and sandwiches ($4-6). Hours vary, but market usually open: Tu and Th 6am-2pm, F 6am-6pm, Sa 6am-3pm, Su 9am-4pm.

aioli, 229 Victoria St. (☎9328 1090), 2 blocks west of QVM. Bright green and red walls only enhance the liveliness that wafts through this classy, healthy culinary establishment. A variety of wraps run $6, while the uniquely blended "aioli cleanser" drink goes for $3.50. Open Tu-Sa 7:30am-4:30pm, Su 10am-3pm.

Annapurna Vegie Hut, 199 Victoria St. (☎9328 5050). After years of catering to carnivores, the friendly vegetarian owner decided to follow his dream and serve what he believes in. Tasty vegetarian curries and pastas are cheap ($4.50-6.50), but the "thali" special, including 2 curries, naan or roti, and pappadum, is the real bargain ($6). Dine-in or takeaway. BYO. Open M-Sa 10:30am-2:30pm and daily 5-10pm.

CARLTON

The best known street in Carlton is **Lygon St.,** where tons of chic Italian pizzerias, cafes, and gelaterias combat budget but tasty Thai and Vietnamese joints along the five-block stretch between Queensberry St. to the south and Elgin St. to the north. The eclectic nature of the area decidedly draws in a diverse crowd; and despite its attendant student traffic from the nearby University of Melbourne, most of the Italian eateries remain out of the budget traveler's range. There are, however, a fair number of affordable non-Italian places, and a few cafes where you can find cheap dishes. Not much exploration is necessary to find a fine eatery.

Threshermans Bakehouse Café, 221 Faraday St. (☎9349 2319). The lunch and dinner at this casual eatery-baker are probably the best value in Carlton: $6 for a large plate of Asian stir-fry, $3.80 for a foccacia pizza. With all the money you've saved on dinner, head over to the other counter for a delicious canoli ($2.50) or an enormous slice of cake ($4.20). Fresh, creative fruit juices ($3.70) are squeezed before your very eyes. Open daily 6am-11pm; hot food served 11am-11pm.

Tiamo, 303 Lygon St. (☎9347 5759). Dark and flavorful, this pasta palace dishes out a range of Italian fare. Its next-door sequel, **Tiamo2** (☎9347 0911) serves a more sophisticated selection in a lighter, classier setting. Cooked-to-perfection pasta $10-12, creamy tiramisu $6, breakfast until noon $4-10.50. *"Ti amo"* means "I love you" in Italian, and perhaps you'll fall in love with this place. If you do, you're utterly desperate. It's just a restaurant–get a grip. Licensed and BYO. Tiamo open M-Sa 7am-11pm, Su 8am-10pm; Tiamo2 open M-Sa 9:30am-10:30pm.

Toto's, 101 Lygon St. (☎9437 1630). Big and busy, Toto's serves a range of meals (from pasta to sirloin to fish-of-the-day), but their pizza's the real sensation. 3 sizes and about a dozen combinations, all hot, chewy, and flavorful ($7-11). Licensed and BYO wine. Open M-F noon-9pm and Sa 11:30am-11pm. V.

Jive, 131 Lygon St. (☎9347 6666). Very popular with the uni crowd, Jive's walls are splashed with big bold colors, and its food is good and cheap. Sound system reverberates to accompany the Asian noodles, pastas, and pizzas of all venues ($6-13). Dine-in or takeaway. The bar gets funky F-Sa. Open Su-Th 4pm-1am, F-Sa until 3am. MC/V.

FITZROY AND COLLINGWOOD

The heart of Melbourne's bohemian scene and cafe society lies in Fitzroy, along **Brunswick St.** between Gertrude and Princes St. Particularly on sunny weekend days, hippies, post-hippies, ferals, and freaks of every ilk frequent the countless artsy coffeehouses and eateries. As always, though, much mainstream and wanna-be chic intermingles with their opposites in an attempt to feel cutting edge. The area gets progressively posher as you go south along Brunswick, closer to the city. The stretch of Johnston St. just west of Brunswick St. is Melbourne's Latin Quarter, with Latin dance clubs, Iberian grocers, and several great—but pricey—tapas bars. There are also dining options galore along **Smith St.** in Collingwood.

Nyala, 113 Brunswick St. (☎9419 9128). The best of East Africa, with some Gambia and Morocco thrown in for kicks. Nyala is all about flavor; meat and vegetable mains ($11-15) retain their natural savory goodness while enhanced by special combinations of season and spice. If you're strapped for cash, try one of the tasty dips, served with the delightfully satisfying thin Mahloul bread ($5.50). You'll have room for one of their rich desserts ($4-6) and still be able to reach the $10 per person minimum (only on F-Sa nights). Open W-Su 11:30am-3pm, Tu-Su 6-10:30pm.

Hideout Café, 389 Brunswick St. (☎9419 6222). Half-cartoon, half-cafe, the Hideout is anything but hiding. If you can see over your unusually high table, you'll find the menu superb: breakfast, mains, and a long list of "Snax" means there's something for everyone. Even the smallest sized nachos ($9.50) could feed a group large enough to fit in the gigantic, colorful booths that line the side wall. The thick milkshakes come in regular ($5.50) and naughty (alcoholic, $12). Open Su-W 7am-1am, Th-Sa 7am-3am.

Vegie Bar, 380 Brunswick St. (☎9417 6935). A converted warehouse where Fitzroy's large meat-averse population gathers to chow guilt-free, single-g "vegie" meals. They promise "food for the body and soul" and serve it up in heaping portions. Mains all under $9.30. Quiet during the day, but evenings draw a crowd. Loads of vegan and wheat-free options. Fully licensed and BYO wine only. Open daily 11am-10pm.

Mario's, 303 Brunswick St. (☎9417 3343). This cafe is hard to spot–a small neon sign bears its name–but it sports some of the best breakfast buys in town ($6.50-10), served all day. Those who spurn the first meal of the day can grab $9-17 pasta dishes or just pop in for a gourmet dessert ($5-7). Fully licensed. Open daily 7am-midnight.

Retro Café, 413 Brunswick St. (☎9419 9103; www.retro.net.au), on the corner of Westgarth St. If you think the bright yellow facade on the building is cool, check out the waterfall and TV-turned-aquarium inside. Meals run the gamut in both price and cuisine, from Mediterranean stuffed grape leaves ($5.50) to the age-old Aussie kangaroo with roasted root veggies ($19). Open daily 8am-1am; breakfast is served until 6pm.

Robert Burns Hotel, 376 Smith St. (☎9417 2233). Just north of Johnston St. Behind the uncharacteristic non-Iberian name hides great value Spanish fare. Eat in the large, simple restaurant, or for a cheaper meal, sit in the bright front bar. Beyond the standard tortilla, the Robbie Burns serves a range of steaks $12-24. Seafood galore from $10. Paella $15 per person, 2-person min. Tapas served from 2:30pm in the bar. Bar open M-Sa 11am-midnight; kitchen open M-Sa noon-2:30pm and 6-10pm. MC/V.

SOUTH YARRA AND PRAHRAN

Preened, pricey South Yarra aggressively markets itself as the place to see and be seen, and its mod-Oz bistros with sidewalk seating see their share of black-clad fashion mavens after a day of shopping on Chapel St. There are some excellent budget options though, particularly south of Commercial St. in more down-to-earth Prahran. The ubiquitous coffee bars are a wallet-friendly way to sample the scene (cappuccino around $2.50). Check out the Prahran Market, on Commercial Rd. at Izett St., for cheap, fresh produce, meat, and ethnic foodstuffs.

Gurkha's Brasserie, 190-192 Chapel St. (☎9510 3325; www.gurkhas.com.au). Delicious Nepalese cuisine comes at a reasonable price in an ornate restaurant bedecked with lanterns and peaceful South Asian music. It might take you a while to figure out what to order, but a good bet is the *Dal Bhat Masu*, which comes with your choice of meat curry (the goat is wonderfully tender), soup, and rice or bread for only $13.50. Licensed and BYO wine ($1 corkage per person). Open daily 5:30-10:30pm.

Afrakico Cafe-Bar, 67 Green St. (☎9529 3590), off Chapel St. in Prahran. This one-time cafe/hair salon (no joke!) now specializes in toasted wraps of all varieties, from Mexican to tropical to the elusive "magic wrap" ($5.50-7). Tons of veggie options go well with refreshingly thick "jungle-juice" smoothies ($3.90). Zebra-print couches, scattered wooden elephants, and upbeat African tunes make Afrakico simultaneously kitchy and cultural. Fully licensed. Open Su-W 8:30am-6pm, Th-Sa until 1am.

Jamon Sushi, 205 Greville St. (☎9510 2928). Around the corner from the bustle of Chapel St., this place is not cheap, but the sushi is absolutely divine. After two bites of the sushi and roll combo platter, the $20+ you just forked over will be but a distant memory. Sushi or sashimi platters $13.50-22.50; sushi and nori roll lunch boxes $12-20. Fully licensed. Open daily 6:30pm-late.

Gelato Bar, Shop 3, 534 Chapel St. (☎9824 0099). Offering some of the cheapest meals in South Yarra, this new and colorful cafe is a good break from shopping or people-watching. Deli-style foccacia sandwiches, filled pastries, and calzones ($5.90); homemade gelati ice cream indulgence ($3-5.50). For a substantial snack, try one of their enormous seasoned breadsticks, served hot ($1). Open daily 8am-late.

That Little Noodle Place, 565 Chapel St. (☎9827 3148). The name says it all: noodles, done in a ton of Asian varieties. Design your own from a selection of all kinds of meat, veggies, and sauce. Soups and noodle dishes $9.50. Young waitstaff provide lightning-fast service. Fully licensed. Dine-in or takeaway. Open daily 11:30am-10:30pm.

ST. KILDA

With all the hipness of South Yarra and Chapel St. but far less pretentious, St. Kilda offers diverse and exciting menus in quality affordable eateries interspersed with many decidedly non-budget options. The result is a delightful mix of value and vogue. You can't go wrong with the holes-in-the-wall or fancier bistros on Fitzroy St.; the Barkly St. end of Acland St.—legendary among locals for its divine cake shops—also has a menagerie of great cuisine of all ethnic stripes. Coles 24hr. **supermarket** is located in the Acland Court shopping center near Barkly St.

Chinta Ria, 94 Acland St. (☎9525 4666). The point of "soul" in a local Malaysian restaurant triangle (its sister fares are home to the "jazz," 9/176 Commercial Rd., Prahran; and "blues," 6 Acland St., St. Kilda). New York chic but still contemplative, Ria matches its delectable $15-19 mains with comparable-quality. Fried rice and noodle selections $8-12. The changing dessert menu is sweet and sinful ($7-10). Open M-Sa noon-2:30pm and 6-10:30pm, Su noon-2:30pm and 6-10pm. MC/V.

Monarch Cake Shop, 103 Acland St. (☎9534 2972). The oldest cake shop on Acland St. (est. 1934 in Carlton, moved to St. Kilda late 1930s) and still the best. Their famous plum cake is the most popular seller ($3 slice), but the chocolate *kugelhopf* is near orgasm ($13-14). Open daily 7-9am to 10pm.

Wild Rice, 211 Barkly St., or 159 Chapel St. (☎9534 2849). This place doesn't look like much, but enter to find an imaginative vegan selection. Meals are based on the principle of "macrobiotics": basically, they only use seasonal produce in order to "balance the body's energy." Rice, veggie, and noodle mains $10-14, but pakhoras and tofu pockets fall under $7. Lush garden courtyard out back. Open daily noon-10pm.

Big Mouth, 168 Acland St. (☎9534 4611). On the corner of Barkly St. Hip and happening, Big Mouth serves bountiful breakfast deep into the afternoon to satisfy its late-rising, young clientele. The upstairs restaurant, complete with colorful couches, only opens evenings and Su, but the loud and lively main cafe serves all day long. Breakfast, lunch, and dinner $7-13. Fully licensed. Open daily 10:30am-late.

Seafood Shack, 47 Fitzroy St. (☎9534 7777). Not too romantic, but offers a gigantic fish'n'chips "shack pack" for a mere $5.70. Open daily noon-10pm.

Hard Wok Cafe (☎9534 6803), next door to the Seafood Shack, hosts the backpackers banquet: curry, rice, asian greens, prawn crackers, spring rolls, chips, roti, and a glass of wine ($8.95 per person, 2 person minimum). Open Su-F noon-late, Sa 5pm-late.

SIGHTS

CITY CENTER

RIALTO TOWERS. Rising 253m above the city, the Rialto Towers is the tallest office building in the Southern Hemisphere. The 55th floor observation deck provides spectacular 360° views of the city and surrounds. The assuredly addictive "Zoom City" live-action video cameras allow you to zoom in and literally see people crossing the street all the way across town. **Rialtovision Theatre** plays a 20min. film, *Melbourne, the Living City* that highlights Victoria's tourist spots with cheesy music and dramatic, wide-angle shots. *(525 Collins St. 1 block east of Spencer St. Station between King and William St. ☎9629 8222; www.melbournedeck.com.au. Open Su-Th 10am-10pm, F-Sa 10am-11pm. Film every 30min. Film and deck admission $10.50, concessions $8, child $6, family $29.50.)* To those without the deep pockets, **Hotel Sofitel,** at the opposite end of Collins St., at the intersection with Exhibition St., offers a similar view, free of charge. Ascend to the 35th floor bathroom, lean out the window with care, and stare into the abyss of the Melbourne skyline.

IMMIGRATION MUSEUM. Chronicling the 200 years of Australian immigration, the museum combines excellent pictures and interactive technology with compelling testimony. A mock ship in the main room shows typical living quarters aboard ocean-going ships from the 1840s to the 1950s. Recent efforts have also begun to explore the Aboriginal experience as a struggle to maintain a sense of continuity among a foreign culture. Ground-floor resource center contains links to immigrant ship listings as well as a genealogy database. *(400 Flinders St. In the Old Customs House on the corner of William St. A City Circle Tram stop. ☎9927 2700; www.immigration.museum.vic.gov.au. Open daily 10am-5pm. Entry $7, concession and YHA $5.50, child $3.50, family $17.50; resource center free. Wheelchair accessible. AmEx/DC/MC/V.)*

ST. PAUL'S CATHEDRAL. The Anglican cathedral, completed in 1891, impresses not in its scale but in the intricacy of its detail. The beautifully stenciled pipes of the 19th-century Lewis organ are easy to miss; look up to the right of the altar. Evening song services echo throughout the hallowed hall M-F 5:10pm and Su 6pm. *(Presides over the corner of Flinders and Swanston St., diagonal Flinders St. Station. Enter on Swanston St. Open daily 7am-6pm. Free.)*

MELBOURNE CENTRAL MALL. This six-level megamall houses some of Australia's swankiest boutiques and cafes alongside tourist shops selling koala-and-kangaroo merchandise at outrageous prices. In the central atrium stands the 50m-tall Coop's Shot Tower, built in 1889-90, then Melbourne's highest structure. Today it houses shops and is enclosed by a soaring 20-story, 490-ton glass cone, the largest glass structure of its type in the world. A huge fob watch in the atrium in front of the Shot Tower has an automated Waltzing Matilda display on the hour—that tourists love and locals hate. A central stage enraptures hordes of schoolkids with shows and sing-alongs; Sundays see local caricature artists working their magic. *(At La Trobe and Swanston St. Open M-Th and Sa 10am-6pm, F 10am-9pm, Su 11am-6pm.)*

STATE LIBRARY OF VICTORIA. A great space to read or work, with a variety of international newspapers, the State Library is worth a visit if just for the interior design. The whole place is undergoing a $200 million renovation (completion date set for 2004) that will most notably reinstate glass to the roof of the Domed Reading Room, a spectacular octagonal space soaring 35m high. An eastern section, formerly the home of the Museum of Victoria (see p. 511), holds a fraction of the permanent collection of the **National Gallery of Victoria** (p. 526) while the gallery undergoes renovations. *(At La Trobe and Swanston St. ☎9669 9888; www.slv.vic.gov.au. Free tours M-F and every other Sa 2pm. Open M-Th 10am-9pm, F-Su 10am-6pm.)*

CHINATOWN. The pagoda gates at the corner of Swanston and Little Bourke St. indicate your arrival at a two-block stretch of Asian restaurants, groceries, and bars that was first settled by Chinese immigrants in the 1870s. A block and a half east, the back-alley **Chinese Museum** houses *Dai Loong* (Great Dragon), the **biggest imperial dragon in the world** (not the longest, which is in Bendigo VIC) and a staple of Melbourne's Moomba festival (p. 531) that is so huge it has to be wound around two entire floors. The third floor provides a brief but honest look at ethnic discrimination as well as some great photographs of influential Chinese community members in the early 20th century. *(22 Cohen Pl. ☎9662 2888. $6.50, concessions $4.50. Open daily 10am-4:30pm. Wheelchair accessible.)*

PARLIAMENT OF VICTORIA AND OLD TREASURY. Victoria's parliament is a stout, pillared 19th-century edifice every bit as stolid and imposing as a seat of government should be. Free tours detail the workings of the Victorian government and the architectural intricacies of the parliament chambers. *(Spring St. north of Bourke St. A City Circle Tram stop. ☎9651 8568; www.parliament.vic.gov.au. Tours when Parliament is not in session 10, 11am, noon, 2, 3, and 3:45pm. No self-guided tours.)* Designed in Italian Palazzo style by a 19-year-old prodigy, the **Old Treasury Building** contains a museum chronicling Melbourne's past, including some great stories about the idiosyncrasies of the city's first years. The gold vaults in the basement were built to prevent a crime wave that plagued the Treasury during the Victorian Gold Rush; now they house a multimedia exhibit detailing daily life and events of Melbourne's gold-rush era. *(Spring St., at Collins St. ☎9651 2233; www.oldtreasurymuseum.org.au. Open M-F 9am-5pm, Sa-Su 10am-4pm. $7.70, concessions $3.80, seniors $5.50.)*

FITZROY GARDENS. These gardens, originally laid out in the shape of the Union Jack, bloom year round. On the south end is Cook's Cottage, a small stone home constructed by Captain James Cook's family in England in 1755 and moved to Melbourne in 1934 to celebrate the city's centennial. Cook never actually reached the site and may not even have spent time in this house, but the information room has a concise but complete history of Cook's voyages. Next door is the Conservatory, a colorfully stocked greenhouse with seasonal plants and flowers. Weekends in Dec.-Jan. often bring concerts and other summer events to the gardens. *(Gardens bordered by Lansdowne, Albert, and Clarendon St., and Wellington Pde. Tram #48 or 75 from Flinders St. Free garden tour W 11am, starting from the conservatory. Cook's Cottage ☎9419 4677. Entry $3.30, concessions $2.20. Conservatory ☎9419 4118. Free tour W 12:30pm. Both open daily 9am-5pm. For more info, go to www.fitzroygardens.com.)*

ST. PATRICK'S CATHEDRAL. A beautiful product of Gothic revival, St. Patrick's comes replete with grotesque gargoyles, stained glass, and a magnificent altar. Among the traditional Catholic relics you'll also find an Aboriginal message stick and stone inlay, installed as a welcoming gesture to Aboriginal Catholics and a reconciliation for past wrongs against their people. The cathedral is most spectacular by night, when its 106m spires are illuminated by floodlights. *(West of the Fitzroy Garden's northwest corner on Cathedral Pl. ☎9662 2332. Open 7:30am-6pm. Free guided tour M-F 10am-noon. No tourists during mass M-Sa 7-7:30am and 1-1:20pm, Sa 8-8:30am, Su 7am-12:30pm and 6-7:30pm.)*

YARRA PARK AND THE MELBOURNE CRICKET GROUND (MCG). First established in 1853 and expanded in 1956 for the Olympics and again in 1992 to seat 92,000, the MCG functions as the sanctum sanctorum of Melbourne's robust sporting life. It houses Australian Rules Football (AFL) every weekend in winter, including the Grand Final the last Saturday in September. There are also, of course, cricket contests, from Oct.-Apr., highlighted by test matches between Australia and South Africa, England, New Zealand, Pakistan, and the West Indies. The north side of the MCG contains the **Australian Gallery of Sport and Olympic Museum** further celebrating Australia's love for sport. The venue houses the **Australian Cricket Hall of Fame** (which requires some understanding to appreciate), an AFL exhibition, a new feature on extreme sports, and the **Olympic Museum,** with a focus on Australian achievements and the '56 Melbourne games. The best way to see the stadium and gallery is by a guided tour from the northern entrance, which offers unique insight into the MCG's history, allowing you to step inside the player's changing rooms, the **Melbourne Cricket Club Museum,** and onto the hallowed turf itself. Entertaining guides make the 1hr. tour worth the price even if you don't have the slightest idea what the hell a wicket, over, or googlie are. *(Take the Met to Jolimont. ☎9657 8888; www.mcg.org.au. Tours run on all non-event days on the hour, and often every 30min. 10am-3pm. $16, concessions $10, families $40. Admission includes tour and access to galleries with audiocassette guide.)* **AFL games** are also a must, allowing you to experience firsthand an essential aspect of Melburnian culture. To achieve, or at least mimic, authenticity, order a meat pie and beer, choose a favorite team, and blow out your vocal chords along with the passionate crowd. *(All in Yarra Park, southeast of Fitzroy Gardens across Wellington Pde. Accessible via trams #48, 70, and 75. Tickets $15-22, concessions about half; prices vary by entrance gate, so search around.)*

MELBOURNE PARK (NATIONAL TENNIS CENTRE). To the west across the railroad tracks from the MCG and Yarra Park sits the ultramodern tennis facility, **Melbourne Park.** The entire complex, composed of the domed Rod Laver Arena, the new and sleek Vodafone Arena, and the numerous outer courts, hosts the **Australian Open** Grand Slam event every January. You can wander around and see the trophies and center court for free or take a 40min. guided tour. Though you can't follow in their footsteps on the center court, the outer courts give proximity to greatness for a $16-24 hourly playing fee. During the **Open,** a $20 ground pass will get you into every court except center; go during the first week and you'll see all the big-names beating up on the freshmen in the outer courts. *(Take tram #70 from Flinders St. Open M-F 9am-5pm. Tours $5, concession $2.50. Australian Open tickets ☎9286 1600. To hire a court, book at ☎9286 1244.)*

NORTH OF THE CITY CENTER

CARLTON GARDENS AND MELBOURNE MUSEUM. Spanning three city blocks, the verdant gardens criss-crossed with pathways and spectacular fountains offer peaceful repose and potential possum sightings. Standing within the gardens is the grandiose **Royal Exhibition Building,** which was home to Australia's first parliament and now hosts major expositions and temporary exhibits. Behind the Exhibition Building stands the multimillion dollar **Melbourne Museum,** a new, stunning facility that contains a range of science-related galleries, including a forest, an Aboriginal center, a children's museum, a new mind and body gallery, and an IMAX theatre (see **Film,** p. 529). *(Bordered by Victoria, Rathdowne, Carlton, and Nicholson St., on the city circle tram. Museum ☎8341 7777; www.melbourne.museum.vic.gov.au. $15, concessions $11, children 3-16 $8, families $35. Open daily 10am-6pm. Public tours of Royal Exhibition Building 2pm daily, $5 or $3 with museum admission. Wheelchair accessible.)*

OLD MELBOURNE GAOL. This stalwart prison was completed in 1845 and housed a total of 50,000 prisoners in its 84 years. The main structure has three levels of cells linked by iron catwalks. The tiny cells each house small displays about everything from the history and specifications of the jail to fascinating stories about **Ned Kelly's gang,** though the creepiest displays feature the stories and death masks of the most notorious criminals executed here. Kelly, Australia's most infamous bushranger, was hanged in the jail in 1880, and a scruffy wax likeness approaches his fate on the original trap door and scaffold. Downstairs is the suit of armor that Kelly—or one of his cohorts—wore in the gang's final shoot-out with police. Wonderfully spooky evening tours led by professional actors provide a chillingly vivid sense of its past horrible. Or satiate your thirst with a Ned Kelly soda in the gift shop on your way out and be thankful you've escaped—no criminal ever did. *(On Russell St. just north of La Trobe. ☎9663 7228; click on "properties" at www.nattrust.com.au. Admission $9.90, concessions $7.70, children $6.60, family $27.50. Night tours W, F, Sa, Su 7:30pm. $18.70, children $11, family $45.65. Bookings essential for night tours; call Ticketmaster 13 61 00. Open daily 9:30am-4:30pm.)*

QUEEN VICTORIA MARKET. The modernizing development that brought the rest of Melbourne into the 20th century somehow passed over the Market. It remains an old-fashioned, open-air market, abuzz with hundreds of vendors hawking their wares to the thousands of Melburnians who pack in for excellent bargains on produce, dairy products, and meat. Saturdays and Sundays see the market at its frenetic best. Don't be afraid to bargain with the vendors; good deals can turn into amazing ones after noon, when sellers are anxious to empty their stock. Walking tours explore the market's history and cultural importance, and include plenty to eat. From late Nov. to early Mar., the market is also open at night from 6-10pm and the focus becomes multicultural. *(On Victoria St. between Queen and Peel St. Open Tu, Th*

6am-2pm, F 6am-6pm, Sa 6am-3pm, Su 9am-4pm. ☎9320 5822; www.qvm.com.au. Tours depart from 69 Victoria St., near Elizabeth St. Food tour Tu, Th-Sa 10am: $22. History tour 10:30am: $16.50. Book ahead ☎9320 5935.)

MELBOURNE ZOO. Many sections of this world-class zoo are expertly recreated native habitats that allow visitors to view animals much as they live in the wild. The African Rainforest—with pygmy hippos, arboreal monkeys, and gorillas—is first-rate, and a new and elaborate Asian elephant exhibit is set to be completed in late 2002. Of course, you won't want to miss the Aussie fauna, which includes echidnas, wombats, goannas, emus, and red kangaroos with whom visitors can play—if the 'roos feel like it, that is. *(On Elliott Rd., north of the University of Melbourne. M-Sa take tram #55 from William St. to the Zoo stop; on Su take tram #68 from Elizabeth St. ☎9285 9300; www.zoo.org.au. Free tours for the elderly and disabled M-F 10am-3pm and Sa-Su 10am-4pm. Open Mar.-Dec. daily 9am-5pm, Jan. M-W 9am-5pm, Th-Su 9am-9:30pm, Feb. M-Th. 9am-5pm, F-Su 9am-9:30pm. $15.30, concessions $11.40, ages 4-15 $7.60, families $41.40.)*

SOUTH OF THE YARRA RIVER

SOUTHBANK. The riverside walk that begins across Clarendon St., Southbank, has an upmarket shopping and sidewalk-dining scene. It's most crowded on sunny Sundays, when an odd mix of skater kids, toned health nuts, and the Armani-clad gather here to relax, show off, and conspicuously consume. The area extends along the Yarra for two very long city blocks. While you could easily squander your entire budget here within a day, you can window-shop, people-watch, and get some great views of Flinders St. Station and the city skyline for free. There are also a slew of expensive but enjoyable river ferry rides, as well as really cool fountains, wacky sculptures, and endlessly-imaginative sidewalk chalk drawings.

SHRINE OF REMEMBRANCE. A wide walkway lined with tall, conical Butan cypresses leads to this imposing temple, with columns and a ziggurat roof, that commemorates fallen soldiers from WWI. The central space is crowned by a stepped skylight and the **stone of remembrance,** which bears the inscription "Greater Love Hath No Man." The skylight is designed so that at 11am on November 11 (the moment of the WWI armistice), a ray of sunlight shines onto the word "Love" on the stone. Don't worry about missing this impressive solar-architectural feat: the effect is simulated a bit anti-climactically every 30min. with artificial light, after which volunteer guides give excellent talks about the site's significance. Lining the outer corridor are books listing names of the Australian heroes who perished in WWI. Ascend to the shrine's balcony for spectacular views of the Melbourne skyline and the neighboring suburbs. Or venture down into the crypt and view the colorful division flags and memorial statue. Outside, veterans of subsequent wars are honored with a memorial that includes the **perpetual flame,** burning continuously since Queen Elizabeth II lit it in 1954. *(St. Kilda Rd. www.shrine.org.au. Open daily 10am-5pm. $2 donation.)*

VICTORIAN ARTS CENTRE. This enormous complex is the central star of Melbourne's performing arts galaxy. The 162m white-and-gold latticed spire of the **Theatres Building** is a landmark in itself, and inside there's more room for performance than most cities can handle. This eight-level facility holds three theatres (see Performing Arts, p. 528) that combined can seat over 3000 and are home to the **Melbourne Theatre Company, Opera Australia,** and the **Australian Ballet.** The Theatres Building also serves the visual arts, as its private **Performing Arts Museum** sets up regular exhibits of performing arts-related clothing, pictures, and memorabilia in the building's foyers. Next door is the 2600-seat **Melbourne Concert Hall,** which hosts the renowned **Melbourne Symphony** and the **Australian Chamber Orchestra**; its chic new **EQ Cafebar** is a bit pricey but offers award-winning meals and great views of the Yarra. Finally, the **Sidney Myer Music Bowl** is the third tier of the Victorian Arts conglomerate, located across St. Kilda Rd. in King's Domain Park. After extensive renovations set to be completed before 2002, the bowl will be the largest capacity outdoor amphitheater in the southern hemisphere, sheltering numerous

WHAT'S THAT ON THE SIDEWALK? Part of Melbourne's oft-cited liveability is the attention paid to public art. Deb Halpern's **Ophelia** on Southbank, is the fat-lipped, multi-colored, Y-shaped visage that has become one of the city's most prominent icons. On the pavement in front of Halpern's work, look for the ephemeral chalk drawings of Bev Isaac. North along Swanston St. in front of the State Library of Victoria, a stone cornice with part of the word **"library"** protruding from the pavement. This random work of Petroneous Sponk will keep you guessing "What the...? Why?" Nonetheless, it draws a crowd for its astounding uniqueness and quirky street artistry. Perhaps the most popular of the sculptures is the group of **three businessmen** cast in bronze standing at the corner of Swanston and Bourke St. Their emaciated frames and wild-eyed expressions inspire amusement in most onlookers, though the work was originally underwritten by the government of Nauru and meant to reflect the greed and spiritual impoverishment of the Australian businessmen who plundered the tiny Polynesian country's natural resources.

free and not-so-free summer concerts. Its "Carols by Candlelight" in the weeks before Christmas draws Victorians by the sleighloads. *(100 St. Kilda Rd. At the east end of Southbank, just across the river from Flinders St. Station. ☎9281 8000; www.vicartscentre.com.au. Open M-Sa 9am-11pm, Su 10am-5pm. Free. Guided tours leave from Arts Center shop, Level 6, Theatres Building. M-Sa noon and 2:30pm. $10, concessions $7.50. Special Su 12:15pm backstage tour $13.50.)*

NATIONAL GALLERY OF VICTORIA. This massive gallery had to adopt the confusing post-phrase "of Victoria" when the Australian National Gallery was built in Canberra. Still considered to house the finest collection in the Southern Hemisphere, the NGV is undergoing a $136 million renovation with an announced completion date of mid-2003. In the meantime, a surprisingly large 1% of the collection can be viewed at the Russell St. entrance of the **State Library of Victoria** (p. 522). In mid-2002, the Australian portion will be moved into the modern facilities of the **Ian Potter Centre NGV: Australian Art** in the new Federation Square building at Swanston and Flinders St. Most of the major international pieces will be in Victorian regional museums, or maybe even in your home town abroad, until the distant grand reopening. *(180 St. Kilda Rd. Temporary location 285-321 Russell St. ☎9208 0222; www.ngv.vic.gov.au. Gallery open daily 10am-5pm. Free guided tours M, W-F 11am, 1, 2pm; Tu 1, 2pm; Sa 2pm; Su 11am, 2pm. Admission to permanent collection free. Wheelchair accessible.)*

ROYAL BOTANIC GARDENS. Over 50,000 plants fill the 36 acres stretching along St. Kilda Rd. east to the Yarra and south to Domain Rd. The gardens first opened in 1845, and the extensive array of mature species reflects 150 years of care and development. Stately palms unique to Melbourne share the soil with twisting oaks, rainforest plants, possums, wallabies, and a pavilion of roses. A number of walking tracks highlight endemic flora. There's also a steamy **rainforest glasshouse** and lake where you can have tea and feed the ducks and geese. *(Open daily 10am-4:30pm.)* Special events, such as outdoor film screenings, take place on summer evenings (see **Cinema,** p. 529). The **Aboriginal Heritage Walk** explores the use of plant-life by local Aboriginal groups in ceremony, symbol, and food. *(Heritage walks Th 11am and alternate Su 10:30am. $15.40, concession $11, child 12-16yrs. $6.60. Book ahead.)* Near the entrance closest to the Shrine of Remembrance are the **Visitor's Centre** and the **observatory.** The Visitor's Center houses an upscale cafe and a garden shop. *(Open M-F 9am-5pm, Sa-Su 10am-5:30pm.)* The observatory includes an original 1874 telescope only accessible by day tours, which give a close-up look at the 'scopes; night tours allow visitors to use the instruments with the help of qualified astronomers. *(Tours W 2pm. $6.60, concession $4.40. Night tour Tu 7:30pm, $15.40, concessions $11, family $37.40. Book ahead.)* The small cottage by Gate F is the **La Trobe Cottage,** home of Victoria's first lieutenant governor, Charles Joseph La Trobe. *(Open M, W, Sa-Su 11am-4pm. $2.)* Tours from the cottage to **Government House,** the Victorian Governor's home and the Queen's appointed representative. *(4 Parliament Pl.*

☎9654 4711. Tours $11, concessions $9, children $5.50. Book ahead. Gardens ☎9252 2300. Open daily Nov.-Mar. 7:30am-8:30pm; Apr.-Oct. 7:30am-5:30pm. Free. Tours of the garden depart the Visitors Centre Su-F 11am and 2pm. $4, concessions $2. Wheelchair accessible.)

MELBOURNE AQUARIUM. Focusing on species of the Southern Ocean, this high-class facility offers a unique look at Australia's less talked-about wildlife. Three levels of fishtastic fun, from an open-air billabong to a 2.2 million liter "Oceanarium," featuring a glass tunnel that allows visitors to walk beneath roaming sharks and giant rays. Don't miss the car-turned-aquarium wittily dubbed "A fish called Honda." *(On King St., across from the Crown Casino. ☎9620 0949; www.melbourneaquarium.com.au. Open daily in Jan. 9:30am-9pm, Feb.-Dec. 9:30am-6pm; last admission 1hr. before close. $19.90, concessions $13, children $9.50, families $49.50. MC/V.)*

ST. KILDA

Bayside St. Kilda lies just far enough away from the city to be relaxed, but close enough to maintain a lively vibe during the day; at night more of the same citywide scene of black-clad bar hoppers appear. St. Kilda has recently undergone a repolish of its former seedy image of drugs and prostitution; although reverberations of the past still linger, a new attitude is coming to life. There aren't a lot of tourist sights per se, but the offbeat shops, gorgeous sandy shoreline, and comfortably mixed population of the weird and the ordinary are indeed a sight to behold. St. Kilda Beach is easily accessed by any number of trams (see **Orientation,** p. 503), and swarms with swimmers and sun-worshippers during summer. The **Esplanade,** along the length of the strand, is a great place for in-line skating and jogging. On Sundays, the Esplanade craft market sells art, toys, housewares, and everything else, all impressively handmade by the stall holders.

LUNA PARK. The entrance gate of this St. Kilda icon is a grotesque, mammoth fun-house face. Venture through its mouth to find classic carnival rides all permanently protected by the historical commission. Its highlight is the largest wooden roller coaster in the world, which circles the park. Extensive renovations ready for 2002 promise some new rides as well. *(On the Lower Esplanade. ☎9525 5033; www.lunapark.com.au. Free entry. Unlimited ride tickets $29.95, children 4-12 $19.95; single rides $6.50, children 4-12 $5, ages 1-3 $3. Open F 7-11pm, Sa 11am-11pm, Su 11am-dusk. Public and school holidays M-Th 11am-5pm, F-Sa 11am-11pm, Su 11am-7pm.)*

ALBERT PARK. Adjacent to Fitzroy St. on the north lies Albert Park, the southern extension of Melbourne's vast park system, with ample green space, free BBQs, tennis courts, and groups of kids playing footy. The Grand Prix course is here, which you can drive on, abiding by speed limits of course (see **Recreation,** p. 529). The huge interior lake is great for sailing or paddleboating, but no swimming is allowed. *(For info call Parks Victoria ☎13 19 63.)*

JEWISH MUSEUM OF AUSTRALIA. The Jewish Museum outlines both the history of the Jewish people as a whole and the experience of Australia's 90,000 Jews from the time of the First Fleet. A stunning hallway draws a timeline of Jewish history, complete with fascinating and state-of-the-art multimedia displays. The Belief and Ritual Gallery provides a thorough overview of Judaism's basic tenets, including a painfully detailed French woodcut of a circumcision ceremony. There are also rotating displays of art and Judaica. *(26 Alma Rd. East of St. Kilda Rd. by stop 32 on tram #3 or 67. ☎9534 0083; www.jewishmuseum.com.au. Museum open Tu-Th 10am-4pm, Su 11am-5pm. $7, child and student concessions $4, family $16. 30-40min. tours of the adjacent synagogue are free with admission and take place Tu-Th 12:30pm and Su 12:30 and 3pm. Wheelchair accessible.)*

OUTSKIRTS OF THE CITY

SCIENCEWORKS. This extension of the Museum of Victoria is a big hit with kids, who arrive in droves on weekends and school holidays. The displays are designed to trick children into thinking learning is fun (two words: fake feces). There are multiple exhibitions, including one called Sports Works that affords the opportunity to engage in simulated competition against Olympians. (Don't try too hard; you will lose, and the kids will laugh at you for taking it too seriously.) The digital planetarium, the only one in the Southern Hemisphere, brings the stars as well as special shows to your comfortably seated self, but requires a few more dollars. *(2 Booker St. 5km from downtown in the suburb of Spotswood. Take the Werribee or Williamstown line from Flinders St. Station, get off at Spotswood, and follow the ample signs; the walk takes about 10-15min. A better option on a sunny day is to take the Williamstown Seeker ferry (☎9506 4144; www.williamstownferries.com.au) from Southgate walk; departs every 2hr. 11am-5pm; $12 return. Scienceworks: ☎9392 4800; www.scienceworks.museum.vic.gov.au. Open daily 10am-4pm. $9, with Planetarium $15, concessions $7/$11.50; children 3-16yrs. $4.50/$8; family $23/$38.50.)*

MUSEUM OF MODERN ART AT HEIDE. A meeting place for artists, writers, and poets during the emergence of Australian modernism in the 1930s and 40s, the Museum of Modern Art has since been converted into an excellent venue for contemporary Australian and international art. Featuring work by Charles Blackman, Arthur Boyd, Joy Hester, and Sidney Nolan, the museum also has rotating exhibits of cutting-edge art from international makers. Perhaps most impressive is the five-hectare sculpture park. *(7 Templestowe Rd. In the northern suburb of Bulleen, via the Bulleen Rd. exit off the Eastern Fwy. By train, take the Hurstbridge line from Flinders St. Station 20min. to Heidelberg Station; then take National Bus 291 to the corner of Manningham and Templestowe, then a 5min. walk up the hill. ☎9850 1500; www.heide.com.au. Open Tu-F 10am-5pm, Sa-Su noon-5pm. $10, concessions $6.70. Sculpture park free.)*

ENTERTAINMENT

Melbourne prides itself on its style and cultural savvy, and nowhere is this more evident than in its entertainment scene. The range of options can seem overwhelming: there are world-class performances at the Victorian Arts Centre, edgy experimental drama in Carlton and Fitzroy, popular dramas and musicals in opulent theatres, and a panoply of independent and avant-garde cinema. The definitive website for performance events is www.melbourne.citysearch.com.au.

PERFORMING ARTS

Book for larger shows through **Ticketek** (☎13 28 49 or 1800 062 849; www.ticketek.com), or try **Halftix** for half-price same day tickets (see **Ticket Agencies,** p. 511); for smaller productions, call the theater companies directly. The **Victorian Arts Centre,** 100 St. Kilda Rd. (☎9281 8000; www.vicartscentre.com.au)— is hard to miss with its Eiffel-like spire right on the Yarra across from Flinders St. Station. The center houses five venues: the **State Theatre** for major dramatic, operatic, and dance performances; the **Melbourne Concert Hall,** for symphonies; the **Playhouse,** largely used by the **Melbourne Theatre Company** for plays; the **George Fairfax Studio,** similar to the **Playhouse,** only smaller; and the **Black Box,** for cutting-edge, low-budget shows targeted at an under-35 audience. (Tickets range from free-$180. Box office open M-Sa 9am-9pm.)

La Mama, 205 Faraday St., Carlton (☎9347 6948). About halfway up Lygon St., head east on Faraday; it's very near the intersection, hidden down an alleyway and behind a parking lot. New, esoteric Australian drama in a diminutive, black-box space. Similar cutting-edge work is performed at the affiliated **Carlton Courthouse Theatre,** 349 Drummond St. (☎ La Mama), just around the corner in the old courthouse building, across from the police station. Tickets $10-14. Free tea and coffee at performances.

Last Laugh at the Comedy Club, 380 Lygon St., Carlton (☎9348 1622). In Lygon Ct. Melbourne's biggest comedy club scene, with big-name international jokesters. Ticket prices vary depending on the act.

National Theatre (☎9534 0224; www.nationaltheatre.org.au), on the comer of Barkly and Carlisle St., St. Kilda. Offbeat, cosmopolitan fare, like modern dance, drama, opera, and "world music." Tickets prices depend on the show, but generally fall between $10-60.

Palais Theatre (☎9537 2444), on the Esplanade, St. Kilda. The Palais holds the largest chandelier in the southern hemisphere. Seats 3000. Tickets $40-60.

Princess' Theatre, 163 Spring St. (☎9299 9850). Popularly successful musicals in a 1500 seat venue. Tickets $40-80. Book through Ticketek (☎13 28 49).

Regent Theatre, 191 Collins St. (☎9299 9500). Just east of Swanston St. Once a popular movie palace, the dazzlingly ornate theater now hosts big-name touring musicals and international celebrity acts. Seats 2000. Tickets $50-80. 2hr. tours of Regent and Forum every Tu: $18, students $15. Book ahead.

The Forum, 150 Flinders St. (☎9299 9700). Looks like a combination of an Arabian palace and Florentine villa, with a few gargoyles thrown in for good measure. Big-budget dance and drama ($50-80), as well as periodic concerts ($20-30).

Dracula's (☎9347 3344; www.draculas.com.au), on the corner of Victoria and Cardigan St., north Melbourne. 2hr. cabaret shows with a vampire horror-comedy theme. Tickets $40-60 and include show, dinner, and a "ghost train" ride.

CINEMA

Melbourne has long been the center of Australia's independent film scene, and there are tons of old theaters throughout the city that screen artsy and experimental fare as well as old cinema classics. The arthouse crowd logs on to www.urbancinefile.com.au, which features flip reviews of the latest stuff. The annual **Melbourne International Film Festival** (see **Festivals,** p. 530) showcases the year's indie hits, and the **St. Kilda Film Festival** (see **Festivals**) highlights short films of all shapes and sizes. Plenty of cinemas in the city center show mainstream first-run movies as well. **Movieline** (☎13 34 56) has a ticketing service and recorded info on showtimes and locations. At the theater, try a "choc-top," the chocolate-dipped ice-cream cone that's a staple of Melbourne movie-going ($2-3).

Astor Theatre, (☎9510 1414; www.astor-theatre.com), on the corner of Chapel St. and Dandenong Rd., St. Kilda. Spectacular 1936 Art Deco theater that still bears many of its original furnishings and all of its stately beauty. Mostly repertory and re-issues. Seats 1100. Many double features. $11, concessions $10, child $9; book of 10 tickets $80.

Cinema Nova, 380 Lygon St., Carlton (☎9349 5201). In Lygon Court. Indie and foreign fare. Claims the oxy-moronic title of "second-largest art-house megaplex in the world." $13, concessions $10.50, child $7.50. Special M $4.50 before 4pm, $7 after.

IMAX, Melbourne Museum, Carlton (☎9663 5454; www.imax.com.au). Off Rathdowne St. in the Carlton Gardens (see p. 524). Gigantic movie screen (23m x 31m) located in a mammoth subterranean theater. Shows are short on content (50min.) but more than make up for it with astounding visuals—some even offer 3-D action viewed through space-age liquid crystal glasses. Slate of films changes seasonally. $15, concessions $12, children $10, family $42; 3-D shows $1 extra ($4 for families). Daily screenings of 5 films happen on the hour Su-Th 10am-10pm, F-Sa 10am-11pm. YHA 20% discount, RACV 20%, NOMADS 10%.

Moonlight Cinema (☎9428 2203; www.moonlight.com.au), in the Royal Botanic Gardens. From mid-Dec.-early Mar., movies play on the central lawn, with a licensed bar and gourmet catering. Films start at sundown, approximately 8:45pm; tickets can be purchased at the gate from 7:30pm. $13.50, concessions $10.50, children $9.

The Kino, 45 Collins St. (☎9650 2100). Downstairs in the Collins Place complex. Quality independent and foreign films. $13.50, concessions $10.50. M special $8.50.

SPORTS AND RECREATION

Melburnians refer to themselves as "sports mad," but it's a good insanity, one that causes fans of footy (Australian Rules Football), cricket, tennis, and horse racing to skip work or school, get decked out in the costumery of their favorite side, and cheer themselves hoarse. Their hallowed haven is the **Melbourne Cricket Ground (MCG),** adjacent to the world-class **Melbourne Park** tennis center (see p. 523). A new ward, **Colonial Stadium,** right behind Spencer St. Station, has begun to share footy-hosting responsibilities with the more venerable MCG, and also hosts the majority of local rugby action. The lunacy peaks at various yearly events: the **Australian Open,** a Grand Slam tennis event in late January; the **Grand Prix** Formula-One car-racing extravaganza in March; the **AFL Grand Final** in late September; the **Melbourne Cup,** a "horse race that stops a nation" in early November; and cricket's **Boxing Day Test Match** on Dec. 26 (see **Festivals,** p. 530).

Melbourne's passion for sport is not limited to spectator events. City streets and parks are packed with joggers, skaters, and footy players. The newly refurbished, crushed gravel tan track that circles the Royal Botanic Gardens is best for **running;** stick to the track, as recreational activities are strictly prohibited in the Gardens proper. Other great routes include the pedestrian paths along the Yarra, the Port Phillip/St. Kilda shore, and the Albert Park Lake. All of these wide, flat spaces make for excellent **in-line skating** as well. **City Skate,** Wednesday at 9pm, draws local bladers together at the Victorian Arts Centre near the waterfall; folks convene and break into smaller groups based on preferred city route and skill level. You can rent equipment at the **Skate Warehouse,** 354 Lonsdale St. (☎9602 3633. $7.50 per hr., $12.50 per 3hr., $17.50 per day, $27.50 per weekend (F-M). Open M-Th 10am-6pm, F 10am-9pm, Sa 9am-5pm, Su 10am-5pm.)

If you're not quite so active, and the weather is agreeable, there is a **beach** in St. Kilda accessible by tram #16 and 96. It's not Australia's finest, but it'll do for sun and swimming. **Albert Park** (see p. 527) has a lake good for sailing, but not for swimming. Just inside the Clarendon St. entrance to the park, **Jolly Roger** rents sailboats for $26-38 per hr., rowboats for $32 per hr., and aquabikes for $13 per 15min. (☎9690 5862. Open Tu-Su 8:30am-4:30pm.) The **Melbourne City Baths,** 420 Swanston St., on the corner of Franklin St., offer two pools, sauna, spa, squash courts, and a gym in a restored Neoclassical building. (☎9663 5888. Open M-Th 6am-10pm, F 6am-8:30pm, Sa-Su 8am-6pm. Pool $3.30; sauna and spa $7.70.)

GAMBLING

The Australian penchant for "having a flutter" (betting) reaches its neon-lit apotheosis at **Melbourne's Crown Casino,** 8 Whiteman St., at the western end of Southbank. A little slice of Las Vegas down under, this $1.6 billion complex houses the most gaming tables of any casino in the world (which could translate to a gathering of many losers...see **That's What It's All About,** p. 307), plus five-star accommodations, luxury shopping, Elvis impersonators, fog-filled, laser-lit jumping fountains, a perennially packed Planet Hollywood, and three **nightclubs:** Heat, Club Odeon, and the Mercury Lounge. The evening pyrotechnic displays out front on the Yarra are not to be missed; every hour, starting at 7pm, you'll think it's some sort of independence day celebration. Independence from gambling? Not likely. Minimum bets are around $5, though the more cautious can start at the less cut-throat "how to play" tables. (☎9292 8888. Open 24hr., and busy just about every one of those hours.)

FESTIVALS

Melburnians create excuses for city-wide street parties any time of the year. Below are the city's major events. For a complete guide, grab a free copy of *Melbourne Events* at any tourist office, or look under "Festivals and Events" at www.visitmelbourne.com. All dates listed are for 2002.

Midsumma Gay and Lesbian Festival, *Jan. 12-Feb. 3* (☎9415 9819; www.midsumma.org.au). 3 weeks of homosexual hijinks all over the city ranging from the erotic (a "Mr. Leather Victoria" contest) to the educational (a Same-Sex Partners Rights workshop), with lots of parades, dance parties, and general pandemonium.

Australian Open, *Jan. 14-27* (for tickets ☎9286 1175; www.ausopen.org). One of the world's elite 4 Grand Slam tennis events, held at Melbourne Park's hard courts.

Qantas Australian Grand Prix, *Feb. 28-Mar. 3* (for tickets ☎13 16 41; www.grandprix.com.au). Albert Park, St. Kilda. Formula One frenzy holds the city hostage.

WorldPhone. Worldwide.

MCI℠ gives you the freedom of worldwide communications whenever you're away from home. It's easy to call to and from over 70 countries with your MCI Calling Card:

1. Dial the WorldPhone® access number of the country you're calling from.
2. Dial or give the operator your MCI Calling Card number.
3. Dial or give the number you're calling.

• Australia 1-800-730-014 AAPT
1-800-551-111 OPTUS
1-800-881-100 TELSTRA

Sign up today!

Ask your local operator to place a collect call (reverse charge) to MCI in the U.S. at:

1-712-943-6839

For additional access codes or to sign up, visit us at www.mci.com/worldphone.

www.mci.com/worldphone

© 2001, WorldCom, Inc. All Rights Reserved.

It's Your World...

© 2001, WorldCom, Inc. All Rights Reserved.

Moomba, *Mar. 8-11.* (☎9650 9744; www.melbournemoombafestival.com.au). Named after the Aboriginal word for "party," Moomba is basically a non-stop 4-day citywide fête amid food, performances, and events.

Melbourne Food and Wine Festival, *Mar. 14-Apr. 4* (☎9412 4220; www.fmelbfoodwinefest.com.au), Collins St. A free and delicious way to celebrate Melbourne as Australia's "culinary capital" or just an excuse to get drunk and stuffed, and more drunk.

International Comedy Festival, *Mar. 28-Apr. 21* (☎1900 937 200; www.comedyfestival.com.au). Huge 3-week international and Aussie laugh-fest, with over 1000 gut-busting performances.

International Flower and Garden Show, *Apr. 10-14* (☎9639 2333). Royal Exhibition Building and Carlton Gardens, Carlton.

Anzac Day Parade, *Apr. 25 each year* (☎9650 5050). ANZAC vets in the Commemoration March head down Swanston St. and St. Kilda Rd to the Shrine of Remembrance.

St. Kilda Film Festival, *late May-early June* (☎9209 6711). Palais Theatre and George Cinemas, St. Kilda. Australia's best short films: documentary, experimental, and comedy.

International Film Festival, *mid-July-early Aug.* (☎9417 2011; www.melbournefilmfestival.com.au). 2001 marked the 50th anniversary of the cream of the international cinematic crop (plus top-level local work) and 2002 is likely to top.

Royal Melbourne Show, *Sept. 19-29* (☎9281 7420; www.royalshow.com.au). At Ascot Vale. Sideshow alleys, rides, entertainment, animal exhibitions for judging.

Melbourne Fringe Festival, *Sept. 29-Oct. 20* (☎9481 5111; www.melbournefringe.org.au). Centered around local artists, the festival opens with a parade on Brunswick St., Fitzroy. Performance and parties all across town.

Melbourne Festival, *Oct. 17- Nov. 2* (☎9662 4242; www.melbournefestival.com.au). A 3-week celebration of the arts, attracting world-famous actors, writers, and dancers for over 400 performances, workshops, and parties in 30 different venues.

Qantas Australian Motorcycle Grand Prix, *late Oct.* (☎9258 7100; www.grandprix.com.au). Phillip Island. Fast bikes (instead of fast cars). Going around a track. Fast.

Spring Racing Carnival, *Oct.10-Nov.22, 2001; dates for 2002 are TBA* (☎9258 4666; www.racingvictoria.net.au). Flemington Racecourse. Australia's love for horse racing reaches fever on the pitch.

Chapel St Festival, *Nov. 3* (☎9529 6331). 250,000-300,000 people crowd Chapel St from Dandenong to Toorak Rd for entertainment and mayhem.

Melbourne Cup Day, *Nov. 6, 2001.* On the first Tuesday every November, Melburnians, along with the rest of Australia, put life on pause to watch, listen, or talk about the most hyped-up and fashionable horse race in the country. Ladies, gents, and Australia's elite come dressed to impress for a comical and entertaining day at the races.

Melbourne Boxing Day Test Match, *Dec. 26* (☎9653 9999; www.baggygreen.com.au). More than 100,000 cricket fans pack the MCG to root for the boys in green and gold against top cricketers from around the world.

NIGHTLIFE

Melbourne pulses with a world-class nightlife scene. Only a handful of venues play the standard bass-heavy club remixes of familiar mainstream dance hits. Most feature DJs (some of whom have international followings) who spin funky, mind-bending original selections of techno, house and deep house, trance, drum 'n' bass, jungle, garage, and breakbeats. You probably won't recognize any of it, but it's eminently danceable. Tons of retro nights feature 70s and 80s faves, with crowds in campy period wear. Covers are ubiquitous outside of Fitzroy and range up to $20, but you get your money's worth—few clubs close earlier than 3am, and some rage non-stop from Thursday all the way until Sunday night.

IF HE HAD ONLY CALLED HER... The upstairs of Young & Jackson bar across from Flinders Street Station is called Chloe's Bar, after the subject of the titillating painting of a nude 14-year-old girl that was unveiled at the 1880 Melbourne Exhibition. It caused a great stir at the time, which was later surpassed when its maker, Jules Lefebvre, ditched Chloe for her sister, and the distraught model killed herself by drinking a cocktail of match heads and champagne. Always remember the "half your age +7" year rule for dating legitimacy.

There are three main areas for **nightclubs.** Downtown tends to be straighter (as in less gay and more mainstream), though you'll find a little bit of everything. South Yarra and Prahran have the trendiest venues and the best **gay scene.** Though most clubs in the area are gay-friendly, predominantly gay places are concentrated along Commercial Rd., with a smattering in Collingwood. Fitzroy and St. Kilda are pretty much the anti-Chapel St.—much more casual, tending toward grungy but good music shows and charging the cheapest covers, if any at all. Melburnians take their nightlife seriously—the more you pay and the trendier the venue, the more attitude you get at the door. Nonetheless, rude treatment comes free of charge at fading venues as well. Another curiosity is that even places that are gritty during the day are, at night, host to black-clad hipsters seeking the ever-changing cutting edge scene. Venues, genres, and cover charges change with bewildering rapidity. To keep up, read *In Press* and, to a lesser extent, *Beat* magazines, both of which are free, released every Wednesday, and have exhaustive weekly listings. For music shows, the best coverage is in The Age's *Entertainment Guide* (*EG*) or the Herald-Sun's *Gig Guide*, both of which come out in their Friday papers.

There is a blurry but important distinction between **bars** and **pubs** in Melbourne. The bars tend to be a bit more chill but no less slick than their nightclub cousins; bars don't have covers, though. Drinks are expensive (beer bottles $4-4.50, wine and mixed drinks $4.50-5.50), and wine and spirits are the intoxicants of choice; many bars don't have beer taps at all. Most pubs, on the other hand, charge less for drinks (half-pint pots $2.30-2.80, pints $4.50-5, mixed drinks (called spirits) $3.50-4.50), are loud and raucous, and have live entertainment on weekends (cover $3-8), making the distinction between pub and club somewhat blurry as well. Most venues try to lure backpackers with cheap drink specials (pots as low as $1-1.50) and often keep taps flowing until early in the morning, or even 24 hours. Basically, almost anywhere you go you're bound to have a damn good time.

BARS AND PUBS

CITY CENTER

Rue Bebelons, 237 Little Lonsdale St. (☎9663 1700). There's no sign outside; you have to be in the know. The consummate Melburnian bar, relaxed and understatedly stylish, with an excellent selection of wines ($3-4) and spirits ($4.50-6). The deep house music and dim lighting create the ideal atmosphere for a silent, brooding solitary drink or an intimate *tête-a-tête.* Open Tu-F 8am-3am, Sa 11am-3am, Su 2-8pm.

Club UK, 169 Exhibition St. (☎9663 2075). Perhaps more British than Britain itself, Club UK quivers with ubiquitous Union Jacks, strikingly accurate Prince Charles cartoons, and pulsating Brit beats. Particularly popular among uni students and backpackers, this club attracts outrageous dress and a notably young, mixed gay-straight crowd. W draws a huge crowd for $2 pints. Cover W $2 after 9pm, Th $5 after 10pm. Open W-Th 4pm-3am, F-Sa until 5am.

Up Top Cocktail Bar, 1st floor, 163 Russell St. (☎9663 8990). Enter via the alleyway off Russell St. Slick and smooth, Up Top's lounge plays host to a regular after-work crowd by day; but when the dance floor opens it's all about dedicated clubbers busting a move. Spirits from $5, bottled beer from $4.50; fruity-sweet drink specials are dangerously tempting ($3). Happy Hours Th-F 4-8pm. No cover. Open W 4pm-midnight, Th until 3am, F-Sa until 5am. Dance floor open F-Sa from 10pm.

Pugg Mahones, 106-112 Hardware St. (☎9670 6155), between Little Lonsdale and Lonsdale St. Irish pub packs in a lively all-ages crowd with live music on weekends. Take the time to study their selection of Irish beers on tap, and their decorative farm equipment above the door. M: backpacker night, $3.50 pints of the Aussie brews. No cover, but M lines can extend out the door. Open daily 11am-3am.

FITZROY AND COLLINGWOOD

Bar Open, 317 Brunswick St. (☎9415 9601). Edgy urban chic tempered by an air of the totally chill that always draws a good aura. Portraits of the Queen Mum abound on thickly painted red walls. Younger crowd chats comfortably downstairs in intimate environs, including cushy chairs near the fireplace. The mellow purple upstairs grooves W-Sa nights with local jazz and funk talent; Tu night features weekly showings of short films of the "bizarre" genre. No cover. Open daily noon-2am.

Labour in Vain, 197 Brunswick St. (☎9417 5955). 5 self-proclaimed beer lovers started this little joint on the site of an 1850s hotel that bore the same name. Today it hops with locals from every walk of life; talk to the barstaff, and they'll direct you to someone with similar interests. Owner Andrew B. proudly displays his 30yr. collection of old and rare beer bottles and will gladly expound on the history of brewing in Australia. Bar opens anytime from 1:30-3:30pm (really, whenever the staff recovers from the previous night), closes 1am daily.

Planet Afrik, 99 Smith St. (☎9419 2687), near Gertrude St. This colorful bar draws in Melbourne's diverse African crowd on the weekends for some of the city's most authentic Reggae and African music. Energy-filled beats encourage enthusiastic dancing; the more mellow can enjoy it all from the lounge's bar or couches instead. F tends to be more reggae and calypso-driven, while Sa brings soca bands from the Congo and elsewhere. Cover $5 Sa, $8 on special nights. Open Th-Su 6pm-3am.

Builder's Arms, 211 Gertrude St. (☎9419 0818), at Gore St., halfway between Brunswick and Smith St. Large and lively, this versatile bar brings in an all ages and orientations. 3 rooms vary in intensity, from the sedate back seating area to the sweaty velvet-curtained dance room to the always-crowded front bar. Very gay-friendly; popular Th "Q&A" (Queer and Alternative) night. W live alternative music 9pm-midnight; Th-Sa DJs and disco; Su live blues, roots, and soul. Th-Sa arrive by 9:30 if you don't want to wait in line. Open M-Th 5pm-1am, F-Sa 5pm-1am, Su 3-11pm.

The Tote, 71 Johnston St. (☎9419 5320), at Wellington St., one block east of Smith St. A somewhat seedy front bar masks the vitality of the back room, which hosts energetic aussie indie rock almost every night of the week. Music is almost always original and ranges in style from punk to metal to girl-rockers; call ahead to find out who's playing. Bar area is free but to go to the back will run you $4-12 if anyone is actually manning the door. Open M-Th noon-1am, F-Sa noon-3am, Su 6-11pm.

The Peel Hotel (☎9416 4762), corner of Peel and Wellington St. An institution in Melbourne's gay nightlife, the Peel is more down-to-earth than its Commercial Rd. counterparts. The club pumps out commercial house to an almost exclusively gay-male crowd. The attached pub is more laid-back and straight-friendly, with cheap drinks (pots $1.40-2.80, spirits $3.50-5.50) and relaxed conversation. Club cover $5-7. Open Th-Su 11:30pm-8am. Pub open M-Tu 5pm-3am, W-Sa until 5am, Su until 1am.

Glasshouse Hotel, 51 Gipps St. (☎9419 4748). Just down the road, off Wellington St. Historically a gay bar, the Glasshouse has recently shifted focus to become Melbourne's only lesbian venue. Its predominantly female crowd varies comfortably in age, dress, and attitude; while some may spend the evening playing pool, others can be found dancing on the bar. Th pool competition; F-Sa retro DJs. Cover $3, $5 F-Sa after 11pm. Open Th 7pm-1am, F-Sa 7pm-5am, Su 7pm-midnight.

SOUTH YARRA AND PRAHRAN

Bridie O'Reilly's, 462 Chapel St. (☎9827 7788). Bringing rural Ireland to posh South Yarra, Bridie's is always busy and a guaranteed good time. Live cover bands every night; Irish folk Su-Th, more contemporary covers F-Sa. A new beer takes the emerald limelight each month, served to well-dressed young patrons for $5.50 a pint (normally $6.80). St. Patrick's Day is Guinness-drinking mayhem, with lines extending several blocks down Chapel St. No cover. Open Su-Th 11am-1am, F-Sa until 3am. AmEx/DC/MC/V.

Xchange, 119 Commercial Rd. (☎9521 2620). Relaxed gay pub-lounge gets rowdy W-Su after 10:30pm, when regular drag queens take control in the small back "show bar." Come see the famous Lucy, BananaDrama, and the Dynamic Duo. Happy Hour daily 5-7pm. $5 cover after 10pm W-Su. Free internet access for patrons. Open noon-2am Su-Th, noon-3am F-Sa. MC/V.

Frost Bites, 426 Chapel St. (☎9827 7401). By day a pizza and pasta restaurant, by night a blaring club that attracts a mainstream young crowd and long lines. Cover bands, generally Top-40s, W, Th, Su; commercial dance DJs F-Sa. Backpacker night W, featuring $2 pots, $3.50 spirits, and $4 alcoholic slurpees. Free bus pickup at many city hostels (arrange ahead). $5 pizzas Tu until 9:30pm. Neat casual dress. No cover. Open daily noon-3am. AmEx/DC/MC/V.

ST. KILDA

Esplanade Hotel, 11 Upper Esplanade (☎9534 0211). Multifaceted seaside hotel, known fondly as the "Espy." Down-to-earth Lounge Bar carries 3-4 live music acts every night and live reggae Su afternoons. Beneath is a gritty pub that hosts live country and old blues Sa nights. Upstairs is the ornate Gershwin Room, where crowds flock to bigger-name live music acts Sa (cover $8-10) and comedy acts Tu and Su (cover $10) Happy Hour with $1.50 pots in pub 3 days a week, 5-7pm. Pub open M-Th 11am-9pm, F-Sa 11am-midnight, Su noon-9pm. Lounge Bar open M-Th noon-midnight, F-Sa noon-1:30am, and Su noon-11:30pm; in summer, daily until 1am.

The Elephant and Wheelbarrow, 169 Fitzroy St. (☎9534 7888). Twin brother of the E&W on the corner of Bourke and Exhibition St., CBD. A very fun "traditional English pub" where the snazzily-dressed drink and flirt with impunity. M nights bring the infamous "*Neighbors* Night," where cast members of this popular Aussie soap opera mingle with patrons and help with trivia games...for $27. Live classic rock, oldies, and jazz W-Su nights. No cover. Open 10am-3am daily.

The George Public Bar, 125 Fitzroy St. (☎9534 8822). Not to be confused with the next door **George Melbourne Wine Room** that carries over 500 wines ($18-500), the George Public bar is a well-lit subterranean neighborhood bar that perfectly follows St. Kilda's unpretentious attitude, even with its popularity. The message here is that "Beauty is in the eye of the Beer Holder." Try their "world-famous" chili mayo chips; only $4 for a big basket. Live music Sa 4-7pm and Su 6-9pm; trivia night M 7:30pm.Open Su-Th noon-1am, F-Sa noon-3am.

Sunset Strip, 16 Grey St. (☎9534 9205). Popular late-night, mainly because it's the only place still open, and near the St. Kilda backpacker cluster. DJs prompt emphatic dancing, M gay night. Su, Tu, Th $1 pots until midnight. Open daily 8pm-5am.

Prince of Wales, 29 Fitzroy St (☎9536 1177; www.theprince.com.au). Longstanding local haunt divided into two downstairs bars: the corner bar attracts a blue collar, grungy crowd, while the other side is a popular gay bar. M nights are a backpacker haven with $1 pots 8pm-1am. Tu night pool competitions start at 7:30pm; entry $2, winner takes all. Upstairs, 1st F of every month is a "girlbar" for lesbians only. Downstairs bar opens noon daily, until 2am Tu-Th and Su, until 3am M, F-Sa.

Mink, 2b Acland St. (☎9536 1199). The elusive red door next to the Prince of Wales. Considered one of Melbourne's best cocktail bars, Mink has enough vodka variations to make you sing like an old Russian sailor. Open daily 6pm-2 or 3am.

NIGHTCLUBS

CITY CENTER

Metro, 20-30 Bourke St. (☎9663 4288; www.metronightclub.com). Simply unbelievable. The largest club in the Southern Hemisphere, the Metro packs in a younger (18-25), straight crowd on weekends for a major scope-and-scam scene. 9 bars and 5 levels of dance action; the ground floor's the most frenetic, with fog, flashing lights, and a triangular plane of green laser that cuts above heads in the main dance pit. 2nd floor has live music and catwalks, 3rd floor an observation deck with plush and private booths. Marble staircases, brass banisters, and Victorian ceilings spared since the building's theatre days form an odd but idiosyncratic juxtaposition with Metro's space-age glitz. "Goo," alternative-grunge on Th; "Pop," mainstream dance hits on Sa. Phone ahead for dress code, and come before midnight. Cover $5-11. Open Th 9pm-5:30am, F 10pm-2:30am, Sa 9pm-6am. Accepts all major credit cards; ATM inside.

Scubar, 389 Lonsdale St. (☎9670 2400). Shagadelic, baby! Prototype for the tacky bachelor pad, this smallish downstairs venue is befitted with red velvet walls, big plush pillows, beaded curtains, a ceiling aquarium with tropical fish, and candles galore. Most active Th-Sa, with DJs spinning through the night and occasionally a live band: Hip-hop on Th, Funk on F, Techno on Sa, and sometimes African-style percussion. Tapas bar serves light food. Cover $5 after 10pm Th-Sa. Open W-Sa 4pm-3am; may close earlier W if crowd is light.

Club 383, 383 Lonsdale St. (☎9670 6575). Pool tables and a big dance space on the 1st floor; a more intimate dance area and black-lit lounge in the neon-painted labyrinth upstairs. Slightly older crowd busts a move to F "80s Retro"; Sa "Noir" goth night draws a younger, subculture slew. Cover $7. Open F-Sa 10pm-5am.

Inflation, 60 King St. (☎9614 6122). Throws the city's biggest backpacker party Tu nights with free hostel pick-up, a pool competition, and free 1-liter buckets of beer from 9-10pm and 11pm-midnight. Ladies only Sa nights until 11pm. Cover $6-10.

SOUTH YARRA & PRAHRAN

Revolver, 1st floor, 229 Chapel St. (☎9521 5985). One of the most happening alternative clubs in the city, with a mixed crowd of uni kids, black-clad club-goers, and edgy, multiple-pierced, skate-punk, dred-heads, and you. Dance area frequented by various alternative bands on weekends; afterwards a DJ takes over for groovy late-night dancing. The calmer mega-lounge has pool, campy table arcade, retro furniture, and mini-chandeliers. Lines can get long; don't worry, once you're in you can stay the weekend. Cover Th-Sa after 9pm $5-10. Open M-Th noon-3am, F noon-Su 3am nonstop.

Salt, 14 Claremont St. (☎9827 8333). Shrouded in a crowd of mist inside, the Salt's narrow dance floor pumps penetrating bass as the scantily-clad young crowd get their groove on. Featured in Madison Avenue's "Who the Hell are You?" music video. Retro on W, Uni night on Th, Asian techno on F. Dress sharply and come early. Cover $7-15. Open W 11pm-5am, Th 10pm-3am, F 11pm-7am, Sa 10pm-7am.

The Market, 143 Commercial Rd. (☎9826 0933). Melbourne's hippest gay club (straight-friendly), The Market changes faces each night. Th alternates between drag and cabaret, while F is a self-titled "Meat Market," featuring beefy brawny male pole dancers. The weekend "straightens" out a bit, with two commercial DJs on Sa and a funk-soul-R&B DJ for "Burning" Su. Big circular dance floor is the main scene for grinding, though on busy nights crowds throb all the way to the upstairs balcony. Cover Th $5, F-Sa $8, Su $10 after 10pm. Open 9pm-3am Th and Su, 9pm-7am F-Sa. MC/V.

Diva, 153 Commercial Rd. (☎9824 2800). Small but very popular gay bar (straight-friendly) with tons of themes and drink specials. "Diva Angels" drag show on W, "Sex, Drugs, and Pop Music" on Th, "Happy Days" on F, "Retro" (80s and 90s) on Sa with our famous lady Lucy (see **Xchange,** p. 534). No cover. Lines after 1am, especially Sa. Open W-Sa 9:30pm-3am. MC/V.

Dome, 19 Commercial Rd. (☎9529 8966). Melbourne's most popular and expensive nightclub, and the place to be seen. The main arena is a vast, crowded, sweaty vortex of dance action, where box-dancing glowstick mavens bump-and-grind to progressive house. Off to the side is "Jane's Bar," where the gay/lesbian crowd generally congregates; drag shows start at 3am. Cover $15. Dress sharply. Open Sa only 11pm-9am.

DAYTRIPS FROM MELBOURNE

HEALESVILLE SANCTUARY. An open-air zoo, the Healesville Sanctuary lies in the Yarra Valley, 65km from Melbourne. Its minimum-security and daily "Meet the Keeper" presentations allow visitors to interact with and ask questions about the native creatures; keeper talks start at 11am and occur roughly every half hour. *(From Melbourne, take the Met's light rail to Lilydale, then take McKenzie's tourist service bus #685. for about 35min. Only 2 buses go directly from the station weekdays at 9:40 and 11:35am. McKenzie's ☎5962 5088. Sanctuary, ☎5957 2800; www.zoo.org.au/hs. Open daily 9am-5pm. $14.90, concessions $11.10, children ages 4-15 $7.40, families of 6 $40.40.)*

WERIBEE PARK AND OPEN RANGE ZOO. For a relaxing daytrip from Melbourne, the mansion at **Werribee Park** is a good bet, with serene sculptured gardens, an imposing billiards room, and an expansive nursery wing. Built between 1874-77 by a Scottish sheep tycoon determined to move beyond his working-class heritage, the estate fell into disrepair after the owner's death and was taken over by a monastery. Since being purchased by the Victorian government, it's become a popular tourist stop. *(K Rd. 30min. west of Melbourne along the Princes Hwy. ☎9741 2444. Open M-F 10am-4pm, Sa-Su 10am-5pm in winter; daily 10am-5pm in summer. $10.30, concessions $6.60, children 3-14 $5.20, families $26.70. Wheelchair accessible.)* You can go on safari among animals from the grasslands of Australia, Africa, and Asia at Victoria's **Open Range Zoo,** just behind the mansion on K Rd. To explore on your own, take the two 30min. walking trails; a tour of the 200-hectare park takes about 3hr. *(☎9731 1311. Open daily 9am-5pm; entrance closes at 3:30pm. 50min. safaris daily 10:30am-3:40pm. $12.20, concessions $9.10, children 3-15 $6.10, families $33.10. Wheelchair accessible.)*

ORGAN PIPES NATIONAL PARK. Australia is all about unique geological formations, and the Melbourne area features one of its own: the Organ Pipes National Park. Although the 6m metamorphic landmarks look more like french fries than organ pipes, they're still a good daytrip or stop en route to the central Goldfields. Look for the **Rosette Rock,** which resembles a flowing stone frozen in time (400m past the Organ Pipes). The park is also a laboratory for environmental restoration and has been largely repopulated with native plants and trees since the early 1970s, when weeds concealed the pipes. The park has picnic and BBQ facilities and charges no entrance fee. *(Just off the Calder Hwy. (Hwy. 79), 20km northwest of Melbourne. Public transport from Melbourne is slightly tricky: take tram #59 from Elizabeth St. to Essendon Station, then switch to bus #483 to Sunbury. ☎9390 1082. Open daily 8am-4:30pm and until 6pm on weekends and public holidays during daylight savings. Wheelchair accessible.)*

HANGING ROCK RESERVE. It's more than just a movie. The unique rock formations on this bit of crown land featured in the famous *Picnic at Hanging Rock* are nearly as curious as the protagonists' fate. *(Enter from Calder Hwy., past Organ Pipes National Park; follow the signs and enter at the south gate on South Rock Rd. Or take V/Line from Spencer St. Station to Wood End, and walk or take a cab the 7km from the station. ☎5427 0295. Open daily 8am-6pm. $8 per car.)*

PUFFING BILLY STEAM RAILWAY. The train is a relaxing way to see the interior of northeast Victoria's Dandenong Ranges. The billowing vapor reminds of simpler times, but quickly dissipates in the verdant rainforest terrain. *(40km east of Melbourne on the Burwood Hwy. to Belgrave. Or, take a 70min. Connex Hillside Train (☎13 16 38) from Flinders St. Station. Train from Belgrave to Lakeside: 1hr., 2-5 per day; $24.50, concessions $19.50, children 4-16 $11.50, families $50; from Belgrave to Gembrook: 1¾hr., 1-2 per day, $34.50/$27.50/$16.50/$70. ☎9754 6800; www.puffingbilly.com.au.)*

NEAR MELBOURNE

YARRA VALLEY WINERIES

Though not as well-known or as heavily visited as the Hunter Valley, NSW (p. 146) or the Barossa Valley, SA (p. 431), the Yarra Valley produces some top-grade wines. Located about 60km from Melbourne, the Yarra's vineyards were started in 1835 with 600, um, procured vinecuttings from the Hunter Valley. After a depression in the 1890s decimated wine demand, the Yarra basically shut down. Grapes were replanted in the 1960s, and today the Yarra has more than tripled its size from its peak in the 1800s. The Yarra's cool climate makes it ideal for growing Chardonnay, Pinot Noir, and Cabernet Sauvignon grapes; virtually every one of the over 30 wineries produces wines of these varieties. Quality sparkling wines abound, as the Chardonnay and Pinot Noir grapes are two of the principal grapes used to make the bubbly. For more information on touring wineries see p. 434.

PRACTICAL INFORMATION. Public transportation options to the wineries are limited; Lilydale, 10-20km outside the Yarra, is on the Met train line, but after that there's no way to get to the wineries without hiring a car (remember *Let's Go* does not recommend drinking and driving, and perhaps more importantly, neither do the police). Pick up a free *Wineries of the Yarra Valley* or *Wine Regions of Victoria* at the Melbourne tourist office, or check out www.yarravalleywineries.asn.au. There are several tour options from Melbourne, though the best and most affordable is the unimaginatively named **Backpacker Winery Tours** (☎9877 8333; www.backpackerwinerytours.com.au). The $75 tour runs virtually every day, offers pickup at major hostels, free tastings at four wineries, and a gourmet lunch overlooking the valley, not to mention knowledgeable commentary and lessons on wine quality and tasting technique from guides who have worked in the winemaking and tasting industries themselves.

WINERIES. You can't go wrong with any of the options, especially at the normal price of $2 for a taste of their whole selection (tasting fee usually refundable upon purchase). Hours vary, but wineries are generally open daily 10am-5pm. Call and arrange a walk-through with the winemaker.

Yering Station, (☎9730 1107; www.yering.com). 1hr. east of the city. On the site of Yarra's 1st vineyard, Yering's tasting area has a delightful art gallery, and the multi-million dollar complex next door has a top-notch restaurant with a huge glass wall overlooking the Valley. Bottles $12.50-45. Open M-F 10am-5pm, Sa-Su 10am-6pm.

St. Huberts (☎9739 1118), on St. Huberts Rd. Founded in 1863 by Hubert de Castella, this small winery offers a very popular Cabernet. It is also 1 of only 4 Australian wineries to produce the Rhone River Valley Roussane, a unique flavor great for mixing or variety. Bottles $19-30. Open M-F 9:30am-5pm, Sa-Su 10:30am-5:30pm.

Oakridge Estate, 864 Maroondah Hwy. (☎9739 1920; www.oakridgeestate.com.au). Having a more modern feel than many of its Yarra neighbors, Oakridge carries several award-winners, including its 1997 Cabernet Sauvignon voted "Best Red Wine in Australia," not to mention best cabernet sauvignon in the world for that season. Bottles $18-40. Open daily 10am-5pm.

Yarra Ridge, 179 Glenview Rd. (☎9730 1022). Even with award-winning wines, these humble winemakers don't boast their success on their labels. They're all about quality, and you'll find it particularly in their Pinot Noir. Bottles $16-45. Open daily 10am-5pm.

Domaine Chandon (☎9739 1110; www.chandon.com.au), "Green Point," Maroondah Hwy. The most polished spot in the Yarra, with a walk-through exhibit on the process of producing sparkling wine. No free tastings–only $5.50 flutes with a free bread plate, or $20-40 bottles to go. Open daily 10:30am-4:30pm. Free tour 3pm.

PORT PHILLIP AND WESTERNPORT BAYS

Two pincers of land curve south from Melbourne around Port Phillip and Westernport Bays: the Bellarine Peninsula to the west and the Mornington Peninsula to the east. The bays were the site of the first European settlement in Victoria in 1803 (near Sorrento), a squalid effort that lasted less than a year. By the late 19th century, though, spectacular coastal views and a sunny, temperate climate made the bays the site of choice for summer homes of the goldfield-spawned *nouveau riche.* With the exception of Phillip Island and its notorious Little Penguins, this area remains largely a wealthy getaway, a fact that deters most backpackers. There are, however, enough budget opportunities here to allow everyone to enjoy the awesome scenery, sandy beaches, and excellent surfing.

PHILLIP ISLAND ☎03

Phillip Island has become synonymous with the endearing Little Penguins that inhabit its southwest corner and scamper back to their burrows nightly in a "Penguin Parade." The Parade is massively popular—drawing some 3.5 million visitors each year—so be prepared for a touristy crowd. A plethora of other wildlife, including koalas, wombats, seals, and hundreds of species of birds, also calls Phillip Island home; spot the animals in the wild on one of a number of nature walks, or visit the island's two wildlife centers. Large breakers crashing against the island's southern shore create a surfers' mecca in summer, and the Grand Prix motorcycle race draws racers and their fervent followers in early October. Despite the crowds, the rolling hills and vibrant blue Bass Strait waters make Phillip Island a great place to relax for a few days.

TRANSPORTATION. Phillip Island lies across a narrow strait from **San Remo,** 145km southeast of Melbourne. Numerous backpacker-oriented tours take groups to the island. The best value is the **Duck Truck Tours,** run by the folks at Amaroo Park Hostel (see below). The tour includes Melbourne transfers, up to three nights at the hostel, a guided tour of the Penguin Parade and the whole island, meals, and a half-day of bike use. (☎5952 2548. $125, VIP/YHA $115.) By car, Phillip Island is just two hours from Melbourne; take the South Eastern Arterial (M1) to the Cranbourne exit to the South Gippsland Hwy. (M420), then turn onto the Bass Hwy. (A420), and finally onto Phillip Island Tourist Rd. (B420). This road leads straight into **Cowes,** the island's biggest township, where it turns into Thompson Ave. **V/Line buses** serve Cowes from Melbourne (3hr.; 1 per day, Dec.-Apr. F-Su 2 per day; $15.20). To purchase V/Line tickets in town, head to **Cowes Travel** (☎5952 2744; open M-F 8:30am-5:30pm, Sa 9-11am) or **Going Places Travel** (☎5952 3700; open M-F 9am-5:30pm), both on Thompson Ave.

PRACTICAL INFORMATION. Once on Phillip Island, you'll see the **Phillip Island Information Centre** over the bridge. (☎5956 7447; www.phillipisland.net.au. Open daily 9am-5pm.) Buy tickets for the Parade here to avoid long queues. Other services include: **police** (☎5952 2037); **hospital** (☎5952 2345); **ATMs** on Thompson Ave.; **laundry** at **Cheap Smokes,** 14 The Esplanade; **Internet** at **Waterfront Internet Services,** 130 Thompson Ave., next to Cowes Travel (see above, $1.50 per 15min.); **post office,** 73 Thompson Ave. (open M-F 9am-5pm). **Postal code:** 3922.

ACCOMMODATIONS AND FOOD. The most popular budget lodging on Phillip Island is the **Amaroo Park Hostel (YHA),** 97 Church St., Cowes; head down Thompson Ave. and hang a left on Church St. Though mostly a trailer park, the backpacker accommodations are lovely, with nice wooden furniture, a pool table, a **pub** with cheap drinks, and an outdoor veranda with BBQ. The friendly staff runs all kinds of tours (including ones to the Penguin Parade) and serves a $6 dinner

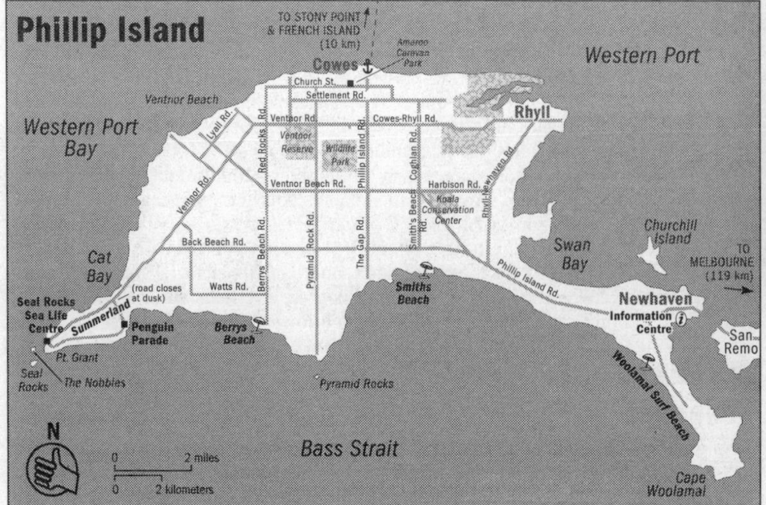

and a $5 cooked or $3 cold breakfast. (☎5952 2548; amaroo@waterfront.net.au. Internet. Swimming pool. Call to inquire about pickup in Melbourne. Mention *Let's Go* to get a free bike for the afternoon. Book ahead. Sites $11; dorms $17.50, non-YHA $21; doubles $42, $50.) For cozy accommodations, head for **Jocks Place Backpackers,** 33 Chapel St., Cowes. There's a homey living room with TV and international newspapers. There's also a free BBQ, car park, local discounts, cheap Internet ($3 per 30min., $5 per hr.), pool tables, book exchange, free pickup from the bus stop, and late check-out. (☎5952 1655 or 0414 494 569; www.home.waterfront.net.au/~jocksplace. Dorms $17; doubles $35. Discounts for longer stays.)

For all-day breakfast, head for the **One Stop Shop,** 58 Chapel St. (☎5952 1439. Open daily 7am-8:30pm.) Your best bet for lunch is the **Phillip Island Bakery,** at the corner of Thompson Ave. and Chapel St.; sandwiches and hot pies are under $3. (☎5952 2027. Open M-F 7am-5pm, Sa-Su 7am-4:30pm.) For more upmarket eats, sample **Café Terrazzo,** 5 Thompson Ave., a whimsically painted bistro with a range of pasta and wood-fired pizza. (☎5952 3773. Meals $8-15. Open daily noon-3pm and 5-9pm; winter daily 5-9pm.) An IGA **supermarket** is at the corner of Thompson and Chapel St. (☎5952 2244. Open 7:30am-5:30pm, summer until 7pm.)

ACTIVITIES AND WILDLIFE. Phillip Island's tourist magnet is the **Little Penguin Parade,** at the Phillip Island Nature Park. Each night, anywhere between a handful and 1000 penguins return to their burrows after lengthy fishing expeditions to rest or attend to their hungry chicks. The **Information Centre** provides extensive information about the penguins, including interactive exhibits on their life cycle, diet, and behavior. A boardwalk provides beach access from the center and allows you to watch the penguins burrow after they arrive. People await the penguins from a large grandstand along the boardwalk at sunset; after a 30min. to 1hr. wait, the penguins emerge, and their parade lasts nearly an hour. (☎5951 2800; www.penguins.org.au. Open daily from 10am-10:30/11pm. $12.50, children $6.50, families $31.40. Wheelchair accessible.)

Although the penguins are the main draw, several other animals make cameos. On the island's western extreme, past the penguin parade, Australia's largest colony of **Australian fur seals** lives just offshore from the **Nobbies** rock formation. A boardwalk approaches the Nobbies, enabling you to take in the beautiful eroded hills and crashing sea (open 7:30am-dusk). The **Seal Rocks Sea Life Centre** is costly for the experience. Inside you'll find displays on local marine life, a video of the seals, and a Disneyesque boat ride past animated displays tracing the area's seal hunting and conservation history. If you pop $1 in the binoculars on the boardwalk, you'll see the coolest thing this place has to offer—the seals themselves. (☎1300 367 325. Open 10am-dusk. $16, students $13, children $8, families $40.) The **Koala Conservation Centre,** south of Cowes on Phillip Island Rd., is a sanctuary housing 23 koalas in eucalypt canopies. The nocturnal marsupials are most active at feeding time, 1½ hours before dusk. (☎5952 1307. Open daily 10am-6pm, until 7pm in the summer. $5, children $2, families $12.)

Throughout the year—but particularly in summer—Phillip Island offers great outdoor recreation. Surfers swarm to the island's southern coast; ask the staff at the information center for the *Surfing Guide to Phillip Island.* **Island Surfboards,** 147 Thompson Ave. and 65 Smith's Beach Rd., can set you up with a board and provides excellent instruction. (☎5952 3443. Boards $10 per hr., $30 per day. 2hr. lesson $30.) **Cape Woolamai,** on the southeast corner, has the island's highest point, numerous walking trails, and a patrolled beach for swimming between the flags. Bushwalking trails cover the island, ranging from casual to hard; the info center's pamphlet *Discover Phillip Island Nature Park* is a good place to start.

SORRENTO ☎03

Though home to a year-round population of only 1500, the small town of Sorrento brims with activity in summer, as travelers seek out history-rich parklands, rocky cliffs, and fine surfing—all just minutes from the town's old limestone buildings. Near the very tip of the Mornington Peninsula's long sweep down from Melbourne, the resort affords visitors the chance to relax in a charming coastal environment.

TRANSPORTATION AND PRACTICAL INFORMATION. From Melbourne, take a **train** to Frankston (1hr., $10), then **bus** #788 to stop 18 (1½hr.; M-F 10 per day, Sa 5 per day, Su 4 per day; $7.30). If you're coming from the Great Ocean Rd., you can reach Sorrento via **ferry** from Queenscliff, on the Bellarine Peninsula (1hr.; 6-7 per day; $7; cars $34-36). The **Information Centre** (☎5984 5678) is on St. Aubins Way, on the shore next to the boat launch. Along **Ocean Beach Rd.,** Sorrento's main street and a traffic nightmare, you'll find numerous **ATMs** and a **post office,** 16 Ocean Beach Rd. (open M-F 9am-5pm). **Postal code:** 3943.

ACCOMMODATIONS AND FOOD. From the roundabout at the inland end of Ocean Beach Rd., follow the YHA signs up Ossett St. to the **Sorrento Backpackers YHA,** 3 Miranda St. Only five minutes from Back Beach, this backpacker retreat has an outdoor patio with BBQ, kitchen, basic groceries, and Internet ($2 per 10min.). The hostel operators will eagerly lead you to beautiful walking tracks and can secure discounts on everything from horse rides to swims with dolphins. (☎5984 4323; fax 5984 2430. Dorms $18, non-YHA $23. Book 1 week ahead in summer.)

Ocean Beach Rd. is lined with eateries. **Stringer's Cafe,** 2-8 Ocean Beach Rd., offers made-to-order sandwiches and salads. (☎5984 2010. Meals $3-8. Open daily 8am-5pm.) There's also a **supermarket** next door. (Open Su-F 8:30am-5:30pm, Sa 8:30am-6pm; in summer M-Th 8am-7pm, F-Sa 8am-7:30pm, Su 8am-6pm.) For Danish hot dogs ($4) and ice cream so good as to make a Viking slobber, head for **The Little Mermaid,** 70 Ocean Beach Rd. (Open daily in summer 11am-10pm; in winter only Sa-Su.) Perched atop the hill, **Hotel Sorrento,** 5 Hotham Rd. (☎5984 2206), provides a chance to enjoy a beer ($2.50) while watching the sunset on the bay.

SIGHTS. The town's main attraction is its bottle-blue bay at the bottom of Ocean Beach Rd., popular for swimming and sailing in summer. Take caution: the riptides here change rapidly. For an unforgettable experience, swim with dolphins and seals with **Polperro Dolphin Swims.** The Muir family runs this eco-friendly service to help fund their dolphin research, promoting conservation through education. (☎5988 8437. 4hr.; Sept.-Apr. 2 per day; $60, YHA $54.) The most popular area to hang out and **surf** is **Back Beach,** on the west of the peninsula. You can learn to surf with the **Sorrento Surf School,** on Ocean Beach Rd. (☎5988 6143. 2hr., $25.)

NEAR SORRENTO: MORNINGTON PENINSULA

Mornington Peninsula National Park spans across more than 40km of coastline and bush country. The park is separated into different regions. **Point Nepean,** located on the western tip of the peninsula, consists of 6km of nearly undeveloped land only recently opened to the public. The best way to see this part of the park is by bus from the **Visitors Centre,** located at the end of Pt. Nepean Rd. (☎5984 4276. Open daily 9am-5pm, Dec.-Feb. until dusk. Buses depart daily every 30min. in summer, every hr. in winter, from 9:30am-3pm. $8, concessions $4.50; park fees included.) Disembark at the first stop and walk the rest of the way (allow 2hr.) to **Fort Nepean,** a military base, and take the bus back home from there.

There are also a plethora of **vineyards** on the peninsula. The **Dromana Estate Vineyards,** on Harrisons Rd. in Dromana, is open for tastings. (☎5987 3800. Daily 11am-3pm. $2.) Pick-your-own fruit farms also abound; check out **Sunny Ridge,** on the corner of Mornington-Flinders Rd. and Shands Rd. (☎5989 6273. Open Nov.-Apr. daily 9am-5pm; May-Oct. weekends only 10am-5pm. $6-8 per kg of strawberries.)

QUEENSCLIFF ☎03

Rustic, relaxing, and maybe even a little romantic, tiny Queenscliff perches perilously on the easternmost tip of the **Bellarine Peninsula,** 120km southwest of Melbourne, overlooking one of the most dangerous stretches of water on the seven seas. Swathed in grand old architecture, the town offers visitors a leisurely ambience well-suited to beach-sitting and twilight strolls. Queenscliff has undergone a series of incarnations, first as fishing village, then as a military outpost, and finally as a resort. Today, many travelers use Queenscliff as a peaceful place to start, or end, their journey on the Great Ocean Rd. (see p. 543).

Reach Queenscliff from Melbourne by taking the **train** to Geelong (1hr.; M-F 25 per day, Sa 18 per day, Su 9 per day; $13.20), and then a **bus** from there (1hr.; M-F 10 per day, Sa 5 per day, Su 4 per day; $5-6). Or take a **ferry** from the Sorrento Pier, just across the bay (1hr.; 6-7 per day; $7, cars $34-36). The **Visitor Information Centre** is at 55 Hesse St. (☎5258 4843. Open M-Tu 2-5pm, Th 10am-1pm and 2-5pm, F 10am-1pm and 2-6pm, Sa 9:30am-noon.) The **Marine Discovery Centre** runs informative events during the summer. (☎5258 3344. Tours $4.) Services include **hospital** (☎5266 7111) and **post office,** 47 Hesse St. (open M-F 9am-5pm). **Postal code:** 3225.

The jewel in the crown of hosteling, YHA-affiliated **Queenscliff Inn B&B,** 59 Hesse St., offers an elegant but affordable taste of the town's luxury. In a red brick 1906 Edwardian building, the Inn is centered around a gorgeous drawing room with an open fire. The delectable breakfast ranges from home-baked breads ($6) to full cooked meals ($13.50). There's a kitchen and laundry available, too. (☎5258 3737. Linen $2.50. Dorms $18; singles $30; doubles $22; family rooms $75.) If you can't get a bed here, some of the scuba diving outfits rent out bunkbeds. Try the **Queenscliff Dive Centre,** 37 Learmonth St., opposite Town Hall. (☎5258 1188. Bunks from $28; private rooms from $55.) Queenscliff Dive Centre conducts snorkeling tours to swim with a colony of playful fur seals and dolphins. They also run scuba certification classes. (☎1800 814 200. Book ahead. 2hr. tour from $35.)

For a light lunch starting at $5 or a $3 milkshake, rub elbows with locals at the **Promenade Cafe,** 1 Symonds St. (☎5258 2911. Open daily 8am-5:30pm, winter 10am-5pm.) The grand **Queenscliff Hotel,** presiding regally over the bay with stained glass and intricately patterned tiles, has served as a summer resort since the town's earliest days. You probably can't afford the rooms or the main dining room, but the casual restaurant, **Mietta's,** 16 Gellibrand St., provides a chance to pretend you can. Menu options range from a delicate tomato bruschetta to a hearty meat lasagna. (☎5258 1066. Meals $9.50-12. Open daily 10am-8pm.) There's a **supermarket** at 73 Hesse St. (☎5258 1727. Open M-F 9am-6pm, Sa-Su 9am-5pm.)

A "HAREY" SITUATION. It doesn't take very long for most visitors to Australia to realize how hated cute little bunny rabbits can become. The presence of rabbits down under owes itself to one very foolish Thomas Austin, of Barwon Park. On Christmas Day, 1859, Austin imported 10 pairs of the little hopping buggers via the waters of Corio Bay off the shores of Geelong. Little did he know that ecological catastrophe was near at hand—in the absence of predators they multiplied quickly, causing widespread destruction of native crops. Farmers have tried everything from the 1950 introduction of the Myxoma virus to the less scientific means of poisoned carrots and rifle rounds to wipe the bouncing blight off the Australian landscape.

GEELONG ☎03

Geelong ("jah-LONG"), an hour southwest of Melbourne on the Princes Hwy. (Hwy. 1) at the western end of Port Philip Bay, is an important transportation hub for the **Great Ocean Road** and other points west. While most people just pass through, there are a few pleasant attractions, including a revamped waterfront, as befits the second-largest city in Victoria.

TRANSPORTATION AND PRACTICAL INFORMATION. The **V/Line Station** (☎13 61 96), on Brougham St., remains Geelong's most important building for most travelers. **V/Line** runs **trains** to Melbourne (1hr., departs daily every hr., $9.50) and Warrnambool (2¼hr.; M-F 3 per day, Sa 2 per day, Su 3 per day; $27). V/Line also sends **buses** to Ballarat (1½hr.; M-Sa 3 per day, Su 2 per day; $10.80). The Princes Hwy. runs north-south through town, and assumes the alias of Latrobe Tce. while in the metropolis. Moorabool St. also runs north-south, from the pier; its intersection with Malop and Little Malop St. host most of the town's action. The **Tourist Centre** is in the Wool Museum. (☎5222 2900. Open daily 9am-5pm.) Other services include **banks** with **ATMs** on Moorabool and Malop St. and a **post office,** 99 Moorabool St. (Open M-F 9am-5:30pm, Sa 9am-noon.) **Postal code:** 3220.

ACCOMMODATIONS. **Irish Murphy's,** 30 Aberdeen St., has small but clean kitchen facilities and a deck with a fabulous view. The pub down below with beautiful wood finishing is a classic hot-bed of Irish fun. (☎5221 4335; fax 5223 3055. Pub open M-Th 11am-midnight, F-Sa 11am-1am, Su 11am-11pm. Bunks $18; doubles $48.) The **National Hotel,** 191 Moorabool St., on the corner of Little Ryrie and Moorabool St., has a worn-looking hostel with complete facilities upstairs, while downstairs, the pub serves up wok-prepared noodle dishes and live music. (☎5229 1211. Key deposit $10. Dorms $19, doubles $44.) Many B&Bs and motels exist southwest of the V/Line station on Aberdeen St.

FOOD. Right on the waterfront, the easy-going **Wharf Shed Cafe,** 15 East Beach Rd., offers a wide-ranging menu for decent prices. (☎5221 6645. Open daily 9am-11pm.) **Gilligan's,** 100 Western Beach Rd., across from the Cunningham Pier, has cheap seafood meals from $7-13. (☎5222 3200. Open daily 11am-8pm.) **Pizza Lovers,** 87 Ryrie St., offers excellent pizza from $5. (☎5221 8858. Free delivery. Open M-Th 11:30am-11:30pm, F-Sa 11:30am-4am, Su 5-11:30pm.) At the corner of Gheringhap and Little Melop St., the **Courthouse Cafe** is a cool spot with outstanding salads and free **Internet.** (☎5229 3470. Open M-F 7am-5pm.)

SIGHTS. The main attraction in town is the large **Wool Museum,** 26 Moorabol St., east along Brougham St. It's surprisingly fascinating, with live weaving demonstrations and interactive displays illustrating the centrality of the wool industry in Australian history and folklore. (☎5227 0701. Open daily 9:30am-5pm. $7.30, concessions $5.90, children $3.90.) An old-fashioned **carousel** overlooks the town's waterfront. ($3, children $2— hey, if there's an adult price then we're meant to ride it!) **Geelong Art Gallery,** in **Johnston Park,** specializes in Australian art. (☎5229 3645. Open M-F 10am-5pm, Sa-Su 1-5pm. $3.) Head down Moorabal to the family **beach** on your right after you pass the Wool Museum on your left.

GREAT OCEAN ROAD

The Great Ocean Road is one of the world's greatest vehicular experiences. The Victoria government, in tribute to Australians who died in World War I, commissioned the coastal highway with this intention in mind. They succeeded, carving a route that winds between misty temperate rainforests and the unearthly pillars, stone arches, and gorges sculpted by the Southern Ocean. The entire serene and spectacular southwestern coast of Victoria, from Torquay to Portland, is encompassed by the Great Ocean Road region, though the road itself is just the 200km stretch that links Torquay to Warrnambool before being absorbed by the Princes Hwy. Almost too notable, the road attracts heavy tourist traffic.

Heading west, the first part of the Great Ocean Road is called the **Surf Coast,** stretching from Torquay to Lorne, where, unsurprisingly, surfers enjoy the excellent breaks. Swimmers can also enjoy the water if they stick to the safer beaches near the towns. Moist ocean winds confront the forest barrier of the **Otway Ranges** on the 73km stretch from Anglesea to Apollo Bay. This cool, rainy climate nurtures tree ferns, large pines, waterfalls, and a range of fauna; a stop here promises an extensive network of walking trails. After Apollo Bay, the hub of the Otways, the drive turns inland across Cape Otway, rejoining the shoreline at the **Shipwreck Coast.** Here, unrelenting winds, unpredictable offshore swells, and inconvenient limestone formations turned the region into a graveyard for 19th-century vessels, but also shaped the famous **Twelve Apostles** rock formations. Moving farther west, discover whales off **Warrnambool,** mutton birds in **Port Fairy,** and estuary fishing in **Lower Glenelg National Park.**

TRANSPORTATION ON THE GREAT OCEAN ROAD

If you have a **car** to explore the Great Ocean Road, you're lucky, as public transport probably won't get you everywhere you want to go. **Bicycling** along the highway is a possibility, but make sure you are in shape for it: the hilly topography between Torquay and Lorne will tone your butt faster than you can say "billabong." **V/Line** (☎13 61 96) **buses** from Melbourne stop in Geelong, from which they head west to Apollo Bay (M-F 3 per day, Sa-Su 2 per day) and Lorne and Torquay (M-F 4 per day, Sa 6 per day, Su 4 per day). On Fridays year round and also Mondays in Dec.-Jan., the special **"coast link" V/Line bus** services Lorne, Apollo Bay, Port Campbell, and Warrnambool, with brief stops at tourist lookouts along the Shipwreck Coast. You thus stand a good chance of getting stranded in Lorne until Friday if you arrive early in the week. **Bellarine Transit** (☎5223 2111) sends about three **buses** a day from Geelong to Torquay.

Several **bus tours** from Melbourne to Adelaide allow travelers to take their time sampling the southwest coast, with layovers en route. **Wayward Bus** runs to Adelaide via the Great Ocean Rd. and allows up to six months of jumping on and off. (☎08 8232 6646 or 1800 882 823; www.waywardbus.com.au. $180 includes lunches, planned pitstops, and accommodations.) **Oz Experience** runs one-day or multi-day tours, including Mornington Peninsula or the Grampians. The Road is also part of their regular journey from Melbourne to Adelaide, allowing you to hop on and off for up to six months. (☎1300 300 028; www.ozexperience.com. Daytrip $55, 2-day with Mornington $149, 3-day with Grampians $245; accommodation included. 5% YHA discount on shorter tours.) **Autopia Tours** runs structured 1- and 3-day return tours as well as 3-day Melbourne-Adelaide trips that incorporate the Great Ocean Rd. and Grampians. (☎9326 5536 or 1800 000 507; www.autopiatours.com.au. 1-day $54, 3-day $140, Melbourne-Adelaide $150.) **Wildlife Tours** runs a highlight tour of the Great Ocean Rd., as well as longer trips. (☎9534 8868; www.wildlife-tours.com.au. Highlights $35, 1- to 3-day tours $50-135, Adelaide link $129-199. ISIC/NOMADS/VIP/YHA.) Short day and overnight trips that cover lots of ground quickly are also very popular. **Let's Go Bush Tours** gives you dinner, breakfast, and accommodation on a 2-day tour. (Cool name, but no affiliation. ☎9662 3969. Tours depart W and Sa. $99.) Tours are highly useful along the Great Ocean Rd. if you don't have a car; public transportation is very limited and infrequent in the area.

Several useful publications on the Great Ocean Rd. are available at tourist offices and bookstores throughout Victoria. The free glossy *The Great Ocean Road* provides just the facts, ma'am, just the facts. The National Park Service's *Map Guide: SouthWest* has reliable maps and sample short-term itineraries. *Great Ocean Road: A Traveller's Guide* is another option. General tourist info can be found at www.greatoceanrd.org.au.

TORQUAY ☎03

Wave seekers and beach bums who feel like they've wandered too far from Byron Bay, take heart: there's great surfing in Victoria, and Torquay ("tor-KEY"), at the eastern end of the Great Ocean Road, is the center of the action.

TRANSPORTATION AND PRACTICAL INFORMATION. **V/Line buses** (☎13 61 96) leave from outside the Bernell Caravan Park by the Bell's Beach hostel on the Great Ocean Rd. to: Geelong (45min.; M-F 4 per day, Sa-Su 2 per day; $5.40); Lorne (1hr., $9.50); Melbourne (1½hr., 4 per day, $12.30); and points west. **Bellarine Transit** (☎5223 2111) provides buses to Geelong. Most commercial activity takes place along the aptly named Surfcoast Hwy., a continuation of the Great Ocean Rd., or just off the highway on Gilbert St., where there is a well-marked shopping district with **ATMs** and food options. The town's **Visitor Centre,** 120 Surfcoast Hwy. in Surfworld Museum, has **Internet.** (☎5261 4606. Open daily 9am-5pm.)

ACCOMMODATIONS AND FOOD. Book in advance for the Easter surfing competition. **Bell's Beach Backpackers,** 51-53 Surf Coast Hwy., is a brightly-painted, bungalow-style bunkhouse with a pronounced surfing mood set by posters, magazines, and nearly constant screenings of surf documentaries. Bell's Beach also has immaculate bathrooms, lockers, bikes, and good vibrations. (☎5261 7070 or 1800 819 883. Key and linen deposit $15. Reception roughly 8-10am and 4-10pm. Dorms $19; doubles $45; higher during school holidays. NOMADS.) Close to Bell's Beach and Jan Juc, but correspondingly farther from town, is **Pointbreak Backpackers,** 185 Addiscott Rd., about 8km southeast via the Great Ocean Rd. Tucked away down a quiet road, this 15-bed hostel has a full kitchen, BBQ, and a courtesy bus to town center and the beach. (☎5261 5105 or 0418 521 855. Dorms $17; winter rates lower. No doubles.) **Bernells Caravan Park,** 55 Surfcoast Hwy., is right in town, near the huge range of surfing stores. It's a two-minute drive from the beach, and it has a pool, spa, and tennis court. (☎5261 2493. Powered sites $18; cabins from $43.)

Hordes of surfers with the munchies provide a large market for the takeaways and chippers that dominate Torquay's food scene, centered on Gilbert St. **Spooner's,** 57 Geelong Rd., a cheap and friendly coffeehouse, provides a dash of the oh-so-popular cafe scene. (☎5261 3887. Open daily 9am-5pm.) There's a Food-Works **supermarket** on Gilbert St. (Open daily 7am-midnight.)

SURFING AND BEYOND. Peak **surfing** season is from March to August. The reef breaks at **Bells Beach** attract top professional surfers for the Easter **Rip Curl Pro Classic.** It's a 10min. drive from town, a 30min. bike ride, or a 1hr. walk along the **Surf Coast Walk** past stunning cliff to **Airey's Inlet.** The walk also passes **Jan Juc,** the second-best surfing site around (also safe for swimmers). For closer swimming beaches, cross the highway from Bells Beach Backpackers and continue straight for 10min. to **Cozy Corner, Torquay Front Beach,** or **Fisherman's Beach.**

The colossal **Rip Curl World Headquarters,** 101 Surfcoast Hwy., is just the beginning of a string of surf retailers. (☎5261 0000. Open daily 9am-5:30pm in winter, 9am-9pm in summer.) Hang a left before the big buildings to find the bargains at one of several secondhand shops, which sell "imperfect" goods at closer to perfect prices. (Most open M-Sa 9am-5pm, Su 11am-5pm.) At the back of the plaza, **Surfworld** has a hall of fame of Australia's most venerated surfers, as well as interactive displays on wave physics, different kinds of breaks, and surfing history. (☎5261 4606. Open daily 10am-4pm. $6.50, concessions and NOMADS $4.50.)

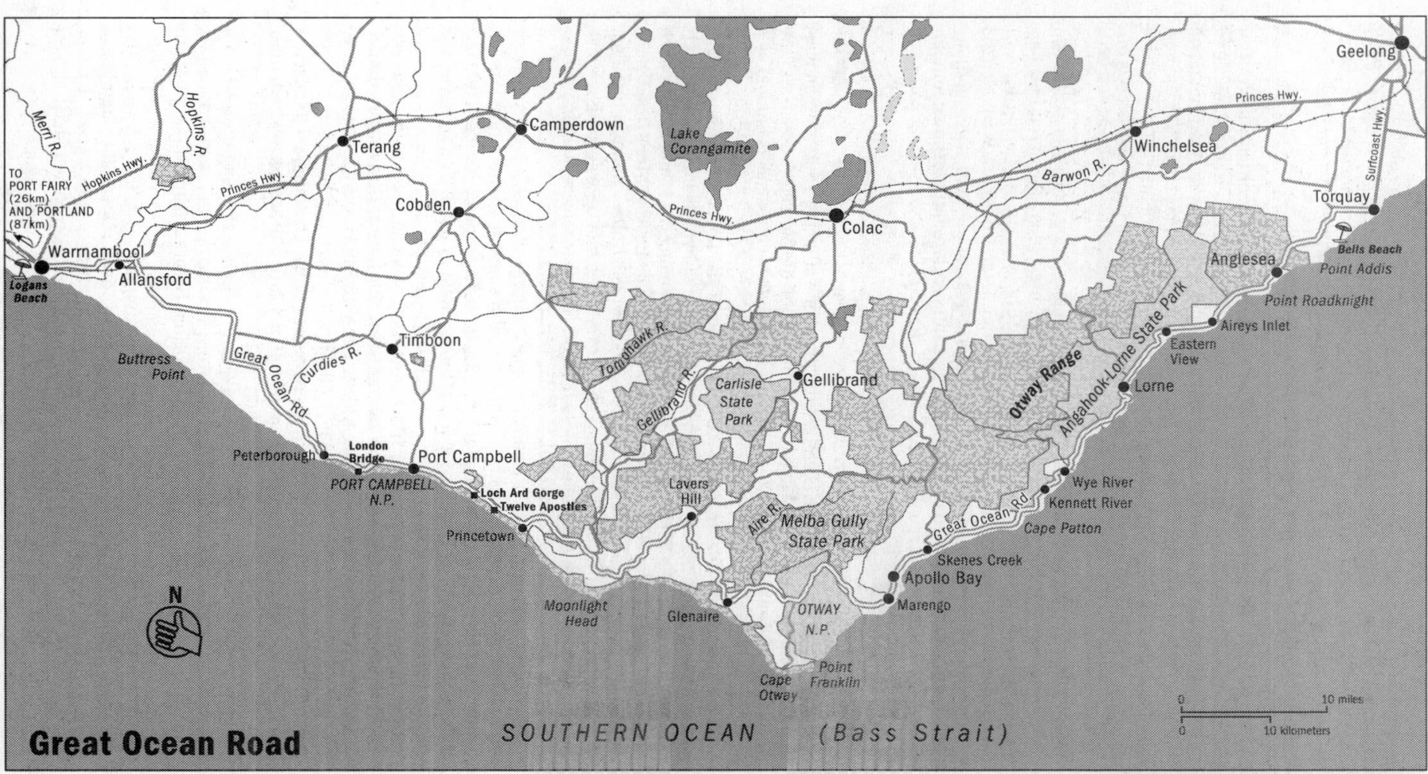
Great Ocean Road
Geelong
Princes Hwy.
Surfcoast Hwy.
Torquay
Bells Beach
Point Addis
Anglesea
Point Roadknight
Aireys Inlet
Eastern View
Lorne
Angahook-Lorne State Park
Otway Range
Wye River
Kennett River
Cape Patton
Great Ocean Rd.
Skenes Creek
Apollo Bay
Marengo
OTWAY N.P.
Point Franklin
Cape Otway
Melba Gully State Park
Aire R.
Glenaire
Lavers Hill
Moonlight Head
Carlisle State Park
Gellibrand
Gellibrand R.
Tomahawk R.
Winchelsea
Barwon R.
Colac
Princes Hwy.
Lake Corangamite
Camperdown
Terang
Cobden
Timboon
Curdies R.
Port Campbell
London Bridge
PORT CAMPBELL N.P.
Loch Ard Gorge
Twelve Apostles
Princetown
Peterborough
Great Ocean Rd
Buttress Point
Hopkins R.
Hopkins Hwy.
Merri R.
Princes Hwy.
TO PORT FAIRY (26km) AND PORTLAND (87km)
Warrnambool
Allansford
Logans Beach
N
SOUTHERN OCEAN (Bass Strait)
0
10 miles
0
10 kilometers

If surfing's not your stuff, then take to the sky. **Skydive Torquay,** run from Tiger Moth World Adventure Park 3km north of Torquay, offers tandem jumps from 10,000 ft. above the beautiful Great Ocean coastline. (☎9432 2419 or 0413 863 929; www.skydivingassoc.com.au. $315, 5% credit card fee. Arrange ahead for pickup.)

FROM TORQUAY TO LORNE

POINT ADDIS. The turn-off to **Point Addis** appears abruptly about 5km out of Torquay. The point offers outstanding views of Victoria's western coast, serrated by silty clay and gray cliffs. Between Point Addis and the highway is the beginning of the recently cleared **Koorie Walk,** (2km; 1hr. return) which leads through the **Ironbark Basin Reserve.** Displays along the way elucidate the history of the Koorie Aborigines who once inhabited the area. Red ironbarks and peregrine falcons are natural highlights; the park is best in the early morning or late afternoon.

ANGLESEA. Between Lorne and Torquay, Anglesea (pop. 2000) is still close enough to the surf for plenty of aquatic action, but is less touristed and less quaint than its more famous neighbors. Surfing lessons, including loan of boards and wetsuits, can be had at short notice from **Go Ride A Wave** (☎5263 2111), with one lesson at $30 or a four lesson package for $100. The company also operates out of Torquay and Lorne. For immaculate but sterile accommodation, try **Anglesea Backpackers,** 40 Noble St. (☎5263 2664. Dorms $22, off-peak $18; with bath from $50.)

LORNE ☎03

Someone once decided to sell Lorne as "the place of well-being"; that tourism mastermind could just as easily have chosen "the place of the well-dressed" or "the place of the well-to-do." This trendy town, with a stylish cafe scene, is flanked by a popular beach and a temperate rainforest.

Qdos Gallery and Artzbar, Allenvale Rd., is one of the finest arts venues in this part of Victoria. The gallery and sculpture garden host ever-changing modern art exhibits. The **Qdos Film Society** has free, outdoor screenings of 16mm movies such as *Bonnie and Clyde* or *The Maltese Falcon.* The cafe has daily fresh food and a constantly changing menu (mains $12-20). (☎5289 1989. Gallery open daily except W 10am-6pm; Easter-Oct. F-M 10am-5pm. Bar open 'til 1am on weekends, Sa live music.) **Meridian Kayak Adventures** offers trips off the treacherous coastline in one- or two-person kayaks. (☎9596 8876. Half-day $50, full-day $90.)

The Great Ocean Rd. morphs briefly into the Mountjoy Pde. as it passes through town. **Buses** depart daily from the Commonwealth Bank at 68 Mountjoy Pde. to: Apollo Bay (1hr., $5.40); Geelong (1½hr., $12.30); Melbourne (2½hr., $24.10). The **Visitor Centre,** 144 Mountjoy Pde., is a few blocks west of the V/Line stop. (☎5289 1152. Open daily 9am-5pm.)

Great Ocean Backpackers (YHA), 10 Erskine Ave., is a colony of treehouse-like wooden cabins set on a hillside in the midst of the forest. Birds of all shapes and colors fly in to share your breakfast. The extremely knowledgeable staff give guests a lift to trailheads. (☎5289 1809. Book ahead. Dorms $18, non-members 21; twins and doubles $42, non-members $50.) **Erskine Backpackers,** 4 Mountjoy Pde., is at the bend at the west end of town. The sincere owners offer shared rooms that open on to a veranda. (☎5289 1496. Doonas $3. Bunks $20.) **Campgrounds** without amenities are available inside the Angahook-Lorne National Park (☎5289 1732; $6, payable to a roving ranger), or for free just behind the town (check in at the Tourist Office before setting up). Complete camping facilities are available 10km west of town at the beautiful **Cumberland River Camping Reserve.** (☎5289 1790. Sites $17; cabins from $59.) Pick up the best fresh fish on the **pier** toward the west end of town. (Open daily 9am-6pm.) Cafes and bakeries line the Great Ocean Rd. Ridgeway's **supermarket,** 1 Great Ocean Rd., is on the Melbourne side of the Erskine River. (Open M-Th and Su 8am-7pm, F 8am-8pm, Sa 7am-8pm.)

VICTORIA

NEAR LORNE: ANGAHOOK-LORNE STATE PARK

Mountains meet the sea with incredible drama and grace in the **Angahook-Lorne State Park,** a 21,000-hectare reserve known for its waterfalls. Several gentle walking trails abound, most notably **Teddy's Lookout,** a sweeping view of the countryside and **Erskine Falls** both in the Lorne forest reserve. Teddy's is a 30min. walk up Bay St. and left on George St. in Lorne. Erskine Falls is a more ambitious (3hr.) 300-step descent, five-minutes from the carpark via William St. and Erskine Falls Rd.

Various simple tracks begin at the **Sheoak Picnic Area,** a 1hr. walk or 15min. drive up Allenvale Rd. from Lorne; off the main road, take the first right after the bridge and turn off the rotary after circling 270°. The walk to **Sheoak Falls** follows a gentle track by the creek, and eventually reaches the ocean (1½hr.), while the **Lower Kalimna Falls Walk** (1hr.) leads beneath a waterfall, which can be seen from above on the **Upper Kalimna Falls Walk** (1½hr.). A fairly easy walk (1½hr. return) connects the **Blanket Leaf** carpark to **Cora Lynn Cascades.**

For a mild challenge, hikers tackle the **Coral Lynn Creek,** a section of track between the Coral Lynn Falls and the Coral Lynn carpark (1½hr.); the terrain is rocky and uneven. The **Castle Rock** hike (2hr.) involves serious hills and stunning views over the ocean. If time is limited then hike down from the Blanket Leaf carpark or the Erskine Falls carpark (3hr.).

There are a number of **free camping sites** in Angahook-Lorne (the biggest being on Hammonds Rd.); camping in picnic areas or carparks results in a fine. **Allenvale Mill,** a 200m walk-in from the carpark, has toilets. The **Wye River Rd.** has 15 sites and all are accessible by car. For a full list, contact the Lorne tourist office.

APOLLO BAY ☎03

Apollo Bay is aptly named after the god without whom the town is lifeless: the sun. The town is the gateway to Otway National Park and Cape Otway to the west.

TRANSPORTATION AND PRACTICAL INFORMATION. The Great Ocean Rd. is the main street through town, with side streets running north off it. **Buses** leave from the front of the visitors centre to: Geelong (2½hr., $19.80); Lorne (1hr., $5.40); Melbourne (3½hr., $27.90). Buses to other points along the Great Ocean Rd. operate on Friday only. The above average **Tourist Information Centre,** 157 Great Ocean Rd., books accommodations and tours. This is a good place to begin planning a trip to the Otways, as they advise on road closures and help with campsite availability. (☎5237 6529; fax 5237 6194. Open daily 9am-5pm.) The stretch of highway through town contains two 24hr. **ATMs,** and an **Internet** cafe ($5 per 30min.).

ACCOMMODATIONS AND FOOD. The small **Surfside Backpackers,** on the corner of the Great Ocean Rd. and Gambier St. at the west end of town, has a record player instead of a TV, and one of the friendliest, most helpful hostel owners around. Some of the bunkbeds are from the Olympic Village (see p. 123), so you might end up in Cathy Freeman's bed if you're lucky. (☎5237 7263 or 1800 357 263. Book ahead. Reception daily 8-10am and 5-10pm. Sites $4; dorms $13; doubles $32-42. Non-YHA $3 more. MC/V.) Farther from the beach is **Apollo Bay Backpackers,** 47 Montrose Ave., a place on a quiet residential street. (☎0419 340 362; backpack@vicnet.net.au. Dorms $16; singles $40, doubles $45.) Twenty kilometers west of Apollo Bay, 7km south of the Great Ocean Rd. on the Cape Otway Rd., stands a hostel ideally located for those hoping to explore the Otway Ranges. **Cape Otway Backpackers,** part of the accommodation menagerie at **Bimbi Park,** puts its guests right on the edge of the great outdoors; the beach is a 20min. walk through the national park, and horseback riding can be arranged. (☎5237 9246. Book ahead. Sites from $12.50; dorms $16.50.)

Raj's, 151 Great Ocean Rd., at the intersection with Hardy St., has inexpensive meals that are justifiably popular. (☎5237 6452. Open daily from breakfast time.) Steps away from the main road, **New Roman Racket Court Restaurant,** 1 Moore St., offers both Italian and Greek fare. (☎5237 6551. Open daily 5-10:30pm, takeout 'til

WHY LONDON BRIDGE FELL DOWN The bizarre rock formations around Port Campbell are a relatively recent geological phenomenon. Port Campbell National Park is founded upon layers of soft limestone which have amassed from marine animal remains. In the process of forming the Twelve Apostles, waves curling into the sides of jutting cliffs bored tunnels, which in turn left archways. The archways eventually collapse, leaving the solitary stacks that still stand. The London Bridge formation displays an intermediate stage of this erosion process. It was once conjoined with a second arch that linked it to the mainland. In 1990 the other arch collapsed—leaving two tourists stranded (see p. 549)—explaining why it's no longer a bridge. So before you climb carelessly about, remember: Peter may have been called the Rock, but these Apostles represent only the shakiest of foundations.

2am.) **The Sandy Feet Cafe,** 139 Great Ocean Rd., is a health-nut's paradise, with veggie burgers ($5.50), salads ($4-6), and crepes galore. (Open daily 9am-5pm.) On the Great Ocean Rd. as it goes through town, there are two **supermarkets,** both open M-Sa 9am-7pm and Su 10am-6:30pm.

SIGHTS. Apollo Bay's most luminating feature are its **glow-worms,** which are actually the larval stage in the life-cycle of a local fly. To witness this enlightening experience, meditate in Otway National Park, or take a tour and be led right to them. **The Glow Worms Tour Co.,** 71 Costin St., runs a tour that brings you close to the action. (☎5237 6080. 1½hr. $17, children free.) **Triplet Falls,** a quiet getaway near Laver's Hill (40km west of Apollo Bay on the Great Ocean Rd.), is a three-tiered waterfall reached by taking Beech Forest Rd. from Lavers Hill, turning right onto Phillips Rd., then following signs on unsealed roads. BBQ facilities are available. Annually, the town grooves to the folksy sounds of the **Apollo Bay Music Festival** (Mar. 24-26th), with acts ranging from Shep Huntley to the Gyuoto Monks of Tibet.

NEAR APOLLO BAY: THE OTWAYS

The Otway Range stretches 60km west of Apollo Bay and encompasses three major parks: **Otway National Park, Otway State Forest,** and **Melba Gully State Park.** Within the cool, temperate rainforest, myrtle beech trees provide shade while tree ferns dominate the eye-level scenery, occasionally animated by wallabies, possums, and gray kangaroos. Waterfalls cascade down steep hillsides to form clear creeks. The walk through Melba Gully is short (30min. return), but promises exposure to a unique, fragile environment. **Mait's Rest** walk (30min.) is one of the best known rainforest walks in Victoria, beginning 17km west of Apollo Bay along the Great Ocean Rd. It's a Disneyesque approach to the bush: informative, convenient, clean, and touristy. Shortly after Mait's Rest is the turn-off for the **Cape Otway Lightstation,** built in 1848. (☎5237 9240. Open daily 9am-5pm. $8, concessions $5.)

Maps for Otways' well-marked walks are available at the Apollo Bay Tourist Info Centre. A 4WD can make the pot-hole filled tracks much easier to navigate. For camping, check into the vast Bimbi Park (see p. 547), or use one of the five **camping** areas in Otway National Park. In summer, pitch at **Blanket Bay;** follow Lighthouse Rd., then watch signs for a left turn. (☎5237 6889. Sites $10.20.) The **Aire River** camping areas are reached from the Great Ocean Rd., another 5km west by way of the Horden Vale turn-off. The Aire River is suitable for swimming, and three walks diverge from the grounds. (☎5237 6889. Sites $10.20.) Both **Parker Hill** and **Point Franklin** have small camping areas with few facilities. (☎5237 6889. Sites $4.20.) **Johanna Beach** has a basic campsite and the best **surfing** in the area. Take the sealed Johanna Rd. from the Great Ocean Rd. (☎5237 6889. Sites $10.20.)

PORT CAMPBELL ☎03

Port Campbell, the only safe harbor from Apollo Bay to Warrnambool, is a sleepy fishing village on one of the nastiest yet most picturesque coastlines in the world. This most treacherous stretch of the Shipwreck Coast was once feared by mari-

LONDON BRIDGE PART II When London Bridge fell in 1990, the couple stranded (see p. 548) on the remaining stack had to wait awhile to be rescued. After about an hour a helicopter came by and circled the high and dry pair. As they began to rejoice, they realized that it was a news 'copter seeking an interview. The couple refused to give one, and so the news 'copter just filmed them from a distance and flew off. Later that day, the six o'clock news reported the story. Apparently the guy had called in sick to work, so when his boss saw him stranded on the London Bridge, he was in big trouble...but even worse was that his WIFE was watching the news at home. Serves the bastard right.

ners around the world. Providing a good base for diving, fishing, or scenic boat charters, the town holds the headquarters of the Port Campbell National Park, which preserves the wondrous rock formations of the Twelve Apostles.

TRANSPORTATION AND PRACTICAL INFORMATION. The Great Ocean Rd. becomes Lord St. in town, and is the center of all the action: takeaway joints, restaurants, tourist attractions, and the beach. **Buses** arrive from Melbourne once a week, on F (also M Dec.-Jan.), and from Warrnambool and points west on Th. The **Visitor Information Centre,** on the corner of Morris and Tregea St. one block south of Lord St., is a wealth of data for all things related to the Great Ocean Road. (☎5598 6089. Open daily 9am-5pm.) There's a pricey, coin-operated **Internet** booth at the **Seafoam Cafe,** on the corner of Lord and Beach St. (Open daily 11am-7pm. $2 for 10min.) The **post office** is in the **Port Campbell General Store,** Lord St., which also has groceries. (☎5510 6255. Open daily 8am-8pm.) **Postal code:** 3269.

ACCOMMODATIONS. Near the beach, **Ocean House Backpackers,** Lord St., is clean and simple. (☎5598 6231. Check-in next door at the Southern Ocean Motor. $20.) The **YHA Hostel,** 18 Tregea St., one block south of Lord St., has a large kitchen and a lounge with a wood stove. (☎/fax 5598 6305. Key deposit $5. Internet $2 per 15min. Reception 8-10am and 4-9pm. Dorms $16, non-YHA $19.50.) The **Port Campbell National Park Cabin and Camping Park,** with BBQ, showers, and laundry is next to the information center on Morris St. (☎5598 6492. Reception 8:30am-9pm. Sites for 2 $15; cabins with bath from $72, extra person $5.)

FOOD AND ENTERTAINMENT. The best place to get some casual eats is downstairs at the **Koo-aah Shop,** Lord St., with fish, lentil, and beef burgers for $7. (☎5598 6408. Open daily 10:30am-late.) More upscale, **Emma's** is right across the street with good value homemade tucker. (☎5598 6458. Open daily 10am-5pm. BYO). The only local **pub** is on the corner of Morris and Lord St.

SIGHTS. The **Twelve Apostles** are the most famous of the rock formations in the area (there *are* twelve, it's just tough to see them all at once). Try to see them at sunset—though you'll have to jockey aggressively for prime photo-ops. The Interpretive Centre (free) is open daily 10am-8pm. **Gibson Steps,** just before the Twelve Apostles, allow a descent and a view from sea level. Other eroding sandstone monoliths dance between the waves. The **Razorback,** for example, is a long spine of rock, perforated in many places and serrated along the top.

The **Bay of Martyrs** and **Bay of Islands** have many tall columns of rock which, like some of the Apostles, occasionally tumble into the sea. The gentle Port Campbell **Discovery Walk** (2.5km) begins at the cliff base at the western end of the beach or at the carpark west of the bay. Or, just hang on the town's beach—a calm, picturesque place to take a dip. **Port Campbell Boat Charters** offers crafts for diving, fishing, or sightseeing expeditions; book through the Tourist Office ☎5598 6089 or the Mobil Service Station. Two companies offer **helicopter tours** of the Twelve Apostles, both for the same high price (12 Apostle Helicopters ☎5598 6161; PremiAIR ☎5598 8266; both $70 for 15min., $90 for 20min.).

WARRNAMBOOL ☎03

Warrnambool is the self-proclaimed capital of the Shipwreck Coast. Despite lacking the historical charm of burgs further west, the city has the stunning beach scenery, plus a lively scene back in town after the sun goes down. From May to October, southern right whales are visible without even leaving the docks. The whales combine with the sand, surf, and (oh yeah) that highway to make Warrnambool a popular holiday destination.

TRANSPORTATION. The **West Coast Railway Station** (☎5561 4277) is just north of Lake Pertobe on Merri St., with **V/Line trains** to Melbourne (3½hr., 3 per day, $37.70) and Geelong (2½hr., 3 per day, $27). V/Line **buses** run to: Ballarat (2½hr., M-F 1 per day, $19.80); Mt. Gambier (2½hr., 1 per day, $29.70); Port Fairy (30min., M-F 1 per day, $4.70); Portland (1½hr., 1 per day, $13.40). From Dec.-Jan. service extends to eastern towns including Apollo Bay, on M and F.

In town, **Transit Southwest** runs six bus routes across the city, with stops at each location roughly on the hour; pick up a timetable from the visitors centre. (☎5562 1866. $1.20, concessions $0.75.) For a **taxi,** call 5561 1114.

ORIENTATION AND PRACTICAL INFORMATION. The city is built around the Princes Hwy., which becomes **Raglan Pde.** in town. The bay is bounded by the Merri River on the west and the Hopkins River on the east. The town is set back from the bay, and is bisected by the main drag, **Liebig St.,** with most of the restaurants, pubs, **banks,** and **ATMs.** The **Visitor Information Centre,** 600 Raglan Pde., provides free maps of the area. (☎5564 7837. Open daily 9am-5pm.) Services include: **laundry,** on 234 Timor St. (open daily 6am-10pm; $4 wash, $1 dry); **police,** 214 Koroit St. (☎5560 1179); **RACV** (24hr. ☎5561 5444); **hospital** (☎5563 1666); **library,** Liebig St., with free **Internet** (☎5502 2258; open M-Th 9:30am-5pm, F 9:30am-8pm, Sa 9:30am-noon); **post office,** corner of Timor and Gilles St. **Postal code:** 3280.

ACCOMMODATIONS. Book accommodations ahead November through March. **Warrnambool Beach Backpackers,** 17 Stanley St., offers clean and colorful rooms with close proximity to the beach. The management runs free penguin- and whale-sighting tours if they are not busy. The front room has a licensed bar, TV with DVD surround sound, and a pool table; back bunkrooms are spacious and quiet. (☎/fax 5562 4874; johnpearson@hotmail.com. Key deposit $10. Reception 7:30am-10pm. Internet $5 per hr. Dorms $18; doubles $44. No credit cards.) The **Western Backpackers and Motel,** has doubles with spotless shared bathrooms, kitchen, laundry, and TV lounge with wood fireplace. The motel section has sparkling singles and doubles with bath, heat, A/C, fridge, tea and coffee, and TV. (☎5562 2011; thewestern@ansonic.com.au. Key deposit $2. Singles $18, weekly $93; doubles $33. Motel singles $45; doubles $55.) The **Stuffed Backpacker,** 52 Kepler St., is in town, near Raglan Pde.; reception is in the candy shop next to the cinema. It's a no-nonsense, no-frills establishment with clean showers, small kitchen, TV lounge, and a *laissez-faire* attitude. Leo, the manager, helps guests find jobs. (☎5562 2459. Key deposit $5. Reception 9am-midnight. Dorms $18; doubles and twins $45.) The **Backpackers Barn,** 90 Lava St., at the Victoria Hotel, has basic pub accommodations right in the heart of Warrnambool. (☎5562 2073; fax 5561 3775. Dorms, singles, and doubles $16. VIP/YHA. AmEx/DC/MC/V.)

FOOD AND NIGHTLIFE. For a sit-down meal, you can't go too wrong in any of the restaurants at the bottom of Liebig St. Brunch is fantastic at hip **Fishtales,** 63-65 Liebig St., which specializes in fish, vegetarian pasta, and Asian food for under $10. (☎5561 2975. Licensed and BYO. Open daily 7:45am-late. AmEx/DC/MC/V.) The inventive woodfire pizzas for $13-16, or $10-12 takeout, at **Bojangles,** 61 Liebig St., are piled high with delicious creative combinations. (☎5562 8751. Open daily 5pm-late.) **China City,** on the corner of Leibig and Koroit St., has the cheapest meal with all-you-can-eat lunch for $7.50. (Delivery ☎5561 5338. Open daily 11:30am-3pm and 5-10pm.) The 24hr. Coles **supermarket** is on Lava St.

The neighborhood around Leibig St. is also where Warrnambool hits the pubs. Perennial favorites include **Taco Bill's,** on the corner of Leibig and Timor St., promising a fun night with a latin flavor (☎5562 9753; open daily 5pm-1am), and **Seanchai Irish Pub** across from Bojangles, where the Guinness flows like water (very thick, golden-brown water). Open a bit later, **The Whaler's Inn,** across the street, is the same scene with stubbies of VB replacing the Guinness. Later on, the party-hearty move on to **The Gallery Nightclub,** at the corner of Keplar and Timor St.

SIGHTS AND ACTIVITIES. The most popular thing to do in Warrnambool is to watch whales. The info center has booklets on the continuously tracked **southern right whales.** Every winter in late May or June, a population of whales stops just off **Logans Beach,** to the east of Lady Bay, to give birth to their calves. They stay until September or October, when they return to the Antarctic to break their five-month fast. To watch the beasts roll, blow, and breach, tourists gather on viewing platforms built above the beach to protect the delicate dune vegetation. These right whales used to be hunted in large numbers all along the Victorian coastline, but have been protected for several decades. Whale watching is much more fun if you have some sort of visual amplification.

Warrnambool's other tourist attraction is the **Flagstaff Hill Maritime Museum,** on Merri St. Fascinating even for those not intrigued by nautical history, the 10-acre museum is an outdoor re-creation of a late 19th-century coastal village, including a coopers' factory, dockyards, a pub (surprisingly familiar), a sail-making store, and not least, a lighthouse keeper's toilet. The stunning, masthead **Loch Ard peacock,** taken from the wreck of the *Loch Ard* in 1878, is located in the Public Hall. Only two people survived the wreck, but this giant ceramic fowl escaped with just a tiny chip. The museum's collection of 1920s and 1930s short maritime films are shown in the theater daily. (☎5564 7841. Open daily 9am-5pm; last entrance 4pm. Lighthouse open 11am-noon and 1-2pm. $12, concessions $9, children $5.)

Boasting ample beach-space and parks, Warrnambool is a great spot for outdoor recreation. The 3.4km **Promenade** lining Lady Bay is popular with cyclists, roller bladers, and evening strollers. Families will enjoy the new **Adventure Playground,** adjacent to Lake Pertobe. The park, built over 35 hectares of former swampland, features a maze, giant slides, and lots of children screaming in joy. **Great Ocean Road Trail Rides** offers day or evening horse rides on the beach and nearby trails. (☎5562 8088; www.warrnambool.com/beach trail rides. 1hr. $27.50; 2hr. $44.)

NEAR WARRNAMBOOL

TOWER HILL

Between Warrnambool and Port Fairy, the main attraction is the Tower Hill State Game Reserve, situated in a volcanic crater. It swarms with the normal Aussie animals. It is possible to drive right through the crater, but to really get a good look at the wildlife, try one of the many walking paths around the reserve.

CHILDERS COVES

This secluded set of beachy coves, a.k.a. **The Cove,** nestled among cliffs, are good for swimming, sun-tanning, and escaping the crowds in the towns along the Great Ocean Rd. It's surprising that more don't drop by here, considering it's barely a deviation from the road itself. (Leave the Great Ocean Road shortly after Mepunga West and rejoin it just before Nirranda, or vice versa.)

PORT FAIRY ☎03

Port Fairy is like your kid brother becoming captain of the football team: it's far more hip than it should be given its size. The three main streets are lined with chic cafes and quirky stores, and the town hosts Victoria's biggest folk and jazz festival every March. In 1826, Captain James Wishart sailed the cutter *Fairy* into the mouth of the River Moyne in search of potable water. From the 1850s to the 1880s, Port Fairy was the busiest Australian port outside Sydney, loading ships headed for the Motherland. Activity has, however, slowed considerably since the late 1800s, but Wishart might still be proud of what remains.

WANTED! REWARD $250,000 In 1522, **Cristovao de Mendonca,** a Portuguese adventurer, may have sailed a mahogany caravel along the east coast of Australia and mapped much of the coastline. Thus, some historians argue that the Portuguese were in fact the first Europeans to discover Australia. But thanks to 16th-century diplomatic arguments and the Lisbon earthquake of 1755, the Portuguese records are lost forever. A French map of a southern land called Java la Grande was published in Dieppe in 1547, but since many of the names appear in Portuguese, some think that the French map was actually plagiarized from de Mendonca's original charts. But de Mendonca lost more than his potential claim to the first map of Australia; his ship crashed on the coast somewhere between Warrnambool and Port Fairy. Since the first sighting of the wreck in 1836, many claim to have spied it, but the constantly shifting coastline has kept it obscured and it has drifted into legend. So when walking this stretch of coastline, keep alert, and perhaps the legend will be verified. The ship's finder, after all, can collect the $250,000 reward still posted by authorities.

TRANSPORTATION AND PRACTICAL INFORMATION. Buses leave from the Tourist Information Centre on Bank St. to: Melbourne (1 per day, $36); Geelong (1 per day, $29); Portland (3 per day, $9); Warrnambool (3 per day, $5). Historical details and a walking tour map are available from the **Tourist Information Centre,** on Bank St. (☎5568 2682. Open daily 9am-5pm.) Services include: **police,** (☎5568 1007); **RACV,** (☎5568 2700, after hours 5568 1017); **hospital,** (☎5568 0100); **post office,** 25 Sackville St., which has **Internet.** (Open M-F 9am-5pm. $5 per hr.)

ACCOMMODATIONS AND FOOD. In a house built by Port Fairy's first official settler, William Rutledge, the **YHA Hostel,** 8 Cox St., has TV, Internet, and a kitchen. (☎5568 2468. Book ahead for March. Reception daily 8-10am and 5-10pm. Beds $16, non-YHA $19.50.) **Eumarella Backpackers** is 20km west of Port Fairy in Yambuk, 200m south of Hwy. 1. The remote hostel, in a converted 19th-century schoolhouse, is run by the Peek Whurrong people of the Framlingham Aboriginal Trust. It's next to the Deen Maar, Victoria's first Indigenous Protected Area. (☎5578 4204 or 5567 1003. Kitchen, laundry, and canoe hire. $15; children $10.)

Rebuking the fishing culture, the town has recently become an artists' haven, and has a fledgling artsy cafe scene, particularly on Bank and Sackville St. The sticky date pudding at **Cobb's Port Fairy Bakery,** 25 Bank St., will change your life for the better. (☎5568 1713. Open daily 8am-5pm.) The **IGA Everyday** on Sackville St. is both grocery store and bottle shop. (Open M-Th 8am-8pm, F-Su 8am-10pm.)

SIGHTS. Visits can be arranged to **Lady Julia Percy Island,** 19km out in the Bass Strait, where seals, fairy penguins, and peregrine falcons dwell. Contact **Mulloka Cruises** (☎5568 1790) stationed at the harbor. **Kitehouse,** 27 Cox St., sells any kind of kite or wind sock a windy day deserves and rents bicycles. (☎5568 2782. Open daily 10am-4:30pm.) Almost every bed on the Shipwreck Coast is hired out in March during the **Port Fairy Folk Festival,** held over Australia's Labor Day weekend. (☎5568 2227. Order tickets months in advance.)

NEAR PORT FAIRY: MT. ECCLES NATIONAL PARK.

Some 20,000 years ago, igneous activity formed Mt. Eccles, and the volcanic turbulence continued until about 7000 years ago. Because the volcano is relatively young, many of its topographical features are in excellent condition, not yet muted by time. In the volcanic crater, Lake Surprise is a beautiful place to walk or swim—although if the volcano decided to erupt again, any swimmers would be quickly boiled alive. Maybe that's the surprise. The park is well known for its koala population; these crabby creatures like to live in the thick manna gum woods near the lake and are most active around dusk. The brush-tailde phasogale, an almost-extinct, tiny marsupial, also calls Mt. Eccles home.

Macarthur, the point of entry to the park, is about 40km north of Port Fairy and 30km south of **Hamilton** on Hwy. A200. Within the park, well-marked walking tracks lead to several relics of the mountain's volcanic past. About 50 years ago, the northwest slope of the mountain was quarried for scoria (the porous volcanic rock that makes up much of the slope); this destructive land use was put to an end when the area was declared a national park in 1960. The **Crater Rim Nature Walk** (1hr. return) passes all of the topographical features, and is detailed in a pamphlet available from the tourist info center, but is not the most interesting or rewarding hike in the park. The **Lake Surprise** trail (45min.) descends from the parking lot into the crater, making a loop around the water. The walk isn't challenging, except for the ascent out, which is fairly steep. For the more adventurous visitor, the **Natural Bridge Walk** or the **Lava Canal Walk** (both 4hr. return) follow the broad, deep lava canal south through a clear forest with little undergrowth for about 1.5km, and then get wild. The Natural Bridge trail follows the canal and a stone wall, so it's difficult to get lost, but it looks overgrown and untraveled. The Lava Canal trail visits Dry Crater and ascends Mt. Eccles to an excellent view of the terrain just covered: from the head of the canal, to the dense forest, to the crater at the end. Rangers can provide camping permits and info about the bushland around the park (sites for up to 4 people Dec.-Jan. $12, other times $9; self-serve registration.

PORTLAND ☎03

Maritime history buffs may take pleasure in Portland's storied past, but most travelers focus more on the beds and parking spaces that make it a hub for the Great South West Walk, Discovery Bay National Park, and Lower Glenelg National Park. This area was once a base for whalers, sealers, and escaped convicts, before the Henty brothers and their sheep enterprise permanently settled it in 1834.

TRANSPORTATION AND PRACTICAL INFORMATION. Two **V/Line buses** per day connect to Port Fairy (1hr., $9.50) and Warrnambool (1½hr., $13.40); the bus stop is on Henty St., just west of Percy St. On F (and M Dec.-Jan.), buses run to: Apollo Bay (4hr., $38); Lorne (5hr., $42.50); Port Campbell (2½hr., $23.40). The two main streets in town are the water-front **Bentinck St.,** with cafes and pubs, and **Percy St.,** which has the majority of the town's commercial activity. Percy and Bentinck St. are connected by Gawler, Julia, and Henty St., all of which have cafes, cinemas, and hostels. On Lee Breakwater St., down the hill toward the water from Bentinck St., is the **Portland Maritime Discovery Centre** has informative displays on the region, as well as a cafe with nice views of the water. (☎5521 7708. Open daily 9am-5pm. $7.70; concessions $5.50.) The **Portland Visitor Information Centre** is in the same building as the Maritime Discovery Centre. (☎5523 2671; fax 5521 7287. Open daily 9am-5pm.) More info on the Lower Glenelg and Discovery Bay can be obtained from the **Parks Victoria** office, 8-12 Julia St. (☎5523 1180. Open M-F 9am-4:30pm.) Other services include: **police** (☎5523 1999); **hospital** (☎5521 0333); **RACV** (24hr. ☎5523 2111); **taxis** (☎5523 2022); **post office** 108 Percy St. **Postal code:** 3305.

ACCOMMODATION AND FOOD. Right in the middle of town, **Portland Backpackers,** 14 Gawler St., is more relaxed than a 60s rock star in Amsterdam. The historic building has a jumble of beds (none of them bunks), all different—look around and take your pick. (☎5523 6390. Internet $5 per hr. Linen included. Dorms $17.) Close to the waterfront, the **Gordon Hotel,** 63 Bentinck St., provides standard pub accommodation with a regal balcony (☎5523 1121. Singles $25; doubles $40.) **Bellevue Backpackers,** Sheoke Rd. (on the way to Cape Nelson), offers bunks in caravans, right next to a sheep farm. (☎5523 4038. $15.) **Port O' Call,** 85 Bentinck St., has good coffee, great views, and a variety of fresh fish options. (☎5523 1335. Open daily from 7am until late.) **Sunstream,** 49 Julia St., is a healthy choice with bins of oddities, a tasty lentil burger, and salad roll-ups for under $5. (☎5523 4895. Open M-F 9am-5:30pm, Sa 10am-12:30pm.) The **IGA supermarket** (open M-Sa 7am-9pm, Su 8am-8pm) is behind the Gordon Hotel, on Percy St.

SIGHTS AND HIKING. Though this stretch of waters is far safer today than in the 1800s, many ships once came to grief in or near the Portland Harbor. They are now memorialized along **Historic Shipwreck Trail,** which begins at Moonlight Head and stretches to the South Australia border (brochures available at the info center). The trail is signposted with road-side brown, blue and white anchors.

Shipwrecks, kelp forests, and delicate corals make the waters near Portland a delight for snorkelers and **divers.** Many shops, including **Duck Dive Scuba,** 57 Bentinck St. (☎/fax 5523 5617), offer equipment and instruction. For a very different kind of tour, check out the **gigantic aluminum smelter** cunningly landscaped to soften the aesthetic blow delivered by metal-processing plants. This "Smelter in the Park" is a great example of environmentally conscious design. (☎5523 2671. 2hr. tours M, W, F at 10am and 1pm. Free.)

Starting and ending at Portland's information center, the looping, 250km **Great South West Walk** rambles along the coast, then doubles back through the Lower Glenelg National Park. The walk traverses a variety of terrains and provides a grand introduction to the wildlands of southwest Victoria. Daytrips access sections ranging from 8-20km in length. For safety, register with the info center.

NEAR PORTLAND

CAPE NELSON STATE PARK

Cape Nelson State Park, a 243-hectare reserve southwest of Portland, provides some beautiful bush walks as well as good surfing beaches, and the **last manned lighthouse** in Victoria (entrance daily 10am-5pm, $2). The black-emu-marked Great South West Walk intersects the park, but other trails, marked with red triangles, abound; one of the best is the **Enchanted Forest** walk (3km return). The car park is just off Sheoke Rd., about halfway to the lighthouse. As you wander through the groves of short claw-like trees, with the edges clothed in vines, the plant life shifts abruptly, and it doesn't take much imagination for this place to become magical. The small white butterflies turn into gossamer-winged fairies; the scrambling sounds of lizards in the underbrush become the teasing giggles of puckish elves; the small caves in the steep seaside cliffs are the stomping grounds of goblins; and one can never be certain if the voices around the next bend are fellow travelers or scurrilous brigands. Anyway, even for the realists who prefer Henry James to Alfred Lord Tennyson, this is a good walk. The **Sea Cliff Nature Walk** (a 3km loop) and the **Lighthouse Walk** (6km) both start from the lighthouse, and show the more typical flora of the area; the lighthouse walk also has spectacular cliff views.

Yellow Rock in Cape Nelson is an experienced **surfers'** dream. For more info, beach boys and girls can consult with *Surfs Up in Portland* compiled by the Portland *Observer*, available at the Maritime Centre. There's no camping in the park itself, but the **lighthouse keeper's cottage** has good rates for groups in dorms ($27 per person for 6 or more; call Parks Victoria ☎13 19 63), and the small **Bellvue Backpackers** (see **Accommodations,** above) is near the edge of the park.

LOWER GLENELG NATIONAL PARK

By 4WD, visitors can access Lower Glenelg National Park via the Nelson Winnap Rd., which intersects with the Princes Hwy. southeast of Dartmoor and northeast of Portland. Limestone dominates the topography of the park and many caves have been formed by percolating rainwater or underground watercourses. The largest and most spectacular of these (and the only ones open to the public) are the **Princess Margaret Rose Caves,** 2km east of the South Australia border and about 15km south of the Princes Hwy. (☎8738 4171. Tours daily 10, 11am, noon, 1:30, 2:30, 3:30, and 4:30pm. $6, concessions $4.50, children $2.50.) This area also features a few nature walks, a large, wooded picnic area with BBQ, and limited camping facilities. Camping arrangements must be made before 5pm with the ranger at the **Caves Information Center** (sites for 4 people $9.50; on-site cabins $40).

The **Glenelg estuary,** the longest in Victoria, is one of the prime **fishing** spots in the country, populated by mulloway, bream, mullet, salmon, trout, and perch. Boats can be rented in **Nelson,** the nearest settlement to the park, though fishing gear is less easy to attain. **Nelson Boat Hire** (☎8738 4048) rents canoes, kayaks, and boats and can help plan trips along the river. The Glenelg River is usually calm, deep, and wide, making it ideal for tranquil canoeing. Four days of paddling will bring the water-born from Dartmoor, on the Princes Hwy., to the mouth of the river at Nelson. This 75km stretch of river supports 11 campsites, only three of which can be reached by automobile. The **Department of Conservation,** at the **Forests and Lands Information Center** (☎8738 4051), on Forest Rd., Nelson, provides camping permits and answer questions about river conditions and canoe rental.

The main **information centre** (☎8738 4051) is on Glenelg Dr., a largely unsealed road that runs through most of the length of the park. The Princess Margaret Rose Caves building (see above), also has helpful information. The road, heading east from the info centre, is unsealed but very smooth for the first 8km, and a good deal bumpier for the last 14km; this is a rewarding drive, despite shaking automobiles. The tracks that branch off are in considerably worse condition.

DISCOVERY BAY COASTAL PARK

Discovery Bay Coastal Park stretches 55km from Portland to the South Australia border. Red emu markers point the way along the Great South West Walk. The park has plentiful **surf fishing** at **Nobles Rocks,** 7km from Nelson. Connecting the sea to freshwater lakes and swamps are mobile dunes up to 20m high; be sure to stay on the marked walking tracks. An extensive lakes system also welcomes fishing, as well as swimming, boating, and views of pelicans, swans, and ducks. Look for Bridgewater Lakes by the Bridgewater Lakes Rd. from Portland; Swan Lake, up a steep gravel road off the Portland-Nelson Rd.; and Long Swamp, 3km from Nobles Rocks. Fickle weather makes it important to plan adventures carefully.

A few kilometers west of Portland at Cape Bridgewater, the Great South West Walk passes through an occasionally steep, always undulating cliff trail leading to a **seal colony.** The access point is a 17km drive west of Portland, heading up Otway St. and out of town on Bridgewater Rd. Just after the town of Bridgewater and its awesome beach, there is a parking lot on the left for the **Spindrift Tearoom,** which is the best carpark for a direct, but occasionally steep walk (2hr. return) to the seal colony. **Seals By Sea** tours run 45min. cruises from Cape Bridgewater, but you see seals for less than 5min. (☎5526 7247 or 1800 267 247. $17 per person.) Though only a tiny town, Bridgewater has backpacker accommodation up hill from the beach at the **Cape Bridgewater Holiday Camp.** (☎5526 7267. Dorms $22.)

At the end of Bridgewater Rd. is a parking lot with access to the three other sights for which the park is chiefly known: the **Springs,** the **Blowholes,** and the **Petrified Forest.** There is an information board here, and bathrooms, but no ranger station. Walking between the sights, the landscape becomes strangely lunar as the persistent waves and seaspray make it nearly impossible for plant life to colonize the local environment. The volcanic cliffs and surf facing directly west make this a superb place to watch the sunset. To the left is the Petrified Forest (20min.), eerie rock formations in cavities left behind when trees rotted away. Back toward the carpark, the Blowholes are at the foot of the sea cliffs. These can be spectacular if the tidal and meteorological conditions are right. Or they can, well... blow. The Springs (1hr.) are virtually indistinguishable from tidal pools, but in fact are freshwater springs caused by rainwater seeping through the limestone farther inland.

THE GRAMPIANS AND OUTBACK VICTORIA

Outback Victoria exemplifies the natural diversity that makes Victoria one of the only places in Australia where so many varying ecosystems are only a daytrip away. Several ill-defined, overlapping regions, Outback Victoria encompasses mountains, lakes, swamps, wildlife reserves, rich farmland, and rugged bushland. West of the Goldfields, inland Victoria rises among the rugged peaks of Grampians National Park before slowly settling into an immense plain that stretches west into South Australia and north into New South Wales. The **Wimmera** region draws its name from the river that finds its source in the Grampians and wanders north past the surprisingly lush Little Desert National Park. In neighboring South Australia, the Coonawarra wine region, the Naracoorte cave system, and Mt. Gambier (see p. 439) are also traditionally considered part of the Wimmera. West of Horsham on the Wimmera Hwy. **Mt. Arapiles** draws rock climbers to its 1300 thrilling ascents. North of Little Desert and west of the Sunraysia Hwy., all the way up to Mildura, lies the semi-arid expanse of the **Mallee,** named for the *mallee eucalypt*, a hardy water-hoarding tree that thrives in the rugged plains. Agricultural pressure, increasing salinity, and the introduction of alien species like goats, cats, and bees are steadily eroding the once vast areas of mallee scrub. The Big Desert Wilderness Park, Wyperfield National Park, Murray Sunset National Park, and Hattah Kulkyne National Park seek to preserve this seemingly doomed habitat.

GRAMPIANS (GARIWERD) NAT'L PARK

In 1836, Major Mitchell, in command of a British expedition, "discovered" the range of mountains he designated as the Grampians, after a range in his home country of Scotland. Ensuing hordes of settlers steadily pushed the Koori Aborigines out of their ancestral home of Gariwerd. A visit to the park now promises both the rich history of Aboriginal culture with 80% of the Aboriginal rock art sites in Victoria, as well as breathtaking ranges, abundant wildlife, rare birds, a springtime carpet of technicolor wildflowers.

THE GRAMPIANS AT A GLANCE

AREA: 167,000 hectares.

WHERE: The end of the Great Dividing Range. 260km west of Melbourne.

FEATURES: Koori rock paintings, the Balconies (Jaws of Death), MacKenzie Falls, climbs in the Wonderland Range and Hollow Mountain.

GATEWAYS: Halls Gap, at it's eastern edge; Horsham in the north.

CAMPING, HIKING, CLIMBING: 13 sites, 160km of walking track, and a variety of rockclimbs. (See **Hiking,** p. 559).

FEES: Camping $8.60 for up to 6 people per car. $3.70 per additional cars.

ORIENTATION AND TRANSPORTATION

The northern approach passes through the seemingly empty town of **Horsham,** at the junction of Western and Henty Hwy., roughly 80km north of the park. From the south, the town of **Dunkeld,** on the Glenelg Hwy., provides access via Mt. Abrupt Rd. From the east, the closest town is **Stawell,** 26km away. The **most convenient point of entry** is on the eastern edge of the park at **Halls Gap.** This is the park's only town, and it's a small one; but it has the basic amenities and is within walking distance of many of the park's points of interest. When reading about the town's offerings remember that, unless otherwise noted, everything is bunched together in a small strip on Grampians Rd., also called Dunkeld Rd., which runs from Halls Gap to (you guessed it) Dunkeld. One **V/Line** bus per day leaves across from the newsagent for: Ararat (1hr., $12); Ballarat (2½hr., $25); Melbourne (4½hr., $40); Stawell (30min., $8). Several companies also run multi-day tours from Melbourne and Adelaide, often incorporating the Great Ocean Rd. along the way.

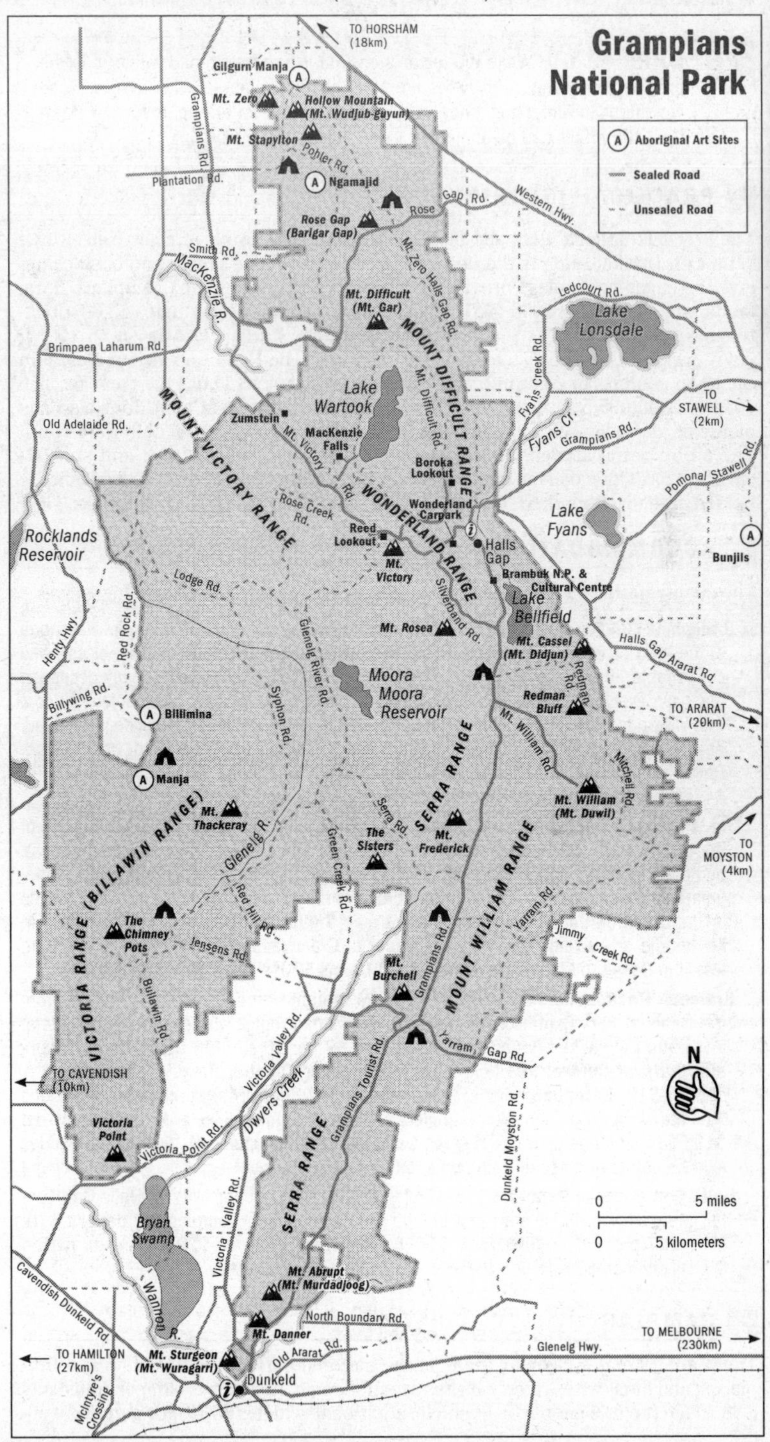
Grampians National Park
Aboriginal Art Sites
Sealed Road
Unsealed Road
TO HORSHAM (18km)
Gilgurn Manja
Mt. Zero
Hollow Mountain (Mt. Wudjub-guyun)
Mt. Stapylton
Ngamajid
Rose Gap (Barigar Gap)
Mt. Difficult (Mt. Gar)
MOUNT DIFFICULT RANGE
Lake Wartook
Zumstein
MacKenzie Falls
Boroka Lookout
Wonderland Carpark
WONDERLAND RANGE
MOUNT VICTORY RANGE
Reed Lookout
Mt. Victory
Halls Gap
Brambuk N.P. & Cultural Centre
Lake Bellfield
Lake Lonsdale
Lake Fyans
TO STAWELL (2km)
Bunjils
Rocklands Reservoir
Mt. Rosea
Mt. Cassel (Mt. Didjun)
Redman Bluff
Moora Moora Reservoir
TO ARARAT (20km)
Billimina
Manja
Mt. Thackeray
VICTORIA RANGE (BILLAWIN RANGE)
SERRA RANGE
The Sisters
Mt. Frederick
Mt. William (Mt. Duwil)
MOUNT WILLIAM RANGE
TO MOYSTON (4km)
The Chimney Pots
Mt. Burchell
TO CAVENDISH (10km)
Victoria Point
Bryan Swamp
Mt. Abrupt (Mt. Murdadjoog)
Mt. Danner
Mt. Sturgeon (Mt. Wuragarri)
Dunkeld
TO HAMILTON (27km)
TO MELBOURNE (230km)
McIntyre's Crossing
0 5 miles
0 5 kilometers
N

WHEN TO GO. While the region's climate is somewhat mild, winter poses a problem for anyone who hates the cold, as nights can get rather chilly. Road conditions in winter might not be as suitable or safe for driving. In the Dry (May-Oct.), waterfalls can be somewhat, well, dry and not as exciting.

PRACTICAL INFORMATION

The **Brambuk National Park and Cultural Centre,** 2.5km south of Halls Gap's town center on Dunkeld Rd., is the best resource for would-be hikers and bush-campers. The engaging displays provide excellent information on the Grampians' flora, fauna, and history. (☎5356 4381. Open daily 9am-5pm. Hiking maps $3.30; donations appreciated.) From outside Halls Gap, **Parks Victoria** (☎13 19 63; www.parks.vic.com.au) is an excellent resource. The Halls Gap **Visitors Centre** in the town center has great info and can answer questions about the park. (☎5356 4616 or 1800 065 599. Open daily 9am-5pm.) The **newsagent** next door also has plenty of maps, as well as an **Internet** kiosk. ($2 per 10min. Open daily 7am-7pm.) The Mobil **petrol station** has camping supplies, basic provisions, and an **ATM.** (☎5356 4206. Open daily in summer 6am-10pm; winter 7am-8pm.) The **post office** is hidden in the well-marked "Coffee Shop." (Open M-F 9am-5pm.) **Postal code:** 3381.

ACCOMMODATIONS

The quality of the accommodations here is as high as the Grampians themselves.

Grampians YHA Eco-Hostel (☎5356 4544; grampians@yhavic.org.au). A 10min. walk north of the town center on Grampians Rd., at the corner of tiny Buckler St. Clean, classy, and comfortable, this energy-efficient hostel is more luxurious, scenic, and sharply decorated than your everyday budget digs. State-of-the-art kitchen, dining area, plush sofas, TV room with VCR, adventure booking office, laundry, Internet ($2 per 15min.), and linens included. Key deposit $10. Reception daily 8-10am and 5-10pm. Busy year-round; book ahead. Dorms with lockers and heaters $19, under 18yrs. $15; singles $42; twins and doubles $47; family rooms $64; non-members pay extra $3.50 Apr.-Dec., $5 Jan.-Mar. MC/V.

Tim's Place (☎5356 4288; www.timsplace.com.au). On Grampians Rd., 500m north of the town center. The most central of the 3 hostels, Tim's is easily the smallest, coziest, and most intimate, and attracts the most diverse group of travelers. Free tea and coffee, unlimited breakfast, and linens. Internet $3 per hr. Mountain bike use and free tickets to the Brambuk Centre Dreaming Theatre (see **Sights,** p. 559). Arrange for pickup in Melbourne or Adelaide that includes a tour of Grampians sights. (Around $70 return; less if in transit to Melbourne or Adelaide.) Dorms $20; singles $35; doubles $46.

Brambuk Backpackers (☎5356 4250; www.brambuck.tourvic.com.au). Across from the National Park Centre on Dunkeld Rd. Very clean rooms all have lockers, heaters, and bath. Big kitchen, laundry, BBQ, Internet $2 per 10min. Affiliated with the **Brambuk Cultural Centre;** free tickets to the Dreaming Theatre. Breakfast included. Key deposit $10. Reception 9am-12:30pm and 3:30-7:30pm (4-8pm in summer). Dorms $19 May-Aug., $20 Sept.-Apr.; singles $35/$40; doubles $45/$48; children 10-16 $12/ $14; children under 10 $7/$8. Campsites $10 per site for 1, $15 for 2; includes light breakfast and use of bathrooms. MC/V.

Halls Gap Caravan Park (☎5356 4251; hgcp@netconnect.com.au). In Halls Gap center. Many walking trails start just behind the campground. Camping key deposit $10. Linens $7 per person. Sites for 2 $16, holidays $19; powered $20/$22; extra person $5. On-site caravans for 2 $45/$50. Discounts for longer stays. MC/V.

CAMPING

There are 13 major **camping** areas in the national park, all with toilets and fireplaces, and most with water. All sites are first-come, first-serve; campers must pay a $8.60 fee (up to 6 people or 1 vehicle, additional vehicles $3.70) for permits available at the National Park Centre and at most camping areas. Rangers advise stopping at the Centre first for a complete map of the park's campsites and new relevant information. Bush camping is free but is forbidden in the Wonderland Range, the Lake Wartook watershed, and any other areas demarcated accordingly on maps. Go to the Park Centre for details.

FOOD

The cheapest eats are at the **pub** 3km north of town on Grampians Rd. (meals until 8pm) and at **Ralphy's** in the center of town. (☎5356 4348. Open daily 8:30am-8:30pm.) **Suzie's Halls Gap Tavern,** toward the Brambuk Centre on Dunkeld Rd., has expensive mains but daily specials. (☎5356 4416. Open daily 8am-10:30pm. $4 breakfast special 8:30-11am, $10 3-course set menu noon-2:30pm and 5-7pm.) The **Friendly Grocer** next to the newsagent in the town center has terribly unfriendly prices. (Open daily 8am-9pm.) Some food items can be purchased at the Mobil station or at YHA reception; otherwise, buy food before arriving.

SIGHTS AND LOOKOUTS

Before you head into the park, go to the **Brambuk Aboriginal Culture Centre,** behind the National Park Centre 2.5km south of Halls Gap, which has small but excellent displays on the culture and history of the **Koori,** southwest Victoria's native people. The **Dreaming Theatre** shows a 15min. light-and-sound show of a traditional Koori story. Periodic workshops and evening activities include boomerang throwing, didgeridoo-playing and Koori traditional dancing. (☎5356 4452. Open daily 9am-5pm. Free entry. Theatre $4.40, concessions $2.80, family $16.40.)

Unfortunately, most are a good distance from Halls Gap and require a car to reach. Many tourists frequent the spots though—hikers report finding rides at the Park Centre or at their accommodations. *Let's Go* does not recommend hitchhiking. Alternately, **Halls Gap Taxis** (☎0429 943 691) offers pickup and drop off at almost anywhere around the park. The **Balconies** (Jaws of Death), the Grampians' predominant icon, lie about 1km up from the Reed Lookout carpark off Mt. Victory Rd. The mostly flat approach (20min.) ends in sweeping panoramas. The Balconies themselves, a pair of parallel slabs of sandstone, jut out over the steep sides of Mt. Victory. Those who brave the steep, slippery path to **MacKenzie Falls,** which begins at the carpark just off Lake Wartook Rd., are rewarded with one of Victoria's most spectacular waterfalls—an 11m wall of crashing water. A new wheelchair-accessible approach was recently opened. **Zumstein picnic area,** west of Lake Wartook on Mt. Victory Rd, is extremely popular because it crawls with kangaroos, but you can see herds of hopping 'roos just about everywhere in the park. Five **Aboriginal art sites** are open to the public but are considerably far apart. **Touring Downunder** runs a full-day **Aboriginal Culture and Art Sites Tour** from the Brambuk Centre that includes informational talks, a bush tucker lunch, and visits to three art sites. (Book through Brambuk ☎5356 4452. Tour runs 9:30am-5:30pm. $69.)

HIKING

Although extremely rugged, the Grampians is a very user-friendly national park; most of its highlights can be reached via relatively easy walking trails, without the need to camp overnight in the bush. Thus it's a favorite among families and nature lovers of the less-hardcore variety, while at the same time catering to the hardcore hiker with more difficult tracks. The **Wonderland Range** adjacent to Halls Gap in the park's eastern end holds a number of the park's main attractions. The strip of **Mt. Victory Rd.,** in particular, is loaded with phenomena to impress even the staunchest urbanite. Pick up the indispensable *Wonderland Walks* map ($3.30) in the Park Centre for details on hiking and driving routes.

Some Wonderland walks lead to serene waterfalls, curious rock formations, and the occasional hookah-smoking caterpillar. To the south, **Victoria Valley** is carpeted with redgum woodlands and is home to emus and kangaroos. **Manja** and **Billimina,** at the park's western border, contain some of the Grampian's best **Aboriginal art sites.** Experienced hikers might want to tackle some of the steep trails on the Gramps' highest peak (1168m), **Mt. William,** at the park's extreme eastern end; the actual "trail" to the summit is disappointingly fully-paved and well-traveled.

The hikes vary by difficulty and duration (from 30min. to 6hr. to several days). The following trails start near Halls Gap. All distances reflect return trips:

Wonderland Loop, (9.6km; 5hr.). Starts in back of the town center carpark. Cross the suspension bridge and turn left before the Botanical Gardens. Of medium difficulty, this hike traverses many of the most touristed sites, though strenuous detours abound off the track. A perfect family outing, the half-day loop along well-formed tracks leads first to the photogenic **Splitters Falls** and the **Venus Baths,** a series of rock pools popular for swimming in summer. The trail continues through the lush forest along a river to the carpark, then up the spectacular **Grand Canyon** and eventually to the narrow rock tunnel called **Silent Street** (not recommended for the claustrophobic). At the awe-inspiring **Pinnacle,** sweeping views of three valleys reward every breathless hiker. The quick descent through stringy-bark forests offers unobstructed ridge-line views, when you're not looking down to avoid rocks and tree roots.

Boronia Peak Trail, (6.6km; 2-3hr.). Starts past the kangaroo fields next to the Brambuk Centre, or alternately from the narrow path by the bridge just north of Tim's Place. A little harder than the Wonderland Loop, but shorter. The dense trees add to the tranquil solitude of this much less touristed route, yet don't obscure bird and other fauna watching. The mostly medium-grade terrain ends in a short unmarked rock scramble to the peak. With a large lake to the south, flat bush country to the east, and the jagged Wonderland range to the west, the view is worth the haul to the top.

Boroka Lookout Trail, (12.4km; 4-5hr.). Same starting location as Wonderland Loop; turn right off the trail just before Splitters Falls. The toughest hike from Halls Gap. An unrelentingly steep ascent to this lookout in the **Mt. Difficult Range** rewards with spectacular views of the **Fyans Valley** and the **Mt. William Range,** the rough slopes of which have been aptly named the Elephant's Hide (also viewable from the nearby carpark).

Chatauqua Peak Loop, (5.6km; 2-3hr.). Starts from behind the Recreation Oval on Mt. Victory Rd., 100m from the intersection with Grampians Rd. The hike opens with an up-close view of the tranquil Clematis Falls, best after rain. The final 400m boulder climb to the peak is long and strenuous, but the views of Halls Gap and the valley are perfect. Those less mobile can skip the boulder hop; the main trail continues on through to **Bullaces Glen,** a lush fern gulley, and ends in the botanical gardens in Halls Gap.

OTHER ADVENTURES

There are opportunities galore and plenty of companies around to book your next requisite adrenaline rush. All outfits offer free pickup in Halls Gap, and often cheaper group rates. The **Adventure Company** (☎5356 4540; www.adventureco.com.au), in the Grampians YHA, offers adventure in every length and level, including 1½hr. canoe trips ($35), 22km downhill bike rides ($45), and a range of full and half-day rockclimbing and abseiling courses ($35-95). The advanced abseil drops you 60m over **The Ledge.** It's all 10% off if you stay at the YHA (see p. 558). Climbing pioneers **Base Camp & Beyond** (☎5356 4300; www.grampians.net.au/basecamp), have specialized in rockclimbing and abseiling since 1982. They provide guided instruction for all skill levels as well as free bushcamping on their private property for clients ($70-180; individual price lower when group size increases). The above two companies can be booked directly or through the **Grampians Central Booking Office,** in the Halls Gap newsagent. (☎5356 4654; www.grampianstours.com. Open daily 9am-5pm, but desk may be unattended during tours.)

The Booking Office also runs the **Grampians Bushwalking Tours,** which focus on wildlife or visual highlights (4WD nature or highlights tour: $49 per half-day, $79 per day; 4WD mountain sunset tour $69; discovery bushwalk $29 per half-day, $49 per day; nocturnal spotlight walk $9, family $29). **Grampians Adventure Services,** in Shop 4 of the Stony Creek stores in Halls Gap center, runs a number of activities and tours and also rents mountain bikes. (☎5356 4556; www.grampians.org.au/gas. Open daily 10am-5pm. Climbing and abseiling $25-65; astronomy evenings $10, families $30; bike tours $30-35, night $20. Bike rental $35 per day, includes drop off with the bike anywhere in the Wonderland Range.)

LITTLE DESERT NATIONAL PARK

The Little Desert is not, in fact, a desert. So-christened because early settlers found the land ill-suited for farming, the Desert's 132,000 hectares are covered with diverse vegetation and wildlife. In the late 1960s, the government announced that 80,000 hectares of the park would be subdivided and cleared for farmland, sparking one of Australia's first major preservation campaigns, which the environmentalists won. The harsh landscape won't wow you with sweeping vistas or spectacular wonders like the Grampians, but it beckons with a subtle beauty: a delicately blooming wildflower here, a rare species of bird there.

TRANSPORTATION

The Little Desert is best approached from **Nhill** ("nil"—guess why? pop. 1900), north of the central parkland; or from **Dimboola** (pop. 1500), on the Wimmera River to the east. Two **V/Line** (☎13 61 96) buses per day Sunday to Friday, and one Saturday, depart Nhill from the stop opposite **Rintoule's Travel Service,** 37 Victoria St. (☎5391 1421. Open M-F 9am-5pm.) Service to: Ararat (2-4hr., $25.70); Ballarat (4-5hr., $40.30); Dimboola (30min., $4.70); Horsham (1-2hr., $9.50); Melbourne (5½-6½hr., $49.90); Stawell (2-3hr., $21.50). Trips from Dimboola are 30min. shorter and include an additional departure Monday to Saturday. Dimboola's bus station is on the corner of Lochiel and Hindmarsh St.; the bus also stops at the Caltex Roadhouse on the corner of High and Horsham St. The daily V/Line Daylink service from Melbourne to Adelaide runs through both Nhill and Dimboola and stops in, among other places: Adelaide (4hr., $48.80); Bendigo (4hr., $32.30); Horsham (1¼hr., $9.50); Melbourne (6¼hr., $49.90).

PRACTICAL INFORMATION

The **ranger station** on Nursery Rd. in **Wail,** is 5km south of Dimboola on the Western Hwy. (☎5389 1204. Open M-F 8am-4:30pm.) Or call **Parks Victoria.** (☎13 19 63; www.parkweb.vic.gov.au.) A few **tourist information centres** can be found in Nhill, on Goldsworthy Park along Victoria St. (☎5391 3086; open daily 10am-4pm); and Dimboola, 119 Lloyd St. (☎5389 1290. Open W-F 9:30am-5:30pm, Sa 9:30am-4pm.) **Commonwealth Bank,** 14 Victoria St., Nhill, has a 24hr. **ATM.** (☎5391 1033. Open M-Th 9:30am-4pm, F 9:30am-5pm.) Dimboola has no ATMs. **Nhill Online Solutions,** 121 Nelson St., has **Internet access.** (☎5391 1910. Open M-Tu and Th 9am-6pm, W 9am-9pm, Su 2-6pm. $2.50 per hr.) The **post offices** are in Nhill, 98 Nelson St. (☎5391 1256; open M-F 9am-5pm; **postal code:** 3418) and Dimboola, 61 Lloyd St. (☎5389 1542; open M-F 9am-5pm; **postal code:** 3414).

ACCOMMODATIONS AND FOOD

The complete experience can be had at **Little Desert Lodge**, set on over 600 acres of bush and owned and operated by Malleefowl expert Whimpey Reichelt and his wife Maureen. Take Nhill-Harrow Rd. 16km south of the Nhill town center; signs point the way. Dinners when there's a full house $18-24. (☎5391 5232; littledesertlodge@wimmera.com.au. Book well ahead. Bunk with no linens $19; single with linens $48, twins/doubles $66; campsites $11.50, powered $14. MC/V.) The lodge and aviary are also a bird- and nature-lover's mecca (see **Sights and Activities,** p. 562).

CHICKS IN THE OVEN Most birds sit on their eggs and use the heat of their bodies to warm their unborn young. But the endangered **Malleefowl** (*Leipoa ocellata)* have come up with a way to save on baby-sitting and still get out of the nest. Of the family *Megapodiidae*, meaning "large feet," these grey, beautifully patterned, pheasant-like birds use their great clonkers to build mounds out of dirt, sticks, and tree litter, in which the females deposit their eggs. Each mound takes weeks or months to build, and the fowl often reuse mounds that have been around for over a century. Once completed, the mound garners warmth from the sun and the fermentation of the tree litter. Over the next few months, dad and mom build-up and repair the natural incubators until they are nearly one meter high and five meters wide. By changing the depth of the sand and litter layers, the Malleefowl can control the temperature of the eggs. In studies of the Malleefowl hatching cycle, researchers have found that the temperature of a mound's interior varies by fewer than two degrees over a span of several months. Once the eggs hatch, the chicks dig themselves out of their nurseries and are immediately on their own.

The **Union Hotel,** across from the info centre in Nhill, is basic. (☎5391 1722. Singles $22. Free continental breakfast. MC/V.) In Dimboola, along Horshoe Bend Rd., 4km from the Dimboola post office, **Little Desert Log Cabins and Cottage** is right in the bush, and a stone's throw from the park entrance. Self-contained cabins with the works. (☎5389 1122. From $70 per double. Group discounts. MC/V.)

There are two **camping areas,** one just south of **Kiata,** a hamlet on the Western Hwy. between Nhill and Dimboola, and the other at **Horseshoe Bend** and **Ackle Bend,** south of Dimboola. Both campgrounds have fireplaces, tables, and toilets. The $10.20 fee covers six people and one vehicle (additional vehicle $4.40; payable at any ranger station, or in the pay receptacles at the campsites). Bush camping is allowed in the western and central blocks only and must be vehicle-based.

Nhill's restaurant pickings are slim. Get **groceries** at the Foodway, 17 Victoria St. (Open M-F 8:30am-6:30pm, Sa 8:30am-6pm, Su 9am-6pm.) In Dimboola, the **Victoria Hotel,** Wimmera St. (☎5389 1630) makes a mean pizza Su and F 6-8pm (from $8). For **groceries,** Kay's Foodworks is at 15-19 Lochiel St., Dimboola. (Open M-F 8am-6pm, Sa 8:30am-12:30pm, Su 9am-12:30pm.).

SIGHTS AND ACTIVITIES

Little Desert's unique ecology is best explored on foot, although 4WD drivers can usually use the rough, unpaved roads (often closed in winter) to reach remote corners. An excellent 30min. introductory walk leads to the lookout on **Pomponderoo Hill,** showing off typical Little Desert terrain. Go through the gate marked "Gateway to Little Desert" at Dimboola (not the official park entrance), turn left immediately after crossing the Wimmera River bridge, and go south, following the "National Park" signs; the trailhead is 1km past the actual park entrance. Other **walks** begin at the campground south of Kiata and at Gymbouen Rd., south of Nhill; large map boards at each campground show the trails. The truly hard-core may wish to take on the 84km **Desert Discovery Walk,** a one- to four-day trek across the eastern section of the park that can be tackled in parts or all at once. Detailed brochures on all the walks are available at ranger stations and tourist offices. The well-marked walk is best attempted in spring, when the weather is mild and the wildflowers are in bloom. Overnight campers should register at Wail's Park Office (☎5389 1204).

The **Little Desert Lodge** (☎5391 5232) provides direct access to bushwalks, including the Lodge Loop (1hr.) and the Stringybark Loop (45min.). They also run 4WD tours, including a visit to Whimpey's **Malleefowl Sanctuary,** a stretch of protected land that attracts international birdlovers. (See **Chicks in the Oven,** above. half-day tour $30, full-day (6-person min.) $66.) The **Malleefowl Aviary,** at the Little Desert Lodge offers a more pampered, up-close view. (Open M-Sa 9:30am-4:30pm, Su 1:30-4:30pm, or by appointment. $5.50, child $3.)

Oasis Desert Adventures, at the eastern entrance of the park in Dimboola, offers many activities, including day tours, flower walks, fishing trips, boomerang and spear throwing, raft and hut building, orienteering, yabbying and canoe hire. Owner Paul Lehman, a local boy, will tailor tours and activities to your interests. (☎0419 394 912; oda@netconnect.com.au. Book ahead. From $15; prices vary based on type and duration of activity.)

GOLDFIELDS

In 1851, the first year of Victorian statehood and just two years after the California gold rush, this most precious of metals was discovered in the unassuming burg of Clunes. A year later, the *London Times* reported that 50,000 diggers had already converged on Victoria's goldfields. To the chagrin of Victorians, who had taken pride in the fact that free persons had settled in Victoria before convicts had, ex-convicts from Van Diemen's Land (present-day Tasmania) floated over to join the crowds. Gold was to prove the great equalizer of classes, as convicts hardened by years of manual labor and rugged immigrants from all corners of the world dug-up ore more efficiently than their effete bourgeois counterparts, and the silk-clad landed gentry soon found themselves having to rub elbows with an unpedigreed nouveau riche. The established classes did not allow this social shake-up willingly, forcing the government to invoke mining taxes and grog prohibition, factors that ultimately led to the brief and bloody Eureka Rebellion of 1854 (see p. 12). The Victorian prospectors eventually extracted more ore than even the Californian '49ers, but by the end of the 19th century, the mines were largely exhausted, and most of the boom towns withered away to ghost towns. A few, such as Ballarat and Bendigo, remain substantial cities, and others, such as Castlemaine and Maldon, have been preserved as historical relics. These remaining cities and townships of the goldfields region, occupying the central area of western Victoria, afford travelers the opportunity to enjoy the recreated gold rush spectacles, a handful of wineries, and the hurly-burly frontier spirit that grew out of this short wave of settlement but went so far in shaping Australia's national character.

BALLARAT ☎03

Victoria's second largest inland city (pop. 83,000), Ballarat is the self-appointed capital of the Goldfields and the birthplace of Australian democratic idealism as the site of the Eureka Rebellion. The most important of the boom towns during the gold rush, it clings to its gracious yet boisterous 1850s image. When miners first started working the Ballarat goldfields, the pickings were easy; alluvial gold, weathered from upstream rocks, was visible to the naked eye in the riverbeds. Although the gold is long gone, much of the 19th-century architecture has been preserved, and the city's golden past has been channeled into a bustling tourist trade that centers on Sovereign Hill, a replica of an old gold town, replete with townspeople dressed in period attire. Huge, elegant Victorian buildings line the main street, and the begonias win the town fame among gardeners.

TRANSPORTATION

Trains/Buses: V/Line (☎13 61 96) services both buses and trains, depending on destination, from **Ballarat Station,** 202 Lydiard St. N, reached by bus #2 from Curtus St. Service to: **Ararat** (1¼hr., 6 per day, $12.30); **Bendigo** (2¼hr., 2 per day, $19.80); **Castlemaine** (1½hr., 1 per day, $15.20); **Daylesford** (40min., 1 per day, $9.50); **Geelong** (1¾hr., 3 per day, $10.80); **Maryborough** (1hr., 1 per day, $10.80); **Melbourne** (1½hr., 12 per day, $15.20). Frequency varies Sa-Su.

Public Transportation: (☎5331 7777), most **bus** routes depart from behind Bridge Mall, on Curtis St. $1.55 ticket valid for 2 hours of unlimited use. Purchase from driver. Helpful transit guide (20¢) from tourist office or on bus. Services typically run every 35min. M-F 7am-6pm; Sa limited schedule. **Ballarat Taxis** (☎5331 3355) line up in the city center and run personal tours of Ballarat and nearby wineries.

Car Rental: Avis, 1104 Sturt St. (☎5332 8310). $49/200km per day. **Budget,** 106 Market St. (☎5331 7788). $55/200km per day.

ORIENTATION AND PRACTICAL INFORMATION

Ballarat straddles the Western Hwy., called **Sturt St.** as it runs through town east to west. The **train station** is a few blocks north of Sturt on **Lydiard St.** From the station, turn left on Lydiard and cross Mair St. to get to Sturt St. At its eastern end, Sturt becomes **Bridge Mall,** a pedestrian mall with shops, restaurants, and supermarkets.

Tourist Office: 39 Sturt St. (☎5320 5741 or 1800 648 450; www.ballarat.com.) From the V/Line station, walk left along Lydiard to Sturt St., turn left, and walk 1 block downhill to the corner of Albert St. Signs point the way. Free maps. Open daily 9am-5pm.

Banks: Banks and **ATMs** line Sturt St.

Laundromat: Ballarat Laundry, 711 Sturt near Raglan St. Wash $2.40, dry $1 for 7min. Open daily 6am-10pm.

Police: (☎5337 7222). On the corner of Dana and Albert St., behind the tourist center.

Hospital: St. John of God, 101 Drummond St. N (☎5331 6677).

Internet Access: Free at the **library,** 178 Doveton St. N. (☎5331 1211), but you must sign up for borrowing privileges. Book ahead. Open Tu-Th 9:30am-6pm, F 9:30am-7pm, Sa 10am-1pm, Su 1:15-4pm, closed M. Places on Peel St. have pay options.

Post Office: (☎5336 5736; fax 5336 5737), in the Central Square Marketplace. **Fax** services. Open M-F 9am-5pm, Sa 9am-noon. Poste Restante. **Postal Code:** 3350.

ACCOMMODATIONS

Ballarat's accommodation market aims mostly at Melburnian families on weekend trips, but there a re a fair number of budget options. Rooms tend to be in short supply because of the city's popularity with school groups, so book well in advance.

Sovereign Hill Lodge YHA, (☎5333 3409; www.sovereignhill.com.au), on Magpie St. at Bourke St. Take bus #9 or #10 from Bridge Mall to Sovereign Hill; or walk for about 20min. up a steep hill by following Peel St. south at the eastern end of Bridge Mall; take a left on Grant St., and then right on Magpie St. By car, follow signs to Sovereign Hill, then to the lodge from Geelong Rd., a continuation of Main Rd. The buildings retain an 1850s style but have recently been refurbished and are in excellent condition. Laundry, kitchen, TV lounge, and bar. Heat, but no A/C. Linens included. Courteous staff issues discounted tickets for all Sovereign Hill events. Reception 24hr. except Su-M 7am-10:30pm. Book in advance due to hordes of school groups. Dorms $17.50, non-YHA $20.50; $5.50 extra to have room alone. Limited wheelchair access.

Irish Murphy's, 36 Sturt St. (☎5331 4091; ballarat@irishmurphys.com.au). A popular Aussie pub chain with live music Th-Su nights (F-Sa after 10pm cover $3). Clean, unadorned doubles at the top of the stairs might be a tad loud for the light dozer. Solution: drink downstairs until the bar closes. Communal unisex bathroom. No heat or A/C. $5 Key deposit. Check in after noon. $16 per person, $19 with linens and doona.

Robin Hood Hotel, 33 Peel St. N. (☎5331 3348). Fairly basic pub bunk accommodations with good location one block from Bridge Mall. Not quite as clean as Irish Murphy's, but you can spend most your time at the billiards bar and award-winning bistro downstairs. No heat or A/C. Book several days in advance on holidays and weekends. Bunks $22.50; singles $25.

Ballarat Goldfields Holiday Park, 108 Clayton St. (☎5332 7888 or 1800 632 237; www.ballarat.com/goldfields_holiday.htm). Campsites and cabins 300m from Sovereign Hill. Kitchens, recreation rooms, playground, heated pool. New heated communal bathrooms. Internet kiosk $2 per 10min. Reception daily 8am-8pm. Reserve cabins in advance. Sites for 2 $18; powered $20.50; powered with bath $26; cabins with bath, heat, A/C, kitchenette, and color TV $54 and up.

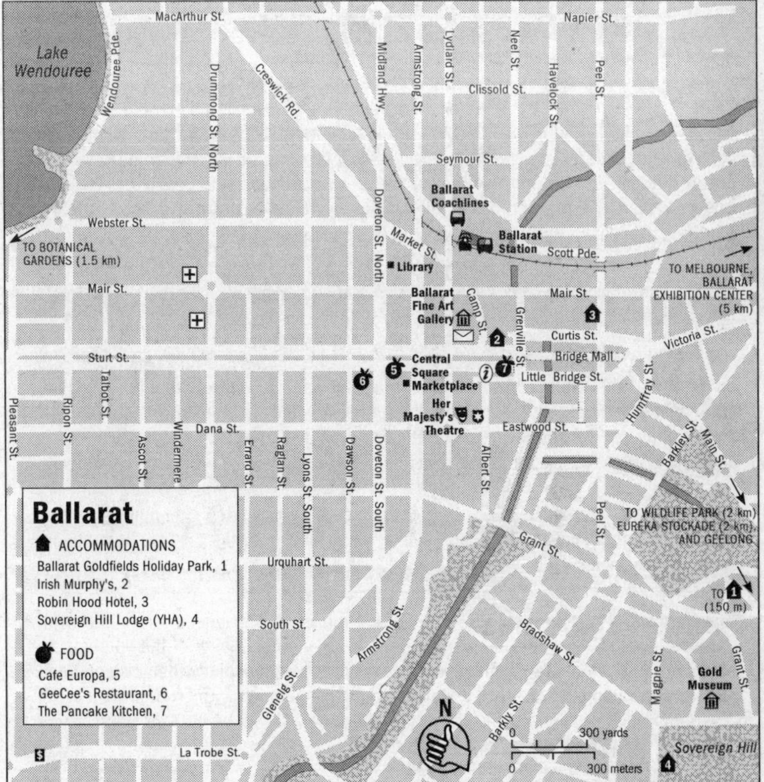

FOOD

Sturt St. is lined with fish'n'chips shops, bakeries, and other takeaway places. The best cafes are up the hill, especially between Dawson and Doveton St. Lake Wendouree provides a serene view for numerous cafes as well. Coles 24-hour **supermarket**, a produce shop, and a bakery are at the far eastern end of Sturt St. behind the Bridge Mall. Several cheap eats sit just east of Sovereign Hill.

The Pancake Kitchen, 2 Grenville St. S (☎5331 6555). This restored 1870s building. dishes out pancakes and crepes in assorted fruit or meat incarnations ($8-14). The bottom floor has a gigantic chess set. Samples W 6-10pm. Takeaway. Fully licensed or BYO. Open M 10am-10pm, Tu-Th 10am-late, F-Sa 7:30am-late, Su 7:30am-10pm.

Gee Cees, 427 Sturt St. (☎5331 6211). Bright, big, and busy, Gee Cees serves gourmet food in an informal yet stylish setting. Order food (mains $13-22, pastas $11-15, pizzas $10-17) at the counter and drinks at the bar, while a youthful waitstaff maintains fast service. Go early on weekends, as it's crowded with locals and tourists alike. Food served daily until 9:30pm; bar open Su-Th until 11pm, F-Sa until midnight.

Restaurante Da Uday, 7 Wainwright St. (☎5331 6655). A quick hop away from Sovereign Hill, this one-room establishment serves Indian, Thai, and Italian cuisines ($6-12). It's not often that you can order tortellini with a side of spring rolls and a mango lassi. They also have a cheaper takeaway menu. Reservations compulsory F-Su. Fully licensed or BYO (wine only). Open daily noon-2pm, Su-W 5:30pm-1am, Th-Sa until 11pm.

OUR PROUDEST DEFEAT. The story of Ballarat's involvement in Australia's closest brush with civil war, the Eureka Rebellion (see p. 12), is told ad nauseum. When the alluvial hype hit this sleepy goldfield's town, the colonial government in Melbourne set up a system to milk the hard-working miners of their daily spoils. The miners had to pay a license fee regardless of whether they found gold, and the governor ordered regular license hunts to make his pockets a bit heavier. The police, though, were not the enlightened, civilized patrolmen of our day, but ex-convicts who were drafted to "keep order" in the bustling gold towns. When a digger was found without a license, he was ordered to pay a fine of £10 or was chained to a log until he could pay (to keep the arrested man's hands in the cuffs, they often smashed them with a mallet so they would bruise and swell). Needless to say, the miners were less than pleased. When James Scobie, a Scottish miner, was murdered outside the hotel of a government supervisor, the already tense situation began to boil over. The miners formed a reform league to abolish the licenses and soon set up a stockade on the Eureka Lead. They burned their licenses, swore allegiance to the Southern Cross flag, and defended themselves valiantly—albeit briefly—when government forces attacked the next day. On December 3, 1854, tensions exploded when thirty miners were killed and 114 taken prisoner. The brutal invasion outraged the rest of Australia, and reforms were soon passed abolishing the licenses and giving miners representation and the right to vote. All those charged with High Treason were acquitted. The miners' leader, Peter Lalor, later became Australian Speaker of the House. Ballarat retains a stronghold on its past by billing itself "the birthplace of Australian democracy."

Europa Café, 411 Sturt St. (☎5331 2486). A mix of Mediterranean fare and New York artistic mood. Chalkboard menu changes weekly–an informality of the youthful staff. Most meals around $10. The large window counter is a great place to try one of their 79 Aussie wines. Fully licensed or BYO. Open Su-W 8:45am-6pm, Th-Sa 8:45am-late.

ENTERTAINMENT

On weekends, the **Bridge Mall** at the east end of Sturt St. fills with pedestrians and street musicians. Numerous hotels and pubs serve as venues for live bands. The **Bridge Mall Hotel,** fondly known as **The Rat,** 92 Bridge Mall (☎5331 3132) encourages up-and-coming musicians and draws university students from the area. Locals report the night scene hops at **Irish Murphy's** (see Accommodations) for drink, **Rattle and Hum** (Peel St.) for live music, and **21 Arms** (Armstrong St.), **Extremity** (Camp St.) and **The Chapel** (Dana St.) for dance. The historic **Her Majesty's Theatre,** 13 Lydiard St. (☎5333 5888; www.hermaj.com), presents live drama nightly. **Blood on the Southern Cross,** a twice-nightly 80min. sound and light show under the open night sky at Sovereign Hill, is worth the price. It introduces diggers' lives on Sovereign Hill and recounts the bitter Eureka Rebellion, with a deep-voiced recorded narrator and delightfully melodramatic music. (☎5333 5777. M-Sa, and Su during holiday periods. $29, concessions $22.50, family $79.50. Book ahead.)

SIGHTS

The Ballarat tourism network offers a *Welcome Pass* that includes two-day unlimited entry to Sovereign Hill, the Gold Museum and the Eureka Stockade and Fine Art Gallery. ($29, concessions $20, child $13.50, families $75. Purchase from tourist office or at attractions.) Several companies offer tours of Ballarat's historic areas, including **Timeless Tours** which specialize in nature and heritage tours but will personalize them depending on your interests. (☎5342 0652. Free pick up from your hotel.) The **Ballarat Begonia Festival,** in early March, is an open-air arts and crafts fair. The **Royal South Street** music, debate, and performance competitions attract top talent (Aug.-Oct.) Locals recommend walking through the tree-lined pathways of Victoria Park, south of Lake Wendouree, or hiking up to the lookout on Black Hill (from Chisholm St., north off Peel St.) for quiet nighttime views.

SOVEREIGN HILL. While a reconstructed gold town built around a mine won't make you rich, Sovereign Hill will at least give you a taste of the past. Actors play the roles of miners and townfolk, milling about in period garb and staging mock events. Exhibits include gold-pouring, candle-making, smelting, musket-firing, and a 40min. tour of the mine that reveals the harsh conditions of mining life. Pan for gold yourself or ride the horse-drawn carriage past shops masquerading as old frontier stores. *(Take bus #9 or 10. Signs point the way. ☎5331 1944. Open daily 10am-5pm. Combined admission with Gold Museum $23, concessions $16, families $59.)*

GOLD MUSEUM. Declaring "The story of gold is firmly linked to the story of man," this Sovereign Hill appendage traces the importance of gold across time and cultures. It also houses an expensive collection of gold coins, ornaments, and replicas of the two largest gold nuggets ever found. If, somehow, you grow tired of gold, the museum also features some interesting but unrelated exhibits, including a section on Chinese in Australia, an Aboriginal display with an assortment of boomerangs, and the Ballarat Sports Hall of Fame, containing the Sydney 2000 Olympic torch. *(Adjacent to Sovereign Hill, on Bradshaw St. ☎5331 1944. Open daily 9:30am-5:20pm. Admission to museum alone $5.80, concessions $3.60, children $2.90.)*

EUREKA STOCKADE. This sleek $4 million multimedia adventure commemorates the miners' resistance in the Eureka Rebellion on the site of the original stockade. Slightly gaudy for its east-Ballarat residential neighborhood, the modern stockade complex dons a giant Southern Cross flag in the shape of a sail. If you've already seen **Blood on the Southern Cross** (see p. 566), the 1hr. self-guided tour may be a little redundant. *(Eureka St. at Rodier St. Take bus #8. ☎5333 1854; www.sovereignhill.com.au/eureka.htm. Open daily 9am-5pm. $8, concessions $6, children $4, family $22.)*

BALLARAT FINE ART GALLERY. The Eureka rebels fought under the Southern Cross flag, the remains of which are kept here. For many years, foreign dignitaries who visited Ballarat were presented with pieces of the flag. The gallery also houses a comprehensive collection of regional and national artwork, notably a large collection of art from or about the goldfields. Keep your eyes peeled for the one Picasso lithograph; it's inconspicuously mixed in with the rest of the lesser-known works. Among the half dozen traveling exhibits expected is "Two laws, One spirit," a modern Aboriginal collection slated for November 2002. The gallery, Australia's oldest, has recently undergone a $5 million expansion. *(40 Lydiard north of Sturt St. ☎5331 5622; www.balgal.com. Open daily 10:30am-5pm. $4, concessions $2, under 16 free. Guided tours 2pm daily. Wheelchair accessible.)*

BALLARAT WILDLIFE PARK. The park's 14 acres of open bush are home to some of Australia's diverse fauna, including fearsome saltwater crocodiles and Tasmanian devils, and less imposing emus, goannas, wombats, koalas, and free-roaming 'roos. The weekend crocodile feed is a particular thrill. *(York at Fussel St. Take bus #8 or 9 or drive down York St. off Main Rd midway between Sovereign Hill and Eureka St. ☎5333 5933; wildlife@lin.cbl.com.au. Tours at 11am. Open daily 9am-5:30pm. $13.50, students $11.50, children $7.50, families $38.)*

DAYTRIPS FROM BALLARAT: WINERIES

Most vineyards in the Ballarat wine region began production in the 1980s. With cool climate Chardonnays becoming increasingly popular, this region is regarded as an up-and-coming area. Pick up the *Wine Regions of Victoria* booklet in local tourist offices. At **Dulcinea Vineyard,** owner Rod Stott says: "I believe in education." He is on site to answer questions and urge visitors to roam through his small cellar and vineyard, tasting his delectable blends on the way. Take the Midland Hwy. from

Ballarat north 11km toward Creswick. (☎5334 6440. dulcinea@cbl.com.au. Open daily 10am-5pm. Bottles $16-18.) **St. Anne's Vineyards** is 22km east of Ballarat and 77km from Melbourne off the Western Hwy. Free tastings are available in a cool, blue stone cottage. A peppery red Shiraz and a fortified tawny port top the list. (☎5368 7209. stannes@hyperlink.net.au. Open M-Sa 9am-5pm, Su 10am-5pm.)

MIDLAND HIGHWAY TO CALDER HIGHWAY

The Midland goes from Ballarat to Bendigo changing names at Castlemaine.

DAYLESFORD AND HEPBURN SPRINGS. Daylesford is 107km northwest of Melbourne and 45km northeast of Ballarat. Visitors come to Daylesford to soak in the curative waters of its neighbor, Hepburn Springs, which contains the largest concentration of curative mineral springs in Australia. Aborigines revered the springs before European settlement, but the many guest cottages and B&Bs have sprung up recently. New Age commercialism has infused these quiet communities with healing crystals, essences, oils, and aromatherapy. While most of the restaurants and services are in Daylesford, the spa complex is in Hepburn Springs, 4km north. Buses run between the towns, but it is a pleasant 40min. walk, if you're up for it. The **Hepburn Regional Park** lets you pump your own mineral water, but take care to avoid falling into abandoned mine shafts (maps at info center, see below).

Most of the area's lovely guest cottages and B&Bs will set you back $80-100 per night. **Continental House,** 9 Lone Pine Ave. (☎5348 2005), described by some of its patrons as a living work of art (and by others as a hippie hideout), is secluded behind an impressively dense 5m tall hedge just a few hundred meters from the spa. Refresh yourself at this strictly vegetarian, strictly relaxed guest house with tranquil common areas and basic bunkrooms. The **Hepburn Spa Resort,** in Hepburn Springs, provides the works. Services range from the normal pool and spa (weekdays $8.80, weekends $11) to massages (45min., $49.50-55) to floatation tanks (30min., $32.50-38.50). Use of spring waters is free. (☎5348 2034. www.hepburnspa.com.au. Open M-Th 10am-7pm, F 10am-8pm, Sa 9am-10pm, Su 9am-7pm.)

MALDON. A veritable ghost town by weekday, Maldon (pop. 1200) attracts weekend Victorian tourists looking for history, antiques, or just plain peace and quiet. If it does not offer much nightlife, at least it can provide an enjoyable respite for the tired traveler. After all, it has been declared "Australia's First Notable Town," as the first town recognized for its historical value. Main Street's 19th-century buildings with corrugated iron roofs and hand-painted wooden signs are the best preserved array of gold rush era buildings in the state.

Historic-looking B&Bs ($60-90), though pricey, are scattered throughout town. A more affordable option, **Central Service Centre Accommodations,** is situated right where Main and High St. merge. This garage-recently-turned-hotel features heating and A/C, bathroom, TV, fridge, and coffee and tea in every room. Laundry machines ($3 wash, $1 10min. dry) and public pay-showers in the lobby. (☎5475 2216. Reception 8:30am-5:30pm. Singles $30; multiple $20 per person.) The **Maldon Caravan and Camping Park,** on Hospital St., northwest along High St., has toilets and BBQs. (☎/fax 5475 2344. $7 per person; powered sites $17; on-site caravans for 2 $35; cabins for 2 $52.)

Maldon abounds with preserved structures from the 19th century; pick up the *Town Walk* from the information center for a detailed list of buildings and sites. Amateur historians may also enjoy the **Maldon Museum and Archives,** which displays local artifacts from the 1850s to the early 20th century. (☎5475 1633. Adjacent to the visitor's center. Open M-F 1:30-4pm, Sa-Su 1:30-5pm. $2, children 50¢.) For a hearty workout, hike the steep trail (a 25-45min. walk starting at Fountain St.) up **Mt. Tarrangower,** 571m above sea level. If you have any breath left, the panoramic views of the bush will take it away.

CASTLEMAINE. Castlemaine, 120km northwest of Melbourne in the central Goldfields, peaked early as a boom town in the heady gold rush days. Since then, with a fairly static population of 7500 for the last 140 years, it has faded into a sleepy, provincial town. Fantastic gardens blossom in the spring, adding to its quiet charm and array of art displays and boutiques.

If you've got money to spare, the **Old Castlemaine Gaol,** on Bowden St., overlooks the town atop the hill to the west of the railroad station. The 1861 jail held felons, lunatics, and later juvenile offenders until 1990, when it was renovated as a well-heated and ventilated B&B. The Gaol primarily hosts conventions and groups over 20, and won't take individual guests unless another large group is staying and there's room. The dungeons, once the site of horrific torture, now house a wine bar and lounge. If you're not staying here, it's worth taking a self-guided tour anyway. (☎5470 5311; www.castlemaine.net.au/~gaol. Tours $4. Call ahead for availability. Doubles $75 per person.)

The **Castlemaine Art Gallery and Historic Museum,** 12 Lyttleton St., between Kennedy and Barker St., houses a collection devoted entirely to Australian artists. Ten temporary exhibits visit throughout the year; September 2002 brings selections representing the 100th anniversary of the Melbourne Society of Women Painters and Sculptors. Downstairs, the historic museum has some interesting old photographs of the Castlemaine area. (☎5472 2292. Open M-F 10am-5pm, Sa-Su noon-5pm. $4, concessions $3, family $8.) Just 4km east of town toward Chewton is the wild and popular **Dingo Farm Australia**. Here you can witness an attempt to keep purebred dingoes from becoming extinct. Although these animals are a danger in the wild, owner Bruce Jacobs domesticates, shelters, and breeds nearly 100 of these canines. (☎5470 5711; www.ins.net.au/dingofarm. Book in advance.) In November, the **Garden Festival** celebrates the blossoming of the city, while Castlemaine **Arts Festival,** held at the end of March in odd years, rings in the spring.

BENDIGO ☎03

Like almost all the towns in the Victorian goldfields, Bendigo (pop. 85,000) sprung into existence in the 1850s when scores of miners flooded in, lured by the promise of success. But while many of its neighbors were tossed from prosperity to obscurity by the boom and bust cycle, Bendigo continued to prosper into the 20th century thanks to its seemingly endless supply of gold-rich alluvial quartz. Bendigo still holds rank as the second highest gold producer in the country, even though it stopped mining commercially in 1954. Such abundance lured gold-seekers from across the globe, notably a significant Chinese population, resulting in a period of harsh discrimination. However, the town's early diversity has created a sense of progressive tolerance in a nearly homogenous nation. The large quantities of gold also encouraged the settling of many gold magnates, who used their early fortunes to turn the fledgling city into a Victorian showcase. Grandiose Gothic buildings and wide thoroughfares with names like Pall Mall ("Pell Mell") imbue Bendigo with a certain Anglophilic nostalgia.

TRANSPORTATION

Trains/Buses: Bendigo Station, behind the Discovery Centre at the south end of Mitchell St. **V/Line** (☎13 61 96) has **trains** and **buses**, depending on destination, to: **Adelaide** (8½hr., 1 per day, $57); **Ballarat** (2hr., 1 per day, $19.80); **Daylesford** (1¼hr., 1 per day, $9.50); **Geelong** (3¾hr., 1 per day, $32.30); **Maldon** (2hr., 2 per day, $6.70) via **Castlemaine** (22min., 11 per day, $4.70); **Maryborough** (1hr., 3 per day, $12.30); **Mildura** (5hr., 4 per day, $51.80); **Melbourne** (2hr., 11 per day, $22.90); **Swan Hill** (3½hr., 2-3 per day, $25.70). Infrequent service on Sa-Su. Round trips Tu-Th 30% off.

Public Transportation: Local **buses** leave from the corner of Hargreaves and Mitchell St. **Taxis** line up along Queen St. between Mitchell and Williamson St.

Car Rental: Hertz (☎5443 5088), at the corner of High and Thistle St. Starting at $42 for 300km per day. **Budget,** 150-152 High St. (☎5442 2766), near the Central Deborah Mine. $55 for 330km per day.

MORTAL MINING. The "Stroker" drill, used by Bendigo miners until the 1890s, earned a morbid nickname among the mining community. Unlike the more primitive "hammer and tap" method, this compressed air drill produced a heavy dust as it cut into the underground rock. As quartz rock is made of silicon, the particles that flew from the rock were essentially miniscule glass bits that could penetrate the flimsy cloth barriers the miners wore over their mouths. Because of this, miners using the "Stroker" often developed a lung disease called silicosis, or miners' phthisis, that proved fatal. The "Stroker" quickly became known as the "Widow Maker."

ORIENTATION AND PRACTICAL INFORMATION

Bendigo is a combination of well-planned streets and winding gold gullies originally packed down by diggers' feet. Most points of interest are near the city center, bounded on the south and east by the railroad tracks and on the north by Rosalind Park. The **Calder Hwy.** from Melbourne runs into the center of town becoming **High St.** At **Charing Cross,** High St. becomes **Pall Mall,** which eventually turns into **McCrae St.** and then into **Midland Hwy.,** which leads to Elmore and Echuca. The popular pedestrian **Hargreaves Mall** extends one block along Hargreaves between Mitchell and Williamson St.

Tourist Office, 51-67 Pall Mall (☎/fax 5444 4445 or 1800 813 153; www.bendigotourism.com). Located in the ornate Victorian post office building (no longer a post office). Mini-museum equipped with maps, brochures, and video displays that tell Bendigo's history. Loads of food and accommodations info. Open daily 9am-5pm.

Currency Exchange: National Bank (☎5443 9399), corner of Queen and Mitchell St. Open M-Th 9:30am-4pm, F 9:30am-5pm. $5 exchange commission. 24hr. **ATM.**

Bookstore: Bendigo Bookmark, 29 High St. (☎5441 7866), will buy, sell, and exchange. Alternative living section and large collection of Penguin classics. Open M-F 9:30am-5:30pm, Sa 9:30am-1pm. Also **Book Now** (☎5443 8587) on Farmers' Ln. off Bridge St. carries cheap secondhand. (Open daily 10am-5pm).

Public Library: 251-259 Hargreaves St. (☎5443 5100; www.ncgrl.vic.gov.au). Books, magazines, and free 15min. **Internet access;** for longer access, book ahead for computers upstairs, $3 for 30min. Open M-F 10am-7pm, Sa 10am- 1pm.

Laundromat: View Street Laundry, 41 View St. (☎5441 8877), next to Rosalind Park. Open daily 6am-9pm. Wash $3, dry 10min. $1.

Emergency: ☎000. **Police** (☎5440 2510), on Bull St. behind the law courts.

Hospital: ☎5441 0222, on Lucan St. between Arnold and Bayne St.

Internet Access: In the public library, see above. Also services at **Buzza's YHA** (see **Accommodations,** below).

Post Office (☎13 13 18), corner of Hargreaves and Williamson St. Open M-F 9am-5pm, Sa 9:30am-12:30pm. Poste Restante. **Postal Code:** 3550.

ACCOMMODATIONS

The strip of Hwy. 79 (Calder Hwy.), also known as High St., running south of town is loaded with cookie-cutter chain motels. You can find some nicer motels and B&Bs ($50-90) with historical charm, along McCrae and Napier St. just northeast of the city center. The **Shamrock Hotel** (☎5443 0333; fax 5442 4494), across from the tourist office, offers doubles with shared bathroom ($70; see **Sights,** p. 572).

Nomads Ironbark Bush Cabins, Watson St. (☎5448 3344; www.bwc.com.au/ironbark). Located 5km from the city center, the Ironbark is out of walking distance, but the owners will pick you up from Bendigo station and shuttle you to the cabins. A refreshing and pleasant taste of the bush, 6 small, tidy cabins sleep 5 to 9 people. All cabins have heating, bathrooms, refrigerators, and coffee makers. Free bush breakfast from the bar-

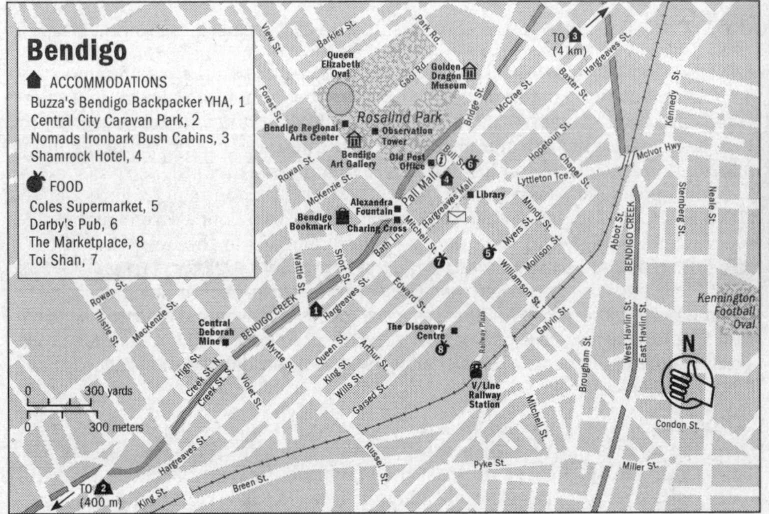

bie; towels and linen included. BBQ (dinner $12) and bar (beer $2.50) in evenings around the campfire. On-site horseback riding ($20 per hr.) Special weekend package deals include horseback riding and meals. Bunks $18; doubles $40.

Buzza's Bendigo Backpacker YHA, 33 Creek St. (☎/fax 5443 7680; buzza@bendigo.net.au). A clean, comfortable, converted house in a quiet residential area close to the center of town. Three individual shower/bathrooms offer some welcomed privacy, while the large dining room with TV, and the reading room with open fireplace allow guests to interact at their leisure. Linens and towels, coffee and tea, and use of kitchen and BBQ included. Laundry $2. Internet 30min. $2. Free parking. Check-in 8-11am and 5-10pm. Dorms $17 (non-YHA $20); singles $19 (non-YHA $24); doubles $40 (non-YHA $47). Family suite also available. Wheelchair accessible.

Central City Caravan Park, 362 High St. at Birch St. (☎/fax 5443 6937). Take bus #1 from Hargreaves Mall. The CCCP, a former YHA affiliate, is the cheapest place around, offering minimalist hostel accommodation, comrade. Hostel $15 per person; sites $14 for two people or $18 with electrical power.

FOOD

Most popular restaurants are near the tourist office, especially on Bull St. and Pall Mall; Main St. also has several options. Budget-friendly restaurants are all around town. The **Hargreaves Mall** has a food court that bustles during lunch hours. **Coles supermarket,** corner of Myers and Williamson St., is open 24hr.

Cafe Kryptonite, 92 Pall Mall (☎5443 9777). Features meals ($6-18) almost as colorful as its interior design, as well as several veggie options and a braggable selection of wine and tea ($3 and up).

Darby O'Gills (☎5443 4916), on the corner of Bull and Hargreaves St. This pub touts itself as "a touch of the Irish, a taste of the world," but their grub outshines their international cuisine. Open M-Sa noon-2:30pm, 6-8:30 M-W, 6-9, Th-Sa till 9:30.

Gillie's Famous Pies (☎5443 4965), on the corner of Hargreaves Mall and Williamson St., features meat pies and sweet cakes ($2-3) either inside or via the "Pie Window" Open M-F 8am-6pm, Sa 8am-5pm, Su 8am-4pm.

Toi Shan, 65-67 Mitchell St. (☎5443 5811). All-you-can-eat "smorgasbor," ($8.50-9.50). Yes, that's without the "d." Convenient self-serve takeaway packs ($3.20-6).

SIGHTS

CENTRAL DEBORAH MINE. Tours take visitors 61m down the last mine to stop operating commercially in Bendigo. Explanations of mining history and techniques are both extensive and interactive; volunteer and you may even get to show off your skill with the drill. It's worth the trip, if only for the geology information and lessons on the harsh lives of miners. True thrill-seekers can try the **Underground Adventure Tour,** in which participants don miner's garb and go down extra levels to use real mine equipment for two hours. Even truer thrill-seekers can plunge into the mine at ungodly speeds in the new Cage Rider, basically a bungee jump in a cage. *(76 Violet St. ☎5443 8322; for advanced bookings 5443 8255,; www.central-deborah.com. Open daily 9am-5pm. Regular Tour, 6 daily, every 70min. $16.50, concessions $14.50. Underground Adventure: with lunch, $49, concession $45, child $26; with morning/afternoon tea $42/$38/$22. Cage Rider $7-8, or included in Underground Adventure. Discounts available for children, families, and groups bigger than six. Prices valid until March 31, 2002.)*

LANDMARKS. Tours, complete with recorded commentary, cover the town using the restored turn-of-the-century tram system (1hr.; $12, concessions $9). Trams run hourly, picking up from the elaborate **Alexandra Fountain** near the tourist office or from the Central Deborah Mine. The late-Victorian feel of Bendigo's architecture is most pronounced along **Pall Mall,** which is littered with more neo-Gothic touches than you can shake a spire at. The most impressive buildings are the **old post office building** (which now houses the visitors center) and the adjacent Bendigo Law Courts, both built with ornate facades on all four sides. The **Shamrock Hotel** at the corner of Williamson St. and Pall Mall originated as a roaring entertainment hall in the golden 1850s. **Rosalind Park,** on the site of the old 1850s police barracks north of Alexandra Fountain, is a vast expanse of greenery scattered with winding pathways, trees, and statues—including a particularly unflattering likeness of Queen Victoria. If you brave the 124-step climb to the top of its observation tower, the reward is a view of Bendigo and the surrounding gold country.

MUSEUMS AND GALLERIES

Golden Dragon Museum, 59 Bridge St. (☎5441 5044). This collection provides a decent overview of both Chinese culture in Australia and its particular impact on Bedigo. Displays offer a look at the Chinese-Australian experience in the place they dubbed "Dai Gum San" (Big Gold Mountain), but do gloss a bit over the racism that Chinese-Australians often faced. The collection's highlight is the fantastically ornate Sun Loong, the longest imperial dragon in the world at just over 100m. Open daily 9:30am-5pm. $7, concession $5, children $4. Garden only: $2.60, children 60¢.

Bendigo Military Museum (☎5443 4013; rslbgo@bigpond.com), across from the tourist office Williamson St. Volunteer military veterans guide the regular tours. Outside, a large monument and wall honor the Australian soldiers who died in World War I, while a nearby statue commemorates those who died fighting for Britain in the 1899-1902 South African War for independence. Open Su-F 10am-4pm. Admission: gold coin.

Bendigo Art Gallery, 42 View St. (☎5443 4991, www.bendigoartgallery.com). The city's major museum houses an extensive national collection, a host of European works, and various rotating exhibits. Bendigo is an artistic haven; studios and galleries can be found all along View St. You probably won't recognize the names of most of the artists, but the modern Aboriginal pieces are some of the most representative of their genre. Open daily 10am-5pm. Free tours daily 2pm. Free admission, donation suggested.

The Capital, 50 View St. (☎5441 5344; www.bendigo.vic.gov.au/thecapital). Formerly Bendigo Regional Arts Center, it houses a full schedule of plays, concerts, and dance exhibitions. Box office open M-F 10am-6pm. Prices vary by show, $12-40.

Discovery Centre, 7 Railway Pl. (☎5444 4400). Kids and kids-at-heart would hate to miss this place where education and adventure go hand in hand. With Australia's only vertical slide (7m high), and frequently changing exhibits, the centre attracts a crowd. Open daily 10am-5pm. $8.25, concessions $7.15, children $5. Wheelchair accessible.

ENTERTAINMENT AND NIGHTLIFE

Pubs are everywhere. Most are tame local hangouts that close around midnight, but weekends can be rowdier when tourists funnel into its small watering holes. The main late-night entertainment options are on the few blocks of Pall Mall and Hargreaves from Williamson to Mundy St. The **Old Crown,** 238 Hargreaves St., is a smoky neighborhood haunt filled with families by day and burly locals at night. Join in some karaoke F-Sa; "real" live music F. (☎5441 6888. Occasional cover $3. Closes Th-F 1-2am, Sa 3am.) **Darby O'Gills,** on the corner of Bull and Hargreaves St., offers a selection of Irish beers on tap ($3.50/pot) and live music W-Sa starting at 10pm. (No cover. Open until 1-2am.) Another live music option is the **Sundance Saloon** on Pall Mall and Mundy St., which hosts Melbourne's top cover bands on Thursdays. (☎5441 8222. Open Th-Sa 8:30pm-late.) The **Golden Vine,** 135 King St., attracts the local twenty-something crowd with its chill music and late nights. (☎5443 6063). If a pub's not your thing, the **Bendigo Cinemas** shows current American movies and houses a fairly substantial video arcade (Queen St. at Short St. Movies before 6pm, $7.50; after 6pm, $12, $9 students.)

MURRAY RIVER

Australia's longest river, the Murray, rambles along the New South Wales-Victoria border for 2600km before meeting the sea in South Australia's Encounter Bay. The river became an essential transportation artery in the late 19th century, its waters plied by giant freight-toting paddlesteamers. But extensive rail and road networks rendered these boats obsolete by the end of the 1930s, and they have since been reincarnated as tourist attractions. Today the river feeds production of vegetables and fruits (including wine grapes) through a complex irrigation system. It's also a favorite spot for picnicking, water sports, and fishing, drawing travelers for a day or a week of relaxation along the banks of the grand old Murray.

ECHUCA ☎03

As the closest point to Melbourne along the Murray, Echuca was once Australia's largest inland port, a clearinghouse for the wool and agricultural products of southern New South Wales. A massive red gum wharf was built to accommodate the paddlesteamers and barges, and a lively array of hotels, brothels, and breweries was built to accommodate the men who sailed them. Although river traffic declined in the late 1800s, many boats have been preserved, and Echuca now possesses the world's largest flotilla of side-wheel paddlesteamers—its major industry is now nostalgia. Old-time facades dominate its main streets, and a late-19th century feel pervades the town. Despite its exterior, Echuca has the bustle of an entirely modern city, and its tourist industry—though not exactly exciting—avoids the theme-park hokiness of other historic river towns, making this the best place to immerse yourself in the Murray riverboat culture.

TRANSPORTATION

V/Line buses run from the Visitors Centre or the Ampole Road House on the Northern Hwy. to: Albury (3-4hr., 1-3 per day, $23-38); Bendigo (1¼hr., 1-3 per day, $6.70); Kerang (1hr., 1 per day M, W, Th, Sa; $12.30); Melbourne (3½-4hr., 4-6 per day, $29.70); Mildura (5½hr.; 1 per day M, W, Th, Sa); Swan Hill (2hr., 1-2 per day, $19.80). A **steam locomotive** (not V/Line) from Melbourne is scheduled to be running by the end of 2001; contact West Coast Railways in Melbourne for details.

ORIENTATION AND PRACTICAL INFORMATION

Echuca, from the Aboriginal word meaning "meeting of the waters," lies about 200km north of Melbourne at the intersection of two rivers, the **Campaspe** (north-south) and the **Murray** (east-west), and of two highways, the **Murray Valley Hwy.** and **Northern Hwy.** Echuca's main drags are **Hare** and **High St.,** parallel roads that run north-south from the Murray River to the Murray Valley Hwy. Follow the **Cobb Hwy.** past the Visitors Centre across the Murray to Echuca's twin city of **Moama** in New South Wales, notable predominantly for its vast array of gambling clubs.

The **Visitor Information Centre,** 2 Heygarth St., is on the Echuca side of the Echuca-Moama bridge. (☎5480 7555 or 1800 804 446; www.echucamoama.com. Open daily 9am-5pm.) **ANZ, National,** and **Commonwealth banks** with **24hr. ATMs** are side-by-side on Hare St. just south of Anstruther St. (All open M-Th 9:30am-4pm, F 9:30am-5pm.) The **library,** at the corner of Heygarth and High St. catty-corner to McDonald's, offers **Internet** access. (Research free, email $2 per 30min. Book ahead at ☎5482 1997. Open M-Tu, Th-F 10am-5:30pm; W noon-8pm winter, 1-9pm summer; Sa 10am-1pm; Su 2-4pm.) There's a **post office** on the corner of Hare and Anstruther St. (Open M-F 9am-5pm, Sa 9am-noon.) **Postal code:** 3564.

ACCOMMODATIONS

Echuca's accommodation scene consists mostly of luxury riverside B&Bs and pricey motels, but there are a few budget options.

Echuca Gardens B&B and Hostel (YHA), 103 Mitchell St. (☎5480 6522; www.echucagardens.com). 8 blocks east from the city center. Think you're well traveled? The engaging owners are more so. Kitchen, cozy lounge, open fireplace, and memorable German Shepherd named Baron. Sauna and spa encourage friendly conversation among guests. Key deposit $10. Reception daily 8-10am and 5-10pm. 4-bed dorms and triples $18; doubles and twins $40, with bath and TV $65. Non-YHA add $3.50. MC/V.

NOMADS Oasis Backpackers, 410-424 High St., on the corner of Pakenham (☎5480 7866; nomads@river.net.au). In town and well-kept, Oasis caters largely to backpackers who come for the fruit-picking seasons. Courtesy bus provides transport to picking sites. Kitchen, TV lounge, and Internet ($5 per hr.). Room key gets discounts around town, including $8.50 cinema tickets and free entry and $2 pots at the **Atomic Bar.** Linens included. Reception 24hr. All dorms 3-12 bed $17, $100 per week. AmEx/DC/MC/V.

Echuca Caravan Park, Crofton St. (☎5482 2157; fax 5480 1551). Due to its idyllic location right on the Murray, this gigantic facility is choked with campervans, especially during holidays. BYO linens. Sites for 2 $20, off-peak $18; powered $22/$20; 5-6 person cabins with bath $73-90/$60-75. Book in advance. MC/V.

FOOD AND NIGHTLIFE

The standard Australian array of chip shops, grub-serving pubs, and fast-food joints line High St., and there are some more upmarket riverfront spots on the Murray Esplanade. Large, cheap meals can be had in the four licensed clubs across the river in Moama. The omnipresent, omni-cheap, budget-friendly **La Porchetta** pizza and pasta chain beckons at 192 Annesley St., attached to the King Pin bowling alley. (☎5480 1130. Open daily 11am-10pm. MC/V.) **Port Precinct Café,** 591 High St., serves inexpensive gourmet burgers ($3.80-5.90) and an all-day breakfast menu ($5-11) by an open fire. Their **Internet cafe** unfortunately is not as cheap. (☎5480 2163. $2.50 per 15min., $5 per 30min., $9 per hr. Open 8am-6 or 7pm daily. AmEx/DC/MC/V.) **River Palace,** 614 High St., offers over 100 Szechuan and Malay dishes. (☎5482 3152. Takeaway daily noon-2:30pm; and dine-in from 5pm. AmEx/DC/MC/V.) For a splurge, visit **Giorgio's On the Port,** 527 High St., which is not actually on the port, but serves awesome Italian meals from $15.50 nevertheless. (☎5482 6117. AmEx/DC/MC/V.) There is also a 24hr. Coles **supermarket** on the corner of High and Darling St.

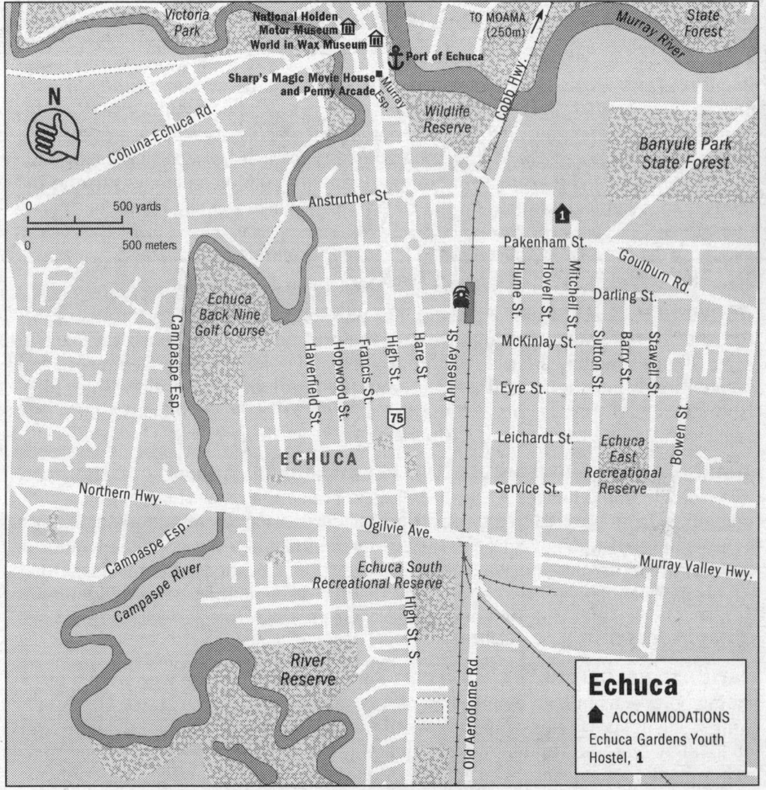

Numerous pubs on High and Hare St. are peopled by friendly locals. The most active are the **Harvest Hotel** at the corner of Hare and Anstruther St., the **Shamrock** on High St. near the port, and the **American Hotel** at Hare and Pakenham St. A younger crowd chills at the **Atomic Pool Bar Cafe,** 207 Darling St., which hosts mellow live music Su afternoons and free pool all day Sa-Su. (☎5480 2227. Open Tu-Th 5pm-1am, F 5pm-2am, Sa noon-2am, Su noon-11pm. F-Sa cover $5 after 10pm.)

SIGHTS

Although most of Echuca's sights center around its paddlesteamer history, the small river-town atmosphere provides some great day-strolls whether or not history is your motivation.

HISTORIC PORT. The main attraction in Echuca is its port, consisting of the wharf and several historic buildings. The 1865 redgum wharf has three levels to accommodate the changing river conditions. Blacksmith and woodturning shops sell handmade wares, and a steam display explains the workings of that portentous invention that brought on the Industrial Revolution. *(Historic Port Area, along Murray Esplanade. ☎5482 4248; www.portofechuca.org.au. Open daily 9am-5pm. $10, concessions $8.50, child $6, family $27.50.)* The port precinct, which is free for strolling, has several old hotels on display. The **Star Hotel** is equipped with every fraternity brother's dream: a secret underground tunnel that allowed drinkers to escape police raids after the place was de-licensed in 1897; the **Bridge Hotel,** Echuca's first, has a carefully preserved suite and gallery upstairs. At the other end, the old **Customs House** where tariffs were exacted from passing watercraft when Echuca was the commercial hub of the Murray. Today, the Customs House building houses **Murray Esplanade Cellars,** which exacts a tariff of zero dollars for sampling its excellent wines and spirits. *(2 Leslie St. ☎5482 6058. Open daily 9am-5pm. Free entry.)*

PADDLESTEAMERS. Several paddlesteamers still ply the waters off the old port, and are now open to the public for leisurely cruises. The Port Authority runs 1hr. cruises on **P.S. Pevensey** or **P.S. Alexander Arbuthnot.** *(Buy tickets at 52 Murray Esplanade. ☎5482 4248. 5 cruises daily: $15.50, concessions $12, child $6. Joint port and cruise: $20/ $17/$11; family $49.50.)* A private company runs the paddlesteamers **Pride of the Murray** and **Emmylou;** a cruise on the Emmylou is worth the slightly higher price. *(Buy tickets at the Custom House Agents or at 57 Murray Esplanade. ☎5482 5244. Pride of Murray: 1hr.; 6 daily cruises; $12.50, seniors $11, children $6, family $35. Emmylou: 5 daily cruises 1hr.; $15, children $7.50; 1½hr. $18, children $9.)*

WORLD IN WAX MUSEUM. Although not particularly relevant to the history of the Murray, the wax museum in front of the port could be the most fun place in town. Figures include dignitaries both foreign and domestic, arranged by era and disposition (amusingly, Stalin, Hitler, and Castro share a case with Churchill). Humorously informative notes line the walls. *(630 High St. ☎5482 3630. Open daily 9am-5:30pm. $8.80, concessions $7.70, children $4.40. $1 YHA discount.)*

SHARP'S MAGIC MOVIE HOUSE AND PENNY ARCADE. Adjacent to the port, this small building houses Australia's largest collection of working penny arcade machines, from strength tests to fortune readers. An array of antique cinematic equipment continuously screens turn-of-the-century newsreels, comedy shorts, and historical documentaries. It's a bit pricey, but kind of cool considering that Australian pennies stopped circulating in 1966. Five pennies are provided with admission. *(☎5482 2361; www.origin.net.au/~nsharp. Open daily 9am-5pm. $12, concessions $10, child $8. Ticket valid all day.)*

NATIONAL HOLDEN MOTOR MUSEUM. For car-lovers or those who want a fascinating perspective on an iconic slice of Australiana, the Holden Motor Museum is a must-see. It showcases over 50 years of "Australia's Own" automobile, with over 40 lovingly restored Holden models including the only one of the space-age 1969 experimental "Hurricane." The amusing video retrospective spotlights not only the car, but also Australia's love for Holden ads. *(7-11 Warren St. ☎5480 2033. Open 9am-5pm. $6, concessions $4.50, children $3, families $14. MC/V.)*

OZMAZE. After living in the past all day, you may want to get lost for awhile. This huge wooden maze is constructed in the form of Australia: Tasmania included, but no 'roos, wombats, or beer. *(On the Echuca side of the Echuca-Moama bridge. ☎5480 2220; ozmaze.com.au. Maze: $7, $5.50 seniors, $25-30 family. Mini golf: $6, children and seniors $5, $20-25 family. Open W-M 10am-4pm.)*

DAYTRIP FROM ECHUCA: BARMAH FOREST

Just 31km from Echuca on the Cobb Hwy., the **Barmah State Park and State Forest** is the largest redgum forest in Victoria. The 22,000 hectares are well-endowed with roads and walking tracks, but rain and high water levels render many impassable. The **Dharnya Centre,** on Sand Ridge Rd. near the park entrance, 9km from the Barmah General Store, provides maps and info on road conditions, and presents an engaging display on white treatment of Aborigines. (☎5869 3302. Open daily 10:30am-4pm.) **Camping** is free and abundant in the park, and fishing is excellent (fishing licenses required for ages 18+). When water levels are high enough, the wetlands can be explored by boat or canoe. **Kingfisher Wetland Cruises** offers 2hr. trips. Purchase tickets from Barmah General Store or from the Pride of the Murray stand on the Esplanade in Echuca. (☎5480 1839. M, W, Th, Sa, Su 12:30pm. $18, child $12.) **Gondwana Canoe Hire,** on Moira Lakes Rd. on the way to the park entrance from Barmah, hires canoes. (☎5869 3347; www.geocities.com/gondwanahire. $25 per hr.; $35 per half-day; $50 per day; $75 per 2 days; $30 per day for

3 or more days.) There is no public transport to the park; **V/Line** has inconveniently-timed service that drops off once per day in Barmah, 10km away. Kind-hearted locals headed toward the park have been known to lend the occasional ride, though *Let's Go* does not recommend hitchhiking. Ask at the youth hostel about ride-sharing or check hostel postings.

MURRAY VALLEY HIGHWAY: FROM ECHUCA TO SWAN HILL

The Murray Valley Hwy. runs along the Murray River becoming the Sturt Hwy.

KERANG. This place is for the birds. Literally. The tiny township of **Kerang,** between Echuca and Swan Hill, has a ratio of about 1000 birds to every human. The entire area comprises one of Australia's most important wetland reserves for avian life. A few kilometers north on the Murray Valley Hwy., **Middle Lake** is a rookery for huge flocks of ibis and has a viewing shelter. The **Gunbower Creek,** a few kilometers east of Kerang off of the Murray Valley Hwy., is another popular area for bird-watching and swamp-rambling. For Kerang info, call **Golden Rivers Tourism,** in Barham (☎1800 621 882; www.goldenriv ers.com.au), or stop in at the **Old Water Tower,** right on the Murray Valley Hwy. on the edge of town. The four-story tower, which costs $1 to climb, houses a **visitor information center** on the ground level. In Kerang, across from the visitors center and set back from the road, the **Kerang Caravan Park** lies along the Loddon River, on Museum Dr. (☎5452 1161. Sites $7.50 per person; on-site caravans $35; standard cabins $40, with bath $50-60.)

SWAN HILL ☎03

Swan Hill, located on the Murray River about 340km northwest of Melbourne, is a tranquil rural town, ideal for families, caravaners, and anybody else who values peace over pace. Swan Hill's style of activities matches its tenor of life; the area is thick with nurseries, craft shops, tea rooms, wineries, and other serene pastimes. This part of the Murray has great fishing, and its relaxing cruises on rented house-boats are especially popular among seniors.

TRANSPORTATION. **V/Line** trains leave daily for Melbourne (4½hr., $47.90) from the station on Curlewis St., between McCrae and Rutherford St., near the Giant Murray Cod. **Bus** service is available to: Adelaide (6hr., 1 per day, $45.30); Albury (5½-7hr., 1-2 per day, $38.20-45.40); Echuca (1½hr. 1-2 per day, $19.80); Kerang (40 min., 2-3 per day, $6.70); Mildura (2½hr., 2-3 per day, $32.30); Sydney (14hr., 1 per day, $75-124).

PRACTICAL INFORMATION. Swan Hill's civic activity centers on the manicured strip of Campbell St. (Murray Valley Hwy.) between Rutherford and McCallum St. The **Swan Hill Development and Information Centre,** 306 Campbell St., on the corner of Rutherford St., is one block west of the river. (☎5032 3033 or 1800 625 373; www.swanhillonline.com. Open daily 9am-5pm.) Heaps of banks with 24hr. **ATMs** are on Campbell St., especially near McCallum St. (All banks open M-Th 9:30am-4pm, F 9:30am-5pm.) The **library,** 53-67 Campbell St., offers **free Internet access** for research and email at $1 per hr. (☎5032 2404. Book ahead. Open Tu, Th-F 10am-5:30pm; W 10am-5:30pm and 7-8:30pm; Sa 10am-noon.) There's a **post office** on 164 Campbell St. (Open M-F 9am-5pm.) **Postal code:** 3585.

ACCOMMODATIONS, FOOD, AND NIGHTLIFE. Budget accommodations are few, as most of Campbell St.'s numerous motels run $40-110 per night. If you're driving, the Commercial Hotel 14km south at Lake Boga may be your best option. The pub accommodation includes continental breakfast, kitchen, laundry, and electric blankets. (On Marraboor St., off Station St. from the highway. ☎5037 2140. Singles $15, doubles $20, family $25. MC/V.) Otherwise, the **Pioneer Settlement,** on Horseshoe Bend, reserves one of its three lodges for backpackers when they're not booked with school groups. There is a kitchen and TV lounge, but only two bedrooms have doors. (☎5032 2410. Linens $5.50. Book ahead. 4- to 6-bed dorms $16.50 first night, each extra night $11; $70 weekly. AmEx/DC/MC/V.) The **Riverside Caravan Park,** 1 Monash Dr., on the river adjacent to the Pioneer Settlement has a pool and spa, BBQ, kitchen, and small grocer. (☎5032 1494. Linens $7. Sites for 2 $15.50-16.50, powered $18-20; on-site caravans $42-50; cabins $56-112. MC/V.) **Cafe Allure,** 147 Campbell St., serves up an eclectic mix of gourmet breakfasts, smoothies, and rich, large foccacias for under $13. Don't be suspicious of the questionably named "Salmonetta" pizzetta. (☎5032 4422. Open M 8am-4pm, Tu-F 8am-5pm, Sa-Su 9:30am-3pm.) For dinner, both the service and the Italian fare at **Quo Vadis,** 255-259 Campbell St., are superb. (☎5032 4408. Open daily 6pm-late.)

SIGHTS. The **Horseshoe Bend Pioneer Settlement,** on Horseshoe Bend, is the oldest outdoor museum in Australia. Heading south on Campbell St., turn left on Gray St. and head across the railroad tracks to the settlement. A full century (1830-1930) of the history of frontier agricultural settlement is represented by original buildings and olde-tyme equipment. Dressed in old-fashioned clothing, the employees perform uproarious slapstick street theater; paddlesteamers cruise the river along the banks of the settlement, and nighttime brings the **Mallee Heritage Sound and Light Show,** a family-friendly, if slightly hokey, cart-ride through history under the southern stars. (☎5036 2410. Open daily 9am-5pm; admission $16, children $9, family $41. Mallee Show: $10, children $6, family $26. Cruise on the paddlesteamer Pyap: $12, children $7, family $31. Joint passes available.) Smaller than the Pioneer Settlement, but almost as engaging, is the **Swan Hill Art Gallery,** housed in a modern mud-brick structure next door. Three rotating galleries showcase local work. There's also a permanent collection of contemporary Australian art, concerts, films, and lectures. (☎5032 9744. Open Tu-F 10am-5pm, Sa-Su 11am-5pm. $3, concessions $2, family $5.)

Swan Hill is also proud of its excellent **fishing.** That pride has resulted in the **Giant Murray Cod.** Towering over its living brethren, it is quite possibly the largest Murray Cod in the world. The statue measures 6m by 11m by 6m, and was originally built as a prop for the movie *Eight Ball.* It now guards the north end of the rail station on Curlewis St. The best fishing holes (mainly cod and carp) are 20min. away; ask for updates at the **Natural Resources and Environment** office, 324 Campbell St. (☎5033 1290. Open M-F 9am-5pm.) The NRE also has information on the town's **required fishing license** ($5 for 3 days, $10 per month, $25 per year).

Swan Hill also has its share of outlying vineyards. **R.L. Buller and Son** is 14km north on the Murray Valley Hwy. (☎5037 6305. Open M-Sa 9am-5pm, during school holidays and long weekends Su 10am-5pm.) **Best's St. Andrews** is to the south near Lake Boga. (☎5037 2154. Open M-Sa 10am-5pm.) Both offer tastings.

MILDURA ☎03

With its wide, palm-lined streets and bustling riverside wharf, Mildura is an oasis in dry Mallee country. The area, in the extreme northwest corner of Victoria, was settled in 1887 by the Chaffey brothers, Canadians who had established irrigation communities in California and repeated their success here. The cleverly harnessed waters of the Murray support thriving citrus groves and make Mildura one of Australia's most productive fruit-growing areas; as such, it attracts hordes of backpackers seeking itinerant work (the best time of year is Feb.-Mar., but every month except May is good). It's also one of the sunniest parts of Australia, and were it not for the massive irrigation system, the landscape would be as arid as the outback that stretches to the horizon. Enjoy it while you're here; Mildura is the last bastion of green for a long, long time.

TRANSPORTATION. The train and bus station is on 7th St., across from the northern end of Langtree Ave. **V/Line** runs to: Albury (10hr., 1 per day Tu, W, F, Su; $61); Echuca (5hr.; 1 per day Tu, W, F, Su; $43.80); Melbourne (7-9hr., 2-3 per day, $59.20), via Bendigo (5-7hr., $51.80) and Swan Hill (3-4hr., $32.30). **Countrylink** runs daily service to Sydney (15hr., 4am, $110). **Tom Evans** coaches (☎5022 1415) services Broken Hill (3½hr.; M, W, F 9am; $49).

ORIENTATION AND PRACTICAL INFORMATION. A well-planned city, Mildura is laid out in a grid on the southern bank of the Murray. In the city center, 7th-10th St. run approximately east-west from the river south; these numeric roads cross the north-south avenues, from the westernmost Olive Ave. through Pine, Lime, Langtree, Deakin, and Madden Ave. The commercial center is the strip of Langtree Ave. from 7th to 10th St., including a **pedestrian mall** from 8th to 9th with speakers blaring an endless array of elevator jazz. The **Mildura Visitor Information and Booking Centre,** 180-190 Deakin Ave. on the corner of 12th St., is housed in the brilliant Alfred Deakin Centre; look for the silver tornado sculpture out front. (☎5021 4424; www.milduratourism.com. Open M-F 9am-5:30pm, Sa-Su 9am-5pm.) Inside, the **library** has **free Internet** access. (☎5023 5011; book ahead.) Those seeking **work** should ask for the thorough and free *Working Holiday and Backpacker Information Sheet* from the info center, or check with the **Mildura Harvest Labour Office** on Deakin Ave. near 10th St. (☎5021 1432. Open M-F 9am-5pm.) Squatter's work can often be found in the *Sunraysia Daily's* employment section. Banks and 24hr. **ATMs** are everywhere. All the major **car rental** companies are located in the airport, 8km out of town on the Sturt Hwy., with rentals from $55-70 per day. The **police station** is on Madden Ave. between 8th and 9th St. (☎5023 9555). A **post office** is on the corner of 8th and Orange Ave., and in the Langtree Ave. Mall (open M-F 9am-5pm). **Postal code:** 3500.

ACCOMMODATIONS. Most of Mildura's budget stays are backpackers designed with the migrant worker in mind. Basic rooms, work placement, and transport to work run about $18 per night ($100-110 per week). The gem of the lot is **Riverboat Bungalow** on Chaffey Ave. near 7th St. A 5min. walk from the train station, this laid-back hostel is complete with a large aquarium and tropical decor throughout, bedrooms named after paddlesteamers, and clean bathrooms. Friendly guests bond through evenings by the backyard campfire and weekend canoe trips on the Murray. (☎5021 5315; www.users.mildura.net.au/bungalow. Linen and cutlery included. Internet $5 per hr. $18 per person, $110 weekly. VIP.) Other centrally located options are the **Zippy Koala,** 206B 8th St. (☎5021 5793) near Cherry Ave. and the **NOMADS Mildura International Backpackers,** 5 Cedar Ave. (☎/fax 5021 0133) off 11th St. If the workers' hostels don't appeal to you, **Hotel Mildura,** at the corner of 8th and Madden Ave., has old-but-clean rooms, a kitchen and TV lounge, and bar and bistro downstairs. (☎5023 0365. Singles $33, with bath $42; doubles and twins $45/$55. V.)

FOOD AND NIGHTLIFE. Mildura's restaurants offer surprising variety. The **Langtree Avenue Mall,** one block west of Deakin Ave. between 8th and 9th St., has a few super-cheap takeaways, while the strip of Langtree between 7th and 8th St. is a veritable international bazaar. **White Monkey,** 26 Langtree Ave., has an extensive pizza list ($10-15) and runs constant promotions, such as "Curry in a Hurry" and the "Beer o'clock" Happy Hour. (☎5022 2900. Open Tu-Sa 6pm-late.) Down the road, **Siam Palace,** 35 Langtree Ave., serves up Chinese and Thai dishes. The steal is the $5 lunch and dinner special, which offers a choice of dishes with steamed rice. (☎5023 7737. Open Su-Th 5:30-10pm, F-Sa noon-2pm and 5:30-late.) A 24hr. Coles **supermarket** is at the corner of 8th St. and Lime Ave. A few nightclubs are at 8th St. and Langtree Ave. The **Sandbar** warms the chilliest of winter nights with its tropical motif. (☎5021 2181. Daily Happy Hour 5-8pm; W-Sa live cover bands 10:30pm. Open Tu noon-midnight, W-Sa noon-3am. F-Sa cover $5 after 1am.)

SIGHTS. Mildura is the base camp for nearby national parks and the outback. The visitors center has info on and books for all the commercial tours. For nearly 30 years Tom Evans has been running tours in the Mildura area, bringing his encyclopedic knowledge on his **Junction Tours** (☎5027 4309) to Mungo National Park (see p. 234; W, F, Su $66); local hotspots (Tu, Th, Sa; $50-68); or Broken Hill (Su-Tu, 3 days and 2 nights of camping for $462). **Mallee Outback Experiences** operates daytrips to Mungo and various local wineries. (☎5024 6007. Mungo W, Sa 8:30am; $55, concessions $53, families $132. Wineries Tu 10:30am. Winery and river cruise Th 9:30am; $49.50, children $33.) **Harry Nanya Tours** runs half- and full-day trips focusing on Aboriginal history and the Dreaming. (☎5027 2076 or 1800 630 864; www.harrynanyatours.com.au. Mungo: $60, concessions $52, family $132. Wentworth: 2 per day; half-day $27.50/22/$66; full-day $55/$52/$132. Canoe tours: 1½hr. $55, 2 nights with camping $185.) A new company, **Jumbunna,** runs trips to Mungo as well as a Mildura nature walk. These tours are guided by an Aboriginal guide and focus on tribal culture and the outback. (☎0412 581 699. Day tour $60, concessions $56, child $29, family $156. Mildura 3hr. nature walk $25/$20/$15/$50.)

The 1881 paddlewheeler **Rothbury** cruises to Trentham Estate winery. (☎5023 2200. 5hr., Th 10:30am, $42, children 5-14 $20. Evening cruise with dinner and live entertainment, 3hr.; Th 7pm, $40, $18; book ahead.) Of the seven local wineries in the immediate area, the most internationally famous is **Lindemans** (☎5051 3285). The easiest way to get there is the Mallee Outback Experiences' river cruise tour (see p. 579; $49.50. Winery open daily 10am-4:30pm).

Mildura Arts Centre, 199 Cureton Ave. just north of 7th St., has a decent permanent art collection as well as rotating Australian avant-garde exhibits. The adjoining museum, **Rio Vista,** was home to W.B. Chaffey, one of Mildura's founders, and is one of Victoria's few examples of Queen Anne's architecture. (☎5023 3733. Open daily 10am-5pm. Gallery and museum $3, concessions $2.) The center also houses a theater complex, which hosts about a dozen imported dance, drama, and music shows per year; prices vary depending on the performance.

Twelve kilometers southeast of town off 11th St., the **Psyche Bend Pump Station** houses the restored steam pumps that kept Mildura alive and irrigated in the early days. Unfortunately it only pumps five days a year, but volunteers from the Steam Preservation Society are on-site the rest of the time to provide commentary. The station is secluded in **King's Billabong,** a bird-filled wetland reserve. (☎5023 2350. Open Tu, Th 1-4pm; Su 11am-1pm. $2, family $5. New Years' Day, Easter Sunday, Queen's birthday, and July and Sept. school holidays; $3, families $8.)

HUME CORRIDOR

The Hume Hwy. links Melbourne and Sydney, shuttling visitors 872km through relatively unspectacular scenery. However, intrepid travelers who venture an hour or two off the Hume will be rewarded with world-class wineries, dusty hamlets, and quietly inviting country towns. Don't blink or you'll miss Glenrowan and Ned Kelly's Last Stand. Stray a bit from the highway, and you can snowboard or ski on Mr. Buller's excellent powdery slopes, or check out the wineries of the Rutherglen Valley. Sun worshipers can laze away by heading west along the Murray Valley Hwy. to fish, swim, or snooze on the Murray's banks in Yarrawonga and Cobram. Across the Murray River, the Hume continues north into New South Wales.

MARYSVILLE AND LAKE MOUNTAIN ☎03

A small town only one and a half hours northeast of Melbourne, Marysville is best known as the closest town (22km) to cross-country ski mecca Lake Mountain.

The Mystic Mountains Tourist Information Centre, on Murchison's main drag Murchison St., posts Lake Mountain snow reports and road conditions, arranges accommodations, and has a list of places to stay. (☎5963 4567; www.mmtourism.com.au. Open daily 9am-5pm.) For local **snow and road conditions,** call 5963 3205 or check www.snowreport.vic.gov.au.

While the area's best lodging lies 21km up the road at Taggerty's Australian Bust Settlement (see below), the **Marysville Caravan Park,** on Buxton Rd., is by the Steavenson River at the end of Murchison St. (☎5963 3443; www.marysvillecaravanpark.com.au. Sites for 2 from $17.50, powered from $21.50; caravans $42; cabins $66; cheaper off-season. MC/V.) The best eats in town are at **Marysville Country Bakery,** on the corner of Murchison St. and Pack Rd., with delectable sandwiches ($3-4.50) and 20 types of pies and pasties for $3-4. (☎5963 3477. Open daily 7am-6pm.)

The 31km of regularly groomed cross-country **ski trails** at Lake Mountain are packed in season (entry fee $20; trail fee $10, children $5). Take the Maroondah Hwy. (Hwy. 34) to Woods Point Rd. (Hwy. 172). Chains are required for the drive up Lake Mountain during winter. Back in Marysville, local shops rent skis, skates, toboggans, chains, and outerwear; just about everything is under $30. Also near Marysville out in the bush, **Steavenson Falls,** 4km down Falls Rd., are spectacular when illuminated at night. There's a 30min. ascent to the top of a nearby peak with a view of the falls, and a 40min. trail downhill through the town.

The real highlight of the town itself is **Bruno's Art and Sculpture Garden,** 51 Falls Rd. Inside Bruno's home is an extensive collection of paintings and collages; outside is a lush garden donned with the creative vitality of Bruno's sculptures. Often whimsical, the subtle creations are powerfully expressive and show great imagination. (☎5963 3513. Garden open daily 10am-5pm. Gallery open Sa-Su 10am-5pm. Gallery and garden $5, ages 12-16 $2; garden alone $3.)

NEAR MARYSVILLE: TAGGERTY

Taggerty is 104km northeast of Melbourne on the Maroondah Hwy. (Hwy. 34), 4km after Buxton. If you ask, the V/Line **bus** from **Melbourne** to **Eildon** will also stop at Taggerty at the 104km marker of the Maroondah Hwy. (daily 3pm, $14). The **Taggerty Australian Bush Settlement** (☎5774 7378; www.green.net.au/australian_bush_settlement), provides a splendorous stay for a one-night guest or a several-month visitor. This 80-acre farm, located near the Cathedral Range National Park, simulates an early pioneer village. The host, Bronwyn Rayner, is the embodiment of selfless sacrifice. She has operated Taggerty for more than 20 years and built it into a combination B&B, hostel, campsite, working farm, classroom, museum, and youth development facility. Rayner cultivates an organic vegetable garden and cares for a variety of unwanted, misfit, or orphaned animals ranging from sheep and horses to wombats and kangaroos. Guests and visitors can interact with the endearing animals, and the working farm and bush settlement serve as a backdrop for educational programs run for both standard classrooms as well as at-risk kids. Taggerty also houses an extensive collection of 19th-century bush memorabilia, including costumes, carriages, and an 1853 Norwegian slab hut. Her latest inspiration is environment-friendly housing, and she hopes to devote a portion of the Settlement property to developing environmentally sustainable buildings and farming.

Lodging comes in four degrees of comfort and privacy: sites ($10 per person); small, rustic cabins ($20); the hostel-like lodge ($20); and the homestead. The cream of the crop, the homestead is richly decorated and recipient of *Home Beautiful*'s 1990 Home of the Year and Design of the Year. A private double room with king-size bed and classic free-standing bath is luxurious ($70); in the next room, the "opium bed" by the fireplace is less private but an interesting experience ($25). All lodgings come with excellent kitchen and toilet facilities in-room or nearby, and all prices include continental breakfast.

For reasonable prices, guests can take advantage of a **board plan.** The Th-Su tour is a fantastic bargain and an unforgettable experience. It includes round trip bus fare from Melbourne, three nights in the Homestead, seven home-cooked meals, a winery tour, Bruno's Sculpture Garden in Marysville, a hike on Cathedral mountain, exploration of the farm and Bronwyn's animal nurture center, and all transportation ($220). If in Victoria, this opportunity is not to be missed.

MANSFIELD ☎03

Mansfield's *raison d'être* is its proximity to Mt. Buller, allowing tourists to stop and rent skis and chains before making the 45km ascent to Victoria's most popular ski resort. The **Mansfield Passenger Terminal** is located at 137 High St. **V/Line buses** (☎13 61 96) serve Melbourne (3hr., 1-3 per day, $30) and Mt. Buller (1hr., 2-3 per day, $34 return) during ski season. Law requires all vehicles heading to Mt. Buller to carry **snow chains** from the Queen's Birthday weekend (usually the second week of June) until the end of the ski season. You can leave them in the trunk, but there are spot checks and hefty fines ($170) for not carrying them at all.

The **Mansfield Visitors Centre** is just out of town at 167 Maroonah Hwy. (☎5775 1464; bookings ☎1800 039 049; fax 5775 2518; reservations@mansfield-mtbuller.com.au. Open daily 9am-5pm.) Heading east into town on **High St.,** the town's main drag, you'll find ski rental places and a few **ATMs.** There is **Internet access** at the **library,** corner of High and Collopy St. (☎5775 2176. Open Tu 2pm-8pm, W 9:30am-1pm, Th-F 9:30am-5:30pm, Sa 9:30am-noon. $2 per 30min.) The **post office** is at 90 High St. (Open M-F 9am-5pm.) **Postal code:** 3722.

Ski Centre Mansfield, 131 High St. (☎5775 2859), and its nearby affiliate, **PJ's Ski Hire,** 149 High St. (☎5775 1624), rent chains (full-day $15) and a wide range of ski equipment and clothing. (Open in season Sa-Th 6am-7pm, F 6am-midnight.) Similar ski hire joints illuminate High St. with attention-grabbing lights. Shopping around is easy, but they all offer comparable deals (full-day skis, boots, poles $25-30; snowboard and boots $45-50).

The best budget beds in town are at the **Mansfield Backpackers Inn,** 116 High St., part of the Mansfield Travellers Lodge. The friendly new owners keep the place very clean and comfortable. They provide a kitchen, lockers, TV, and a pool table. (☎5775 1800; travlodge@cnl.com.au. Reception 24hr. Dorms $17-20; motel room singles $54-60; doubles $66-85; family $115-135. Book 1-2 weeks ahead.) The **Commercial Hotel,** one of the pubs near the intersection of High and Highett St., offers simple lodging. (☎5775 2046. Singles $30; doubles $50.) The **Mansfield Bus Stop Cafe,** 141 High St., is a good quick-eats place with reasonable prices and a twist of culinary class. The Caribbean Banana pancakes ($8) are outrageously good. (☎5775 1277. Hours vary. Open daily 6:30am-7pm during peak ski season.) The **Mansfield Hotel,** on the corner of High and Highett St., creates excellent, gourmet, wood-fired pizzas for $12.50. (☎5775 2101. Open daily 11am-1am.) For more upscale dining and sophisticated ambience, **Mingo's Bistro,** 101 High St., has pasta dishes from $10. (☎5775 1766. Open daily 6pm-late.) For quality fresh produce (some organic), stop by the **Mansfield Fruit Palace,** 68 High St. (☎5775 2239. Open M-F 8:30am-6pm, Sa 8am-2pm.) You can also stock up on food at the **supermarket.** Check out Foodworks, 12 Highett St. (☎5775 2255), or IGA, 47 High St. (☎5775 2014). Both are open daily 8am-8pm.

MOUNT BULLER ☎03

Victoria's largest ski resort, Mt. Buller is a 3hr. drive from Melbourne. Buller's terrain is arguably the best in Victoria, and though it's not the Alps or Rockies, from mid-June through early October, it's a mecca for Aussie skiers and snowboarders.

TRANSPORTATION. Along with **V/Line** (see Mansfield entry), **Mansfield-Mt Buller Bus Lines** (☎5775 2606) operates coach service to Mt. Buller from Mansfield (1hr., 6-8 per day, $34). **Snowcaper Tours** departs from Melbourne and offers tour packages that include return transport, entrance fees, and a full-day lift ticket. Participants leave Melbourne at 4am and return by 9:30pm. (☎5775 2367, reservations ☎1800 033 023. Mid-week $110, weekend $120.) All buses pull into the **Cow Camp Plaza,** in the center of Mt. Buller village.

If going by car, bring **snow chains** (it's the law) and take Hwy. 164 (Buller Rd.) east to Mt. Buller. (Car admission $20 per day; overnight fee Su-Th $3.30 per night, F-Sa $6.60 per night.) Free parking is on the side of the mountain. To get to the village from the parking lot, visitors without luggage can take a free shuttle. Visitors with luggage must take a taxi ($10). Beware: all these daily charges add up fast. Consider taking the bus, especially if you're staying on the mountain for a while.

PRACTICAL INFORMATION. The village is the hub of accommodation, food, and ski services. The Cow Camp Plaza houses lockers, restaurants, and **Cow Camp Alpine Ski Rentals.** (☎5777 6082. Skis, boots, and poles $28; snowboard and boots $40-45.) The **Information Centre,** in a tower opposite the plaza, has maps of the resort and slopes, as well as info on work and long-term accommodations options. (☎5777 7600; reservations ☎1800 039 049; www.mtbuller.com.au. Open daily during ski season 8:30am-5pm. In summer, visit the post office.) The **lift ticket office** sits across the village center from the info tower. (Day pass $60, weekend $70.) For the latest **snow conditions,** call the Official Victorian Snow Report (☎1902 240 523. 24hr. $0.55 per minute), visit www.vicsnowreport.com.au, tune into 93.7FM, or check the local ski shop. La Trobe University, New Summit Rd., has **Internet access.** (☎5733 7080. Reception Office, Level 5. $4 per 30min.) There is a **post office** at the foot of Summit Rd. in the Resort Management Building. (☎5777 6077. Open daily 8:30am-5pm.) **Postal code:** 3723.

ACCOMMODATIONS AND NIGHTLIFE. The **Mt. Buller YHA Hostel Lodge** is the least expensive lodging on the mountain, and you can literally ski to the front door. The lodge has well-heated dorms. Book at least three weeks ahead in July and August. (☎5777 6181; yha@yhavic.org.au. Ski lockers available. Reception daily 8-10am and 5-10pm. Dorms $50, non-YHA $54. 20% midweek discount in June and Sept.) Next door to the YHA, the **Kooroora Hotel** has more intimate, four-person dorms with showers. Guests get breakfast in the fully licensed pub, which also hosts late-night entertainment. There is a 15% guest discount for on-site ski hire. (☎5777 6050; fax 5777 6202. Open only during ski season. Reservations require a 50% deposit. Dorms M-Th $70, F-Su $80. 18+ only.)

ABOM (☎5777 6091), on Summit St., couldn't be further from its full name—Abominable. Despite the menacing Polar Bear lurking next to the doorway, this European-style ski resort is the perfect refuge from the cold, and the bistro fare is affordable. (Pizza slice $4, toasted sandwich $3.50.) The **Cow Camp Plaza** houses two upstairs eateries. The **Pancake Parlour** (☎5777 6503) serves up both typical short stacks ($6) and crazy varieties like Hot Bavarian Apple and Jamaican Banana ($10). The brand new **Moguls Loft Bar and Bistro** is more upmarket, offering pastas ($10-18.50) and meal-size salads for $17.50. (☎5777 6596. Open 4-11pm.)

Kooroora's Pub is hands-down the place to go for nightlife. Bands (W, F, Sa) and DJs (M, Tu, Th, Su) rage into the wee hours of the morning. **Mooseheads Bar,** downstairs at the ABOM, caters to a more laid-back, couch-lounging crowd. With the cheapest spirits on the mountain ($4.50), the Happy Hour from 4-6pm might just be the happiest time to visit. (Open 3pm-1am.)

SKIING. Intermediate runs predominate, though several expert trails are sprinkled on the southern slopes. On the south face, **Fanny's Finish** and **Chute 1, 2, and 3** separate the skiers from the snowbunnies. First-time skiers have plenty of long runs to choose from, as well as numerous lesson packages. The lift capacity is excellent and lift lines are usually not long. Those ready for an aerobic challenge will find 75km of cross-country skiing trails (30km groomed) and an entire mountain, **Mt. Stirling,** set aside for their use. (☎5777 3541; www.mtstirling.com.au. Open during daylight hours. No overnight accommodations on the mountain. Car entry $20; trail $9; cross country ski hire $27; telemark $37.)

MOUNTAIN BIKING AND HIKING. In the summer, mountain biking is the thing to do at Buller, with a plethora of tracks and lift access to the top. Lifts operate daily from December 26 to the end of January, then on long weekends until Easter. **Raw NRG** (☎5777 6887; www.rawnrg.com.au), will set you up with information and equipment. (Front suspension bike 1hr. $18; up to 4hr. $40; over 4hr. $60. Dual suspension bike 1hr. $25; up to 4hr. $55; over 4hr. $75.) Downhill initiation tours, including dual suspension bike, lift ticket, full monty body armor, and insurance cost $155; $65 with your own bike. Once initiation is completed, "expression sessions" using the lift cost $45 per day. Cheaper biking without the chairlift is possible, as are free hikes. The **Summit Walk** (1½hr. return, moderate difficulty), beginning and ending at the clock tower, rewards hikers with views of the High Country below. A longer hike, popular with mountain bikes, to **Mt. Stirling via Corn Hill and Howqua Gap** (5-7hr. return, moderate difficulty) offers a grand perspective of Mt. Buller. The Information Centre has maps and details.

GLENROWAN ☎03

A small stop heading north up the Hume Hwy. (Hwy. 31) between Benalla and Wangaratta, Glenrowan owes its fame entirely to the notorious bushranger Ned Kelly and the authorities who finally corralled him here. Upon entering the town, visitors are greeted by the 6m-tall Kelly statue, clad in an iron mask like the one he wore on that fateful day. The primary attraction is the $2.5 million animatronic tourist extravaganza, **Ned Kelly's Last Stand,** located at the **Glenrowan Tourist Centre,** a corny, cultish narrative presentation—entertaining to kids and at least appreciated by adults—in which Ned's outlaw exploits are presented in a self-described "40 minutes of rip-snorting action." (☎5766 2367. Every 30min. 9:30am-4:30pm. $16, concession $14, ages 5-15 $10.) Next door, the **Ned Kelly Memorial Museum and Homestead** offers a small gold prospector style shack as a re-creation of Kelly's headquarters. (☎5766 2448. $2.75, children 60¢.)

WANGARATTA ☎02

Referred to endearingly as "Wang" by locals, Wangaratta (pop. 25,000) is a quiet, river-strewn neighborhood seated conveniently at the junction of the Hume Hwy. and the Great Alpine Road. Although the town has few tourist attractions, it can be a sound base for exploring Victoria's alpine country and the nearby vineyards.

TRANSPORTATION AND PRACTICAL INFORMATION. **V/Line** (☎13 61 96) runs from the station on Norton St. to: Melbourne (2½hr., 4-6 per day, $32.30); Albury-Wodonga (50min., 4-6 per day, $10.80); Bright (1½hr., 1 per day, $10.80); Rutherglen (30min.; W, F, Su evenings and daily 3:45pm during school holidays; $4.70). **Countrylink** runs to Sydney (8hr., 2 per day, $90.40).

The Hume Hwy. from Melbourne runs into town as Tone Rd., which becomes Ryley St. then **Murphy St.** for the stretch through the city center. Murphy intersects Ford, Ely, Reid, and Faithfull St. as it runs northeast. **Ovens St.** runs parallel to and northwest of Murphy St. The **Visitors Centre** is on Tone Rd. 1km southwest of the city center. (☎5721 5711. Open daily 9am-5pm). The **library,** 62 Ovens St. (☎5721 2366) has free Internet use; email is $2 per 30min. Book ahead. The **post office** is at the intersection of Murphy and Ely St. (Open M-F 9am-5pm.) **Postal Code:** 3677.

ACCOMMODATIONS AND FOOD. The **Billabong Motel,** 12 Chisholm St., at the end of Reid a block east from Murphy St., has basic heated rooms with linens and TV. (☎5721 2353. Singles $30, with bath $35; doubles $40-45/$45-55). **Wangaratta Backpackers** is 5km north of town on the Old Hume Hwy. but has bike hire and free daily pick-up and drop-off in town (☎5721 2624. Dorms $18, linens included). Across the Ovens River on Pinkerton, just north of Faithfull St., is **Painters Island Caravan Park.** (☎5721 3380. Reception 8am-8pm. Sites $6.60 per person, powered for 2 $15.40; on-site caravans $27.50; cabins $38.50, with bath $55.)

Scribbler's Cafe, 66 Reid St., has cheap deluxe sandwiches ($6.50-8.50) as well as cuisine from across the globe. (☎5721 3945. Open daily 8am-5:45pm. Kitchen closes around 5pm. BYO. AmEx/MC/V.) **Vespa's Cafe,** at Reid and Ovens St., has a bar specializing in local wine and a delightfully eclectic menu; live music every weekend and themed event nights once a month. (☎5722 4392. Open Su-Th 10am-11pm, F-Sa 10am-1am, Su 10am-5pm. MC/V.) Safeway **supermarket** is on Ovens St. between Reid and Ford St. (open daily 7am-midnight), and Coles 24hr. supermarket is on Tone Rd. just south of the city center.

SIGHTS AND WINERIES. The best day trip is 15km southeast via Oxley Flats Rd. at the **Milawa Gourmet Region.** The classy **Brown Brothers Vineyard,** on Snow Rd., could sate a small island nation with its five tasting bars. Every course at its Epicurean Centre restaurant includes its own accompanying wine. (☎5720 5500. Open daily 9am-5pm; restaurant open daily 11am-3pm.) Around the corner on Factory Rd., the lactose-loving **Milawa Cheese Company** has free samples of gourmet cheeses handmade from the milk of local goats, ewes, and cows. (☎5727 3589. Open daily 9am-5pm.) **Milawa Mustards,** at the Old Emu Inn on Snow Rd., concocts an awe-inspiring set of the condiment. (☎5727 3202. Open daily 10am-5pm. Free tastings.) Varieties range from the sweet (honey, ginger, orange) to the hot (chilli, super fine hot) to the alcoholic (bourbon).

Back in Wang, **Kaluna Park** offers ample space for picnic and play just east of Murphy St. A local **bike trail** runs along the One-Mile Creek, but for a longer excursion try the newly-completed "Murray to the Mountains Rail Trail." The 94km paved trail follows historical railway lines and passes through Bowser, Beechworth, and Myrtleford all the way to Bright. (☎03 5751 1238; www.rail-trail.com.au.) Wangaratta's renowned **jazz festival** (☎5722 1666 or 1800 803 944; www.wangaratta-jazz.org.au), the first weekend of November, ranks among Australia's best. Accommodations can be booked out as early as June.

RUTHERGLEN ☎02

At the heart of Victoria's most renowned wine region, Rutherglen is an excellent base for touring the surrounding wineries. The Murray Valley Hwy. (Hwy. 16), called Main St. in Rutherglen, runs from Yarrawonga (45km west) through Rutherglen to Albury (50km east). **V/Line** buses leave Rutherglen's BP service station for Melbourne via Wangaratta (3½hr.; M, W, F 6:35am; $36). Purchase tickets from the newsagency. **Webster** Bus Service shuttles to Albury at 9:30am on weekdays from the BP station west of the city center (☎6033 2459; $7). The **tourist office,** in the Jolimont Cellar building on the corner of Drummond and Main St., is the place to go for a potentially dangerous combination of winery literature and bicycle hire. (☎6032 9166 or 1800 622 871. Open daily 9am-5pm. One-day rental including helmet, pump, and bottled water $22.)

The **Victoria Hotel,** 90 Main St., offers cozy budget rooms with heaters, electric blankets, linens, towels, and breakfast. (☎6032 8610. Singles and twins $27.50 per person; doubles $55, with bath $66. Su-Th stay 2 nights get the third night free. MC/V.) **Rutherglen Caravan Park,** 72 Murray St., has tentspace as well as luxurious cabins by the lake. (☎6032 8577; rutherglencvanpark@iprimus.com.au. Sites for 2 $12, powered $15; fully-furnished cabins $40-70. Wheelchair accessible. MC/V.)

For a real treat, eat at the **Rutherglen Tea Rooms,** 86-88 Main St. Their chicken, cheese, ham, and mustard pie was voted best chicken pie in Australia in 2000; the ultra-friendly staff deserves national recognition as well. (☎6032 9605. Pie $4.20, with large plate of pasta, chips, and potato salad $8.) For less extravagance, the IGA supermarket, 95 Main St., sells **groceries.** (☎6032 9232. Open M-W 7:30am-7pm Th-F 7:30am-7:30pm, Sa 7:30am-5pm, Su 8:30am-5pm.)

NEAR RUTHERGLEN

WINERIES

Rutherglen's temperate climate allows vineyards to keep grapes on their vines longer, favoring full-bodied red wines and fortified varieties like Tokay and Muscat. Choosing from among the excellent local wineries can be quite difficult, especially since they all offer free tastings. For those traveling by car, the *Rutherglen Touring Guide*, available at the visitors center and most wineries, is an indispensable free map. Or grab a free *Muscat Trail Map* for help navigating by bike. For a campier tour, take a horse-drawn stagecoach from **Poachers Paradise Hotel,** 120 Main St. (☎6032 9502. Daily 10am and 1pm; three wineries in 2hr. $15 per person; bookings essential.) **Grapevine Getaways** designs tours based on individual interests and requests. Groups of 20 or more can arrange pick-up from just about anywhere, including Melbourne and Sydney. (☎6032 9224 or 0407 577 241; www.grapevinegetaways.com.au. From $30; bookings essential.) For more information on touring vineyards see p. 434.

The Rutherglen vineyards sponsor several festivals throughout the year. The most popular is the carnival-like **Rutherglen Winery Walkabout** (on Queen's Birthday weekend) featuring food and entertainment at the estates and a street fair downtown. True connoisseurs would probably prefer to skip the big production and instead sample the impressive food and wine combinations during the **Tastes of Rutherglen** (March 10-11 and 17-18, 2002).

All Saints Estate (☎6033 1922; www.allsaintswine.com.au). Head northwest of Rutherglen via Corowa Rd., then north on All Saints Rd. If you're only going one place, go here. The most polished, tourist-oriented winery-going experience around. All Saints confirms romantic visions of what wineries should look like, with towering elms lining the driveway, a red-brick castle tasting room, and a sculptured rose garden with central fountain. A marked, self-guided tour leads past immaculate gardens, huge display casks, and a playground; pick up map from the cellar door. A peek into the **Chinese Dormitory and Gardens** on the grounds gives a sense of the early laborers' living conditions. Just behind the castle, the **Rutherglen Keg Factory** manufactures traditional kegs and offers a number of kegs and wine racks for show or purchase. Free delivery of wine purchases to Rutherglen for cyclists. Winery open M-Sa 9am-5:30pm, Su from 10am. Terrace Restaurant open daily 10am-5pm, Sa until 7pm; book ahead on weekends. Keg factory open daily 9am-5pm. AmEx/DC/MC/V.

Cofield Wines (☎6033 3798). Northwest of Rutherglen on Distillery Rd., just off Corowa Rd. Small family-run winery produces signature bubbly; their sparkling shiraz is fantastic. Enormously popular **Pickled Sisters Cafe** is next door. Cellar door open M-Sa 9am-5pm, Su 10am-5pm; cafe open W-M 10am-4pm. AmEx/MC/V.

Chambers Rosewood Winery (☎6032 8641), is an easy-to-miss building on Barkley St., 1km from the tourist office. Unpretentious and easygoing, the winery's simple tasting area gives no hint of the international praise lavished on its rare Tokays and Muscats. Open M-Sa 9am-5pm, Su 11am-5pm.

Gehrig Estate (☎6026 7296). 22km east of town on the Murray Valley Hwy. Claiming to be Victoria's oldest winery, Gehrig produces a wide range including excellent shiraz and durif. Open M-Sa 9am-5pm, Su 10am-5pm.

Fairfield Vineyard (☎6032 9381), head east from Rutherglen on the Murray Valley Hwy. Their idyllic old cellar building is even better than their selection of wines. Open M-F 10am-4pm, Sa 10am-5pm.

COROWA

Just 10km northwest of Rutherglen in NSW, the quiet hamlet of Corowa boasts a big history. Prior to Federation in 1901, the current Australian states were separate colonies without a federal Parliament. As the population expanded and resources such as gold were discovered, interstate customs and tariffs without standard laws grew complicated. Local leagues promoting Federation sprang up across the continent, but the 1893 Corowa Federation Conference marked the beginning of the common people's involvement in the movement. Today, the **Federation Museum** on the corner of Queen and Mary St. outlines the importance of the Corowa Conference to Australian history. (☎6033 1568. Open Sa-Su 2pm-5pm. More information and maps of key sites can be found at the tourist office ☎1800 814 054 on historic Sanger St. Open M-Sa 10am-5pm, Su 10am-3pm.)

Despite Corowa's critical role in the Australian political past, it is perhaps most notable today as a great place for jumping out of planes. **Skydive Corowa,** at the Aerodrome 2km west of town, offers many jumps for novices and a certification course for more serious beginners. Licensed jumpers pay dirt-cheap rates according to altitude. (☎6033 2435 or 1800 446 448. Tandem jump $299; static line full-day training and next-day jump $310; accelerated free fall full-day training and next-day jump $460; licensed jumpers $60, much cheaper if you bring your own chute.)

HIGH COUNTRY

Victoria's High Country, tucked between the Murray River and Gippsland's thick coastal forest, is a contrast to Australian sights like Surfer's Paradise or the Red Centre. Ancient forests display dazzling autumn leaves, and rambling valleys nurture spring flowers in colors that only the rare sunset can capture. In winter, Mt. Hotham and Falls Creek offer the continent's best skiing. In summer, abseilers, climbers, and mountain bikers taunt the steep slopes and cliffs of Mt. Buffalo.

CHAIN ME. All vehicles heading into the mountains must carry tire chains from Queen's Birthday (June 10, 2002) until October 1.

THE OWENS HIGHWAY TO ALPINE ROAD

From Wangaratta, the Owens Hwy. runs southwest, passing, among several small towns, Mt. Buffalo National Park and the Alpine Rd., which leads to Mt. Hotham.

BEECHWORTH ☎03

Off of the Owen's Hwy. to the northeast, is the gold town of Beechworth. Traces of gold were first discovered here on a cold, February day back in 1852. As news of the strike spread, miners soon swarmed to the area. By 1866, over 4.1 million ounces of the metal were found. Though the mining frenzy has subsided, Victoria's best preserved gold town still draws a crowd.

The bus stop is on Camp St., just west of Ford St. **V/Line buses** (☎13 61 96) run to: Bright (1hr., 1-2 per day, $5); Melbourne (3-4hr., 1-4 per day, $38); Wangaratta (35min., 1-6 per day, $6). The **Visitors Information Centre** is located in beautifully preserved Shire Hall on **Ford St.,** Beechworth's main north-south street.

Beechworth overflows with B&Bs. The visitors center can help you select an accommodation based on price, theme, or amenities. The four-room **Hibernian Hotel,** 40 Camp St., on the corner of Loch St., one block west of the town center carries a B&B charm in a hotel-style setting. (☎5728 1070. Reception at bar 10am-11pm. All rooms $50.) The award-winning **Beechworth Bakery,** 27 Camp St., should not be missed by those who prize anything leavened. A loaf of "Orchard" bread ($5.50) is worth every cent. (☎5728 1132. Open daily 6am-7pm.)

Inquire at the information centre about local **bike rentals** and 1½hr. **walking tours** of historic Beechworth. (Tours 10:30, 11:30am, 2, and 6:30pm. Adults $10; families $25.) Behind the information center, on Loch St., the **Burke Museum** displays gold-rush era artifacts, the oldest and most comprehensive known collection of Aboriginal weapons from Southwest Victoria and various stuffed animal and bird specimens, including the now extinct Tasmanian marsupial wolf known as the Thylacine. (☎5728 1420. Open daily 10:00am-4:30pm. $5.50.) At the Beechworth **cemetery,** north of the town center on Cemetery Rd., you'll find the **Chinese Burning Towers** and rows of simple headstones—reminders of the Chinese presence in gold-rush Beechworth. Chinese miners once outnumbered whites five to one, but their tightly packed grave sites testify to the discrimination they faced. Bushranger **Ned Kelly** was first detained in a cell you can visit behind Shire Hall (admission by donation). Proceedings commenced here against Kelly for the killing of constables Lonigan and Scanlon in the infamous Glenrowan siege before moving to Melbourne in search of an impartial jury. Inside the **Beechworth Historic Court House,** 94 Ford St., the courtroom has been preserved in its 19th-century condition, right down to the dock where Kelly stood during his trials. Renovation slated for 2002 will have new, interactive exhibits. (☎5728 2721. Open daily 10am-3:30pm. $2.50.)

MOUNT BUFFALO NATIONAL PARK

The sheer face of Mt. Buffalo rises imposingly alongside the Great Alpine Rd., signaling the site of a rich sub-alpine ecosystem with plenty of outdoor adventure opportunities throughout the year. Though the mountain's craggy walls look intimidating from a distance, the ski slopes that draw people here in winter are gentle. Mt. Buffalo's slopes are primarily for beginner and intermediate skiers, and are heavily family-oriented.

The **park entrance gate** (☎5756 2328) serves as the primary information source on site, though the actual **Parks Victoria Office** is located 20km beyond the entry. (☎5755 1466 or 24hr. 13 19 63; fax 5755 1802. Open daily 8am-4pm, usually staffed weekday early mornings and late afternoons.) Entrance to the national park is just off the Great Alpine Rd. roundabout by Porepunkah, 5km north of Bright (see p. 589). The entrance fee is waived for guests of mountaintop lodging. ($12.50, off-season $9; concessions $6/$4.50.)

The clean, simple lines of the main lounge and bistro at the **Mt. Buffalo Lodge,** 7km along the main road from the visitors center, overlook the slopes (entrees $4-10). Inside, a ski shop serve visitors for both cross-country and downhill skiing. The rates are comparable to those in Bright (downhill package $26, snowboard and boots $50). Guests have access to laundry, a games room, a small bouldering wall, and a TV lounge. Dorms contain basic bunks without linen, a kitchen, and shared facilities. (☎5755 1988 or 1800 037 038. Dorms July-Sept. $35, less in off-season. Twin lodge units $105, breakfast and dinner included.) Great **campsites** lie beside Lake Catani, 2km beyond the park office. Some are caravan-accessible, and there are toilets, water, hot showers, and laundry. (6-person sites $12-23.50, seasonal. Book at entrance station. Open Nov.-Apr.)

Lift passes are available for the **Cresta Valley site** adjacent to the Mt. Buffalo Lodge, and the price is a steal. (Morning $32, afternoon $37, $39 per day. Ages 8-15 $20/$23/$25. Lift ticket and lesson package $39, under 16 $27.) In the park, a 13km network of marked cross-country ski trails lie across the road from the Mt Buffalo Lodge parking lot at Cresta Valley. There's no fee for cross-country skiing; ask for the information sheet at the entrance gate. (On-site rental of cross-country skis and boots are $16 per day.) The drive up the flanks of Mt. Buffalo is dramatic. In the car, you pass through dense eucalypt forests on the winding mountain road, never knowing what surprise is around the next hairpin turn. The occasional views of **waterfalls** plunging over sheer cliffs into deep gorges are thrilling. Within the park are some spectacular lookouts as well as numerous walking tracks. The most challenging hike is **The Big Walk** (11.3km; 4-5hr. one way from Park Entrance to the Gorge Day Visitor Area). The track ascends over 1,000m in only 9km as it climbs the plateau. The **Eurobin Falls** track (1.5km; 45min. return) is a much shorter hike, with a trailhead approximately 2km past the park entrance. Beginning with an amble and ending in a steep clamber, the walk features spectacular views of the falls careening down the bare rock. At the top of the mountain, adjacent to the Mt. Buffalo Chalet, **Bent's Lookout** dazzles with a panoramic sweep across the Buckland Valley. On clear days, **Mt. Kosciuzsko** is visible.

Driving past the park office toward the Mt. Buffalo Lodge, you'll see numerous marked **walking trails.** The steep, but relatively short, **Monolith Track,** across from the Park Office, leads to a precariously balanced, granite monolith and is definitely worth the effort (1.8km; 1hr. circuit). Mt. Buffalo's warm-weather activities are as popular as its winter ones. **Abseilers** go over the edge near Bent's Lookout year-round. **Rock climbing, caving,** and rugged **mountaineering** expeditions, are run through the **Mt. Buffalo Chalet Activities Centre** (☎5755 1500; www.mtbuffalochalet.com.au). The climbing on the north wall of the Gorge is world renowned. Mt. Buffalo is also excellent for hang-gliding and was the site of the World Championships in 1986. Lake Catani is a man-made lake but perfect for swimming, fishing and canoeing, as well as bushwalking.

BRIGHT ☎03

While it's primarily a base for winter skiing at Mt. Hotham, Falls Creek, and Mt. Buffalo, Bright is an apt name for this town of radiant natural beauty and glowing hospitality. Excellent budget accommodations and proximity to snowfields, wineries, and larger cities, make Bright a great base for outdoor extravaganzas.

Bright is 79km southeast of Wangaratta along the **Great Alpine Rd.** The town center lies hidden off the highway behind a roundabout with an Art Deco clock tower. Both **Barnard** and **Anderson** link the main drag, **Ireland St.,** with the Great Alpine Road (renamed **Gavan St.** as it passes through Bright). The **Bright Visitor Centre** is at 119 Gavan St. (☎5755 2275; fax 5750 1655; brightvc@netc.net.au. Open daily 8:30am-5pm.) Public transportation in and out of Bright is quite limited and expensive, so it helps to have a car. However, **V/Line** (13 61 96) services Melbourne (4½hr., 1-2 per day, $43) and Wangaratta (1½hr., 1-2 per day, $10).

Bright's centrally located backpacker accommodation is the **Bright Hikers Backpackers Hostel (VIP),** 4 Ireland St. on the second floor, across from the post office. There are comfy indoor and outdoor common areas, a drying room, a pool table, a video library, laundry, and a soda machine constructed by the owner from a refrigerator. Guests can borrow a limited selection of snow chains and skiing gear. Kitchen, dorms, and bathrooms are sparklingly clean. (☎5750 1244; fax 5750 1246; hikers@netc.net.au. Linen $3. Suspension mountain bikes $10 per 2hr., $1 per additional hr. Internet $2.50 per 10min. Reception 9am-10pm. Dorms $18, weekly from $105. Doubles $37, $245.) Five minutes outside of town is the **Bright & Alpine Backpackers,** 106 Coronation Ave. To find this old school camp turned hostel/campground, follow the Great Alpine Way east past the information center, turn right sharply onto Hawthorne St., then left onto Coronation St. The backpackers is on the right, just before the small bridge. The facility is filled with nostalgia but does show its age. (☎5755 1154. Kitchen, laundry. Linen $5. Reception 24hr. Sites $7, powered $8. Singles $15; doubles $30.) Bright is blessed with quite a few good restaurants. **Tin Dog,** 94 Gavan St., dishes up Asian, Mexican, and Italian fare, including excellent wood-fired pizza. (☎5755 1526. Open daily 5:30pm-late. Entrees $12-16. Small pizza $9-11.) The **Alpine Hotel** serves full-on breakfast and has a lively bar that gets a little crazy on Saturday nights when local bands perform. (☎5755 1366. Breakfast from 8am. Bar 11am-late.)

Gear shops and businesses cater to adrenaline-junkies. At the center of town, a handful of ski hire establishments will outfit you with ski and snowboard equipment, snow chains, and clothing. **Adina Ski Hire,** 15 Ireland St., offers both new and used, budget skis for rent. (Open Sa-Th 7am-7pm, F 7am-late. Downhill skis, boots and poles $34 per day, $103 per week; budget $26/$84; snowboard and boots $45/$125. 20% YHA discount.) **Bright Ski Centre,** 22 Ireland St. (☎5755 1093), and **JD's for Skis,** on the corner of Burke and Anderson St. (☎5755 1557), offer similar services.

Warm thermal air currents make the valleys surrounding Bright ideal for hang-gliding and paragliding—the area was home to the 1986 World Championships. **Alpine Paragliding,** 6 Ireland St., next to Bright Hikers, offers tandem paraglides. (☎5755 1753. 10-15min., $130.) The **Eagle School of Hang Gliding and Microlighting** (☎5750 1174) offers an introductory "Bright Flight" (15min., $95). The "Mt. Buffalo Flight" takes you over the gorge and then silently glides back to earth (20min., $125). The local ranges are ideal for mountain biking during warm, dry weather. Contact **CyclePath Adventures,** 9 Camp St., about their fully supported, 1- to 5-day high-country, singletrack, and food and wine gourmet bike tours. (☎/fax 5750 1442 or 0427 501 442; cyclepat@bright.albury.net.au.) **Adventure Guides Australia** (☎5728 1804 or 0419 280 614) conducts abseiling (full-day from $120), single and multi-day caving trips from $120, rock climbing (full-day from $180), and bushwalking and camping excursions. All adventure activities are year-round, though they're subject to weather and are much more sporadic in winter.

VICTORIA

MOUNT HOTHAM

With Victoria's highest average snowfall, 13 lifts, and a partnership with nearby Falls Creek (see p. 591), Mount Hotham is Victoria's intermediate and advanced-skiing and snowboarding headquarters. Mt. Hotham is considered the hottest place in Victoria for thrill-seekers, and especially for **snowboarders.** The slopes are more challenging than in the rest of Australia, with short but steep double black diamonds cutting through the trees in the **"Extreme Skiing Zone."** Beginner skiing is limited, though lessons are available. With a constant stream of uni groups filling club lodges in the ski season, the mountain is a little younger and a little more hip than nearby Falls Creek, though *après*-ski offerings are more or less on par with its rival. In the summer, Hotham is relatively quiet, with nature trails and a few shops and lodgings open for visitors.

Info on current road, weather and slope conditions is available at ski rental shops and local-area accommodations, online at www.hotham.net.au, and at ☎1902 240 523 (all Victorian Resorts) or 1902 240 644 (Mt. Hotham & Falls Creek) for a 50¢ per minute fee.

From the north, Mt. Hotham is accessible in the winter by a sealed road. Entrance from Omeo to the south is safer and more reliable, but inconvenient for those in Melbourne or Sydney. To get to Mt. Hotham by **bus,** depart from Melbourne's Spencer St. Station (6¼hr., 1-2 per day, $120 return); Wangaratta Railway Station (3¼hr., 1-2 per day, $85 return); or Bright's Alpine Hotel (1½hr., 2-3 per day, $40 return). Contact **Trekset Tours** (☎9370 9055 or 1800 659 009; www.buslines.com.au/trekset) to book.

There's a fee to enter the resort, not covering lift tickets, payable at the tollbooth located 1½hr. from Bright on the Great Alpine Rd. (Cars 3hr. $10; 1-day/1-night $21; 2-days/2-nights $42; season pass $175.) If you're driving through without stopping at the resort, it's free. From mid-October to the Queen's Birthday in June, resort admission is free. Drivers heading from Bright can rent mandatory **snow chains** from **Hoy's A-Frame Ski Centre,** on the right just after the school bridge in Harrietville. (☎5759 2658. $22, with a $30 deposit.) These can be returned to **Les and Betty's Mobil Service Station** in **Omeo,** on the south side of Mt. Hotham.

The resort is constructed around the Great Alpine Rd., which climbs the mountain. The lodges cluster to the south, with ski lifts and services farther north. Village buses transport folks for free around the resort. The **information centre** is on the first floor of the Resort Management building, just above the Corral carpark. (☎5759 3550; www.mthotham.net.au.) Directly across the street, Hotham Central houses a **snow sports school office** (☎5759 4444), ski rental places (downhill package $27; snowboard and boots $55), a small **grocery store** and a **lift ticket** office, which sells passes valid both here and at Falls Creek. (Full-day ticket $59-75, children $33-39; lift and lesson packages start at $85-105.) Tickets for round-trip **helicopter rides** to Falls Creek are $59 with a valid lift ticket; $99 without. Trips must be booked in person on the day of travel. The Big D lift hosts night skiing. (Open W and Sa 6:30-9:30pm. $11, upgrade from valid lift ticket $6.)

Lodging on Mt. Hotham is pricey, and Bright's excellent hostels offer an inexpensive alternative. **Mt. Hotham Accommodation Service** (☎5759 3636) can sometimes place you in a club lodge cheaply.

To the south of both the resort and the Big D chairlift sits **Big D,** a complex housing both a ski boutique and the **Isobar,** a trendy joint with meals for dine-in or takeaway. (☎5759 3066. Mains $15-$19. Open daily 9am-late.) Next door sits **The General,** a general store with a mini-market, pub, bistro, and mailbox. (☎5759 3523. Market open daily in ski season 8am-7pm; bistro noon-2:30pm, 6-10pm; bar 11am-late.) The 11km **cross-country track** to Dinner Plain begins just beyond the store. The **Swindler's Balcony Bar & Restaurant,** downstairs in the back of Hotham Central, serves hearty meals by its open fireplace; the bar is a post-ski hotspot with live music on weekends. (☎5759 3436. Open daily 7am-late. Pizza $4 per slice, full meals $11-15.) A couple of good **bars** are opposite Hotham Central. The **Summit** bar, in the Snowbird Inn, features outstanding views, live bands (W, Th, Sa), happening crowds, and 5-drink jugs for $8 from 4:30-6:30pm. (☎5759 3503. Open daily noon-2am.) The **Irish Bar**, also in the Snowbird Inn, attracts a mellower crowd.

FALLS CREEK ☎03

An hour's drive from Bright, along roads with sweeping views of the Victorian Alpine country, **Falls Creek Ski Resort** (☎5758 3733; www.skifallscreek.com.au) takes guests as high as 1842m. **Lift ticket** prices are comparable with other resorts. ($75 per day, $144 per 2 days, $420 per week; children $39/$74/$218. Lifts plus lesson $105, students $78, children $70). The ample snowfall, both natural and man-made, is a selling point, and the spread of trails means that bad weather conditions from one direction leave good skiing elsewhere on the mountain. Few trails are very long and most are intermediate runs. Advanced skiers can expect to spend more chairlift time than snow time. As snowfall permits, an area of black diamond trails, known as **The Maze**, is opened, as is a snowboarding terrain park with a **half-pipe.** A Kat service transports skiers in heated Kassbohrers up the backcountry slopes of **Mt. McKay** (1842m) for thrilling black and double-black diamond bowl runs ($59 with lift pass). Falls' ambience is more family-oriented than nearby Mt. Hotham (see p. 590), though their partnership gives multi-day skiers the chance to try both (lift tickets are priced the same and allow access to both resorts).

Driving to the slopes in winter requires carrying **snow chains** (24hr. rental in Tawonga and Mt. Beauty $18-22) and paying a hefty entrance fee (overnight $20; $29 not including lift tickets). It is not practical to stay in Bright and use public transport to reach the resort for the day. **Pyle's Falls Creek Coach Services** (☎5754 4024) runs a ski-season service from Melbourne (6hr., 1-2 per day, $115 return), Albury (3½hr., 1-3 per day, $63 return), and Mt. Beauty (50min., 2-4 per day, $33 return). All prices include entrance fee.

Activity is concentrated at the edges of the village. The **Falls Creek Information Centre** sits at the bottom of town, opposite the day parking lot, and keeps information on lessons, lift packages, and accommodations. (☎5758 3490; fax 5758 3585; fallsinfo@fallscreek.albury.net.au. Open daily 9am-5pm.) Staying on the mountain will let you sleep longer, party later, and make snow angels outside, but the privilege does not come cheap. A horde of small, independent lodges offers varying styles of accommodation. The folks at **Central Reservations** (☎5758 3733 or 1800 033 079) can direct you to the kind you're after.

Quiet stays in the delightfully swanky **Alpha Lodge,** 5 Parallel St., are available year-round. It has Excellent kitchen and roomy commons area. (☎5758 3488; fax 5758 3643; manager@alphaskilodge.com.au. Drying room, laundry, BBQ garden, and sauna. 4-share bunk room $23-81; 2-3 bed with bath $29-93.) The **Frying Pan Inn,** 4 Village Bowl Circle, offers basic, motel-style dorms at the base of the Summit and Eagle chairlifts. The location is excellent. It's also the place to be on weekends, when there are live bands, dance parties, and drink specials to fuel the debauchery. (☎5758 3390; fax 5758 3695. Drying closet, no kitchen. Pub open daily 5pm-late; bistro 8am-8pm. Dorms with bath $40-75.) **The Man,** 20 Slalom St., is the heart of the nightlife, serving up food and beer, live bands, multiple bars, pool tables, fusbol, and even Internet access. (☎5758 3362. Open daily 6pm-late.)

Also on Slalom St., next to the Halley's Comet quad chair, is the **Snowland** complex, housing the **Wombat Cafe** (☎5758 3666; open daily 9am-6pm; light meals $6-8), a **mini-market** (☎5758 3318), and the **post office** (open M-F 9am-5pm, Sa 9am-noon). **Postal code:** 3699.

An active summer resort as well, Falls Creek has bushwalking, horseback riding, tennis, and water activities from October to June. A smaller number of lodges are open for housing during the summer (call Central Reservations for current openings and tariffs), but prices are lower. During Victoria school holidays in summer, conditions permitting, one lift is opened for mountain biking. Take the chair up and then bike down the snow-free trails ($15).

GIPPSLAND

Southeast of Melbourne and on its way to the border of New South Wales, the Princes Hwy. loosely follows the contours of the Victoria coast through verdant, rolling wilderness interspersed with extensive lake systems and small towns. Undeveloped and sparsely populated, this belt hosts eco-tourists and inspires frequent struggles among developers, loggers, and environmentalists. National parks pepper the region; highlights include backpacking through Wilsons Promontory and Croajingalong, boating on the Snowy River, and paying homage to the Den of Nargun in Mitchell River.

FOSTER

☎03

From gold rush to gateway, Foster has long been a place where people come looking for supplies and a warm bed. Most of today's visitors are headed to the park; its entrance is just 30km to the south. While in town, take a moment to relax by the creek, or head up the hill behind the hotel for a lovely view of the land.

To reach Foster by car from Melbourne (170 km), take the South Eastern Arterial (M1) to the South Gippsland Hwy. (M420), following signs first to Phillip Island, then to Korumburra (changing numbers to A440), and finally to Foster. Alternatively, **V/Line** (☎13 61 96) **buses** run from Melbourne (2¾hr.; M-F 4:30pm, Sa 6:50pm, Su 5:40pm; returns M-Sa 7:49am, Su 3:25pm; $25), requiring that you spend the night in Foster before shuttling to the Prom with the **Foster-Tidal River Bus Service** (see below). **Tourist information** is available inside the Stockyard Gallery at the end of Main St. toward the Prom. (☎5682 1125. Open Th-Su 10am-4pm.) **Parks Victoria** staffs an office in the same building. (☎5682 2133. Open M-F 8am-4:30pm.) Other services include: **Internet** at Raider's Pizza, 10 Station Rd. ($6 per hr.); **laundromat,** 6 Station Rd. ($4 wash and dry; open daily 8am-9pm); **police** (☎5682 2407); **hospital** (☎5683 9777); **post office,** corner of Main and Bridge St. (☎5682 2597; open M-F 9am-5pm, Sa 9am-noon). **Postal code:** 3960.

The cozy **Foster Backpackers Hostel,** 17 Pioneer St., is the most affordable option, with shared kitchen and outdoor BBQ. (☎5682 2614. Dorms $17; triples and quads from $50.) You can also rent **camping gear** ($10 per night). Ask the owners about their **farm hostel** (dorms $20, doubles $50). Arriving from the S. Gippsland Hwy., turn right onto Main St., then left on Bridge St.; Pioneer St. is on the right and the hostel on the right side. Margaret, from the tourist information office, also kind-heartedly rents out the "Rose Cabin" behind her house, which is surrounded by grapefruit groves and blueberry bushes and includes a solar-powered shower. (☎5682 2628. 1 person $35, 2 people $70.)

The best option for meals is one of the town's two bakeries. **Sally's Bakery,** 18 Main St., makes good sandwiches for $1.50-4. (☎5682 2903. Open M and W-F 6:30am-5:30pm; Sa-Su 6:30am until sometime in the afternoon.) Or try **Foster Hot Bread,** 33 Main St. (Open M-F 6am-5:30pm, Sa 6am-1:30pm.) Foodway, on the corner of Main St. and Station Rd., sells **groceries.** (Open daily 8am-8pm.)

WILSONS PROMONTORY NATIONAL PARK

Whether it's an echidna sighting in the woods, or the 360° view of granite headlands from Mt. Oberon, chances are you will leave Wilsons Promontory with some unforgettable experiences. Though one of Australia's most famous parks, annually receiving 400,000 visitors, **the Prom** is also one of the most unspoiled and diverse natural reserves in the world. Jetting out to form the continent's southernmost extreme, tidal flats and marshland meet clusters of heath and towering gum forests, while rich fern gullies follow the shape of the land. This diversity of flora creates habitats for scores of native marsupials, reptiles, birds, insects, and sea creatures. Partly preserved as a national park back in 1898 and now declared a UNESCO World Biosphere Reserve, the Prom is off-limits to human settlement and most transportation.

The Boonerwrung tribe believed that this area was sacred, protected by Lo'han, the ancient guardian spirit, and visited only for special occasions. English Naval Officer Tobias Furneaux was the first European to spot the coastline, in 1773. In the early days of Australia's settlement, sealers and whalers exploited the waters offshore. The immigration booms of the gold rush (1850s) and Federation (1900s) brought an active forestry industry, as timber was needed to support new development elsewhere in Victoria. During World War II, the government sealed off the Prom for commando training. Now connected to the mainland by parallel sandy ridges, at various points in its history the peninsula was an island, while at another time, these ridges extended south all the way to Tasmania. For more **information** on Wilsons Promontory, call 1800 350 552, or visit the Parks Victoria website (www.parks.vic.gov.au).

THE PROM AT A GLANCE	
AREA: 490km² of parkland; 83km² of marine parks.	**GATEWAYS:** Foster and Yanakie.
FEATURES: A UNESCO World Biosphere; home to Mt. Oberon and Sealers Cove.	**CAMPING:** Must register with the ranger (p. 593). Fees vary through the park.
HIGHLIGHTS: Easy to challenging hikes and walk, from day to overnight routes.	**FEES:** $8 per vehicle. Fishing permits are required; all payments and inquiries at Tidal River.

TRANSPORTATION AND PRACTICAL INFORMATION. Coming from Foster, turn left at the end of Main St. onto the **Foster Promontory Rd.,** which snakes 30km to the park entrance, nearly 10km past Yanakie (entry $8 per car; free if you have arranged for accommodations at Tidal River, but not for outstation campers). Without access to a car, the only transport option into the park is by the **Foster-Tidal River Bus Service,** run by Anne at the Foster Backpackers Hostel (see above), which delivers passengers from Foster to Tidal River. (☎5682 6614. Travels on request. $15 each way, $20 each way if single traveler; park entrance fee included.) Some touring companies offer daytrips into the park; try Duck Truck Tours, which carts people over from Phillip Island. (☎5952 2548. $60; see p. 538.)

From the entrance station, the park's only sealed road, **Wilsons Promontory Rd.,** winds 30km along the Prom's western extremity, providing many opportunities to turn off for picnics, pictures, and hikes. The road ends at **Tidal River,** a township that does little justice to the park's natural splendor. Many take overnight hikes or daytrips from this area. During its busiest periods, the park runs a **free shuttle bus** between the Norman Bay carpark, at the far end of Tidal River, and the Mt. Oberon carpark (leaves Norman Bay every 30min. from 8am-7pm, arriving at Mt. Oberon for drop off and pickup 15min. later).

Visitors who wish to stay overnight, obtain a fishing license, or get weather updates should go to the **Tidal River Information Centre,** at the end of the main road. The Centre also has exhibits and a video on the Prom's geology and diverse plant and animal populations. All visitors must **register** bushwalking and camping plans with park officials here. (☎5680 9555. Open Nov.-Easter Sa-Th 8am-7:30pm, F 8am-9:30pm; Easter-Oct. daily 8am-5pm.) Tidal River also has the last toilets, pay phones, and food before setting off into the bush. During peak season, Tidal River's amenities include an **open-air cinema,** with a 9:15pm nightly screening of a recent release. Purchase tickets at the cinema 45min. before showtime ($7.50, children $5). A 24hr. **Blue Box** phone for contacting a ranger is outside the info center.

ACCOMMODATIONS AND CAMPING. Finding accommodation in the Prom during the summer months is notoriously difficult, though significantly easier for overseas travelers than locals. While Victorian residents lottery for spots, the park reserves last-minute, first-come **campsites** for non-residents of Victoria at Tidal River (2 nights max; $15.50 peak, off-peak for up to 3 people $13.50). For outstation camping, there's usually no need to book in advance, but you must obtain a permit and pay nightly fees ($4.40, children $2.20). All sites have a one-night max. stay, except **Roaring Meg** campsite and northern sites (2-night max.). You can bounce from site to site, though this must be registered with the info center. Toilets in outstation sites have no toilet paper, and no sites are powered.

Finding an accommodation other than one with a canvas roof in the summer months is hard to come by. Try to reserve three to six months in advance, and even sooner for summer weekends. There are **cabins** all over the park with bath, kitchen, and living room (singles and twins Sept.-early Apr. $115, late Apr.-Aug. $105); bunk-style **units** (Su-F $36, Sa $56), and 4- to 6-bed **huts** ($44 and $66). Book through the **Tidal River Info Centre** (☎5680 9555; wprom@parks.vic.gov.au).

HIKING. To best experience the Prom, tackle a few bushwalking trails and take a dip in its crystal-clear water. Although most visitors sample the Prom in a day, allow three to five days to savor it. The information center's *Discovering the Prom* ($13) details the over-100km of trails that criss-cross the Prom, and *Down Under at the Prom* ($17) points to dive sites for scuba and snorkeling. One of the most popular swimming beaches is at **Norman Bay,** past Tidal River.

SHORT HIKES. Past the Yanakie entrance to the park, the first left leads to the **Five Mile Track Car Park,** accessing the less-visited northern reaches traversed mostly by overnight hikers. A short detour along the Five Mile Track leads to the **Miller's Landing Nature Walk.** The easy walk (4km; 1½hr.) leads through banksia woodlands to the dwarf mangroves and mudflats of Corner Inlet. Several short walks (1-2km) depart from Tidal River, including: **Whale Rock** (0.7km; 30min.), a loop track winding gradually uphill to a delightful view of Mt. Oberon; and **Loo-ern Track** (2km; 1hr.), a boardwalk designed for those with limited mobility, leading through swamp paperbark to an overlook. For a slightly longer hike, try **Squeaky Beach Nature Walk** (5km; 1½hr.), which passes through dunes, coastal scrub, and beautiful granite outcroppings. Look for wombats in the scrub, and once on the beach, slide your feet to hear the remarkably uniform white-grained quartz sand squeak. **Lilly Pilly Gully Nature Walk** (4.7km; 3hr.), starting from the Lilly Pilly carpark 2km up the road from Tidal River, follows a slight incline through coastal woodlands into the rainforest. This walk can be extended by leaving from Tidal River (6.7km; 4hr.); the section between Tidal River and Lilly Pilly Gully is wheelchair accessible. About 5km up the main road is a turn-off for the Mt. Oberon carpark, where the **Mt. Oberon Nature Walk** begins. The walk (6.8km; 2-3hr.) climbs steadily up to the summit, leading to one of the best sunrise spots in the park.

DAY-HIKES. For more ambitious hikers, three incredible day-hikes cover some of the most beloved spots in the Prom. In the southern half of the park, **Tongue Point Track** (11.2km; 4hr.) starts from Darby Saddle (6.7km north of Tidal River) and proceeds, sometimes steeply, past two sweeping lookouts to a small granite peninsula with a stunning view of the coast. The **Oberon Bay Track** (12.4km; 5hr.) leaves from Tidal River, mirroring the scenic coastline along yellow-sand beaches of the western bays. In the opposite direction, departing from the Mt. Oberon carpark, the **Sealers Cove Track** (19km; 5-6hr.) takes you across nearly every environment in the Prom. This popular route passes through eucalypt, stringy bark, and Messmate forest, rising up to Windy Saddle, 3km from the carpark, before descending into **Sealers Swamp** and through fern gullies en route to **Sealers Cove.** The park bills this as one of the most spectacular beaches in the world—it's hard to disagree.

OVERNIGHT HIKES. The overnight hikes in the south are absolutely worth the time and extra preparation, as they allow hikers to savor the multitude of terrains and spectacular secluded spots. The most popular two- to three-day hike sweeps 36km around the eastern coastal areas along well-maintained trails to Sealers Cove (9.6km, see above), Refuge Cove (16.6km), and Waterloo Bay (24km). From Sealers, the track rises to a steep, stunning overlook of the sea before descending into Refuge Cove. This campsite is popular with **boaters** from around the world, and also offers **diving** opportunities. The next bit up Kersops Peak (2.3km) is chal-

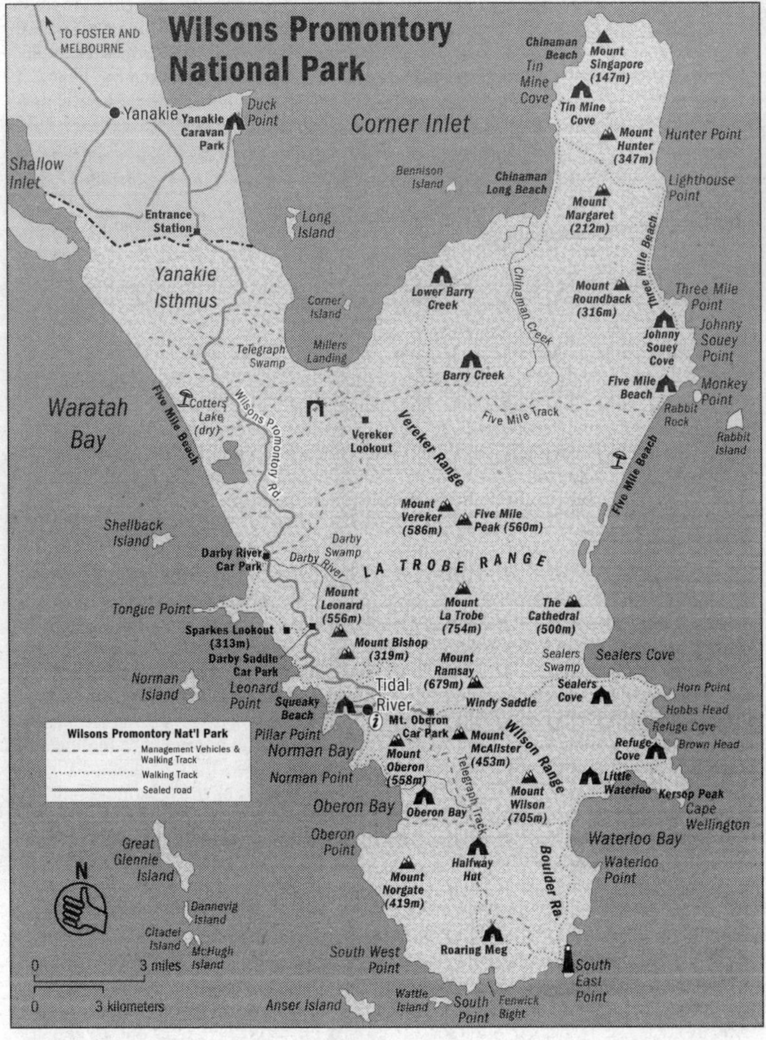

lenging, but short; it's worthwhile to take the 300m detour up to the summit, with views extending all the way to the lighthouse. The track then dips back down and shadows the coastline, where the varying hues of azure, sapphire, and turquoise water will continue to have you agape. Turning from the sea, you go along a flat section of boardwalks through swampy areas until meeting up with the **Telegraph Track** (29.4km), where it follows this dirt road up to the carpark. It is possible to do this walk in two days, but it's far more enjoyable to spend two nights—preferably at **Refuge Cove** and **Little Waterloo**—to spread the hiking out. There are toilets and drinking water at each site. And don't forget your bathers—the bays are great for **swimming** and offer a well-earned treat after a day on the track. To slip off the beaten path for a truly invigorating experience, try the **Lighthouse Walk** (33km). Departing the Mt. Oberon carpark, head south on the **Telegraph Track** past the **Half-way Hut** through stands of eucalypts. From here, a rugged walking trail through tea-tree groves and temperate rainforest, and over a wind-blown plateau, goes past

VICTORIA

LEGENDS OF THE GUNAI For at least 18,000 years, the Gunai (or Kurnai) Aboriginal people have inhabited Gippsland. According to legend, Borun, "the Pelican," was the first Gunai. He descended from the northwest mountains carrying his canoe on his head. As he crossed the Tribal River by Wayput (now Sale), a tapping noise began to follow him. Finally, he reached the ocean inlet, still bothered by the incessant tapping. When he put down the canoe, Borun found sitting in it the woman he would wed–Tuk, "the Musk Duck," who would become the mother of all Gunai people. In order to discourage their children from disobeying tribal laws, the Gunai told them fables. One explains the fallen link between Tasmania and the mainland (at Wilsons Promontory). One day, the story goes, two children at play removed a sacred object from the land and brought it back to their mother. The ground rapidly crumbled into the sea, breaking up families and drowning many Gunai. The moral of this story for you: don't remove anything from Australia's National Parks.

Roaring Meg before making a final steep descent along the old telegraph line. The fury of gale and surf combine with the majestic 1858 vintage lighthouse to frame an unparalleled bushwalk. If you can get a bed at the lighthouse, it's doubly worthwhile (bookings through Tidal River). The lighthouse can also be reached via a new track from Waterloo Bay (14.4km; 4½hr.), though this section is difficult and quite steep, allowing you to do both these popular overnights routes in one trip.

PORT ALBERT ☎03

Bring two things with you to Port Albert: an interest in maritime antiquity and a hunger for fish'n'chips. The oldest fishing town in Victoria, and one of the few still working, Port Albert is 50km east of Foster and 15km south of Yarram off the S. Gippsland Hwy. (A440). Walk around town and soak up the salty seafaring aura. The **Maritime Museum,** on Tarraville Rd. (☎5183 2520), attests to the town's deep connection to the sea, containing details on the famous *Clonmel* shipwreck of 1841 (which led to the settlement of Port Albert), old navigational instruments, and a fabulous collection of sea-shells. Take a walk by the **Nooramunga Marine and Coastal Park,** which extends along the coast near town. This park protects a fragile wetland environment, full of marine sediments that support a wonderland of worms, sand fleas, burrowing crabs, mollusks, sea anemones, and other jelly-like translucent creatures. To access the park on foot or bike, pick up the **Old Port Trail** across from Port Albert Fish'N'Chips. The track winds toward Seabank along inlets and coastal wetlands (11.3km; 4hr. return). By car, look for the anchor on the roundabout outside the town and take the nearest road, labeled "No Through Road." Though unsealed, the first 2km to the park is adequate for 2WD vehicles.

The portside **Port Albert Hotel,** on Wharf St., claims to be the oldest licensed hotel in Victoria. Though perhaps showing its age, the hotel has a lovely veranda. (☎5183 2212. Bunks from $15.) For something a bit newer, try **Port Albert Caravan Park,** 9 Bay St. (☎5183 2600. Sites for 2 from $16, powered $17; self-contained units from $58.) The **Port Albert Fish'N'Chips** shop (☎5183 2431), at the end of Wharf St., serves outstanding fish'n'chips. If you'd rather catch your dinner, rent **fishing** gear and a boat from **Winch House,** on Wharf St. along the pier. (☎5183 2022. Open daily 6:30am-dusk. Tackle $5 per day; canoe $30; kayak $20.)

YARRAM ☎03

Yarram's most outstanding feature is its proximity to the **Tarra-Bulga National Park.** A 15km turn-off in Toora, about a third of the way between Foster and Yarram, will lead you to **Agnes Falls,** the highest single-span waterfall in Victoria, dropping 59m into the Agnes River. In the other direction, about 30km east of Yarram, you can access the southern portion of **Ninety Mile Beach,** an unusually long, and quite exceptional, stretch of white-sanded coastline extending past Lakes Entrance. To reach **Woodside Beach,** popular for **swimming** and **surfing,** follow the S. Gippsland Hwy. to Woodside and turn right onto Woodside Beach Rd.

Yarram is 50km east of Foster on the S. Gippsland Hwy., which turns into Commercial Rd. as it passes through town. The **Toppa Coffee Lounge,** 275 Commercial Rd., sells **V/Line bus** tickets to Melbourne via Foster. (☎5182 6066. 3½hr.; departs M-Sa 7am, Su 2:35pm; $29.) The **Tourist Information Centre** is in the old Court House, at Commercial Rd. and Rodgers St. (☎5182 6553. Open M-F 10am-4pm, Sa-Su 10am-2pm.) **Banks** and **ATMs** are everywhere. The **library,** on Grant St., has **free Internet.** (☎5182 5135. Open M-Tu 2-6pm, Th-F 10am-6pm, Sa 10am-noon. Book ahead.)

For accommodations, head 1km south of town to the **Ship Inn Motel,** on the S. Gippsland Hwy. Though these pleasant, flowery rooms may be a bit over your budget, they're your best bet for a comfortable night's sleep. (☎5182 5588. Singles $59, doubles $69). For food, the **Federal Coffee Palace,** 305 Commercial Rd., is definitely the hippest place in town, with cushioned chairs, books, and board games. (☎5182 6464. Open W-F noon-10pm, Sa 9am-10pm, Su 9am-4pm. Great latte $2.50; chicken fillet with apricots and camembert $14.) There's an IGA **supermarket** inside the Yarram Plaza. (☎5182 6033. Open M-F 8am-6pm, Sa 8am-1pm.)

TARRA-BULGA NATIONAL PARK

At Tarra-Bulga National Park, if it's a sizzler of a day, the fronds of overhanging fern trees nod their welcome and wave away the oppressive heat of the valley. Driving west on the S. Gippsland Hwy., turn left at the edge of **Yarram,** following signs to the national park. From here, take either the **Tarra Valley Rd.** through the Tarra Valley, or the unsealed **Balook Yarram Rd.,** which passes through the Bulga Forest. Both roads connect to the perpendicular **Grand Ridge Rd.,** forming a great loop through the forest. The ascent through the **Tarra Valley,** along a narrow and windy 25km stretch of sealed road, passes through lush fern and eucalypts, with occasional patches of yellow wildflowers. Unless you've got a 4WD, don't take any unmarked roads, as they are rarely patrolled and conditions are variable. About 20km up the road lies the superb **Tarra Falls,** visible just after getting out of the car. Another kilometer up the road at the Tarra Valley picnic area, follow the easy **Tarra Valley Rainforest Walk** (1.2km) through the rainforest to **Cyathea Falls.**

At the junction of the Grand Ridge Rd. and the Balook Yarram Rd. is the **Tarra Bulga Visitor Centre,** with maps and info on day-walks and driving tracks. (☎5196 6166. Open Sa-Su and holidays 10am-4pm.) From here you can follow the Lyrebird Ridge Track to the Ash Track (1km) to access the **Fern Gully Nature Walk** (500m). This short walk is the site of the **Suspension Bridge,** which enables you to stand high above a breathtaking fern gully housing birds, wallabies, bats, and bush rats. To reach the Fern Gully Walk directly, head down Grand Ridge Rd. about 1km past the Visitor Centre to the Bulga carpark. A slightly longer but moderate walk through the park, from the Visitor Centre, is the **Forest Track** (4.3 km; 1½hr.).

Tarra-Bulga fills a section of the **Strzelecki Ranges,** named after the neurotic Polish explorer Count **Paul Strzelecki.** During his 1840 expedition from New South Wales to the Victoria coast, the Count insisted on maintaining a direct line through any and all terrain by using a compass, sextant, and chronometer. His Aboriginal guide, **Charlie Tarra,** saved the expedition from starvation. For his help, the Tarra Valley is named for him ("bulga" is an Aboriginal word for mountain).

There is no bush camping in the park, but there are two **caravan parks** along the Tarra Valley Rd. inside the forest. Coming into the park from Yarram, the first one you'll hit is the **Nangeela Tourist Park,** 1369 Tarra Valley Rd. (☎5186 1216. Sites for 2 $13, $16 powered; cabins for 2 $55, for families $61-79.) About 2km further up the road, the **Tarra Valley Caravan Park,** 1385 Tarra Valley Rd., is slightly plusher. (☎5186 1283. Sites for 2 $13-15; cabins for 2-10 from $50.) Both parks have powered sites, bathrooms, showers, laundry, game room, and a small grocer in the office.

BAIRNSDALE ☎03

Though perhaps not a fascinating destination itself, Bairnsdale is a useful place to refuel before venturing into **Mitchell River National Park** or the **Australian Alps.** About 275km east of Melbourne and 35km west of Lakes Entrance, Bairnsdale is accessible by the Princes Hwy. (A1), called **Main St.** in town. Bairnsdale is the starting point of the **Great Alpine Rd.,** a 300km drive that takes you through the **Australian Alps,** near the **Falls Creek Ski Resort,** to **Wangaratta.** You can also walk in the Alps on the **Australian Alps Walking Track,** which begins in Walhalla (approximately 50km from Bairnsdale) and goes all the way (655km) to Mt. Tennent, outside Canberra. This massive bushwalk over many of the area's highest mountains can be completed in 10 weeks. For more info, call the **Parks Victoria** (☎13 19 63).

Bairnsdale has a **train station with no trains,** though there are plenty of **V/Line buses,** on MacLeod St. (☎5152 5592), across from the tourist office and down Pyke St. Buses run to Melbourne (4hr.; M-F 3 per day, Sa-Su 2 per day; $38) via Sale where you switch to an actual train (1hr.) and Lake's Entrance (30min.; M-F 4 per day, Sa-Su 1 per day; $8.20). **Bairnsdale Visitors Centre,** 240 Main St., between McDonald's and the church, has a knowledgeable staff. (☎5152 3444. Open daily 9am-5pm.) In the same building, you can surf the **Internet** at **Gateway Cafe.** (☎5152 6444. $8 per hr. Open M-F 7:30am-5pm, Sa-Su 9am-5pm.)

The accommodations in Bairnsdale aren't so great. Try camping in **Mitchell River National Park** (below) or stay at the **Espas Arts Resort** on Raymond Island (below). Locally, you can try **Mitchell Gardens Holiday Park,** at the eastern end of Main St., where there are clean showers, kitchen, laundry, and a pool. (☎5152 4654. Sites $14-22 depending on season; cabins from $40.) An IGA **supermarket** is behind McDonald's. (Open M-W 8am-7pm, Th 8am-8pm, F-Sa 8am-9pm, Su 9am-7pm.)

NEAR BAIRNSDALE

RAYMOND ISLAND

If you're looking for a bit of solitude, Raymond Island is the place. **Buses** run from Bairnsdale to nearby Paynesville (30min.; M-F 4-5 per day, Sa 1 per day; $6.50), from where you can take a 2min. **ferry** to the island. (☎0418 517 959. Ferry runs Su-Th 7am-7pm and 9:30-9:55pm, F-Sa 7am-7:10pm and 10:30-11:55pm. Cars $3.) This tiny island serves as a wonderful retreat for bushwalking, cycling, and spotting koalas. And though Raymond Island has no stores, there is the good fortune of the **Espas Arts Resort,** a sparkling but pricey facility. From the ferry, head left toward the yellow complex. (☎5156 7275. Doubles $80. Call ahead.)

METUNG

There's something about Metung. Perhaps it is the uniformity of structure and color in the architecture, or the stylish, oblique plane of the condos with sun-streaked sliding doors opening onto a blue lake. Or it may just be that it's easy to lose track of time strolling by the yachts or lying on the beach. Whatever the reason, Metung is a perfect place to rig up and unwind. From Bairnsdale, drive 20km east on the Princes Hwy. (A1) and 10km south on Metung Rd. (C606). A good diversion in this quiet hamlet is to hire a boat; visit **Metung Cruisers** at the jetty. (☎5156 2208 or 5156 2400. Open daily 8:30am-5pm. 3m inboard with half-cabin $50 per half-day, $90 per day.) Most people take a boat out to the beaches and wilderness islands; the bird observatory **Rotamah Island** (☎5156 6398) is a full-day trek. If you want to stay closer, **Back Beach,** along the coast in town, is a popular area for swimming, prawning, floundering, waterskiing, and parasailing. **Legend Rock,** in the waters by the yacht club, is the last standing of three rocks that, according to Gunai/Kurnai Aboriginal lore (see p. 596), were hunters turned to stone for hoarding their spoils.

Though not a tourist hot-spot, Metung is a popular holiday retreat, so there are many more up-scale rental units than budget accommodations. Try the **Metung Tourist Park,** at Mairburn and Stirling Rd., a right off Metung Rd. just before town. (☎5156 2306. Open daily 8am-9pm. Sites $16-25; cabins for 4 $70-120. Reserve 5 months in advance for Christmas.) When hunger strikes, you'll find an ice-creamery, a bakery, and a posh cafe in town; pick up essentials at the **Village Store** on Metung Rd. (Open daily 7:30am-6pm.) The **post office** is across the street from the general store. (Open M-F 9am-5pm.) **Postal code:** 3904.

MITCHELL RIVER NATIONAL PARK

The Mitchell River flows from the alpine high country down to the Gippsland Lakes, bisecting the 11,900 hectares of rainforest that comprise the park. Canoeing, rafting, and hiking through the **Mitchell River Gorge** is the best way to see the park's splendors. To reach the park from Bairnsdale (45km), turn right about 3km west of town onto Lindenow Rd., which becomes Dargo Rd.; a number of well-labeled right-hand turns leads from here. Most roads through the park are unsealed and navigated more safely in a 4WD.

Beside the gorges and high cliffs looming over the river, most daytrippers venture into the park to pay respect to the **Den of Nargun.** Gunai legend (see p. 596) describes Nargun as a giant stone female creature who destroyed intruders with spears or boomerangs and abducted children who strayed from camp. The cave is said to have been used for initiation ceremonies for women. To reach the Den, turn right off Dargo Rd. onto Waller Rd., and then follow a 15min. downhill track through the forest. Sit by the side of the water and absorb this site's mystical energy, but please **do not enter** the cave because it contains fragile stalagmites.

There are two places to **camp** in the park. One is at **Angusvale,** reached by turning right off Dargo Rd. onto the unsealed Mitchell Dam Rd. (River water only; pit toilets. Free.) The other, at **Billy Goat Bend,** is accessible only by foot; turn right off Dargo Rd. onto Billy Goat Bend Rd., follow to picnic area, and then hike in about 1km (free). Bairnsdale Parks Victoria (☎5152 0400) has information.

LAKES ENTRANCE ☎03

Lakes Entrance is the unofficial capital of the Gippsland Lakes region, the largest inland waterway in the Southern Hemisphere. Lakes Entrance is extremely touristy, crowded during summer holidays, and full of caravan parks and mini-golf courses. Fortunately, its expansive beaches, excellent fishing, and numerous boating opportunities enable land-locked visitors to get out of town and into the water.

TRANSPORTATION AND PRACTICAL INFORMATION. V/Line buses leave near the post office and head to Narooma, NSW (5½hr., 1 per day, $51) and Melbourne (5hr.; M-F 2 per day, Sa-Su 1 per day; $45-60) via Bairnsdale (30min.; M-F 4 per day, Sa-Su 1 per day; $8.20). **Greyhound** runs to Melbourne (daily 12:15am, $50). For reservations, call **Esplanade Travel,** 309 Esplanade. (☎5155 2404. Open M-F 9am-5pm.)

The Princes Hwy., called the **Esplanade** in town, becomes a waterfront strip full of less-than-quaint shops. The **Lakes Entrance Visitors Centre,** on the western end of the Esplanade, has plenty of regional information. (☎5155 1966. Open daily 9am-5pm.) The part of town a few blocks east from the visitors center houses most **banks** and **ATMs.** There's a **launderette** on Carpenter St. (Open daily 8am-7pm.) The **library,** 55 Palmers Rd., up the hill at the east end of town, offers **free Internet** access. (☎5150 9100. Book ahead. Open M-F 8:30am-5pm.) Or try **Lakes Post,** 505 Esplanade. (Open M 8:30am-5pm, Tu-F 9am-5pm, Sa 9am-noon; $2.50 per 15min., $4.50 per 30min., $8 per hr.) The **post office** is at 287 Esplanade. (☎5155 1809. Open M-F 9am-5pm.) **Postal code:** 3909.

ACCOMMODATIONS. Beach camping is fun, but it's illegal, and the area is frequently patrolled.

Riviera Backpackers (YHA), 5 Clarkes Rd. (☎5155 2444; riviera@net-tech.com.au), off the eastern end of the Esplanade. Ask the bus to stop at the hostel bus stop. This excellent motel-style YHA earns high marks for its sparkling new facilities. Large lounge with TV, solar-heated pool, billiards, bike rental ($1 per hr., $5 per day), laundry, kitchen, Internet ($2 per 15min.), and safe storage. Book a few weeks ahead for Dec.-Jan. Reception 24hr. Heated dorms, twins, and doubles all $17 per person, weekly $102.

Echo Beach Tourist Park, 33 Roadknight St. (☎5155 2238), across from the Esplanade. 4-star park with kitchen, BBQ, laundry, pool, spa, TV, and billiards. Reception 8am-10pm. Powered sites $30, off-season $18; cabins $50-103.

Silver Sands Tourist Park, 33 Myer St. (☎5155 2343; ssands@b150.aone.net.au), 1 block from the Esplanade. Friendly and clean. Pool, kitchen, BBQ, laundry, linen from $2. Single travelers must have their own tent; van accommodations not available. Sites $14, for 2 $18; beds $16 per person (only in groups of 2 or more).

FOOD. The Esplanade is overflowing with take-away food shops, and the hotels in town tend to have good bistros in the mid-price range. Get **groceries** at Foodworks, 30-34 Myer St. (☎5155 1354. Open daily 8am-7:30pm). Or for **bulk foods,** try Lakes Health Bar, 10 Myer St. (Open M-F 8am-5pm, Sa 9am-noon.)

Caffe 567, 567 Esplanade (☎5155 1144). Some of the best coffee this side of the Pacific. Sip a cafe latte ($2.40), while indulging in a devilishly divine dessert, like cherry cheesecake ($4.50). Or enjoy sun-dried tomato and olive bread ($3.50) and—of course—a bottle of beer. Open daily 11am-10pm.

Pinocchio Inn Restaurant, 569 Esplanade (☎5155 2565). Noch's usually has a special: all-you-can-eat pasta or 2 large pizzas for $22. 10% YHA discount. Open daily in summer noon-3am; otherwise Su-M 5-10pm, Tu-Th 5-11pm, F-Sa 5pm-midnight.

Riviera Ice Cream Parlour (☎5155 2972), opposite the footbridge on the Esplanade. Award-winning farm-produced ice cream in 35 flavors. Try the "frog on a log." Generous portions $2-4.40. Open daily 9am-5pm, in summer until 11pm.

SIGHTS AND ACTIVITIES. The **Jemmys Point Lookout** at the western end of town affords a perfect view of the patchwork Gippsland Lakes. The town's biggest attraction is its expansive beachfront. To reach **Ninety Mile Beach,** cross the footbridge opposite Myer St. From the snack bar and toilet area, a walking track (1hr.) follows the coast to the man-made boat entrance to the deep, blue waters of the Bass Strait. Most visitors **hire boats** from one of the jetties along Marine Pde. Try **Victor Hire Boats,** on the north arm of Marine Pde. (☎5155 3988. 8-passenger cabins $20 per hr., each extra hour $15.) A bit further down, **Portside Boat Hire** has more options. (☎5155 3832. 6- to 8-passenger cabins $25 per hr., $50 per 3hr. 12-passenger BBQ boat $30 per hr. plus fuel; canoes $10 per hr.) Both places are generally open during daylight hours. **Barrier Landing** is the western strip of land created by the entrance. Only accessible by boat, the landing has great fishing and rests by both a lake beach and a **surf beach.** Contact **Mulloway,** on the Marine Pde., for a 3hr. **fishing trip.** (☎0427 943 154. Trips 9am-noon and 1-4pm. $35.) To find out where to fish, pick up the *East Gippsland Fishing Map* ($7) at the visitors center. For action on land, the **Lakes Entrance Wilderness Trail Rides,** on the corner of Princes Hwy. and Bruces Rd. in Kalimna West, 10km west of Lakes Entrance, provides horse riding in the Colquhoun Forest. (☎5156 3288. 1hr. beginner bush ride $25, 2hr. $45; overnights also arranged.)

The **Wyanga Park Winery,** on Baades Rd., provides for less active entertainment. Drive there by following the signs from Myer St. or take a cruise to the vineyard on *The Corque* for lunch or dinner at **Henry's Cafe.** (☎5155 1508. Open Su-W 9am-5pm, Th-Sa 9am-8pm for free tastings. Cruises 2-5hr. including tea or meal $20-50; book ahead.) **Lake Tyers Boat Trips,** 10km east of town in Lake Tyers, offer relaxing and virtually silent afternoon cruises on Victoria's largest electric boat. (☎5155 1283. $18.50, children $11.) The **Griffith Sea Shell Museum,** just west of Centrepoint on the Esplanade, is a fantastically bizarre rainy-day stop with shells in an unbelievable number of shapes, colors, and sizes. Don't miss the psychedelic, black-light coral exhibit. (☎5155 1538. Open daily 9am-5pm. $4.40, children $2.20.)

BUCHAN ☎03

Just 58km north of Lakes Entrance and 50km northeast of Bruthen, Buchan (rhymes with "tuckin'"; pop. 200) is surrounded by rolling hills at the base of the Snowy River Valley. Buchan is best known for its spectacular Buchan Caves.

TRANSPORTATION AND PRACTICAL INFORMATION. No public transport serves Buchan, so most backpackers arrive on touring buses, such as **Oz Experience** (☎1300 300 028) or **Wayward Buses** (☎1800 882 823), bound for Melbourne or Sydney. Driving from Lakes Entrance, take the Princes Hwy. 23km east to Nowa Nowa, turn left onto C620, then right onto C608, following signs to Buchan.

Just south of the Buchan Caves, the small town center contains a **general store** with basic food and **tourist information.** (Open M-F and holidays 8:30am-6pm, Sa 8:30am-1pm, Su 9am-1pm.) The **Parks Victoria office** has the most info on camping and the national parks area, as well as tickets for the caves and reservations for the 100 closely-packed campsites in the area. (☎5155 9264. Sites $11-14.50, powered $15.50-19.) The **Buchan Outreach-Resource Centre,** 6 Davidson St., over the bridge onto Orbost Rd. and then right again onto Davidson, has **Internet** access. (☎5155 9294. Open M-Th 9am-4:30pm. Internet $3 per hr.) The **post office** is across from the general store. (Open M-F 9am-5pm.) **Postal code:** 3885.

ACCOMMODATIONS AND FOOD. The **Buchan Lodge,** left after the bridge on Saleyard Rd. just north of the town center, provides outstanding budget accommodation in a beautifully constructed wooden building. The grand main room houses a lounge, dining area, wheelchair facilities, and a well-equipped kitchen. Guests can swim, watch for platypuses in the Buchan River, play volleyball, practice the piano, or just relax and have a laugh with Dick, the proprietor, and Casey, his dog. (☎5155 9421. Breakfast included; complimentary tea and coffee all-day. Bunks $17.) **Willow Cafe,** the muralled house a few doors down from the post office, has tasty meals. (☎5155 9387. Open daily 9am through dinner.) Afterward, amble across the street to the **Caves Hotel,** a.k.a. the **pub.** (☎5155 9203. Open M-Sa 11am-between 10pm and 1am, Su noon-8pm.)

SIGHTS. The 260-hectare **Buchan Caves** reserve just past the town center before the bridge is up to 25 million years old, reaches depths of over 50m, and will definitely dazzle with stalactites and stalagmites. The two big caves, **Fairy Cave** and **Royal Cave,** are open for guided tours (1hr.; 3-5 tours daily 10am-3:30pm; $11, children $5.50, families $28). For a bit more of a challenge without all the railings and floodlights, you can book a group tour of Federal Cave ($15; min. 5 people; book through Parks Victoria or Buchan Lodge).

SNOWY RIVER NATIONAL PARK

Shrouded in mythic Australiana, Snowy River National Park surrounds the once mighty Snowy River with jagged hills dressed in green. This is some of the most extreme wilderness in Australia. The rugged beauty of the landscape inspired Banjo Paterson, author of *Waltzing Matilda,* to pen his bush ballad *The Man From Snowy River,* which idealizes the harsh bush life and those who choose to take on the challenge among these "pine-clad ridges." Once an underwater landmass, the park stretches across vastly distinct ecosystems, from rainforest to rainshadow. Many rare species call it home, including the brush-tailed rock wallaby and the tiger quoll. Whether you bushwalk, white-water raft, camp, or canoe, the Snowy River and its surrounding mountainside remain an impressive wonder.

TRANSPORTATION. A car can circumnavigate the park in 6hr. The park road is mostly unsealed, and becomes increasingly windy and narrow as it heads north. It is suitable for 2WD vehicles, depending on your confidence as a driver, and weather and road conditions. Call **Parks Victoria** in Orbost (☎5161 1222) or Buchan

SNOWY RIVER NATIONAL PARK AT A GLANCE	
AREA: 98,700 hectares **FEATURES:** Snowy River, Bowen Range, Gelantipt Plateau, Mountain Creek, and Rodger River. **HIGHLIGHTS:** Bushwalking, Canoeing, and Scenic driving.	**GATEWAYS:** Buchan (above) and Orbust (p. 603). **CAMPING:** Allowed throughout the park (free); main sites are around Mackillop Bridge ($8). **FEES:** None

(☎5155 9264) for up-to-date reports. If you are driving from Buchan, you can take either the **Buchan-Gelantipy Rd.** (C608) through the countryside, or the unsealed **Tulloch Ard Rd.** through the forest, both of which end in Gelantipy. To reach the Tulloch Ard Rd., head north out of Buchan and take a right on Orbost Rd., continuing straight on Basin Rd., then left on Tulloch Ard Rd. The Buchan-Gelantipy Rd. leads through **Wulgulmerang,** the last place to get petrol and supplies until you reach Bonang east of the park. About 1km down the road, take the right fork onto Bonang-Gelantipy Rd., which follows a steep descent to **MacKillop Bridge,** and continues east until its intersection with **Bonang Main Rd.** You can either take this all the way to Orbost, or turn right onto **Yalmy Rd.** to reach the eastern sections of the park. **Eastour,** out of Orbost, drives people through the Snowy River region. (☎5154 2969. 1-day $120; for more info see **Errinundra National Park,** p. 604.)

ACCOMMODATIONS. The **Karoonda Park YHA,** 1½hr. from the Princes Hwy. and 40km north of Buchan on the Buchan-Gelantipy Rd. (C608), has a swimming pool, ping-pong, billiards, darts, tennis, bar, wheelchair facilities, and Internet access. After two nights as a paying guest, useful hands can stay longer as farm workers in exchange for room and board. The YHA has many adventure options: overnight rafting trips (seasonal; $110, backpackers $75); overnight horseback trips ($110, backpackers $75); abseiling (intro $10, full 40m $25); and indoor rock climbing ($5). Oz Experience stops here. Call ahead for pickup from Lake's Entrance. (☎5155 0220. Rooms $17, non-YHA $19, with board $32; non-backpackers $48. Motel singles $28; doubles $48.) About 30km farther north along the dirt track en route to Suggan Buggan and Jindabyne, NSW (see p. 210), is the tranquil mountain retreat of **Candlebark Cottage,** at "Springs" along the Snowy River-Jindabyne Rd. On a hill 1km from the main house, this secluded cottage sleeps eight, with a double bed and six loft bunks. Popular with cyclists and families, the cottage is ideal for bushwalking, trout fishing, or winter expeditions. (☎5155 0263. $25, for 2 $50, each extra person $20.) The most popular places to **camp** within the park are **MacKillop Bridge, Raymond Falls,** and **Hicks Campsite.** Raymond Falls and Hicks Campsite can be reached off Yalmy Rd., on dirt tracks suitable for 2WD. All sites have pit toilets, and only MacKillop Bridge has a fee ($8).

SIGHTS AND HIKING. The Snowy River region is well worth a few days' exploration. From Buchan along Tulloch Ard Rd., start your journey at **Ash Saddle,** halfway to **Gelantipy.** From here, the **Betts Creek Track** (1-2km, 30min.) begins an easy loop through a magnificent stand of massive, old-growth mountain ash. Follow the Betts Creek 4WD track to the sign for Snowy River National Park, then look on your left for a narrow trail leading through a break in the trees. Continuing further north, the **Seldom Seen Track** is a left-hand turn 15km north of Gelantipy. This 7km uphill track is suitable for 4WD vehicles or walkers only, and leads to the **Mt. Seldom Seen Fire Tower.**

Heading into the park on **Bonang-Gelantipy Rd.,** the first sight is Little River Falls. A 400m walking track leads to a viewing platform. Back on the main road, just over the bridge, a sign for **Alpine National Park** leads left to a steep unsealed road. This road goes to **Hanging Rock,** or World's End, one of the most fantastic and least known lookouts in the park. To reach Hanging Rock, turn left after the bridge (Milky Creek Track), left at Rocky River Ridge Track, and left again at Hanging Rock Track (5km, 4WD vehicles only). The rock is a 10min. descent, jutting out

THE MAN FROM SNOWY RIVER The wild brumbies of the Snow Mountains and the hard men who braved the unforgiving land inspired the legendary Australian ballad, *The Man from Snowy River.* A.B. Paterson, writing under the pen name of Banjo, wove the story of a young horseman who outrode even the most experienced mountain riders to round up a herd of wild mountain horses. While Banjo wasn't writing with a particular rider in mind, once the ballad was released, dozens of stories came pouring in—as he had expected—about men exactly fitting the description. It is widely believed in the Upper Murray country in Victoria that Jack Riley was the man forever immortalized in the epic tale.

over a 400m valley with a 270° view of the countryside. Back on the main road, 1km further into the park lies the 400-million-year-old **Little River Gorge,** the steepest gorge in Victoria (500m). A 400m trail leads down to the gorge from the carpark. MacKillop Bridge, spanning the Snowy at the north of the park, is the starting point of the busiest walking track in the park (which isn't too busy at all). The Silver Mine Walking Track (18km, 6hr.) allows glimpses of the glimmer of silver in the surrounding hills, and spectacular views of the river and mountains to the west. The track starts along the 4WD **Deddick Track,** passing through native pine stands, rising steadily to viewpoints, then dropping down on a walkers-only track as it follows the banks of the Snowy. There is a campsite here for overnight hikers. The walk ascends again to a lookout before heading back down toward the bridge. For the less ambitious, the **Snowy River Track** (1.5km, 30min.), leaving from MacKillop Bridge, is a self-guided nature walk along the Snowy.

MacKillop Bridge is the second structure to span the banks of the Snowy. The original bridge rose 22m above the river, but on the day before the scheduled opening, the great river flooded it out. The current bridge soars 30m above the luxuriously warm and clear waters, though damming for hydroelectricity has cut water flow to less than 5% of its original levels; it is unlikely the Snowy will ever tackle another bridge. This is the source of some debate in the vicinity, as community activists rally to "Let the Snowy Flow Again!" Even so, the beauty depicted in the legendary film *The Man From Snowy River* (actually filmed in Mansfield, p. 581) is only slightly muted. Whitewater rafting, canoeing, and kayaking are quite popular, water levels permitting. Contact Snowy River Expeditions, run out of Karoonda Park YHA (see **Accommodations,** p. 602).

ORBOST ☎03

Orbost is a logging town 60km northeast of Lakes Entrance that mostly serves only as a pitstop on the way to nearby beaches and national parks. About an hour from Orbost are two worthy sights, neither of which gets many visitors. To the north, **Errinundra National Park** houses Victoria's largest stand of rainforest. To the south, **Cape Conran** offers beautiful beaches away from the tourist hubbub. Ensuring minimal tourism, no buses go to either.

V/Line buses run to Orbost from: Bairnsdale (1½hr., 1-2 per day, $19.80); Canberra (5hr., 2 per week, $50); Melbourne (5½hr., 1-2 per day, $51.80). Buy tickets at **Orbost Travel Centre,** 86 Nicholson St. (☎5154 1481. Open M-F 9am-5:30pm, Sa 9am-noon.) By car, Orbost is just off the Princes Hwy. via Lochiel St. or Salisbury St.; both exits intersect with **Nicholson St.**

The **Snowy River Orbost Visitors Centre,** on Lochiel St., just off the Princes Hwy., creates an all-senses-activating experience, including comparative forest displays, an audiovisual show, info on East Gippsland's national parks, and two outdoor paths that snake through manicured rainforest. (☎5154 2424. Open daily 9am-5pm.) In town, there are **ATMs;** the Business Centre library, just off Nicholson on Ruskin St., with **free Internet** (☎5150 9100; open M-F 8:30am-5pm); more **Internet** at East Gippsland Computers, 124 Nicholson St. (☎5154 1492; open M-Tu and Th-F 9:30am-5:30pm, Sa 9:30am-noon; $6 per hr.); **post office,** on the corner of Nicholson and McLeod St. (open M-F 9am-5pm). **Postal Code:** 3888.

The **Orbost Club Hotel,** 63 Nicholson St., an average budget stay with standard Australian-Chinese menu options (☎5154 1003. Singles $25; doubles $30; twins $35.) The **Snowy River Kingfruit Shopping Complex,** 28 Salisbury St., is the best option for food and supplies. (☎5154 1577. Open M-Sa 8:30am-5:30pm.) **The Snowy River Cafe,** 100 Nicholson St., has basic cheap food. (☎5154 1054. Open M-F 7:30am-5pm, Sa 7:30am-3pm.) Or try Foodway, on Nicholson St. opposite the hotel for **groceries.** (☎5154 1206. Open M-Th and Sa 8:30am-6:30pm, F 8:30am-9pm, Su 9am-6:30pm.)

NEAR ORBOST

ERRINUNDRA NATIONAL PARK

Normally, cool rainforests like the Errinundra are dominated by ancient myrtle beeches, as in the Otway Ranges of southwestern Victoria. Here, however, black olive berry and cinnamon-scented sassafrass cover the forest floor, while a wet eucalypt overstory extends through much of Errinundra Plateau. Approach the forest either by the winding **Bonang Rd.** from the north (from Snowy River), or by the Princes Hwy. from the south. About 11km south of Bonang and 54km east of Orbost, these roads intersect with the two ends of Errinundra Rd., which leads into the park. Most of the roads in the park are unsealed, but navigable in a 2WD vehicle on a good day. However, they can be closed after a lot of rain; call the **Parks Victoria** office in Orbost. (☎5161 1222. Open M-F 8am-5pm.) There are a few operators in Orbost with tours to Errinundra, but they tend to be pricey. **Eastour** leads trips upon request, including an Errinundra 4WD day tour. (☎5154 2969. $120.)

To tackle the park independently, get a map and the *Guide to Walks and Tours* at the Info Centre in Orbost and inquire about which tracks are in good condition. Most visitors make their first stop at **Errinundra Saddle,** where Errinundra Rd. passes through the plateau. For more of an uphill challenge, climb to the top of **Mt. Ellery,** more than 1000m above sea level, for a grand view of the forest (2.5km return). To get there, take Errinundra Rd. to Big River Rd. at the Mt. Morris picnic area, and follow signs to Mt. Ellery. The **Coastal Range** track (25km; 6hr.) is an easy-moderate day trip along an old 4WD track that shows off the forest's unique features. Farther down the road, you'll hit the **Goonmirk Rocks** track (1km; 30min.), which leads through mountain plum pines, silver wattle, and in springtime, the red flowers of the Gippsland waratah. The most popular place to **camp** near the park is **Ada River,** on the southern section of Errinundra Rd. If you want to be within the park, go to **Frosty Hollow,** a remote camping area in the park's eastern reaches; take Bonang Rd. to Gap Rd. to Gunmark Rd. to Goonmirk Rocks Rd. to Hensleigh Creek Rd. Both locations are **free** and have pit toilets and a water source.

CAPE CONRAN

Cape Conran and its Coastal Park are just 35km southeast of Orbost through Marlo. This area offers a solitary and rugged melange of dunes, heath, wetlands, swamps, and woods. From Orbost, go south down Nicholson St. to **Marlo-Cape Conran Rd.** and follow it to the end. From points farther east, turn left off the Princes Hwy. onto Cabbage Tree Rd., 30km east of Orbost, and avoid the right fork to Marlo. The road ends at the Marlo-Cape Conran Rd.

Coming from Orbost, there are some serene spots on the road past **Marlo.** One of the best is **French's Narrows,** where the Snowy River meets the sea, about 5km east of Marlo. Two thin strips of land divide the murky river's end from its shallow estuary and the breaks of the Bass Strait. Five kilometers farther down the road is **Point Ricardo,** a secluded beach popular for fishing. A short jaunt from the accommodations options is the main **East Cape Beach.** The two primary walking options both begin at the carpark on the beach at the end of the road, where there is a map. The mainly coastal **Dock Inlet Walk** is for the fit and ambitious (25km; 6-8hr.). The **Cape Conran Nature Trail** goes inland (2.5km; 1hr.). Because of occasional **flooding,** check with rangers (☎5154 8438) before setting out. The **Yeerung River** is popular for **fishing** and **swimming.** The best places to **swim** are **Sailors Grave** (East Cape Beach) and **Salmon Rocks** (near West Cape Beach).

If you plan to spend the night on the Cape itself, the only options are the Parks Victoria **cabins** or **camping** at **Banksia Bluff,** left off Cape Conran Rd. onto Yeerung River Rd., just before East Cape Beach. The eight self-contained cabins are comfortable, and one is handicapped accessible. Bring sleeping gear, towels, and food, though the Marlo supermarket drops by daily around 11:30am with groceries. (☎5154 8438. Book well in advance. Cabins for 4 $70, peak $100.) **Campsites,** though more plentiful, are also in demand (sites for 4 $13, peak $17). If they're booked, try the **Burbang Caravan Park,** tucked in the forest about 3km back up the road toward Marlo. (☎5154 8219. Sites $12-14; vans for 6 $26-40; cabins $50-80.)

CANN RIVER AND MALLACOOTA

East of Lakes Entrance, the coast of Victoria becomes a seemingly endless stretch of wilderness punctuated by secluded lakes and estuarine inlets. The Princes Hwy. surrenders the coast to this length of wild and retreats 10-20km inland. The highway passes through Cann River and Genoa before crossing the border into New South Wales; a smaller highway winds south to Mallacoota. Cann River and Mallacoota are good bases for a venture into the park if you are unprepared to camp.

Cann River is a one-road-town with nary a red light to stop the **bus** to Melbourne (6½hr., 1 per day, $55) or Canberra (4hr.; 1 per day M, Th; $43). The handy **Parks Victoria Information Centre,** on the Princes Hwy. near the east end of town, has info on accommodations and the park's road conditions. (☎5158 6351. Open daily 9am-5pm, shorter hours off-peak.) **Cann River Hotel,** on the Princes Hwy. toward the west of town, is a standard pubstay. (☎5158 6221. Singles $22.) **Pelican Point Coffee Lounge,** a few doors down from the Info Centre, offers perfect pre-wilderness meals. (☎5158 6328. Open daily 9am-4:30pm.) There is a **supermarket** across from the hotel. (Open M-F 8am-6pm, Sa 8am-1pm, Su 9am-1pm.)

Mallacoota stays true to its slogan as "Victoria's hidden treasure"—public transportation approaches only as close as **Genoa,** 23km north on the Princes Hwy. The town does, however, have a **Parks Victoria Office,** on the corner of Buckland and Allan Dr. (☎5158 0219. Open M-F 9:30am-3:30pm, closed noon-1pm.) A 24hr. **laundromat** is at 57 Maurice Ave.

The **Mallacoota Lodge YHA,** 51-55 Maurice Ave., is a motel-style hostel connected to a bistro and a pub that fills after 9pm. (☎5158 0455. Swimming pool. Bunks $14, non-YHA $17.) There is also the 600-site **Mallacoota Camp Park,** at the bottom of Maurice Ave. on Allan Dr., with waterfront lookouts at the Howe Range. (☎5158 0300. Sites $13-19, powered $16-23.) For eats, your best bet is **Corner Cafe and Take-Away,** 43 Maurice Ave., which uses many ingredients from their farm in Genoa. (☎5158 0998. Meals $4-5. Open M-Sa 9am-3:30pm, longer holiday hours.) There are two **supermarkets** at the top of Maurice Ave. (both open daily 8:30am-6:30pm).

GABO ISLAND ☎03

To really head off the beaten path, go to **Gabo Island,** 13km from Mallacoota. Connected to the mainland until the isthmus eroded away at the turn of the century, Gabo Island's vibrant, red granite composes Victoria's easternmost isle. Quarried from the island in a Herculean feat in 1862, the **lighthouse** (Australia's second-tallest at 47.5m) continues to steer ships clear of the coast. Gabo Island also houses the world's largest colony of **Little Penguins,** with over 40,000 adult birds. Accommodation is at the **Light Station,** which can hold up to eight people (for 6 people $70, peak $90; each additional person $10). Book through Parks Victoria in Mallacoota (☎5158 0219). Transport to the island can be tricky. If you don't want to sea-kayak, the **Mallacoota Air Service** (☎5158 0102) will take three adults for $60, or try **Gabo Island Tours** (☎6495 2958), with daytrips from Merimbula, NSW to the island

CROAJINGOLONG NATIONAL PARK

Tickling Victoria's eastern coastline from the New South Wales border to Sydenham Inlet is Croajingolong ("crow-a-JING-a-long") National Park. Scamper amid boulders lodged into the park's sandy beaches, frolic in one of the rivers that empties into the ocean, hike out to (and maybe even stay at) the lighthouse, or tumble down one of the massive sand dunes. This phenomenal park, recognized by UNESCO as a World Biosphere Reserve, extends nearly 100km and covers 87,500 hectares. Busy during peak season, it remains uncrowded the rest of the year.

If you're unprepared to tackle the bush alone, the best way to navigate the park from Mallacoota is with **Natural Adventures,** which coordinates activities from kayaking and bushwalking to 4WD adventures and evening spotlight walks. (☎5158 0166. Full-day $100; self-guided kayak trip $50.) If you are going solo, your first stop should be the **Parks Victoria Office** in Cann River or Mallacoota (see above) to pick up maps and check the road conditions.

From Cann River it's a 45km drive down unsealed roads (the Tamboon Rd. and then left on Pt. Hicks Rd.) to the **Thurra** and **Mueller Rivers,** where you can splash about, head to the beach, or **camp** ($12 per night). The campgrounds are now run by the folks at Point Hicks Lighthouse, so Parks Victoria has no info on availability. Both campgrounds have fireplaces, pit toilets, and river water; Thurra is more popular because of its private sites and overnight parking. Highlights include the 2.2km easy walk out to **Point Hicks Lighthouse,** built in 1888, with a great beach to **swim** at on the way. You can also stay at one of two cottages beside the lighthouse. (☎5158 4268. Linen $10. Call to arrange vehicle access. Cottages for 8 $160-190.) Another great walk (4km; 2hr.) leads through tea-tree forest to 150m high dunes, the second highest in the Southern Hemisphere. There are no sign-posts in the dunes, however, so you've either got to play Hansel and Gretel with your footprints on the way back, or return along the river.

In between Cann River and Genoa, there is the turn-off for **Wingan Inlet,** another campsite with popular bushwalking. These sites also have fireplaces, pit toilets, a water source, and fantastic fishing (inquire at Parks Office for permit; sites $10-12). Out of Wingan, there is the idyllically named **Lake Elusive Walk** (4km, 2hr.), which heads to the lake through **wildflowers.**

Fifteen kilometers southwest of Mallacoota, heading out along Betka Rd., is the **Shipwreck Creek Campsite** (fireplaces, pit toilets, limited tank water; sites $7.50-10). While there aren't many bushwalking tracks out of this site, you can always head out to the beach for the day (not a recommended swimming beach), or start the **Wilderness Coast Walk.** This walk takes you along the beautiful, sandy shoreline, punctuated by grassy outcroppings and immense algae-coated boulders at the water's edge. There are 10 campsites along the 70km trek, starting with Shipwreck Creek and terminating at Bemm River. Do a piece, or, if you're lucky, do it all. To minimize impact on the environment, all overnight hikers must receive a **permit** from the Parks Victoria office in Cann River or Mallacoota before hitting the trail.

WESTERN AUSTRALIA

Western Australia is distinct from the rest of the country in many ways, but the most glaring is its overwhelming size. WA covers about a third of Australia, which seems like an obvious and useless observation, but visitors soon realize that simply getting from place to place will occupy much of their time in the state. Tiny pieces of the map translate into full, draining days of driving or busing on empty roads. The upside of WA's immensity is a collection of landscapes and activities that no other area in Australia can match. Yet most visitors, like most Australians, don't bother to explore the West, believing that it's just a desolate backwater. Even native Westralians usually only see a fraction of their state. Of WA's 1.8 million people, 1.4 million live in the Perth area, and most of the rest are close to the coast, along the vineyards of the south or the surf-pounded capes of the north. Perth, WA's capital, is a modern city complete with shiny skyscrapers, four universities, and several suburbs. People in Perth and throughout the state have a friendly, relaxed interest in the hardy tourists that do make it out west, and with good reason: tourism has become one of the state's economic mainstays, and a lot of effort has gone into making WA a tourist-friendly destination.

From quokkas in the south to camels and saltwater crocs in the north, WA is home to a range of Australian wildlife. The state's interior is covered with miles of bushland, spinifex grass, and sandy plains, and between August and November the land comes alive as carpets of 8000 wildflower species bloom along the coast south from Exmouth into the Great Southern. The Southwest is the domain of old-growth forests. One of the world's largest trees, the majestic karri reaches heights of 80m, for which it is subject to the state's thriving woodchipping industry. In the north, the desert gives way to the rugged tropical vegetation of the Kimberley. A few rough roads carve through the huge expanses of rainforest, around unearthly rock formations, and past waterfalls that cascade into the Indian Ocean.

Because of the isolation from the rest of the country, Westralians have developed an independent nature. In 1933, a state referendum revealed a two-to-one preference to separate from the Commonwealth of Australia. Secession never became a political reality, but the self-sufficient spirit remains an undercurrent. While many Westralians depend on heavy industry for their livelihood, a growing number are fighting to protect their state's natural resources. Ecotourism and promotion of natural attractions have begun to edge out the fishing and animal husbandry industries; the dolphins at Monkey Mia have replaced the massive open-pit mines of the outback as state treasures. Best of all, West Australia has for the most part avoided the overdevelopment and tourist saturation that some find so distasteful about the east coast. With that in mind, the time is right to go West.

TRANSPORTATION

Because of the distances between attractions, and the dearth of long-haul transportation, many travelers—even budget travelers—**buy a car** for long visits (see **Buying and Selling Used Cars,** p. 66). A thriving gray market exists for used cars, 4WDs, and campervans, fueled by hostel message boards and the *West Australian* classifieds. **Used car dealerships** line Beaufort St. several kilometers north of Northbridge, outside Perth. Before paying, have the car checked by a mechanic. Some unscrupulous car dealers prey on backpackers and don't honor warranties. Be wary and do your homework before investing. The **Royal Automobile Club (RAC),**

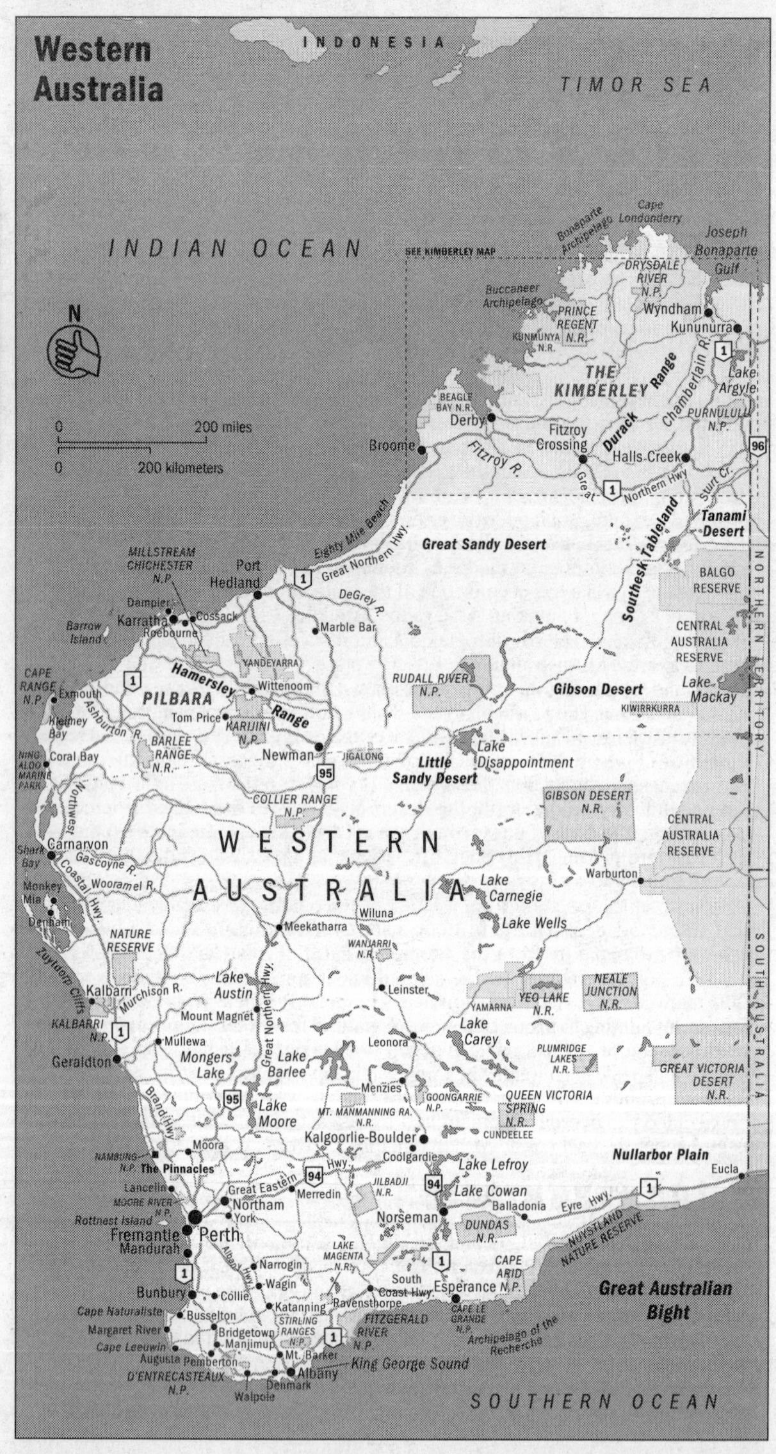

Western Australia
INDONESIA
TIMOR SEA
INDIAN OCEAN
N
0
200 miles
0
200 kilometers
SEE KIMBERLEY MAP
Cape Londonderry
Bonaparte Archipelago
Joseph Bonaparte Gulf
DRYSDALE RIVER N.P.
Buccaneer Archipelago
PRINCE REGENT N.R.
KUNMUNYA N.R.
Wyndham
Kununurra
THE KIMBERLEY
Range
Chamberlain R.
Lake Argyle
PURNULULU N.P.
BEAGLE BAY N.R.
Derby
Broome
Fitzroy R.
Fitzroy Crossing
Durack
Halls Creek
Great Northern Hwy
Sturt Cr.
Tanami Desert
Eighty Mile Beach
Great Northern Hwy.
Great Sandy Desert
Southesk Tableland
MILLSTREAM CHICHESTER N.P.
Port Hedland
DeGrey R.
Dampier
Karratha
Cossack
Roebourne
Barrow Island
Marble Bar
BALGO RESERVE
CENTRAL AUSTRALIA RESERVE
YANDEYARRA
CAPE RANGE N.P.
Exmouth
Hamersley Range
PILBARA
Wittenoom
RUDALL RIVER N.P.
Gibson Desert
Lake Mackay
Ashburton R.
Tom Price
KARIJINI N.P.
KIWIRRKURRA
Coral Bay
BARLEE RANGE N.R.
Newman
JIGALONG
Lake Disappointment
Little Sandy Desert
NORTHERN TERRITORY
COLLIER RANGE N.P.
GIBSON DESERT N.R.
WESTERN AUSTRALIA
CENTRAL AUSTRALIA RESERVE
Carnarvon
Shark Bay
Gascoyne R.
Northwest Coastal Hwy.
Monkey Mia
Wooramel R.
Denham
Lake Carnegie
Warburton
Wiluna
Meekatharra
Lake Wells
NATURE RESERVE
WANJARRI N.R.
Zuytdorp Cliffs
Lake Austin
Leinster
NEALE JUNCTION N.R.
Kalbarri
Murchison R.
YAMARNA
YEO LAKE N.R.
SOUTH AUSTRALIA
KALBARRI N.P.
Mount Magnet
Lake Carey
Mullewa
Leonora
PLUMRIDGE LAKES N.R.
Geraldton
Mongers Lake
Lake Barlee
GREAT VICTORIA DESERT N.R.
Brand Hwy
Menzies
GOONGARRIE N.P.
QUEEN VICTORIA SPRING N.R.
Lake Moore
MT. MANMANNING RA. N.R.
Kalgoorlie-Boulder
CUNDEELEE
Moora
NAMBUNG N.P.
The Pinnacles
Coolgardie
Lake Lefroy
Nullarbor Plain
Lancelin
MOORE RIVER N.P.
Great Eastern Hwy.
Merredin
JILBADJI N.R.
Lake Cowan
Eucla
Northam
York
Rottnest Island
Norseman
Balladonia
Eyre Hwy.
Fremantle
Perth
Mandurah
DUNDAS N.R.
NUYSTLAND NATURE RESERVE
Albany Hwy.
LAKE MAGENTA N.R.
Narrogin
CAPE ARID N.P.
Wagin
South Coast Hwy.
Esperance
Great Australian Bight
Bunbury
Collie
Ravensthorpe
Katanning
Cape Naturaliste
Busselton
STIRLING RANGES N.P.
FITZGERALD RIVER N.P.
CAPE LE GRANDE N.P.
Archipelago of the Recherche
Margaret River
Bridgetown
Manjimup
Cape Leeuwin
Augusta
Pemberton
Mt. Barker
King George Sound
D'ENTRECASTEAUX N.P.
Albany
Denmark
Walpole
SOUTHERN OCEAN
1
95
94
96

WESTERN AUSTRALIA HIGHLIGHTS

CABLE BEACH. The sunset camel rides in Broome never fail to impress (p. 659).

THE VALLEY OF THE GIANTS. Walk among the clouds on the Treetop Walk (p. 631).

GERALDTON. You might think this place to be windsurfing capital of the world. Test you skills against the year-round winds that sweep its coast. (p. 642).

EXMOUTH. Head to Ningaloo Reef for a swim with whale sharks (p. 648).

THE PINNACLES. The Pinnacles, at Nambung National Park, are wind-eroded limestone pillars that rise from desert-like sand dunes (p. 642)

THE GIBB RIVER ROAD. Stumble upon a tropical gorge and other surreal wonders along the untouched desert track. (p. 664).

AUGUSTA. Humpback whales jump past your boat off the coast of Augusta (p. 628).

228 Adelaide Tce., Perth, at the corner of Hill St., offers inspections for members. As WA's branch of AAA, RAC also provides roadside assistance. (☎13 17 04, roadside assistance ☎13 11 11. One-year membership $86.90; inspections from $100.) For more information see **On the Road,** p. 67.

If you plan to **drive through the desert,** bring plenty of water, petrol, a spare tire, a beacon, and a fanbelt. Winter and early spring are the safest times of year to drive the Great Northern Hwy. because temperatures are lower and traffic more frequent. Throughout WA, you'll share the highway with **road trains,** massive tractor-trailers. Don't assume their turn signal is an attempt to communicate that it's ok to pass them; several people have been killed making this mistake. *Let's Go* does not recommend **hitchhiking,** but some people do it. The most reliable way to get a ride is to check **hostel message boards.**

With the exception of the Kalgoorlie and Perth stops on the *Indian Pacific* line, passenger **rail** service is essentially non-existent. **South West Coach Lines, Westrail,** and **EasyRider** operate **bus services** south of Perth and Kalgoorlie. **Greyhound Pioneer** (☎13 20 30) is the only bus company that runs north of Exmouth. The seasonal Greyhound timetable book is indispensable. Try to book at least a day ahead; space may be limited and the bus might not even stop unless the driver knows you're waiting. If you plan on a lot of bus travel, Greyhound has cheaper passes. For more information see **By Bus,** p. 65.

Portions of Western Australia can be toured by **bicycle,** but you must carry significant amounts of water. In northern WA, it's not advisable to bike in the hotter, wetter months. Advise regional police and the **Royal Flying Doctor Service** of your itinerary. The **Ministry of Sport and Recreation** (☎9387 9700) has more info.

A bewildering range of guided group **tours** are available around Perth and throughout the state. Tourist officials, travel agents, and hostel managers can help narrow the options. Standard prices for four- to five-day tours through the Southwest are around $450. This sum will also get you to Monkey Mia, Kalbarri, and the Pinnacles. Longer and pricier tours are also available.

PERTH ☎08

Western Australia has been informally called the land of "no worries"—rumor has it that WA spurns daylight savings time so that folks can fit in a quick surf before work. This mellow attitude culminates in Perth, the state's capital. Set in a landscape of green hills and quite farming communities, Perth serves as the west coast's only metropolis. Perth carries the weight of being the world's most isolated capital city (Adelaide is at least two days away by car), but isolation does not mean desolation. Perth is home to 88% of the state's population, and continues to grow steadily. This development is easy to understand given the clean air, accessible beaches, gorgeous sunsets, and mild climate. However, there are those who miss the slower pace of the city's past, and these folks look to Fremantle to provide a link to the way life used to be. Fondly referred to as "Freo," money has been poured into historic, restorative face-lifts rather than skyline highrises. Whether in the city's center or traveling through its outskirts, pride carried by happy souls will open you to a lifestyle for which Perth is famous.

INTERCITY TRANSPORTATION

BY PLANE. Flights arrive at and depart from **Perth Airport,** east of the city. The international terminal is 8km away from the domestic terminals; keep this in mind if you're planning a connection. **Qantas** (☎13 13 13) and **Ansett** (☎13 13 00) fly daily to: Adelaide (2¾hr., $468-661); Darwin (3½hr., $534-759); Melbourne (3¼hr., $518-734); Sydney (4hr., $579-819); Cairns (indirect, $567-806). Qantas flies to Brisbane daily (4½hr., $596-847), and Ansett flies there twice a week. For trips within the state, try Ansett, Qantas, or regional carrier **SkyWest.** The **Qantaslink** network offers direct flights between Perth, Broome, Kalgoorlie, Karratha, and Port Hedland.

There are many transport options between the city and airport. **TransPerth buses** #200, 201, 202, 208, and 209 run between the domestic terminals and St. Georges Tce. in the city center (35min.; every 30-50min.; $3, concessions $1). The bus from Perth to the airport leaves from the north side of St. George Tce., stop 39. An **Airport City Shuttle** (☎9479 4131) runs frequently to a number of stops in Perth from both the domestic ($9) and international ($11) terminals, and also picks up travelers from accommodations. The **Fremantle Airport Shuttle** goes to both Perth Airport terminals, departing daily from the Fremantle Railway Station regularly until midnight; pickup at Fremantle accommodations is available 24hr. when booked in advance. (☎9383 4115. $15.) A **taxi** from the airport to the city center costs around $18-21 from domestic terminals and $25-30 from the international terminal.

BY TRAIN. Intercity trains run from the **East Perth Terminal,** off Lord St. on Summer St., a 25min. walk northeast from the Perth tourist center. TransPerth trains transport between the station and the city center every 15min. on weekdays and every 30min. on weekends. **Westrail** (☎13 10 53; www.westrail.wa.gov.au) has service to Bunbury (2hr., 2 per day, $20) and Kalgoorlie (8hr., 1-2 per day, $54) via Midland. The **Indian Pacific** runs to Sydney (65hr.,$459).

BY BUS. **Westrail** (☎13 10 53) runs buses from the East Perth Terminal. The more expensive **Greyhound** departs from Perth Station in the city center. (☎13 20 30. VIP/YHA 10% discount, students 20%.) **Southwest Coach Lines** (☎9324 2333) departs from the Perth City Bus Port, Mounts Bay Rd. See the Table on p. 612.

BY CAR. There are several cheap **car rental** agencies in town, but beware: those rock-bottom rate quotes have 100km limits, and many agencies won't allow their cars to go up north. **Bayswater,** 160 Adelaide Tce. (☎9325 1000), or 13 Queen Victoria Ave., Fremantle (☎9430 5300), rents to drivers age 20 and up and allows north-bound trips. **Cottesloe Car and Ute Hire,** 2 Servetus St., Swanbourne (☎9383 3057), rents to drivers 21 and up but does not allows its cars to go north. **Atlas Rent-a-Car,** 36 Miligan St. (☎9481 8866 or 1800 659 999), sometimes has backpacker specials. Although costs will vary depending on distances and vehicle, rates in the city are reasonable: between $30 and $40 per day ($20 off-season); weekly rates are cheaper. An $8-13 per day surcharge generally applies to drivers under 25. It will cost $45-60 per day to head north with unlimited mileage, and unsealed roads may be off limits without a bigger, more expensive set of wheels. 4WD vehicles generally start at $70 per day, with $20 extra for unlimited miles and, in most cases, 25+ age restrictions. **ATC,** 145-151 Adelaide Tce. (☎1800 999 888), and **Action Hire Cars,** 343 Great Eastern Hwy. (☎1800 627 688), rent 4WD. The **Travellers' Club,** 499 Wellington St. (☎9226 0660), across from the train station, helps backpackers with rentals. Many hostels have deals with local companies for lower rates. The **Royal Auto Club,** 228 Adelaide Tce. (☎9421 4400), offers roadside assistance (☎13 11 11) to members of RAC or several automobile associations from other countries.

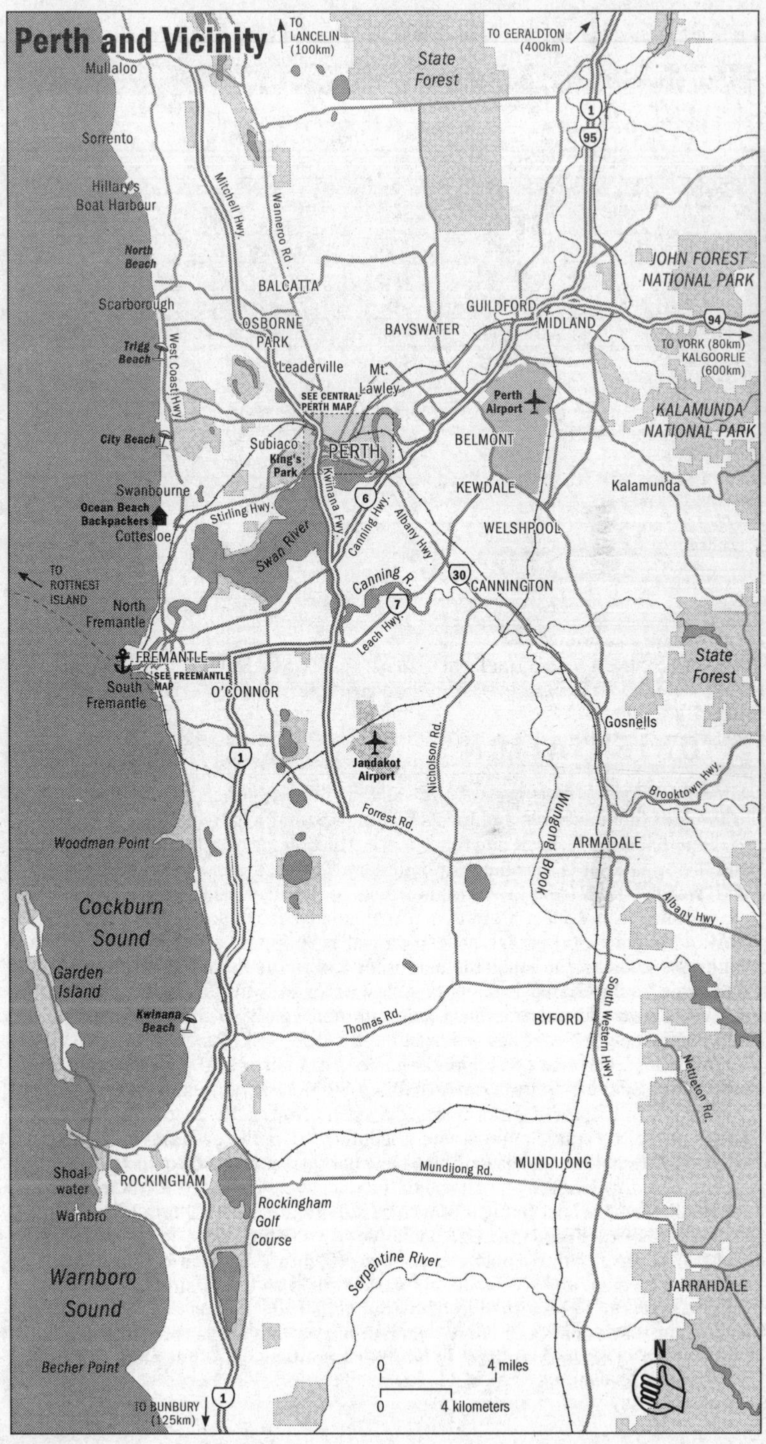
Perth and Vicinity
TO LANCELIN (100km)
TO GERALDTON (400km)
State Forest
Mullaloo
Sorrento
Hillary's Boat Harbour
North Beach
Scarborough
Trigg Beach
City Beach
Swanbourne
Ocean Beach Backpackers
Cottesloe
TO ROTTNEST ISLAND
North Fremantle
FREMANTLE
SEE FREMANTLE MAP
South Fremantle
Mitchell Hwy.
Wanneroo Rd.
BALCATTA
OSBORNE PARK
Leaderville
Mt. Lawley
SEE CENTRAL PERTH MAP
West Coast Hwy.
Subiaco
King's Park
PERTH
Stirling Hwy.
Swan River
Kwinana Fwy.
Canning Hwy.
Albany Hwy.
Canning R.
Leach Hwy.
O'CONNOR
BAYSWATER
GUILDFORD
MIDLAND
Perth Airport
BELMONT
KEWDALE
WELSHPOOL
CANNINGTON
JOHN FOREST NATIONAL PARK
TO YORK (80km)
KALGOORLIE (600km)
KALAMUNDA NATIONAL PARK
Kalamunda
State Forest
Gosnells
Jandakot Airport
Nicholson Rd.
Forrest Rd.
Wungong Brook
Brookton Hwy.
ARMADALE
Albany Hwy.
Woodman Point
Cockburn Sound
Garden Island
Kwinana Beach
Thomas Rd.
BYFORD
South Western Hwy.
Nettleton Rd.
MUNDIJONG
Mundijong Rd.
Shoalwater
ROCKINGHAM
Warnbro
Rockingham Golf Course
Serpentine River
Warnboro Sound
JARRAHDALE
Becher Point
TO BUNBURY (125km)
0 4 miles
0 4 kilometers
N
1
95
94
6
30
7
1
1

BUSES AND TRAINS FROM PERTH TO:

DESTINATION	COMPANY	DURATION	TIMES	PRICE
Adelaide	Greyhound	36hr.	M-W, F, Su 6:30am	$226
Albany (via Bunbury)	Westrail	6-8hr.	1-2 per day	$38
Albany (via Mt. Barker)	Westrail	6hr.	1-2 per day	$38
Augusta	Southwest	5-5½hr.	2 per day	$30
Broome	Greyhound	32hr.	1 per day (F, Su 2)	$266
Bunbury	Southwest	2½hr.	3 per day	$17
Busselton	Southwest	4hr.	3 per day	$21.50
Carnarvon	Greyhound	12hr.	1 per day (W, F, Su 3)	$103
Darwin	Greyhound	56hr.	1 per day	$496
Dunsborough	Southwest	4½hr	1 per day	$24
Esperance	Westrail	10hr.	Su-F 2 per day	$58
Exmouth	Greyhound	16½hr.	1 per day	$200
Geraldton	Greyhound Westrail	6hr. 6-8hr.	1 per day (W, F, Su 3) 1-2 per day	$37 $40
Kalbarri	Greyhound Westrail	8hr. 8hr.	1 per day (W, F, Su 2) M,W,F 8:30am	$76 $49
Kalgoorlie	Greyhound Westrail	8hr. 8hr.	M-W, F, Su M,W,F	$101 $54
Margaret River	Southwest	4½hr.	2 per day	$25
Monkey Mia	Greyhound	12-14hr.	1 per day (W, F, Su 3)	$134
Pemberton (via Bunbury)	Westrail	5½hr.	1-2 per day Su-F	$34
Port Hedland	Greyhound	24hr.	1-2 per day	$186
York	Westrail	1½hr.	1-2 per day Su-F	$10

ORIENTATION

Although Perth's streets are not quite aligned north-south and east-west, it helps to think of them as such, and locals will understand what you mean if you refer to them that way. The rail line functions as the boundary to the north of the city, and the **Swan River** is the southern boundary. The east-west avenues run parallel with **Wellington St.** from the railroad tracks to the river. The north-south streets run parallel with **William St.** Between William and Barrack St., east-west streets Hay and Murray St. become **pedestrian malls.** Shopping arcades and overhead walkways connect the malls to each other and to the **Perth Railway Station.** The **Wellington St. Bus Station** is one block west of the railway station, across William St. Downtown Perth is relatively safe, but not well-lit. **It's probably best not to walk alone at night.**

Northbridge, the city's cosmopolitan nexus of culture and nightlife, is a 2min. walk north of Perth Station down William St. Most activity and budget accommodation are clustered in a square formed by Newcastle St. on the north and James St. on the south, and between Beaufort St. on the east and Russel Sq. on the west. Great, green **Kings Park** rises just southwest of downtown, overlooking the city and the Swan River. Although technically its own city and 30min. away, **Fremantle (Freo)** is best thought of as a part of greater Perth. Perth is the central business district, Freo is the laid-back, lucrative fishing port. TransPerth buses and trains run regularly between the two (30min.). **Subiaco** is a hot spot for cafes and cuisine, and has weekend market stalls on either side of the Subiaco train stop on the Fremantle line. The Fremantle train also passes through **Swanbourne** and **Cottesloe,** both lively beach suburbs. **Leederville,** one stop north of Perth on the Currambine line, is another popular area, with plenty of pubs, cafes, and funky shops.

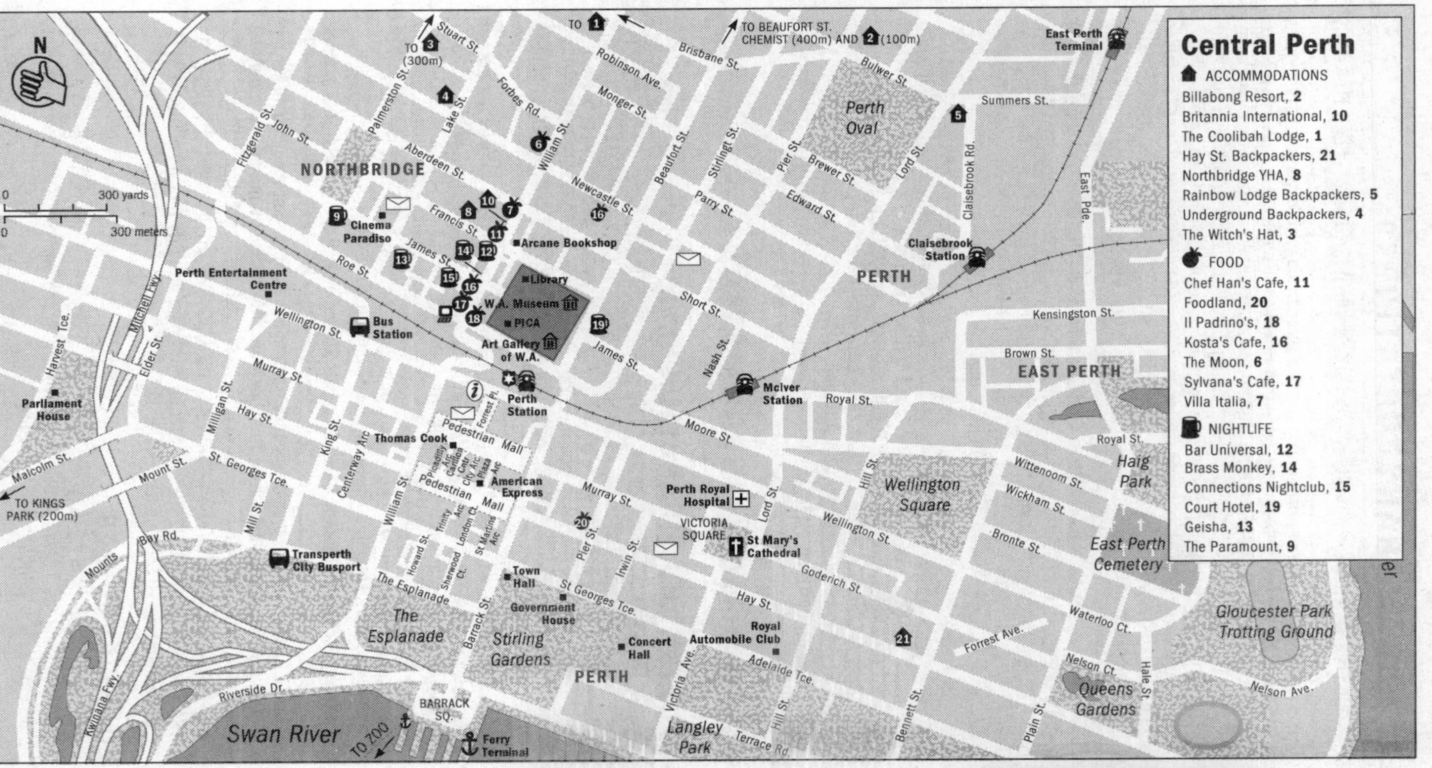
Central Perth
ACCOMMODATIONS
Billabong Resort, 2
Britannia International, 10
The Coolibah Lodge, 1
Hay St. Backpackers, 21
Northbridge YHA, 8
Rainbow Lodge Backpackers, 5
Underground Backpackers, 4
The Witch's Hat, 3
FOOD
Chef Han's Cafe, 11
Foodland, 20
Il Padrino's, 18
Kosta's Cafe, 16
The Moon, 6
Sylvana's Cafe, 17
Villa Italia, 7
NIGHTLIFE
Bar Universal, 12
Brass Monkey, 14
Connections Nightclub, 15
Court Hotel, 19
Geisha, 13
The Paramount, 9
N
0
300 yards
0
300 meters
TO 3 (300m)
TO 1
TO BEAUFORT ST. CHEMIST (400m) AND 2 (100m)
TO KINGS PARK (200m)
TO ZOO
East Perth Terminal
Claisebrook Station
McIver Station
Perth Station
Bus Station
Transperth City Busport
Ferry Terminal
NORTHBRIDGE
PERTH
EAST PERTH
PERTH
Perth Oval
Wellington Square
Haig Park
East Perth Cemetery
Gloucester Park Trotting Ground
Queens Gardens
Langley Park
Stirling Gardens
The Esplanade
Swan River
BARRACK SQ.
VICTORIA SQUARE
Perth Royal Hospital
St Mary's Cathedral
Royal Automobile Club
Concert Hall
Government House
Town Hall
American Express
Thomas Cook
Library
W.A. Museum
PICA
Art Gallery of W.A.
Arcane Bookshop
Cinema Paradiso
Perth Entertainment Centre
Parliament House
Stuart St.
Robinson Ave.
Brisbane St.
Bulwer St.
Summers St.
Palmerston St.
Lake St.
Forbes Rd.
Monger St.
John St.
Fitzgerald St.
William St.
Beaufort St.
Stirlingt St.
Pier St.
Brewer St.
Lord St.
Claisebrook Rd.
East Pde.
Aberdeen St.
Newcastle St.
Parry St.
Edward St.
Francis St.
James St.
Roe St.
Short St.
Kensington St.
Brown St.
Nash St.
James St.
Wellington St.
Mitchell Fwy.
Harvest Tce.
Elder St.
Murray St.
Milligan St.
Hay St.
Forrest Pl.
Pedestrian Mall
Royal St.
Moore St.
Royal St.
King St.
Centerway Arc.
Piccadilly Arc.
Carillon Arc.
City Arc.
Plaza Arc.
Pedestrian Mall
Malcolm St.
Mount St.
St. Georges Tce.
William St.
Hill St.
Witteenoom St.
Wickham St.
Murray St.
Lord St.
Wellington St.
Mill St.
Trinity Arc.
London Ct.
St Martins Arc.
Howard St.
Sherwood Ct.
Pier St.
Irwin St.
Bronte St.
Bay Rd.
Mounts
The Esplanade
Barrack St.
St Georges Tce.
Goderich St.
Hay St.
Waterloo Ct.
Forrest Ave.
Adelaide Tce.
Victoria Ave.
Nelson Ct.
Hale St.
Nelson Ave.
Kwinana Fwy.
Riverside Dr.
Hill St.
Bennett St.
Plain St.
Terrace Rd.

LOCAL TRANSPORTATION

Like all cities of a million plus people, Perth takes up quite a bit of space. However, the downtown area is compact and easy to navigate on foot. Most sights are within walking distance of one another, and the **CAT bus service** whisks passengers around downtown for free. The **blue** CAT runs in a north-south loop from the Swan River to Northbridge, and the **red** CAT runs east-west from West Perth to East Perth. (☎13 62 13. Blue CAT: every 5-15min.; M-Th 7am-6pm, F-Sa until 1am; Su 10am-5pm. Red CAT: every 5min.; M-Th 7am-6pm; F-Sa, hourly 10am-6pm.)

The **TransPerth** network of **buses, trains,** and **ferries** is divided into eight **fare zones** connecting to outlying areas; a two-zone ride costs $2.70 and will get you from the city center to the airport or Fremantle. Save your **ticket stub**—it can be used to transfer between bus, train, and ferry services. Tickets for up to four zones are valid for 1½hr. **All-day passes** and **multi-ride cards** are available at TransPerth InfoCentre machines and newsagents and can save you up to 25% (unlimited usage day pass $7). Additional info, as well as maps and timetables for bus and rail service, is available by phone (☎13 62 13) or at all four TransPerth InfoCentres: Plaza Arcade, Wellington St. Bus Station, City Busport, and the train station.

It's also easy to get around by taxi; a **taxi** ride between the international airport terminal and Northbridge costs between $25 and $30. Swan Taxi, 1008 Wellington St. (☎13 13 30), or Black and White Taxi (☎13 13 88) can be hailed around the city, especially along Wellington St. or William St., but it's best to call. **Bikes** are also a good option. The tourist office has free maps of bike routes. The **Bicycle Transportation Alliance,** 2 Delhi St. (☎9420 7210), also has info, maps, and advice on bike routes. Bikes can be rented from Kings Park or at stands around the city.

PRACTICAL INFORMATION

TOURIST AND FINANCIAL SERVICES

Tourist Offices: Perth Visitors Centre, on the corner of Wellington and Forrest Pl. (☎1300 36 13 51; fax 9481 0190), has free bus and tour booking. Open M-Th 8:30am-6pm, F 8:30am-7pm, Sa 8:30am-5pm, Su 10am-5pm; off-season M-Th 8:30am-5:30pm, F 8:30am-6pm, Sa 8:30am-4:30pm, Su 10am-3pm. **Fremantle Tourist Bureau** (☎9431 7878), on the corner of High St. and William St., Kings Sq. Open M-F 9am-5pm, Sa 9am-4pm, Su noon-5pm.

Budget Travel: Travel agencies hawk tours and airfares for backpackers on every block of the city center. **YHA Western Australia,** 236 William St., Northbridge (☎9227 5122; www.yha.com.au), arranges travel with YHA discounts. Membership info available (international travelers $32). **STA Travel,** 100 James St. (☎9227 7569), Northbridge. Open M-W, F 9am-5pm, Th 9am-6pm, Sa 10am-3pm. Another branch at 53 Market St. (☎9430 5553), Fremantle. Open M-F 9am-5pm, Sa 10am-3pm, Su 11am-3:30pm.

Currency Exchange: Thomas Cook, Piccadilly Arcade on Hay St. (☎9481 7900). Open M-F 8:45am-4:45pm, Sa 10am-2pm. **American Express,** 645 Hay St. Mall (☎9221 0777), London Court. Foreign exchange open M-F 9am-5pm, Sa 9am-noon. **ATMs** and banks are everywhere, especially on William St. in Northbridge and on Hay St. in the mall area between Barrack and William St. Most machines accept Cirrus/Plus.

Embassies and Consulates: Britain, 77 St. Georges Tce. (☎9221 5400); **Canada,** 267 St. Georges Tce. (☎9322 7930); **Ireland,** 10 Lilika Rd., City Beach (☎9385 8247); **United States,** 16 St. Georges Tce. (☎9231 9400).

LOCAL SERVICES

Outdoors Information Centers: CALM (☎9334 0333) has a customer service center at 17 Dick Perry Ave., near the corner of Hayman Rd. and Kent St., Kensington. Take bus 33 east to stop 19. Open M-F 8am-5pm.

Employment Agencies: Perth is a great place to find temporary work in WA. **Workstay,** 158 Williams St., 1st floor (☎9226 0970), at Wellington St., is a new employment service for working travelers. Membership $15 per year. Open M-F 10am-4pm.

Public Markets: Subiaco has markets at the Pavilion at the corner of Rokeby and Roberts Rd. on Th-F 10am-9pm, Sa-Su 10am-5pm; **Fremantle** has markets at 84 South Tce. F 9am-9pm, Sa 9am-5pm, Su 10am-5pm.

Library: The Alexander Library Building (☎9427 3111), at the north end of the Perth Cultural Centre. **Internet** for research only. Open M-Th 9am-9:45pm, F 9am-5:30pm, Sa-Su 10am-5:30pm. Wheelchair accessible.

Ticket Agencies: For sporting events, try **Ticketmaster** (☎13 61 00; www.ticketmaster7.com), Perth Entertainment Centre, at Wellington St. and Miligan St., and in the underground at 713 Hay St. Mall. Open M-F 9am-5:30pm, Sa 9am-1pm. For theatrical and musical events, reach **Bocs Tickets,** Perth Concert Hall, 5 St. George's Tce. (☎9484 1133; fax 9221 2241). Open M-F 8:30am-5:30pm.

MEDIA AND PUBLICATIONS

Newspapers: *The West Australian* (88¢).

Nightlife: *XPress* and the mainstream *Hype* come out weekly (free). For gay nightlife, try the weekly *Shout* (free). *WOW* is a lesbian monthly ($3.85).

Radio: Rock, 96FM and 92.9FM; News, ABC 720AM; Tourist Info, 88FM.

EMERGENCY AND COMMUNICATIONS

Emergency: ☎000.

Police: ☎9222 1111; Fremantle: ☎9430 1222.

Hotlines: Sexual Assault (24hr. ☎1800 199 888). **Crisis Line** (☎1800 199 008). **AIDS/STD Line** (☎9429 9944). **Sea, Search, and Rescue Line** (maritime ☎1800 641 792, aviation ☎1800 815 257).

Late Night Pharmacy: 24hr. Chemist, 647 Beaufort St., Mt. Lawley (☎9328 7775).

Hospital: Royal Perth Hospital (☎9224 2244), on Wellington St. near Lord St. **Northbridge Medical Centre,** 252a William St. (9227 1199). **Fremantle Hospital,** on the corner of South Tce. and Alma St. (☎9431 3333).

Internet Access: Student Uni Travel, 513 Wellington St. (☎9321 8330), offers 15-20min. free. Open M-F 8am-6pm, Sa 11am-3pm. The going rate for the 'net in Northbridge is $3 per hr. Fast connections include: **Internet Go Go,** 150 William St., Northbridge (☎9226 3282). $3 per hr. **net.CHAT,** shop 14, Wesley Way Arcade, Market St., Freo (☎9433 2011). 10¢ per min, $4 per hr. Open daily 8-11am and 9-11pm.

Post Office: General Post Office (GPO), 3 Forrest Pl. (☎9237 5460). Poste Restante pickup M-F only. Open M-F 8am-5:30pm, Sa 9am-12:30pm, Su noon-4pm. **Fremantle GPO,** 13 Market St. (☎9335 1611). Open M-F 8:30am-5pm. **Postal Code:** 6000.

ACCOMMODATIONS

There are an inordinate number of backpacker pads around Northbridge and the city center. If you are in town for more than a few weeks, check the classified section of the *West Australian* for listings of rooms and flats to lease; they can be cheaper than hostels. All hostels listed offer free luggage storage, on-site laundry facilities, and kitchens. There are no lock-out times, but it's a good idea to call ahead with your estimated time of arrival so someone will be there to greet you.

CITY PROPER

Ocean Beach Backpackers, 1 Eric St. (☎9384 5222), at Marine Pde., Cottesloe. Take the Fremantle train to Grant St., head south to Eric St., and turn right to hit the beach. Bright, new ocean-front complex has dorms with bath and bikes for hire, surfboards, even 4WD. Dorms $19, Apr.-Oct. $17; singles $45; doubles $55.

The Coolibah Lodge, 194 Brisbane St., Northbridge (☎9328 9958; fax 9227 6231). A maze of lounges, dorms, and kitchens in a remodeled colonial home. The bathrooms get a bit cramped, but otherwise it's a great spot. Free pickup. Internet $2 per 20min. Dorms $17.50; singles $30; doubles $46-48. VIP.

The Witch's Hat, 148 Palmerston St., Northbridge (☎9228 4228; fax 9228 4229; witchs_hat@hotmail.com). This beautiful pointed building has hardwood floors, leather couches, free tea and coffee, and an adorable dog. Internet $4 per hr. Dorms $19; singles $45; twins and doubles $49. VIP.

Underground Backpackers, 268 Newcastle St. (☎9228 3755; fax 9228 3744). Huge dorms with big windows and high ceilings. Bar, pool, and brick basement lounge area just a few steps from the best of the city's nightlife. Internet $5 per hr. Dorms $18; singles, twins, doubles $55. NOMADS.

Britannia International, 253 William St., Northbridge (☎9328 6121; fax 9227 9784; britannia@yhawa.com.au). Between Aberdeen and Francis St. A massive place with nice rooms and dining space located "right in the heart of it." Internet $4 per hr. No smoking. Reception 24hr. Dorms $19; singles $27; doubles $52. YHA.

Northbridge YHA, 46 Francis St., Northbridge (☎/fax 9328 7794). Fun crowd livens up basic rooms. Beware, sappy pop tunes seep out of the intercom. Internet $4 per hr. Reception 7am-10pm. Dorms $17, weekly $102; twins, doubles, and triples $48. YHA.

Hay St. Backpackers, 266-268 Hay St., East Perth (☎9221 9880). Clean and freshly painted rooms with heat and A/C are nice, but far from the bustle of Northbridge; often attractive to working travelers. Two kitchens, pool table, and small swimming pool. Internet $4 per hr. Dorms $15-18, weekly $84-98; doubles $40-45, with bath $50.

Rainbow Lodge Backpackers, 133 Summers St., Northbridge (☎9227 1818; www.rainbowlodge.com.au). East of the Perth Oval, cross Lord St. to Summers St., 3min. from the East Perth Terminal. Take the free train from Perth Station to Claisebrook Station and walk up Claisebrook Rd. Caters to working travelers. Colorful and social. Kitchens, Internet, free in-line skates, bicycles, fishing rods, and didgeridoos. Free pickup. Dorms $15, weekly $90; singles $25/$150; twins $21 per person/$126. ISIC/VIP/YHA.

Billabong Resort Backpackers, 381 Beaufort St. (☎9328 7720). The newest, swankiest NOMADS megaplex. An old college dormitory renovated into a state-of-the-art, 220-bed hostel with gym, game room, library, and pool. Internet $4 per hr. Dorms with bath $18; twins with fridge and TV $69; large group accommodation available.

FREMANTLE

YHA Backpackers Inn Freo, 11 Pakenham St. (☎9431 7065; fax 9336 7106). From the train station, turn right onto Phillimore St., then left onto Pakenham. The renovated warehouse space is beautiful. Relaxed atmosphere and normally quiet. Reception 7am-11:30pm; 24hr. check-in available. Dorms $16; singles $25; doubles $49. YHA.

Cheviot Marina Backpackers, 4 Beach St. (☎9344 2055; fax 9433 2066). Turn left down Elder St. from train station (becomes Beach St.). A big, sunny place offers a beautiful lounge upstairs and discounted drinks at the bar next door. Internet $1 per 20min. Dorms $12; singles $32; twins and doubles $40. Peak season, $10 more. VIP/YHA.

Old Firestation Backpackers, 18 Phillimore St. (☎9430 5454; fax 9335 6828), at Henry St. Turn right from the train station. Easy-going management. The rooms are basic, but where else can you try an original firepole? Free Internet and washing machines. Dorms $16.50; twins and doubles $44.

FOOD

The multicultural cornucopia of Northbridge delivers a spicy selection of seafood noodle soups and garlicky pasta specials. To craft your own culinary masterpiece, grab meats and produce at **City Fresh Fruit Company,** 375 William St. (open M-Sa 7am-8pm, Su 7am-7pm), or hike to the more-comprehensive **Food-**

land, 556 Hay St. (open M-Th 8am-6:30pm, F 8am-8pm, Sa 9am-6pm, Su 10:30am-6pm). For cheap, quality, imported bulk pasta, cereals, and deli foods, you can elbow your way through the crowds into **Kakulas Brothers Wholesale Importers,** 185 William St. (Open M-F 8am-5:30pm, Sa 8am-5pm.) In Fremantle, **Kakulas Sister** emulates her Perthite sibs on the corner of Market and Leake St. (open M-F 9am-5:30pm, Sa 9am-2pm), and **Coles,** corner of Cantonment and Queen St., meets basic grocery needs (open M-W, F 8am-7pm, Th 8am-9pm, Sa 8am-5pm, Su noon-6pm).

A number of pubs and clubs cater specifically to the backpacker set (vegetarian-friendly), enlivening the crowds with free meals and drink specials. The determined can find free food almost every night. M: **The Deen,** 84 Aberdeen St. (☎9227 9361); Tu and Th: **hip-e-club** (☎9227 8899), on Newcastle and Oxford St. in Leederville; W: **The Post Office,** (☎9228 0077), on Aberdeen and Parker St.

CITY PROPER

Chef Han's Cafe (☎9328 8122), on the corner of Francis and William St. With a few locations in central Perth, Chef Han is the emperor of local budget cuisine. Delicious, fast heaps of vegetarian-friendly noodle and stir-fry for $6-8. Open daily 11am-10pm.

Il Padrino, 198 William St. (☎9227 9065). Known for the best pizza in Perth. Dinner Tu half-price pizza and $7.50 pasta. Open Tu-F 11am-late, Sa-Su 5pm-late.

The Moon, 323 William St. (☎9328 7474). The young, black-clad, and trend-setting pour into this glistening, space-age diner. Pasta, seafood $11-15; several veggie options. Open daily 5pm-late.

Villa Italia, 279 William St. (☎9227 9030). The best of the area's numerous Italian restaurants, with a casual atmosphere and flamenco music in the air. Pasta dishes $12-16 and great dessert. Open M-F 7am-late, Sa 8am-late, Su 5pm-late.

Sylvana's Cafe, 297 William St. (☎9328 6691). A small den with cheap, satisfying Lebanese food. Vegetarian plates $5, omelette with salad $4.50, pastries $1-2. Open Su-Th noon-10:30pm, F-Sa noon-midnight.

Kosta's Cafe, 67 James St. (☎9328 4779). Family-run, neighborhood-oriented joint in the heart of Northbridge. Southern European regulars feast on lasagne ($11), foccacia ($6.50), and sandwiches ($4-5.50) on the sidewalk outside. Open Su-F 6:30am-5:30pm, Sa 6:30am-4pm.

FREMANTLE

Cicerello's, 44 Mews Rd. (☎9335 1991). One of Western Australia's classic fish'n'chips joints. Greasy, succulent goodness of well-fried seafood ($5-10). Eat on the docks out back for the full harborside experience. Open daily 10am-8:30pm.

Hara Cafe, 33 High St. (☎9335 6118). Good, cheap vegetarian meals. Thalis $6-9, teas $3.50 a pot. Open M-Tu 11am-4pm, W-F 11am-9pm, Sa-Su noon-9pm.

Fiorelli, 19C Essex St. (☎9430 6119). Tasty Italian restaurant with all-you-can-eat pizza/pasta special Tu and W nights for $10.90. Open daily noon-late.

SIGHTS

CITY PROPER

THE ART GALLERY OF WESTERN AUSTRALIA. Sharing the **Cultural Centre** complex with the **Alexander Library,** the **Perth Institute of the Contemporary Arts (PICA),** and the **Western Australian Museum,** the art gallery has several collections of Australian and international art, including some beautiful Aboriginal carvings and paintings. Exhibits in 2002 feature Aboriginal art (May 2-July 21) and the works of Max Ernst from April 13-June 9. *(North of the railway station between William St. and Beaufort St. Open daily 10am-5pm. Free guided tours Tu-F, Su 1pm, F 12:30pm, Su 10:30am. Free, except for special exhibitions.)*

PERTH INSTITUTE OF THE CONTEMPORARY ARTS (PICA). PICA shows contemporary and student art and hosts evening performances. Pick up a booklet of events or call for current happenings. *(☎9227 6144. Open Tu-Su 11am-8pm. Gallery free, but performance prices vary.)*

THE WESTERN AUSTRALIAN MUSEUM. The museum has exhibits on WA's natural history and culture. The Discovery Center has drawers of shells, jewelry, bugs, old shoes, and anything and everything else. Don't miss the blue whale skeleton, Aboriginal exhibit, or butterfly gallery. *(☎9427 2700. Open daily 9:30am-5pm. Free.)*

PERTH ZOO. The zoo houses native and exotic fauna and conducts endangered species breeding programs. The Australian section has frilled lizards, crocodiles, and wallabies, while the African Savannah has lions, meerkats, and rhinos. If you can avoid all the strollers it's a pretty good time. *(On Labouchere Rd. in South Perth. Take the blue CAT to stop #19 and then ferry across the river (ferry $1.10). ☎9367 7988. Open daily 9am-5pm. $13.20, children $6.60, under 4 free.)*

AQUARIUM OF WESTERN AUSTRALIA. Leafy sea dragons, saltwater crocodiles, and four kinds of sharks make AQWA their home. Walk through a tunnel surrounded by fish and feed animals in a pool. Adults can book ahead to dive with the sharks for $85, or swim with the seals for $75. *(North of Perth along the West Coast Hwy. at Hillary's Harbour, off the Hepburn Ave. exit. Take the Joondalup train to Warwick, then the #423 bus to Hillary's. $3. ☎9447 7500. Open daily 9am-5pm, Nov.-Apr. W 9am-9pm. $19, concessions $15, children $9, under 3 free.)*

KINGS PARK. A welcome retreat just outside the city center, the 400 hectares of King's Park are criss-crossed with foot and bike paths and, in spring, covered with wildflowers. Perched atop **Mt. Eliza,** the park offers a great view of the Swan River and the city below. Within the park, the **Botanic Gardens,** next to the **War Memorial,** are home to 1700 native species; free walks depart from the karri log opposite the memorial. There is an info center near the karri log and a restaurant on Fraser Ave. *(20min. walk by foot west from the city center up St. George's Tce. Bear left as St. George's Tce. becomes Malcom St. and head to the roundabout at the north end of the park. Otherwise, take the free red CAT to stop #25. Free parking. Info center ☎9480 3600. Open daily 9am-4pm. Walking tours daily 10am; also W, Su 2pm July-Oct.)*

BEACHES. The Perth beach experience is calm and carefree, and numerous clusters of shops and cafes thrive on the patronage of those who track in sand from the ocean playground at their doorstep. Families flock to **Cottesloe Beach,** on the Fremantle train line, for swimming and mild surf, while the teenage boys wander just north to **Swanbourne Beach,** in order to ogle the nudists who occasionally sunbathe there. **City Beach** is a swimming spot with a long shore and good facilities. **Scarborough** has bigger surfing waves and crowds of 20-somethings that make for excellent people-watching. *(Take bus #400 from Wellington St. Station.)* Surfers rip through the tubes at **Trigg Beach,** just north of Scarborough; the waves here can get a bit rough for swimming.

ABOVE AND BEYOND THE CITY. A **river cruise** from Perth or Freo features local sights along the river and a view of the city skyline from the water. *(Captain Cook Cruises departs Pier 3, Barrack St. Jetty, daily 9:45am and 2pm; departs East St. Jetty, Fremantle, daily at 11am and 12:25pm. ☎9325 3341. $27, children under 14 $13, families $67.)* Rent catamarans and windsurfs on the south bank off Mill Point Rd., opposite the city center, to further enjoy Swan River. **Malibu City Dive** has diving tours to **Rottnest Island** (see p. 621), noted for its unique corals and fish, and also offers scuba certification classes. *(126 Barrack St. ☎9225 7555. Rottnest trips start at $135.)* **Planet Perth** has several tour options, including a night tour of a wildlife park with kangaroos, koalas, and Tasmanian devils. *(☎9342 2829. Tours start at $40.)* For **Pinnacles** tours (see **Nambung NP,** p. 642), the most popular options are **West Coast Explorer** *(☎9418 8835)*, **Redback Safaris** *(☎9275 6204)*, and **Travelabout Outback Adventures.** *(☎9244 1200. Tours from $90.)* **W.A. Skydiving Academy** offers tandem jumps. *(193 William St., Northbridge. ☎9227 6066 or 1800 245 066. From $215.)*

> **PRIDE GOETH BEFORE THE ESCAPE** Although its colonial keepers regarded Fremantle Prison as escape-proof, one man managed not only to escape but to dramatically embarrass British authorities in the process. John Boyle O'Reilly and six of his comrades were sentenced to imprisonment at Fremantle for their role in the 1868 Fenian uprising in Ireland. O'Reilly broke out of the prison and hitched a ride to North America aboard a whaling ship. He moved to Boston, where the Irish-American community raised money for him to outfit a new ship, the *Catalpu.* O'Reilly then sailed for Australia to rescue his brethren. When British ships fired on the *Catalpu* off Fremantle, O'Reilly raised the American flag, reminding his attackers that they were in international waters, whereupon his aggressors grudgingly backed off. O'Reilly made his rendezvous with his fellow Fenians and returned to Boston.

FREMANTLE

FREMANTLE PRISON. Get a thorough look at a maximum security prison without committing a felony. The prison was closed in 1991, three years after nearly burning down during a prisoner-incited riot. *(Along Hampton Rd., take Parry to Fairbairn St. ☎9430 7177. Tours every 30min., last tour 5pm. Spooky candlelight tours W and F; book ahead. Open daily 10am-6pm. $12, concession $10, children $4.80, families $28.80.)*

FREMANTLE MARKETS. One can find just about anything in the markets, from clothing to a massage. Fresh veggies abound; produce prices hit rock bottom around closing time on Sunday. *(On the corner of South Tce. and Henderson St. Open F 9am-9pm, Sa 9am-5pm, Su 10am-5pm.)*

MARITIME MUSEUM. The Western Australia Maritime Museum traces the history of Fremantle, port trading, and marine archaeology, with several pieces from area shipwrecks. The museum also runs tours of the *HMS Ovens*, a decommissioned Australian submarine. *(At the corner of Cliff St. and Marine Tce. ☎9431 8444. Open daily 10:30am-5pm. Tours M-F 11:30am and 2pm. Admission by donation, tours $9.)*

TOURS. The **Fremantle Trams** runs on several different routes through the city. *(Depart on the hour from in front of Town Hall on High St. $8, concessions $7, children $3.)* **Fremantle Ghost Walks** offers evening tours of the old asylum and the West End of town, both of which are reputed to be haunted. *(Old asylum tour departs from main gate at Finnerty St.; West End tour departs from Town Hall. ☎9336 1916. Asylum tour M 8pm, West End tour W 8pm. $15, concessions $12, children $10.)*

NIGHTLIFE

Perth has heaps of good pubs, clubs, and cafes, with laid-back, friendly crowds. The best of the budget scene is in Northbridge, but **Subiaco** swings with a ritzier, more-upscale scene. The free entertainment weeklies *XPress* and *Hype* dish the lowdown on what's happening, and can be picked up at news agents, record stores, and hostels. The website *perthtribe.com* is another resource for nightlife listings. Covers and dress codes are rare, but a few places will give you nasty looks if you're in jeans, and most places require closed-toed shoes.

Fast Eddy's Cafe is a cheap, cool 24hr. diner with locations in both Perth (454 Murray St; ☎9321 2552) and Fremantle (13 Essex St.). Perth is a reasonably **gay- and lesbian-friendly** city; for up-to-date event info, listen to *Sheer Queer*, a gay and lesbian radio program on 92.1FM (W 9-10am) or check out the free *Shout*, a gay and lesbian newspaper. The lesbian publication *WOW* comes out monthly ($3.85). The **Arcane Bookshop,** 212 William St., is immensely helpful and full of info and publications on Perth's gay scene. (☎9328 5073; www.arcbooks@highway1.com.au. Open M-W 10am-6pm, Th-Sa 10am-9pm, Su noon-5pm.)

NORTHBRIDGE AND CITY PROPER

The Grosvenor, 339 Hay St. (☎9325 3799). Perth's premier venue for original live music. Relaxing house music on W; live band Th until 11:15pm. Weekly local band contest F-Sa; live bands Su. Open daily for dinner, W-Sa until midnight, Su until 10pm.

The Brass Monkey (☎9227 9596), on the corner of James and William St, Northbridge. A big, fun place for drinking brews. It makes a good beginning or end to the Northbridge pub crawl. Pool tables downstairs; indoor courtyard; mellow upstairs with fireplace and balcony. Adjoined to suave wine bar. Open M-Sa 11am-midnight, Su noon-10pm.

Bar Universal, 221 William St., Northbridge (☎9227 9596). Classy dive with live jazz, *sake,* and a slightly older, more sophisticated crowd. Dress code. Open M-Tu 11:30am-midnight, W-Th 11:30am-1am, F 11:30am-2am, Sa 4pm-2am.

Connections Nightclub, 81 James St., Northbridge (☎9328 1870). A popular gay-owned club with DJ-spun dance, house, and techno beats. Theme nights like Hawaii night, and shows F and Su. Cover: M-Th $3, F-Sa $10, Su $5. Open Tu-W, F 10pm-6am, Sa 9pm-6am, Su 9pm-1am.

The Court Hotel, 50 Beaufort St., Northbridge (☎9328 5292), near the corner of James St. Check out the drag queens at the Dive Bar or seek out the off-the-wall theme nights like "bears' night"—for big hairy men and their fans. During summer, live bands play outside in the beer garden. Open M-Sa 11am-midnight, Su 3pm-10pm.

Metropolis Club (☎9228 0500). 2 locations at 146 Roe St., Perth and 58 South Tce., Fremantle. Glitzy, multi-level dance clubs. Cover $5 F after 11pm, Sa after 10pm. Open F 9pm-5am, Sa 9pm-6am. Freo location also open Th 9pm-6am.

Geisha, 135a James St. (☎9328 9808). Pulsates with underground and house, sometimes from celebrity guest DJs. Free passion pop Th. Open Th-Su 10pm-late.

Paramount, 163 James St. (☎9228 1344). Heavy on noise, smoke, and live music. Also has an outdoor bar. Dressy. Open F 6pm-6am, Sa 7pm-6am.

FREMANTLE

The Bog, 189 High St. (☎9336 7751). Away from the main scene of South Tce., but there's almost always something happening here. Free food, $6 jugs of beer, and $4 bourbons on Tu. Open M 6pm-4am, Tu-Sa 6pm-6am, Su 8pm-1am.

Sail and Anchor, 64 South Tce. (☎9335 8433). British pub with a wide variety of intoxicating poisons. Freo is the home of Redback beer; this is a good place to hoist one. Open M-Th 11am-midnight, F 11am-1am, Sa 11am-1am, Su 10am-10pm.

The Newport, 2 South Tce. (☎9335 2428). Pool room, an outdoor area, and a dark smoky area. Cover Su for local original music varies. Open M-Th 11am-midnight, F-Sa 11am-1am, Su noon-10pm.

NEAR PERTH

ROTTNEST ISLAND

Called a "rat's nest" by Dutch explorers who mistook the island's quokkas (wallabies) for giant rats, Rottnest Island is a hunk of limestone about 19km off the coast near Fremantle (30min. by ferry). The island was settled by farmers in 1830 but was turned into a prison for Aborigines in 1838. Today, the island is a class-A nature reserve, and tourists and locals flock there to cycle, swim, snorkel, surf, and relax. The quokkas, Rottnest's unofficial mascot, roam about the island unafraid of humans.

TRANSPORTATION. Several companies offer **ferry service** to Rottnest from Perth, Fremantle, and Hillary's Harbour. The cheapest is **Oceanic Cruises** (☎9325 1191), which departs from Pier 2 of the Barrack St. Jetty (daily 8:45 and 10am; $53, children $16) and from the East St. Jetty or B Shed on Victoria Quay, Fremantle (daily 9:45 and 11:45am; Fremantle $40 same-day return, children $13; extended-stay $5 more). They offer free pickup from Perth hotels and the Freo train station. **Rottnest Express** has several daily departures from Victoria Quay, Fremantle. (☎9335 6406. Same-day return $40, children $15; extended stay $5 more.) Both ferries offer $5 VIP/YHA discounts. Courtesy buses depart from the main jetty roughly every hour and head to the accommodations in Geordie Bay, Kingstown, and the airport. The **Bayseeker Bus** is a good way to get around the island (45min. loop around the island; every hr. 8:30am-4:30pm; day-ticket $5.50). The best way to see Rottnest is by bike—the island is only 11km by 4½km, though Rottnest's rolling hills can be tough to navigate. **Rottnest Island Bike Hire** has a wide selection, including bike buses for family groups. (☎9292 5105. 1-speed $15 per day; 18-speed $20. Locks and required helmets included; $25 deposit. Open daily 8am-5pm.)

PRACTICAL INFORMATION, ACCOMMODATIONS, AND FOOD. The **Visitors Information Centre** is 150m to the left of the jetty at Thomsons Bay. (☎9372 9752; fax 9372 9775. Open daily 8am-5pm.) To the right of the jetty is a pedestrian mall with an **ATM,** the **post office,** the general store, and the bakery. 400m north of the mall is the **nursing post.** (☎9292 5030. Open daily 8am-4:30pm.) The **YHA Kingstown Barracks Youth Hostel** is in Kingstown, a 20min. walk or a quick bike ride from the Visitors Centre. A free shuttle bus runs from the island every 30min. The hostel is inside an old army barracks with simple, spacious rooms. (☎9372 9780; fax 9292 5141. Reception 8am-5:30pm. Dorms $18; family rooms $42; non-YHA members $21/$49.) Though there are meals available in the barracks complex ($7), it's a good idea to bring food to the island. The Thomsons Bay settlement has a general store with **groceries** in the pedestrian mall north of the visitors center, but prices are considerably higher than on the mainland.

ACTIVITIES. Rottnest's beaches become emptier as you head away from the settled areas—go far enough and you may have the luxury of a cove all to yourself. **Narrow Neck** and **Salmon Bay** offer good **fishing,** and **The Basin, Pinky Beach,** and **Par-**

TOURS, TOURS, TOURS The best way to see Western Australia is to toss the eskie and camping gear in the back of the 4WD truck and go about conquering the bushlands, beaches, gorges, and reefs on your own. Unfortunately, many don't have sufficient time, patience, or material resources for such an excursion, and that's where adventure tours come into play. Booking agents on every street corner in Perth hawk excursions for as brief as one day and as long as one month to nearby towns as well as to the farthest reaches of the continent.

For those who just need wheels, **Easyrider Backpackers** offers lengthy tours allowing you to hop off the bus in a town and hop back on the next tour a few days later. (☎9226 0307. 5-day tour $329.) But for an all-inclusive experience, a mind-numbing selection of outfitters offer guided 4WD tours, mostly up north to Exmouth (5-6 days, $500-600) and Broome (8-10 days, $900-1100), or even to Alice Springs (6 days, $730). For cheaper tours with high adventure quotients, **West Coast Explorer** is highly recommended, and **Travelabout Outback Adventures** and **Adventure Tours Australia** are also popular. Whatever your preference, the important factors to consider in choosing a tour are the degree of physical exertion involved, the ritziness or rustic-ness of food and accommodation, and of course, whether the seats in the vehicle face forward or to the side–you don't want to spend the whole trek puking.

akeet are among the many good swimming spots close to the settlement. **Little Salmon Bay** and **Parker Point** have good snorkeling, and **Strickland Bay** has good surfing. Whales and dolphins are frequently seen from the windy cliffs at **West End.** Ask at the visitors center for a booklet of "snorkel trails" in the island's bays ($5.50). **Rottnest Malibu Dive** is the only dive shop on the island, offering tours and equipment rentals. (☎9292 5111. Snorkel gear $16.50; 1 dive $60, 2 dives $110.)

THE DARLING RANGE, YORK, AND THE AVON VALLEY

Heading east from Perth, the city's suburbs gradually give way to the gently rolling orchards and verdant forests of the **Darling Range** (also called **Perth Hills;** take the M1 train from Perth to Midland, then buses #317-320 or #327-330 from Midland Station). **John Forrest National Park,** just off the Great Eastern Hwy., offers miles of shaded hiking trails, a colorful **wildflower** season, and wildlife galore. **Wayunga National Park** is filled with walking trails, wallabies, and Aboriginal sites, and is known for its whitewater rafting. **Avon Valley National Park** is also in the area, with more trails and rivers for canoeing. (Each park has a $9 per day entrance fee.) For questions on the national parks, check with the Mundaring **CALM** office, 51 Mundaring-Weir Rd. (☎9295 1955. Open M-F 8am-5pm.) **Lake Leschenaultia** offers peaceful swimming, canoeing, BBQ, walking trails, and **camping.** (☎9572 4248. Gate open until anywhere from 4:30 to 9pm. Day entry $5 per car; book ahead.)

Undulating hills, misty dales, and wildflower fields make the **Avon Valley,** 100km east and somewhat north of Perth, and 35km from the Great Eastern Hwy., a great place for a drive. WA's first inland settlement, **York** is home to several restored historical buildings and makes a good lunch spot. Westrail **buses** leave for **Perth** from the railway station (2hr., 1 per day, $11). The **tourist bureau** is in the Town Hall on Avon Tce. (☎9641 1301; www.yorkwa.com.au. Open daily 9am-5pm.)

YALGORUP NATIONAL PARK

About 100km south of Perth is Yalgorup National Park, marked by a sign 500m before you reach the turn-off. If coming from the north, do not mistakenly turn at Yalgorup Eco Park or Yalgorup Park Rd., which come before the correct turn-off. There is an obvious sign for the National Park. The park, featuring sites, nature reserves, miles of dunes, and a forest of jarrah and tuart trees with peppermint undergrowth, is a popular summer weekend destination for Perth residents. Emus, grey kangaroos, and wallabies frolic here, and in the winter the beaches make for good bird-watching, when the speedboats aren't scaring off the wildlife.

SOUTHWEST

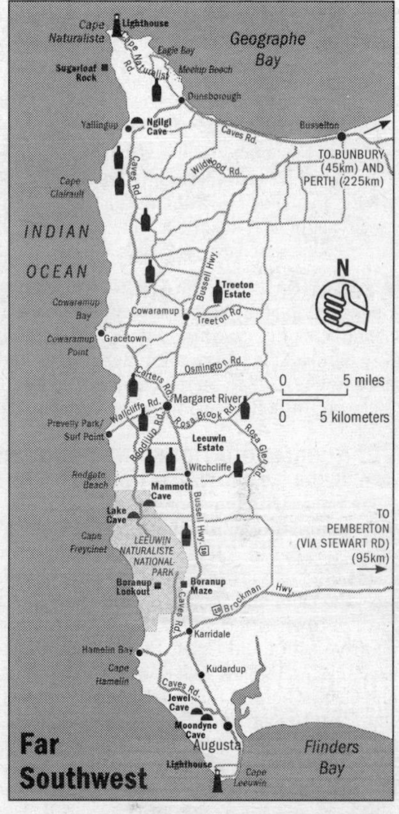

The Southwest coast of Australia is experiencing a boom in both tourism and year-round residency. It's not hard to understand why—Mother Nature has indeed been kind to the Southwest. Its spectacular scenery and abundant variety of wildflowers, make it a favorite for travelers. Hikers rave about the Stirling and Porongurup Ranges, and surfers swear by the Southwest's gorgeous beaches and pounding waves. Visitors can bushwalk in the region's karri and jarrah forests, and spot whales from the shore or from a tour boat in the winter. The climate is ideal for vineyards; it's worth a trip just to tour area wineries and try native vintages.

TRANSPORTATION

The easiest way to see the Southwest is by car; many sights are well off the bus routes, and public transportation in many of the towns is either nonexistent or inadequate. Once you get completely out of the city, the 3hr. drive south from Perth toward Margaret River takes you past shoreline, forests, farms, cattle stations, and the occasional limestone quarry. Several options exist for the autoless. Some travelers use the **Easy Rider Backpackers** bus. A 3-month pass ($200) covers bus service between most regional hostels. (☎9226 0307. Dec.-Feb., 6 per week; Sept.-Nov. and Mar.-May, 4 per week; June-Aug., 2 per week. 24hr. notice for pickup.) Another option is **Westrail's** (☎13 10 53) 28-day Southern Discovery Pass ($134). The pass allows for bus and train travel to most southern and eastern destinations including Albany, Esperance, and Kalgoorlie.

BUNBURY ☎08

Two hours (180km) south of Perth, Bunbury (pop. 28,000) revels in West Australia's obsession with dolphins. Over one hundred bottle-nosed sea critters swim and play just offshore, and visitors come here to frolic with them. Bunbury offers a calm and convenient base camp from which to tour the coast and nearby parks.

TRANSPORTATION. If heading south by train, Bunbury is 3km from Wollaston, the southern terminus of WA's **train** network. Transit buses will honor a train ticket stub for a free lift to Bunbury. **South West Coachlines,** in the Old Railway Station at Carmody and Haley St., (☎9791 1955; open daily 8am-7pm) runs to Perth (2½hr.; 3 times per day; $17.20, students $8.60) and Augusta via Busselton and Margaret River (2½ hr.; departs 6:20am daily, also 4:20pm on weekends; $28, students $14). Also run by South West Coachlines, **local transit** buses circle the city regularly. (M-F 7am-6pm, Sa 7am-1:15pm; $1.80, $2.70 for outlying areas.)

BIBBULMUN TRACK For the rugged and diehard hiker, the popular Bibbulmun Track goes from Kalamunda, outside Perth, to Albany, passing through North Bannister, Dwellingup, Collie, Balingup, Bridgetown, Manjimup, Pemberton, Northcliffe, Walpole, and Denmark along the way. If the whole 964km trek seems a bit daunting, it is easy to hike a smaller section, or even do short day hikes. The trail passes campsites, shelters with bunks, and nearby towns with hostels and B&Bs that will pick up hikers from the trail. Contact the **Bibbulmun Track Office** (☎9334 0265; fax 9334 0100; www.calm.wa.gov.au).

PRACTICAL INFORMATION. The old rail station at Carmody Pl. and Haley St. houses the **Bunbury Visitor Information Centre** (☎9721 7922; open M-Sa 9am-5pm, Su 9:30am-4:30pm), the bus station, and the **Bunbury Internet Cafe** (☎9791 1254; open M-Sa 8am-4:30pm; $4 per hour). Services include: several **banks** along Victoria St.; **police** (☎9791 2422), on the corner of Wittenoom St. at Stephen St.; **hospital** (☎9722 1000), on Bussell Hwy. following Blair St. south out of town.

ACCOMMODATIONS AND FOOD. There are plenty of standard motels in town. Better yet, the **Wander Inn YHA,** 16 Clifton St., near Wittenoom St., is friendly and popular, with ping-pong and pool tables, BBQ, and bright rooms. (☎9721 3242; yhabunbury@hotmail.com. Dorms $18; singles $29; doubles $49; family rooms $65. Internet $4 per hr. VIP/YHA.) The hostel provides **snorkel gear,** rents **bikes** and **surf boards,** and can arrange **dolphin tours, bushwalking,** and **kayaking.** For a change of pace, the calm and secluded **Castlehead Bed and Breakfast,** 44 Elinor Bell Rd., 8km north of town, offers a few beautiful rooms overlooking an estuary. Take the scenic drive off of Old Coast Rd. in Australind and turn inland onto Elinor Bell Rd. (☎9797 0272. Singles $40; doubles $65; under 16 $20 extra.) The Centrepoint Shopping Center behind the tourist office houses Coles **Supermarket** (open M-W and F 8am-6pm, Th 8am-9pm, Sa 8am-5pm). The main strip, on Victoria St. between Wellington and Symmons St., has numerous restaurants and cafes.

SIGHTS. Sleepy Bunbury has generally managed to avoid the crowds that plague dolphin-addled **Monkey Mia**, but it may not stay quiet for long. The town is growing rapidly, new houses are springing up, and public spaces are being revitalized and expanded. The **Dolphin Discovery Centre,** on Koombana Dr., features the main local attraction: **dolphin-sighting tours**, and even a chance to swim with the popular creatures. The center also has a theater and interactive exhibits. (☎9791 3088. Open daily Oct.-Apr. 8am-5pm; May-Sept. 9am-3pm. $5, children $2, families $12.) The boat tours are run by **Naturaliste Charters** from the jetty on Koombana Dr. (☎9755 2276. 1½hr. daily 9:30, 11am, 2pm. $25, students $22, children $18.) The swim tours cost a hefty $90.

Across from the Dolphin Discovery Centre, the **Mangrove Boardwalk** weaves through an aqueous mangrove ecosystem. Over 70 species of birds reside at the **Big Swamp Estuary** on Prince Philip Dr., and you can see the white kangaroo at the **Big Swamp Wildlife Park.** From Ocean Dr., turn onto Hayward St. and look for the sign at the next roundabout. (☎9721 8380. Open daily 10am-5pm. $5, pensioners $4, ages 2-12 $3.) The **Marlston Hill Lookout,** near the oceanside end of Koombana Dr., has a good view. Along Ocean Drive, **Back Beach** is popular, but the stretch of sand below the dunes further south is much more beautiful.

MARGARET RIVER AREA ☎08

Around Margaret River, dramatic rock formations rise out of the pounding surf, vast cave systems weave through the subterranean depths, and celebrated vineyards court every viticultural taste. Small towns speckle Caves Road between Cape Naturaliste and Cape Leeuwin. In the north, the oceanside settlements of

Bussleton, Yallingup, and Dunsborough all loll in small-town bliss. Further south, Margaret River itself (pop. 7,000) comprises a small community of wine makers, artisans, and surfers, and is an ideal place from which to explore the area.

ORIENTATION AND TRANSPORTATION

Margaret River lies 100km south of Bunbury on the **Bussell Hwy.** (Hwy.10). The scenic **Caves Road** branches from the Bussell Hwy. at the town of **Busselton,** 52km from Bunbury, and continues on its separate course to Margaret River. Fantastic wineries and beaches, as well as the towns of **Yallingup** and **Dunsborough,** sit along Caves Rd. between Bussleton and Margaret River.

The vast expanse of untouched regions in WA makes transportation rather difficult for the lone traveler. The best way to get around is by car (see **Transportation,** p. 610), or by checking at hostels. **South West Coachlines** stops at Charles West St., two blocks from the Bussell Hwy., Margaret River. and goes to Perth (4½hr., 2 per day, $23). **Westrail** (☎13 10 53) uses **Harvey World Travel,** 109 Bussell Hwy. (☎9757 2171), as its Margaret River agent. (Open M-F 9am-5pm, Sa 9am-noon.)

PRACTICAL INFORMATION

Tourist Offices:

- **Margaret River Tourist Bureau** (☎9757 2911; www.margaretriverwa.com), corner of Bussell Hwy. and Tunnbridge St. Has maps, countless fliers, and a wine showroom. Open daily 9am-5pm.
- **Busselton Tourist Information Centre** (☎9752 1288; fax 9754 1470), at Peel Tce. and Causeway Rd. Aboriginal garden out back. Open M-F 8:30am-5pm, Sa 9am-4pm, Su 10am-4pm, May-Sept. 10am-2pm.
- **Dunsborough Tourist Bureau** (☎9755 3299), in the shopping center on Seymour Blvd., Margaret River. Books tours.
- **Caves Park Store** (☎/fax 9755 2042), on Yallingup Beach Rd. near Caves Rd., gives the down-low on Yallingup.
- **CALM.** Busselton office, 14 Queen St. (☎9752 1677). Margaret River office (☎9757 2322), on the Bussell Hwy. near town. Gives info on hiking and camping in Leeuwin-Naturaliste National Park. Open M-F 8am-5pm.

Police: 42 Willmott Ave. (☎9757 2222), Margaret River.

Hospital: (☎9757 2000), on Farrelly St. off Wallcliffe Rd., Margaret River.

Internet Access: River Video, 103 Bussell Hwy., Margaret River. $2 per 15min.

Post office: 53 Townview Tce. (☎9757 2250; open M-F 9am-5pm), one block up Willmott Ave. from Bussell Hwy., Margaret River.

ACCOMMODATIONS AND CAMPING

Though hostels are cheaper, the area has many wonderful B&Bs, which can be a good deal for those traveling in pairs or larger groups. Rooms in the area fill up quickly from October to March; be sure to book in advance for summer weekends. From June to August, bargains abound. Contact CALM (see p. 625) about camping in Leeuwin-Naturaliste National Park.

MARGARET RIVER

Surf Point Lodge (☎9757 1777; fax 9757 1077), on Riedle Dr. south of Prevelley, just above Gnarabup Beach and within walking distance of the Rivermouth area. Clean and spacious. Free pickup from bus station, bike and boogie board rental, BBQ. Internet $5 per 30min. Book ahead in summer. Dorms $21; doubles $52, off-season $47; with fridge and bath $68, off-season $63.

Margaret River Lodge (☎9757 9532; fax 9757 2532), 1½km southwest of the Bussell Hwy. off Wallcliffe Rd. on Railway Tce. Free pickup from bus station, bike and bodyboard rentals, swimming pool, and vegetable garden. Internet $3 per 30min. Dorms $18; doubles $49, with from $65. VIP.

Matan's Lodge (☎/fax 9757 2936), on Caves Rd., after a right turn-off from Wallcliffe Rd. going away from town. Beautiful, bohemian, relaxed place. Nice rooms for 3-4 people $85. From June-Aug., rooms fill up dorm style for $18 per person.

Prevelly Park Beach Resort (☎9757 2374; fax 9757 2790), on the way into Prevelly Park taking Wallcliffe Rd. west out of town. Sites $8-12; van sites $45-55; $7 for each extra person; cabins $50-75.

BUSSELTON, YALLINGUP, AND DUNSBOROUGH

Three Pines Beach YHA, 285 Geographe Bay Rd. (☎9755 3107), Dunsborough. Excellent location right on beach. Buses between Augusta and Perth drop off in Dunsborough upon request. Hostel books tours. Dorms $17-19; doubles $44-49. YHA.

Busselton Backpackers, 14 Peel Tce. (☎9754 2763), Busselton. Simple, clean, and friendly. A small place with laundry and kitchen facilities. Dorms $18; singles $20; doubles $35; family room $40.

Hideaway Holiday Homes, 24 Elsegood Ave. (☎9755 2145), Yallingup. Big cabins with baths. Simple and cheap with several bedrooms and a kitchen, but no linen. Doubles from $45, 6-bed from $85.

Dunsborough Lakes Caravan Park, 2-48 Commanage Rd. (☎9756 8300; fax 9756 8333), off the Bussell Hwy. just north of Dunsborough. Sites $15 per person, off-season $11; cabins $30-130.

FOOD AND NIGHTLIFE

Reflecting the refined tastes of its vintners, Margaret River's restaurants are good but pricey. Many are BYO, perfect for enjoying the fruit of the local vineyards. Dewson's Supermarket, next to the tourist office on the Bussell Hwy. in Margaret River and Newmart Supermarket along Dunn Bay Rd. both sell **groceries.** In Dunsborough, small restaurants line Dunn Bay Rd., which runs through the center of town. In Busselton, restaurants line Queen St. Several of the vineyards on Caves Rd. towards Yallingup also have restaurants.

Sails Cafe, 117 Bussell Hwy. (☎9757 3573). The place to go for breakfast—at any time of the day. Complete breakfast with eggs, sausage, bacon, mushrooms, and tomatoes $11. So good at times it's hard to get a table. Open daily 8am-5pm.

Caffe 111, 111 Bussell Hwy. (☎9758 7222). Features a constantly changing gourmet menu, which usually includes seafood or pasta ($10-16). No set hours. Usually open daily 8am-4ish. Sometimes open with live music F and Su nights.

Goodfellas Café Woodfire Pizza, 97 Bussell Hwy. (☎9757 3184). Offers huge bowls of pasta and exotic pizzas in a candlelit setting. Meals $10-15. Open daily 5:30-9:30pm.

Settler's Tavern, 97 Bussell Hwy. (☎9757 2398). Live bands of all sorts frequent this popular booze spot every night. Pool tables, big screen TV. 21+. Cover varies. Open M-Th noon-midnight, F noon-2am, Sa 10am-1am, Su noon-10pm.

SIGHTS

WINERIES. There are about 70 wineries in the Margaret River area; many offer free tastings and spectacular grounds to picnic. The first stop on any wine tour should be the tourist office (see p. 625), which provides maps and listings, and has a wine showroom. Most of the wineries are clustered in the area bordered by Caves Rd. and Johnson Rd. between Yallingup and Margaret River. For an enjoyable tour, mix older vintners, such as **Cullen,** which are usually more personable and more prestigious, with the many newcomers to the region, such as **Howard Park,** which tend to have magnificent estates and excellent views.

For those staying in Margaret River without a car, several wineries are accessible by bike or foot from town. **Chateau Xanadu** features an award-winning chardonnay and an elegant setup. *(3km southwest of town off Boodijup Rd. ☎9757 2581. Open daily*

10am-5pm.) The **Cape Mentelle** winery was one of the first in the area; it remains a relaxed, personable place. *(Just off Wallcliffe Rd. south of town. ☎9757 3266. Open daily 10am-4:30pm.)* For those more inclined toward other forms of drink, **Bootleg Brewery** is a "beer oasis in a desert of wine." *(Off Caves Rd. near Willyabrup. ☎9755 6300. Open daily 10am-4:30pm.)*

WINE TOURS. Numerous agencies run wine tours, which generally cost about $45 for a half day and $80 for a full day, and can be booked at the tourist office. One of the most popular is the **Great Wine, Food, Forest Bushtucker Tour.** In five hours, this tour packs in a drive through the karri forest, a gourmet lunch, and a tour of six local vineyards. *(☎9757 9084. Tours daily at noon.)* **Milesaway Tours** *(☎1800 818 102)* departs from a number of towns in the region; call for details.

FOOD TASTINGS. The Margaret River area offers a variety of free food tastings to complement its famous wines. **Fonti Farm** provides the cheese *(on the Bussell Hwy. near Cowaramup; open 9:30am-5pm)*; **The Berry Farm** offers jams *(222 Bessell Rd.; 10km east of the Bussell Hwy. off Davis Rd. south of Margaret River; ☎9757 5054; open daily 10am-4:30pm)*, and the **Fudge Factory** doles out small, scrumptious helpings *(152 Bussell Hwy., Margaret River; ☎9758 8881; open daily 10am-5pm)*.

OTHER SIGHTS. The two-kilometer-long **Busselton Jetty** is a thin plank jutting way out into the Indian Ocean. It's a good hike to the end of the jetty, and waters below are a popular seasonal diving area. *(At the end of Queen St. in Busselton. $2.20, children $1.10.)* The **Eagles Heritage Raptor Wilderness Centre,** on Boodjidup Rd. near Margaret River, is Australia's largest collection of birds of prey and is dedicated to education, rehabilitation of injured birds, and breeding projects. (*☎9757 2960. Open daily 10am-5pm. Flight displays daily 11am and 1:30pm. $8, seniors $6, children $4, families $20. Wheelchair accessible.*)

OUTDOOR ACTIVITIES

Margaret's beaches and surf are a major tourist draw. Caves Rd. south of Margaret's is one of the area's most spectacular drives. Winding through the karri forests of Leeuwin-Naturaliste National Park, the road passes hundreds of hidden caves, though only four are open to the public. **Biking** is a good way to travel in and around Margaret River. **Gull's Petrol Station,** 111 Bussell Hwy. in Margaret River rents bikes, including a helmet, chain, and water bottle. (☎9758 7038. $7 per hr., $15 per half-day, $20 per day, $70 per week. $50 deposit.)

LEEUWIN-NATURALISTE PARK. Spanning much of the coast from Cape Naturaliste to Cape Leeuwin, Leeuwin-Naturaliste National Park encompasses wild forests, untouched beaches, and jagged rock formations rising from the waters. At the northern tip of **Cape Naturaliste,** a number of short trails lead from the lighthouse to breathtaking expanses of sand. *(12km north of Dunsborough on Naturaliste Tce. Lighthouse open daily 9:30am-4pm; last tour leaves at 3:30pm. Tours $6.50, children $2.50.)* About 25km south of Margaret River on the left side of Caves Rd. is the **Boranup Maze,** a massive shrub labyrinth that is best visited in summer. *($2.20, children $1.10)*. Nearby, the **Boranup Lookout,** off Caves Rd. just south of the maze, is a windy spot with views of the Indian Ocean. Technically, you need a National Parks Pass to visit these sights, but there is rarely anyone checking. On the other hand, a hefty $50 fine awaits those who are caught. *(Passes $9 per day, 4-week $22.50, 1-year $51. Available at CALM offices and some tourist bureaus.)*

SURFING. Packs of grommets (young surfers) learn the ropes in the relatively tame surf at **Rivermouth** and **Redgate** near Margaret River; more experienced surfers delight in the breaks off **Surf Point,** or head further north to **Gracetown.** There are tons of other surf spots in the area, but levels of safety and difficulty vary; stop at **Beach Life Surf Shop** for information and advice, or to set up a surfing lesson. *(117 Bussell Hwy., just up from the tourist office. ☎9757 2888; 24hr. surf report ☎1900 922 995. $30 for group lessons, $75 for individual.)*

90-TON THREESOME If you do take a whale-watching trip in the Southwest, look for groups of Humpback whales traveling in threes. Why three? These mammals, each weighing around 30 tons as adults, are too big for private sexual intercourse. Male sexual organs are too large and unwieldy; they are 14% of the length of their entire body. Thus, an interested couple must get help from another whale for everything to work properly. Perhaps that's what true friends are for.

Further north, **Yallingup Beach** was one of the first breaks surfed in WA in the 1950s and remains famous among surfers. The best time for surfing is Oct.-Apr., though it gets very crowded, especially in Dec. and Jan. The two best spots in the Yallingup area are Yallingup Beach itself, right in front of Yallingup's Surf Shop at the bottom of Yallingup Beach Rd., and **Smith's Bay,** just south of Yallingup Beach.

DIVING AND SNORKELING. In Dunsborough, Eagle and Meelup Bays both have great beaches for snorkeling and surfing; turn-offs are well marked on Cape Naturaliste Rd., north of town. **Bay Dive and Adventures,** in Dunsborough, offers diving, diving classes, and snorkeling trips. *(26 Dunn Bay Rd. ☎9756 8846.)* **Cape Dive** is one of a few outfitters that run diving trips to the wreck of the HMS Swan off Cape Naturaliste. *(☎9756 8778.)* **Hamelin Bay** (see p. 628), near Augusta, is another good dive and snorkel spot.

CAVES. Cave systems run throughout the Margaret River area. They're difficult to access without a car; a taxi from Margaret's to Mammoth Cave (the nearest to town) costs about $25 each way, and hostels can usually help arrange transport. Still, the caves are amazing natural phenomena, and worth the trouble of getting there. The **Cave Works Eco Centre,** at **Lake Cave** about 15km south of Margaret, has educational exhibits, but the caves themselves are much more interesting. *(☎9757 7411. Open daily 9am-5pm. $3, children $2. Exhibit free with cave entrance fee.)* Tours at Lake Cave and **Jewel Cave,** which is the real gem of the four caves, take about an hour each. *(1 hr., every hour 9:30am-3:30pm. $14, children $5.50, families $37.)* The Cave Works **Grand Pass** covers all the caves except for Moondyne, and is valid for seven days. *($33, children $13, families $92.)*

Up north near Yallingup, **Ngilgi's Cave,** also known as Yallingup Cave, was named after an Aboriginal legend about two battling spirits. It is part of a cave system that descends as much as 37m below the surface. *(At end of well-marked turn-off to the right off Caves Rd. between Dunsborough and Yallingup. ☎9755 2152. Tours daily every 30min. from 9:30am-3:30pm. $12, children $5, family $34. Adventure tours of more difficult sections of the caves available with 24hr. advance booking for $35.)*

OUTDOOR TOURS. Several companies organize half- or full-day adventure tours, most of which can be booked through tourist bureaus. **Naturaliste Charters** runs **whale-watching** tours that bring sight-seers to the Humpback whales off Augusta (see below) and Dunsborough from June to August. *(Departs daily from Boat Ramp on Geographe Bay Rd. in Dunsborough. ☎9755 2276. 3hr., $45, children $25, under 4 free.)* **Boranup Eco Walks** gives guided walks through karri and jarrah forests. *(☎9757 7576. Daytime walks 1½-3hr. $10-15, children $5-8; night walks 1½hr. in summer $12, children $6. Book ahead.)* **Outdoor Discoveries** organizes abseiling outings and other adventurous expeditions. *(☎0407 084 945. From $65 per person.)*

AUGUSTA ☎08

About 45km south of Margaret River lies the small, pleasant community of Augusta. It's a good base for exploring the surrounding area and, from June through August, for cruising on a whale-watching tour. The **tourist office** is on Blackwood Ave., which is the end stretch of the Bussell Hwy. and the main drag in town. (☎9758 0166; fax 9758 0174. Open M-F 9am-5pm, Sa-Su 9am-1pm; off-season M-F 9am-4pm, Sa-Su 9am-1pm.) There is a **fruit market** and **grocery store** on Blackwood Ave., north of the tourist office.

PROTECTING THEIR OWN Rangers around the world erect fire towers to spot signs of forest fire as early as possible, but those in WA decided to construct cabins in the tops of the trees themselves. The rangers drove pegs into the karri trunks so that they could climb to these treetop dwellings. From here, the fearless (and vertigo-resistant) firefighters remained vigilant from the 1930s to 1970s, when they switched to aircraft. Today, the towers are open to visitors. Tremendous views reward those who can muster the courage to ascend a mammoth eucalypt. The highest such treehouse, at 75m, is in the **Bicentennial Tree** in Warren National Park.

The best lodging in town is the **Baywatch Manor Resort YHA,** 88 Blackwood Ave. There are no busty Southern Californian beauties here—only nice people and spacious, perfectly maintained quarters, where visitors tend to relax and enjoy the ocean rather than partying. The friendly owners arrange whale-watching and tours. (☎9758 1290; fax 9758 1291. Dorms $17; doubles $42, with bathroom $53. Non-YHA members $2 more.) The **Hamelin Bay Caravan Park** north of town has camping and van sites by the beach. (☎9758 5540. Sites $18, powered $22.)

Nine kilometers south of town is **Cape Leeuwin,** Australia's southwestern-most point, where the Indian and Southern Oceans meet. A **lighthouse** built in 1895 stands guard over the spot. (Open daily 9am-5pm. Last tour leaves at 4pm. $6, children $3.) **Whales** can often be spotted off the coast from June-Aug., stopping in Flinders Bay on their way to the warm waters of the north. Humpback, Southern Right, and the occasional Pygmy Blue Whale are abundant in season, and at times there are as many as 80 whales in the bay. **Naturaliste Charters** runs whale-watching tours from Augusta in the winter; 3hr. tours depart daily at 10am. (☎9755 2276. $45, children $25.) Confirm the tour to make sure the weather isn't too rough.

About 12km north of Augusta on Caves Rd. lies **Hamelin Bay,** which has a lovely beach. Indeed, the bay may be beautiful to the point of distraction—the area has seen 11 shipwrecks since 1882. Independent scuba and snorkeling outings to the four visible wrecks are welcome, but there's no boat, so you have to swim from shore. Check with someone before going on a dive; the wrecks are old and shift around a bit. Swimming here is sheltered, and fishing in the area is superb. Stingrays often cluster below the boat ramp to feed on the remains left by fishermen. **Augusta Hardware and Scuba Supplies,** on the main Blackwood Ave. stretch across from the post office, has information on dives, renting gear, and filling tanks. (☎9758 1770. Open M-F 8:30am-5:30pm, Sa 8:30am-4:30pm, Su 9am-1pm.)

PEMBERTON ☎08

The **Gloucester Tree,** one of the tallest fire lookouts in the world, is a prime attraction in Pemberton. Steel dowels wind 61m up the trunk to the platform, from which the brave-hearted get a breathtaking view of the forest canopy and distant sand dunes. Miles of walking trails criss-cross the surrounding **Gloucester National Park** ($9 per vehicle). Scenic rail tours of the area on the **Pemberton Tramway** may be booked in the tourist office or by phone. (☎9776 1322. Tours 1¾-5½hr. Prices start at $14, children $7.50.) **Pemberton Hiking Company** (☎9776 1559) offers guided hikes, including wheelchair accessible options.

West of Pemberton on the road to Augusta is **Beedelup National Park,** home to the **Beedelup Falls** and a karri tree with a hole cut in its middle through which you can walk. Roads inside the park are unsealed; the road to the falls is very smooth, but not elsewhere. The ascent to the falls is quite dangerous after dark.

The eastern spur of Hwy. 10 runs from Karridale, north of Augusta, out to Pemberton, a good 1½hr. drive. Make sure the tank is full before you leave Karridale, and watch for signs—an easily missed right turn onto Stewart Rd., about 40km from Karridale, leads to the last 69km stretch to Pemberton.

Westrail buses (☎13 10 53) stop once per day in Pemberton on the Bunbury-Albany line. The **Karri Visitors Centre** has information on the surrounding forest, a pioneer museum, and a "Discovery Centre" ($2, children $1, families $5). More practically, it has pay showers and toilets for campers. The Visitors Centre sells useful bushwalking guides and car passes for the nearby national parks. (☎9776 1133; fax 9776 1623. Open daily 9am-5pm.) There is a **CALM office** on Kennedy St. (☎9776 1207. Open M-F 8am-5pm.)

Pemberton Backpackers, right on the main strip, offers small, cheery rooms in a friendly atmosphere, and rents mountain bikes. (☎9776 1105. Internet $5 per 30min. Dorms $16.50; twins $19; doubles $49.50.) **Pemberton YHA,** on Stirling Rd. in the middle of the forest, has clusters of rooms in small cabins that share a kitchen and bathroom. It's charming, but town is 10km away. (☎9776 1153; fax 9776 1819. Towels, linen $2. Internet $3 per 30min. Dorms $16; twins $35; doubles $40; families $55; non-YHA members $3-$6 extra.) There are a number of **campsites** in the surrounding national parks; check the tourist bureau or the CALM office for details. A SupaValu **grocery store** is just off the highway on Dean St.

GREAT SOUTHERN

Sprawling karri and tingle forests, rugged mountain ranges, and the vast nothingness of the Nullarbor Plain are all part of the diverse and beautiful region known as the Great Southern. The South Western Hwy. links the region's many parts together, and the ecological variance along the drive is fascinating. Albany functions as an urban hub for the sparsely populated southern coast, but by the time you reach Esperance, Perth's cosmopolitanism seems a world away.

The largely agricultural Great Southern is home to a number of respected vineyards, many of which offer complimentary wine-tastings. Tourism has become an economic mainstay, peaking in the spring wildflower season and in the summer, when the beaches around Denmark, Albany, and Esperance are most inviting. Winters in the Great Southern can be chilly, so be sure to bring a warm jacket.

WALPOLE ☎08

Tiny and congenial, Walpole (pop. 450) is experiencing a tourism boom primarily because of its proximity to **Walpole-Nornalup National Park** and the highly popular **Valley of the Giants** Tree Top Walk, 17km out of town.

PRACTICAL INFORMATION. **Westrail** (☎13 10 53) **buses** stop once per day en route to Albany and Bunbury. The friendly, volunteer-run **Walpole-Nornalup Visitors Centre,** on the north side of the highway, hands out information on the surrounding tingle and karri forest and the beautiful coast of Walpole and Nornalup Inlets, and also sells Tree Top Walk tickets. (☎9840 1111; fax 9840 1355. Open M-F 9am-5pm, Sa-Su 9am-4pm.) The local **CALM office,** on the Western outskirts of town, has info on hiking and camping in the national parks. (☎9840 1027. Open M-F 8am-5pm.) There's **Internet access** at Telecentre on Vista Ave. (☎9840 1395. Open Tu-F 9am-5pm. $8 per hr.) There are **groceries** and **camping supplies** at the Foodland and the BP gas station and a **post office** (☎9840 1048; open M-F 9am-5pm) on Nockolds St.

ACCOMMODATIONS AND FOOD. **Walpole Backpackers,** on Pier St. off Vista Ave., is laid-back and user-friendly. The staff is filled with forestry experts who give 4WD tours of the area on demand and fees are negotiable. (☎/fax 9840 1244. Laundry and kitchen facilities. Reception 24hr. Dorms $17.50; singles $25; twins and doubles $45; family rooms $60.) **Tingle All Over YHA,** on Nockolds St., has a BBQ, and a huge chess set with two-foot-high wooden pieces in the yard. All rooms have sinks, but showers are a short walk outdoors. (☎9840 1041. Dorms $17.50; singles $32; twins and doubles $45. Non-YHA add $2.) **Coalmine Beach Caravan Park,** at Coalmine Beach just east of town, offers camping right on the banks of the inlet and rents canoes. (☎9840 1026. Sites for 2 people $16; powered $18, $6.50 per extra person; cabins $75-95.) Camping in the national parks is available at Mt. Frankland, Crystal Springs, near Mandalay Beach, and at other locations. For info, head to the tourist bureau or the CALM center.

POISON 1080 RISK! Signs all over the south of Western Australia warn of the poison risk from fox baits. What's going on? When Englishmen first came to Australia, the homesick chaps brought along some foxes to keep them company. The foxes took a liking to each other and made more little foxes. Pretty soon there was a rampant fox infestation, preying local fauna into extinction. An Australian plant, to which indigenous creatures had grown immune, was observed to kill foreign species with extreme prejudice. Biologists managed to isolate the unique poison, synthesized the toxic chemical in the plant, injected it into pieces of kangaroo meat, and air-dropped them all over the southern wilderness regions of Western Australia. The project has been working well, so if you happen upon a tasty meat morsel along the Bibbulmun Track, DON'T EAT IT.

ACTIVITIES. The area's biggest draw is the **Tree Top Walk,** a 600m metal catwalk passing through the canopy of tingle trees. The views are incredible, but those scared of heights be forewarned—the swaying walkways reach as high as 40m. (☎9840 8200. Open daily 9am-5pm, last admission 4:15pm. $6, children $2.50; families $14.) The **Ancient Empire** boardwalk, a short, pleasant walk, departs from the Tree Top Walk info center and passes through a grove of giant red tingle, which can reach 16m in circumference.

Fifteen kilometers east of Walpole is the right turn down Conspicuous Beach Rd. that leads to **Conspicuous Cliff,** a splendid stretch of beach with an information board, picnic space, and public restrooms. It is wheelchair accessible up to the first lookout. About 6km east of town is the left-hand turn-off to the **Giant Tingle Tree,** 24m in diameter and the largest known living eucalypt in the world. Twelve kilometers west of Walpole is the popular **Mandalay Beach,** good for swimming and camping (but a fee may apply). Walpole is also famous for its diversity of **wildflowers,** including more than 90 species of orchids; prime viewing runs from Aug.-Nov.

WOW Wilderness Services offers cruises through the Walpole Inlet to a beach and some coastal forest. (☎9840 1036. 2½hr.; daily 10am, in January also 2pm; $22, children $11.) **Walpole-Nornalup National Park** has several hiking trails. The Tree Top Walk is a good place to meet up with the **Bibbulmun Track.** The 17km hike back to Walpole passes through a variety of beach and forest zones. Check with CALM about path conditions and other area hikes along the track. Some shorter hikes around the area include the **Coalmine Beach Heritage Trail,** a flat 3km hike from the tourist bureau in Walpole through melaleucas, ferns, and sheaoak to Coalmine Beach (2hr.); a short but steep hike (1½hr.) through wildflowers to the top of **Mount Frankland,** 12km from town; turn off the highway just east of Walpole.

DENMARK ☎08

Located 66km east of Walpole along the South Coast Hwy., Denmark's coastline has good fishing, surfing, boating, and swimming. A number of beaches lie along William Bay Rd. off the South Coast Hwy. west of Denmark. The shores of **William Bay** are the most scenic, but **Waterfall Beach** to the east runs a close second. In addition, **Greens Pool, Elephant Rocks,** and **Madfish Bay** are all sheltered enough to swim. Denmark has an active **arts and crafts** scene around Strickland St. The Denmark area is also an important **winery** region. For some free tastings, grab a wine lovers' guide from the tourist office and head for the 34km Scottsdale Rd., off Mt. Shadforth Rd., where most of the wineries are clustered.

Winner of the 1998 national "Tidy Town" title for its appearance and progressive environmental policies, Denmark has a thriving organic farming scene. Denmark has more than a small town's fair share of organic produce shops, health food stores, and whole-grain bakeries, and a friendly population to boot.

Westrail buses run from the tourist office to Albany (40min., $7) and Perth (7hr.; daily 8:47am, M and Th 9:22am; $45). **Strickland St.,** Denmark's main thoroughfare, intersects the **South Coast Hwy.** Heading east, turn right on Strickland to reach the **Denmark Visitors Centre.** (☎9848 2055; fax 9848 2271. Open daily 9am-5pm.)

PICK ON SOMEONE YOUR OWN SIZE If you are walking along a sandy path and find a very small mound with a few large holes in it, you may be foolishly inclined to knock gently with your foot to see who is home. But stand back, because it's likely the home of the bull ant—or several bull ants, to be more exact. Each ant is over one inch long, extremely aggressive, and has the ability to inflict excruciating pain. When they figure out where you are, they will stand facing you in a fighting stance. If they do manage a sting, the pain is terrible, and lasts a week.

The **Denmark Waterfront,** 63 Inlet Dr., off of Hollings Rd., contains simple rooms for backpackers near the shores of the inlet and on the Bibbulmun Track. (☎9848 1147; fax 9848 1965. Laundry, kitchen, BBQ, and Internet access $5 per 30min. Rooms $17, weekly $84. VIP.)

MOUNT BARKER ☎08

Mt. Barker (pop. 1700), 47km north of Albany along Albany Hwy., is the sleepy gateway to the floral paradise of Porongurup National Park. The park is filled with rocky peaks, karri trees, and the region's renowned wildflowers.

TRANSPORTATION AND PRACTICAL INFORMATION. Lowood Rd., the main street in Mt. Barker, branches off of the Albany Hwy. and winds to intersect the Muir Hwy., which becomes Langton Rd. as it enters town from the west. **Westrail buses** (☎13 10 53) run to Perth and Albany once per day. The **tourist office** is in the old train station on the Albany Hwy. (☎9851 1163; fax 9851 1919. Open M-F 9am-5pm, Sa 9am-3pm, Su 10am-3pm.) Barker Home Video provides **Internet access.** (☎9851 1880. $5 per hr. Open M-Sa 11am-8pm, Su noon-8pm.)

ACCOMMODATIONS AND FOOD. Most lodging and restaurants are located along the Albany Hwy. and the Muir Hwy. **Chill Out Backpackers,** 79 Hassell St., off the very start of Porongorup Rd., is in a beautiful wooden A-frame building. (☎9851 2798. Dorms $16.50; singles $20; doubles $35.) About 20km outside of town on Porongurup Rd. and within walking distance of the main hikes in the Porongurups is the **Porongurup Shop and Tearoom,** which offers backpacker accommodations, a homey, lived-in atmosphere, and fresh vegetables from the garden. Upon request, owners will try to arrange pickup from Mt. Barker or Albany. (☎9853 1110. Internet $5 per hr. Rooms $16.) The **Mt. Barker Caravan Park** is at the north end of town. (☎9851 1691. Backpackers singles $17, weekly $90; park homes for 2 $44.) The food options in town are somewhat limited. The **Mt. Barker Hotel** (☎9851 1477), at the corner of Lowood and Langton Rd., has daily lunch noon-2pm and dinner 6-9pm. SupaValu, on Lowood Rd., sells **groceries.**

PORONGURUP RANGE. The Porongurup Range is one of the oldest volcanic formations in the world, dating back more than 1100 million years. To get there from town, follow Lowood Rd. north and turn right on Albany Hwy., then left on Porongurup Rd. (Tourist Dr. 252). Two of the most popular hikes are the short but very photogenic Castle Rock walk (1½hr.), which requires some nerve and agility over the last 300m, and the longer Tree in the Rock hike (2½hr.; $9 per vehicle). Both are accessible by right-hand turns from Porongurup Rd. Hundreds of varieties of wildflowers have been identified in Porongurup and the nearby Stirling Range National Park (see p. 632). Peak season is Sept.-Nov., but in the high mountains there are still flowers in December.

STIRLING RANGE NATIONAL PARK

The Stirling Range National Park should not be missed. The rugged, rocky 1000m peaks are a dramatic contrast to vast farmlands, making the drive from Albany undoubtedly one of the Great Southern's most scenic routes. The Stirling Range is the only place in Western Australia that regularly sees snow, high winds, and rain at higher altitudes—be sure to carry food, water, and warm clothing.

The hikes such as Talyuberlup Peak, Mt. Hassell, and Mt. Trio, lead to spectacular scenery through 1600 species of **wildflowers.** The most popular is the 3.1km ascent to **Bluff Knoll,** the highest peak in southwestern Australia and rated as one of Australia's top 25 climbs. The Aborigines labeled this knoll *Bullah Meual* (Great Many Face Hill) for its mercurial climate and face-like appearance. Though marked as a 3-4hr. return, experienced hikers can make the moderately strenuous ascent in an hour. For Bluff Knoll, visitors must buy a $9 day pass to the park at an honor box on the road to the trail. Enter yourself in the registration book, but don't forget to fill out the time on your way out—unless you want to dispatch a search team. Four-week holiday passes, valid at all of Western Australia's parks, are available from a park ranger ($22.50 per car). A rocky, but rewarding trail ascends to **Toolbrunup,** the range's second highest peak (3hr.; difficult).

Though a shuttle (☎9827 9229) travels to Bluff Knoll from the Stirling Range Retreat ($11), the best way to see the area is by car. Car rental is easily arranged in Albany: try **King Sound Vehicle Hire** (☎9841 8466), 145 Albany Hwy., **Crossroads Autos** (☎9842 2993), 42 Sanford Rd., or **Albany Car Rentals** (☎9841 7077), 386 Albany Hwy. Prices range from $40-50 per day.

Along Chester Pass Rd., 90km north of Albany and just across the road from the turn-off to Bluff Knoll, the **Stirling Range Retreat** has immaculate rooms and a swimming pool out back. Owners have slide shows and guided nature walks in wildflower season ($10). The trailers are well-heated and roomy. (☎9827 9229. Book ahead Sept.-Nov. Campsites $8 per person; on-site vans $35, for 2 $43, for 3 $51; backpacker units $17; cabins for 5-6 with kitchen $84-94.) Camping is permitted in the national park at Moingup Spring (No showers or power. Sites $10, $5.50 per additional person).

There are **ranger stations** at Moingup Spring (☎9827 9320) and Bluff Knoll (☎9827 9278). The nearest **hospital** is in Gnowangerup (☎9826 1003).

ALBANY ☎08

Established in 1826, Albany was the first colonial settlement of Western Australia., and is proud of its past. As the commercial center of this region, Albany has all the conveniences of a small city, with the traffic to match. Fortunately the coastline remains pristine, and a lovely view waits around each corner.

TRANSPORTATION.

Westrail buses (☎13 10 53) depart from in front of the tourist office to: **Bunbury** (6hr., 1 per day, $36) via **Walpole, Pemberton, Augusta,** and **Margaret River**; **Esperance** (6hr., M and Th, $46); **Perth** (6hr., 1-2 per day, $37). *Let's Go* does not recommend hitchhiking. Hitchhikers usually wait by the "Big Roundabout" on the Albany Hwy, 2km west of the north end of York St. The two hostels in town also have a steady stream of travelers sharing rides. For the lazy, Love's Bus Service provides **city transport** for $2 a trip (☎9841 1211. Open M-Sa.) But it's not hard to get around Albany on foot.

PRACTICAL INFORMATION.

York St. runs north-south through the center of town. The **tourist office** is in the Old Railway Station, just east of the southern end of York St. near Stirling Tce. (☎9841 1088; fax 9842 1490. Open M-F 8:15am-5:30pm, Sa-Su 9am-5pm.) There is **Internet** at Argyle's Bistro, 42 Stirling Tce. (☎9842 9696, daily 7am-7pm, $4 per 30min.).

ACCOMMODATIONS AND FOOD.

Albany has two hostels near the center of town. The **Albany Backpackers** is on Spencer St., around the corner from Stirling Tce. and one block east of York St. It has colorful, ragtag joint rooms, and provides info about tours of local sights, including snorkeling and kite flying. (☎9842 5255. Internet $4.40 per 30min. Reception 8am-9pm. Dorms $18; doubles $44. ISIC/NOMADS/VIP/YHA.) The **Albany Bayview YHA,** 49 Duke St., two blocks west of York St., is another good option with a nice view of the bay and free movies. Visitors can rent bikes, boogie boards, and fishing gear. (☎/fax 9842 3388. Dorms $19; twins

$38.) The **Cruize-Inn,** 122 Middleton Rd., is one step up from hostelling with beautiful, home-style accommodations complete with kitchen and TV lounge. (☎9842 9588. Singles $33; doubles $55.) **Middleton Beach Holiday Park,** at the end of Middleton Rd., is farther from the center of town, but right on the beach. (☎9841 3593; fax 9842 2088. Sites $21, powered $22; off-season $18/$19.)

Dylan's on the Terrace, 82 Stirling Tce. whips up sandwiches and burgers for $4-6. (☎9841 8270. Open M-Th 7am-11pm, F-Su 7am-midnight.) SupaValu, on at York St. near Stirling Tce. has **groceries.** (Open daily 7am-9pm.)

SIGHTS. Albany has the distinction of being home to the world's largest whaling museum. **Whaleworld,** on Frenchman Bay Rd. past the Gap and Blowholes, is on the site of Australia's last whaling station, which closed in 1978 because it was no longer profitable. Check out the former blubber vats, harpoons, and the docks where whales were processed. (☎9844 4021. Open daily 9am-5pm. 30min. tours every hr. 10am-4pm. $11, concessions $9, families $25.) If live whales are more your speed, try **whale watching** from May-Oct.; peak season is June-Sept. Several outfits run cruises; book at the hostels. **Southern Ocean Charters** (☎0409 107 180), a.k.a. **Big Day Out,** departs daily at 9:30am ($35).

Apart from whales, Albany's most impressive sight is the **Natural Bridge,** a rock formation bridging 24m above crashing waves located in **Torndirrup National Park,** 20km south of town along Frenchman Bay Rd. Nearby **blowholes** only work in rough weather, when spray from below the rock shoots out through a crack. *Do not go beyond the blowholes; people have died trying to get a good photo.* No Kodak moment is worth that. Another natural beauty, the protected **Middleton Beach,** lies just outside of town. The **Middleton Bay Scenic Path** is a pretty walk from the beach out to Emu Point. For those with access to a 4WD vehicle, **West Cape Howe National Park** (about 30km west of Albany) is worth exploring. The roads, which are more like trails, are treacherous even with 4WD, but for 2WD vehicles, **Shelley** and **Dunsky** beaches are near perfect. There is good snorkeling and common dolphin sightings in the waters around the rocks to the left of gorgeous Little Beach at **Two Peoples Bay Reserve,** 35km east of town.

FROM ALBANY TO ESPERANCE

As the South Coast Hwy. slices eastward, rolling farmland slowly gives way to brush, and massive trucks known as road trains comprise most of the traffic. Give them a wide berth; they're unlikely to do the same for you. Petrol stations only appear every 50 to 75km, so fuel up in Albany before heading out. The highway is low and fast, and the temptation to speed will be great, but take care: the 500km stretch to Esperance is subject to high crosswinds and winter flooding. The small towns of Jerramuhgup and Ravensthorpe are good rest stops along the way.

Westrail buses (☎9326 2813, 13 10 53) run between Albany and Esperance via Ravensthorpe (M and Th $41). The **Ravensthorpe/Hopetoun Tourist Bureau,** on the South Coast Hwy. in Ravensthorpe, periodically publishes a guide to the area; check the tourist offices in Albany or Esperance. (☎9838 1277. Open daily when possible; summer 9am-5pm; winter 9am-4:30pm.) **EFTPOS** is at most petrol stations and at the **Hopetoun General Store.** (☎9838 3052. Open daily 7:30am-6pm.)

About halfway between Albany and Esperance lies the enormous **Fitzgerald River National Park.** This park has two main access points, one at **Bremer Bay** (the western end) and one at **Hopetoun** (the eastern end); several unsealed roads run south from the South Coast Hwy. to the park. To get to Bremer Bay from the South Coast Hwy., turn right onto Bremer Bay Rd. about 120km east of Albany, then travel 65km east. Hopetoun is 50km south of Ravensthorpe on Ravensthorpe Hopetoun Rd. Hammersley Rd. cuts through the park from the highway to Hopetoun.

Named a "Biosphere Reserve" due to the abundance and diversity of wildlife, Fitzgerald River National Park hosts rare creatures like the **Malleefowl** (p. 562), a bird that builds nests out of mounds of dirt that can reach 1m high and 4m wide, the **Chuditch,** a carnivorous marsupial, and the **Dibbler,** a marsupial once thought to be extinct. **Whales** can also be seen from the reserve. The park is also home to thousands of species of plants and wildflowers in spring (Sept.-Nov.). Hikes for all skill levels abound; the **East Mount Barren Walk** (3hr.), starting about 12km west of the Hopetoun entrance, is of medium difficulty with great views of the beach.

Parts of the park require a 4WD, but many areas are reachable on 2WD unsealed roads. Caravans should not attempt park roads. Passes for the park are available at **CALM** offices in Albany (☎9842 4500) or Esperance (☎9071 3733) and the tourist office in Ravensthorpe. Day passes can be deposited in an honor box at the entrance ($9 per vehicle). For camping, **Four Mile Beach** (just west of Hopetoun) and **Saint Mary Inlet** (at Point Ann) are the easiest to access by car (2 people $10, each extra adult $5.50, children $2). To reach **Point Ann,** a particularly good whale-watching spot, take Pabelup Dr. from the north, or Devils Creek Rd. from the west. Fires are not allowed, but gas barbecues are available free of charge at Mylies, Point Ann, Quoin Head and Fitzgerald Inlet. There are no reliable sources of water in the park, so be sure to bring enough. **Mt. Madden, Mt. Short,** and **Mt. Desmond** are not in the park itself, but are all near Ravensthorpe, and offer excellent views of the area. **Cheynes Beach** in **Waychinicup National Park** is also highly recommended. There are **ranger stations** in the park at East Mt. Barren (☎9838 3060) and on Murray Rd. (☎9837 1022), toward Bremer Bay.

WESTERN AUSTRALIA

ESPERANCE ☎08

Esperance (pop. 13,000) may be rather remote from other major settlements, but it is blessed with some of the best beaches and diving in all of Australia. In summer, the town hops with tourists who flock to the area to swim, fish, dive, and explore nearby Stokes, Cape Le Grand, Peak Charles, and Cape Arid National Parks. Esperance itself is a pleasant, though rather ordinary, town—the key to enjoying your stay is to escape to the natural splendor of its surroundings.

TRANSPORTATION. **Westrail buses** (☎13 10 53) stop near the tourist office and run to: Albany (6-10hr.; Tu-W, F-Sa 8am; $43); Kalgoorlie (5hr.; Tu, F 8:35am, Su 2pm; $36); Perth (10hr., M-Sa 8am, $56). Arriving by **car** from the west, the South Coast Hwy. (Monjingup Rd.) intersects Harbour Rd., which runs south into town. Several **car rental** companies have offices in town: **STOPOVER** (☎9071 0312) and **Avis** (☎9071 3998), have various deals for around $45 to $55 per day. While *Let's Go* does not recommend hitchhiking, **hitchhikers** report luck at the north end of Dempster St. and on Norseman Rd.

ORIENTATION AND PRACTICAL INFORMATION. The **Esplanade** flanks the bay, and **Dempster St.** snakes along roughly parallel to it. The **tourist office** is near the center of town on the corner of Dempster and Kemp St. (☎9071 2330; fax 9071 4543. Open M-F 8:45am-5pm, Sa-Su 9am-5pm, May-Aug. close at 4pm.) **Internet access** is at Computer Alley, 69c Dempster St. (☎9072 1293. Open M-F 9am-5pm, Sa 9am-noon.)

ACCOMMODATIONS AND FOOD. The **Esperance YHA Blue Waters Lodge,** 299 Goldfields Rd., is across the street from the ocean. Formerly a R.A.A.F. building in Kalgoorlie, the entire edifice was transported to Esperance, reassembled, and spruced up. The hostel is a 15min. walk from the city center along the harbor bike path. Perks include pool table, ping-pong table, Internet ($4 per 30min.), and book exchange. (☎/fax 9071 1040. Free bus station pickup and drop off. Dorms $16; singles $23; twins $40; families $55. Non-YHA $3 extra.) **Esperance Backpackers,** 14 Emily St., just outside the end of town, has spacious rooms and a comfy lounge. Even the kitchen has personality with a huge slab of local wood as the table. They can arrange a wide variety of tours at reasonable prices. (☎9071 4724. Internet $4 per 30min. Free pickup from the bus stop. Dorms $16; twins and doubles $42. NOMADS/VIP/YHA.) **NOMADS Shoestring Stays,** 23 Daphne St., is also a good option. Clean and ready to please, this hostel offers lockers in the rooms, Internet, a hot tub in summer, tours, free bike rental, and free pickup and drop off. (☎9071 3396. Dorms $17; singles $30; doubles $41. NOMADS/VIP/YHA.)

PRETTY IN PINK Why are many lakes in Western Australia pink? The *Dunaliella salina* algae and a bacteria called *Halobacterium cutirubrum* thrive along the salt crusts at the bottom of lakes, living in water with salinity as high as 35% sodium chloride–over 10 times the salinity of seawater. When salinity, temperature, and sunlight are at high levels, the bacteria produce beta carotene to protect themselves, breaking out into natural pink hues. The algae is even farmed in some places to make food coloring or dietary supplements.

There is good **camping** in Cape Le Grand National Park, 60km east of town ($9 per car entry fee; sites $12.50 for 2, $5.50 per extra person), and on **Woody Island** in Esperance Bay (sites from $9 per person). **Mackenzie's Island Cruises,** 71 The Esplanade, runs daily cruises to Woody, if enough people show up on the dock. (☎9071 5757. $53, 16 and under $20.)

The Tin Shed, on Andrew St., is a great place for a sandwich ($7-10) or a simple dinner from $13-16. (☎9071 2172. Open M-Th 9am-5pm, F-Sa 9am-9pm.) **Merivale Farm,** 25km east of Esperance along Merivale Rd., serves lush desserts and coffees. (☎9075 9020. Open only in summer Sa-W 10am-5pm.) Duncan's SupaValu **supermarket** is in the shopping center at the corner of Andrews St. and Dempster St. (Open M-W, F 8am-6pm, Th 8am-8pm, Sa 8am-5pm.)

SIGHTS AND ACTIVITIES. Drivers or bikers with strong legs should try the 38km loop along the **Great Ocean Dr.,** which snakes along the coast and by the algae-tinged **Pink Lake.** The tourist office has a decent map and the road is clearly marked. Take care if biking: the road can be narrow and curvy, and with such stunning costal views, drivers will have a hard time keeping their eyes on the road. The drive begins at the southern end of Dempster St. and turns right onto Twilight Beach Rd., passing great beaches; **Blue Haven** and **Twilight** are especially pretty.

Cape Le Grand National Park lies 60km east of Esperance and should not be missed. Take Goldfields Rd. north to Fisheries Rd., turn right onto Marivale Rd., and right again onto Cape Le Grand Rd. For transportation to the park, ask at Esperance Backpackers or Shoestring Stays about tours. However, the drive to the park along a 40km stretch of beach is beautiful. At Cape Le Grand, try the short (3km; allow 1½hr.) but direct ascent up **Frenchman Peak** for completely sheltered views of coast and sea. Down the road, **Lucky Bay** offers incredible white sands and glowing aquamarine water, some surf, and very friendly 'roos. **Hellfire Bay** is equally stunning. In summer there is good snorkeling, possibly with dolphins. *Beware of riptides and undertows, and if you are driving on the beach, do not park your car above squishy patches of sand that can suck in your car.*

Diving around Esperance is quite good. **Sanko Harvest,** the second largest **wreck dive** in the world, is popular among experienced divers. **Esperance Diving and Fishing** guides dives and charter fishing trips. (☎9071 5111. Diving from $80. Fishing charters from $145.) **Sea lions** put on a show below the big tanker jetty on the main beach in town. **Peak Charles National Park,** north of Esperance along the Coolgardie Esperance Hwy., has **rock climbing;** ask at the CALM office, 92 Dempster St. for details. (☎9071 3733. Open M-F 8:30am-4:30pm.)

GOLDFIELDS

Hundreds of kilometers east of Perth, a handful of towns cling tenaciously to a precarious existence in the middle of WA's harsh interior. Two things keep these towns from disappearing altogether: water, piped in from the coast, and gold. In 1893 a group of Irish prospectors stumbled onto an area that would become the Golden Mile, and the city of Kalgoorlie was born. Today, would-be miners continue to migrate to "Kal," now the unofficial capital of the Goldfields, in search of work. For the casual traveler however, Kal is a long way from anything and not much of a destination. The Goldfields are barren and dry, and if you're heading west to Perth from Eyre, you may consider heading south along the South Coast Hwy. to avoid them: the scenic coastal towns make for a more enjoyable trip.

KALGOORLIE-BOULDER ☎08

The twin towns of Kalgoorlie and Boulder (total pop. 30,500) cling together as if to escape the isolation of the surrounding outback. Their reason for survival is simple—more than a century after panning began here, the region's gold mines are still going strong. These days, folks don't come to town hoping to stumble upon a lode, stake a claim, and strike it rich—gold doesn't come in chunks anymore; it's in microscopic particles. Mammoth mining interests run the show, and the work is dirty. However, pay can be quite high, so workers flood the area and its hostels, creating an atmosphere that backpackers may find a bit gritty.

HI HO HI HO, OFF TO WORK I DON'T GO

The main reason people come to Kal is to work, but finding a job in mining is not as easy as one might expect. Many mining companies will only hire employees with previous experience, and require safety training and certification, which takes time and costs money. It can be done, but it isn't a breeze. Non-mining jobs may be easier to come by.

TRANSPORTATION

The **airport** is south of Boulder off Gatacre St. **Qantaslink, Ansett, and Skywest** offer daily service to Adelaide (Sa-Su) and Perth (1-3 times per day, times and prices vary; check with tourist centre). The **bus stop** is between the tourist office and the post office on Hannan St. Greyhound Pioneer heads to Perth (8hr., daily 10:45am, $102, book at tourist office). From the tourist office, **Westrail's Goldfields Express** serves Perth (8hr.; M, W, and F 10:05pm, T and Th 2pm; $77, with YHA $59). **Westrail Prospector trains** depart from the train station on the corner of Forrest and Wilson St. for Perth (8hr., 1-2 per day, $53) and Esperance via Norseman (5hr.; departs M, W, F 5pm; $34).

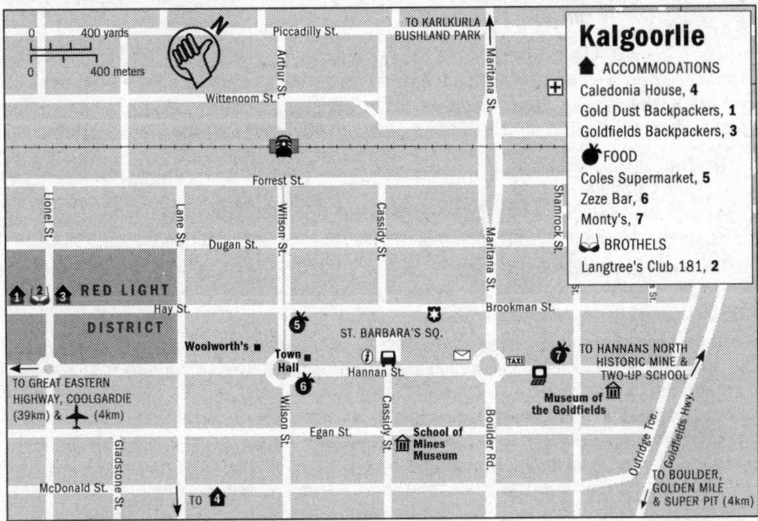

FOURTEEN CARAT ASPHALT Kalgoorlie, like all cities, originally had dirt streets, and one of the city's biggest problems was that whenever it rained, the streets immediately turned into impassable mudpits. Meanwhile, the town's miners were digging up huge amounts of a black stone called telluride in their search for gold, and didn't know what to do with it all. Eventually it occurred to the town's leaders that the telluride could be used to pave the streets, thereby killing two birds with one stone. It wasn't until after the job was done that a prominent scientist determined that telluride itself was composed largely of gold. Kalgoorlie's street had literally been paved with gold, but it didn't take them long to become unpaved once word got out. The town had to wait a little longer to solve its mud problem for good.

ORIENTATION AND PRACTICAL INFORMATION

Where the Great Eastern Hwy. (National 94 from Coolgardie) ends at the Goldfields Hwy., tumbleweeds roll by. A hard-looking man with a ruddy complexion exits a saloon here on **Hannan St.,** Kalgoorlie's main commercial boulevard, spits out some blood from the brawl he just won, and sidles over to the brothels on the parallel **Hay St.** Hannan St. looks like a movie set for an old Western and it is about as warm and welcoming as its story hero. Lionel St., Wilson St., and **Boulder Rd.** run perpendicular to Hannan and Hay St. along the main stretch. The residential district of Boulder lies several kilometers southeast. To reach Boulder from downtown Kalgoorlie, turn right on Boulder Rd. at the north end of Hannan St. and follow it into **Lane St.**

The **tourist office** is at 250 Hannan St. (☎9021 1966; fax 9021 2180. Open M-F 8:30am-5pm, Sa-Su 9am-5pm.) **Internet** is available at Matrix Internet Services, 87 Hannan St. (☎9022 3111. Open M-F 9am-5pm; $6 per hr.) There is a **post office** on Hannan St., south of city center. (Open M-F 8:30am-5pm.)

The police maintain that no areas of Kalgoorlie-Boulder are particularly unsafe, although they do warn to be careful of deep mining holes when bushwalking. Much of the city is poorly lit, and it is a good idea to exercise caution after dark. The center of Kal's red-light district, **Hay St.,** with neon-adorned tin shacks advertising sauna and spa services, is home to three working brothels. **Women may not want to walk alone in this area after dark.**

ACCOMMODATIONS

Most budget accommodations are geared toward those who have come to town for work and to stay several weeks or months. The two hostels on Hay St. are smack in the middle of Kal's red-light district, an area that tends to be noisier at night. Both offer tours or at least transportation around the city for a small fee.

Goldfields Backpackers, 166 Hay St. (☎9091 1482 or 0412 11 00 01; fax 9091 1484), near the intersection with Lionel St. Dingy place with shared kitchen, laundry, lounge, and swimming pool. Call the cell phone if nobody is at reception. More oriented towards travelers than long term workers. Dorms $16; singles $22; doubles $38.

Gold Dust Backpackers, 192 Hay St. (☎/fax 9091 3737). Clean, with kitchen and nice lounge spaces. Slightly rowdier crowd. Internet $8 per hr. Dorms $16; twins and doubles $40. ISIC/NOMADS/VIP/YHA.

Caledonia House, 122 Piesse St. (☎9093 1413), Boulder. Simple, clean singles with well-kept, communal kitchen and lounge area. Singles $20; doubles $40.

FOOD AND NIGHTLIFE

Monty's, at the corner of Hannan and Porter, is open 24hr. and has various deals (Tu $9 pasta). The **Zeze Bar** in the Kalgoorlie Hotel, at the corner of Hannan and Wilson St., crafts excellent woodfire gourmet pizzas from $12-17. (☎9021 3046.

Open daily noon-2:30pm, 6-9:30pm.) **Cafes** line Hannan St. and many open early and close late. Kal is a hard-working, hard-drinking town. Many **pubs** cluster near the corner of Hannan and Maritana St. **Coles supermarket** is at the corner of Wilson and Brookman St. (Open M-W, F 8am-6pm, Th 8am-9pm, Sa 8am-5pm.)

SIGHTS

Hannans North Historic Mining Reserve, a right turn off Goldfields Hwy., 2km north of Hannan St., offers demonstrations of gold panning and underground mining techniques. The gold pouring and drilling demonstrations are worthwhile, but don't plan on striking it rich panning for gold. The underground tour gives some insight into just how demanding mining work is; plug your ears tight for "the screamer" and the drill. A brand-new, multi-million-dollar Mining Hall of Fame adds to the proceedings. (☎9091 4074. Open daily 9am-4:30pm. $16.50, concessions $12, children $8.50, families up to 6 $42.) The **Super Pit,** an immense open-pit working mine, is the largest hole in the Southern Hemisphere. Do not miss this amazing look into the heart of Kalgoorlie; you will be awed by its size. For an added treat, they often set off explosions daily at 1pm and 5pm. The lookout is just outside town; turn towards Boulder on the Goldfield's Hwy., then turn left at the sign for the pit. (Open daily 6am-7pm, except when closed for further blasting. Free.) The **Western Australian Museum,** on Hannan between Porter St. and Outridge Tce., offers info about the history of gold mining in the area, tools, and samples of the product. (☎9021 8533. Open daily 10am-4:30pm. Suggested donation $2.) For a unique experience, you can visit one of Kalgoorlie's **brothels. Langtree's Club 181,** 181 Hay St., recently received a $2.5 million dollar face-lift (but no boob job) and the tour shows just what that money bought. Yes, $25 is steep for views of a few bedrooms, but it's a lot cheaper than the "hands-on" tours. (☎9026 2181. 18+. Tours daily 11am, 3pm, 7pm, and Sa-Su 1pm.)

There are a few mining ghost towns north of Kalgoorlie, but in most, not even much rubble remains. The exception is **Gwalia,** a two-hour drive north on the Goldfields Hwy., adjoined to the present-day settlement of Leonora. Several outfits have **bush tours;** Aboriginal guide Geoff Stokes (☎9093 3745; Geoffstokes@bigpond.com) runs day tours ($80) and camping trips ($170 per night) focusing on Aboriginal culture and native plants and animals.

NORSEMAN ☎08

About 100 years ago, "Hardy Norseman" was tethered overnight in this area as his rider slept. The restless horse pawed at the dusty ground, uncovering a chunk of gold. Prospectors rushed to the area, and the town of Norseman was born. Today, however, Norseman serves more as a waystation than a destination. For travelers heading north from Esperance, Norseman is the first encounter with the Goldfields. For those heading east across the desolate Nullarbor Plain, it is the last taste of civilization for over 1000km.

The **tourist office** on Robert St., one block east on the highway between Sinclair and Richardson St., has information about Norseman and traveling the Eyre Hwy. They also offer free showers, which is a dream come true for Nullarbor survivors. (☎9039 1071. Open daily 9am-5pm.) Next to the office is a small welcome park, one of the few green spots in town. (Open daily 8am-6pm.) The people of Norseman were shocked when ANZ bank recently installed an **ATM.** "What do we do with this new-fangled gadget?" an bank customer cried. There is **Internet** at the Telecentre on Robert St. (☎9039 0538. Open M-F 10am-11:30am. $2.50 per 15min.)

The family-run **Norseman Guest House and Backpackers Lodge** on Prinsep St. offers comfortable accommodations for visitors who are inevitably on their way somewhere else. Backpackers can use a small kitchen and an outdoor sheltered lounge area. (☎9039 1541. Dorms $16.50; singles $27.50; twins $44.) The town's hotels and motels have restaurants, but there are no great budget options. The SupaValu, 89 Robert St., has **groceries.** (Open M-F 8:30am-6pm, Sa 8:30am-5pm, Su 9:30am-1pm.) The **BP 24-hour Travelstop,** north of town at the exit for the Eyre Hwy., has a diner, convenience store, and **petrol.**

TYRANNY OF DISTANCE The Nullarbor spans bewildering expanses of nothingness, punctuated by a few isolated outposts where passersby gas-up or take a breather—and these are some of the most isolated settlements in the world. How do a few hundred residents spread out over these thousands of kilometers cope with emergencies, or even their basic medical needs? Australia's **Royal Flying Doctor Service** provides vital medical services to 80% of continental Australia from 20 air bases spread out across the country. For 70 years, doctors have flown into remote communities in planes outfitted as medical centers, setting up makeshift clinics in homesteads and carting trauma victims up into the skies. The Flying Doctor has become an Australian icon for overcoming the "tyranny of distance".

CROSSING THE NULLARBOR

The **Eyre Hwy.**, running between Norseman and Adelaide across the **Nullarbor Plain** (p. 458) is a grueling desert haul by car or bus; on a Greyhound **bus,** it's a mind-boggling 26hr. trek ($225, 10% discount with YHA card). The one noteworthy sight is the pink **Lake McDonald** near Penong. **90 Mile Straight,** the longest completely straight stretch of highway in Australia and possibly the world, begins just west of Cocklebiddy. For questions on what is allowed across the border into SA, call the agriculture department (☎9039 3227 in WA, ☎8625 2108 in SA; www.agric.wa.gov.au). The **tourist office** in Norseman has helpful info and handles bus bookings. When you reach **Ceduna** at the eastern corner of SA's **Eyre Peninsula,** pick up a Nullarbor certificate of completion at the tourist office. That's a keeper. (For more info on this highway, see p. 458.)

GREAT EASTERN HIGHWAY

The drive from Perth to Kalgoorlie along the Great Eastern Highway is long (nearly 600km) and uneventful. The first hour heading east from Perth winds through the city's suburbs and the **Swan River Valley;** travelers may encounter nasty **traffic** near the city. Driving through the **Darling Range** offers beautiful fields and forests full of wildflowers in season. Road trains rule the road; beware of wide loads bearing machinery, farm equipment, and even buildings. The last stretch between the tiny town of **Southern Cross** (really no more than a wide spot in the highway) and **Coolgardie** is a very desolate 200km. This part of the highway is not as well maintained, so fuel up whenever possible. **Merredin** (pop. 3700), home of the world's longest road train (over 600m), is the largest town on the Great Eastern between Coolgardie and Perth. The tourist office, post office, bank, and supermarket all lie within one block of each other on Barrack St., which is just one block north of the highway. It's a good spot for lunch—the comfortable **Hay Loft Coffee Lounge,** next to the tourist office, is one of several nice spots in town.

Coolgardie has exceedingly little to offer the average traveler. It's a dusty frontier town that serves mainly as a residential satellite for families of Kalgoorlie miners. The main street, 94 Hwy. (Bayley St. in town) houses a **tourist bureau** (☎9026 6090; open daily 9am-5pm). There are no **ATMs** in town, but most roadhouses have **EFT-POS** and the post office does banking. If you must spend the night in Coolgardie, the **Caltex Roadhouse,** on Bayley St., rents simple, clean rooms. (☎9026 6049; fax 9026 6756. Singles $38.50; doubles $49.50.)

BATAVIA COAST AND MIDLANDS

Renowned as much for its seas of bright autumn wildflowers as for its beautiful coast, this region depends upon fishing, agriculture, and tourism to earn its keep. The Batavia Coast stretches from just north of the Pinnacles as far as the red cliffs of Kalbarri, and takes its name from the most famous of the many shipwrecks that litter its waters. The wheat-growing Midlands extend hundreds of kilometers

ENGINEERING A TRAGEDY Ask any Western Australia local for the story of the Kalgoorlie pipeline, and you'll likely hear a popular Westralian yarn. The tale concerns an engineer who claimed he could build a conduit which would carry water from Perth all the way to Kalgoorlie. Since Kalgoorlie is over 500km away from Perth and over 400m higher in elevation, no one believed that it could be done. But he insisted, and finally someone gave him the money to try. The local legend relates that after he designed and built this huge pipeline, the engineer went to Kalgoorlie and turned on the tap. When nothing happened, the broken man shot himself in the head. No one bothered to turn off the tap, and about an hour later, water flowed out of the pipe and into Kalgoorlie. This account is a myth, but the real story of the engineer's death is tragic as well. After proposing the project in 1898, C. Y. O'Connor, frustrated by delays in construction and plagued by faithless critics, took his own life in 1902, one year before his visionary pipeline became a successful reality.

inland. The Brand Hwy. is the main artery of the region, and runs north from Perth a few dozen kilometers from the coast. A sealed, scenic highway (Hwy. 60) runs through sloping dunes and heathland along the coast from Perth to Lancelin, and then continues again past fishing shacks from Cervantes to Dongara as Indian Ocean Rd. The stretch from Lancelin to Cervantes is unsealed and only accessible to 4WD. The area has offerings for all seasons: the mind-blowing wildflowers peak in autumn, the world-famous windsurfing is best in summer, and the jagged gorges of Kalbarri are busy in winter.

LANCELIN ☎08

Lancelin (pop. 800), 126km north of Perth, might just be the windsurfing capital of Australia. The Aborigines called the area *Wangaree*, meaning "Good Fishing Place," and this small fishing village still thrives upon the ocean's bounty. Yet Lancelin is equally a place of good winds, and thrill-seekers flock here from October through March to ride the air currents. The high point of the season is the famed Ledge Point Sailboard Classic held in the second week in January, but even in the off-season, there's almost always some good breeze.

TRANSPORTATION AND PRACTICAL INFORMATION. There is no public transportation to Lancelin, but **Coastal Coachlines** runs **buses** from Perth to nearby Regans Ford. (☎9652 1036. 2hr.; departs the Perth train station M-F 4:30pm; $14. Book ahead.) Better yet, the YHA will pick up its guests from Perth for $25. The easiest way to reach Lancelin is by car; from Perth, take Bulwer St. to Charles St., which becomes Hwy. 60 (Wanneroo Rd.). A **4WD vehicle** can drive the beach, and it's possible to drive along the dunes up the coast to **Cervantes.** Proceed with caution, and check with the **tourist information centre,** 102 Gingin Rd., to see if the beach is suitable. (☎9655 1100. Open daily 9am-6pm.) Lancelin has one small shopping strip on Gingin Rd., which includes a surfshop, two bakeries, a **supermarket** (☎9655 1172; open daily 7am-7pm), and a Telecentre, 127 Gingin Rd., with **Internet.** (☎9655 2033. Open M-F 10am-4pm, Sa 10am-1pm. $8 per hr.)

ACCOMMODATIONS. The sparkling, well-run **YHA Lancelin Lodge,** 10 Hopkins St., has a comfy lounge, free bikes, boogie boards, fishing rods, and a lovely kitchen. It's only a short walk to Lancelin's beautiful beach, and the people couldn't be nicer. (☎9655 2020; fax 9655 2021. Internet $6 per hr. Dorms $17; doubles $45; family rooms $60; rates higher in peak season.) **Lancelin Holiday Accommodations** can be a good deal for groups, offering well-maintained private units with full kitchen and bath. Inquire at the tourist office. (☎9655 1100. Double $64, $320 weekly; suite for up to six $75/$480.) The other budget alternative is the **Lancelin Caravan Park,** just down Hopkins St. from the YHA—you can't miss the sign. (☎9655 1056. Sites $8.80, powered $11; on-site vans $22.)

ACTIVITIES. **Windsurfing** is Lancelin's major draw. **Werner's Hotspot** (☎9655 1553) rents equipment and gives windsurfing lessons. Another Lancelin attraction is its sand dunes, which extend for miles to the north and east of town. The dunes are a 4WD playground, and also a practice area for the Australian **military.** They're accessible by car, and many tour operators out of Perth bring travelers here to sandboard (like snowboarding, but on... well, you get the idea). **Bigfoot Bus Adventure Tours** offers a veritable rollercoaster ride over the dunes in a schoolbus with monster truck tires and an equally monster stereo. You don't crush any cars, but it's a fun trip all the same. (☎9655 2550. $28, children $18.)

There are several coastal **nature walks** in the area, primarily to view wildflowers in bloom; pick up trail maps at the hostel or tourist center. Lancelin's coral reefs are unusually close to shore, which makes for good snorkeling and diving. The lagoon on the far side of **Lancelin Island,** a bird sanctuary within swimmable distance, is one of the best spots. Very experienced divers enjoy the **Key Biscayne Dive** around an old drilling rig, 19km northwest of Ledge Point. **Lancelin Surfsports,** 127 Gingin Rd., rents scuba, snorkeling, sandboarding, and surfing gear. (☎9655 1441. Dive gear $55 per day; sandboards, surfboards, snorkels $11 for 2hr. or $22 per day. Open daily 8am-4pm, later in summer.) Fishing in the area is also good; casual anglers cast right off the jetty.

NAMBUNG NATIONAL PARK: THE PINNACLES

The over-hyped Pinnacles Desert, located in Nambung National Park, may disappoint those who fork over $100 for a day trip from Perth, but it's still a worthwhile stop on the great trek northward. The park isn't really a desert at all, but an expanse of sand dunes with thousands of wind-eroded limestone pillars, up to 4m tall. Dutch sailors sighting the jagged rocks from the sea mistook them for the ruins of an ancient city. From up close the park looks more like a graveyard, and is quite beautiful in its own desolate way. The Pinnacles are best viewed at sunrise or sunset, or under the light of a full moon.

The park is a good 250km north of Perth, and driving is definitely the easiest way to get there. The primary base for exploring the park is the small coastal town of **Cervantes. Greyhound-McCafferty's** (☎13 20 30) drops off at the Cervantes turnoff from the Brand Hwy. (2hr., 1 per day, $20). **HappyDay Tours** picks up from there for a 3hr. walking tour of the Pinnacles. (☎9652 7244. Departs daily 8am. $33, from Cervantes $20.) The friendly **Pinnacles Beach Backpackers,** 91 Seville St., on the corner of Seville and Barcelona St., offers beautiful, sunny rooms up the street from the beach. Baby pinnacles decorate the garden. (☎9652 7377; fax 9652 7318. Dorms $18, doubles 45.) In Cervantes, the Shell Gas Station acts as the official **tourist bureau** (☎9652 7041; open daily 8am-6pm), but in a town this size, any local can probably point you in the right direction.

Some popular one-day and over-night packages to the Pinnacles are given by **West Coast Explorers** (☎9418 8835), which arrives at sunset, and **Redback Safaris** (☎9275 6204). Prices range from $90-110. If you're driving, allow one hour for the drive west to Cervantes from the left turn off the Brand Hwy., about 20km north of the Cataby Roadhouse. The last stretch of road before the Pinnacles is unsealed but relatively smooth ($9 vehicle fee). **Camping** is not allowed in the park, but there are picnic areas and a beach at **Hangover Bay,** a few kilometers from the Pinnacles site. **Turquoise Coast Enviro Tours** unveils the area's other natural attractions with 4WD treks to the **Stockyard Tunnel Cave,** which descends 270m underground, and **Lake Indoom,** a nice waterskiing and swimming spot. (☎9652 7047. 10hr., $100.)

GERALDTON ☎08

For a town sprawled along the stunning Indian Ocean, Geraldton (pop. 24,000) pays surprisingly little attention to its coastline. Most restaurants, shops, and hotels in town actually face away from the beach. Windsurfers eager to test their skill in the strong southerly winds flock to Geraldton every summer, but there aren't many sights worth noting back on land. Nevertheless, the many restaurants, several movie theaters, and budget accommodations make Geraldton a good place to stop for a day on your way somewhere else.

THE LITTLE PRINCIPALITY Along the North Coast Hwy. between Geraldton and Kalbarri, Australia takes a hiatus. **Hut River Province** is a $75km^2$ area that claims to be its own principality. This island of royalty was created by Prince Leonard George Casley with a few twists of the law for a few benefits of tax evasion. Visitors of Prince Leonard (a former farmer) and his very own principality can get a special stamp in their passport, Hut River postage stamps (that need additional Australian stamps to work), and Hut River currency. If you happen to bump into the prince around town, ask him to show you his realm; he is said to be brilliant and talkative—if perhaps a bit eccentric.

WESTERN AUSTRALIA

TRANSPORTATION AND PRACTICAL INFORMATION. If you're arriving by car from the Brand Hwy., head straight through the rotary up Cathedral Ave. to get to the town center. The town's main drag, Chapman Rd., and the shop-lined Marine Tce. both run parallel to the coast and intersect Cathedral Ave. **Greyhound** and **Westrail** run **buses** to Perth (1-2 per day, 6hr., $40). Greyhound also runs to Broome (daily 4:15pm, $280) via Carnarvon ($63) and Exmouth ($154). The **tourist office** is located inside the Bill Sewall Complex at the corner of Bayly St. and Chapman Rd., about 1km north of Cathedral Ave. (☎9921 3999; fax 9964 2445. Open M-F 8:30am-5pm, Sa 9am-4:30pm, Su 9:30am-4:30pm.)

ACCOMMODATIONS AND FOOD. **Batavia Backpackers,** next to the tourist office, is a friendly, convenient place to stay with basic rooms and a view of the ocean. (☎9964 3001; fax 9964 3611. Dorms $15.50; singles $20; twins $34. ISIC/VIP/YHA.) **Geraldton YHA Foreshore Backpackers,** 172 Marine Tce., one block southwest of Cathedral Ave., has a musty flavor and a refreshing lack of bunk beds. (☎9921 3275; fax 9921 3233. Free pickup and drop off. Internet $7 per hr. Dorms $15; singles $22; twins and doubles $37; family rooms for 2 adults $37, each child $5.50). Woolworth's, in the Stiling Shopping Centre on Sanford and Durlacher St., has cheap **groceries.** (Open M-F 8am-6pm, Th 8am-9pm, Sa 8am-5pm.)

SIGHTS AND ACTIVITIES. Most people come to Geraldton for one reason: **windsurfing.** The best conditions are Oct.-Nov. and Mar.-Apr., though it is good year-round. Bring your own gear or pay the price at **Sailwest,** at the Point Moore Lighthouse on Chapman Rd. south of town. (☎9964 1722. Windsurfing gear $90 per day, surfboards $30, lessons $25 per hr. Open M-F 9am 'til 20 knots, Sa-Su 10am 'til 20 knots.) The best windsurfing in the area is at **Point Moore,** the windiest spot around. **St. George's Beach** has tamer winds, but also a shallow reef that can be dangerous. In the town itself, **Back Beach** is the surfing hot spot and also has reasonably good swimming. The **Abrolhos Islands,** an archipelago about 60km off of Geraldton, were the site (and cause) of the Batavia wreck. These islands are rich in marine life; some say the diving is as good as on the Great Barrier. With a fast new boat, **Oddysey Abrolhos** (☎042 838 250) runs daytrips to the islands, and both the Oddysey and **Eco Abrolhos Tours** (☎9964 7887) offer extended tours. **Abrolhos Air** (☎9923 3151) takes visitors on sight-seeing flights from $66.

KALBARRI ☎08

Originally home to some of Australia's earliest Europeans—two Dutch settlers marooned just south of town for their role in the Batavia mutiny—Kalbarri (pop. 1700) is the gateway to the wonderland of Kalbarri National Park. Here, multi-colored bluffs soar out of the ocean swells and the Murchison River snakes through the plunging gorges of the park's interior. During rock lobster season (Nov.-June), crayfishing boats bob in the calm waters off the mouth of the Murchison River, and year-round travelers weave in and out of town on their way to and from the surrounding natural splendor.

The access road from the North West Coastal Hwy. becomes Clotworthy St. in town and connects from the east to **Grey St.,** which skirts the coast and runs to the town center. A new, paved **scenic road** enters Kalbarri from the south, having branched from the North West Coastal Hwy. at Northampton. The **tourist bureau** is on Grey St. to the left of Woods St. when facing the ocean. (☎9937 1104; fax 9937 1474. Open daily 9am-5pm.) The **Department of Conservation and Land Management (CALM)** office (☎9937 1140) is on the Ajana-Kalbarri Rd., 1km east of town.

Kalbarri Backpackers, 52 Mortimer St., offers decent rooms, a pool, BBQ, bike rental ($9 per day), 4WD rental (ages 25+, $77 per day), and free use of snorkel gear and boogie boards. From the tourist bureau, turn right on Grey St., then right on Woods St. (☎9937 1430; fax 9937 1563. Dorms $17; doubles $42. 7th night free. Non-VIP/YHA $2 extra.) **Kalbarri Anchorage Caravan Park,** across from the jetty at the north end of Grey St., is in a scenic location with an enclosed kitchen facility. (☎9937 1181; fax 9937 1806. Sites for 2 $14, on-site vans $36; $5 per extra person.)

Finlay's Fresh Fish BBQ, on Magee Crescent, serves healthy portions of tasty seafood for $10 to $18 in a huge outdoor shed with picnic tables and campfires. To get there from Grey St., turn left at Porter St., right on Walker St., then right onto Magee Crescent. (☎9937 1260. Open Tu-Su 5:30-8:30pm.) Foodland **supermarket** is in the Ampol station on Grey St. (☎9937 1100. Open daily 7am-6pm.)

KALBARRI NATIONAL PARK

The town of Kalbarri is dwarfed by the surrounding 18.3km^2 of dramatic oceanside cliffs, red river gorges, and wildflowers. Eleven kilometers east of town, an unsealed access road runs 25km off the highway to **The Loop** and **Z Bend,** which are stunning overlooks onto the Murchison River. Don't miss **Nature's Window,** at the Loop lookout, a red rock outcropping that frames the scenery behind it. Further east, near the North West Coastal Hwy., is the access road for the less-visited **Ross Graham Lookout** and **Hawks Head.** The park also has a coastal section south of town, where turnoffs lead from Red Bluff Rd. to **Red Bluff Lookout, Mushroom Rock, Eagle Gorge,** and **Natural Bridge,** all of which overlook the sea and, frequently, passing dolphins and whales.

The park's unsealed roads are generally in good condition and 2WD-accessible, but check with **CALM** (☎9937 1140) for updates. Admission to the inland river gorge area costs $9 per vehicle; the machine doesn't accept bills, so bring $1 and $2 coins. Camping is not permitted in the park.

Perhaps the best hike in the area is **The Loop** (8km; 4hr.), which runs east along the cliff top from Nature's Window to the riverbank, and then down along the ledges and floodplain at water level. Be sure to keep the river to your right. Along the coast, the cliffside hike (one-way 10km; 4hr.) from **Eagle Gorge** to the **Natural Bridge** skirts banded sandstone and limestone cliffs that have been worn into fantastic formations. A **Cycle Shuttle** drops hikers off daily at the Natural Bridge for the one-way trip back toward town. (☎9937 1161. Departs daily 9:30am. $9.) The 38km trek from the **Ross Graham Lookout** to the Loop is for the diehard hiker. It takes about four days, and CALM recommends hiking with at least five people. If you plan an overnight hike in the area, alert CALM beforehand.

For those without wheels, tours are plentiful and provide access to otherwise-unreachable areas of the park. **Kalbarri Adventure Tours** has a day-long "Canoe the Gorges" trip stopping at Nature's Window and the Z Bend. The hikes in and out are tough at parts but worth the sweat. (☎9937 1677. M, Tu, Th, Sa; $60.) **Kalbarri Safari Tours** runs a full-day trek along Z Bend. (☎9937 1011. Tu, W, F, Su; $60.) **Kalbarri Bush and Wildflower Tours** offers half-day tours to the Z Bend and Nature's Window. (☎9937 1742. $40.) For more outlandish thrills, you can try abseiling down the gorges with **Kalbarri Abseil** (☎9937 1618; daily, $60) or **sandboard** 280ft. down the superbowl with **Kalbarri Safari Tours** (M, Th, Sa; $60).

Kalbarri Explorer Ocean Charters has sunset dolphin and whale trips, morning whale watching trips from August to November, and deep sea fishing on demand. (☎9937 2027. Sunset 2hr., $44. Morning $49. 6hr. fishing., $130.) Plant lovers will appreciate the herbarium and nature trail at the **Kalbarri Wildflower Centre** on the North West Coastal Hwy., 1km before Kalbarri. (☎9937 1229. Open June-Nov. daily 9am-5pm. $2. Free bus service daily 10am from tourist office. Guided 1hr. walks Aug.-Oct. daily 10am, $6.) **Rainbow Jungle,** on Red Bluff Rd. about 3.5km south of town, is a parrot breeding center. (☎9937 1248. Open Tu-Sa 9am-5pm, Su 10am-5pm; last entrance 4pm. $8.50, ages 4-16 $3.50.)

OUTBACK COAST AND GASCOYNE

The Outback Coast is an unfathomable expanse of bushland, broken up only by termite mounds and the occasional befuddled emu crossing the road. Although the distances between towns are daunting, the desolate landscape holds its own sense of wonder. The dazzling ocean that abuts this semi-desert counters its sparseness with a lush flowering of marine life, from the dolphins and dugongs of Shark Bay to the whale sharks and coral of the Ningaloo Marine Park. Winter is peak season, when caravanning Perthites park themselves along the sunny coast to wait out the chill of the southlands.

SHARK BAY

Shark Bay, Western Australia's much-touted World Heritage area, was the site of the earliest recorded European landing in Australia. In 1616, Dutch Explorer Dirk Hartog came ashore at Cape Inscription on the island that now bears his name. Today, Shark Bay is known mainly for the dolphins at Monkey Mia, tranquil shell beaches, and the "living fossils" (stromatolites) at Hamelin Pool. The best way to see the area is by car or on a tour; buses are infrequent.

DENHAM. With around 500 permanent residents, the westernmost town in Australia is just a speck on the Peron Peninsula. The main street, **Knight Tce.,** runs parallel to the town's narrow beach. It seems as though you can see the ocean from any point in town. Most travelers stay here because it's the closest town to Monkey Mia, but the area's natural beauty makes it worthwhile.

The Greyhound **bus** departs for the Overlander Roadhouse on the North West Costal Hwy. from the Shell station on Knight Tce. (M, Th, Sa 5am, 6pm). The area is best seen by car; **Shark Bay Car Hire** (☎9948 1247), on Knight Tce., rents cars. The **tourist bureau,** 71 Knight Tce., a few doors down from the Shell station, is very helpful and has **Internet** access. (☎9948 1253; fax 9948 1065. Internet $5 per 30min. Open daily 9am-6pm.) A few doors down, the **Department of Conservation and Land Management (CALM),** 67 Knight Tce., advises on Monkey Mia and the area's parks, and sells National Park passes. (☎9948 1208. Open M-F 8am-5pm.)

The **YHA Denham Bay Lodge,** on Knight Tce., 100m south of the bus stop, has nice facilities—dorms are shared units with bath and kitchen. (☎9948 1278; fax 9948 1031. Free bus to Monkey Mia daily 7:45am, returning at 4:30pm. Dorms $18.50; twins and doubles $48. ISIC/VIP/YHA.) Tradewinds **Supermarket** is at the BP Station. (Open daily 7am-7pm.)

MONKEY MIA. At Monkey Mia, the Indian bottlenose dolphins of Shark Bay swim right up to the shore to be fed by herds of tourists. The dolphins have been visiting Monkey Mia since the time it was nothing but a sheep-farming area, but in the past ten years, the playful creatures have become an international sensation. Some think Monkey Mia provides an unparalleled opportunity to interact with intelligent, sociable animals; others find it a contrived, exploitative, and downright tacky show. You'll have to come here to decide the issue for yourself.

One-day access to the site is $6; a family pass costs $12, and four-week passes are $9, although it only takes an hour or two to "do" the Monkey Mia dolphin bit. Generally there are three feedings between 8am and 1pm each day; it's best to get there early in the morning. The reserve is home to an **information centre** and the **Department of Conservation and Land Management (CALM) office,** which has displays, videos, and talks. (☎9948 1366. Open daily 8am-4pm.) **Aristocat 2** offers cruises to see marine life, with underwater windows and a short talk about the dugong, an endangered species of seacow. (☎9948 1446. $29-49, children $14-20.)

The **YHA Monkey Mia Dolphin Resort,** right next to the dolphin interaction site, has backpacker beds in cramped, aging campervans, and sites. (☎9948 1320; fax 9948 1034. Campsites $8; dorms $16.) Bring food to Monkey Mia; the restaurants and mini-mart food shop (open 7am-6pm; Internet $6 per 30min.) are expensive.

FAMILY FEUD The infamous Vegemite that pops up all over Australia for breakfast—just when you think you are safe with plain toast and butter—was not always vegemite. It was originally called Parwill, as a competitive move against Marmite, another splendid spread of yeastiness. When you've got an Australian accent, Marmite sounds like "Ma might." And Parwill sounds like "Pa will," as though whatever confidence Ma lacks, Pa possesses. Nobody got this complicated joke, though, so the spread was renamed vegemite.

OTHER SITES. About 100km south of Denham and 34km west of the Overlander Roadhouse lies **Hamelin Pool,** with a white shell beach and **stromatolites.** Stromatolites are formed over thousands of years by microbes, and are the oldest known form of life on Earth. To reach these sights, you need a car or tour. **Shark Bay Coaches** gives tours to the Stromatolites and Shell Beach. (☎9948 1601. $44.)

Though not the most thrilling of sights, the Hamelin Pool stromatolites are one of only two living colonies in the world. A short boardwalk extending into the pool's crystal clear, salty waters allows for a closer look. Back on shore, a short walking trail winds along the beach and through a small quarry where chunks of sedimentary shell "rocks" were cut and used to construct many of the area's early buildings. **Camping** is available at the **Hamelin Pool Caravan Park.** (☎9942 5905. Sites for 2 $12, powered $13, each extra adult $6, extra child $2.) For **info** on the area, inquire at the tea rooms in the caravan park. (Open daily 8:30am-5:30pm.)

Fifty kilometers north of the turn-off to the Hamelin Pool along the Denham-Hamelin Rd. is the turn-off for **Shell Beach,** a dazzling 60km expanse of tiny white shells, up to 10m deep. Bring something to sit on if you want to do any sunbathing.

In the northern reaches of Shark Bay, 4WD tracks lead to **Steep Point** and the tip of **Cape Peron North,** which are great coastal areas for swimming and fishing. **Camping** is available in Peron National Park, but only 4WD vehicles can access the sites ($10 for 2, $5.50 per extra person, $2 per extra child).

CARNARVON ☎08

Even though it's near the ocean, Carnarvon (pop. 7000) is at best a place to catch your breath and break up the long distances between destinations on the west coast. Most people come here looking for work at the many local fruit plantations.

ORIENTATION AND PRACTICAL INFORMATION. **Greyhound-McCafferty's** buses depart from the tourist bureau for: Broome (1 per day; $143); Darwin (1 per day); Exmouth ($97); Perth (1-2 per day, $108). Integrity has buses to Exmouth (8:30am M, F; $75) via Coral Bay ($60) and Perth (M, W, F; $100). A big yellow plastic banana welcomes visitors to Carnarvon as they head into town along Robinson St. from the North West Coastal Hwy. The center of Carnarvon is **Robinson St.** between **Babbage Island Rd.** and **Olivia Tce.,** which passes along the water. The **tourist bureau** is at 11 Robinson St., in the Carnarvon Civic Centre at the corner of Stuart St. (☎9941 1146; fax 9941 1149. Open M-F 8:30am-5pm, Sa 9am-noon.)

ACCOMMODATIONS AND FOOD. **Carnarvon Backpackers,** 9790 Olivia Tce., south of Robinson St., has small, self-contained units that were built for American scientists on the Apollo and Gemini missions. With a large contingent of working travelers, the management has heaps of info on jobs, and the atmosphere is warm and social. There's BBQ, off-street parking, A/C or fans, and canoe use. (☎/fax 9941 1095. Internet $1 per 10min. Dorms $18-19, weekly $102; doubles $45/$270.) The **Carnarvon Tourist Centre Caravan Park,** 108 Robinson St., is five blocks down Robinson St. from the tourist office. (☎9941 1438. Book ahead in winter. Sites $15, powered $17; clean cabins with TV and A/C for 2 $50; each extra person $5.)

Woolworth's, in the Carnarvon Boulevard Shopping Center on Robinson St., has cheap **groceries.** (☎9941 2477. Open F-W 8am-8pm, Th 8am-9pm.) There is a weekly **produce market** on Robinson St. across from the tourist bureau (Sa 8:30am-noon).

SIGHTS. Babbage Island Rd. runs along the coast to **Pelican Point,** and makes for a pleasant bike ride among mangroves. Along the way, the mile-long jetty has good fishing and crabbing. A drive or bike ride east of town, on the back roads just north of the North West Coastal Hwy., passes many banana and mango **plantations.** Fresh fruit and veggies are plentiful and cheap; ask if you can collect the non-saleable fruits lying on the ground. **Carnarvon Bus Charter** visits the plantations, as well as the shrimp factory, boat harbor, salt mine, blowholes, jetty, and the OTC—the out-of-use NASA communications center on the outskirts of town. (☎9941 1146. Town tour $20, children $16.50; saltmine and blowholes $50, children $39.)

The Blowholes, 73km north of town, are water jets that reach as high as 20m in choppy weather; a lovely beach is 1km south. To get there, go 24km north on the North West Coastal Hwy. and turn left at the sign. The limestone access road can get pretty choppy; ask after conditions at the tourist bureau.

Carnarvon is a popular base for trips to **Mt. Augustus,** the largest rock in Australia; it's twice the size of Ayers Rock. The trip is 460km by car on Gascoyne Junction, a 2WD unsealed road that can get rough; check on road conditions at the tourist bureau before leaving. **Stockman Safaris** runs treks to the **Kennedy Range** and a sheep station. (☎9941 3116. 1 day $110, 2 days $250-300.)

CORAL BAY ☎08

Coral Bay is one of two gateways (Exmouth is the other) to the splendid Ningaloo Marine Park. The Ningaloo Reef, over 250km long, starts south of Coral Bay and stretches north around the Northwest Cape and back into Exmouth Gulf. The town itself is just a small collection of dive shops and caravan parks right on the reef. The beach is a good spot for snorkeling and swimming.

There are four main non-dive outfitters in Coral Bay, offering a wide-range of activities from scenic flights to dune buggy tours, in addition to those listed here. **Coral Bay Adventures** (☎9942 5955), with a booking agent at Mermaid's Cave in the shopping arcade on the east side of town, has whale shark tours (Mar.-June; $275) and glass-bottom boat tours ($25). The **Bayview Caravan Park** (☎9942 5932) has similar options and 4WD tours. With a kiosk in the People's Park Caravan Village, **Ningaloo Experience** (☎9942 5887) runs manta ray tours ($95) and fishing charters (from $140). A few doors down, **Coral Bay Dive Centre** (☎9942 5830) has whale-watching ($60), sunset cruises ($35), manta ray tours ($90), and snorkel tours ($110). Divers flock to Ningaloo in droves, and while they'll find more options in Exmouth, Coral Bay proves a good alternative destination. **Ningaloo Reef Dive Centre,** in the shopping arcade, offers two-dive trips from $132, and a certification course that starts Saturdays for $335. **Power Dive** offers tours for people who want to dive but aren't certified; an air hose connects you to the surface and you can go down to 6m. (☎9942 5889. $50.)

The Perth-Exmouth **Greyhound** bus (☎13 20 30) and **Integrity buses** (☎1800 226 339) head to Perth (Integrity Su and Th, $150; Greyhound $189) and Exmouth (Integrity M and F $35; Greyhound $56). The shopping arcade on the right side of the road as you enter Coral Bay houses a small **supermarket** (☎9942 5988; open daily 8am-6pm), Coral Bay News and Gifts, which doubles as the local **post office** (☎9942 5995; open M-F 8:30am-5pm) and a **bakery** (open M-F 7am-5:30pm). **The Mermaid's Cave,** also in the shopping center, is a good resource for tourist info and books tours for Coral Bay Adventures. (☎9942 5955. Open M-Sa 9am-1pm and 2-5pm, Su 9am-1pm.) In the People's Park Caravan Village, the **Fins Cafe** is popular for pricey seafood and **Internet access.** (Open 7:30am-10pm. $5 per 30min.)

The friendly **Bayview Coral Bay Backpackers** has small but colorful twins and doubles, with a BBQ and a large resident lizard. The resort also has cabins, self-contained duplexes, and chalets that can be a good deal for groups. They plan to open a new backpacker complex in April 2002. (☎9942 5932. Book ahead. Twins and doubles $18 per person; caravans from $60. VIP.)

EXMOUTH ☎08

The scuba diving epicenter of the west coast, Exmouth (pop. 3500) is the place to swim with giant, easy going whale sharks and manta rays. The wonders of the colorful Ningaloo Reef are complemented on land by the dry, dramatically beautiful Cape Range National Park. The main township area is inland and not much to look at, but as a diving and fishing destination Exmouth can't be beat.

TRANSPORTATION AND PRACTICAL INFORMATION. Most action takes place around **Maidstone Crescent,** which intersects **Murat Rd.** at both ends. **Greyhound** (☎13 20 30) **buses** run to Perth (1-2 per day, $211) and Broome (1 per day, $259). **Integrity** (☎1800 226 339) also runs to Perth ($165). The Exmouth Tourist Village provides **car rental.** (☎9949 1101. 21+ from $33 per day; 4WD 25+ $100 per day). The **tourist bureau** is on Murat Rd. (☎9949 1176; fax 9949 1441. Open M-Sa 8:30am-5pm.) The **CALM office,** on Nimitz St. just off Murat Rd., has more detailed info on the Cape Range. (☎9949 1676. Open M-F 8:30am-5pm.) **Challenge Bank,** on Learmouth St., is home to Exmouth's only **ATM.** The shopping center just off Maidstone houses a **pharmacy** (open M-F 9am-5:30pm, Sa 9am-12:30pm) and a SupaValu **supermarket** (open Tu-F 7am-7:30pm, Sa-M 7am-7pm). The **hospital** is two blocks west, on Lyon St. near Fyfe St. (☎9949 1011. Dive medicals $60 cash; call ahead.) **Internet** is available at **Blue's Net Cafe,** in the back of the shopping center. (☎9949 1119. $5.50 per 30min. Open daily 10am-7pm.)

ACCOMMODATIONS AND CAMPING. Most of the backpacker joints in Exmouth are part of sprawling tourist villages, which have their own dive shops and tours in addition to sites, cabins, or in some cases hotel rooms. Many people stay wherever they're doing their diving course—some places even offer package deals. Fierce competition between Exmouth's tourist parks has led them to offer guests lots of freebies, including free bike use, BBQ, swimming pools, and A/C. **Exmouth Base Lodge,** 6km north of town inside the refurbished Holt Naval Base (next to Diving Ventures), is out of the way, but offers the best facilities around. The twin rooms, bathrooms, and kitchens are spotless, and there is free use of the tennis courts and gym. (☎9949 1474; fax 9949 1440. Internet $6 per hr. Laundry. Free pickup and drop off and frequent transport to town. Rooms $18. VIP/YHA.) **Excape Backpackers,** within the Potshot Resort on Murat Rd., has somewhat small rooms, but tons of space outdoors and a nice lounge area. Reception is at the Exmouth Diving Center on Payne St. (☎1800 655 156. Dorms $16, with a SCUBA package $13; twins $50. VIP/YHA.) **Winston's Backpackers,** in the Ningaloo Caravan and Holiday Resort on Murat Rd., along with Coral Coast Dive, has tiny rooms in a well-kept building with a kitchen, pool table, and boat hire. (☎9949 2377; fax 9949 2577. Dorms $16.50.) If you're really into sealife, the Exmouth Cape Tourist Village packs 'em like sardines into the camper-vans of **YHA Pete's Exmouth Backpackers,** on Truscott Cr. between town and the beaches. Village Dive operates out of the same building. (☎9949 1101; fax 9949 1402. Internet $6 per 30min. Reception until 7pm. Sites $8; dorms $16.50; twins and doubles $40. Non-VIP/YHA $2-3 more.) **Camping** is permitted in designated sites within Cape Range National Park (2 people $10 per night, $5.50 each additional person; not including vehicle entry fee), but don't camp elsewhere—rangers patrol. Fires are strictly prohibited and there is no water in the park, so come prepared.

FOOD AND NIGHTLIFE. The **Rock Cod Cafe,** just after the Ampol station on Maidstone Crescent, has seafood specials, pasta, and burgers for $8-18. (☎9949 1249. Open M-F 5-9:30pm, Sa-Su 4-9:30pm.) Behind the shopping center, **Whaler's Restaurant** does delicious gourmet food ($10-20) in an upscale setting. (☎9949 2416. Open daily 8am-4pm, 6:30pm-late.) Another popular choice is the **Golden Orchid Chinese Restaurant** (☎9949 1740), in the shopping complex with its Thursday $16.50 all-you-can-eat buffet from 5:30-9pm.

There are two nightlife options in town. **Grace's Tavern,** on Murat Rd. across from the Exmouth Tourist Village, is a pleasant hangout with indoor and outdoor areas. (Open M-Sa 10am-midnight, Su 10am-10pm.) The **Potshot Resort,** on Murat Rd., has a complex of nightspots with an elegant main bar, the Bamboo Room (called "the bimbo bar" by locals), and the more-crowded Vance's Bar. Friday is the big night, when beer flows until the wee hours. (☎9949 1200. Open M-Th 10am-midnight, F 10am-1:30am, Sa 9:30am-1:30am, Su 10am-10pm.)

NINGALOO MARINE PARK. Most people come to Exmouth to see the impressive Ningaloo Reef, and the town is full of dive shops catering to all experience levels. Introductory PADI courses are as cheap as they come at $300-330; they take four or five days and include four ocean dives. Arrange a diving medical in advance, or put up $60 in cash at the local clinic (see **Practical Information,** p. 648). Shop around before choosing a dive shop; all have certified instructors, good equipment, and a specified instruction regime, but class size and quality of instruction vary. For veteran divers, there are many great dives in the area, including **Lighthouse Bay, Navy Pier, Muiron Islands,** and the **Hole-in-the-Wall,** on the outside of the reef near the North Mandu campsite.

The cheapest PADI course in town is run by **Coral Coast Dive,** near Winston's Backpackers in the Ningaloo Caravan Resort, with training facilities at the naval base; it has computer-oriented PADI classes with a maximum class size of six. (☎9949 1004. Dives from $90; classes $295.) **Diving Ventures** (☎9949 2300) is a big, Perth-based operation with four-day PADI courses ($330; starts M, Th) and two reef dives for $120. **Village Dive** has resort pier dives and well-organized PADI classes. (☎9949 1101. Pier dive $70; PADI $330.) **Exmouth Dive Centre** (☎9949 1201) has a sleek boat, good upper-level classes, and pier and island dives from $121.

Whale shark snorkeling is inordinately expensive (about $275, 1 dive $50 extra), but also a unique experience you won't get any other way. The Ningaloo is one of the few areas in the world where the world's biggest fish visit consistently; they appear most frequently between March and June. **Ningaloo Blue** (☎9949 1119) does a great whale shark tour, as do a number of the dive shops listed above. The best surfing is found at **Surfers Beach** at Vlamingh Head, at the northern end of the cape.

Several operators run tours of the Exmouth area and Cape Range National Park. **Ningaloo Ecology Cruises** offers snorkeling and coral-viewing tours on glass-bottom boats. (☎9949 2255. 1hr. tours from $25; 2hr. snorkeling trips from $35, backpackers $30, children $10.) **Neil MacLeod's Ningaloo Safari Tours** (☎9949 1550) and **Exmouth Cape Tourist Village** offer tours including snorkeling at Turquoise Bay, a boat cruise up Yardie Creek, and a 4WD trek over the top of Cape Range, as well as longer tours to Karijini and Mt. Augustus. **Ningaloo Reef Retreat** (☎9949 1776) has day tours from $50-80 and an overnight package for $135 within the national park.

CAPE RANGE NATIONAL PARK. The rugged limestone cliffs, canyons, and gorges of **Cape Range National Park** lie to the west of Exmouth on Yardie Rd., providing a haven for bungarras, emus, and Stuart's desert peas. The solar and wind-powered **Milyering Visitor Centre,** 52km from Exmouth, hands out maps and info on the parks. (☎9949 2808. Open daily 10am-4pm. National Park day pass $9 per car. No water.) The sealed main road into the park leads to the north to the tip of the cape and then south along the west coast of the cape to Yardie Creek, which makes it a relatively long trip. Unsealed roads (Shothole Canyon Rd. and Charles Knife Rd.) run across the cape into the eastern section of the park, but they can be rough going—check with CALM before heading in this way. If you don't have a car, try the Cape's excellent shuttle service, **Ningaloo Reef Bus,** which stops at the lighthouse, Yardie Creek, Turquoise Bay, Reef Retreat, the Milyering Visitor Centre, and Tantabiddi Reef. (☎9949 1776. F-W $22 to Turquoise Bay, children $11; includes park entry.)

The park has several walking trails, from the **Yardie Creek Track** (1.5km) and the **Mandu Mandu Gorge Route** (3km, 2hr.; take the 2WD track 15km south of the Milyering Visitor Centre) to the more difficult **Badjirrajirra Route** (8km, leaves from the

Thomas Carter Lookout carpark on Charles Knife Rd., 23km south of Exmouth along the Minilya-Learmonth Rd.). **Turquoise Bay** is a popular snorkeling spot, but acquaint yourself with the strong current before jumping into the water. The Exmouth Cape Tourist Village (☎9949 1101) will get set you up with snorkel gear and transportation to Turqoise Bay for $33.

THE PILBARA

The Pilbara is a harsh land. Hundreds of kilometers of arid, undeveloped outback separate the region's small, industrial towns; bumpy dirt roads weave through its mountainous, mineral-rich interior; the searing temperatures of summer can hold dangers for those who don't come prepared. Yet the hardness of the Pilbara merely protects its remote and unheralded treasures, for the region holds some of Australia's most dramatic scenery. White-barked gum trees glow through the dusty red twilight across the Pilbara's quiet plains. The lush Dampier Archipelago rises from its crystalline coastal waters. Among the peaks of the Hammersley Range, an oasis of delicate pool grottoes form in the enclosing depths of Karijini's spectacular gorges. As rewarding to explore as it is difficult to navigate, the imposing Pilbara is a land ripe for adventure.

KARRATHA ☎08

The commercial and administrative center of the Pilbara, Karratha (pop. 10,500) was born in the late 1960s as a base for local industrial projects. Today, it houses WA's largest shopping center north of Perth and all the services of a small city. Travelers can find work around town and on the trawlers and prawn

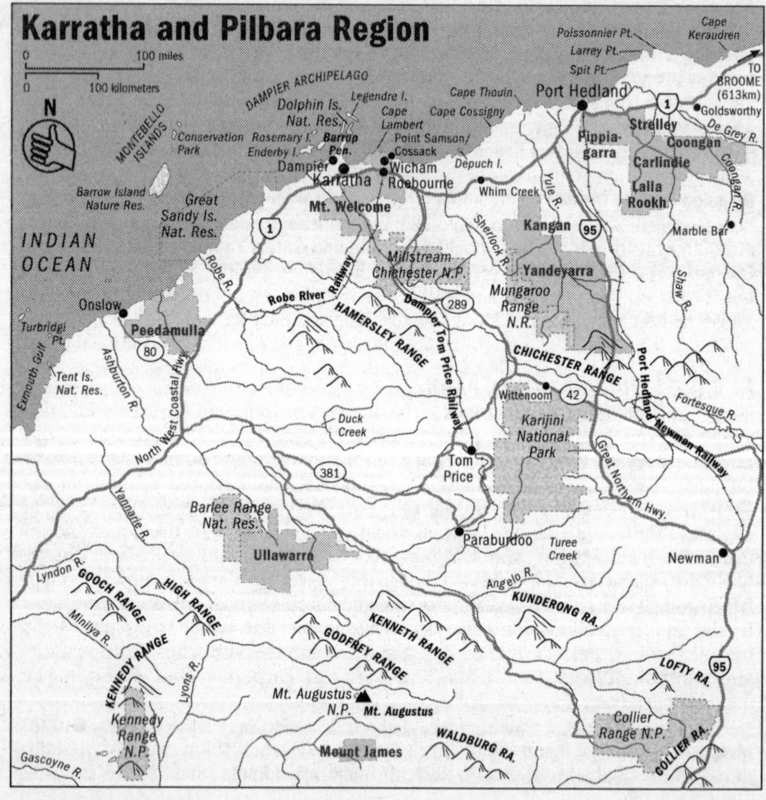

TAKE ME TO YOUR LEADER Deep Gorge is a remarkable site with dozens of Aboriginal engravings on the rust colored rocks. There are pictures of people dancing, and indications that emu were present in the area, which is no longer the case. Among the garden-variety pictures however, are two mysterious engravings. The first is of a man who seems to be wearing a sort of wide brimmed hat. The hat is reminiscent of the silly hats that European mariners used to wear (picture the stereotypical pirate—yeah, that's the one). Some people think that this could be a picture of an early European visitor, and a sign that Aboriginal culture was about to change dramatically. The other remarkable picture is of a man with a dome covering his head who looks exactly like an astronaut. Perhaps the Aborigines had visitors from much farther away than Europe?

boats operating off-shore. From Karratha you can explore the nearby Burrup Peninsula, Dampier Archipelago, Point Samson, and Millstream-Chichester National Park.

TRANSPORTATION AND PRACTICAL INFORMATION. **Greyhound buses** leave Karratha daily from the Shell station at the corner of Searipple and Welcome Rd. (northbound 7:30am, southbound 7:30pm; book at the tourist bureau). Karratha is a good place to rent a car for exploring the Pilbara. **Free Car Hire** may not live up to its name, but you can get a car for local use from $35 per day, or a two-seater 4WD with 100km free from $110 per day (☎9185 1003; 21+). **McLaren Hire** is a reputable local company (☎9185 6383), and **Budget** (☎13 27 27), **Avis** (☎9144 4122), and **Thrifty** (☎9143 1711) also service the area.

Most of Karratha's services are clustered in the town center, bounded by Warambie Rd. to the north, Searipple Rd. to the east, Welcome Rd. to the south, and Balmoral Rd. to the west. The **tourist bureau** is on Karratha Rd., 1km south of town toward the highway. (☎9144 4600; fax 9144 4620. Open Apr.-Nov. M-F 8:30am-5pm, Sa-Su 9am-4pm; Dec.-Mar. M-F 9am-5pm, Sa 9am-noon.) The largest **shopping center** (☎9185 4288) in WA north of Perth takes up a block on Welcome Rd. and Sharp Ave.

ACCOMMODATIONS AND FOOD. The **Karratha Backpackers,** 110 Wellard Way, off of Searipple Rd. across from the shopping center, is a pleasant, workingman's joint with a courtyard. (☎9144 4904. Free bus pickup. Dorms $16.50; singles $33; twins and doubles $44.) The shopping center has two **supermarkets,** Woolworth's (open daily 7am-9pm) and Cole's (open daily 5am-midnight).

SIGHTS. The major natural attraction in the area is the **Dampier Archipelago.** The 42 islands are fringed by coral reefs and the ocean floor is littered with shipwrecks, making for excellent fishing and snorkeling. Unfortunately there is no regular transportation to any of the islands; the only way to get there is a tour or hired boat. There are several local tour operators, including **Deck'em Charters** (☎9185 2691), which offers fishing, diving, snorkeling, and whale-watching cruises.

Northwest of Karratha, the **Burrup Peninsula** was originally the home of the Yaburrara people, and their legacy remains in over 10,000 rock carvings on piles of loose rocks and boulders. The Burrup also has a handful of safe **swimming beaches,** and a drive out to the peninsula makes a good daytrip from Karratha. There is **no public transport** to the Burrup Peninsula, but you can rent a car in Karratha. To get there, head toward Dampier on the Dampier Rd. and after about 18km turn right on the Burrup Rd. (at the sign for the Dampier Port Authority). The turn-off for **Hearson's Cove** is marked on the right. On this beach you can see the "staircase to the moon," a natural phenomenon that occurs when a full moon rises over a low tide: the ripples on the water look like steps running up to the moon. About 1km before Hearson's Cove, a dirt track heads into **Deep Gorge,** an area rich in Aboriginal engravings (see **Take Me Your Leader** above).

ROEBOURNE AND COSSACK ☎08

Roebourne and, Cossack are east of Karratha and quite close to each other. To get to this area from Karratha take the Karratha Rd. south, back to the North West Coastal Hwy., and then go east about 35km to Roebourne. Cossack is north of Roebourne; take the Point Samson-Roebourne Rd. north from the highway. The turn-off for Cossack is about 11km down this road.

The oldest existing town in the Pilbara and once a thriving capital of the north-west, Roebourne is a now shadow of its former self. The Roebourne **tourist bureau,** inside the old jail on the east side of town, has info on Roebourne, Cossack, and Pt. Samson. (☎9182 1060. Open Mar.-Oct. M-F 9am-5pm, Sa-Su 9am-4pm; Nov.-Feb. M-F 9am-3pm, Sa 9am-noon.) **Sandy's Shellhouse,** west of the Roebourne-Point Samson Rd. just north of Roebourne, is a fun place to stop. Overrun by birds, kangaroos, emus, and marine life, it's a museum, gift shop, and rehab center for orphaned or injured animals. (☎9182 1510. Open daily 9:30am-5pm.)

Twelve kilometers north of Roebourne lies historic Cossack, the first port to be established in the Northwest and once the center of a thriving pearling industry; today it's more a historic relic than a living town. **Settler's Beach** is gigantic and has safe swimming; Aboriginal carvings can be found in the surrounding cliff faces. The town's **hostel** building, dating back to 1897, has pleasant, quiet accommodations and hilarious proprietors who are almost as historic as the town itself. (☎9182 1190; fax 9182 1132. Beds $13.50; rooms for 2-6 $38.50.) There are no groceries in Cossack. The nearest supermarket, post office, and bank are a few kilometers north in the town of Wickham. **Getaway Boat Hire** (☎9182 1190) will get you on the water from $35 per hour or $110 per day. 10km north on the main road past Cossack lies sleepy little **Point Samson** and its beach. Just east around the point is **Honeymoon Cove,** a beach that is well attended on nice days.

MILLSTREAM-CHICHESTER NATIONAL PARK

Once a watering hole for weary Afghan camel drivers, Millstream is a lush green oasis in the midst of thousands of acres of rock and dry, spinifex-covered hills. Millstream palms thrive in and around the park's freshwater pool (CALM is trying to control the imported water lillies, cotton, and date palms that also thrive here), and the surrounding wetlands support a diverse range of fauna. For ages, the Aboriginal Yinjibarndi peoples of the Pilbara would gather here to make laws, and thrived off of the area's "living water."

The turn-off to Millstream-Chichester is 28km east of Roebourne and 175km southwest of Port Hedland on the North West Coastal Hwy.; head 60km south along the unsealed but well-maintained Roebourne-Wittenoom Rd. You can also take the shorter, unsealed rail service road from Karratha or Tom Price with a free permit from the Hammersley Iron Company; ask for specifics at the tourist bureau in Karratha (p. 650) or the **Shell Garage** (☎9189 1301) on Mine Road in Tom Price (p. 653). The park's roads are 2WD-accessible in good weather, except where the Fortescue River crosses the Millstream-Yarraloola Rd., but this stretch can be avoided by driving along the scenic roads. Still, this area is more suited for 4WD.

The **CALM** regional office, at the corner of Mardie and Lambert Rd. in the industrial area of Karratha, is a vital source of info on the park. (☎9143 1488. Open daily 8am-5pm.) It's especially important to check in with CALM in the summer months, when temperature extremes can be dangerous and trails, campsites, and roads may be subject to flooding. The park has **no petrol.** The **Millstream Homestead,** near the southwest corner of the park, is the park's unstaffed **visitors center,** with displays on local flora and fauna, early settler life, and the culture of the Yinjibarndi Aborigines. (Open daily 8am-4pm.) The homestead also has untreated **water** (treating recommended) and a **phone** booth.

Camping is permitted in the park only at the designated sites of **Crossingpool, Deep Reach Pool,** and **Snake Creek.** (Entrance fee $9 per car. Sites for 2 $10, $5.50 per extra person). **Python Pool,** about 25km to the north along the Wittenoom-Roebourne Rd., is a beautiful spot to swim. The **Cameleers Trail** (4km, 1½hr return)

HOLD YOUR BREATH About 40km west of the Auski Roadhouse lies the town of Wittenoom, incorporated in 1947 as a home for asbestos miners. Asbestos tailings were used extensively as landfill in town, and the road from Wittenoom through Wittenoom Gorge is actually paved with the stuff. Despite the early warnings of health researchers, asbestos mining continued until 1966. Many residents of Wittenoom have contracted mesothelioma, and government officials still warn against travel to the area. Despite this, a handful of die-hard Wittenoomans continue to hang on. The government ordered the shut-off of water, electricity, and phone service to the 25 or so remaining residents on January 1, 1997. But the holdouts arranged a deal with Telstra for phone service, and a court challenge has kept power and water flowing. Though area tourist bureaus refuse to distribute information about Wittenoom or even to give directions, a handful of still-healthy residents push Wittenoom as a destination, trying to preserve the memory of the town that Western Australia would like to forget.

uphill from the pool and the trek up **Mt. Herbert** (600m, 45min. return) have rewarding views. The **Murlunmunyjurna Track** connects the homestead with Crossing Pool; trailside plaques explain Aboriginal uses of the area's plants (6.8km, 2hr. return). **Nor-west Explorer** runs day-tours from Karratha. (☎9144 1056. $99.)

TOM PRICE ☎08

Tom Price is becoming part of the tourist circuit as the closest town to the amazing Karijini National Park. At 747m above sea level, it's the tallest town in Western Australia. Named after an American mineral surveyor, the town gained its independence from the Hamersley Iron Company in 1988 and since then has worked hard to turn itself into a popular destination. It's a tidy little place that bears no resemblance to the rough and tumble mining towns of the Goldfields. The park is easily explored by car and maps are available in town. Two companies offer cushy bus tours of the park. **Design-A-Tour** has daytrips from both Tom Price and the Auski Roadhouse, east of Karijini. (☎9188 1670. May.-Oct. daily 7:30am $95, children $45.) **Lestok Tours** daytrips depart from the Tom Price Caravan Park and the tourist bureau. (☎9189 2032. $93, children $45.)

There is **no public transportation** to Tom Price, though **Easyrider Backpackers** (☎9226 0307) drops off there once weekly on its Exmouth-to-Broome tour. The town lies about 300km east of the Nanutarra Roadhouse and 250km south of the Millstream visitors center. From the Northwest Coastal Hwy., head east on Hwy. 136 just north of Nanutarra. The well-maintained, paved road passes through some spectacular country, but no services are available until **Paraburdoo,** 276km away, so fuel up before you go. After about 220km, the road forks. Both ways are 2WD-accessible except after heavy rain; the right fork is paved, and the left fork is 70km shorter but unsealed. From Millstream take the Roebourne-Wittenoom Rd. to the Nanutarra-Wittenoom Rd. or get a permit from Hammersley Iron in Dampier to take their shorter, private route (inquire at tourist bureau in Karratha, see p. 650).

The friendly **tourist bureau,** on Central Rd., offers **Internet** access. (☎9188 1112. $5 per 30min. Open M-F 8:30am-5pm.) The cheapest beds in town are at the **Tom Price Tourist Park,** 4km west of town. Showers and a swimming pool will wash off the dust of Karijini. They plan to install a backpackers unit sometime in 2002. (☎9189 1515. Sites $8 per person, powered $20 per site; cabins for 6 $83; chalets for 4 $99.)

KARIJINI NATIONAL PARK

Once an ancient sea floor, Karijini National Park is now a rugged and magnificent wonderland in the heart of the Pilbara. Within Karijini's domain, sheer gorges slice through the mountains, revealing colorful bands of rock and harboring cool freshwater pools and waterfalls. Homeland to the Banjima, Innawonga, and Kurrama Aboriginal people, the park takes its name from their traditional word for the Hamersley Range. Aboriginal legend has it that the gorges of Karijini were formed by *Thurru,* giant serpents that once snaked through the rocks and now reside within the glistening waters of Karijini. The park hasn't received the publicity of some other parks in WA, and the lack of tourists only adds to its allure.

KARIJINI NATIONAL PARK AT A GLANCE	
AREA: 100,000km²	**HIGHLIGHTS:** Hiking the expansive gorges. Swimming in the rock pools.
FEATURES: Junction Pool, Dales Gorge, Kalmina Gorge, the Hancock and Weano Gorges, and Fortescue Falls.	**CAMPING:** Sites for 2 $10.
GATEWAY: Tom Price.	**FEES:** $8 per vehicle entry fee.

TRANSPORTATION. It will take a car or a tour to conquer Karijini. **Cars** can be rented in Karratha (p. 650) and Port Hedland (see p. 655). Karijini is easily reached by car from both Tom Price (p. 653) and the Great Northern Hwy.; a sealed access road bisects the park south of the gorges. The park's northern entrances, through Yampire Gorge and Wittenoom, are closed. Both are contaminated by asbestos, inhalation of which can cause cancer or death (see **Hold Your Breath,** above). The other park roads are unsealed but mostly well-kept and 2WD-accessible. There are rough spots, especially after rains, so a 4WD is safer. Check the statewide road condition report (☎1800 013 314; www.mrwa.wa.gov.au) before tackling the area.

Numerous tour operators frequent Karijini. From the Karratha area, **Snappy Gum Safaris** offers a variety of tours into the park, including a three-day adventure that scales the perilous 25m waterfall in the Weano Gorge area. (☎9185 3141. $350.) From Port Hedland, **Dingo's Desert Trek Adventure Tours** (☎9173 1000; 3-day tour every Tu and Sa $380) and **Pilbara Outback Safaris** (☎9172 2428) cover the area.

PRACTICAL INFORMATION. Karijini is a big place with fairly scant infrastructure, so make sure you come prepared. The one-day park entrance fee is $9 per car. Untreated **water** is available in the park at a turnoff near the visitors center and on Banjima Dr. near the turnoff for Weano gorge (treating recommended), but it's best to carry a lot when you arrive. **Petrol** and supplies are available west of the park in **Tom Price** (p. 653) and at the **Auski Roadhouse** (see below) to the northeast. **Maps,** updates on **road conditions,** and **weather** forecasts can be found at area tourist bureaus, as well as at Karijini's **Visitors Centre** near Fortescue Falls.

The impressive, multi-million-dollar new **Visitors Centre** has exhibits on local flora and fauna, geology, and both Aboriginal and colonial history, and has showers (20min. $2; ☎9189 8121; open daily 9am-4pm). For more practical park know-how, ask attendants at park entrances and campsites, or contact the **CALM ranger station** (☎9189 8157; after-hours emergency ☎9189 8102). There is an emergency radio in the Weano gorge day-use area, and the good people of Tom Price (p. 653) provide the nearest medical and rescue services.

ACCOMMODATIONS AND CAMPGROUNDS. Camping is permitted in the rocky, designated areas near Weano Gorge, Joffre Falls, and Fortescue Falls (sites for 2 $10). For more comfy quarters, head to Tom Price or the basic rooms at the **Auski Roadhouse,** on the northeastern corner of Karijini, just before the dusty turn-off to Wittenoom. (☎9176 6988. Singles $45; doubles $50.)

HIKING. There are impressive lookouts in the park, especially at **Junction Pool,** where four gorges converge. But don't be content to stop at the vista points, take some photos, and go home. The tops of Karijini's mountains may be dusty and remote, but cradled in the gorges are rocky mazes of the cool, damp, and wild. If you're prepared to wade, climb, swim, and scramble, you'll find blissful adventures here in the heart of the Hammersley. Wet suits are recommended, and both traveling companions and **prior consultation with a park ranger** are absolutely essential. Make sure you know what you're doing before you go. **Dales Gorge** and **Kalamina Gorge** are pleasant introductions to the gorge system with relatively easy trails. At Dales Gorge, a short, steep path (3km, 3hr. return) plummets to **Fortescue Falls,** weaves along the gorge floor to the **Circular Pool,** and returns along the rim of the gorge. The stair-lined descent into the **Kalamina Gorge** is one of the easier ones in the park, and the subsequent trail through the grassy gorge explores **Kalamina Falls** and the **Rock Arch Pool** (3km, 3hr. return). **Joffre and Knox Gorges** have waterfalls, deep pools, and more rigorous hikes. At Joffre Gorge, a rugged trail descends to Joffre Falls (3km, 3hr. return). The **Hancock and Weano Gorges** prove a spectacular gateway to fantastic and, if you're not careful, precarious adventures. The best routes in the park are the rugged scrambles through Hancock Gorge to **Kermit Pool** (1.5km, 3hr. return) and through Weano Gorge to **Handrail Pool** (1km, 1½hr. return). You'll either have to get wet or employ some inventive bouldering skills, but the dramatic dimensions and narrow spaces of the gorges are worth the effort. The Weano Gorge can be scaled as far as the top of the 25m waterfall before Red Gorge (but no farther), and Hancock Gorge actually connects with Joffre Gorge through Junction Pool on a six-kilometer route. Agile and determined adventurers can pursue the gorge areas beyond Handrail Pool, Kermit Pool, and Joffre Falls. However, these are **level-two treks,** requiring significant climbing and swimming. Farther afield are the great views from the summit of **Mt. Bruce** (9km, 6hr. return), the second tallest peak in the area, and the demanding **Hammersley Gorge route** (1km, 3hr. return) to a fern-lined grotto.

PORT HEDLAND ☎08

Industry is definitely king in Port Hedland: salt mines, refineries, shipping docks, and red dust rule the skyline of this narrow city sandwiched between the Indian Ocean and the Great Northern Hwy. Most visitors to the city are looking for work, passing through en route to Broome or Exmouth, or gearing up for an excursion into the fantastic Karijini National Park (p. 653).

Pretty Pool, a massive tidal mud-flat 8km east of the town center, is a popular shell-collecting and swimming spot—but wear shoes, as toxic rockfish hide in rocky areas. In the summer, several species of **sea turtles** may be seen, especially Aug.-Oct., at the Pretty Pool, Cooke Point, and Cemetery Beach.

The town centers around the intersection of **Wedge** and **Richardson St. Greyhound buses** bound for Broome (11am, $81), Darwin (11am, $311), and Perth (3:55pm, $196) stop beside the **Port Hedland Welcome Centre,** 13 Wedge St., near the corner of Anderson St. (☎9173 1711; fax 9173 2632. Internet $5.50 per 30min. Open M-F 8:30am-5pm, Sa 8:30am-4pm, Su noon-4pm; Nov.-May Sa closes 1pm, Su closed.) Port Hedland has an infrequent **bus service.** (☎9172 1394. M-F 7am-5pm; $2.50 one-way to South Hedland.) National rental car agencies may be a surer bet. (**Avis** ☎9140 1877; **Budget** ☎13 27 27; **Thrifty** ☎9140 2411.) There is a shopping center, 3km from Wedge St. east along Wilson St., with an Action **supermarket.** (Open M-W and F 8am-8pm; Th 8am-9pm; Sa-Su 8am-5pm.)

The two backpacker places in town are very friendly. **Dingo's Oasis Backpackers,** 59 Kingsmill St., has a unisex bunkhouse in a great view of the ocean. (☎9173 1000; fax 9173 5149. Free bus pickup. Internet $2 per 15min. Dorms $17; twins and doubles $45; A/C extra.) **Port Hedland Backpackers,** 20 Richardson St., has basic rooms, some with A/C. (☎/fax 9173 3282. Internet $2.50 per 30min. Dorms $16; twins $32.)

GREAT NORTHERN HIGHWAY: PORT HEDLAND TO BROOME

Six hundred kilometers of empty Great Northern Hwy. separate Port Hedland and Broome. By bus, the trip takes 7hr. ($85); by car it's a bit less. It's nearly 300km between the Sandfire Roadhouse and the Roebuck Roadhouse outside Broome, so it is essential to fuel up at either end of this stretch and bring plenty of water. Many travelers head from Port Hedland to Broome, and there's only a few hostels in Port Hedland, so it's not hard to find traveling companions. The surrounding scrubland is full of driving perils, including cows, sheep, goats, kangaroos, and a camel or two. Pardoo Station, about 130km east of Port Hedland, offers simple rooms in a delightfully calm setting; call ahead. (☎9176 4930. Singles $33; doubles $50.)

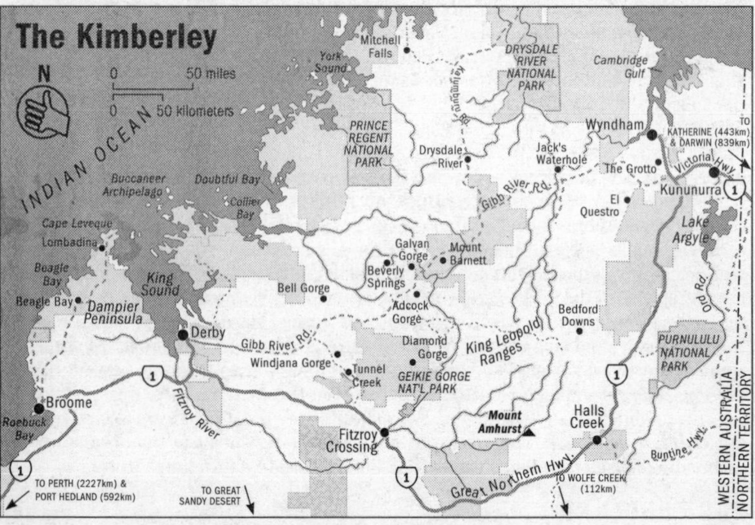

THE KIMBERLEY

The Kimberley's 320,000 square kilometers of raw, semi-desert bush has hardly changed since its settlement by non-Aborigines a century ago. Pressed between the Indian Ocean and the Great Sandy Desert, entire sections of the vast open cattle land have remained uncharted until recent decades. Driving through the strikingly barren landscape, one wonders how anything could live here, or how Aborigines could thrive here for so many centuries. Yet, hidden away on the boulder-stacked cliffs, unpredictable rivers and gorges, and the proud pockets of settlement lie the Kimberley's deceptive wealth. Occupying the northernmost reaches of Western Australia, the Kimberley is accessible from the rest of the state by flights to Broome or via the long, lonely desert highway from Port Hedland. From the east, Routes 1 and 96 branch off the Stuart Hwy. of the Northern Territory. The region's only paved road is the Great Northern Hwy. Most others, including the Gibb River Rd. and its offshoots in the north, are unsealed 4WD tracks. Rainfall levels change drastically between the Kimberley's two seasons; flooded rivers during the Wet (Nov.-Mar.) often close these roads. Call ahead for road conditions (☎1800 013 314), and register with the police before leaving. The Kimberley's high season is the Dry (Apr.-Oct.).

BROOME ☎08

You know you're likely to enjoy a place, when the airport bears a sign claiming, "Relax now, you're in Broome." Sprawling gracefully between the ocean and mangroves, Broome (pop. 14,000) has an immaculate shoreline and a carefree aura that feels surreal after driving through the dusty interior of the Kimberley. The tropical town's fame grew as a result of a thriving pearling industry in the 1880s. Today, the seaside mecca attracts vacationers seeking to sink their toes into the cool sands of its pristine beaches. Visitors may find themselves lingering over an iced cappuccino or strolling at twilight down endless Cable Beach, reluctant to leave the romantic oasis.

TRANSPORTATION

Airport: Broome International Airport (☎9193 5455). Follow the signs from Coghlan St. in the city center to McPherson St. **Ansett** and **Qantas** fly direct to: **Perth** (3hr., $621); **Darwin** (2hr., $451); **Alice Springs** (2hr., $466); **Uluru (Ayers Rock)** (2hr., $466).

Buses: Greyhound (☎9192 1561), next door to the Tourist Bureau. Service to **Perth** (32½hr., daily 8:30am, $266) and **Darwin** (27hr., daily 7:15pm, $230).

Public Transportation: Town Bus (☎9193 6585) connects **Chinatown, Cable Beach,** and several hotels. (Daily on the hr. 7:10am-6:30pm, every ½hr. 10am-3pm, except Su.) First bus of the day reaches **Gantheaume Point** with no return service (prepare for the 5km walk to Cable Beach). Fare $2.70, children $1; day pass $8.50, children $4.

Taxis: Broome Taxis (☎9192 1133). **Roebuck Taxis** (☎1800 880 330). 24hr. service.

Car Rental: Budget, at the airport (☎9193 5355 or 1800 649 800), **Hertz,** 69 Frederick St. (☎9192 1428 or 1800 655 972), and **Broome Broome** (☎9192 2210), corner of Harmersley St. and Frederick St., each offer one-way rental options from $400. Broome Broome also has a YHA discount of $5 per day. **Woody's 4WD Hire,** Lot 24, Dampier Tce. in Chinatown (☎9192 1791), and **Broome Discount Car Hire,** 100km from the airport on McPherson St. (☎9192 3100), have no one-way option. All of the above prefer drivers 25+; all except Hertz will rent to 21+ for an additional fee. Book ahead in the high season from Apr.-Oct. **Note:** car rentals vary drastically in prices, availability, and model, due to weather concerns and road closures, especially during the Wet.

ORIENTATION

Broome occupies a peninsula, with the business area tucked on Roebuck Bay to the east and the beach sprawled on the Indian Ocean to the west. The **Great Northern Hwy.** (**Broome Hwy.** in town), curls into Roebuck Bay from the north, becoming **Hamersley St.** at its intersection with **Napier Tce.** This is **Chinatown,** the oldest part of Broome and the closest thing it has to a downtown. **Paspaley Shopping Centre, Johnny Chi Ln.,** and most restaurants and services are scattered on a few blocks of **Carnarvon St.** A block south of Napier Tce., Frederick St. heads west; a right on Cable Beach Rd. East, a right on Gubinge Rd., and a left on Cable Beach Rd. West leads to **Cable Beach** on the other side of the peninsula. East of Broome, the Great Northern Hwy enters the Kimberley proper and commences its grueling haul toward the Northern Territory.

PRACTICAL INFORMATION

Tourist Office: Broome Tourist Bureau (☎9192 2222; www.ebroome.com/tourism). Well marked on the corner of Broome Rd. and Bagot St. Open during Apr.-Sept. 8am-5pm, Sa-Su 9am-4pm; Oct.-Mar. M-F 9am-5pm, Sa-Su 9am-1pm.

Budget Travel: Harvey World Travel (☎9193 5599). Paspaley Shopping Centre in Chinatown. Serves as the broker for Qantas and other carriers. Open M-F 8:30am-5:30pm, Sa 9am-1pm. **Traveland,** 9 Johnny Chi Ln. (☎9193 7233), off Carnarvon across from the movie theater. Open M-F 8:30am-5pm, Sa 9am-1pm.

Currency Exchange: ANZ Bank, 16 Carnarvon St. (☎13 13 14). Open M-Th 9:30am-4pm, F 9:30am-5pm. **Commonwealth Bank** (☎9192 1103). On Hamersley and Barker St. Open M-Th 9:30am-4pm, F 9:30am-5pm.

Books: Woody's Book Exchange (☎9192 8999), on Johnny Chi Ln. in Chinatown. Open M-F 9:30am-4:30pm, Sa 9:30am-2pm, Su 10am-1pm. **Kimberley Bookshop,** 6 Napier Tce. (☎9192 1944). Just east of Carnarvon. Open M-F 10am-5pm, Sa 10am-2pm.

Markets: Courthouse Market, near the courthouse on the corner of Hamersley and Frederick St. Open Sa 8am-1pm. **Sunday Market** on Johnny Chi Ln. is open Su 9am-1pm.

Laundromat: Broome Laundromat, Paspaley Plaza, Chinatown (☎9192 2130). Open daily 6am-10pm. Most hotels have laundry.

Emergency: ☎000.

Police: (☎9192 1212), at the corner of Frederick St. and Carnarvon St.

Pharmacy: Chinatown Pharmacy, Shop 2, Paspaley Shopping Centre (☎9192 1399). Open M-F 8:30am-5:30pm, Sa 8:30am-2pm, Su 10am-1pm.

Hospital: Broome District Hospital (☎9192 1401), on Robinson St., between Barker and Anne. **HealthDirect** offers 24hr. health advice (☎1800 022 222).

Internet Access: Telecentre, 40 Dampier Tce. (☎9193 7153). $8.40 per hr. Open M-F 9am-5pm, Sa 9am-1pm. **Munchies** (☎9192 5572), on the corner of Cable Beach and Murray Rd. $10 per hr. Open daily 7am-8pm.

Post Office: Australia Post (☎9192 1020), in Paspaley Shopping Centre. Open M-F 9am-5pm. **Postal Code:** 6725; Cable Beach 6726.

ACCOMMODATIONS AND CAMPING

During the high season (Apr.-Oct.), it is essential to book in advance, even at campgrounds. Most of Broome's backpackers have their own in-house bars, which means that BYO is strictly prohibited. All hostels in Broome are very communal, and most host an international mix of enthusiastic young backpackers.

Kimberley Klub (☎9192 3233; fax 9192 3530), on Frederick St. between Robinson and Herbert, a 5min. walk from Chinatown. Free pickup from Greyhound depot. Have inserted a bit of luxury into budget travel. The Klub is social and family-friendly, with an enormous sparkling pool, bar, ping-pong, billiards, TV lounge, and sand volleyball court. Kitchen, laundry, coin operated A/C for some rooms. $10 deposit each for cutlery and linen. Reception daily 6:30am-7pm. Dorms $17; quads $19 per person; twins and doubles $65. NOMADS $1 discount.

Roebuck Bay Backpackers (☎9192 1183; fax 9192 2390), on Napier Tce. This busy hostel is planted right next to Chinatown and the nightlife action. Luggage storage, kitchen, laundry, pool. 12-bed $12-13; 8-bed $14-16; 4-bed $14-16; doubles $55; twins $60. VIP/YHA.

Cable Beach Backpackers, 12 Sanctuary Rd. (☎9193 5511; fax 9193 5532; meyo@tpgi.com.au). An ideal location for those who can't get enough beach time. Kitchen, bar, laundry, pool, billiards. A free shuttle makes the rounds to Chinatown, Greyhound, and the airport. 4-bed dorms $17; twins $58. VIP/YHA.

Broome's Last Resort (☎9193 5000; fax 9193 6033), on the left at the cul-de-sac at the end of Bagot St. Patrons relax in the pool by day and chill at the in-house bar by night. Kitchen, cafe, free luggage storage, coin-op A/C, laundry. Dorms $16-18; twins and doubles $50-55. VIP/YHA.

Camping is popular around Cable Beach, and most popular is the **Cable Beach Caravan Park** on Millington Rd., where the good location compensates for the crowds, with laundry, pool, and kitchen. (☎9192 2066; fax 9192 1997. Sites $7.50-8.50 per person, powered sites for 2 $18-20; 12min. to the beach.) **Tarangau Caravan Park,** 994 Millington Rd., at the corner of Millington and Lullfitz Dr., is quiet, spacious, and much less crowded, but you should allow for a full 20min. walk to get to Cable Beach. (☎9193 5084; fax 9193 7551. Sites for 2 $15.40, powered $22.)

FOOD

Chinatown possesses only a smattering of Chinese restaurants, but the area is packed with tasty outdoor cafes. Coles **supermarket** (☎9192 6299), in the Paspaley Shopping Centre, is open 24 hours.

Cable Beach Sandbar and Grill (☎9193 5090) on Cable Beach Rd. West, adjacent to pedestrian access to the beach. The sandy and sunburned patrons of Cable Beach come crawling for this super-snackbar. From tasty nachos ($9.90) to pasta carbonara ($15.50) to Lebanese wraps ($8.50), the extensive menu includes light and hearty meals from around the world, vegetarian and meat-lover options, and a kids menu as well as a full bar. Open daily 7am-9pm.

Fong Sam's Cafe (☎9192 1030), on Carnarvon St. across from the cinema. Delicious baked goods for bargain-basement prices make this street cafe in the heart of Chinatown all the rage. Various pies and pasties run from 70¢. Fresh quiche and salad are $8.50; pasta of the day $9.50. Open daily 6:30am-5pm.

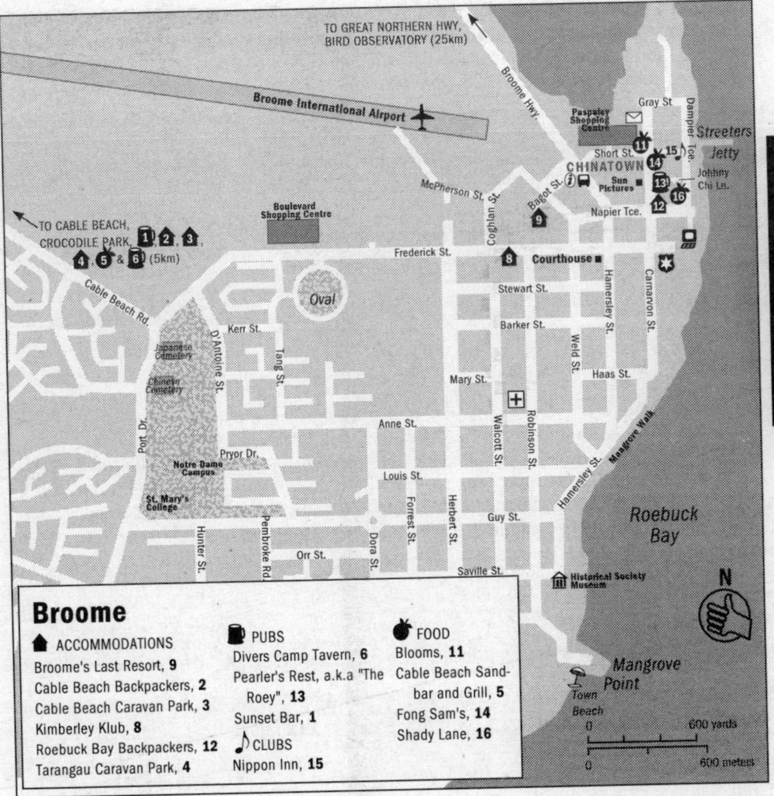

Blooms Cafe and Restaurant, 31 Carnarvon St., Chinatown (☎9193 6366). Despite your best efforts to finish a meal, you'll find yourself thwarted by large portions. Choose from pastas, pizzas, and Thai curries, all in the $10-$16 range. At lunch grab a sandwich with intriguing ingredient combinations ($8.50-10). BYO. Open 7:30am-10pm.

Shady Lane Cafe (☎9192 2060), on Johnny Chi Ln. off Carnarvon. Perfect relief from the midday sun. Flap jacks for $6.50, 4-filling toasted foccacia for $8, and fruity smoothies for $4 make it a wallet-friendly eatery. Open daily 7am-4:30pm.

SIGHTS AND ACTIVITIES

CABLE BEACH. At Broome's paradise, 22km of clear Indian Ocean laps against the pearly white sand. Despite the claims of camel, sailing, hovercraft, and 4WD tours alike, the superlative-defying sunsets are always free. Other sources of visual stimulation can be found in the clothing-optional portion of the beach, just past the rocks to the north.

WATER ACTIVITIES. If lounging the day away on the beach makes you itch to get moving, you may have too much sand in your bathing suit. If that's not the case, then Cable Beach offers plenty of activities. Surfboard rental *($8 per hr.)* is available on the beach. Parasailing, jet skiing, and tubing operators work out of the vans that stop by the beach to rent out equipment. Would-be mermen, or those who are just curious, visit **Workline Dive & Tackle** *(☎9192 2233)* on Short St. in Chinatown for all there is to know about scuba diving in Broome.

REPTILES OLD AND NEW. Do crocodiles scare you? How about 1500 of 'em? Throw in countless warning signs and more chain-link fence than you can shake a stick at, and you've got **Malcolm Douglas Broome Crocodile Park.** *(200m from the beach access on Cable Beach Rd. ☎9192 1489. Feedings W-Su 3pm. Guided tours M-Tu 3pm. Open M-F 10am-5pm, Sa-Su 2-5pm. $15, concessions $12, children $8, families $38.)* These crocs ancestors might be long gone, but pieces of them still reside at **Gantheaume Point,** where a set of **dinosaur footprints** is preserved among the rocks. Found on the western tip of the Broome Peninsula about 4km from Cable Beach, the 120-million-year-old prints surface at very low tide (check at the tourist bureau) and can be difficult to find, so a plaster replica is at the top of the cliff. Beyond the fossils, get a spectacular view of the Cable Beach expanse from above. *(Take a left onto Gubinge Rd., where Cable Beach Rd. turns to the right.)*

OTHER BEACHES. Town Beach is farther south on the Roebuck Bay shore, at the end of Robinson St. To the left of the jetty, for three consecutive days each month from March to October (check at the tourist bureau for exact dates), Broome's massive 10m tide is so low that the exposed mudflats stretch for miles, reflecting the light of the full moon in a staircase pattern. The city celebrates with the **Staircase to the Moon Market** at Town Beach. At the lowest tides, the waters off Town Beach recede to uncover the skeletons of boats sunk in WWII. **Reddell Beach,** at the southern tip of the peninsula, is covered with rocky outcroppings and red cliffs. The **Mangrove Walk,** on the east coast between Chinatown and the Historical Society, weaves its way through a forest of mangroves.

BIRD OBSERVATORY. The **Broome Bird Observatory** is an excellent place to spy 40% of Australia's total bird species—it's one of only four such observatories in the country. *(Located 25km outside of town. Take Broome Rd. for 9.2km and watch for the turn-off. ☎9193 5600. Open daily Apr.-Oct. 7am-5pm, Nov.-Mar. Tu-Su 8am-5pm. Self-guided tours by donation; half-day tours $28, with pickup $50. Book ahead June-Aug.)*

TOURS. Ride camels down Cable Beach at sunset, threading your way up the dunes to reach the hilltop at twilight. **Ships of the Desert** has morning, sunset, and twilight camel tours. *(☎9192 6383. $30 per hr., full-day $75.)* Also try **Red Sun Camel Safaris** *(☎9193 7423; 2:15pm and 4pm tours, $33 per hr.).* **Land tours** are costly, but if you lack a strong 4WD, they may be the best way to see the rugged terrain of the Kimberley and the remote shorelines to the north. **Discover the Kimberley Tours** runs daytrips to the pristine beaches of the Dampier Coast, north of Broome. *(☎1800 636 802. 8hr. tours depart W and F. $165, with Pearl Farm tour $195.)* **Over the Top Adventures** offers tours to the Dampier Peninsula and the Gibb River Rd. *(☎9192 5211. Dampier 1-day $195, 2-day $295; Windjana Gorge and Tunnel Creek 2-day $320. 5-day trip along the Gibb River Rd. $795.)* **Australian Pinnacle Tours** runs similar treks throughout the Kimberley. *(☎9192 8080. Windjana Gorge and Tunnel Creek 1-day $169. Dampier 1-day $185.)* The priciest tours are **scenic flights,** some of which travel all the way to Mitchell Falls and the Buccaneer Archipelago. Soar through the air with the greatest of ease—thanks to a much lighter wallet—on flights from **Broome Aviation** *(☎1300 136 629)* or **King Leopold Air** *(☎1800 637 155);* pricing starts at $285 *(2½hr.).*

NIGHTLIFE

No visit to Broome is complete without catching a feature at the charming **Sun Pictures Outdoor Cinema,** on Carnarvon St., the oldest operating outdoor film theater in the world. It spun its first reel in 1916 and flicks still spin every night. Curl up on the distinctive benches under the stars. (☎9192 1077. $12, concessions $10.)

Brief affairs with beer and fellow backpackers are the staple of after-hours life in Broome, and many **accommodations** have in-house bars that encourage it. In town, **Pearler's Bar** a.k.a. **"The Roey,"** in the Roebuck Hotel on Carnarvon, is the spot for live music and partying backpackers, where you can down a pitcher of beer with the young and spirited crowd. (☎9192 1221. Open M-W 10am-midnight,

Th-Sa 10am-1am, Su noon-10:30pm.) **Nippon Inn,** on Dampier Tce. near Short St., is Broome's only nightclub. When the other bars wind down around midnight, this club is just getting started. Immerse yourself in purple walls and techno beats. (☎9192 1941. Open M, W, F, Sa 9pm-4am.)

At Cable Beach, locals play pool at **Divers Camp Tavern,** on Cable Beach Rd., a bar and bistro where all the campers let loose on weekends. (☎9193 6066. Open M-Sa 10am-midnight, Su 11am-10pm. Brews from $4.) At the **Sunset Bar** at the Cable Beach Resort right on Cable Beach, for $10.50, the cocktails better be as heavenly as the view. (☎9192 0400. Beers $5. Open daily 4pm-midnight.)

FESTIVALS

The **Easter Dragon Boat Regatta** is featured in mid-April at the Town Beach. Horse racing is big throughout July when the town starts hopping for the **Broome Cup.** For 10 days in early September, the **Shinju Matsuri Pearl Festival** celebrates the natural beauty of pearls. The **Mango Festival,** (Nov.) pays homage to the mango harvest with a Mardi Gras celebration and a "Great Chefs of Broome Mango Cook Off."

NEAR BROOME: DAMPIER PENINSULA

North of Broome, pristine white beaches stretch all along the Dampier Peninsula. 4WD-only access roads promise striking views of the Indian Ocean. Ask the tourist center in Broome for road and weather conditions, maps, and tide charts before leaving. Allow at least two days to visit, as the roads are tricky; carry plenty of spare parts, water, and rations. Alternatively, several tour companies run one- or two-day trips to the area (see p. 660).

From Broome heading north, **Beagle Bay,** 118km up a rough 4WD track, has a petrol station and houses the **Beagle Bay Church,** with an unusual mother-of-pearl altar. (☎9192 4913. Open M-F 7am-4pm, Sa 8am-noon.) Fifty kilometers farther north, the mellow waters of the **Middle Lagoon** offer swimming, snorkeling, and accommodations. (☎9192 4002. Sites $12 per person, powered $15; beach shelters for 2 $40; cabins for 4 $100.) The **old mission church,** built from corrugated iron and paperbark, is the highlight of **Lombadina,** 200km from Broome near the northern tip of the peninsula. You can fuel up, buy **groceries,** and sleep here. (☎9192 4936. Dorms $38.50; cabins $132.) At **Kooljaman,** the end of the Peninsula, tourists can swim, fish, and dive. (☎9192 4970. Sites $11 per person, powered $14.50; beach shelters $30.) Once the sites of Catholic missions, several Aboriginal communities also inhabit the Peninsula, welcoming travelers with a glimpse into a rich history. (Entry to most sites $5. Open M-Sa.)

GREAT NORTHERN HIGHWAY

Crossing the Kimberly on the way to the Northern Territory, you have two options. The Great Northern Hwy. leaves Broome, continuing along in a tame, mostly sealed fashion. However, the unparalleled Gibb River Rd. (see p. 664) is the more adventurous route. It cuts west-east across Western Australia, from Derby to Kunanurra; or the other way around, if you please.

DERBY. "As the sun sank below the horizon, he stared out into the distance, and as far as he could see, it was all mud. And yet it was beautiful." Okay, we made that quote up, but such is life in Derby (pop. 5000). The expanse of mudflats and water make **sunsets** at the Derby wharf sparkle with a golden-brown hue; you too might be inspired to create such wondrous prose. Home to the regional headquarters of the **Royal Flying Doctor Service** (☎9191 1211) on Clarendon at Fairbairn St., all is up in the air in Derby. For a view from above, you can book a flight to **Horizontal Falls** through **Aerial Enterprises** (☎1800 006 132. From $132.) The falls, due to a water displacement phenomenon and the area's especially low tides, change drastically throughout the year.

A BOAB FOR BAD BOYS 7km south of Derby, on the Derby hwy., lies the gargantuan Boab Prison Tree. Though it may resemble a plastic cave, you'd find at a theme park, this extraordinary natural treehouse is believed to be over 1500 years old and is a long-time site of Aboriginal religious significance. With a girth of 14.7m (exceeding the size of most hostel dorm rooms, we might add), there was plenty of space for European oppressors to hold Aboriginal prisoners here. When visiting "The Big Boab" today, stay out of the immediate vicinity of the tree, as it is disrespectful to traditional native beliefs. Plus, there are snakes inside with a stronger bite than you'll ever have.

Greyhound (a McCafferty's affiliate) **buses** stop here twice daily and continue on to Darwin (10pm, $196) and Perth (4:55pm, $309). The Derby Hwy. becomes **Loch St.,** the town's main thoroughfare. The **tourist office,** with **Internet access** ($8 per hr.), is at the end of **Clarendon St.,** which runs parallel to Loch St. (☎9191 1426. Open Apr.-Sept. M-F 8:30am-4:30pm, Sa-Su 9am-1pm, until 4pm June-Aug.; Oct.-Mar. M-F 8:30am-4:30pm, Sa 9am-noon.)

The **West Kimberley Lodge,** at the corner of Sutherland and Stanwell St., has quiet rooms with A/C and fridge; the lodge has a kitchen and laundry facilities. (☎9191 1031. Twins $60; suites $75.) The grassy **Kimberley Entrance Caravan Park,** on Rowan St., around the curve from the tourist office, overlooks mudflats. (☎9193 1055. Sites $9, powered $15, for 2 $21.)

FITZROY CROSSING. Fitzroy Crossing (pop. 1500), near the **Fitzroy River** right off the Great Northern Hwy. 270km east of Derby, is used primarily as a base for nearby **Geikie Gorge.** 18km from town on the sealed Russ Rd., Geikie Gorge ("GEEK-ee"), is a set of awe-inspiring sheer faces of black, white and rust-colored rock towering over the Fitzroy River. **Boat tours** take you right up to the rock faces and allow a close-up of freshwater crocs. Buy tickets in the gorge parking lot. (☎9168 4200. 1hr.; June-Sept. 3 per day, Apr.-May and Oct.-Nov. 1-2 per day.) A few walks (from 1-3hr.) offer a more panoramic perspective of the gorge, though no camping is permitted. (Open daily in the Dry 6:30am-6:30pm.) 43km east of Fitzroy Crossing, on the Great Northern Hwy. lies the 4WD-only turn-off to **Tunnel Creek** (68km), **Windjana Gorge** (103km), and the **Gibb River Rd.** (see p. 664). Day tours for Windjana gorge and Tunnel Creek leave from Fitzroy Crossing ($85); book at the tourist office.

The **Greyhound bus** runs daily to Perth (1:45am, $360) and Darwin (1:20am, $153). The **Tourist Centre,** left off the highway at Forrest Rd., has maps of the gorges. (☎9191 5355. Open in the Dry daily 9am-5pm; in the Wet M-F 9am-5pm, Sa 9am-1pm.) Farther down Forrest Rd. is the **supermarket** (open M-F 8:30am-5:30pm, Sa-Su 8am-1pm)

A resort community unto itself, the **Fitzroy River Lodge,** right off the highway, offers motel rooms, "safari lodges," and camping. (☎9191 5141. Sites for $9.75, powered $22; motel rooms and lodges from $126.) **Darlngunaya Backpackers** is 4km down Forrest Rd. and a right onto Russ Rd. A $5 shuttle from the bus stop will also get you here. It's colorful, well-kept, and soothing, with high ceilings, porches, kitchen, and laundry. (☎9191 5140. Sites $10; dorms $16.50.).

HALLS CREEK. The next settlement along the Great Northern Hwy., 280km east of Fitzroy Crossing, is the low-key desert town of Halls Creek (pop. 1300). It can act as a somewhat distant base to see **Purnululu National Park** (the turn-off is 109km north on the highway) or the second largest meteorite crater in the world, the **Wolf Creek Crater** (the turn-off is 16km south on the highway, then 132km on the unsealed Tanami Rd). Considerably closer is the unsealed **Duncan Hwy.** just north of town, which has a series of worthwhile sites. The best are found 16km away, where the scattered remains of **Old Halls Creek** mark the origin of the gold rush in Western Australia, and another 52km, where **Sawpit Gorge** promises swimming and secluded camping beneath a dramatic stone cliff.

TERMITE BE GIANTS When crossing through the lonely plains of the Kimberley, at times, you are likely to feel like you have intruded upon the barren fields of some distant planet. Such a feeling might come at the point when you cross through the curious array of upright stones, resembling an abandoned cemetery or our long-lost alien friends. But, alas! You *are* on Earth, and those curious mounds are actually the work of colonies of hardworking termites. The mounds, which can measure up to 6m in height, serve as an essential part of the desert eco-system, diligently consuming dead trees and other debris. Formed from a delicate mixture of termite food, saliva, feces, and round-the-clock efforts, we ask you: an architectural wonder or a big pile of shit? Nonetheless, impressive for the small little buggers.

The **Tourist Centre** (☎9168 6140; open M-F 7am-6pm, Sa-Su 8am-5pm) has the most space-age toilets in Western Australia. Other services on the highway include: **grocery store** (☎9168 6186; open M-F 8am-6pm, Sa 8am-noon, Su 9am-noon); **Shell station** (☎9168 6060; open daily 6am-10pm).

While most travelers stop in Halls Creek just long enough to fill the petrol tank, accommodations do exist. For an overnight stay among the town's ruins, **The Lodge** is located at Old Halls Creek. (☎9168 8999. Sites $7; caravan sites $12, powered $15; singles $25.) The **Shell** has beds and A/C but no linen (dorms $18.50; singles $55; doubles $82.50). **Halls Creek Caravan Park** is a block south of the highway on Roberta Ave. (☎9168 6169. Sites for 2 $15.40; powered $17.60.)

PURNULULU (BUNGLE BUNGLE) NAT'L PARK

A collection of beehives? A carton of eggs? The sight of the striking and mysterious orange sandstone formations, striped with black bands of algae, regularly lends itself to such strange comparisons. The inaccessibility and remoteness of Purnululu kept it hidden from the public until the 1980s. The Kija Aboriginal people have inhabited the area for over 20,000 years and the park is packed with Aboriginal cultural sites. The awkward name "Bungle Bungle" is thought to be either a corruption of the Kija word *purnululu*, meaning "sandstone," or a misspelling of a commonly found grass in the area, *Bundle Bundle.*

PURNULULU AT A GLANCE

AREA: 209,000 hectares.

FEATURES: Bungle Bungle Range, Ord River.

HIGHLIGHTS: Scenic helicopter flights, walks through the gorges (see Tours, below).

GATEWAYS: Kununurra (p. 666), Halls Creek (p. 662), Warmun (below).

CAMPING: At Walardi and Kurrajong campsites, or registered overnight bush camping ($9 per night per person).

FEES: Entry $9 per vehicle.

TRANSPORTATION AND PRACTICAL INFORMATION. To drive to Purnululu, you need a high clearance 4WD (no caravans). Bring a spare tire, jack, water, food, and chutzpah. The unsealed access road, **Spring Creek Track,** is located on the Great Northern Highway 250km south of Kununurra or 109km north of Halls Creek. For 53km Spring Creek Track rumbles, splashes, bumps, and grinds its way to the Visitors Centre; allow five hours driving time from Kununurra or four hours from Halls Creek to reach the park. The vehicle **entry fee** is $9; fees are payable at the **Visitor Centre** near the entrance to the park.

Vehicular access to the park is closed during the Wet (Jan.-Mar.), but temporary closure due to rain is possible at other times. Call the **Department of Conservation and Land Management** office in Kununurra for conditions (☎9168 4200). Topography maps are available in Kununurra at the **Department of Land Administration** on Messmate Way at the roundabout. (☎9168 0255. Open M-F 8am-4:30pm.) Camping is $9 per person per night. Toilets and untreated water are available in the park; but no food or fuel can be brought in.

If you're in need of a fuel stop, **Warmun** (formerly Turkey Creek) is located less than 100km north of the Spring Creek Track on the Great Northern Hwy. to Kununurra. The **Turkey Creek Roadhouse** offers petrol, takeaway, and a variety of accommodations. (☎9168 7882. Key deposit $10. Reception daily 6am-8pm. Dorms and singles $20; sites $6; on-site caravans $17, powered $22.)

TOURS. Signing up for a tour can be cheaper than renting a car, but the options might be overwhelming. **Scenic flights** offer unparalleled views of the range that are inaccessible by car or by foot. **Slingair** offers an on-site helicopter flight for those who drive themselves ($180).

BY AIR.

Slingair Heliwork (☎9169 1300 or 1800 095 500; www.slingair.com.au). From Kununurra: 2hr. flight, no landing in the park $185; 3½hr. helicopter $380; 8hr. helicopter and ground tour $580. From Warmun: 45min. $165, window seat $190.

Alligator Airways (☎9168 1333 or 1800 632 533). From Kununurra: 2hr. 15min. $185; full day air/ground, minimum 2 persons $425; 2 gorges $540; overnight $650.

East Kimberley Tours (☎9168 2213 or 1800 682 213; www.eastkimberleytours.com). Fly in and out from Kununurra: 1-day $395; 2-day $685; 3-day (2-night) $785.

BY LAND.

East Kimberley Tours (☎9168 2213 or 1800 682 213; www.eastkimberleytours.com). Drive in/drive out from Warmun: 1-day $160; 3-day $451.

Desert Inn 4WD Adventures (☎9169 1257 or 1800 805 010; kimberleyadventure.com). Drive in and out from Kununurra or Warmun: 2-day $290; 3-day $430.

Kununurra Backpackers Bungle Bungle Adventures (☎9169 1998 or 1800 641 998; www.adventure.kimberley.net.au). Drive from Kununurra 2-day $286, 3-day $427).

CAMPING AND WALKING TRAILS. The two campsites available within the park have untreated water, toilets, and firewood. Seven kilometers to the left of the Visitor Centre is the **Kurrajong campsite,** and 13km to the right is the **Walardi campsite** (all sites $9). These are the only sites where fires are allowed. Camping is allowed only at established campsites.

While the sandstone of the range is too fragile to allow people to climb to the tops, a handful of **walking tracks** meander along the edge of the Purnululu massif. From the Piccaninny Gorge carpark, 25km south of the Visitor Centre, three walks are available. The easiest is the **Domes walk** (1km) that loops through the smaller formations. The **Cathedral Gorge walk** (3km) is a reasonably easy, popular hike that leads to a massive rock chamber with astounding acoustics. The **Piccaninny Gorge hike** (30km) requires more stamina and a night in the bush. Register with the rangers before setting out. The fairly easy **Echidna Chasm walk** (2km) starts 21km north of the ranger station and scrambles over some large boulders. Two walks leave from a carpark 2km south of Echidna Chasm: the more challenging **Froghole** walk (1.4km, 1-2hr.) leads to a small seasonal pool, and the **Mini Palms** (5km, 3hr.) walk ends at a natural amphitheater surrounded by palms.

GIBB RIVER ROAD

The Gibb River Road is a rugged and unforgettable 4WD track that crosses the heart of the Kimberley. By day, wander the bumpy road to a series of national parks, gorgeous gorges, Aboriginal camps, cattle stations, and waterholes. By night, sleep under the stars in isolated wilderness. For the true adventurers who long to conquer the bush first-hand, the challenge awaits.

GIBB RIVER ROAD AT A GLANCE	
LENGTH: 647km. **FEATURES:** Windjana Gorge, Tunnel Creek Nat'l Park, King Leopold Range. **HIGHLIGHTS:** Dips into pristine, saltie-free gorges, unpopulated walks, and cliff jumping for the super-brave.	**GATEWAYS:** Derby (p. 661), Kununurra (p. 666), Fitzroy Crossing (p. 662). **DURATION:** It will take 4-5 days to enjoy the primary gorges, and longer to tackle the several turn-offs.

ORIENTATION AND PRACTICAL INFORMATION. The Gibb River Road begins 8km south of Derby off the Derby Hwy. and ends at the Great Northern Hwy. between Wyndham (48km away) and Kununurra (45km). A series of access roads and tracks lead to the main attractions. The only through-road connection is at the Winjana/Tunnel Creek turn-off 119km from Derby, which eventually stretches to the Great Northern Hwy. and Fitzroy Crossing.

Emergency: ☎000.

Guides: Tourist offices in Derby and Fitzroy Crossing sell copies of the *Traveller's Guide to the Gibb River and Kalumburu Roads*, which has detailed information on distances, limited services along the roads, and what to do in case you encounter a bush fire ($3; write to Derby Tourist Bureau, PO Box 48, Derby WA 6728; ☎9191 1426; derbytb@comswest.net.au; www.comswest.net.au/~derbytb).

Tours: Many people do the Gibb River Rd via small group tours, which can actually be cheaper than renting your own 4WD. From Kununurra or Broome, **Desert Inn 4WD Adventures** (☎9169 1257 or 1800 805 010; kimberleyadventure.com) offers a 7-day trip ($980), while **Kimberley Wilderness Adventures** (☎9192 5741 or 1800 804 005; www.kimberleywilderness.com) does it in 5 or 6 days ($1050, $1595). From Darwin to Broome and vice-versa, **Kimberley Adventure Tours** (☎9168 3368 or 1800 083 368; www.kimberleyadventure.com) makes a 9-day trek ($1195).

WHEN TO GO. Traveling the Gibb River Road is not recommended from Dec.-Apr. due to Wet season floods. **Road conditions** should be checked at any time of year (☎1800 013 341). Even though the **climate** is dry and arid, it can get cold at night (Mt. Elizabeth has recorded the coldest temperatures in WA).

TRANSPORTATION. The Gibb is severely corrugated in parts, and many of the turn-offs to the gorges are bumpy and hole-filled. Rental companies in Broome (see p. 657, Derby (see p. 661), and Kununurra (see p. 666) will rent 4WDs that can do most of the road. Travelers should be well-prepared and have a hearty helping of grit and self-sufficiency. Travelers should register with tourist offices at either end before starting the journey and consider renting a walkie-talkie, CB radio, or cell phone. Traffic can be scarce and you could get stuck for a while without help.

HIKES, GORGES, AND CAMPING.

Camping is allowed only in designated areas; much of the property along the road is privately owned. Listed after sight names are turn-off distances from Derby.

WINDJANA GORGE. *123km.* The limestone crevasse looms as high as 100m over the Lennard River and is part of the 250-million-year-old Devonian Reef, but the freshwater crocs are the main attraction (swimming is not recommended). A sandy 3.5km walk skirts the river to the right, past the sheer walls of the gorge. *(Off 21km access road. Camping with showers, toilets and water $9.)*

CHIA-CROC You may be frightened out of your wits when you visit one of Australia's numerous crocodile farms, but these reptile gardens are capitalizing on more than the terror of tourists. The big business of crocs extends all the way to the fashion industry of Italy and France ("I'm too sexy for my croc-skin vest"). Every part of the croc–skin, bones, and everything in between (except the stomach)–can be packaged and sold. And even though each croc farm holds several thousands of the green guys, the farms still struggle to keep up with the huge demand. In captivity, the most vicious predators are turned into breeding machines, and the money keeps rolling in.

TUNNEL CREEK. *158km.* A flashlight and shoes are essential for wading through the thigh-deep water of the 750m tunnel in pitch-black darkness. If you're lucky, you might see one of the five species of bats that make their home in this cave. The opposite end of the tunnel is the site where Jandamarra, the famous Pigeon outlaw of the Bunuba people, was shot and killed in 1897.

BELL GORGE. *214km.* A series of falls meet a deep plunge pool at popular and perfectly shaped Bell Gorge, accessed via a 1km walk from the carpark. *(Off a rough 29km on access road. Camping at Silent Grove or Bell Creek on the turn-off; $9.)*

OLD MORNINGTON. *247km.* Nearby Bell Gorge, Diamond Gorge and Sir John Gorge are worthwhile, and there is riverside camping ($8). Back on the Gibb, the tropical Adcock Gorge and the intimate Galvans Gorge are at 267km and 286km respectively with short turn-offs. *(Allow 2.5hr. on 90km access road. ☎9191 7035).*

MT. BARNETT ROADHOUSE. *306km.* Owned and operated by the Kupungarri people, the roadhouse provides access to the Manning Gorgehike (1hr.) which warrants a stop. Camping ($8) and groceries available. *(☎9191 7007.)*

KALUMBURU RD. *406km.* An entire 267km journey after its intersection with the Gibb River Rd., the Kalumburu branches north towards the Mitchell Plateau and Mitchell Falls (a four-cataract waterfall plunging into the Indian Ocean). This region is one of the most isolated and stunning sights in the Kimberley, but is even more bone-jarring than the Gibb—complete self-sufficiency is an absolute must.

JACK'S WATERHOLE. *524km.* Swimming, canoeing, fishing, and camel rides are available, as are sites and hot showers. *(Off a 1km access road; ☎9161 4324.)*

EL QUESTRO STATION. *614km.* You will need a Wilderness Park Permit ($12.50 per week) to get to the boat tours on Chamberlin Gorge, bushwalks to El Questro, and Amalia Gorges. *(Off a 16km access road. ☎9161 4318. Sites $12.50.)*

EMMA GORGE. *623km.* The crescent, fern-covered cliffs are high above a perfect pool, and a droplet waterfall gives the semblance of rain. No camping, but pricey cabins are available. *(Off a 2km access road; from here it is only 24km to the end of the Gibb. Permit $5.50 for 7 days. Cabins ☎9169 1777. $66-91 per person.)*

KUNUNURRA ☎08

Five-hundred kilometers west of Katherine, NT, the little pocket of civilization known as Kununurra ("kuh-nah-NUR-ah") sleeps beneath the sandstone formations of the eastern Kimberley. The name means "big waters," appropriate for a town that accesses the Ord River and grew in the 1960s and 70s during the effort to reroute that river for irrigation. Most travelers use Kununurra (pop. 5000) as a base to explore the dramatic attractions in the eastern Kimberley region, such as Purnululu (Bungle Bungle) National Park, Lake Argyle, and the Gibb River Rd.

TRANSPORTATION

Flights: The airport is 5km down the Victoria Hwy towards Wyndham. **Ansett** (☎13 13 00) flies daily to **Broome** ($294), **Darwin** ($200), and **Perth** ($677).

Buses: Buses arrive at the tourist bureau at the corner of Coolibah Dr. and White Gum St. **Greyhound Pioneer** (☎13 20 30) departs for **Broome** (14hr., daily 4:55pm, $156) and **Darwin** (12hr., daily 10:05am, $117).

Cars: Budget, 947 Mango St. (☎9168 2033), and at the airport. **Avis,** 12 Coolibah Dr. (☎9169 1258), and at the airport. **Thrifty Territory Rent-a-Car,** 596 Bandicoot Dr. (☎9169 1911), at the BP service station. **Handy Rentals** (☎9169 1188), at the corner of Messmate and Bandicoot Dr. **Hertz** (☎9169 1424).

Taxis: Spuds Taxis ☎9168 2553. **Alex Taxi** ☎13 10 08.

ORIENTATION AND PRACTICAL INFORMATION

Messmate Way turns off the Victoria Hwy. at a petrol station and heads into town, where it crosses **Konkerberry Dr.** and ends at Coolibah Dr. The **Kununurra Shopping Centre** is on Konkerberry Dr. Most restaurants and the two hostels are on or near Konkerberry as it heads away from Messmate.

Tourist Office: Tourist Bureau (☎9168 1177), on Coolibah Dr. Open in the Dry daily 8am-5pm; in the Wet M-Sa 9am-4pm.

National Park Information: Conservation and Land Management (☎9168 4200). On Messmate Way at the traffic circle. Open M-F 8am-4:30pm. Sells Western Australia park vehicle passes ($51 per year; $22.50 per month). Across the hall is the **Department of Land Administration** (☎9168 0255), which sells topographic maps of the Kimberley ($7.50). Open M-F 8am-4:30pm.

Banks: Commonwealth Bank (☎13 22 21), on the corner of Coolibah Dr. and Cotton Tree Ave., has a 24hr. **ATM.** Open M-Th 9:30am-4pm, F 9:30am-5pm.

Laundry: Laundromat available 24hr. on Banksia St.

Police: (☎9166 4530), at Coolibah Dr. and Banksia St. 24hr.

Kimberley Road Conditions: ☎1800 013 314.

Hospital/Ambulance: (☎9168 1522), on Coolibah Dr., toward Ivanhoe Rd.

Internet Access: Telecentre (☎9169 1868), at the corner of Banksia St. and Collibah Dr. $9.90 per hr. Open M-F 9am-5pm, Sa 10am-2pm.

Post Office: (☎9168 1395), across from the police station at Coolibah Dr. and Banksia St. Open M-F 9am-5pm. **Postal Code:** 6743.

ACCOMMODATIONS

The options for backpackers are limited in Kununurra, so the motto during the Dry (Apr.-Nov.) is: "If you want a bed, book ahead."

Desert Inn (☎9168 2702), 2 blocks from the shopping center near the corner of Konkerberry and Tristania St. This cozy place performs hip decorating feats with scrap metal and the color purple. Friendly staff, pool, patio, shaded lounge areas, spacious kitchen, laundry. Free transport to and from the bus station and to Kelly's Knob for sunset. Dorms $18; doubles $46; triples and quads $19 per person. VIP/YHA.

Kununurra Backpackers, 24 Nutwood Crescent (☎9169 1998). A 10min. walk from the tourist office; follow Konkerberry away from the highway, then turn right on Nutwood. In a quiet neighborhood but quite social, with A/C, pool, kitchen, VCR, and laundry. Free transport to and from the bus station and Kelly's knob for sunset. Key deposit $10. Dorms $18; twins and doubles $46. NOMADS/VIP/YHA.

Camping is available along the Victoria Hwy. The **Red Gum Caravan Park** (☎8972 2239) is 1km from town (10min. walk). Laundry, pool, and BBQ. (Sites $13.50, for 2 $18, powered $20; cabin $60, $12 each extra person). The **Riverview Caravan Park and Motel** (☎8972 1011) has a pool and spa, and is located at the hot springs. Laundry, BBQs. (Sites for 2 $16, powered $19; singles $20; doubles and twins $25, budget cabins for 2 $50.)

FOOD AND ENTERTAINMENT

Kununurra's scenery may be spectacular, but the food is not. For **groceries,** head to **Coles** in the shopping center. (☎9168 2711. Open daily 5am-midnight.) **Farmers Fruit and Vege-mart,** at the corner of Konkerberry Dr. and Ebony St., have cheap but tasty sandwiches for $3.50 and milkshakes for $2.80. (☎9168 3583. Open M-F 6am-5:30pm, Sa 6am-noon.) At **Rumours Patisserie,** in the shopping center, the burger bar does it all, from barra to lentil, from $5.80. (☎9168 2071. Open M-F 7am-5:30pm; Sa, Su 7am-4pm.) The main pub in town is **Gulliver's Tavern,** on Konkerberry Dr. at Cotton Tree Ave. Relax on the patio with Aussie pints for $5.70. (☎9168 1666. Open M-Th noon-11pm, F noon-1am, Sa noon-midnight, Su 1-9pm.)

SIGHT AND ACTIVITIES

Kelly's Knob, the mini-mountain, looks down over the stunning topography of Kununurra. Take Konkerberry Dr. to the end; turn left on Ironwood, right on Speargrass, and right again at the large stone tablet reading "Kelly's Knob." **Mirima (Hidden Valley) National Park,** 2km east of town, looks like a miniature Purnululu range (but without the 6hr. drive). Three short paths wind past the 350-million-year-old formations. The **Derdebe-gerring Banan** lookout trail (800m) ascends a steep hill for a view over the Ord Valley and nearby sandstone ranges. Ranger-led walks meet at the carpark at the end of Hidden Valley Rd. **Wild Adventure Tours** (☎0409 456 643; wildtour@yahoo.com) offers abseiling tours and instruction at local sites, including Kelly's Knob ($60) and the Grotto ($110).

DAYTRIP FROM KUNUNURRA: LAKE ARGYLE

The largest freshwater body in the southern hemisphere was created by humans. Sandwiched between ancient orange sandstone hills and dotted with approximately 90 islands, the 850 sq. km lake was created in the early 1970s as part of the ambitious Ord River Irrigation Project. While it looks eerily out of place, Lake Argyle is brilliantly blue and still strikingly massive (it can hold 18 Sydney Harbours). To get there, drive 35km south of Kununurra on the Victoria Hwy. and turn onto the access road. 35km more brings you to the **Lake Argyle Tourist Village.**

Cruises are a popular way to see a fraction of the lake. Though expensive, they are a worthwhile splurge for the amazing views. **Lake Argyle Cruises** has a booking office at the Lake Argyle Tourist Village on the lake. (☎9168 7361. Tours daily May-Sept., by demand in the Wet; 2hr. wildlife morning cruise $35; 2½hr. sunset cruise $44; 6hr. mountain and island cruise $105. Pickup in Kumunurra $15.) **Triple J Tours** provides cruises of Lake Argyle and the Ord River. (☎9168 2682. Full-day from $85, including pickup.) To try your hand at navigating the Ord River on your own from Lake Argyle to Kununurra, **Kimberley Canoeing** offers a three-day self guided tour ($135, includes drop-off/pickup, canoe/camping equipment; minimum 2 persons.)

The **Lake Argyle Tourist Village** has accommodations. The **caravan park** has showers and laundry. (☎9167 1050. Sites $7, powered $11.50.) The **motel** next door has a pool and restaurant. (☎9167 7360. Singles $71.50; doubles $77.)

WYNDHAM ☎08

A 20m-long crocodile statue welcomes you to the tiny port town of Wyndham (pop. 800). The northernmost point on the Great Northern Hwy., Wyndham is isolated but more charming than Kununurra (100km south). Here the pioneer spirit thrives in the dramatic backdrop of the Bastion Range and the Cambridge Gulf.

Wyndham is neatly divided into two clusters. Most shops and services (and the big croc) are found in the southern section, including the **tourist office** in the Mobil station (☎9161 1281; open daily 6am-6pm), and **Internet access** at **Telecentre,** 6 O'Donnell St. (☎9161 1161), opposite the Boab gallery. The cheerful staff at the **Wyndham Caravan Park,** near the Mobil station, will be more than glad to show you their giant 2000-year-old boab tree. (☎9161 1064. Sites $8, powered $11.) **Gulf Breeze Guest House,** on the highway before the wharf, has a kitchen, TV, and shady patio. (☎9161 1401. Singles $20, doubles $45, families $50.)

Follow the signs east from the highway for the **Five River Lookout,** 7km up a steep road, with a tremendous view of the wharf, mudflats, and the Ord, Forrest, King, Durack, and Pentecost rivers emptying into the gulf. At the **Wyndham Zoological Gardens and Crocodile Park,** just north of the wharf, you can munch on a croc-covered fudge bar ($2.50) or get up close to the name-tagged crocs, which read "Hi! I'm David. I'm 6m long and I eat people and tip over boats. I mate with all the females." The park also houses six endangered Komodo Dragons. (☎9161 1124. Open daily in the Dry 8:30am-4pm, feedings at 11am; call ahead in the Wet. $14.) The bronze **Dreamtime Statues,** across from the Mobil station, stand as a reminder of the heritage of Wyndham's Aboriginal population (50%).

Thirty kilometers south of Wyndham on the way to Kununurra, an unsealed 1km access road leads to **The Grotto,** but you will have to descend 140 stone steps to reach the perfectly peaceful swimming hole. It is worth a trip at any time of year but looks best during the Wet when the waterfall is in full force.

APPENDIX

BEER TERMINOLOGY

Nothing's more Australian than beer, and accordingly, the language used for it has an Aussie twist too. Because of the hot climate, Australian pubs generally eschew the British pint in favor of smaller portions which stay cold until you're done. Thus, size is a major variable in the argot of ale. If you're too drunk to think of the proper terms, ordering by size, in ounces, usually works. On the mainland, try a "5," "7," "10," or "15." In Tasmania, order using the numbers "6," "8," "10," or "20." Most importantly, don't forget to **shout** your new-found mates a round, that is, to buy them all a drink.

BRING ME A...	
Australia:	**Handle** 285mL (10 oz.) glass with handle, **Long Neck** 750mL (25 oz.) bottle, **Stubbie** 375mL (12 oz.) bottle, **Tinny** 375mL (12 oz.) can, **Slab** case of 24 beers
New South Wales:	**Pony** 140mL (5 oz.), **Beer / Glass** 200mL (7 oz.), **Middy** 285mL (10 oz.), **Schooner** 425mL (15 oz.)
Northern Territory:	**Darwin Stubbie** 1.25L (40 oz.) bottle
Queensland:	**Beer / Glass** 200mL (7 oz.), **Pot** 285mL (10 oz.), **Schooner** 425mL (15 oz.)
South Australia:	**Butcher** 200mL (7 oz.), **Middy / Schooner** 285mL (10 oz.), **Pint** 425mL (15 oz.)[smaller than the British or American pint], **Real Pint** 560mL (20 oz.)
Tasmania:	**Real Pint** 560mL (20 oz.)
Victoria:	**Beer / Glass** 200mL (7 oz.), **Pot** 285mL (10 oz.)
Western Australia:	**Bobby / Beer** 200mL (7 oz.), **Middy** 285mL (10 oz.), **Pot** 425mL (15 oz.)

GLOSSARY OF 'STRINE

'Strine is 'stralian for "Australian." The first trick to speaking Australian slang is to abbreviate everything: **Oz** for Australia, **brekkie** for breakfast, **cuppa** for cup of coffee, **sammy** for sandwich (for more help on how to **Abbreviate Till You Drop,** see p. 352). The term **pommy,** meaning English person, has a debatable origin. Some say it comes from "pomegranate," referring to stereotypically rosy cheeks, while others point to the acronym worn on the early convicts' uniforms: POME, or Prisoner Of Mother England. The second, less ubiquitous aspect of Aussie slang is **rhyming. Noahs** are sharks (shark rhymes with ark, Noah built an ark), while **I'm on the dog** means "I'm on the phone" (bone rhymes with phone, and then the whole dog-bone thing). Get it? American travelers may be disturbed to be called **seppos,** for good reason: Yanks rhymes with tanks, and the worst kind of tanks are septic tanks. Ouch! Australian **pronunciation** is harder to learn than the lingo—with Aboriginal words especially, but even with English-derived proper nouns it can seem impossible. Americans and Canadians generally have particular difficulties, as much of 'strine has distinctly Anglo origins. Smile, and don't be embarrassed—yes, you're a tourist, but in Australia that's not such a mark of shame. One rule to note: when Australians spell a word out or pronounce a number, they always use the expression "double" (or "triple"), as in the phone number "nine-three-double-seven-five-triple-one" (9377 5111).

ablution block: shower/toilet block at a campground
abseil: rappel
ace: awesome
ANZAC: Australia-New Zealand Army Corps
ANZAC biscuits: honey-oat cookies
arvo: afternoon
Aussie: Australian (pronounced Ozzie– thus, Australia is Oz)
backpackers: hostel

barbie: barbecue
bathers: bathing suit/swimsuit
belt bag: fanny pack (don't say "fanny" in Oz: it's a crude word for a part of the female anatomy)
beyond the black stump: *really* far away
billabong: a water hole
biro: pen
biscuit: cookie
bitumen: a rough black asphalt used to pave roads (BICH-uh-min)
bloke: guy, man (familiar)
bludger: moocher, grifter, lazy person; weak drinker who can't finish a full cycle of shouts
bluey: someone with red hair (seriously)
bonnet: hood of a car
book: make reservations
boot: trunk of a car
bottle shop: liquor store
brekkie: breakfast
bush: wilderness
bush tucker: traditional Aboriginal wild foods
bushwalking: hiking
busk: (verb) to play music on the street for money
BYO: bring your own alcohol
campervan: mobile home, RV
capsicum: bell peppers
caravan: trailer, like a cab-less campervan
carpark: parking lot
chap: guy, man; see **bloke**
chazzwazzer: bullfrog
chips: thick french fries, often served with vinegar and salt
chippers: fish and chips or fish and chips shops
chockerblock: very crowded
chook: chicken
chunder: vomit
coffee: beer (yes, Marge)
coldie: a cold beer
concession: discount; usually applies to students, seniors, or children, sometimes only to Australian students and pensioners
cordial: concentrated fruit juice
dag: one who is daggy (usage is common, often benevolent)
daggy: unfashionable, unhip, goofy, silly
damper: traditionally unleavened bread
dear: expensive
Devonshire tea: tea and scones, often served in the late afternoon
dodgy: sketchy
doona, duvet: comforter, feather blanket
dramas: problems. "No dramas" is interchangeable with "no worries."
drink driving: driving under the influence of alcohol
drier than a dead dingo's donger: very thirsty
ensuite: with bath
entree: appetizer ("main" is a main dish)
esky: a cooler (originally from the brand name Eskimo)
excess: deductible (as in car insurance)
fair dinkum: genuine
fair go: equal opportunity
fairy floss: cotton candy
fancy: to like; as in "would you fancy...?"
feral: wild, grunge-style (a common slang term)
flash: fancy, snazzy
flat out like a lizard drinking: doing nothing
flat white: coffee with hot milk and a touch of foam
free call: toll-free call
franger: condom (colloquial, somewhat crude)
fossicking: gem-hunting and gold-sifting
furphy: tall tale, exaggerated rumor (tell a furphy)
g'day: hello
good onya: good for you
glasshouse: greenhouse
grommet: young surfer
ground floor: American first floor ("first floor" is second floor, etc.)
grog: booze
hire: to rent
hitching: hitchhiking
hoon: loud-mouth, show-off
icy-pole: popsicle (sweet frozen treat on a stick)
jersey: sweater, sweatshirt
jackaroo: stationhand-in-training
jillaroo: female jackaroo
jug: pitcher of beer
jumper: see jersey
keen: term of respect ("a keen surfer")
Kiwi: New Zealander
lad: guy, man; see **chap**
licensed: serves alcohol
like hen's teeth: rare (when did you last see a hen with teeth?)
lollies: candies
magic: really wonderful, special: "that beach is magic"
mate: friend, buddy (used broadly)
milk bar: convenience store
moke: an open-air, golf-cart-esque vehicle
mozzie: mosquito
nappy: diaper
newsagent: newsstand/convenience store
no worries: sure, fine, or "you're welcome"
ocker: hick, Crocodile Dundee-type
odds and sods: odds and ends
off like a bucket of prawns: something has a bad smell
ordinary: bad; an "ordinary" road is full of potholes.
Owyergoin'?: How are you?
Oz: Australia
pavlova: a creamy meringue dessert garnished with fruit
pensioner: senior citizen
petrol: gasoline
piss: beer (usually)
pissed: drunk (usually)
pokies: gambling machines
powerpoint: outlet (also electrical hookup at campsites)
pram: stroller (for a baby)
prawn: jumbo shrimp
pub: bar
publican: bartender
push bike: bicycle
return: round-trip
roadie: takeaway beer
'roo: as in kanga-
roundabout: traffic rotary
rubber: eraser
sandgroper: a West Australian (also Westralian)
sang or sanger: sausage
sauce: usually tomato sauce; closest equivalent to ketchup.
serviette: napkin
sheila: slang for a woman
shout: buy a drink or round of drinks for others. Also a noun, as in an evening's worth of everyone buying rounds for each other.
side: team
singlet: tank top or undershirt
skivvie: turtleneck sweater
spider: ice cream float or nasty arachnid (use context clues here)
squiz: a look (to take a squiz at something)
stone the crows!: an expression of surprise
'strine: Aussie dialect (from Australian)
'straya: Australia
swimmers: swimsuit
suss: figure out, sort out
ta: short for thank you—usually muttered under breath.
ta ta: goodbye
TAB: shop to place bets, sometimes in pubs
takeaway: food to go, takeout
Tassie: Tasmania (TAZ-zie)
that's a boomerang: that's something very important to me I don't want you to steal
torch: flashlight
touch wood: knock on wood
track suit: sweat suit, jogging suit
tucker: food.
uni: university (YOU-nee)
unsealed: unpaved roads, usually gravel, sometimes dirt
ute (yute): utility vehicle, pick-up truck
upmarket: upscale, expensive
Vegemite: yeast-extract spread for toast and sammies
vejjo: vegetarian
walkabout: to spontaneously set off across the countryside
Waltzing Matlida: Oz's unofficial national anthem
wanker: jerk (very rude term)
XXXX: pronounced four-ex, a brand of beer
yakka: hard work
zed: Z (American "zee")

TEMPERATURE CHARTS

To convert from °C to °F, multiply by 1.8 and add 32. For a rough approximation, double the Celsius and add 25. To convert from °F to °C, subtract 32 and multiply by 0.55. For a rough approximation, subtract 25 and cut it in half.

°CELSIUS	-5	0	5	10	15	20	25	30	35	40
°FAHRENHEIT	23	32	41	50	59	68	77	86	95	104

Av. Temp. lo/hi Precipitation	January			April			July			October		
	°C	°F	mm	°C	°F	mm	°C	°F	mm	°C	°F	mm
Adelaide	16/28	61/82	19	12/22	54/72	43	7/15	45/59	65	10/21	50/70	43
Alice Springs	21/36	70/97	40	13/28	55/82	17	4/19	39/66	12	15/31	59/88	20
Brisbane	21/29	70/84	161	17/26	63/79	89	10/20	50/68	57	16/26	61/79	77
Cairns	24/31	75/88	407	22/29	72/84	200	17/26	63/79	27	20/29	68/84	38
Canberra	13/28	55/82	58	7/20	45/68	53	0/11	32/52	40	6/19	43/66	67
Darwin	25/32	77/90	393	24/33	75/91	103	20/31	68/88	1	25/34	77/93	52
Hobart	12/22	54/72	48	9/17	48/63	52	4/12	39/54	54	8/17	46/63	64
Melbourne	14/26	57/79	48	11/20	52/68	58	6/13	43/55	49	9/20	48/68	68
Perth	18/30	64/86	9	14/25	57/77	46	9/18	48/64	173	12/22	54/72	55
Sydney	18/26	64/79	98	14/23	59/72	129	8/16	46/61	100	13/22	55/72	79

HOLIDAYS AND FESTIVALS

PUBLIC HOLIDAYS AND FESTIVALS IN 2002	
January 1	New Year's Day
January 28	Australia Day
January 18-27	Tamworth Country Music Festival, NSW (see p. 352)
January, 3 weeks	Sydney Festival, NSW (see p. 126)
February 16-18	WOMADELAIDE (World Music Art Dance) Adelaide, SA (see p. 418)
February 8 - March 2	Sydney Gay and Lesbian Mardi Gras, NSW (see p. 126)
March 29 - April 1	Good Friday through Easter Monday
April 25	Anzac Day
June 10	Queen's Birthday
July 13	Camel Cup Carnival, Alice Springs, NT (see p. 276)
Mid-July to Early August	Melbourne International Film Festival, VIC (see p. 531)
November 5	Melbourne Cup Races. Gold Coast, QLD
December 25	Christmas Day
December 26	Boxing Day

For some Australian "holidays" everything closes down—see **Sport, p. 25.**

Major regional festivals are also included within the state capitals. Banks, museums, and other public buildings are often closed or operate with reduced hours during these times. Vacations differ between schools and regions, but as a general rule, tourism peaks when school is out of session. **Summer holidays** for primary and secondary schools generally include December and January; for universities, they're from the end of November to the middle of February. **Winter break** runs from the end of June through early July. From Christmas to New Year's is ultra-peak season.

Travel Cheep.

Visit **StudentUniverse** for real deals on student and faculty airline tickets, rail passes, and hostel memberships.

StudentUniverse.com

Real Travel Deals

800.272.9676

INDEX

INDEX

C

D

H

I

J

K

L

INDEX

O

P

Q

R

S

T

INDEX

MAPS

DOWNLOAD

Let's Go: Amsterdam
Let's Go: Barcelona
Let's Go: Boston
Let's Go: London
Let's Go: New York City
Let's Go: Paris
Let's Go: Rome
Let's Go: San Francisco
Let's Go: Washington, D.C.

For Your PalmOS™ PDA

Pocket-sized and feature-packed, Let's Go is now available for use on PalmOS-compatible PDAs. **Full text, graphical maps,** and **advanced search capabilities** make for the most powerful and convenient Let's Go ever.

PalmOS is a registered trademark of Palm, Inc.

Yahoo! Travel

Do You Yahoo!?™

CHOOSE YOUR DESTINATION SWEEPSTAKES

No Purchase Necessary.

Explore the world with Let's Go® and StudentUniverse!
Enter for a chance to win a trip for two to a Let's Go destination!

Separate Drawings! May & October 2002.

GRAND PRIZES:

Roundtrip StudentUniverse Tickets

✓ Select one destination and mail your entry to:

- ☐ Costa Rica
- ☐ London
- ☐ Hong Kong
- ☐ San Francisco
- ☐ New York
- ☐ Amsterdam
- ☐ Prague
- ☐ Sydney

* Plus Additional Prizes!!

Choose Your Destination Sweepstakes
St. Martin's Press
Suite 1600, Department MF
175 Fifth Avenue
New York, NY 10010-7848

Restrictions apply; see offical rules for details by visiting Let'sGo.com or sending SASE (VT residents may omit return postage) to the address above.

Name: ________________

Address: ________________

City/State/Zip: ________________

Phone: ________________

Email: ________________

Grand prizes provided by:

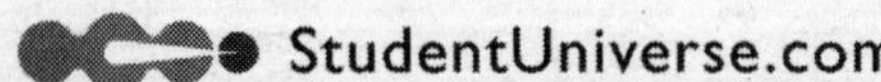

Real Travel Deals

Drawings will be held in May and October 2002. NO PURCHASE NECESSARY. These are not the full official rules, and other restrictions apply. See Official Rules for full details.
To enter without purchase, go to www.letsgo.com or mail a 3"x5" postcard with required information to the above address. Limit one entry per person and per household.

Void in Florida, Puerto Rico, Quebec and wherever else prohibited by law. Open to legal U.S. and Canadian residents (excluding residents of Florida, Puerto Rico and Quebec) 18 or older at time of entry. Round-trip tickets are economy class and depart from any major continental U.S. international airport that the winner chooses.
All mailed entries must be postmarked by September 16, 2002 and received by September 27, 2002.
All online entries must be received by 11:59 pm EDT September 16, 2002.